THE ROUTLEDGE INTERNATIONAL HANDBOOK OF RACE, CULTURE AND MENTAL HEALTH

This handbook presents a thorough examination of the intricate interplay of race, ethnicity, and culture in mental health – historical origins, subsequent transformations, and the discourses generated from past and present mental health and wellness practices.

The text demonstrates how socio-cultural identities including race, gender, class, sexual orientation, disability, religion, and age intersect with clinical work in a range of settings. Case vignettes and recommendations for best practice help ground each in a clinical focus, guiding practitioners and educators to actively increase their understanding of non-Western and indigenous healing techniques, as well as their awareness of contemporary mental health theories as a product of Western culture with a particular historical and cultural perspective. The international contributors also discuss ways in which global mental health practices transcend racial, cultural, ethnic, linguistic, and political boundaries.

The Routledge International Handbook of Race, Culture and Mental Health is an essential resource for students, researchers, and professionals alike as it addresses the complexity of mental health issues from a critical, global perspective.

Roy Moodley is associate professor of counselling and clinical psychology at the University of Toronto, Canada.

Eunjung Lee is associate professor at the Factor-Inwentash Faculty of Social Work, University of Toronto, Canada.

Routledge International Handbooks

Handbook of Urban Mobilities
Edited by Ole B. Jensen, Claus Lassen, Vincent Kaufmann, Malene Freudendal-Pedersen and Ida Sofie Gøtzsche Lange

The Routledge Handbook of French Politics and Culture
Edited by Marion Demossier, David Lees, Aurélien Mondon and Nina Parish

The Routledge Handbook of British Politics and Society
Mark Garnett

The Routledge Handbook of Integrated Reporting
Edited by Charl de Villiers, Pei-Chi Kelly Hsiao and Warren Maroun

The Routledge International Handbook of Global Therapeutic Cultures
Edited by Daniel Nehring, Ole Jacob Madsen, Edgar Cabanas, China Mills and Dylan Kerrigan

Routledge Handbook of Street Culture
Edited by Jeffrey Ian Ross

The Routledge International Handbook of Simmel Studies
Edited by Gregor Fitzi

Routledge Handbook of Counter-Narratives
Edited by Klarissa Lueg and Marianne Wolff Lundholt

Routledge Handbook of Art, Science, and Technology Studies
Edited by Hannah Star Rogers, Megan K. Halpern, Kathryn de Ridder-Vignone, and Dehlia Hannah

Routledge Handbook of Bounded Rationality
Edited by Riccardo Viale

Routledge International Handbook of Charisma
Edited by José Pedro Zúquete

Routledge International Handbook of Working-Class Studies
Edited by Michele Fazio, Christie Launius, and Tim Strangleman

For more information about this series, please visit:
www.routledge.com/Routledge-International-Handbooks/book-series/RIHAND

THE ROUTLEDGE INTERNATIONAL HANDBOOK OF RACE, CULTURE AND MENTAL HEALTH

Edited by Roy Moodley and Eunjung Lee

LONDON AND NEW YORK

First published 2021
by Routledge
2 Park Square, Milton Park, Abingdon, Oxon OX14 4RN

and by Routledge
52 Vanderbilt Avenue, New York, NY 10017

Routledge is an imprint of the Taylor & Francis Group, an informa business

© 2021 selection and editorial matter, Roy Moodley and Eunjung Lee;
individual chapters, the contributors

The right of Roy Moodley and Eunjung Lee to be identified as the authors
of the editorial material, and of the authors for their individual chapters,
has been asserted in accordance with sections 77 and 78 of the Copyright,
Designs and Patents Act 1988.

All rights reserved. No part of this book may be reprinted or reproduced or
utilised in any form or by any electronic, mechanical, or other means, now
known or hereafter invented, including photocopying and recording, or in
any information storage or retrieval system, without permission in writing
from the publishers.

Trademark notice: Product or corporate names may be trademarks or
registered trademarks, and are used only for identification and explanation
without intent to infringe.

British Library Cataloguing-in-Publication Data
A catalogue record for this book is available from the British Library

Library of Congress Cataloging-in-Publication Data
Names: Moodley, Roy, editor. | Lee, Eunjung, editor.
Title: The Routledge international handbook of race, culture and
mental health / edited by Roy Moodley and Eunjung Lee.
Other titles: International handbook of race, ethnicity and culture in
mental health | Routledge international handbooks.
Identifiers: LCCN 2020018868 (print) | LCCN 2020018869 (ebook) |
ISBN 9781138279995 (hardback) | ISBN 9781138280007 (paperback) |
ISBN 9781315276168 (ebook)
Subjects: MESH: Mental Health–ethnology | Culturally Competent Care |
Ethnic Groups–psychology | Minority Groups–psychology |
Cultural Diversity | Ethnopsychology
Classification: LCC RC455.4.E8 (print) | LCC RC455.4.E8 (ebook) |
NLM WA 305.1 | DDC 362.196890089–dc23
LC record available at https://lccn.loc.gov/2020018868
LC ebook record available at https://lccn.loc.gov/2020018869

ISBN: 978-1-138-27999-5 (hbk)
ISBN: 978-1-138-28000-7 (pbk)
ISBN: 978-1-315-27616-8 (ebk)

Typeset in Bembo
by Newgen Publishing UK

CONTENTS

Editors' biographies	*x*
Contributors' biographies	*xi*
Acknowledgements	*xxi*
Foreword by Jaswant Guzder	*xxii*

Introduction   1
Roy Moodley and Eunjung Lee

PART A
Coloniality, globalization, and mental health   7

1   Configurations of race and culture in mental health   9
Roy Moodley and Sandra Osazuwa

2   Coloniality, indigeneity, and mental health   19
Tony B. Benning

3   A postcolonial critique of mental health: Empire and psychiatric
     expansionism   32
Bruce M. Z. Cohen

4   Culture and the globalization of mental health   43
Vishal Bhavsar, Antonio Ventriglio and Dinesh Bhugra

5   The politics of the global governance of mental health   54
Lindsay L. Miller and China Mills

Contents

PART B
Race and culture in mental health practices — 67

6 Culture in counselling psychology — 69
Farah A. Ibrahim, Jianna R. Heuer and Noreen G. Khan

7 Culture and psychoanalysis — 81
Ruth M. Lijtmaer

8 Race and culture in psychiatry — 92
Suman Fernando

9 Race, culture and group psychotherapy — 103
Fred Bemak and Rita Chi-Ying Chung

10 Culture and nursing in mental health — 115
Josephine Etowa

11 Culture and social work in mental health — 128
Eunjung Lee and Marjorie Johnstone

PART C
Culture and multiple identities in mental health — 139

12 Culture and gender in mental health — 141
Charmaine C. Williams

13 Culture and social class in mental health — 151
Yu Chak Sunny Ho, Laurence Chan and William Ming Liu

14 Culture and disability in mental health — 162
Fabricio E. Balcazar, Kristine M. Molina and Nev Jones

15 Culture and sexual orientation in mental health — 174
Joanna Semlyen and Sonja Ellis

16 Culture and religion in mental health — 187
Ayesha Ahmad and Simon Dein

17 Culture, transgender individuals, and mental health — 200
T. Dawson Woodrum, Trenton Owens, and Lauren Mizock

Contents

PART D
Religion and healing in mental health 213

18 Atheism and healing in mental health 215
 G. Eric Jarvis and Rob Whitley

19 Buddhism and healing in mental health 226
 Michel Ferrari and Jessica Carmichael

20 Christianity and healing in mental health 238
 Abrahim H. Khan and Sandra Dixon

21 Hinduism and healing in mental health 250
 Meetu Khosla, Roy Moodley and Erica Killick

22 Islam and healing in mental health 262
 Amina Mahmood

23 Judaism and mental health 273
 Devora Shabtai and David H. Rosmarin

PART E
Special populations and culture in mental health 287

24 Culture, mental health, and children and adolescents 289
 Dominika A. Winiarski, Nisha Dogra, and Niranjan Karnik

25 Culture, mental health, and older people 301
 Amanda Grenier and Blessing Ojembe

26 Culture, mental health, and immigrants 314
 Rachel Tribe and Claire Marshall

27 Culture, mental health, and refugees 326
 Sophie C. Yohani

PART F
Culture and mental health in a global context 339

28 Culture and mental health in Brazil 341
 Francisco Ortega and Leandro David Wenceslau

vii

Contents

29 Culture and mental health in Chile 353
Cristina Pastén Peña and Leonor Villacura Avendaño

30 Culture and mental health in (the greater) China 365
Yu-Te Huang

31 Culture and mental health in Egypt 377
Michael Elnemais Fawzy

32 Culture and mental health in India 387
Satheesh Varma M.

33 Culture and mental health in Jamaica 399
Samantha Longman-Mills, Patrice Whitehorne-Smith, Carole Mitchell,
Lester Shields and Wendel D. Abel

34 Culture and mental health in Kenya 411
Elijah M. Marangu

35 Culture and mental health in Nigeria 422
Aneneosa A. G. Okocha, Henrietta Alika, and Olamojiba O. Bamgbose

36 Culture and mental health in Pakistan 434
Humair Yusuf

37 Culture and mental health in Peru 445
David M. R. Orr

38 Culture and mental health in the Philippines 458
Antover P. Tuliao, Angelica V. Ang, Melissa R. Garabiles,
Minerva D. Tuliao and Maria Cristina Samaco-Zamora

39 Culture and mental health in South Africa 470
Edmarie Pretorius and Sharon Moonsamy

PART G
Indigenous and traditional healing in mental health 483

40 Indigenous North American healing 485
Roderick McCormick

41 Indigenous African healing 496
Olaniyi Bojuwoye

viii

Contents

42 South Asian healing 505
    Baiju Gopal

43 Caribbean healing 517
    Shivon Raghunandan and Roy Moodley

44 Māori indigenous healing practices in Aotearoa (New Zealand) 530
    Rebecca Wirihana, Cherryl Smith, and Takirirangi Smith

Glossary *541*
Index *544*

EDITORS' BIOGRAPHIES

Roy Moodley, PhD, is an associate professor in Clinical and Counselling Psychology at the University of Toronto. Roy is also the Director of the Centre for Diversity in Counselling and Psychotherapy. His research and publications include critical multicultural counselling and psychotherapy, race and culture in psychoanalysis, global south psychologies; traditional healing and mixed-race relations.

Eunjung Lee, PhD, MSW, RSW, is an associate professor and Endowed Chair in Mental Health and Health at the Factor-Inwentash Faculty of Social Work, University of Toronto. Using critical theories in language, discourse and power, her research focuses on cross-cultural clinical practice and training in community mental health, immigration, and politics of multiculturalism and democracy.

CONTRIBUTORS' BIOGRAPHIES

Abrahim H. Khan, PhD, is a professor in the Faculty of Divinity, Trinity College, and Graduate Department for the Study of Religion, University of Toronto. The span of his research and teaching interests includes philosophy of religion, cross-cultural and comparative studies in religion, and religion, healing and medicine, and Kierkegaard studies.

Amanda Grenier, PhD, is a professor and Norman and Honey Schipper Chair in Gerontological Social Work at the University of Toronto and Baycrest Hospital. Amanda is an inter-disciplinary scholar focused on aging and inequality. Her forthcoming books focus on *Late Life Homelessness* and *Precarity and Late Life*.

Amina Mahmood, PhD, is a licensed psychologist at HPA/LiveWell in Albany, NY. She teaches graduate and undergraduate courses on an adjunct basis. Her clinical and research interests include working with the Muslim population, and multicultural issues in psychology. She is active in creating and providing psycho-educational workshops and programs to the local Muslim community.

Aneneosa A. G. Okocha, PhD, NCC, LPC, is a professor of Counselor Education at the University of Wisconsin Whitewater, USA, where she served as department chairperson and program coordinator. She also served on editorial boards of some counselling journals. Her research and teaching interests encompass career development, multicultural counselling, and global mental health.

Angelica V. Ang, PhD, is an assistant professor of Psychology at the Ateneo de Manila University, Philippines. Her research interest includes culture and psychopathology, social construction of mental illness, trauma, grief, and attachment. She is a licensed clinical psychologist and a practicing psychotherapist.

Antonio Ventriglio, MD, PhD, is a psychiatrist in the Department of Mental Health, and Department of Clinical and Experimental Medicine, University of Foggia, Foggia, Italy. He is honorary member of the World Psychiatric Association

Contributors' Biographies

Antover P. Tuliao, PhD, is an assistant professor in the Community, Family, and Addiction Sciences Department of Texas Tech University. His research interests lie in the intersection of substance abuse and related harmful and risk behaviors, culture, and decision-making.

Ayesha Ahmad, PhD, is a lecturer in Global Health, St Georges University of London and Honorary Lecturer at the Institute for Global Health, University College London. Ayesha's research interests include mental health and gender-based violence in conflict, and she works on developing trauma therapeutic interventions for survivors of violence using traditional storytelling.

Baiju Gopal, PhD, is an associate professor of Psychology at CHRIST (Deemed to be University) Bangalore. He is also the Project Director of the 21st century US-Indo Knowledge initiative award in partnership with Miami University, USA, funded by USIEF. His research interests include cultural psychology; qualitative research, theatre, and psychoanalysis.

Blessing Ojembe, PhD (candidate), in Social Gerontology at McMaster University, Canada. Her research focuses on loneliness and social isolation among older immigrants in Canada, specifically focusing on the influence of age, race and ethnic factors as contributory factors to loneliness, social isolation, and social exclusion.

Bruce M. Z. Cohen, PhD, is a senior lecturer in sociology at the University of Auckland. He teaches courses on the sociologies of mental health, cultural studies, and education, and his publications include the critically-acclaimed monographs, *Mental Health User Narratives: New Perspectives on Illness and Recovery* (2008) and *Psychiatric Hegemony: A Marxist Theory of Mental Illness* (2016).

Carole Mitchell, PhD, is a lecturer in the Faculty of Medical Sciences at the University of the West Indies. Carole is also a consultant Clinical Psychologist at the University Hospital of the West Indies. Her research interest includes culture and mental health, adolescent mental health, substance misuse, and sexual harassment.

Charmaine C. Williams, PhD, is the vice-dean of Students, School of Graduate Studies and Associate Professor in the Factor-Inwentash Faculty of Social Work, University of Toronto. Her research bridges practice and access and equity issues that affect various populations including racial minority women, LGBTQ individuals in local and international context, and individuals and families affected by serious and persistent mental illnesses.

Cherryl Smith, PhD, is a senior researcher for Te Atawhai o te Ao and Te Runanga o Nga Wairiki/Ngati Apa. She has worked extensively for her tribe and for Māori organizations. Strong interests in revival of Māori knowledge and application to health, education, and environmental settings.

China Mills, PhD, is a senior lecturer in public health at City, University of London. China carries out research into different facets of the global mental health assemblage. Her work looks into how the psy-disciplines and psychotropic drugs function in local and global contexts of entrenched inequality, chronic poverty, (neo)colonial oppression, border imperialism, and increasingly under the politics of austerity.

Contributors' Biographies

Claire Marshall, BSc, Cert, PGCert, MRes, MA, DPsych (CPsychol, HCPC, FHDA), is a Counselling Psychologist currently on the psychology faculty at the University of East London, where she teaches on the Professional Doctorate in Counselling Psychology and MSc International Humanitarian Psychosocial Intervention. She is consulted by immigration lawyers, working within immigration removal centres (IRCs) to provide medico-legal reports, as well as a Senior Psychologist in a service specialising in developmental trauma. Dr Marshall is on the editorial board for the Journal of Psychological Therapies, Existential Analysis Journal and the Journal of Ethnic and Migration Studies. With over ten years of experience in public, private and third sectors, she supervised psychosocial workers stationed in North African camps and her work in Central Africa has contributed to projects running in collaboration with international bodies such as the United Nations and the European Commission. Her special interests include responses to forced migration from state and non-state actors, with a focus on policy, co-ordination, and intervention.

Cristina Pastén Peña, MA, is a clinical psychologist trainer and staff at the Psychological Unit of the Student and Community Affairs Department of Medicine Faculty at the University of Chile. Her research and teaching interests include philosophy of psychotherapy, existential psychology, and existentialism.

David M. R. Orr, PhD, is a senior lecturer in Social Work at the University of Sussex, UK. His primary research interests focus on culture and mental health; literary representations of mental disorders; and safeguarding policy and practice. He co-edited the *Palgrave Handbook of Sociocultural Perspectives on Global Mental Health* (2017).

David H. Rosmarin, PhD, ABPP, is an assistant professor in the Department of Psychiatry at Harvard Medical School, and Director of McLean Hospital's Spirituality & Mental Health Program.

Devora Shabtai, PhD (candidate), is a therapist at Transformations Substance Abuse and Mental Health Treatment Center in South Florida where also serves as Program Director for their Jewish Faith Based program. She is currently a doctoral candidate in the University of Warwick, UK where she is examining relationships between psychological variables and Jewish spiritual/religious development.

Dinesh Bhugra, PhD, FRCPsych, is a professor emeritus of Mental Health and Cultural Diversity at King's College London. Past President of the Royal College of Psychiatrists, World Psychiatric Association and British Medical Association. His research interests include culture and mental health, primary care psychiatry and social justice, and well-being of doctors and medical students. See http://dineshbhugra.net/.

Dominika A. Winiarski, PhD, is an assistant professor in the Department of Psychiatry and Behavioral Sciences at Rush University Medical Center. Her research and clinical interests converge on understanding the biopsychosocial mechanisms by which early life adversity influences the development of psychopathology across childhood and adolescence, and in using this information to develop future iterations of trauma-informed interventions for youth.

Edmarie Pretorius, PhD, is a social worker by profession and an associate professor in the Department of Social Work in the School of Human and Community Development at the

University of the Witwatersrand. Her professional experience, fields of teaching and research are mental health, community and social development, school social work, research methodology, and education.

Elijah Marangu, PhD, RN, MPH is a lecturer in the School of Nursing & Midwifery at Deakin University in Melbourne, Australia. His research interests are capacity building strategies for mental health care in low income settings, assessment of gaps in mental health care in Kenya, and a mental health literacy survey among health workers in primary health care settings.

Erica Killick, PhD (candidate), in the Department of Applied Psychology and Human Development at the University of Toronto. Her research interests include yoga education for children and contemplative practices in childhood. Erica's research is on how children in pre-school experience yoga from the point of view of the child.

Fabricio E. Balcazar, PhD, is a professor in the Department of Disability and Human Development at the University of Illinois at Chicago. His primary interest is in developing methods for enhancing consumer empowerment and personal effectiveness among individuals with disabilities. Fabricio is the director of the Center on Capacity Building for Minorities with Disabilities Research.

Farah A. Ibrahim, PhD, LP (CO) is a professor in the School of Education and Human Development at the University of Colorado Denver. Her research interests include: Cultural and social justice issues in counselling and psychotherapy, group work in diverse settings, and working effectively with cultural non-dominant groups and individuals.

Francisco Ortega, PhD, is a full professor in the Institute for Social Medicine of the State University of Rio de Janeiro and Research Director of the Rio Center for Global Health. He is also Visiting Professor at the Department of Global Health and Social Medicine of King's College, London

Fred Bemak, EdD, is a Professor Emeritus at George Mason University and Founder and Director of Counselors Without Borders. His research interests focus on cross-cultural psychology, social justice and human rights, group psychotherapy, race relations, and refugees and immigrants.

G. Eric Jarvis, MD, is an associate professor of Psychiatry at McGill University, and a research associate of the Lady Davis Institute. His main research interests are the relation between psychosis and culture, language barriers to psychiatric services, and the process of cultural consultation.

Henrietta Alika, PhD, is an associate professor of Counselling at the University of Benin, Benin City, Nigeria. She is a member of the Counselling Association of Nigeria and participated in various conferences on counselling and mental health. Her research interests encompass, psychology, mental health issues, career guidance, and sexuality education.

Humair Yusuf, EdD, is a visiting faculty at the Department on Social Sciences and Liberal Arts at the Institute of Business Administration, Karachi, Pakistan. His research and teaching interests include cognitive psychology, cross-cultural psychology and critical multicultural counselling, and psychotherapy.

Contributors' Biographies

Jaswant Guzder, MD, is a professor at McGill University, Montreal. She is the founding co-director of the Cultural Consultation Service at McGill; former head of child psychiatry at the Jewish General Hospital; and active internationally in training and teaching. She is currently engaged with global mental health work with Jamaica and Nepal, Indigenous child and family health and her art practice.

Jessica Carmichael, PhD (candidate), in the School and Clinical Child Psychology program at the Ontario Institute for Studies in Education (OISE), University of Toronto. She is currently studying how therapists influence treatment outcomes for children and youth in therapy, and the professional and personal development of therapists.

Jianna R. Heuer, MSW, LCSW, is a psychotherapist in private practice in New York City. Her research and clinical interests include feminist psychology, group theory, and race, culture, and immigration issues in mental health.

Joanna Semlyen, PhD, is a British Psychological Society Chartered Psychologist and Senior Lecturer based at Norwich Medical School at the University of East Anglia, UK. She has particular expertise in mental health in sexual minorities and publishes both qualitative and quantitative research focusing on LGBTQ health outcomes, experiences, and disparities.

Josephine Etowa, PhD, RN, RM, FWACN, FAAN, is a professor of Nursing and past holder of Loyer–DaSilva Research Chair in Public Health Nursing (2012–2019), University of Ottawa. Josephine is a founding member, and past president of the Health Association of African Canadians (HAAC). Her clinical practice, research, and teaching address health inequities in health and health care.

Kristine M. Molina, PhD, is an associate professor of Psychological Science at the University of California, Irvine. Her research focuses on investigating how different dimension of inequality (e.g., discrimination, resource inequality) become embodied at multiple levels to affect health across the life course.

Lauren Mizock, PhD, is the director of the Social Justice and Diversity concentration and a core faculty member in the Clinical Psychology PhD Program at Fielding Graduate University. Dr. Mizock is also a Program Developer for the Center for Psychiatric Rehabilitation at Boston University. Dr. Mizock is in private practice as a licensed psychologist in San Francisco.

Laurence Chan, PhD (candidate), in the Counseling Psychology program at The University of Iowa. His research interests are in examining white supremacist extremism and developing recommendations for psychotherapy and countering violent extremism (CVE) interventions. His additional research interests include racial identity and classism.

Leandro David Wenceslau, MD, PhD, is an assistant professor of Family Medicine in the Department of Nursery and Medicine of Federal University of Viçosa (UFV), Brazil. He is a member of the Mental Health Working Group of the Brazilian Society of Family Medicine (SBMFC) and of the World Organization of Family Doctors (WONCA).

Leonor Villacura Avendaño, MA, is the director at the Psychological Unit of the Student and Community Affairs Department of Medicine Faculty at the University of Chile. Her research and teaching interests include mental health, quality of life and psychopathology in higher education students, phenomenological integrative model, critical thinking, and education method.

Lester Shields, PhD, is a mental health counsellor at the University of the West Indies Health Centre. His client population comprises nationals from the Caribbean and from different socioeconomic background. He has lived and worked in inner-city communities in Jamaica, the United States and Mexico; and has lived in a village in Ghana. He supervises counselling interns including those in deaf community.

Lindsay Lee Miller, PhD (candidate), in the School of Education at the University of Sheffield, UK. Through utilizing an arsenal of abolition-based healing arts Lindsay's thesis is an anarchival study of a [settler] colonial psy-archive that moves at the limits of madness and poethically breaks down with the deep implicancy of border and psy-imperialisms.

Maria Cristina Samaco-Zamora, PhD, is an adjunct faculty at the University of San Francisco and Golden Gate University. Her research interest includes personality, mindfulness, and wellness.

Marjorie Johnstone, PhD, is an assistant professor at the School of Social Work, Dalhousie University in Canada. Her research focuses on critical feminist perspectives, the history of Canadian social work, community mental health, citizenship, immigration, and globalization.

Meetu Khosla, PhD, is an associate professor in the Psychology Department, University of Delhi. She is a Fulbright Fellow, Erasmus Mundus Fellow, Shastri Fellow and ICSSR Fellow. Meetu has published 57 articles, and a book on Physiological Psychology. Meetu has presented 130 keynote addresses in Indian and International Conferences in the United States, Canada, France, Poland and Lithuania.

Melissa R. Garabiles, PhD, RPsy, is an assistant professor and licensed clinical psychologist at Ateneo de Manila University. Her publications are on mental health, positive psychology, and labor migration. Other research interests include men and masculinities and family relationships.

Michael Elnemais Fawzy, PhD, is a consultant child psychiatrist at El-Abbassia Mental Health Hospital, and a Lecturer at the Continuous Medical Education Committee, Egyptian Medical Syndicate. He founded 'Hope Foundation' to promote resilience in high-risk, underserved children in Egypt. His research and teaching interests include patients' rights; stigma; mental health policies; laws; and child psychiatry.

Michel Ferrari, PhD, is a professor in the Department of Applied Psychology and Human Development at the University of Toronto. As Director of the Wisdom and Identity Lab, he is currently studying wisdom and acculturation in Islamic immigrants and refugees, and the wisdom in emerging adults with Autism.

Minerva D. Tuliao, PhD, is an adjunct faculty at the College of Education, Texas Tech University. Her research focuses on the education, training, and human resource development of underrepresented populations in the context of higher education and community partnerships.

Contributors' Biographies

Nev Jones, PhD, is an assistant professor in the Department of Mental Health Law and Policy; and faculty affiliate with the Louis de la Parte Florida Mental Health Institute.

Niranjan Karnik, MD, PhD, is The Cynthia Oudejans Harris, MD, Professor of Psychiatry and Associate Dean for Community Behavioral Health at Rush University Medical Center. His research focuses on community-based interventions for high-risk youth with psychiatric and substance use disorders. He is collaborating with community partners on the westside of Chicago to develop community-based approaches to reducing mental health disparities.

Nisha Dogra, PhD, MRCPsych, is Emeritus Professor in Psychiatry Education at the University of Leicester. She is involved in educational research in cultural diversity and psychiatric education and in issues of cultural competence in health care. She was also until her retirement a consultant child and adolescent psychiatrist.

Noreen Gul Khan, MA, recently graduated in multicultural clinical counselling. Her interests include multiracial identity development connected to mental health, prevention work, and working with youth.

Olamojiba O. Bamgbose, PhD, NCC, is an assistant professor at the University of Wisconsin Whitewater. She teaches clinical mental health and school counselling graduate courses. Her research interests include global mental health and school counsellor professional identity. She is on the editorial board for the *Journal of Child and Adolescent Counseling*.

Olaniyi Bojuwoye, PhD, Olaniyi Bojuwoye is a professor at the Department of Special Education, Kwara State University, Malete-Ilorin, Nigeria. His research and publication interests include cross-cultural psychology, African indigenous knowledge systems and healthcare and special education needs. He is a member of several psychology-related associations including the International Council of Psychologists (ICP), International Association for Special Education and Counselling Association of Nigeria.

Patrice Whitehorne-Smith, PhD (candidate), in Public Health at Curtin University in Western Australia. Her areas of research interests including the accessibility of public health services, culture, and mental health, and substance use in the Caribbean.

Rachel Tribe, PhD, is a professor at the School of Psychology, University of East London. She is a Chartered Psychologist and trustee of two international mental health charities. She has published and consulted nationally and internationally. She recently set up a mental health and well-being web portal for refugees and those working alongside them www.uel.ac.uk/Schools/Psychology/Research/Refugee-Mental-Health-and-Wellbeing-Portal.

Rebecca Wirihana, PhD, is tribally affiliated to Ngarauru kii tahi, Ngati Maniapoto, Tainui, Te Rarawa, Ngāpuhi and Te Aupouri. She is a clinical psychologist who specializes in working in mental health services by applying kaupapa Māori and clinical methods of healing in both her research and clinical practice.

Rita Chi-Ying Chung, PhD, is a Professor Emerita at George Mason University. Her research and teaching focuses on human rights and social justice, refugees and immigrants, cross-cultural psychology, human trafficking, and race relations.

Contributors' Biographies

Rob Whitley, PhD, is an associate professor of Psychiatry at McGill University, and a research scientist at the Douglas Hospital Research Centre. His main research interests are recovery, stigma, and men's mental health.

Roderick McCormick, PhD, is a professor of Mental Health at Thompson Rivers University. Rod is also a Research Chair in Indigenous Health and the Director of the All My Relations Indigenous Research Centre. His research interests include Indigenous mental health, traditional healing practices, and research capacity building.

Ruth M. Lijtmaer, PhD, is a senior supervisor, training analyst and faculty at the Center for Psychotherapy and Psychoanalysis of New Jersey. Ruth's private practice is in Ridgewood, New Jersey. She is a board member of IFPE from 2015 to the present. Ruth has presented her research nationally and internationally.

Samantha Longman-Mills, PhD, is a clinical psychologist at the University of the West Indies, Jamaica and Consultant at the University Hospital of the West Indies. Samantha is a former Director of Advocacy for the Jamaican Psychological Society and a former Vice President for the West Indies Group of University Teachers (Jamaica). Her research interests include cultural and intergenerational trauma; substance use, and childhood maltreatment.

Sandra Dixon, PhD, RPsych, is a registered psychologist in Alberta and an Assistant Professor of Counselling Psychology in the Faculty of Education, University of Lethbridge. Her main interests are in multicultural counselling practices, religion/spirituality, social justice, ethnocultural diversity issues, and cultural identity reconstruction.

Sandra Osazuwa, MA (candidate), in Clinical and Counselling Psychology at the University of Toronto. Her research is in the intersectional analysis of race, culture and psychotherapy and mental health; critiquing the mental health care for marginalized groups; and the therapeutic effects of cultural and indigenous healing practices, particularly African healing traditions.

Satheesh Varma M., PhD, is an assistant professor of Psychology at School of Philosophy, Psychology and Scientific Heritage, Chinmaya Vishwavidyapeeth, Deemed to be University. Ernakulam, Kerala, India. His research and teaching interests include culture and mental health, indigenous psychologies, Indian wisdom on mental health and counselling, transpersonal psychology, industrial and organizational psychology, the psychology of advertisements and media, service-learning, and eco-psychology.

Sharon Moonsamy, PhD, is a speech-language therapist and remedial education consultant. She is an Associate Professor in the Department of Speech Pathology at Wits University and the Acting Head of the School of Human & Community Development. Language and cognition are her teaching and research interests. Sharon is a member of local and international associations, including SASLHA and IALP.

Shivon Raghunandan, EdD (candidate), in counseling and psychotherapy at the University of Toronto; and is a Registered Psychotherapist at Humber College in Toronto, Canada. Her clinical interests include trauma and attachment; diversity, race/culture and mental health. Her research interests include Caribbean healing practices; issues of racism in mixed-race relationships.

Contributors' Biographies

Simon Dein, PhD, is a professor and Consultant Psychiatrist in Essex, UK, specializing in rehabilitation and liaison psychiatry. His doctoral degree is in social anthropology from University College London. He is an honorary Clinical Professor at Queen Mary College, London and Visiting Professor Goldsmiths College, London.

Sonja Ellis, PhD, is an associate professor in Te Kura toi Tangata/School of Education at The University of Waikato, New Zealand. Her research and teaching interests include gender, sexuality, and mental health. She has published widely in the field of LGBTQ Psychology.

Sophie C. Yohani, PhD, is a psychologist and an associate professor of Counselling Psychology at the University of Alberta. She has served as co-director of the Division of Clinical Services, a training clinic for graduate students in the Counselling, School and Child Clinical Psychology programs at the University of Alberta. Her interests lie in critical multicultural counselling, community-based participatory research, and refugee/migrant mental health.

Suman Fernando, MD, FRCPsych, formerly a consultant psychiatrist, is now Emeritus Professor of Social Sciences within the School of Social Sciences, London Metropolitan University, London, UK. His research and academic interests explore transcultural critiques of psychiatry and psychology that engage with the topic of institutional racism in these disciplines. See www.sumanfernando.com.

Takirirangi Smith, PhD, is an esteemed carver and Māori knowledge expert. He has expertise in Māori language manuscripts written during the early years of colonization. He has also spent many years on tribal research.

T. Dawson Woodrum, PhD (candidate), in Clinical Psychology at Fielding Graduate University and a Doctoral Intern in the Counseling and Psychological Services department at Oregon State University.

Tony B. Benning, PhD, MBChB, MRCPsych, FRCPC, is a general adult psychiatrist in Maple Ridge, BC, Canada. He is also a clinical instructor at the University of British Columbia. For the last seven years he has contributed to the provision of psychiatric services to First Nations throughout British Columbia's Fraser Valley.

Trenton Owens, PhD (candidate), in Clinical Psychology at Fielding Graduate University and a Doctoral Intern in the Aggie Health & Wellness Center at New Mexico State University. He is also a Licensed Professional Counselor Associate in North Carolina.

Vishal Bhavsar, PhD, MRCPsych, is an epidemiologist and psychiatrist at the Maudsley Hospital. Currently NIHR Postdoctoral Fellow in Women's Mental Health at IOPPN, King's College London. He carries out epidemiological investigations of the impact of gender, violence, and discrimination on the design/delivery of mental health services, and on public health interventions.

Wendel D. Abel, PhD, is a professor of Mental Health Policy at the University of The West Indies, Mona, Jamaica. Professor Abel is the Chair of the Department of Community Health & Psychiatry His research and teaching interests include mental health policy, suicide, alcohol and substance abuse, and culture in mental health.

Contributors' Biographies

William Ming Liu, PhD, is a professor of Counseling Psychology at the University of Maryland at College Park and Chair, for the Department of Counseling, Higher Education, and Special Education. His research is in White privilege and White supremacist ideologies, men and masculinities, and social class and classism.

Yu Chak Sunny Ho, PhD (candidate), at the University of Iowa's Counseling Psychology Program. He is currently a pre-doctoral intern at the Rutgers University Counseling Center. His research interests are international students' mental health issues, social justice issues, culturally responsive psychotherapies, and international trainees' supervision and training.

Yu-Te Huang, PhD, is an assistant professor at Department of Social Work and Social Administration in the University of Hong Kong. His research interests cover adolescent mental health, sexual and gender minority youth, and immigrants' cross-cultural experiences. Prior to working in academia, he was a psychiatric social worker in Taiwan.

ACKNOWLEDGEMENTS

Our sincere thanks go to all of the authors and co-authors for sharing their research and scholarship in this book. All the chapters were dedicated to the issues currently preoccupying us in the mental health field. All the authors and co-authors made this book come to reality through their efforts, time and patience; we are extremely grateful and deeply appreciative.

Also particular thanks to Routledge for permission to republish two articles that were revised as book chapters. Fred Bemak and Rita Chi-Ying Chung (2019): 'Race Dialogues in Group Psychotherapy: Key Issues in Training and Practice', published in the *International Journal of Group Psychotherapy*, 69 (2): 172–191. This paper has been revised and updated as Chapter 9 in this book; and Michael Elnemais Fawzy (2017): 'Mental Health Care in Egypt: Review of Current State, Policy, and Needs', published in the *Routledge International Journal of Mental Health*, 46 (4): 339–345. This paper has been revised and updated as Chapter 31 in this book.

Finally, our sincere thanks and appreciation to Joanne Forshaw, Susannah Frearson, Heather Evans, Laura Lawrie and Flora Kenson at Routledge for the help and support we received during the writing of this book.

FOREWORD

Global movements of populations and the increasing ethnic diversity across the continents has underlined the relevance of culture impacting mental health. However, despite the wide recognition that cultural factors are fundamental to shaping mental wellness, identity, suffering, and delivery of mental health care, the dominance of ethnocentric euro-North American assumptions continues to bias frameworks of the mental health literature, research publications, institutional policies, and training approaches especially relevant to global mental health and minorities. The variations of cultural frameworks relevant to mental health in other regions of the world than the West as well as the limited recognition of differences in the predominant values, life cycle experiences or premises evident across collectivist, indigenous and minority groups has evoked a long-standing counter-narrative and inter-disciplinary dialogue. In this timely volume, Roy Moodley and Eunjung Lee have brought together a group of exceptional scholars and creative clinicians who contributed to this rich offering of critical contemporary discourses on race, culture, and mental health. These collected writings address the implications of race and intersectional theory on clinical, theory, and policy. The shifts from primarily Western frameworks has been enriched by the gathering impact of ethnographies, divergent clinical experience, socio-political realities, and international variables relevant to the vast populations of non-Western, marginalized and indigenous subjects. These essays are particularly relevant to current practices promoting cultural safety, challenges of institutional racism, innovative community partnerships, alliance building across dissonant cultural spaces, addressing the mhGAP (mental health gap in resources) for unserved and vulnerable populations and creative partnerships between healers and local clinicians. These explorations of emerging pathways reconsider aspects of clinical care and intervention paradigms in an era when task shifting and community engagement are expanding, and professionals revisit the vertical hierarchies of 'expert' medical models with possibilities of horizontal partnerships relevant to diverse global realities.

The pioneers of this clinically relevant discourse include the outstanding works of Frantz Fanon who engaged with questioning his own hybridity and identity quandaries positioned as a black Martinique psychiatrist trained in France while treating a population of oppressed and colonized Others in Algeria, Edward Said as an Egyptian American tracing the social and historical creation of 'Orientalism' and Stewart Hall's work on hybridity, acculturation and migration grounded in his own life experience as a Jamaican origin British immigrant. Many

Foreword

anthropologists, social scientists, philosophers and mental health scholars including the philosopher Michel Foucault, the Afro-American sociologist W. E. B. Du Bois and the Sri Lankan anthropologist Ganath Obesekeyere, have contributed to this important discourse over the previous decades. These stimulating revisions of ethnocentrism are concerned with culture as essential to our clinical lens and our approach to training. While grappling with cultural meaning and translation of symptoms in unique contexts of practitioner, client, and community narratives, mental health often evokes a deeper listening implicating the deconstruction of meaning and interpretation of mental states. We are enriched by an exploration of cultural factors operating at multiple levels of psyche, collectives, migration, acculturation, identity, socio-political influences, and historical context. Many scholarly works have offered relevant input to this discourse including the possibilities of community and systemic intervention as well as the strains and successful adaptation processes of families encountering the dissonant collectivist or individualistic paradigms.

Culture in relation to mental health has been benefitted from ethnographic and qualitative studies, socio-political historical deconstruction, philosophical commentary, understanding variables of collectivist frameworks, acknowledging spiritual or religious influences, researching developmental variations, and expanding parameters of resilience essential to healing pathways. The territories of mental health indeed embrace a wide canvas including the vicissitudes of oppression, racism, acculturation dissonances, resilience, complex identity agendas, mourning, spiritual frameworks, adaptations to culture change, and challenges of intergenerational trauma. In view of the continuing dynamics arising from power imbalances, inequalities, human rights disparities, poverty, massive global movements of populations and fluctuating tensions toward minorities, these discussions are increasingly relevant to advocacy and human rights currents in mental health intervention and policy. The cultural axis components are simultaneously interactive with practitioner, client, and institutional variables that invite innovative approaches to empathic listening, diagnosis, access and intervention planning. Cultural factors interacting with political biases and institutional responses have often influenced priorities in mental health delivery and leave room for expanding attention to community partnerships, school-based programs and a focus on women's health. Children remain amongst the most invisible in mental health budget allocation and planning in indigenous communities and the low- and middle-income nations despite the wide research data on the 'first thousand days' or child abuse epidemiology surveys. Cultural factors and institutional responses have often influenced priorities and leave room for expanding attention to community partnerships, school-based programs and a focus on women's health.

Therapeutic spaces require the client and therapist to enter an uncertain territory motivated by the partnerships of healing. Empathic listening and cultural attunement facilitate bridges across the divides of cultural dissonances and dynamics of hybridity which remain highly relevant for populations moving from rural to urban contexts, caught in social class mobility, crossing borders, migrating, and enduring upheaval or traumatic loss. The cultural frameworks indeed alter constantly with migration, unexpected social upheavals or embedded traumas of historical, religious or collective memory, requiring a continuous process of translation across psychological, social, cultural, epigenetic, and external variables. Cultural knowledge remains a pillar of resilience and wellness possibilities, and broadly informs healing interventions. Skills in cultural formulation are seminal to promoting alliance building, deconstructing practitioner bias and finding constructive solutions for vulnerable, marginal or subaltern populations. Cultural agendas are often fundamental to approaching successful engagement with largely underserved communities, the populations of many low- and middle-income country (LMIC) populations

Foreword

or indigenous groups who have endured generational trauma or exclusion yet retain a bedrock of unrecognized mythic repertoires of spiritual strength which have sustained their communities. Contemporary social preoccupations fluctuate between emphasis on cultural difference or race despite the wider embrace and emergence of cultural hybridization.

The long-standing conceptual conflation of race and culture has been addressed by many authors including Suman Fernando who tracing the Western historical arc of race and psychiatry with its implications for mental health care. The relevance of intersectional theory to identity and suffering, expanded practitioner skills as well as reframing individuation agendas across generations. Understanding cultural embedding is also significant for primary health care workers who do the majority of mental health intervention in community partnerships. Global and local initiatives have expanded capacities for mutual exchange of knowledge, skills and sustained respectful mental wellness partnerships. Several chapters in this volume, have elaborated experiences with marginalized or minority populations and the practitioner's integration of mental health skills with aspects of cultural specificity of development, life cycle tasks, systemic dynamics, and socio-political realities leading to evolving pragmatic solutions to resistances, obstacles or dynamic contexts. The stigma of 'madness', 'badness', and incarceration whether in childhood or adulthood has reinforced fear or avoidance of mental health care for a range of psychiatric disorders and remained a challenge of community mental health access. Mental health training could provide stronger support to professionals to increase their confidence in dealing with diversity and resistance to engagement. The wider framework of culture in problem solving and intervention involves an appreciation of practitioner, institution, and client gestalts. Building a mutual dialogue of client and practitioner is often furthered by a respectful humility in approaching the unique context of individuals, communities or family systems. The ethnographic understanding of each community reaches to the core of meaning systems, embedded in their mythic or core beliefs of life cycle and development aims unravelled within the dynamic context of the communities. Navigating cultural parameters, symptom interpretation, and systemic dynamics progresses with a clinical focus on co-constructing meaning, aims and eliciting emotional maps of strengths or deficits guided by distressed individuals or communities.

The history of colonization, slavery, genocides, war, and civil conflict is another essential reality that is often denied as significant to the domain of cultural spaces. The inequities of class, caste, tribal hierarchies, or embedded histories may be silenced, implicit or evident, yet essential to problem solving in mental health. In addition, the cultural realities of religious and spiritual beliefs have long been ignored or minimized in clinical practice but remain significantly implicated in defining a sense of belonging, contributing to constructing gender identity, to power structures or roles, establishing group boundaries or awakening possibilities that may have undermining and positive aspects to support resolution of distress. Spirituality and religious parameters are often left aside as territory of traditional healers yet can be essential to understanding strengths or vulnerabilities.

The construction of hope for populations at risk remains essential to recovery and a prominent implicit cultural axis ingredient. Research on international cohorts confirming that the trajectories of clients who suffer chronic severe mental illness such as schizophrenia have shown better outcomes and quality of life in collective societies than in the Western context underlined the importance of cultural factors in well-being. Though social or interpersonal stigma may be a variable across cultures, caretaking capacity and protective care provided by a familial or community solidarity, may also be a significant variable, undermined or more fragile in urban, highly

xxiv

Foreword

individualistic or highly mobile societies. In order to promote innovative pathways to healing and considerations of both the obstacles and possibilities for resilience and hope, comprehending the transformative opportunities of integrating cultural axis knowledge may move practitioners towards a more wholistic inter-disciplinary and bio-psychosocial model.

Jaswant Guzder, MD

INTRODUCTION

Roy Moodley and Eunjung Lee

The theory and practice of mental health care globally is not a new phenomena, nor one that arises in the modern era. All cultures and communities have been engaging in health, mental health and well-being of its people throughout its history. This means that it has been happening long before the rise of European psychology and psychoanalysis. One could say that it began with the dawn of civilization, and not just European civilization as is erroneously felt throughout the symbolic representations, academic and intellectual texts, and indeed the knowledge production of Western literature and science about health and mental health. Non-Western traditions of healing the body, mind and soul is as much a science of the Global South as it is in the Western world. Christian theology is replete with narratives of healing and well-being; so do many of the world religions. With enlightenment came the possibility of rationality and madness. Michel Foucault in *Madness and Civilization* (1961[1967]:3), offers a poignant reminder of the dehumanizing culture that was experienced in Europe, when he states that:

> at the end of the middle ages leprosy disappeared from the Western world … in the margins of the community, at the gates of the city there stretched wastelands … the leper vanished … structures remained. Often in the same places, the formulas of exclusion would be repeated … with an altogether new meaning in a very different culture.

Michel Foucault, as Simone Fullagar (2018: 39) suggests has an understanding of

> how 'madness' or 'mental disorder' has been problematized and made thinkable as an historical category within particular regimes of truth and are configured through power-knowledge relations … not as zero sum game nor was it a matter of ideology; rather power was understood as relational … implicated in the production of certain ways of knowing and being that could be both regulatory and normalizing, as well as resistant and subversive.
>
> *(Faucault 1980)*

Throughout the centuries those who suffered mental illness or mental ill health or psychological pain became 'abjects' (Kristeva 1982), marginalized, outcasts and driven outside the city walls. In the exploration of race, culture and mental health there appears to be strong evidence that those who suffer displacement, fragmentation and subjugation, alienation and diaspora come to experience a certain kind of exclusion 'often in the same places, the formulas of exclusion would be repeated'. The 'power-knowledge relations' has been dominated by Eurocentric ways of knowing. Suman Fernando (2017: 30–31), argues that since disciplines such as psychology, psychiatry, psychotherapy and clinical mental health developed in a Western context, "drawing little, if anything, from 'other' cultural traditions, the question arises as to its suitability *culturally* for informing mental health services meant for people whose backgrounds may not be culturally *Western*", So it may not be a matter where one is born or where one resides but that the mental health tools and processes are themselves inherently uni-cultural.

Therefore, this book represents a critical exploration of the intricate interplay of culture and mental health – its historical origins, subsequent transformations, and the discourses generated from past and present mental health and wellness practices. The focus is to examine critically the variety of ways in which socio-cultural identities of race, ethnicity and cultures, and their intersectionality with sexuality, disability, and social class are intersected in clinical and wellness work; its position in the global context and how they are part of the process of psychopathology or resilience in health and wellness. The various chapters in this book discuss ways in which global mental health practices includes and at the same time also transcend racial, cultural, ethnic, linguistic and political boundaries. As a Western cultural product, current mental health theories, practices and research reflect a particular historical, philosophical and cultural perspective; these ideas have been a major influence in determining mental health care around the world. Intersecting and juxtaposing ethnicity and race as cultural paradigms can displace, disturb and disrupt this dominance allowing for a restructuring and reformulation of existing theories and practices.

Many Global South countries and cultures find that their traditional healing practices are often silenced or viewed as the antithesis of European science; this disavowal goes back to the Colonial period and have since remained in their 'post-colonial' states. Many of the traditional healing practices are viewed or are represented as exotic, marginal, powerless, forbidden, devious, and sometimes dangerous. Indeed, while tensions will always exist between cultural and indigenous healing traditions and post-modernist clinical discourses of current mental health practices, emphasis needs to be placed on examining how these various and multifaceted ways of engaging mental health and well-being be a part of the mainstream, especially where the many of the community members are from the Global South.

De-centering a current global mental health paradigm

In exploring race, culture and mental health this book will contribute to our understanding of the nature of current shifts in professional and clinical practice, particularly in the mental health professions. Through a critical interrogation of the dominant discursive regimes of Western conventional health and mental health care theories in various clinical discourses, the volume will explore the nature of research, theory and practice in relation to all clients. Given that Western health care models and practices have evolved in one cultural frame and are now required to perform in another – a multicultural context – a crisis of theory and practice is facing mental health care in the West. These dilemmas are facing scholars, researchers, practitioners, and students in training in the various health and mental health fields, viz., mental health clinicians, nurses, doctors, psychiatrists, counselors, psychotherapists, social workers and others. While the focus is on how minoritized and racialized individuals and groups construct illness perceptions and the kinds of treatments, the larger project is to disturb, dislodge, and disengage the medical

Introduction

model of mental health, the Eurocentric and individualistic psychologies of the Euro-American capitalistic mental health industrialization of health and mental health, and focus on Global South Psychologies (Fernando and Moodley 2018). It also attempts to recover from the subjugation by colonialism the indigenous knowledge/s and healing practices that has been available for the alleviation of human suffering since 'pre-history'.

Through a critical analysis of Western psychologies and mental health practices this book will present a range of critical, theoretical and empirical accounts of the philosophies, psychologies and healing practices which have intersected with issues of the Big 7 socio-cultural identities race, gender, class, sexual orientation, disability, religion and age (Moodley 2011). Indeed, the history of psychology in history is a troubling one. Psychology was responsible through the pseudo-scientific theories (such as measuring skulls of different group to determine intelligence; using facial and skin tones to categorize humans; essentially to dehumanize one group of people over another). These ideas and theories provided the foundation for the eugenic movements, towards a justification of Colonialism, Genocides of the aboriginal peoples; the holocaust, and many others.

In an ever-increasing global mobility, immigration and globalization can be defined as the growing interconnectedness between people around the world with regards to social, political, economic, technological and cultural exchanges. Particularly in the last two decades with the growth of the internet and social media, health care ideas, theories and practices have constructed the world into a global village; within which there has been an increasing consciousness of what works clinically in what contexts for whom. Of significance are the research and practices of global mental health and its focus on diversity, differences and culturally sensitive services. In mental health care, the processes of immigration and globalization have also increased the need for countries to look beyond their borders in order to promote effective health and mental care treatments. Indeed, we are now witnessing worldwide changes in the mental health care systems brought about by the global mental health movement. For example, radical changes have been made to health care policies that are informed by randomized control trials (RCTs) and other evidence-based treatments (EBTs); or the growth of multiple therapeutic orientations endorsed by practitioners, and engaged by clients across ethnicities, sexualities and religions.

However, the global mental health movement has generally led to the domination of Western views of mental health, as well as the policies and interventions associated with it. In other words, the integration of Western Eurocentric healing strategies into the health and well-being of non-dominant communities has offered very little opportunity for other forms and formulations of healing and wellness practices to engage productively in research and theory building. For example, cultural, traditional and indigenous psychologies are not part of the paradigm of health care generally but have a strong significance in mental health practices where culturally diverse clients can appropriately seek psychic and spiritual retreats. This is due in part to the established dominant status and specialty of Western health and mental health theories as the standard approach to health and well-being. One way to address these shortcomings is to facilitate a critical discussion on ethnicity, race, culture and mental health as this book aims to do.

Many professionals in both national and private health care institutions are now sympathetic towards alternative and complementary healing practices. Minority communities have long been engaging in cultural and indigenous healing practices alongside modern medicine, but especially in relation to mental health concerns. Alongside these practices there seems to be a growing awareness of spirituality and religion as a force in healing care. However, the development of these cultural and traditional healing practices has been the philosophical, cultural and religious texts informing how if any culture, race, and ethnic historical experiences can be part of current healing traditions. While the growth and practice of indigenous psychologies is not prevalent in the West, it has been an area of recent interest in many parts of the world; some of which will be articulated in this book.

As immigration continues to characterize change in the Western world, it is imperative for practitioners, clinicians, educators, and those in training to abandon their sense of self-sufficiency and actively increase their understanding of non-Western healing traditions and practices as they exist across cultures globally. Thus through the critical exploration of ethnicity, race, and culture in mental health care this book will make a significant contribution to the already growing awareness, understanding, knowledge and practices of the current culture sensitive practices, racial identity theories, cultural competency frameworks, and many others; as well as the rich, centuries old healing traditions of the 'third world', including indigenous peoples of the West, such as the Native Americans, First Nations of Canada and Aboriginals of Australia.

Given that Western health care models and practices have evolved in one cultural frame and are now required to perform in a multicultural context, a crisis of theory and practice is facing mental health care in the West. These dilemmas are facing scholars, researchers, practitioners, and students in training in the various health and mental health fields, viz., mental health clinicians, nurses, doctors, psychiatrists, counselors, psychotherapists, social workers and others.

In sum, this book not only critically examines Western Eurocentric mental health care but defines the processes and practices of Indigenous Psychologies to explain the historical and philosophical basis of 'third world' cultural knowledge/s and how they are part of the healing repertoire of 'racialized' communities. Moreover, in connecting with current debates concerned with health, the analysis of indigenous and cultural healing practices of communities of the 'Third World' may provide a critical point of departure for highlighting challenges and transformations within the field of health and mental health for Black and Minority Ethnic (BME) groups and immigrant communities in the West. This book also engages Western practitioners to seriously consider integration of issues of race, ethnicity, and culture into mental health care and to develop and sustain a strong research culture of collaboration with traditional and contemporary forms of Global South endeavors to evolve new approaches in current health and mental health care.

How the book is organized

The various sections of the book are as follows.

Part A: Coloniality, globalization, and mental health

This section starts with re-configuring the construct of culture and race to anchor the book and then offers a comprehensive critique of the Eurocentric psychologies of the West; its roots in colonialism; its limitations; and its race and gender bias/based practices. Under the whiteness dominance, talking about race and culture and its impact on mental health of racialized people are also discussed within the white space and colonial languages. The failure of Western European mental health to meet the needs of all patients in a multicultural society is explored. Drawn from historical, geopolitical and/or post-colonial perspectives, the chapters attempt to illustrate how the Eurocentric values are marked as a norm and become dominant yet implicit in current global mental health practices. Each chapter then explores ways to de-centralize the Eurocentric values and to end epistemic injustice in mental health. Shifting and globalizing the mental health knowledge away from Eurocentric views will position anti-colonial practice into the center and shine a light for future research and practice that are grounded in indigenous cultural knowing and healing in mental health.

Introduction

Part B: Race and culture in mental health practices

The chapters in Part B discuss theories, research, and practice concerning the roles of cultural, ethnic, and racial diversity in relation to specific mental health disciplines and related professions. Organized around the development of cultural competence in clinical practice, each chapter attempts to draw on research and professional expertise to highlight important considerations regarding cultural differences, social identities and their associated strengths and risk factors, and their relationships to theory and practice in each discipline. These are illustrated through the use of two or three short case vignettes per chapter. The chapter in this section also offer recommendations for best practice with culture and discourse, highlighting unique theoretical concerns and pertinent differences in practice with respect to other mental health professions.

Part C: Culture and multiple identities in mental health

This part focus on specific identities and their relationship with mental health. The specific ways in which illness and psychological distress are represented and made meaning of through the lenses of multiple identities are discussed. Each chapter also make connections between the presenting issues and the complex ways in which diversity as a socio-cultural and psychological paradigm enters the clinical space; and, offer two or three short case vignettes to illustrate the ideas and discussion of how culture intersects with diversity and multiple socio-cultural identities and mental health.

Part D: Religion and healing in mental health

The chapters in this section explore the beliefs, practices, and experiences of specific religious groups and their relationship with mental health. The ways in which illness, psychological distress, and healing are represented and understood through the lenses of each religion are discussed, with consideration for within-group diversity, intersectionality and multiple ways of knowing. Short case vignettes are interweaved onto the chapter to illustrate the beliefs, values, practices, and experiences of each religious group as they enter the clinical space. The unique challenges and complexities of each religion's embeddedness in contemporary socio-cultural landscapes are discussed in light of their implications for mental health.

Part E: Special populations and culture in mental health

In Part E, the chapters discuss marginalized populations and their unique features and challenges in mental health. The focus is on how race, culture and ethnicity contribute to shaping mental health practices with some of these special populations. Some of the chapters also explore how human mobility and displacement from home to host nations provide a site where voluntary or forced migrants revisit representations and meanings of mental health and illness. As in the rest of the book chapters in this section also offer short case vignettes to illustrate how each special population negotiates presenting issues and struggles to make changes within their socio-cultural contexts.

Part F: Culture and mental health in a global context

These chapters explore the mental health practices of several countries. The chapters discuss the demographic context, a brief history and philosophy of mental health; how illness is conceptualized culturally in different country contexts, and the kinds of mental health care that is practiced in each country. The chapters also offer short case vignettes to illustrate the relationship between culture and mental health.

Part G: Indigenous and traditional healing in mental health

The final group of chapters discuss indigenous, cultural and traditional healing as they are practiced in contemporary mental health settings. Chapters explore traditional healing: its history, philosophy and its contemporary evolution. Some of the chapters also discuss the training of healers, their accreditation, licensure, and certification and the ways in which indigenous healing is practiced.

References

Fullagar, S. (2018). Foucauldian theory. In Cohen B. (Ed.) *Routledge International Handbook of Critical Mental Health*. Abingdon: Routledge.

Foucault, M. (1961/1967) *Madness and Civilization*. London: Routledge.

Foucault, M. (1980) *Power/Knowledge*. C. Gordon (Ed.), New York: Pantheon Books.

Kristeva, J. (1982) *Powers of Horror*. Trans. L. Roudiez. New York: Columbia University Press.

Fernando, F. (2017) *Institutional Racism in Psychiatry and Clinical Psychology: Race matters in mental health*. London: Palgrave Macmillan.

Fernando, S. and Moodley, R. (Eds.) (2018) *Global Psychologies. Mental Health and the Global South*. London: Palgrave Macmillan.

Moodley, R. (2011) *Outside the Sentence: Readings in Critical Multicultural Counselling and Psychotherapy*. Toronto: CDCP.

PART A

Coloniality, globalization, and mental health

1

CONFIGURATIONS OF RACE AND CULTURE IN MENTAL HEALTH

Roy Moodley and Sandra Osazuwa

In an age of internationalization and globalization, various terms such as race, culture, ethnicity, immigration, multiculturism, transnationalism, transculturalism, and diversity have gained popularity. Since definitions of these nomenclatures are constantly changing to match our ever-evolving societies, these terms and concepts are becoming more complex and confounding as they become increasingly politicized (Hong and Cheon 2017). According to Williams, this presents an issue as "the categories race, culture, black, have been problematized as a base on which to construct analysis" [and] "leads to a reductionist's aggregation of ethnic differences … confus[ing] practice through oversimplification, generating stereotypes and fostering ethnocentrism" (Williams 1999: 213).

Race, culture, ethnicity, multiculturalism, and many other concepts that describe cultural differences are often made complex by oversimplifying generalities and stereotypical representations of what constitutes race and ethnic cultures within a Western Eurocentric discourse. This results in social and cultural identities that are constantly enacted and manifested within socio-economic and political arenas. Indeed, meanings attributed to race, culture, and ethnicity are not fixed and constant. Rather, they are fluid and flexible, resulting in the growth of numerous ideologies, policies (e.g. social, health, etc.), and practices through the dominance of the socio-economic, political and cultural discourses prevalent within particular geopolitical spaces. Thus, attempts at engaging in discussions of race, culture, and ethnicity in health and mental health offers a discourse that is heavily laden with ideological projections and ethnic group investments where imagined cultural positions are fantasized and enacted both consciously and unconsciously through a paradigm of colonial history, individual and national struggles for independence and current Western multiculturalism. Thus, the whole enterprise of race, culture, and mental health becomes a very *thorny problem* – proposed by Solomos and Back (1995: 16), the 'thorny problem' of race presents "the question of how political identities are shaped and constructed is through the meanings attributed to race, ethnicity and nation".

In this chapter, the concepts of race and multiculturism in mental health will be discussed. Historical complexities such as slavery, colonialism, indentureship, contemporary imperialism, as well as socio-economic and cultural racism have legacies that are engrained within the systems of Western societies and the psyches of their racialized citizens (Moodley 2011). While mental health interventions can be used to support this specialized group, it is important to examine how race and scientific domains have interacted historically. Once influenced by enlightenment rhetoric and natural science methodologies, the past of supporting racist pseudo-scientific practices, ethnocentric and individualistic theories have continued implications within the field of psychology, counselling, psychotherapy, and mental health generally (see Thomas and Sillen 1972, for discussion). The central tenants of critical race theory will also be explored as it forms the foundation for any critique in relation to Western mental health care and race and culture. Through this lens, the tensions, contradictions and challenges that mental health discourses face as it moves and meanders through the complexities and confusions of multiculturalism, diversity and the intersectionality of the multiple and multicoloured matrices of the socio-cultural identities of race, culture, ethnicity, gender, sexual orientation, disability, age, and religion will be explored.

Configuring race and culture

The current usage of the term 'race' as a concept to define people from various parts of the world, is either based on a genetic, skin colour–based and pseudo-scientific understanding or one that is sociological and political. Since its first appearance in the English language in 1508, race simply referred to a category or class of persons, without any reference to anything biological (Miles 1982), and by the late eighteenth century it was tagged with a physical connotation, and by the early-nineteenth-century specific theories of racial types began to emerge (Alderman 1985; Moodley 2011). As Brantlinger (1985: 205) notes: "social darwinists were offering 'scientific' justifications for genocide as well as imperialism". From the late nineteenth century, the classification of race as a set of biological and physical meanings facilitated pseudo-scientific discussions of racially-based primal differences, with many scientists scouring for links between intelligence and certain physiological attributes (Moodley, Mujtaba, and Kleiman 2017).

Popularized by Darwin's evolution theories, scientific tools and methods were developed to determine racial superiority through physiological examinations. An example of this was cranial capacity data and skull and brain measurements concluding that blacks possessed traits associated with low-functioning brain activity, hyper-sexuality, and susceptibility to disease and insanity – which coincidentally worsened when given freedom (Stepan 1986). With white bodies performing at gold-standard in virtually every domain, scientific testing 'proved' that Europeans had a genetically superior advantage. Gaining rapid popularity, these findings were considered gospel. The data's integrity and validity rarely underwent ridicule as it confirmed what the empires already knew – Europeans were the pinnacle of humanity. What followed was an agenda of colonial and imperial dominance seeking to dehumanize, enslave, and exploit non-European peoples and lands (Moodley et al. 2017). Eugenics and Social Darwinism movements emerged with goals of strengthening the human gene pool through genocidal actions (Brantlinger 1985). Ideologies regarding genetic and racial differentiations were socially perpetuated into the twentieth-century through biblical interpretations of the curse of Ham, genetic fallacies, the mark of oppression, slavery, and segregation (Thomas and Sillen 1972; Moodley et al. 2017). These pseudo-scientific theories are now largely discredited (Moodley and Curling 2006).

An individual comes into race rather than is born of one. Indeed, one is historicized and politicized through cultural, social, and economic ideology. It is these same ideologies that are permeated with the politics of identity and relations of power. Ferber argues that if we take race for granted, "we obscure the relations of power which constitute race as a foundation. Rather than taking race for granted, we need to begin to explore the social construction of race and the centrality of racism" (Ferber 1998: 60). According to Richard T. (1993: 33), racism could be defined as:

> the inability to accept and acknowledge difference without attempting to control and dominate the object that is felt to be different and separate. The control and domination aim to reinforce the phantasy that the quality of separateness does not exist. To put it another way, the object is perceived to be similar, leading to a distorted omnipotent feeling of similarity. The creation of similarity in this way is based on infantile phantasies of introjective controlling of the object as well as projective identification with it … Because this is such a primitive and omnipotent infantile level of functioning, development is often obstructed in this area.

When deconstructing race this way, we begin to see that race enters the discourse of mental health through its creative manipulation of the *other* as an exotic, aesthetic, sensual, and primitive object. It does this while simultaneously reproducing and reinforcing two myths: the homogeneity of white and the myth of purity of the white race. Consequently, the concepts of culture and multiculturalism tend to construct the iconography of whiteness as a bland palate within which its participants are indistinguishable as opposed to the diversity concept of *'people of colour'* – a North American term that includes a wide variety of possibilities of multiple ethnicities. By constructing a global white category, an erasure takes the place of the particular ethnicities that constitute whiteness while in the process making individual subjects invisible by dismissing ethnic and cultural histories. In mental health and cultural care, this was often perpetrated by the 'multiculturalists' who privileged black and ethnic minorities and excluded white people from the process as clients by constructing the skin colour of the participants as the chief determining characteristic for selection. In addition to reinforcing pseudo-scientific racist notions and maintaining a colonial relationship as a healer and expert of the other, this practice also has serious consequences for those who are employed to work with racial, cultural, and ethnic minority clients.

More recently, it appears that the de-centring of whiteness has begun to take place. Attempting to 'colour-in-the-white', an increasing number of Europeans are starting to engage in methods that allow them to recognize their ethnic, cultural heritage – a process that has interrogated the concept of multiculturalism. In other words, it appears that the discourse of ethnicity has now entered the white word (world) and infused it with a memory of distinctive European ethnicities. Evidently, recent literature depicts the 'colouring-in-the-White' movement as one that is having a profound effect on the deconstructed forms of multiculturalism. For example, a Roth and Ivemark study that focused on the impact of genetic ancestry testing on the racial and ethnic identities of consumers indicated that "white respondents aspired to new identities more readily" (2018: 150) and "used the tests to claim multiracial or non-white identities" (2018: 153). However dubious, ideological and suspicious as an idea the concept of race tends to be, it appears it has begun to shift its meaning and is no more the prerogative of the visible minorities nor just a black attachment concept (Moodley 2011).

Race is now a white word. Now that ethnicity, race, and culture are becoming part of the white imagination, it is critical to consider what feminist scholar Sara Ahmed calls the *'declarations of whiteness'* and *'the rainbow'* view of multiculturalism which suggests that "the transformation of whiteness into a colour can work to conceal the power and privilege of whiteness" (Ahmed 2004: 10). Indeed, this rainbow view is illusionary. As white becomes more diverse, we are no longer able to measure the 'non-white' against the 'white' as the norm or yardstick – the value system to which one aspires to be accepted, to emulate and to perform the 'civilization project'. A new comparison becomes possible. No more is Black set against White. 'Colouring-in-the-white' presents a new colour scheme that sets up a palate of multicultural colours – shades of white, brown, yellow, olive, pink, and so on. With the comparison now being between Black and this new shade of multiculturalism, a rainbow with its many different colours is now set against notions of anti-blackness which tends to be consistently prominent among the different races. Social, economic and political acceptance of the 'multicultural citizen' is not based on norms of whiteness but on how different one is from Black (Moodley 2011). In other words, "you are accepted as long as you are one of us; as long as one is not black" (see Kymlicka 1998 for discussion). This experience was highlighted in writings by Kymlicka (1998) in which he uses the Canadian social situation to talk about the existence of a type of anti-Black racism where some visible minority groups create opposition to Blackness in an attempt to be part of a multicultural Canadian society (Moodley 2011).

As, culture – like race – is neither fixed nor static, it is critical to consider the ways in which it constantly changes in different times and spaces within a given society especially when approaching the topic of mental health (Moodley and Palmer 2005). Culture tends to cover a wide spectrum of meaning from customs, morals, myths, laws, art, literature, architecture, and many other attributes and artefacts related to individuals and groups within a social and geo-political constituency. Its breadth along with the general inclusion of the symbolic, physical and spiritual aspects of a community allows for culture to be filled in with whatever preconceptions a theorist manages to bring to it (Halton 1992). Related terms such as subculture, popular culture, counterculture, high culture, ethnic culture, organizational culture, mass culture, political culture, feminist culture, deaf culture, and others, have been indicative of the complexity, dynamism, and the evolving nature of the concept of culture. By not treating culture as a global entity, more nuanced meanings can be produced. This allows for it to be disaggregated into several discrete variables (e.g., values, ideologies, beliefs, preferences) to avoid any vagueness, multiple meanings, and circular definitions. Indeed,

> stripped of its dynamic social, economic, gender and historical context, culture becomes a rigid and constraining concept which is seen somehow to mechanistically determine peoples' behaviour and actions rather than provide a flexible resource for living, for according meaning to what one feels, experiences and acts to change.
>
> *(Ahmad 1996: 190)*

It is the global characterization of culture that offers methodological difficulties when an attempt is made to link it causally with phenomena in individual behaviour (Smelser 1992). This latter point is particularly important when attempting to understand mental health care. A contemporary critique of psychiatry would contend that the psychiatric discourse tends to link culture with the now outdated pseudo-scientific theories on race (see Thomas and Sillen 1972) and the Western socio-biology of culturally different clients or patients. These approaches have often resulted in particular treatments for black and minority ethnic patients, some of which would now be seen as racist (see Fernando 1988).

Culture and cultural diversity – or the 'multiplicity of cultures', are defined in various ways across the socio-economic, cultural, and political spectrum with no consensus on a single or precise definition, making it all the more difficult to ascribe meanings outside its specific set of (con)texts. Through its judicious use of the hyphen with its associated terms such as: cross-cultural, inter-cultural, trans-cultural, ethnocultural, inter-racial, trans-racial, and inter-ethnic, the diversity of cultures constructs a particular relationship between the individuals and groups who occupy this space and those who do not. Moreover, there appear to be other terms that by association attach themselves to the concept of culture, such as immigrant, inner-city, cultural food and ethnic music, post-colonial, third world, and many others; these also reinforce the prevailing notions of racialized or minoritized people as mad, bad, and sad with no interplay or creativity that is afforded to the dominant culture.

Acknowledging the potential for negative associations to form, the only way to address and responsibly circumvent this issue is to establish the multicultural field by encouraging the engagement of cultures. Parekh (2006: 338–339) defines culture and the multiplicity of cultures as a perspective that is composed of a creative interplay of:

> the inescapability and desirability of cultural diversity ... to illuminate the insights and exposé the limitations of others and create ... a vital in-between space, a kind of immanent transcendentalism, from which to arrive at a less culture-bound vision of human life and a radically critical perspective.

Yet reflecting on our current system, it seems that "a less culture-bound ... and a radical critical perspective" is far from the way in which mental health research and practice are undertaken. On the contrary, it has historically polarized cultural groups, set up binary divisions, and contributed to creating prejudices and discrimination amongst clinicians and patients alike (Moodley, 2011).

The attachment of race and culture to black and minority ethnic people has, in one way or another problematized the theory and development of mental health care. First, it constructs meanings within particular stereotypical spaces and places. This limits the opportunities for growth and newer meanings to emerge in the representations and presentations with respect to mental health. Second, it reinforces group cultures as hegemonic entities, instilling the notion that one is superior to the other and project what Dalal (2006) calls *culturalism* (akin to racism). Supporting beliefs and rhetoric that uphold the 'my culture is morally superior to yours' sentiments, cultural hegemony is often the result as it is constructed by the world view of people who identify within these categories. These ideologies tend to surpass a point that even the polarized dualism of the 'us and them' dichotomy is eclipsed by the 'us without them' dichotomy. This shift also emerges for Martin Buber's (1958) 'I and Thou', as it is reduced to the 'I without Thou' subjectivity. Both instances demonstrate that the lack of space for both subjects to simultaneously exist as the ideologies that form make it so that one becomes possible only as a result of the disavowal of the other. Within a historical context, the Aboriginal genocide in North America and Australia, the Atlantic slave trade, the Holocaust, the Rwandan genocide and many more have shown that engaging in this pursuit has often required the total extermination, annihilation, domination, and obliteration of a people using calculated means.

Critical race theory

Despite slavery and discriminatory legislation (such as, in the United States, the Jim Crow Laws; and in the race-based exclusionary immigration policies of the United Kingdom, Australia, and Canada) being overturned, racism and racial disparity has continued to operate in nuanced forms, such as income inequality, redlining, standardize testing, and race-neutral legislation (Delgado and Stefancic 2001). Recognizing these racist and systemic disadvantages that were oppressive and burdening racialize minorities, Critical Race Theory (CRT) was developed to interrogate and engender an agency of action, disruption or resistance against systemic race-based social, economic, and political racist practices.

Formally established in the mid-1970s by Derrick Bell, Richard Delgado, and Alan Freeman, CRT served as a practical change movement after the progressions of the American 1960s civil rights era ended (Delgado and Stefancic 2001). Decades after passing the Civil Rights Act, racialized citizens continued to find themselves within society's margins (Winant 1998). In response, academics, practitioners, and activists attempted to address the government's unfulfilled promise of essential civil rights statutes for minorities, and critique liberal and positivist legislative approaches. Using radical feminism and critical legal studies frameworks, CRT analyzes racial constructs within societies by theoretical exploring the thoughts of significant philosophers, radicals, and movements for racialized people. Due to its fluid nature and multiple perspectives, alternative movements have adopted CRT-inspired frameworks (e.g. Asian-American Jurisprudence, Latino-Critical Theory, Queer-Critical Theory, and Critical Indigenous Theory). Each serving unique audiences, key pieces of literature and principles are rightfully developed while continually acknowledging the strengths and validity of CRT's core principles, perspectives and methodologies.

Developing a CRT perspective: Race, culture, and mental health

With CRT providing a space for individuals and groups from a variety of backgrounds to exchange thoughts and narratives, the experiences of the underserved are being validated through extensive documentation. To encourage meaningful conversations surrounding issues of diversity and inclusion within the field of psychology, critical theorists ask academics and professionals to recognize and consider the role of several factors within Western societies:

The permanence of racism

Within the context of CRT, the permanence of racism speaks to the degree to which it is deeply ingrained into the social, political, and economic fabric of society (Hiraldo 2010). Evolving from overt occurrences to one that is subtle and ambiguous, black and other minority ethnic (BME) people continue to experience racist rhetoric (Delgado and Stefancic 2001). An example of racism that is perpetrated on a regular basis is the use of *racial microaggressions* – "brief and commonplace daily verbal, behavioural, or environmental indignities, whether intentional or unintentional, that communicate hostile, derogatory, or negative racial slights and insults toward people of colour" (Sue et al., 2007: 271). With the perpetrators being often unaware of its delivery and the receivers often left feeling conflicted as to whether they should respond at the risk of being perceived as 'overreacting', its ambiguous and their compounding nature "serve to negate one's experiences and afford narrower possibilities with one's self and others" (Moodley et al. 2017: 84).

CRT's interest in racial permanence allows for the *intersectional* examination – an assessment of social variables and how their compounding effects play out in various settings of class, power, and laws in our society (Delgado and Stefancic 2001). This approach focuses on the "multidimensionality and complexity of oppressions while addressing how multiple forms of inequity and identity interrelate in different contexts" (Moodley et al. 2017: 81). Within it, the concept of *differential racialization* – that every race has its own unique origin and developing history – is expanded to acknowledge that "no person has a single, easily stated, unitary identity. Everyone has potentially conflicting, overlapping identities, loyalties, and allegiances" (Delgado and Stefancic 2001: 9). This allows seemingly fixed constructs to be thought of as complex when discussing how oppression manifests and operates.

Liberalist ideologies

CRT encourages us to challenge current ideologies that are dominant within our society by examining the effects of the refined systematic racism that has been embedded in various societal sectors. Theorists take on the assertion that the traditional claims of objectivity, meritocracy, colour and gender blindness, law neutrality, and equal opportunity serve as fronts for the self-interest, power, and privilege of dominant groups and are not reality-based (Solórzano 1998; DeCuir and Dixson 2004). A concept that is rooted in traditionalist claims is 'colour-blindness'. Rather than advocating for an 'equality-over-equity' mindset, CRT theorists maintain that in reality, it perpetuates social inequality by disregarding individual differences and cultural backgrounds, while upholding policies rooted in racism (DeCuir and Dixson 2004). This and other problematic equality notions serve as vehicles for oppression by those at the top of society through supporting legislation that is systemically disenfranchising in addition to enacting policies that call for blanketed treatment rather than ones sourced from flexible needs-based models (Delgado and Stefancic 2001).

White dominance

CRT explores the property interest that society has placed on whiteness (DeCuir and Dixson 2004). Afforded only through inheritance, the preference of 'whiteness-over-otherness' is a societal driving-force due to its association with prosperity and freedom rights (i.e. possession, use and enjoyment, disposition, exclusion) (Hiraldo 2010). Racism perpetuated by white preference has been historically used to advance the material interests of white elites and the physical interests of the working-class (Delgado and Stefancic 2001). Our systemic reality consistently clashes with aims for diversity and inclusion because our society still supports the embedded racist paradigms it was built upon (Hiraldo 2010). Participation in this practice causes certain groups to be inherently restricted from obtaining certain goods and privileges, while whites continue to invest towards the ever-appreciating stock of whiteness to continue a streak of dominance that serves their best interests. Due to the exclusivity placed on whiteness, CRT proponents challenge barriers constructed as a means of its protection.

Interest convergence

When there is a lack of progression within a societal system, it is often found that a dominant group has little to no incentive to enact social change. CRT theorists label this occurrence as *interest convergence* and recognize whites as the historic and current primary beneficiaries of North American civil rights legislation (Hiraldo 2010). This notion becomes even more apparent when taking into consideration the purpose of the civil rights movement, where starting in the 1950s in Canada and the 1960s in the United States the racialized community worked to obtain constitutional rights that were readily afforded to white people. Additionally, as the movement adopted several minority groups that experienced oppression differently, a socially-based hierarchy of privilege emerged within it resulting in white feminists becoming the ultimate beneficiaries. A controversial example of this occurrence is the enactment of affirmative action laws. Originally developed to encourage equal opportunity and employment, affirmative action has acquired mixed reactions among whites. While much of the pushback comes from the argument that these policies disadvantage whites, reports have shown that white women have gained the most from them (Unzueta, Gutiérrez, and Ghavami 2010). This has been shown through studies examining the *glass ceiling* – a set of career advancement resistant barriers put in place for women and people of colour (Jackson and Callaghan 2009). Although women and BME people are both recognized by the US government as victims of its effects, a taxonomy of glass ceiling-related documents performed by Jackson and Callaghan (2009: 468) indicated that "only 33.3% of the definitions explicitly defined the glass ceiling in relation to race or ethnicity". CRT theorists acknowledge that while white feminists experience glass ceilings in their careers, BME groups continue to battle against several concrete barriers (Cotter et al. 2001). For this reason, proponents place importance on identifying who-benefits-from-what within societal domains.

The value of counter-narratives

Finally, CRT calls for the acknowledgement of experiential knowledge and voices of people of colour. As the accounts of Western history were recounted from the perspective of the dominant group, it is important to recognize that the history taught within our education system and disseminated through media presents a conqueror-based narrative. Rather than exclusively accepting an indoctrinated narrative, CRT calls for its advocates to legitimize the voices of marginalized people. Due to the uniqueness, complexity, and multidimensionality of their histories and experiences in relation to oppression, its theorists maintain that having a minority status affords the competency to speak on racial issues (Delgado and Stefancic 2001). Having BME people communicate their personal and communal realities to white dominant groups is crucial for developing conversations that can lead to change. With a variety of delivery methods that include storytelling, family histories, biographies, scenarios, parables and more, these narratives work together to analyze and validate the cultural climates and experiences of racial minorities (Solórzano 1998).

Conclusion

Considering the race-driven transgressions experienced by cultural groups historically, CRT serves as a pillar of cultural significance and tool of necessity. Through the movement, complex conversations of race in relation to mental health concepts can be formulated in attempts to address the ambiguities and complications that make common appearances in the domains of psychology and psychotherapy. The euro-centric origin of the field and low rates of minority practitioners raises concerns about the competency levels of clinicians when working with racialized clients.

Applying a critical race perspective provides a starting point for practitioners who may be unfamiliar with the unique struggles experienced by their minority clients, where they could adopt new insights. In turn, time and space within the therapy room could be used to discuss culture and ethnic issues (e.g. immigration, assimilation versus acculturation) as well as issues that centre around the topic of race (e.g. colourism, microaggressions, racial climate). These discussions foster client-practitioner rapport, allowing clinicians to spark conversations of histories revealing circumstances like transgenerational trauma or deeply ingrained internalized racism. This fosters the practitioner's ability to explore elements of racism and misogyny within the social constructs of race, while also exhibiting consideration for clients' intersectional identity (Moodley et al. 2017). The developing relationship between CRT perspective and the mental health field continues to facilitate healthy nuanced discussions that ultimately work to generate new spaces and opportunities that allow for a more inclusive health care system.

References

Ahmad, W. I. U. (1996) Trouble with culture, in D. Kelleher and S. Hillier (eds), *Researching cultural differences in health*. London: Routledge.

Ahmed, S. (2004) Declarations of whiteness: The non-performativity of Anti-racism. *Borderlands*, 3(2): 1–16.

Alderman, G. (1985) Explaining racism. *Political Studies*, 33: 129–135.

Brantlinger, P. (1985) Victorians and Africans: The genealogy of the myth of the dark continent. *Critical Inquiry*, 12(1): 166–203.

Buber, M. (1958) *I and thou*. New York: Scribner.

Cotter, D. A., Hermsen, J. M., Ovadia, S., and Vanneman, R. (2001) The glass ceiling effect. *Social Forces*, 80(2): 655–681.

Dalal, F. (2006) Culturalism in multiculturalism psychotherapy, in R. Moodley and S. Palmer (eds), *Race, culture and psychotherapy*. London: Routledge.

DeCuir, J. T. and Dixson, A. D. (2004) 'So when it comes out, they aren't that surprised that it is there': Using critical race theory as a tool of analysis of race and racism in education. *Educational Researcher*, 33(5): 26–31.

Delgado, R. and Stefancic, J. (2001) *Critical race theory: An introduction*. New York: New York University Press.

Ferber, A. L. (1998) Constructing whiteness: The intersections of race and gender in US white supremacist discourse. *Ethnic and Racial Studies*, 21: 48–63.

Fernando, S. (1988) *Race and culture in psychiatry*. Kent: Croom Helm.

Halton, E. (1992) The cultic roots of culture, in R. Munch and N. J. Smelser (eds), *Theory of culture*. Berkeley/Los Angeles: University of California Press.

Hiraldo, P. (2010) The role of critical race theory in higher education. *The Vermont Connection*, 31(1), 7.

Hong, Y. Y. and Cheon, B. K. (2017) How does culture matter in the face of globalization? *Perspectives on Psychological Science*, 12(5): 810–823.

Jackson, J. F. and O'Callaghan, E. M. (2009) What do we know about glass ceiling effects? A taxonomy and critical review to inform higher education research. *Research in Higher Education*, 50(5): 460–482.

Kymlicka, W. (1998) *Finding our way: Rethinking ethnocultural relations in Canada*. Oxford: Oxford University Press.

Miles, R. (1982) *Racism and migrant labour*. London: Routledge & Kegan Paul.

Moodley, R. and Curling, D. (2006) on culture (pp. 129–130), ethnicity (pp. 189–190), multiculturalism (pp. 385), race (pp. 324–325), in Y. Jackson (ed.), *Encyclopedia of multicultural psychology*. Thousand Oaks, CA: Sage.

Moodley, R. and Palmer, S. (Eds) (2005) *Race, culture and psychotherapy: Critical perspectives in multicultural practice*. London: Routledge.

Moodley, R., Mujtaba, F., and Kleiman, S. (2017) Critical race theory and mental health, in M. Z. Cohen (ed), *Routledge international handbook of critical mental health*. London: Routledge.

Moodley, R. (2011) *Outside the sentence: Readings in critical multicultural counselling and psychotherapy*. Toronto: Centre for Diversity in Counselling and Psychotherapy.

Moodley, R. (2014) Ethno-racial representations and the burden of 'Otherness' in mental health, in R. Moodley and M. Ocampo (eds), *Critical psychiatry and mental health*. London: Routledge.

Parekh, B. (2006) *Rethinking multiculturalism: Cultural diversity and political theory* (2nd edn). London: Palgrave Macmillan.

Richard, T. (1993) Racism and similarity: Paranoid-schizoid structures, *British Journal of Psychotherapy*, 10(1): 33–43.

Roth, W. D. and Ivemark, B. (2018) Genetic options: The impact of genetic ancestry testing on consumers' racial and ethnic identities. *American Journal of Sociology*, 124(1): 150–184.

Smelser, N. J. (1992) Culture: Coherent or incoherent, in R. Munch and N. J. Smelser, (eds), *Theory of culture*. Berkeley and Los Angeles: University of California Press.

Solomos, J. and Back, L. (1995) *Race, politics and social change*. London: Routledge.

Solórzano, D. G. (1998) Critical race theory, race and gender microaggressions, and the experience of Chicana and Chicano scholars. *International Journal of Qualitative Studies in Education*, 11(1): 121–136.

Stepan, N. L. (1986) Race and gender: The role of analogy in science. *Isis*, 77(2): 261–277.

Sue, D. W., Bucceri, J., Lin, A. I., Nadal, K. L., and Torino, G. C. (2007) Racial micro aggressions and the Asian American experience. *Asian American Journal of Psychology*, 5(1): 88–101.

Thomas, A. and Sillen, S. (1972) *Racism and psychiatry*. New York: Brunner/Mazel.

Unzueta, M. M., Gutiérrez, A. S., and Ghavami, N. (2010) How believing in affirmative action quotas affects White women's self-image. *Journal of Experimental Social Psychology*, 46(1): 120–126.

Williams, C. (1999) Connecting anti-racist and anti-oppressive theory and practice: Retrenchment or reappraisal, *British Journal of Social Work*, 29: 211–230.

Winant, H. (1998) Racism today: Continuity and change in the post-civil rights era. *Ethnic and Racial Studies*, 21(4): 755–766.

2

COLONIALITY, INDIGENEITY, AND MENTAL HEALTH

Tony B. Benning

This chapter's principal contribution to the present volume of writings on race, culture, and mental health lies in its discussion of the relevance of post-colonial thought as well as settler colonial studies to the interface between indigeneity and the Western mental health professions. The latter category encompasses counselling, clinical psychology, and psychiatry. Many scholars in the emerging field of colonial settler studies argue that post-colonial theory, either because it is too broad in its scope, or for other reasons, is inclined to understate the incorrigible persistence of the colonial dynamic in the contemporary world. Notwithstanding the existence of important areas of overlap between post-colonial and colonial settler studies, the latter can bring into especially sharp clarity – for mental health clinicians – colonialism's persisting imprint on the relationship between Western mental health professions and indigeneity.

Thurner (2003) argues that the binary colonizer/colonized relationship that characterized the era of European political colonialism continues to manifest in the contemporary world, despite the formal period of colonialism having ended. The purported persistence of that binary renders the term *post-colonial* problematic because of its semantic implication that colonialism *was* a historical event that has since been consigned to the past (Mishra and Hodge 1991). Childs and Williams (1997) also call attention to the problematic nature of the term post-colonial, doing so by pointing out that the colonial scenarios in the British and French empires and those of Spain and Portugal, are very different from those of Latin America, which in turn are different from that of the United States and so forth.

The Peruvian sociologist Anibal Quijano (2000) is an influential exponent of the idea that colonialism has not been super-ceded by some sort of *post*-colonial historical stage, certainly in the Americas. Quijano prefers the term 'coloniality of power' (2000:536) to capture the idea that those 'Eurocentric' (2000:534) power hierarchies that characterized political colonialism continue to be alive and well – as contemporaneous facts. Such broadly-endorsed sentiments find expression in the emerging field of settler colonial studies (Wolfe 1999; Veracini 2011) and in the use of the term colonialism by contemporary commenters on indigeneity (see, for example, Alfred and Corntassel 2005; Cannon and Sunseri 2011; Coulthard 2014).

Terms such as *indigenous* and *indigeneity* are not devoid of controversy either (Kuper 2003), but for the purposes of this chapter, the term indigeneity is understood – in keeping with an influential definition from convention 169 of the International Labour Organization (1989) – to refer to peoples 'whose ancestors have lived in the area before the settlement or the formation of modern state borders' (article 1). The author of the present chapter, as a psychiatrist who works with indigenous communities in British Columbia in Canada, is committed to understanding the nature of the relationship between indigeneity and the Western mental health professions. This chapter seeks to understand how post-colonial theory and the new settler colonial studies can contribute to the understanding of that relationship. By way of foregrounding that inquiry the chapter will begin with a presentation of the basic proposition that the inherent reductionism within modern Western models of mind and mental illness fail to adequately grasp the sociogenic basis of mental illness among indigenous peoples. That idea was in fact one to which the Martiniqean psychiatrist Frantz Fanon subscribed, and the initial section will be followed by a necessarily abbreviated discussion of some of Fanon's major ideas as well those of post-colonial theorists Gayatri Spivak, Homi Bhabha and Edward Said. There will also be a discussion of a body of literature that sought to overturn so-called progressivist theories of socio-historical development. That will be followed by an overview of some models of service provision that followed in the wake of independence, in Nigeria and in Jamaica. Some theoretical models as well as models of service provision that transcend the colonizer/colonized dialectic will be highlighted. Given the contention by scholars in the emerging field of settler colonial studies (Wolfe 1999; Veracini 2011) that the circumstances of indigenous people fall in the peripheries of the concerns of post-colonial studies, this chapter will ask what settler colonial studies might add to the understanding of the indigeneity/mental health interface.

Critique of Western explanatory models and conceptualizations of mental illness

Implicit in the writings of several authors (see, for example, Duran and Duran 1995; Tatz 2001) is an assertion that any etiological theory of indigenous psycho-pathology is unlikely to have merit if it is not grounded within a suitable ecological paradigm. That means that in the absence of an ecological paradigm that goes beyond the mere neuroscientific level of explanation, justice is not likely to be done to the pathogenic role of socio-historical trauma in accounting for the burden of indigenous mental illness. Tatz's (2001) indictment of biological reductionism and determinism in his discussion of Aboriginal suicide speaks to the intersectionality of ethics, politics, and medical/psychiatric explanation. He argues that biochemical and genetic levels of explanation have limited explanatory power given that they overlook the etiological role of socio-historical factors in suicide. But Tatz (2001: 143) goes further, by asserting that explanations at the biological level are 'damaging to the people under scrutiny'. This assertion is supported by his citing of a report on high rates of infant mortality in Australia's Northern territory in the 1970s in which the significance of environmental factors was all but elided in favor of a discussions about Aboriginal women's purportedly high 'genetic predisposition in Aboriginal women to see their babies die' (Tatz 2001: 143). Similar sentiments – questioning the legitimacy of Western explanatory paradigms to in purporting to explain indigenous psychopathologies – are echoed by Duran and Duran (1995) in their critique of the dominant theories of alcoholism within native communities. Their critique is a balanced one in that they avoid the temptation of jumping off one totalizing explanatory band-wagon onto another; they are cognizant and critical of the positivistic underpinnings of Western theories of psycho-pathology, but they are at pains not to entirely jettison either the medical model or the psychodynamic explanatory paradigm. It is just that neither of those explanatory paradigms on their own do justice to the etiological significance of socio-historical factors in the etiology of alcoholism. In fact, purely medical or psychological theorizing is likely to deflect from an appreciation of the fact that such factors as degree of social disintegration are posited as being correlated to rates of alcoholism.

Post-colonial theory and indigenous mental health

What is the essence of post-colonial theory? What are the field's major ideas and theoretical commitments? Who are the field's major contributors? The notion of a post-colonial *canon* is rendered somewhat problematic by the fact that post-colonial theorists are given to paying close attention to that which is silenced and that which is given voice. That said, there is no denying the fact that there is a cohesive (albeit still evolving) body of work and a set of ideas that help to define the field of post-colonial theory. Of significance to the concerns of the present chapter is the fact that one of the most important post-colonial thinkers, Frantz Fanon (1994a, 1994b, 2007, 2008) was a psychiatrist; Fanon grew critical of the psychologism that he saw as being inherent to psychiatry and psycho-analysis (Adams 1970). For Fanon, the *intra-psychic* level of analysis to which psychiatry and psycho-analysis are inclined, downplays the etiological significance – with respect to mental illness – of such *social* ills as poverty and racial discrimination. Fanon's contention was that the language of *psycho*-pathology, in locating pathology *intra*-psychically, overlooks its *extra*-psychic origins.

As superintendent of the hospital in Bilda, Algeria, it came to Fanon's attention that indigenous Arabic men were disinclined to participate in the dominant modes of therapy that were being offered at the institution. This observation helped Fanon to understand that therapy is laden with cultural assumptions that may render it alien to patients from certain backgrounds. Robertson and Walters (2009) cite Fanon's ideas about the sociogenic nature of mental illness and his calling of attention to psychiatry's complicity in the imposition on colonized peoples of Western cultural hegemonies, as being among those ideas that have the most relevance for contemporary psychiatry. Fanon's writing engenders an awareness of the colonial commitments within Western mental health discourse, and of the fact that Western mental health professions remain characterized by a psychologism that downplays the role of socio-historic trauma in its conceptualizations of illness causation. Fanon's basic insight can engender a greater awareness among clinicians of reductive explanatory paradigms in general, not only psychologism. The reductionistic biologism of today is no less problematic and no less a cause for concern for, like psychologism, it marginalizes the sorts of socio-historical levels of explanation that are essential to understanding the etiology of mental illness among indigenous peoples (Marsella 2010). For the above reasons, Fanon remains highly relevant to contemporary clinicians engaged in the project of delivering mental health services to indigenous peoples (Benning 2017).

Like Fanon, the figures of Edward Said (1978) and Gayatri Spivak (1988) loom large over contemporary post-colonial thought. Spivak's (1988) most celebrated essay *Can the subaltern speak?* was considered by Byrd and Rothberg (2011:1) to have been an 'inaugurating moment of post-colonial studies in the US ...' Spivak asserts that the West produces knowledge of the subjects of the third world in a way that entails the former speaking *about* the latter for the former's benefit in a manner that is akin to the production of knowledge during the European colonial project (Morris 2010). As Spivak is to the *subaltern* Said is to the *Oriental* subject. The very concept of *the Orient,* for Said, represents a European construction of the non-European *other* in a manner that also sub-serves and is rooted in European imperialist agendas. Said was influenced by Foucault's writings on the relationship between power and knowledge but was critical of Foucault for 'neglecting the possibilities of resistance' (Kennedy 2000:30).

Byrd and Rothberg (2011:1) assert that Spivak's most famous publication has 'important implications for those working in indigenous studies'. The same can be said of Said's Orientalism.

This othering that is of central concern to both Said and Spivak is predicated on an uneven power relationship between the European *representer* and the non-European *represented*. That power differential is something that indigenous activists are trying to resist in the contemporary colonial setting, and they are doing so by reclaiming the right to represent themselves (Battiste 2011). Said and Spivak can serve as conceptual touchstones for mental health clinicians working with indigenous people – reminding them of the importance of listening more and talking less (Carey and Dudgeon 2017). As well, Said and Spivak can remind clinicians of the need to cultivate a self-reflexive awareness of the huge power-gradient separating mental health professions and indigeneity and how one way in which that power-gradient is manifest is in the way that the former has a unidirectional power to represent the latter. As well, there has been a growing interest among indigenous people to reclaim ownership of research activities, which means not only indigenous involvement in every step of the research process but the use of research methods that are congruent with indigenous ethics and cosmologies (see for example, Wilson 2008). Clinicians need to facilitate and be respectful of these processes.

A new historicity

An assumption that has sat at the core of the Western psyche for centuries is that Western civilization represents the top rung of a socio-historical developmental ladder which indigeneity is situated at the bottom of. Homi Bhabha (1988: xxiv), in his introduction to Fanon's *Black Skin White Masks* notes that the disruption of such *progressivist* narratives of Western history constitutes a central characteristic of the anti-colonial struggle. Western mental health discourses have been complicit in reproducing and perpetuating such progressivist models of socio-historical development. This is to say that indigenous worldviews, conceptualizations of mind, healing practices and so forth have all been pathologized and as well as otherwise deprecated at the hands of Western mental health professions (Benning 2014; Waldram 2004).

However, an important turning point came in recent decades with the publication of several texts. They include *Colonial Psychiatry and the African Mind* (McCulloch 1995), *Imperial Bedlam* (Sadowsky 1999), *Colonial Madness* (Keller 2007), *Psychiatry and Empire* (Mahone and Vaughan, 2007), and *Revenge of the Windigo* (Waldram 2004). The significance of those texts is that they reflected a new awareness of mental health professions' (principally psychiatry's) complicity in the colonial deprecation of indigenous peoples. As such, those texts contributed to a revised understanding of history (a new historicity) that was no longer able to blindly endorse progressivist depictions of the history of either the Western mental health professions or of Western civilization. One of Aimé Césaire's (1972) great insights about the legacy of colonialism was that it forced a re-evaluation of Europeans' benign self-image. For Cesar, one of the legacies of colonialism is that it led to self-confrontation on the part of the colonizing powers that changed, irrevocably, their understanding of themselves. And this is exactly what the texts achieved for the Western mental health professions.

Western psychology's progressivist commitments continue to be exposed. Celia Brickman (2003), for example, in her *Aboriginal populations in the mind* argues that Freudian psychoanalysis perpetuates colonial assumptions of racial hierarchy by conflating racialized notions of primitivity with pathology. Acknowledging her indebtedness to the historian of anthropology George Stocking (1968), Brickman identifies and is critical of the assumptions of the comparative method in anthropology, assumptions which, as she contends, suffuse Freudian psychoanalytic theory. In *C.G. Jung and the Sioux Traditions*, Vine Deloria Jr. (2009) finds a similar commitment (to a comparative anthropological method) in Jung's writings. On the one hand, Jung had a deep interest in North American indigenous culture, something that was reflected

Coloniality, Indigeneity, and Mental Health

and catalyzed by his visit to the Taos Pueblo in New Mexico in the winter of 1924. But Jung was also influenced by the prevailing attitudes of his time concerning about human evolution – such as those that were espoused by the Belgian anthropologist Levi-Bruhl – which understood so-called primitive peoples to belong to 'an undeveloped position in an evolutionary trajectory' (Vine Deloria Jr. 2009:37).

Psychiatry after colonial withdrawal

Following Jamaica's gaining of independence from Britain in 1962 and Nigeria's in 1960, psychiatrists in both of those countries aspired to re-envision mental health services not only so that they would be in line with indigenous worldviews and belief systems of those two respective countries but also that they would take into consideration the way in which the experience of colonialism colors patients' clinical presentations. By looking at the work of Thomas Lambo (Asuni 1967; Sadowsky 1999) in Nigeria and Fred Hickling (2007) in Jamaica, the focus of this section is to suggest that there are important parallels between different post-colonial contexts. The significance for that for mental health professionals working in indigenous settings is that mental health professionals may be informed by other post-colonial contexts.

Key to understanding Hickling's (2007) psycho-historiographic model of brief cultural psychotherapy is to appreciate the context in which it was developed. In that regard, Hickling writes that the model was created in a Jamaica newly independent from Britain while also acknowledging his indebtedness to the writings of Frantz Fanon. Echoing Fanon, Hickling is critical of the lack of attention given to cultural factors in Freudian therapy. A central concept in Hickling's model is an understanding of the nature of the self that encompasses familial as well as social dimensions. Such a multi-layered conceptualization of self is pictorially represented with the individual self at the center of a circle which is surrounded by a series of concentric circles (depicting the familial self, social self and so on). The entirety of the concentric circles is traversed by a series of what Hickling (2007:196) refers to as 'dialectics' that include black/white, colonizer/colonized, oppressor/oppressed, and so forth. As a way of rehabilitating indigenous approaches to healing, poetry, story-telling, and folk traditions are all recognized for their potential therapeutic role in the psycho-historiographic cultural therapy model. A particularly instructive vignette concerned the case of a mixed race (black father and white mother) 14-year-old boy presenting with conduct problems and anti-authoritarianism. In his formulation of the case, Hickling identifies the boy's experience of oppression at the social level as a key etiological factor in explaining the boy's rebellious nature. A key strategy in Hickling's (2007:195) therapeutic work with the boy included encouraging the boy to facilitate 'the encouragement of his understanding of the historical struggles of the Jamaican people'.

In Nigeria, as Sadowsky (1999:42) notes, psychiatrists including Lambo and Asuni were 'were critical of colonialism in both explicit and implicit ways'. Lambo was very much invested in 'the decolonization of psychiatric practice in Nigeria' (Heaton 2013:77) and his creation of the 'village system' (Asuni 1967:764) as part of the development of the famous Aro hospital would bring him national and international recognition. In the village system mentally ill patients' and their relatives stayed as lodgers in houses in the villages surrounding the hospital. It was acknowledged that the environment of psychiatric hospitals could be alienating for many Nigerians and so residing in the village afforded those patients the opportunity to access hospital treatment while they essentially continued to live with family members, in benign environments. Traditional healers were also used within the village system at Aro (Heaton 2013; Sadowsky 1999), and that, as Sadowsky (1999:43) writes, was regarded by Lambo as a 'retort to the arrogance of Western medical science and its assumption that it alone provides the keys to health'.

Different (post)colonial mental health contexts

The present author's contention in this section is that insights derived from any given post(colonial) mental health context have the potential to inform the understanding of other post(colonial) mental health contexts. That is to say that there is great potential for a kind of mutual illumination to take place when we consider one or more contexts in the light of others.

This point will be illustrated by a discussion in what follows of the writings of two psychiatrists from the United Kingdom, Suman Fernando (1991) and Begum Maitra (2008) warrant mention insofar that their insights and analyses, though from an ostensibly non-indigenous *post-colonial* context, can inform the indigenous *colonial* context. As emigres to the United Kingdom from the Indian subcontinent Fernando (from Sri Lanka) and Begum (from India) redefined what was considered permissible to write about and speak about in British psychiatry. Fernando (1991), in his acclaimed *Race, Culture, and Mental Health* critiqued the unacknowledged universalist pretensions of psychiatry and was one of the first to bring attention to institutional racism within British psychiatry. Maitra brought attention to cultural difference in healthcare settings arguing that while it often plays out in psychiatrist-patient interactions as well as in interdisciplinary interactions, these issues are rarely the subject of scholarly reflection. In addition to those discussions, Maitra's cautions about essentialist interpretations of traditional identity as well as her cautions about the uncritical adoption of Western conceptualizations about health outcomes remain relevant to the work of mental health professionals working with indigenous communities.

Transcending the colonizer-colonized dialectic

At least as insofar as the Western mental health professions are concerned, one of the ways on which Western thought assumes a position of dominance over non-Western, traditional, and indigenous forms of knowing is to peddle the often-unacknowledged assumption of universality (Benning 2016). In the previous section we saw how the exposing of this fallacy of universalism within the Western mental health theory and practice and its critical deconstruction constitute important strategies in the work of contemporary post-colonial mental health scholars (Duran 2006). Universalism overlooks and denies differences between Western and non-Western cultures and is given to deliver a one size fits all conceptual framework. Given that fact, it is not surprising that post-colonial theorists have sought to bring attention to the *differences* between cultures and, therefore, between systems of psychology that the universalizing tendencies of Western psychology have all but conspired against. The danger, however, is this: in countering the denial of difference that is implicit to universalism, there is a risk of the pendulum swinging too far in the opposite direction to such an extent that an equally unsatisfactory scenario results, one in which similarities and continuities between cultures come to be overlooked and differences overstated. What we are left with in such a scenario is the creation of a binary that itself runs the risk of recapitulating and reinforcing, rather than mitigating, the dichotomous colonizer-colonized dynamic.

This dilemma is in fact one with which post-colonial thinkers have engaged, with Chamberlin (2000:132) acknowledging that 'there are certainly hazards in relying on binary oppositions'. In the present author's opinion, a satisfactory solution can only come from an acknowledgement that though there are differences, they must be understood as being underpinned by a substratum of commonality, one that is able to transcend the differences without denying them. In other words, the ideal understanding of the relationship between Western thought and indigeneity is one that can simultaneously embrace the polarizing motifs of *sameness* and *difference*; of *universalism* and *particularism*, in way that avoids over-identification with either position.

For several contemporary writers who are grappling with the theoretical and pragmatic issues pertaining to the delivery of mental health services to indigenous communities, either/or constructs tend to be eschewed in favor of both/and hybrid ones. This is the case at conceptual and pragmatic levels. Overmars (2010), for example, offers a balanced discussion of the issue of psychiatric diagnosis in relation to mental illness among indigenous people. He certainly calls for cautious approach but also acknowledges the usefulness of diagnosis. Similarly, Gone (2009) acknowledges the utility of Western rationality in furthering the cause of indigenous people without being oblivious to its limitations. Discussions of adapted cognitive behavior therapy (see, for example, Bigfoot and Schmidt 2010; Nowrouzi et al. 2015), and two-eyed seeing (Martin 2012) reflect the same conciliatory principle.

In discussing Aboriginal health in hospital settings, Walker et al. (2009:11) endorse a hybrid model too: 'Genuine cross-cultural competency in health requires the effective integration of traditional and contemporary knowledge and practices' and in fact, such blended models of mental healthcare delivery aiming to blend contemporary and traditional approaches are increasingly held up as the ideal for indigenous mental health care delivery, around the world (see, for example, Benning et al. 2017; Crowe Salazar 2007; Maar and Shawande 2010; Marsh et al. 2015; Menzies et al. 2010; NiaNia et al. 2017).

The idea of 'hybridity' (Bhabha 1994: 277) that the above formulations evoke, is central to late-twentieth and early-twenty-first-century post-colonial discourses. It is an idea that emphasizes the inherent mutuality within the inter-cultural encounter (Ashcroft et al. 1998). It is also an idea that does justice to the inter-dependent nature of the relationship between colonizer and colonized – permitting the emergence of a non-oppositional 'third space' (Bhabha 1994:53). Note the resonance here with Willie Ermine's (2007:194) concept of 'ethical space' which, similarly, affords space in which collaborative dialogue can emerge between parties who would otherwise relate only antagonistically. Hybridity is therefore an inherently optimistic idea, allowing, as Bettez (2012:33) puts it, for the possibility of 'empowerment for the colonized agent'. Further, hybridity implies a post-essentialist cultural identity that does not assume individuals to be ossified black boxes, devoid of agency, subject to the externally determining influence of their socio-historical circumstances (Kirmayer et al. 2008). To the contrary, a post-essentialist view of culture and identity retains the role of agency and self-determination as an individual navigates her way through a veritable smorgasbord of possible cultural identifications.

Writing to transgress

The colonial predicament should engender moral outrage. It was in an atmosphere of outrage, after all, that post-colonial theory initially emerged. Bhabha's (1994:58) description of Fanon as 'the purveyor of transgressive and transitional truth' captures very well the essence of post-colonial theory – as a body of ideas that problematize the status quo with the intention of demanding change. The work of contemporary post-colonial theorists arguably reflects the same values; akin to a sort of ethical watchdog they are ever-vigilant to the persisting colonial imprimatur and are willing to speak up with intention of exposing inequities. Post-colonial theory allows for a defiance (Rukundwa and Van Aarde 2007) that is necessary to resist established power hierarchies and its language is therefore often uncompromising (Young 2003).

The focus of this chapter is mental health and indigeneity. Arguably, there is not enough moral outrage on the part of government or society-at-large in response to the inordinately high rates of psychiatric morbidity and suicide throughout indigenous communities, globally. Equally outrageous is the assumption that the biological reductionist of contemporary Western psychiatry is a suitable paradigm within which to conceptualize the epidemic of mental illness and suicide in indigenous communities.

Settler colonial studies and the indigeneity/mental health interface

What are the distinctive characteristics of settler colonial studies? What are that field's implications for mental health practice? How should the relationship between post-colonial studies and colonial settler studies be understood? Settler colonial studies and fields with which it has close relationships, such as indigenous studies and subaltern studies (Byrd and Rothberg 2011), paint uncompromisingly candid portraits of the contemporary indigenous situation and its socio-historical antecedents. In comparison to post-colonial studies, one finds within settler colonial studies a greater commitment to identifying and resisting institutionally entrenched power differentials by calls for self-determination and self-governance (Coulthard 2014) and assertion of indigenous paradigms (Turner 2006). For its deep attunement to the power hierarchies within the contemporary colonial encounter, the field of colonial settler studies remains unrivalled. So much so that the criticism levelled against Bhabha's post-colonial hybridity theory, that it 'usually implies negating and neglecting the imbalance and inequality of the power relations it references' (Ashcroft et al.1998:119) is unlikely to acquire any traction whatsoever if made against settler colonial studies.

There are several implications of settler colonial studies for mental health clinicians. First, clinicians need to be cognizant of the fact that the very fact of being colonized, as Fanon understood, is of etiological significance with respect to mental illness. Contemporary commentators (see, for example, Richmond and Ross 2009) often discuss this point by invoking the rubric of *determinants of health* given that factors such as low income and poor housing (all of which have consistently been shown to be higher in indigenous communities) correlate with poor mental health. Further, there is an increasing appreciation of the intergenerational legacy of socio-cultural trauma, as the high rates of suicide among descendants of survivors of Canada's residential school system attest (Elias et al. 2012).

The second implication – following on from and closely related to the first – is that clinicians need to be aware of the way in which institutional structures and practices reproduce the colonial dynamic. The multifarious manifestations of that are akin to an interlacing web of such elements as racism and discrimination (Goodman et al. 2017; Menzies et al. 2010) within healthcare services, cultural insensitivity, and various other forms of structural violence (Hole et al. 2015).

The third implication can be articulated as follows; the history of colonial subjugation of indigenous paradigms casts a long shadow and so the assertion of indigenous paradigms cannot be considered in isolation from the anti-colonial struggle. It is especially non-indigenous clinicians who needs to be mindful of the play of such dynamics in the cultural transference since clinicians are likely to encounter patients who are suspicious that Western mental health professions reflect a form of cultural domination vis-à-vis the imposition of a Western worldview. The following case vignette illustrates these issues: An 18-year-old male suffering from anxiety and drug addiction had come from Vancouver to stay at a First Nation in the Fraser Valley to participate in the longhouse ceremonies over the winter. The ceremonialists were concerned about him enough to suggest that he see a psychiatrist, but the patient was reluctant to see a 'Western doctor'. The patient agreed to see a psychiatrist on the condition that a traditional healer be present at the meeting. To minimize the barriers to care, the psychiatrist visited the First Nation and there indeed was a 3-way meeting between the patient, traditional healer, and the psychiatrist. The traditional healer acted as an ally and an advocate for the patient and his presence helped significantly to lessen the power differential between patient and psychiatrist. Within a few sessions, the patient felt comfortable enough to disclose some culturally congruent beliefs he held about local indigenous mythology. He disclosed that his reticence about seeing a psychiatrist stemmed from a fear that his beliefs would be pathologized as 'delusions'. The patient felt reassured that the traditional healer's presence would buffer against such inappropriate pathologization.

The fourth implication is that clinicians ought to cultivate a hyper-sensitive awareness of the asymmetry (Benning 2016) that is liable to attend all aspects of the Western mental health professions/indigeneity dyad. Examples include the privilege that is likely to be accorded to Western explanatory models/conceptualizations of mental illness at the expense of indigenous ones and the uncritical deployment, in indigenous settings, of research and evaluative methods that are rooted within Western positivist paradigms. It is incumbent upon mental health clinicians, if they are going to play a role in identifying and dismantling those asymmetries, to exercise integrity, humility, and self-reflexivity. Without those values, the asymmetries – and the colonial dynamic underpinning them – remain unchecked. The recent apology made to Australian Aboriginal and Torres Strait Islander people by the Australian psychological society (Carey et al. 2017) represents a good recent example of humility. The acknowledgement of psychology's complicity in the colonial subjugation of Australian Aboriginal peoples (through, for example, inappropriate diagnoses and the use of culturally-insensitive rating instruments, etc.) contained within that apology set a precedent that one hopes will be replicated in other colonial contexts. The following case demonstrates how the flattening of the hierarchy between Western and indigenous explanatory models of illness can contribute to a favorable clinical outcome. A 50-year-old lady from a First Nation near the town of Chilliwack in BC presented with a 6-month history of depressed mood and such symptoms as sleep disturbance, poor appetite, diminished motivation, loss of interest and so on. As the patient's narrative unfolded, her psychiatrist was able to ascertain from her the that a local elder had informed her that what she was experiencing amounted to a spirit sickness and that she would be advised to undergo initiation as a spirt dancer in the upcoming winter ceremonials. A key role here for the psychiatrist was to respect her and the elder's explanatory model. Such a respectful approach facilitated rapport and was thought to be a factor that influenced the patient to undergo antidepressant treatment and to continue seeing the psychiatrist for supportive psychotherapy. The positive outcome seen over the ensuing months was thought to have been brought about by the patient's simultaneous acceptance of Western treatments and traditional spiritual/healing practice.

This section has emphasized the distinctive characteristics of colonial settler studies and has sought to examine some of its implications for mental health clinicians. This is not to say, though, that there are not overlaps between colonial settler studies and post-colonial studies. There are; just consider the fact that Fanon is discussed under the auspices of both post-colonial and colonial settler studies and the fact that both are undergirded by a strong transgressive ethos (Krautwurst 2013). As well, the insights from post-colonial theorists Said, Bhabha, and Spivak remain highly relevant to the contemporary colonial situation, in which they have a potent power to engender a hyper-reflexive awareness among clinicians of the way in which mental health practice produces knowledge about the colonized subject.

Consider, as well, the fact that the major principles of Hickling's psycho-historiography in Jamaica as well as Lambo's decolonized psychiatry in Nigeria have clear relevance to settler colonial mental health settings. The same is true for the writings and thought of Suman Fernando and Begum Maitra. Such observations speak to the existence of equivalences between many (post)colonial settings, internationally, across time and space. Cognizance of those equivalences need not imply a lack of appreciation of the uniqueness of local factors and can greatly inform the work of clinicians.

Future directions

In terms of potential future research directions, there is a dearth of either qualitative or quantitative empirical literature examining and documenting indigenous people's experience of mental health services. Several questions therefore remain unanswered: *Are clients who self-identify as indigenous likely than non-indigenous patient populations to be offered psychotherapy? To be incarcerated under the mental health act? Do indigenous people perceive that mental health professionals inquire into their worldviews and explanatory models in respectful ways and then incorporate that information into treatment planning?*

As well, a potentially profitable theoretical area to pursue would be to examine the relationship between the Western mental health professions and indigeneity from an overtly epistemological perspective. One specific focus could be an inquiry into the implications of Western mental health professions' positivist underpinnings for its relationship to traditional/indigenous cultures. At its bare-boned core, the encounter between the Western mental health professions and indigeneity is an encounter between divergent epistemologies. The challenge, though, stems from positivism's intolerance towards non-positivist ways of knowing, a characteristic that the philosopher of science Michael Polanyi referred to as epistemic totalitarianism (as cited in Gelwick 2004). In addition to impeding the possibility of meaningful and effective mutually respectful collaborative relationships, the epistemic totalitarianism inherent to Western epistemology can occasion tremendous harm when it encounters traditional/indigeneity worldviews. In this respect, renowned Polanyi scholar, Richard Gelwick (2004:46), speaks of '... the dangers of a philosophy that tries to eliminate all traditional beliefs and to base our knowledge only upon the testimonies of the senses ...'. The history of the colonial encounter with indigenous peoples is replete with examples of such elimination or attempted elimination of traditional beliefs by Western mental health professions. That relationship of domination and deprecation needs to be urgently replaced with one of parity and equity.

Conclusion

This chapter has attempted to characterize the nature and scope of post-colonial theory, especially as it pertains to the relationship between the Western mental health professions and indigeneity. While the ideas of Frantz Fanon remain unsurpassed for the relevance that they have for the contemporary mental health/indigeneity interface, the contributions of Spivak, Bhabha, Said and others also remain highly relevant to the post-colonial critique of the Western mental health professions. Post-colonial studies' evolving, and inter-disciplinary nature means, first, that the concept of a post-colonial *canon* does not seem very suitable, and second, that its insights pertaining to the post-colonial condition can bring into greater clarity dynamics at the indigenity/mental health interface. This chapter has also ventured to undertake a preliminary glance at the field of colonial settler studies – an emerging discipline whose existence is justified by the sharp light it throws specifically on indigenous issues – and to inquire about its relationship to post-colonial studies. Mental health clinicians working in indigenous populations stand to profit a great deal from engaging with the emerging and evolving colonial settler studies scholarship, but they would be advised to acknowledge that field's close relationship with the inter-disciplinary field of post-colonial studies.

References

Adams, P. (1970). 'The social psychiatry of Frantz Fanon'. *American Journal of Psychiatry*, 127(6), 809–814.

Alfred, T. and Corntassel, J. (2005) 'Being indigenous: Resurgences against contemporary colonialism', *Government and Opposition: An International Journal of Comparative Politics*, 40(4): 597–614.

Asuni, T. (1967) 'Aro Hospital system in perspective', *American Journal of Psychiatry*, 124(6): 763–770.

Ashcroft, B., Griffiths, G., and Tiffin, H. (1998) *Key concepts in postcolonial studies.* New York: Routledge.

Battiste, M. (2011). *Reclaiming indigenous voice and vision.* Vancouver: UBC Press.

Benning, T. B. (2014) 'Before and after psychopathology: A Foucault-inspired perspective on western knowledge concerning the shaman', *Fourth World Journal*, 13(1): 59–67.

Benning, T. B. (2016) 'Envisioning deep collaboration between psychiatry and traditional ways of knowing on a British Columbia First Nation: A personal reflection', *Fourth World Journal*, 15(1): 54–64.

Benning, T. B. (2017) 'Frantz Fanon and the decolonization of psychiatry', *Canadian Journal of Native Studies*, 37(2): 1–10.

Benning, T. B., Hamilton, M., Isomura, T., Kuperis, S., Mussell, B., Nozinan, S. and Peters, V. (2017) 'Sts'ailes mental wellness clinic: Description of the first 15 months of a service development journey on a St'olo First Nation in British Columbia, Canada', *Journal of Community Medicine and Health Education*, 7(3): 1–8.

Bettez, S. C. (2012) *But don't call me white: Mixed race women exposing nuances of privilege and oppression politics.* Rotterdam: Sense Publishers.

Bhabha, H. K. (1988) *Introduction to black skin white masks* (Translated by Charles Lam Markmann). London: Pluto Press. (Originally published in 1952 as Peau Noire, Masques Blanc).

Bhabha, H. K. (1994) *The location of culture.* New York: Routledge.

Bigfoot, D. S. and Schmidt, S. R. (2010) 'Honoring children, mending the circle: Cultural adaptation of trauma-focused cognitive-behavioral therapy for American Indian and Alaska Native children', *Journal of Clinical Psychology: In session*, 66(8): 847–856.

Brickman, C. (2003) *Aboriginal populations in the mind: Race and primitivity in psychoanalysis.* New York: Columbia University Press.

Byrd, J. A. and Rothberg, M. (2011) 'Between subalternity and indigeneity: Critical categories for post-colonial studies', *Interventions: International Journal of Postcolonial Studies*, 13(1): 1–12.

Cannon, M. J. and Sunseri, L. (Eds) (2011) *Racism, colonialism, and indigeneity in Canada: A reader.* Toronto, ON: Oxford University Press.

Carey, T. A., Dudgeon, P. and Hammond, S. W., Hirvonen, T., Kyrios, M., Roufeil, L. and Smith, P. (2017) 'The Australian society's apology to Aboriginal and Torres Strait Islander People', *Australian Psychologist*, 52(4): 261–267.

Césaire, A. (1972) *Discourse on colonialism* (Translated by Joan Pinkham). New York: Monthly Review Press (Originally published as Discours sur le colonialisme by Editions Presence Africaine, 1955).

Chamberlin, E. J. (2000) 'From hand to mouth: The postcolonial politics of oral and written traditions' in M. Battiste (Ed), *Reclaiming indigenous voice and vision* (pp. 124–141). Vancouver: UBC Press.

Childs, P. and Peters, W. (1997). *An introduction to post-colonial theory.* London: Prentice Hall/Harvester Wheatsheaf.

Coulthard, G. S. (2014) *Red skin, white masks: Rejecting the colonial politics of recognition.* Minneapolis: University of Minnesota Press.

Crowe-Salazar, N. (2007). 'Exploring the experiences of an elder, a psychologist and a psychiatrist: How can traditional practices and healers complement existing practices in mental health?' *First Peoples Child & Family Review*, 3(4), 83–95.

Duran, E. (2006) *Healing the soul wound: Counseling with American Indians and other native peoples.* New York: Teachers College Press.

Duran, E. and Duran, B. (1995). *Native American postcolonial psychology.* Albany: SUNY Press.

Elias B, Mignone, J., Hall, M., Hong, S. P., Hart, L., and Sareen J. (2012) 'Trauma and suicide behaviour histories among a Canadian indigenous population: An empirical exploration of the potential role of Canada's residential school system', *Social Science & Medicine*, 74(10):1560–1569.

Ermine, W. (2007) 'The ethical space of engagement', *Indigenous Law Journal*, 6(1): 193–203.

Fanon, F. (1994a) *A dying colonialism* (H. Chevalier, Trans.). New York: Grove Press (Original work published 1959).

Fanon, F. (1994b) *Toward the African revolution: Political essays.* New York: Grove Press (Original work published 1964).

Fanon, F. (2007) *The wretched of the earth* (R. Philcox, Trans.). New York: Grove Press (Original work published 1963).

Fanon, F. (2008) *Black skin white masks* (R. Philcox, Trans.). New York: Grove Press (Original work published 1952).

Fernando, S. (1991) *Mental health, race, and culture.* Basingstoke: Macmillan Palgrave.

Gelwick, R. (2004) *The way of discovery: An introduction to the thought of Michael Polanyi.* Eugene, OR: Wipf & Stock Publishers.

Gone, J. (2009). 'Encountering professional psychology: Re-envisioning mental health services for native North America' in L. Kirmayer and G. G. Valaskakis (Eds), *Healing traditions: The mental health of Aboriginal peoples in Canada* (pp. 419–439). Vancouver: UBC Press.

Goodman, A., Fleming, K., Markwick, N., Morrison, T., Lagimodiere, L., Kerr, T., and the Western Aboriginal harm reduction society (2017) '"They treated me like crap and I know it was because I was Native": The healthcare experiences of Aboriginal peoples living in Vancouver's inner city', *Social Science and Medicine*, 178(1): 87–94.

Heaton, M. H. (2013). *Black skin, white coats: Nigerian psychiatrists, decolonization, and the globalization of psychiatry.* Athens: Ohio University Press.

Hickling, F. W. (2007) *Psychohistoriography: A post-colonial psychoanalytic and psychotherapeutic model.* London: Jessica Kingsley.

Hole, R. D., Evans, M., Berg, L. D., Bottorff, J. L., Dingwall, C., Alexis, C., Nyberg, J., and Smith, M. L. (2015) 'Visibility and Voice: Aboriginal People experience culturally safe and unsafe care', *Qualitative Health Research*, 25(12): 1662–1674.

International Labour Organization (ILO), Indigenous and Tribal Peoples Convention, C169, 27 June 1989, C169, available at: www.refworld.org/docid/3ddb6d514.html [accessed 24 June 2018].

Keller, R. C. (2007) *Colonial madness: Psychiatry in French North Africa.* Chicago: University of Chicago Press.

Kennedy, V. (2000) *Edward Said: A critical introduction.* Cambridge, UK: Polity Press.

Kirmayer, L. J., Fletcher, C., and Watt, R. (2008) 'Locating the ecocentric self: Inuit concepts of mental health and illness' in L. J. Kirmayer and G. Valaskakis (Eds), *Healing Traditions: The Mental Health of Aboriginal Peoples in Canada* (pp. 289–314). Vancouver: UBC Press.

Krautwurst, U. (2003) 'What is settler colonialism? An anthropological meditation on Frantz Fanon's "concerning violence"', *History and Anthropology*, 14(1): 55–72.

Kuper, A. (2003) 'The return of the native', *Current Anthropology*, 44(3): 389–402.

Maar, M. A. and Shawande, M. (2010) 'Traditional Anishinabe healing in a clinical setting: The development of an Aboriginal interdisciplinary approach to community-based Aboriginal mental health care', *International Journal of Indigenous Health*, 6(1): 18.

Mahone, S. and Vaughan, M. (2007) *Psychiatry and empire.* London: Palgrave Macmillan.

Maitra, B. (2008) 'Postcolonial psychiatry: The empire strikes back? Or, the untapped promise of multiculturalism' in C. I. Cohen and S. B. Timimi (Eds), *Liberatory psychiatry: Philosophy, politics, and mental health* (pp. 183–204) Cambridge: Cambridge University Press.

Marsella, A. J. (2010) 'Ethnocultural aspects of PTSD: An overview of concepts, issues, and treatments', *Traumatology*, 16(4): 17–26.

Marsh, T. N., Coholic, D., Cote-Meek, S., and Najavits, L. M. (2015) 'Blending Aboriginal and Western healing methods to treat intergenerational trauma with substance use disorder in Aboriginal peoples who live in northeastern Ontario, Canada', *Harm Reduction Journal*, 12(1):14.

Martin, D. H. (2012) 'Two-eyed seeing: a framework for understanding indigenous and non-indigenous approaches to indigenous health research', *Canadian Journal of Nursing Research*, 44(2): 20–42.

McCulloch, J. (1995). *Colonial psychiatry and the 'African mind'.* New York: Cambridge University Press.

Menzies, P., Bodnar, A., and Harper, V. (2010) 'The role of the elder within a mainstream addiction and mental health hospital: Developing an integrated paradigm', *Native Social Work Journal*, 7(1): 87–107.

Mishra, V. and Hodge, B. (1991) 'What is post (-) colonialism?', *Textual Practice*, 5(3): 399–414.

Morris, R. (2010) *Can the subaltern speak: Reflections on the history of an idea.* New York: Columbia University Press.

Nowrouzi, B., Manassis, K., Jones, E., Bobinski, T., and Mushquash, C. J. (2015) 'Translating anxiety-focused CBT for youth in a First Nations context in Northwestern Ontario', *Journal of the Canadian Academy of Child and Adolescent Psychiatry*, 24(1): 33–40.

Overmars, D. (2010) 'Diagnosing as a naming ceremony: Caution warranted in the use of DSM-IV with Canadian Aboriginal peoples', *First Peoples Child and Family Review*, 5(1): 78–85.

Quijano, A. (2000) 'Coloniality of power, Eurocentricism, and Latin America', *Nepantla: Views from South*, 1(3): 534–580.

Richmond, C. A. M. and Ross, N. A. (2009) 'The determinants of First Nation and Inuit health: A critical population health approach', *Health and Place*, 15(2): 403–411.

Robertson, M. and Walter, G. (2009) 'Frantz Fanon and the confluence of psychiatry, politics, ethics and culture', *Acta Neuropsychiatrica*, 21(6): 308–309.

Rukundwa, L. S. and van Aarde, A. G. (2007) 'The formation of postcolonial theory', *HTS Teologiese Studies/Theological Studies*, 63(3): 1171–1194.

Sadowsky, J. (1999) *Imperial bedlam: Institutions of madness in colonial Southwest Nigeria*. Berkeley: University of California Press.

Said, E. W. (1978) *Orientalism*. London: Routledge and Kegan Paul.

Spivak, G. (1988). *Can the subaltern speak?* Basingstoke, UK: Macmillan.

Stocking, G. (1968) *Race, culture, and evolution: Essays in the history of anthropology*. New York: Free Press.

Tatz, C. (2001) *Aboriginal suicide is different: A portrait of life and self-destruction*. Canberra: Aboriginal Studies Press.

Thurner, M. (2003) 'After Spanish rule: Writing another after' in M. Thurner and A. Guerrero (Eds), *After Spanish rule: Postcolonial predicaments of the Americas* (pp. 12–57). Durham, NC: Duke University Press.

Turner, D. A. (2006) *This is not a peace pipe: Towards a critical indigenous philosophy*. Toronto, ON: University of Toronto Press.

Veracini, L. (2011) 'Introducing settler colonial studies', *Settler Colonial Studies*, 1(1): 1–12.

Vine Deloria, Jr. (2009) *C. G. Jung and the Sioux traditions: Dreams, visions, nature and the primitive*. New Orleans, LA: Spring Journal Books.

Waldram, J. B. (2004) *Revenge of the Windigo: The construction of the mind and mental health of North American Aboriginal peoples*. Toronto: University of Toronto Press.

Walker, R., Cromarty, H., Kelly, L., and St. Pierre-Hansen, N. (2009) 'Achieving cultural safety in Aboriginal health services: Implementation of a cross-cultural safety model in a hospital setting', *Diversity in Health and Care*, 6(1): 11–22.

Wilson, W. (2008) *Research is ceremony: Indigenous research methods*. Fernwood Black Point, NS: Fernwood Publishing.

Wolfe, P. (1999) *Settler colonialism and the transformation of anthropology: The politics and poetics of an ethnographic event*. New York: Cassell.

Young, R. J. C. (2003) *Postcolonialism: A very short introduction*. Oxford: Oxford University Press.

3

A POSTCOLONIAL CRITIQUE OF MENTAL HEALTH

Empire and psychiatric expansionism

Bruce M. Z. Cohen

With growing calls from the World Health Organization (WHO) and the Movement for Global Mental Health (MGMH) to 'scale up' Western mental health provision to meet a supposed 'treatment gap' in the Global South (Patel et al. 2007; World Health Organization 2010), this chapter offers a timely postcolonial critique of the historical imposition of such medical practices and discourse. Utilizing postcolonial theory in the area of mental health allows us to appreciate that the contemporary arguments of such professional institutions for the expansion of their enterprise are far from new. Instead, the claims forwarded that there is an 'epidemic' of mental illness in the Global South (Patel et al. 2007; World Health Organization 2010), that Western psychiatry has a 'moral imperative' to act (Patel et al. 2006), and that – despite recognition of 'cultural bound' variations in symptoms – mental illness is a universal phenomenon with well-established biological markers (Patel et al. 2007; World Health Organization 2010) can all be found in the ideas of nineteenth-century colonial psychiatry.

More specifically, the socio–historical analysis covered in this chapter will demonstrate three distinct parallels: first, a racialization of the Global South within psychiatric discourse which marks such populations as more susceptible to mental disease than those in the Global North; second, a medical imperialism which claims the superiority of Western psychiatric ideas and practice over local, Indigenous understandings of distress and healing; and third, Western psychiatry's ability to pathologize resistance to Western imperialism and the expansion of capital. As I have outlined previously (Cohen 2016), the Western system of mental health serves specific roles in aiding the expansion of capitalism: it encourages consumption; it opens up new markets for products (most obviously in contemporary society, the markets for psychopharmaceuticals); it medicalizes resistance to capitalism; and, perhaps most importantly, it naturalizes and reproduces the norms and values of capitalism as common sense and take-for-granted conceptions of how the world should be. For this reason, we should not be so surprised when we find evidence of such processes taking place within the dynamics of colonialism and neocolonialism.

The chapter begins by defining and explaining postcolonialism and the rare engagements with such theory in previous mental health literature. This is followed by a summary of the 'official narrative' of Western mental health interventions in colonial and 'post-colonial' societies which forwards the position that psychiatry's social control function in colonial times was less than systematic, and that their work has ultimately had a positive impact on the local population.

This view will then be challenged by my postcolonial critique which follows for the remainder of the chapter. It will become clear that, whereas reformist scholars focus on the *practices* of psychiatry in the Global South, they ignore the far more influential *ideas* of the profession on the 'native mind' which remain crucially important in understanding their role in facilitating Western imperialism today.

Postcolonial theory and mental health

The origins of postcolonial theory can be located in the critical ideas of Franz Fanon (1986), Albert Memmi (1990), and Aimé Césaire (1972) (Mayblin 2017: 160–162). While often disparate in their focus, such scholarship was inspired by post-war anticolonial struggles to consider a number of common issues surrounding the colonial project including the political dynamics and philosophies of Western imperialism, the cultural and political processes which embedded and maintained colonial authority, and the potential forces which could displace such colonial rule. Following the key scholarship of Edward Said (1978; 1994), Gayatri Spivak (1990), and Homi Bhabha (1994), these critical writings on colonialism and decolonization were formulated under the umbrella term of 'postcolonial theory.' As opposed to the former writings which had a more specific focus on the processes which would lead to the geo-political reality of independent, 'post-colonial' statehood, the latter more centrally theorized colonialism as an ongoing process of Western imperialism rooted in power disparities and material relations between the Global North and the Global South. This is the reason why the hyphen is purposely dropped in postcolonial theory (as it is in this chapter); as McLeod (2010: 6, emphasis original) has outlined, 'post-colonialism' suggests a specific historical period, one which we might imagine to have a definite end-point, whereas 'postcolonialism' is a set of ideas and practices which 'can circulate *across* the historical border between colonial rule and national independence.' This broad area of study is summated in the definition of postcolonialism offered by Quayson (2000: 2) who suggests:

> it involves a studied engagement with the experience of colonialism and its past and present effects, both at the local level of ex-colonial societies as well as at the level of more general global developments thought to be the after-effects of empire. … The term is as much about conditions under imperialism and colonialism proper as about conditions coming after the historical end of colonialism.

Of note within this direction of study is an understanding that Western imperialism is realized not only through the physical colonization of territory and peoples, but also through a cultural and political hegemony which produces representations of the colonialized 'other' for appropriation and consumption by the West (Said 1978). As Joseph (2015: 1032) summarizes of Said's argument, colonization has a 'strong ideological component.' 'Although formal colonization may come to an end,' he states (2015: 1032), 'the ideological influences remain (Said 1994). Through art, literature, music, and science, the discourse of empire and domination persist.' In this way, an important focus for postcolonial analysis is the way in which the Western discourse on colonization 'naturalizes' Western interventions while silencing the competing experiences and knowledges of the colonized. A good example offered by Said (1994) is the colonizers use of the language of 'civilization' to separate the 'civilized' Westerners from the 'uncivilized' 'natives,' in turn aiding the construction of a hierarchy in the colonized space which legitimates colonial rule as benign, 'rational,' 'progressive,' and just

To adequately contextualize postcolonialism and the discussion on mental health that follows, the central drivers of the colonial project require identification and recognition. As McLeod (2010: 9, emphasis added) argues:

> Colonialism was first and foremost a lucrative commercial operation, bringing wealth and riches to Western nations through economic exploitation of others. It was pursued for economic profit, reward and riches. Hence, *colonialism and capitalism share a mutually supportive relationship with each other.* Indeed, the birth of European modernity was in many ways parented by this partnership of capitalism and colonialism, a fact which should remind us that colonialism is absolutely at the heart of Europe's modern history.

He further notes, however, that colonialism is but '*one form of practice, one modality of control,* which results from the ideology of imperialism' (McLeod 2010: 9, emphasis original). Imperialism has been defined by Childs and Williams as 'the extension and expansion of trade and commerce under the protection of political, legal, and military controls' (cited in McLeod 2010: 9); whereas colonialism specially involves the issue of *settlement,* this is not necessarily required for imperialism to function (McLeod 2010: 9). Hence, the argument supported by many postcolonial scholars that Western nations continue to engage in imperial acts despite the formal end of colonialism in many parts of the world (McLeod 2010: 9). Indeed, the increased global flow of ideas, people, information, and capital as part of the process of globalization has been theorized by scholars such as Hardt and Negri (2001) as a new phase of 'Empire,' where Western imperialistic exploitation of the Global South has become more brutally efficient than before (McLeod 2010: 307).

Regarding the intersection in contemporary scholarship between the processes of colonialism and the Western mental health system, Keller (2007c: 35) has commented that, '[w]hile fascinating recent studies have exposed how colonialism shapes scientific development, and how science informs colonial expansion, they have largely ignored exploring psychiatry in the same light.' To broadly separate what literature there is into two (a large proportion of which appears in this chapter), there is, firstly, a number of contemporary and original historicized accounts which form what might be considered the 'official narrative' from medicine on colonial psychiatry, and, secondly, a more critical literature which draws, to a greater or lesser extent, on postcolonial and critical race theory to consider the imposition of the contemporary mental health discourse on the Global South as an example of neo-colonialism. That said, specific postcolonial analyses of the mental health field remains rare and is less than comprehensive (Penson 2014: 176). This chapter aims to fill that gap by centrally applying a postcolonial critique to the practices, priorities and discourse of the Western mental health system in the Global South. In doing so it is necessary to critically engage with both historical writings and contemporary debates on mental health to discern the role that Western psychiatry might play in forwarding the objectives of colonialism, capitalism, and, ultimately, Western imperialism over time. Postcolonial theory, then, requires that we critically contextualize the changing approaches to psychiatric care and treatment in the colonial space alongside analyzing the production of medical knowledge on the 'other' as it may aid empire. Before presenting such a critique, the following section outlines the official narrative from medical historians, which emphasizes Western psychiatry's trajectory in colonial and post-colonial spaces as fundamentally 'progressive' in meeting the mental health needs of the local population.

The official narrative of Western psychiatry in the Global South

More so than writing on psychiatry in the West, when medical historians are reflecting on colonial psychiatry, they cannot avoid contemplating the awkward question of the profession's role in the policing of oppressed peoples. In their case studies of various colonial sites, scholars have had to weigh-up the extent to which the imposed system of mental health supported colonial interests rather than followed the fundamental goals of a modern medical profession to offer humane care and treatment to people facing mental distress. To this extent one might claim that all contemporary histories of colonial psychiatry have a 'critical' dimension to them. However, utilizing a postcolonial lens, we can detect a distinctly reformist narrative being forwarded throughout the seemingly diverse collection of writings on the subject. While there is little denial that psychiatry could be used at times as a 'tool of empire' (to borrow Headrick's (1981) phrase), scholars suggest that the evidence demonstrates a less than systematic social control of the colonized and, instead, the development of improved mental health services over time which better met the needs of the Indigenous population. Thus, despite critical aspects, we can detect an underlying conservative tone which reinforces the idea of colonial medicine as essentially benign and the institution of psychiatry as fundamentally progressive. As will be discussed in further detail below, this narrative is forwarded through the premise that, while there was a lack of significant benefit to colonial powers in doing so, the psychiatric care and treatment of the local mentally ill population significantly improved under colonialism.

When contemplating colonial psychiatry as a form of social control of the local population, medical historians often compare nineteenth-century incarceration rates in Western asylums to those in the colonies. It has generally been found that much lower rates existed in the colonies. For instance, Swartz (2010: 166) notes that an 1862 audit of asylums in the British Empire recorded over 33,000 lunatics present in England and Wales compared to much smaller figures in the colonies such as 156 in Cape Colony, 339 in the West Indies, and 744 in Australia. Additionally, it has been found that the vast majority of those in colonial asylums were settler populations rather than the colonized (Cohen 2014; Ernst 2011: 537; Roman et al. 2009: 36). As Wig (2015: 6) has noted of India, for example, '[i]n the beginning, asylums were meant for European patients only'; while the first asylum in the country was built in 1745 for the European servants of the colonizers who went mad, Indian patients were only accepted for admittance after 1817 (Cohen 1988: 37). As the number of asylums and the overall inmate population grew throughout the nineteenth century, so too the proportion of Indian residents grew, though Mills (2001: 435) notes that the comparative rates of confinement remained relatively small (in the low thousands) in relation to the total population of the country (in the hundreds of millions). On the basis of such evidence, these scholars argue that there was no 'great confinement' of colonial populations in asylums as there was in Europe and America (Ernst 2011: 537; Mills 2001: 435; Swartz 2010: 172; Vaughan 1991: 101), thus offering a significant rebuke to the Foucauldian (1988) notion of the asylum as an increasing instrument of social control for deviant, local populations throughout the nineteenth century.

In contrast, it is detailed that colonial authorities are at first slow to accept that Indigenous populations might have mental health needs similar to Europeans, and then to resource the necessary building of asylums to provide for such treatment. As Sadowsky (2003: 211) has argued of colonial psychiatry in Africa, there was 'no demonstrable economic benefit' for the colonies to provide asylums, and this led to 'half-measures' and eventual over-crowding of the existing institutions. Nevertheless, as in the mother country, the pressure from medical authorities and political reformers to extend available health care and treatment to all citizens of the empire meant that there was eventually an increase in the resourcing of local mental health provision and, overtime, an increased number of local people seeking such treatment (Desrouelles and Bersot 1996: 560). For instance, the first of a number of mental hospitals in the Dutch East Indies (now Indonesia) was built in 1882, fifty years after mental health care reforms in the Netherlands (Pols 2006: 363); while, later in the 1930s, a number of modern psychiatric hospitals fashioned on the provision available in France was established in French-occupied North Africa (Keller 2007c: 21–22).

In the early decades of the twentieth century, colonial asylums increasingly included (and occasionally were overseen by) Indigenous staff who had received training in Western psychiatry. In the case of India, Mills (2001: 450–451) speaks of an 'Indianization' of the psychiatric profession happening from the 1930s onwards, with the first generation of Indian psychiatrists being mainly trained in the UK (Malhotra and Chakrabarti 2015: v). The ultimate success of colonial psychiatry in India for scholars such as Ernst (2011) and Mills (2001) is summed up by the latter's statement that 'when the period after 1947 is briefly compared with that immediately before Independence, the similarities rather than the differences seem the most striking' (453). Rather than the abandonment of the asylum and Western psychiatry following Independence in 1947, India further advanced mental health care along Western lines, initially extending institutional care, followed by the extension of psychotherapeutic and drug treatments, and eventually moving from hospital to community care (Wig 2015). And India's case is far from exceptional: Pols (2006: 367) notes that not only did institutional care remain after Indonesian Independence in 1949, but the number of mental hospitals was subsequently doubled during the 'golden age' of Indonesian psychiatry in the 1970s and 1980s (of which Penson (2014: 181) ruefully comments, '[w]hile the Dutch had left, their exports remained and grew'); similarly, Brennan (2018) finds that rather than incarceration rates decreasing following Irish Independence in 1922, the local population confined in psychiatric institutions steadily increased until the mid-1950s; while Ibrahim (2014: 397) highlights that approximately 60 per cent of African nations still continue to use the same Mental Health Act as introduced by their colonial powers. Additionally, since Independence, many nations have established their own institutions for the training of local professionals in Western psychiatric methods (Malhotra and Chakrabarti 2015: v; Pols 2006: 367) and, despite ongoing complaints of the under-resourcing of mental health provision in such societies (Pols 2006: 368–369), Western psychiatry is understood by reformist writers to be now firmly rooted in such post-colonial contexts.

The official narrative of colonial psychiatry then, while not discounting 'that military violence, social denigration and an ideology of subjugation in the name of "civilization" were part and parcel of the colonial project,' is keen to focus on the pragmatics of 'institutional practices and practitioners' concerns' including psychiatrists' ambitions 'to provide medical care and cure (rather than merely confinement and control)' in the colonial setting (Ernst 2011: 544). It is this moral imperative within the Western medical discourse which allows historians of psychiatry to justify not only colonial interventions into the lives of the colonized as benign and progressive but, ultimately, rationalizes the post-colonial *continuation* of such activities. From the mythical 'emancipation' of the colonized mad with the introduction of the more 'civilized' colonial asylum system (see, for example, Keller 2007b: 21) to the contemporary global mental health campaigns by the WHO and MGMH, the official version argues that there were (and continues to be) 'gaps' in the effective treatment of the Indigenous mentally ill which justifies the continuation of Western interventions. This narrative will now be questioned through engaging a post-colonial critique which interrogates both the ideas and practices of colonial and post-colonial psychiatry as they might serve Western imperialism.

A postcolonial critique

It is noteworthy that reformist scholars focus on rates of asylum incarceration as their key measure for the (lack of) social control of the colonized because it conveniently ignores the more significant ideological role that Western psychiatry has played in justifying the subjugation of Indigenous peoples – thereby legitimating colonial rule – through medicalizing the natural state of the 'other' as abnormal. As Vaughan (1991: 125) has documented, 'relatively little' time and effort was devoted to 'the practice of psychiatry or the institutionalization of the insane' in the colonies. In contrast, '*the views* colonial psychiatrists expressed about the nature of the normal Indigenous mind were *far more influential*' (Pols 2006: 364, emphasis added). These views, adds Sadowsky (1997: 110, emphasis original), 'represented *colonial* anxieties and preoccupations' to a degree that even colonial psychiatrists themselves 'could not acknowledge.' In the specific case of East African psychiatry, for instance, Mahone (2007: 42) notes that it was through their 'intellectual rationale for colonial rule' that psychiatry proved its worth to empire. Similarly, Swartz (2010: 172) confers that while the mental health profession in the Caribbean can be considered 'a negligible force in the creation of docile bodies,' its most significant contribution was the development of racialized theories on the colonized. Summating these arguments with reference to French-occupied North Africa, Keller (2007b: 9) explains that psychiatric theories on the Indigenous mind appeared to confirm the inherent inferiority of the colonized, thus legitimizing colonialism on moral and humanitarian grounds – the European invader is promoted through such theories as most suited to rule and to progress 'primitive' societies towards 'civilization.' In this way, 'colonial psychiatry functioned as "screens" that concealed political agendas with medical language' (Keller 2007b: 22); it attempted to naturalize the colonizers as 'superior' while medicalizing dissent and resistance to their rule (Mills 2018: 210).

The theories on the Indigenous mind which informed colonial psychiatry were heavily influenced by philosophers of the Enlightenment such as Immanuel Kant who argued that the '"primitive man" rarely experienced mental disorder because he was "free in his movements",' though 'maladaptation' in the environment could lead to greater vulnerability to such disease (Mahone 2007: 49). Under this idea, comments Keller (2007c: 23), 'madness marched in step with modern progress'; as the 'father of psychiatry,' Philippe Pinel, suggested, 'madness was the price Europeans paid for living in civilization' (Keller 2007c: 23). In contrast, the colonized were considered as living at a more 'primitive' state of evolution (Mills 2018: 210; Pols 2007: 175), possessing less intellect (De Leeuw et al. 2010: 287). Therefore, unburdened by the demands and complexities of modern 'civilization,' psychiatry understood the 'native' as less prone to mental illness. Swartz (2010: 165), for example, notes a typical image of the colonized Caribbean subject as 'a childlike innocent, in need of both civilizing influence and humane care' (for a similar picture of First Nations Indigenous peoples in Canada, see De Leeuw et al. 2010: 287). As with children, the Indigenous were theorized as possessing 'infantile psyches,' being highly egocentric, untrustworthy, and lacking social responsibility (Pols 2007: 175). When episodes of madness were identified within the local population, these were explained as 'cultural bound' violent pathologies (see, for example, Pols 2006: 364) rather than the more 'complex' neuroses and anxieties found among Europeans (Keller 2007a: 827). In this way, colonial psychiatry's construction of the colonized as 'simple' or 'backward' (Cohen 2014: 324, 329) justified 'scientifically' the fundamental inequalities imposed on Indigenous populations by colonial authorities (Pols 2006: 365) including the moral rationalization for the colonized to serve their colonial masters as slaves, servants, low-wage laborers, and so on (Ibrahim 2014: 394–395).

This dominant view of the Indigenous as less prone to mental illness also explains the low numbers found in colonial asylums in the mid-nineteenth century; the asylums were not established for the local population and, under such theories of the 'primitive,' it was not expected to house many. Those locals who did end up incarcerated were only those who proved a big enough nuisance or threat to public order (Pols 2006: 364), such inmates being considered a significant 'burden' to staff despite their low numbers (Roman et al. 2009: 36). However, as the asylum rates for Indigenous populations increased in the latter half of the nineteenth century and into the twentieth century, this too was explained under the same racialized theory – the introduction of 'civilization' with colonialism was driving the colonized mad due to their inability to adapt to the new environment. As colonial psychiatry appeared to predict, Indigenous people were ill-equipped for the necessary 'acculturation' to a more advanced society (Cohen 2014: 328; Kirkby 1999: 199; Mahone 2007: 51; Vaughan 1991: 112).

While medical historians may claim that such increases were the result of the extension of care and treatment to the local population, it can be more precisely explained as a result of the profession's expanding jurisdiction over the area of madness as the nineteenth century progressed (Swartz 2010). As Swartz (2010) has detailed, the poor conditions witnessed in many nineteenth-century asylums led to a more regulated environment where, from the 1860s onwards, colonial psychiatry assumed direct control for the operations of the institution. This led to an increase in the authority and power of psychiatry over time, and with it an increase in the local population being incarcerated; asylums became places where the burgeoning profession could study and experiment upon local subjects with almost impunity (see, for example, Keller 2007c: 28–30) in the name of advancing knowledge on what the 'father of modern psychiatry,' Emil Kraepelin, described as 'comparative anthropological psychology' (Pols 2007: 175). In this way, colonial psychiatry aimed to demonstrate their worth not only to colonial authorities (in continuing to 'innovate' with their theories on the Indigenous mind), but also to their professional colleagues back in Europe. Over time, colonial psychiatry also moved to extinguish local spiritual and health practices through pressing for legislation to outlaw Indigenous healers (see, for example, Cohen 2014: 322–323).

As detailed by Sadowsky (1997: 109), colonial psychiatry's 'policing of the cultural boundary' between the colonized and colonizer became increasingly crucial the more it was threatened; as the struggles for Independence progressed into the twentieth century, colonial psychiatry moved to further essentialize racial differences, to pathologize resistance to colonial rule, and to incarcerate increasing numbers of the local population. Giving Kenya as an example, 'where colonial rulers sought to suppress a violent uprising,' reports Sadowsky (1997: 110), it 'occasioned a psychiatric literature that was noticeably more racist.' It is during this period of severe colonial anxiety that psychiatry really proved its worth to empire.

Strongly influenced by eugenicist theories (see, for example, Galton 1892) of an inherent racial hierarchy in which the white European race was 'naturally' superior to all others (Cohen 2016: 176; Fernando 2017: 46–54), colonial psychiatry attempted to add further medical and scientific credibility to colonial authority by arguing that the colonized were fundamentally 'unfit' to govern their own countries. Colonial doctors and psychiatrists such H. L. Gordon and J. C. Carothers carried out detailed studies of Indigenous groups in Africa and concluded that the 'native intelligence' was inherently lower than the European (Swartz 2010: 172); the former suggested that there was an 'inferior durability' of the brain cells, while the latter infamously argued that the normal brain of the African was comparable to a leucotomized European (Mahone 2007: 43, 46; see also Sadowsky 1997). Similarly, the French psychiatrist Antoine Porot in Algiers theorized that the 'North African mind' was 'inherently puerile and incapable of coping with the realities of modern civilization' (Keller 2007c: 25). As Keller remarks of this move by French North African psychiatry towards a eugenicist discourse, rather than seeing their patients as sick individuals, psychiatrists instead saw them as 'representing dangerous tendencies that were inherent to North Africans' mentality' (2007c: 25). With the rise of African nationalism, such psychiatric theories of 'mass instability' among colonial populations proliferated and found 'its most extreme application' (Mahone 2007: 59) in Carothers' 1954 government-commissioned report, *The Psychology of the Mau Mau*.

Reporting on the Mau Mau rebellions by the Kikuyu tribe against the British in 1950s Kenya, Carothers suggested that, rather than the continued British occupation and exploitation of stolen lands, the root cause of the uprising was due to a general psychological disturbance in the local population. Writers such as A. S. Cleary argue that this was highly useful to British colonialism in suggesting that the uprising was 'perhaps the symptom of some form of mass psychosis' (cited in Sadowsky 1997: 106), an irrational act of disordered minds rather than a popular uprising signaling a fundamental – and, as it turned out in Kenya, terminal – threat to colonial rule. These biological theories on the colonized changed colonial government attitudes towards the Indigenous: instead of believing in the continued potential for 'rehabilitation' among the natives, the colonized were more and more seen as a threat to social order and civilization in general (Keller 2007c: 25). Consequently, dissent to colonialism was increasingly met with brutal measures of policing and punishment. As Ibrahim (2014: 396) confirms, colonial Mental Health Acts were more frequently used in Africa during this period 'for suppressing rebellion and detaining individuals or groups who appeared to be a threat to the colonial establishment.' For instance, notable Independence activists Nonthetha Nkwenkwe and Elijah Masinde were labeled as insane and incarcerated in asylums in South Africa and Kenya respectively, while freedom fighter Mohamed Abdullah Hassan was pathologized by the colonial rulers as 'Mad Mullah' in Somalia (Ibrahim 2014: 396). Additionally, one of the most popular diagnoses used to label Africans in early-twentieth-century asylums was 'persecutory delusions,' despite the obvious point 'that colonialism was, in fact, a form of persecution' (Sadowsky 2003: 213). For Fanon (1965: 200), this was a clear example of how colonial psychiatry sought to 'pacify' an entire population who had been traumatized by colonial rule. Meanwhile, in settler societies such as Aotearoa New Zealand, similar acts of resistance were met with increased levels of psychiatric incarceration and labeling of Indigenous groups with serious mental illnesses such as schizophrenia (Cohen 2014).

As we have seen, the formal end of colonization did not mark the end of the influence or intervention of Western psychiatry in Independent territories, but rather – as medical historians are keen to point out – a continuation. This was not however due to any realization from the newly Independent states that psychiatry had improved the mental health of their nation (as Penson (2014: 181) notes, for instance, native Indonesian recovery rates had been good *despite* the introduction of Western psychiatric practice in the Dutch East Indies), but instead because the mental health system – especially the colonial asylum system – had proved useful as a system of social control. Other colonial institutions of social control such as the education system, the police services, the church, the army, and the criminal justice system remained in place after the colonizers left and became part of the apparatus of Independent nations, so the maintenance of Western medical institutions in such places is far from surprising. Less surprising still, given the critical history recounted here, is that the mental health system continues to aid Western imperialism in its exploitation of the Global South through the same tried and tested methods as originally used by colonial psychiatry: namely, by imposing an ideology of Western superiority on former colonized peoples which pathologizes them as more susceptible to mental illness, individualizes socio-economic and political issues, and devalues Indigenous beliefs systems, customs and practices, and forms of healing as 'primitive' and 'backward.'

Through a postcolonial critique, the claims of the WHO and the MGMH can be understood as having a number of distinct parallels to colonial psychiatry's previous imperialist work. First, there is a continued racialization within the Western psychiatric discourse: claims continue to be made that mental illness is more prevalent in the Global South, that local populations are more 'at risk' of such conditions, and that more cases go 'untreated' than in the Global North (Patel et al. 2007; World Health Organization 2010). And while there is reference made in the WHO literature to higher rates of socio-economic disadvantage in such societies, biological factors are still very much considered as the 'root cause' for this 'global burden of disease' (Summerfield 2012); the inference again being that the populations of the Global South are inherently less stable and more prone to mental disorder. Ironically, the Western mental health system can even utilize a discourse of 'post-colonial trauma' with which to further pathologize Indigenous groups in contemporary settler societies. This discourse acknowledges the persecution of the colonized at the hands of the colonizers while usefully side-stepping the role of mental health workers within this process (see, for example, Carey and McDermott 2017). This way, acts of collective resistance by former colonized groups can be effectively neutralized by psychiatrists, psychologists, and other mental health workers as part of an ongoing, intergenerational pathology which can affect *all* members of the group.

Second, there is a continued medical imperialism implicit within the ideology of such health movements (Mills 2018; Summerfield 2014; Tribe 2014): the claims forwarded reflect the 'civilizing' mission of the empire builders which reject any validity to Indigenous understandings of distress in the face of the supposed 'universalism' of Western psychiatric knowledge (Summerfield 2014: 407). This is despite Western knowledge on mental illness itself having yet to produce any scientifically valid results on the subject (see, for example, Burstow 2015; Cohen 2016: 9–17; Summerfield 2014; Whitaker and Cosgrove 2015). As with the mythical 'unchaining of the mad' in the colonies, Western psychiatry is again forwarding a moral argument that it is in the 'best interests' of the colonized to impose 'progressive' Western methods on these societies. In this way, Summerfield (2012: 7) has rightly referred to global mental health workers as 'the new missionaries.'

Third, Western psychiatry continues to depoliticize and individualize socio-economic and political issues: as colonial psychiatry previously attempted to pathologize resistance to colonial rule, so the discourse continues to be a significant tool in neutralizing the effects of globalization and any threats to profit extraction from the Global South. For example, rather than suffering from malnutrition, drought-ridden villagers in 1960s Brazil, can be diagnosed as having *delirio de fome* or 'hunger madness' (Mills 2014: 41). Similarly, a spate of farmer suicides due to the increased volatility of global agrarian markets in the first decade of the twenty-first century in Vidarbha, India, can be medicalized by local psychiatrists as the local population suffering from a collective genetic fault for which more anti-depressant treatment is necessary (Mills 2014: 36–37).

Conclusion

Whether as practitioners or scholars, when we contemplate issues of 'race' and 'culture' within the area of mental health we are often asked to consider what the nature of appropriate treatment and care for people from different backgrounds than our own would look like. We are encouraged to consider different meanings given to experience so as not to misinterpret culturally-acceptable behavior as pathology, we are made aware of the need for 'culturally-sensitive' services and 'cultural awareness' training, and to understand the issues of racism, poverty, disability, and general socio-economic disadvantage as they may affect different communities (see, for example, Bhui 2013). While these discussions have their merits, without a simultaneous engagement with critical theories on colonialism, race, ethnicity and culture, there remains the tendency to lose sight of the discourses and practices of power which continue to operate at the very heart of the Western mental health system. Engaging with postcolonial theory in the field of mental health then, has allowed us to understand the imposition of Western psychiatric ideas and practices on the Global South as an ongoing system of ideological oppression of Indigenous populations, rather than an aspect of medical enterprise confined to the past. As we have seen in this chapter, it is the ideas on the 'native mind' which have been of most significance to aiding the expansion of capital in both colonial and neocolonial times. The claims from medical scholars that psychiatric interventions in the Global South are benevolent, moral, and serve no economic benefit to Western imperialism does not stand up to close scrutiny. On the contrary, the mental health system continues to facilitate financial globalization and the authority of corporations and ruling elites through pushing biomedical ideology, pharmaceutical products, and therapizing technologies on the Global South while silencing opposition through the increased labeling of local populations with seemingly ever-expanding categories of 'mental illness.'

References

Bhabha, H. K. (1994) *The Location of Culture*. London: Routledge.
Bhui, K. (Ed.) (2013) *Elements of Culture and Mental Health: Critical Questions for Clinicians*. London: RCPsych Publications.
Brennan, D. (2018) 'The Myth of the Irish Insanity Epidemic'. In Cohen, B. M. Z. (Ed.), *Routledge International Handbook of Critical Mental Health* (pp. 133–140). Abingdon: Routledge.
Burstow, B. (2015) *Psychiatry and the Business of Madness: An Ethical and Epistemological Accounting*. New York: Palgrave Macmillan.
Carey, T. A. and McDermott, D. R. (2017) 'Engaging Indigenous People in Mental Health Services in Australia'. In R. G. White, S. Jain, D. M. R. Orr, and U. M. Read (Eds.), *The Palgrave Handbook of Sociocultural Perspectives on Global Mental Health* (pp. 565–588). London: Palgrave Macmillan.
Césaire, A. (1972) *Discourse on Colonialism*. New York: Monthly Review Press.
Cohen, B. M. Z. (2014) 'Passive-Aggressive: Māori Resistance and the Continuance of Colonial Psychiatry in Aotearoa New Zealand', *Disability and the Global South*, 1(2): 319–339.
Cohen, B. M. Z. (2016) *Psychiatric Hegemony: A Marxist Theory of Mental Illness*. London: Palgrave Macmillan.
Cohen, D. (1988) *Forgotten Millions: The Treatment of the Mentally Ill – A Global Perspective*. London: Paladin.
De Leeuw, S., Greenwood, M. and Cameron, E., (2010) 'Deviant Constructions: How Governments Preserve Colonial Narratives Of Addictions And Poor Mental Health To Intervene Into The Lives Of Indigenous Children And Families In Canada', *International Journal of Mental Health and Addiction*, 8(2): 282–295.
Desrouelles, M. and Bersot, H. (1996) 'Care of the Insane in Algeria since the Nineteenth Century', *History of Psychiatry*, 7(28): 549–561.
Ernst, W. (2011) 'Crossing the Boundaries of "Colonial Psychiatry": Reflections on the Development of Psychiatry in British India, c. 1870–1940', *Culture, Medicine, and Psychiatry*, 35(4): 536–545.
Fanon, F. (1965) *The Wretched of the Earth*. Harmondsworth: Penguin.
Fanon, F. (1986) *Black Skins White Masks*. London: Pluto Press.
Fernando, S. (2017) *Institutional Racism in Psychiatry and Clinical Psychology: Race Matters in Mental Health*. London: Palgrave Macmillan.
Foucault, M. (1988) *Madness and Civilization: A History of Insanity in the Age of Reason*. New York: Vintage Books.
Galton, F. (1892) *Hereditary Genius: An Inquiry into its Laws and Consequences*, 2nd edn. London: Macmillan.
Hardt, M. and Negri, A. (2001) *Empire*. Cambridge, MA: Harvard University Press.
Headrick, D. R. (1981) *The Tools of Empire: Technology and European Imperialism in the Nineteenth Century*. New York: Oxford University Press.
Ibrahim, M. (2014) 'Mental Health in Kenya: Not yet Uhuru', *Disability and the Global South*, 1(2): 393–400.
Joseph, A. J. (2015) 'The Necessity of an Attention to Eurocentrism and Colonial Technologies: An Addition to Critical Mental Health Literature', *Disability & Society*, 30(7): 1021–1041.

Keller, R. C. (2007a) 'Clinician and Revolutionary: Frantz Fanon, Biography, and the History of Colonial Medicine', *Bulletin of the History of Medicine*, 81(4): 823–841.

Keller, R. C. (2007b) *Colonial Madness: Psychiatry in French North Africa*. Chicago: University of Chicago Press.

Keller, R. C. (2007c) 'Taking Science to the Colonies: Psychiatric Innovation in France and North Africa'. In S. Mahone and M. Vaughan (Eds.), *Psychiatry and Empire* (pp. 17–40). Basingstoke: Palgrave Macmillan.

Kirkby, K. C. (1999) 'History of Psychiatry in Australia, pre-1960', *History of Psychiatry*, 10(38): 191–204.

Mahone, S. (2007) 'East African Psychiatry and the Practical Problems of Empire'. In Mahone, S. and Vaughan, M. (Eds.), *Psychiatry and Empire* (pp. 41–66). Basingstoke: Palgrave Macmillan.

Malhotra, S. and Chakrabarti, S. (2015) 'Preface'. In S. Malhotra and S. Chakrabarti (Eds.), *Developments in Psychiatry in India: Clinical, Research and Policy Perspectives* (pp. v–iv). New Delhi: Springer.

Mayblin, L. (2017) 'Postcolonial Theory'. In W. Outhwaite and S. Turner (Eds.), *The Sage Handbook of Political Sociology* (pp. 157–171). London: Sage.

McLeod, J. (2010) *Beginning Postcolonialism*, 2nd edn. Manchester: Manchester University Press.

Memmi, A. (1990) *The Colonizer and the Colonized*. London: Earthscan.

Mills, C. (2014) *Decolonizing Global Mental Health: The Psychiatrization of the Majority World*. Hove: Routledge.

Mills, C. (2018) 'The Mad Are Like Savages and the Savages Are Mad: Psychopolitics and the Coloniality of the Psy'. In B. M. Z. Cohen (Ed.), *Routledge International Handbook of Critical Mental Health* (pp. 205–212). Abingdon: Routledge.

Mills, J. (2001) 'The History of Modern Psychiatry in India, 1858–1947', *History of Psychiatry*, 12(48): 431–458.

Patel, V., Araya, R., Chatterjee, S., Chisholm, D., Cohen, A., De Silva, M., Hosman, C., McGuire, H., Rojas, G. and van Ommeren, M. (2007) 'Treatment and Prevention of Mental Disorders in Low-Income and Middle-Income Countries', *The Lancet*, 370(9591): 991–1005.

Patel, V., Saraceno, B. and Kleinman, A. (2006) 'Beyond Evidence: The Moral Case for International Mental Health', *American Journal of Psychiatry*, 163(3): 1312–1315.

Penson, W. J. (2014) 'Psy-Science and the Colonial Relationship in the Mental Health Field', *Mental Health Review Journal*, 19(3): 176–184.

Pols, H. (2006) 'The Development of Psychiatry in Indonesia: From Colonial to Modern Times', *International Review of Psychiatry*, 18(4): 363–370.

Pols, H. (2007) 'The Nature of the Native Mind: Contested Views of Dutch Colonial Psychiatrists in the Former Dutch East Indies'. In S. Mahone and M. Vaughan (Eds.), *Psychiatry and Empire* (pp. 172–196). Basingstoke: Palgrave Macmillan.

Quayson, A. (2000) *Postcolonialism: Theory, Practice or Process?* Cambridge: Polity Press.

Roman, L. G., Brown, S., Roman, L., Brown, S., Noble, S., Wainer, R. and Young, A. E. (2009) 'No Time for Nostalgia!: Asylum-Making, Medicalized Colonialism in British Columbia (1859–97) and Artistic Praxis for Social Transformation', *International Journal of Qualitative Studies in Education*, 22(1): 17–63.

Sadowsky, J. (1997) 'Psychiatry and Colonial Ideology in Nigeria', *Bulletin of the History of Medicine*, 71(1): 94–111.

Sadowsky, J. (2003) 'The Social World and the Reality of Mental illness: Lessons from Colonial Psychiatry', *Harvard Review of Psychiatry*, 11(4): 210–214.

Said, E. W. (1978) *Orientalism*. London: Routledge and Kegan Paul.

Said, E. W. (1994) *Culture and Imperialism*. London: Vintage.

Spivak, G. C. (1990) *The Postcolonial Critic: Interviews, Strategies, Dialogues*. New York: Routledge.

Summerfield, D. (2012) 'Afterword: Against "Global Mental Health"', *Transcultural Psychiatry*, 49(3–4): 519–530.

Summerfield, D. (2014) 'A Short Conversation with Arthur Kleinman about His Support for the Global Mental Health Movement', *Disability and the Global South*, 1(2): 406–411.

Swartz, S. (2010) 'The Regulation of British Colonial Lunatic Asylums and the Origins of Colonial Psychiatry, 1860–1864', *History of Psychology*, 13(2): 160–177.

Tribe, R. (2014) 'Culture, Politics and Global Mental Health', *Disability and the Global South*, 1(2): 251–265.

Vaughan, M. (1991) *Curing their Ills: Colonial Power and African Illness*. Cambridge: Polity Press.

Whitaker, R. and Cosgrove, L. (2015) *Psychiatry under the Influence: Institutional Corruption, Social Injury, and Prescriptions for Reform*. New York: Palgrave Macmillan.

Wig, N. N. (2015) 'The Beginnings of Psychiatry in India'. In S. Malhotra and S. Chakrabarti (Eds.), *Developments in Psychiatry in India: Clinical, Research and Policy Perspectives* (pp. 3–12). New Delhi: Springer.

World Health Organization (2010) *Mental Health Gap Action Programme: MhGAP Intervention Guide for Mental, Neurological and Substance Use Disorders in Non-Specialized Health Settings*. Geneva: World Health Organization.

4

CULTURE AND THE GLOBALIZATION OF MENTAL HEALTH

Vishal Bhavsar, Antonio Ventriglio and Dinesh Bhugra

Globalization itself is not novel – people, ideas and resources have moved across the world often in relation to the need for economic and political survival. Today, there seems to be no end to types of things that can be considered globalized, that is, subject to trans-cultural exchange and influence (Al-Rodhan and Stoudmann, 2006). In this chapter, we present a description and critique of the accordingly complex global mental health (GMH) movement, before discussing other manifestations of global exchange/material and culture flows in mental health. It is important to add, as disclaimer, that the authors, as *psychiatrists,* hold a particular perspective on global mental health. Moreover, the authors assert their "globality", as human beings, and clinicians – our work is framed in a global context, because our patients are international, and the social networks of our patients are far-reaching. This is important not only for describing the substantive issues, but also for making sense of existing literature – critiques of global mental health programmes adopt sceptical positions towards the biological basis of mental disorders, the pervasive benefit of international socioeconomic development, and the utility of epidemiological approaches to understanding why and how things happen. On the other hand, we are interested whether psychiatry affects global mental health, and possible consequences.

Definitions of mental health, global mental health, and the campaign for, and against global mental health

We take "globalization of mental health" to refer to themes in the description, ascription and attribution of mental health and well-being. A necessarily broad, but recurring concept is the prevailing brand of scientific empiricism in health research, which emphasizes evidence over lived experience and, thereby, privileges settings where large scale data is available, of appropriate extent/quality. On the other hand, "global mental health" (GMH) is a term with increasing cachet as a descriptor of a spatially and historically localized *movement* (Collins et al. 2011). It has a particular set of stakeholders, terms of reference, and a management structure. There may be no neutral positions on this topic, and allegiances one way or another often reflect broader theoretical alignments on critical psychiatry, the medical model, and broader psychiatric practice. We recognize that the GMH movement benefits from a defined set of aims, including improving the disparity, or gap, in the treatment of mental illness around the world. Such an approach rests on the assumption that these same treatments are themselves effective, and that there already exist frameworks for equitable provision in the high-income settings where these interventions were developed, which could be strong assumptions (Kirmayer and Pedersen 2014). Political analyses suggest medical power lies at the common root of both health inequity in high-income countries, and disparity in provision between rich and poor countries. It has been supposed that the global contribution of alternative medical practitioners and other forms of healing is underplayed (Mills 2014).

In examining these issues, we must keep in mind the availability of evidence to support the claims of the GMH movement, and realities of the current development and health space. It would appear that GMH is the only game in town. Beyond a rehearsal of age-old arguments between universalist/positivist and localist/relativist perspectives, we ask what work *could* exist as part of GMH that does *not*. The World Health Organization (WHO)'s 1948 definition of health as "a state of complete physical, mental and social well-being and not merely the absence of disease or infirmity" has been criticized for ignoring the presence and complexity of co-morbidities, and the influence of wide-scale demographic and socioeconomic shifts. Furthermore, it ignores "well-being", fuels suspicion that it facilitates an undue over-medicalization of lives (because nobody is completely healthy all the time, according to that definition), and inherent difficulties in operationalizing and measuring "completeness" (Huber et al. 2011) of well-being. Although this definition has stood for seventy years, the WHO has specified a definition of mental health in particular, as: "*a state of well-being in which the individual realises his or her own abilities, can cope with the normal stresses of life, can work productively and fruitfully, and is able to make a contribution to his or her community*" (WHO, 2005).

Despite this broad, non-disease-driven definition, grand epidemiological projects such as the global burden of disease project (Whiteford et al. 2013) and the world mental health surveys (Kessler and Üstün 2004) adopt *diagnostic* definitions to classify those with and without mental illness. Indeed, mental health research globally has tended to adopt a disease-driven approach to the classification of individuals as mentally ill or not – clinical relevance criteria (the need for professional treatment) are part of most definitions within the DSM-5 (American Psychiatric Association 2013). This is reflected in the widely shared *Nature* article entitled "Grand Challenges in Global Mental Health" (Collins et al. 2011), considered by many as the rallying call for the GMH initiative. Compounding difficulties around definitions of health and mental health themselves, are important differences in local definitions of particular mental illnesses. A recent review of qualitative studies reported significant differences in features of depression across 170 different study populations (Haroz et al. 2017). And, although articulated as a resource to mitigate effects of intensification, increasing employment insecurity, and an increasingly competitive world, well-being is now packaged similarly to mental health (Kirkwood, Bond, May, McKeith, and Teh 2014), with perhaps less marked asymmetry between research on rich and poor populations (Camfield 2006; Camfield, Crivello, and Woodhead 2009; White 2010).

The ascent of the campaign for global mental health

Proponents for the GMH movement understandably adhere to a historicist view of its development – as a linear story from a defined starting point, leading inexorably to current strength. On the other hand, this kind of assessment risks downplaying the extent to which GMH programs have been a product of distinct and (partially) randomly allocated sets of circumstances. Historical approaches also cement the notion of a thing, or process itself, separate from the local arguments of a particular piece of research's validity.

Patel and Prince (2010) examine four contributions to the advancement of the campaign for global mental health (CMGH), deriving from the assumption that mental disorders are "real" causes of human suffering and not a figment of Western imaginations, nor a colonial exportation. First, mental disorders are partly socially driven, and occurrence of mental disorders is shaped by disadvantage, poverty, violence and trauma. Second, the operationalization of morbidity and disease burden in the form of disability adjusted life years and others (Murray et al. 2012), has allowed a case to be made for depression, for example, as a global health concern *per se*. Third, evidence that interventions into mental disorders, developed, defined and operationalized in Western countries, can be safe and effective in LAMIs, has emboldened these efforts. Fourth is recognition that, aside from influences of disadvantage and adversity described in the first point, mental disorders are associated with social and medical costs – including those reflecting discrimination, coercion, restraint, and indignity. These points focus around a key, reproducible and declarative problem in global health, the *mental health treatment gap*, abbreviated throughout much of this literature to "mhGAP" (WHO 2017). Symmetrically, four goals are outlined by Patel. They are to synthesize evidence on treatment effectiveness, to build evidence on optimal delivery of these treatments, establishing a social movement to mobilize political will, and organization of ongoing research priorities. In 2008, WHO launched a mental health gap action plan, aimed at producing evidence-based guidelines for the management of mental disorders by non-specialist health worker in poorer countries. Patel proposes that this document was important because it crossed traditional boundaries between mental, substance-related and neurological disorders, that it was holistic, and deliverable by professionals without specific mental health training.

The notion of a treatment gap has been influential, however we should not overlook the fact that the existence of gaps depends on where you look – treatment gaps are noted for addictions (Bartlett, Garriott, and Raikhel 2014), psychosis, and a range of other mental health problems, including in high-income countries (Weich et al. 2017). By taking the effectiveness of interventions as read, barriers to progress according to GMH proponents lie in *implementation*, not in evidence on effectiveness. Delivery of researched interventions into clinical practice is limited by the availability of staff, salaries, and physical spaces for providing care, which might be overcome by re-purposing existing staff, facilities, and training programmes (McInnis and Merajver 2011). Critics argue that this focus on delivery and scalability involves discounting social determinants in interventions, delivery and the experiences of mental health itself. Building international presence for CMGH has required a secretariat, the establishment of a social media presence, and regular meetings, grounded within an increasingly elaborate framework of global psychiatric epidemiology, e.g. in the world mental health survey (Kessler and Üstün 2004) and global burden of disease projects (Murray, Lopez, and Organization 1996). Therefore, it is clear that one thing that identifies CMGH is its emphasis on delivery alongside "discovery". In this sense therefore, it is dynamic, muscular, and effective and yet very Western.

Background of GMH in evidence-based medicine

Criticism of modern biomedical science is everywhere, not only in mental health research (Lancet 2018). Evidence-based medicine, a historically circumscribed body of methods and theory borrowed from different branches of scientific research, prioritizes the causes of illness, effective treatments for this illness, and groups at greatest risk (Sackett, Rosenberg, Gray, Haynes, and Richardson 1996). It has derived energy over the past 50 years from an interest in randomized trials for inferences regarding effective treatments. These methods and their derivatives are in wide use within GMH and deserve further consideration. For example, it is evident that disease and illness concepts are different, both in terms of their underlying drivers, and the balance of the two in clinical consultations (Eisenberg 1977). GMH circumvents these issues, which locate as central the illness role in shaping experiences of ill health in low-income countries; instead what is assumed is equivalent illness experience in different settings. This lumping risks obscuring important information for improving services.

Accompanying expansion in health research has been expansion in the terms capturing good health – well-being, resilience, functioning are all in common parlance today, reflecting an interest not only in the variegated aspects of health, but also the diverse impacts which good health might, have on a person's life – for example, good health in the context of extreme poverty, or natural disaster, might result in poor quality of life or well-being (Farmer, Nizeye, Stulac, and Keshavjee 2006). Increasingly effective care, the widening scope of medical practice in human life, and improved childhood health globally has resulted in a greater emphasis on a happy, as well as a healthy population. Much anthropologically-guided work has addressed local conceptions of healing, and meaning given to mental and behavioural phenomena, including the meaning of suffering. It is pointed out that such nuances have yet to find their way into the CGMH discourse, and psychiatric disorders themselves continue to be defined in terms of sets of phenomenologically defined criteria, although recent investment in Research Domain Criteria (RDoC) suggests an attempt to move away from this.

Key to this stability and influence is the institutional basis of psychiatry and its link to WHO. In this sense, the institutionalization of psychiatry has also happened commensurately with its globalization. The ICD-10 is a WHO document, enshrining not only a global definition of mental disorder but also a classification system. In contrast, prevailing models of causation and intervention in mental disorders reflect an interest in identifying the universal mechanisms (usually, but not exclusively, biological) for mental disorders, leading some to argue that there exists a neurobiological hegemony in psychiatric research and treatment, facilitated by global diagnostic documents and global psychiatric institutions – although these are not psychiatric institutions in the traditional sense (Scheper-Hughes 1990). More positively, social sciences have seen increasing academic and policy interest in social inequality, violence, conflict, and injustice around the world. There has been an internationalization of social policy, and the integration of global social policy with mental health policy may be a matter of time, rather than of inter-necine differences. Both global social policy and global mental health research have highlighted the importance of reducing stigma, social injustice, restraint and violence towards people with mental illness across the world.

Many worlds of global de-institutionalization

De-institutionalization has been a central change in the lives of people with mental illness in the West, occurring in the past thirty or so years. Coercion and restraint have for the most part declined. We need to see this change in low and middle-income countries; however, it is unclear if this is properly within the sights of CGMH, in terms of concrete action. Addressing stigma, violence towards people with mental illness, and coercion requires understandings of psychiatric labels and their function. Therefore, labels are necessary for dismantling psychiatric power, if only to understand where the "enemy", if that is what they are, are coming from. Again, it remains unclear how CGMH will address this. Neither does CMGH address global variation in practices of healing around the world. Global healing is complex, embedded, and not simply understandable with simplistic empirical approaches, including epidemiological studies. There is a risk of incorrectly transporting Western values when it comes to service design, for example, in relation to the moral and other benefits of "de-institutionalization" to settings where existing structures may appear to be functioning pretty well, and where priorities may lie elsewhere (Bhugra et al. 2018). Moreover, such an approach risks undermining its own efforts to universalize mental health, by particularizing seclusion, restraint, rights abuses, and social injustice as LAMI problems (Shukla et al. 2012).

Global mental health and cultural psychiatry

Psychiatrists are perennially interested in mental states of locals in other countries, and less interested in themselves *as* locals. There has been difficulty for psychiatry in accommodating local experiences of individuals seeking medical care within some kind of general framework. This is in effect also a concern of globalization theory, which seeks to understand globalization both as a process of homogenization and also of localization. Collectively, we know much more about the shape of distress around the world, and yet consider that cultural referents to distress, such as depression, mental health "issues" and others, are in more common use than ever, and promise to "unify" human distress. A perhaps under-recognized development is increasingly embedded integration of internal medical research with psychiatric research, both methodologically (in terms of the onward march of neuroimaging modalities, genetic studies, and metabolic methods) and substantively (the increasing recognition of mental disorders as a cause of mortality differences in society). This has incorporated increasing attention to physical health care of people with mental illness, and an increasing accommodation of mental disorders in a global disease framework (Millard and Wessely 2014). These interests are defined in terms of Western reference point – for example, Kraepelin's Indonesians investigations were considered cross-cultural because Indonesia lay outside of Europe.

Global mental health critics reiterate the accusation, levelled against Western psychiatric practices, that they are inherently colonial (Mills 2014). Coloniality, like globalization, might explain everything (Motyl 2006) and nothing at the same time. Moreover, the accusation is *not* that CMGH does not contend *correctly* with these perspectives, but that no attempt is made to do this. In this respect, we advocate a greater inclusivity of disciplines by the CGMH, and a greater appreciation of Western psychiatry as an indigenous system of knowledge. There should be attention to theoretical models developed with epidemiological and "localized" disciplines, including those approaches which involve service users, qualitative researchers, and "critical" psychiatrists (Bracken, Giller, and Summerfield 2016). There needs to be attention not only to common mental disorders in LAMIs, but also risk factors, such as abuse, drugs, and partner-related violence. Good information on prevention, treatment, and broader public health policy for mental disorders remains urgently necessary. There needs to be investment in infrastructure for these measurements, and for inferences on what works.

It is not clear whether the ease with which critics are able to blame CGMH for neglecting social determinants translates easily, given the limited extent to which the framing of social determinants of health has in itself impacted world health – in this respect again, it seems that these critiques are aspects of broader biomedicine, rather than of CGMH *per se*. Micro-identities, intersectional identities, and identity politics have shaped the global mental movement, and responses thereto, reflecting the complex interplay between evidence-based medicine, and its own methodological critiques. Critical disciplines from social sciences have engaged more directly with identities and their complex ramifications into social, family, and working life. Criticism of global mental health has proven discursive rather than empirical, has been clearly external rather internal, and apparently fragmented rather than coherent.

The assertion of GMH critics, that major psychiatric corporations aim for the reduction of all mental and behavioural disorders to brain pathologies, and targets for drugs is to ignore a body of other opinion and evidence which locates social and other factors as important factors on causal pathways to mental illness, and to help-seeking for mental health problems (Goldberg and Huxley 1992; Kleinman et al. 1978). To say, as others have done, that psychiatric ignores anthropology is to downplay decades of interaction between the two disciplines, and the attempts of some anthropologists to understand psychiatry through the anthropologic lens. The either–or nature of this argument betrays concrete thinking – in fact, naïve empiricism and etic anthropologic approaches are part of the same game; data must be understood as a societal and cultural product if it is to properly used, processed, and summarized to guide policy, practice and the design of health care services.

In many critiques of global mental health, including that of Bracken, global mental health is portrayed as a homogeneous system of research activity, guided by clearly laid out principles, but ones that are nevertheless palpably and demonstrably false and misguided. At the same time, criticism is levelled that global mental health manifests a medical scientific hegemony over academic discourse, with GMH adopting the accouterments of modern medical research. However, medical research evidence is today evidently and overwhelmingly varied, multi-stranded and, indeed, incomprehensibly massive – in a sense then, GMH is a microcosm of globalization as a whole – homogenizing on the one hand, and generating massive novelty, diversity, and quantity on the other. The CGMH is considered a well-delineated movement in these critiques, whilst also accused of pushing these boundaries that are so clearly defined. There is reference to institutional and editorial support for the campaign for global mental health – frequent references to WHO, the Lancet and the Global Burden of Disease project – and yet, these critics describe extensive and increasingly vehement attacks from critical psychiatrists, service users, and the public, in the next breath. How can this be so? Whitley's focus is on the coloniality of psychiatry, vocabulary, psychiatry self-definition as a medical field, the elision of non–Western models and modes of healing, and the evidence that psychiatric illness outcomes are better outside richer countries. Alternatives are closer collaboration with medical anthropologists, greater attention to systematic social inequalities that drive poor mental and physical health. Whitley accuses psychiatrists of scientific racism in many of his critical articles on the campaign for global mental health. It is clear that, in citable journal articles of a handful of pages, simplistic accusations of scientific racism belie the complex, historically sensitive, and scientifically important concept of racism itself. Equating yesteryears' proponents of eugenics with an ethnically diverse group of Western-trained psychiatrists who are (perhaps misguidedly) trying to reduce the global gap in psychiatric provision is perhaps a little far-fetched. If couching GMH as a "movement" is a device for proponents, then it is used also as such by opponents, who point to the passion and energy of "enthusiasts", inevitably and perhaps deliberately downplaying the role of evidence and methodological critique. In this respect as in many others, it is perhaps the same foibles, oversights, and preoccupations that make global mental health suspect that have made it a successful player as far as grants, publications and influence are concerned.

Different structures of knowledge, and its production

Kirmayer (2014) asserts that some critiques against GMH can be obviated by improving methods of evidence production, but that deeper problems exist – diagnostic and conceptual frameworks used to classify, and local epistemologies that are not necessarily the same as causal inference approaches employed in classical evidence-based medicine, prioritizing for example, randomized trial evidence. We can extend this critique by considering GMH to be a problem of medicine and globalization, not of psychiatry. Over decades, psychiatry has made collective efforts to bring itself into line with medicine, in its methods, skills, attitudes, and knowledge base, and modes of enquiry. Accordingly, medicine argues mental illness to be vertically segmented into disorders, such as common mental disorders, dementias, addictions, and psychotic disorders, while globalized solutions such as GMH are inevitable aggregated into single issue frameworks, separating GMH from global adversity, global cardiovascular health, global addictions, and so on. Of course, the problem of cultural extinction as a bad thing to be prevented, is the paradox of globalization as homogenization *and* as diversification (of rich countries of psychopathology, etc.). Insufficient attention has been paid to the way in which GMH works as an evidence-based practice – it may be fair to say that GMH is in fact the logical extension of EBM practices, and it is the primacy of causal understandings (which may be n themselves cultured, globalized and hegemonic) which are problematic. It is not quantitative research, but evidence-based medicine itself, which is at the heart of the GMH movement, and it is the causal framework of such work that is at stake. But perhaps this is not clearly put. The service use stuff is obviously equally relevant in England too. Derek Summerfield concludes a critical article on CGMH (Summerfield 2013) with: "*A humanity which refuses to recognize that what is philosophically false cannot be scientifically true is not worthy the name*" [Thomas Mann].

This quote is telling – Summerfield is highlighting that there is no point something being scientifically true, if it is not philosophically so. But what does this mean? Could it be that CGMH critics must concede that the approach of much GMH research and implementation is grounded in widely used empirical methods (including qualitative methods) that are used in branches of medicine such as cardiology and pathology, and the discussion at hand here is a moral and political one, rather than one of evidence? And if so, how does a field built on this empirical basis counter these criticisms? CGMH critiques consistently paint GMH as blithe, indifferent, narcissistic, uncaring, and biological. However, the inconsistency of this rendering with the scientific process requires examination.

It must be understood that as doctors we accept and appreciate the evidence-based model of practice, but in particular are comfortable with qualitative approaches to the gathering of evidence on distress and well-being. Definitions and measurements are necessary. One has to start somewhere. Viable alternatives should be tested, in the crucible of the Journals. Research on effectiveness and the nature of disease should be critiqued openly, on a level playing field. Some of this is a question of time – public engagement, evaluating social measurements and risk factors, cultural factors within disease models, are limited by the availability of the data necessary to do this work – this is changing. For mental health professionals, criticisms of the CGMH in the literature may appear to rest on a number of well-ploughed furrows. It is not the intention of this chapter to contend with any of these, but to try and present some alternative viewpoints, and to suggest that concrete, conflationary, and straw-man approaches to confronting CGMH do a disservice to both proponents and critics. Too often critiques are framed as attacks, accusations of invalidity are made, and blame is attached for propagating a neoliberal consensus which, to be fair, is far from being only psychiatry's problem. A more fruitful approach to refining, and indeed checking the expansion of CGMH programmes may lie in proposing challenges for the campaign, and for the campaign itself to be sensitive to the challenges that are laid down.

It might also be expedient for CMGH to accommodate its own possible shortcomings within those of wider modern biomedicine – where repeated testing, poor reproducibility, post-hoc inferences, overemphasis on intervention designs, a focus on proximal biological, as opposed to distal and social, determinants of health, and over-technologization of health care are considered to be problems in some disciplines. A common understanding of these challenges as issues for CGMH as well as health research and policy more generally, could be useful in unravelling the sense that CGMH is panacea. Mendenhall and others (2014) examine the feasibility and acceptability of using non-specialist mental health workers to deliver mental health care in a group of low- and middle-income countries. Scaling up of services in these settings is considered to require human resources, supportive infrastructure, and training and compensation for workers who are involved in the sharing of skills. Account of socio-cultural context is necessary in order to identify which local personnel can assist in the detection of mental illness and facilitate treatment, training, supervision, and service delivery. The authors advocate recognition of systemic challenges and socio-cultural nuances which might influence the effectiveness of tasks sharing between mental health professionals.

Such a reading reinforces an interest in cultural factors that influence health systems but does not really advance theoretical frameworks for doing so. Nevertheless, the authors do press the importance of avoiding concretized/dichotomous understandings of what locals want from their mental health professionals – in some instances, rather than advancing traditional health practitioners, they opt for effective solutions (Khoury, Kaiser, Keys, Brewster and Kohrt 2012) – belief in *vodou* was not a barrier to accepting psychiatric treatment in a small Haitian study (Khoury et al. 2012). Local studies need to examine in detail how traditional healing systems (or social support systems) might appropriately intersect with what are described as "biomedical systems of care".

The problem is that the validity of research may be differently perceived by different groups, and the sense is that bias, prior interests, and political/theoretical affiliations can come into play into arguments over the effectiveness of interventions. A recurring critical theme is the distinction between biomedical approaches which individualize, and thereby lead to a erasure of the social and more upstream determinants of health. It is important to recognize these as issues for the global research world to deal with, and not as specific issue with mental health in particular. Moreover, a cursory examination of Western medical research suggests categorically that any privileging of biomedical understandings of health reflects underlying asymmetries in training, education, research funding, and the availability of data on important social, as opposed to biological determinants, of health – too often social determinants are considered to be messy, noisy, complicated, or sensitive, to collect, when actually such information could provide useful starting points for the development of policy and interventions, and help to contextualise biomedical research findings about what is effective.

Secondly, such a dichotomy underplays both the connections of GMH critiques to critiques of Western biomedical psychiatry, which are in themselves "global" (see the "Mad in ..." series of websites) and the increasing emphasis given by funders and universities on involving stakeholders and the public in the design of research, and in the implementation of services. Such shifts suggest that CMGH does not suffer from specific or particular epistemological problems, but that, as a practical set of efforts, it reflects underlying structural tensions within science and health research as a whole. Turning to social interventions, it has been asserted that Western biomedical psychiatry proposes psychopharmacological interventions at the expense of social integration. While this may be true as a general point, much mental health care delivered in the West is delivered within private health care frameworks, or within social security funded health systems within extremely resource-limited health systems, where evidence-based interventions for social integration, such as befriending, occupational placements with support, and social participation interventions, have been de-invested. Given funding environments for mental health care in rich countries, long-running debates over the effectiveness of psychological therapies *in general*, become particularly relevant when considered in a global context – are psychological therapies likely to be effective for people in low and middle-income countries, even fi locals do want them?

An underestimated aspect of CGMH critiques is the lack of validity in estimates of burden, due to incomplete data, and a perceived lack of methodological rigour. This might point towards a need for CGMH to accommodate theoretical public health perspectives which locate data availability as subject for empirical enquiry. No one seems to disagree that war, poverty, employment and discrimination are important for health, including mental health. Global mental health programmes are focused on deliverable practical changes to the mental health care landscape of poorer countries. It is difficult to assert the relevance of structural violence, for example, without good data for health planners on these aspects. Another aspect which links the possible tensions within CGMH with Western health research is that the notion of local factors influencing the effectiveness of delivered interventions is a universal issue with randomized controlled trials, and with population-based health research more generally – what works and for whom remains a critical issue for most types of health problem, and mental health is no different. We argue that paying greater to consideration to the social and cultural context within which intervention s are delivered when they are evaluated could be useful in guiding how interventions might be delivered in other settings or might be modified for particular populations.

Kirmayer's assertion that the inappropriate application of diagnostic boundaries in poor country settings could result in misdiagnosis has some truth to it, but as with many truths, this is a general issue for all provision of mental health care – diagnoses are working hypotheses and descriptive summaries, and should be used to guide management where they are helpful – moreover, it is not only "mis" diagnosis that can have huge impacts on patients' lives – a diagnosis which is inappropriately emphasized at the expense of social or family relational factors, or medical health factors, can also limit a person's health (Kirmayer and Pedersen 2014). Greater attention to social determinants of mental health within a social epidemiological methodological framework will assist the global mental health program to deliver strategies that are locally nuanced and attentive to structural and proximal drivers of mental health. However, in itself CGMH, and the challenges it faces in implementation, are manifestation of these self-same relations, complicating the way forward for CGMH. For example, if mental health stigma is a crucial driver of the treatment gap, and a key target for interventions in low and middle-income countries, then the fundamental drivers of stigma must be considered to be, and conceptualized as, societal, cultural, and historically produced. Moreover, we think that although CGMH cannot be blamed for lack of research evidence of social determinants of health to date, important organizations driving research work and funding applications need to pay attention to the broader set of forces that are shaping mental health in all countries – in this regard, CGMH should be seen as a reflection of a globalized mental health, and a part of a broader structure (Lancet 2018).

Conclusion

There remain no good solutions to the question of how to improve dialogue between CGMH and its critics. But perhaps, by changing the focus from "us vs them", to "systems of evidence and explanation" and "the influence on help-seeking behaviour and pathways to care", we can begin to produce more integrated and helpful critiques of GMH, and more socially sensitive GMH research and interventions. Perhaps it is the role of service users and the public in guiding the questions that scientists and policy makers ask, and in a sense returning research and policy to democracy; and perhaps this might be a bridge between the global and the local. Structural violence describes the social, often unseen, and context factors which drive avoidable harm occurring to people. Whether the Campaign for Global Mental Health's "treatment gap" is an

Vishal Bhavsar et al.

instrument for the magnification of structural violence, or a crucial instrument to limit this violence, remains up for debate.

References

Al-Rodhan, N. R., and Stoudmann, G. (2006) Definitions of globalization: A comprehensive overview and a proposed definition. *Program on the Geopolitical Implications of Globalization and Transnational Security, 6:* 1–21.

American Psychiatric Association (2013) *Diagnostic and Statistical Manual of Mental Disorders* (5th ed.). Washington, DC: Author.

Bartlett, N., Garriott, W., and Raikhel, E. (2014) What's in the 'treatment gap'? Ethnographic perspectives on addiction and global mental health from China, Russia, and the United States. *Medical Anthropology, 33*(6): 457–477.

Bhugra, D., Pathare, S., Joshi, R., Kalra, G., Torales, J., and Ventriglio, A. (2018) A review of mental health policies from Commonwealth countries. *International Journal of Social Psychiatry, 64*(1): 3–8.

Bracken, P., Giller, J., and Summerfield, D. (2016) Primum non nocere. The case for a critical approach to global mental health. *Epidemiology Psychiatric Sciences, 25*(6): 506–510.

Camfield, L. (2006) Why and How of Understanding 'Subjective' Well-being: Exploratory work by the Wellbeing in Developing Countries (WeD) Research Group, Economic and Social Research Council. Bath, UK.

Camfield, L., Crivello, G., and Woodhead, M. (2009) Wellbeing research in developing countries: Reviewing the role of qualitative methods. *Social Indicators Research, 90*(1): 5.

Collins, P.Y., Patel, V., Joestl, S.S., March, D., Insel, T.R., Daar, A.S., Bordin, I.A., Costello, E.J., Durkin, M., Fairburn, C. and Glass, R.I., 2011. Grand challenges in global mental health. *Nature,* 475(7354), pp.27–30.

Eisenberg, L. (1977) Disease and illness distinctions between professional and popular ideas of sickness. *Culture, Medicine and Psychiatry, 1*(1): 9–23.

Farmer, P. E., Nizeye, B., Stulac, S., and Keshavjee, S. (2006) Structural violence and clinical medicine. *PLoS Medicine, 3*(10): e449.

Goldberg, D. P., and Huxley, P. (1992) *Common mental disorders: A bio-social model*: Tavistock London: Routledge.

Haroz, E., Ritchey, M., Bass, J., Kohrt, B., Augustinavicius, J., Michalopoulos, L., . . . Bolton, P. (2017) How is depression experienced around the world? A systematic review of qualitative literature. *Social Science & Medicine, 183*: 151–162.

Huber, M., Knottnerus, J.A., Green, L., van der Horst, H., Jadad, A.R., Kromhout, D., Leonard, B., Lorig, K., Loureiro, M.I., van der Meer, J.W. and Schnabel, P., 2011. How should we define health?. *BMJ,* 343.

Kessler, R. C., and Üstün, T. B. (2004) The world mental health (WMH) survey initiative version of the world health organization (WHO) composite international diagnostic interview (CIDI). *International Journal of Methods in Psychiatric Research, 13*(2): 93–121.

Khoury, N. M., Kaiser, B. N., Keys, H. M., Brewster, A.-R. T., and Kohrt, B. A. (2012) Explanatory models and mental health treatment: Is Vodou an obstacle to psychiatric treatment in rural Haiti? *Culture, Medicine, and Psychiatry, 36*(3): 514–534. doi:10.1007/s11013-012-9270-2

Kirkwood, T., Bond, J., May, C., McKeith, I., & Teh, M.-M. (2010). *Mental capital and wellbeing through life: Future challenges.* In C. L. Cooper, J. Field, U. Goswami, R. Jenkins, & B. J. Sahakian (Eds.), *Mental capital and wellbeing* (p. 3–53). Wiley Blackwell. Oxford.

Kirmayer, L. J., and Pedersen, D. (2014) Toward a new architecture for global mental health: London: Sage.

Kleinman, A., Eisenberg, L., and Good, B. (1978) Culture, illness, and care: Clinical lessons from anthropologic and cross-cultural research. *Annals of Internal Medicine, 88*(2): 251–258.

Lancet. (2018) UK life science research: Time to burst the biomedical bubble. *The Lancet, 392*(10143): 187. doi:10.1016/S0140-6736(18)31609-X.

McInnis, M. G., and Merajver, S. D. (2011) Global mental health: Global strengths and strategies: Task-shifting in a shifting health economy. *Asian Journal of Psychiatry, 4*(3): 165–171.

Mendenhall, E., De Silva, M.J., Hanlon, C., Petersen, I., Shidhaye, R., Jordans, M., Luitel, N., Ssebunnya, J., Fekadu, A., Patel, V. and Tomlinson, M., 2014. Acceptability and feasibility of using non-specialist health workers to deliver mental health care: stakeholder perceptions from the PRIME district sites in Ethiopia, India, Nepal, South Africa, and Uganda. *Social science & medicine,* 118: 33–42.

Millard, C., and Wessely, S. (2014) Parity of esteem between mental and physical health. *BMJ: British Medical Journal (Online), 349.*

Mills, C. (2014) Decolonizing global mental health: The psychiatrization of the majority world. *London and New York: Routledge.*

Motyl, A. J. (2006) Is everything Empire? Is Empire everything? [Empire: The rise and demise of the British world order and the lessons for global power, Niall Ferguson; Colossus: The price of America's Empire, Niall Ferguson; Empire, Michael Hardt, Antonio Negri; Multitude, Michael Hardt, Antonio Negri]. *Comparative Politics, 38*(2): 229–249. doi:10.2307/20433991.

Murray, C.J., Lopez, A.D. and World Health Organization, 1996. *The global burden of disease: a comprehensive assessment of mortality and disability from diseases, injuries, and risk factors in 1990 and projected to 2020: summary.* World Health Organization. Geneva, Switzerland.

Murray, C.J., Vos, T., Lozano, R., Naghavi, M., Flaxman, A.D., Michaud, C., Ezzati, M., Shibuya, K., Salomon, J.A., Abdalla, S. and Aboyans, V., 2012. Disability-adjusted life years (DALYs) for 291 diseases and injuries in 21 regions, 1990–2010: a systematic analysis for the Global Burden of Disease Study 2010. *The lancet,* 380(9859): 2197–2223.

Organization, W. H. (2001) *The World Health Report 2001: Mental health: new understanding, new hope:* World Health Organization. Geneva, Switzerland.

Patel, V., and Prince, M. (2010) Global mental health: A new global health field comes of age. *Journal of the American Medical Association, 303*(19): 1976–1977.

Sackett, D. L., Rosenberg, W. M., Gray, J. M., Haynes, R. B., and Richardson, W. S. (1996) Evidence based medicine: What it is and what it isn't: British Medical Journal Publishing Group. London, UK.

Scheper-Hughes, N. (1990) Three propositions for a critically applied medical anthropology. *Social Science & Medicine, 30*(2): 189–197.

Shukla, A., Philip, A., Zachariah, A., Phadke, A., Suneetha, A., Davar, B., and Srinivasan, C. (2012) Grand challenges to global mental health. *Economic and Political Weekly, 47*(42): 4–5.

Summerfield, D. (2013) "Global mental health" is an oxymoron and medical imperialism. *BMJ: British Medical Journal (Online), 346.*

Weich, S., McBride, O., Twigg, L., Duncan, C., Keown, P., Crepaz-Keay, D., . . . Bhui, K. (2017) Variation in compulsory psychiatric inpatient admission in England: A cross-classified, multilevel analysis. *The Lancet Psychiatry,* 4(8): 619–626.

White, S. C. (2010) Analysing wellbeing: A framework for development practice. *Development in Practice, 20*(2): 158–172.

Whiteford, H.A., Degenhardt, L., Rehm, J., Baxter, A.J., Ferrari, A.J., Erskine, H.E., Charlson, F.J., Norman, R.E., Flaxman, A.D., Johns, N. and Burstein, R., 2013. Global burden of disease attributable to mental and substance use disorders: findings from the Global Burden of Disease Study 2010. *The lancet, 382*(9904): 1575–1586.

WHO. (2017) mhGAP training manuals for the mhGAP intervention guide for mental, neurological and substance use disorders in non-specialized health settings: mental health Gap Action Programme (mhGAP). World Health Organization. Geneva, Switzerland.

World Health Organization, (2005) Promoting mental health: concepts, emerging evidence, practice: a report of the World Health Organization, Department of Mental Health and Substance Abuse in collaboration with the Victorian Health Promotion Foundation and the University of Melbourne. World Health Organization. Geneva, Switzerland.

5

THE POLITICS OF THE GLOBAL GOVERNANCE OF MENTAL HEALTH

Lindsay L. Miller and China Mills

This chapter focuses on governance in global mental health policy-making, taking as its starting point that current dominant conceptions of mental health have always been global, have always been about governance, and have always been tied to racialization. Focusing on the connections between governance of madness, racialized and colonial governance, and global governance (Howell 2012), we aim to show how the seemingly new governance of global mental health is linked to long established global governance *of* madness *through* the psy-disciplines (and so is neither 'new' nor simply a recurrence of the same 'old' imperialism). Thus, "the psy disciplines ... are heavily implicated as technologies of governance used to manage the social danger purportedly posed by the untamed mad" (Howell 2010: 352). In this way, according to Foucault (2004: 276), psychiatry is found 'wherever there is power', from the school to the prison. Taking this further, this chapter is interested in diffuse logics of governance as the strategic imposition of systemic alteration/correction that are 'talked' about, through, within, and between institutions as embodiments of capitalist modernity. Or as Harney and Moten (2013: 57) put it: "the hospital talks to the prison which talks to the university which talks to the NGO which talks to the corporation through governance, and not just to each other but about each other". These connections occur through and about governance and are often spoken in the language of the psy-disciplines. The politics of these connections and entanglements – their colonial histories and contemporary coloniality – are the topic of this chapter.

After documenting the construction of the need for governance within the global mental health assemblage, the chapter traces the assumption of globality (universality) already inherent in 'western' conceptions of madness, and the way that enumerative logic (metrics) enable and consolidate classificatory politics. Categorization as a form of psycho-power (Orr 2006) illuminates the role of the psy-disciplines as technologies of security and governance, where governance is not seen as displacing sovereign power on a linear scale of 'progress', but instead complements it through employing a range of strategies that co-exist, including forced treatment, incarceration, rehabilitation and recovery (Howell 2010: 356–7). This shows the need to attend to different manifestations of governance, i.e. governance through the asylum, through diagnosis, through psychopharmaceuticals, through community, and self-governance. Delving further, we explore how presumed inability to self-govern among colonized peoples and mad peoples (and the danger this implies) was/is used to justify the rule of law (something still seen as central to 'good' governance), and contemporary forms of therapeutic governance. This means that rule of law provides a central link in both saneist and racist projects of governance.

Throughout the chapter, as a method to expose multiple entanglements and historical conditions of possibility between global governance and mental health, we take up Stoler's (2016) invitation to refuse the linearly limited imaginaries constricted within Western/Euro-American notions of time and space. Instead, we consider global governance within what Stoler calls a recursive analytic that both challenge the seemingly naturalized notions of historicity (pre)occupied with progressive trajectories typical of development discourses of nation-states/ economies and human/child, and their inherent racial logic where 'underdevelopment' equals *dangerous* and *at-risk*.

We argue that one cannot approach a discussion of global governance without discussing power. We cannot discuss power without discussing knowledge. As the knowledge that has legitimized what is conceived of as 'mental health' and 'global' and 'governance' is and has always emerged out of (and is constitutive of) power as a relationship of force, one which entangles each of these concepts together and exposes how they were always already of the same substance. Here power is conceptualized as more than brute force, and as a microphysics – tactical, technical, subtle, and exercised through an intricate network of implicated relations. This Foucauldian view of power-knowledge as a 'relationship of force' opens up the possibility, according to da Silva (2007), for violence (both symbolic and productive) to be considered as an aspect of the political. Policy as a political endeavour, then, can be viewed as a violent form of correction, "forcing itself with mechanical violence upon the incorrect, the uncorrected" (Harney and Moten 2013: 80). The notion of 'good governance', as promoted by global mental health advocates, "requires the translation of mental health policies into implementable plans" (Petersen et al. 2017: 706). Policy as an apparatus of normalization, a plan to 'correct' the disruption of business as usual, is mixed up in recursively enduring 'civilizing missions' of colonialism and conquest, important components of the materialization and proliferation of institutions for the 'insane' and psychiatrization more generally (Mills 2014).

While it has been pointed out that Orr's (2006) theorization of psycho–power in *Panic Diaries* is limited in that it does not include a necessary analysis of racialization or colonialism (see Tam 2012 and further elaborations that include these analytical contexts in Orr's subsequent work; 2010, 2013), it is useful here when thinking about the specific expressions of power within the politics of the global governance of mental health. Psycho-power, as a sort of psycho-scientific (psy-entific) reason/rationale to mitigate risk and danger, attempts to

> project a persuasive empirical outline across the surface of symptomatic terrors that it promises to both name and erase...both make and manage...multiplying the possible surfaces of contact between psychic processes and their regulation by legitimating power *itself* as a kind of therapeutic activity.
>
> *(p. 12, emphasis added)*

The 'multiplying of possible surfaces' in the making and managing of the mind can be thought of within a fractal imaging that is not historically/temporally bound; where power does not have a 'place'; where attention is given to the iterative features of (a)symmetrical patterns that – through folding and refolding back on themselves – expose both "previous and future repetitions of the founding violence of capital" deeply implicated in conquest (colonization/settlement) and slavery (da Silva 2016a). These considerations will be expanded on throughout this chapter.

Governance of (mental) health

Global health governance is usually understood as complex and multifaceted, and involving multiple 'factors, forces, and actors' (Fidler 2002: 7). The WHO's 2000 World Health Report describes governance as 'stewardship': "setting and enforcing the rules of the game and providing strategic direction for all the different actors involved" (viii). Alongside stewardship, global governance often refers to management, governability, and implementation of policies and practices (Díaz-Castro et al. 2017).

Typologies of governing (national, international and global) are seen as intertwined, with global governance (while linked to national governance) seen as distinct because it involves (or talks to) non-state actors, such as non-governmental organizations (NGOs) and multinational corporations (MNCs) (Fidler 2002: 9). More recently, global mental health governance has come to the fore, given sustained advocacy by international organizations and networks, such as the WHO and the Movement for Global Mental Health, to frame mental health as a development priority and as vital to the global health agenda (Mills 2018). Following the inclusion of mental health in the Sustainable Development Goals (SDGs) in 2015, the World Bank and the International Monetary Fund (IMF) have started to take mental health seriously as a development issue, for example, hosting the 2016 event – *Out of the Shadows: Making Mental Health a Global Development Priority* (April 2016), which aimed 'to move mental health from the margins to the mainstream of the global development agenda' (World Bank, online) and to build a "collaborative response to tackle mental health as a development challenge" (Kleinman et al. 2016: 2274).

This growing interest in mental health systems governance is embedded within a broader health systems strengthening agenda, seen as important for ensuring accountability, transparency, and to improve performance (Upadhaya 2017). 'Poor governance' is conceived of as a "barrier to effective integration of mental health care in low- and middle-income countries [LMICs]", and as a failure to protect and promote mental health (Petersen et al. 2017: 699). Governance folds into and emerges out of a broader global mental health assemblage, consisting of the following intersecting (yet inseparable) components (and more): the production of metrics (prevalence and burden; predictive capacity of risk assessments); the idea of a 'treatment gap'; calls to scale up access to mental health services in low- and middle-income countries; attempts to increase monitoring and standardization of psychopharmaceuticals; and embedding mental health within primary healthcare (Hanlon et al. 2017). The WHO's Mental Health Gap Action Programme (mhGAP 2008), and the mhGAP intervention guide version 2.0 (mhGAP) (WHO 2016) are important mechanisms in this global mental health assemblage, particularly in their use of algorithmic diagnostic tools to expand the 'reach' of mental health diagnostic practices and treatments. This 'reach' can be viewed within the context of psycho-power, as an empirical projection that seeks to multiply "the possible surfaces of contact between psychic processes and their regulation by legitimating power itself as a kind of therapeutic activity" (Orr 2006: 12).

Much of the multiplying literature on mental health governance comes out of the 'Emerging mental health systems in LMICs' (EMERALD) programme, which works across six countries, and "focuses specifically on the health system functions of financing, service delivery, information and governance" (Hanlon et al. 2017: 3), aiming to strengthen health systems for the scale up of mental health care. Governance here is talked about as key to successful scale up and to the expansion of mental health care at regional, district and global levels (Hanlon et al. 2017). The literature produced from EMERALD suggests a number of challenges in relation to governance, including low demand for mental health care (seen as due to stigma and lack of awareness); inadequacy of mechanisms at country-level for monitoring and evaluation; lack of mental health laws and policies; unreliable supply of psychopharmaceuticals; and human resources issues (Hanlon et al 2017; Petersen et al. 2017; Upadhaya et al 2017).

Missions in the 'global' making and managing of madness/normality

Metrics are key tools in constructing and making visible the global scale of mental health ('prevalence' and 'burden'), and thus in justifying the need for the global governance of mental health. Quantification has played a central role in the formulation of a 'treatment gap' that is a central figure within global mental health advocacy. Counting things requires stripping them of their context, history and meaning (decontextualization and oversimplification), in an attempt to make them commensurate (homogenization) and thus comparable within a space of equivalence (Merry 2016). In this way, the production of statistics for international comparison "unify the global space through measurement" (Lingard 2011: 369), making nations legible for governing (Scott 1998). The interpretative work involved in the production of mental health metrics is often overlooked, replaced by seemingly objective numbers used to justify need for governance to measure effectiveness of governance strategies. Yet the social, cultural and political processes that underlie quantification are important because how these numbers are "created, produced, cast into the world, and used has significant implications for the way the world is understood and governed" (Merry 2016: 5), and in relation to this chapter, for the way that mental health is understood and governed.

The governance of mental health through metrics is now new. The asylum as a space of surveillance enabled large amounts of data to be generated through observation of patients, making use of and producing new techniques of categorization and classification. This then provided the conditions of possibility for techniques of quantification now used (from the individual body to the body politic), and the proliferation of data. Concerns with calculating deviance, and particularly the enumeration of sickness and of suicide, were central to the development of statistics as a 'moral science' used to know and govern the population, and thus, to the formation of the nation state (Hacking 1982: 281).

Orr (2006) shows that from the 1970s onwards, the pressure to produce statistics for inter/national comparison of mental disorder shaped the design of psychiatric classification systems. For example, the criteria within the *DSM-III*, and the development of rating scales and structured diagnostic interviews, were specifically designed to systematize how people report 'symptoms', to enable commensurability between diagnosis in different contexts, and ultimately to make psychiatric decisions more data driven (Orr 2006: 226). For example, the Diagnostic Interview Schedule (DIS) (1981) was developed as a structured interview tool designed to be administered by trained non-clinicians and was used to carry out the first large-scale survey of prevalence rates of mental disorder among the population of the United States. The statistical data produced was seen as necessary to enable design of public mental health policies which framed mental health as a national public health concern in the United States, as well as globally (linked to pharmaceutical company UpJohn's cross national studies on panic) and can thus be implicated in the conditions of possibility that put movement in the current global mental health agenda.

But, thinking recursively, metrics in mental health were already in motion, already contributing to the current (of the) Movement for Global Mental Health and already part of the pattern that made standardized diagnosis in the 1970s United States make sense. For example, attempts to quantify prevalence of mental illness in India (while ongoing) have a long genealogy that links calculation and enumeration to domestic and colonial forms of governance. In 1871, the quantification of mental health led to the publication of two censuses calculating rates of insanity: one in England and Wales, and one in colonized India. According to this, India had one-eighth the level of insanity than England and Wales, as insanity was seen to be associated with being civilized (Sarin and Jain 2012). Enumerating mental illness through the census can be folded back to the United States' sixth national census of 1840, the first census that attempted to calculate, through the coding of medical knowledge, the 'mentally defective' – 'insane and idiots' within the context of racial difference and comparison. Published in 1841, the census claimed to find that "the incidence of mental illness among freed blacks was eleven times higher than for slaves and six times higher than for the white population", providing anti-abolitionists with "scientific proof that Blacks were congenitally unfit for freedom", providing early claims of the statistical link between blackness and madness (Gilman 1982/2014: 11). Or, "Put differently, the Census of 1840 invites us to think about mathematics not as an objective reflection of the external world, but as a premiere tool for fantasies, power and imaginings" (Warren 2016: 118).

Considering the above, and thinking about fracticality, it becomes possible to see that the politics of the governance of mental health have always been global and have always been caught up in the modern grammar of universality, historicity, and self-determination (da Silva 2007). As noted, with power-knowledge as a relationship of force, each of these concepts ('global' 'governance' 'mental' 'health') are always already of the same substance with nothing 'new' per se but rather a process of constant recalibration when seemingly 'hidden' surfaces are disproportionately exposed, 'made' into something that can be managed (psycho-power as a form/technology of global governance).

Similarly, Ajana (2013) points out that governance through biometrics, classification, measurement and surveillance has long been underway (2013: 45). Different bodies have been subjected to different kinds of governance, making it important to note, in relation to this disproportionality, that colonized and racialized peoples have long experienced their very being as framed by more powerful others as 'madness' and as an inter/national security threat. Thus, for some groups, the global governance of mental health through security is neither 'new' nor 'increasing'. Beer (2015) makes this point in showing how data are already implicated in shaping our social world and thus "rather than seeing this as a sudden rupture or a moment of change" we need to explore a longer and older history of metrics – one which may take old and new forms and coalesce in different ways with different intensities (p. 1).

Thus, techniques of governance through quantification create 'mental disorder' as they also seek to govern it, meaning that enumeration constructs mental disorder in specific ways, i.e. as universal and as commensurable across cultures, and that enumerative logic constitutes and consolidates a classificatory politics of mental health. The hierarchical scale of (mental) difference – with classification and measurement (order) as a tool of governance – has been sustained through comparison wherein "the conception of 'the global' that underpins the modern subject institutes regions not covered by the ideals of universality and self-determination" (Gorman 2017: 311). Gorman, thinking with da Silva, links this further to Western representations of madness and the production and reproduction of the white subject. This normative/naturalized (social) scientific order of knowledge production which the modern (white/Euro-American/sane) subject has sole self-determining access to through universal reason, is mapped onto the idea of the globe and is sustained only in reference to 'other' regions who have the power to enforce the 'rules of the game' (da Silva 2007). The making up of madness as a constellation of knowable, classifiable (and thus manageable) illnesses through the joining of the emerging field of psychiatry with the already racialized anatomical-pathological scientific standard in the 19th century was always a global project of comparison sustained by force/violence (see Emile Kraepelin and his development of psychiatric nosology and the field of comparative psychiatry; Jilek 1995).

This comparative cataloguing of minds is revealed in skull anatomist (craniometrist) Samuel George Morton's illustrative volume *Crania Americana; or, A comparative view of the skulls of various aboriginal nations of North and South America* published in 1839 which documented and hierarchized racial difference through measurements of cranial capacity (the measure of the volume of the interior of the skull) as a proxy of brain size and thus mental capacity/intelligence. These measurements that separated what was determined to be, following Johann Blumenbach, five distinct races were compared against the 'made up' gold standard of white/Caucasian skulls. Morton's work was incredibly influential throughout the transatlantic world and was taken up in a multitude of ways, especially significant to the formation and legitimation of the psy-disciplines (e.g. phrenology; Rusert 2017; Poskett 2015; Davies 1955) as well as the formation and legitimation of the settler colonial state, where it was used as justification for the continuation of slavery, the domination and dispossession of American Indians, and policies that were anti-black and anti-native.

The notion that knowledge can be secured through the self-determining ability to produce concepts through comparison, classification and measurement (order), which can then be used to determine truth, is the 'stuff' that modern thinking is made of. This Kantian thinking is deployed in the process of assigning value to a universal a priori determining force which can then be used as a governing mode of measurement and comparison that mediates the understanding of difference or deviance (this process being a legitimating force that is 'reached' internally through universal reason) (da Silva 2016b). This desire to tell the difference, this desire to 'make up' the criteria from which one can develop the scientific expertise to tell the difference (Mills 2014), is intimately implicated in (psy)imperial effects and formations of "regimes of truth that rely on and reproduce the pathologization of racialized populations, the feminine, the queer, and purportedly unsound minds and bodies" (Howell 2011: 17). The "Four D's" of diagnosis that are embedded within the DSM's (2013, 2000) definition of 'mental disorders': *deviant, dysfunctional, distressed and dangerous* (heuristically used to 'conceptualize mental disorders' and determine 'abnormality'; Davis 2009), are inseparable from the politics of global governance of mental health where pathologization (and criminalization) of racialized blackness, indigeneity, queerness and immigration is nested in a larger context wherein disorder threatens the security of the ordered life of 'humanity' as we *know* it, threatens the continuation of 'the world' as we *know* it, while simultaneously (and paradoxically) this disorder is required in order to give normality/sanity/humanity coherence.

Psy-disciplines as technologies of security and governance

The psy-disciplines have long been recognized as technologies of security both claiming to provide social security in national settings (Miller and Rose 1986), and "increasingly harnessed in international security imperatives" (Howell 2010: 347–8; Pupavac 2001). Yet as has been expressed throughout this chapter thus far, the harnessing of psy-expertise in global governance is not a new phenomenon and is situated within the *long durée* of colonial violence. Tracing mental health governance in post 2003 Iraq, Howell (2010) sees psychiatry as a 'technology of security', a discipline and practice that "has instantiated its authority through a claim to provide social security within national spaces, both through methods of sovereign confinement and through liberation and governance" (p. 347). This promise of security is bound together with the construction of madness as dangerous (to both the individual and social body) and its codification as a potential security threat (Howell 2010: 351).

Singer and Weir (2006: 448) challenge those, such as Rose (1999), who figure all forms of power as governance, arguing that this overlooks sovereign power (which is not geared towards optimization of subjects). Sovereign power needs to be recognized as distinct from governance in order to see the multiple relations and interactions between different forms of power, and the ways they are articulated together and complement one another (Singer and Weir 2006: 459). Howell (2010) navigates this by referring to 'sovereign incarceration' "to denote a form of institutionalization that is marked by the absence of a will to improve" (p. 356), examples of which include the incarceration of those deemed unrecoverable, such as detainees in extra-judicial sites, asylum seekers and undocumented migrants in immigration detention, and the incarceration of mad people deemed dangerous. These groups expose the entanglements of border imperialism and psy-imperialism.

Here mental health governance is tied to the "ability of the psy-disciplines to divide up the mad – to assess who can be governed through community, who will be rehabilitated, and who is dangerous and thus subject to sovereign incarceration – functions to continually shore up the authority of the psy-disciplines as technologies for the defence of society and, increasingly, security in the international realm" (Howell 2010: 358). Thus, classificatory power not only attempts to divide what is perceived as the mad from the sane and the abnormal from the normal (delineations which are constantly shifting) but extends to internal categorization "between those considered ready for community governance, those not yet ready (but potentially ready in the future), and those who are simply removed from such consideration (the forensic patients)" (Howell 2010: 356).

The (psycho)power relations that frame observations aimed at telling the difference, categorizing the difference, and governing the difference are what are fundamentally violent, with the discriminatory hierarchy being simply a consequence of that inaugural violence. The psycho-power of the psy-disciplines as a forceful process of making and managing is reflected in

> both he who can state the truth of the illness through the knowledge he has of it, and he who can produce the illness in its truth and subjugate it in reality through the power his will exerts on the patient…the function of all of this was[/is] to make the medical figure the master of madness: the person who makes it appear in its truth (when it is hidden, when it remains buried and silent) and the person who dominates it, pacifies it, and gradually makes it disappear after having artfully unleashed it.
>
> *(Foucault 2003: 340)*

The 'master of madness' as the medical figure, however, has indeed become more diffuse and less discernable with the task of 'mastery' distributed throughout a multiplicity of institutions and communities that talk (utilizing modes of global governance) about, through, within and between each other. While we do not share Rose's stance on a linear move from incarceration to governance, his work points to the increasing shift in Western liberal democratic market-based societies to the governance of mental health through community (1999: 173–6). According to Rose (1999: 175), it is the rendering of community as technical that enacts governance, such as in the making of responsible citizens through training and awareness raising in the community (Ilcan and Basok 2004).

Governance through community extends now to the push for community mental health care in the so-called Global South, which is seen as central to 'good governance' (Petersen et al. 2017), and includes training community health workers in mental health diagnosis and treatment ('task-sharing'), and the development of algorithmic diagnostic tools such as the WHO mhGAP Intervention Guide (2016) and e-mhGAP. Within mainstream global mental health literature, these mechanisms are positioned as humane alternatives to 'irrational' alternative forms of healing (often positioned as 'traditional'), to chaining of people who are framed as undiagnosed within the community and within families, or to older psychiatric institutions/asylums (often described as punitive and as violating human rights) – all described as practices in need of 'weeding out' (Patel et al. 2011b: 1442). Yet the governance of mental health through the community a) does not necessarily replace incarceration in institutions (i.e. for those deemed unable to improve), and b) enables different forms of incarceration (Mills 2014). For example, the 'tranquil prisons' of chemical incarceration powerfully documented by Fabris in reference to Community Treatment Orders (the mandatory administration of medication to those deemed 'mentally ill' within their own homes) in Canada (2011).

Underlying the discussion so far is the assumption "that the mad need to be governed at all … particularly when such governance is positioned as a security measure in the defence of a society, nation or international stability" (Howell 2010: 355). Nested within this assumption, and particularly within the 'will to improve' (Li 2007), is a concern for the capacity for self-governance. Dean (2002) shows how groups of people come to be classified according to those seen capable to self-govern, those 'in need of' training and interventions to achieve self-governance, and those who will never be seen as able to self-govern. The construction of self-governance is deeply racialized and saneist, also closely tied to the idea of the child and to imaginaries of linear developmental stages.

A key part of the colonial apparatus (still present in ongoing patterns of coloniality) was/is the construction of colonized, racialized, and/or indigenous peoples as 'savage' – close to nature and thus as child-like (see Mills and LeFrancois, 2018, for a detailed discussion), where the idea of the child functions to make thinkable the colonial apparatus of 'improvement' used to justify subjugation (Wallace 1994:176). The construction of colonized peoples as 'permanently child-like' worked to frame European imperialists as 'permanent guardians' or stewards (McEwan 2008: 136), masking 'colonial ambitions to achieve global sovereignty under the rhetorical banner of a duty of care' (Barker 2011:7). That 'savages were made developmentally equivalent to children' (Castañeda 2002:26), has key implications in terms of paternalistic colonial domin-ance. Indeed, Reed (2014) notes that the 'compounding of the idiot, child, madman and slave is an essential part of the production of the proper US subject' (p. 97). This has echoes and linkages with the 'race-thinking' that was made possible by, and also a condition of possibility for, psychiatric classifications; the institutionalized whiteness of the psy-disciplines (Kalathil and Jones 2016; Fernando 2017); and societal denigration of Mad knowledge and ways of knowing (Leblanc and Kinsella 2016).

The questionability of the colonized subject's capacity for both self-governance and self-care and the necessity for 'benevolent' guardianship is highlighted in John C. Calhoun's statement in response to the (erroneous) results of the 1840 census which he used in an attempt to garner support for the annexation of Texas as a slave territory which would apparently be of benefit to the wellbeing of 'Africans' and would also serve to protect civil society (Warren, 2016): "Here is proof of the necessity of slavery. The African is incapable of self-care and sinks into lunacy under the burden of freedom. It is a mercy to give him guardianship and protection from mental death" (Deutsch, 1944, p. 473).

This exposes the developmental logic underlying white supremacist narratives of pro-gress linked to the nineteenth-century nation state and used to further justify colonialism as a civilizational and economic project that legitimizes various regimes of ruling through the sub-ordination of certain groups, often in the name of their 'best interests'.

Understanding 'the importance of rules to the process of governing societies' – legal systems and rule of law – is seen as central to the architecture of global health governance (Fidler 2002: 7). This was exemplified throughout the 1990s in policies of the World Bank and International Monetary Fund, which equated 'good governance' with the development and institution of domestic rule of law (World Bank 1994; IMF 1997; Carothers 1998), thus imposing worldwide, through loan conditionalities and sometimes military intervention, the ideals of 'western' liberal democracy (Santos 2014: 169). Rule of law was in fact "one of the most vigorously advertised aspects of British Empire", which portrayed itself as "planting the principles of the Magna Carta in foreign soils around the globe" (McBride 2016: 10). The framing of rule of law as key to health governance not only overlooks the coloniality of rule of law and how it relies upon and develops unequal political and economic systems, but also deflects how "the violence of imperialism was legitimated in its being exercised through law" (Fitzpatrick 2011:19). Linking back to the regimes of ruling enabled through developmental narratives that invoke racialized and colonized people as 'child-like', we can see how interventions of the World Bank and IMF in imposing rule of law, equates with the parental role taken on by the so-called Global North more generally (enabled by the continued infantilization of the so-called Global South that has always been vital to the colonial imagination).

Rule of law as key to governance strategies thus challenges claims that mental health governance is somehow an innocent space that is being securitized (Howell 2014; Howell 2018) or psychologized (Klein and Mills 2017), showing that the psy-disciplines have emerged entangled with inter/national security, and continue to operate as a form of what Pupavac (2001) calls 'therapeutic governance' where, through the pathologization of distress, certain populations are labelled as psychologically dysfunctional and traumatized.

Conclusion

Through a recursive analysis that refuses to historicize mental health governance within a linear developmental trajectory, this chapter has aimed to trace the always already global and racialized nature of mental health and its governance, where governance, race and madness are tightly and inextricably bound. Thus, we examined how the governance of mental health and the classificatory politics of psychiatry were made possible by, and also a condition of possibility for, racialized and racist modes of thinking and governing.

Instead of seeing governance as replacing sovereign power, or understanding shifting forms of governance (self-governance, or governance through the community) as evolving from one to the next, we emphasize instead how multiple forms of governance operate to complement one another in the governance of mental health. This process we relate to psycho-power as the multiplying of possible surfaces of governance that, in its fragility, requires to iteratively fold and refold back on itself in order to legitimate power itself as a kind of therapeutic (and yet often still carceral and/or violent) activity. This approach allows us to take seriously the burgeoning literature and attention to mental health as an issue for global governance, especially given the framing of mental health as a global health and development *priority*. Yet it also allows us to see how the governance of mental health is not 'new' per se, evident in its intimate entanglements with coloniality (intimacies that can be viewed as monstrous when thinking with Christina Sharpe, 2017). This is particularly exemplified in the central role that rule of law is seen to play in 'good governance' in more recent global mental health literature and the key role played by rule of law more recursively, as an ongoing tool of colonial governance. Yet global mental health governance is not and never has been monolithic nor entirely rationalistic, meaning that further attention needs to be paid to the 'messy actualities' of mental health governance projects (i.e. how governance strategies are taken up, appropriated, resisted, or refused). Particular attention must also be given to the scholarship (variously understood) and/or experiential expressions of those who know the intricacies of the governance of mental health well and for whom the governance of mental health not being new will come as no surprise. This includes those who identify as mad people of colour, and/or as psychosocially disabled people of the Global South. This is central in a project of un/in-disciplining the psy-disciplines (whether or not this is even possible) and refusing the epistemic injustices that devalue Mad knowledge.

References

Ajana, B. (2013) *Governing through Biometrics – The Biopolitics of Identity*. Basingstoke: Palgrave Macmillan.

American Psychiatric Association. (2013) *Diagnostic and Statistical Manual of Mental Disorders* (5th ed.). Washington, DC: Author.

American Psychiatric Association. (2000) *Diagnostic and Statistical Manual of Mental Disorders* (4th ed., text rev.). Washington, DC: Author.

Ashcroft B., Griffiths, G., and Tiffin, H. (1989) *The Empire Writes Back: Theory and Practice in Post-Colonial Literatures*. London: Routledge.

Barker, C. (2011) *Postcolonial Fiction and Disability: Exceptional Children, Metaphor and Materiality*. London: Palgrave Macmillan.

Beer, D. (2015) Productive measures: Culture and measurement in the context of everyday Neoliberalism. *Big Data & Society*, 2(1): 1–12.

Carothers, T. (1998) The rule of law revival. *Foreign Affairs*, Mar./Apr. 1998; 77: 95–106.

Carr, Helen. (1985) Woman/Indian, the "American" and his others. In F. Barker, P. Hulme, M. Iversen and D. Loxley (Eds.), *Europe and Its Others, Vol. 2*. Colchester: University of Essex Press.

Castañeda, Claudia. (2002) *Figurations: Child, Bodies, Worlds*. Durham, NC: Duke University Press.

da Silva, D.F. (2016a, April 27) *Fractal Thinking*. Retrieved June 29, 2020, from https://accessions.org/article2/fractal-thinking/.

da Silva, D.F. (2016b) On difference without separability. *32nd Bienal De São Paulo Art Biennial, "Incerteza viva" (Living Uncertainty)*. Retrieved June 29, 2020, from https://issuu.com/amilcarpacker/docs/denise_ferreira_da_silva.

da Silva, D.F. (2007) *Toward a Global Idea of Race*. Minneapolis: University of Minnesota Press.

Davies, J.D. (1955) *Phrenology, Fad and Science: A 19th-Century American Crusade*. New Haven, CT: Yale University Press.

Davis, T. (2009) Conceptualizing psychiatric disorders using "Four D's" of diagnosis. *The Internet Journal of Psychiatry*, 1(1): 1–5.

Dean, M. (2002) Liberal government and authoritarianism. *Economy and Society* 31(1): 37–61.

Deutsch, A. (1944) The first U.S. census of the insane (1840) and its use as proslavery propaganda. *Bulletin of the History of Medicine*, 15: 469–482.

Díaz-Castro, L., Arredondo, A., Pelcastre-Villafuerte, B.E. and Hufty, M. (2017) Governance and mental health: Contributions for public policy approach. *Rev Saúde Pública*, 51(4): 1–13.

Fabris E. (2011) *Tranquil Prisons: Chemical Incarceration under Community Treatment Orders*. Toronto: University of Toronto Press.

Fernando, S. (2017) *Institutional Racism in Psychiatry and Clinical Psychology: Race Matters in Mental Health*. London: Palgrave Macmillan.

Fidler, D. (2002) Global Health Governance: Overview of the role of international law in protecting and promoting global public health. Discussion Paper 3. London and Geneva: Centre on Global Change and Health, London School of Hygiene World Health Organization & Tropical Medicine, and WHO Dept. of Health and Development. Retrieved June 29, 2020, from https://apps.who.int/iris/handle/10665/68936.

Fitzpatrick, P. (2011) Terminal Legality: Imperialism and the (De)Composition of Law. In D. Kirkby and C. Coleborne (Eds.), *Law, History and Colonialism: The Reach of Empire*. Manchester: Manchester University Press.

Foucault, M. (2004) *Abnormal: Lectures at the Collège de France, 1974–1975*, eds Valerio Marchetti & Antonella Salomoni; trans. Graham Burchell. New York: Picador.

Foucault, M. (2003) *Psychiatric power: Lectures at the Collège de France, 1973–74*. Arnold I. Davidson (Ed.), Graham Burchell (Trans), Houndmills: Palgrave Macmillan.

Gilman, S.L. (1982/2014). *Seeing the insane: A visual and cultural history of our attitudes towards the mentally ill*. Brattlero, VT: EchoPoint Books.

Gorman, R. (2017) Quagmires of affect: madness, labor, whiteness, and ideological disavowal. *American Quarterly*, 69(2): 309–313.

Hacking, I. (1982) Biopower and the avalanche of printed numbers. *Humanities in Society*, 5: 279–295.

Hacking, I. (1990) *The Taming of Chance*. Cambridge: Cambridge University Press.

Hanlon, C., Eshetu, T., Alemayehu, D., Fekadu, A., Semrau, M., Thornicroft, G., Kigozi, F., Leigh Marais, D., Petersen, I., and Alem, A. (2017) Health system governance to support scale up of mental health care in Ethiopia: A qualitative study. *International Journal of Mental Health Systems*, 11(38): 1–16.

Harney, S. and Moten, F. (2013) *The Undercommons: Fugitive Planning & Black Study*. Brooklyn and Wivenhoe: Minor Compositions Press.

Howell, A. (2012). Toward an international political sociology of health and medicine. *International Political Sociology*, 6(3): 315–316.

Howell, A. (2018) Forget "militarization": Race, disability and the "martial politics" of the police and of the university. *International Feminist Journal of Politics*, DOI: 10.1080/14616742.2018.1447310.

Howell, A. (2014) The global politics of medicine: Beyond global health, against securitization theory. *Review of International Studies*, 40: 961–987.

Howell, A. (2011) *Madness in International Relations: Psychology, Security, and the Global Governance of Mental Health*. New York: Routledge.

Howell, A. (2010) Sovereignty, security, psychiatry: Liberation and the failure of mental health governance in Iraq. *Security Dialogue*, 41(4): 347–367.

Ilcan, S. and Basok, T. (2004) Community government: Voluntary agencies, social justice, and the responsibilization of citizens. *Citizenship Studies*, 8(2): 129–144.

International Monetary Fund (1997) *Good Governance: The IMF's Role*. Washington, DC: International Monetary Fund.

Jilek, W. G. (1995) Emil Kraepelin and comparative sociocultural psychiatry. *European Archive of Psychiatry and Clinical Neuroscience*, 245: 231–238.

Kalathil, J. and Jones, N. (2016). Unsettling disciplines: Madness, identity, research, knowledge. *Philosophy, Psychiatry, & Psychology*, 23(3/4): 183–188.

Klein, E. and Mills, C. (2017) Psy-Expertise, therapeutic culture and the politics of the personal in development. *Third World Quarterly*, 38(9): 1990–2008.

Kleinman, A., G.L. Estrin, S. Usmani et al. (2016) Time for mental health to come out of the shadows, *Lancet* 387: 2274–7225.

Leblanc, S. and E. Kinsella (2016) Toward epistemic justice: A critically reflexive examination of 'sanism' and implications for knowledge generation. *Studies in Social Justice*, 10 (1): 59–78.

Li, T. (2007) *The Will to Improve: Governmentality, Development and the Practice of Politics*. Durham, NC: Duke University Press.

Lingard, B. (2011) Policy as numbers: Ac/counting for educational research. *Australian Educational Research*, 38: 355–382.

McBride, K. (2016) *Mr. Mothercountry: The Man Who Made the Rule of Law*. Oxford: Oxford University Press.

McEwan, C. (2008) *Postcolonialism and Development*. London: Taylor and Francis.

Miller, P. and Rose, N. (Eds.) (1986) *The Power of Psychiatry*. Cambridge: Polity.

Merry, S. E. (2016) *The Seductions of Quantification*. Chicago and London: University of Chicago Press.

Mills, C. (2018) 'Invisible problem' to global priority: The inclusion of mental health in the Sustainable Development Goals (SDGs). *Development and Change*. 49(3): 843–866.

Mills, C. and LeFrancois, B.L. (2018) Child as metaphor: Colonialism, psy-governance, and epistemicide. *World Futures: The Journal of New Paradigm Research*, 74(7–8): 503–524.

Mills, C. (2014) *Decolonizing Global Mental Health: The Psychiatrization of the Majority World*. London: Routledge.

Morton, S. (1839) *Crania Americana: Or, Comparative View of the Skulls of Various Aboriginal Nations of North & South America*. Philadelphia: Dobson. Retrieved June 29, 2020, from https://archive.org/details/Craniaamericana00Mort.

Orr, J. (2010) The 'soul of the citizen,' the invention of the social Governing mentalities. In J. R. Hall, L. Gindstaff, and M. -C. Lo (Eds.), *Handbook of Cultural Sociology*. New York: Routledge, 547–556.

Orr J. (2013, June 17) a possible history of oblivion. Retrieved from: https://socialtextjournal.org/periscope_article/a-possible-history-of-oblivion/.

Orr, J. (2006) *Panic Diaries: A Genealogy of Panic Disorder*. Durham, NC, and London: Duke University Press.

Patel, V., Boyce, N., Collins, P.Y., Saxena, S. and Horton, R. (2011) A renewed agenda for global mental health. *The Lancet*, 378: 1441–1442.

Petersen, I., Marais, D., Abdulmalik, J., Ahuja, S., Alem, A., Chisholm, D., Egbe, C., Gureje, O., Hanlon, C., Lund, C., Shidhaye, R., Jordans, M., Kigozi, F., Mugisha, J., Upadhaya, N. and Thornicroft, G. (2017)

Strengthening mental health system governance in six low- and middle-income countries in Africa and South Asia: challenges, needs and potential strategies. *Health Policy and Planning*, 32: 699–709.

Petras, J. and Veltmeyer H. (2001) *Globalization Unmasked: Imperialism in the 21st Century*. London: Zed Books.

Poskett, J. (2015) National types: The transatlantic publication and reception of *Crania Americana* (1839). *History of Science*, 53(3): 264–295.

Pupavac, V. (2001) Therapeutic governance: Psycho-social intervention and trauma risk management. *Disasters*, 25(4): 358–372.

Reed, A.M. (2014) Mental Death: Slavery, Madness and State Violence in the United States (Doctoral Dissertation). Retrieved from UC Santa Cruz Electronic Theses and Dissertations. Retrieved June 29, 2020, from https://escholarship.org/uc/item/79r782m7.

Rose, N. (1999) *Powers of Freedom: Reframing Political Thought*. Cambridge: Cambridge University Press.

Rusert, B. (2017) *Fugitive Science: Empiricism and Freedom in Early African American Culture*. New York: New York University Press.

Sander, G. (1982/2004) *Seeing the Insane: A Visual and Cultural History of Our Attitudes Toward the Mentally Ill*. Battleboro, VT: Echo Point Books and Media.

Santos, B. S. (2014) *Epistemologies of the South: Justice Against Epistemicide*. Colorado: Paradigm.

Sarin, A. and Jain, S. (2012) The census of India and the mentally ill. *Indian Journal of Psychiatry*, 54(1): 32–36.

Scott, J. C. (1998) *Seeing Like a State: How Certain Schemes to Improve the Human Condition Have Failed*. New Haven: Yale University Press.

Sharpe, C. (2017) *Monstrous Intimacies: Making Post-Slavery Subjects*. Durham, NC: Durham University Press.

Singer, B.C. J. and Weir, L. (2006) Politics and sovereign power: Considerations on Foucault, *European Journal of Social Theory*, 9(4): 443–465.

Stoler, A.L. (2016) *Duress: Imperial Durabilities in Our Times*. Durham, NC: Durham University Press.

Tam, L. (2012) *Governing through competency: Race, pathologization, and the limits of mental health outreach* (Unpublished MA Thesis). University of Toronto, Toronto, Canada.

Upadhaya, N., Jordans, M.J.D., PokhreL, R., Gurung, D., Adhikari, R.P., Petersen, I. and Komproe, I.H. (2017) Current situations and future directions for mental health system governance in Nepal: findings from a qualitative study. *International Journal of Mental Health Systems*, 11(37): 1–12.

Wallace, J. (1994) De-Scribing the Water-babies: "The Child" in Postcolonial theory. In C. Tiffin and A. Lawson (Eds.), *De-scribing Empire: Postcolonialism and Textuality*. London and New York: Routledge. pp. 171–184.

Warren, C. (2016b) Black interiority, freedom, and the impossibility of living. *Nineteenth-Century Contexts*, 38(2): 107–121.

WHO (2008) Mental Health Gap Action Programme (mhGAP): Scaling up Care for Mental, Neurological and Substance Abuse Disorders. Geneva: WHO.

WHO (2016) mhGAP Intervention Guide – Version 2.0: for mental, neurological and substance use disorders in non-specialized health settings. Geneva: WHO.

World Bank (1994) Governance: The World Bank's Experience. Washington, DC: The World Bank.

PART B

Race and culture in mental health practices

6

CULTURE IN COUNSELLING PSYCHOLOGY

Farah A. Ibrahim, Jianna R. Heuer and Noreen G. Khan

This chapter considers the recognition of culture as an important variable in counselling psychology from an historical perspective. The earliest attention was focused on race and it's positive and negative effects on the counselling process. Slowly, several other dimensions of diversity were included, to ultimately result in a focus on intersectionality, power, and privilege; a much more complex picture emerged that researchers and practitioners are still working on addressing in the counselling process.

Given the brief history of psychology, it is surprising that cultural issues were not incorporated from the beginning of the process, it was assumed that counselling was generic and it should work with everyone (Holliday and Holmes 2003; Sumari and Hanim 2008). People have always had biases, stereotypes, and assumptions about every culture in the world, probably based on the basic need for survival; however, these were based on speculation. Psychology set out to apply scientific methods to the study of human behavior, thoughts, and emotions. However, the pioneers were quite sure that they were the most advanced of the human species, therefore, they become the template for normal behavior, thoughts, and emotions (Holliday and Holmes 2003). Any variation indicated less evolved members of human species! Even writing this seems laughable, and impossible!

Research on cultural factors and their relationship to mental health, illness, and cure began in earnest after World War II. It has gained significant momentum due to globalization, advances in technology, especially communication and the media, and global migrations (American Psychiatric Association 2013). The relationship between mental health and cultural context was recognized by mental health professionals who worked in cultural contexts that were dissimilar from their own (Marsella 1978). They noticed that the presentation, and cure of psychological problems varied by context; this was not what they had learned or were exposed to in their training and education (Prince and Acosta 2006). This led to the development of transcultural psychiatry as an area of study spearheaded by Eric Wittkower and the creation of Montréal's Transcultural Psychiatry Research Unit after World War II (Delille 2018). The Civil Rights Act (1964) in the United States prohibited discrimination on the basis of race, and gender in hiring, promotion, and firing, it helped in augmenting the age of ethnicity, race, and gender, in Psychology, and fueled the work of non-dominant cultural group psychologists, mostly African Americans initially, with help from several White psychologists committed to social justice and ethics (Holliday and Holmes 2003). Psychology in general was confronted with the missing piece of the puzzle, i.e., culture, which served as a wake-up call for American Psychology in 1976, with the publication of "Even the rat was White," by Robert V. Guthrie (1976; 1998). Transcultural psychiatry had a nearly 35-year head start on studying how culture informed mental illness and mental health among the cultures of the world. Somehow, this research was not incorporated in mainstream psychology and it remained blissfully ignorant of the emerging research in transcultural psychiatry (Holliday and Holmes 2003).

Today, there are many claimants to the title of "father" or "mother" of cross-cultural/multi-cultural counselling movement in counselling and clinical psychology, one scholar stands out as the parent of this movement in counselling psychology, namely Clemmont Vontress (Walcott 2010). He initiated the dialogue on the implication of White therapists working with African American clients (Vontress 1967). Vontress pioneered multicultural psychology when he published "Counseling Negro Adolescents" in 1967, which brought attention to the White counsellor/Black client counselling relationship. His work has significantly influenced counselling and psychotherapy and has shaped and guided the application of Existential coun-selling and psychotherapy to cross-cultural encounters. Vontress focuses on the humanity of a client before race, nationality, etc. He emphasizes understanding client-specific variables, along with culture-specific, and culturally universal variables. This complex schema was also operationalized in the theory of cultural identity and worldview to understand the complex-ities of an individual's world (Ibrahim 1991; 2010). In counselling psychology, research by Clemmont Vontress (1967; 1968; 1971) on counselling African Americans was the first instance of attention to non-dominant populations of the United States. His pioneering work brought the issue of counselling individuals with different cultural and sociopolitical contexts *within* the larger dominant cultural context, prior to his work, African philosophers and thinkers such as Frantz Fanon, W. E. B. DuBois, Angela Davis, and others, influenced thinking on the oppression and exclusion of Africans in the Caribbean and other colonized nations, including the United States.

Interest in understanding the influence of culture on the symptoms, and cure of mental illness was evident among scholars, however, even when culture was attended to, there were problems with methodology and interpretation. Anthony Marsella (1978) a prominent clinical psychologist who engaged in several epidemiological studies conducted in various countries on mental illness, studied how the symptoms, and the treatments varied by cultural contexts. He noted that the research methods used to study mental illness in various cultures were not pro-viding adequate information from a research perspective, and were not rigorous.

Clinical and counselling psychology was forced to confront their training models and questioned what they had overlooked. It was determined that the goal of a psychology training model was to educate applied psychology students to be scientist-practitioners. Culture was not the focus and was not brought into the picture until much later due to the efforts of non-dominant cultural group psychologists who kept agitating for change and asking for relevance of therapeutic interventions for the culturally different. This movement led to the emergence of multicultural psychology, which also relied on cross-cultural studies on culture, mental health, and cure in different geographical settings as evidence (Holiday and Holmes 2003). Two major criticism of psychology and its lack of understanding and acceptance of cultural variables as critically important in studying human behavior were that scientific racism (using science to discriminate against humans who were seen as less evolved based on Darwinian thinking); and the lack of attention to social justice issues, focusing on the psyche, without acknowledging the role of society, environmental variables, poverty, racism, and exclusion and so on (Holiday and Holmes 2003; Ibrahim and Heuer 2016; Weikart 2004).

Holliday and Holmes (2003) note that evolutionary thinking gained momentum during the 20th century as colonialization of most non-European countries was the goal of Western Europe and contact with colonized nations increased. Further, they state that given that normal was the White European yardstick, cultures, values, beliefs and assumptions that were not similar to Western European assumptions were considered inferior. Similarly, ethnic and racial non-dominant cultural groups in the United States when judged by European assumptions were found lacking. This thinking supported by "science" was used to enslave, exclude, oppress, conduct genocides, and other atrocities on people of color in the United States. Psychology maintained and continued with scientific racism into the 1940 and kept "inferior" humans out of positions of power in psychology, and from institutions of higher learning (Guthrie 1976, 1998; Holliday and Holmes 2003).

The latter part of the 20th century in the United States saw a resurgence in confronting issues of culture, a movement led primarily by non-dominant cultural group psychologists, with White allies who started to publish articles focusing on ethnic non-dominant cultural groups and their mental health needs. Professional organizations established task forces, and divisions to address the needs of ethnic non-dominant cultural groups. Ethnic non-dominant psychologists (from both clinical and counselling psychology) organized professional organizations to address the mental health needs of non-dominant cultural groups. Multicultural training during the civil rights movement was nonexistent when Black psychologists began to discuss the paucity of Black psychologists, lack of diversity of students in graduate programs, lack of publications on racism and its impact on people subjected to it, and diversity in the APA governing body. The following case example highlights the concerns regarding lack of understanding of culture, power, privilege, and social marginalization.

Elsa, a psychologist, has been practicing in her own private practice for 40 years in Hialeah, FL. She has upheld a great reputation in her community and has had a successful business. Elsa's spouse recently acquired a new job in Oakland, CA. Consequently, Elsa relocated with her spouse and opened her private practice in Oakland, CA. Her client population had changed drastically in terms of diversity, but Elsa continues practicing as usual. She has recently been seeing a new client, Daniel who is a Black male in his early 40s. Daniel presented with symptoms of depression. Elsa has been treating clients with depression throughout her career and treats Daniel as she would most of her other clients. She utilizes a behavioral approach, as she has seen progress among her clients when they change their behavior related to their depression. After several sessions, it was evident that Daniel is not making any progress with his depressive symptoms. Elsa thinks she has tried everything she can to help Daniel and decides that he is too resistant to make a change in therapy.

What has Elsa overlooked in this case? Is her educational training (from the 1970's) and experience relevant to treat Daniel? What does Elsa need to know to work effectively with Daniel? Education and training in the 1970's did not consider cultural or contextual factors, nor the effect of the sociopolitical history of African Americans in the United States, or the ongoing racism, the micro and macro aggressions that African Americans face on a daily basis. Neither was the status of African American males in US society, and the degree of hate and prejudice directed at them considered.

The fourth and fifth force in counselling and clinical psychology

Culture-centered interventions in the field of counselling and clinical psychology have been labeled as the "fourth force" (Pedersen 1999). Pedersen (1999) notes that the first force was psychoanalytic, the second force was behavioral, the third humanistic, and the fourth was culture-centered. Some may view the fourth dimension as a competing force, however, it is meant to complement existing theories. It was as early as the 1930s that human behavior was viewed as reciprocal, i.e., the individual acts upon the environment and the environment acts upon the individual, famously stated as behavior is a function of the person in an environment (Lewin 1936, 1938). When culture was first implemented in the psychology, it was mostly defined as race, ethnicity, and nationality (Gallardo and McNeil 2009). This is a very narrow view of culture; we cannot effectively implement cultural variables in the field of applied psychology with such a limited perspective (Ibrahim 1984, 1985). We need to also consider the intersections of all the identity variables (such as race, gender, sexual orientation and so on, along with power and privilege of both the helper and the client!). Culture encompasses more than ethnographic variables, it also includes sexual orientation, age, gender, ability status, social class, education, migration status, religion, etc., and the intersections of these variables (Gallardo and McNeil 2009; Ibrahim 2007; Ibrahim and Heuer 2016).

Although the fourth force of multicultural psychology in clinical psychology has been around for decades, little has been done to implement the perspective into actual practice (Essandoh 1996); efforts were made to include multicultural psychology into the field, little was done to include it into the profession and the practice of clinical work, which was still conducted from an intrapsychic perspective. According to Essandoh (1996), multicultural issues were emphasized to be politically correct, instead of requiring acceptance of cultural issues as ethical mandates and morally right. In addition, although, several institutions implemented a course on multicultural counselling, but continued to go about their business as usual, in other courses. It took years of arguing to implement just one course on the topic of culture and mental health; currently, integrative models exist in several graduate programs, meaning that multicultural psychology is incorporated throughout the entire curriculum in both counselling and clinical psychology. Berg-Cross and So (2011) maintain that the competencies and guidelines did not provide the results such as enhanced cultural competence. They note that there is only one study that compares the effectiveness of multicultural competence. It found that the multicultural competencies (ACA 1992) were unrelated to therapeutic outcomes, however, clients perceived their therapist as having cultural competence, and the outcome of therapy was positive. Overall, when therapists were able to understand the presenting problem from a cultural perspective, clients were more satisfied (Owen, Leach, Wampold, and Rodolfa 2011). Although, applied psychology programs have moved to an integrative model in graduate programs, Holliday and Holmes (2003) note that counselling psychology seems to incorporate multicultural psychology more than clinical psychology programs in the United States, which indicates that the field of clinical psychology continues to be resistant.

Essandoh (1996) discusses the importance of culture-specific and cultural universals in understanding clients in both clinical and counselling psychology. Theorists and researchers have had a difficult time determining which variables would be relevant, and to whom, and under what conditions (Vontress 2015). However, all seem to agree that eventually both approaches need to be combined to fully understand an individual. Essandoh argues that it makes sense to continue the work from an emic perspective and to later include the etic approach.

The fifth force in counselling and psychotherapy was identified by Ratts (2009) by recognizing a change in applied psychology fields, such as intersectionality and social justice issues emerged as critically important in providing mental health services to oppressed populations. To focus on social justice issues, the American Counselling Association put forth Advocacy Competencies (ACA, 2003). The Advocacy Competencies provide guidance on identifying and addressing social justice issues for individuals, groups, and communities/institutions. Once again, the competencies are not a new theoretical framework, like the first three forces in counselling and psychotherapy; they are similar to multicultural psychology as they complement the original three schools of thought in counselling and psychotherapy and help clarify and identify client concerns from intersectionality of identity, culture, and context, and a social justice perspective to make therapeutic interventions meaningful to clients.

Cultural education and training in counselling and clinical psychology

According to the American Psychological Association, multicultural competencies have been an integral part of both psychological practice and thinking for about 50 years (DeAngelis 2015). It is not only a part of thinking and practice within the field of psychology, but a core competency (DeAngelis 2015). Although multicultural competencies are emphasized in the field of psychology, DeAngelis explained that there has been a lack of funding for research, and disagreement on how to implement multicultural competencies within the field. In 1985 the concept of cultural diversity was first implemented as a component of effective training, following the American Psychological Association's Vail conference in 1973 when culture was first mentioned as a clinical variable (DeAngelis 2015). Finally, in 1992 the revision of the *APA Ethics Code* Principle D, noted that "Psychologists are aware of cultural, individual, and role differences, including those related to age, gender, sexual orientation, race, ethnicity, national origin" (1992: 1599). Despite the fact that it was stated during the Vail conference that it would be unethical to treat diverse populations without proper knowledge, skills, and training on cultural issues, many institutions resisted implementing cultural information pertaining to mental health and treatment into their graduate programs (Holliday and Holmes 2003). The argument was that the competencies were too vague, when the guidelines in response to this criticism became more specific, there were complaints that the criteria was too specific. According to Mio (2003), this exemplified that the real issue was resistance to incorporating multicultural issues, although it was unethical not to do so.

Training on multicultural issues in clinical and counselling psychology originally focused on teaching about different cultural and ethnic groups and increasing cultural knowledge of the clinician. This approach although much more useful than ignoring culture altogether, did not address the implicit biases and prejudices that the socialization process created, and in effect posed the danger of stereotyping people based on clinicians' perspective on a cultural group. Although, the multicultural competencies and guidelines (ACA 1992; APA 2002) emphasized "understanding own and client worldview and culture" there was no specific strategy provided to access these competencies and assess them. Two studies confirmed that using worldview assessment and Ibrahim's training model for clinicians increased client trust, and credibility of the clinicians as rated by clients (Cunningham-Warburton 1988; Ibrahim 1982; Sadlak 1986).

Multicultural counselling training requires an increase in self-awareness of the professional and recognizing implicit biases, resulting from the socialization process.

Cross-cultural education and training recognizes that mental health professionals must confront their own worldview (values, beliefs, and assumptions), socialization process, and the influences that shape their identity, along with the biases and the prejudices that they grew up with (socially and culturally), and understand social justice issues of privilege, and oppression as the most important aspects of cross-cultural training (ACA 1992; AMCD 2015; APA 2002; Ibrahim 1991; Ibrahim and Arredondo 1986). The goal is to come to terms with one's identity and culture, and to develop a nonracist (non-homophobic, nonsexist, non-classist, etc.,) identity.

Internationally, various countries have incorporated local cultural traditions in counselling and clinical psychology, along with Western theories of counselling and psychotherapy (Hohenshil, Amundsen, and Niles 2013). These countries included: Argentina, China, India,

Kenya, Mexico, the Philippines, and Switzerland (Hohenshil, Amundsen, and Niles 2013; Jennings, D'Rozario, Goh, Sovereign, Brogger and Skovholt 2008; Leung, and Chen 2009). In addition, Canada and the United Kingdom has made significant progress in addressing counselling from an indigenous and cultural perspective (Collins and Arthur 2007; Hussein and Cochrane 2002; Moodley 2007, 2009; Shariff 2009).

The emphasis on intersectionality and identity

The focus on intersectionality and identity of mental health professionals asks them to confront their own socialization, to understand their similarities and differences from their clients, and reduce cultural mishaps and malpractice. Further, identity research has highlighted the need for understanding intersectionality, and the implications of non-dominant status in a society (Bauer 2014; Seng, Lopez, Sperflich, Hamama, and Reed Medrum 2012; Viruell-Fuentes, Miranda, and Abdulrahmin 2012). Identity development scholarship originated with William Cross (1971) theory of "Nigrescence." It brought the attention of psychology to identity development among oppressed non-dominant cultural group members and presented a whole new perspective on identity development for research and psychological interventions. Later, Helms (1984, 1990) developed assessment measures for both Black and White racial identity. Several identity development models followed, including Feminist (Downing and Roush 1985), Ethnic non-dominant adolescents (Phinney 1989), Gay, Lesbian (Bilodeau and Renn 2005; McCarn and Fassinger 1996; Troiden1989), and Transsexual identity (Devor 2004; Morgan and Stevens 2012). Models for ethnic cultural identity followed, specifically: Biracial Identity (Poston 1990), Pilipino (Nadal 2004), South Asian (Ibrahim, Ohnishi, and Sandhu 1997), Marianismo/Machismo (Nuñez, González, Talavera, Sanchez Johnsen, Roesch, Davis et al. 2016), and Latinx cultural identity (Felix-Ortiz 1994). These models were primarily designed to assist with identity development and empowerment interventions. They also proved useful in therapeutic work for assessing clients phase of identity development to ascertain the best strategies for therapeutic interventions (Helms and Cook 1999).

Intersectionality is critical to understanding how identity variables interact with marginal status and the implications for counselling (Seng, Lopez, Sperflich, Hamama, and Reed Medrum 2012; Viruell-Fuentes, Miranda, and Abdulrahmin 2012).

> Intersectionality is a term used to describe the intersecting effects of race, class, gender, and other marginalizing characteristics that contribute to social identity and affect health. Adverse health effects are thought to occur via social processes including discrimination and structural inequalities, i.e., reduced opportunities for education and income.
>
> *(Seng et al. 2012: 2347)*

Recognizing power and privilege issues inherent in identity variables as they pertain to the mental health professionals and clients is important. This aspect was completely overlooked in the initial cultural movements in counselling and psychotherapy. Recently, issues of marginality and power and privilege are now being addressed in US professional associations' ethical principles and competency statements (AMCD 2015; ACA 2015; APA 2017).

Although multicultural psychology in clinical and counselling psychology is a core component, Vera and Speight (2003) maintain that the concept itself does not address or resolve racial issues in the United States, but can actually camouflage them, given that professionals can learn and practice culturally responsive therapeutic work, without taking responsibility for changing the hierarchical dynamics of society. This indicates that it is imperative that mental health training programs include social justice advocacy as a component of cross-cultural training in both clinical and counselling psychology (Ibrahim and Heuer 2016).

Counselling interventions

This section explores what is needed to provide effective cross-cultural/multicultural counselling and psychotherapy. It also addresses the changing role of therapists given professional guidelines. The issue of arriving at the best psychological interventions for cultural and non-dominant cultural group is still not resolved (Chu, Leino, Pflum, and Sue 2016). Meta-analytic studies show that culturally mediated psychotherapy is effective, and therapy conducted in the client's language is highly effective (Griner and Smith 2006). However, we still have controversies about evidence-based practices and we are still wondering about effective interventions for non-dominant populations! Research and funding is needed to study which interventions, will work for whom under what conditions. Kaplan, Johnson, and Kobor (2017) report that funding for psychological research has been limited from 1980 to 2016. Given the burden of mental illness, especially on the most vulnerable populations, the profession and professionals must advocate for funding for research to study within group and between group variations and the most meaningful psychological interventions for diverse cultural groups.

Another issue that needs attention is that counselling and clinical psychology needs to address intersectionality of identity and recognize that all diversity categories must be addressed, there has been an overemphasis on race/ethnicity, gender, and sexual orientation with limited attention to age, disability, immigrant and refugee status, religion/spirituality, etc. Considering identity from a singular perspective, limits our ability to recognize and understand the intersections of multiple identities, especially when there are several oppressed identities involved (Ibrahim and Heuer 2016; Ratts, Singh, Nassar-McMillan, Butler, and McCullough 2016; Shin 2015).

The final issue concerns the changing role of psychologists and mental health professionals as social justice advocates. This means we cannot simply dispense services when someone reaches out for help, but also function as a community resource and help educate the public about the importance of mental health and its relationship to intersectionality, and social justice and provide public service information to our communities, along with grass root efforts to identify and stop emotional and psychological abuse perpetuated by racism, sexism, homophobia, classism, ableism, ageism, etc. It is important for us to help stop psychological abuse and recognize that emotional and psychological stress leads to both mental and physical disorders (Ibrahim and Heuer 2016; Ratts et al. 2016)

Future directions

Considering the case presented earlier in this chapter, the issues that stand out are: (a) training and philosophical differences among the various generations of professionals providing services to clients who are culturally different even within the same country; and (b) recognition of intersectionality of identities in hierarchical social systems and a movement away from a unimodal perspective on identity (such as just race, or gender) (Bauer 2014; Seng et al. 2012). The profession needs to address how guidelines and competency statements about culture will be implemented in educational programs, and for the several generations of therapists and clinicians that are already in the field. It is up to us as professionals to continue to work on behalf of the public to ensure that services provided are culturally meaningful and improve mental health locally, nationally, and globally. Leong, Pickren, and Vasquez (2017) note that an early historical analysis of the activities of psychological associations reveals that efforts regarding human rights and social justice were not consistently positive. It was the leadership of ethnic non-dominant psychologists that led to changes by addressing issues of cultural oppression in counselling and clinical psychology. Furthermore, they identify that the last two decades had seen significant positive changes in policy and practice as it pertains to culture in counselling and clinical psychology, e.g., with the provision of ethical and cultural guidelines that incorporate social justice concerns and integrative training models (APA 2002; ACA 2015). Leong et al. (2017: 787) also note that that counselling and clinical psychology face critical challenges, which include: "health disparities; violent extremism; social problems associated with culture, race and ethnicity."

Conclusion

A significant issue that needs attention if we are to move toward stronger societies is eradication of prejudice and hate, based on race, ethnicity, gender, sexual orientation, age, disability, migration status, religion/spirituality, and social class (Wilkinson and Pickett 2010). These external variables are responsible for significant human misery and lead to mental and physical disorders, suicide, depression and anxiety (Jun 2010). Recognition of these external stressors has ignited the social justice movement in psychology and the helping professions (Ibrahim and Heuer 2016; Ratts 2009). The UN (2015) recognizes that violent extremism is the root of hatred and prejudice.

To address health disparities, we need political action to provide health care access to everyone (Phelps, Bray, and Kearney 2017). This is a charge for mental health professionals and professional associations. Constant political instability based on party lines hurts the most vulnerable, and social justice requires that we are politically active on behalf of vulnerable populations to prevent mental health crises created by lack of services, or services that are not culturally adapted, and provided in the client's language (Griner and Smith 2006).

Finally, we need curricula that internationalizes psychology and decolonizes it (Leong, Pickren, Leach, and Marsella 2012; Goodman and Gorski 2015). The impact of Western colonialization has deep roots in psychology (Goodman and Gorski 2015). Incorporating cultural information relevant to global communities is critical in making clinical and counselling psychology relevant for education, training, and practice. Shin (2015) also argues for educating for critical consciousness and intersectionality to decolonize racial/ethnic identity models in counselling and clinical psychology.

Another related concern identified by Tomlinson (2013) is that existing competencies and guidelines are limited to the US context, and counsellors in global communities cannot use them. This concern is also voiced by Leong and Ponterotto (2003), Leung (2003), and Sumari and Jalal (2008) call for globalization of cultural competencies. A unique model for collaboration and exchange of ideas has been active in a global context for decades, i.e., the International Round Table for the Advancement of Counselling (Lee, 1997). Similar collaboration are needed to increase the exchange of ideas for counselling and clinical psychology, and research collaborations.

Although, we have come a long way in recognizing the role of culture in counselling and clinical psychology; we still have a long way to go to address global mental health needs. Cultural competencies must be developed for a global context. Culture, intersectionality and social justice must become the mediating variables to guide us in working with diverse populations as advocated by mental health professionals, and generating critical consciousness among psychology professionals is needed for education and training to address issues of culture, intersectionality, and social justice to reduce health disparities.

References

American Counseling Association (ACA). (1992) *Multicultural Competencies*. Alexandria, VA: American Counseling Association.

American Counseling Association (ACA) (2003) *Advocacy Competencies*. Alexandria, VA: American Counseling Association.

American Counseling Association (ACA) (2015) *Multicultural and Social Justice Competencies*. Alexandria, VA: American Counseling Association.

American Psychiatric Association (2000) The Diagnostic and Statistical Manual of Mental Disorders (DSM-IV; Text Revised). Washington, DC: American Psychiatric Association.

American Psychiatric Association (2013a) *Resource Document on Cultural Psychiatry as a Specific Field of Study Relevant to the Assessment and Care of all Patients*. Washington, DC: American Psychiatric Association.

American Psychiatric Association (2013b) The Diagnostic and Statistical Manual of Mental Disorders (DSM-5). Washington, DC: American Psychiatric Association.

American Psychological Association (1992) *Ethical Code* . Washington, DC: American Psychological Association.

American Psychological Association (2002) *Ethical Code*. Washington, DC: American Psychological Association.

American Psychological Association (2017) *Ethical Code*. Washington, DC: American Psychological Association.

Association for Multicultural Counseling and Development (AMCD) (2015) *Multicultural and Social Justice Counseling Competencies*. Alexandria, VA: Association for Multicultural Counseling and Development.

Bauer, G. R. (2014) Incorporating Intersectionality Theory into Population Health Research Methodology: Challenges and the Potential to Advance Health Equity. *Social Science & Medicine*, 110: 10–17. https://doi.org/10.1016/j.socscimed.2014.03.022.

Berg-Cross, L., and So, D. (2011) Evidence-Based Multicultural Therapies: The Start of a New Era. *The National Register*. Retrieved from: www.nationalregister.org/pub/the-national-register-report-pub/the-register-report-fall-2011/evidence-based-multicultural-therapies-the-start-of-a-new-era/?pri… 14/14.

Bilodeau, B. L., and Renn, K. A. (2005) Analysis of LGBT Identity Development Models and Implications for Practice. *New Directions for Student Services*, 111: 25–39.

Collins, S., and Arthur, N. (2007) A framework for Enhancing Multicultural Counselling Competence. *Canadian Journal of Counselling*, 41(1): 31–49.

Chu, J., Leino, A., Pflum, S., and Sue, S. (2016) A Model for the Theoretical Basis of Cultural Competency to Guide Psychotherapy. *Professional Psychology: Research and Practice*, 47(1): 18–29. http://dx.doi.org/10.1037/pro0000055.

Cunningham-Warburton, P. A. (1988) A Study of the Relationship Between Cross-Cultural Training, the Scale to Assess World Views© and the Quality of Care Given by Nurses in a Psychiatric Setting. Unpublished doctoral dissertation, University of Connecticut, Storrs.

Cross, W. E. (1971) The Negro-to-Black Conversion Experience. *Black World*, 20(9): 13–27.

DeAngelis, T. (2015) In Search of Cultural Competence. *Monitor on Psychology*, 46(3): 64.

Delille, E. (2018) Eric Wittkower and the Foundation of Montréal's Transcultural Psychiatry Research Unit after World War II. *History of Psychiatry*. Retrieved from: https://doi.org/10.1177/0957154X18765417.

Devor, A. H. (2004) Witnessing and Mirroring: A Fourteen Stage Model of Transsexual Formation. *Journal of Gay and Lesbian Psychotherapy*, 8(1–2): 41–67.

Downing, N. E., and Roush, K. L. (1985) From Passive Acceptance to Active Commitment: A Model of Feminist Identity for Women. *Counseling Psychologist*, 13(4): 695–709.

Essandoh, P. K. (1996) Multicultural Counseling as the "Fourth Force." *The Counseling Psychologist*, 24(1): 126–137.

Felix-Ortiz, M. (1994) A Multidimensional Measure of Cultural Identity for Latino and Latina Adolescents. *Hispanic Journal of Behavioral Sciences*, 16: 99–116.

Gallardo, M. E., and McNeill, B. W. (2009) *Intersections of Multiple Identities*. New York: Routledge

Goodman, R. D., and Gorski, P. C. (2015) *Decolonizing "Multicultural Counseling" through Social Justice*. New York: Springer.

Griner, D., and Smith, T. B. (2006) Culturally Adapted Mental Health Intervention: A Meta-Analytic Review. *Psychotherapy: Theory, Research, Practice, Training*, 43(4): 531–548. http://dx.doi.org/10.1037/0033-3204.43.4.531.

Guthrie, R. V. (1976) *Even the Rat was White: A Historical View of Psychology*. Boston: Allyn and Bacon.

Guthrie, R. V. (1998) *Even the Rat was White: A Historical View of Psychology* (2nd ed.). Boston: Allyn and Bacon.

Helms, J. E. (1984) Toward a Theoretical Explanation of the Effects of Race on Counseling: Black and White Model. *Counseling Psychologist*, 12(4): 163–165.

Helms, J. E. (1990) *Black and White Racial Identity: Theory, Research, and Practice*. Westport, CT: Greenwood.

Helms, J. E., and Cook, D. A. (1999) *Using Race and Culture in Counseling and Psychotherapy: Theory and Process*. Needham, MA: Allyn & Bacon.

Hohenshil, T. H., *Amundsen, N. E., & Niles, S. G. (2013). Counseling around the world: An international Handbook*. Alexandria, VA: American Counseling Association.

Holliday, B. G., and Holmes, A. L. (2003) A Tale of Challenge and Change: A History and Chronology of Ethnic Minorities in Psychology in the United States. In G. Bernal, J. E. Trimble, A. K. Burlew, and F. T. L. Leong (Eds.), *Handbook of Racial & Ethnic Minority Psychology* (pp. 15–64). Thousand Oaks, CA: Sage.

Hussain, F. A., and Cochrane, R. (2002) Depression in South Asian Women: Asian Women's Beliefs on Causes and Cures. *Mental Health, Religion, & Culture*, 5(3): 285–311. doi: 10.1080/13674670210130036.

Ibrahim, F. A. (1982) *Cross-Cultural Counseling: Graduate Course*. Storrs, CT: University of Connecticut.

Ibrahim, F. A., (1984) Cross-Cultural Counseling and Psychotherapy: An Existential-Psychological Perspective. *The International Journal for the Advancement of Counseling*, 7: 159–169.

Ibrahim, F. A. (1985) Effective Cross-Cultural Counseling and Psychotherapy: A Framework. *The Counseling Psychologist*, 13: 625–638.

Ibrahim, F. A. (1991) Contribution of Cultural Worldview to Generic Counseling and Development. *Journal of Counseling and Development*, 70: 13–19.

Ibrahim, F. A. (1999) Transcultural Counseling: Existential World View Theory and Cultural Identity: Transcultural Applications. In J. McFadden (Ed.), *Transcultural Counseling* (2nd. ed., pp. 23–57). Alexandria, VA: ACA Press.

Ibrahim, F. A. (2007) *Cultural Identity Check List-Revised[©]*. Denver, CO: Copy written document.

Ibrahim, F. A. (2010) Clemmont Vontress: Reflections of a Long-Distance Mentee. In R. Moodley and R. Walcott (Eds.), *Clemmont Vontress: Pioneer of Cross-Cultural Counseling* (pp. 87–96). Toronto, ON: University of Toronto Press.

Ibrahim, F. A., and Heuer, J. R. (2016) *Cultural and Social Justice Counseling: Client Specific Interventions*. New York: Springer Science+Business Media.

Ibrahim, F. A., and Arredondo, P. M. (1986) Ethical Standards for Cross-Cultural Counseling: Preparation, Practice, Assessment and Research. *Journal of Counseling and Development*, 64: 349–351.

Ibrahim, F. A., and Helms, B. J. (2008, November) *A Paradigm Shift for Evaluation Research: Incorporation of Cultural Dynamics in the Evaluation Process*, at the National Evaluation Association conference, Denver, CO.

Ibrahim, F. A., and Kahn, H. (1984) *Scale to Assess World View[©]*. Unpublished document, Storrs, CT.

Ibrahim, F. A., and Kahn, H. (1987) Assessment of World Views. *Psychological Reports*, 60: 163–176.

Ibrahim, F. A., Ohnishi, H., and Sandhu, D. S. (1997) Asian American Identity Development: A Culture-Specific Model for South Asian Americans. *Journal of Multicultural Counseling and Development*, 25(1): 34–50.

Jennings, L., D'Rosario, V., Goh, M, Sovereign, A., Brogger, M., & Skovholt, T. (2008). Psychotherapy expertise in Singapore: A qualitative investigation. *Psychotherapy Research*, 18(5), 508–522.

Jun, H. (2010) *Social Justice, Multicultural Counseling and Practice*. Thousand Oaks, CA: Sage.

Kaplan, R. M., Johnson, S. B., and Kobor, P. C. (2017) NIH Behavioral and Social Science Research Support: 1980–2016. *American Psychologist*, 72(8): 808–821.

Lee, C. C. (1997) The Global Future of Professional Counseling: Collaboration for International Change. *International Journal of Intercultural Relations*, 21(2): 279–285.

Leong, F. T. L., Pickren, W. E., Leach, M. M., and Marsella, A. J. (Eds.) (2012) *Internationalizing the Psychology Curriculum in the US*. New York: Springer.

Leong, F. T. L., Pickren, W. E., and Vasquez, M. J. T. (2017) APA Efforts in Promoting Human Rights and Social Justice. *American Psychologist*, 72(8): 778–790.

Leong, F. T. L., and Ponterotto, J. G. (2003) A Proposal for Internationalizing Counseling Psychology in the United States: Rationale, Recommendations, and Challenges. *The Counseling Psychologist*, 31: 381–395.

Leung, S. A. (2003) A Journey Worth Traveling: Globalization of Counseling Psychology. *The Counseling Psychologist*, 31: 412–419.

Leung, S. A., & Chen, P-H. (2009). Counseling psychology in Chinese communities in Asia: Indigenous, multicultural, and cross-cultural considerations. *The Counseling Psychologist*, 37(7), 944–966.

Lewin, K. (1936) *Principles of Topological Psychology*. New York: McGraw-Hill.

Lewin, K. (1938) *The Conceptual Representation and Measurement of Psychological Forces*. Durham, NC: Duke University Press.

Marsella, A. J. (1978) Thoughts on Cross-Cultural Studies on the Epidemiology of Depression. *Culture, Medicine, and Psychiatry*, 2(4): 343–357.

McCarn, S. R., and Fassinger, R. E. (1996) Revisioning Sexual Minority Identity Formation: A New Model of Lesbian Identity and its Implications for Counseling and Research. *Counseling Psychologist*, 24(3): 508–534.

Mio, J. S. (2003) On Teaching Multiculturalism. In G. Bernal, J. E. Trimble, A. K. Burlew, and F. T. L. Leong (Eds.), *Handbook of Racial and Ethnic Minority Psychology* (pp. 119–146). Thousand Oaks, CA: Sage Publications

Moodley, R. (2007) (Re)placing Multiculturalism in Counselling and Psychotherapy. *British Journal of Guidance and Counselling*, 35(1): 1–22.

Moodley, R. (2009) Multi(ple) Cultural Voices Speaking "Outside the Sentence" of Counselling and Psychotherapy. *Counselling Psychology Quarterly*, 22(3): 297–307. doi: 10.1080/09515070903302364.

Morgan, S. W., and Stevens, P. E. (2012) Transgender Identity Development as Represented by a Group of Transgendered Adults. *Issues in Mental Health Nursing*, 33: 301–308. doi: 10.3109/01612840.2011.653657.

Nadal, K. L. (2004) Pilipino American Identity Development Model. *Journal of Multicultural Counseling and Development*, 32(1): 45–62.

Nuñez, A., González, P., Talavera, G. A., Sanchez Johnsen, L., Roesch, S. C., Davis, S. M., Arguelles, W., Womack, V. Y., Ostrovsky, N., Ojeda, L., Penedo, F. J., and Gallo, L. C. (2016) Machismo, Marianismo, and Negative Cognitive Emotional Factors: Findings from the Hispanic Community Health Study/Study of Latinos Sociocultural Ancillary Study. *Journal of Latino Psychology*, 4(4): 202–217. doi: 10.1037/lat0000050.

Owen, J., Leach, M. M., Wampold, B., and Rodolfa, E. (2011) Client and Therapist Variability in Clients' Perceptions of Their Therapists' Multicultural Competencies. *Journal of Counseling Psychology*, 58(1): 1–9.

Pedersen, P. (1999) *Multiculturalism as a Fourth Force*. Philadelphia, PA: Brunner/Mazel.

Phelps, R., Bray, J. H., and Kearney, L. K. (2017) A Quarter-Century of Psychological Practice in Mental Health and Health Care: 1990–2016. *American Psychologist*, 72(8): 822–836.

Phinney, J. S. (1989) Stages of Ethnic Identity Development in Minority Group Adolescents. *Journal of Early Adolescence*, 9(1–2): 34–49. https://doi.org/10.1177/0272431689091004.

Pope-Davis, D. B., Reynolds, A. L., Dings, J. G., and Ottavi, T. M. (1994) Multicultural Competencies of Doctoral Interns at University Counseling Centers: An Exploratory Investigation. *Professional Psychology: Research and Practice*, 25: 466–470.

Poston, W. S. C. (1990) The Biracial Identity Development Model: A Needed Addition. *Journal of Counseling and Development*, 69: 152–155.

Prince, M., & Acosta, D. (2006). Aging and dementia in low- and middle-income countries-the work of the 10/66 Dementia Research Group. *International Psychiatry*, 3(4), 3–6.

Ratts, M. J. (2009) Social Justice Counseling: Toward the Development of the Fifth Force among Counseling Paradigms. *The Journal of Humanistic Counseling*, 48(2): 160–172.

Ratts, M. J., Singh, A. A., Nassar-McMillan, S., Butler, S. K., and McCullough, J. R. (2016) Multicultural and Social Justice Counseling Competencies: Guidelines for the Counseling Profession. *Journal of Multicultural Counseling and Development*, 44(1): 28–48.

Sadlak, M. J. (1986) *A Study of the Impact of Training in Cross-Cultural Counseling on Counselor Effectiveness and Sensitivity*. Doctoral dissertation, University of Connecticut, Storrs.

Seng, J. S., Lopez, W. D., Sperflich, M., Hamama, L., and Reed Medrum, C. D. (2012) Marginalized Identities, Discrimination Burden, and Mental Health: Empirical Exploration of an Interpersonal-Level Approach to Modeling Intersectionality. *Social Science and Medicine*, 75: 2437–2445. https://doi.org/10.1016/j.socscimed.2012.09.023.

Shariff, A. (2009) Ethnic Identity and Parenting Stress in South Asian Families: Implications for Culturally Sensitive Counselling. *Canadian Journal of Counselling*, 43(1): 35–46.

Shin, R. Q. (2015) The Application of Critical Consciousness and Intersectionality as Tools for Decolonizing Racial/Ethnic Identity Development Models in the Fields of Counseling and Psychology. In R. D. Goodman and P. C. Gorski (Eds.), *Decolonizing "Multicultural" Counseling through Social Justice* (pp. 11–22). New York: Springer.

Sue, D. W., Bernier, J. E., Duran, A., Feinberg, L., Pedersen, P., Smith, E. J., et al. (1982) Position Paper: Cross-Cultural Counseling Competencies. *Counseling Psychologist*, 10: 45–52.

Sue. S., Zane, N., Nagayama Hall, G. C., and Berger, L. K. (2009) The Case for Cultural Competency in Psychotherapeutic Interventions. *Annual Review of Psychology,* 60: 525–548. doi:10.1146/annurev.psych.60.110707.163651.

Sumari, M., and Jalal, F. H. (2008) Cultural Issues in Counseling: An International Perspective. *Counselling, Psychotherapy, and Health*, 4(1): 24–34.

Tomlinson-Clarke, S. (2013) Multicultural Counseling Competencies: Extending Multicultural Training Paradigms toward Globalization. 2, article 60.

Troiden, R. R. (1989) The Formation of Homosexual Identities. *Journal of Homosexuality*, 17: 43–73.

United Nations General Assembly. (2015) *Plan of Action to Prevent Violent Extremism.* Retrieved from: www.shareweb.ch/site/Conflict-and-Human-Rights/tools/Documente%20Shareweb%20von%20Excelliste/UN_ActionPlan_PVE_def.pdf.

Vera, E. M., and Speight, S. L. (2003) Multicultural Competence, Social Justice, and Counseling Psychology: Expanding Our Roles. *The Counseling Psychologist,* 31(3): 253–272.

Viruell-Fuentes, E. A., Miranda, P.Y., and Abdulrahmin, S. (2012) More than Culture: Structural Racism, Intersectionality Theory, and Immigrant Health. *Social Science & Medicine*, 75: 2099–2106. https://doi.org/10.1016/j.socscimed.2011.12.037.

Vontress, C. E. (1967a) Counseling Negro Adolescents. *The School Counselor*, 15: 86–91.

Vontress, C. E. (1967b) The Culturally Different. *Employment Service Review*, 4: 35–36.

Vontress, C. E. (1968, April) *Cultural Differences: Implications for Counseling.* Presentation at the Personnel and Guidance Association National Conference, Detroit, MI.

Vontress, C. E. (2015, March) Cross-Cultural/Multicultural Counseling: A Historical Perspective. Presentation in a Symposium, Chair, Farah A. Ibrahim, *Cross-Cultural/Multicultural Counseling: Past, Present, and Future* at the American Counseling Association annual conference. Orlando, FL.

Walcott, R. (2010) A Theory of Apprehension?: Fanon, Vontress, and Cultural identity; or how not to get Stuck There. In R. Moodley, and R. Walcott (Eds.), *Clemmont Vontress: Pioneer of Cross-Cultural Counseling* (pp. 57–69). Toronto, Canada: University of Toronto Press.

Weikart, R. (2004) *From Darwin to Hitler: Evolutionary Ethics, Eugenics, and Racism in Germany.* New York: Palgrave Macmillan.

Wilkinson, R., and Pickett, K. (2010) *The Spirit Level: Why Greater Equality Makes Stronger Societies.* New York: Bloomsbury.

7

CULTURE AND PSYCHOANALYSIS

Ruth M. Lijtmaer

Psychoanalysis has a long history as a progressive movement devoted to the common good. Psychoanalysis asks us to examine the processes of self-deception that perpetuate both individual unhappiness and social structures that are inequitable and oppressive. However, it is necessary for psychoanalysis to remember that it is a minority discipline in relation to the rest of the world. Until recently, psychoanalysis has focused on training and treating the relatively privileged. Yet the psychoanalytic community at large is composed of very different individuals, particularly in terms of culture and race.

Appearances provide the first information about the individual to others in the context of face-to-face social interaction. It helps define the identity of the individual and to express their self-identification. It is in this process that identities are negotiated and either validated or invalidated. Therefore, it is impossible to think of identity without its cultural and racial nature (Lijtmaer 2006). Race as a psychological experience may well challenge the distinction we make between social reality and psychic reality. Typically, psychoanalytic discussions of race emphasize race as racism (Holmes 1992; Leary 1997), race as a focal point for representations of unacceptable or unacknowledged aspects of the self projected elsewhere (Holmes 1992; Leary 1997). Strongly grounded in each individual by a growing assemble of symbolic rituals where specific cultural values are transmitted, racial attitudes are learned and a culturally influenced worldview is established (Javier and Rendon 1995). These basic belief systems and culturally specific ways of relating are programmed providing the foundation for the development of identity.

This chapter will examine both the resistances to, and the necessity for psychoanalytic engagement of issues of otherness, difference and diversity included in the concept of culture and race. It will also discuss the cultural and racially imposed trauma that affects people's lives.

Culture-free psychoanalysis

Culture is our shared illusion (Winnicott 1951, 1971). It is the transitional space in which we interact. Within a culture there are beliefs about the purpose of life, symbolic rituals, concepts of time and space, causation of events, the individual's responsibility for those events and how mind and body work. Viewing culture in this way, we can think of culture as having defensive hierarchies that result in cultural patterns and ethnic characters. There is a commonality of defenses and conflicts that are both provided and facilitated by a particular culture. Considering the above statements, what it means and how the treatment space is experienced depends on the sensitivity of the clinician to awareness of the patient's and the therapist ethnicity and culture (Lijtmaer 2006). Therefore, the clinician comes to the consulting room with a set of predetermined ideas about the characters of these respective patients. The clinician's cultural assumptions may be correct or incorrect; however, the point here is that to think that the clinician is transferentially neutral or "culturally free" is inaccurate. For those cultural assumptions will quickly serve to guide the clinician's judgments about such things as the patient's human values, likeability, personal threat, amenability to treatment, capacity for insight and change and other judgments that will influence the course of treatment (Perez-Foster 1999).

Culture and ethnicity are something found at the very deepest level of psychic life because growing up requires socialization in the diverse array of human societies, each with its own distinctive beliefs and practices for guiding us through life (Layton 2013). This is reflected in the consulting room, where different nationalities and languages are communicated, as dialects, accents and intonations offer clues to the analyst's and patient's origins (Lijtmaer 2013).

It is around difference real or imagined that our earliest and most primitive defenses gather to split our objects into them and us, the feared and the safe, the loved and the hated, the privileged and the excluded, the envied and the denigrated. It can also provoke unconscious guilt, or the reaction formation of overcurious interest and identification. These categories evolve in profoundly individual ways, and, as with any trauma, external reality reinforces and shapes fantasy. By the time we see their manifestation in the transference/countertransference they appear as complex structures, each with its own mix of aggressive, erotic, defensive, and self-punitive components that applies to both patient and analyst. In the clinical setting, Susan, an American female patient, after being in therapy for a while told the author that she chose her because her accent reminded the patient of a Hispanic housekeeper who worked for the family. Susan had become very attached to her. When the housekeeper left suddenly, my patient still a child, was very sad. Therefore, for her, the therapist being of the same ethnicity as the housekeeper, helped her to work through the complex feelings attached to the early caretaker who abruptly left her. The positive transference developed. However, this attachment figure was privately adored but publicly denigrated. Susan's parents treated the housekeeper with respect but there was an underlying tone of disdain. The author realized that underlying this closeness, was a power differential, the therapist was the "servant" and the patient was the "boss" (Lijtmaer 2013). This brief vignette demonstrates the power of being the "other" and how it can affect the therapeutic relationship. The ability to consider the relationship between psychic and social realities necessarily refers us to the connotations of the therapist's social position and the relationships they establish with their patients, and therefore to the ways in which the social context affects the development of the treatment.

The Western Eurocentric point of view

Psychoanalysis and psychotherapy from its conception, have functioned from a Western ethnocentric viewpoint. In instances of individuals whose self-identity was influenced by a society that demands a different level of interaction than the values of the Western culture, the nature of the transference-countertransference will be affected by these factors. The clinician needs to exercise particular caution against applying his or her personal assumptions and metapsychology about minds at large. Whether the therapists' attitudes fall within the range of despondency, sadness or guilt over the patient's life circumstances, or whether the therapist's reactions run the spectrum of puzzlement, fear, ethnic prejudice or dislike, they will be detectable by our patients.

These reactions demand scrutiny and can be a critical point of contact with the patient's transference, conflicts and resistance. Confronted with a patient of different ethnic background compelled the therapist to look at assumptions and fantasies about the other and not to rely on the therapist's own ethnicity as the primary source of identity (Lijtmaer 2001).

The issue at stake is that Western psychology and psychoanalysis had until quite recently focused on the White population being therapy a treatment for the powerful and the few (Altman 2006).

Laungani (2004), an Indian psychotherapist, stated that "The therapist operates from a Eurocentric model, which posits a 'horizontal', non-hierarchical, but formal interpersonal relationship that emphasizes individualism". Laungani (2004: 201) cautions to therapists' "playing out" their own internalized value system that will influence his/her work. This fact is true particularly, when we think of some cultural values like individualism, materialism, secularism compared to communalism, religiosity, determinism, emotionalism and spiritualism that are tenets of Eastern cultures. As a clinical example, I personally experienced conflict when I, a Latina/Hispanic therapist working in the eastern United States treated my first Chinese patient. My metapsychology and the Western values of mental health with which I trained, were shaken by this patient. I had to adjust my treating modality to fit the patient's needs. For example, I frequently had to question the patient in order to clarify cultural practices and meanings related to her ethnic background. My candid ethnic illiteracy and attunement to "difference" constituted a powerful vehicle toward effecting psychic change. I also had to be more didactic and assumed the role of teacher which went against the psychodynamic philosophy in which I was trained (Lijtmaer 2001).

Roland (1988, in Alperin 2001), who in his psychoanalytic anthropological research compared American and Western culture to the cultures of India and Japan, contended that this has resulted in a developmental emphasis in American society on separation-individuation, a strong I-self with firm outer ego boundaries, and an intense need for privacy. He contrasted this with the Indians and the Japanese (the "collective man"), whose child-rearing patterns foster capacities for intense dependence and interdependence, resulting in a we-self with permeable outer boundaries and a much higher degree of empathy and sensitivity to others. Western trained mental health professionals, not aware of these cultural and ethnic differences may misjudge, misunderstand or pathologize the patient. Moreover, it can bring to the therapist feelings of anger and discomfort since he/she is unaware of how the Western values conflict with the ones of the East.

More recently, relational psychoanalytic approaches have challenged these Western Eurocentric ideals of human development (Comas-Díaz 2011; Layton 2006; Roland 1996; Tummala-Narra 2015). For example, the concept of healthy attachment in early relationships are based in Western values of individualism and independence, whereas conceptualizations of healthy attachment in most other cultures emphasize collectivistic values of interdependence and family unity.

Psychotherapy has been conceived as involving enactments when the therapist and the patient are unconsciously drawn to sociocultural norms that are problematic for the patient's well-being. As such, cultural conflict is not openly discussed, and aspects of the patient's identity remain hidden (Layton 2006). Supporting the above statements is to think what constitutes sensitive, responsive child-rearing practices. Those notions reflect indigenous values and goals, which are apt to differ from Eastern and Western cultures. For example, Japanese parents prefer to anticipate their infants' needs by relying on situational cues. Sometimes this means identifying situations that may stress their infants and taking anticipatory measures to minimize the stress. Parents in Western cultures, by comparison, prefer to wait for their infants to communicate their needs before taking steps to meet those needs. The different expressions of sensitivity and responsiveness suggest that for Japanese caregivers, responsiveness has more to do with emotional closeness and the parent's role in helping infants regulate their emotional states, whereas for caregivers in the Western world, responsiveness has more to do with meeting children's need to assert their personal desires and, wherever possible, respecting children's autonomous efforts to satisfy their own needs. What I am arguing is that the image of the self taken in by the infant from its caregivers is, from the first moments, intrinsically social. This means that one may no longer draw a dichotomy between a social self and a personal one, because the personal self is intrinsically social (Dalal 2006).

Culture, intersectionality and mental health

The term "intersectionality theory" was first coined in an essay by Crenshaw in 1989. In her work she specifically discussed the idea of "black feminism". According to the *Oxford English Dictionary*, "intersectional" means pertaining to or characterized by intersection. Here, this refers to the intersection of race, gender, culture and class in the development of identity.

Smith and Tang (2006) define different categories of social identity, some innate and visible (such as race and gender), some innate and invisible (sexual orientation), and some acquired or achieved (marital status and political affiliation). They then show how each category affects what mental health professionals disclose, wittingly and unwittingly, in the clinical situation. To better understand the regressive and foreclosing use of identity categories Layton (2006) coined the concept *normative unconscious processes*. This term refers to the psychological consequences of living in a culture in which many norms serve the dominant ideological purpose of maintaining a power status quo, stressing the consequences of living within particular class, race, sex, and gender hierarchies. Her assumption is that these hierarchies, which confer power and exist for the benefit of those with power, tend not only to idealize certain subject positions and devalue others, but tend to do so by splitting human capacities and attributes and giving them class, race or gender assignations. This demonstrates the inextricable link between the psychic and the social: the regimes of power that define relations between the genders, between the races and classes, and between those with different sexual desires condition the very way we experience dependence and independence, separation and individuation, for example, not usually thought of in social terms (p. 5).

All these comments raise the following questions: What do we mean when we speak of racial and/or ethnic identities? Do we refer to categories that are coherent, socially constructed, and inherently oppressive? Do we then focus politically on redressing long histories of systemic prejudice and discrimination? Or, as "colorblind" adherents claim, do racial and ethnic identities rest on cultural and/or biological differences that ought not to be taken into account. Finally, does it even make sense to speak of racial identities without simultaneously speaking of the way they intersect with class, gender, and other identity categories (Williams 1997, in Layton 2006). Therefore, race and culture exists on a continuum comprised of multiple variables, including skin color, education, income, and geographic location. The implication of these concepts in clinical work is that the therapist who must ask himself/herself which aspects of identity feel more salient when working with a patient of any particular sociocultural background, and which social identity issues the therapist is more comfortable addressing with a patient. The therapist's ability to engage with not only the patient's internal conflicts concerning social identity but also to bear the anxiety of not knowing or experiencing difference from the patient's cultural identification is critical for a therapeutic relationship that is collaborative and productive. From this perspective, the therapist is required to refrain from the tendency to minimize difference and universalize experience. The therapist's ability to bear anxiety helps to facilitate the patient's willingness to negotiate the multiplicity of his or her identity and to explore shared fantasies of sameness and the other, and to "face reality together" (Benjamin 2011, in Tummala-Narra 2015).

In summary, race, ethnicity, culture, sexual orientation, socioeconomic class, religious and spiritual orientations have little meaning in and of themselves. It is the social context in which these dimensions are perceived, experienced, understood and defined that makes them salient. Their salience is determined by how much of a difference these differences actually make in people's lives, at a given time and what they mean (Greene 2007).

Culture, race and resistance

Patients who are descendants of Holocaust survivors; African-Americans (in the United States); refugees or immigrants, they all suffer some kind of social-cultural trauma. This is another topic in the psychoanalytic discourse that has been neglected for many years. There are reasons why there has been scant attention given to issues of culture that is embedded in every psyche and frequently is the cause of trauma. Guralnik (2016) identifies three key reasons that psychoanalysis maintains an institutionalized resistance to addressing socio-political-cultural issues: First, as a group, mental health professionals are still overidentified with our forefathers. The early theorists were struggling to establish the legitimacy of a new discipline during a time of tremendous world struggles. They feared that attending to the horrific historical realities of their time (World War II or slavery) would weaken their claims to objective, empiricist truths by appearing to be biased by subjective pain. Second, the hierarchical structures of our discipline, the rigid training norms and the particular ways the discipline operates as a society that discouraged independent critical thinking. This limitation has created conformity and silence. Third, our aversion of pain and horror, expressed through the tendency to avoid inconvenient truths through denial and projective identification. Destructive cultural realities and traumas are particularly difficult to deal with (Guralnik 2016; Holmes 2016). Clinicians may feel powerless in the face of poverty, trauma and a culturally different population to treat. Fear of the "other" different from us makes psychoanalysts uncomfortable, sometimes about "white privilege", other times being different due to skin color, social class and language, that is felt threatening to the perceived and wished status quo of the clinician's comfort zone (Leary 2012; Lijtmaer 2001). As a result of this, there are still resistances in including cultural awareness courses or in supervision, to create more cultural sensitive future psychoanalysts. The student's and the teacher's inability to tolerate anxiety, fear, and narcissistic vulnerability, which accompany the discussion of topics and clinical material related to race and ethnicity can prevent the exploration of these topics in the overall learning process. What complicates this matter is that the fear is frequently linked to a desire to be like them; therefore fear and envy can be intertwined (Kuriloff 2014; Lijtmaer 2001, 2006, 2013).

Inclusion of culture and race in the psychoanalytic discourse

There is now a growing literature on understanding how psychoanalysts and psychoanalysis have responded to the greater accessibility of cultural traumas in terms of recognizing and addressing the psychical harm done by culturally imposed trauma (Holmes 2016). The interpersonal school influenced psychoanalysis to contextualize the person within their culture. The works of the so-called interpersonalists and culturalists such as Fromm (1941, 1955), Sullivan (1953), and Horney (1967, in Skelton 2006), were re-discovered. Fromm saw a tension between the individual and society. His vision was that the society failed to provide the conditions under which the individual could actualize the potential for love and productive activity. He spoke about the social character (1953, 1956). This concept recognizes the influence of social factors on the psyche. In conceiving of this influence as a deformation of the psyche, drawing a distinction between the psyche per se and the psyche as shaped by certain kinds of social influence.

Sullivan (1953) believed that early interactive patterns with others are internalized and responsible for the structuring of the self. Sullivan's "I" is structured around constraints of significant others; "Not-me" experiences originate in responses to intense forbidding gestures by the mother. His interpersonal approach emphasized the vicissitudes of interpersonal relationships. This was exemplified by his concept of "participant observer" in that the therapist is an active member of the dyad. A pioneering effort in the field of intersubjectivity comes from Sullivan's observation that humans change from biological animals into social and cultural beings through their membership in interpersonal relationships.

Horney's (1967 in Skelton 2006) seminal papers on feminine psychology, presented cultural influences as an alternative to biological bases of development, and in the process, questioned the centrality of the oedipal complex, the role of penis envy in feminine development, and the origin of masochism. Influenced by the writings of cultural anthropologists, she made her own observations on the impact of the North American milieu on character development. She believed in fundamental changes in human development resolving multiple intrapsychic and interpersonal conflict. Another development in the inclusion of culture in psychoanalysis, was a new interest in intergenerational transmission of trauma. This was another shift from a preoccupation with intrapsychic conflict and fantasy to the impact of "real" events on people's psyches. Trauma gradually replaced drives as an explanatory factor, and dissociative mechanisms have become an alternative model of mind to the repressive mechanisms relied on by earlier theory (Bromberg 1998, in Guralnik and Simeon 2010).

Other explanations are the influence of the Human Rights and feminist movements and the change in the ethnic composition of the countries. Additionally, the new look at the role of psychoanalysis at the intersection of three cultures: Psychoanalysis, African-American/Asian/Latino identity (or other ethnicities) and that of the dominant Euro-American culture. Significant clinicians contributed to this development (Holmes 2016; Javier and Rendon 1995; Javier and Herron 2002; Javier and Moskowitz 2002; Leary 2000; Lijtmaer 2010; Moskowitz 1995; Perez-Foster 1998; Suchet 2004). They showed an increase interest in cultural-social-racial-linguistic differences in the clinical setting including the role of transference and countertransference when the dyads are of the same or different ethnicity, culture and race. The development of a two-person psychoanalysis started as an observation of the role of sociocultural and socio-economic differences, exploring how the external world of the patient and therapist are a very important component on how they feel internally.

Another important advance in the inclusion of culture and race was the development of the relational school, in that the mechanism of change is located in the relationship between patient and therapist, rather than insight of the patient. This point of view makes for a more democratic therapeutic situation taking into account the social identities of the members of the dyad which include culture and race.

The relational school has conceptualized the concept of race reflecting deeper unconscious material, and as a stereotype that holds meaning in the context of racism, from a classical perspective (Dalal 2006; Holmes 2006). Object relations and relational theories suggest that social location and racial positioning is reflected and reproduced in the transference (Altman 2010; Leary 2012). When compared with other psychoanalytic traditions, intersubjective, and relational approaches tend not to separate intrapsychic experience from social experience (Aggarwal 2011; Altman 2010; Leary 2012). Although the study of race and racism in psychoanalysis has focused on racial tensions and dynamics between Whites and African-Americans (in the United States) recent scholarship has begun to explore racial dynamics across other cultural groups. For example, the concept of ethnocultural transference developed by Comas-Díaz and Jacobsen (1991) highlighted the ways that sociocultural histories and realities of the patient and therapist influence therapeutic dynamics.

From a perspective that integrates psychoanalytic, feminist, multicultural, and liberation psychologies, challenges the decontextualized approaches to traumatic stress.

Included in the relational theorizing is the concept of the "analytic third" (Odgen 2004, in Aggarwal 2011) representing the analytic significance of the racial, cultural, and social class status of patient and therapist, as well as the institutional context of their work. The "third person" representing the social context frames both therapist and patient attitudes about socioeconomic issues as well as the attitudes, feelings and concerns about race, culture and social class (Altman 2006, 2010). Differences such as language barriers and sexual orientation can trigger fears and anxieties among health professionals. As a result of these imposed identities, patients become identified in ways that may violate their self-images. "Culture powerfully influences cognition, feelings and self-concept as well as the diagnostic process and treatment decisions" (Lu, Lim and Mezzich, 2007: 118, in Aggarwal 2011). These concepts included the idea of intersubjectivity showing how shared and diverse meanings are co-constructed, offering new ways to think about culture between clinician and patient.

As currently framed, clinicians and patients possess their own cultures, but how does identity transpire in clinical settings? How does the therapeutic relationship produce new identifications unique to the clinician-patient interaction? How can clinicians mobilize these identifications to further therapeutic work? Many articles characterize the races and cultures of patients and clinicians, such as African-America; Chinese, Latino and so on. Some clinicians may extrapolate experiences with a limited number of patients perceived to be similar to members of an entire group. Such generalizations minimize intragroup differences and ignore how individuals negotiate identities with multiple cultural references. Moreover, a reverse generalization occurs if clinicians make faulty assumptions about patients because recommendations exist for the entire cultural class. In addition, this outlook presumes a separation of cultural groups even though information technology and globalization have allowed people to physically and psychologically accumulate cultural influences beyond their immediate surroundings. Indeed, intraethnic, and not just interethnic, dyads can produce significant transference and countertransference (Comas-Díaz and Jacobsen 1991). In fact, psychoanalysis has minimized how its theories remain culture-bound and tested mostly with European and the United States. populations (Perez-Foster 1998). From a subversive perspective, the above literature review also exposes anxieties concerning accepting new cultural and ethnic groups within society. In this manner, transference and countertransference refer to the subjective experience of the clinical relationship through self and object representations and their associated affects for the patient and clinician, respectively (Stolorow, Atwood and Ross 1978 in Aggarwal 2011).

The fields of psychological anthropology and cultural psychology have amply demonstrated how culture constructs ideas about the self, others, values, and beliefs, which constitute the very contours of therapy through transference and countertransference (Bonovitz 2009). Intersubjectivity allows for an inquiry into how culture might organize experience.

Internal and external reality and culture

The inclusion of the outside world into the consulting room has helped clinicians deal with patient's difficulties in a diverse way. Issues of ethnic discrimination, poverty, immigration and deportation, wars, dictatorial regimes to name a few, are traumatic events for all individuals. The emergence of narcissistic populist leaders around the world has created an age of anxiety based on these leaders' responses to people's existential needs, creating social trauma. Brothers and Lewis (2012: 183) have suggested that trauma results when the systemically emergent certainties that organize psychological life are exposed as false by some devastating experience. When these certainties are destroyed the traumatized individual is likely to experience a shattering loss of all that once seemed familiar. As Armstrong (2000) indicates, it is:

> a violent uprooting, which takes away all normal props, breaks up our world, snatches us forever from places that are saturated in memories crucial to our identity, and plunges us permanently in an alien environment, can make us feel that our very exist-ence has been jeopardized.

This "social trauma" is reflected in the situation of immigrants around the world. In Europe, for example, the immigration of Syrian and other refugees had created a pattern of fear in the popula-tion. Immigrants and refugees are conceived as alien invaders creeping through porous boundaries penetrating and threatening to destroy a vulnerable self, because immigrants generate hysteria, mass hysteria. Boundaries must be firmed up: walls erected to protect against not-self-others seeking to become parasitic upon the body politic: to drain the self of its substance (Koenigsberg 2016). Because of this, they become a threat and have to be discarded. They are considered non-humans by the "host" country. Therefore, mental health professionals treating this population have to be careful in diminishing the trauma experienced by these populations (Lijtmaer 2017b, 2018).

Cultural and religious violence in the world is another source of the influence of the external reality influencing the mental health of the population. These occurrences of mass violence wherein specific groups of a population are brutally killed, raped, and tortured by another group that considers its own behavior morally justifiable. There are social, economic, and political crises that lead to the scapegoating of one group. An ideology is put forth that promises a better life and designates the scapegoated group as the enemy. It represents a mental instrument that validates dehumanizing the chosen enemy and gives "meaning" to the extermination of dan-gerous "elements" as part of a battle between good and evil.

Another feature of the trauma suffered by a survivor of political repression or war is the victim's feeling of helplessness to affect the environment interpersonally so as to elicit a sense of mutuality and justice. Therefore, the link between self and other has been effaced by the failure of empathy. The traumatized person, in order to "survive" and live on among the riches of life around him/her has to take flight into a certain kind of deadness. What gets killed off is imagin-ation, empathy, curiosity, desire, and kindness. All these are present in the consulting room with these traumatized patients.

The outside world expressed through history, culture, race and politics influence character formation and consequently transference and countertransference. Taking this position into the therapeutic dyad, the therapist can be aware of how race, class, gender, sexual orientation and so on have an effect on character formation and thus on the therapeutic dyad. The inevitable sense of "otherness" requires additional levels of meaning in the vicissitudes of the patient and therapist's ability to identify with one another.

Future directions

Focusing on cultural traumas is less familiar and is less articulated in our psychoanalytic clinical theories, supervision, and practice. In particular, what is less focused on is an acknowledgment and articulation of the layer within the psyche that contains secret dehumanization and discrimination in society. Scholarship and clinical teaching in psychoanalysis continue to take a too narrow view of what history we should focus on when working with our patients and what freedoms we should help them to achieve. Psychoanalysis in general has largely excluded cultural history and its traumas from what it is on which we are to concentrate on (Holmes 2016). The therapist lives in the reality of multiple cultures in a clinical space where, to be authentic, all aspects of the self must be available for use in the work. The anxiety and discomfort engendered by the "other" contributes to a therapeutic impasse that can only be resolved when the therapist can be free to bring to the treatment the multidimensional aspects of self that evolve from life at the intersection of multiple cultures. Psychoanalysis has only recently added culture and race to the understanding of the patient's life including the social the social psychology of racial and cultural experiencing (Lippman 2003, in Bennett 2006).

A true observation will require some immersion in literatures and with methods outside of our own. This will likely leave us feeling a bit unfamiliar to ourselves. This is the nature of the adaptive work we ask of our patients and that we must ask of our field. Substantive change always requires us to renegotiate our loyalties, to redefine ourselves, and this makes new conversations possible. Enhancing clinical practice with respect to race and culture obliges us to expand our analytic pedagogy beyond that of the intrapsychic, the intersubjective, or even the relational. Although struggling with issues of race and culture sometimes feels like being caught in an out of control and immobilized situation, by raising the question of "who we are" in all our aspects allows us to explore new perspectives. On the other hand, there may be a fear of overemphasizing race and culture. This stance may incline some therapists not only to avoid making racial or cultural differences explicit, but to become deaf to allusions in the material to other ethnic groups, to other apparent differences between therapist and patient, or to material that may represent a displacement of reaction to their cultural differences.

Conclusion

Clinicians and scholars need to make a more collaborative effort to deconstruct stereotypes or prejudices acknowledging the role of culture and race in personality development in the consulting room, and in teaching, supervising or writing about human beings at an individual and group level.

In the consulting room it is crucial for the therapist to become familiar with his or her own racial attitudes and feelings, including racism in the interaction with the patient, Otherwise, these subjective states can seriously impact, derail, and even truncate the treatment. If as therapists we are blind to difference and sameness, we will leave untouched critical aspects not only of our patients but also of ourselves (Gump 2010). To train the new generation of psychoanalysts we must focus on issues of culture and race that include social justice, child-rearing practices, religion, treatment of women, amongst others, to make more meaning living in this diverse society. The listening of the therapist apparatus is not neutral; rather, it operates with manifold screening device – the institutions that constitute it. The ability to contemplate the relationship between psychic and cultural-social realities necessarily refers us to the connotations of the clinician's social position and the relationships they establish with their patients, and therefore to the ways in which the social context affects the development of the treatment. We must also consider how therapists are interwoven with their practice within a social structure that assigns them a place from where to listen. The traditional view presumes that clinicians are apolitical and beatifically neutral, that they are beyond good and evil. The political is thus reduced either to a set of materials illuminated by unconscious fantasy or to pure subjectivity – to an externality foreign to treatment. This dynamic stems from an approach rooted in a theoretical tradition that sees clinicians as "inhabiting" an extraterritorial place. From this perspective, therapists may neglect the therapist–patient bond and the constituting effects of cultural, racial and social history.

Clearly, from the conceptual framework of the therapist's involvement, the analytic device is not a set of neutral techniques that allow therapists to listen. Rather, in its development and construction, this device participates in the same socio-historical field as other social practices. It may, therefore, produce similar effects to those of these practices (we may recall here the relationship between the analytic device and psychiatry's function as a mechanism of social control or, from an epistemological perspective, the relationship between heredity and a certain medical model). Furthermore, when striving to account for a "specific psychoanalytic discourse", we overlook and ignore the influence of the social-racial- political-economic structure that gives rise to the creation and development of a certain type of analytic device.

References

Aggarwal, N. K. (2011) Intersubjectivity, Transference, and the Cultural Third. *Contemporary Psychoanalysis*, 47(2): 204–223.

Alperin, R. (2001) Barriers to Intimacy. *Psychoanalytic Psychology*, 18(1): 137–156.

Altman, N. (1995; 2010) *The Analyst in the Inner City: Race, Class and Culture through a Psychoanalytic Lens.* Hillsdale, NY: The Psychoanalytic Press.

Altman, N. (2006) How Psychoanalysis Became White in the United States, and How that Might Change. *Psychoanalytic Perspectives*, 3(2): 65–72.

Armstrong, K. (2000) *The Battle for God: The 4000-Year Quest of Judaism, Christianity, and Islam.* New York: Knopf.

Bennett, J. O. (2006) The Analyst at the Intersection of Multiple Cultures. *Psychoanalytic Perspectives*, 3(2): 55–63.

Bonovitz, C. (2009) Mixed Race and the Negotiation of Racialized Selves: Developing the Capacity for Internal Conflict. *Psychoanalytic Dialogues*, 19(4): 426–441.

Brothers, D. and Lewis, J. (2012) Homesickness, Exile, and the Self-Psychological Language of Homecoming. *International Journal of Psychoanalytic Self Psychology*, 7(2): 180–195.

Comas-Díaz, L. (2011) Multicultural Approaches to Psychotherapy. In L. Comas-Díaz (Ed.), *History of Psychotherapy: Continuity and Change* (2nd ed., pp. 243–267). Washington, DC: American Psychological Association. http://dx.doi.org/10.1037/12353-008.

Comas-Díaz, L. and Jacobsen, F. (1991) Ethnocultural Transference and Countertransference in the Therapeutic Dyad. *American Journal of Orthopsychiatry*, 6(13): 392–402.

Crenshaw, K. (1989) Demarginalizing the Intersection of Race and Sex: A Black Feminist Critique of Antidiscrimination Doctrini, Feminist Theory and Antiracist Politics. *University of Chicago Legal Forum*, 139–167. Retrieved June 6, 2018, from www.google.com/search?num=40&source.

Dalal, F. (2006) Racism: Processes of Detachment, Dehumanization, and Hatred. *The Psychoanalytic Quarterly*, 75(1): 131–161. http://dx.doi.org/10.1002/j.2167-4086.2006.tb00035.x.

Fromm, E. (1941) *Escape from Freedom.* New York: Avon.

Fromm, E. (1955) *The Sane Society.* Greenwich, CT: Fawcett.

Greene, B. (2007) How Difference Makes a Difference. In J. C. Muran (Ed.), *Dialogues on Difference: Studies of Diversity in the Therapeutic Relationship* (pp. 47–63). Washington, DC: American Psychological Association. http://dx.doi.org/10.1037/11500-005.

Gump, G. (2010) Reality Matters. *Psychoanalytic Psychology*, 27: 42–54.

Guralnik, O. (2016) Sleeping Dogs: Psychoanalysis and the Socio-Political. *Psychoanalytic Dialogues*, 26(6): 655–663.

Guralnik, O. and Simeon, D. (2010) Depersonalization: Standing in the Spaces between Recognition and Interpellation. *Psychoanalytic Dialogues*, 20(4): 400–416.

Holmes, D. E. (1992) Race and Transference in Psychoanalysis and Psychotherapy. *International Journal of Psychoanalysis*, 73, 187–219.

Holmes, D. E. (1999) Race and Countertransference: Two "Blind Spots" in Psychoanalytic Perception. *Journal of Applied Psychoanalytic Studies*, 1(4): 319–332.

Holmes, D. E. (2006) The Wrecking Effects of Race and Social Class on Self and Success. *The Psychoanalytic Quarterly*, 75(1): 215–235. http://dx.doi.org/10.1002/j.2167-4086.2006.tb00038.x.

Holmes, D. E. (2016) Culturally Imposed Trauma: The Sleeping Dog has Awakened. Will psychoanalysis Hake Heed? *Psychoanalytic Dialogues*, 26(6): 641–654.

Javier, R. A. and Moskowitz, M. (2002) Special Section: Underserved Populations. *Psychoanalytic Psychology*, 19(1): 144–148.

Javier, R. A. and Rendon, M. (1995) The Ethnic Unconscious and its Role in Transference, Resistance and Countertransference: An introduction. *Psychoanalytic Psychology, Special Section: Ethnicity and Psychoanalysis*, 12(4): 513–520.

Koenigsberg, R. A. (2016) A Human Body Becomes a Body Politic. *Library of Social Science. E-Bulletin*, 3: 21–16.

Kuriloff, E. A. (2014) *Contemporary Psychoanalysis and the Legacy of the Third Reich: History, Memory, Tradition*. New York: Routledge.

Laungani, P. (2002) Cross-Cultural Psychology: A Handmaiden to Mainstream Western Psychology. *Counseling Psychology Quarterly*, 15(4): 385–397.

Laungani, P. (2004) Counseling and Therapy in a Multicultural Setting. *Counseling Psychology Quarterly*, 17(2), 195–207.

Layton, L. (2006) Racial Identities, Racial Enactments, and Normative Unconscious Processes. *Psychoanalytic Quarterly*, 75: 237–269.

Layton, L. (2013) Enacting distinction: Normative unconscious process in the clinic (Personal communication).

Leary, K. (1997) Race, Self-disclosure, and "forbidden talk": Race and Ethnicity in Contemporary Clinical Practice. *Psychoanalytic Quarterly*, 66: 163–189.

Leary, K. (2000) Racial Enactments in Dynamic Treatment. *Psychoanalytic Dialogues*, 10(4): 639–653.

Leary, K. (2012) Race as an Adaptive Challenge. *Psychoanalytic Psychology*, 29: 279–291.

Lijtmaer, R. (2001) Countertransference and Ethnicity: The Therapist's Psychic Change. *Journal of the American Academy of Psychoanalysis*, 29(1): 73–84.

Lijtmaer, R. (2006) Black, White, Hispanic and Both: Issues in Bi-racial Identity and Its Effects in the Transference–Countertransference. In R. Moodley and S. Palmer (Eds.), *Race, Culture and Psychotherapy: Critical Perspectives in Multicultural Practice* (pp. 130–138). London: Brunner-Routledge.

Lijtmaer, R. (2010) Migration, Cultural Values and the Medical Model: Pittu Laungani and Psychotherapy. In R. Moodley, A. Rai and W. Alladin (Eds.), *Bridging East-West Psychology and Counseling* (pp. 220–230). Delhi: Sage.

Lijtmaer, R. (2013) When the Analyst Is the Other. Paper presented at the Psychology and the Other Conference. Lesley University in Cambridge, Massachusetts, USA.

Lijtmaer, R. (2017a) Re-Making the History of Psychology and Psychoanalysis: Awakening the Political in the Consulting Room. Paper presented at the International Psychohistory Association, New York, USA.

Lijtmaer, R. (2017b) Variations on the Migratory Theme: Immigrants or Exiles Refugees or Asylees. *Psychoanalytic Review*, 104(6): 687–694.

Lijtmaer, R. (2018) Social Trauma, Nostalgia and Mourning in the Immigrant Experience. Paper presented in the panel: The Migration of Ideas a la Ferenczi. International Ferenczi Conference, Florence, Italy.

Moskowitz, M. (1995) Ethnicity and the Fantasy of Ethnicity. *Psychoanalytic Psychology, Special Section: Ethnicity and Psychoanalysis*, 12 (4): 547–555.

Moskowitz, M. (1996) The Social Conscience of Psychoanalysis. In R. Foster, M. Moskowitz, and R. Javier (Eds.), *Reaching Across Boundaries of Culture and Class: Widening the Scope of Psychotherapy* (pp. 21–46). Northvale, NJ: Aronson.

Perez Foster, R. (1998) The Clinician's Cultural Countertransference: The Psychodynamics of Culturally Competent Practice. *Clinical Social Work*, 26(3): 253–270.

Perez-Foster, R. (1999) An Intersubjective Approach to Cross-Cultural Clinical Work. *Smith College Studies in Social Work*, 69(2): 269–291.

Roland, A. (1996) Cultural pluralism and psychoanalysis: The Asian and North American experience. New York, NY: Routledge.

Skelton, R. (Ed.) (2006) The Edinburgh International Encyclopaedia of Psychoanalysis.

Smith, B. and Tang, N. (2006) Different Differences. Psychoanalytic Quarterly, 75: 295–321.

Suchet, M. (2004) A Relational Encounter with Race. *Psychoanalytic Dialogues*, 14(4): 423–438.

Sullivan, H. S. (1953) *The Interpersonal Theory of Psychiatry*. New York: Norton.

Sullivan, H. S. (1956), *Clinical Studies in Psychiatry*. New York: Norton.

Tummala-Narra, P. (2015) Cultural Competence as a Core Emphasis of Psychoanalytic Psychotherapy. *Psychoanalytic Psychology*, 32(2): 275–292.

Winnicott, D. W. (1951, 1971) *Playing and Reality*. New York: Routledge.

8

RACE AND CULTURE IN PSYCHIATRY

Suman Fernando

Notions about the terms race and culture in relation to mental health and how they impact on the theory and practice of psychiatry are often talked about loosely in popular discourse – so loosely that the terms sometimes give rise to confusion and misunderstandings – for example, about what constitutes cultural and/or racial *difference* and what cultural sensitivity means. Further, there have been marked changes during the past two or three decades in what these terms imply: Pieterse (2007, 2009), a foremost commentator in the field, points out that, as a result of complex social changes in many societies in the West during the first decade of the twenty-first century cultural *hybridity* rather than cultural *difference* has become a leading paradigm in social and cultural studies; and several commentators on the political and social significance of 'race' (for example, Bonilla-Silva 2014; Kendi 2017) have pointed out that although the notion of race that seemed in the late 1990s to have lost its importance – Western societies being seen as having become 'post-race' – racism has returned in full force in the post-Trump, post-Brexit era, 'race' once again becoming a leading parameter denoting individual and group differences between people in the West.

Psychiatry is a discipline that came into being in tandem with clinical psychology following the cultural changes in Western Europe of the late seventeenth and eighteenth centuries generally referred to as 'The Enlightenment' (see Outram 1995). Although originally based on academic studies of madness seen as 'mental illness', psychiatry and clinical psychology (the 'psy-disciplines'), today dominate much of the knowledge about mental health in the global North. Although historian Edward Shorter (1997) states that "there was no such thing as psychiatry" (1997: 1) before the end of the eighteenth century – by which he meant that even when medical doctors cared for inmates of institutions (which had existed in Europe from the middle ages) housing people deemed to be 'insane', they did not work to a *medical* system, any care being given to them being purely custodial. However, it is now clear (see Fernando 2014) that the medieval *māristāns* (Islamic hospitals) in the Islamic empire (Middle East, North Africa and southern Spain) used established *medical* treatments, based largely in the (Greek) Galenic medical tradition (Dols 1992); and that some asylum 'lunatics' in France in the 1790s were given psychological therapy called '*traitement moral*' (Davidson et al. 2010).

This chapter describes (a) the meanings of the terms culture, race and ethnicity as used today in the field of mental health; (b) the background of psychiatry and clinical psychology, that currently underpin mental health services and how psychiatry is currently practiced in the West; and (c) recent critiques of psychiatry that have emerged; before making some concluding remarks on the place of race and culture in psychiatric system in the future.

Deconstructing race, culture and ethnicity in psychiatry

What is considered in this chapter are *Western* notions of culture and race – modes of thinking around what we currently mean by the terms are different in non-Western cultural traditions but, generally speaking, the Western modes of thought (on race and culture) are now universally accepted in the field of mental health. Although derived from original notions of race being perceived as something *physical*, culture as *sociological* and ethnicity as *psycho-social*, the concepts have undergone complicated changes and continue to change in both academic and popular discourse.

Race and culture

The term 'race' entered the English language in the sixteenth century at a time when the Bible was accepted as the authority on human affairs, and was used originally in the sense of lineage, supposedly ordained at the creation of the world (Banton 1987). From then, well into the nineteenth century, race as lineage referred to groups of people connected by common descent or origin, implying a biological definition of race. Later, as Darwinian concepts were accepted in European thinking, race was seen as subspecies, and finally sociological theories of race led to the notion of races as populations. More recently, as a result of what are called the 'new racisms' (Fernando 2017: 64), the term has taken on a social definition (closely linked to the understanding of institutional racism) exemplified by that given by Omi and Winant (2015: 110, emphasis in original): "*Race is a concept that signifies and symbolizes social conflict and interests by referring to different types of human bodies*".

Presently, the various notions about race exist together in the West and have penetrated many parts of the world through the use of the English language, giving rise to considerable confusion because the corollaries of these different notions are very different. For example, race as lineage may explain why people *look* physically different, and seem culturally different as groups, but race as population does not do so; and race as lineage may be a satisfactory explanation of physical differentiation of populations that are relatively isolated from each other, but cannot interpret cultural differentiation except by assuming that ecological forces governing unconscious behaviour determine human culture in the way it determines social life of animals. It is this muddled idea of 'race' (varying from the old-fashioned biological meaning to the modern social meaning) that is spreading worldwide and being incorporated into ideas about people's identities, even cultural identities – see 'conflation of the concepts of race and culture', as discussed below.

A firm notion of culture as an individual characteristic was evident in late-nineteenth- and twentieth-century social anthropology – for example, Leighton and Hughes (1961) talked of "shared patterns of belief, feeling and adaptation which people carry in their [individual] minds' and pass on through the generations" (1961: 447); and group cultures were attributed to people in terms of their geographical home. This idea of culture as "a unique way of life ... usually that of the 'uncivilized'" took hold in anthropology during colonialism in order to separate Europeans, white people, from (what the West saw as) uncivilized natives of (mainly) Asia, Africa and pre-Columbian America (Eagleton 2000: 26) and so it could not last. What emerged after de-colonization, and more so in the postmodern terrain of the late twentieth century, is the notion of culture as malleable and changeable, not just depending on traditions that people inherit but also on historical and political influences in a context of power relations. Homi Bhabha's (1994) *Location of Culture* emphasizes the hybridity of cultural forms and the ways in which cultural arrogance, associated with racism, is evident as societies become cultural diverse in many parts of the Western world; and Edward Said's (1994) *Culture and Imperialism* unravels the intimate connections between understandings of culture presented in Anglo-American literature and European domination of the rest of the world during the past 300–400 years.

Although there is a perception sometimes of cultures of people in particular locations (such as a geographical region or country) being 'pure', in actual fact, cultural interchanges and mingling have always taken place – at times very extensively, resulting in mixtures seen as 'new' cultures or termed (sometimes pejoratively) creole or hybrid cultures. Historian J. J. Clarke (1997) points out that "commercial and cultural intercourse between East and West was well established at the time when philosophical foundations of Western thought [that fed into the cultures of Europe] were being laid down in Greece" (1997: 37); that it continued along the silk routes between the Middle East and Asia; and that links between Europe and Asia (curtailed by the imposition of the Islamic empire) resumed after the thirteenth century. Then, "[p]artly because of empire [colonialism] all cultures [became] involved in one another … [so that] … none is single and pure, all are hybrid heterogeneous, extraordinarily differentiated, and nonmonolithic" (Said 1994: xxix). This mixing of cultures has been greatly accelerated during the past four or five decades as a result of better communication, easier travel and migration from East to West driven by post-colonial poverty in parts of Africa and Asia.

The discourse on culture that is applicable to psychiatry mainly concerns the culture of the individual because emphasis on the individual – a characteristic of Western thinking – dominates psychiatry and psychology (which are Western disciplines). But even here, it is recognized that individual culture rests on a bed of traditional family culture, the culture of the community they are part of and the wider body of people they feel attached to through personal connections or even 'imagined communities' (Anderson 1991). These ramifications of culture determine – or more correctly are reflected in – people's behaviour, social systems, religious systems and beliefs, world-views, and, most importantly their concept of the human condition, the meaning of life itself. In other words, diverse traditional cultures have generated a diversity of psychologies (see Fernando and Moodley 2018) to form the background to people's lived experience, how they perceive and make sense of their lives, what they see as natural, and so on. Since (as discussed above) culture is not a fixed entity but subject to almost constant change, it is difficult to pin down. Thus, it is quite complicated and problematic to work out at any given time, what particular aspects of their traditional culture affects any one person or cultural group – differences are always there, so are similarities. Today, culture (applied to an individual) is seen as something that is dynamic; a flexible system of values and world-views that people live by, and through which they define identities and negotiate their lives (for fuller discussion, see Fernando 2010). But in the mental health field, we talk also of family cultures, or cultures of whole communities in addition to the culture of an individual. When we say that a society is 'multicultural', we imply that there are broad cultural differences between groups of people within the society. And we refer to cultures of professional groups, for example, 'medical culture', 'police culture', or to institutional cultures – for example in the health service or in psychiatry.

Conflation of race and culture

It would be seen from earlier paragraphs that the term 'culture' lacks precision and its meaning is both variable and dynamic. As a result, culture is often confused with race and thence gets involved in matters to do with racism – most obviously in the political field in the United Kingdom and North America where opposition to immigration is often attributed to the *cultures* of migrants, when in fact it is more about their perceived 'race'. In spite of this conflation in popular discourse – or perhaps because of it – the concept of ethnicity (briefly discussed later in this chapter) has achieved popularity in the United Kingdom. Yet, the race–culture conflation (and the problems arising from it) is best seen in making sense of so-called 'ethnic statistics' from the (British) Census (2001). In the question on ethnicity, under the heading 'What is your ethnic group?', the question asked about *cultural background* not race; and national statistics about numbers of people in ethnic groups are interpreted both as differences in 'culture' *and* differences in race – the latter being used to promote racist political propaganda and the former to measure degrees of 'cultural diversity' in a population. Another problem that arises from the conflation of race and culture is that, when people are identified in 'ethnic' terms (with both 'cultural' and 'racial' connotations), there may be a tendency to impose 'cultural' categories on people because of the way they look ('racially' in the sense of old-fashioned biological 'race') instead of allowing people to find their own position in the stream of changing and varied cultural forms. This creates resentment against the concept of multiculturalism itself. Even more importantly, some aspect of culture, like religious practice or belief, may be taken as a marker of racial difference, resulting in Muslims and Jews being racialized – that is seen *as if they are races* (see Fernando, 2017: 96), and subjected to forms of racism (in the instances quoted anti-Semitism and Islamophobia).

Ethnicity

The notion of 'ethnicity' (often used as an alternative to race or culture in categorizing people for census purposes – see earlier) includes elements of both race and culture but additionally, taps into a sense (that many people have) of belonging to, and identifying with, a particular group of people – an 'ethnic group'. According to British sociologist Stuart Hall "The term ethnicity acknowledges the place of history, language and culture in the construction of subjectivity and identity, as well as the fact that all discourse is placed positioned, situated, and all knowledge is contextual" (1992: 257). In a multiracial and multicultural society the perception of belonging to a group emerges in complex ways through various pressures, social, political, economic, and psychological (Fernando 2012). The ethnicity that is promoted and crystallised by mainly social forces has been called an emergent ethnicity (Yancey et al. 1976); and sociologists refer to 'new ethnicities' having emerged in British society during the 1980s and 1990s (Cohen, 1999) as a result of African, Caribbean and Asian diasporic communities being perceived as 'different' to the majority white population.

Psychiatry: Background and current practice

In the sixteenth century, Descartes established the 'Cartesian concept' (Gold 1985) of a strict division between mind and body (psyche and soma) – what Ryle (1963) calls the

> official doctrine which hails chiefly from [the Cartesian concept of] … the Ghost in the Machine … [that] … maintains that there exist both bodies and minds; that there occur physical processes and mental processes; that there are mechanical causes of corporal movements and mental causes of corporal movements.
>
> *(1963: 13–23)*

The confinement of 'the mad' (the insane), together with other socially undesirable people, in asylums – 'the great confinement' according to (Foucault 1967: 38) – gathered pace in the eighteenth century throughout Western Europe, resulting in large numbers of people being excluded from society and being perceived as suffering 'mental illness'. Medical doctors who treated madness, or "mental alienation" as it was called sometimes, were called "alienists", initially called "mad doctors" in England (Shorter 1997: 17). As they grappled with madness, they established power over the mentally ill and also made it possible for them (medical doctors), later together with psychologists, to study mental pathologies and aspects of mentally normal functioning of the mind. Psychologists who worked in the 'clinic', *clinical* psychologists, became associated to varying degrees with psychiatrists in treating and controlling the 'mad' as well as accumulating knowledge about normal psychological functioning and psychological therapies for mental health problems. Since then, (Western) psychology and psychiatry have led the thinking around madness and mental illness – and to some extent, mental health in general – at first in the West but gradually all over most of the world as Western culture was imposed across the world on the back of colonialism (see Fernando 2014). It should be noted that concepts of 'mind' and ideas about normal and abnormal mental functioning, developed very differently in non-Western cultural traditions (Kirmayer et al. 2018).

During the nineteenth century, various medical explanations were developed for mental illness and 'pathologies' were proposed that allegedly caused a variety of different illnesses – of emotion, intellect, beliefs, feelings, thinking and so on. By the early part of the twentieth century, biological causation (largely genetic) took centre stage. Models of mental illness (with various subdivisions) were built up over the years in Euro-America embodying a Western (cultural) world-view – the "culture of psychiatry", such as Mind-body dichotomy, Mechanistic view of life, Materialistic concept of mind, Segmental approach to the individual, Illness equals bio-medical change, and Natural cause of illness (see Fernando 1995: 13). In the face of criticism of this overdependence on biological causation of mental illness, a paper by Engel (1977) suggested a model that tried to broaden thinking in psychiatry, calling it the "biopsychosocial model" (1977: 135) that postulated causes of mental illness in terms of a variety of factors, psychological, biological, social, cultural and so on – the multi-factorial approach – but most psychiatrists continued to put their trust in the narrow bio-medical model.

Major changes occurred in the practice of psychiatry in most Western countries in the period between the mid-1960s and the late 1980s. Asylums were phased out, and organized supervision of patients in community settings instituted as 'community care'. However, powerful psychotropic drugs became available at about the same time and got used both in community and institutional settings. Whereas asylum psychiatry looked to drugs mainly for sedation and behaviour control, the newer medications were popularized as cures – or at least symptom relief or control – for mental illness and later various other psychological problems seen as 'disorders' of the mind. Although an appreciation of impact of social conditions on illness, both in relation to physical and mental health, are now recognized (see Wilkinson and Picket 2010), mainstream systems of psychiatry in the global North, together with clinical psychology as formulated in Euro-America, continue as a predominantly *medical* disciplines geared to finding cures and/or remedies for what are constructed as illnesses/disorders; and so-called 'treatments' for emotional/psychological distress and deviations from social norms of behaviour seen as conditions (such as personality disorders) bordering on illness. In practice, the need to address social and cultural elements of mental illness and mental health problems (seen as factors impinging on the illness itself) get pushed to the sidelines; the ability to make specific diagnoses (the bio-medical approach) being the standard by which the expertise of psychiatrists are judged by their peers and often also by the general public; and medication (with or without other less important psycho-social approaches developed by clinical psychologists) is the main approach in treatment. Meanwhile, the shift in psychiatry – the "medication revolution" (Fernando 2014: 83) – that took place in the 1970s and 1980s had profound effects in shaping modern psychiatry with far-reaching effects on society at large, so far mainly in the West, but spreading rapidly to the global South (see later).

Yet, in spite of the doubts about the effectiveness of psychiatric practice in the West (see later), some positive developments should be noted on the fringes but still falling within the basic tenets of the original psychiatric models of mental illness – an example being *Recovery* postulated by users of mental health services as a sort of psycho-social journey as an alternative to the treatment and rehabilitation model for mental/psychiatric illness. Recovery as a journey is aimed at regaining a sense of purpose and self-worth after a major life disruption such as admission to a psychiatric facility and/or administration of psychotropic medication (Kloos 2005) – a model for a process that could follow any period of extreme distress or suffering. The journey itself subsumes the pursuit of personal goals of maintaining hope, making sense of experiences, understanding and empowerment (Repper and Perkins 2003). Allied to the concept of recovery is the term 'recovery approach' which is about the role of services and systems in supporting the journey of recovery. It is about partnership between service providers and service users to develop support networks, promote hope and enable integration of service users into the mainstream of wider society (social inclusion).

Recent critiques of psychiatry

Apart from criticism of psychiatry from an experiential perspective by people who have used mental health services – sometimes called 'experts by experience' (see Rose 2019) – several critiques have emerged since the early 1950s from academic and professionals circles in Europe and North America. Some of these are considered briefly below as being of particular relevance to matters of race and culture.

Critical psychiatry of Fanon

Franz Fanon, a black man from the Caribbean who trained in France to become a psychiatrist and then worked in both France and Algeria before leaving the field of mental health to become a freedom fighter in Algeria, died of leukaemia in 1961, aged just 36. Although best known for writings that inspired the Black Power Movement during the American civil rights movement (Ehlen 2000; Macey 2000), Fanon's contributions to critical psychology and psychiatry are only recently becoming known, partly because he wrote in French – much of it banned in France for many years – and his work not being translated into English until the mid-1960s, some only in 2018. Although attracted to psychoanalytic theories early on in relation to sexuality and 'race', Fanon was later an outspoken critique of many psychoanalytic ideas; turned to study problems faced by North African immigrants in France from a psycho-social perspective (Bulhan 1985); and became a firm adherent of the sociocentric approach to psychological and mental problems. Fanon saw the primary problem in mental illness as (psychological) "alienation", the status of being a (psychiatric) patient being tied up with "societal and political conditions" (Gordon and Paris 2018: 226). For Fanon, the way out of illness was a process of *disalienation* through both "self-reflection similar to that associated with psychotherapeutics" and "education and popular culture … [in association with] … direct attack upon the oppressive socioeconomic conditions under which the African lives" (McCulloch 1983: 77).

In 1953, Fanon was appointed as chief psychiatrist at a psychiatric hospital in Blida-Joinville (in Algeria, then under French colonial rule) that catered for both expatriate French-European and indigenous Muslim patients (Macey 2000). Jean Khalfa (2018), who with Robert

J. C. Young, has edited the latest collection of Fanon's work, writes that once he took up his post at Blida-Joinville, Fanon studied "ways in which mental illnesses were conceptualized in local [Algerian] cultures" (2018: 191) and reorganized the institutional structures in the hospital to enable 'social therapy' consisting of regular ward meetings, collective psychotherapy sessions and discussions of topical events and news – a way of working similar to 'therapeutic community' approaches in asylums in the United Kingdom in the 1960s (Martin, 1968). When Fanon found that the therapeutic system he introduced benefitted Europeans but not Muslims (the wards were racially segregated) he reorganized the ward for Muslim men to include a form of social therapy *that suited the social and cultural background of the Muslim patients,* while addressing the political predicament they found themselves in under colonialism. Thus, apart from instituting a Muslim cultural environment, Khalfa (2018) quotes Fanon as saying "I had to show … that Algerian culture carried other values than colonial culture; that these restructuring values ought to be taken on board confidently by those who bear them, that is, by Algerian patients or staff. To gain support of the Algerian staff I had to arouse in them a feeling of revolt of the sort: 'We are just as able as the Europeans'". Khalfa describes how Fanon incorporated Algerian staff to participate in the therapeutic process and quotes Fanon as saying: *"Psychiatry must be political"* (2018: 190, italics inserted).

Unfortunately, Fanon's early death, the banning of his books in France for many years, and political turmoil in Algeria at the time he worked there, meant that the critical psychology and psychiatry that he founded did not develop into a full-blown system. But his work shows how social therapy (of the type that Fanon established in the 1950s) could incorporate issues of power linked to racism – something that may well be copied in many European cities if it is politically possible to establish (see transcultural critiques later below).

Critiques in the United States and the United Kingdom

In the 1960s, Thomas Szasz (1962) in the *Myth of Mental Illness* and sociologists such as Thomas Scheff (1966) challenged the traditional biological view of mental illness. Similar views developed into the so-called anti-psychiatry movement – better named the Laingian movement led by R. D. Laing and Esterson (Laing and Esterson 1970) – that 'blossomed between 1965 and 1970' at a residential establishment, Kingsley Hall in the East End of London (UK) (O'Hagan 2012), although here illness, particularly schizophrenia, was not denied as an individual reality but was perceived as a label signifying '*a political event*' (Laing, 1964: 64, italics in original) in power struggles within families represented by concepts such as the 'double-bind' (Bateson et al. 1956). The work of this critical movement is described vividly in *Two Accounts of a Journey Through Madness* (Barnes and Berke 1971).

In the 1980s, racial inequalities in mental health service provision led to study of racial bias and cultural insensitivity resulting in social injustice affecting mainly diasporic communities derived from immigrants from non-Western cultural backgrounds in Asia and Africa; and fed into the growth of a critical movement within transcultural psychiatry (see Fernando 1988, 2010, 2017; Fernando and Keating 2009; Littlewood and Lipsedge 1982; Rack 1982) largely voiced by members of the Transcultural Psychiatry Society (TCPS) (see Vige 2008). Critiques centred on diagnostic practices resulting from racist stereotyping; the failure to appreciate cultural diversity in matters to do with 'mind'; and the exclusion of spirituality and religion in the models of psychology with which psychiatry is closely associated. The theorizing underlining it was largely *anti-racist* inspired by sociological studies (for example, Hall et al. 1978; CCCS, 1982), together with studies of how psychiatry and psychology were part of a socio-political system oppressing people who are 'othered' and racialized (see Fernando

2017: 95–96), thus similar in some respects with ideas proposed in the 1950s by Fanon. The influence of British anti-racist transcultural psychiatry did not have the political power to become widely accepted in the United Kingdom, although its ideas extended far and wide (Moodley and Ocampo 2014).

Critiques of medication

In the early part of the twenty-first century, questions were raised in the United States and the United Kingdom about the efficacy of psychotropic medications and the bio-medical model of mental illness (referred to as 'Kraepelian' or 'neo-Krapelian' – Donald 2001) codified in the Diagnostic and Statistical Manual (DSM) (APA 2013) and the International Classification of Diseases (ICD) (WHO 1992). A review by Marcia Angell (2011a), former editor of the prestigious *New England Journal of Medicine,* came to signify concerns among professionals from disciplines of both psychology and psychiatry about: (a) Pharmaceutical companies "that sell psychoactive drugs through various forms of marketing … determine what constitutes a mental illness and how these disorders should be diagnosed and treated" (Angell 2011a: 3); (b) the validity of assuming that "mental illness is caused by a chemical imbalance in the brain" (2011a: 3); and (c) convincing evidence that psychoactive drugs are not just useless but may actually cause harm. Commending a book by Carlat (2010), Angell (2011b) criticized damningly the collusion between the American Psychiatric Association and the pharmaceutical industry in spreading the use of psychoactive drugs in the American population, condemning "the 'frenzy' of diagnosis, the overuse of drugs with sometimes devastating side effects, and the widespread conflict of interests [of people involved in the trade of making diagnoses and providing drugs]" (2011b: 7). In the United Kingdom, too significant disquiet has been voiced about the efficacy of much of the psychiatric practice in the West, largely to do with the misuse of medication (see Moncrieff 2009, 2013).

Critiques of the Movement for Global Mental Health

During most of the colonial period of the mid-eighteenth to mid-twentieth century, indigenous medical systems and systems of religious healing in much of Asia and Africa were underdeveloped and sometimes actively suppressed by the European colonial powers. Colonialism imposed the asylum model for mental health services in Asia and Africa but colonial psychiatry was confined to asylums that were few and far between; and psychiatry and its counterpart clinical psychology, failed to connect with the needs of people in colonized countries of Asia and Africa. On the whole, ordinary people in the colonies followed their own ways of dealing with (what psychiatry terms) 'mental illness', possibly no less effectively as the West did at the time (Fernando 2014). After political liberation was achieved (ex-colonial) developing nations were gradually enticed to adopt Western systems of bio-medical psychiatry linked to community care often helped by Western-financed agencies (NGOs).

In the early 2000s, a project called the Movement for Global Mental Health (MGMH) appeared (Collins et al. 2011; Horton 2007; Patel and Prince 2010), arguing that problems to be tackled in mental health in the global South should be seen in terms of psychiatric and neurological diagnoses as described in Western psychiatry and remedies promoted as remedies being consistent with evidence-based medicine (EMB). Opposition to the MGMH has grown both in the global North and the South (for example, Bemme and D'souza 2012; Campbell and Burgess 2012; Das and Rao 2012; Mills 2014; Shukla et al. 2012); suspicions of economic interests being involved have surfaced (Fernando 2011); and the very idea that there is a globally valid concept called 'mental health' and that there are global remedies for what amount to social suffering in all cultural settings has been criticized (Summerfield 2012). For a full discussion of the disputes over the MGMH and the problems involved in developing mental health services in the global South, the reader is referred to the book *Mental Health Worldwide; Culture, globalization and Development* (Fernando 2014).

Conclusion

In describing and discussing the terms 'race' and 'culture' in psychiatry, and to some extent in clinical psychology (the psy-disciplines), this chapter indicates the importance of considering their relevance in both theory and practice in the field of mental health. However, the chapter also indicates (for example in describing current practice of psychiatry) what little part they play in relation to clinical systems in mental health services. The section on critiques of psychiatry indicates that much of the dissatisfaction of users of mental health services and the criticisms (of mental health services) voiced by 'critical' professionals often relate to the failure of both psychiatry and clinical psychology to address race and culture issues. In the view of the author, it is important to redress this situation.

If there is to be a discipline of psychiatry that is *universally* applicable and, incidentally, better suited to multicultural societies in the West, psychiatry in the West must adapt to the range of cultural diversity across the world as well as deal adequately with issues of bias that arise from institutional racism in its structures. In other words, psychiatry must address most, if not all, the critiques of psychiatry described in brief in this chapter – perhaps getting close to the system of psychiatry implemented by Fanon. The critical psychiatry movement in the United Kingdom, in a special article (Bracken, Thomas Timimi et al. 2012), points to a way forward on a road that would result (eventually) in a paradigm change that may allow this to happen. However, judging from recent shifts of mainstream psychiatry (as put forward in a paper by Craddock et al. 2008) to turn away from socio-political considerations towards becoming more rigorous in looking for universally valid brain diseases that correspond to psychiatric diagnoses and looking to the neurosciences to produce new biological models of illness.

References

Anderson, B. (1991) *Imagined Communities, Reflections on the Origin and Spread of Nationalism*. London and New York: Verso.
Angell, M. (2011a) The epidemic of mental illness: Why? *The New York Review of Books*, 23 June 2011.
Angell, M. (2011b) The illusions of psychiatry, *The New York Review of Books*, 14 July 2011.
APA (American Psychiatric Association) (2013) DSM 5: *Diagnostic and Statistical Manual of Mental Disorders*, 5th edn. Washington, DC: American Psychiatric Publishing.
Banton, M. (1987) *Racial Theories*. Cambridge: Cambridge University Press.
Barnes, M. and Berke, J. (1971) *Two Accounts of a Journey through Madness*. London: MacGibbon and Kee.
Bateson, G., Jackson, D., Haley, J. and Weakland, J. (1956) Toward a theory of schizophrenia, *Behavioural Science*, 1: 251–264.
Bemme, D. and D'souza, N. (2012) Global mental health and its discontents, *Somatosphere*. Retrieved 10 May 2013 from: http://somatosphere.net/2012/07/global-mental-health-and-its-discontents.html.
Bhabha, H. K. (1994) *The Location of Culture*. London: Routledge.
Bonilla-Silva, E. (2014) *Racism without Racists: Color-Blind Racism and the Persistence of Racial Inequality in America*, 4th edn. New York, Toronto and Plymouth: Rowman and Littlefield.
Bracken, P., Thomas, P., Timimi, S., Asen, E. and Yeomans, D. (2012) Psychiatry beyond the current paradigm, *British Journal of Psychiatry*, 201: 430–434.
Bulhan, H. A. (1985) *Frantz Fanon and the Psychology of Oppression*. New York: Springer Science+Business Media.

Campbell, C. and Burgess, R. (2012) The role of communities in advancing the goals of the movement for global mental health, *Transcultural Psychiatry*, 49(3–4): 379–395.

Carlat, D. (2010) *Unhinged: The Trouble with Psychiatry – A Doctor's Revelation about a Profession in Crisis*. New York: Free Press.

CCCS (Centre for Contemporary Cultural Studies) (1982) *The Empire Strikes Back. Race and Racism in the 70s Britain*. London: Hutchinson.

Census (2001) *Resident Population Estimates for Local Authorities, All Persons, and June 2003 – (for Total population)*. London: Office for National Statistics. www.statistics.gov.uk/census2001 (retrieved on 15 October 2006).

Clarke, J. J. (1997) *Oriental Enlightenment. The Encounter between Asian and Western Thought*. New York and Abington: Routledge.

Cohen, P. (1999) *New Ethnicities, Old Racisms?* London: Zed Books.

Collins, P. Y., Patel, V., Joestl, S. S., March, D., Insel, T. R. and Dar, A. (2011) Grand challenges in global mental health, *Nature*, 475: 27–30.

Craddock, N., Antebi, D., Attenburrow, M-J., Bailey, A., Young, A. and Zammit, S. (2008) Wake-up call for British psychiatry, *British Journal of Psychiatry*, 193: 6–9.

Das, A. and Rao, M. (2012) Universal mental health: Re-evaluating the call for global mental health, *Critical Public Health*, 22(4): 183–189.

Davidson, L., Rakfeldt, J. and Strauss, J. (Eds.) (2010) *The Roots of the Recovery Movement in Psychiatry. Lessons Learned*. Chichester: Wiley-Blackwell.

Dols, M. W. (1992) *Majnūn: The Madman in Medieval Islamic Society* D. E. Immisch (Ed.). Oxford: Clarendon Press.

Donald, A. (2001) The wal-marting of American psychiatry: An ethnography of psychiatric practice in the late twentieth century, *Culture, Medicine and Psychiatry*, 25(4): 427–439.

Eagleton, T. (2000) *The Idea of Culture*. Oxford: Blackwell.

Ehlen, P. (2000) *Frantz Fanon. A Spiritual Biography*. New York: Crossroad Publishing.

Engel, G. L. (1977) The need for a new medical model: A challenge for biomedicine, *Science* New Series, 196 (4286): 129–136.

Fernando, S. (1988) *Race and Culture in Psychiatry*. London: Croom Helm.

Fernando, S. (1995) Social realities and mental health. In S. Fernando (Ed.), *Mental Health in a Multi-ethnic Society: A Multi-disciplinary Handbook*. London and New York: Routledge, pp. 11–35.

Fernando, S. (2010) *Mental Health, Race and Culture*, 3rd edn. Basingstoke and New York: Palgrave Macmillan.

Fernando, S. (2011) A 'global' mental health program or markets or Big Pharma? *Openmind*, 168: 22.

Fernando, S. (2012) Race and culture issues in mental health and some thoughts on ethnic identity, *Counselling Psychology Quarterly*, 25(2): 113–123.

Fernando, S. (2014) *Mental Health Worldwide; Culture, Globalisation and Development*. Basingstoke: Palgrave Macmillan.

Fernando, S. (2017) *Institutional Racism in Psychiatry and Clinical Psychology; Race Matters in Mental Health*. New York and London: Palgrave Macmillan.

Fernando, S. and Keating, F. (2009) *Mental Health in a Multi-ethnic Society. A Multi-disciplinary Handbook*, 2nd edn. London and New York: Routledge.

Fernando, S. and Moodley, R. (2018) *Global Psychologies. Mental Health and the Global South*. London: Palgrave Macmillan.

Foucault, M. (1967) *Madness and Civilization. A History of Insanity in the Age of Reason*. Transl. Richard Howard. London: Tavistock.

Gold, J. (1985) Cartesian dualism and the current crisis in Medicine – a plan for a philosophical approach: Discussion paper, *Journal of the Royal Society of Medicine*, 78: 663–666.

Gordon, L. R. and Parris, L-R, T. (2018) Frantz Fanon's psychology of black consciousness. In S. Fernando and R. Moodley (Eds.), *Global Psychologies. Mental Health and the Global South* (pp. 252–259). London: Palgrave Macmillan.

Hall, S. (1992) New ethnicities. In J. Donald and A. Ratansi (Eds.), *Race, Culture and Difference*. London: Sage.

Hall, S., Critcher, C., Jefferson, T., Clarke, J. and Roberts, B. (1978) *Policing the Crisis. Mugging, The State, and Law and Order*. Basingstoke: Macmillan.

Horton R. (2007) Launching a new movement for mental health, *Lancet*, 370: 806.

Kendi, I. X. (2017) *Stamped from the Beginning. The Definitive History of Racist Ideas in America*. London: Bodley Head (Random House).

Khalfa, J. (2018) Fanon, revolutionary psychiatrist. In J. Khalfa, and R. J. C. Young (Eds.), trans. S. Corcoran. *Alienation and Freedom. Frantz Fanon* (pp 168–202). London: Bloomsbury Academic.

Kirmayer, L. J., Adeponle, A. and Dzokoto, A. A. (2018) Varieties of global psychology: Cultural diversity and constructions of the self. In S. Fernando and R. Moodley (Eds.), *Global Psychologies. Mental Health and the Global South* (pp. 21–37). London: Palgrave Macmillan.

Kloos, B. (2005) Creating new possibilities for promoting liberation, well-being, and recovery: Learning from experiences of psychiatric consumers / survivors. In G. Nelson and I. Prilleltensky (Eds.), *Community Psychology: In Pursuit of Well-being and Liberation* (pp. 426–47). Basingstoke: Palgrave Macmillan.

Laing, R. D. (1964) What is schizophrenia? *New Left Review*, 28: 63–69.

Laing, R. D. and Esterson, A. (1970) *Sanity, Madness and the Family. Families of Schizophrenics.* Harmondsworth: Penguin Books. (First published Tavistock Publications, 1964.)

Leighton, A. H. and Hughes, J. M. (1961) Cultures as causative of mental disorder, *Millbank Memorial Fund Quarterly*, 39(3): 446–70.

Littlewood, R. and Lipsedge, M. (1982) *Aliens and Alienists.* Harmondsworth: Penguin.

Macey, D. (2000) *Frantz Fanon. A Life.* London: Granta Books.

Martin, D. V. (1968) *Adventure in Psychiatry: Social Change in a Mental Hospital.* Oxford and London: Cassirer.

McCulloch, J. (1983) *Black Soul White Artefact. Fanon's Clinical Psychology and Social Theory.* Cambridge: Cambridge University Press

Mills, C. (2014) *Decolonizing Global Mental Health; The Psychiatrization of the Majority World.* London: Routledge.

Moncrieff, J. (2009) *The Myth of the Chemical Cure. A Critique of Psychiatric Drug Treatment.* New York and Basingstoke: Palgrave Macmillan.

Moncrieff, J. (2013) *The Bitterest Pills. The Troubling Story of Antipsychotic Drugs.* New York and Basingstoke: Palgrave Macmillan.

Moodley, R. and Ocampo, M. (2014) (Eds.) *Critical Psychiatry and Mental Health.* New York: Routledge.

O'Hagan, S. (2012) Kingsley Hall: RD Laing's experiment in anti-psychiatry, The Guardian online US edition, Accessed 8 August 2018 at: www.theguardian.com/books/2012/sep/02/rd-laing-mental-health-sanity.

Omi, M. and Winant, H. (2015) *Racial Formation in the United State*, 3rd edn. New York & London: Routledge.

Outram, D. (2005) *The Enlightenment*, 2nd edn. Cambridge and New York: Cambridge University Press.

Patel, V. and Prince, M. (2010) Global mental health: A new global health field comes of age, *Journal of the American Medical Association*, 303: 1976–1977.

Pieterse, J. N. (2007) Ethnicities and Global Multiculture: Pants for an Octopus Plymouth, New York and Toronto: Rowman and Littlefield.

Pieterse, J. N. (2009) *Globalisation and Culture: Global Mélange.* Plymouth, New York and Toronto: Rowman and Littlefield.

Rack, P. (1982) *Race, Culture and Mental Disorder.* London and New York: Tavistock.

Repper, J. and Perkins, R. (2003) *Social Inclusion and Recovery: A Model for Mental Health Practice.* London: Ballière Tindall.

Rose, N. (2018) *Our Psychiatric Future. The Politics of Mental Health.* Cambridge: Polity.

Rose, N. (2019) *Our Psychiatric Future. The Politics and Mental Health.* Cambridge: Polity.

Ryle, G. (1963) *The Concept of Mind.* London: Penguin Books.

Said, E. W. (1994) *Culture and Imperialism.* London: Vintage.

Scheff, Thomas J. (1966) *Being Mentally Ill: A Sociological Theory.* Chicago: Aldine.

Shorter, E. (1997) *A History of Psychiatry from the Era of the Asylum to the Age of Prozac.* New York: John Wiley.

Shukla, A., Philip, A., Zachariah, A. and Shatrugna, V. (2012) Critical perspectives on the NIMH initiative 'Grand Challenges to Global Mental Health', *Indian Journal of Medical Ethics*, 9(4): 292–293.

Summerfield, D. (2012) Afterword: Against 'global mental health', *Transcultural Psychiatry*, 49(3), 1–12.

Szasz, Thomas S. (1962) *The Myth of Mental Illness.* London: Secker and Warburg.

Vige, M. (2008) (Ed.) *Goodbye TCPS.* London: Diverse Minds Special Edition, 33.

WHO (World Health Organization) (1992) *ICD-10 Classification of Mental and Behavioural Disorders.* Geneva: WHO.

Wilkinson, R. and Picket, K. (2010) *The Spirit Level.* London: Allen Lane.

Yancey, W. L., Erickson, E. P. and Julian, R. N. (1976) Emergent ethnicity: A review and reformulation, *American Sociological Review*, 41: 391–402.

9

RACE, CULTURE AND GROUP PSYCHOTHERAPY

Fred Bemak and Rita Chi-Ying Chung

As the world becomes more globally connected, xenophobia and intolerance of cultural, ethnic, racial, and religious differences have become more intensified. Contributing to this is the global mass movement of people as a result of ongoing wars, conflicts, and natural disasters. As formerly homogeneous communities, regions, and countries increasingly become racially and ethnically heterogeneous, potential social and psychological problems can arise. Long-standing racism combined with contemporary issues and attitudes about minorities promulgate xenophobia and intolerance while policies perceived as discriminatory and exclusionary heighten racial tensions. In the United States (US), for example, the response to migrants has magnified conflictual race relations by emphasizing the criminality of undocumented migrants and accentuating that refugees are potential terrorists, leading to a governmental Muslim travel ban and the push for "building a wall" between the US and Mexico to prevent undocumented migration. Globally the increase of White nationalism and attacks towards migrant groups in places such as New Zealand, France, Spain, Australia, the United Kingdom (UK), and the US, contributes to growing hate crimes and violence (Levin 2019). Adding to this volatile situation is historical, sociopolitical, and contemporary racism. For example, in the US there have been numerous reports of law enforcement officers killing unarmed Black men and the rise of public demonstrations and expression of racism by White supremacy groups, while in the UK hate crimes dramatically increased following the Brexit vote (O'Neill 2017). These complex issues create, exacerbate, and ignite racism, xenophobia, and a growing fear of those who are different from oneself. As the world spirals to higher degrees of xenophobia and intolerance, we believe group therapists can play an active role in preventing and intervening in issues of bigotry, prejudice, and racism by incorporating race dialogues during group psychotherapy.

We believe that race, ethnic, and cultural dialogues in group psychotherapy can play a major role in reducing racial tensions and promoting racial harmony. Although we are fully aware of and understand and acknowledge the distinction, as well as the overlap between race, ethnicity, and culture that results in an interchangeability of these terms, for the readability of this article we will use the term race to denote racial, ethnic, and cultural groups (Cardemil and Battle 2003; Day-Vines et al. 2007). Race dialogues have been identified as an effective strategy to prevent xenophobia and racism (Chung, Bemak, Talleyrand, and Williams 2018; Sue 2013; Sue 2015; Sue, Lin, Torino, Capodilupo, and Rivera 2009). Race dialogues involve intense and challenging interactions about race between members from diverse groups that incorporate discussions about prejudice, biases, worldviews, power, and privilege, oftentimes resulting in strong emotional reactions (e.g., Chung et al. 2018; Sue 2013; Sue 2015; Sue et al. 2009) and can be easily embedded in group psychotherapy. Bohm (1996) described dialogues as free flowing, open, transparent, and honest group conversations where members equally share their viewpoints without judgement in an attempt to find a common and deeper understanding. This would be consistent with race dialogues with sharing views and attitudes about race, racism, and discrimination. Bohm's principles form a basis for race dialogues that promote a unique way of examining and discussing differing perspectives of group members and acquiring an awareness that can change one's perceptions, biases, assumptions, and stereotypes (Sue 2015), despite conflict, disagreement, uncertainty, risk, and anxiety (Chen, Thombs, and Costa 2003).

Given the goals of race dialogues described above and that 70%–80% of the world's population are from collectivistic cultures that emphasize family, friends, and community as compared with Western individualistic cultures that primarily focus on the individual and self (Pilch 1997; Triandis 1995), we believe that incorporating race dialogues in group psychotherapy provides a unique response to the intersection of mental health and racism. Consequently, given the current racial climate, greater systematic attention to racial issues in group psychotherapy may be vital in addressing mental health problems that are a result of racism, discrimination, and oppression (Cardemil and Battle 2003; Corrigan et al. 2003; Day-Vines et al. 2007; Office of the US Surgeon General 2001), and subsequently in promoting more harmonious interracial interethnic communities. We suggest that group psychotherapists have a major responsibility to readapt and redesign training and practice so that group psychotherapy becomes a culturally responsive intervention that responds to the psychological impact of changing demographics and contemporary race issues, as well as the potential to support psychological healing, understanding, and appreciation of differences through the facilitation of difficult race dialogues (Bemak and Chung 2004).

To provide a foundation for understanding the critical need for group psychotherapy to address race relations through difficult race dialogues, we will describe changing racial demographics in the US as an example that is representative of countries worldwide, especially in the global north. This will be followed by a discussion of seven key factors that we have found to be effective in addressing race in group psychotherapy: (1) encouraging race dialogues in group psychotherapy; (2) involving the racial interpersonal process as a core element of group psychotherapy; (3) acknowledging racial identity as a key element in group psychotherapy; (4) dealing with and facilitating emotionally charged difficult race dialogues in group psychotherapy; (5) engaging the group psychotherapist as a role model for how to honestly and courageously raise and engage in difficult race dialogues; (6) incorporating political countertransference in group therapy race dialogues; and (7) emphasizing the importance of redefining cultural ethical boundaries in group therapy race dialogues. Recommendations on how group psychotherapists can effectively facilitate race dialogues will be integrated in these seven factors.

Diversity issues: The US example

As previously noted, the US provides a good example of what is happening globally in a number of countries. Immigration is a major factor in the increasing diversity in numerous countries including the US. Projections are that in the upcoming decades many areas in the US will become majority-minority regions with a number of states and jurisdictions having populations with less than 50% non-Hispanic Whites (Colby and Ortman 2015). By 2020 it is projected that foreign-born populations will increase to nearly 20% (Colby and Ortman

2015) as immigration continues to surpass US birth rates (US Census Bureau 2013). Estimates are that one in five persons in the US has foreign-born parent(s) (US Census Bureau 2013). Projections are that biracial and multiracial populations are the fastest-growing groups, tripling from 8 million to 26 million between 2014 and 2060, an increase of 226%, while Asians, the second fastest-growing group, increasing 128%, and Latina/os, the third fastest-growing group, increasing 115% (Colby and Ortman 2015). Muslims (1% of the US population) are estimated to double to 3.3 million by 2050 (Mohamed 2016). Given the increasing racial diversity in the US and with the current tense racial climate, we believe it is essential that group psychotherapists address race issues in group psychotherapy through race dialogues. This requires cultural competence as well as the ability to recognize one's own racial biases and the conspiracy of silence about race (Sue 2015), as well as the intense emotional reactions and potentially threatening responses of group members (DeLucia-Waack and Donigian 2004; Sue et al. 2009). We recommend seven key factors, outlined below, therefore, that we have found to be essential in facilitating effective difficult race dialogues in group psychotherapy.

Seven key issues for facilitating difficult race dialogues in group psychotherapy

Facilitating difficult race dialogues in group psychotherapy is to encourage expressing and examining issues of power, privilege, status, biases, prejudice, oppression, racism, discrimination, marginalization, cultural mistrust, systematic oppression, and the influence of dominant culture on racial group members, all of which have an impact on mental health. For example, group members from diverse backgrounds who experience depression may have countless incidents of discrimination and racism in their daily lives, leading to feelings of hopelessness and helplessness. In addressing these issues, it is important that group psychotherapists are able to recognize both individual and societal, overt and intentional, and covert and unintentional, racism while being acutely aware of the dynamics and reenactment of dominant-minority dynamics in the group (Billow 2005; Eason 2009). Portera (2014) argued that these types of dynamic interactions present opportunities for all groups to break down racial, ethnic, religious and cultural stereotypes and myths leading to different perspectives about race and race relations that have a significant influence and impact on psychological well-being. For example, historically in the US the dominant White culture has been the majority culture with privilege and power (Sue 2015). Not having life experiences based on their race and skin color may cause a lack of understanding of racial profiling, being routinely stopped in their cars by law enforcement, being the target of strangers' direct and indirect racial slurs, being denied home mortgages or access to housing in certain neighborhoods, or being discriminated against in education, employment, health, and legal systems, in contrast to people from diverse backgrounds who may experience these types of encounters on a daily basis. Race dialogues assist in understanding these different experiences based on race and dispel myths, stereotypes, and misperceptions that significantly contribute to healing.

Consequently, diverse groups have both recipients and perpetrators of racism, discrimination, oppression, and marginalization that have a significant impact on mental health and group dynamics. Race-based experiences are carried into group therapy sessions. If the group psychotherapist encourages and cultivates a safe and supportive environment where issues of race and racism can be respectfully and honestly discussed, group therapy can become a place where individuals have the opportunity to examine the psychological impact of these issues on their lives and relationships. For example, the Latina who describes being taunted to "go back home where you belong," or the Black man who describes his humiliation at being stopped and harassed by the police for no apparent reason, or the White man who describes a time in his life when he and his friends taunted a Muslim woman, all have impact on how each of them are behaving in the group, interpersonal dynamics in the group, and intrapsychic issues that may be helpful to address with diverse clients in the group therapy sessions. We believe that it is incumbent on the group psychotherapist to embolden the group members to open up to these sensitive race issues in treatment in a respectful, honest, and open manner.

Racial interpersonal process as a core element in group psychotherapy

Group psychotherapy has utilized interpersonal process as an important aspect in personal and social development. Racial diversity and the race issues within groups have been found to have significant impact on interpersonal process (Zaharopoulos 2014). With increasing diversity combined with greater access to social media, it is inevitable that group members will come from or have exposure to diverse racial and ethnic populations. It is important, therefore, that group therapists understand racial dynamics and racism from multiple perspectives that include historical and sociopolitical values (implicit and explicit), biases, prejudices, power, and privileges, and understand how these variables relate to mental health issues that are present in group therapy with diverse clientele. Helms (1995) provides a useful guideline in understanding the complexities of racial interactional patterns within groups, outlining four types of interactions: parallel interaction – when group members agree and foster harmony through shared racial perspectives; progressive interaction – when group members share views about race that are more complex and promote deeper connections among group members; regressive interaction – when there is a less complex expression about race creating distance and tension within the group; and crossed interaction – when group members directly oppose others' beliefs about race, causing friction, antagonism, and disunity. The values, biases, power, and prejudices that are inherent in these four racial interactional patterns are oftentimes buried in "political correctness," so that expressing one's true beliefs and values about race may be socially unacceptable (Chung, Bemak, Ortiz, and Sandoval-Perez 2008; Chung et al. 2018; Sue 2013; Sue 2015). It is important, therefore, that the group therapist acknowledges that there is a fundamental interpersonal process that has roots in race relations, racial dynamics, systemic oppression, racism, and political correctness and is able to address these issues as they present themselves within groups.

When facilitating race dialogues in groups, one must acknowledge that cultural mistrust exhibited by group members from racially and ethnically diverse backgrounds has an impact on group dynamics (Terrell, Taylor, Menzise, and Barrett 2009). The historical sociopolitical mistreatment and systemic oppression and racism experienced (both directly and indirectly) by individuals, families, and diverse communities may have a dramatic negative and transgenerational impact on their attitudes and trust toward mainstream systems, organizations, and White people in general (Jones et al. 2013; Terrell et al. 2009). Stories of racism, mistreatment, and oppression, such as the unethical US 40-year (1932–1972) Tuskegee experiment, where African American men were not treated for syphilis nor informed that they had syphilis, are talked about and passed down from generation to generation creating cultural mistrust of mainstream organizations and systems, including mental health services, within the African American community (Chung et al. 2018; Jones 1993; Marcella and Wanamaker 2017; Thomas and Quinn 1991). Similarly, for Asian Americans, the US Chinese Exclusion Act of 1882 and the US internment of Japanese Americans during World War II (Takaki 1989) are historical sociopolitical events that remain in the US Asian psyche.

It is vital that group therapists are aware of, sensitive to, and appreciate the origin and relationship between cultural mistrust and mental health and how it manifests in group race dialogues. For example, a Black woman may share in group therapy about the discrimination she experienced when she attended a predominately White school and talks about her deep distrust of schools and other systems to protect her from harassment. Her sharing may stimulate emotional reactions by other group members who also experienced discrimination and distrust as well as those who lack an understanding of her experience and feel offended by the criticism of White people and systems. These issues affect group interpersonal dynamics both consciously and unconsciously, and they may have bearing on the interpersonal dynamics in the group.

When understanding these complex race issues and dynamics within group therapy, it is helpful to look at the composition of American Psychological Association's (APA's) Division 49, the Society of Group Psychology and Group Psychotherapy. Division 49 has an overwhelming majority of members who identify as White (73.1%), with only 5.2% of the total membership identifying as people of color or multiracial/multiethnic, and the remaining 21.7% as non-specified (APA 2016). Given that almost three-quarters of Division 49 group psychotherapists identify as White, it is critical that they, as well as group psychotherapists from all races, fully understand the impact of microaggressions, implicit biases, racial stereotyping, sociopolitical bias and discrimination, oppression, cultural mistrust, and racism that group members harbor. Furthermore, it is essential that group psychotherapists are aware of the conscious and unconscious expression of power and privilege by White group members and simultaneously expressions of oppression, racism and discrimination by diverse group members, all of which contribute to heightened interpersonal dynamics and emotionality in difficult race dialogues in group psychotherapy.

In group therapy one can see examples of these issues when a Black woman passionately expresses her resentment about a comment that was made at her worksite that all lives, not just Black lives, matter, followed by a White group member's comment that she sees the Black woman as "being angry, and not everything is about race." Similarly, in another group a White group member asks a Latino group member, without any apparent reason, about his status in the US, or an Asian American group member is repeatedly asked where she is "really" from, even though she had answered that she is a third-generation American from California, USA. These three examples represent a combination of racial stereotyping, microaggressions, implicit bias, and cultural mistrust and have significant influence on psychological health and group dynamics. Subsequently, it would be important for group psychotherapists in an open and non-defensive way to understand and respond to the interpersonal dynamics and perceptions of group members within the context of these historical, sociopolitical, and current race-based issues (Chung et al. 2008).

Racial identity as a key element in group psychotherapy

Understanding and acknowledging one's own and group members' racial identity is instrumental in facilitating difficult race dialogues in group therapy (Bemak and Chung 2004). Racial identity has been a key element contributing to one's personal and social development in a dominant White racially diverse society. The nature of how one incorporates an understanding of one's own and others' racial and cultural identity plays a critical role in one's psychosocial development and impacts one's socioracial socialization (Helms and Cook 1999), shaping how one views, interacts, and relates to the world around them. Personally understanding the intersection of race and racial identity can buffer the negative effects of discrimination and foster healthy social and emotional development (Else-Quest and Morse 2015). Related to possible application in group therapy, research has found that successful mental health treatment correlates with helping diverse clients deconstruct their racial and cultural identities (Portera 2014).

Subsequently racial identity can be a useful tool in understanding group members' conscious and unconscious attitudes of privilege, power, racism, and oppression (Hardiman, Jackson, and Griffin 2013) and help shape interpersonal interactions that can be examined in psychotherapy groups (Singh and Salazar 2014). Within a psychotherapy group it is likely that members have different statuses of racial identity. One group member may have a more advanced racial identity status, being more aware of racial issues, having a stronger racial identity, and actively working to educate and advocate against racism, while another member may have a beginning racial identity status and be oblivious to race issues believing there is no longer a problem with race and there is full equity, citing a former African American US president as proof of racial equality. Using racial identity to identify the different racial statuses helps understand factors of race and perspectives of group members (Chung et al. 2018). Having a clear understanding of racial identity theory provides the group psychotherapist with a deeper sensitivity about the impact of race on interpersonal and group behaviors (McRae and Dias 2014) and affords a theoretical foundation for understanding the intense emotional interactions and psychological issues of diverse racial and ethnic group members during difficult race dialogues.

Dealing with and facilitating emotionally charged difficult race dialogues in group psychotherapy

The literature shows that interactions focusing on race, power, oppression, and privilege, may provoke strong emotional interactions (Marbley et al. 2015). Our experiences support these findings where honest and open dialogue about race and racism creates highly emotionally charged interactions in group therapy sessions, especially given the very sensitive nature of race in today's society. Some may view race dialogues as threatening and offensive, as privileges and biases are exposed within the group therapy context. Touching on deeply rooted racial experiences evokes personal and interpersonal reactions related to being the recipients, perpetrators, or observers of discrimination, racism, and prejudice. In our experience, race dialogues in group therapy oftentimes unleash deeply buried memories and life events that are associated with strong and unresolved psychological issues. An example of touching the deepest emotional pain when discussing race in group therapy was evident when an African American client shared an early repressed childhood memory growing up in the Southern part of the US when as a 4-year-old he and his father watched a White man shoot and kill his dog for no apparent reason. Tearfully, he described to the group how hard he was crying while his father stood next to him looking at their dog on the ground and apologizing to the shooter. As a result of this early experience he learned not to speak out against racism. This painful experience, rooted in racial hatred, deeply touched other group members and their own experiences, causing several group members to recall personal experiences of racial encounters and feelings of anger, hurt, pain, frustration, and empathy. Simultaneously, some White group members perceived the discussion about race and racism as frightening, highly uncomfortable, and unpleasant, resulting in fear of revealing their own biases and prejudices and being called a "racist," triggering intense emotional responses and reactions of defensiveness, fear, denial, guilt, and shame (Chung et al. 2018; Sue 2013; Sue 2015).

It is critical that the group psychotherapist understands the emotional intensity that accompanies this kind of race dialogue and is receptive to facilitate an honest and open examination of group members' racial experiences and strong emotional reactions. To be effective in this type of highly charged interaction, group therapists should be clear about their own emotional reactions to racism and have clarity about how their experiences and reactions intersect with both the group members and group process. For example, the group therapist listening to the client's story of his dog being killed may trigger memories of witnessing patrons at a restaurant degrading a Latino worker that stimulates feelings of helplessness and regret about her passivity. In this situation, it would be important for the group therapist to understand the impact of their personal experiences and their own racial identity to effectively respond to such a powerful story and group members' reactions. In turn, a lack of awareness may create difficulty in facilitating an honest emotionally charged discussion of conscious and unconscious processes that may be exhibited in the group, and may even cause avoidance to address issues of race and racism. Consequently, it would be important for group therapists to undergo in-depth self-examination of their own racial identity, biases, prejudice, power, and privilege (Chung et al. 2018; Sue 2013; Sue 2015) to assist in diminishing defensiveness, overreactions, and personalization of group members' comments. Furthermore, monitoring one's countertransference helps to objectively understand the group members' processes and cultivate safe spaces for highly charged race dialogues in group psychotherapy (Chung et al. 2018).

Group psychotherapists as role models

Research has shown that group psychotherapists significantly influence groups (Bechelli and Santos 2004). What they say, what they do, and how they interact influences group members. Similarly, the group therapist's impact on the group will have substantial effect during difficult race dialogues (Meeussen, Otten, and Phalet 2014). How the therapist responds to issues of power, privilege, discrimination, racism, prejudice, oppression, and injustice impacts how group members will participate and respond to one another in the group. For example, in a group facilitated by an Asian psychotherapist, an African American client painfully shares how an Asian shopkeeper followed him and then without cause yelled racial slurs and told him to leave the store. The group may watch carefully to see how the Asian therapist responds to the client's feelings of hurt, violation, and discrimination. What tone of voice does the therapist use to respond; does the therapist objectively facilitate open discussion among all group members, and does the group therapist welcome and explore or avoid emotional responses from group members? Is there openness to discussing racial stereotypes, anger, and distrust, or are these issues avoided or deflected? The modeling by the Asian therapist to address the race issues in this situation affects group members and impacts how efficacious these dialogues will be within the group. Through modeling, the group therapist can demonstrate a genuine receptivity to difficult race issues and by example demonstrate how to responsibly, openly, and respectfully discuss race. Replying in an open manner gives the group permission and courage to share these deeply challenging and emotionally intense issues.

Political countertransference in group race dialogues

Political countertransference has a major influence in facilitating difficult race dialogues in group process (Chung et al. 2008). As a result of accessibility, frequent usage, and reliance on technology, we are bombarded with a deluge of information from both mainstream and social media through smart phones and other technological devices. The information we receive instantaneously through sound bites in tweets, livestreaming videos, and so on, enables anyone and everyone to be a journalist and critic and share personal opinions and perspectives about contemporary issues such as race relations, immigration, health care, poverty, terrorism, education, gun violence, gun control, climate change, and so on (Bemak and Chung 2017a, 2017b).

Group psychotherapists, similar to others, receive a continuous barrage of information that influences and affects their values and perspectives of the world and, subsequently, their clinical work. This would be particularly heightened in group therapy that incorporates difficult race dialogues because some media addresses issues specific to race, ethnicity, and culture. We suggest that group psychotherapists may have explicit and implicit reactions to this barrage of information that may impact their values and attitudes about racial issues and therefore their ability to effectively and openly facilitate race dialogues in group psychotherapy. Take, for example, the Muslim client in group therapy that is quiet, soft spoken, and dogmatic in his beliefs, while at the same time distraught about the discrimination he experiences. During the months that the group is meeting, a series of terrorist attacks occur in the New Zealand, Europe and the US, promoting a high terrorist alert. Despite having no indication or sense that the Muslim client has leanings toward violence or terrorism, the group psychotherapist, who has been bombarded and subliminally impacted with news media about Muslim terrorists, may arrive at an erroneous conclusion that the Muslim client could be dangerous and even potentially violent. This is an example of political countertransference where the group therapist, influenced by the media bombardment, may "rethink" or "overthink" the client's sharing feelings of alienation and distress and wonder if the client's comments may lead him to explore terrorist connections and activities despite the lack of any information or clinical evidence to support this notion. We consider this type of clinical misinterpretation based on politics and media information as political countertransference and believe that group therapists have to be keenly aware of the influence of public and social media on their clinical work.

Redefining cultural ethical boundaries in group therapy race dialogues

Given the importance of considering cultural and racial backgrounds and oppressive life situations as a context for group-based race dialogues, it is important to redefine ethical boundaries within the context of culture. Ethical standards used by mental health practitioners are based on Western European American cultural values (Barnett, Lazarus, Vasquez, Moorehead-Slaughter, and Johnson 2007; Bemak and Chung 2015a, 2015b; Eason 2009) and may not be applicable in group psychotherapy that incorporates difficult race dialogues. There has been long-standing confusion over ethical standards, evident in the 1992 national survey in the US that found that the second major concern in counseling was the misunderstanding regarding dual relationships and unclear boundaries (Pope and Vetter 1992). Although group psychotherapists adhere to the International Association for Group Psychotherapy and Group Process Ethical Guidelines and Professional Standards for Group Psychotherapy (2009) that specifically address race by noting the inclusion of equality and tolerance between people and prohibiting discrimination against clients based on race, the question remains about how culturally responsive the ethical codes are as they specifically relate to facilitating difficult race dialogues in group psychotherapy.

Of course, certain therapist–client boundaries are universal and applicable to difficult race dialogues in group therapy, such as not abusing one's power as a therapist; not exploiting, abusing, undermining, or harassing group members; and not engaging in inappropriate behaviors that involve intimate and sexual relationships (Barnett et al. 2007). Beyond these universal basics, we would concur with Lazarus (cited in Barnett et al.) who suggests that some ethics and boundaries are open for reconsideration. Being responsive to racial and cultural differences correlates with understanding how and when ethical standards of psychological practice align with cultural variance. Eurocentric individualistic ethical guidelines may lack cultural sensitivity and result in group psychotherapists losing stature and credibility to facilitate difficult race dialogues as well as negatively impact the therapeutic relationship (Chung and Bemak 2012), thus potentially hindering a genuine examination of race and racism. Pope and Vasquez (2016) noted the danger of harming clients by applying Western therapeutic boundaries grounded in legality rather than being culturally responsive. We would propose that ethical boundaries are less clear when working from a cross-cultural framework and need to be reassessed when incorporating challenging race dialogues in group therapy.

In our opinion, culturally responsive modifications to ethical standards may be important when conducting race dialogues in group therapy. We have identified three key ethical issues that we believe are helpful for group psychotherapists to reassess when incorporating challenging race dialogues in group therapy sessions. First, it is important to reexamine self-disclosure. In many diverse communities and with marginalized populations, openness and sharing by the group therapist has helped establish more meaningful and open relationships with clients (Langseth 2014), which helps clientele open up more readily (Bitar, Kimball, Bermúdez, and Drew 2014; Langseth 2014). Thus, group therapists who facilitate difficult race dialogues may cultivate trust and openness by sharing their own experiences to model authentic and truthful discussions, helping group members have the courage and take risks sharing both their racial experiences and honest reactions to those experiences (Chung et al. 2018). Group psychotherapists' self-disclosure has the potential to be a powerful tool building connections with and between clientele who may share histories of their own experiences related to marginalization, privilege, power, oppression (Burnes and Ross 2010), discrimination, and racism. Second, many cultures are founded on the principle of gift-giving as a means of expressing gratitude and appreciation. Rather than a gift being a violation of ethics, in many cultures gift-giving is an important means to show respect and thankfulness (Sue and Sue 2016). An example of this in group therapy was with a Latina who was very appreciative of the progress she was making in the sessions. To express her gratitude, she made a special food for the group psychotherapist as a gift. For the group therapist to reject her offering would have been insulting and culturally insensitive. Although the food was given specifically to the therapist, it was suggested (and gratefully accepted) that the food be shared with all the group members. Third, as group therapists our ethical standards delineate clear boundaries about relationships with clients. When working with issues of race and race relations, part of being culturally responsive may involve accepting invitations to major events such as funerals, birthdays, special cultural holidays, weddings, and graduations (Bemak and Chung 2015b). Let us imagine for a moment that during an intense and painful race dialogue an ethnically or racially diverse client shared the sudden death of a loved family member because of a hate crime incident and announced a community gathering to mourn the loss of this person, inviting the group therapist. For the group psychotherapist to refuse the invitation could be seen as a rejection and culturally insensitive in light of the group's very personal race dialogues. It is significant if the group psychotherapist attends the ceremony rather than defines the relationship with group members by Western European ethical standards.

Conclusion

With growing diversity and racial tensions globally, there is an increased need for racial healing. Race dialogues have been found to be an effective means of addressing psychological issues inherent in racism, xenophobia, and bigotry. Group psychotherapy is in a unique position to incorporate race dialogues in treatment. This chapter defines critical areas of awareness, cultural sensitivity, and skills in which group psychotherapists can be effective in embracing and facilitating difficult race dialogues outlining seven key issues necessary for effective race dialogues in group psychotherapy that promote psychological healing.

References

American Psychological Association (2016) 'Demographic Characteristics of Division 49 Members by Membership Status 2016.' Retrieved October 3, 2017, from (www. apa.org/about/division/officers/services/div49-2016.pdf).

Barnett, J. E., Lazarus, A. A., Vasquez, M. J. T., Moorehead-Slaughter, O., and Johnson, W. B. (2007) 'Boundary Issues and Multiple Relationships: Fantasy and Reality'. *Professional Psychology: Research and Practice*, 38(4): 401–410.

Bechelli, L. P. D. C., and Santos, M. A. D. (2004) 'Psicoterapia de Grupo: Como Surgiu e Evoluiu [Group Psychotherapy: How it Emerged and Evolved]'. *Revista Latino-Americana De Enfermagem*, 12(2): 242–249.

Bemak, F. and Chung, R. C.-Y. (2004) 'Teaching Multicultural Group Counseling: Perspectives for a New Era'. *The Journal for Specialists in Group Work*, 29: 31–41.

Bemak, F. and Chung, R. C.-Y. (2015a) 'Critical Issues in International Group Counseling'. *Journal for Specialists in Group Work*, 40(1): 1–21.

Bemak, F. and Chung, R. C.-Y. (2015b) 'Cultural Boundaries, Cultural Norms: Multicultural and Social Justice Perspective'. In B. Herlihy and G. Corey (Eds.), *Boundary Issues in Counseling: Multiple Roles and Responsibilities* (3rd ed., pp. 84–91). Alexandria, VA: American Counseling Association.

Bemak, F. and Chung, R. C.-Y. (2017a) 'Refugee Trauma: Culturally Responsive Counseling Interventions'. *Journal of Counseling and Development*, 95: 299–308.

Bemak, F. and Chung, R. C.-Y. (2017b) 'The Psychological Impact of Terrorism on Refugees'. In C. E. Stout (Ed.), *Terrorism, Political Violence, and Extremism: New Psychology to Understand, Face, and Defuse the Threat* (pp. 260–283). Santa Barbara, CA: ABC-CLIO.

Billow, R. (2005) 'The Two Faces of the Group Therapist'. *International Journal of Group Psychotherapy*, 55: 167–187.

Bitar, G., Kimball, T., Bermúdez, J., and Drew, C. (2014) 'Therapist Self-disclosure and Culturally Competent Care with Mexican-American Court Mandated Clients: A Phenomenological Study'. *Contemporary Family Therapy: An International Journal*, 36(3): 417–425.

Bohm, D. (1996) *On Dialogue*. New York: Routledge.

Burnes, T. R., and Ross, K. L. (2010) 'Applying Social Justice to Oppression and Marginalization in Group Process: Interventions and Strategies for Group Counselors'. *The Journal for Specialists in Group Work*, 35(2): 169–176.

Cardemil, E. V., and Battle, C. L. (2003) 'Guess Who's Coming to Therapy? Getting Comfortable with Conversations about Race and Ethnicity in Psychotherapy'. *Professional Psychology: Research and Practice*, 34(3): 278–286.

Chen, E. C., Thombs, B. D., and Costa, C. I. (2003) 'Building Connection through Diversity in Group Counseling: A Dialogic Perspective'. In D. B. Pope-Davis, H. L. K. Coleman, W. M. Liu, and R. Toporek (Eds.), *Handbook of Multicultural Competencies in Counseling and Psychology* (pp. 456–477). Thousand Oaks, CA: Sage.

Chung, R. C.-Y. and Bemak, F. (2012) *Social Justice Counseling: The Next Steps Beyond Multiculturalism*. Thousand Oaks, CA: Sage Publications.

Chung, R. C.-Y., Bemak, F., Ortiz, D. P., and Sandoval-Perez, P. A. (2008) 'Promoting the Mental Health of Migrants: A Multicultural-Social Justice Perspective'. *Journal of Counseling and Development, Multicultural and Diversity Issues in Counseling*, 38: 310–317.

Chung, R. C.-Y., Bemak, F., Talleyrand, R. M., and Williams, J. M. (2018) 'Challenges in Promoting Race Dialogues in Psychology Training: Race and Gender Perspectives'. *The Counseling Psychologist*, 26: 213–240.

Colby, S. L., and Ortman, J. M. (2015) 'Projections of the Size and Composition of the U.S. Population: 2014 to 2060.' Population Estimates and Projections Current Population Reports, Washington, DC: U.S. Census Bureau. Retrieved August 30, 2017, from (www.census.gov/content/dam/Census/library/publications/2015/demo/p25-1143.pdf).

Corrigan, P., Thompson, V., Lambert, D., Sangster, Y., Noel, J. G., and Campbell, J. (2003) 'Perceptions of Discrimination among Persons with Serious Mental Illness'. *Psychiatric Services*, 54(8): 1105–1110.

Day-Vines, N. L., Wood, S. M., Grothaus, T., Craigen, L., Holman, A., Dotson-Blake, K., and Douglass, M. J. (2007) 'Broaching the Subjects of Race, Ethnicity, and Culture during the Counseling Process'. *Journal of Counseling & Development*, 94(1): 123.

DeLucia-Waack, J. L., and Donigian, J. (2004) *The Practice of Multicultural Group Work*. Belmont, CA: Brooks/Cole, Thompson Learning.

Eason, E. A. (2009) 'Diversity and Group Theory, Practice, and Research'. *International Journal of Group Psychotherapy*, 59(4): 563–574.

Else-Quest, N. M., and Morse, E. (2015) 'Ethnic Variations in Parental Ethnic Socialization and Adolescent Ethnic Identity: A Longitudinal Study'. *Cultural Diversity and Ethnic Minority Psychology*, 21(1): 54–64.

Hardiman, R., Jackson, B. W., and Griffin, P. (2013) 'Conceptual Foundations'. In M. A. Adams, W. J. Blumfeld, C. R. Castañeda, H. W. Hackman, M. L. Peters, and X. Zúñiga (Eds.), *Readings for Diversity and Social Justice* (3rd ed, pp. 26–35). New York: Routledge.

Helms, J. E. (1995) 'An Update of Helms White and People of Color Racial Identity Models'. In J. G. Ponterotto, J. M. Casas, L. A. Suzuki, and C. M. Alexander (Eds.), *Handbook of Multicultural Counseling* (pp. 181–191). Thousand Oaks, CA: Sage.

Helms, J. E., and Cook, D. A. (1999) *Using Race and Culture in Counseling and Psychotherapy*. Needham Heights, MA: Allyn & Bacon.

International Association for Group Psychotherapy and Group Process (2009) *Ethical Guidelines and Professional Standards for Group Psychotherapy*. Retrieved October 1, 2017, from (www.iagp.com/about/index.htm).

Jones, J. (1993) *Bad Blood: New and Expanded Edition*. New York: Simon and Schuster.

Jones, P. R., Taylor, D. M., Dampeer-Moore, J., Van Allen, K. L., Saunders, D. R., Snowden, C. B., and Johnson, M. B. (2013) 'Health-Related Stereotype Threat Predicts Health Services Delays among Blacks'. *Race and Social Problems*, 5(2): 121–136.

Langseth, M. (2014) 'Maximizing Impact, Minimizing Harm: Why Service-Learning Must More Fully Integrate Multicultural Education'. In C. R. O'Grady (Ed.), *Integrating Service Learning and Multicultural Education in Colleges and Universities* (pp. 247–262). New York: Routledge.

Levin, B. (2019, March). 'Why White Supremacist Attacks Are on the Rise, Even in Surprising Places'. *Time*. Retrieved October 31, 2019, from (https://time.com/5555396/white-supremacist-attacks-rise-new-zealand/).

Marbley, A. F., Stevens, H., Taylor, C. M., Ritter, R. B., Robinson, P. A., Mcgaha, V., and Li, J. (2015) 'Mental Health Consultation: An Untapped Tool for Facilitating Volatile Intercultural Diversity Group Dialogs'. *Multicultural Education (San Francisco)*, 22(2): 8–15.

Marcella, A., and Wanamaker, M. (2017) *Tuskegee and the Health of Black Men* (Working Paper 22323). National Bureau of Economic Research. Retrieved November 3, 2017, from (www.nber.papers/w22323).

McRae, M. B., and Dias, W. V. (2014) 'In the Boardroom/Out of the Loop: Group and Organizational Dynamics'. In M. L. Miville and A. D. Ferguson (Eds.), *Handbook of Race-Ethnicity and Gender in Psychology* (pp. 295–309). New York: Springer New York.

Meeussen, L., Otten, S., and Phalet, K. (2014) 'Managing Diversity: How Leaders' Multiculturalism and Colorblindness Affect Work Group Functioning'. *Group Processes & Intergroup Relations*, 17(5): 629–644.

Mohamed, B. (2016, January) 'A New Estimate of the U.S. Muslim Population. FACTANK. News in the numbers.' Retrieved August 23, 2017, from (www.pewresearch.fact-tank/2016/01/06/a-new-estimate-of-the-u-s-muslim-population/).

Office of the U.S. Surgeon General (2001) *Mental Health: Cultural, Race, Ethnicity: Surgeon General's Report*. Washington, DC: U.S. Department of Health and Human Services.

O'Neill, A. (2017, October) 'U.K. Home Office Hate Crime, England and Wales, 2016/2017'. Statistical Bulletin 17/17. Retrieved October 31, 2019, from (https://assets.publishing.service.gov.uk/government/uploads/system/uploads/attachment_data/file/652136/hate-crime-1617-hosb1717.pdf).

Pilch, J. J. (1997) 'Psychological and Psychoanalytical Approaches to Interpreting the Bible in Social-Scientific Context'. *Biblical Theology Bulletin*, 27(3): 112–116.

Pope, K. S., and Vasquez, M. J. T. (2016) *Ethics in Psychotherapy and Counseling: A Practical Guide for Psychologists* (5th ed). Hoboken, NJ: Wiley.

Pope, K. S., and Vetter, V. A. (1992) 'Ethical Dilemmas Encountered by Members of the American Psychological Association: A National Survey'. *American Psychologist*, 47(3): 397–411.

Portera, A. (2014) 'Intercultural Competence in Education, Counselling and Psychotherapy'. *Intercultural Education*, 25(2): 157–174.

Singh, A. A., and Salazar, C. F. (2014) 'Using Groups to Facilitate Social Justice Change: Addressing Issues of Privilege and Oppression'. In J. L. DeLucia Waack, C. R. Kalodner, and M. T. Riva (Eds.), *Handbook of Group Counseling and Psychotherapy* (2nd ed, pp. 288–300). Thousand Oaks, CA: Sage.

Sue, D. W. (2013) 'Race Talk: The Psychology of Racial Dialogues'. *American Psychologist*, 68(8): 663–672.

Sue, D.W. (2015) *Race Talk and the Conspiracy of Silence: Understanding and Facilitating Difficult Race Dialogues.* Hoboken, NJ: Wiley.

Sue, D. W., Lin, A. I., Torino, G. C., Capodilupo, C. M., and Rivera, D. P. (2009) 'Racial Microaggressions and Difficult Dialogues on Race in the Classroom'. *Cultural Diversity and Ethnic Minority Psychology*, 15: 183–190.

Sue, D.W., and Sue, D. (2016) *Counseling the Culturally Diverse: Theory and Practice.* Hoboken, NJ: John Wiley.

Takaki, R. (1989) *Strangers from a Different Shore: A History of Asian Americans.* New York: Penguin Books.

Terrell, F., Taylor, J., Menzise, J., and Barrett, R. K. (2009) 'Cultural Mistrust: A Core Component of African American Consciousness'. In H. A. Neville, B. M. Tynes, and S. O. Utsey (Eds.), Handbook of African American Psychology (pp. 209–309). Thousand Oaks, CA: Sage.

Thomas, S. B., and Quinn, S. C. (1991) 'The Tuskegee Syphilis Study, 1932 to 1972: Implications for HIV Education and AIDS Risk Education Programs in the Black Community'. *American Journal of Public Health*, 81(11): 1498–1505.

Triandis, H. C. (1995) *Individualism and Collectivism.* Boulder, CO: Westview Press.

U.S. Census Bureau (2013, May 15) *International Migration is Projected to Become Primary Driver of U.S. Population Growth for First Time in Nearly Two Centuries.* Retrieved August 22, 2017, from (www.census.gov/newsroom/pressreleases/2013/cb13-89.html).

Zaharopoulos, M. (2014) 'Racial-Cultural Events in Group Counseling as Perceived by Group Therapists.' Unpublished doctoral dissertation, Fordham University, New York, NY.

10

CULTURE AND NURSING IN MENTAL HEALTH

Josephine Etowa

Caring for people with mental and behavioural disorders has always reflected the prevailing social values related to the perception of mental illness (WHO 2001). Indeed, there is no doubt that culture affects people's mental health particularly because it influences the course and outcome of mental health problems, health seeking, response to health promotion, prevention and treatment interventions (Kirmayer 2012). Canada, like other Western countries, is becoming increasingly diverse. Over 20 percent of Canadian residents are foreign-born and about 20 percent are ethnocultural and racialized sub-populations. More than 200,000 immigrants and an estimated 25,000 refugees make Canada their home every year (Citizen and Immigration Canada [CIC] 2013). While Canada draws strength from its ethnocultural and racial diversity, research evidence suggests these immigrant, refugee, ethnocultural and racialized (IRER) groups have less access to mental health services than their White and Canadian-born counterparts (Kirmayer 2012). They are less likely to receive needed care, and they face numerous barriers to good quality care when they seek it. Thus, they bear a greater burden from unmet mental health needs and overall poor health.

There is mounting evidence in health literature of the impact of violence, racism, discrimination, and the social determinants of health on the mental health of the IRER population. In a review of the literature, Guruge and Butt (2015) found that experiences of collective and personal violence or trauma, discrimination, and refugee status contributed to higher rates of depression, stress, anxiety and conduct disorders among immigrant and refugee youth. Similarly, Beiser and Hou (2016) found that refugee youth who have experienced pre-immigration trauma and post-immigration discrimination report higher incidences of aggressive behaviours and emotional problems. These findings have been echoed with the South East Asian refugees (Noh et al. 1999), the Aboriginal population (Kafele 2004), for immigrant women (Crooks et al. 2011), and those experiencing social inequalities (WHO 2014).

Members of the IRER population face additional barriers to accessing health care and mental health services. These barriers could be individual, systematic, cultural, or economic. Thomson et al. (2015) in a scoping review of the literature, categorized the barriers to access into three groups. The first set of barriers were related to the uptake of existing health information and services and included a lack of awareness and knowledge of the services available and cultural barriers of stigma, gender roles, and adherence to alternative therapies, among others. The second set of barriers were related to the immigration and settlement experience itself and the resulting socioeconomic consequences and experiences of discrimination. The third set of barriers is related to the linguistic and cultural inappropriateness of mental health services. This chapter underscores the importance of cultural competence in mental health nursing to curtail the influence of culture-related barriers and their intersection with other social determinants of health on mental health nursing.

Historical background

In the past, the mentally ill were treated both humanely and inhumanely. For example, during the Greek and Roman era, they were cared for in temples, but were mistakenly thought to be possessed by the devil and they were whipped and starved to exorcise the evil spirit (Taylor 2008). During the 16th and 17th centuries, they were imprisoned in almshouses, which were a combination of jail and asylum. The 18th and 19th centuries saw the beginnings of the current psychiatric nursing care with the introduction of attendants to care for the mentally ill as part of the "moral therapy" introduced in France and England. Moral therapy was founded on the belief that mental illness was due to faulty upbringing and immorality and that it can be corrected with the provision of a therapeutic environment in which patients were kept busy with work and other diversions (Wasserbauer and Brodie 1992). Hotel Dieu in Quebec was the first hospital in Canada to dedicate a ward for women who were mentally ill in 1714, and the first asylum was built in 1835 in Saint John, New Brunswick.

Although the original purpose of the asylums was to use Moral Therapy to treat and discharge the mentally ill patients, they were almost never discharged. As the institutions became crowded, Moral Therapy was no longer practical as a treatment and, by the late 1800s, these institutions deteriorated into abysmal environments with a terrible public image. In an effort to improve the conditions within these institutions, physicians adopted strategies to improve patient care that included hiring graduate nurses instead of attendants and incorporating science-based treatments. This marked a drastic shift from containment to caring for the mentally ill.

As the 20th century dawned, the book *A Mind That Found Itself* by Clifford Beers (1908, as cited in Kirby and Keon 2004), that described his experience of being a mentally ill person, led to reforms in psychiatry that called for prevention and early intervention. Additionally, Sigmund Freud's work provided the foundation for the scientific study of human behaviour and many of his concepts continue to be embedded into mainstream culture even though much of his theory is no longer embraced by the scientific community. The increased knowledge about the causes of mental illness including damage to the brain and congenital and hereditary causes "led to an era of pessimism regarding the possibility of treatment" (Kirby and Keon 2004: 135). It was only when thousands of people suffered from psychological, emotional and physical stress due to World War I that the scientific community became aware of the vulnerability of individuals to such stressors and that scientific and psychological treatment of mental illness is possible. As a result, there was increased funding for research and education of mental health professionals in the disciplines of psychology, psychiatry, psychiatric social work, and psychiatric nursing.

The deplorable conditions in the asylums and the advances in pharmacology and mental health knowledge and treatments led to the de-institutionalization of mental health patients between the 1960s and the 1990s. Currently, mental health interventions and treatments are provided by multidisciplinary teams that include psychiatrists, clinical psychologists, psychiatric mental health nurses, social workers, and occupational or behavioural therapist. Services are provided in out-patient and community settings as well as in in-patient hospitals and psychiatric and mental health centres. As mental health clients and the health care providers became more integrated with the rest of health care, there was a notable lessening in the stigma associated with mental illness and psychiatry (Kirby and Keon 2004). This also highlighted the need for mental health to be incorporated into the curricula of all schools of nursing.

In the later part of the 1900s, mental health nurses quickly moved from being hand-maidens to the psychiatrist to accountable professionals with the educational preparation and credentials that allow them to practice autonomously and as part of mental health care teams. Nurses in a mental health practice use the fundamental basics of the psychiatric interviewing process to collect vital information; utilize the nursing process in the assessment, diagnosis, planning, implementation, and evaluation of psychiatric care; and practice the artful use of self in the therapeutic relationship in order to promote positive patient outcomes through the use of therapeutic communication (American Nurses Association [ANA] 2014; Registered Psychiatric Nurse Regulators of Canada [RPNRC] 2014). Mental Health Nursing has become a specialty in nursing with a preferred baccalaureate level preparatory education and specialty credentialing in Mental Health.

While any registered nurse can practice in a mental health setting in Canada, Registered Psychiatric Nurse (RPN) is a protected title in the provinces of Manitoba, Saskatchewan, Alberta, and British Columbia, and in the Yukon Territory. To carry the title, a nurse must have graduated from a recognized psychiatric nursing program or has had her/his knowledge, skills and abilities assessed to be equivalent to the Canadian Registered Psychiatric Nursing Entry-Level Competencies (RPNRC 2014). The scope of practice of an RPN is based on the Health Professions Act that governs the regulation of all health care professions in Canada (CIHI 2017; CRPNBC 2017; RPNRC 2014).

Despite the current advances in mental health treatments and support, major challenges continue to exist. One of which is the social aspect of mental illness that cannot be addressed by health care. Homelessness is a case in point. Furthermore, considering the social determinants of health and their impact on mental health, there is a need for "major collaborative cross-sectoral and multi-pronged approach from the still poorly coordinated mental health, health care, social services, education, correctional, recreational, vocational and addiction systems" (Kirby and Keon 2004: 143). Additionally, in the ethnically diverse global village reality of today's societies, there is an increased need to provide mental health services in a culturally competent and relevant manner. The next section will highlight the cultural context within which nursing care is provided to mentally ill clients by exploring how culture impacts the presentation, meaning, and outcomes of mental illness and the clients' satisfaction with the care they receive.

Cultural considerations in nursing care

Culture and social context are among the determinants that shape the mental health of minorities as well as their access to health services (US Department of Health and Human Services [DHHS] 2001: 25). Beliefs about health and even the definition of health differ among cultures. While the Western medical system distinguishes physical and mental health, this is not the case for many cultures who have a more holistic view of health that incorporates the physical, social, spiritual, and mental dimensions (Gorman and Cross 2011; Debs-Ivall 2016). These beliefs influence mental health and access to, utilization of, and satisfaction with mental health services. Mental health nurses need to be aware of these beliefs and give them due considerations as they assess their clients; plan, implement and evaluate the plan of care; and build a therapeutic relationship with their clients. The following section of this chapter will address these issues under the categories of: (a) causation and prevalence; and (b) presentation and help-seeking.

Causation and prevalence

Mental health is a product of a complex interaction of biological, psychological, social and cultural factors (DHHS 2001). The prevalence of certain mental illnesses such as schizophrenia, bipolar disorder, and panic disorder, has been found to be fairly consistent across countries. Furthermore, the global consistency of symptoms and prevalence of these diseases point to the high role hereditary factors, rather than social and cultural factors, play in their causation (DHHS 2001).

Cultural and social factors, including poverty and trauma, however, have been found to play a more prominent role in the causation of depression. Similarly, cultural and social factors such as war, violence, racism, and threats of death and injury, have been found to have a direct causation of post-traumatic stress disorder (American Psychiatric Association 2013; DHHS 2001). This impact is seen not only in the generation that has experienced the trauma or violence, but also in the following generations should healing not take place (Brokenleg 2012).

Traumatic experiences are common among refugees and immigrants arriving from countries that have experienced civil war and political and social turmoil leading to increased rates of post-traumatic stress disorder (PTSD) in this population. Additionally, experiences of racism and discrimination that are considered traumatic during the transition and following arrival in the host country, have a similar impact. This could be due to increased vulnerability during a time when the social network is not as strong (McKenzie et al. 2010). Rates of PTSD, for example, were found to be higher in refugees that had been detained in immigration holding centres in Canada than those who had never been detained (Cleveland and Rousseau 2013).

Of interest, in their review of the literature on intergenerational trauma, Hudson and colleagues (2016) identified six themes that a psychiatric mental health nurse would need to optimize in their care of mental health clients who have experienced trauma. These include silence and nondisclosure of the experience, communication patterns in the transmission of traumatic experiences, adaptation to the new environment, remembering and recalling past trauma to aid healing, relationship-building with family members and the extended community, and national redress or public acknowledgement of past wrongs. This becomes especially important when caring for members of groups that have experienced historical and systemic violence, racism, and discrimination.

Presentation and help-seeking

As symptoms have culture-specific meanings, clients from diverse backgrounds will describe their symptoms differently (DHHS 2001), will have different ideas about what might have caused it, and will differ in their acceptance of it (Ballard 2008). Some clients, for example, will express emotional symptoms with somatic manifestations which are more culturally acceptable (Kleinman 1988). Other clients could attribute their disorder to evil spirits, racism, or divine retribution (Ballard 2008). This adds a level of complexity when the cultures of the nurses and clients are different. Not only would they have to cross linguistic barriers, they will also need to interpret the culture-specific meaning attributed to symptoms and disorders. Consequently, the meaning a person attributes to the illness will influence help-seeking behaviours and outcomes.

It is well documented that Immigrant, Refugee, Ethnocultural, and Racialized (IRER) populations are less inclined than the native-born and White population to seek help for mental disorders, and will delay until symptoms are more severe (Durbin et al. 2014; Jimenez et al. 2013). They will, more often, turn to other more culturally acceptable resources such as folk and family healers, religious leaders, or primary care providers (Ballard 2008; DHHS 2001). It is therefore important that nurses caring for these IRER populations must appreciate the perspective of the client and support the incorporation of culturally relevant interventions and treatments into the plan of care.

Evidence points to mistrust and stigma as underlying barriers to seeking mental health services. Mistrust in the healthcare providers and the health care system arise, for the most part, from historical and present-day practices of discrimination against people with mental illness (DHHS 2001). IRER populations commonly report experiences of racism and discrimination. These experiences are stressful and have been linked to poor mental and physical health (Guruge and Butt 2015; Ginieniewicz and McKenzie 2014; Reitmanova and Gustafson 2009).

Stigma, whether experienced, internalized, or perceived, is another barrier to help-seeking among people with mental illness (Clement et al. 2015). The historical discriminatory treatment of people with mental illness and their segregation in mental asylums has contributed to a public view of them as dangerous and not competent. Clients from IRER populations would be reluctant to seek help for mental illness because of their fear of compounding the discrimination they already experience because of their minority status with that of being mentally ill (Gary 2005). Mental health nursing services must be accessible and appropriate to all and should address culture-related needs.

Cultural competence and mental health nursing

Nursing was one of the first health professions to recognize and address health inequities related to ethnocultural and racial practices and develop the theories to guide nurses in the provision of culturally competent care. Madeleine Leininger was the first nursing theorist to lead this charge with the Theory of Cultural Care Diversity and Universality (Leininger and McFarland 2002). With the increasing diversity of the client population and the escalating awareness of health inequities and the impact of cultural and social factors on population health, several other cultural care and cultural competence nursing theories emerged. Most stress the importance of the interpersonal relationship between the client and the mental health nurse and the therapeutic impact of the relationship on the client.

Cultural competence has been described as the ability of nurses "to provide effective health care taking into consideration the people's cultural beliefs, behaviours, and needs" (Papadopoulos 2006: 10). It is the result of the synthesis of skills and knowledge that nurses continue to acquire through their personal and professional experiences. According to Papadopoulos et al. (1998), cultural competence develops through four stages including cultural awareness, cultural knowledge, cultural sensitivity, and cultural competence. Cultural awareness begins with the examination of one's own beliefs and values, especially pertaining to health and health practices. Since our own cultural beliefs and values are the lens through which we view and assess others and the world around us, self-awareness allows us to view commonalities with others as well as areas of potential conflict (Etowa and Adongo 2007). Additionally, it helps the nurse to identify any potential sources of stereotyping, ethnocentrism and prejudice. Cultural knowledge is acquired through study, research, and experience. It is based on the knowledge that health inequalities have a basis in the social and cultural determinants of health. Cultural sensitivity allows the building of partnerships between nurses and clients through trust, acceptance, and respect. Sensitivity to the culture and context of the client will impact on how power is negotiated and the relationship facilitated. During the encounter, the nurse exercises interpersonal communication skills to build the therapeutic relationship with the client. The communication skills involve both verbal and non-verbal variations, as well as time orientation and forms of address. The last stage is cultural competence, which "requires the synthesis and application of previously gained awareness, knowledge, and sensitivity" in order to assess the clients' needs; select nursing diagnoses; and develop, implement and evaluate culturally appropriate and relevant plans of care (Papadopoulos 2006: 18). Rather than a clinical detachment in the relationship, the nurses exhibit genuine interest in the clients as they listen to and learn from them.

Throughout their professional lives, nurses acquire generic cultural competencies of knowledge, awareness, skills and attitudes that enable them to provide care to people from diverse backgrounds. These competencies, which include the knowledge of how culture impacts health and the structural processes that impact health equity, are foundational to clinical cultural competence (Pottinger, Perivolaris and Howes 2007). In the field of mental health nursing, the generic knowledge would include whether a culture is high or low context; the culture's time orientation or perspective (past, present, or future); how the relationship between humanity and the environment is perceived; how emotions are expressed; where the locus of control is perceived to be (internal or external); how a culture views and expresses mental health and emotional and affective expressions; and whether there are any culture bound syndromes such as the impact of the "evil eye" and the somatization of affective and emotional symptoms (Lo and Pottinger 2007).

Nurses utilize generic cultural competencies to acquire specific cultural competencies particular to specific cultural groups and clients from within these groups (Pottinger et al. 2007). These competencies in mental health nursing include the culture's unique mental health diseases, symptoms and interventions; and the client's usual rules of interaction, worldview, and view of mental illness (Lo and Pottinger 2007). The nurse needs to take into account the immigrant or refugee experiences of the clients as these experiences have a direct impact on their mental health status.

The psychiatric nurse will utilize both generic and specific cultural competencies in the three-fold role of caring for clients with mental illness: (a) using the fundamental basics of the psychiatric interviewing process to collect vital information; (b) utilizing the nursing process in the assessment, diagnosis, planning, implementation, and evaluation of psychiatric care; and (c) practicing the artful use of self in the therapeutic relationship in order to promote positive patient outcomes through the use of therapeutic communication.

Cultural formulation interview: Collecting vital information

A culturally competent nurse's assessment of a client presenting with a mental health problem has to start with a self-assessment of her/his own culture and its impact on the interaction. The nurse would then utilize the generic cultural competencies to assess for the specific cultural perspective and presentation of the client (Etowa and Adongo 2007).

The American Psychiatric Association's fifth reiteration of the *Diagnostic and Statistical Manual of Mental Disorders* that was published in 2013 (APA 2013), included a cultural formulation interview guide for use by clinicians in assessing the needs of their clients. Psychiatric nurses are encouraged to use the interview guide with *all* their patients, not only those whom they deem *cultural* as every client has a unique and individual culture that will impact the presentation, progression, and outcome of their illness (Lo and Pottinger 2007). Several other cultural assessment tools exist that could support the collection of this vital information including Leininger's Inquiry Guide for Kinship and Social Factors (Leininger and McFarland 2002). "Effective communication is vital to an accurate psychiatric assessment" (Lo and Pottinger 2007: 250). Mental health nurses are to conduct their assessment with curiosity, respect, and compassion and are to listen carefully to the responses while observing for non-verbal cues in order to better understand the many cultural and social aspects that are at play in the presentation of the client.

Mental health nurses are also encouraged to utilize interpreters in the assessment interview to bridge the linguistic gap that may exist with non-dominant language speakers. Nurses might also consider working with cultural navigators or consultants who will help them contextualize the assessment findings within the cultural background of the client (Lo and Pottinger 2007). This resource can also be utilized in formulating treatment plans to honour and integrates the cultural values of clients. Finally, nurses need to understand the client impact of specific social processes such as anti-immigrant and racist sentiments against immigrants and refugees, colonization and racism in the case of the Aboriginal population, and stigma and discrimination in the case of the lesbian, gay, and transgendered groups, to name a few.

Utilizing the nursing process

Meyer and Zane (2013) found that mental health clients were less satisfied with the care they received when cultural elements that were important to them were not incorporated into their treatment plans. Interestingly, this was the case for ethnic minority clients only, not for White clients. Whether considering psychopharmacology or psychoanalysis, the treatment plan needs to be customized with the cultural perspective of the client in mind. The nurse needs to be aware of the culturally specific treatments and resources (such as family members, folk healers, or herbal remedies) that the client is already accessing and their potential impact on any recommended course of action. Nurses also need to also be aware of the diverse metabolic and cultural reaction to psychiatric drugs and the need to adjust dosages or negotiate acceptance as the need arises.

Leininger and McFarland (2002) recommend three courses of action for nurses when planning the care for their clients. First is cultural preservation intended for clients whose cultural practices do not have any negative physiological impact on them and are positively impacting their experiences. They are to be supported to retain and maintain these practices. Second, cultural negotiation is recommended for the clients whose choice of a course of action or culturally relevant practice does not sufficiently address their condition or symptoms. In this case, the nurse would respectfully negotiate the additional use of medications, treatments, and practices. Third, cultural re-patterning or re-framing is a strategy recommended to redirect a client to change certain decisions or practices that are harmful. The nurses should respectfully and compassionately provide alternate practices. When planning the care and evaluating the outcomes of their clients, psychiatric nurses need to appreciate that psychopharmacology and psychoanalysis are Western Medicine practices that might not be well researched or accepted in other cultures and subcultures (Lo and Pottinger 2007). As such, nurses need to consider the careful incorporation of some cultural, spiritual, and herbal remedies into the care plan, as well as the potential use of family or group therapy which are more acceptable in some cultures.

Lo and Pottinger (2007) recommend the addition of four fields or columns to the case formulation tool in order to capture the cultural assessment of the client and guide the plan of care. The fields would include: (a) *spiritual* issues, (b) *presenting* clinical features, (c) *protective* strengths, and (d) a *plan* column to indicate any potential interventions.

The artful use of self in the cultivation of the therapeutic relationship

The therapeutic pairing of psychiatric nurse and client in a therapeutic relationship and the resulting transference and counter-transference will be impacted by the existence of cultural and power dynamics. Nurses will need to be sensitive to these dynamics and utilize cultural competence strategies to address them.

Intersectionality and mental health nursing

The success of mental health nursing programs is affected by the intersectionality of various factors related to culture. For example, research by Chiu et al. (2018) on ethnic differences in mental health status and service utilization in Ontario Canada among the White, South Asian, Chinese, and Black sub-populations found that self-reported physician-diagnosed mood and anxiety disorders and mental health service use were generally higher among the White respondents compared with the South Asian, Chinese, and Black respondents. The wide variation of the prevalence of mental health factors and mental health service use across ethnic groups suggests the possible existence of ethnicity or cultural related barriers to service use. Consistent with the above is the contention of Mental Health Commission of Canada (MHCC) (2016) that IRER populations in Canada seek help for mental health problems less frequently compared with others. Race has therefore been associated with mental health status and help-seeking behaviours.

Additionally, other aspects of culture have also been found influential to mental health. The role played by the power relations between the patient and clinician and how these relations affect the clinical encounter due to differences in cultural knowledge, identity, language, religion and other aspects of cultural identity was highlighted by Kirmayer (2012). Moreover, the general social structure including the health care system regulates the various kinds of ethnic or cultural differences that are considered worthy of attention. MHCC (2016) identified cultural incompatibility of services as a pertinent barrier to accessibility of services by IRER populations. Other barriers include long wait lists, complicated procedures, and shortage of medical professionals. Additionally, language proficiency is a barrier for some IRER groups who are unable to read and understand instructions, prescriptions and instructions written in English and French (Lai and Surood 2013). Also, in some ethnocultural groups, mental health problems and illnesses are stigmatized and this may delay seeking help (MHCC 2016). Various aspects of culture therefore intersect in ways that intricately compound the barriers to access, help-seeking and response to treatment and care. For example, belonging to an IRER group in which mental illness is either stigmatized or not recognized as a health issue, coupled with inability to read and understand English and French would further undermine a person's prospects not only of seeking help but also responding appropriately to treatment and care. Culture is therefore one of the social determinants of health that intersects with others such as age, gender, social economic status, to influence one's mental health or access and response to services. The intersectionality of culture with other social determinants of health therefore calls for a multi-pronged approach for people from varying ethnic groups, gender, age, social economic status, language, religion, and living in different contexts.

Future directions

According to WHO (2014), people's mental health is a result of various conditions in their daily lives throughout the different stages of the human life cycle. Strategies to improve population mental health and to reduce the risk of those mental disorders that are associated with social inequalities should therefore be targeted at improving these conditions. The Mental Health Commission of Canada (MHCC) 2016 report, has acknowledged the need for health providers to respond appropriately to mental health needs of the diverse population and the social determinants of health at play in their lives. Consideration should be made to the intersection of cultural and social factors and their multiplicative impact on the experiences of mental health and illness by the clients and on their affective and emotional well-being (Rossiter and

Morrow 2011). Regarding practice and education, nurses providing care for and within these populations need the cultural competence to respond appropriately. MH nurses need a thorough understanding of the complexity of the cultural and social factors that influence health and illness grounded in the experiences of the MH clients for it to be appropriate (Burr and Chapman 1998).

The findings of a study by Meyer and Zane (2013) show that ethnocultural people consider racial match and provider knowledge of discrimination/prejudice to be important in their mental health. Ethnocultural and racialized clients view providers of similar background as more credible sources of help because of the shared values and worldviews (Meyer, Zane and Cho 2011). As such, the racial matching of clients and providers might be an appropriate strategy to help provide culturally and linguistically appropriate services. However, as that is not always possible, it is imperative that nurses providing mental health services to clients be culturally competent and appropriate in their approach. Additionally, material about mental health services ought to be made available in multiple languages in order to be accessible to the client population (Gorman and Cross 2011). Furthermore, strategies ought to be undertaken to increase the diversity within psychiatric and mental health nurses to reflect the increasing diversity of the population. Mental Health nurses ought to be educated in cultural and cross-cultural communication competency. Besides, there is need to develop more empirically validated clinical strategies for addressing issues related to race and ethnic minority client with a focus on how to manage and cope with life experiences involving prejudice and discrimination (Meyer and Zane 2013). This would imply changes not only to the curriculum, but also to the way the education is delivered and the experiences of the students in the clinical setting are tailored (Thomson et al. 2015).

Pertaining to research, there is a need for additional studies into the low uptake of mental health services by the IRER population and the different approaches that could be taken to improve access. There is a need as well additional research into the rates and incidences of mental health in the sub-populations within the IRER population and the intersection and multiplicative impact of the social determinants of health on their mental health status. Furthermore, considerations should also be made to intergenerational expressions of trauma in refugees and their children (Hudson et al. 2016). "If one generation does not heal, problems are transmitted to subsequent generations" (Brokenleg 2012: 10).

There is need to put in place and/or strengthen the existing policy framework in order to increase the promotion of mental health services for the IRER population groups. Specifically, such policies ought to "strengthen and support ethnic communities, attack racism, and provide access to the development of required skills" (Thomson et al. 2015: 1900). Policies also need to also address the systemic barriers that IRER groups face, including credentialing, socio-economic disparities, settlement, loss of social capital, and fragmentation of services. Policies ought to also address the specific needs of the sub-groups within this population, such as the youth, women, and elderly and so on.

Conclusion

Culture influences many aspects of mental health, including how the people express the disorder, their coping style, willingness to seek services and how social support is mobilized. Similarly, the cultures of health professionals such as nurses and the health care system influence diagnosis, treatment, and service delivery. These factors play important role in mental health service utilization for racialized people. There is an overwhelming amount of evidence of the inequities experienced by the IRER population and the resulting impact on their physical and mental health. Nursing like many disciplines in the Western world has struggled with effective health care for racialized people. While it has made some strides to address mental health through cultural competence models, there remains a void in terms of targeted efforts to effectively address the mental health of ethnocultural/racialized people in Canada through critical social theories. Nursing cannot continue to ignore the pathways through which the social determinants of health including culture intersect to create poor health for racialized people. Nursing practice, research, education and policy has to be informed by critical social theories on race, colonialism, ethnicity and culture in order to deconstruct the structures and power dynamics nested within Western health care system. Critical theory lens provides the upstream and intersectional analysis necessary for health and social services grounded in social justice. The strategic use of a critical lens will help nurses to discover the root cause of precarious mental health issues. It is rooted in an understanding that systemic and structural barriers are most complicit in creating inequities in mental health outcomes. This approach will help nurses to understand and address the social cultural circumstances, and structural barriers that renders racialized people vulnerable or 'at risk'.

Nurses must challenge behavioural approaches that individualizes health problems and opt rather for the strong evidence that inequities in mental health outcomes are greatly influenced by unequal access to conditions and resources necessary for healthy living and by biologic effects of stress that result from these unequal opportunities to be healthy. Attempts to change behaviour without changing its social context is unlikely to be successful. They must look for solutions for 'why some people are healthy and others not', in a way that refuses to accept simplistic and individualized responses that blame people for 'poor choices'. In addition to addressing material conditions, efforts to address mental health must include interventions to empower racialized communities and confront the harmful processes of marginalization and exclusion (e.g. systemic discrimination and stigmatization) rooted in power and privilege.

References

American Nurses Association (2014) *Psychiatric-Mental Health Nursing: Scope and Standards of Practice* (2nd ed.). Silver Springs, MD: Author.

American Psychiatric Association (2013) *Diagnostic and Statistical Manual of Mental Disorders* (5th ed.). Washington, DC: Author.

Ballard, K.A. (2008) 'Issues and trends in psychiatric-mental health nursing'. In O'Brien, P.G., Kennedy, W.Z., and Ballard, K.A. (2008/2013). *Psychiatric mental health nursing: An Introduction to theory and practice* (1st ed., pp. 21–23). Sudbury, MA: Jones and Bartlett Publishers.

Beiser, M. and Hou, F. (2016) 'Mental health effects of premigration trauma and postmigration discrimination on refugee youth in Canada'. *The Journal of Nervous and Mental Disease*, 204(6): 464–470.

Brokenleg, M. (2012) 'Transforming cultural trauma into resilience'. *Reclaiming Children and Youth*, 12(21): 9–13.

Burr, J.A. and Chapman, T. (1998) 'Some reflections on cultural and social considerations in mental health nursing'. *Journal of Psychiatric and Mental Health Nursing*, 5(6): 431–437.

Canadian Federation of Mental Health Nurses (2014) *Canadian Standards for Psychiatric-Mental Health Nursing (4th Ed.)*. Toronto: CFMHN.

Canadian Institute of Health Information (2017) *Registered Psychiatric Nurses*. Retrieved from www.cihi.ca/en/registered-psychiatric-nurses.

Chiu, M., Amartey, A., Wang, X., and Kurdyak, P. (2018) 'Ethnic differences in mental health status and service utilization: a population-based study in Ontario, Canada'. *The Canadian Journal of Psychiatry*, 63(7): 481–491.

Citizen and Immigration Canada (2014) Facts and Figures 2013: Immigration Overview – *Permanent Residents*. Retrieved from http://publications.gc.ca/collections/collection_2015/cic/Ci1-*8-9-2013*-eng.pdf.

Clement, S., Schauman, O., Graham, T., Maggioni, F., Evans, Lacko, S., Bezborodovs, N., Morgan, C., Rusch, N., Brown, J.S.L., and Thornicroft, G. (2015) 'What is the impact of mental health-related stigma on help-seeking? A systematic review of qualitative and quantitative studies'. *Psychological Medicine*, 45: 11–27. doi:10.1017/S0033291714000129. Retrieved from: www.cambridge.org/core/services/aop-cambridge-core/content/view/E3FD6B42EE9815C4E26A6B84ED7BD3AE/S0033291714000129a.pdf/what_is_the_impact_of_mental_healthrelated_stigma_on_helpseeking_a_systematic_review_of_quantitative_and_qualitative_studies.pdf.

Cleveland, J. and Rousseau, C. (2013) 'Psychiatric symptoms associated with brief detention of adult asylum seekers in Canada'. *The Canadian Journal of Psychiatry*, 58(7): 409–416.

College of Registered Psychiatric Nurses of British Columbia (2012) Consultation Report for Registered Psychiatric Nurses' Scope of Practice. Port Moody, BC, Canada: Author. Retrieved from www.crpnbc.ca/wp-content/uploads/2012/02/2012-02-15-Scope-of-Practice-Consultation-Report-FINAL.pdf.

College of Registered Psychiatric Nurses of British Columbia (2017) Scope of Practice for Registered Psychiatric Nurses: Standards, Limits, and Conditions. Port Moody, BC: Author. Retrieved from www.crpnbc.ca/wp-content/uploads/2017/02/2016-03-15-Revised-Scope-with-disclaimer-updated-Feb-13-2017.pdf?v=831.

Crooks, V. A., Hynie, M., Killian, K., Giesbrecht, M., and Castleden, H. (2011) 'Female newcomers' adjustment to life in Toronto, Canada: sources of mental stress and their implications for delivering primary mental health care'. *GeoJournal*, 76(2): 139–149.

Debs-Ivall, S. (2016) *The Lived Experiences of Immigrant Canadian Women with the Healthcare System* (Unpublished Doctoral Dissertation). Walden University.

Durbin, A., Lin, E., Moineddin, R., Steele, L.S., and Glazier, R.L. (2014) 'Use of MH care for non-psychotic conditions by immigrants in different admission classes and by refugees in Ontario Canada'. *Open Medicine*, 8(4): e136–e146.

Elias, A. and Paradies, Y. (2016) 'Estimating the mental health costs of racial discrimination'. *BMC Public Health*, 16(1): 1205.

Etowa, J. and Adongo, L. (2007) 'Cultural competence: Beyond culturally sensitive care for childbearing Black women'. *Journal of the Association for Research on Mothering*, 9(2): 73–85.

Etowa, J., Keddy, B., Egbeyemi, J., and Eghan, F. (2007) 'Depression: The "invisible grey fog" influencing the midlife health of African Canadian women'. *International Journal of Mental Health Nursing*, 16(3): 203–213.

Finch, B.K., Kolody, B., and Vega, W.A. (2000) 'Perceived discrimination and depression among Mexican origin adults in California'. *Journal of Health and Social Behavior*, 41: 295–313.

Gary, F.A. (2005) 'Stigma: Barriers to mental health care among ethnic minorities'. *Issues in Mental Health Nursing*, 26(10): 979–999. DOI: 10.1080/01612840500280638.

Ginieniewicz, J. and McKenzie, K. (2014) 'Mental health of Latin Americans in Canada: A literature review'. *International Journal of Social Psychiatry*, 60(3): 263–273. doi: 10.1177/0020764013486750.

Gorman D. and Cross W. (2011) 'Cultural issues in mental health'. In K-l. Edward, I. Munro, A. Robins, and A. Welch (Eds.), *Mental health nursing: Dimensions of praxis*, (pp. 427–442). South Melbourne: Oxford University Press.

Guruge, S. and Butt, H. (2015) 'A scoping review of mental health issues and concerns among immigrant and refugee youth in Canada: Looking back, moving forward'. *Canadian Journal of Public Health*, 106(2): e72-e78. doi: 10.17269/cjph.106.4588.

Hansson, E. K., Tuck, A., Lurie, S., and McKenzie, K. (2012) 'Rates of mental illness and suicidality in immigrant, refugee, ethnocultural, and racialized groups in Canada: a review of the literature'. *The Canadian Journal of Psychiatry*, 57(2): 111–121.

Hansson, E., Tuck, A., Lurie, S., and McKenzie, K., for the Task Group of the Services Systems Advisory Committee, Mental Health Commission of Canada (2009) *Improving mental health services for immigrant, refugee, ethno-cultural and racialized groups: Issues and options for service improvement*. Retrieved from www.mentalhealthcommission.ca/sites/default/les/Diversity_Issues_Options_Report_ENG_0_1.pdf.

Hudson, CC, Adams, S., and Lauderdale, J. (2016) 'Cultural expressions of intergenerational trauma and mental health nursing implications for US health care delivery following refugee resettlement: An integrative review of the literature'. *Journal of Transcultural Nursing*, 27(3): 286–301. doi: 10.1177/1043659615587591.

Jimenez, D.E., Cook, B., Bartels, S.J., and Alegria, M. (2013) 'Disparities in Mental Health Services use among racial/ethnic minority elderly'. *Journal of American Geriatric Society*, 61(1): 18–25. doi:10.1111/jgs.12063.

Kafele, K. (2004) *Racial discrimination in mental health: Racialized and Aboriginal communities*. Report for Ontario Human Rights Commission.

Kleinman, A. (1988) *Rethinking psychiatry: From cultural category to personal experience*. New York Free Press.

Kirmayer, L. J. (2012) 'Rethinking cultural competence'. *Transcultural Psychiatry*, *49*(2): 149–164. DOI: 10.1177/1363461512444673.

Lai, D. W. L. and Surood, S. (2013) 'Effect of service barriers on health status of aging South Asian immigrants in Calgary, Canada'. *Health and Social Work*, *38*(1): 41–50.

Leininger, M. and McFarland, M.R. (2002) *Transcultural nursing: Concepts, theories, research & practice* (3rd Ed.). New York: McGraw-Hill Medical Publishing Division.

Lo, H. and Pottinger, A. (2007) 'Mental health practice'. In R. Strivastava (Ed.), *The healthcare professional's guide to clinical cultural competence* (pp. 247–263). Toronto: Elsevier Canada.

McGibbon, E. and Etowa, J. (2009) *Anti-racist health care practice*. Toronto: Canadian Scholars Press.

McKenzie, K., Hansson, E., Tuck, A., and Lurie, S. (2010) 'Improving mental health services for immigrant, refugee, ethno-cultural, and racialized Groups'. *Canadian Issues*, 65–69.

Mental Health Commission of Canada (2016) *The Case for Diversity: Building the Case to Improve Mental Health Services for Immigrants, Refugees, Ethno-cultural and Racialized Populations*. Ottawa: Mental Health Commission of Canada.

Meyer, O.L. and Zane, N. (2013) 'The influence of race and ethnicity on clients' experiences of mental health treatment'. *Journal of Community Psychology*, *41*(7): 884–901.

Meyer, O.L., Zane, N., and Cho, Y.I. (2011) 'Understanding the psychological processes of the racial match effect in Asian Americans'. *Journal of Counseling Psychology*, *58*: 335–345.

Noh, S., Beiser, M., Kaspar, V., Hou, F., and Rummens, J. (1999) 'Perceived racial discrimination, depression and coping: A study of Southeast Asian refugees in Canada'. *Journal of Health and Social Behavior*, *40*(3): 193–207.

Papadopoulos, I. (2006) 'The Papadopoulos, Tilki and Taylor model of developing cultural competence'. In I. Papadopoulos (Ed.), *Transcultural health and social care: Development of culturally competent practitioners*, pp.7–24. London: Elsevier.

Papadopoulos, I, Tilki, M., and Taylor, G. (1998) *Transcultural care: A guide for health care professionals*. Wilts: Quay Books.

Pottinger, A., Perivolaris, A., and Howes, D. (2007) 'The end of life'. In R. Strivastava (Ed.), *The healthcare professional's guide to clinical cultural competence* (pp. 227–246). Toronto: Elsevier Canada.

Purnell, L. (2002) 'The Purnell model for cultural competence'. *Journal of Transcultural Nursing*, *13*(3): 193–196.

Registered Psychiatric Nurse Regulators of Canada (2014) *Registered Psychiatric Nurse Entry-Level Competencies*. Edmonton, AB: Author. Retrieved from www.rpnc.ca/sites/default/files/resources/pdfs/RPNRC-ENGLISH%20Compdoc%20%28Nov6-14%29.pdf.

Reitmanova, S. and Gustafson, D. L. (2009) 'Primary mental health care information and services for St. John's visible minority immigrants: Gaps and opportunities'. *Issues in Mental Health Nursing*, *30*(10): 615–623. doi: 10.1080/01612840903033733.

Ren, X. S., Amick, B. C., and Williams, D. R. (1999) 'Racial/ethnic disparities in health: the interplay between discrimination and socioeconomic status'. *Ethnicity and Disease*, *9*(2): 151–165.

Rossiter, K.R. and Morrow, M. (2011) 'Intersectional frameworks in mental health: Moving from theory to practice'. In O. Hankivsky (Ed.), *Health inequities in Canada: Intersectional frameworks and practices* (pp. 312–330). Vancouver: University of British Columbia Press.

Sareen, J., Jagdeo, A., Cox, B.J., Clara, I., Have, M., Belick, S.L., de Graaf, R., and Stein, M.B. (2007) 'Perceived barriers to mental health service utilization in the United States, Ontario, and The Netherlands'. *Psychiatric Services*, *58*(3): 357–364.

Statistics Canada (2013) Immigration and ethnocultural diversity in Canada. Ottawa (ON): Author. www12.statcan.gc.ca/nhs- enm/2011/as-sa/*99-010-x/99-010-x2011001-eng*.cfm.

Taylor, C. M. (2008) 'Introduction to psychiatric-mental health nursing'. In O'Brien, P.G., Kennedy, W.Z., and Ballard, K.A., *Psychiatric mental health nursing: An introduction to theory and practice* (1st ed., pp. 3–20). Sudbury, MA: Jones and Bartlett Publishers.

The Standing Senate Committee on Social Affairs, Science, and Technology (2004) Kirby, J. L. and Keon, W.J., *Interim Report, Mental health, Mental Illness and Addiction: Overview of policies and Programs in Canada*. Ottawa: The Senate of Canada.

Culture and Nursing in Mental Health

Thomson, M. S., Chaze, F., George, U., and Guruge, S. (2015) 'Improving immigrant populations' access to mental health services in Canada: A review of barriers and recommendations'. *Journal of Immigrant and Minority Health*, 17(6): 1895–1905. doi: 10.1007/s10903-015-0175-3.

U.S. Department of Health and Human Services (2001) *Mental Health: Culture, Race, and Ethnicity – A Supplement to Mental Health: A Report of the Surgeon General.* Rockville, MD: U.S. Department of Health and Human Services, Substance Abuse and Mental Health Services Administration, Center for Mental Health Services. Retrieved from www.ncbi.nlm.nih.gov/books/NBK44243/pdf/Bookshelf_NBK44243.pdf.

Wasserbauer, L. I. and Brodie, B. (1992) 'Early precursors of psychiatric nursing, 1838–1907'. *Nursing Connections*, 5: 19–25.

World Health Organization (2001) *Mental Health: New Understanding, New Hope.* Geneva: Author.

World Health Organization and Calouste Gulbenkian Foundation (2014) *Social Determinants of Mental Health.* Geneva: Author.

11
CULTURE AND SOCIAL WORK IN MENTAL HEALTH

Eunjung Lee and Marjorie Johnstone

Social work engages in multiple levels of the system from individuals to families to institutions and to sociocultural structures. The International Federation of Social Workers (IFSW 2018) defines social work as "a practice-based profession and an academic discipline that promotes social change and development, social cohesion, and the empowerment and liberation of people" and highlights principles of "social justice, human rights, collective responsibility and respect for diversities" as the core of social work. Social work approaches to mental health are contextualized within this view. The Council on Social Work Education (CSWE 2019) highlights the critical roles social workers play for mental health recovery, by noting how social workers' training in direct practice, systems change and policy practice enables simultaneous interventions at the micro, mezzo and macro levels which enriches the recovery of individuals with lived experience of psychiatric struggles. It further notes that "[T]his focus on activism; social justice; and civil and human rights at the organizational, local, state, tribal, territorial, federal, and global level distinguishes social work from other behavioral health disciplines" (CSWE 2019:3). Decentering mental suffering from individual illness and shortcomings, social workers focus on (1) mental health and the well-being of people by promoting social changes and social cohesion despite the presence of mental illness; and (2) addressing the sociocultural aspects that precipitate and maintain their mental health struggles impeding their well-being.

Scholars in the social determinants of health (SDH) research (Craig, Bejan and Muskat 2013) illustrate the detrimental impacts of unmet social needs on clients' health treatment outcomes. It is inevitable that addressing social needs (e.g., food and job security, safe housing, proper education, etc.) while connecting 'the individual' to 'the social' (i.e., mediating discrimination and oppression embedded in the system) is an essential component of mental health care. This is a site where social workers contribute to the mental health field. Social workers in the mental health field move beyond the dichotomy between macro-politics and micro-practice and acknowledge that 'the personal is political' in social work practice (Mullaly 2007; Roets et al. 2012).

From the emergence of profession in the early 20th century to the present, social workers have served marginalized population, such as immigrants and refugees, socioeconomically deprived populations, and/or people with health and mental health struggles and disabilities, often marginalized racially, ethnically and culturally (Jennissen and Lundy 2011). The noble idea of placing a person-in-their-social environment (PIE) embedded in the social work profession, however, has been an ongoing negotiation in the everyday practice of social workers. When social justice values are entrenched under the name of law and policies in the system, social workers have been caught between upholding professional values and being an arm of state control (Jennissen and Lundy 2011). For example, deinstitutionalization of mental health care in the 1960s in many Western countries increased the roles of social workers in community mental health practice. This systemic change in mental health care positioned social workers to be constantly negotiating with the state agenda – namely social control of the mentally ill.

Critical social work scholars note that this shift in mental health care should be understood from the underlying ideology of the *neoliberal attack on mental health care*. This has left one of our most vulnerable populations – the severely mentally ill (SMI) – located even further in the margins of society thus compromising their psychic and social well-being (Finkel 2013). Among the mentally ill population, those who are most lacking social resources are often members of the population who are racially and economically marginalized or dislocated, such as those immigrating from the Global South to the Global North, and indigenous populations who move from their own communities to cities due to the destruction of their own land (Neckoway and Brownlee 2015).

This observation thus echoes the argument that neoliberalism and colonialism are two edges of the same sword that supports Western dominance including Western psychiatry. The dominance of one form of understanding well-being that claims to be universal is a form of colonization or 'cognitive injustice' while denying the legitimacy of other forms of ethno-psychiatry and cultural values and norms (Santos 2014). While Western psychiatry has diverse forms, biopsychiatry dominates the psy disciplines (Mills 2017). Psychiatry was used as a postcolonial tool to subjugate and control indigenous populations as Fanon (1963: 245) documents "the lay-out of the cerebral structures of the North African" were seen as explanations of their laziness, ineptitude, slowness and impulsivity, in other words such observed behavior was deemed to be "biologically organized." In the context of colonization, resistance was pathologized and oppressive social conditions were overlooked while the focus was on the psychopathology of the individual (Mills 2017). Biomedicalism and neoliberal capitalism both support individualistic explanations and understandings of social problems. Neoliberalism promotes individualistic understandings of distress or responsibilization (Braedley and Luxton 2010) as well as the increased use of market techniques in mental health care service delivery (Dustin 2007) and fiscal stringency with reduced services and calls for sustainability and self reliance (Morrow and Malcoe 2017). What is disturbing is that these ideological stances that continue to construct, perpetuate and reify social injustice for racialized people with mental struggles are often out of sight, at times even being legitimized within the systems and described as desirable practice to promote the welfare and well-being of people in distress. This rhetoric pre-empts efforts to closely investigate, critique and change the vicious cycle of marginalization and injustice being done to the racialized mentally ill and erases their cultural norms and beliefs around well-being and suffering.

This chapter has two objectives. The one is to unveil this cycle of marginalization by critically reviewing how the implicit state agenda of social control of the mentally ill population is obscured in the rhetoric of human rights and self-care and even presented as 'best' practice and 'self-determination' in the global neoliberal welfare states. The other is to illustrate how this neoliberal agenda affects social workers' ongoing negotiation in working with clients with SMI and in what ways this practice can be, though unintended, oppressing culturally marginalized clients. Using critical theories of neoliberalism (Bradley and Luxton 2010; Morrow and Malcoe 2017), social workers' everyday practice with culturally diverse clients will be illustrated with community case examples in outpatient mental health settings. The chapter will close with a discussion around how to achieve socially just ways to promote well-being for culturally marginalized people with mental health struggles.

Social work and marginalized populations in community mental health

Alarmed by multiple aspects of industrial capitalism such as increased gaps in class and poverty, the settlement house program started in England and the United States in the late 1890s to provide social assistance to the poor. Similarly, the first settlement program in Canada was set up in Toronto in 1902 which corresponded with an increase in immigration and the rapid growth of large cities as Canada moved from a largely agricultural economy to an industrialized urban economy. Associated city problems such as homelessness, slums, prostitution and unemployment became a focus for faith-based organizations and the emerging profession of social work (Jennissen and Lundy 2011). The mother of American social workers Mary Richmond (1917:25) wrote a seminal book, *Social Diagnosis*, to highlight the significance of assessing the social contexts of a person, instead of diagnosing an individual illness alone: "Mass betterment and individual betterment are interdependent, however, social reform and social casework of necessity progress together." The social work profession has always distinguished itself by considering the wider social and political context in concert with the personal troubles of an individual.

Along with the civil right movement in the 1960s, the deinstitutionalization movement shifted the care of the mentally ill from an institution-based approach to a community-based approach where many social service workers and social workers were called into the center of mental health services in Britain, Canada, the United States, and other Western countries (Morrow and Malcoe 2017). The approach called 'care management' in Britain and 'case management' in Canada and the United States became prevalent to address the social needs of the mentally ill who were deinstitutionalized (Dustin 2007). This approach has still been the most prevalent community mental health approach, and it has expanded its contents into various programs such as the Assertive Community Treatment (ACT) approach and clinical case management (Morrow and Malcoe 2017). Despite the contribution that case management has made to the everyday social needs of the mentally ill in community living, this approach has been criticized in creating a dichotomy between psychiatric service and 'other' services, while positioning a biomedical model of mental illness as superior and a social approach by social workers as secondary mainly working to support psychiatric treatment (Morley 2003). The biomedical construction of mental struggles continues to constitute the authoritarian dominant meta-narrative and to position responsibilities for mental struggles as individual deficits and shortcomings (Karapanagiotidis and Kilkeary 1997), while depoliticizing the social determinants of mental struggles and denying the impact of structural factors. In fact, critical scholars note that the whole ideal of 'managing a case' means giving up 'providing care' to people who need services and this change was a direct reflection of the neoliberal welfare state where public services are framed into a business model called New Public Management (NPM) and a pervasive practice of 'case management' in mental health services is such an example of NPM (Dustin 2007). Bainbridge (1999: 187) thus attests that "psychiatry serves the interests of patriarchal capitalism." Although there has been ample critical discussion around the biomedical approach and its underlying eugenics and colonial agenda (Mills 2017), there has been comparatively limited discussion around capitalism and neoliberalism and their impacts on mental health services (Morrow and Malcoe 2017). Thus, this chapter attempts to conduct a 'social diagnosis' of current community mental health services especially around the neoliberal agenda, while illustrating how social workers reify or resist dominant discourses in mental health services in serving culturally diverse others.

A workfare-as-welfare regime in the neoliberal state

Neoliberalism promotes the autonomy of individuals from the state and asks individuals to assume the roles and risks of the state, such as unemployment, poverty and homelessness (Braedley and Luxton 2010). This discourse is internalized by neoliberal subjects as the freedom to choose how to compete for economic effectiveness and as an individual right. Citizens' human rights are reframed as consumer rights and citizens' responsibilities are reframed as contributions/obligations to work for the economic prosperity and its measurable outcomes. Even the state responsibilities for the well-being and welfare of citizens are reframed as contributing to the nation's economic prosperity, which Roets and colleagues (2012) call the workfare-as-welfare regime. Critical social work scholars have observed this transformation of Western welfare states into liberal workfare regimes over the preceding decades (Dustin 2007; McDonald and Marston 2005). In these neoliberal policy contexts, the states "attempt to increase efforts to employ economically inactive individuals, such as people with chronic 'mental health problems', through a wide range of activation strategies" (Roets et al. 2012: 94) and "the investment in the welfare of citizens is translated into moving inactive individuals into employment as a social obligation" (95).

Roets and colleagues explore a recent research project in Belgium, where social workers are positioned to manage labor market training programs and guide us to re-think the pervasive international debate about the un/employability of people with SMI in the regular labor market. They argue that the discourse around people with mental health struggles as dangerous, deviant and unproductive has been pervasively circulated as "frames of reference in social policy and social practices in public employment services" (Roets et al. 2012: 97). In workfare-as-welfare regimes, dichotomous discourses are embedded (McLaughlin 2003): constructing individuals in paid employment as economically valued and deserving rights, whereas individuals who are inactive economically as less valued with few safeguarded rights. This assumed inability to work then reifies "a priori perceived and socially constructed un-employability" of people with chronic mental health struggles in the public services and Roets and colleagues (2012: 97) call this dynamic as "losing the game before it starts." Here, social workers and other mental health professionals can get caught up in this dominant discourse where "the objective of the employment trajectory is a pre-described outcome" (Roets et al. 2012: 106). Instead of pointing fingers to individual clients and/or social workers, it would be critical to analyze the current dominant sociopolitical order (i.e., neoliberal governing principles) that impacts everyday interactions between clients and social workers, and their ongoing negotiation in the neoliberal subject making process where clients with SMI are positioned as less desirable and less worthy neoliberal subjects. This dynamic of positioning individuals with SMI as the lesser is further complicated when a client comes from racially and culturally marginalized populations.

To illustrate, we draw case examples from our community mental health research data (see Lee et al. 2019, 2018 for details). Client A is a second-generation Vietnamese female in her 40s with a diagnosis of psychosis in remission for years. The therapist has a Master's degree in social work, in his 40s, self-identified as White British/Canadian, and has more than 15 years of postgraduate experience in community mental health. In the first session, the client and the social worker converse about independent living options in the community and her potential career plans. The client clearly expresses her interest in becoming a paralegal and discusses an educational program with this goal in mind. However, this stated educational interest was not an entry for exploration in sessions. Rather, the social worker advises and explains repeatedly (i.e., uses forms of soft coercion) that the work adjustment program staff would help the client to determine which educational program, which work and career path would be most appropriate for her rather than exploring how to pursue the career path that the client set out. In this session and across all of the 32 weekly sessions in the original data set, there is little information about this client's work experience prior to her psychotic breakdown, or any exploration of what led her to choose this line of career interest.

One might wonder, then, why the social worker chose to question and invalidate the client's choice of this career path and its educational program. One may speculate that the social worker might hold some bias around the occupational and educational capacities of people with a severe mental health diagnosis. Although the client's psychotic symptoms have been in remission and managed with medications for years, and her talk appears coherent across the transcripts, the social worker in the study seems to doubt her capacities of even thinking about her own career path, and further subscribes to the idea that the professionals should decide what education programs were best for her and when she could attend.

In addition to the social control of people with SMI, we also wonder how the social worker's bias of the client's gender and ethnic identities may influence this professional intervention to the point of discouraging the client from pursuing her dreams. Harley and colleagues (2002: 225) also articulate how vocational and psychological counsellors "either did not counsel people of Color to enter the professions of their choice, excluded consumers of Color altogether, or matched these consumers to the types of employment that they were likely to be able to get." Given the client's gender, race and ethnicity in this case, we wonder if the therapist would question and invalidate her choice of education program if she contemplated and expressed her desire to be a cleaning person, nanny, or personal aid worker – vocations that many female Asian immigrants serve in urban Canadian cities. Transnational feminist scholars critically analyze how the mobility of female migrants from the Global South to the Global North have (re)produced a global chain of social provisioning services, which has perpetuated a gender inequality and has further positioned female migrants in the margins of class, race, ethnicity, and culture in a neoliberal global economy (Lee and Johnstone 2013). This pervasive theme of systemic xeno-racism and racialized occupational choices in the neoliberal global economy could have influenced therapists' minds, unconsciously positioning female Asian migrants as less intelligent, less professional, and more prone to domestic work (i.e., the less valued neoliberal subject), rather than the professional office work as a paralegal which the client wanted to try.

Social control of the racialized mentally ill under the neoliberal state

Individuals with severe mental health struggles have been "one of the few remaining groups that may be legally denied basic human rights" (Perry et al. 2018: 109) and have been subject to state and professional control. Perry and colleagues (2018) noted that historically people with SMI and others with disabilities have been subjected to explicit forms of legal and medical control. They examined the relevance of 'soft coercion' in contemporary mental health treatment settings with respect to clients' sexual behavior and contraception use, and found that most clients' experiences reflect "elements of ambiguous or limited autonomy" using four types of soft coercion - coercion, enabling, education, and conciliation, "wherein compliance is achieved by invoking therapeutic goals" (Perry et al. 2018: 108). This finding is similar to Lee and colleagues' studies (2018, 2019), where social workers invoke consensus and collaboration by using ongoing explanation/education to influence and persuade clients to continue on income assistance or stay within assigned community living under the name of treatment goals and the 'best' services under current welfare policy regulations. They argue, although rehabilitation and recovery are noted as the central goals for community mental health services, these goals are often centered around economic self-sufficiency and independent living, which ironically work to keep people with SMI in the economic margins and subject to ongoing professional control and management.

In these studies, "desired behavioral outcomes are often obtained by framing conformity as adherence to cooperatively developed treatment plans" (Horwitz 1982: 108). What is tricky here is that the various forms of soft coercion occur under the name of 'therapeutic' goals and 'best' practice for clients, thus looping back to ongoing social control through conformity to the dominant values and norms. Critical scholars thus warn that the social control of individuals with SMI in contemporary mental health practice is often disguised by discourses of self-determination, where compliance is framed as evidence of self-care and progress toward recovery rather than obedience and subjugation, thus often blinding many people into keeping the status quo of the marginalization process (Perry et al. 2018).

In his early book, *The Social Control of Mental Illness*, Horwitz (1982) described two distinct types of therapeutic social control: the one is coercion where a decision (e.g., medication regimen, etc.) is forcefully imposed on clients by others (e.g., families, professionals, states, etc.); and the other is conciliatory 'soft' control, which appears to permit clients with mental health struggles to have ambiguous but limited decision power. Horwitz notes that there has been an ongoing criticism for the former with respect to its embedded eugenic thinking and a violation of human rights. If the latter is still present in the current mental health services, it is an area of debate. Over three decades later, we contend that, although it is not explicitly forceful, many decisions are still imposed onto clients with SMI by others, and this social control and systemic marginalization has been even framed as the 'best practice' (e.g., New Public Management) in community mental health. We also argue that the line between the first and second types of therapeutic social control is very tenuous, and both are in the continuum, and in both types the governing values and ideologies (i.e., neoliberalism) are reified in everyday service encounters. Although individuals with SMI have been historically subject to professional and state control, what we are concerned with is that the contemporary soft coercions are further legitimized and marked as the *norm* in mental health practice under the global neoliberal economy. At the same time, while marking neoliberal values in the forefront of mental health practice, honoring and exploring cultural understanding of illness and well-being are pre-empted from community mental health practice and becomes even non-existent in therapists' minds.

As another case example, Client B is a single, second-generation Japanese Canadian in his forties, living in the basement of his parents' home in an urban city of Canada. He was diagnosed with schizophrenia in his 20s, the positive symptoms having been in remission for years and had a history of suicidal attempts years ago. Also, there was the history of his parents being interned by Canada after the Second World War. The therapist has a Master's degree in social work (MSW), self-identifies as white, in his forties, with over ten years of post-graduate clinical experience in community mental health settings. Services related to income security and stability are important parts of case management in community mental health. In the past, the client saved this welfare fund he received, thus jeopardizing his eligibility due to his accumulated assets. Previously he had a record of not completing the disability form and had not had any income assistance for a while. To avoid similar disservice situations and to discuss how to secure the client's disability check so that he can be self-sufficient, the social worker invited the client and his parents into the second session. Most of the session the social workers and the parents brainstormed various ways to have his disability check secured – e.g. the parents to monitor his spending and his savings and so on. Although the client repeatedly asserted that he didn't need the disability pension and preferred saving to spending, and expressed his hope that he would get a new job while now saving for 'rainy days', all his assertions were not even acknowledged by the social workers and the parents. At the end of the session, there has been little exploration of how the client constructs the meaning of receiving a disability pension.

Here, the neoliberal value of self-sufficiency is already "a pre-described outcome" (Roets et al. 2012:106) of the mental health service provision. Even before the session, the client is positioned as a less desirable neoliberal subject who is not active in the economic market. A forefront of the focus in the session was the pre-described neoliberal task of securing financial independence as the marker of being healthy, while the client's needs/aspects of the services and the other tasks of the social worker (e.g., listening to the client in making meaning of the client's experiences) have already disappeared. The client's voice/meaning making process (e.g., why he wants to save the money?) is excluded by the therapist from early in the session. Perry and colleagues (2018:117) warn that "it is worth noting that many of the arguments leveled by treatment providers and family members about clients' inability to effectively parent or be financially independent are direct reflections of pervasive stigmatizing attitudes toward people with SMI." Meanwhile, the client is positioned as a lesser productive individual in the neoliberal state, thus producing and consolidating the pre-determined division between who is up to the expectation of the neoliberal agenda and who is not (Dustin 2007).

Out of 19 audio-taped sessions in this case, there have been recurring pervasive conversations related to case management topics (e.g., education training for job search and preparation, how to manage finances, daily activities and time management to be effective an efficient for future work, etc.). Meanwhile, it was noteworthy to see that there was little exploration of his own meaning making of receiving the welfare check and more importantly little attention to any cultural values and experiences. For example, there was no conversation around the critical family history of Japanese Internment and its impact on the family. For example, do his suicidal ideations and ongoing self-surveillance around managing money and his episodes of paranoia around being a good responsible person have anything to do with his parents being interned, and the deep scar of intergenerational trauma? Any of these consideration around culturally relevant topics were not even introduced into the therapeutic conversation and the focus is consistently on the case management goals/tasks.

Discussion

Critical scholars note that common values (e.g., self-sufficiency) and service approaches (e.g., psychoeducation) that are pervasively used for clients with SMI appear to be ostensibly noncoercive and value-neutral, at times even appear to be empowering the client and to be framed as consumer rights, but nonetheless they reify dominant values and norms in society (Horwitz 1982; Perry et al. 2018). This critical scholarship in the current mental health field articulates how dominant and pervasive soft power tactics are in working with individuals with SMI. However, there has been little focus on meta-discourses such as neoliberal governance in mental health.

While prioritizing the role of the neoliberal agenda in the designation of therapy tasks and the resulting selected interventions, what is dismissed and pre-empted in therapy is, as illustrated in both cases, the clients' own voice and culturally embedded experiences. In their cross-cultural process research project, Lee and colleagues (Lee et al. 2018, 2019) thus illustrate that, although racialized clients critically reflect on their own immigrant and racist experiences and the impacts of these on their mental health struggles and even initiate culturally relevant dialogues in therapy, these dialogues soon become monologues because therapists dismiss them by changing the topic into individual pathology-focused conversations as if cultural issues are of little relevance to clinical issues, and as a result, the clients' culturally embedded experiences become placed in the periphery or don't even enter into the therapy conversation, whereas more task-oriented and seemingly apolitical and acultural topics are centered in the conversation. What we contend here is that this is not a mishap of individual therapists only, but rather a structure of dominant neoliberal governing principles around 'effective', 'evidence-based', and 'outcome-driven' treatment approaches that pre-empts professional values that honor clients' culturally centered voices and social justice issues.

Petersen and colleagues (2015: 10) note that "[T]he primary goal of recovery-oriented rehabilitation is not only to facilitate individual change and create a culture of healing within services, but also to bring about opportunities to live in an inclusive society." In the current neoliberal workfare-welfare regime, the dichotomy present between less and more desirable neoliberal subjects based on one's economic contributions positions the people with SMI in a losing place even before they start, which limits their recovery and mental health. Although they participate in the neoliberal project which aims to make them active in economic markets, the clients' desires, wishes and hopes are often dismissed using soft controls by professionals, and societal biases and systemic discriminations around race, gender and (dis)abilities are often reified in therapy encounters.

Lavie-Ajayi and Nakash (2017: 74, italics added) underline that:

> Gender, ethnicity, class, and other social identity dimensions often translate to asymmetric power relations in society that seep into the therapeutic encounter. … Still, what was missing is an understanding of social marginalization as *an everyday process* embedded in unequal power relations in society (Prilleltensky et al. 2008), as well as awareness to the *unquestioned psychological, social, and cultural discourses*, and the structural features of *bureaucratic hierarchies*.

We agree with Lavie-Ajayi and Nakash (2017: 62) in that "psychotherapy can no longer be viewed as politically neutral, in the sense of 'political' as related to distribution of societal power and resources." Rather, psychotherapy is "a field of political action, a place where power is exercised and contested, as therapists try to affect clients' lives and clients acquiesce, resist or do both at the same time" (Totton 2006: XV). As illustrated in our case examples, the unequal power relations during the clinical encounter become even more pronounced when the client is from a culturally and racially disadvantaged social group.

Future directions

We wondered then in what ways we could utilize this mental health practice space to negotiate with governing dominant social orders and make changes for individual and systemic liberation to highlight social justice, inclusion and empowerment in working with culturally diverse clients. Foucault (1979) offers a transformative model of power and the subject describing a capillary osmotic process where social power (dominant discourses) construct the subject but the subject also has the agency to construct alternative discourses. Therefore, during the therapeutic encounters with racialized clients with mental health struggles, both the client and therapist, who have themselves been socialized into the biomedical model and neoliberal governance of mental health field, can intentionally interact by rejecting pathologizing labels given the underlying neoliberal and postcolonial values. In other words, the therapists can collaboratively work with clients to have them construct their own meaning and interpretation of their culturally embedded experiences. Then, "this practice also directly challenges the dominant ideological view of mental health and thus demonstrates how personal liberation is inherently connected with social change" (Morley 2003: 65).

We echo Lavie-Ajayi and Nakash's assertion (2017: 74, italics in original) in that "Clinical empathy is not enough. What is needed is *political empathy.*" Teghtsoonian (2017: 249) also suggests that it is empowering to understand neoliberalism as temporal governing programs, which are "tenuous and incomplete, rather than permanent and secure." This conceptualization allows us space to question and critique the pervasive dominance of neoliberal attack on community mental health practice, and to push for change, to document inadequacies and omissions and to demand improvement. Our everyday practice can become a site for epistemic resistance and a source of empowerment for personal validation and social advocacy.

Conclusion

The National Institute of Mental Health (NIMH) and Health Resources and Services Administration (HRSA) identify social work as one of the five core professions of the mental health workforce in the United States (CBHSQ 2015). A survey conducted by the National Association of Social Workers in the United States found that 96% of social workers work with clients with mental illness, 87% work with clients with substance use disorders, and 93% work with clients with co-occurring substance use and mental health disorders (Whitaker et al. 2006). Social workers are thus well positioned to assess and intervene in mental health related issues and they are often the first professionals to assess and treat individuals seeking treatment (Kourgiantakis et al. 2019). However, critical social work scholars note that that "the majority of social work practice conducted in mental health settings reflects an uncritical embrace of the medical model of psychiatric illness, and therefore largely neglects social work approaches which utilize critical principles" (Morley 2003: 61) such as, social justice, inclusion and empowerment.

Reflecting on this criticism, we attempted in this chapter to envision the community mental health field where social workers practice, as a mirror of the social order and a site of socio-political conflicts and resistance. Our case examples illustrated how the neoliberal rhetoric that reframes therapy tasks and interventions in seemingly apolitical realms, in fact pre-empts discussion of the impact of sociopolitical factors on mental suffering. Therefore, this chapter and our ongoing cross-cultural research in social work contribute to these epistemic gaps by (1) fostering the understanding of social marginalization as an everyday therapy encounter reifying social inequity; and (2) by promoting critical reflexivity on the unquestioned and often normatively positioned psycho-socio-political-cultural discourses of biopsychiatry, and the structural features of bureaucratic hierarchies and neoliberal ideology.

References

Bainbridge, L. (1999). 'Competing paradigms in mental health practice and education'. In B. Pease and J. Fook (Eds.), *Transforming Social Work Practice: Postmodern Critical Perspectives* (pp. 179–194). St Leonards: Allen & Unwin.

Braedley, S. and Luxton, M. (Eds.) (2010) *Neoliberalism and Everyday Life*. Montreal and Kingston, McGill-Queens University Press.

Center for Behavioral Health Statistics and Quality (CBHSQ, 2015) *Behavioral health trends in the United States: Results from the 2014 National Survey on Drug Use and Health* (HHS Publication No. SMA 15–4927, NSDUH Series H-50). Retrieved from www.samhsa.gov/data.

Council on Social Work Education (2019). Advanced social work practice competencies in mental health recovery. Retrieved from www.cswe.org/getattachment/Centers-Initiatives/Institutional-Research/Recovery-to-Practice-Initiative/AdvancedSocialWorkPracticeCompetenciesinMentalHealthRecovery.pdf.aspx.

Craig, S. L., Bejan, R. and Muskat, B. (2013) 'Making the invisible visible: Are Canadian medical social workers addressing the social determinants of health?' *Social Work in Health Care*, 52(4): 311–331.

Dustin, D. (2007) *The McDonaldization of Social Work*. New York: Routledge.

Fanon, F. (1963). *The Wretched of the Earth* (C. Farrington, Trans.). London: Penguin Books.

Finkel, L. (2013) '"They should not be allowed to do this to the homeless and mentally ill": minimum separation bylaws reconsidered'. In LeFrancois, B., Menzies, R. and Reaume, G. (Eds.), *Mad Matters. A Critical Reader in Canadian Mad Studies* (pp. 221–239). Toronto: Canadian Scholars Press.

Foucault, M. (1979) *Discipline and Punish*. New York: Vintage Books.

Harley, D., Jolivette, K., McCormick, K. and Tice, K. (2002) 'Race, culture and gender: A constellation of positionalities with implications for counselling', *Journal of Multicultural Counselling and Development*, 30(4): 216–238.

Horwitz, A. V. (1982) *The Social Control of Mental Illness*. New York: Academic.

International Federation of Social Workers (2018). *The global definition of social work*. Retrieved on July 17, 2018, from www.ifsw.org/what-is-social-work/global-definition-of-social-work/.

Jennissen, T. and Lundy, L. (2011) *One Hundred Years of Social Work: A History of the Profession in English Canada 1900–2000*. Waterloo: Wilfrid Laurier University Press.

Karapanagiotidis, K. and Kilkeary, S. (1997). A Human Rights Model for Mental Health. In *Social Work Influencing Outcomes: 25th Australian Association of Social Workers National Conference Proceedings*, 21–24, September. Australian National University ACT, Canberra, Australia, 387–393.

Kourgiantakis, T., Sewell, K., Lee, E., Adamson, K., McCormick, M., Kuehl, D. and Bogo, M. (2019) 'Enhancing social work education in mental health, addictions, and suicide risk assessment: Teaching note', *Journal of Social Work Education*, Online First. https://doi.org/10.1080/10437797.2019.1656590.

Lavie-Ajayi, M. and Nakash, O. (2017) '"If she had helped me to solve the problem at my workplace, she would have cured me": A critical discourse analysis of a mental health intake', *Qualitative Social Work*, 16(1): 60–77.

Lee, E. and Johnstone, M. (2013) 'Global inequities: A gender-based analysis of the Live-in Caregiver Program and the Kirogi phenomenon in Canada', *Affilia: Journal of Women and Social Work*, 28(4): 401–414.

Lee, E., Tsang, A. K. T., Bogo, M., Johnstone, M. and Herschman, J. (2019) 'Clients and case managers as neoliberal subjects? Shaping session tasks and everyday interactions with severely mentally ill (SMI) clients', *European Journal of Social Work*, 22(2): 238–251.

Lee, E., Tsang, A. K. T., Bogo, M., Johnstone, M. and Herschman, J. (2018) 'Enactment of racial microaggression in everyday therapeutic encounters', *Smith College Studies in Social Work*, 88(3): 211–236.

McDonald, C. and Marston, G. (2005) 'Workfare as welfare: Governing unemployment in the advanced liberal state', *Critical Social Policy*, 25(3): 374–401.

McLaughlin, J. (2003) *Feminist Social and Practical Theory: Contemporary Debates and Dialogues*. New York: Palgrave Macmillan.

Mills, C. (2017) Global psychiatrization and psychic colonization: the coloniality of global mental health. In M. Morrow and L. Malcoe (Eds.), *Critical Inquiries for Social Justice in Mental Health* (pp. 87–113). Toronto: University of Toronto Press.

Morley, C. (2003) 'Towards critical social work practice in mental health', *Journal of Progressive Human Services*, 14(1): 61–84.

Mullaly, B. (2007). *The New Structural Social Work* (3rd ed.). Don Mills, ON: Oxford University Press.

Morrow, M. and Malcoe, L. (Eds.) (2017) *Critical Inquiries for Social Justice in Mental Health*. Toronto: University of Toronto Press.

Neckoway, R. and Brownlee, K. (Eds.) (2015) *Child Welfare in Rural Remote Areas with Canada's First-Nations Peoples: Selected Readings*. Winnipeg: Hignell Book Printing.

Perry, B. L., Frieh, E. and Wright, E. R. (2018) 'Therapeutic social control of people with serious mental illness: An empirical verification and extension of theory', *Society and Mental Health*, 8(2): 108–122.

Petersen, K. S., Friis, V. S., Haxholm, B. L., Nielsen, C. V. and Wind, G. (2015) 'Recovery from mental illness: A service user perspective on facilitators and barriers', *Community Mental Health Journal*, 51(1): 1–13.

Poole, J. and Ward, J. (2013) '"Breaking open the bone": Storying, sanism, and mad grief'. In B. LeFrancois, R. Menzies and G. Reaume (Eds.), *Mad Matters: A Critical Reader in Canadian Mad Studies* (pp. 94–105). Toronto: Canadian Scholars' Press.

Richmond, M. (1917) *Social Diagnosis*. New York: Russell Sage Foundation.

Roets, G., Roose, R., Clases, L., Vandekinderen, C., Van Hove, G., and Vanderplasschen, W. (2012) 'Reinventing the employable citizens: A perspective for social work', *The British Journal of Social Work*, 42(1): 94–110.

Santos, B.S. (Ed.) (2014) *Epistemologies of the South: Justice Against Epistemicide.* Boulder, CO: Paradigm.

Teghtsoonian, K. (2017) 'Depression in workplaces: Governmentality, feminist analysis, and neoliberalism'. In M. Morrow and L. Malcoe (Eds.), *Critical Inquiries for Social Justice in Mental Health* (pp. 229–255). Toronto: University of Toronto Press.

Totton, N. (2006) 'Power in the therapeutic relationship'. In N. Totton (Ed.), *The Politics of Psychotherapy: New Perspectives* (pp. 83–93). Berkshire: Open University Press.

Whitaker, T., Weismiller, T., and Clark, E. (2006) *Assuring the Sufficiency of a Frontline Workforce: A National Study of Licensed Social Workers.* Executive summary. Washington, DC: National Association of Social Workers.

PART C

Culture and multiple identities in mental health

12
CULTURE AND GENDER IN MENTAL HEALTH

Charmaine C. Williams

Although there may have been a time in the history of mental health when gender and culture were not recognized as issues that warranted particular attention, that is not the case now. I would argue, however, that gender and culture are somehow hyper-visible in mental health as indicators of deviation from a universalized norm, and invisible because of their exclusion from mainstreamed discourses in mental health. These states of hyper-visibility and invisibility are revealed when one examines the literature surrounding gender, culture and mental health.

This chapter addresses the question of how gender and culture should be addressed in mental health and how we evolve beyond current discourses that treat them as markers of peculiarity or ignore them. The current state of knowledge and practice regarding gender, culture and mental health is problematic, but may not be recognized as such. In 1971, Herbert Blumer wrote:

> A social problem does not exist for a society unless it is recognized by that society to exist. In not being aware of a social problem, a society does not perceive it, address it, discuss it, or do anything about it. The problem is just not there.
>
> *(Blumer 1971: 301–302)*

Blumer's (1971) quotation reminds us that the issues taken up in any social space are dictated by what those who have power in the group determine to be perceivable, recognizable, discussable and actionable within that social space. The same process can just as easily subvert the perception of an issue, rendering it unrecognizable, undiscussable and unactionable. Therefore, in presenting the state of knowledge on gender, culture and mental health as a problem, this chapter presents ideas about how we as mental health professionals and researchers can make that problem something that is perceivable, recognizable, discussable, and actionable.

Gender, culture and mental health

Gender is the social corollary to ideas of biological sex that are currently in flux, focusing attention to the social and cultural distinctions between people who occupy various gender identities. Existing mental health knowledge lags in adapting to contemporary spectrum-based notions of gender. Instead, the literature is largely focused on the long-established position that the important gender issue in mental health is the treatment of women made vulnerable by their specific biological, psychological and social deviances (Chandra and Satyanarayana 2010; Clarke and Miele 2016; Kira et al. 2015). There is a striking inertia in knowledge building for women's mental health. In the 1980s, McCannell (1986) identified violence and exploitation as priority issues for women's mental health, and 30 years later the only modification of these priorities is that they are embedded in a life course perspective (Rondon 2013). Further evidence of stagnancy, or even regression, in the sphere of gender and mental health is the ongoing proliferation of research directed at comparisons between men and women, attempting to explain why there are differences, or if there are differences, in psychological functioning (Hill and Needham 2013). The problem here is not that these may not be important questions, but rather, that they continue to be the questions that preoccupy a gendered perspective on mental health.

Recent shifts to align gendered mental health with genders other than woman seem to contribute to reinforcement of the same conventional tropes. Masculinity research presents men as suffering due to improper enactment of a masculine role, potentially complicated by sexual or cultural identities that frustrate their efforts to emulate a mentally healthy masculine norm (Affleck et al. 2018; Emslie et al. 2006; Fischgrund, Halkitis, and Carroll 2012). Individuals occupying trans and other gender identities are also suffering; they are a new vulnerable population for mental health practice and research to examine and classify, despite the removal of gender identity disorder from the Diagnostic and Statistical Manual (Dhejne et al. 2016). Therefore, it seems the gender problem that mental health literature has determined to be perceivable, recognizable, discussable and actionable is the traditional problem; gendered bodies that are dysfunctional or malfunctioning.

Culture has not fared much better with regard to evidence of progression from the preoccupations of the previous century. The historical focus of cultural psychiatry and, by extension, culture-focused mental health, has been the cross-cultural study of mental disorder, cultural variations in mental illness, and study of migrant populations (Kirmayer and Minas 2000). These are agendas that guided the work of psychiatrists and mental health professionals from the times that colonizing nations were venturing into the world and seeking tools to keep Indigenous and migrant populations under control (Fernando 1991). Since that time, the literature on culture and mental health has often been a cataloguing of exotic and barbaric practices that convey the inherent pathologies of populations with culture, contrasted against the idealized and universalized cultural arrangements of White, Western-based experts viewed as authorities on mental health (Williams 2005). The mental health and deviations of particular cultural (ethnic and racial minority) populations still remains of interest in contemporary mental health literature (Ai, Pappas, and Simonsen 2015; Diane Sookyoung and Amado 2014; Lorenzo-Blanco et al. 2012). The literature on culture and mental health remains focused on culture-specific idioms of distress, culture-specific syndromes, and techniques for interacting with cultural others (Karthick and Barwa 2017). This mirrors what we have seen with gender; a failure to progress beyond traditional preoccupations.

With culture and mental health, however, there is another layer of preoccupation with the extension of Western approaches to mental health to bodies outside of the Western space, under the auspices of movements like transcultural psychiatry and global mental health. Opportunities that could be taken up to increase literacy of culture and its impact on mental health are taken up as opportunities to separate universal from exotic mental disorders (Kirmayer and Minas 2000) and establish the necessity of North American psychiatric knowledge to alleviate global burdens associated with mental health (Kirmayer and Pedersen 2014). This instersects with gender and mental health discourses that assert the presumed leadership of North America in defining emancipatory mental health practices for women (Williams 2005). Practice-specific interventions like cultural formulation (Lewis-Fernandez 1996, 2009) and cultural competence (Pope-Davis et al. 2002; Williams 2006) are a gesture toward transforming practices to integrate culture, but are relegated to the sidelines of mainstream mental health. Transcultural and global mental health may be important, but the preoccupation with these century-old issues and the exclusion of others is problematic. At the moment, the problem that appears to be perceivable, recognizable, discussable and actionable in the sphere of culture and mental health is the need to render cultural differences into a form that can be expropriated by Western-based mental health knowledge.

The failures to progress with regard to gender and mental health and culture and mental health have points of convergence. A first point of convergence is that these bodies of work have points of contact, for example, in the previously cited work that pathologizes racial and ethnic minority men, and in parallel work that explores female psychopathologies within specific cultural contexts (Andermann 2010; Eagle and Long 2011; Kim et al. 2014). A second and more troubling convergence, however, is what Barn (2008) identifies as a 'culturalist perspective' in mental health that centres on the behaviours and beliefs of bodies associated with gender and culture while ignoring the connections between race, ethnicity, gender, social class and social exclusion. The literature is an outcome of over a century of knowledge-buildling about gender, culture and mental health that identifies deviance, peculiarity and perplexity as what is perceivable, recognizable, discussable and actionable.

Gender, culture and oppression

The problem with past-still-present conceptualizations of gender, culture and mental health is that they dramatically oversimplify how gender, culture and mental health intersect. A benign interpretation of that oversimplification would be that gender and culture are too complex, too dynamic to ever be effectively or comprehensively understood, and the reliance on culturalist perspectives represents the best efforts of the field. A less benign interpretation of that oversimplification would be that gender and culture have been used to veil and euphemize issues that are more appropriately named as White supremacy/racism and cisnormativity/sexism, and to support the development of knowledge and practices that are racist and sexist by association. With either of these interpretations there is a question to be answered about whose interests are served by the current state of knowledge on gender, culture and mental health. The Blumer quotation reminds us that problems and their recognition are based on social determinations about what is important, knowable, and actionable. If we understand mental health to be a social space in which decisions are made about what is important and how it should be known, then the current state of gender, culture and mental health knowledge must be interpreted with attention to the values and political interests of the community that has created that state (Hill and Needham 2013). Furthermore, there is a necessity to end the concealment of systemic racism, sexism and other oppressions that underlie mental health problems and problematic mental health practices with particular populations.

This is an opportunity to create an intellectual and clinical space in which the focus is not on identities and associated pathologies, but rather the operation of identity-based oppressions and their mental health consequences. The groundwork for this approach has been established in literature that shifts the focus from individual to social factors as determinants of mental health (Allen et al. 2014; Shim and Compton 2018) and structural, institutionalized social inequality as a further determinant of mental health (Denton, Prus, and Walters 2004; Sturgeon 2012). I propose that viewing gender, culture and mental health through a lens that recognizes the overarching consequences of oppressions for mental health and inequitable mental health practices guides us toward new ways of thinking about how to work with gender and culture.

A potential entry point for engaging with the mental health consequences of oppression is the five faces of oppression as described by Iris Young (1990). In this classic work, Iris Young provides a qualitative description of how oppression works in the lives of individuals and groups (Shlasko 2015). The work is revolutionary in that it makes the link between structural processes of racism, sexism, class exclusion, heterosexism, etc. and individual suffering while transcending the identity-based, minoritized categories that are conventionally assigned to bodies that are not aligned with dominance. Her focus is not race-based, gender-based, class-based oppression but, instead, the tools that are used to manifest these various oppressions in the lives of people who are not White, not male, not heterosexual, not able-bodied, or otherwise not included in groups that hold power.

Some of these faces of oppression are easily recognized as experiences that pervade the lives of people who are members of stigmatized and disempowered groups. For example, she names powerlessness as a face of oppression, pointing to the ways in which certain groups are barred from making decisions that affect the conditions of their lives. We can think of many oppressed groups that have been acted on by powerful others and prevented from controlling the circumstances of their lives – action that I prefer to describe as disempowerment, rather than powerlessness. Violence is another face of oppression that we know can be ubiquitous in the lives of oppressed groups, both through acts of violence visited on bodies and through actions and inactions that place people in situations of danger, risk and harm. Young (1990) extends our thinking about violence by challenging us to recognize that violence becomes systemic when acts of violence against certain individuals and groups unfold in a context in which it is inherently possible, acceptable and unremarkable. She also names marginalization as a manifestation of oppression that touches lives, noting that certain groups are excluded from participation in social life. Her work, however, extends ideas of marginalization as a purely social phenomenon of exclusion from the mainstream or the dominant. Young emphasizes that being positioned outside boundaries of privilege and perceived usefulness is linked to material consequences of poverty and underclass status.

The remaining two faces of oppression are perhaps less obvious because they are so commonplace that they do not catch attention. The first, exploitation, refers to practices in which the results from certain groups' labour is used to benefit other dominant groups. This is more than just the concentration of oppressed groups in labour sectors like serving and caregiving that attend to the needs and wants of elites. This exploitation is arrangements that reify class relations that keep oppressed groups in positions of precarity and dependence on the will/needs/wants of a ruling class. This exploitation is the unequal exchange of labour to the point of exhaustion for meagre, precarious or no benefit. The final face, cultural imperialism, refers to the universalizing of experiences and meanings in society so that groups who are outside of this universal are rendered invisible or hyper-visible. This manifests in the circulation of images and ideas that centralize the dominant as the norm, and the propagation of stereotype-based images and ideas that situate others as inferior, problematic anomalies. This fifth face of oppression is especially insidious as it is propagated by both the output of dominant groups concreting their superiority and the internalization of meanings and expectations that persuade both dominant and oppressed to accept that superiority as natural.

Young writes in the context of economics, so her emphasis is on material and political outcomes. Reading from mental health, we emphasize the psychological and social outcomes. The five faces that Young identifies are easily recognized as pillars of everyday experiences of microaggressions that affect the mental health of oppressed groups (Sue et al. 2007). As Dover

(2016) asserts, these microaggressions are more specifically named as microassaults, microinsults, and microinvalidation connected to the macro operation of systemic oppression. The five faces of oppression make appearances in practice every day, but do we recognize them? Or, do we see the fear, anger, heartbreak, despair and rage that are the outcomes of systemic oppression, outcomes of being targeted for systemic aggression, and redefine them as depression, anxiety, anger management, chronic fatigue and a host of other diagnostic labels that shift the gaze away from oppression and toward the inherent dysfunctions and malfunctions of gendered and racialized bodies? The rewriting of oppression-based distress as individual psychopathology runs deep through the past-still-present of mental health. Drapetomania diagnosed slaves who dared to flee slavery (Fernando 1991). Hysteria diagnosed women who dared to speak of their sexual abuse (McOmber 1996). Gender dysphoria diagnoses trans people who dare to exist (Dhejne et al. 2016). The people who live these experiences are not well served by systems of knowledge that would shape intervention based on pathologies of their genders and cultures.

The proposal here is that we continue to recognize gender and culture as things that must be perceived, discussed and addressed in mental health, but we give equal or greater space to perception, discussion and intervention for the mental health consequences of oppression. This means recognizing exploitation, marginalization, disempowerment, cultural imperialism, and violence as determinants of mental health, supplementing, or possibly supplanting language about social and structural determinants that distance us from the humanity of people who live with systemic threats to mental health and well-being. Exploitation, marginalization, disempowerment, cultural imperialism, and violence are embedded in systems but they are acted on people, human beings, that bring their suffering to mental health practitioners who must be prepared to perceive, discuss and address what they are experiencing.

Oppression as a determinant of mental health

Mental health theorists have grappled with how gender and culture shape health and health behaviours but a full understanding of these influences is not possible without also grappling with the links between identities formed by gender and culture and exposures to oppression as manifested in those five faces identified by Young (1990). Although we all live gendered and cultured existences, we are not all exposed to exploitation, cultural imperialism, marginalization, disempowerment and violence, because oppression is not distributed evenly or randomly. Writers in intersectionality theory have articulated that as beings with simultaneous memberships in multiple identity groups, some people face augmented and more pervasive exposures to oppression (Hancock 2007) or through alignment with privilege, can be insulated from those exposures (Williams et al. 2017). An important contribution of intersectionality theory (Carbado et al. 2013; Choo and Ferree 2010; Crenshaw 1991) has been to complicate our understandings of how oppression is manifested in vectors of racism, sexism, class exclusion, heterosexism, ableism, and other exclusions that converge to preserve privilege for those in dominant groups and activate the five faces of oppression against those in disempowered and stigmatized groups. The network of institutions that define and provide mental health care are one of many contexts which shape permutations of privilege and oppression that create possibilities for individuals and groups to move through social environments safe and healthy or unsafe and at risk. It is this complex interaction of oppressive ideologies and institutional processes that determine a myriad of possibilities for mental health and well-being across the range of cultural and gender identities. If we practice with awareness of gender-based and culture-based oppression as determinants of mental health, then we begin to think differently about why people become unwell and what barriers prevent them from being healthy.

145

For example, imagine a student who has come to counselling services seeking help to resolve a conflict that has emerged in one of her student group activities. She has been an active member of a Black LGBTQ Student Alliance since her first year and the group has been important for establishing a sense of belonging in the university, where she feels quite isolated as a racial minority, queer woman from a working-class background. Recently, she clashed with one of her male peers because he asserted that men needed to be foregrounded in the work of the group because they were the main targets of anti-Black violence and homophobia, while queer women 'just deal with the stuff that other Black women do'. She is seeking help to deal with the anger, resentment and pain that now taints her work with this group that she considered vital to her life as a university student.

This example presents us with a woman who is feeling distressed about an interpersonal conflict that has unfolded in the context of a group that is very important to her feelings of well-being. It does not describe a situation of psychopathology, but instead, the kind of emotional pain and sorrow that erodes mental health. The situation is one in which in which gender and culture matter. She is a woman in conflict with an agenda defined by men and that conflict threatens her connection to a group that helps her navigate her position as a Black woman in an environment where she is a minority in many ways. An exploration of gender and culture might raise questions for us about how she has learned to manage conflict, or what roles women have in her cultural context that are problematic for negotiating the current situation. A counsellor's interventions may be to help her assert herself within the group or find her way toward integration with the wider university environment to reduce her dependence on it. Such interpretations, however, give short shrift to the pain that has prompted her to seek help. Is the problem her assertiveness skills and her isolation, or is there more? Considering oppression as a determinant of her mental health in this situation introduces the possibility that what she is experiencing is pain, anger, and grief that arise from feeling exploited by a group that expects her to serve the interests of others, feeling marginalized within that group, and feeling disempowered to affect change within that group. Further, these experiences of exploitation, marginalization and disempowerment are likely repetitions of experiences had elsewhere, but especially painful in the context of this group that has been so precious to feeling affirmed as a Black queer woman in the university space. Her positioning as a Black queer woman in the Black LGBTQ alliance is a further complication, as her peer is asserting her marginalization within the marginalized group, referencing her 'prototypical invisibility' (Sesko and Biernat 2009; Thomas, Dovidio and West 2014) as a Black woman who is not centred in representations of Blackness or queerness, and assumed to be less relevant in facing the harms of oppression or charting advocacy against those harms. Gender and culture may be part of a conversation to be had with this woman about her distress, but it is incomplete without also considering how oppression-associated microaggressions are a further threat to her emotional well-being.

Similar analysis can promote insight into situations that are not as immediately associated with experiences of oppression. Imagine a young, male veteran of the war in Afghanistan referred for help with symptoms of post-traumatic stress disorder. He has been part of several violent experiences during his deployments, but he is particularly shaken by an incident in which men in his unit were killed by an explosive device smuggled into the camp by a child. When he recounts the events, he is factual, as if providing testimony in a court, but his hands shake and his language is peppered with profanities that telegraph tension always very close to the surface. He has sought help for the PTSD – attending veteran support groups, educating himself about the signs and symptoms, and taking prescribed medications. The group sessions help with feelings of isolation, but he thinks they are not doing anything to make him feel 'more normal'.

Culture and Gender in Mental Health

This example presents a situation that is more immediately recognizable as related to psychopathology; a diagnostic label is already in place. Given that diagnosis, do gender and culture matter here? It is possible to approach this situation as a pharmacological dilemma, a search for the right combination of medications to reduce symptoms. Yet, his involvement in support groups with other former soldiers is an indication of the importance of culture, military culture, to his attempts to recover from traumas experienced during his deployments. His attempts to heal may require his connection with a variety of cultures, but he has found some relief by seeking help within a context where the culture of the military, its knowledge, expectations, behaviours, symbols and so on, are understood. Gender matters here as well. It is likely the support groups that he attends would include mostly or only men (although women in Canada can serve in armed conflict), and a male-centred space could be further beneficial to recovery. However, considering oppression as a determinant of mental health introduces other possibilities. Adam's anxiety about not feeling 'normal' reveals the concurrent influence of oppression on his current mental health. Most apparent is that cultural imperialism, a dominant idea of what 'normal' looks like after exposure to war trauma, is contributing to his level of distress. As a former soldier who is not well, his struggles with mental health are affected by ideologies, perhaps from society at large or from the military specifically, that communicate that his current state is not right, not normal. This is known to be a significant stressor for men returning from military service, exacerbated by hegemonic masculine ideals that further reinforce feelings of inadequacy (Green et al. 2010). With more knowledge about his identities and more details of the path that took he to serving in the armed forces and going to Afghanistan, we might find that there are other ways in which he has been exposed to aggressions and assaults that align with the five faces of oppression. However, starting with this idea of 'normal' and the oppressive ideologies that underlie his feeling that he is failing to achieve it, there is much that can be discussed about what is undermining his mental health.

For both of these examples, awareness and sensitivity to issues of culture and gender create pathways for understanding of the mental health problems that are presented. Attention to oppression as a determinant of mental health, and the mental and emotional toll of exposure to exploitation, marginalization, disempowerment, cultural imperialism and violence, creates additional pathways for understanding and healing. If people come to us seeking help and we are not prepared to perceive, address, discuss and act on the ways in which their emotional well-being is undermined and threatened by the operation of oppression in their lives, or we try to sanitize those experiences by reframing them as problems of culture and gender differences, then we are not only providing incomplete intervention; we are perpetuating and driving systematic devastation of their emotional well-being.

Future directions

As the field moves forward, mental health practitioners and researchers need to find ways to make oppression perceivable, discussable and actionable items for mental health care. It is possible that the solution to stagnation of work on culture and gender in mental health may be integration of attention to oppression, and the development of interventions based on processing the exposures to the five faces of oppression and building resilience against their negative effects on mental health. The resources available for anti-oppressive clinical practices are growing. For example, a recent overview of literature on clinical strategies for anti-racist practice identified categories of work for clinicians to do on self-awareness and consciousness raising, and strategies for validation, education, and positive connection with identities and communities for clients (Miller et al. 2018). Other writers concerned with integrating attention to oppression in mental health care advocate for open discussion of experiences of oppression and social injustice (Gillies, Tolley, and Wolstenholme 1996; Waldegrave 2005), confrontation of dominant narratives that undermine feelings of self-respect and empowerment (Loveday 2009; McKenzie-Mohr and Lafrance 2017; Wright et al. 1999), cultivating resistance and resilience (Harrison 2000; Wade 1997), and transmuting experiences of oppression through arts-based expression (Jackson 2003; Wright and Wright 2017). These are promising practices, but incomplete without also transforming the systems in which mental health care is embedded through specific attention to organizational factors that contribute to experiences of oppression as described in Young's work (Ramsundarsingh and Shier 2017).

Conclusion

There is an important distinction between asserting oppression as a determinant of mental health and asserting gender and culture as important issues to address in mental health. An agenda to perceive, address, discuss and act on oppression in mental health care is an agenda that prioritizes equitable, ethical, effective and accessible care to racialized and gendered bodies that have been poorly served by the system. This is an agenda that starts by acknowledging that everyone has culture and gender, but there are specific remediations needed because particular bodies with culture and gender are treated unequally in the mental health care system and elsewhere.

References

Affleck, W., U. Thamotharampillai, J. Jeyakumar, and R. Whitley (2018) '"If one does not fulfil his duties, he must not be a man": Masculinity, mental health and resilience among Sri Lankan Tamil refugee men in Canada', *Culture, Medicine and Psychiatry*, 42 (4): 840–861:https://doi.org/10.1007/s11013-018-9592-9s.

Ai, Amy L., Cara Pappas, and Elena Simonsen (2015) 'Risk and protective factors for three major mental health problems among Latino American men nationwide', *American Journal of Men's Health*, 9 (1): 64–75.

Allen, J., R. Balfour, R. Bell, and M. Marmot (2014) 'Social determinants of mental health', *International Review of Psychiatry*, 26 (4): 392–407.

Andermann, Lisa (2010) 'Culture and the social construction of gender: Mapping the intersection with mental health', *International Review of Psychiatry*, 22 (5):501–512.

Barn, Ravinder (2008) 'Ethnicity, gender and mental health: Social worker perspectives', *International Journal of Social Psychiatry*, 54 (1): 69–82.

Blumer, H. (1971) 'Social problems as collective behavior', *Social Problems*, 18 (3): 298–306.

Carbado, D. W., K. W. Crenshaw, V. M. Mays, and B. Tomlinson (2013) 'Intersectionality: Mapping the movements of a theory', *Du Bois Review Social Science Research on Race*, 10 (2): 303–312. doi: 10.1017/S1742058X13000349.

Chandra, Prabha S., and Veena A. Satyanarayana (2010) 'Gender disadvantage and common mental disorders in women', *International Review of Psychiatry*, 22 (5): 513–524.

Choo, H.Y., and M.M. Ferree (2010) 'Practicing intersectionality in sociological research: A critical analysis of inclusions, interactions, and institutions in the study of inequalities', *Sociological Theory*, 28 (2): 129–149.

Clarke, Juanne N., and Rachelle Miele (2016) 'Trapped by gender: The paradoxical portrayal of gender and mental illness in Anglophone North American magazines: 1983–2012', *Women's Studies International Forum*, 56: 1–8.

Crenshaw, K. W. (1991) 'Mapping the margins: Intersectionality, identity, and violence against women of color', *Stanford Law Review*, 43 (6): 1241–1300.

Denton, M., S. Prus, and V. Walters (2004) 'Gender differences in health: A Canadian study of the psychosocial, structural and behavioural determinants of health', *Social Science & Medicine*, 58 (12): 2585–2600.

Dhejne, C., R. Van Vlerken, G. Heylens, and J. Arcelus (2016) 'Mental health and gender dysphoria: A review of the literature', *International Review of Psychiatry*, 28(1): 44–57.

Culture and Gender in Mental Health

Diane Sookyoung, Lee, and M. Padilla Amado (2014) 'Acculturative stress and coping: Gender differences among Korean and Korean American university students', *Journal of College Student Development*, 55(3): 243–262.

Dover, M.A. (2016) 'The moment of microaggression: The acts of oppression, deumanization, and exploitation', *Journal of Human behavior in the Social Environment*, 26 (7–8): 575–586.

Eagle, Gillian, and Carol Long (2011) 'In our culture, in our gender: Implications of the culture/gender interface for South African psychotherapists', *Feminism & Psychology*, 21 (3): 336–353.

Emslie, Carol, Damien Ridge, Sue Ziebland, and Kate Hunt (2006) 'Men's accounts of depression: Reconstructing or resisting hegemonic masculinity?', *Social Science & Medicine*, 62 (9): 2246–2257.

Fernando, S. (1991) *Mental health, race and culture*. London: Macmillan Press.

Fischgrund, B.N., P.N. Halkitis, and R.A. Carroll (2012) 'Conceptions of hypermasculinity and mental health states in gay and bisexual men', *Psychology of Men and Masculinity*, 13 (2): 123–135.

Gillies, P., K. Tolley, and J. Wolstenholme (1996) 'Is AIDS a disease of poverty?' *AIDS Care*, 8: 351–365.

Green, G., C Emslie, D. O'Neill, K. Hunt, and S. Walker (2010) 'Exploring the ambiguities of masculinity in accounts of emotional distress in the military among young ex-servicemen', *Social Science & Medicine*, 71 (8): 1480–1488.

Hancock, A.M. (2007) 'When multiplication doesn't equal quick addition: Examining intersectionality as a research paradigm', *Perspectives on Politics*, 5: 63–79.

Harrison, N. (2000) 'Gay affirmative therapy: A critical analysis of the literature', *British Journal of Guidance & Counselling*, 28 (1): 37–53.

Hill, T.D., and B.L. Needham (2013) 'Rethinking gender and mental health: A critical analysis of three propositions', *Social Science & Medicine*, 92 (2): 83–91.

Jackson, V. (2003) 'In our own voice: African-American stories of oppression, survival and recovery in mental health systems', *Off Our Backs*, 33 (7/8): 19–21.

Karthick, S., and S. Barwa (2017) 'Culture and mental health: A review of culture related psychiatric conditions', *Psychology and Behavioral Science*, 5 (5):1–6.

Kim, Eunha, Ingrid Hogge, Peter Ji, Young R. Shim, and Catherine Lothspeich (2014) 'Hwa-Byung among middle-aged Korean women: Family relationships, gender-role attitudes, and self-esteem', *Health Care for Women International*, 35 (5): 495–511.

Kira, Ibrahim A., Andrea Z. Omidy, Mounir Fawzi, Kenneth G. Rice, Mohab Fawzi, Linda Lewandowski, and Mireille Bujold-Bugeaud (2015) 'Are the negative mental health effects of gender discrimination (GD) salient across cultures? Does self-esteem mediate these effects: GD as a continuous traumatic stress and the pathways to its negative dynamics?', *Psychology*, 6 (1): 93–116.

Kirmayer, L.J., and D. Pedersen (2014) 'Toward a new architecture for global mental health', *Transcultural Psychiatry*, 51 (6): 759–776.

Kirmayer, L.J., and H. Minas (2000) 'The future of clinical psychiatry: An international perspective', *Canadian Journal of Psychiatry*, 45: 438–446.

Lewis-Fernandez, R. (1996) 'Cultural formulation of psychiatric diagnosis', *Culture, Medicine and Psychiatry*, 20 (2): 133–144.

Lewis-Fernandez, R. (2009) 'The cultural formulation', *Transcultural Psychiatry*, 46 (3): 379–382.

Lorenzo-Blanco, Elma I., Jennifer B. Unger, Lourdes Baezconde-Garbanati, Anamara Ritt-Olson, and Daniel Soto (2012) 'Acculturation, enculturation, and symptoms of depression in Hispanic youth: The roles of gender, hispanic cultural values, and family functioning', *Journal of Youth and Adolescence*, 41 (10): 1350–1365.

Loveday, H. (2009) 'From oppression, resistance grows', *International Journal of Narrative Therapy & Community Work*, 1: 3–13.

McCannell, K. (1986) 'Special issue: Women and mental health', *Canadian Journal of Community Mental Health*, 5 (2): 5–6.

McKenzie-Mohr, S., and M.N. Lafrance (2017) 'Narrative resistance in social work research and practice: Counter-storying in the pursuit of social justice', *Qualitative Social Work*, 16 (2): 189–205.

McOmber, J.B. (1996) 'Silencing the patient: Freud, sexual abuse, and "the etiology of hysteria"', *Quarterly Journal of Speech*, 82 (4): 343–363.

Miller, M.J., B.T. Keum, C.J. Thai, Y. Lu, N.N. Truong, G.A. Huh, X. Li, J.G. Yeung, and L.H Ahn (2018) 'Practice recommendations for addressing racism: A content analysis of the counseling psychology literature', *Journal of Counseling Psychology*, 65 (6): 669–680. Advance online publication http://dx.doi.org/10.1037/cou0000306.

Pope-Davis, D. B., R. L. Toporek, L. Ortega-Villalobos, D. P. Ligiero, C. S. Brittan-Powell, W. M. Liu, M. R. Bashshur, J. N. Codrington, and C. T. H. Liang (2002) 'Client perspectives of multicultural counseling competence: A qualitative examination', *Counseling Psychologist*, 30 (3): 355–393.

Ramsundarsingh, S., and M.L. Shier (2017) 'Anti-oppressive organisational dynamics in the social services: A literature review', *British Journal of Social Work*, 47 (8): 2308–2327.

Rondon, M.B. (2013) 'Priority issues in women's mental health', *World Psychiatry*, 12 (3): 275–276.

Sesko, A.K., and M. Biernat (2009) 'Prototypes of race and gender: The invisibility of Black women', *Journal of Experimental Social Psychology*, 46: 356–360.

Shim, R.S., and M.T. Compton (2018) 'Addressing the social determinants of mental health: If not now, when? If not us who?' *Psychiatric Services*, 69 (8): 844–846.

Shlasko, D. (2015) 'Using the five faces of oppression to teach about interlocking systems of oppression', *Equity & Excellence in Education*, 48: 3.

Sturgeon, S. (2012) 'Stigma and marginalisation: Structural violence and the impact on mental health', *Social Work*, 48 (1): 58–67.

Sue, D.W., C.M. Capodilupo, G.C. Torin, J.M. Bucceri, A.M.B. Holder, K.L. Nadal, and M. Esquilin (2007) 'Racial microaggressions in everyday life: Implications for clinical practice', *American Psychologist*, 62 (4): 271–286.

Thomas, E.L, J.F. Dovidio, and T.V. West (2014) 'Lost in the categorical shuffle: Evidence for the social non-prototypicality of Black women', *Cultural Diversity and Ethnic Minority Psychology*, 20 (3): 370–376.

Wade, A. (1997) 'Small acts of living: Everyday resistance to violence and other forms of oppression', *Contemporary Family Therapy*, 19 (1): 23–29.

Waldegrave, C. (2005) '"Just therapy" with families on low incomes', *Child Welfare,* 84 (2): 265–276.

Williams, C.C. (2005) 'Chapter 2 commentary: A feminist perspective', in S.E. Romans and M.V. Seeman (Eds.), *Women's Mental Health: A Life Cycle Approach*. Philadelphia: Lippincott, Williams & Wilkins.

Williams, C. C. (2006) 'The epistemology of cultural competence', *Families in Society: The Journal of Contemporary Social Services*, 87 (2): 209–220.

Williams, C. C., D. Curling, L. S. Steele, M. F. Gibson, A. Daley, D. C. Green, and L. E. Ross. (2017) 'Depression and discrimination in the lives of women, transgender and gender liminal people in Ontario, Canada', *Health Soc Care Community*, 25 (3): 1139–1150. doi: 10.1111/hsc.12414.

Wright, L. K., J.V. Hickey, K. C. Buckwalter, S. A. Hendrix, and T. Kelechi (1999) 'Emotional and physical health of spouse caregivers of persons with Alzheimer's disease and stroke', *Journal of Advanced Nursing*, 30 (3): 552–563.

Wright, T., and K. Wright (2017) 'Exploring the benefits of intersectional feminist social justice approaches in art psychotherapy', *The Arts in Psychotherapy*, 54: 7–14.

Young, I. M. (1990) *Justice and the Politics of Difference*. Princeton: Princeton University Press.

13

CULTURE AND SOCIAL CLASS IN MENTAL HEALTH

Yu Chak Sunny Ho, Laurence Chan and William Ming Liu

Social class and classism are difficult social phenomena to discuss due to the complexities in capturing classist experiences, idiosyncratic definitions, and strong emotional responses (e.g., embarrassment, guilt, shame) created for clients during therapy sessions. In some cultures, it is a taboo topic to talk about. As mental health clinicians, we need to understand how social class and classism impact everyone's lives to a certain extent. Scholars believe that discussing individuals' social class and classism experiences in therapy can help improve clients' psychological well-being and reduce their psychological symptoms, such as depression and anxiety (Baum et al. 1999; Smith 2005). Research suggests that classism usually occurs concurrently with other -isms (Liu et al. 2007). White middle-class males oftentimes have the privilege in society to achieve job stability, engage in decision-making processes, and obtain flexibility in life. For instance, they can take vacations during big holiday seasons to celebrate and relax, however, they may not be able to recognize their colleagues who are people of color still need to work during holidays and earn extra income for the family. A large proportion of people of color in America live under poverty and regularly face conditions including noise and air pollution, crime, and overcrowding (Smith 2005). This could be considered as classism because these individuals are segregated from the majority of White middle-class males and live a poor quality of life. They do not have freedom of choice, access to good quality of food and necessities, and stability in life (Liu et al. 2007). Even though they would like to move upward on the social ladder, they do not have adequate resources and opportunities to search for a desired career and maximize their potentials. Due to the constant stress burdens low-socioeconomic-status individuals need to face on daily basis, they are very likely to develop health concerns, such as chronic physical diseases and mental health problems (Baum et al. 1999).

The term *social class* will be used intentionally in this chapter instead of other commonly referenced terms such as *social status* or *socioeconomic status*. *Social class and classism* illustrates how people classify themselves and others into categories and not on a spectrum or gradient (Liu and Ali 2008). The definition provides room for individual subjectively when people consider their social class positionality.

Using discrete and objective indicators to categorize social standing belies an often assumed yet unchallenged notion that people can be easily classified into discrete categories (e.g., upper class, middle class, and lower class) (Liu and Ali 2008). Not only is the concept of having solely objective indicators to define social class impossible, these indicators are susceptible to inaccurate self-reporting and can change depending on an individual's mood (Duncan 1988; Liu 2008, 2013). Objective classification measures such as educational level and income make problematic assumptions that overgeneralize the experiences of groups of people, does not accurately explore intersectionality (e.g., race, gender, sexual orientation) (Smith 2005) and the difficulties of determining the number of social classes one can create (e.g., lower middle class) (Liu 2008). Therefore, we propose social class standing to be a self-identified subjective experience.

In some cultures, it may be taboo and disrespectful topic to bring social class discussion up in conversations. Individuals may feel offended when prompted to discuss social class in social settings because discussing the topic may often violate cultural norms and rules. In this chapter, we will discuss four worldviews of lateral classism: *Crabs-in-a- Barrel Mentality*, *Selling Out*, *Proxy Kids*, and *Materialism*. We will illustrate each concept with case vignettes to deepen our understanding on how social class interacts with other social identities and how clinicians can respond in those situations.

Defining social class

"What is your social class?" "Have you experienced classism in your life?" These are two questions infrequently addressed in counseling sessions. In this chapter, we will first define social class and classism according to the existing literature. Second, we will explore the reasons why mental health practitioners are hesitant to mention social class and classism within the therapeutic setting. Third, we will explain the importance of discussing the role of social class and classism in counseling sessions, which can be helpful to foster clients' psychological well-being. Research suggests mental health clinicians may not have the necessary knowledge and skills to discuss social class and classism with clients nor do they believe it is an important topic when compared to other presenting concerns, such as interpersonal relationships and family/psychiatric backgrounds (Kim and Cardemil 2012; Liu, 2013; Smith 2009).

According to Liu (2013) and Smith (2009), psychologists may have a limited understanding about how to talk about social class and classism in therapy sessions. Many graduate psychology training programs may not include social class and classism as one of the discussion topics in their curriculum even if multicultural counseling courses were offered in most of the programs (Pieterse et al. 2009; Smith et al. 2008). As a result, trainees, and even fully-trained counselors and psychologists may feel unprepared and incompetent to discuss the topic with their clients (Smith 2008). According to the American Psychological Association (APA) Ethical Standards, psychologists have the responsibility to offer sufficient training opportunities for students to equip knowledge and skills to serve clients with a wide range of psychopathologies in different contexts (APA 2017). This includes responding to clients' presenting concerns in culturally appropriate ways in therapy. Process and outcome research demonstrates the therapeutic alliance and clinicians' effectiveness can be strengthened by discussing social class at the early stages of counseling sessions (Smith et al. 2011). Therefore, it is crucial for psychologists to be ready to initiate discussions with clients regarding their lived social class experiences. If clients are encouraged to talk about their social class and classism in therapy sessions, it is more likely for them to develop trust and confident in the therapy process, thus having better therapeutic outcomes.

Research suggests it is common for an individual to face classism at some point in one's life (Russell 1996; Smith 2008). Therefore, it is very likely for mental health practitioners in their career to run into clients who come from low-socioeconomic-status families or poverty and many of them may have experienced some degrees of classism in their lives. However, psychologists may struggle to conceptualize and empathize with clients because social class is not always only directly related to variables obviously tied to social class (i.e., occupational prestige) (Liu 2013). Research also suggests that classism contributes to many psychological and physical health symptoms: Chronic physical pain is positively associated with exposure to residing near high-stake living environments for prolonged periods of time (Krieg 2005; Liu 2013). Depression and apprehension are often developed in an environment where classism occurs (Smith 2009). For instance, people who live under poverty may not be able to get access to certain basic life-sustainable resources, such as good quality of food and water. These individuals may reside within environments where there are higher crime and unemployment rates. The safety of their living environments may need to be compromised in exchange of meeting basic needs, such as food and utilities, in lives. If the basic needs were not met, people often feel distressed and worried.

There are many different definitions of social class in scholarship, which can make it confusing and difficult to comprehend (Liu 2013; Smith 2009). We argue that scholars tend to discuss social class using perceived objective terms, i.e., education level, income, and occupation, in existing literature; however, we suggest that mental health counselors and researchers need to study social class and classism in parallel with privileges, marginalization, discriminations, and microaggression (Collins and Andersen 2007). This is because social class is a self-constructed and subjective term and people would have different definitions attached to it (Liu 2013). In addition, scholars believe that social class is not simply a perception by an individual but rather, it is related to systems of power and institutionalized discrimination (Collins and Andersen 2007). In other words, social class is a societal-determined experience, which helps people navigate in different contexts. This can potentially lead to marginalization and experiences with classism. Mental health practitioners need to recognize that individuals develop and conceptualize their own definitions of social class differently and there is no one absolute standard to classify people in different social class groups. According to Liu (2013), self-defined social class may vary across different geographic locations and times, and different levels of consumptions. For instance, two individuals can earn the same income in two different cities, but they may have very different quality of life. The median income in New York City is higher than the median income in some other rural areas or even other cities in the United States because the price of living is much higher in New York City. In terms of times, people's spending habits are so much different now than 50 years ago. People are able to save a majority of income couple decades ago, however, people today may use credit cards to pay off debts. Furthermore, consumers had greater spending power decades ago than now due to inflation. All of these conditions make it difficult for individuals to determine their own socioeconomic status and it can be fluid throughout their lives and time. It also adds another extra layer of difficulty for mental health clinicians to determine one's socioeconomic status in counseling sessions.

It is also problematic to study class and classism without studying the intersection of other social identities. Research study participants can potentially feel stressed and stereotyped when they were inquired about social class (Croizet and Claire 1998). As mentioned, people often feel embarrassed and uncomfortable when they are asked about social class. Using the Social Class Worldview Model (SCWM) as a framework to understand social class, the theory posits individuals identify and interpret their capital demands and learn how to respond to them (Liu 2013). People learn about their social class through two different channels: socialization messages and social class-consciousness. One can interpret and understand their social classes through interaction with family, peers, and friends and this shapes individual's worldviews towards social class. Liu (2013) further explains that individuals might have different levels of awareness towards social class. According to the Social Class and Classism Consciousness Model (SCCC), there are three stages of social class awareness: no social class-consciousness, social class self-consciousness, and social class-consciousness. Within these levels, there are ten statuses: unawareness, status position saliency, questioning, exploration and justification, despair, the world is just, intellectualized anger and frustration, reinvestment, engagement, and equilibration. Mental health clinicians can utilize the two models to help initiate conversations with clients about how they might perceive themselves as a social classed person and what the functions of social class are in their lives. Going through the models, clinicians can have a better understanding of clients' social class and classism experiences within different contexts.

Significance of discussing classism in mental health practice

To fully understand the impact of social class and individual's subjective social class experiences, practitioners and researchers must also recognize the impact of classism (Liu et al. 2004). Like race and racism, and sex and sexism, class and classism are co-constructed, interdependent constructs (Liu et al. 2004). In other words, one cannot study social class without examining classism, such as there cannot be a complete understanding of race and racial identity without exploration of racism. We continue Liu's (2013) definition of classism as macro and micro interpersonal forms of prejudice and discrimination and acknowledge the deleterious effects of classism on an institutional and systemic level (e.g., big banks).

Classism, like racism and sexism continue to serve and uphold a social hierarchy in which people in the dominant cultural group (White, heterosexual, upper-class men) hold positions of power through domination and social control (Smith 2005). Classism can be viewed as the physical manifestation of social class privilege and is often expressed as a means of policing those in different and similar social classes who "step out" of their expected social circles. This policing ensures that the status quo remains (Smith 2005). Some scholars believe classism is a form of oppression and therefore can only be practiced by the dominant class (Lott 2002) and the authors agree. However, the authors assert individuals of any social class group (Liu et al. 2004) can practice classist prejudice and forms of discrimination informed by classist values.

Research examining classism often assumes a unilateral direction and focus. In other words, research tends to examine class-related negative attitudes, behaviors, and values from individuals in higher social classes towards individuals in lower social classes. This pattern is perpetuated by the frequency of research calling for additional mental health services for individuals in lower social classes whenever discussion of social class are held (Smith 2005). Therefore, counselors and psychologists tend to conceptualize social class and classism as a lower-class issue. However, classism can be understood in terms of the directions they may be projected, and are categorized into four domains: upward, downward, internally, and laterally (Liu 2002).

Downward classism, as described, is the most commonly thought of direction of classism. Consistent with the myth of meritocracy, *downward classism* attributes individual responsibility to social and financial success. Meritocracy can be deconstructed into four dimensions: (1) merit, (2) distributive justice, (3) equality of opportunity, and (4) social mobility. Merit and distributive justice are the test of individual ability (Conrad 1976; Liu 2011). For instance, persistent stereotypical characteristics upper-class individuals may have of lower-class individuals include lacking education, exploitation of the welfare system, and hyper-sexuality. A person in any social class can enact *downward classism*, however, as no matter what social class standing an individual is in, there is always a belief that someone else is in an inferior position (Liu 2002).

Upward classism, on the other hand, is prejudice and discriminatory attitudes and behaviors towards individuals in a perceived higher class standing (Liu 2002). Cognitions may include thoughts that these individuals are "out of touch" with common folks, are elitist, snobby, or have not experienced "true struggles." Perceivers' affective-emotional reactions in enacting *upward classism* may include anger, resentment, and self-pity.

Internalized classism refers to the internalized beliefs and thoughts an individual should have in order to belong to their social class (Liu 2002). Worries of being "found out," caught as a fraud, or inability to "keep up" result in distressful affective responses such as anger, anxiety, depression, guilt, and disappointment when unable to maintain one's social class standing.

Finally, *lateral classism*, which will make the bulk of the following case vignettes and discussion, is the prejudice and discrimination people hold towards others perceived to be in similar social class standings (Liu 2002). Individuals perceiving others within the same social class engaging in actions and behaviors attempting to increase their social class upward mobility utilize lateral classist prejudice and discrimination as a tool. Transgressors of *lateral classism* attempt to police another's social class standing and to exert control to ensure an individual realigns to their shared social class (Liu et al. 2004). The successful coercion of an individual to stay within their group standing allows the transgressor of *lateral classism* to avoid the negative feelings of seeing another become more successful than themselves (Smith 2005).

While this chapter primarily focuses on the negative impacts of *lateral classism* in the hopes of enabling mental health providers to better understand how these issues affect clients, it is important to recognize the human tendency to categorize individuals into larger social groups is not inherently negative. *Allocentrism*, a trait of collectivism in which individuals are focused on the people around them in a community, has been linked with lower levels of isolation and positively correlated with social support (Triandis et al. 1985). Being in the presence of others that hold similar worldviews have been associated with increased self-worth through appraisal by valued groups, (Cialdini and Richardson 1980), social belonging, and interconnectedness (Correll and Park 2005). Individuals within the ingroup experiencing distress may become motivated to utilize classist prejudice and discrimination as power and dominance to maintain a hierarchical status quo.

Social class, intersectionality, and mental health

This section explores the nuanced ways in which *lateral classism* may appear and hold racial and ethnic subtleties. *Lateral classism* is complex and intersectional by nature - race, gender, sexual orientation, and other social identities impact the forms of *lateral classism* an individual may face (Liu et al. 2004). The felt impact of poverty and environmental racism – institutional, environmental forms of racism (e.g., the storage of toxic chemicals and dysregulation of smog in predominately African American and Latinx communities) – showcase the interdependence of race and social class (Allen 2001; Liu et al. 2004). Liu (2002) also describes the importance of understanding the intersection of gender and social class by analyzing men's self-perceptions in their ability to provide financially as assessments of success. We conceptualize four categories or worldviews in which *lateral classism* occurs: *Crabs-in-a-Barrel Mentality*, *Selling Out*, *Proxy Kids*, and *Materialism*. These headings are not intended to be fully comprehensive, as we expect variations and additional forms of *lateral classism* may be established in future research. Instead, these categories allow the reader to begin the organizational framework of *lateral classism* across cultures, specifically racial and ethnic groups. Case vignettes are utilized to describe some examples of *lateral classism* as due to the complexity of intersectionality of cultural factors. Each case vignette discusses some form of social identity (e.g., race, sex, gender, social class, sexual orientation), introduce culturally relevant language, and identify ways in which these forms of *lateral classism* continue to perpetuate the social status quo. We will first describe and explain what the four categories are, then we will further illustrate the concepts by providing some case examples. At the end of each case study, we will discuss mental health implications.

Crabs-in-a-barrel mentality worldview

Strong feelings of competition, denying of rights to others, and feelings of resentment arise from observing others obtain success and status amongst peers. This phenomenon is known as crab mentality and is observed across cultural groups. As one example within Filipino culture, *Kanya-Kanya Syndrome* references one's sense of envy at the belief that another person's success is their own downfall (Dy 1994). Crab mentality has been associated with poverty and post-colonial society (Sweetman 1997), although it has also been used to describe the mentality of individuals across cultural and ethnic groups (Miller 2015; Sarangi 2013; Shanker 1994; Sweetman 1997), suggesting it is not related to any one specific cultural or ethnic group. Crab mentality can be demonstrated in Terry's story. Terry is a Filipino American high school student who resides in a predominantly Filipino neighborhood within the United States. While his childhood friends frequently engaged in truancy and devalued formal education, Terry was drawn to school. Intrigued by the science fields, he achieved high grades across classes. As teachers noticed Terry's hard work and active engagement in classes, his biology teacher began talking to him about the possibility of attending college. Terry began experiencing bullying by his old peers due to his rising interest in nursing. They jeered and suggested his chosen profession was for women only and made effeminizing and homophobic comments towards Terry. The persistent bullying has resulted in Terry feeling increasingly isolated, especially as his peers began to exclude him out of social activities. Consequently, Terry began to go straight home immediately after school. He contemplated giving up on attending college and working in an auto-repair shop with his male cousins upon graduation. Terry reasoned his peers will more likely socially accept auto-repair work as a man's work and it would be easier for him to be accepted by others then. In this case vignette, Terry is experiencing his peers' perceptions and sense of feeling threatened by his academic success. Their disparaging comments reflect their own insecurities of not being successful and reflect the lateral classist projection that an individual attempting to achieve success for themselves may view themselves as better than others. The saying "They think they're better than us" reflects this mentality.

Threatened ingroup members police individuals to stay in their place through the lashing out at any individuals seemingly preparing to advance their social standing with disparaging remarks and insults (Liu and Ali 2008). In this vignette, Terry's peers utilize inscribed hegemonic masculinity norms to suggest Terry may not be a "real" man for liking schoolwork and nursing via usage of homophobic and effeminacy-laden terms (Connell 1998; Frank 1987). Therefore, to be a real man, he must abandon these interests. While it is important to understand ingroup and outgroup attitudes may swing on a continuum from socially-positive to socially-detrimental, holding positive attributes towards one's ingroup increases one's sense of belonging (Allport 1954). *Pakikipagkapwa-tao* is the prescribed belief within Filipino culture that one must treat others in manners of shared-identities, equality, respect, concern for well-being, and shared sense of moral responsibility (Mina Jr. 2015). When working with individuals from collectivistic cultures, highlighting the strengths of culturally appropriate positive attributes of belonging are associated with decreasing isolation (Brewer 1999). If a mental health practitioner was working with Terry, they may be able to validate his struggles with lateral classism through familiarizing themselves with the psychological phenomena of *karka-karka syndrome* and how Terry's current incongruence with his values and exclusion from peers is creating distress.

"Selling out" worldview

"Selling out" is a social context often associated with being White and obtaining academic success for people of color, especially African Americans (Fordham 2008; Fordham and Ogbu 1986). In fact, Fordham and Ogbu (1986) argued successful school learning is antithetical to the normative expectation of being Black. A pervasive myth is that academically successful African American students have sacrificed some aspect of their racial identity or belonging (Welch et al. 1989). This disparaging comment is a form of *lateral classism* directed at other people of color who are striving for academic success. "Selling out" and "acting White" are especially powerful forms of criticism in ensuring individuals stay within their social class. Smitherman (2000) describes "selling out" as a tool for individuals to label fellow African Americans as people who do not support Black causes but instead seek to gain power for themselves – often betraying their communities and race in the process.

Accused of being White can be psychologically distressing due to the complex history of slavery and slave drivers who were Black. For example, calling an African American an Uncle Tom (i.e. a Black person is eager to serve Whites and viewing Blacks as racially inferior) is viewed as questioning their authenticity, sense of Blackness and understanding of race (Alim et al. 2010). The implication suggests individuals who "sold out" or are "acting White" are not aware of their own actions or how they themselves are being manipulated by the dominant culture. This is in contrast to the concept of "playing the game"; when people of color are aware of the issues and follow along with the system with an ulterior motive (Urrieta 2005). It is important to note because pervasive stereotypes in American society view African Americans as unable to succeed academically, accusations such as "selling out" and "acting White" are especially detrimental to the success of African American students (Fordham and Ogbu 1986). For example, the case vignette, we discuss below illustrates the benefit from gaining awareness of how harmful these stereotypes can be and speak with successful African American role models who have experienced similar forms of teasing.

Gregory is a young African American male born and raised in an upper-middle-class suburban area. His parents both grew up lower class in a nearby city. Gregory's parents hold successful jobs while their relatives remain lower class; his father works as an engineer and his mother is a pharmacist. Most of Gregory's neighbors and friends are White and upper middle class. Each year, Gregory's parents host their extended relatives for a family gathering during the holidays. During the most recent gathering, an uncle suggested Gregory's parents had "sold out" for choosing to leave their hometown and pursue academic work. In his tirade, much of this uncle's resentment was directed to Gregory's parents for obtaining graduate degrees and living in a White suburban neighborhood. This uncle claimed Gregory's parents act "White" in the ways their family spoke and dressed. This greatly infuriated Gregory. Soon, he was resentful towards his relatives and above all, the notion that his parents "sold out" and "act White" caused Gregory to begin doubting his own way of speaking and dressing, causing him to feel anxious and self-conscious.

A mental health practitioner may work with Gregory develop his own sense of racial identity and lessen the cognitive dissonance he may experience between being Black and the way he dresses and speaks. Due to being raised in a predominantly White environment, much of Gregory's social support are White individuals. Allport (1954) states that while holding negative attitudes towards outgroup members may facilitate an attachment towards one's ingroup, this does not necessarily need to be the case. Brewer (1999) reports having ingroup identification does not require the holding of discriminatory views towards an outgroup. Therefore, development of Gregory's sense of his racial identity may not need to include the removal or detachment of his current social support.

Proxy kids worldview

According to Kohn (1963), differences in social class within parent–child relationships demonstrate struggles and conflicts. A person can be very successful in life with a very prestigious job. However, their values and worldviews could be so different when compared to their parents. Parents may take on honors and accomplishments of their children to enhance their social status in their community. In Asian cultures, individuals may incorporate their traditional Asian values in their parenting, i.e., hard work is the only key to prestigious career and comfortable life. Asian parents may often expect their children to behave in certain ways to align with traditional Asian values and norms. Asian children may disagree with their parents because they may have a different set of values and perspectives in life growing up in a different country and culture. When foreign-born Asian children were asked to go back to their home country with parents, they would feel embarrassed and uneasy to manage their situation when their parents used them as a "proxy" to compare them with other cousins and family friends. Intergenerational conflicts can stem from two separate belief and value systems as well as miscommunication. This is clearly seen in John's example: John is a 26-year-old Asian American male born in the United States. He recently graduated with a Master's degree in business from a prestigious university and works at a famous, well-paying firm. He comes from a working-class family, in which his parents work 12 hours a day to make a living. John's parents immigrated to a small town in Virginia from China in the 1990s. Even though John's parents did not have time to spend with him, John always strove to excel academically to make his family proud of him. He received straight As throughout his education. Since enrolling in graduate school at this prestigious university, his parents have been receiving many compliments from relatives and friends back in China and from Chinese neighbors. When John's parents get together with their relatives in China, especially when John is present, John's parents would use John as a "proxy" to demonstrate how successful the family has been doing in the United States. John's parents also always use John as a "proxy" to compare him with other cousins in China to show how "superior" and "different" he and his family are. This reflects a high social status and prestige in the society. In those situations, John would feel embarrassed and unnecessary. John's family feels very much needed to demonstrate how smart and accomplished John is in order to gain respect and reputation within the family; lineage matters.

Research showed that people from the middle-class and people from the working class have different life priorities (Kohn 1959). Author believes that working classed individuals focus on respectability and success/accomplishment, whereas middle classed individuals focus more on internalized standards of conduct. Based on the above example, John's family come from different cultural and educational background and intergenerational conflicts arise when there's a misunderstanding of personal values between the two generations. When working with Asian families, mental health practitioners ought to understand their family dynamics and value systems and discuss ways to enhance communication between the older and younger generations.

Materialistic worldview

Based on the SCWM model, there are three social class worldview considerations: attitudes towards materialism, social class behaviors, and lifestyle considerations (Liu 2013). Materialism emphasizes on relationships being evaluated by possessions and assets. Social class behaviors are shaped by one's social class norms and behaviors, for example, etiquette, accents, and language. Lifestyle considerations explain the ways in which individuals spend their time. A person may look up to and respect someone simply because the person is wealthy. In Chinese culture, it is important for individuals to show "what you get" upfront, social network can thus be formed. Classism can certainly occur much frequently in this culture because people from working class and under poverty would not be able to meet middle classed friends. Individuals from the working class would not be valued and respected by the middle-class group because of material deficiencies. It can be very problematic and contributing to working classed person's psychological distress. The following example illustrates the concept of materialism in Asian culture. In most of the Asian cultures, owning properties and wealth can help you move upward on the social ladder and suggest that you own power and privilege. David, a 30-year-old Chinese man, recently bought a house in the most expensive neighborhood in Shanghai. He is currently working as an investment banker in a world-famous financial institution. Besides residing in a well-known expensive neighborhood, he has several successful investment properties, and by most relative cultural accounts, is perceived by others as financially wealthy. Because of his accomplishments and successful career, his friends and family are always proud. Despite this, David's cousins are often envious about what David has achieved in his life. David's colleagues, family, and friends in Shanghai often feel inferior when hanging out with David because he is very successful and wealthy. David's friends always allow David to make decisions and look up to him. David's parents and relatives understand that David has prestigious social class status in the society through witnessing on what "materials" he owns, i.e., this is what people see, perceive, and evaluate success, knowledge, and power/privilege in this community. In this case vignette, David's parents and friends look up to David because of the assets that he owned. His family feels he is successful and accomplished based on David's stimulus value of financial wealth. David gains power, privilege, respect, and acceptance from people around him and he can make decisions in his family, work, and among his friends. Materialism, in this case, can bring David infinite resources, power, and relationships. On the other hand, he may perpetuate classism and oppress individuals who are under poverty and working class.

Future directions

Greater research needs to be conducted that examines how effective culturally relevant treatments look within the framework of social class and race. As clinicians and scholars, we do not wish to pathologize clients who come from different cultural backgrounds. Researchers need to understand what culturally acceptable behaviors entail when talking about social class and classism. We suggest mental health clinicians to engage in ongoing reflection practices about their own biases and assumptions with colleagues and supervisors to promote the best welfare of clients. We also need to provide relevant community resources that can help client connect with local organizations to further address their concerns outside of counseling.

Conclusion

Social class and classism have been challenging topics for clinicians and scholars to discuss in their professional work. In some cultures, as discussed in the chapter, social class is a taboo and disrespectful topic to bring up in daily conversations. Counselors and psychologists are often given the message to focus on clients' intersection of identities, such as race, gender, social-economic status, sexual orientation and so on, however, we seldom engage in dialogues to address our personal power and privilege, biases, and assumptions towards these social justice issues. It is more difficult to engage with clients in discussions of social class and classism if we do not feel comfortable sharing our own personal reactions, experiences, and perspectives with peers and colleagues. We may have explored social justice issues briefly in academic training, but it rarely allows trainees to reflect and confront their personal biases and assumptions in depth. As we have discussed in this chapter, it is crucial to explore social class and race together because resources and physical spaces are sometimes allocated unevenly across racial groups. To better address issues of class and classism, we suggest mental health practitioners equip awareness, knowledge, and skills to confront the system of oppression and advocate for racial minorities' needs.

References

Alim, H. S., Lee, J., and Carris, L. M. (2010) '"Short Fried-Rice-Eating Chinese MCs" and "Good-Hair-Havin Uncle Tom Niggas": Performing Race and Ethnicity in Freestyle Rap Battles', *Journal of Linguistic Anthropology*, 20(1): 116–133.

Allen, D. W. (2001) 'Social Class, Race, and Toxic Releases in American Counties, 1995', *The Social Science Journal*, 38(1): 13–25.

Allport, G. W. (1954) *The Nature of Prejudice*. Cambridge, MA: Addison-Wesley.

American Psychological Association. (2017) *Ethical Principles of Psychologists and Code of Conduct* (2002, Amended June 1, 2010, and January 1, 2017), Retrieved from www.apa.org/ethics/code/index.aspx.

Baum, A., Garofalo, J. P., and Yali, A. N. N. (1999) 'Socioeconomic Status and Chronic Stress: Does Stress Account for SES Effects on Health?', *Annals of the New York Academy of Sciences*, 896(1): 131–144.

Brewer, M. B. (1999) 'The Psychology of Prejudice: Ingroup Love or Outgroup Hate?', *Journal of Social Issues*, 55(3): 429–444.

Cialdini, R. B. and Richardson, K. D. (1980) 'Two Indirect Tactics of Image Management: Basking and Blasting', *Journal of Personality and Social Psychology*, 39: 406–415.

Collins, P. H. and Andersen, M. (2007) *Race, Class and Gender: An Anthology*. Belmont, CA: Wadsworth.

Connell, R. W. (1998) 'Masculinities and Globalization', *Men and Masculinities*, 1(1): 3–23.

Conrad, T. R. (1976) 'The Debate about Quota Systems: An Analysis', *American Journal of Political Science*, 20(1): 135–149.

Correll, J. and Park, B. (2005) 'A Model of the Ingroup as a Resource', *Personality and Social Psychology Review*, 9: 341–359.

Croizet, J. C. and Claire, T. (1998) 'Extending the Concept of Stereotype Threat to Social Class: The Intellectual Underperformance of Students from Low Socioeconomic Backgrounds', *Personality and Social Psychology Bulletin*, 24(6): 588–594.

Duncan, G. J. (1988) 'The Volatility of Family Income over the Life Course'. In P. Baltes and R. M. Lerner (Eds.), *Life Span Development and Behavior* (pp. 317–358). Hillsdale, NJ: Erlbaum.

Dy, M. B. (1994) *Values in Philippine Culture and Education*. Washington, DC: Office of Research and Publications and the Council for Research in Values and Philosophy.

Fordham, S. (2008) 'Beyond Capital High: On Dual Citizenship and the Strange Career of "Acting White"', *Anthropology and Education Quarterly*, 39(3): 227–246.

Fordham, S. and Ogbu, J. U. (1986) 'Black Students' School Success: Coping with the "Burden of Acting White"', *The Urban Review*, 18(3): 176–206.

Frank, B. (1987) 'Hegemonic Heterosexual Masculinity', *Studies in Political Economy*, 24(1): 159–170.

Kim, S. and Cardemil, E. (2012) 'Effective Psychotherapy with Low-Income Clients: The Importance of Attending to Social Class', *Journal of Contemporary Psychotherapy*, 42(1): 27–35.

Kohn, M. L. (1959) 'Social Class and Parental Values', *American Journal of Sociology*, 64(4): 337–351.

Kohn, M. L. (1963) 'Social Class and Parent-Child Relationships: An Interpretation', *American Journal of Sociology*, 68(4): 471–480.

Krieg, E. J. (2005) 'Race and Environmental Justice in Buffalo, NY: A ZIP Code and Historical Analysis of Ecological Hazards', *Society and Natural Resources*, 18(3): 199–213.

Liu, A. (2011) 'Unraveling the Myth of Meritocracy within the Context of US Higher Education', *Higher Education*, 62(4): 383–397.

Liu, W. M. (2002) 'The Social Class-Related Experiences of Men: Integrating Theory and Practice', *Professional Psychology: Research and Practice*, 33(4): 355–360.

Liu, W. M. (2013) 'The Oxford Handbook of Social Class in Counseling'. In W. M. Liu (Ed.), *Introduction to Social Class and Classism in Counseling Psychology* (pp. 3–20). New York: Oxford University Press.

Liu, W. M. and Ali, S. R. (2005) 'Addressing Social Class and Classism in Vocational Theory and Practice: Extending the Emancipatory Communitarian Approach', *The Counseling Psychologist*, 33(2): 189–196.

Liu, W. M. and Ali, S. R. (2008) 'Social Class and Classism: Understanding the Psychological Impact of Poverty and Inequality'. In S. D. Brown and R. W. Lent (Eds.), *Handbook of Counseling Psychology* (pp. 159–175). Hoboken, NJ: John C. Wiley.

Liu, W. M., Pickett, T., and Ivey, A. E. (2007) 'White Middle-Class Privilege: Social Class Bias and Implications for Training and Practice', *Journal of Multicultural Counseling and Development*, 35(4): 194–206.

Liu, W. M., Soleck, G., Hopps, J., Dunston, K., and Pickett, T. (2004) 'A New Framework to Understand Social Class in Counseling: The Social Class Worldview Model and Modern Classism Theory', *Journal of Multicultural Counseling and Development*, 32(2): 95–122.

Lott, B. (2002) 'Cognitive and Behavioral Distancing from the Poor', *American Psychologist*, 57: 100–110.

Miller, C. D. (2015) 'A Phenomenological Analysis of the Crabs in the Barrel Syndrome', *Academy of Management Proceedings*, 2015(1): 1.

Mina, M. O., Jr. (2015) 'Cultural Influences on Attitudes toward the Criminal Justice System: A Focus on the Filipino American Community', available from ProQuest Dissertations & Theses Global. Retrieved from http://proxy.lib.uiowa.edu/login?url=https://search proquest-com.proxy.lib.uiowa.edu/docview/1717322372?accountid=14663.

Pieterse, A. L., Evans, S. A., Risner-Butner, A., Collins, N. M., and Mason, L. B. (2009) 'Multicultural Competence and Social Justice Training in Counseling Psychology and Counselor Education: A Review and Analysis of a Sample of Multicultural Course Syllabi', *The Counseling Psychologist*, 37(1): 93–115.

Russell, G. (1996) 'Internalized Classism: The Role of Class in the Development of Self', *Women and Therapy*, 18(3–4): 59–71.

Sarangi, S. (2013) 'Capturing Indian 'Crab' Behaviour', *The Hindu*. Retrieved from www.thehindubusinessline.com/opinion/capturing-indian-crabbehaviour/article4570414.ece

Shanker, A. (1994) 'Where We Stand: The Crab Bucket Syndrome', *The New York Times*. Retrieved from http://source.nysut.org/weblink7/DocView.aspx?id=1012.

Smith, L. (2005) 'Psychotherapy, Classism, and the Poor: Conspicuous by Their Absence', *American Psychologist*, 60(7), 687.

Smith, L. (2008) 'Positioning Classism within Counseling Psychology's Social Justice Agenda', *The Counseling Psychologist*, 36(6): 895–924.

Smith, L. (2009) 'Enhancing Training and Practice in the Context of Poverty', *Training and Education in Professional Psychology*, 3(2): 84.

Smith, L., Foley, P. F., and Chaney, M. P. (2008) 'Addressing Classism, Ableism, and Heterosexism in Counselor Education', *Journal of Counseling and Development*, 86(3): 303–309.

Smith, L., Mao, S., Perkins, S., and Ampuero, M. (2011) 'The Relationship of Clients' Social Class to Early Therapeutic Impressions', *Counselling Psychology Quarterly*, 24(1): 15–27.

Smitherman, G. (2000) *Talking That Talk: Language, Culture, and Education in African America*. New York: Routledge.

Sweetman, C. (1997) *Men and Masculinity*. Oxford: Oxfam.

Triandis, H. C., Leung, K., Villareal, M. J., and Clack, F. I. (1985) 'Allocentric versus Idiocentric Tendencies: Convergent and Discriminant Validation', *Journal of Research in Personality*, 19(4): 395–415.

Urrieta Jr, L. (2005) '"Playing the Game" Versus "Selling Out": Chicanas and Chicanos Relationship to Whitestream Schools'. In B. K. Alexander, G. L. Anderson and B. P. Gallegos (Eds.), *Performance Theories in Education: Power, Pedagogy, and the Politics of Identity* (pp. 173–196). New York: Routledge.

Welch, O. M., Hodges, C., and Warden, K. (1989) 'Developing the Scholar's Ethos in Minority High School Students: The Vital Link to Academic Achievement', *Urban Education*, 24(1): 59–76.

14

CULTURE AND DISABILITY IN MENTAL HEALTH

Fabricio E. Balcazar, Kristine M. Molina and Nev Jones

There has been a limited amount of research on the topic of disability culture as it relates to mental health areas including counseling, psychotherapy, and psychology. This has been due in part to a lack of awareness among clinicians about the way in which many individuals with disabilities identify themselves as having their own cultural identity. Culture implies an integrated and complex pattern of human behavior that includes thoughts, communications, actions, customs, beliefs, values, and institutions of a given racial, ethnic, religious, or social group. In fact, the degree of complexity of every culture has implications for the classification and treatment of mental health. The U.S. Department of Health and Human Services (U.S. DHHS 2001) supplemental report on Mental Health, Culture, Race and Ethnicity documented the existence of striking disparities for minorities in mental health services and the underlying knowledge base. One of the main conclusions of this report was that "racial and ethnic minorities bear a greater burden from unmet mental health needs and thus suffer a greater loss to their overall health and productivity" (U.S. DHHS 2001: 3). Indeed, these issues still remain today (Alegría et al. 2018). Given that many minority individuals are poor, a factor to consider is that lower socioeconomic status – in terms of income, education, and occupation – has been strongly linked to the development of psychiatric disabilities (Regier et al. 1993). The authors found that people in the lowest socioeconomic strata are about two and a half times more likely than those in the highest strata to have a mental disorder. However, vulnerability alone may not be sufficient to cause a mental disorder; rather, the causes of most mental disorders lie in some combination of genetic and environmental factors, which may be biological or psychosocial.

All people are shaped by culture, and usually by more than one culture. The phrase "cultural identity" refers to the culture with which someone identifies and to which he or she looks for standards of behavior (Cooper and Denner 1998). A key aspect of any culture is that it is dynamic—culture continually changes and is influenced both by people's beliefs and the demands of their environment (Lopez and Guarnaccia 2000). Ward (2001) defined the term "acculturation" as the socialization process by which minority groups gradually learn and adopt selective elements of the dominant culture. Ward explains that at the individual level, the process of acculturation refers to the socialization process by which foreign-born individuals adopt the values, customs, norms, attitudes, and behaviors of the host culture. Yet that dominant culture is itself transformed by its interaction with racial and ethnic minority groups; and to make matters more complex, the immigrant group may form its own syncretic culture, distinct from both its country of origin and the dominant culture; so a culture is not homogeneous but fluid and there are enormous variations within a given culture. These variations are influenced by multiple factors, including racial and ethnic groups, socio economic status, levels of education, disability, and experiences of oppression, among others.

With regards to the definition of disability, Braddock and Parish (2001: 11) proposed that "throughout Western history, disability has existed at the intersection between the particular demands of a given impairment, society's interpretation of that impairment, and the larger political and economic context of disability." The World Health Organization (1980) defined impairment as any loss or abnormality of psychological, physiological, or anatomical structure or function. However, the difference between disability and impairment has become a central point of divergence between what is now known as the medical model and the social model of disability. Disability scholars favor the social model of disability, which characterizes disability as "a product of the interaction between the individual and the environment" (Hahn 1993: 41). According to this framework, the disabling experience is related to the degree of functioning of individuals in their particular environments. Disability-related challenges are seen primarily as a product of limiting environments and negative societal attitudes (Gill 2001). From this perspective, individuals with disabilities need enabling and accessible environments that provide them with the resources and opportunities for full participation in everyday life activities and achievement of personal goals (Albrecht 2007). Balcazar and Suarez-Balcazar (2017) concluded that the capacity of the individual with a disability to fully participate in the community and be integrated into the fabric of society is a reflection of the environment's accessibility and the supports available for him/her to function and perform effectively, rather than his/her individual 'deficits'. One example refers to the way in which we speak about people with disabilities. For instance, People with Disability Australia (nd) suggest that a person isn't defined by their disability – they are a person before anything else, therefor they advise to put the person first. However, in England, many scholars and activists often refer to 'disabled people' in the way they talk, which illustrates the lack of consensus in the field. As mentioned, there is limited research in the psychology and mental health literature on the experiences of people with disabilities with regards to their cultural identity and the social model of disability. In this chapter we are going to examine in some detail the interaction between the constructs of culture, disability, and mental health.

Diagnosing mental health

Mulvany (2000) pointed out that the social model of disability demands an identification and analysis of the social, political and economic conditions that restrict the life opportunities of those experiencing impairment. Central to this work is a focus on the rights of people with disabilities and the consequences of the development of a collective identity for social action and social change. The application of the social model of disability to the study of mental health helps focus research and theoretical developments towards an analysis of the complexity and multiplicity of social restrictions faced by people diagnosed as mentally ill, and the social disadvantages and oppression they face. Proponents of the social model like Shakespeare and Watson (2001) warned about the potential ascendancy of the medical model, with its focus on blaming the victim, which could lead to the dissipation of the disability political movement. On the other hand, theorist like Barton (1993) and Lloyd (1992), contend that the conceptualization of disability often ignores differences that exist between people with disabilities based on class, gender, race and ethnicity, sexual orientation and age among other factors. In addition, Crow (1996) and Hughes and Paterson (1997) are concerned about ensuring that the social model incorporates an analysis of impairment. They argue that to ignore impairment is to ignore the 'reality' of the lived experiences of people with disabilities.

The diagnosis of a mental disorder is arguably more difficult than diagnoses in other areas of medicine and health because there are usually no definitive lesions (pathological abnormalities) or laboratory tests. Rather, a diagnosis depends on a pattern, or clustering of symptoms (i.e., subjective complaints), observable signs, and behaviors associated with distress or disability. In fact, diagnostic assessment can be especially challenging when a clinician from one ethnic or cultural group uses the fifth edition of the *Diagnostic and Statistical Manual on Mental Disorders Classification* (*DMS-5*) to evaluate an individual from a different ethnic or cultural group. As Aggarwal et al. (2013) pointed out, a clinician who is unfamiliar with the nuances of an individual's cultural frame of reference may incorrectly judge as psychopathology normal variations in behavior, beliefs, or experience that are particular to the individual's culture. This suggests that there is a clear need for mental health professionals to become familiar with their patients' cultural background and the cultural interpretations of disability. Here is a case that exemplifies some of the consequences of being diagnosed among minority individuals:

> A young Latino man, experiencing bipolar mania for the first time, walks into a department store and, believing he is God, attempts to leave with a high dollar cell phone without paying. Store clerks call 911 and he is arrested; while the judge considers his psychiatric condition a mitigating circumstance, he is nevertheless charged with a felony. Subsequently, he experiences tremendous difficulty getting a job, and when asked to explain his felony, he is not sure whether including an explanation of his psychiatry disability will make things better or worse. His ethnic identity exacerbates the tendency of potential employers to assume to worst.

In an effort to improve diagnosis and care to people of all backgrounds, the *DSM-5* (American Psychiatric Association [APA] 2013a) incorporated greater cultural sensitivity throughout its educational resources manual (APA 2013b). Different cultures and communities exhibit or explain symptoms in various ways. Because of this, it is important for clinicians to be aware of relevant contextual information stemming from a patient's culture, race, ethnicity, religion or geographical origin. The APA (2013b) produced a cultural formulation interview guide to help clinicians assess cultural factors influencing patients' perspectives of their symptoms and treatment options. It includes questions about patients' background in terms of their culture, race, ethnicity, religion or geographical origin. The interview provides an opportunity for individuals to define their distress in their own words and then relate this to how others, who may not share their culture, see their problems. This gives the clinician a more comprehensive foundation on which to base both diagnosis and care (APA 2013b). According to the APA (2013b) guidelines, areas to be addressed include examining the cultural definition of the problem; the cultural perceptions of cause, context and support; the cultural factors affecting self-coping and past help seeking; and the cultural factors affecting current help seeking. The guidelines also suggest that the evaluator should address possible barriers to care or concerns about the clinic and the clinician–patient relationship raised during the interview. This strategy should also consider efforts to identify the individual's sense of empowerment and his/her degree of understanding of disability rights. The following section examines some critical elements of the construct of disability culture and its intersectionality with the construct of mental health, including some of the experiences of exclusion of people with disabilities that have contributed to its development.

Intersectionality of disability culture and mental health

The construct of disability culture assumes a sense of common identity and interests that unite people with disabilities and separate them from people without disabilities. The potential for developing disability consciousness varies across individuals and is usually enhanced when people share their experiences of social exclusion. Disability culture often rejects the notion of impairment/difference as a symbol of shame or self-pity and emphasizes instead solidarity and positive identification. Brown (1996: 1) argues that "people with disabilities have forged a group identity and we share a common history of oppression and a common bond of resilience; but most importantly, we are proud of ourselves as people with disabilities."

However, moving from an impairment-based self-perception to a disability identity is not necessarily one-directional or even shared by all individuals with disabilities. One important aspect of this process is whether the disability community is based on those who share a range of impairments or is restricted to a particular impairment like deafness or blindness. This often becomes the basis for differentiating a general disability culture from disability subcultures that function among specific groups of people with disabilities. The fact is that disability culture has been built as part of a political struggle to promote people with disabilities' independence and self-reliance, yet every person has multiple dimensions which influence his/her identity.

The construct of intersectionality has been suggested to address this reality in a more accurate way. For example, Warner and Brown (2011) examined racial/ethnic/gender differences in intra-individual change in functional limitations (disability) among White, Black and Mexican American men and women, and the extent to which differences in life-course account for group disparities in initial health status and rates of change with age. The authors reviewed data from a nationally representative sample (1994–2006) in the U.S. Health and Retirement Study. Their results support an intersectionality approach, with all demographic groups exhibiting worse functional limitation trajectories than White men. Whereas White men had the lowest disability levels at baseline, White women and racial/ethnic minority men had intermediate disability levels and Black and Hispanic Women had the highest disability levels. These health disparities remained stable with age – except among Black women who experience a trajectory of accelerated disablement. These findings highlight the utility of an intersectionality approach to understanding health disparities. On the other hand, many service providers encounter challenges when dealing with individuals with multiple identities that could lead to discrimination. Here is a case example:

> An African American woman in her mid-40s suddenly collapses and her family rushes her to the nearest ER. An ER nurse searches her purse and finds antipsychotic medication. In fact, the woman has had a stroke but when she awakens, disoriented, they assume that she is experiencing a psychiatric relapse and because no psychiatric beds are available, they put her in restraints. The truth of the situation is not learned for another 6 hours. She strongly suspects that both the presence of antipsychotics and her race contributed to the way she was miss-treated. Subsequently, she is afraid to return to an ER for physical health emergencies.

Roberts and Jesudason (2013) concluded that intersectional analysis does not apply only to the ways in which identity categories or systems of power intersect in individuals' lives. Nor must an intersectional approach focus solely on differences within or between identity-based groups. It can also be a powerful tool to build more effective alliances between movements to make them more effective at organizing for social change. Therefore, the intersectional construct may be a way to better represent the diversity of experiences and circumstances of people with disabilities. In the case of individuals with mental health symptoms, the interaction of minority status and poverty makes it more difficult for these individuals to access appropriate treatments and supports. The following section examines in more detail instances of exclusion that many individuals with mental health experience and then we discuss the strategies that they are using to cope with these challenges.

Exclusion

Historically, mental illness has been a source of fear and misunderstanding in many cultures. For example, Corrigan et al. (2004) conducted a survey analysis of several English-speaking newspapers (from Canada, Britain and the United States) and found that news stories frequently frame mental illness in a stigmatizing manner. Most articles discuss people with mental illness in terms of dangerousness or violent criminals. They point out that notably absent are positive stories that highlight the recovery of many persons with even the most serious mental illnesses.

Sue (2010) argued that members of any marginalized group can easily become targets of micro-aggression which are often tacit, unintentional manifestations of subtle exclusion or marginalization. Given this definition, people diagnosed with mental illnesses would qualify as a socially marginalized group. Gonzales et al. (2015) conducted a series of focus groups with adult mental health consumers and college students with a mental illness diagnosis in order to explore their experiences with micro-aggression. They found several themes: *invalidation* (no matter what you do or how you feel, people are going to either minimize your problems, symptomatize your behavior or become patronizing); *assumption of inferiority* (you are assumed to have lower intelligence, being incompetent, or not having agency to function independently); *fear of mental illness* (being dangerous, unpredictable and placing others at risk of "contamination"); *shaming of mental illness* (it is better not to disclose it); and *becoming* a *second-class citizen* (lack of control over your own treatment and recovery). Participants indicated that the perpetrators of micro-aggressions were most commonly identified as being close friends, family members, and authority figures. Importantly, participants reported experiencing more overt discrimination experiences than subtle micro-aggression experiences and reported negative outcomes related to micro-aggression experiences such as isolation, negative emotions, and treatment non-adherence. Here is an example:

> People in my family, if I actually start being happy, they're like "Are you sure you're okay? You look happy today." It's like I'm allowed to be happy sometimes. Or if I do a lot of activities or if I stay up late, I'll have people call me up and say "Maybe you're manic, you stayed up really late. You've done a lot more things than you usually do."
> *(cited by Gonzales et al. 2015: 4)*

Disability culture has been built to a great extent as a response to the multiple forms of exclusion experienced by individuals with disabilities. Ravaud and Stiker (2001) described several types of exclusionary practices. Here are some of the most relevant experiences reported by individuals with psychiatric disabilities:

Exclusion through elimination. This is of course, the most extreme form of social exclusion and it has played a role in discussions about quality of life and the price of human life. The argument is that life under certain conditions in not worth living, which then justifies a number of medical practices like eugenics, sterilization of mentally disabled women, selective abortion on the basis of genetic screening, and more recently euthanasia and assisted suicide. Another manifestation of structural 'elimination' that should be mentioned is the high risk of premature death that people with mental illness in the United States, and in particular low-income African Americans and Latinos – experience at the hands of police officers who are often poorly trained to deal with individuals who are experiencing a crisis. 'Suicide by cop' (SbC) is a phenomenon of importance to understanding death among persons with psychiatric disabilities. In fact, Hutson et al. (1998) found that this type of events accounted for 11 percent of all officer-involved shootings in a large metropolitan law enforcement agency. More recently, Dewey et al. (2013) added that reducing fragmentation between law enforcement and mental health service providers might be a crucial goal for suicide intervention and prevention, at least among cases of SbC. In another study, Lamb et al. (2002) concluded that there is a need for police officers to have training in recognizing mental illness and knowing how to access mental health resources. Collaboration between the law enforcement and mental health systems is crucial, and the very different areas of expertise of each should be recognized and should not be confused.

Exclusion through social abandonment. This practice often takes place as children and people with disabilities are left in the hands of a state agency, hospital or institution by their families or caretakers. Isaac and Armat (1990) pointed out that a short walk through any American community today reveals the utter failure of de-institutionalization policies: our sidewalks and parks have become open-air mental wards – but without treatment for their inmates. It is too easy to call this population "homeless" for the hard truth is that affordable housing, even if available, does not treat mental illness. Finally, for both homeless individuals and those with psychiatric disabilities more broadly, the criminal justice system in many large cities has become the largest "system of care" for the treatment of severe mental illnesses in the United States, which in effect is not prepared or designed to do (Raphael and Stoll 2013; Al-Rousan et al. 2017).

Exclusion through segregation. Throughout history, segregation has been one of the most widespread forms of exclusion experienced by individuals with disabilities and those with mental illness have experienced it to a great extent. Even today, institutions continue to exclude people with disabilities from the mainstream of society and reinforce negative stereotypes of dependency and hopelessness. Exclusion through abandonment and segregation highlight the paradox that people with mental illness experience: on the one hand, they want to leave institutions that are oppressive and de-humanizing, and, on the other hand, they should not be abandoned in the streets without access to treatment or services. Indeed, research suggests that even when housed in the community, persons with psychiatric disabilities continue to experience de-facto segregation in low-income service ghettoes (Metraux et al. 2007).

Exclusion through discrimination. To discriminate is to single out, to place a social group to one side and restrict its rights. In modern societies, the principle of equality of citizens before the law is the moral ideal of a democratic nation. This includes the right to receive identical treatment, the right to equal access, the right to equal opportunities, and the right to an identical quality of life for all citizens. The exclusion in this context refers to the various ways in which individuals with impairments are not able to achieve their rights. Indeed, there are significant differences from country to country and even from the places in which people with disabilities live. All these negative experiences of people with a mental health diagnosis have led to their efforts to organize and become more active in defending their rights and advocating for change. Some of these efforts are summarized in the next section.

Coping strategies

Many professionals in the field of mental health service delivery perceive engagement in disability organizations and advocacy as acts of resistance against their treatments and interventions.

Professionals are often concerned about treatment compliance and do not want to see their patients challenge their expertise. People with mental illness founded the *"mental patients' liberation movement"* in the 1970s because they felt rejected and stigmatized by society and robbed of decisions regarding their own treatment and normal lives. This has been and continues to be an ongoing argument in the field of mental health. Stroman (2003) pointed out that the early movement was militant – typically against laws favoring involuntary commitment, against the use of electro-convulsive and antipsychotic medication treatments, and against coercive psychiatry. Members were survivors or ex-patients of the system, who organized in homes and churches to help others locate community-based services, advocate for self-determination, access services and try to reform oppressive and ineffective systems (Frese 1998).

Among the main goals shared by much of the individuals in the consumer movement are to overcome stigma and prevent discrimination in policies affecting persons with mental illness; to encourage self-help and a focus on recovery from mental illness; and to draw attention to the distinct needs associated with a particular disorder or disability, as well as the age, gender or racial and cultural identity of those who have mental illness. In the past several decades, as Stroman (2003) pointed out, the consumer movement has expanded and diversified, with some groups and networks choosing to align with the public mental health system and work for change from within (e.g. through the integration of peer support staff and recovery-oriented principles), while others focus on particular intersections (for example, Youth-MOVE, a large national network focused on systems-involved youth with mental health), and groups focused on mental diversity and/or "mad pride" (for example, the Icarus Project or the International Hearing Voices Movement).

Fisher and Shapiro (2010) argued that recovery, wellness, and complete community reintegration are attainable goals for persons labeled with mental illness through advocacy training programs designed and carried out by peers/consumers/survivors. These authors point out that this process reflects a paradigm shift that emerged through self-help groups where individuals labeled with mental illness move away *"from considering ourselves the objects of neuro-chemical forces to being empowered agents who are finding the freedom to begin to creatively and effectively run our own lives"* (Fisher and Shapiro 2010: 214). Fisher and Shapiro describe an advocacy training developed by the National Empowerment Center that utilizes the following principles: develop personal connections; work with passion; learn the principles of recovery; develop a positive view of the future; have a clear purpose; be persistent and be patient; and have a well developed advocacy plan, among others. The other components that have also played a central role in the development of the consumer movement around the world are self-determination and peer support.

The construct of *self-determination* refers to people with disabilities controlling their own lives to achieve self-defined goals and participate fully in society. Cook and Jonikas (2002) added that self-determination encompasses concepts that are central to existence in a democratic society, including freedom of choice, civil rights, independence, and self-direction. Copeland (2003) listed a number of values and ethics that support self-determination and recovery from a consumer's perspective. Some of the most relevant include: treating each other as equals, with dignity, compassion, mutual respect and high regard; unconditional acceptance of each person as they are, unique, special individuals, including acceptance of diversity; avoidance of judgments, predictions, put downs, labels, blaming and shaming; validation of personal experiences; each person being recognized as the expert on him/herself and having a sense of their own personal value; and concentrating on the strengths of each person and away from perceived deficits.

Copeland (2003) argues that only with these values and ethics, we can overcome the powerlessness, fear, insecurity, sadness, isolation, worry and low self-esteem, as well as the internalized discrimination, prejudice, and/or stigma which so easily become the trademark for those of us who experience these difficult symptoms. On the other hand, Cook and Jonikas (2002) pointed out that many individuals with psychiatric disabilities have not experienced the levels of self-determination achieved by many other disability groups. Their lives in unwelcoming or unsafe neighborhoods are often difficult, stressful, and unrewarding to the extent that their lifestyles could be as disabling as their mental illnesses. Clearly, it seems that context continues to play a critical role in the way individuals cope with their disability and that context is even more critical for minority individuals who live in low-income communities.

The other coping mechanism that has been extensively studied is *peer support*. Peer support services are an evidence-based mental health model of care that consists of a qualified peer support provider who assists individuals with their recovery from mental illness and substance use disorders (Center for Medicare and Medicaid Services, 2007). As Jones (2015) emphasizes, as individuals, peers stand to benefit from greater participation (across domains) through a heightened sense of personal empowerment and self-efficacy and the development of concrete skills and work or volunteer experience. Here is how a person characterized her experience with peer support:

> Those of us who experience psychiatric symptoms were told that we should not associate with others who experience similar symptoms. Now we know that others who have experienced psychiatric symptoms can often be the best of supporters. We can understand each other and support each other in ways that are really helpful. We can "be" with our discomfort rather than needing to "fix" it immediately, and support each other through recovery. We can challenge each other to take risks and create change that would be difficult to accomplish alone.
>
> *(Copeland 2003: 73)*

From a more interpersonal perspective, the peer-to-peer relationships have been widely understood to exemplify the so-called helper-helpee principle, which holds that both helpers and helpees (roles which often alternate over time) reciprocally benefit from the helping (Repper and Carter 2011). According to Solomon (2004), individuals are likely to benefit from access to peer mentors – i.e., individuals with similar struggles but who are further along the path to recovery who can serve as guides or models of what might be possible in the future (a process known as "upward social comparisons"). Importantly, the benefits of peer "mentors" hold not just for direct clinical services, but for peers occupying any number of different roles with whom newer clients might come into contact. Strong peer involvement in general (and, specifically, in outreach efforts) is also likely to increase the engagement of both current and prospective clients (Davidson et al. 2012). Peer-led groups or programs may provide additional incentives to attend appointments, for instance, or help prospective clients feel more comfortable about seeking services (Jones et al. 2013).

Future directions

People diagnosed/labeled with a mental health disability experience many challenges in their lives, and yet many of them are making significant improvements in many areas. The focus on disability culture suggests that further attention should be placed in examining contextual and systemic barriers and how those barriers could be reduced or eliminated. Some researchers (Simpson and Thomas 2015) are urging clinicians to consider the social context in which people with mental illness function and take more efforts to understand that distress should not just include individual factors but also incorporate the psychological impact of stresses caused by societal barriers preventing inclusion. The prevalence of homelessness among individuals with mental illness in the United States represents both a systemic failure and a challenge. There are many local efforts that try to address this issue with housing options. One such effort is Oxford House (see Jason and Ferrari 2010), which involves rented homes managed by previously homeless individuals with drug addiction and community reentry challenges. These are self-run dwellings where participants find jobs, pay the utility bills, and learn to be responsible citizens. The individuals receive stable housing without any limits on the length of stay, a network of job opportunities, and peer support for abstinence. Future research could examine what other housing models appear to be effective and how can those models be replicated and disseminated.

The issue of availability of appropriate mental health services and supports involves the development of advocacy efforts at the local and state levels. Budgetary constraints are often cited as main reasons for the failure to provide such services. This is an area that requires the involvement of consumers themselves in advocating for their needed services and supports. Important progress has been made in this area (see Fisher and Shapiro 2010), yet the need for wider consumer involvement and dissemination of advocacy training persist. Future research could continue to examine effective strategies for promoting consumer engagement and self-advocacy, particularly among individuals recently diagnosed who have no experience or understanding of the systemic barriers they are about to face.

With regards to the issues of intersectionality, Alegría et al. (2008) developed an intervention designed to train Latino individuals with mental health diagnoses to identify and make questions to providers that would help them understand their role during treatment, the process for decision making and the reasons for those decision, and become empowered to take charge of their care. The results suggested the intervention potential to increase patient activation, retention, and attendance to mental health services. Finding ways to increase the effectives in which individuals with mental health issues engage the system should continue to be pursued in future research. Finally, efforts to educate the public should remain a priority, given the persistence of negative attitudes and perceptions towards individuals with mental illness. New interventions perhaps with social media as a way to reach out younger generations may be called for.

Conclusion

The culture of the consumer of mental health services influences many aspects of mental health treatment, perceptions of mental illness, and patterns of health care utilization (Alegría et al. 2018). We are calling attention to the construct of disability culture as an additional factor that can play an important role in the way individuals with mental illness engage the health care system. Mental health professionals and practitioners could benefit from developing a clearer understanding of the role that disability culture can play in the process of empowering consumers of mental health services. The implications are similar to those pursued by Alegría et al. (2008) designed to empower consumers to advocate for their rights and remain engaged in their treatment.

The intersectionality of factors like race, social class, and gender were examined here, although we recognize that additional factors like age, sexual orientation and even religious affiliation can also play an important role in mental health access and the quality of the services received. Culture reflects the beliefs and attitudes of members of a given group or society. Regarding the perceptions of individuals with mental health symptoms, our societies have still a long way to go in efforts to develop more positive perceptions and attitudes towards those individuals. We have to start early and educate children to understand disability, its causes and most

Culture and Disability in Mental Health

importantly the potential of individuals who experience it to become contributing members of the communities in which the live. The task for researchers is to seek and promote interventions that contribute to the enhancement of consumer empowerment and the education of the general public, so individuals with disabilities can pursue their dreams and aspirations like any individual in the society.

References

Aggarwal, N. K., Nicasio, A. V., DeSilva, R., and Lewis-Fernandez, R. L. (2013) 'Barriers to implementing the DSM-5 Cultural Formulation Interview: A qualitative study', *Culture, Medicine, and Psychiatry*, *37*(3): 505–533.

Albrecht, G. (2007) 'Disability values, representations and realities'. In P. Devlieger, F. Rusch, and D. Pfeiffer (Eds.), *Rethinking Disability* (pp. 27–43). Antwerp: Garant Publishers.

Alegría, M., Nakash, O., and NeMoyer, A. (2018) 'Increasing equity in access to mental health care: A critical first step to improving service quality', *World Psychiatry*, *17*(1): 43–44.

Alegría, M., Polo, A., Gao, S., Santana, L., Rothstein, D., Jimenez, A., Hunter, M. L., Mendieta, F., Oddo, V., and Normand, S. L., (2008) 'Evaluation of a patient activation and empowerment intervention in mental health care', *Medical Care*, *46*(3): 247–256.

Al-Rousan, T., Rubenstein, L., Sieleni, B., Deol, H., and Wallace, R. B. (2017) 'Inside the nation's largest mental health institution: A prevalence study in a state prison system', *BMC Public Health*, *17*(1): 342–358.

American Psychiatric Association (2013a) *Diagnostic and Statistical Manual of Mental Disorders*, 5th edition. Arlington, VA: American Psychiatric Publishing.

American Psychiatric Association (2013b) *Educational resources: DSM–5 Fact Sheets, Cultural concepts – Cultural Formulation Interview*. Retrieved from: www.psychiatry.org/psychiatrists/practice/dsm/educational-resources/dsm-5-fact-sheets.

Balcazar, F. E. and Suarez-Balcazar, Y. (2017) 'Promoting empowerment among individuals with disabilities'. In M. A. Bond, C. B. Keys, and I. Serrano-García (Eds.), *Handbook of Community Psychology* (Vol. 2, pp. 571–585). Washington, DC: American Psychological Association.

Barton, L. (1993) 'The struggle for citizenship: the case of disabled people', *Disability, Handicap and Society*, *8*(3): 235–248.

Braddock, D. L. and Parish, S. L. (2001) 'An institutional history of disability'. In G. L. Albrecht, K. D. Seelman and M. Bury (Eds.), *Handbook of Disabilities Studies* (pp. 11–68). Thousand Oaks, CA: Sage Publications.

Brown, S. E. (1996) *Disability Culture: A Fact Sheet*. Las Cruces, NM: Institute on Disability Culture. Retrieved from: www.independentliving.org/docs3/brown96a.html.

Center for Medicare and Medicaid Services (2007) *Dear state Medicaid director letter*. Retrieved from http://downloads.cms.gov/cmsgov/archived-downloads/SMDL/downloads/ SMD081507A.pdf.

Cook, J. A. and Jonikas, J. A. (2002) 'Self-determination among mental health consumers/survivors: Using lessons from the past to guide the future', *Journal of Disability Policy Studies*, *13*(2): 88–96.

Cooper, C. R. and Denner, J. (1998) 'Theories linking culture and psychopathology: Universal and community-specific processes', *Annual Review of Psychology*, *49*: 559–584.

Copeland, M. E. (2003) *Self-determination in mental health recovery: Taking back our lives*. University of Illinois at Chicago, NRTC National Self-Determination and Psychiatric Disability Conference Papers. Retrieved from www.cmhsrp.uic.edu/download/sdconfdoc06.pdf.

Corrigan, P. W., Markowitz, F. E., and Watson, M. C. (2004) 'Structural levels of mental illness stigma and discrimination', *Schizophrenia Bulletin*, *30*(3): 481–491.

Crow, L. (1996) 'Including all of our lives: Renewing the social model of disability'. In C. Barnes and G. Mercer (Eds.), *Exploring the divide: Illness and disability* (pp. 55–72). Leeds: The Disability Press.

Davidson, L., Bellamy, C., Guy, K., and Miller, R. (2012) 'Peer support among persons with severe mental illnesses: A review of evidence and experience', *World Psychiatry*, *11*(2): 123–128.

Dewey, L., Allwood, M., Fava, J., Arias, E., Pinizotto, A., and Schlesinger, L. (2013) 'Suicide by cop: Clinical risks and subtypes', *Archives of Suicide Research*, *17*: 448–461.

Fisher, D. and Shapiro, L. (2010) 'Finding and using our voice: How consumer/survivor advocacy is transforming mental health care'. In L. D. Brown and S. Wituk (Eds.), *Mental Health Self-help* (pp 213–233). New York: Springer Science + Business Media.

Frese, F. J. (1998) 'Advocacy, recovery and the challenges of consumerism for schizophrenia', *Psychiatric Clinics of North America, 21*: 233–249.

Gill, C. J. (2001) 'Divided understanding: The social experience of disability'. In G. L. Albrecht, K. D. Seelman and M. Bury (Eds.), *Handbook of Disability Studies* (pp. 351–372). Thousand Oaks, CA: Sage Publication.

Gonzales, L., Davidoff, K. C., Nadal, K. L., and Yanos, P.T. (2015) 'Microaggressions experienced by persons with mental illnesses: An exploratory study', *Psychiatric Rehabilitation Journal, 38*(3): 234–241.

Hahn, H. (1993) 'The political implications of disability definitions and data', *Journal of Disability Policy Studies, 4*(2): 41–52.

Hughes, B. and Patterson, K. (1997) 'The social model of disability and the disappearing body: Towards a sociology of impairment', *Disability and Society, 12*(3): 325–340.

Hutson, H. R., Anglin, D., Yarbrough, J., Hardaway, K., Russell, M., Strote, J., Canter, M., and Blum, B. (1998) 'Suicide by cop', *Annals of Emergency Medicine, 32*(6): 665–669.

Isaac, R. J. and Armat, V. C. (1990) *Madness in the Streets: How Psychiatry and the Law Abandoned the Mentally Ill.* New York: Free Press.

Jason, L. A. and Ferrari, J. R. (2010) 'Oxford house recovery homes: Characteristics and effectiveness', *Psychological Services, 7*(2): 92–102.

Jones, N. (2015) *Peer involvement and leadership in early intervention in psychosis services: From planning to peer support and evaluation.* Technical Assistance Material Developed for SAMHSA/CMHS. Reference: HHSS283201200002I/Task Order No. HHSS28342002T.

Jones, N., Corrigan, P. W., James, D., Parker, J., and Larson, N. (2013) 'Peer support, self-determination, and treatment engagement: A qualitative investigation', *Psychiatric Rehabilitation Journal, 36*(3): 209–214.

Lamb, H. R., Weimberger, L. E., and DeCuir, W. J. (2002) 'The police and mental health', *Psychiatric Services, 53*(10): 1266–1271.

Lloyd, M. (1992) 'Does she boil eggs? Towards a feminist model of disability', *Disability, Handicap, and Society, 7*(3): 207–221.

Lopez, S. R. and Guarnaccia, P. J. (2000) 'Cultural psychopathology: Uncovering the social world of mental illness'. *Annual Review of Psychology, 51*: 571–598.

Metraux, S., Caplan, J. M., Klugman, D., and Hadley, T. R. (2007) 'Assessing residential segregation among Medicaid recipients with psychiatric disability in Philadelphia', *Journal of Community Psychology, 35*(2): 239–255.

Mulvany, J. (2000) 'Disability, impartment or illness? The relevance of the social model of disability to the study of mental disorder', *Sociology of Health and Illness, 22*(5): 582–601.

People with Disability Australia (nd). *A Guide to Reporting on Disability.* Retrieved from: http://pwd.org.au/library/guide-to-reporting-disability.html.

Raphael, S. and Stoll, M. A. (2013) 'Assessing the contribution of the deinstitutionalization of the mentally ill to growth in the US incarceration rate', *The Journal of Legal Studies, 42*(1): 187–222.

Ravaud, J. F. and Stiker, H. J. (2001) 'Inclusion/exclusion: An analysis of historical and cultural meanings'. In G. L. Albrecht, K. D. Seelman and M. Bury (Eds.), *Handbook of Disability Studies* (pp. 490–514). Thousand Oaks, CA: Sage Publications.

Regier, D. A., Narrow, W. E., Rae, D. S., Manderscheid, R. W., Locke, B. Z., and Goodwin, F. K. (1993) 'The de facto US mental and addictive disorders service system: Epidemiologic Catchment Area prospective 1-year prevalence rates of disorders and services', *Archives of General Psychiatry, 50*: 85–94.

Repper, J. and Carter, T. (2011) 'A review of the literature on peer support in mental health services', *Journal of Mental Health, 20*(4): 392–411.

Roberts, D. and Jesudason, S. (2013) 'Movement intersectionality: The case of race, gender, disability, and genetic technologies', *Du Bois Review, 10*(2): 313–328.

Shakespeare, T. and Watson, N. (2001) 'The social model of disability: An outdated ideology?'. In S. N. Barnarrt and B. M. Altman (Eds.), *Exploring Theories and Expanding Methodologies: Where are We and Where do We Need to Go? Research in Social Science and Disability* (Vol. 2, pp. 9–28). Amsterdam: JAI.

Simpson, J. and Thomas, C. (2015) 'Clinical psychology and disability studies: bridging the disciplinary divide on mental health and disability', *Disability and Rehabilitation, 37*(14): 1299–1304.

Solomon, P. (2004) 'Peer support/peer provided services underlying processes, benefits, and critical ingredients', *Psychiatric Rehabilitation Journal, 27*(4), 392–401.

Stroman, D. F. (2003) *The Disability Rights Movement: From Deinstitutionalization to Self-determination.* Lanham, MD: University Press of America.

Sue, D. W. (2010) 'Microaggressions, marginality, and oppression: An introduction'. In D. Sue (Ed.), *Microaggressions and Marginality: Manifestation, Dynamics, and Impact* (pp. 3–25). Hoboken, NJ: Wiley.

U.S. Department of Health and Human Services (2001) *Mental Health: Culture, Race, and Ethnicity – A Supplement to Mental Health: A Report of the Surgeon General*. Rockville, MD:

Ward, C. (2001) 'The A, B, Cs of acculturation'. In D. Matsumoto (Ed.), *The Handbook of Culture and Psychology* (pp. 411–445). Oxford: Oxford University Press.

Warner, D. F. and Brown, T. H. (2011) 'Understanding how race/ethnicity and gender define age-trajectories of disability: An intersectionality approach', *Social Science and Medicine*, 72(8): 1236–1248.

World Health Organization (1980) *International Classification of Impairments, Disabilities and Handicaps*. Geneva: WHO. Retrieved from http://whqlibdoc.who.int/publications/1980/9241541261_eng.pdf.

15

CULTURE AND SEXUAL ORIENTATION IN MENTAL HEALTH

Joanna Semlyen and Sonja Ellis

Mental health continues to be a significant public health concern. Recent considerations focus on social stress as an important factor in determining mental health outcomes. In particular, social stigma in relation to sexual orientation (e.g. homophobia; victimization; discrimination) has been identified as placing lesbian, gay, and bisexual (LGB) persons at risk of psychological distress (Hatzenbuehler 2009). While much psychological work has focused on mental health in LGB persons, limited attention has been paid to the interface between race/ethnicity/culture and mental health in this particular subgroup of the LGB community. The context of the chapter's consideration of minority sexuality and minority racial/ethnic population forms part of a wider, broader, intersectional context recognising the cumulative aspects of multiple minority identities throughout.

Historically, understanding psychological distress and mental health in LGB people has been difficult due to the way in which 'homosexuality' was regarded as a mental illness until its removal from the *Diagnostic and Statistical Manual of Mental (DSM)* in 1973 (see Kitzinger and Coyle 2002). While much has changed, the Euro-Western construction of psychological distress as a 'disorder' or 'dysfunction' of the mind – termed 'mental illness' – has in itself been problematic for understanding mental health in LGB people. In particular, it decontextualizes mental health, ignoring the social determinants of psychological distress arising from prejudice and marginalization. Furthermore, it ignores the ways in which for LGB people from diverse racial, ethnic and cultural groups mental health may be viewed more holistically (Rountree and Smith 2016).

This chapter focuses on the interface between sexual orientation and mental health, with particular attention to mental well-being of racial and ethnic minority adult LGB persons. As well as providing an overview of the theory and research in relation to LGB mental health, some implications for research and practice with racial/minority ethnic LGB persons is also considered. We have framed our discussion around 'mental well-being' to indicate that we are discussing mental health in a much broader sense than is typically the case elsewhere. In the interests of simplicity, throughout this chapter we use the phraseology 'LGB persons' as a collective term for all those whose sexual identity/orientation differs from the heterosexual norm. However, we are aware that many racial/minority ethnic persons may use culturally specific terms (e.g. *Takatāpui wahine* [Gowlett and Rasmussen 2014]) to describe sexual orientation.

Sexuality and mental health

It is well evidenced that LGB persons face societal discrimination and stigma and continue to experience poorer mental health than their heterosexual counterparts. For example, LGB persons are more likely to experience depression and anxiety (Semlyen et al. 2016); substance misuse disproportionately affects lesbian and bisexual women (Hagger-Johnson et al. 2013); and there is a clear increased risk of suicidality in LGB persons, especially gay and bisexual men (King et al. 2008). Other health disparities exist in these groups but there is limited data available on sexual minority health outcomes. With no current data collection within health services admissions, cancer registry data or coronary care, health outcomes for LGB depend on national health surveys using self-report data which itself is likely to result in under-reporting of sexual orientation at data collection. Moreover, sexual orientation is complex and variously defined in relation to dimensions of attraction, identity and behaviour resulting in a lack of comparability between different data sources. Coherent health outcome data, especially longitudinal data, is made possible only with ongoing data collection and health surveillance through sexual orientation monitoring data (Semlyen 2017; Sell 2017).

Health and well-being of LGB persons is impacted throughout the lifespan, however adolescence is a key period in terms of mental well-being for LGB persons. Characterised by self-identity formation (Meeus 2011), adolescence is a period when LGB persons may well be negotiating their sexual orientation and contending with disclosing this to family, friends and peers; making them a particularly vulnerable group. Identifying as LGB, and potentially 'coming out' to significant others can be especially challenging in a highly heteronormative world (Rosario, Schrimshaw, and Hunter 2004). A combination of a lack of positive affirmation, rejection by family/friends, and social stigmatization can result in an increased risk of isolation (Harrison 2003). Furthermore, there is widely accepted evidence that LGB youth often experience homophobic bullying at school, impacting on academic achievement (Haas et al. 2011). All of these factors place LGB youth at higher risk of depression and suicidality (e.g. see Birkett, Espelage, and Koenig 2009); the negative effects demonstrating a trajectory into adulthood (Needham 2012; Marshal et al. 2013).

There is emerging evidence of differently experienced health disparities within this group. LGB populations are heterogeneous groups with diverse identities and differing health needs, experiences, and outcomes (Mulé et al. 2009) and who experience a range of different health issues, health care experiences and health risks. Racial and minority ethnic populations have been shown to have high psychological distress and co-morbidity (Balsam et al. 2011; O'donnell, Meyer, and Schwartz 2011) however this risk becomes greater in those who are racial/ethnic minorities and also identify as LGB. Suicide attempts among racial/ethnic minority LGBs have been found to have higher prevalence than both heterosexual racial/ethnic persons (Cochran et al. 2007) and white LGB persons (O'donnell, Meyer, and Schwartz 2011). Young racial/ethnic people's loss of family may be additionally detrimental as often the family provides cultural support to protect that young person against the racist oppression they may be experiencing (Frost, Meyer, and Schwartz 2016).

These health disparities continue into both health care experience (Durso and Meyer 2013) and health-seeking behaviour (Phillips and Malone 2014). LGB persons have a history of experiencing bias within health care. Reparative 'therapy', linked to earlier considerations of homosexuality as a mental health disorder, and listed in the *DSM* until 1973, was designed to 'cure' homosexuality. Although recently rejected in many countries, it is yet to become illegal. Given that minority groups' experiences of marginalization as LGB or as 'racial/ethnic minority have been shown to be associated with poorer health care experiences, it may well be that this is an outcome of particularly low trust of the medical professions leading to delay in presentation or avoiding health services altogether(e.g. see Williams and Chapman 2011).

Theoretical perspectives: Minority stress

In the psychological literature, a number of theories have been presented to explain the relationship between marginalization and poor mental health. Early theoretical work suggested a relatively simple relationship existed between being LGB and experiencing mental health issues. For example, Sophie's (1987) research with lesbians resulted in the theory of 'internalized homophobia': the idea that LGB persons experience psychological trauma as a result of the negative views of homosexuality prevalent in society. While the construct 'internalized homophobia' is still widely used (e.g. see Pepping and Halford 2014; Sineath et al. 2016) it could be seen as a simplistic, individualistic, and pathologising explanation for psychological distress in LGB persons. Consequently, the theory itself has largely been superseded by Meyer's theory of 'minority stress' (Meyer 1995, 2003).

Minority stress theory (MST) offers a much more complex explanation for poor mental health in LGB persons based on the premise that like members of other minority groups, LGB persons are subjected to chronic stress related to stigmatization (Meyer 2003). In contrast with earlier explanations, MST focuses on both distal (external) and proximal (internal) factors as contributing to minority stress. Since its development, the model has been extensively employed to assess and explain mental health issues in the LGB population; and is widely used today, including in research with racial/ethnic minority LGB persons (Szymanski and Sung 2010). The following case study illustrates the way in which minority stress contributes to psychological distress according to Meyer's model.

Ramira is an older lesbian of Afro-Caribbean descent who lives in London and is experiencing ongoing bouts of depression. Although British born, she grew up in a time when being lesbian was not readily accepted in the United Kingdom. Her parents (who were first generation migrants) have never accepted her as a lesbian and forced her to leave home when they found out. Being London-based in the late 1970s, Ramira found solace in lesbian feminism and the thriving gay community that arose from this. She made many long-standing friends through the groups she belonged to and refers to these women as her 'family of choice'. Ramira reports that when she was young it was these women who gave her strength to stand up to both homophobic and racist prejudice.

Essentially, MST suggests that psychological distress results from the experience of conflict in the social environment between majority and minority group values. Based on a rigorous scientific study with gay men, Meyer (1995) demonstrated that three components –internalized homophobia, stigma (i.e. expectations of rejection/discrimination), and prejudice (i.e. actual events of discrimination and violence) – individually and in combination produce psychological distress. In his later work, Meyer (2003) extended his research to include lesbian, gay, and bisexual persons; additionally focusing on the effects of concealing one's sexual orientation, and on the role of coping processes in mitigating against the effects of stress. The findings of this study pointed to a two-to-threefold risk of psychological distress resulting from minority stress. For Ramira, being both lesbian and 'non-white' at a time when neither was socially condoned in mainstream British society would likely mean that she grew up with a negative sense of self-worth, low expectations that others would like/accept her, and actual experiences of homophobia and racism. According to Meyer's model, these factors – combined with the need to conceal her sexuality from her family – have undoubtedly contributed to her experiencing persistent depression.

Despite its widespread adoption, minority stress theory has remained largely uncritiqued (Riggs and Treharne 2017) but is by no means unproblematic. For example, Meyer (2003) claims that the model is underpinned by a social stress framework, and while it makes reference to certain social processes (i.e. stigma; prejudice) the focus is primarily on individual processes (i.e. internalized homophobia; concealment of identity) and the effect these have on the *individual*. Essentially, it focuses on the impact of one person's negative regard on another and is "largely devoid of an account of the role of social norms in shaping how particular individuals may be rendered legitimate targets of negative regard" (Riggs and Treharne 2017). In this respect, it fails to acknowledge and explain the role that institutionalized, systematic oppression (e.g. lack of legal recognition; insensitivity to, and ignorance of, sexual minority perspectives/experiences; social exclusion) may have on well-being of LGB persons individually and collectively. Therefore in explaining Ramira's depression, the emphasis is on her own actions (internalizing homophobia and/or racism; concealing her sexuality; expecting to be marginalized) and experiences at the expense of understanding the way in which *systematic* homophobia and racism has impacted on her as a person, in turn resulting in psychological distress.

The model is further limited by its lack of accounting for intersectionality – the combination of different aspects of identity – and the way in which LGB persons are differentially impacted (Riggs and Treharne 2017). For example, it doesn't explain why some LGB persons experience poor mental health while others may not, nor why those who occupy multiple marginalized positions (e.g. gay and racial/ethnic minority) may be at greater risk of poor mental health than those occupying just one marginalized subject position. For example, why is Ramira experiencing ongoing bouts of depression when other lesbian women are not? In particular, why is it that Ramira and other racial/ethnic minority lesbian women feel more marginalized than 'white' lesbian women?

Although carrying many of the same issues as MST, a different perspective is offered by Hatzenbuehler (2009) in the form of the Psychological Mediation Framework (PMF). In contrast with MST where 'stress' is seen as a mediator between minority status and mental health, the PMF views stigma-related stress as the catalyst which triggers general psychological processes around coping and affect which in turn impact mental health. From this perspective, Ramira's persistent depression would be seen as a state of failing to deal effectively with stress arising from her minority status as both lesbian and racially/ethnically marginalized. While in many ways an elaboration on MST, it offers a potential explanation for how individual differences mediate stigma-related stressors and mental health, it too is not without issues. While it acknowledges the role that stigma-related stress plays in the poor mental health of (many) LGB persons, it individualizes psychological distress by attributing it to psychological factors such as poor coping skills and an inability to regulate emotions, and failing to address the primary issue of minority stress itself; and its social determinants.

Riggs and Treharne (2017) offer an alternative theory for explaining psychological distress in marginalized groups: decompensation. They suggest that when living in a society where one is marginalized, there is a need to compensate for wrongdoings, injuries and harms (e.g. microaggressions, stigma, discrimination) enacted against the individual – and/or the group(s) with which they identify – on a daily basis. From this perspective, psychological distress occurs when an individual is no longer able to compensate for the daily discrimination, the ideologies that question their right to exist, and the experience of repeated marginalization that their protective resources no longer work. This framework is consistent with research highlighting the importance of social norms rather than subjective appraisals in affecting well-being in individuals marginalized by ideologies of gender and sexuality (e.g. see Pachankis and Bernstein 2012). This particular approach is therefore more useful for understanding the mental health of those with multiple oppressed identities in that it highlights the way in which aspects of the social world (e.g. cultural values of families/communities) impact on the well-being of LGB persons. Within this theoretical framework, Ramira's ongoing depression would be explained in terms of her having to carry the burden of prejudice (i.e. societal stigma; discrimination) from both family and society for too long. Therefore, her psychological distress is a manifestation of no longer being able to cope with the burden of 'homophobia' on top of prejudice and marginalization around her racial/ethnic minority status.

Other, theoretical considerations beyond the scope of this chapter include Queer theory. Emerging in the 1990s, Queer theory offered a sociological perspective on the diversity of identities (beyond those of gay and lesbian) and offering a postmodern lens through which to observe and understand sexual minority experience (Halperin 2003) and that of mental health (MacBride-Stewart 2007).

Sexual orientation, intersectionality and mental health

Although LGB ethnic and racial minorities have been shown to have poorer mental health than their white counterparts, these disparities are not universally found in the data (Balsam et al. 2015). The risk hypothesis suggests racial/ethnic minority LGB persons are at greater risk of psychological distress because they are exposed to both homophobia and racism. This means that they may endure anti-LGB prejudice within their ethnic community and racial prejudice within the predominantly white LGB community; a phenomenon sometimes referred to as 'double jeopardy' (Greene 1997).

The problem with understanding mental well-being from the perspective of double jeopardy is that it assumes an additive approach whereby marginalized identities (i.e. as racial/ethnic minority; as LGB) are treated as independent of each other (Parent et al., 2013). As highlighted by Riggs and das Nair (2012: 14) just as treating psychological distress among LGB people as simply related to sexuality is reductionist; "simply adding on more identities (while treating them all as separable) will also fail to recognise the complexities of clients' lives". Consequently, in order to understand the mental well-being of racial/ethnic minority LGB people it is necessary to take an intersectional approach. That is, to understand the individual holistically rather than as a function of each of their various subject positions. The following case study illustrates the way in which intersectionality operates to impact mental health.

Mohammad is a young gay Muslim who has been experiencing depression on and off for the last few years. He broke up with his partner a few weeks back and has been drinking too much and struggling to sleep. He knows he would benefit from talking about things with someone, but his GP doesn't know he is gay and he wouldn't want him to find out about his sexuality and anyway he would feel stupid talking to him. He also doesn't feel he can talk to his family or close friends because they are Muslim and homosexuality is taboo within Islamic teachings. So, he thought about going to the local LGBT centre who run a gay men's drop in but he's walked past that a few times and everyone there is either white or have gym bodies or both. He doesn't feel like he fits in, in his two-year-old trainers and jeans. He does not seek support for his difficulties and subsequently his mental health issues escalate.

An intersectional approach is based on the premise that multiple identity categories combine to produce distinct – or relatively unique – experiences of marginalization (Choo and Ferree 2010; Parent, DeBlaere, and Moradi 2013). Consequently, psychological distress will be experienced differently as a result of each individual's particular combination of subject positions. So, for Mohammad, because his marginalization arises from being both gay and Muslim, his psychological distress is not simply the combination of homophobia and racism (i.e. homophobia + racism) but the *interaction* between the two. From this standpoint there is no one experience of being LGB or being a racial/ethnic minority or being both as each aspect of identity is intertwined and cannot be separated. Intersectional theory proposes it is the accumulation of oppression from a disadvantage conferred by these multiple marginalized identities that is most important for us to consider (Crenshaw 1989) and to understand (Graham et al. 2011). In Mohammad's case this manifests in his not feeling able to talk to his GP due to him not being out to his GP, and not wanting to be (perhaps because it feels risky given the need to maintain secrecy due to Muslim taboos about homosexuality) and the way in which he would feel stupid talking to a GP about mental health (perhaps because within his culture men are not meant to show 'weakness'; or perhaps the GP is white and he would feel even more racially marginalized presenting with mental health issues). Furthermore, his unease at seeking out help from the local LGBT centre appears to foreground racial difference ('everyone there is white') and also appearance (e.g. clothing; body shape/fitness). Consequently, marginalization is not a set of discrete characteristics and contexts; it is experienced individually. The privilege afforded by certain aspects of one's identity can be eclipsed by other aspects. For instance, lesbian and bisexual women experience both sexism (as women) and homophobia (as lesbians) creating a particular experience of marginalized sexual identity (i.e. one that is gendered). Similarly, a middle-class black man may have significant advantage by being middle class but at the same time be marginalized as someone from a racial/ethnic minority background. It is the way that aspects of identity such as these combine that creates particular experiences of being LGB.

While one's cultural background and sexual orientation may intertwine to create a particular experience of being, for example, racial/ethnic minority and gay; the addition of mental well-being adds another layer to that intersectionality. LGB persons may have myriad marginalizations such as class, gender, having different geographies, cultures, behaviours and beliefs. For example, because Mohammad is experiencing bouts of depression his sense of not fitting in may be more acute. These overlapping multiple positions can create health (dis)advantage differently, linking directly to and yet impacting diversely on their lived experience of mental well-being (Nash 2008). The importance of multiple identities and their link to health cannot be overstated (King 1988) yet little research to date has focused on questions of intersectionality in relation to health inequalities in LGB persons (Cole 2009; Cho, Crenshaw and McCall 2013).

Risk, resilience and protective factors

The interplay of culture, ethnicity and sexuality has an important role to play in protection and resilience in sexual minority populations. As already highlighted, LGB persons are at high risk of experiencing mental health issues (e.g. anxiety, depression, self-harm, suicidality); primarily attributable to factors associated with stigma and prejudice. In the psychological literature, the construct 'resilience' is widely used to describe positive adaptation in the face of substantial adversity (Luthar, Cicchetti, and Becker 2000); arising from a complex interrelationship between risk and protective factors (de Lira and de Morais 2017). Many contemporary researchers have undertaken studies to identify risk and protective factors among LGB persons with a view to better understanding how fostering resilience can minimise/prevent psychological distress.

A growing body of research has focused on understanding resilience and identifying 'protective factors' which might mediate the relationship between risk factors (i.e. homophobia, victimization, discrimination) and mental health. While some individual factors (e.g. coping skills; sense of self-worth) have been suggested, resilience is primarily seen as a function of social factors such as the ability to get married (see Buffie 2011) and having a sense of social connectedness. For example, some studies have indicated that technology is an important factor in fostering connectedness (Ybarra et al. 2016). Importantly, isolation, especially that due to ageing, (Westwood 2016) often contributes to a lack of connectedness for older LGB persons. Many studies (e.g. Fredriksen-Goldsen et al. 2013; McConnell, Birkett, and Mustanski 2016) echo this, identifying social support as the most important protective factor in reducing psychological distress. For example, McConnell et al (2016) found that for LGB youth, those with low levels of support from both family and non-family networks exhibited high levels of psychological distress; while those with good support from family, non-family sources (including 'families of choice'), or both fared much better. The ability to feel comfortable in disclosing one's sexual orientation has also been seen as an important protective factor in preventing poor mental health in LGB persons (see Meckler et al. 2006).

Consistent with the theories described above, the empirical literature (e.g. see de Lira and de Morais 2017) indicates that various forms of homophobia including victimization, microaggressions, rejection by family (and/or significant others) (Ryan et al. 2009), and heterosexism (institutionalized prejudice) put LGB persons at high risk of psychological distress. Similar effects may also be found where communities to which a person belongs have a negative outlook on homosexuality. For example, for some faith/cultural groups (e.g. Pentecostal Christians, Muslims) homosexuality is generally rejected as a viable way of life (e.g. see Siraj 2006; Kligerman 2007); so LGB persons within those communities may experience a negative sense of self in relation to their sexuality; placing them at risk of experiencing mental health issues. racial/Ethnic minority communities may also place a premium on cultural connections resulting in LGB persons from those communities needing to conceal their sexual orientation (Bowleg et al. 2009) and this may play out in healthcare settings as demonstrated in a qualitative study looking at gay Muslim men and their experiences with health care practitioners (Semlyen, Ali, and Flowers 2018).

Often it is suggested that the interplay between heterosexism in one's racial/ethnic minority community and the suppression of one's sexual orientation can be detrimental to the mental health of racial/ethnic minority LGB persons (Balsam et al., 2011). However, some (e.g. Meyer 2010; Moradi et al. 2010) have suggested that the collective orientation of many cultural groups, together with experience in coping with racism, means that racial/ethnic minority LGB persons may have *more* social and personal resources to cope with adversity; and therefore a greater level of resilience. Furthermore, it has been suggested that moving between identities – for example, concealing sexual orientation only in some contexts – may indicate greater resilience in that it is a reflection of psychological flexibility (Moradi et al. 2010). This approach offers the opportunity to benefit from social support from both ethnic and LGB communities in relation to each aspect of identity rather than prioritising one aspect of identity at the expense of another (Bowleg et al. 2003). There is, however, a limited research evidence to substantiate that this is indeed the case.

For those from cultures that prohibit homosexuality – including LGB persons who are asylum seekers – developing resilience may be a much more substantive journey. The lived experience of concealment, and the dilemma presented by holding incommensurate identities (Semlyen, Ali, and Flowers 2018), together with the experience of fleeing torture inflicted from one's home country (Piwowarczyk, Fernandez, and Sharma 2017) may act as very real barriers to accessing LGB culture and mental health services. With no data collected on sexual orientation of asylum seekers, there is no prevalence estimate available but it is safe to assume that the specific pre-migration stressors for forced LGB migrants (e.g. trauma experienced prior to fleeing; grief at having to leave one's homeland and/or family), add to the already significant mental health impacts arising from identifying as LGB in a non-western context (Shidlo and Ahola 2013). Resilience is an important part of mediating the impact of stress. Protective factors

Culture and Sexual Orientation in Mental Health

such as social support are key. In this case we can see how the gay community itself is a key factor is producing resilience.

Future directions

While the importance of institutional and structural cultural competence requires policy and governmental interventions, clinical competence can and needs to be effectively addressed (Betancourt et al. 2016). Positive relationships with mental health services/providers are vital for improving mental health as poor communication can lead to poor outcomes. In particular, it is important for mental health professionals to understand their clients' previous experiences of prejudice in relation to ethnicity and sexuality and that this may have been experienced from within and outwith their own cultural or ethnic communities. It is also important to remember that LGB clients may hold religious beliefs and that these may impact on therapeutic effectiveness (Bartoli and Gillem 2008). Understanding specific experiences allows a closer reading of different ways of relating to the world and may go some way to address assumptions held (Powell Sears 2012).

Heteronormative assumptions render the LGB individual invisible and have discriminatory impact. Creating opportunities for disclosure of sexuality in a health care setting would allow improved practitioner understanding resulting in appropriate care. Homophobia is highly impactful. We know that health professionals report feeling uncomfortable treating sexual minority patients (Stein and Bonuck 2001) and that lesbian, gay and bisexual patients receive sub-standard care (e.g. Kelley et al. 2008) yet we know that LGB persons seek treatment for mental health at higher rates than heterosexuals (King et al. 2007; Grella et al. 2011). Health care professional education is a key route through which culturally competent healthcare practice might best be developed (Obedin-Maliver et al. 2011) and this is an area that needs significant development as it has been reported that in training, for a range of healthcare professionals, LGB content is significantly limited (Semlyen 2015). Moreover, mental health professionals need to be knowledgeable about sexual orientation but also actively gay-affirming. Gay-affirmative therapy can be defined as

> the integration of knowledge and awareness by the therapist of the unique development and cultural aspect of LGBT individuals, the therapist's self-knowledge, and the translation of this knowledge and awareness into effective and helpful therapy skills at all stages of the therapeutic process.
>
> *(Perez 2007: 408)*

Not all mental health care is provided or sought within clinical settings and this has been found to be different within different sexual minority racial/ethnic groups. For example, black LGB persons are more likely to seek mental health treatment in religious or spiritual settings (Meyer, Teylan, and Schwartz 2015). However, there is little or no regulation of these interventions. We know that conversion or reparative therapy is now considered a harmful and unethical practice within any clinical setting (BPS 2017) and that LGB persons are protected under the Equality Acts in several countries, yet heteronormative and homophobic views are commonly found within faith groups and some religious groups have links with reparative therapy provision (Grace 2008). Importantly, research shows that even after controlling for prior suicidality, seeking treatment from a religious or spiritual advisor has been shown to be associated with increased odds of attempting suicide in LGB adults (Meyer, Teylan, and Schwartz 2015). Thus we need to look at promoting gay-affirming religious support in our communities (Gattis, Woodford, and Han 2014).

There are ongoing limitations in our knowledge of both the prevalence and the experience of LGB persons mental health as there is minimal inclusion of LGB as a demographic within national research and very rarely is there any explicit mention of sexual diversity within most research findings. With the limited inclusion of LGB in research that we do have, there is little we know about this beyond small community-based samples and qualitative studies. There is some emergent representative data (Semlyen et al. 2016) but this is dependent on ongoing data collection through national and state health surveys which requires ongoing political and financial commitment which is not readily available. Small samples within these surveys mean that only through statistical techniques such as pooling (Semlyen 2017) can we create statistical power sufficient to demonstrate findings.

There is even more limited research of multiply marginalized groups. For example, only small samples of racial/ethnic minority LGB persons are included in research studies (DeBlaere et al. 2010) and only limited research on racial/ethnic minority LGB health care experience (Kinsler et al. 2007; Burgess et al. 2008, Grant et al. 2010). The small samples limit any disaggregation by ethnicity or other relevant characteristics. Until then, the experiences of all LGB are assumed the same. An inclusive approach using intentional recruitment and researching of broad cultural groups also acknowledges barriers to taking part in research and finding ways to overcome this.

For the broadest possible understanding of the intersectional experience and health of racial/ethnic minority LGB persons, there also needs to be a mixed methods approach. Research designs that capture voice along with policy impactful evidence are both important to address and will go some way to address tensions between impact and intersectionality.

Conclusion

In this chapter, we draw attention to the influence and interaction between culture, mental health and sexual orientation emphasising intersectional aspects of this particular experience. We highlight the importance of understanding diverse identities within individuals and the importance of prioritising understanding of multiple intersecting factors within mental health service provision and academic research.

In developing services, culture and sexuality should not be separated from each other or from mental health – they are inter-related in complex and inseparable ways generating an individuality of experience. Consequently, those working with racial/ethnic minority LGB persons need to ensure that culturally competent mental health practice includes an understanding of intersectionality and the way in which different aspects of a person's subjectivity (e.g. sexuality, race/ethnicity, socio-economic status) combine to produce an individual – and unique – experience of marginalization. It is this experience that underpins the manifestation of mental health in LGB people.

Moreover, we need to promote the development of sensitive, meaningful, impactful mental health interventions that do not conflate race/culture and marginalized sexuality with pathological models of mental health but promote a framing of the richness of individualized experience. Adopting approaches that situate mental health within a Euro-Western framework runs the risk of constructing psychological distress arising from prejudice and marginalization as 'disorder' or 'dysfunction' at an individual level. To address specific needs of racial/ethnic minority LGB persons and mainstream services that improve the inclusion of marginalized groups it is important to ensure a wide investment in education and training is warranted enabling practitioners to become culturally aware and competent to ensure the best possible healthcare be provided

References

Abreu, Roberto L, Siobhan Brooks, Lawrence O Bryant, Candice Crowell, Sannisha K Dale, Rahwa Haile, Angelique Harris, Tfawa T Haynes, Lashaune P Johnson, and Jane A McElroy (2016) *Black LGBT Health in the United States: The Intersection of Race, Gender, and Sexual Orientation*. New York: Lexington Books.

Balsam, Kimberly F., Yamile Molina, Blair Beadnell, Jane Simoni, and Karina Walters (2011) Measuring multiple minority stress: The LGBT People of Color Microaggressions Scale. *Cultural Diversity and Ethnic Minority Psychology*, 17 (2):163.

Balsam, Kimberly F., Yamile Molina, Blair Beadnell, Jane Simoni, and Karina Walters (2015) Racial/ethnic differences in identity and mental health outcomes among young sexual minority women. *Culture Diversity and Ethnic Minority Psychology*, 21 (3):380–90. doi: 10.1037/a0038680.

Bartoli, Eleonora, and Angela R Gillem (2008) Continuing to depolarize the debate on sexual orientation and religion: Identity and the therapeutic process. *Professional Psychology: Research and Practice*, 39 (2):202.

Betancourt, Joseph R, Alexander R Green, J Emilio Carrillo, and II Owusu Ananeh-Firempong (2016) Defining cultural competence: A practical framework for addressing racial/ethnic disparities in health and health care. *Public Health Reports*.

Birkett, M., D. L. Espelage, and B. Koenig (2009) LGB and questioning students in schools: The moderating effects of homophobic bullying and school climate on negative outcomes. *Journal of Youth and Adolescence*, 38 (7): 989–1000. doi: 10.1007/s10964-008-9389-1.

Bowleg, Lisa, Gary Burkholder, Michelle Teti, and Melynda L Craig (2009) The complexities of outness: Psychosocial predictors of coming out to others among Black lesbian and bisexual women. *Journal of LGBT Health Research*, 4 (4):153–166.

Bowleg, Lisa, Jennifer Huang, Kelly Brooks, Amy Black, and Gary Burkholder (2003) Triple jeopardy and beyond: Multiple minority stress and resilience among Black lesbians. *Journal of Lesbian Studies*, 7 (4):87–108.

BPS (2017) *Memorandum of Understanding on Conversion Therapy in the UK*.

Buffie, William C. (2011) Public health implications of same-sex marriage. *American Journal of Public Health*, 101 (6):986–990.

Burgess, Diana, Richard Lee, Alisia Tran, and Michelle Van Ryn (2008) Effects of perceived discrimination on mental health and mental health services utilization among gay, lesbian, bisexual and transgender persons. *Journal of LGBT Health Research*, 3 (4):1–14.

Cho, Sumi, Kimberlé Williams Crenshaw, and Leslie McCall (2013) Toward a field of intersectionality studies: Theory, applications, and praxis. *Signs: Journal of Women in Culture and Society*, 38 (4):785–810.

Choo, Hae Yeon, and Myra Marx Ferree (2010) Practicing intersectionality in sociological research: A critical analysis of inclusions, interactions, and institutions in the study of inequalities. *Sociological Theory*, 28 (2):129–149.

Cochran, Susan D., Vickie M. Mays, Margarita Alegria, Alexander N. Ortega, and David Takeuchi (2007) Mental health and substance use disorders among Latino and Asian American lesbian, gay, and bisexual adults. *Journal of Consulting and Clinical Psychology*, 75 (5):785.

Cole, Elizabeth R. (2009) Intersectionality and research in psychology. *American Psychologist*, 64 (3):170–80.

Crenshaw, Kimberle (1989) Demarginalizing the intersection of race and sex: A black feminist critique of antidiscrimination doctrine, feminist theory and antiracist politics. University of Chicago Legal Forum: 139.

de Lira, Aline Nogueira, and Normanda Araujo de Morais (2017) Resilience in Lesbian, Gay, and Bisexual (LGB) populations: An integrative literature review. *Sexuality Research and Social Policy*: 1–11.

DeBlaere, Cirleen, Melanie E. Brewster, Anthony Sarkees, and Bonnie Moradi (2010) Conducting research with LGB people of color: Methodological challenges and strategies. *The Counseling Psychologist*, 38 (3):331–362.

Durso, Laura E., and Ilan H. Meyer (2013) Patterns and predictors of disclosure of sexual orientation to healthcare providers among lesbians, gay men, and bisexuals. *Sexuality Research and Social Policy*, 10 (1):35–42.

Fredriksen-Goldsen, K. I., H. J. Kim, S. E. Barkan, A. Muraco, and C. P. Hoy-Ellis (2013) Health disparities among lesbian, gay, and bisexual older adults: results from a population-based study. *American Journal of Public Health*, 103 (10):1802–9. doi: 10.2105/AJPH.2012.301110.

Frost, D. M., I. H. Meyer, and S. Schwartz (2016) Social support networks among diverse sexual minority populations. *American Journal of Orthopsychiatry*, 86 (1):91–102. doi: 10.1037/ort0000117.

Gattis, M. N., M. R. Woodford, and Y. Han (2014) Discrimination and depressive symptoms among sexual minority youth: Is gay-affirming religious affiliation a protective factor? *Archives of Sexual Behavior*, 43 (8):1589–99. doi: 10.1007/s10508-014-0342-y.

Gowlett, Christina, and Mary Lou Rasmussen (2014) The cultural politics of queer theory in education research. *Discourse: Studies in the Cultural Politics of Education*, 35 (3), 331–334.

Grace, André P. (2008) The charisma and deception of reparative therapies: When medical science beds religion. *Journal of Homosexuality*, 55 (4):545–580.

Graham, Robert, Bobbie Berkowitz, Robert Blum, Walter Bockting, Judith Bradford, Brian de Vries, Robert Garofalo, Greg Herek, Elizabeth Howell, and Daniel Kasprzyk (2011) The health of lesbian, gay, bisexual, and transgender people: Building a foundation for better understanding. edited by Institute of Medicine. Washington, DC: *Institute of Medicine* 10: 13128.

Grant, Jaime M, Lisa A Mottet, Justin Tanis, Jody L Herman, Jack Harrison, and M Keisling (2010) *National transgender discrimination survey report on health and health care*. Washington, DC: National Center for Transgender Equality and the National Gay and Lesbian Task Force.

Greene, Beverly (1997) Ethnic minority lesbians and gay men: Mental health and treatment issues. *Journal of Consulting and clinical Psychology* 62 (2): 243.

Grella, Christine E, Susan D. Cochran, Lisa Greenwell, and Vickie M. Mays (2011) Effects of sexual orientation and gender on perceived need for treatment by persons with and without mental disorders. *Psychiatric Services*, 62 (4):404–410.

Haas, A. P., M. Eliason, V. M. Mays, R. M. Mathy, S. D. Cochran, A. R. D'Augelli, M. M. Silverman, P. W. Fisher, T. Hughes, M. Rosario, S. T. Russell, E. Malley, J. Reed, D. A. Litts, E. Haller, R. L. Sell, G. Remafedi, J. Bradford, A. L. Beautrais, G. K. Brown, G. M. Diamond, M. S. Friedman, R. Garofalo, M. S. Turner, A. Hollibaugh, and P. J. Clayton (2011) Suicide and suicide risk in lesbian, gay, bisexual, and transgender populations: Review and recommendations. *Journal of Homosexuality*, 58 (1):10–51.

Hagger-Johnson, Gareth, Rafik Taibjee, Joanna Semlyen, Isla Fitchie, Julie Fish, Catherine Meads, and Justin Varney (2013) Sexual orientation identity in relation to smoking history and alcohol use at age 18/19: Cross-sectional associations from the Longitudinal Study of Young People in England (LSYPE). *BMJ Open*, 3 (8). doi: 10.1136/bmjopen-2013–002810.

Halperin, David M. (2003) The normalization of queer theory. *Journal of Homosexuality*, 45 (2–4):339–343.

Harrison, Therese W. (2003) Adolescent homosexuality and concerns regarding disclosure. *Journal of School Health*, 73 (3):107–112

Hatzenbuehler, Mark L. (2009) How does sexual minority stigma 'get under the skin'? A psychological mediation framework. *Psychological Bulletin*, 135 (5):707.

Kelley, Leah, Calvin L Chou, Suzanne L Dibble, and Patricia A Robertson (2008) A critical intervention in lesbian, gay, bisexual, and transgender health: Knowledge and attitude outcomes among second-year medical students. *Teaching and Learning in Medicine*, 20 (3):248–253.

King, Deborah K. (1988) Multiple jeopardy, multiple consciousness: The context of a Black feminist ideology. *Signs: Journal of Women in Culture and Society*, 14 (1):42–72.

King, Michael, Joanna Semlyen, Helen Killaspy, Irwin Nazareth, and David Osborn (2007) A systematic review of research on counselling and psychotherapy for lesbian, gay, bisexual & transgender people. *British Association for Counselling and Psychotherapy.*

King, Michael, Joanna Semlyen, Sharon See Tai, Helen Killaspy, David Osborn, Dmitri Popelyuk, and Irwin Nazareth (2008) A systematic review of mental disorder, suicide, and deliberate self harm in lesbian, gay and bisexual people. *BMC Psychiatry*, 8:70.

Kinsler, Janni J, Mitchell D Wong, Jennifer N Sayles, Cynthia Davis, and William E Cunningham (2007) The effect of perceived stigma from a health care provider on access to care among a low-income HIV-positive population. *AIDS Patient Care and STDs*, 21 (8):584–592.

Kitzinger, Celia, and Adrian Coyle (2002) Introducing lesbian and gay psychology. *Lesbian and Gay Psychology: New Perspectives*, 1–29.

Kligerman, Nicole (2007) Homosexuality in Islam: A difficult paradox. *Macalester Islam Journal*, 2 (3):8.

Luthar, Suniya S., Dante Cicchetti, and Bronwyn Becker (2000) The construct of resilience: A critical evaluation and guidelines for future work. *Child Development*, 71 (3):543–562.

MacBride-Stewart, Sara (2007) Que(e)rying the meaning of lesbian health: Individual(izing) and community discourses. In *Out in Psychology: Lesbian, Gay, Bisexual, Trans and Queer Perspectives*, edited by Victoria Clarke and Elizabeth Peel, (pp. 427–443). New York: John Wiley.

Marshal, Michael P., Sarah S. Dermody, JeeWon Cheong, Chad M. Burton, Mark S. Friedman, Frances Aranda, and Tonda L. Hughes (2013) Trajectories of depressive symptoms and suicidality among heterosexual and sexual minority youth. *Journal of Youth and Adolescence*, 42 (8):1243–1256.

McConnell, Elizabeth A., Michelle Birkett, and Brian Mustanski (2016) Families matter: Social support and mental health trajectories among lesbian, gay, bisexual, and transgender youth. *Journal of Adolescent Health*, 59 (6):674–680.

Meckler, Garth, Marc Elliott, David Kanouse, Kristin Beals, and Mark Schuster (2006) Nondisclosure of sexual orientation to a physician among a sample of gay, lesbian, and bisexual youth. *Archives of Pediatrics & Adolescent Medicine*, 160 (12):1248–1254. doi: citeulike-article-id:13616520.

Meeus, Wim (2011) The study of adolescent identity formation 2000–2010: A review of longitudinal research. *Journal of Research on Adolescence*, 21 (1):75–94.

Meyer, I. H. (1995) Minority stress and mental health in gay men. *Journal of Health and Social Behavior*, 36 (1):38–56.

Meyer, Ilan (2003) Prejudice, social stress, and mental health in lesbian, gay, and bisexual populations: Conceptual issues and research evidence. *Psychological Bulletin*, 129 (5):674–697.

Meyer, Ilan H. (2010) Identity, stress, and resilience in lesbians, gay men, and bisexuals of color. *The Counseling Psychologist*, 38 (3):442–454.

Meyer, Ilan H., Merilee Teylan, and Sharon Schwartz (2015) The role of help-seeking in preventing suicide attempts among lesbians, gay men, and bisexuals. *Suicide and Life-Threatening Behavior*, 45 (1):25–36.

Moradi, Bonnie, Marcie C. Wiseman, Cirleen DeBlaere, Melinda B. Goodman, Anthony Sarkees, Melanie E. Brewster, and Yu-Ping Huang (2010) LGB of color and white individuals' perceptions of heterosexist stigma, internalized homophobia, and outness: Comparisons of levels and links. *The Counseling Psychologist*, 38 (3):397–424.

Mulé, Nick J., Lori E. Ross, Barry Deeprose, Beth E. Jackson, Andrea Daley, Anna Travers, and Dick Moore (2009) Promoting LGBT health and wellbeing through inclusive policy development. *International Journal for Equity in Health*, 8 (1):1–11.

Nash, Jennifer C. (2008) Re-thinking intersectionality. *Feminist Review*, 89 (1):1–15.

Needham, Belinda (2012) Sexual attraction and trajectories of mental health and substance use during the transition from adolescence to adulthood. *Journal of Youth and Adolescence*, 41 (2):179–190. doi: citeulike-article-id:13577708.

O'donnell, Shannon, Ilan H Meyer, and Sharon Schwartz (2011) Increased risk of suicide attempts among Black and Latino lesbians, gay men, and bisexuals. *American Journal of Public Health*, 101 (6):1055–1059.

Obedin-Maliver, Juno, Elizabeth S. Goldsmith, Leslie Stewart, William White, Eric Tran, Stephanie Brenman, Maggie Wells, David M. Fetterman, Gabriel Garcia, and Mitchell R. Lunn (2011) Lesbian, gay, bisexual, and transgender–related content in undergraduate medical education. *JAMA*, 306 (9):971–977.

Pachankis, John E., and Laura B. Bernstein (2012) An etiological model of anxiety in young gay men: From early stress to public self-consciousness. *Psychology of Men & Masculinity*, 13 (2):107.

Parent, Mike C., Cirleen DeBlaere, and Bonnie Moradi (2013) Approaches to research on intersectionality: Perspectives on gender, LGBT, and racial/ethnic identities. *Sex Roles*, 68 (11–12):639–645.

Pepping, Christopher A., and W. Kim Halford (2014) Relationship education and therapy for same-sex couples. *Australian and New Zealand Journal of Family Therapy*, 35 (4):431–444.

Perez, Ruperto M. (2007) The "boring" state of research and psychotherapy with lesbian, gay, bisexual, and transgender clients: Revisiting Barón. (1991). In Bieschke, Kathleen J., Ruperto M. Perez, and Kurt A. DeBord (Eds.), *Handbook of Counseling and Psychotherapy with Lesbian, Gay, Bisexual, and Transgender Clients* (2nd ed., pp. 399–418). Washington, DC: American Psychological Association.

Phillips, Janice M., and Beverly Malone (2014) Increasing racial/ethnic diversity in nursing to reduce health disparities and achieve health equity. *Public Health Reports*, 129 (1, suppl2):45–50.

Piwowarczyk, Linda, Pedro Fernandez, and Anita Sharma (2017) Seeking asylum: Challenges faced by the LGB community. *Journal of Immigrant and Minority Health*, 19 (3):723–732.

Powell Sears, Karen (2012) Improving cultural competence education: The utility of an intersectional framework. *Medical Education*, 46 (6):545–551.

Riggs, Damien W, and Roshan das Nair (2012) Intersecting identities. *Intersectionality, sexuality and psychological therapies: Working with lesbian, gay and bisexual diversity*, 9–30.

Riggs, Damien W, and Gareth J Treharne (2017) Decompensation: A novel approach to accounting for stress arising from the effects of ideology and social norms. *Journal of Homosexuality*, 64 (5):592–605.

Rosario, Margaret, Eric W Schrimshaw, and Joyce Hunter (2004) Ethnic/racial differences in the coming-out process of lesbian, gay, and bisexual youths: A comparison of sexual identity development over time. *Cultural Diversity and Ethnic Minority Psychology*, 10 (3):215.

Rountree, Jennifer, and Addie Smith (2016) Strength-based well-being indicators for Indigenous children and families: A literature review of Indigenous communities' identified well-being indicators. *American Indian and Alaska Native Mental Health Research*, 23 (3):206–220.

Ryan, Caitlin, David Huebner, Rafael M. Diaz, and Jorge Sanchez (2009) Family rejection as a predictor of negative health outcomes in white and Latino lesbian, gay, and bisexual young adults. *Pediatrics*, 123 (1):346–352.

Sell, R L. (2017) LGBTQ health surveillance: Data = power. *American Journal of Public Health*, 107 (6):843.

Semlyen, Joanna (2015) Health psychology. In Christina Richards and Meg John Barker (Eds.), *The Palgrave Handbook of the Psychology of Sexuality and Gender* (pp. 300–315). Basingstoke: Palgrave Macmillan.

Semlyen, Joanna (2017) Recording sexual orientation in the UK: Pooling data for statistical power. *American Journal of Public Health*, 107 (8):1215–1217. doi: 10.2105/AJPH.2017.303910.

Semlyen, Joanna, Atif Ali, and Paul Flowers (2018) Intersectional identities and dilemmas in interactions with health care professionals: An interpretative phenomenological analysis of British Muslim gay men. *Culture, Health and Sexuality* 20 (9):1023–1035.

Semlyen, Joanna, Michael King, Justin Varney, and Gareth Hagger-Johnson (2016) Sexual orientation and symptoms of common mental disorder or low wellbeing: Combined meta-analysis of 12 UK population health surveys. *BMC Psychiatry*, 16 (1):67. doi: 10.1186/s12888-016-0767-z.

Shidlo, Ariel, and Joanne Ahola (2013) Mental health challenges of LGBT forced migrants. *Forced Migration Review*, (42):9.

Sineath, R. C., C. Woodyatt, T. Sanchez, S. Giammattei, T. Gillespie, E. Hunkeler, A. Owen-Smith, V. P. Quinn, D. Roblin, R. Stephenson, P. S. Sullivan, V. Tangpricha, and M. Goodman (2016) Determinants of and barriers to hormonal and surgical treatment receipt among transgender people. *Transgender Health*, 1 (1):129–136.

Siraj, Asifa (2006) On being homosexual and Muslim: Conflicts and challenges. In L. Ouzgane (Ed.), *Islamic Masculinities* (pp. 202–216). London: Zed Books.

Sophie, Joan (1987) Internalized homophobia and lesbian identity. *Journal of Homosexuality*, 14 (1–2):53–65.

Stein, Gary L, and Karen A Bonuck (2001) Physician–patient relationships among the lesbian and gay community. *Journal of the Gay and Lesbian Medical Association*, 5 (3):87–93.

Szymanski, Dawn M, and Mi Ra Sung (2010) Minority stress and psychological distress among Asian American sexual minority persons. *The Counseling Psychologist*, 38 (6):848–872.

Westwood, S. (2016) Dementia, women and sexuality: How the intersection of ageing, gender and sexuality magnify dementia concerns among lesbian and bisexual women. *Dementia (London)*, 15 (6):1494–1514. doi: 10.1177/1471301214564446.

Williams, K. A., and M. V. Chapman (2011) Comparing health and mental health needs, service use, and barriers to services among sexual minority youths and their peers. *Health and Social Work*, 36 (3):197–206.

Ybarra, M. L., M. Rosario, E. Saewyc, and C. Goodenow (2016) Sexual behaviors and partner characteristics by sexual identity among adolescent girls. *Journal of Adolescent Health*, 58 (3):310–6.

16

CULTURE AND RELIGION IN MENTAL HEALTH

Ayesha Ahmad and Simon Dein

Religion and spirituality have had a tumultuous relationship with the emergence of psychiatry into mainstream clinical discourses (Koenig 2008: 201–203; Dein et al. 2010: 63–64). The contemporary expansion of psychiatry into the global mental health movement (Prince et al. 2007) is offering further challenges. The global mental health movement is a call by mental health professionals and organisations to drive political action towards creating mental health infrastructure in all countries. The initiative has gained momentum through an evidence base of the global burden of disease of mental health, namely the impact of mental illness on health, mortality, and morbidity as well as economic development. Given that understanding of mental illness varies from a cultural lens and causation, help-seeking behaviour, and treatment is subject to pluralistic beliefs, psychiatry is coming face to face with traditional, faith-based and culturally contextualised spirituality and the ethical challenges that originate from ensuring sensitive psychiatric practice when involving religious and spiritual beliefs (Sperry and Peteet 2016).

Changing discourses are creating fruitful spaces to reflect and evaluate on the role of religion and spirituality in mental health against the backdrop of developing understandings of the importance of socio-cultural identities of both patients and psychiatrists for help-seeking behaviour and treatment responses, which has been particularly recognized in the mental health care of traumatised refugees (Groen et al. 2018; Bhugra and Bhui 2018). The narrative of religion and spirituality in mental health is experiencing challenging perspectives due to the movement of global mental health and the emergence of different discourses of mental health in the clinical setting due to globalization and changing patterns of migration. Refugee and asylum mental health care remains under-researched and needing greater understanding especially with regards to the ways that trauma impacts on an individual in a new society or in humanitarian responses (Affleck et al. 2018). In this chapter, we detail the relationship of religion and spirituality with mental health and the way mental health is shaped by our understanding of various socio-cultural identities.

Spirituality, religion and personal beliefs are highly correlated with the World Health Organisation's quality of life instrument (WHOQOL SRPB Group, 2006: 1486) whereby an international study involving 18 countries revealed the importance of inner peace, faith, hope and optimism for quality of life.

In effect, the goal is to present mental health in a revised light whereby there is a greater space for pluralism and dialogue through belief-systems and world-view perceptions.

Critical overview of mental health findings: Religion, spirituality, and mental health

A historical account of psychiatry is fraught with multiple perspectives and theories about the changing turn in the approach to mental illness following the enlightenment (Fernando 2014). The differences are ontological, that is, to say that the nature of the way to understand mental illness underwent a historical transition. This transition has been questioned quite dramatically, for example, in the form of "should the emergence of psychiatry in the late 18th century be viewed as the triumph of the Enlightenment, ushering a rational approach to mental illness and overturning the primitive and barbaric ideas of previous eras?" (Beveridge 2012: 431). Furthermore, the challenge continues of how to view contemporary psychiatry. The biomedical model is the dominant paradigm for understanding all aspects of illness.

In the development of the bio-psycho-social model of health and disease following critics of the medicalization or Westernization of illness by Michel Foucault (Foucault and Dreyfus 1987) or Ivan Illich (1975), for example, psychiatry remains in the tense struggle to maintain authority over mental illness by conforming to the viewpoint it can only be explained and understood using the biomedical explanation. Yet, the rupture soon enters whereby psychiatry cannot be sustained purely by the biomedical model of mental illness, due to the representation of lived experiences, cultural notions and theories of the mind, and altering concepts of the self that affect the presentation, manifestation, help-seeking behaviour and treatment of forms of mental distress.

However, a critical overview of the relationship with biomedical models must also account for both the positive and negative ways that religion and spirituality can demonstrate for mental health. Miscommunication and misunderstanding are ways that religion and spirituality can be negative coping mechanisms in psychiatric settings, thus the spiritual needs of believers need to be carefully assessed by practitioners (Weber and Pargament 2014).

In Koenig's review (2009) of research on spirituality, religion, and mental health, the role of religion in society overall and more specifically, the intricate ways that religious ways of coping are linked with the experience of mental illness are highlighted. He points out that: "Among 93 observational studies, two-thirds found significantly lower rates of depressive disorder or fewer depressive symptoms among the more religious" (Koenig 2009: 285). Furthermore, among 68 studies that examined the religion-suicide relation; "57 found fewer suicides or more negative attitudes toward suicide among the more religious" (Koenig 2009: 287). Considering the embodiment, then, of mental illness and religion, is vital for understanding the way for effective response to recovery as well as prevention of suicide. Religion, for some individuals, is a healing practice similar to the ethos of psychiatry.

A cross-sectional study of American adults (Abu-Raiya et al. 2016) identified the multifaceted ways that religious ways of coping affects the ability to manage life-stressors. Four religious factors were examined (religious commitment, life sanctification, religious support, and religious hope). Higher levels resulted in increased buffering between religious and spiritual struggles and predicting happiness or depressive symptoms. Nevertheless, the impact of religious and spiritual views of patients with severe mental illness on clinical outcomes remains controversial (Mizuno et al. 2017). Resilience plays a significant role in managing such negative stressors and religious coping has been identified as an external factor for supporting resilience in patients with schizophrenia (Gooding et al. 2017). Again, this highlights the necessity to bridge gaps between religion and spirituality with psychiatric interventions.

Divine discourses – the emergence of religion and spirituality in mental health

While the area of religion and spirituality in mental health remains under-researched, there is an increasing focus on religious beliefs and the role of spirituality in psychiatric research (Koenig 2009). Mental health pertains to the lived experience of an individual and due to a globalized stigma and taboo of varying degrees towards mental illness, psychiatrists are also treating symptoms of society and the ways that the individual experiences their surrounding environment. Yet, there is a discrepancy in achieving a balance between a mental health care system that accommodates religion and spirituality and a mental health care system that is aligned with the paradigm of a positivistic framework of biomedicine. Globally, the emergence of religion and spirituality in mental health offers some interesting views for the direction that the future of mental health may develop.

Cultural interpretations and traditional forms of treatment for the mentally ill have in recent decades gathered attention in human rights circuits and ethnographic analysis. The guidelines for spirituality and mental health by the Royal College of Psychiatrists in the United Kingdom state that spirituality and psychiatry "on the face of it, do not seem to have much in common" but that there is growing awareness "of ways that some aspects of spirituality can offer real benefits for mental health" (Royal College of Psychiatrists' Spirituality and Psychiatry Special Interest Group Executive Committee 2017).

Spirituality and religion are the basis for understanding distress and suffering in many contexts around the world and the spiritual positionality plays a role in creating and maintaining a person's situatedness in their sense of self and surrounding world regardless of the location of the suffering in the person's past. To illustrate, in an interview conducted by one of the authors in rural Nepal, in a region deeply affected by the 2015 earthquake that killed over 9,000 people, a 75-year-old man was attending a local health clinic with his wife. Whilst he was there, he began to talk to the physician about some thoughts he has been having. He had been remembering the time he was arrested by Maoist during the Nepalese civil war of 1996–2006. He related his experience to the recent earthquake and reflected on how the earthquake symbolised punishment from God. He stated how punishment occurs when a quota of 150,000 sins have been committed and was using the earthquake as motivation for addressing grievances that he felt he contributed to with his family. He believed that disasters occur as spiritual tests. Furthermore, he seemed to be deeply reflective at this stage and felt comforted by his religious understanding of suffering. Any form of clinical intervention for the long-term traumatic effects of past experiences would need to facilitate the spiritual needs that underpinned the way suffering was perceived and expressed. Yet, questions emerge about the relationship of mental health from a paradigm of psychiatry with spirituality.

The relationship rupture: Psychiatry and spirituality

Despite the coherence of psychiatry and spiritual sharing concepts of healing, the nature of their relationship shows spaces of rupture, which has been the source of some scholarly study. In an editorial by William R. Breakey (2001) on 'Psychiatry, Spirituality, and Religion', he describes a *mutual suspicion* from psychiatry and religion based on the commonalties that both these modes for understanding the experiencing of the mind share. He argues that "psychiatry and religion have so much in common that perhaps it is not surprising that they have often viewed each other as rivals" (Breakey 2009: 61).

Psychiatry has faced challenges to conform to the positivistic framework of biomedical science to understand, diagnose and treat disorders of the mind. At the time of Freudian theory, God was argued to be an illusion and represent a desired fatherly figure and became an important representation for understanding human attachments (Kirkpatrick and Shaver 1990). The abandonment of religion as a viable form of inquiry into the human condition, then, served psychiatry badly. When compared to religion, psychiatry was subject to negative and ridiculing viewpoints about its validity (Kleinman 2008). Psychiatry then needed to reinforce its role in clinical medicine and bracketed non-clinical influences from its portrayal of mental disorders. Mental disorders developed as a malady or symptom of pathological processes.

However, the unprecedented growth of scientific advancements in examining the human body, including the brain, have created new dynamic discourses to construct the psychiatric patient. Concepts from the positivist paradigm have been accused of medicalizing existential meanings of the human condition. The transgression for example of traditional terms such as melancholia or acedia into depression has been heavily criticized and attempts have been made to 'transcend the medicalization of sadness' by using non-clinical terms to express suffering (Dura-vila 2017: 38). Whether depression captures a diagnostic category that is universal across time and cultures has implications for the role of spirituality in explaining and responding to the experiences that are defined as depression as well as other diagnostic categories in psychiatry.

Mental health and religious experiences

As understanding about religion in relation to mental health has emerged, a more nuanced, pluralistic nature of religion has been developed including both healthy and unhealthy ways that religious values impact on mental health. In this sense, it has been suggested that mental health professionals should receive education and training on religious issues and values to be able to address the mental health needs of religious patients (Bergin 1991). The internalization of religious values can prevent mental illness (Payne et al. 1991). For example, religiosity and spirituality has been linked to positive mental health indicators such as subjective well-being and personality dimensions and offer a protective mechanism against addictive or suicidal behaviours (Unterrainer et al 2014).

The below case relating to mental health and religious experience is from Simon Dein's work as a cultural psychiatrist with a background in anthropology:

> I first met Grace while working in London. She was a thirty-year old woman from Jamaica who had migrated to the UK to study business. She had no previous psychiatric history or drug history. Shortly after coming to the UK, Grace joined a black Charismatic church in North London. Over a period of several months her religious practice intensified to the point that for a couple of weeks she was awake almost day and night reading the Gospels and preaching on the streets. This culminated in an episode where she was involved in a skirmish with a passer-by. Interestingly, due to the combined religious and cultural aspects with Grace's behaviour, the police were called because she was thought to be mentally ill. Subsequently, Grace was taken to hospital under the Mental Health Act (Section 136).
>
> On her arrival in the Accident and Emergency department, Grace was dishevelled, excited, had pressure of speech and repeatedly stated "I am a sister of Christ" and "Jesus

is the Lord, Come to him". It was very difficult to distract her from these themes and she was unable to give any relevant history. She was placed on Section 2 of the Mental Health Act and administered an intramuscular antipsychotic, following which she slept for twelve hours.

The following morning, Grace was coherent and cooperative. She recounted that she was in the UK to study and that after her arrival here she had become involved in a local Charismatic church. Both she and her pastor maintained that her behaviour had been inappropriate and that she had taken her religious beliefs too far. She reiterated that she was a sister of Christ (meaning a disciple rather than the biological sister). She remained settled on the ward for the next day (without any medication). The following evening, she again became excitable and started preaching on the ward. About midnight she went to her room. About two hours later she jumped from the window and subsequently died.

The concept of taking religious beliefs too far, to the extent that her expression of her religion strayed into the domain of mental illness, was a potent reflection. Perhaps this reductionism to fit her experience into a confined category of behaviour limited her insight into her experience. Lacking is the narrative that drew Grace to a charismatic church. Of course, the charismatic church conforms to her cultural narrative in terms of race, identity and socio-historic situated-ness. However, an important question is whether the church offered Grace a space to explore or free any existential struggles she may have been encountering, perhaps as a form of religious coping. At the point of Grace's death, Grace's experiences had been placed in religious and in mental health frameworks, which are both responding to the trials and tribulations of the human condition. Is it the incompatibility between the expression of her struggles in a religious form and the subsequent ways that such behaviour was translated into mental illness in a clinical context an insurmountable barrier for Grace to mediate; in the sense, that she found a physical barrier, namely the window, to try to overcome even though the very act of overcoming led to the cessation of her life? These reflections open up the discourse for religion and mental health to find ways to work together.

For example, religious leaders play an important role in the recognition and acknowledgement of mental distress and to facilitate coping strategies and can create new pathways to promoting mental health utilization amongst marginalized groups (Cauce et al. 2002). The Black church in the United States, for example, act as gatekeepers to a disadvantaged population group dealing with mental health issues (Farris 2007). Pastors are on the frontline of society, akin to healthcare professionals in clinical settings, and represent initial points of contact for parishioners who require mental health support and understanding positive and negative forms of religious coping (Avent et al. 2015).

Positive and negative religious coping

Positive and negative religious coping reflect the complexity of embodying faith as part of lived experiences, which, of course, vary throughout cultural contexts. Understanding both positive and negative religious coping is important to reflect on ways societies may be able to draw on and utilize resources during crises and also ways that sufferings may be enhanced by harmful belief-systems or processes. There is recent evidence that individuals in each of the major world religions deploy religious resources to cope with life events. While Hindus may emphasise karma, yoga and detachment (Tarakeshwar, Pargemon and Mahoney 2003), Muslims may emphasise religious behaviours such as giving alms in the name of Allah. Jews may rely on community involvement (Rosmarin, Pirutinsky, Pargemon and Krumrei 2009).

While there are commonalities in religious coping amongst different faith groups, there are also differences. However, the functions of religious coping are generally similar across the three faith groups, i.e. gaining meaning and control, feeling closer to God, comfort and life transformation. Studies on Muslims (Khan and Watson 2006) and in Jews (Rosmarin, Pargament et al. 2009) found that both groups used positive and negative religious coping. A study of Hindus found the use of negative coping alongside two other forms of positive coping, God focussed and spirituality focussed (Tarakeshwar, Pargament, and Mahoney 2003). Typically, greater use of positive religion as coping resulted in better outcomes, whilst negative coping strategies worsened mental health

Overall findings of improved mental health outcomes among religious persons indicate that those who are religious have better prognosis (Dein 2013). Religious activities and beliefs can alleviate severe symptoms of psychiatric disorders (Tepper et al. 2001). However, religious coping can have both positive or negative outcomes depending on whether the religious coping itself is characterised by positive or negative ways of practicing religion (Olson et al. 2012).

Religious variables that can affect whether coping is positive or negative include "beliefs in a just benevolent God, the experience of God as a supportive partner in coping, involvement in religious rituals, and the search for support through religion" (Pargament et al. 1990). The basis that positive religious coping following negative events can help mediate the symptoms of psychiatric disorders demand two important areas be focussed on; namely, a closer look at religion and potential ways it impacts on an individual, and an integrated approach to mental health that has space for religious forms of coping. Contributions of religious coping to mental health also have potential for regulating aspects of identity that could be harmful depending on the context, for example, gender (Zukerman et al. 2017). In a study with 1,016 participants to assess relationships between religious coping, gender, posttraumatic stress disorder (PTSD) and posttraumatic growth (PTG), positive religious coping was more strongly linked to PTG and negative religious coping more associated with PTSD, and, in addition, positive religious coping helped to control the relationship between gender and PTG (Gerber et al. 2011).

Religious experience and mental health across cultures

In traditional systems of treating mental illness, religion and spirituality frequently inform and provide the foundation for how the patient is perceived and treated. In this sense, religion and spirituality is entwined with the way that mental health is viewed; the divisions and separations that we have been discussing so far in this chapter are not so evident. Compared to beliefs, practices and coping, religious experiences are quite elusive and can be deeply embedded into cultural traditions, which deviate away from the focus of mental health.

Explanations of mental illness in terms of spirit possession are a global phenomenon (Boddy 1994). Cultures that are structured on deep-rooted beliefs about spirits are linked to human rights violations in terms of the persecution and physical abuse of individuals who are suffering from distressing psychological symptoms and are not offered support or treatment other than potentially harmful traditional practices (Ae-Ngibise et al. 2010). The phenomena associated with mental disorders fit into the schema of a world-view where different forms of spirits exist and are related to higher rates of psychological distress and suicide (Neuner et al. 2012).

Spirit possession in the context of mental illness is considered involuntary (Ahmad and Dein 2016). Involuntary spirit possession is when a person is considered as possessed by a spirit caused by witchcraft or other supernatural forces such as ancestors or ghosts. In this sense, the spirit needs to be expelled. An individual's agency and autonomy during the period of spirit possession is reduced and overcome by the presence of the spirit. The possessed individual is viewed in terms of "instrumental agency" (Keller 2005), which is to say that he/she obtains their identity as possessed from their community's view that they are no longer an autonomous agent. Without autonomy, an individual is understood as not having capacity and cannot consent to treatment. Spirit possession is not considered to be a mental disorder but as spirit possession is an integral part to global cultural narratives, a person possessed by a spirit needs healing. In this sense, spirit possession is a unique situation juxtaposing agency and pathology (Ahmad and Dein 2016).

The person experiencing the spirit possession is viewed as weak and unable to overcome the possession individually. By virtue of understanding spirit possession as part of a cultural narrative, the person possessed by a spirit is under the hold of a more powerful force and refers to "an integration of spirit and matter, force or power and corporeal reality, in a cosmos where the boundaries between an individual and her environment are acknowledged to be permeable, flexibly drawn, or at least negotiable" (Boddy 1994: 407). This understanding of the role of spirits in society reflects an overall understanding about a wider world-view that incorporates different elements of the tangible and intangible and that these are potentially very different from other societies such as the United Kingdom, which is premised on a rationalistic and positivist view of the human body.

Exorcisms are a traditional practice for treating spirit possession (Sanford 2016). An exorcism is a religious or cultural practice governed to expel an evil spirit from an individual's body (Laycock 2015). Exorcisms are violent procedures in order to overcome the possessive force that is subsuming the individual. The method includes frequent physical attacks on the individual's body by another party, often the traditional healer or a religious leader, including torture, flogging, and starvation. Exorcism is a common treatment because spirit possession is also linked to religious discourses such as Christianity and Islam (Hanwella et al. 2012). A pre-existing psychiatric diagnosis does not prevent the use of localized religious and cultural treatments such as exorcisms – exorcisms take place even in cases of individuals who have been recognized as having a mental illness (Tajima et al. 2011).

Exorcisms take place over a prolonged period of time and can recur if the perceived signs of spirit possession occur. Due to the exposure to traumatic situations and significant impact on health, exorcisms can exacerbate pre-existing psychiatric symptoms and in turn lead to an increased likelihood of the individual being viewed as possessed by a spirit. Spirit possession is a form of "instrumental agency" (Keller 2005). In other words, an individual loses their autonomy during episodes of spirit possession and is not viewed as a person who is able to consent to treatment. Exorcisms thus take place without the consent of the individual and are a form of forced treatment with harmful and potentially fatal consequences.

A person experiencing the spirit possession is viewed as weak and unable to overcome the possession individually. By virtue of understanding spirit possession as part of a cultural narrative, the person possessed by a spirit is under the hold of a more powerful force and refers to "an integration of spirit and matter, force or power and corporeal reality, in a cosmos where the boundaries between an individual and her environment are acknowledged to be permeable, flexibly drawn, or at least negotiable" (Boddy 1994: 407). This understanding of the role of spirits in society reflects an overall understanding about a wider world-view that incorporates different elements of the tangible and intangible and that these are potentially very different from other societies such as the United Kingdom, which is premised on a rationalistic and positivist view of the human body. In this sense, there are extreme divisions between biomedical paradigms of mental health and religion. However, within the paradigm of human rights argumentation, religion and mental health are intrinsically embodied in these examples of cross-cultural contexts.

The treatment of conditions like schizophrenia relies on an understanding of their causation and in particular the meaning and representation that the presentation of this illness expresses for the society. Cultural beliefs are paramount in shaping the experience of a mental illness and play an integral role in the "aetiology, diagnosis, preventative measures and regiments of healing" (Rubel 1977: 119) of certain phenomena. Hearing voices and talking to voices that are not experienced by others is recognized as talking with an ancestral spirit (Duijl et al. 2005). In this sense, it is possible that individuals who are known to be hearing voices are subject to responses appropriate for the particular cultural context. Witchcraft and spirit possession are understood to influence an affected individual through altering their behaviour to resemble that of a mentally ill person (Ally and Laher 2008). The notion of treatment in such cases of spirit possession or curses from witchcraft refers to the need to expel the spirit and/or curse that is understood to be inhibiting the person and causing their abnormal behaviour. Treatment for spirit possession is sought for both physical and mental illnesses, which reflects an explanatory model of understanding the mind and body as separate concepts, although "many African cultures do distinguish between the mind and the body" (Patel 1995: 1291).

African traditional medicine is a significant health-delivery system and forms part of the cultural expectations of local populations seeking healthcare (Kajawu et al. 2016). From a Western scientific medicine approach, African indigenous medicine is viewed as idiosyncratic and unpredictable (Hewson 2015). African concepts of health and healing for both physical and psychospiritual problems are viewed within a paradigm situated in particular historical, geographic, linguistic, religious and cultural contexts (Hewson 2015). There is a significant divide, therefore, between approaches to mental illness in global contexts as well as the efficiency of treatments.

A health care system about mental illness that is rooted in beliefs about spirits and witchcraft as causal agents has a bearing on the mode of treatment given. A patient's cultural background is integral for their experience and attitudes towards treatments in pluralistic societies. For example, there is a strong correlation between beliefs in supernatural causes of mental illness and poor drug compliance as well as follow-up care when mental health facilities are available (Razali et al 1996). For example, there is a global burden of disease reflecting that there is a severe lack of mental health resources and in the absence of westernized psychiatric treatments, traditional medicine is the dominant framework and point of entry for an individual requiring healing.

Modern magic: Religion and mental health systems

Treating mental health through medications and other psychotherapeutic practices are modern transitions of scientific knowledge about how to respond to illnesses of the mind that may traditionally have been viewed as the malevolent products of magic. However, at the same time, the image of traditional healers as belonging to the terrain of anthropologists exploring healing practices and rituals in communities is transforming into systematic and structured mental health care interventions. The convergence of religion and spirituality with mental health is stemming from the parallel development of empirical based evidence on the prevalence of mental illness with recognition and greater adherence to respecting the right to have freedom of thought and belief in pluralistic healthcare contexts, with the aim to developing effective collaborations with traditional systems of medicine to treat mental health disorders (Gureje et al. 2015: 168).

The United Arab Emirates (UAE) is a prime example of a high-income country with one-fifth of the global burden of disease constituting neuropsychiatric disorders. However, 'religious viewpoints' were strongly associated with the UAE citizens' reluctance to seek professional mental health care (Chowdhury 2016), illustrating the role of religion in determining the nature of a mental health system. For example, current approaches in addressing the gap between mental illness and treatment involve positioning mental illness and treatment in the context of Islamic jurisprudence and includes working with Imams of mosques as well as training primary healthcare doctors and nurses in mental health. Religion, therefore, acts as a centralizing locale for drawing attention to the role of mental health care providers in treating mental illness.

However, on a global scale, culture is entwined with religion and spirituality in healing practices for mental-health-related suffering. Traditional healers are estimated to be consulted by 70%–80% of the population in Africa (Truter 2007). In South Africa, a setting of limited mental health infrastructure and resources, traditional healers and religious leaders play an integral role in responding to mental health care needs. Mental health is predominantly viewed from a spiritual lens, with traditional healers relating to belief-systems that understand mental illness to be the result of bewitchment or due to ancestors and are more accessible than Western mental health care facilities (Sorsdahl et al. 2009). Thus, accessibility is an integral factor in the decision-making for ways to treat mental illness. In globalized contexts, there will typically by a mix of orthodox and non-orthodox models of mental health care. Yet, is it truly the case that traditional healers appeal because there are limited alternative choices for seeking treatment for mental illness. In addition to the demand for cultural appropriation, traditional healers have been described as contributing to the well-being of a significant proportion of the world's population by acting as "unintended partners in global mental health" (Incayawar et al. 2009: xvii).

Religion, intersectionality, and mental health

Intersectionality theory is an analytic tool that considers how different forms of identity such as religion, ethnicity, gender or age, for example, affects an individual's social and cultural status (Nash 2008). Intersectionality theory provides a framework for understanding identity and society through the modalities of multiple identities in mental health including service use (Cairney et al. 2014) and understanding mental health illness stigma (Oexle and Corrigan 2018). Recognizing identity within a paradigm of spirituality is challenging. However, failure of psychiatrists to address spiritual or religion concerns as pointed out by Dein et al is not "consistent with the objective of gaining a full understanding of the patient's condition and their self-understanding or attracting their full and active engagement with services" (Dein et al. 2010: 63). An individuals' lived experience may be defined by their religious and spiritual identities. Unless these identities are accounted for there will be gaps in patient personal and thus clinical histories.

Socio-cultural identities play a significant role in the juxtaposition of spirituality and psychiatry. Spirituality opens an interesting space for the individual to explore existential meanings relating to their lived experiences. In psychiatry, the endeavour to respond to distress and suffering creates a vulnerability in the need to enter the reflection and need to comprehend how the patient is understanding their situation. Spirituality, then, offers the opportunity for the individual to engage with their cultural bearing on the way that they perceive their sense of self and the surrounding world.

Culture and ethnicity as well as gender, religion, age and disability, shape the content of the psychiatrist-patient relationship. Socio-cultural identities are also a governing factor in the diagnosis and treatment of mental disorders (Schultz 2005) and thus cultural competence is a key aspect of practicing psychiatry. Psychiatric diseases are varied in occurrence and prognosis but are found in every culture (Kastrup and Ramos 2007). However, global mental health critics such as Derek Summerfield argue that global mental health is another form of imperialism (Summerfield 2013). Such strong criticism does raise issues for cultural competency in mental health by questioning the transportation of mental health systems to diverse populations, most notably from the viewpoint of Arthur Kleinman's 'category fallacy', namely that the "reification of a nosological category developed for a particular cultural group that is then applied to members of another culture for whom it lacks coherence and its validity has not been established" (Kleinman 1987: 452). For cultural groups that are part of healthcare systems dominated by religious or spiritual narratives, receiving prescriptions on how to perceive and act on diagnoses and prognoses of mental disorder can thus be harmful. As the global mental health movement continues, Kleinman's 'category fallacy' will be increasingly relevant and important to consider.

Future directions

Practitioners in mental health, particularly in contexts such as North America and Europe, where a biomedical framework of psychiatry is dominant, need to be aware of the relationship between religion and spirituality and mental health. The parallels between the cultural critiques of religion, spirituality, and mental health with the ever-evolving global mental health movement pose exciting new spaces for the fusion of alternative discourses with the medicalization of mental health. Psychiatry needs to draw on wider aspects of lived experiences of religion, spirituality and contextualised within the cultural paradigms of global contexts of mental health. We conclude hereby with the need to explore spaces in the various forms of treatment settings for psychiatric practice, which can accommodate pluralistic beliefs that form the understanding and healing for mental illness.

Conclusion

Culture and religion in mental health continue to be intertwined to the complexity of understanding modals of distress, suffering, as well as coping. The intersectionality of mental health with religious and spiritual beliefs systems magnifies the fluidity of historical and contemporary frames of references towards perceptions of mental illness. Culture and religion in mental health plays a role in diagnosing, treating, and recovery in psychiatry.

References

Abu-Raiya, H., Pargament, K.I. and Krause, N. (2016) 'Religion as problem, religion as solution: Religious buffers of the links between religious/spiritual struggles and well-being/mental health'. *Quality of Life Research*, 25(5): 1265–1274.

Abu Raiya, H., Pargament, K.I., Mahoney, A. and Stein, C. (2008) 'A psychological measure of Islamic religiousness: Development and evidence for reliability and validity'. *The International Journal for the Psychology of Religion*, 18(4): 291–315.

Ae-Ngibise, K., Cooper, S., Adiibokah, E., Akpalu, B., Lund, C., Doku, V. and Mhapp Research Programme Consortium (2010) 'Whether you like it or not people with mental problems are going to go to them: A qualitative exploration into the widespread use of traditional and faith healers in the provision of mental health care in Ghana'. *International Review of Psychiatry*, 22(6): 558–567.

Affleck, W., Selvadurai, A. and Sikora, L. (2018) 'Underrepresentation of men in gender-based humanitarian and refugee trauma research: A scoping review'. *Intervention*, 16(1): 22–30.

Ahmad, A. and Dein, S. (2016) 'Does culture impact on notions of criminal responsibility and action? The case of spirit possession'. *Transcultural Psychiatry*, 53(5): 674–682.

Ally, Y., and Laher, S. (2008) 'South African Muslim faith healers perceptions of mental illness: Understanding, aetiology and treatment', *Journal of Religion and Health*, *47*(1): 45–56.

Avent, J.R., Cashwell, C.S. and Brown-Jeffy, S. (2015) 'African American pastors on mental health, coping, and help seeking'. *Counseling and Values*, *60*(1): 32–47.

Bergin, A.E. (1991) 'Values and religious issues in psychotherapy and mental health'. *American Psychologist*, *46*(4): 394–403.

Beveridge, A., (2012) 'Reading about the History of Psychiatry', *The British Journal of Psychiatry*, *200*(5): 431–433.

Bhugra, D. and Bhui, K. (Eds.) (2018) *Textbook of cultural psychiatry*. Cambridge: Cambridge University Press.

Boddy, J. (1994) 'Spirit possession revisited: Beyond instrumentality'. *Annual Review of Anthropology*, *23*(1): 407–434.

Breakey, W.R. (2001) 'Psychiatry, spirituality and religion'. *International Review of Psychiatry*, *13*(2): 61–66.

Cairney, J., Veldhuizen, S., Vigod, S., Streiner, D.L., Wade, T.J. and Kurdyak, P. (2014) 'Exploring the social determinants of mental health service use using intersectionality theory and CART analysis'. *Journal of Epidemiology and Community Health*, *68*(2): 145–150.

Cauce, A.M., Domenech-Rodríguez, M., Paradise, M., Cochran, B.N., Shea, J.M., Srebnik, D. and Baydar, N. (2002) 'Cultural and contextual influences in mental health help seeking: A focus on ethnic minority youth'. *Journal of Consulting and Clinical Psychology*, *70*(1): 44–55.

Chowdhury, N. (2016) 'Integration between mental health-care providers and traditional spiritual healers: Contextualising Islam in the twenty-first century', *Journal of Religion and Health*, *55*(5): 1665–1671.

Dein, S. (2013) *Religion and Mental Health*. United Kingdom: Royal College of Psychiatrists, pp. 1–5.

Dein, S., Cook, C.C., Powell, A. and Eagger, S. (2010) 'Religion, spirituality and mental health', *The Psychiatrist*, *34*(2): 63–64.

Durà-Vilà, G. (2017) *Sadness, Depression, and the Dark Night of the Soul: Transcending the Medicalisation of Sadness*. Jessica Kingsley Publishers. London.

Farris, K. (2007) 'The role of African-American pastors in mental health care'. *Journal of Human Behavior in the Social Environment*, *14*(1–2): 159–182.

Fernando, S. (2014) 'Transcultural psychiatry and mental health'. In *Critical psychiatry and mental health* (pp. 29–37). London: Routledge.

Foucault, M., and Dreyfus, H. (1987) Mental illness and psychology. University of California Press, United States of America.

Gerber, M.M., Boals, A. and Schuettler, D. (2011) 'The unique contributions of positive and negative religious coping to posttraumatic growth and PTSD'. *Psychology of Religion and Spirituality*, *3*(4): 298–307.

Gooding, P.A., Littlewood, D., Owen, R., Johnson, J. and Tarrier, N. (2017) 'Psychological resilience in people experiencing schizophrenia and suicidal thoughts and behaviors'. *Journal of Mental Health*, *28*: 1–7.

Groen, S.P., Richters, A., Laban, C.J. and Devillé, W.L. (2018) 'Cultural identity among Afghan and Iraqi traumatized refugees: Towards a conceptual framework for mental health care professionals'. *Culture, Medicine, and Psychiatry*, *42*(1): 69–91.

Gureje, O., Nortje, G., Makanjuola, V., Oladeji, B.D., Seedat, S. and Jenkins, R. (2015) 'The role of global traditional and complementary systems of medicine in the treatment of mental health disorders'. *The Lancet Psychiatry*, *2*(2): 168–177.

Haneef Khan, Z.I.A.S.M.A. and Watson, P.J. (2006) 'Religious orientation and the experience of Eid-ul-Azha among Pakistani Muslims'. *Journal for the Scientific Study of Religion*, *43*(4): 537–545.

Hanwella, R., de Silva, V., Yoosuf, A., Karunaratne, S. and de Silva, P. (2012) 'Religious beliefs, possession states, and spirits: Three case studies from Sri Lanka', *Case Reports in Psychiatry*, *2012*: 1–3.

Hewson, M. G. (2015) 'Challenges of Medicine across the Cultural Divide', In *Embracing Indigenous Knowledge in Science and Medical Teaching* (pp. 53–72). Springer: Dordrecht.

Illich, I. (1975) *Medical nemesis* (p. 59). Australian Broadcasting Commission, Science Programmes Unit. Australia.

Incayawar, M., Wintrob, R., Bouchard, L. and Bartocci, G. (2009) *Psychiatrists and traditional healers: Unwitting partners in global mental health* (Vol. 9). London: John Wiley.

Kajawu, L., Chingarande, S. D., Jack, H., Ward, C., and Taylor, T. (2016) 'What do African traditional medical practitioners do in the treatment of mental disorders in Zimbabwe?', *International Journal of Culture and Mental Health*, *9*(1): 44–55.

Kastrup, M. C., and Ramos, A. B. (2007) 'Global Mental Health', *Danish Medical Bulletin*, *54*(1): 42–43.

Keller, M. (2005). *The Hammer and the Flute: Women, Power, and Spirit Possession*. JHU Press. Baltimore, USA.

Kirkpatrick, L.A. and Shaver, P.R. (1990) 'Attachment theory and religion: Childhood attachments, religious beliefs, and conversion'. *Journal for the Scientific Study of Religion*; 315–334.

Kleinman, A. (1987) 'Anthropology and psychiatry: The role of culture in cross-cultural research on illness', *The British Journal of Psychiatry, 151*(4): 447–454.

Kleinman, A. (2008) *Rethinking psychiatry*. New York: Simon and Schuster.

Koenig, H.G. (2008) 'Religion and mental health: What should psychiatrists do'? *Psychiatric Bulletin, 32*(6): 201–203.

Koenig, H.G. (2009) 'Research on religion, spirituality, and mental health: A review'. *The Canadian Journal of Psychiatry, 54*(5): 283–291.

Krumrei, E.J., Pirutinsky, S. and Rosmarin, D.H. (2013) 'Jewish spirituality, depression, and health: An empirical test of a conceptual framework'. *International Journal of Behavioral Medicine, 20*(3): 327–336.

Laycock, J.P. (Ed.) (2015) *Spirit possession around the world: Possession, communion, and demon expulsion across cultures*. United Kingdom: ABC-CLIO. Mind, Body, and Spirit Publishers.

Lim, A., Hoek, H.W. and Blom, J.D. (2015) 'The attribution of psychotic symptoms to jinn in Islamic patients'. *Transcultural psychiatry, 52*(1): 18–32.

Mizuno, Y., Hofer, A., Frajo-Apor, B., Wartelsteiner, F., Kemmler, G., Pardeller, S., Suzuki, T., Mimura, M., Fleischhacker, W.W. and Uchida, H. (2017) 'Religiosity and psychological resilience in patients with schizophrenia and bipolar disorder: An international cross-sectional study'. *Acta Psychiatrica Scandinavica*: 316–327.

Nash, J.C. (2008) 'Re-thinking intersectionality'. *Feminist Review, 89*(1): 1–15.

Neuner, F., Pfeiffer, A., Schauer-Kaiser, E., Odenwald, M., Elbert, T. and Ertl, V. (2012) 'Haunted by ghosts: Prevalence, predictors and outcomes of spirit possession experiences among former child soldiers and war-affected civilians in Northern Uganda', *Social Science and Medicine, 75*(3): 548–554.

Oexle, N. and Corrigan, P.W. (2018) 'Understanding mental illness stigma toward persons with multiple stigmatized conditions: Implications of intersectionality theory', *Psychiatric Services, 69*(5): 587–589.

Olson, M.M., Trevino, D.B., Geske, J.A. and Vanderpool, H. (2012) 'Religious coping and mental health outcomes: An exploratory study of socioeconomically disadvantaged patients', *Explore: The Journal of Science and Healing, 8*(3): 172–176.

Pargament, K.I., Ensing, D.S., Falgout, K., Olsen, H., Reilly, B., Van Haitsma, K. and Warren, R. (1990) 'God help me (I): Religious coping efforts as predictors of the outcomes to significant negative life events'. *American Journal of Community Psychology, 18*(6): 793–824.

Patel, V. (1995) 'Explanatory models of mental illness in sub-Saharan Africa', *Social Science & Medicine, 40*(9): 1291–1298.

Payne, I.R., Bergin, A.E., Bielema, K.A. and Jenkins, P.H. (1991) 'Review of religion and mental health: Prevention and the enhancement of psychosocial functioning', *Prevention in Human Services, 9*(2): 11–40.

Prince, M., Patel, V., Saxena, S., Maj, M., Maselko, J., Phillips, M.R. and Rahman, A. (2007) 'No health without mental health', *The Lancet, 370*(9590): 859–877.

Razali, S. M., Khan, U. A., and Hasanah, C. I. (1996) 'Belief in supernatural causes of mental illness among Malay patients: impact on treatment', *Acta Psychiatrica Scandinavica, 94*(4): 229–233.

Rosmarin, D.H., Pargament, K.I., Krumrei, E.J. and Flannelly, K.J. (2009) 'Religious coping among Jews: Development and initial validation of the JCOPE', *Journal of Clinical Psychology, 65*(7): 670–683.

Rosmarin, D.H., Pargament, K.I., Pirutinsky, S. and Mahoney, A. (2010) 'A randomized controlled evaluation of a spiritually integrated treatment for subclinical anxiety in the Jewish community, delivered via the Internet', *Journal of Anxiety Disorders, 24*(7): 799–808.

Rubel, A.J. (1977) 'The epidemiology of a folk illness: *Susto* in Hispanic America'. In D. Landy (Ed.), *Culture, disease and healing: Studies in medical anthropology* (pp. 119–128). Macmillan: London.

Sabry, W.M. and Vohra, A. (2013) 'Role of Islam in the management of psychiatric disorders', *Indian Journal of Psychiatry, 55*(2): S205–S214.

Sanford, J.R. (2016) 'Facing our demons: Psychiatric perspectives on exorcism rituals', *The Hilltop Review, 8*(2): 87–93.

Schultz, D. (2005) 'Cultural competence in psychosocial and psychiatric care: A critical perspective with reference to research and clinical experiences in California, US and in Germany', *Social Work in Health Care, 39*(3–4): 231–247.

Sorsdahl, K., Stein, D.J., Grimsrud, A., Seedat, S., Flisher, A.J., Williams, D.R. and Myer, L. (2009) 'Traditional healers in the treatment of common mental disorders in South Africa', *The Journal of Nervous and Mental Disease*, *197*(6): 434–441.

Sperry, L. and Peteet, J.R. (2016) 'Ethics and spiritually sensitive psychiatric practice: Introduction and overview. *Spirituality in Clinical Practice*', *3*(3): 153–154.

Spirituality and Psychiatry Special Interest Group. (2017) Newsletter No. 43. Retrieved from www.rcpsych.ac.uk/docs/default-source/members/sigs/spirituality-spsig/newsletter-no-43-june-2017.pdf?sfvrsn=62c314cf_4. Accessed on July 12, 2020.

Summerfield, D. (2013) '"Global mental health" is an oxymoron and medical imperialism', *British Medical Journal*, *346*: 3509.

Tajima-Pozo, K., Zambrano-Enriquez, D., de Anta, L., Moron, M. D., Carrasco, J. L., Lopez-Ibor, J. J., and Diaz-Marsá, M. (2011) Practicing exorcism in schizophrenia. *Case Reports, 2011: 1–3*, bcr1020092350.

Tarakeshwar, N., Pargament, K.I. and Mahoney, A. (2003) 'Initial development of a measure of religious coping among Hindus', *Journal of Community Psychology*, *31*(6): 607–628.

Tepper, L., Rogers, S.A., Coleman, E.M. and Malony, H.N. (2001) 'The prevalence of religious coping among persons with persistent mental illness', *Psychiatric Services*, *52*(5): 660–665.

Truter, I. (2007) 'African traditional healers: Cultural and religious beliefs intertwined in a holistic way', *South African Pharmaceutical Journal*, *74*(8): 56–60.

Unterrainer, H.F., Lewis, A.J. and Fink, A. (2014) 'Religious/spiritual well-being, personality and mental health: a review of results and conceptual issues', *Journal of Religion and Health*, *53*(2): 382–392.

Van Duijl, M., Cardeña, E., and De Jong, J. T. (2005) 'The validity of DSM-IV dissociative disorders categories in south-west Uganda'. *Transcultural Psychiatry*, *42*(2): 219–241.

Weber, S.R. and Pargament, K.I. (2014) 'The role of religion and spirituality in mental health'. *Current Opinion in Psychiatry, 27*(5): 358–363.

WHOQoL SRPB Group. (2006) 'A cross-cultural study of spirituality, religion, and personal beliefs as components of quality of life'. *Social Science and Medicine*, *62*(6): 1486–1497.

Zukerman, G., Korn, L. and Fostick, L. (2017) 'Religious coping and posttraumatic stress symptoms following trauma: The moderating effects of gender', *Psychology of Religion and Spirituality*, *9*(4): 328–336.

17

CULTURE, TRANSGENDER INDIVIDUALS, AND MENTAL HEALTH

T. Dawson Woodrum, Trenton Owens and Lauren Mizock

Historically, conversations about gender have been steeped in language supporting assumptions that were accepted as valid on their face (Hyde et al. 2018). For many years, gender has been viewed as binary, fixed, and biologically determined. Gender was conflated with biological sex. Once declared at birth based on external appearance of genitalia it could never change. There was no other alternative – one's personal feelings about their gender were irrelevant. Anyone challenging these assumptions was ostracized; anyone refusing to conform to behavioral roles consistent with their assigned gender was an anomaly at best or deviant at worst.

Current transgender-focused research cuts across multiple disciplines including psychology, biology, sociology, history, anthropology and archeology. This research also, to a large degree, challenges many long-held assumptions about gender (Hyde et al. 2018). These challenges, in turn, generate significant cultural tension. A number of gender-based assumptions undergird pervasive gender-based power structures in our society (Westbrook and Schilt 2014) and continue to influence how we approach health research for individuals who do not conform with those assumptions (Frohard-Dourlent et al. 2017).

This chapter examines current research addressing the interplay between culture, transgender identity, and mental health. A brief overview of terminology and population size estimates will be followed by an overview of transphobia and its contributory role in creating stressors that may negatively impact mental health. A review of this research landscape would not be complete, however, without also examining protective factors that contribute to the development of coping skills and resilience in this population. Lastly, alternative, less pathologizing constructs – like demoralization and transgender community connectedness – offer clues for developing more effective approaches to promoting transgender mental health.

Transgender population background

Given the evolution of terminology surrounding diverse gender identities, it is important to clarify terms that will be used in this chapter. Transgender is an umbrella term used when one's gender identity and biological sex assigned at birth do not align (although not all genderqueer/non-binary individuals self-identify as transgender) (APA 2015). This misalignment may be subjectively experienced, objectively observed, or both. Genderqueer and non-binary are terms used to denote a variety of identities, including those that fall between or outside of the traditional male-female binary spectrum, actively fluctuate between male and female, or reject gender as an identity (Matsuno and Budge 2017). Gender diversity is an affirming term that refers to the extent to which a person's gender identity differs from culturally prescribed gender norms.

Estimating the size of the population of people who identify as transgender or gender diverse (TGD) is problematic because traditional data collection instruments usually confound biological sex assigned at birth and gender identity. In other words, TGD-identified people forced to choose "Male" or "Female" on documents with significant legal, medical, and psychological ramifications are often rendered invisible in the dominant culture. TGD identity is multifarious and includes those who choose to transition socially and/or medically, as well as those who do not. More recent population studies addressing prevalence data for the TGD population use self-identification measures (Winter et al. 2016).

Researchers have begun to analyze population-based probability samples to more accurately estimate TGD population size. For example, Crissman et al. (2017) conducted a secondary analysis of transgender status data from the U.S. 2014 Behavioral Risk Factor Surveillance System and found self-identified transgender individuals made up 0.53% of the population. Meerwijk and Sevelius (2017), using a meta-regression of population-based probability samples from five recurring U.S. surveys undertaken from 2006 through 2015, found that the current best estimate for the number of transgender adults in the United States is 0.39%. This is 390 adults per 100,000 (or approximately 1 in every 250 adults, giving a total of almost 1 million people). Worldwide estimates of transgender prevalence rates range from 0.3% to 0.5% (Winter et al. 2016). The U.S. Bureau international database of world populations lists the 2017 population of people aged 15 and older at roughly 5.5 billion. Extrapolating these prevalence rates would result in an estimated worldwide TGD population of between 15 and 25 million people, a figure which has largely been underestimated in the past.

Though recent surveys have included questions about transgender identity, the lack of standardized definitions continues to make it difficult to accurately estimate the population size of TGD-identified people. A two-step approach, asking for sex assigned at birth followed by current gender identity, has been recommended as best practice (Lombardi and Banik 2016).

Transphobia

Transphobia is a problem often experienced by TGD individuals. Transphobia is defined as discrimination against TGD individuals that can take place at institutional, societal, and individual levels (Nemoto, Bödeker, and Iwamoto 2011: 1980). This discrimination may include harassment, violence, and denial of basic human rights. Research suggests high rates of transphobic violence enacted toward TGD people. Lombardi et al. (2002: 95) conducted a survey with 402 TGD individuals to determine if they had ever been the victim of violence or harassment in their lifetimes. Over half of the participants reported experiencing verbal harassment and 47% of participants reported being assaulted.

Clements-Noelle, Marx, and Katz (2006: 59) also found high rates of violence and discrimination in their sample of over 500 transgender participants in San Francisco. Fifty-nine percent of participants reported being raped, 62% had experienced discrimination based on their gender, and 83% had received verbal harassment due to their TGD status. Similarly, Nemoto et al. (2011: 1981–1983) found that half of the 573 TGD participants had been physically assaulted, and half reported experiencing transphobia that included distancing themselves from family or friends due to harassment, concealing their TGD identity, and losing a job. Sugano, Nemoto, and Operario (2006: 220) found that during childhood, 80% of their 332 adult TGD participants experienced verbal harassment while 64% reported experiencing physical harassment. Moreover, those over age 25 reported greater levels of exposure to transphobia.

Transphobia is also manifested through laws and regulations that perpetuate discrimination. For example, the state of North Carolina passed House Bill 2 on March 23, 2016. The bill was enacted to allow for single-sex multiple occupancy in public restrooms and changing facilities based on biologic sex. Biologic sex was defined as the physical state of being female or male as expressed by one's birth certificate (North Carolina General Assembly 2016). In other words, TGD individuals were denied the right to use the restroom that aligned with their gender identity in facilities overseen by state agencies if they had not had surgical interventions that allowed them to then change their birth certificate. Non-discrimination laws that include gender identity are in place in other states and with some community agencies, but have not been enacted at the national level and are often poorly enforced (Scout 2016: 378).

TGD individuals may be denied basic protections that offer access to equal and harassment-free treatment in public spaces, such as schools, prisons, shelters, and treatment centers (Anton 2009: 442). In schools, TGD youth may be ridiculed by peers and teachers. Teachers may also balk at using a student's preferred name or encourage them to behave in ways that more closely align with their sex assigned at birth. Teachers and school officials may also ignore complaints of harassment and threats of physical violence (Case and Meier 2014: 64). TGD individuals may be denied civil rights and protections that their cisgender counterparts take for granted. They could be denied the right to marriage, which can provide personal, social, and legal benefits. They may be prevented from acquiring documentation related to their identity or be required to maintain legal documentation that discloses their TGD status post-transition (Anton 2009: 442; Mizock and Hopwood 2018: 66). In recent decades, there has been an increase in visibility of TGD individuals and their related difficulties in popular culture (Appleton 2005: 291). Bockting (2008: 216) believed this change helped TGD youth buffer against the effects of transphobia. While some strides have been made to address the needs of this group as of late, TGD children and adults still face profound inequities.

Internalized transphobia and mental health

Persistent encounters with transphobic stigma, victimization, or discrimination can result in the internalization of stigma (Austin and Goodman 2017: 828). Herek, Gillis, and Cogan (2009: 828) described internalized stigma as accepting strong feelings of disapproval about an aspect of one's identity and incorporating those feelings into one's belief system. Individuals adapt their view of self to overcome the dissonance that exists between their self-concept and societal stigma. For TGD individuals, this internalized transphobia can be directed inward, towards the self, or outward, towards other TGD people. The negative attitudes about other TGD individuals are likely to be secondary to negative attitudes these individuals hold about themselves and their own identities (Scandurra et al. 2018).

A number of studies provide support for the various types of discrimination that TGD individuals may face that can lead to internalized transphobia and negative mental health outcomes (Bockting 2008; Clements-Noelle et al. 2006; Dhejne et al. 2016; Lombardi et al. 2002; Mizock and Mueser 2014; Nadal and Mendoza 2013; Sevelius, Keatley, and Gutierrez-Mock 2011; Sugano et al. 2006). Recent studies suggest that prevalence rates for anxiety, bipolar disorder, and depressive disorders are two to three times higher in the TGD population than in the general population. While poor mental health may be the direct result of gender dysphoria or transphobia, identifying as TGD does not inescapably result in, nor explain, mental health problems (Mizock 2017).

The prevalence of physical and psychological abuse as well as psychological distress related to romantic partnerships has been linked to elevated depression rates. Studies have revealed rates that range from 48% to 62%. Anxiety among this group has an occurrence rate of 26% to 48%. Anxiety may be a response to prejudice, anticipation of stigma, life stress, financial hardship, transition-related difficulties, and loss of loved ones or social support. TGD individuals who have experienced trauma are more susceptible to developing depression, anxiety, and posttraumatic stress disorder. These mental health issues can be exacerbated by substance use (Mizock 2017).

Rates of substance use disorders among TGD individuals vary from 10% to 69%. Substance use may be a form of coping with discrimination, poverty, social isolation, and mental illness. Researchers have suggested the incidence of psychotic disorders and serious mental in the TGD population are similar to the general population. However, serious mental illness may impact how TGD individuals understand and express their gender. Mental health clinicians and treatment programs may also possess limited understanding of an individual's gender variance and how to provide gender affirming care (Mizock 2017). A thorough conceptualization is necessary for the purposes of treatment planning. For TGD individuals, that conceptualization involves developing an understanding of both the external and internal processes that drive mental health concerns.

As mentioned above, TGD individuals experience a variety of mental health difficulties as a result of discrimination and existing in a heteronormative society. The internalization of stigma has also been linked to many negative outcomes. Individuals who experience internalized transphobia are at increased risk for depression and substance abuse (Mizock and Mueser 2014; Morrow 2004). High levels of internalized transphobia have also been associated with increased chances of lifetime suicide attempts (Perez-Brumer, Hatzenbuehler, Oldenburg, and Bockting 2015). Low levels of internalized transphobia have been associated with reductions in suicidal ideation (Bauer, Scheim, Pyne, Travers, and Hammond 2015).

Sánchez and Vilain (2009) also found that TGD individuals who identified negative internal feelings regarding their gender identity endorsed lower well-being scores. Furthermore, TGD people with mental health problems may be more inclined to experience internalized stigma (Mizock and Mueser 2014). Researchers have linked substance use to perceived discrimination, internalized transphobia, and problems with mental health (Reisner, Perkovich, and Mimiaga, 2010; Sevelius 2013; Zimmerman et al. 2015). In addition to having a negative impact on mental health, internalized transphobia can have an adverse effect on the social aspects of the lives of TGD individuals.

Individuals who experience internalized transphobia may expect rejection and/or discrimination. To avoid this experience, they are likely to hide their TGD status or avoid interpersonal interactions (White Hughto, Reisner, and Pachankis 2015). TGD individuals may also experience body shame and self-objectification (Sevelius 2013: 677). Individuals who can "pass" or who are not perceived by others as TGD may choose not to disclose their TGD identity. These individuals may garner benefits associated with the privilege of passing, such as avoiding discrimination and poor treatment. However, they may also encounter anxiety related to disclosure and being out-ed (Sevelius 2013: 680; White Hughto et al. 2015).

Internalized transphobia can breed loneliness and result in risky sexual behaviors (Hendricks and Testa 2012; Sevelius 2013; Sevelius et al. 2011). Higher levels of exposure to transphobia have been associated with becoming infected with HIV (Sugano et al. 2006). TGD individuals may fear that their gender identity will negatively impact their relationships and sex lives. This phenomenon was substantiated by Meier, Sharp, Michonski, Babcock, and Fitzgerald (2013) who studied the prevalence of romantic relationships in transmen. Of the 593 participants studied, 54% reported their relationship ended due to their gender transition. While 51% of participants maintained their relationship post-transition, Meier et al. believed this was an over-estimate due to the length of these relationships. Relationship difficulties based on gender identity can lead to social isolation, which is connected to increased suicide risk (Hendricks and Testa 2012). TGD individuals may not only avoid platonic or romantic interpersonal situations but may avoid seeking professional relationships such as those required for necessary routine or emergency medical care (Cruz 2014; White Hughto et al. 2015). For example, TGD participants in the study by Reisner and colleagues (2010) expressed concerns with finding a suitable partner that would accept them. Participants also disclosed participating in risky sexual activities that they might be uncomfortable with because they felt grateful that a sexual partner was interested. TGD individuals may experience rejection, violence, and explicit or implicit discrimination in romantic relationships.

Pulice-Farrow et al. (2017) found that TGD participants reported microaggressions in their relationships that were divided into four categories: (1) minimization of their identity; (2) their partner(s) forcing their own expectations for the participants' gender onto them; (3) partners behaving less accepting and affirming in public than in private; and (4) microaggressions during milestones, such as coming out, periods of grief, and when a relationship was ending. According to Puckett and Levitt (2015), it is important to understand that internalized transphobia exists within a sociopolitical context. In other words, TGD individuals exist within a heteronormative environment that shapes their views of self as a gender minority. Therefore, the internalization of stigma cannot solely be attributed to their unique personality characteristics that lead to poor self-evaluation based on fear and shame related to their TGD identity but must also be attributed to the external influences that occur within the context of a prejudicial society with laws and regulations that perpetuate the discrimination.

In summary, circumstances like public discrimination, the threat of physical violence, and the denial of basic civil rights are a reality in the lives of TGD individuals. These stressors can impact their general level of functioning as well as fuel the trans-prejudice internalization process. The cognitive-affective processing systems of TGD individuals are heavily impacted by the internalization of stigma, which informs how they view and make sense of themselves, others, and their environments (White Hughto et al. 2015). Having a better understanding of internalized transphobia from the perspective of TGD individuals will inform future interventions and provide necessary information for prevention.

The above section highlighted a number of life domains in which TGD individuals are disproportionately impacted when compared to other populations. Related to mental health, TGD individuals experience higher rates of depression, anxiety, substance use, and risky sexual behavior. The attempted suicide rate of people who identify as TGD is also significantly higher than that of the general population. Unfortunately, these statistics are sometimes used in a pathologizing and stigmatizing manner by health care providers – making it all the more difficult for TGD individuals to acknowledge mental health problems and pursue treatment. It is important, therefore, to highlight the roles transphobia and minority stress likely play in TGD mental health problems in order to avoid the temptation to automatically couple TGD identity with mental health problems.

Mental health protective factors and coping with transphobia

Although the possession of minority status is associated with negative effects, minority status may serve as a protective and coping factor (Hendricks and Testa 2012; Meyer 2003). For instance, minority status is linked to togetherness and in-group acceptance. Coming out, for example, is a common experience among sexual and gender minorities. The coming out process allows sexual and gender minorities an opportunity to develop coping skills and learn how to mitigate the effects of stress. In addition to group resources, individual characteristics such as robustness and resilience help buffer against the effects of internalized transphobia.

Resilience among TGD individuals has been a particular area of focus in TGD research. Faced with an enormous number of stressors, researchers have shown an interest in what resources these individuals can draw upon to help them cope (Singh, Hays, and Watson 2011). However, Meyer (2015) proposed that coping should be distinguished from resilience. He explained that resilience and coping both protect TGD individuals from internalized stigma. However, coping suggests an effort that is made to adapt to or defend against a stressor. Resilience suggests a successful adaptation.

Singh et al. (2011) conducted a phenomenological study to explore the meaning of resilience in the lives of TGD individuals. The researchers uncovered five themes across the participants. One theme that emerged was being able to define their identity using their own language. Another theme they encountered was embracing self-worth. The participants also expressed the need for transgender individuals to be aware of the widespread nature of prejudice and discrimination towards them. This awareness helped participants to identify transphobic messages in an effort to avoid internalizing them. The next resilience theme Singh et al. found was being connected to a supportive community. Participants felt the support of like-minded individuals was an essential factor to combat the stressors associated with being a gender minority. The final theme was fostering the growth of hope for the future. In the face of challenges in a variety of domains, such as family and work, participants were able to look to a more positive future to help them through the difficult present. Two separate themes, social activism and being a positive role model, were common to the majority of participants. Being an advocate and role model helped to buffer the negative effects of discrimination (Singh et al. 2011), thus avoiding internalization of transphobia.

Breslow et al. (2015) surveyed 552 transgender individuals to explore the relationship between internalized transphobia and resilience. The authors also sought to gain an understanding of how engagement in collective action served as a buffer against the negative effects of minority stress. Breslow and colleagues found that resilience was connected to lower levels of psychological distress. Resilience was negatively associated with internalized transphobia, the awareness of stigma, and transphobic discrimination.

The coping strategies utilized by TGD individuals are not strictly the result of innate personality structures, but are often developed as a response to stress (White Hughto et al. 2017). TGD individuals who have experienced high rates of victimization and psychological distress have an increased rate of engaging in avoidant coping (Budge, Adelson, and Howard 2013; White Hughto et al. 2017). Utilizing avoidant coping reduces the strength of the positive correlation between victimization and symptoms of depression (White Hughto et al. 2017). However, rates of depression and anxiety are positively correlated with the use of avoidant coping. TGD individuals whose gender identities are further developed may exhibit less reliance on avoidant coping indicating lower levels of distress (Budge et al. 2013).

In a mixed method study, Mizock and Mueser (2014) found that lower levels of internalized transphobia were linked to higher levels of effective coping. Coping strategies were found at individual, interpersonal, and systemic levels. One particularly unique form of coping that emerged from the data was gender-normative coping. This referred to dealing with a situation in a manner that was consistent with one's gender identity. For example, one participant, a trans woman, who when being discriminated against, thought about her mother and cisgender women who would walk away with their "heads held high" instead of having what she perceived as a more stereotypically masculine response of fighting back. Another key form of coping that emerged was self-affirming coping. This referred to coping through reinforcing an individual's own strengths. This particular style included individual strengths of confidence, perseverance, self-awareness, and genuineness.

Mizock and Mueser (2014) also found that participants used emotional-regulation coping. With this form of coping, individuals exercised the ability to manage their emotions in response to stress. Those who used this coping strategy were able to stay calm, use relaxation, monitor their health regularly, and remain active. Cognitive-reframing coping was another individual strategy that emerged. This included using particular ways of thinking, e.g. positive thinking, reframing, and understanding the situation from various angles, to overcome stress. At the interpersonal level, the researchers noted the following coping skills: social-relational, preventative-preparative, and disengagement. Social-relational coping involved seeking support from close relationships and engaging in the community. The preventative-preparative coping style involved being alert and expecting discrimination so that participants would be prepared to deal with it if/when it occurred. For transgender individuals, this included whether or not to disclose their gender identity based on the safety of the situation and the potential outcome. The disengagement style of coping that emerged showed that participants would emotionally detach themselves from transphobic situations. This strategy also included isolating, ignoring, and hiding their identity from others (Mizock and Mueser 2014).

Finally, on a systemic level, resource-access, spiritual and religious, and political-empowerment styles of coping also emerged in Mizock and Mueser's (2014) study. Participants who used resource-access coping had a tendency to rely on community resources, such as legal advice, social media, and therapeutic services. Spiritual and religious coping referred to drawing on spiritual and religious direction, participating in activities, staying connected to a religious community, and having a relationship with God. Interestingly, roughly 9% of participants were religious leaders. This particular area of coping seems paradoxical as religious communities can also be a source of discrimination and prejudice for the same individuals who look to it for help overcoming stigma. The final coping style in this area, political-empowerment, was associated with becoming involved in activism and other activities that protect the rights of other transgender people and other marginalized groups (Mizock and Mueser 2014). This study illustrated some of the coping strategies utilized by TGD individuals as well as the various levels in which support can be found.

Freese, Ott, Rood, Reisner, and Pantalone (2018) also studied coping strategies among TGD individuals utilizing the Brief COPE coping measure. The largest coping profile endorsed by participants (42.4%) was titled the high-functional/low-dysfunctional (HFLD) profile. Individuals with this profile utilized positive self-efficacy and social support factors, while relying minimally on negative self-directed and substance abuse factors. The low-functional/low-dysfunctional (LFLD) coping profile was the next prominent profile (32.9%) identified in the study. Individuals with this profile rarely utilized any of the four factors (self-help and positive thinking, reaching out to others, denial and blame, and substance abuse) as a coping strategy. About 25% of participants were in the high-functional/high-dysfunctional profile, indicating they participated in all coping strategies. Overall, the findings of Freese and colleagues suggested that TGD individuals may rely on their own personal attributes and strengths as well as the support from social networks to cope with minority stress. TGD individuals utilize a variety of coping strategies, both positive and negative, to mitigate the deleterious effects of a minority existence.

Transgender community connectedness

What risk factors might be related to demoralization in the TGD-identified population, and how might they be mitigated? There are many factors that may, individually or cumulatively, overwhelm the TGD individual, ranging from heightened levels of external stigmatization and isolation, to internal psychological distress about gender identity. The minority stress model, for example, highlights the role external factors (like stigma, prejudice, and discrimination) contribute to the increased levels of psychological distress experienced by marginalized populations (Meyer 2003). In an online survey ($N = 1093$) of U.S. individuals identifying as transgender, Bockting, Miner, Swinburne, Romine, Hamilton, and Colman (2013) found support for the minority stress model: social stigma was significantly and positively associated with psychological distress.

The Bockting et al. (2013) study further revealed that available peer support (specifically from others who also identified as transgender) significantly moderated the relationship between enacted stigma and psychological distress. When the level of available peer support from other transgender people was high, the relationship between enacted stigma and psychological distress became insignificant. Additionally, Budge, Rossman, and Howard (2014) surveyed individuals who self-identified as genderqueer to examine how overall social support (from significant others, friends, and family) interacts with coping and mental health. There was a significant interaction between overall social support and coping factors. Respondents who reported higher levels of social support also used more facilitative coping, such as seeking help, and reported lower anxiety levels. The results of this study also supported the role of social support as a moderating variable; high levels of facilitative coping were not associated with lower anxiety levels if there was also lowered social support.

On the other hand, Austin and Goodman's (2017) survey of TGD-identified adults did not support social connectedness (interpersonal closeness with friends, peers and society) as having a moderating effect on the relationship between internalized transphobia and self-esteem. These differing results – one study supporting the role of social support as a moderating variable and another not – highlight the need for further research. Refining our understanding of when and how social support buffers the impact of various stressors or enhances resilience factors in the psychological well-being of TGD-identified individuals is necessary to develop effective prevention, assessment, and intervention strategies.

Plöderl et al. (2014) did not include gender non-conforming individuals in their study, and it is interesting to note that outness for TGD-identified persons is comprised of a different constellation of issues than for those LGB people who are non-TGD. For example, some of the former may be able to medically transition in a binary fashion: this may remove external cues that trigger enacted stigma and relieve that source of minority stress. For such individuals, outness may be closely akin to LGB outness, because their identity can be simultaneously expressed (in terms of a normative binary gender role) and concealed. That is to say, they can elect where and when assert their TGD identity.

TGD-identified persons may not want nor be able to medically transition, however; others (e.g., genderqueer individuals) may not identify as binary. In these cases, outness is less akin to LGB outness: a non-binary or non "passing" binary gender identity cannot be openly lived and concealed at the same time. Depending on the community where one lives, the risks associated with being out under these circumstances may be much higher.

Bockting et al. (2013) found that, contrary to expectation, concealment (or "passing") was positively associated with enacted stigma. This finding is suspect, however, because of the way concealment ("investment in passing" versus "actual passing") and enacted stigma ("ever experienced" versus "experienced after physical transition was compete") were operationalized in that study. Further research is needed to tease out whether differences in the experiences of outness within the TGD population impact how peer support might operate as a protective factor against stigma.

Testa et al. (2017) recently evaluated suicidal ideation (SI) in a large study of transgender adults. This study showed that factors from the gender minority stress and resilience (GMSR) model, a gender minority-specific model of mental health, and the IPT general theory of suicide are intertwined. The GMSR was developed to account for differences in mental and physical health between transgender and nontransgender populations (Testa et al. 2015). Pathway analysis showed that all seven gender minority stress factors of GMSR (rejection, nonaffirmation, victimization, discrimination, internalized transphobia, negative expectations, and nondisclosure) and the IPT factors of thwarted belongingness and perceived burdensomeness were related to one another, and contributed to risk of SI in TGD-identified individuals (Testa et al. 2017).

In the longer term, coming out seems to have a buffering effect against the negative impact of stigma for both LGB- and TGD-identified people. For example, suicidal ideation may be lowered, as those who are "out" gain access to a broader social support network and experience lower levels of internalized stigma following increased exposure to positive role models. A recent survey of TGD-identified people in Ontario, Canada also revealed that available social support and reduced transphobia were associated with large relative and absolute reductions in suicide risk (Bauer et al. 2015).

These studies shed light on the complex mechanisms by which suicidal ideation develops among those who identify as LGBT. Increased suicidality is, however, just one indicator of demoralization – especially in the TGD population, where the sources and impact of demoralization and social isolation are potentially extensive, and these factors may magnify or attenuate each other in unique ways. A better understanding of these factors and how they relate could inform the development of more effective policies and clinical approaches promoting wellbeing in the TGD population.

For example, Barr, Budge, and Adelson (2016) examined the relationship between transgender community belongingness and well-being in a large online survey of TGD-identified adults. The survey results revealed that the strength of transgender identity was indirectly and positively related to well-being through transgender community connectedness but was not directly related to well-being. Identification of oneself as transgender was not, by itself, related to increased levels of well-being: well-being only increased when trans identification endowed the individual with a sense of belonging to a transgender-identified community.

These findings are consistent with several other studies highlighting the importance of social support, a potential outcome of community connectedness, in buffering the negative impact of stigma (Bauer et al. 2015; Plöderl et al. 2014; Testa et al. 2017). It is unclear, however, whether this is because social support acts as a buffer. For example, in another large online survey of transgender-identified adults, Breslow et al. (2015) found resilience was, as predicted, negatively associated with psychological distress but did not, as predicted, moderate any of the relationships between the minority stressors and psychological distress. Resilience is a protective factor that has been examined across general populations, but it may work differently in the TGD population – especially if it requires establishing ties to a broader community that rejects them and is a source of psychological distress instead of comfort (Beasley, Jenkins, and Valenti 2015).

Historically, research concerning TGD people has tended to medicalize and pathologize their expression of gender diversity, instead of examining the impact marginalization has on otherwise healthy individuals (dickey, Hendricks, and Bockting 2016). Both demoralization and community connectedness seem particularly well-suited to research which seeks to view well-being in a less pathologizing and a more holistic and empowering way, by taking into account important dimensions of the lived experience of TGD-identified people.

Barr et al. (2016) noted that a sense of belonging to a community of peers may be particularly important for TGD-identified people because of their shared experience of alienation from mainstream society and lack of opportunity to experience their identities in a supportive environment as the norm. A sense of feeling connected to a supportive community of peers, in particular, may provide a buffer against minority stress, as well as affording more opportunities to enhance well-being by use of effective coping mechanisms, like seeking help.

Future directions

Basic terminology concerning gender diversity continues to evolve. Capturing gender-related identity data beyond the binary "male" and "female" continues to present a challenge for estimating the size of transgender population and assessing their representation in broader health-related research efforts (Lagos 2018; Mueller, De Cuypere, and T'Sjoen 2017). Candidate methods for standardization are starting to emerge (Lombardi and Banik 2016) but there is still considerable room for improvement in encouraging the routine collection of gender identity demographics (Valentine and Shipherd 2018).

Transphobia plays an important role in creating an environment (both externally imposed and internally experienced) that negatively impacts transgender mental health. There is a considerable body of research demonstrating the positive relationship between transgender identities and mental health concerns; most of these studies point the cultural intolerance, social stigma, discrimination, violence, and victimization as key contributors to this relationship (Sweileh 2018). Recent research, moreover, highlights the positive relationship between transgender mental health and resilience, thereby pointing to the need for more resilience-promoting approaches when treating this population (Matsuno and Israel 2018).

Conclusion

As we have seen in this chapter, minority stress and demoralization contribute to the development of theoretical models that focus on the impact of pervasive negative stressors in moderating and mediating the positive relationship between transgender identity and mental health concerns. American Psychological Association guidelines note that psychologists should provide TGD-affirming care (APA). It is, therefore, vital that psychologists develop culturally competent mental health assessments and interventions that identify and remediate the impact of these stressors instead of over-pathologizing transgender and gender diverse identities.

References

American Psychological Association (2015) 'Guidelines for psychological practice with transgender and gender nonconforming people', *American Psychologist*, 70(9): 832–864.

Anton, B. S. (2009) 'Proceedings of the American Psychological Association for the legislative year 2008: Minutes of the annual meeting of the Council of Representatives', *American Psychologist*, 64(5): 372–453.

Appleton, S. F. (2005) 'Contesting gender in popular culture and family law: Middlesex and other transgender tales', *Indiana Law Journal*, 80(2): 291–440.

Austin, A., Craig, S. L., and D'Souza, S. A. (2018) 'An AFFIRMative cognitive behavioral intervention for transgender youth: Preliminary effectiveness', *Professional Psychology: Research and Practice*, 49(1): 1–8.

Austin, A. and Goodman, R. (2017) 'The impact of social connectedness and internalized transphobic stigma on self-esteem among transgender and gender non-conforming adults', *Journal of Homosexuality*, *64*(6): 825–841.

Barr, S. M., Budge, S. L., and Adelson, J. L. (2016) 'Transgender community belongingness as a mediator between strength of transgender identity and well-being', *Journal of Counseling Psychology*, *63*(1): 87–97.

Bauer, G. R., Scheim, A. I., Pyne, J., Travers, R., and Hammond, R. (2015) 'Intervenable factors associated with suicide risk in transgender persons: a respondent driven sampling study in Ontario, Canada', *BMC Public Health*, *15*(1).

Beasley, C. R., Jenkins, R. A., and Valenti, M. (2015) 'Special section on LGBT resilience across cultures: Introduction', *American Journal of Community Psychology*, *55*(1–2): 164–166.

Bockting, W. O. (2008) 'Psychotherapy and the real-life experience: From gender dichotomy to gender diversity', *Sexologies*, *17*(4): 211–224.

Bockting, W. O., Miner, M. H., Swinburne Romine, R. E., Hamilton, A., and Coleman, E. (2013) 'Stigma, mental health, and resilience in an online sample of the U.S. transgender population', *American Journal of Public Health*, *103*(5): 943–951.

Breslow, A. S., Brewster, M. E., Velez, B. L., Wong, S., Geiger, E., and Soderstrom, B. (2015) 'Resilience and collective action: Exploring buffers against minority stress for transgender individuals', *Psychology of Sexual Orientation and Gender Diversity*, *2*(3): 253–265.

Budge, S. L., Adelson, J. L., and Howard, K. A. S. (2013) 'Anxiety and depression in transgender individuals: The roles of transition status, loss, social support, and coping', *Journal of Consulting and Clinical Psychology*, *81*(3): 545–557.

Budge, S. L., Rossman, H. K., and Howard, K. (2014) 'Coping and psychological distress among genderqueer individuals: The moderating effect of social support', *Journal of LGBT Issues in Counseling*, *8*(1): 95–117.

Case, K. A., and Meier, S. C. (2014) 'Developing allies to transgender and gender-nonconforming youth: Training for counselors and educators', *Journal of LGBT Youth*, *11*(1): 62–82.

Clements-Noelle, K., Marx, R., and Katz, M. (2006) 'Attempted suicide among transgender persons: The influence of gender-based discrimination and victimization', *Journal of Homosexuality*, *51*(3): 53–69.

Crissman, H. P., Berger, M. B., Graham, L. F., and Dalton, V. K. (2017) 'Transgender demographics: A household probability sample of U.S. adults, 2014', *American Journal of Public Health*, *107*(2): 213–215.

Cruz, T. M. (2014) 'Assessing access to care for transgender and gender nonconforming people: A consideration of diversity in combating discrimination', *Social Science & Medicine*, *110*: 65–73.

Dhejne, C., Van Vlerken, R., Heylens, G., and Arcelus, J. (2016) 'Mental health and gender dysphoria: A review of the literature', *International Review of Psychiatry*, *28*(1): 44–57.

dickey, l. m., Hendricks, M. L., and Bockting, W. O. (2016) 'Innovations in research with transgender and gender nonconforming people and their communities', *Psychology of Sexual Orientation and Gender Diversity*, *3*(2): 187–194.

Freese, R., Ott, M. Q., Rood, B. A., Reisner, S. L. and Pantalone, D. W. (2018) 'Distinct coping profiles are associated with mental health differences in transgender and gender nonconforming adults', *Journal of Clinical Psychology*, *74*(1): 136–146.

Frohard-Dourlent, H., Dobson, S., Clark, B. A., Doull, M., and Saewyc, E. M. (2017) '"I would have preferred more options": Accounting for non-binary youth in health research', *Nursing Inquiry*, *24*(1): e12150.

Gamarel, K. E., Reisner, S. L., Laurenceau, J., Nemoto, T., and Operario, D. (2014) 'Gender minority stress, mental health, and relationship quality: A dyadic investigation of transgender women and their cisgender male partners', *Journal of Family Psychology*, *28*(4): 437–447.

Hendricks, M. L., and Testa, R. J. (2012) 'A conceptual framework for clinical work with transgender and gender nonconforming clients: An adaptation of the minority stress model', *Professional Psychology: Research and Practice*, *43*(5): 460–467.

Herek, G. M., Gillis, J. R., and Cogan, J. C. (2009) 'Internalized stigma among sexual minority adults: Insights from a social psychological perspective', *Journal of Counseling Psychology*, *56*(1): 32–43.

Hyde, J. S., Bigler, R. S., Joel, D., Tate, C. C., and van Anders, S. M. (2018) 'The future of sex and gender in psychology: Five challenges to the gender binary', American Psychologist. Advance online publication. http://dx.doi.org.fgul.idm.oclc.org/10.1037/amp0000307.

Kosciw, J. G., Palmer, N. A., and Kull, R. M. (2015) 'Reflecting resiliency: Openness about sexual orientation and/or gender identity and its relationship to well-being and educational outcomes for LGBT students', *American Journal of Community Psychology*, *55*(1–2): 167–178.

Lagos, D. (2018) 'Looking at population health beyond "male" and "female": Implications of transgender identity and gender nonconformity for population health', *Demography, 55*(6): 2097–2117.

Lombardi, E., and Banik, S. (2016) 'The utility of the two-step gender measure within trans and cis populations', *Sexuality Research and Social Policy, 13*(3): 288–296.

Lombardi, E. L., Wilchins, R. A., Priesing, D., and Malouf, D. (2002) 'Gender violence: Transgender experiences with violence and discrimination', *Journal of Homosexuality, 42*(1): 89–101.

Matsuno, E., and Budge, S. L. (2017) 'Non-binary/Genderqueer Identities: A critical review of the literature', *Current Sexual Health Reports, 9*(3): 116–120.

Matsuno, E., and Israel, T. (2018) Psychological interventions promoting resilience among transgender individuals: Transgender Resilience Intervention Model (TRIM). *The Counseling Psychologist, 46*(5): 632–655.

Meerwijk, E. L., and Sevelius, J. M. (2017) 'Transgender population size in the U.S.: A meta-regression of population-based probability samples', *American Journal of Public Health, 107*(2): e1–e8.

Meier, S. C., Sharp, C., Michonski, J., Babcock, J. C., and Fitzgerald, K. (2013) 'Romantic relationships of female-to-male trans men: A descriptive study', *International Journal of Transgenderism, 14*: 75–85.

Meyer, I. H. (2003) 'Prejudice, social stress, and mental health in lesbian, gay, and bisexual populations: Conceptual issues and research evidence', *Psychological Bulletin, 129*(5): 674–697.

Meyer, I. H. (2015). 'Resilience in the study of minority stress and health of sexual and gender minorities', *Psychology of Sexual Orientation and Gender Diversity, 2*(3): 209–213.

Mizock, L. (2017) 'Transgender and gender diverse clients with mental disorders', *Psychiatric Clinics of North America, 40*(1): 29–39.

Mizock, L., and Hopwood, R. (2018) 'Economic challenges associated with transphobia and implications for practice with transgender and gender diverse individuals', *Professional Psychology: Research and Practice, 49*(1): 65–74.

Mizock, L., and Mueser, K. T. (2014) 'Employment, mental health, internalized stigma, and coping with transphobia among transgender individuals', Psychology of Sexual Orientation and Gender Diversity, *1*(2): 146–158.

Morrow, D. F. (2004) 'Social work practice with gay, lesbian, bisexual, and transgender adolescents', *Families in Society, 85*(1): 91–99.

Mueller, S. C., De Cuypere, G., and T'Sjoen, G. (2017) 'Transgender research in the 21st century: A selective critical review from a neurocognitive perspective', *American Journal of Psychiatry, 174*(12): 1155–1162.

Nadal, K. L., and Mendoza, R. J. (2013) 'Internalized oppression and the lesbian, gay, bisexual, and transgender community'. In E. J. R. David (Ed.), *Internalized oppression: The psychology of marginalized groups* (pp. 227–252). New York, NY: Springer.

Nemoto, T., Bödeker, B., and Iwamoto, M. (2011) 'Social support, exposure to violence and transphobia, and correlates of depression among male-to-female transgender women with a history of sex work', *American Journal of Public Health, 101*(10): 1980–1988.

North Carolina General Assembly. (2016, March 23) '*House bill 2/ S. L. 2016-3*', Retrieved from www. ncga.state.nc.us/Sessions/2015E2/Bills/House/PDF/H2v4.pdf.

Perez-Brumer, A., Hatzenbuehler, M. L., Oldenburg, C. E., and Bockting, W. (2015) 'Individual-and structural-level risk factors for suicide attempts among transgender adults', *Behavioral Medicine, 41*(3): 164–171.

Plöderl, M., Sellmeier, M., Fartacek, C., Pichler, E.-M., Fartacek, R., and Kralovec, K. (2014) 'Explaining the suicide risk of sexual minority individuals by contrasting the minority stress model with suicide models', *Archives of Sexual Behavior, 43*(8): 1559–1570.

Puckett, J. A., and Levitt, H. M. (2015) 'Internalized stigma within sexual and gender minorities: Change strategies and clinical implications', *Journal of LGBT Issues in Counseling, 9*(4): 329–349.

Pulice-Farrow, L., Brown, T. D., and Galupo, M. P. (2017) 'Transgender microaggressions in the context of romantic relationships', *Psychology of Sexual Orientation and Gender, 4*(3): 362–373.

Reisner, S. L., Perkovich, B., and Mimiaga, M. J. (2010) 'A mixed methods study of the sexual health needs of New England transmen who have sex with nontransgender men', *AIDS Patient Care and STDs, 24*(8): 501–513.

Sánchez, F. J., and Vilain, E. (2009) 'Collective self-esteem as a coping resource for male-to-female transsexuals', *Journal of Counseling Psychology, 56*(1): 202–209.

Scandurra, C., Bochicchio, V., Amodeo, A. L., Esposito, C., Valerio, P., Maldonato, N. M., Bacchini, D., and Vitelli, R. (2018) 'Internalized transphobia, resilience, and mental health: Applying the psychological mediation framework to Italian transgender individuals', *International Journal of Environmental Research and Public Health*, 15(3): 508e.

Scout, N. (2016) 'Transgender health and well-being: Gains and opportunities in policy and law', *American Journal of Orthopsychiatry*, 86(4): 378–383.

Sevelius, J. M. (2013) 'Gender affirmation: A framework for conceptualizing risk behavior among transgender women of color', *Sex Roles*, 68: 675–689.

Sevelius, J. M., Keatley, J., and Gutierrez-Mock, L. (2011) 'HIV/AIDS programming in the United States: Considerations affecting transgender women and girls', *Women's Health Issues*, 21, S278-S282.

Singh, A. A., Hays, D., and Watson, L. S. (2011) 'Strength in the face of adversity: Resilience strategies of transgender individuals', *Journal of Counseling and Development*, 89(1), 20–27.

Sugano, E., Nemoto, T., and Operario, D. (2006) 'The impact of exposure to transphobia on HIV risk behavior in a sample of transgendered women of color in San Francisco', *AIDS and Behavior*, 10(2): 217–225.

Sweileh, W. M. (2018) 'Bibliometric analysis of peer-reviewed literature in transgender health (1900–2017)', *BMC International Health and Human Rights*, 18(1): 16.

Testa, R. J., Habarth, J., Peta, J., Balsam, K., and Bockting, W. (2015) 'Development of the gender minority stress and resilience measure', *Psychology of Sexual Orientation and Gender Diversity*, 2(1): 65–77.

Testa, R. J., Michaels, M. S., Bliss, W., Rogers, M. L., Balsam, K. F., and Joiner, T. (2017) 'Suicidal ideation in transgender people: Gender minority stress and interpersonal theory factors', *Journal of Abnormal Psychology*, 126(1): 125–136.

Valentine, S. E., and Shipherd, J. C. (2018) 'A systematic review of social stress and mental health among transgender and gender non-conforming people in the United States', *Clinical Psychology Review*, 66: 24–38.

Westbrook, L., and Schilt, K. (2014) 'Doing gender, determining gender: Transgender people, gender panics, and the maintenance of the sex/gender/sexuality system', *Gender & Society*, 28(1): 32–57.

White Hughto, J. M., Pachankis, J. E., Willie, T. C., and Reisner, S. L. (2017) 'Victimization and depressive symptomology in transgender adults: The mediating role of avoidant coping', *Journal of Counseling Psychology*, 64(1): 41–51.

White Hughto, J. M., Reisner, S. L., and Pachankis, J. E. (2015) 'Transgender stigma and health: A critical review of stigma determinants, mechanisms, and interventions', *Social Science & Medicine*, 147: 222–231.

Winter, S., Diamond, M., Green, J., Karasic, D., Reed, T., Whittle, S., and Wylie, K. (2016) 'Transgender people: health at the margins of society', *The Lancet*, 388(10042): 390–400.

Zimmerman, R. S., Benotsch, E. G., Shoemaker, S., Snipes, D. J., Cathers, L., Perrin, P. B., McMillan, D., Pierce, J., McNulty, S. and Heck, T. (2015) 'Mediational models linking psychosocial context, mental health problems, substance use, and HIV risk behaviors in transgender women', *Health Psychology and Behavioral Medicine*, 3(1): 379–390.

PART D

Religion and healing
in mental health

18
ATHEISM AND HEALING IN MENTAL HEALTH

G. Eric Jarvis and Rob Whitley

Recent polls show the nonreligious to be growing in Western European and North American societies (Pew Research Center 2014; Win-Gallup International 2012, 2016). In some countries, such as Canada, the United States and the UK, the nonreligious are the second largest religious category. In yet other countries, such as Japan and China, many endorse atheism. At first glance, one may equate the nonreligious in Europe and North America with atheism, but such is not the case. Nonreligious people include a mixed bag of diverse groups including (i) unaffiliated; (ii) non-participating religious; (iii) agnostics; and (iv) atheists. In fact, the proportion of self-described atheists in most countries, apart from a few exceptions like China, Japan, the Czech Republic and France, remains less than 5% (Pew Research Center 2014). Some atheists prefer to keep a low profile and tolerate, or even support, the religious participation of their fellow citizens, while lacking a belief in the supernatural, a position sometimes known as negative atheism (Martin 2007b). Others attack religious traditions, declare religion to be harmful to human societies, and actively evangelize their cause, a position sometimes known as positive atheism (Martin 2007b). Despite growing numbers and visibility, researchers have paid little attention to the mental health of the nonreligious, especially atheists (Brewster et al 2014), even though there has been a rich historical interplay between culture, atheism and healing over the centuries.

Some scholars consider certain religions, such as Jainism, Therevada Buddhism, and Confucianism to be atheist, at least potentially, although most adherents to these religious traditions would not consider themselves atheists in any formal way (Martin 2007a). Political atheism, on the other hand, is the product of Marxist theories that view religion as a form of social control that would inevitably fade with the onset of socialism. These ideas influence populations in East Europe, France and China where socialist and communist thought became well established in the 20th century (Hyman 2007). Intellectual atheism can trace its roots to ancient Greek and medieval European philosophers who discuss atheism without clearly espousing it as a philosophy – theism was simply too pervasive during those times to permit so complete a rejection of society and its norms (Bremmer 2007; Weltecke 2013). Their writings nonetheless anticipate a modern tradition of intellectual atheism beginning with Diderot and d'Holbach in the 18th century and continuing to the current day (Robichaud 2013). In fact, atheism of this kind is indelibly linked to modernity and seems to emerge specifically in opposition to the conception of God (or gods) as part of the natural world that arises from 14th century Europe and gradually replaces transcendent medieval notions (Taylor 2007). Healing practices in atheist religions, such as Confucianism, take the form of activities and beliefs inherent to the specific tradition, while healing traditions associated with intellectual and political atheism have constituted an enthusiastic endorsement of secular science and secular medicine bereft of religious overtones. This chapter will (i) clarify the position of atheism within the broader category of the nonreligious; (ii) review worldwide trends regarding the nonreligious and atheism; (iii) discuss the intersection of ethnicity, culture, gender, and sexuality in the context of atheism and healing; (iv) chronicle the rise and fall of the New Atheism; and (v) review the religion-mental health association, with a particular emphasis on the mental health of the nonreligious.

The many faces of atheism

Before addressing these questions, some definitions: The nonreligious, sometimes called the "nones", are those who, when asked to identify with a religion, indicate nothing in particular (Putnam and Campbell 2010). For example, the 2011 National Household Survey in Canada asked "what is this person's religion?" and one category of response was "no religion" (Statistics Canada 2011). All those choosing "no religion" in this survey were considered "nones".

The nonreligious include the religiously unaffiliated, the 'spiritual but not religious', self-described agnostics and atheists. Agnostics are not atheists, but persons who hold the view that any ultimate reality (such as God) is unknown and probably unknowable (Merriam-Webster 2017). Atheists, strictly speaking, believe there are no gods or lack a belief in gods (American Atheists 2017). Secularism is often linked to the nonreligious and refers to the absence of religious favoritism at the governmental level i.e. separation of church and state (Taylor 2007).

What do secular, or nonreligious, societies look like? These tend to be societies in which the government functions independent of religion, and the members of the society have low levels of religious identity, belief and participation. Examples of such societies include countries in central and west Europe, Canada, Australia, New Zealand, China and Japan (Zuckerman 2016). In these kinds of societies, the nonreligious are growing in numbers, and atheists have full civil rights and freedoms to criticize religion and may flourish in the absence of state-mandated religious life and obligations.

What are the qualities of the nonreligious as a group and of atheists more specifically? In the Faith Matters survey (Putnam and Campbell 2006), which interviewed 3,108 respondents by telephone about religious beliefs and behaviors in the United States, 17% of the respondents belonged to the "nones". According to Putnam and Campbell (2010), the "nones" have been growing in recent decades while numbers of mainline Protestants have been shrinking, although this growth has not been due to large numbers of self-described atheists or agnostics. In fact, only five of the more than 3,000 respondents chose these labels when the survey was conducted.

In the Religious Landscape Study (Pew Research Center 2014), a nationally representative telephone survey of 35,071 U.S. adults, the unaffiliated category (i.e. no religious connection) included Atheist, Agnostic, and 'Nothing in particular' subgroups. In this study, compared to religious groups, atheists were young, mostly white men, with higher education and income levels. Beit-Hallahmi (2007), reported similar findings: the average atheist was a young white man, married, of high intelligence and education, with a tendency to the scholarly professions, less authoritarian and suggestible, less dogmatic, less prejudiced and more tolerant, law-abiding, compassionate and conscientious. In short, Beit-Hallahmi suggested that the average atheist would make a good neighbor.

Importantly, atheism takes different forms, akin to religious orientation for theists. Positive atheism connotes an active disbelief in all gods, while negative atheism referred to a simple lack of belief (Martin 2007b). Silver et al. (2014) propose a more complex typology with six kinds of nonbelief from being assertively opposed to theism to simply being disinterested or apathetic regarding religion. Hence, the ways of being atheist, or nonreligious, are diverse just like there are many ways of being theist or religious.

Intersectional aspects of atheism

Ethnicity and religion. Ethnicity and religion are intimately connected and often overlap. Healing traditions, including Euro-American medicine, have an extensive historical connection to Christian religious traditions (Ferngren 2014). Atheism, on the other hand, has mostly been absent from the discussion of healing belief systems, perhaps because atheism in many settings has represented those who have rejected traditional religious belief and participation. In fact, in their book, *Religion and Ethnicity in Canada*, Bramadat and Seljak (2009) never mention atheists or the nonreligious, although secularism is discussed mainly in terms of how schools are being affected by secular curricula. The authors affirm, however, that ethnicity and religion are closely tied to the point that it may be impossible to separate them. Putnam and Campbell (2010) make the same observation in the United States, namely that ethnic and religious identity overlap. They also report that being nonreligious in the United States (not necessarily atheist) is more likely among white men who are not from the South, who are raised in nonreligious backgrounds, and are from the center-left political spectrum. In contrast, African Americans are markedly more religious than the U.S. population as a whole and self-identify as atheists at a low rate of about 1% (Sahgal and Smith 2009). When ethnic identity overlaps with religion the number of admitted atheists will be small. In contrast to this trend, India has a long atheist tradition deriving from strands of the Hindu religion and perpetuated in Jain and Buddhist traditions (Frazier 2013). These religious atheists have persisted to modern times as corrective critics of the mainstream religious culture by focusing on material realities and denying the existence of the soul.

Secularism. Charles Taylor (2007) links atheism to secularism, a concept that has gained ground mostly in Euro-American societies over the last 500 years. He posits that atheism will be more common in societies affected by French Republican values, or by Marxist socialism in China and the countries of the former Soviet Union. Data on atheism and religious belief in some of these countries have been difficult to obtain and its quality has been suspect when available.

Gender and sexuality. In Euro-American discourse, the theist-atheist debate is relatively polarized, with the material position requiring a categorical rejection of the Christian god. Atheism of this variety has traditionally been more common among men than women. Brewster (2013) goes so far to say that atheist women are "conspicuous by their absence" (Brewster 2013: 2). She feels that reasons for gender disparities in religious belief are "unsatisfying" (Brewster 2013: 2) but mostly derive from social constructions of femininity and gender roles. Sexual minorities, on the other hand, have been more likely to reject religion due to intolerance by traditional religious communities and better acceptance among atheists. Brewster (2013) notes similarities between atheists and LCBTQ individuals in that both must come out to their social circles in order to live a free and open life.

A growing atheist movement?

Has the number of atheists been growing? According to the Religious Landscape Study (Pew Research Center 2014), the religiously unaffiliated represent 23% of the total population, or 55.8 million adults in the United States, up from 16% in 2007. 3% of the U.S. population define themselves as atheist and 4% as agnostic, up from 1.6% and 2.4%, respectively, in 2007 (Lipka 2015). Just to complicate the picture, 7% of Americans say that their religion is nothing in particular, but also report that religion is important to them (up from 6% in 2007). So, the "nones" is a diverse category that seem to be growing on all fronts, whether atheists or nondenominational believers.

What about in other parts of the world? According to the Global Index of Religiosity and Atheism-2012 (Win–Gallup International 2012), China and Japan led the world in atheism with 47% of Chinese and 31% of Japanese self-identified as atheist. The Czech Republic and France followed, with 30% and 29% respectively, and Canada scored 9%. Globally, religiosity decreased from 2005–2012 by 9% overall, and atheism rose by 3% over the same time period. 23% of respondents said they were not religious, while 13% said they were convinced atheists. How does this compare to the Win–Gallup International survey in 2016? China increased to 67% self-identified atheist, and Canada to 10%, but Japan decreased to 29%, France to 21%, and the Czech Republic to 25%. Globally, 25% of those surveyed said they were not religious, while 9% said they were convinced atheists. When asked the question "Do you believe in God?" even greater numbers of people responded "No", with a global average of 17%. Hence, atheism and the nonreligious may be on the rise overall, with fluctuating numbers in any given year, but the real numbers are difficult to capture due to reluctance to self-identify as atheist in religious societies, and reluctance to self-identify as religious in states where religion is officially discouraged (e.g. China). Still, no matter what the survey numbers may have shown, the average citizen of the world believes in God and considers religion to be an important part of life.

Zuckerman et al. (2016) raised concerns that the sharp division between the religious and the secular in European Christian tradition may have forced an unwanted dichotomy onto peoples from non-European cultures. The authors highlighted some of the difficulties surveying rates of atheism and secularism around the world: poor research methods, social desirability bias, and cultural or linguistic differences in religious terms that may have invalidated responses. Given these problems, the available evidence confirmed previous findings, namely relatively high rates of professed atheism in North Asia (China and Japan) and Western Europe (such as France). The Asian findings, however, were accepted with caution due to a different concept of what it may mean to be religious in countries where there was a relative focus on ritual behavior without a binary religious-secular division. In other words, atheism may have been overestimated in China by surveys conducted by Win–Gallup, the Pew Forum and others. The authors' conclusions were that secularity and atheism were unevenly distributed around the world, but they were cautious about saying that religion was in retreat globally – this may only be the case in Western Europe and possibly in parts of the English-speaking world and former communist countries.

A new atheism

In recent years, an atheism movement, called by some "New Atheism" (Wolf 2006; Stenger 2009), has launched an attack on religious perspectives with a kind of evangelical zeal (van Prag 2010). For example, in 2008–9, an Atheist Bus Campaign in the United Kingdom placed messages about atheism on buses in various cities expressly to counter similar Christian messaging. The first message said, "There's probably no God. Now stop worrying and enjoy your life" (Sherine 2008: 1). A message posted on billboards aimed to limit the effects of religion on children by showing the picture of a child with a caption saying, "Please don't label me. Let me grow up and choose for myself" (Sherine 2009: 1). Atheist and humanist groups promoted campaigns about similar concerns in several other countries (Wikipedia 2017). The stigma associated with atheism (Lipka 2016) may have accounted for the strident rhetoric of New Atheists as they sought wider acceptance and approval. This sometimes involved conscious efforts to awaken quiet atheists from their perceived slumber to participate in the public discourse about religion and secularity. In fact, the title of the first Global Atheist Convention in 2010 was *The Rise of Atheism*, a call to potential delegates (and atheists) to stand up and be noticed. Such assertions unsurprisingly have garnered considerable criticism. In 2015, Nathaniel Comfort summarized (and satirized) the new atheism and its leaders in an article in *Nature* journal about Richard Dawkins. For Professor Comfort, Dawkins and the New Atheists espoused the very religious zeal that they opposed.

In a less assertive approach, the American Atheists website (2017) encouraged the open use of the word atheist. "Don't use those other terms to disguise your atheism or to shy away from a word that some think has a negative connotation. We should be using the terminology that is most accurate and that answers the question that is actually being asked. We should use the term that binds all of us together" (American Atheists 2017: 2). Statements like this encouraged people to self-identify as atheists even if they were reluctant. The tone of the writing carried a sense of urgency, of exhorting people to "out" themselves, to join the larger community of avowed atheists, and not to be afraid. Although traditional atheism is a philosophical position rather than a religious tradition (Martin 2007a), for all the express reliance on the rational, the New Atheism sometimes took on the flavor of a religious movement due to its proselytizing and 'stand up and be counted' zeal.

In spite of initial successes, New Atheism may be running into hard times. Christopher Hitchens, one of the key founders of the movement, died in 2011; Richard Dawkins' newest book, *Brief Candle in the Dark*, has received lukewarm reviews (Comfort 2015; Menaker 2015); and the third meeting of the Global Atheist Convention, entitled *A Reason To Hope*, which was to have taken place in Melbourne in 2018, was cancelled for lack of interest (Prestigiacomo 2017). These developments indicated that New Atheism, as promoted by Richard Dawkins and colleagues, may have gone decline.

Cultures of atheism and healing

As already discussed, different cultural pathways may lead to atheism: (1) material religious traditions stemming from ancient Hinduism, (2) anti-religious political ideologies (societies influenced by communism, for example), and (3) intellectual traditions that explicitly argue against the existence of God (mostly in Europe and North America). Each of these cultures of atheism may predispose to specific mental health problems or may confer resilience, recovery and healing. First, religious atheism may apply to individuals that have espoused Hindu theologies derived from the skeptical and Lokayata schools of antiquity. Although they peaked in the middle ages, and most Hindus today would classify themselves as theist, materialist and skeptical texts continued to act as a critical discourse to the modern period. Given the lack of central orthodoxy in Hindu traditions, there was no explicit pressure to abandon skeptical viewpoints in favor of theism (Frazier 2013). Hence, atheists from religious traditions like Hinduism would likely retain an acceptable place for their beliefs in the culture of origin, with all the benefits of intact social and family networks. We would, therefore, expect religious atheists to be embedded in their culture, with similar mental health profiles as other members of the mainstream society.

Tensions among scholars, scientists and religionists over the last two centuries, especially in the behavioral sciences, contributed to a secularizing movement that has challenged the religious worldview in several countries and societies. Influential thinkers critical of God and religion, such as Charles Darwin, Sigmund Freud and Karl Marx, have shaped political and intellectual discourse and have provided explanatory models of creation and human behavior outside of God and religion. Max Weber (1993) called this secularizing process the 'disenchantment' of the world. Unlike in Hinduism and other Eastern religions, skepticism and materialism were less tolerated by Judaeo-Christian and Muslim religions, with the result that doubters and skeptics in these traditions found themselves in opposition to the theist worldview (rather than enfolded by it). Cultures of political atheism may have arisen from these tensions as a form of protest against heavy-handed religious hegemony. It is unclear what mental health problems may be linked to political atheism, but Zuckerman (2016) reported that secular societies in general tend to have more mental health problems like suicide than religious ones, a finding that may be linked to the proscription, even persecution, of comforting belief systems and traditional social networks.

Intellectual atheism emerged from the writings of ancient Greek and medieval scholars and have gained wide exposure over the last two centuries. The decision to abandon God and religion may appear to be a personal one, however, the role of context should not be ignored. While some individuals may have an inborn lack of receptivity to religious or spiritual experience (van Praag 2010), several environmental factors may predispose to atheism: less emphasis placed on religion in the childhood home, poor relations with parents, an authoritarian style on the part of parents, a less ethnocentric worldview (perhaps implying a less cohesive religious identity), and participation in radical political activity (Beit-Hallahmi and Argyle 1997). Hence, it may be that some individuals who become nonreligious, or eventually declare an atheist position, may have been raised in home environments with less religious structure, more discipline, and strained relationships.

Atheism and mental health

Before examining the relation between atheism and mental health, a brief review of the correlates of religion and mental health will provide needed background. Harold Koenig et al. (2012) have written an exhaustive compendium of the literature entitled Handbook of Religion and Health in which they reported that the majority of studies have found a positive association between religion, mental health and well-being. Studies conducted since 2012 have essentially confirmed these findings. However, Whitley (2010) has pointed out that atheism has not been accurately measured as an individual exposure variable in studies of religion and mental health. Instead, atheists have been lumped together with such disparate categories as agnostics, religiously unaffiliated, spiritual but not religious, and lapsed religious into a catch-all "no religion" category as in the National Household Survey (Statistics Canada 2011). While high levels of religiosity clearly were associated with better mental health, no one knew the granular-level mental health differences between the sub-categories that constituted the "nones" or the "nonreligious".

Some qualitative research indicated that staying in the religion of childhood was stressful and difficult for some people, and that after leaving the religion, there may be a tremendous sense of relief or liberation – and loneliness (Heiner 1992; Smith 2011; Zuckerman et al. 2016). But do these subjective accounts of stress and wellness translate into measurable mental health outcomes? Some authors maintained that the nonreligious were at a disadvantage to the religious (Wulff 1997). Genia (1998) recruited subjects from a university campus in the United States and documented their levels of religiousness and well-being. She reported that devoutly religious students found their lives to be more meaningful and satisfying than their nonreligious counterparts. A later study found that, compared to those who did not believe, a belief in God, but not religious affiliation, correlated with several positive treatment outcomes: response to a day treatment program, reduction in depression and self-harm, and improved psychological well-being (Rosmarin et al. 2013). These studies did not consider the nonreligious as subjects worthy of study in their own right and did not consider atheists as a distinct group among the nonreligious. Ross (1990) reported that early investigators either combined the nonreligious with persons who endorsed weak religious beliefs or entirely excluded them from statistical analyses. Brewster et al. (2014) performed a content analysis of academic scholarship about atheists and atheism from 2001 to 2012 and found broad neglect of the subject across social science disciplines, few relevant empiric studies, and a paucity of studies relating to atheist mental health. Furthermore, the authors expressed concern that there was a tacit message running throughout the religion and mental health literature that if religion/spirituality was linked to better mental health, lack of religious commitment must lead to poor outcomes. Whitley (2010: 191) drew attention to some of these problems and said, "In light of the evident popularity and penetration of the 'new atheism' in the marketplace of ideas, I contend that social scientists and psychiatrists have a socio-moral imperative to further investigate the relationship between atheism and mental health". Progress has been slow: Brewster et al. (2014) found that over the course of their content analysis, the number of articles about atheism increased minimally from zero in 2001 to 20 in 2012. None of these directly compared mental health outcomes between theists and atheists, failing to adopt a precise granular-level approach as suggested by Whitley (2010). However, there have been some advances in the field.

First, some evidence suggested that nonreligious people do not suffer worse mental health than the religiously inclined. Hunsberger et al. (2001) compared mental health and adjustment on eleven measures among students that were raised in no religion, mainline Protestant, conservative Protestant, and Catholic families, and found no differences among the groups. Wilkinson and Coleman (2009) compared the coping of matched groups of elderly, one group with religious beliefs and the other with atheistic beliefs, and found that members of both groups were coping well in the face of loss and other stressors. A later study supported these conclusions: Moore and Leach (2016) administered a questionnaire to an online sample of 4,667 respondents, of which 348 were theistically absolutely certain and 515 were atheistically absolutely certain. The authors anticipated that highly religious respondents would have greater mental health on five measures, but the secular participants (including atheists and agnostics) reported similar overall levels of mental health as the theists in the study, with the exception of gratitude levels, which were significantly higher in the religious. Weber et al (2017) suggested that some mental distress experienced by nonbelievers might be the result of being misunderstood by health care professionals. In other words, some forms of distress traditionally attributed to atheists may be more apparent than real.

Second, there was increasing evidence for a curvilinear relationship between religion, irreligion and mental health, and a positive relationship between mental health and the nonreligious. Ross (1990) was one of the first to report that those who held strong religious beliefs *and* reported no religious beliefs were less distressed than those who scored in the weak to moderate ranges of belief. She felt that since having no religion was a marginal status in the United States, respondents would have to make a determined choice to self-identify in this way, which may mean that they had commitments to nonreligious beliefs and institutions that served to structure their lives and give them purpose. Ross (1990: 243) proposed that "persons who participate in religion without religious conviction were in the worst condition psychologically". Galen and Kloet (2011) continued to challenge a linear relation between religiosity and mental health. In a study designed specifically to compare individuals with varying shades of belief, they predicted that respondents with high levels of certainty on either end of the belief spectrum would show relative mental health (well-being) compared to those who were weakly religious. As predicted, a curvilinear relation emerged for life satisfaction and emotional stability (self-rated), with lowest levels occurring among those who were not sure about God's existence or only somewhat certain there was a God, and highest levels at the ends of the belief continuum. In a second study in the same paper, the authors assessed the mental well-being of the nonreligious according to a range of certainty about their beliefs. Consistent with the previous study, nonreligious subgroups with a greater degree of certainty (atheists and humanists) had greater life satisfaction and emotional stability than those with less confidence about their belief systems and worldviews (i.e. spiritual rather than formally religious, and agnostic rather than atheist). Mochon et al. (2011), while reproducing the curvilinear relationship between religiosity and well-being, suggested that adherents with low levels of belief may be happier abandoning their religion altogether and seeking nonreligious community and friends. In a similar vein, the third National Psychiatric Morbidity Study in England (King et al. 2013) interviewed 7,403 people. Of these, 35% had a religious understanding of life, 19% were spiritual but not religious, and 46% were neither religious nor spiritual. On mental health outcomes, religious people were similar to the nonreligious on all outcomes but substance use (religious people used less), but spiritual people (i.e. not religious but spiritual) reported more drug use, abnormal eating attitudes, generalized anxiety, any phobia, any neurotic disorder, and use of psychotropic medication. The authors concluded that spiritual people without a religious framework are more likely to have mental health problems than their religious or expressly nonreligious peers.

Individual contexts, healing and well-being

Even if the nonreligious and atheists enjoy comparative mental health in research studies, the situation for individuals is always more complicated and demonstrates the need for better theory, tools, and interventions. At the individual level, atheists and the nonreligious who have grown up in a religious family and who have felt the need to leave the religion of their childhood, may be susceptible to several sources of distress, some of which may predispose to mental disorders, such as depression or anxiety, depending on the situation. Forms of distress that may be common in atheists and the nonreligious include cognitive dissonance, loss of worldview, loneliness and isolation, conflict with family and friends, loss of social networks, and discrimination (Heiner 1992; Lipka 2016; Zuckerman et al. 2016). These problems must be acknowledged and addressed by mental health professionals, while at the same time avoiding simplistic approaches, which blindly encourage religiosity because it is "good for your mental health" or will make a person happy. All this should be born in mind when working with the nonreligious in clinical settings.

Some individuals may become nonreligious in the face of overwhelming adversity and stress. They may experience anger toward God because, despite petitions, life problems persist. Sources of distress in such cases may include isolation and conflict with family about lifestyle changes. These issues may contribute to or exacerbate clinical diagnoses such as major depressive disorder. Other individuals may adopt atheism after a period of painful doubt and questioning. In either case, conflict with family and friends, including discrimination by religious community members, may precipitate a complete rupture by the individual with religious communities and families to reduce tension and negative affect, at least in the short term.

Future directions

Research needs to focus on the nonreligious from parts of the world other than North America and Western Europe. Questions need to be adapted for use in Non-Christian settings that will gather more accurate data on questions of belief in God, religious doubt, and atheism. Whitley's suggestions in 2010 remain relevant: first, develop accurate and granular-level measures of atheism as an exposure variable to various mental health outcomes; second, examine the influence of atheism on psychiatry as an institution and on other mental health professions; and third, practical application of atheistic theory to mental health. Qualitative work with nonbelievers would add tremendous value to the surveys that have been done to date. Cross-cultural comparisons of those who have abandoned faith also would be valuable. Most important would be treatment guidelines for clinicians working with patients going through a faith crisis, especially focusing on the loss of worldview, the isolation of withdrawing from family and community, and building a new life with an atheist orientation.

Conclusion

Atheists and the nonreligious are related but not identical. In fact, both groups comprise considerable heterogeneity. Atheists could be religious, political or intellectual in their orientation. Some may think intellectual atheism, the most common form in Europe and North America, to be a secular religion for the nonreligious, but in reality, it represents a guiding philosophy anchored in skepticism, materialism, secular values and scientific rationalism. Nonreligious worldviews, including atheism, have been growing in popularity around the world and constitute approximately 23% of the United States population and 11% of the world population. Most atheists quietly hold to their beliefs, but an active branch of atheism, called New Atheism by some, has been opposed, even hostile, to religion. The movement served a rallying function for the nonreligious in some wealthy countries of the world, but after years of rapid expansion, ground to a halt since 2012.

A growing number of studies refute earlier work that linked atheism with mental illness, and suggest an atheism-mental health relationship similar to some of the health benefits found in the highly religious (King et al. 2013; Moore and Leach 2016). Possible exceptions include substance abuse, feelings of gratitude and suicide, for which outcomes remain better in the religious. Researchers and commentators explain this curvilinear relationship in terms of stability of guiding philosophy such that it is the spiritual without secure religious foundations that suffer the worst mental health. On the other hand, functional neuroimaging of belief, disbelief, and uncertainty (Harris et al. 2008) show that the human brain has been hardwired to accept statements as true rather than false. This may explain, in part, why religious faith has persisted in human populations; and why disbelief in its various forms constitutes a minority position.

Atheism, as with any other paradigm, may provide psychological stability; but the path to a secure non-believing position may be fraught with difficulty, even cognitive disgust and pain as suggested in the Harris et al (2008) study, and may cause significant suffering. Looking forward, mental health risks for atheists may decrease over time, given that their numbers have been increasing in some countries, with less stigma and more social acceptability; on the other hand, the decline of the militant New Atheism, with its promise of community and support for nonbelievers, may leave some doubters in a precarious and isolated position. Mental health professionals need to be aware of these issues and provide appropriate care and support according to clinical need.

References

American Atheists. (2017) 'What Is Atheism?' Retrieved November 16, 2017, from www.atheists.org/activism/resources/about-atheism/.

Beit-Hallahmi, B. (2007) 'Atheists: A Psychological Profile'. In M. Martin (Ed.), *The Cambridge Companion to Atheism* (pp. 300–317). New York: Cambridge University Press.

Beit-Hallahmi, B. and Argyle, M. (1997) *The Psychology of Religious Behaviour, Belief & Experience.* New York: Routledge.

Bramadat, P. and Seljak, D. (2009) *Religion and Ethnicity in Canada.* Toronto: University of Toronto Press.

Bremmer, J.N. (2007) 'Atheism in Antiquity'. In M. Martin (Ed.), *The Cambridge Companion to Atheism* (pp. 11–26). New York: Cambridge University Press.

Brewster, M.E. (2013) 'Atheism, Gender, and Sexuality'. In S. Bullivant and M. Ruse (Eds.), *The Oxford Handbook of Atheism* (pp. 511–524). Oxford: Oxford University Press, DOI: 10.1093/oxfordhb/9780199644650.013.006.

Brewster, M.E., Robinson, A., Sandil, R., Esposito, J., and Geiger, E. (2014) 'Arrantly Absent in Psychological Science from 2001 to 2012', *The Counseling Psychologist*, 42 (5): 628–663.

Comfort, N. (2015) 'Dawkins, Redux', *Nature*, 525: 184–85.

Dawkins, R. (2006) *The God Delusion.* London: Bantam Press.

Ferngren, G.B. (2014) *Medicine and Religion: A Historical Introduction.* London: John Hopkins University Press.

Frazier, J. (2013) 'Hinduism'. In S. Bullivant and M. Ruse (Eds.), *The Oxford Handbook of Atheism* (pp. 367–382). Oxford: Oxford University Press, DOI: 10.1093/oxfordhb/9780199644650.013.015.

Galen, L.W. and Kloet, J.D. (2011) 'Mental Well-Being in the Religious and the Non-Religious: Evidence for a Curvilinear Relationship'. *Mental Health, Religion & Culture*, 14(7): 673–689.

Genia, V. (1998) 'Religiousness and Psychological Adjustment in College Students'. *Journal of College Student Psychotherapy*, 12(3): 67–77.

Harris, S., Sheth, S.A., and Cohen, M.S. (2008) 'Functional Neuroimaging of Belief, Disbelief, and Uncertainty'. *Annals of Neurology*, 63(2): 141–147.

Heiner, R. (1992) 'Evangelical Heathens: The Deviant Status of Freethinkers in Southland', *Deviant Behavior*, 13:1, 1–20.

Hunsberger, B., Pratt, M., and Pancer, S.M. (2001) 'Religion Versus Nonreligious Socialization: Does Religious Background Have Implications for Adjustment?' *The International Journal for the Psychology of Religion*, 11(2): 105–128.

Hyman, G. (2007) 'Atheism in Modern History'. In M. Martin (Ed.), *The Cambridge Companion to Atheism* (pp. 25–46). New York: Cambridge University Press.

King, M., Marston, L., McManus, S., Brugha, T., Meltzer, H., and Bebbington, P. (2013) 'Religion, Spirituality and Mental Health: Results from a National Study of English Households'. *The British Journal of Psychiatry*, 202: 68–73.

Koenig, H., King, D.E. and Benner Carson, V. (2012) *Handbook of Religion and Health, Second Edition.* New York: Oxford University Press.

Lipka, M. (2015) 'A Closer Look at America's Rapidly Growing Religious "Nones"'. Pew Research Center. Retrieved November 16, 2017, from www.pewresearch.org/fact-tank/2015/05/13/a-closer-look-at-americas-rapidly-growing-religious-nones/.

Lipka, M. (2016) '10 Facts about Atheists'. Pew Research Center. Retrieved November 16, 2017, from www.pewresearch.org/fact-tank/2016/06/01/10-facts-about-atheists/.

Martin, M. (2007a) 'Atheism and Religion'. In M. Martin (Ed.), *The Cambridge Companion to Atheism* (pp. 217–232). New York: Cambridge University Press.

Martin, M. (2007b) 'General Introduction'. In M. Martin (Ed.), *The Cambridge Companion to Atheism* (pp. 1–7). New York: Cambridge University Press.

Menaker, D. (2015) 'Sunday Book Review: 'Brief Candle in the Dark'. The New York Times, November 24.

Merriam-Webster Dictionary. (2017) Retrieved November 17, 2017, from www.merriam-webster.com/dictionary/agnostic.

Mochon, D., Norton, M.I., and Ariely, D. (2011) 'Who Benefits from Religion?' *Social Indicators Research*, 101: 1–15.

Moore, J.T. and Leach, M.M. (2016) 'Dogmatism and Mental Health: A Comparison of the Religious and Secular'. *Psychology of Religion and Spirituality,* 8(1): 54–64.

Pew Research Center. (2014) *America's Changing Religious Landscape: Christians Decline Sharply as Share of Population, Unaffiliated and Other Faiths Continue to Grow.* Washington, DC: Pew Research Center.

Prestigiacomo, A. (2017) 'Global Atheist Convention Called 'Reason to Hope' Cancelled Because No One Wants to Go'. Daily Wire, November 15. https://www.dailywire.com/news/global-atheist-convention-called-reason-hope-amanda-prestigiacomo

Putnam, R.D. and Campbell, D.E. (2006) *Faith Matters Survey, 2006*. ICPSR36315-v1. Ann Arbor, MI: Inter-university Consortium for Political and Social Research [distributor], 2016-03-22. http://doi.org/10.3886/ICPSR36315.v1.

Putnam, R.D. and Campbell, D.E. (2010) *American Grace: How Religion Divides and Unites Us*. New York: Simon & Schuster.

Robichaud, J.-J. (2013) 'Renaissance and Reformation'. In S. Bullivant and M. Ruse (Eds.), *The Oxford Handbook of Atheism* (pp. 179–194). Oxford: Oxford University Press, DOI: 10.1093/oxfordhb/9780199644650.013.006.

Rosmarin, D.H., Bigda-Peyton, J.S., Kertz, S.J., Smith, N., Rauch, S.L., and Bjorgvinsson, T. (2013) 'A Test of Faith in God and Treatment: The Relationship of Belief in God to Psychiatric Treatment Outcomes'. *Journal of Affective Disorders*, 146: 441–446.

Ross, C.E. (1990) 'Religion and Psychological Distress'. *Journal for the Scientific Study of Religion*, 29(2): 236–245.

Sahgal, N. and Smith, G. (2009) *A Religious Portrait of African-Americans*. Washington, DC: Pew Research Center.

Sherine, A. (2008) 'All Aboard the Atheist Bus Campaign'. *The Guardian*, October 21.

Sherine, A. (2009) 'Hey, Preacher – Leave Those Kids Alone'. *The Guardian*, November 18.

Silver, C.F., Coleman III, T.J., Hood Jr., R.W., and Holcombe, J.M. (2014) 'The Six Types of Nonbelief: A Qualitative and Quantitative Study of Type and Narrative'. *Mental Health, Religion & Culture*, 17(10): 990–1001. DOI: 10.1080/13674676.2014.987743.

Smith, J.M. (2011) 'Becoming and Atheist in America: Constructing Identity and Meaning from the Rejection of Theism'. *Sociology of Religion*, 72(2): 215–237.

Statistics Canada. (2011) '2011 National Household Survey: Data tables, Religion (108)'. Retrieved December 10, 2017, from www12.statcan.gc.ca/nhs-enm/2011/dp-pd/dt-td/Rp-eng.cfm?LANG=E&APATH=3&DETAIL=0&DIM=0&FL=A&FREE=0&GC=0&GID=0&GK=0&GRP=1&PID=105399&PRID=0&PTYPE=105277&S=0&SHOWALL=0&SUB=0&Temporal=2013&THEME=95&VID=0&VNAMEE=&VNAMEF=.

Stenger, V.J. (2009) *The New Atheism: Taking a Stand for Science and Reason*. New York: Prometheus Books.

Taylor, C. (2007) *A Secular Age*. Cambridge, MA: Harvard University Press.

Van Praag, H.M. (2010) 'God's Champions and Adversaries: About the Borders between Normal and Abnormal Religiosity'. In P.J. Verhagen, H.M. van Praag, J.J. Lopez-Ibor Jr., J.L. Cox, and D. Moussaoui (Eds.), *Religion and Psychiatry: Beyond Boundaries* (pp. 235–252). Chichester: John Wiley & Sons.

Weber, S.R., Lomax II, J.W., and Pargament, K.I. (2017) 'Healthcare Engagement as a Potential Source of Psychological Distress among People without Religious Beliefs: A Systematic Review'. *Healthcare*, 5: 19, doi:10.3390/healthcare5020019.

Weber, M. (1993) *The Sociology of Religion*. Boston: Beacon Press.

Weltecke, D. (2013) 'The Medieval Period'. In S. Bullivant and M. Ruse (Eds.), *The Oxford Handbook of Atheism* (pp. 164–178). Oxford: Oxford University Press, DOI: 10.1093/oxfordhb/9780199644650.013.006.

Whitley, R. (2010) 'Atheism and Mental Health', Harvard Review of Psychiatry, 18: 190–194.

Wikipedia. (2017) 'Atheist Bus Campaign'. Retrieved November 16, 2017, from https://en.wikipedia.org/wiki/Atheist_Bus_Campaign.

Wilkinson, P.J. and Coleman, P.G. (2009) 'Strong Beliefs and Coping in Old Age: A Case-Based Comparison of Atheism and Religious Faith', *Age & Society*, 30: 337–361.

Win-Gallup International. (2012) 'Global Index of Religiosity and Atheism – 2012'. Retrieved May 22, 2014, from www.scribd.com/document/136318147/Win-gallup-International-Global-Index-of-Religiosity-and-Atheism-2012.

Win-Gallup International. (2016) 'End of Year Survey 2016'. Retrieved November 17, 2017, from www.wingia.com/en/services/end_of_year_survey_2016/10/.

Wolf, G. (2006) 'The Church of the Non-Believers'. WIRED, Retrieved on November 18, 2017, from www.wired.com/2006/11/atheism/.

Wulff, D.M. (1997) *Psychology of Religion: Classic and Contemporary, Second Edition*. New York: John Wiley.

Zuckerman, P., Galen, L.W. and Pasquale, F.L. (2016) *The Nonreligious: Understanding Secular People & Societies* New York: Oxford University Press.

19
BUDDHISM AND HEALING IN MENTAL HEALTH

Michel Ferrari and Jessica Carmichael

Buddhism is the world's fourth largest religion after Christianity, Islam, and Hinduism (Vaughan 2020), but unlike the other three, it a non-theistic religion perhaps better understood as a life-guiding philosophy that aims to promote mental health. In fact, the relationship between Buddhism and health care has long been noted and, in his discourses, the Buddha explicitly calls himself a doctor who will help people remove the 'three poisons'(greed, anger, and delusion) (Kalra et al. 2018; Martini 2011). Buddhist practices intersect ethnicity, gender and transnational cultures, more fully than Hinduism, to which it is a principled response, and it has a worldwide following – although over 90% of Buddhists continue to live in South-East Asia (World population review 2020).

For these reasons, Buddhism has attracted much scholarly research in anthropology, psychology, and other social sciences into the efficacy of Buddhist practices in promoting mental health, not always in any systematic way (Kalra et al. 2018; Shonin et al. 2014a). Indeed, given its 2,500-year history, Buddhist beliefs and practices are diverse and sometimes the understanding of people and worldview underpinning these mental health practices radically diverge from those in the West (Eddy 2019); therefore it is critical to consider to what extent Buddhist practices can be incorporated into Western practices and institutions without adverse effects (Compson 2018).

This chapter aims to offer a critical analysis of Buddhist and Buddhist-inspired Psychologies and mental health practices as they intersect ethnicity, gender, religion and transnational cultures. More specifically, we focus on the beliefs, practices, and experiences of culturally main branches of Theravada and Mahayana Buddhism and their relationship to mental health. We also discuss how Buddhists understand physical and mental illness, and what treatments they believe promote health in ways thought to transcend race, gender and culture. At the same time, our analysis of Buddhist healing practices will highlight cultural differences within Buddhism as it interacts with the Western field of mental health. We include a few short case vignettes to illustrate how beliefs, values, practices, and experiences of Buddhists can promote mental health, both as stand-alone practices and as coordinated with Western mental health services.

Different schools of Buddhism and mental health

Each of the main schools of Buddhism has its own understanding of the Buddha's main teachings and how to cultivate them to achieve mental health, and each acknowledges '3 baskets' (Appleton 2014; Armstrong 2001; Gyatso and Chodron 2014):

1 *Suttas (Lectures/sermons; Sanskrit:* **Sutras**), preserved in texts called Nikāyas or Āgamas, are largely shared between all Buddhist denominations.
2 *Vinaya* (monastic rules). Differences in these rules may have divided historical Buddhist communities; generally, they are more elaborate for Mahayana Buddhists.
3 *Abhidhamma/Abhidharma,* philosophical/psychological analysis, later extrapolated from these and other Buddhist writings.

Most recently, Secular, Humanist or Neo-Buddhism claims to return to the historical Buddha as heard through suttas themselves (Batchelor 2012). Engaged Buddhism claims to extend its scope to address contemporary political and social injustice (Queen and King 1996).

Despite these variations, all contemporary branches of Buddhism trace their lineage back to the Historical Gautama Buddha born a Shakya prince, in Kedarnath, in the fifth or sixth century BCE.[1] Full biographies of his life were composed centuries later using several stock scenes that exemplify the Buddhist dharma (Nagao & Blum 1991)[2]. Four scenes were identified by the Buddha himself at the end of his life, as places to visit, and stupas were later erected commemorating them (Digha 1995): his birth, his awakening, his first sermon, and his attainment of parinirvana.[3]

Buddha as Doctor in Theravada Buddhism. *Theravada* (Pāli for "school of the elders" or 'old school') is the oldest extant form of Buddhism. It uses Pāli as its scriptural language (related to that spoken by the historical Buddha) and is prevalent in Cambodia, Laos, Thailand, Sri Lanka, and Burma. Since they rely most heavily on the suttas, those describing the Buddha as doctor convey the Theravada understanding of Buddhism and mental health.

In the Pāli Suttas, Buddha often advocated a holistic approach to combatting physical and mental dis-ease (dukka), one that included Indian Āyurveda, a Chinese and Tibetan medicine (Burton 2010), with nibbana/nirvana as the ultimate goal and expression of what Burton (2010) calls "a therapy of beliefs and desires." Human beings (except Arhants) are thought experience mental dis-ease, since even pleasurable sensations contain mental afflictions (klesas) and unwholesome states (akusala dhammā) that are: (1) mentally unhealthy, (2) morally blameworthy, (3) unskillful, and (4) produce painful results (Nandisena 2011: 16 Dhs. 1). In the Tikicchā Sutta (Anguttara Nikāya [AN] 2012: 108) Buddha explains:

> Monks, doctors give a purgative for warding off [bodily] diseases. [...] I will teach you the noble purgative that ... never fails ... whereby beings ... are freed from birth; ... freed from aging; ... freed from death; ... freed from sorrow, lamentation, pain, distress & despair. [...] In one who has right view, wrong view is purged away, and the many evil, unskillful mental qualities that come into play in dependence on wrong view are purged away as well, while the many skillful mental qualities that depend on right view go to the culmination of their development.
>
> [And the same is true for: right resolve, right speech, right action, right livelihood, right effort, right mindfulness, right concentration, right knowledge, and right release.][4]

Just as a good doctor adapts his treatment to the specific disease of the patient, so the Buddha adapted his teachings to different types of people: Between monks and lay practitioners, and between people afflicted by attachment/greed/lust (rāgacarita), hatred/anger (dosacarita) and delusion (mohacarita) – called the three poisons. For early Buddhists, tranquility meditation was meant to support the development of insight meditation (AN 2012: 10; Martini 2011).

The suttas show the Buddha interacting with many people: some privileged, some very poor and desperate, some who had 'lost their mind' (ummata; Pio 1988). One very popular story is that of Kisa Gotami.[5] Kisa ('frail' or 'lean') Gotami was poor and was not accepted by her husband's family until she had a son. But the young child fell ill and died. Her grief was inconsolable, and someone suggested she see the Buddha. The Buddha said he could help her and told her to first gather mustard seed from a family in which no one had died. Kisa went from house to house, but there was no such family to be found and she came to realize that death is universal. Returning to the Buddha, she became a nun, who eventually became an arahant (Derris 2014; Ohnuma 2007; Tan 2010). Echoing Gautama Buddha's first sermon, she writes of her own transcendence of human suffering:

> I followed the noble eightfold path[6]
> that goes to that which is without death,
> nibbana is known at first hand.
> I have seen myself in the mirror of the dhammā.
> Now I am someone with depravities' darts cut out,
> with burden laid down,
> who has done what needed to be done.
>   (Hallisey 2015: 115)

In the Jakata tales, the Prince of Banaras (a Bodhisatta) learns of eight categories of ummata: possession (yaksha); melancholia (pitta); alcoholism (sura), mental retardation (moha), sexual dysfunction (kama), mania (krodha), hallucination (darshana) and depression (vyasana) (Pio 1988). Being diseases, they were thought to be curable, as we see in the story of Kisa Gotami. Feminist scholars suggest this, and similar,[7] stories show early Buddhist ambivalence about motherly love as both altruistic and worldly attachment (Derris 2014; Ohnuma 2007).

Buddha as doctor in Mahayana Buddhism. *Mahayana Buddhism* (Sanskrit: महायान meaning "Great Vehicle") added additional discourses and made the Buddha a set of universal divine principles, supporting the flourishing of all sentient beings (Eddy 2019; Gyatso and Chodron 2014). It uses Sanskrit and Chinese scripture and is prevalent in China, Japan, Korea, Taiwan, Singapore and Vietnam as well as within Indochina, Southeast Asia and the West – most Southeast Asian Mahayana Buddhists live in Vietnam and Singapore.

Vajrayana Buddhism (Sanskrit: वज्रयान, diamond or thunderbolt vehicle), sometimes considered a separate branch, uses tantric Buddhist literature and associated mantic practices. Mahayana Buddhists consider this an age of decline, in which selfishness and ignorance have become increasingly deep-rooted, so the enlightenment gained by early followers, like Kisa Gotami, is now impossible. Some Pure Land schools believe that our individual efforts are insufficient to achieve spiritual progress and that we need the saving grace of a celestial Buddha (Burton 2010).

The healing Buddha, *Bhaisajyaguru* (Sanskrit for "Master of Healing")[8] is one of the most popular of the Mahayana celestial Buddhas. Originally a bodhisattva in the Lotus Sutra,[9] in China and Japan large crowds still attend beautiful temples dedicated to Bhaisajyaguru (Chen and Chen 2004; Kalra et al. 2018). Buddhist temples monks often help patients with mental health problems through "meditation, physical exercise, counselling, learning of the Buddhist sutras, fasting and retreat" (Nguyen 2015: 1249), practices said to rid them of 'illusions of and attachment to the self'. In some temples, Buddhist monks also perform 'exorcisms' to cleanse people of feelings of guilt, shame and fear (Nguyen 2014).

An illustration of Buddhist treatment of mental illness is offered by a webpage devoted to advice by Tibetan Lama Zopa Rinpoche,[10] which describes the following diagnosis and treatment for a 16-year-old violent, paranoid schizophrenic, said to be a danger to himself and others: The symptoms are said to be due to the karma generated by his having harmed sentient beings in the past, leading to a paranoia caused by an invading spirit. The recommended treatment is to get a geshe whose life is morally pure and is familiar with such situations; in particular, Khadro-la or lamas from India and Nepal with bodhicitta and tantric realizations, who are said to be more powerful. These people should do pujas for him – like the *che-trul* puja, *Liberating from Harm, Black Magic and So Forth*. It is also recommended that he wear a pill from His Holiness the Dalai Lama around his neck, and to burn it a few times a day. He should also be told as to what is happening and counselled not to listen to the voice urging him to do harm. According to Lama Zopa Rinpoche, both problems and happiness (up to and including enlightenment) come from the mind, based on past lives.

Hyeyoung Bang (2018) interviewed a Korean Seon [Zen]-Buddhist monk Ji-Gong about his efforts to promote mental health and was given a very similar account of his healing practices, despite the many cultural differences between Korea and Tibet. Asked how this relates to Western therapy, Ji-Gong claimed that it was closest to hypnotherapy "accessing clients' unconscious to extract the cause of suffering and treat it." However, he then adds that he does not need hypnosis to accomplish this, or even to have people in front of him to treat them. He believes he accesses a spiritual dimension of human life that psychotherapy cannot reach, where karma resides.

What is striking about these accounts is that although they use symptom-based diagnosis to recommend specific treatment plans, they rely on a very different metaphysics and world view than that the one that informs Western medicine, and so use a notion of mental illness as involving spirit possession that has not been dominant in the West since at least the 18th-century enlightenment, if not the middle ages.

Some have argued that in severe cases Buddhist practices can do more harm than good in treating people with mental illness. Haslam (2019) considers herself a survivor of New Kadampa Tradition (NKT) practice. She believes that very vulnerable people are given unsafe and damaging practices at an inappropriate time, because it encourages them to feel nothing, or that 'an impure mind perceives an impure world' making them to blame for their suffering. In fact, research shows that meditation practice can produce adverse reactions in some participants (Compson 2018; Hudson 2014). Joanne Clark (2019) admits that, while Buddhism can complement and support psychotherapy, it can't replace it.[11] Indeed, Buddhism is directly challenged by modern scientific claims that some emotions can be changed only by psycho-pharmaceutical intervention, and that insight and behavioral changes may be of little benefit in treating them (Burton 2010).

Although Dockett and Rahmaan (2006), for example, found that experienced SGI Nichiren Mahayana Buddhist practitioners were more optimistic, resilient, and stress-resistant – compared both with those who had more recently begun their Buddhist practice and with university students and staff (N = 227), and had more self-esteem, an internal locus of control and less perceived stress than did the other groups, some SGI members felt ashamed when their prayers and chanting failed to alleviate mental illness (Phoenix 2014). For this reason, in 2002, the SGI-San Francisco Mental Health Support Group began monthly drop-in meetings open to both SGI members and to non-members interested in learning about Buddhist perspectives on mental health and illness. This group provided social support for everyone who attended, and also promoted an opportunity to discuss mental health issues more openly within the larger SGI Buddhist organization, so members with mental illness could feel less stigmatized and better able to support others (Phoenix 2014).

Another effective North American partnership between Western and Buddhist approaches is a California Mental Health Clinic effectively partnered with a Khmer Buddhist Temple to reach killing fields refugees living in California. After a decade, Reicherter and colleagues (2015) find that the clinical operations, wellness programs, and community activities of the clinic and temple operate seamlessly together, which they attribute to the dedicated partnership between clinicians and monks that allowed them to develop the right community connections and a deep understanding of the experience of members of the community.

We find similar efforts worldwide. The Buddhist counselling approach of Rungre-angkulkij and colleagues (Rungreangkulkij and Wongtakee 2008; Rungreangkulkij et al. 2011) allows psychiatric mental health nurses to integrate therapeutic techniques from Theravada Buddhism, assuming that patients prefer and are more compliant with counselling interventions if the therapeutic framework matches with their own worldview. Chandradasa and Kuruppuarachchi (2019) consider this coordination common practice in Sri Lanka where "the confluence of Western psychotherapy techniques and Buddhist teachings seems to provide a culturally acceptable mental health care to the Sri Lankan population" (1475). However, perhaps because Mahayana Buddhism is more esoteric and deeply rooted in traditional culture, Vietnamese state medical institutions have been slow to incorporate Buddhist techniques, despite the prevalence of Buddhist beliefs, and support for traditional Buddhist healing in temples by both clients and medical practitioners; but they agree that monks also need mental health training (Nyugen 2018; Samuel and Deane 2019).

Modernist Buddhism and Western therapy

Modernist [humanist, secular or neo-] Buddhism rejects the dharmic worldview and focuses on an experiential analysis of the benefits of Buddhist practices (e.g., mindfulness) (Batchelor 2012). Secular Buddhism allows a dialogue with contemporary Western counselling and psychotherapy, beginning with Caroline Rhys Davids' (1900/2003) seminal translation of the Abhidhamma, that has led to many Buddhist-inspired approaches to promoting mental health. Shonin et al. (2014a) identify several reasons why Western health disciplines have increasingly assimilated secular Buddhist practices: Buddhism is philosophical and practice-based (not faith-based or dogmatic); Buddhism parallels aspects of Western therapeutic approaches such as cognitive–behavior therapy (CBT), seeking to improve their own effectiveness; there is also more effort to establish an evidence base about the effectiveness of specific forms of spiritual practice (e.g., mindfulness) for improved psychological health. Furthermore, the worldwide admiration and fame of Buddhist leaders like the Dalai Lama and Thich Nhat Hanh has led to more and better English translations of essential Buddhist writings; and we find a growing number of Western practice centers for most Buddhist traditions. Finally, greater cultural and ethnic diversity among service users due to greater global migration requires more culturally appropriate treatments.

Buddhism-based third-wave therapies. Secular Buddhist traditions have permeated Western psychology through 'third-wave' interventions[12] such as Dialectical Behaviour Therapy (DBT; Linehan 1993), Mindfulness-Based Stress Reduction (MBSR; Kabbat-Zinn 2017), Mindfulness-Based Cognitive Therapy (MBCT; Segal et al. 2001), Acceptance and Commitment Therapy

(ACT; Hayes et al. 2006), and Compassion-Focused Therapy (CFT; Gilbert 2009). The main distinction between Western and Buddhist approaches is the use of Buddhist texts and the dharma to help guide the counselling process (Lee et al. 2017). However, there are many similarities, such as prominent themes of mindfulness, acceptance, and compassion, that are observed across these therapeutic approaches.

Both Buddhist and Western third-wave interventions bring attention and emphasis to the development of *mindfulness*. Murphy (2016) identifies awareness, attention, non-judgment, acceptance, and being in the present moment as key objectives in mindfulness practice, allowing participants to observe their changing internal and external experiences, as well as their behavioral, and physiological reactions to these experiences (Hayes et al. 2006; Huxter 2007; Teasdale et al. 2002). Guided mindfulness activities include yoga exercises, recording of guided meditations to increase self-practice, and silent retreats as examples (Shonin et al. 2013). Mindfulness is considered efficacious for dealing with addiction in a variety of ways that span patient engagement, assessment, diagnosis, and treatment (see Shonin et al. 2016), although Kabbat-Zinn (2017) believes it is too early to tell if mindfulness has contributed significantly to Western mental health.

Through *defusion and decentering*, third-wave therapies help patients distance themselves from cognitive associations underlying their clinical symptoms and develop a healthier view of themselves and their environment (Semple et al. 2010; Hayes et al. 1999). *Metacognitive insight* particularly as it relates to one's experience of psychological symptoms, is another a hallmark feature of modern therapies that strongly links third-wave approaches to their Buddhist roots (Huxter 2007). Observing the significance of internal and external experiences allows patients to develop insight into maladaptive patterns of behavior motivating their psychological symptoms, and to replace them with more adaptive coping strategies, including *compassion toward self and others* – one of the four Buddhist immeasurables and prominent themes in modern therapy (Lee and Oh 2019). Compassion-based therapies disrupt habitual self-criticism, guilt, and shame and other maladaptive patterns of affect regulation (Lee and Oh 2019). Lee and Oh (2019) propose a Buddhist counselling technique that extends compassion-focused therapy based on Mahayana Buddhist teachings beyond mindfulness to other contexts of practice.

For both Buddhist and third-wave therapies, the aim is to help clients develop *wisdom and autonomy* relative to psychological symptoms. For example, DBT skills training assists clients in achieving harmonious balance between emotion and reason, referred to as "Wise Mind" (Linehan 1993). Refinement of these skills is thought to empower the individual to achieve inner peace and resolution of both mental and physical issues.

Consider this case of a woman receiving MBCT to address grief and distress related to fertility issues (Patel et al. 2018) – not unlike that of Kisa Gotami. After three miscarriages, a woman and her husband were diagnosed with secondary infertility and recurrent pregnancy loss, leading her to develop significant distress with mixed symptoms of depression (i.e. ruminative thoughts, excessive worrying, and crying spells), somatic symptoms (i.e. gastrointestinal issues, tension headaches, and palpitations), and negative body preoccupations and guilt surrounding their fertility issues.

MBCT treatment began with normalization of the woman's hardships and psychoeducation around her fertility experiences, before teaching mindfulness skills (e.g., attendance, allowance, acknowledgment of experiences). Adaptive coping strategies were taught in-session, including cognitive strategies targeting her ruminative thinking and anxious/depressive thought patterns. Breathing techniques and sitting meditations were practiced in session to help her accept and tolerate her experience of anxiety and distress related to the unsuccessful fertility attempts. Outside of direct skill development, advice, psychoeducation, and planning for relapse prevention was also provided by the psychologist. The woman's anxiety and depression reduced to subclinical levels and these effects were sustained in the months following treatment, even after the couple experienced additional fertility failures.

General efficacy of Buddhist-based (third-wave) approaches

The incorporation of secular Buddhist practices in modern third-wave psychotherapies holds promise. Studies have shown MBCT to be effective in reducing in anxiety and automatized thinking patterns (Kaviani et al. 2005), psychological distress and relapse rates for clients with depression, as well as reducing negative affect and increasing levels of mindfulness following MBCT (Collard et al. 2008). Improvement of experienced pain, body image, anxiety, and depression have all been demonstrated following participation in mindfulness-based stress reduction (Kabat-Zinn et al. 1985; Kuyken et al. 2016).

Third-wave therapies have also demonstrated promising effects for a wide range of clinical profiles. MBCT, ACT, and compassion-based therapy appear to be especially promising in utilizing Buddhist ideas of mindfulness to reduce symptoms of depression and anxiety – two of the most common mental illnesses affecting present Western societies. Likewise, DBT effectively uses the same ideas to promote self-regulation and stabilization of both thinking and behavior while reducing more severe symptoms of emotional and behavioral dysregulation characterized by borderline personality disorder.

However, not all Western clinicians endorse adopting Buddhist practices. Some clinical psychologists find meditation inappropriate for clinical contexts because of its religious origins (Dimidjian and Kleiber 2013). Monteiro, Musten, and Compson (2015) believe that the "secular mindfulness juggernaut" (276) separates Mindfulness from Buddhist ethics in a way that dilutes and distorts Buddhist teachings "to fit a commercialised version of meditation training, now deemed palatable to the sensibilities of a Westernised non-Buddhist population…divorced from Buddhist ethics [that critics have cynically called 'McMindfulness']" (Monteiro et al. 2015: 276). Furthermore, Buddhist practice is historically culturally situated in a context of spiritual development, aiming ultimately for enlightenment – total liberation and omniscience – whereas clinical practices aim simply to promote favorable treatment outcomes for patients with psychological problems, rather than helping them achieve their full human potential (Shonin et al. 2014b)

Future directions

The Buddhist approach to mental health shows the importance of integrating ethics into treatment plans. We also need to emphasize the phenomenological focus on 1st-person science, while still remaining sensitive to culture specific understanding of mental illness and mental health. Through temples, millions of immigrants and refugees from South-East Asian countries have relied on Buddhism to cope with trauma related to their displacement to America and experiences of cultural assimilation (Canda and Phaobtong 1992). However, Western-based mindfulness and acceptance-based psychotherapy reflects significantly different understandings of self, family, and communication than does Asian Culture, therefore, the effectiveness of culturally enhanced psychotherapies for Asian migrants is moderated by acculturation (Hall et al. 2011). Future research should look at the fine-grained nature of particular meditation and spiritual practice techniques beyond mindfulness meditation, with people who have particular personality profiles, and to study the psychological effects and implications of other Buddhist healing practices, like mindful repentance (Lee et al. 2017), anger management (Ariyabuddhiphongs

2014), or emic concepts like the Tibetan 'rlung' ('psychic wind'), whose proper functioning they consider essential to mental health (Deane 2018).

In particular, it is important to explore ways to integrate Buddhist and Western approaches in a way that values the insights and therapeutic strengths of both. For example, following Zagzebski (2013), we can use bodhisattva exemplars and sutras to articulate therapeutic practices, like teaching the four immeasurables (loving kindness, empathetic joy, compassion and equanimity) to promote mental health in therapeutic settings, adapting practice the bodhisattva path in a way that speaks to contemporary counselling theories and practices (Cheng and Tse 2014).

Finally, an important limitation to Buddhist 'philosophical therapy' (Burton 2010) is its focus on inner individual change to treat suffering, while neglecting role played by broader institutional and social forces in causing human suffering. Some Buddhists argue that the right social conditions are needed to properly transmit and practice Buddhist teachings, through so-called 'socially engaged Buddhism' practiced, most notably, by the Dalai Lama and Thich Nhat Hanh (Hanh 2002; Queen and King 1996). By adapting core Buddhist teachings about interdependence, selflessness, compassion, and right livelihood, both advocate social change to promote mental health that extends beyond what the historical Buddha himself advocated (Burton 2010).

Conclusion

Buddhist practices have been used to address mental health and dis-ease for millenia. Their influence continues in traditional settings like Buddhist temples found in many countries in South-East Asia. Today, Buddhist-inspired ideas such as the teaching of mindfulness and meditation skills are also commonplace in modern third-wave psychotherapeutic approaches and have been used to deliver effective treatment to individuals with a range of presenting problems, including anxiety and depression.

Buddhist and western approaches to psychotherapy have many parallels, including the overarching goal of conceptualizing symptoms causing dysfunction in the individual. Whereas traditional Buddhist practices operate within a spiritual paradigm to classify and treat mental disorders (e.g., karma and spirits), Western theories use neuro/biological, social, cognitive, and behavioral paradigms to inform diagnosis and treatment. Nevertheless, scientific studies of the use of secular Buddhist practices in modern therapeutic intervention provide a strong evidence-based foundation for the efficacy of traditional approaches in Western clinical psychology, promising the continued use of Buddhist practices to address mental health around the world.

Notes

1 Traditionally, Gautama was given the historical dates of c. 563–c. 483 BCE, but these have recently been the revised to c.480–c. 400 BCE by scholars seeking to align it with historical events described in his biographies (Cousins, 1996).
2 For those interested in a fuller account of the many-layered story of the Buddha's life, we recommend reading Armstrong (2001), Penner (2009) and especially Nanamoli (1992).
3 Late Chinese Buddhism proposes eight aspects needed to accomplish the path (Nagao & Blum, 1987).
4 These follow closely the elements of the fourth noble truth: the eight-fold path. When Buddha Gautama gave his first sermon (Saṃyutta Nikāya V.420), he set rolling the wheel of the dharma for a new age, by outlining his realization of a middle way as 'four noble truths':
(1) suffering is all pervasive (dukkha ariyasacca);
(2) suffering has a cause (dukkha samudaya ariyasacca);
(3) that cause can be overcome (dukkha nirodha ariyasacca); and

(4) the way to overcome suffering is an eight-fold path (dukkha nirodhagāminīpaṭipadā ariyasacca) that includes: Right/Wise/Skillful/Ideal (samma) View/Understanding, Right Intention, Right Speech, Right Action, Right Livelihood, Right Effort, Right Mindfulness and Right Concentration.

5 There are several versions of this story; our account relies heavily on Tan (2010).

6 See Note 4.

7 Other examples of women in a similar state include: Patacara, Vasetthi and Uibbiri, queen of Kosala. According to Pio, 1988, p. 128, it is hard to find men mentioned by the early Buddhists who show signs of madness (although the monk Gagga is cited as the cause for several new rules in the Vinaya Pitaka relating to ummada).

8 "The characteristic association with the healing stone lapis lazuli and the myrolaban fruit united two different strands of medicinal thinking/ those of Central Asia and India (ayurvedic medicine)" (Chen and Chen, 2004, p. 240).

9 In this important Mahayana text, the Buddha is compared to a doctor finding a cure from poison for his children.

10 See www.lamayeshe.com/advice/schizophrenia.

11 See https://buddhism-controversy-blog.com/2019/04/18/does-the-dharma-have-a-role-in-recovering-from-mental-health-problems-a-personal-perspective/

12 The first wave was behavioral therapy, that emerged in the 1950s in response to traditional psychoanalytic psychotherapy. The second wave refers to the rise of Cognitive Therapy in the 1960s and 1970s, which focused on cognition as a way to understand clinical problems and interventions, culminating in Cognitive-Behavioral Therapy (CBT) (Fung, 2015).

References

Anguttara Nikāya (AN), in Bhikkhu, B. (Ed.) (2012) *The Numerical Discourses of the Buddha: A Translation of the Anguttara Nikaya*. Boston: Wisdom Publications.

Appleton, N. (2014) 'Buddhist Scriptures: An Overview', *The Expository Times,* 125: 573–582.

Ariyabuddhiphongs, V. (2014) 'Anger Concepts and Anger Reduction Method in Theravada Buddhism', *Spirituality in Clinical Practice,* 1(1): 56–66.

Armstrong, K. (2001) *Buddha.* New York: Penguin.

Bang, H. (2018) 'Buddhism and Up (Karma): A Buddhist Priest's Wisdom to Help Suffering: A Conversation with Ji-Gong Bob-Sa', *Journal of Global Mental Health and Traditional Healing,* 1: 85–102.

Batchelor, S. (2012) 'A Secular Buddhism', *Journal of Global Buddhism,* 1: 87–107.

Burton, D. (2010) 'Curing Diseases of Belief and Desire: Buddhist Philosophical Therapy', 66:197–217.

Canda, E. R. and Phaobtong, T. (1992) 'Buddhism as a Support System for Southeast Asian Refugees', *Social Work,* 37(1): 61–67.

Chandradasa, M. and Kuruppuarachchi, K. A. L. A. (2019) 'Confluence of Western Psychotherapy and Religious Teachings in Mental Healthcare of an Asian Buddhist Community: Sri Lanka', *Journal of Religion and Health,* 58(5): 1471–1476.

Chen, Thomas S, N. and Chen, Peter S. Y. (2004) 'The healing Buddha', *Journal of Medical Biography, 12:* 239–241.

Cheng, F. K., & Tse, S. (2014) 'The use of Chinese Buddhist theories in counselling, psychotherapy, psychology, and mental health research: An integrative review', *International Journal for the Advancement of Counselling, 36*(3): 229–242.

Collard, P., Avny, N. and Boniwell, I. (2008) 'Teaching Mindfulness Based Cognitive Therapy (MBCT) to Students: The Effects of MBCT on the Levels of Mindfulness and Subjective Well-Being', *Counselling Psychology Quarterly, 21*(4): 323–336.

Compson, J. (2018) 'Adverse Meditation Experiences: Navigating Buddhist and Secular Frameworks for Addressing Them', *Mindfulness,* 9: 1358–1369.

Cousins, L. S. (1996) 'The Dating of the Historical Buddha: A Review Article', *Journal of the Royal Asiatic Society, Third Series,* 6(1): 57–63.

Cowell, E. B. (Ed.) (1990) *Jātaka: Stories of the Buddha's Former Births* (Vols. I–VII). New Delhi: Asian Educational Services.

Davids, C. A. F. R. (1900) *A Buddhist Manual of Psychological Ethics or Buddhist Psychology, of the Fourth Century B.C.* London: Royal Asiatic Society.

Deane, S. (2018) *Tibetan Medicine, Buddhism and Psychiatry: Mental Health and Healing in a Tibetan Exile Community.* Durham, NC: Carolina Academic Press.

Derris, K. (2014) 'Interpreting Buddhist Representations of Motherhood and Mothering', *Journal of Feminist Studies in Religion*, 30(2): 61–79.

Digha Nikaya (1995) *The Long Discourses of the Buddha.* Walshe, M. (Trans.) Boston: Wisdom.

Dimidjian, S. and Kleiber, B. (2013) 'Being Mindful About the Use of Mindfulness in Clinical Contexts', *Cognitive and Behavioral Practice*, 20(1): 57–59.

Dockett, K. H. and Rahmaan, A. (2006, August 12) *Are Experienced Buddhists More Resilient than Novice and Non-Buddhists? Empirical findings.* Presented at the Annual Meeting of the American Psychological Association, New Orleans, LA.

Eddy, G. (2019) 'Deity practice in the FPMT: understanding the nature of the Tibetan Buddhist deity from the Western practitioner's perspective', *Culture and Religion*, 20(2): 169–191.

Fung, K. (2015) 'Acceptance and Commitment Therapy: Western Adoption of Buddhist Tenets?', *Transcultural Psychiatry*, 52(4): 561–576.

Gilbert, P. (2009) 'Introducing Compassion-Focused Therapy', *Advances in Psychiatric Treatment*, 15: 199–208.

Gyatso, T and Chodron, T. (2014). *Buddhism: One Teacher; Many Traditions.* Boston: Wisdom Publications.

Hall, G. C., Hong, J. J., Zane, N. W. and Meyer, O. L. (2011) 'Culturally Competent Treatments for Asian Americans: The Relevance of Mindfulness and Acceptance-Based Psychotherapies', *Clinical Psychology: Science and Practice*, 18(3): 215–231.

Hanh, T. N. (2002) 'The Fourteen Precepts of Engaged Buddhism', *Social Policy*, 33(1): 39–40.

Haslam, M. (2019, June) *A Psychological Report on The New Kadampa Tradition.* Retrieved from: www.kalyanamitra.ca/single-post/2019/06/29/A-Psychological-Report-on-TheNewKadampa-Tradition---Dr-Michelle-Haslam#!.

Hayes, S. C., Luoma, J. B., Bond, F. W., Masuda, A. and Lillis, J. (2006) 'Acceptance and Commitment Therapy: Model, Processes and Outcomes', *Behaviour Research and Therapy*, 44: 1–25.

Hayes, S. C., Strosahl, K. and Wilson, K. G. (1999) *Acceptance and Commitment Therapy: Understanding and Treating Human Suffering.* New York: Guilford.

Hudson, J. (2014) *Can Buddhism Cure Mental Illness?* Retrieved from: https://appliedbuddhism.com/2014/04/23/can-buddhism-cure-mental-illness/.

Huxter, M. J. (2007) 'Mindfulness as Therapy from a Buddhist Perspective'. In D. A. Einstein (Ed.), *Innovations and Advances in Cognitive Behaviour Therapy (pp.* 43–55). Sydney: Australian Academic Press.

Joanne Clark (2019) 'Does the Dharma Have a Role in Recovering From Mental Health Problems? – A Personal Perspective', *Tibetan Buddhism – Struggling With Difficult Issues.* (Downloaded 14 August 2020 from: from: https://buddhism-controversy-blog.com/2019/04/18/does-the-dharma-have-a-role-in-recovering-from-mental-health-problems-a-personal-perspective/)

Kabbat-Zinn, J., Lipworth, L. and Burney, R. (1985) 'The Clinical Use of Mindfulness Meditation for the Self-Regulation of Chronic Pain', *Journal of Behavioral Medicine*, 8(2): 163–190.

Kalra S, Priya G, Grewal E, Aye TT, Waraich B K, SweLatt T, Khun T, Phanvarine M, Sutta S, Kaush U, Manilka, Ruder S and Kalra B. (2018) 'Lessons for the health-care practitioner from Buddhism', *Indian Journal of Endocrinology and Metabolism [serial online]*, 22: 812–817.

Kaviani, H., Javaheri, F. and Bahiray, H. (2005) 'Efficacy of Mindfulness-Based Cognitive Therapy in Reducing Automatic Thoughts, Dysfunctional Attitude, Depression andAnxiety: A Sixty Day Follow-Up', *Advances in Cognitive Science*, 7(1): 49–59.

Kuyken, W., Warren, F. C., Taylor, R. S., Whalley, B., Crane, C., Bondolfi, G. ... and Segal, Z. (2016) 'Efficacy of Mindfulness-Based Cognitive Therapy in Prevention of Depressive Relapse: An Individual Patient Data Meta-Analysis from Randomized Trials', *JAMA Psychiatry*, 73(6): 565–574.

Lee, K. C. and Oh, A. (2019) 'Introduction to Compassionate View Intervention: A Buddhist Counseling Technique Based on Mahāyāna Buddhist Teachings', *Journal of Spirituality in Mental Health*, 21(2): 132–151.

Lee, K. C., Oh, A., Zhao, Q., Wu, F., Chen, S., Diaz, T. and Ong, C. (2017) 'Buddhist Counselling: Implications for Mental Health Professionals', *Spirituality in Clinical Practice*, 4(2): 113–128.

Linehan, M. (1993) *Skills Training Manual for Treating Borderline Personality Disorder* (Vol. 29). New York: Guilford Press.

Martini, G. (2011) 'The Meditative Dynamics of the Early Buddhist Appamānas', *Canadian Journal of Buddhist Studies*, 7:137–180.

Monteiro, L. M., Musten, R. F. and Compson, J. (2015) Traditional and Contemporary Mindfulness: Finding the Middle Path in the Tangle of Concerns', *Mindfulness*, 6(1): 1–13.

Murphy, A. (2016). 'Mindfulness-Based Therapy in Modern Psychology: Convergence and Divergance of Early Buddhist Thought', *Contemporary Buddhism*, 17 (2): 275–325.

Nagao, G. and Blum, M. L. (1987) 'The Life of the Buddha: An Interpretation', *The Eastern Buddhist*, 20(2): 1–31

Nagao, G. and Blum, M. L. (1991) 'The Buddha's Life as Parable for Later Buddhist Thought', *The Eastern Buddhist*, 24(2): 1–32.

Nanamoli, B. (1992) *The Life of the Buddha According to the Pali Canon*. Kandy, Sri Lanka: Buddhist Publication Society.

Nandisena, B. (2011) 'Mental Illness According to Theravada Buddhism: Towards a Theory of Mental Illness Based Upon the Buddha´s Teachings', *Journal of the International Association of Buddhist Universities*, 7(2): 137–144.

Nguyen, H. (2014) 'Buddhism-Based Exorcism and Spirit-Calling as a Form of Healing for Mental Problems: Stories from Vietnam', *Journal of Religion & Spirituality in Social Work: Social Thought*, 33: 33–48.

Nyugen, H. (2015) 'Linking Social Work with Buddhist Temples: Developing a Model of Mental Health Service Delivery and Treatment in Vietnam', *British Journal of Social Work*, 45: 1242–1258.

Ohnuma, R. (2007) 'Mother-Love and Mother-Grief: South Asian Buddhist Variations on a Theme', *Journal of Feminist Studies in Religion*, 23(1): 95–116.

Patel, A., Dinesh, N., Sharma, P. S. V. N., Kumar, P. and Binu, V. S. (2018) 'Outcomes of Structured Psychotherapy for Emotional Adjustment in a Childless Couple Diagnosed with Recurrent Pregnancy Loss: A Unique Investigation', *Journal of Human Reproductive Sciences*, 11(2): 202–207.

Penner, H. H. (2009) *Rediscovering the Buddha: Legends of the Buddha and Their Interpretation*. New York: Oxford University Press.

Phoenix, B. (2014) 'Promoting Resilience and Recovery in a Buddhist Mental Health Support Group', *Issues in Mental Health Nursing*, 35: 257–264.

Pio, E. (1988) *Buddhist Psychology: A Modern Perspective*. New Delhi: Abhinav Publications.

Queen, C. S. and King, S. B. (1996) *Engaged Buddhism: Buddhist liberation movements in Asia*. Albany: State University of New York Press.

Reicherter, D., Bay, S., Phen, B., Chan, T. and Lee, Y. S. (2015) 'The Cambodian Lotus Thrives Under a California Sun: How a Mental Health Clinic Partnered with a Khmer Buddhist Temple to Reach Killing Fields Refugees Living in California'. In L. W. Roberts et al. (Eds.), *Partnerships for Mental Health* (pp. 53–67). New York: Springer.

Rhys Davids, Caroline A. F. ([1900], 2003). *Buddhist Manual of Psychological Ethics, of the Fourth Century B.C., Being a Translation, now made for the First Time, from the Original Pāli, of the First Book of the Abhidhamma-Piṭaka, entitled Dhamma-Sangaṇi (Compendium of States or Phenomena)*. London, UK: Royal Asiatic Society Publisher.

Rungreangkulkij, S. and Wongtakee, W. (2008) 'The Psychological Impact of Buddhist Counseling for Patients Suffering from Symptoms of Anxiety', *Archives of Psychiatric Nursing*, 22(3): 127–134.

Rungreangkulkij, S., Wongtakee, W. and Thongyot, S. (2011) 'Buddhist Group Therapy for Diabetes Patients with Depressive Symptoms', *Archives of Psychiatric Nursing*, 25(3): 195–205.

Samuel, G. and Deane, S. (2019) 'Introduction to Special Section of Journal of Religion and Health, Mental Health, the Mind, and Consciousness: Tibetan and Western Approaches', *Journal of Religion and Health*, 58(3): 688–692.

Saṃyutta Nikāya: Kindred Sayings (SN). Vol. I, Davids, R. (Trans.), London: Pāli Text Society, 1979; Vols III–V, Woodward, F. L. (Trans.), London: Pāli Text Society, 1975–1980.

Segal, Z. V., Williams, J. M. G. and Teasdale, J. T. (2001) *Mindfulness-Based Cognitive Therapy for Depression: A New Approach to Preventing Relapse*. New York: Guilford Press.

Semple, R. J., Lee, J., Rosa, D. and Miller, L. F. (2010) 'A Randomized Trial of Mindfulness Based Cognitive Therapy for Children: Promoting Mindful Attention to Enhance Social Emotional Resiliency in Children', *Journal of Child and Family Studies*, 19(2): 218–229.

Shonin, E., Van Gordon, W. and Griffiths, M. D. (2016) (Eds.) *Mindfulness and Buddhist-Derived Approaches in Mental Health and Addiction*. In: Advances in Mental Health and Addiction (Masood Zangeneh, seies editor). New York, NY: Springer.

Shonin, E., Van Gordon, W. and Griffiths, M. D. (2014b) 'Current Trends in Mindfulness and Mental Health', *International Journal of Mental Health and Addiction*, 12: 113–115.

Shonin, E., Van Gordon, W. and Griffiths, M. D. (2016) (Eds.) *Mindfulness and Buddhist-Derived Approaches in Mental Health and Addiction*. In: Advances in Mental Health and Addiction (Masood Zangeneh, seies editor). New York, NY: Springer.

Shonin, E., Van Gordon, W., Slade, K. and Griffiths, M. D. (2013) 'Mindfulness and Other Buddhist-derived Interventions in Correctional Settings: A Systematic Review', *Aggression and Violent Behavior*, 18(3): 365–372.

Tan, P. (2019, downloaded) *Kisa Gotami*, in Dharmafarers Sutta Discovery series, 43.2. Retrieved from: www.themindingcentre.org/dharmafarer/sutta-discovery/sd-40–49).

Teasdale, J. D., Moore, R. G., Hayhurst, H., Pope, M., Williams, S. and Segal, Z. V. (2002) 'Metacognitive Awareness and Prevention of Relapse in Depression: Empirical Evidence', *Journal of Consulting and Clinical Psychology*, 70(2): 275–287.

Therīgāthā: Poems of the First Buddhist Women (T). Hallisey, C. (Trans.). Cambridge, MA: Harvard University Press, 2014.

Vaughan, Don (2020). 'What Is the Most Widely Practiced Religion in the World?' Encyclopedia Britannical (online). https://www.britannica.com/story/what-is-the-most-widely-practiced-religion-in-the-world (Downloaded 10 July 2020).

World population review (2020). Retrieved from https://worldpopulationreview.com/country-rankings/buddhist-countries. Downloaded 10 July 2020.

Zagzebski, L. T. (2013) 'Moral Exemplars in Theory and Practice', *Theory and Research in Education*, 11(2): 193–206.

20

CHRISTIANITY AND HEALING IN MENTAL HEALTH

Abrahim H. Khan and Sandra Dixon

At the core of Christianity is the idea of salvation that is conceptually and theologically related to two other ideas. One is the person and work of Christ Jesus. The other is the healing of the body. The three ideas became interwoven in the first century (CE). According to church historian and theologian Harnack (1908:74), in that period Christianity "deliberately and consciously assumed the form of 'the religion of salvation or healing,' or 'the medicine of soul and bod,' and at the same time recognized that one of its chief duties was to care assiduously for the sick." In its cosmic vision, Christianity holds that the relationship between humanity and God is ruptured through human disobedience or sin. In modern terms it issues in a dis–ease or existential estrangement.[1] Doctrinally, the relationship has become repaired through a salvific act of Jesus as Christ, the God-man[2] understood as simultaneously fully human and divine and integral to Christology.[3] Jesus' sacrificial suffering, death and resurrection compose the salvific act to which the expression "the person and work of Christ," refers. He is then the *salve* for *heal*ing, regaining *heal*th or w*hol*eness, words with a shared meaning element, the Old English "*hæl.*"[4] Christian adherents embrace the core belief that one can regain wholeness of self, be healed, only through the person and work of Christ (Woollcombe 1964: 40–44). Thus, the wholeness of self or health incorporates a relationship of three aspects: spiritual, physical and mental.[5]

The theological view of wholeness or health resonates in contemporary understandings or approaches to well-being. Mental health, according to the World Health Organization (WHO 2014), encompasses a state of complete physical, emotional, psychological, and social well-being and not merely the absence of disease or infirmity. Underlying the definition is a presupposition that religious adherents should be able to adapt and manage their physical, mental and social challenges, including spiritual ones. However, religious ideas of being saved spiritually have at times either elided or obscured the fact that impairments in the psychophysical organism can be painful, and that increasing hope for healing or cure elicits from others empathy for the sick. Healing the spiritual or caring for the soul has pre-empted the idea that physical impairments might arise from demonic interference as evidenced in Jesus's ministry which the Gospels[6] narrate.

Some Christians suffering from mental illness are reluctant to seek the help of mental health practitioners or psychotherapists. A predominant reason is its social implication: mental illness is a stigma of personal sin (Briscoe 2018)). The stigmatizing or the relation of sin and psychopathology requires closer attention amongst mental health counsellors and psychotherapists. Here closer attention is given to the relation without pre-empting benchmark studies by Favazza (1982), Kelsey (1988), Ferngren, (2009), Pargment (1997, 2013), or Duff (2009) on the relation between Christianity, healing and mental health. In fact, it presupposes their work as foundational to moving forward.

This chapter contributes to the discourse of Christian healing traditions and health, referencing particularly the mental health field. It considers the historical and philosophical perspectives of Christen healing, adumbrating an epistemological framework or axiomatic foundation and boundary conditions for knowledge claims in discussing healing in the mental health area. Throughout the chapter runs an argument for recognition of a spirit belief system as beneficial in the psychotherapeutic dialogue or recovery process for religiously oriented clients. Case studies illustrate Christian healing traditions that are non-Eurocentric, and outside of Christian liberalism or mainline Christianity. Future directions for research and practice by mental health professionals interested in Christian healing are highlighted. The conclusion considers a psychoanalytic hermeneutical[7] explanation as accommodative of Christian healing understood as epistemologically useful for mental health professionals working with adherents of that faith tradition.

Historical and philosophical contexts on Christian healing traditions

Regardless of variations, Christian healing tradition emerged from a Hebraic-Greco-Roman cultural background. The theology associated with it shows marks of the historical and biblical traditions of the Hebrew world and the mythological, philosophical and medical traditions associated with Graeco-Roman world-view as Jesus's ministry spread beyond Palestine, encountering different cultures. The biblical Adam and Eve story about innocence, disobedience, Fall[8] of humanity, and experience of suffering succinctly represents the Hebraic background (Genesis 2:15–3:24).[9] Seeking deliverance from bodily and psychic afflictions at the shrines of deities or through consecration of one's life to a deity characterizes the Greco-Roman context (Harnack 1908). Below is a summary of a highly textured historical development of a major theme in early Christianity.

Healing through miraculous encounters have been an active part of the landscape of Christian cultural communities from the time of Jesus' public ministry (*circa*. 26–31 CE) in Palestine. The Gospel narratives Matthew, Mark, Luke, and John provide an appropriate historical starting point for his healing activities. Each portrays him as a healer performing numerous miracles.[10] Matthew (11:4–5) summarizes it in reporting Jesus' answer to the question of whether he is the Coming One, Christ:

> Go and tell John the things which you hear and see. The blind see and the lame walk; the lepers are cleansed and the deaf hear; the dead are raised up and the poor have the gospel preached to them.

Matthew, chapter 9, tells of the healing of the paralytic man (v. 2), and of the blind (v. 29). Then there is the miracle of restoring life to the dead (v. 18), and the cure of the mute by casting out the demon (v. 34). Much of the healing reported is linked to belief, apparently psychosomatic, relating to the restoring of meaning in one's life. His form of healing accords very well with that of professional healers whom Plich (2007: 20) maintains "were actually philosopher-types who healed people through therapeutic regimens of self-analysis, confession, and forming correct beliefs about the world."

Techniques and having faith are crucial for healing to occur. Jesus as healer employed techniques like those of folk healers in Middle Eastern cultures. For example, he used according to Plich (2007: 20) "laying on hands or touching the sick person (Mark 1:41), using spittle (Mark 8:23) or mud (John 9:6), pronouncing powerful words – like *talitha cum* (Mark 5:41) or *ephphatha* (Mark 7:34)." But that similarity did not mean that he considered himself a folk healer. He was understood as being in the tradition of a Hebraic prophetic healer, one that helped to restore meaning to people's lives and in that respect his healing activities were an expression of the power of the spirit or God (Luke 7:9–17). The distinction between being cured and being healed is crucial to appreciate healing as connected with restoring meaning in life and hence well-being. For we cannot be sure of cure scientifically occurring since there might be a condition of remission later (Duff 2009) as with some cancer patients. Further, Jesus' healing activities have an aim: to manifest God's power and proclaim the Gospel or kingdom of heaven.

Crucial for healing to occur are psychological factors. One is that the sick has to have faith in the healer as a holy person, as one filled with divine spirit/power. Having faith is just as important as the healer having to be initiated as a holy person. For the sick to have faith is psychologically possible if the healer exudes the power. Anthropologists identify six steps in the call to be a holy person across cultures (Pilch, 2007: 24). Two of the more evident steps for our purposes are that of being called by the spirit and having ritual skills to deal with the spirit world. The Gospel accounts of Jesus confirm both: spirit descending on him at his baptism (Mark 1:11), and his healing skills (Luke 4:1–13). The sickness problems enumerated by the Gospels are ones connected with impurity in one's relation to the boundary of God's holy community. Or as stated by Pilch (2007:22), sickness problems in the Bible are essentially purity problems, relating to a ruptured relationship with God as often indicated in the Old Testament. Pilch (2007: 22) recollects: "The sick violate God's command and desire: 'You shall be holy [exclusive and whole], for I the Lord your God am holy' (Leviticus 19:2; cf. 11:45 and 20:7)." What sets this holy healer apart from others is that he is an intercessor of God, the source of all healing.

Historically, that healing ethos of the first-century (CE) Middle Eastern culture shaping Jesus as a holy person or prophetic healer presupposes a philosophical view of time. Accordingly, human beings have a temporal awareness of before, *now*, and *after* three categories implying a change in the natural order for all living things (Brandon 1999). *Before* the fragmentation, humankind is in a state of innocence. The Fall is the *now*, a rupturing or change from the state of innocence. *After* the Fall is the experiencing of sin, suffering, old age, physical frailty, and death. The *after*, in short is a change in which sin and evil as the absence of goodness ensue. As already mentioned, reparation must be made to heal the rupture or fragmentation. Considered as part of the natural world the human body is subject to change, but not the soul that is spiritual, eternal, and enfleshed to constitute the human body. This presupposition of time as implicating change underlies the emergence of the dominant healing mode associated with Christian eschatology or view of life after death (Brandon 1999).

The reception of healing and the idea of eschatology in Christianity came on stream in the context of a Greco-Roman world-view of healing associated with the cultic names: Asclepius, Salus, and Hygenia. As reported, Asclepius not only healed but would also reveal the future in cities where his shrine was established (Harnack 1908). Christian eschatology, however, includes a strand that in the hereafter the body will be reconstituted with a soul to enjoy a beatific vision (1 Corinthians 15:35–58). That strand is within the philosophical view of time and concept of Christian salvation and lends support to other healing traditions in Christianity, as shown later below. This body-soul relation stands in strong contrast to the body-mind relation influencing modern medical and mental health practices. For this reason, some acquaintance with the philosophical foundation of the Christian faith tradition is advantageous for mental health professionals to having meaningful dialogues with Christian clients. Dialogue about clients' spiritual experiences of healing that is informed by their faith and that explores how these experiences might intersect with their mental health may help to facilitate positive change in their clients' lives.

Healing in the New Testament context

The New Testament offers a perspective of the healing–salvation relation in the emergence and spread of organized Christianity by the disciples and the apostle Paul. Jesus commissioned his disciplines to do as he did: heal the sick and cast out demons while preaching that the kingdom of heaven is near (Luke 9:1–2, 6). The spreading of the Gospel message beyond local ethnicities and culture, is credited largely to the missionary activities of Paul, recorded in letters to newly formed congregations and reported also by a medical travelling companion in Acts, one of the New Testament books. Reported instances include the disciple Philip casting out demons and healing the paralyzed and the lame (Acts 8:6–7) and the apostle Paul casting out demons but doing no healing (Acts 16:16–18).

However, four relevant notations may follow from the New Testament accounts. One is that healings are done through Jesus' name, thereby implying a connection between the psychophysical and spiritual aspects (Acts 3:16, and 4:7–12). Another is on a difference between healing the sick and casting out demons, as indicated by the account of Philip. A third notation is that Paul lists healing as a gift that God has given the church for its ministry but not exorcism (Ferngren 2009). These notations above are suggestive of a new mood, one in which Paul is referring to mighty works (Greek, *dunamis*) or miracles as that of healing by Jesus and the apostles, compared to exorcism. A fourth notation is that there is less emphasis on healing and more on salvation as a way of strengthening new Christian congregations in new ethno-cultural settings with cultic and folkloric practices posing as a threat to the young faith.

The different perspectives mentioned above and others throughout Christian history chronicled by Porterfiled (2005) are indicative of how multi-layered and complex healing is within the Christian tradition. This is particularly so when healing practices are viewed through a biblical lens where the works of the Holy Spirit[11] is said to be present in the lives of many believers who lean on their faith for strength, healing, and mental health (Koenig, 2005, 2008, 2009). Research studies show that Bible reading, and prayer may help in coping with depression, grief and loss. Studies by Pargament (1997, 2013) provide empirical support for it. This fact may well be an inroad to psychotherapy.

Healing and 20th-century Christianity

The last century is marked by a renewed interest in faith healing as evidenced by Christian adherents hoping that God will answer prayers for relief from pain or healing. Commissions by mainline Christian churches such as Lutherans and Episcopalians/Anglicans seek to reinstate a healing ministry as part of the pastoral vocation or Christian experience (Woollcombe 1964). But there are also Pentecostal groups within Protestantism recognizing that humans in pain seek relief now rather than be edified about spiritual healing and ideas of salvation or atonement (Belcher and Hall 2001; Krause 2014). In North America, for example, some itinerant evangelists and televangelists seek to heal through prayer. Well-known names among them include Aimee Sempel McPherson, Kathryn Kuhlman, Oral Roberts, and Pat Robertson (Kelsey 1988; Robinson 2014).

Furthermore, by mid-20th century, the phenomenon of a spiritual belief system was gaining consideration in the broadening of research areas in psychiatry and the social sciences. Cultural and ethnicity factors were also taken as determinants of the self formerly understood merely as a Cartesian body-mind relationship. Add to that some other developments that lead to the emergence of a new field known as the humanistic sciences. They include the introduction of a concept of comparative psychiatry by Eric Kremlin (Mihanović et al. 2005). Another is the field studies of anthropologists Margaret Mead and Ruth Benedict leading to transcultural psychiatry. Its impetus came from misdiagnosing of minority patients and overcoming of racial bias in treatment (Jenkins 2007) and questioning assumptions of the body-mind interaction model in treating suffering soldiers from two world wars. A further stimulus was developments in the field of psychology with its interest on consciousness in its search for explanation of and/or meaning with respect to syndromes. This new field of humanistic science established by the mid-20th century meant explaining away religious beliefs.

The dissonance between religion and scientific psychiatry and psychology, however, did not dissuade a rapprochement. For contemporary Christian approaches in mainline churches to healing or mental health began relying on psychiatric insights: pastoral counsellors are undergoing clinical training. And psychiatrists interacting with pastoral counsellors or chaplains may integrate Christian symbols in the therapeutic process when dealing with patients having strong Christian beliefs (Fazazza 1982). But, in that harmonizing religion was accorded an adjunctive role compared to that described in the New Testament and early Christian literature. By the turn into the 21st century with diasporic and transnational movements to North America there seemed to be an emphasis on the healing dimension of the Christian faith, transcending culture, race and ethnicity.

Intersectionality of race, culture and mental health in Christian faith

In past years the politics of identity embodied a dominant Eurocentric view of race and gender while ignoring religion as having saliency, especially as it relates to non-dominant groups (Moodley and Barnes 2015: 7). A Eurocentric view positions race and gender within a framework that caters primarily to the dominant Anglo-Saxon, male, heterosexual culture. Confining identity discourse to that framework disadvantages non-dominant groups such as people of African descent and for whom religion is a core aspect of their cultural identity and should not be ignored (Moodley and Barnes 2015: 12–17).

Cultural identity is generally viewed in multicultural research as a broad concept to include not just collectively shared values, beliefs, and expectations, but also race, gender and religion (Arthur and Collins 2010: 317–320). Within a dominant cultural system, one's own cultural heritage may become marginalized, thereby disadvantaging one economically and psychologically to the point of mental health debilitation. Such is the situation for some people of non-European ethnicity that are adherent to Christianity (Moodley and Barnes 2015: 12–17), particularly those in the Black communities across the diasporas. Many Black women are marginalized in various socio-cultural contexts based on racialized features (James 2010: 89). The racialization often creates tension on many different levels, including mental distress and health related problems. They find some degree of relief and sense of meaning through a shared religious world-view and collective identity rather than a singular identity (Nolan and West 2015: 15–17).

In a religiously pluralistic society, the intersectionality between culture, race, and gender presents complex and difficult challenges or conflicts to be confronted (James 2010: 156). Inner conflicts may occasion stress levels that impact overall mental health functioning (Brown 2017: 25–30).

The study by Edge (2013:39) on Black British Caribbean women's mental health found that spirituality, particularly organized religion, can be regarded as an ethno-cultural coping strategy for many members of that population. Emphasis on spiritual theme in mental health coping is found also in similar cross-cultural studies in the North American context. Ethnographic work on spirituality and subjective religiosity among African Americans, Caribbean Blacks, and Non-Hispanic Whites support the fact that high levels of religious involvement play a significant role in enhancing their overall mental health functioning (Chatters et al. 2008:727). Their positive mental health or well-being is shaped by their religious behaviours (e.g., church attendance, worship practices, etc.), cultural values, and ethno-religious identities (McAlister 1998: 134). This is in alignment with studies that investigated English-speaking people of Caribbean origin in Canada and their openness to engage in counselling. The latter studies found that religion and/or spirituality tends to be highly valued as a resource for maintaining optimal mental health in times of distress and hardship for these individuals (McKenzie et al. 2011: 10).

The findings above are important with respect to world-view orientations and mental health connections. To expand the WHO (2014) health definition mentioned earlier, mental health is circumscribed in the West by a psychological framework that considers person as an individual-oriented phenomenon (Sue et al. 2019: 14). Priority to individuality or self-choice is evident in the emphasizing of the principle of autonomy in healthcare and medical ethics. In contrast, Eastern philosophies understands mental health largely from a psychological framework that contextualizes person or self as a holistic phenomenon from which follows a holistic conceptualization of mental health. That is, the self is perceived as a complex of relations harmoniously balanced, an interplay of mind, body, spirituality, and nature interrelationships (Chan et al. 2001: 261). The relations may go out of balance and have to be restored for mental health and well-being.

Nevertheless, Christian and Eastern conceptualizations of mental health have a commonality. For some strands of the Christian tradition emphasize the individual as a holistic being with salient dimensions: mental, physical, social, and psychological through which the healing power of the Holy Spirit may restore brokenness in the individual (Fee 1996: xiii–7). This is in accord with the belief that only God has the power to restore one's brokenness, to make one whole in mind, body, and soul, thus fostering good health (Black Gifford 2016: 210). Many cultures within the Christian tradition have both participated and benefited from miraculous healing, illustrated by biblical examples mentioned earlier.

In modern day Christianity, non-dominant groups across various geographical locations, particularly the United Kingdom and North America, have been documented as being more willing to engage in miraculous healing practice. They find it a source of relief from the stress by systemic barriers and socio-economic plights like racism, unemployment, ethnic discrimin-ation and feeling "othered" in a multicultural society (Krause 2014: 35; Porterfield 2005). It is necessary to draw attention to these issues within the mental health and counselling domains so that practitioners may assist in the healing process for non-dominant groups identifying with Christianity as do some individuals of African and Afro-Caribbean descent (Moodley and Barnes 2015: 7). For such ethnic populations, religion is inextricably tied to their cultural traditions and identities (Worland and Vaddhanaphuti 2013).

Colonized oppression through slavery also has resulted in psychological and generational trauma (Dixon and Arthur 2014: 95), thereby increasing the complexity of the intersectional conflicts. Many of the oppressed have turned to their Christian church community as part of the recovery process from the pain of subjugation. Conditions for the recovery process, according to the recovery model of rehabilitation, include components of hope, empower-ment, healing and group connection (Jacobson and Greenly 2003: 52). Religious performances and beliefs intertwined with cultural practices of non-dominant group assist in creating such conditions. Non-*dominant* refers to groups who have suffered from oppression, marginalization and discrimination, which in turn affect their emotional and psychological health and perhaps can lead to their reasons for seeking therapy (Arthur and Collins 2010: 16). Cultural awareness of the intersectional challenges of race, gender and religion, would augment understanding of mental health practitioners in their sensitivities and treatment offered to clients of a Christian world-view (Brown 2017: 65–69).

To shift from the theoretical to the empirical, consideration is given to different religious case studies influenced by key aspects of culture and connected to religion as a source of healing for non-dominant groups. Dixon's study (2015), described how praying helped immigrants to cope with being "othered" because of their accent at the workplace or lack of Canadian work experience, educational certification or industry level skills. Such reasons were interpreted as discriminatory and signified forms of "othering" amongst this immigrant population (Dixon 2015: 100–153). Despite discriminatory oppression, these individuals found spiritual refuge, healing and strength in the safe spaces of their church communities. And they learned to forgive their oppressors and accepted their new realties and socio-cultural location with newfound gratitude and grace. Refuge and safe space give hope for a sense of belonging and connectedness, on the recovery model of psychosocial rehabilitation mentioned earlier, two pre-conditions for health and well-being.

In an African context, spirituality and religiosity constitute an integral dimension of the cultural heritage (Wane and Sutherland 2010: 339–340). Prevalent in that context or world-view is demonic possession from which the possessed needs to be delivered. For Christians, deliverance is through the healing power of the Holy Spirit (Fee 1996: 140). Two examples are illustrative of the healing power of the spirit. One is an example in which missionary and anthropological goals can merge into "a harmonious and helpful pastoral strategy" in an underrepresented area of research amongst traditional African people: demon-possession (Singleton 1977: 185). The other is a variation that aims at the whole person, and is a community effort rather than a single person healing ministry

To give more context, example one is that of a young girl, who according to Singleton (1977: 185) is presumably possessed by spirits for refusal to marry the man her father designated. During a spirit cleansing session, the girl confessed through a medium to having done nothing wrong to deserve death or be afflicted by diabolical spirits. According to missionary and commentator Shorter (1985: 184), the problem was expressed in terms of a conflict between spirits: those sent by her father, and those controlled by the medium aiding in the cleansing process; that meant having to deal "with morally neutral beings not amenable to Christian categories." Singleton used a client-cantered therapy approach, meaning that he entered the mental world of the client/girl to affirm her objective reality (spirits) and thereby to assist the client (Shorter 1985). However, Shorter's perspective of the case differed from Singleton's point of view. For Shorter viewed the duty of the Christian healer as being in a unique position to offer the sufferer a "direct experience of God's healing love, revealed in Jesus Christ" (1985).

Many Christians believe that the Holy Spirit empowers them for healing ministry, and so they are receptive to God's spiritual leading, to use them as agents for healing practices (Dube et al. 2011: 95). Given the widespread world-view of demon-possession in the African context, many Christian healers operate within an African frame of reference (Brown 2017: 82). They are steeped in the knowledge of Shona taboos, rituals and cosmology and specialize in delivering people from evil spirits. From their perspectives, the spiritual and natural worlds are related as cause and effect; the natural world is "a product of spiritual force that also sustains it" (Dube et al. 2011: 95–96). Such healing ministries are Christ-cantered, caring and compassionate, done on the authority of the Holy Spirit.

Further, Christian healing manifests itself dramatically and creatively in other contexts besides exorcising of demons. For example, it may become manifested through singing to the glory of God or drumming and dancing as in Africa. Comparatively less dramatical, Christian healing may occur at a holy or sacred place as with the flagpole of the Church of St. Anthony of Padua at Puliampatti, in Tamil Nadu, South India (John 2014). Healing may occur also within the congregational setting of Pentecostal movements in Latin America or other parts of Asia, or at healing ministry rallies. Moreover, healing–salvation variations may involve a paradigm shift, not exclusive either to a particular ethnicity, colour politics, or to colonized people.

Example two, illustrating further the healing power of the spirit, is that of Christian healing associated with a community support ministry, identified as a Whole-Person Healing Center approach and initiated by the Bethel Baptist Church in Jamaica[12]. The approach works on a paradigm that liberates those of slave ancestry from a "black self-hate" identity (Allen 2001). That is, from the ambivalence of being Black/African on the outside and White/European on the inside while being economically and politically marginalized. Known for having members experience divine healing, the Bethel Baptist church also became the centre for integrative or a Whole-Person healing approach: addressing social, spiritual, and medical aspects of illness, instead of relying on a Western medicine mind/body dualism. In the church's prayer ministry, conducted by adherents of the faith, sudden recovery from illness has occurred (Allen 2001).

As evidenced by the descriptions above, religious and spiritual healing can be a tool of resilience, liberation and coping for many non-dominant groups cross-culturally. The examples cited underscore the centrality of religious beliefs in fostering psychological healing, resilience and meaning-making to socio-cultural struggles (Moodley and Barnes 2015). It is important to note that in the highlighted cases, where the integrity of a culture might be threatened, religion can provide a source of healing and wholeness since it represents an integral component of one's cultural identity (Dixon 2015:32–36). Familiarity with Christian healing practices or the epistemological framework for such practice can be a powerful psychological tool for holistic health and well-being (Allen and Khan 2014).

The variations above of the healing in North America, India, Africa, and the Caribbean are indicative of a worldwide phenomenon with respect to Christianity and healing: a reclaiming of healing by faith in God as part of the Gospel message. It is a response to two prevailing conditions. One is a perceived deficiency in a dominant stream of the Western Christian tradition on healing as also the work and activity of the Holy Spirit. That deficiency extends to the mission field, issuing in neglect by mainstream churches to recognize the reality of spirit possession and related infirmities. It may arise from a narrow understanding of Christianity: a *Christus victor* view of winning souls for Christ and neglecting the painfulness of afflictions and illnesses. The other condition is the total reliance on medical science to cure a disease. That science operates with an interpretative schema defined by testability, falsifiability, cause and effect, randomized clinical trials, diagnosis and treatments confined to the pharmacopeia and the latest *Diagnostic and Statistical Manual*. Further, associated with the reliance is the expansion of knowledge, resulting largely from research funded by stakeholders in a healthcare market economy. Unlike preaching or science, healing is a helping-caring art whose canvas is the person as a wholistic being.

Future directions

Movement towards understanding the person as being more than a psychophysical organism viewed according to either a medical or psychotherapeutic model of the self is occurring. The models, naturalistic explanatory schemata, exclude consideration of a healing–salvation relation. But the receptivity of anthropological emphases by epistemological psychiatry (Jenkins 2007: 21; Mihanović 2005) may produce an annealing of naturalistic explanatory schemata to consider healing–salvation symbol system as a factor. Already discussion and dialogue, warranted by the social challenges of diasporas to Europe and North America, are indicating renewed receptivity to a religion and mental health connection.

For future work four investigative suggestions are proposed: (1) devise projects that consider the ethical involvement of the most marginalized people in faith communities; (2) investigate the ethical role and responsibility that mental health professionals have to honour worldviews and religious backgrounds of clients; (3) proactively encourage public mental health providers to become more aware of the spiritual and correlated epistemological background of clients as an aid in the healing process; and (4) incorporate in the graduate training programs workshops on spirituality, religious beliefs, and cultural identities to widen meaningful dialogue with clients during the counselling session. The suggestions cohere with the importance of using good clinical judgment and to seek supervision and consultation when appropriate to best support religiously pluralistic clientele seeking to regain mental health and well-being,

Conclusion

Christian healing practices are premised on a defined spirit belief system, occur in specific social contexts and operate through a sympathetic imagination. As a social construct, illness symptoms are culturally determined, and occasioned by the texture or fissures in the social fabric of the patient. Moods, emotions, and stressful social expectations come into play as in the cases mentioned. An element of subjectivity is present. For one must listen to the client as to what ails, for terminology that is ambiguous, and to grasp sympathetically what is happening. That includes a longing for wholeness and a conviction of a healing or divine power that wells up in the innermost heat of the client. In Britain, the tendency is to integrate the client's spirituality into the therapeutic process to increase the possibility of successful outcomes. A similar approach is in connection with the Whole-Person Healing Center, discussed above. In its approach, health and illness beliefs are more easily framed or renamed, for illness does not exist unless one can perceive, name and respond to it. Perhaps the wholistic approach is a step forward to Jesus' command to his disciples to preach and heal and does not exclude medical intervention and sympathy.

Clearly though, the wholistic healing approach is not the same as a sudden recovery from an illness, as in miraculous healing. It operates with a psychoanalytic hermeneutical explanation whose epistemological implicates allow for introducing religious insights and practices in mental health services. For the explanation involves seeing culture as a way of being in the world, choosing a reasoning pattern, discerning, and judging about what is going one with the client. Further, the approach is not exclusive to Christianity. Thus, the argument underlying the chapter is for openness to epistemological significance of religious or spirit belief system for a more useful mental health model of the self, for clients of a religiously plural society.

Notes

1 It is a human condition or experience Kierkegaard and existential thinkers referred to as *angst*, anxiety, or dread. Expression of the estrangement or ontological disconnect is manifested differently by each belief system or religion.
2 In this chapter, the term "God" refers to the Judaic-Christian being, creator and sustainer of all. The term is capitalized to distinguish it from reference to a deity among many in a pantheon, or one god single out for worship form aong many. The God-man means simultaneously fully God and fully human with reference to God becoming incaarnate,

3 For more information see Brandon, S. G. F (rev. 2012) 'Salvation' online *Encyclopaedia Britannica* accessed June 4, 2019, at www.britannica.com/topic/salvation-religion#ref33997.

4 See *Oxford English Dictionary* (1974).

5 Based on the New Testament Greek affirmation by Paul, an apostle of Christ, who refers to keeping the spirit, soul and body sound *(holokleron)*. He distinguishes the natural man *(psychikos)* from the spiritual man *(pneumatikos)* as in 1 Corinthians 2:14, associating the natural with the outward or that which is of *sarx* (flesh), as in Romans 8:1–11, while the inward is aligned with *soma* (body), the fullness of human life, self or person as in 1 Corinthians 6:15–19. Paul's Greek usage yields the following antithesis for the human wholeness: inward/outward, spiritual/natural, and body/flesh. For more details, see Kenneth Woollcombe (1964: 40–44), a publication of a commission report on healing, presented to the General Convention of the Episcopal Church. St. Louis Missouri.

6 "Gospels" refers to the first 4 of the 27 books of the New Testament which together with the Old Testament (39 books) compose the Christian Bible (66 books) The Gospel books are Matthew, Mark, Luke, and John.

7 A methodological interpretation of the outcome of human actions understood as having also an inner meaning. This line of approach, seeing actions as text to be interpreted, has for its theorists Dilthey, Heidegger, and Gadamer who represent a philosophical existential branch of hermeneutic

8 The Fall in Christianity refers to the Adam and Eve story that represent disobedience of Creator by creature and later because the original sin of all humanity. See old Testament book (Genesis 3:1–8) for the story.

9 Biblical reference are to the New English King James version of the *Bible* accessed at www.biblegateway.com/versions/New-King-James-Version-NKJV-Bible/

10 Studies show 41 healing instances are identified according to illness, where found in parallel gospels, and the method by which the healing is done. See Table 3.11 (Healing World of Jesus) in Swartley (2012: 67–68).

   See, for example, of healing in crowds, Matthew 4:23, 8:16, 9:35; Mark1:32, 3:16, 6:55; Luke 6:17, 9:11, and John 6.2.

11 In Christianity holy spirit references one of three persons or energies of God. The two others are God as Father, and as Son (Jesus), instancing theologically one triune God.

12 The Whole Person Healing approach is simply a variation of a wholistic approach developed in Jamaica – a partnership of a local Christian congregation and health care services to attend to the whole person as discussed by Allen (2001, 2004).

References

Allen, E. A (2001) 'Whole person healing, spiritual realism, and social disintegration', *International Review of Missions*, 90(356–357): 118–133. doi: 10.1111/j.1758–6631.2001.tb00267.x.

Allen, E.A. and Khan, A. H. (2014) 'Christian spirituality, religion and healing in the Caribbean' 153–163. In P. Sutherland, R. Moodley, and B. Chevannes, (Eds.), *Caribbean healing traditions*. New York: Routledge.

Arthur, N. and Collins, S. (Eds.) (2010) *Culture-infused counselling* (2nd ed.). Calgary, AB: Counselling Concepts.

Belcher, J. R. and Hall, S. M. (2001) 'Healing and psychotherapy: The Pentecostal tradition,' *Pastoral Psychology*, 50(2), 63–75. doi:10.1023/A:1012253630417.

Black Gifford, C. (2016) *Heart made whole: Turning your unhealed pain into your greatest strength*. Grand Rapids, MI: Zondervan.

Brandon, S. G. F (rev.2012) 'Salvation'. In *Encyclopaedia Britannica*, accessed June 4, 2019 at www.britannica.com/topic/salvation-religion#ref33997

Briscoe, B. (2018) *Educating the conservative Evangelical church about mental illness*. Retrieved from https://cmda.org/educating-the-conservative-evangelical-church-about-mental-illness/.

Brown, J. (2017) *Counseling diversity in context*. North York, ON: University of Toronto Press.

Bruner, F. D. (1997) *A theology of the Holy Spirit: The Pentecostal experience and the New Testament Witness*, Reprinted edn. Eugene, OR: Wipf & Stock Publisher.

Chan, C., Ho, P., and Chow, E. (2001) 'A body-mind-spirit model in health: An Eastern approach', *Social Work in Health Care*, 34(3–4), 261–282. Retrieved from www.researchgate.net/publication/11148479_A_body-mind-spirit_model_in_health_an_Eastern_approach.

Chatters, L. M., Taylor, R. J., Bullard, K. M., and Jackson, J. S. (2008) 'Spirituality and subjective religiosity among African Americans, Caribbean Blacks, and non-Hispanic whites', *Journal for the Scientific Study of Religion*, 47(4), 725–737. doi:10.1111/j.1468-5906.2008.00437.x.

Dixon, S. (2015) *Reconstructing cultural identities: The lived experiences of Jamaican.* (Unpublished dissertation). University of Calgary, Calgary, Alberta, Canada. Retrieved from https://prism.ucalgary.ca/handle/11023/2635.

Dixon, S. and Arthur, N. (2014) 'Creating space to engage Black Pentecostal clients in multicultural counselling practices', *International Journal for the Advancement of Counselling*, 37(2): 93–104. doi:10.1007/s10447-014-9228-x.

Dube, L., Shoko, T., and Hayes, S. (2011) *African initiatives in healing ministry.* Pretoria, SA: UNISA Press.

Duffin, J. (2009) *Medical miracle: Doctors, saints, and healing in the modern world.* Oxford: Oxford University Press.

Edge, D. (2013) 'Why are you cast down, o my soul? Exploring intersections of ethnicity, gender, depression, spirituality and implications for Black British Caribbean women's mental health', *Critical Public Health*, 23(1):39–48. doi:10.1080/09581596.2012.760727

Este, D. and Bernard, W. T. (2006) 'Spirituality among African Nova Scotians: A key to survival in Canadian society', *Critical Social Work*, 7(1):1–23. Retrieved from www.uwindsor.ca/criticalsocialwork/spirituality-among-african-nova-scotians-a-key-to-survival-in-canadian-society.

Favazza, A. R. (1982) 'Modern Christian Healing of Mental Health', *American Journal of Psychiatry*, 139(6):728–735.

Fee, G. D. (1996) *Paul, the Spirit and the people of God.* Peabody, MA: Hendrickson Publishers.

Ferngren, G. B (2009) *Medicine and health care in early Christianity.* Baltimore, MD: Johns Hopkins Press.

Hall, S. (1990) 'Cultural identity and diaspora', 222–237. In J. Rutherford (Ed.), *Identity: Community, culture, difference.* London: Lawrence & Wishhart.

Hanser, M. (2012) *Healing the spiritual dimension: A Christian perspective.* National Center of Continuing Education, Inc. Retrieved from www.nursece.com/courses/68-healing-the-spiritual-dimension-a-christian-perspective.

Harnack, A. (1908) *The Mission and expansion of Christianity in the first three centuries.* New York: Harper and Row. Retrieved from www.ntslibrary.com/PDF%20Books/Christianity%20in%20First%20Three%20Centuries.pdf.

Jacobson, N. and Greenley, D. (2003) 'What is a recovery model? A conceptual model and explication', *Psychiatric Services*, 52(4): 482–485.

James, C. E. (Ed.) (2010) *Seeing ourselves: Exploring race, ethnicity and culture* (4th ed.). Toronto, ON: Thompson Educational Publication.

Jenkins, J. H. (2007) 'Anthropology and psychiatry: the contemporary convergence'. In E. Bhugra, and K. Bhui (Eds.), *Textbook of pultural psychiatry* (pp. 20–32). Cambridge: Cambridge University Press.

John, S. S. (2014) 'Traditional healing rituals in Tamil Nadu, South India', *South Asian Anthropologist*, 14(1): 1–9. Retrieved from www.mukpublications.com/resources/14-1-1.pdf.

Kelsey, M. D. (1988) *Psychology, medicine, and Christian healing.* New York: Harper & Row.

Khan, A. H. (2011) 'Contemporary integration of spirituality and healthcare delivery: An Indi-Caribbean case perspective referencing an Islamic influenced healing therapy', *Voice of Intellectual Man*, 3(1): 1–32.

Koenig, H. (2005) *Faith and mental health: Religious resources for healing.* Philadelphia, PA: Templeton Foundation Press.

Koenig, H. G. (2008) 'Religion and mental health: What should psychiatrists do?', *Psychiatric Bulletin*, 32:201–203. doi:10.1192/pb.bp.108.019430.

Koenig, H. G. (2009) 'Research on religion, spirituality, and mental health: A review', *Canadian Journal of Psychiatry*, 54(5): 283–291. doi:10.1080/01459740.2013.846339.

Krause, K. (2014) 'Space in Pentecostal healing practices among Ghanaian migrants in London', *Medical Anthropology*, 33(1), 37–51. doi:10.1080/01459740.2013.846339.

McAlister, E. (1998) 'The Madonna of 115th street revisited: Vodou and Haitian Catholicism in the age of transnationalism'. In R. S. Warner and J. G. Wittner (Eds.), *Gatherings in diaspora: Religious communities and the new immigration* (pp. 123–160). Philadelphia, PA: Temple University Press.

McKenzie, K., Khenti, A., and Vidal, C. (2011) *Cognitive-behavioural therapy for English-speaking people of Caribbean origin: A manual for enhancing the effectiveness of CBT for English-speaking people of Caribbean origin in Canada.* Toronto, ON: Centre for Addiction and Mental Health (CAMH).

Mihanović, M., Babić, G., Kezić, S., Šain, I., and Longčar. Č. (2005) 'Anthropology and psychiatry', *Collegium Antropologicum*, 29(2): 747–751.

Moodley, R., and Barnes, C. (2015) 'Multiculturalism, religion and counselling: Freedom to heal'. In G. Nolan, and W. West, (Eds.), *Therapy, culture and spirituality: Developing therapeutic practice* (pp. 7–23). New York: Palgrave Macmillan.

Nolan, G., and West, W. (2015) 'Researching therapy, culture and spirituality'. In G. Nolan, and W. West, W. (Eds.), *Therapy, culture and spirituality: Developing therapeutic practice* (pp. 221–231). New York: Palgrave Macmillan.

Oxhandler H and Pargament, K (2014) 'Social work practitioners' integration of clients' religion and spirituality in practice: A literature review', *Social Work*, 59(3): 271–279. Retrieved from https://academic.oup.com/sw/article/59/3/271/2261296.

Pargament, K. I. (1997) *The psychology of religion and coping: Theory, research, practice*. New York: Guilford Press.

Pargament, K. I. (2013) 'What role do religion and spirituality play in mental health?' American Psychological Association. Retrieved from www.apa.org/news/press/releases/2013/03/religion-spirituality.aspx.

Pilch, J. J. (2007) 'Jesus as healer,' *Health*. Center for Christian Ethics at Baylor University, pp. 19–26 Retrieve from www.baylor.edu/ifl/christianreflection/HealthArticlePilch.pdf.

Porterfield, A. (2005) *Healing in the history of Christianity*. Oxford: Oxford University Press.

Robinson, J. (2014) *Divine healing: The years of expansion, 1906–1930* . Eugene, OR: Pickwick. Publications.

Shorter, A. (1985) *Jesus and the witchdoctor*. New York: Orbis Books.

Singleton, M. (1977) 'Spirits and spiritual direction: The pastoral counselling of the possessed', *Missiology: An International Review*, 5(2):185–194. doi: 10.1177/009182967700500204.

Singleton, M. (2001) '"Your faith has made you well": The role of storytelling in the experience of miraculous healing', *Review of Religious Research*, 43(2): 121–138. doi:10.2307/3512058.

Statistics Canada. (2016) *Immigration and ethnocultural diversity in Canada*. Retrieved from www12.statcan.gc.ca/nhs-enm/2011/as-sa/99-010-x/99-010-x2011001-eng.cfm#a3.

Sue, D. W., Sue, D., Neville, H. A., and Smith, L. (2019) *Counseling the culturally diverse: Theory and practice*, 8th edn. Hoboken, NJ: John Wiley & Sons, Inc.

Volf, M. and Bass, D. C. (2002) *Practicing theology: Beliefs and practices in Christian life*. Grand Rapids, MI: W. B. Eerdmans.

Wane, N. and Sutherland, P. (2010). 'African and Caribbean Traditional Healing Practices in Therapy'. In R. Moodley and A.S. George (Eds.), *Building Bridges for wellness in counseling and psychotherapy*, (pp. 335–347). Bangalore: CDCP and Backlog Press.

Woollcombe, K. (1964) 'Biblical meaning and use of the words flesh, body, soul, spirit, and Mind'. In *The Episcopal Church's ministry of healing* (pp. 40–44). New York: George McKay Press.

World Health Organization. (2014) *Mental health: A state of well-being*. Retrieved from Retrieved from www.who.int/features/factfiles/mental_health/en/.

Worland, S., & Vaddhanaphuti, C. (2013). "Religious expressions of spirituality by displaced Karen from Burma: The need for a spiritually sensitive social work response'. *International Social Work*, 56(3), 384–402.

21

HINDUISM AND HEALING IN MENTAL HEALTH

Meetu Khosla, Roy Moodley and Erica Killick

Hinduism as a culture and religion is integral to the evolution and development of Indian society and not unlike other Eastern cultures it is family based and community centred (Laungani 2005). Hinduism can be seen as a way of life, not separating the secular from the sacred; religious from the scientific; or the individual from the collective. According to Laungani (2005), at the simplest level Hinduism can be seen as a 'revealed' religion (in the same way that Judaism, Christianity and Islam is understood), or has evolved over the centuries into a complex philosophical and religious phenomena.

Hinduism is based on ancient texts and scriptures – the Upanishads, the Vedas, and the Bhagvad Gita – which has informed the history and philosophy of every aspect of Hindu life (Mysorekar 2006). These writings are the material and spiritual texts that has influenced Indian cultural practices, value systems and beliefs about mental health and well-being (Juthani 2001). Its emphasis on Karma yoga (or theory of action) and Jnana yoga (theory of pursuit of knowledge, sacrifice and service to the society) towards liberation from material desires tend to inform the very existence of a Hindu (Chekki 1996). It is also believed that a confused state of consciousness (ignorance, fear, and false beliefs) is the root cause of pain and suffering; and mental and psychological distress. Hinduism provides the basic knowledge about how to live life meaningfully, the concept of God or gods and the path to reach God or the gods; social norms, and customs and traditions. During a time of psychological distress or mental ill health, Hindus prefer to resort to believe in the karma theory in understanding the aetiology of the illness (Dalal and Misra 2011) and then resort to faith in God (Dalal 2016) and the use of Indian cultural and traditional healing practices (Khosla and Das 2019).

There are certain beliefs among the Hindus, such as Karma (good, bad or evil karma in the past life or the present one) that is the conceptual basis for the ways in which mental health and illness and notions of well-being are understood (Padayachee and Laher 2014). Hinduism tends to view mental health and well-being through a holistic system of beliefs; and not in terms of Cartesian dichotomies and binaries (Narendra 1999). Individuals are seen as holistic and interdependent, where concepts about mental health cannot be separated from the beliefs of physical, mental and spiritual health are integrated and interdependent (Fowler 1997). Therefore, culture shapes the expression of mental illness, and the pathways for health care (Komiti, Judd and Jackson 2006; Matsumoto and Juang 2004; Saravanan et al. 2008). The effectiveness of health care practices depends upon the extent to which there is cultural sensitivity in the healing practices as well as knowledge about the traditional beliefs and values so that they can be integrated into the modern Western healing systems (Chong et al. 2007; Khosla 2018; Moodley, Lo and Zhu 2018).

In this chapter, we will discuss religious beliefs and practices in Hindu culture; the way Hinduism influences the perception and attitudes towards mental health and illness; the various healing approaches and treatment methods. How this has influenced or can influence clinical work in mental health care.

Religious beliefs and practices: Karma and Dharma

The roots of Hindu religious beliefs and practices can be traced to its vast philosophical and religious literature and other treatises, – such as, the Vedas, the Upanishads, the Puranas, the Dharma Sutras, the Ramayana, the Mahabharata, and the Bhagavad Gita (Ramisetty-Milker1993). These texts inculcate values and religious beliefs which are deeply engraved in the hearts, minds and souls of Hindu people forming an integral part of their identity and worldview (Krishnamurthy 1989). Two concepts that are key to Hinduism are Karma and Dharma. These are discussed below.

Karma or Sanskrit Karman ('act') or Pali Kamma is a philosophy of universal causal theory that constructs an understanding that one's present or future mode of existence is based on the good or bad deeds or actions of one's past life. The concept of karma stipulates that one will have to bear the fruits of their actions, when the time is appropriate. If a person is flourishing or suffering it is therefore due to past karma (Kumar 2000; Rama 2007). Illness could also be related to past evil karma (Juthani 2001), where one may have, for example, hurt another person for personal benefit or harmed the society for selfish reasons (Balodhi 1990; Khosla and Das 2019). These bad intentions and bad deeds would then contribute to bad karma and future suffering (Khosla and Joshi 2019). This theory or philosophy informs the ethical dimension of the process of Samsara (a process of rebirth) and allows individuals to be released from the limited and restricted cycle of birth and death (moksha). It also provide individuals with the motivation to live a moral life; thus, karma is seen as the moral law of causality in one's life (Rama 2007).

Dharmais the duty and the moral rules of the society (Jayakar 1994) that must be performed by virtue of belonging to a social group, caste or gender. The values enforced by dharma are not restrictions or burdens but instead are the duties that build social order, justice and maintain harmony and integrity. If one is not following their *dharma* appropriately then it may cause bad karma (Kurian 1986). Meditation, pilgrimages and prayer are believed to reduce the impact of the negative consequences of bad karma (Kumar 2000).

Hinduism, mental health perceptions and illness representations

Hindu religion and philosophy are the principal texts and constructs that inform how illness is perceived, represented and presented. Beginning with an anti-Cartesian concept where the individual is seen as a whole in which the mental, physical and spiritual aspects of the self is not divided into separate categories (Kakar 1982), the debates surrounding mental health take on a very different perspective than the West. Although viewing health and illness as dichotomous is a mere artefact of language (Radley 1994), it has nevertheless contributed largely to the ways in which mental health and well-being professional have been trained and identified, while Dalal (2016) proposed that health and illness are on a continuum and the distinction between them depends upon the perception of the placement on this continuum, the fact is that Western models of healing are conceptualized to address the problem in the Cartesian individual where body, mind and spirit is seen as separate entities. It seems that either extremes are not conclusive in a complex and nuanced way that modernity interacts with mental health. This complexity can be understood by some of the principles of Hinduism. For example, *Swastha* (Svastha) is a Sanskrit word (my own self that is situated); in other words, for being in one's natural state healthy, devoid of any abnormality (Tripathi 2000); or put another way: that which is situated in one's ownself but considers one's whole existence (Dalal 2016). This concept suggest that health and mental health depends upon the level of awareness (*mansa*) and mental status (*ahara* and *vihara*) of the person.

Hinduism proposes a holistic system of beliefs where mental health is mediated by mental factors, physical factors and socio-cultural influences (Dalal and Misra 2011; Ramakrishna and Weiss 1992). Prolonged illness may cause pain, suffering, discomfort and lead to crisis in the family or feelings of loneliness or guilt (Sharma and Misra 2009). A synchronisation between the *ahar* [nutrition], *vihar* [leisure], *vichar* [thoughts] leads to health.

The conceptualization of mental health and well-being is somewhat closer to that of the concept of happiness, contentment, satisfaction with experiences in life, sense of belongingness, and utility (Verma and Verma 1989). In the traditional Indian thought, health is viewed in a broader sense of complete well-being and happiness (Sinha 1998). Health is perceived as not merely an absence of pain and suffering but cultivation of personality attributes, intellectual capacities, self-knowledge, inner peace, truthfulness and moral values. Health and well-being of a person is also contingent upon the health and happiness of other people or living beings around them Sinha (1998). Hinduism views illness and health as determined by karma or supernatural elements (Salagame 2013).

In Hinduism, spiritual illnesses are associated with witchcraft, evil eye, and spirit possession. These spiritual illnesses may exist along with mental illness or in solitude. Evil spells are believed to cast 'bad luck' causing a person to, for example, suffer from dizziness, nausea, convulsions, crying, fatigue and illness (Khosla, Parvez and Verma 2019) or even death. Spirit or ghost possession is another ailment caused by a persons' karma. If there is an untimely death or unfinished karma then the person may experience ghost from the previous birth causing symptoms of ill health (for example, shaking, trance like state, strange speech, hallucinations, changes in the body, epilepsy etc.).

Hinduism and healing

Hinduism's concept of healing is holistic involving psychological factors, such as the experience of the inner sense of well-being, harmony, balance, peace and between the mind and body (Dalal 2016: 40). If there is an imbalance or distress or dis-function then healing may not change the situation or eliminate the symptoms completely, but it may enable the individual to cope with the illness or crisis, engender a sense of hope and resolve the conflicts associated with the causal attribution of illness providing relief from anxiety or stress, feelings of guilt, fear, loneliness and depression associated with the illness (Dalal 2016: 40). While, Khosla and Das (2019) found that psychological recovery of the disabled accident victims was significantly correlated with their karmic attributions which reduced the intensity of the burden they experienced in their present life of their perceived 'wrong' behaviours. This motivated them to gain control of their present situation and seek medical treatment. This benevolent religious reframing was perhaps a kind of positive coping (Pargament 1997). There are other types of religious coping too that help in healing such as collaborative religious coping and congregational support. In a study (Khosla and Kaur 2019) comparing Hindu and Sikh community members with their quality of life and happiness, it was found that sharing of religious views with friends, visiting a temple, engaging in pro-religion behaviours as altruistic behaviours, sharing of the *prasadam* or offering to God, chanting, reading religious texts all help to enhance positive mood, social support as well as coping with stressful and personally traumatic events.

Sometimes during a series of unfortunate events in ones' life, such as losing a job, a grievance in the family, illness all happening simultaneously people think it is God's punishment for their bad deeds or negligence of their moral duties. This belief will often encourage people to take part in religious activities more rigorously, such as keeping a religious sermon at home, visiting temples more frequently, praying more, and asking God or the gods for forgiveness, giving more donations, offering food to animals, performing religious rituals and ceremonies to ward off the evil spirits, visiting religious places or sprinkling holy water from the Ganges to purify the home or person suffering. Some of these ways in which people engage in seeking readdress against physical or mental illness they experience is shown in Tarakeshwar, Pargament and Mahoney's (2003) study. They examined religious coping and mental health among Hindu Asian Indians in the United States. They found that religious coping was associated with finding meaning, achieving a life transition, gaining control, comfort, and closeness to God, enhancing personal well-being, relationship well-being and reducing psychological distress.

Guru–Chela relationship

The *Guru–Chela* relationship is evident in many healing processes. The spiritual preceptor or the teacher is considered the *guru* while the follower or the student is called *chela* or disciple. According to Kumar, Bhugra and Singh (2005: 118), "the guru acts as a physician of mind and soul with objectivity and competence"; whose main role is to encourage the development of self-discipline and harmonious relationship with the society. When the relationship between the guru and the disciple is close, similar to that of a parent–child relationship, then healing takes place (Kakar 1982, 1991). The chela becomes aware of the faulty patterns of their thoughts and behaviours, which need to be rectified to feel better (Kumar, Bhugra and Singh 2005). Gurus primarily use religious sermons, chanting, *bhajans* and spiritual lectures to heal. Often people seek help from the guru more readily than seeking out a medical practitioner or psychiatrist due to the social stigma. If a patient has sought treatment for depression from a temple priest at *Balaji* instead of seeking psychiatric help, there will be a better chance of being accepted by the society (Khosla, Parvez and Verma 2019).

Ritual healing

Rituals have been described as patterned and ordered sequences of words indulged repeatedly making appeal to extraordinary beings (Sax, Weinhold and Schweitzer 2010). Ritual healing is used in healing physical or mental illnesses, such as infertility, restlessness, chronic pain, economic difficulties, absconding children, marital problems, failure in business or work, and childhood illnesses (Sax 2010), and restructuring social relationships (Sax 2009). Generally, one seeks help from a healer for any kind of problem or physical trouble, *pareshani* (Khosla and Das 2019). It is perceived that there is an imbalance between the physical, social and spiritual worlds, probably in some state of *adharma* [disharmony with the nature of things]. The patient visits the *ashram* or the shrine of the village goddess to worship. Ritual healing brings about personal transformation (Ranganathan 2015), a change in meaning of experience, and the way reality is perceived (Csordas 1994).

Hinduism and traditional healing

Traditional healing is the oldest form of method of treatment that is based on the underlying philosophy and it is practices on the basis of certain specific principles (Ramashankar and Sharma 2015). The earliest evidence of healing practices can be traced to artefacts obtained from Mohenjodaro and Harappa which were in accordance with the social and cultural practices, and beliefs of that time (Dalal 2016: 41). Harapan people used to worship animals, mostly bull, engaged in ritualistic purity and hygiene. Shamans belonged to the urban Harappa community and healed various kinds of diseases. The healing involved magical and religious rituals in combination to ward off evil spirits (Chattopadhay 1982; Zysk 1998). These rituals involved dancing, using herbs, and sacrificing animals which are still being adhered to by some tribal groups in India (Khosla and Keya 2019). Traditional healing is practiced more often in the villages and rural areas of India where psychiatric care is limited. It is often used as the first resort to treat any mental illness before seeking help form a medical practitioner since traditional healers are culturally sensitive, easily accessible and affordable (Khosla and Das 2019; Shankar, Sravanan and Jacob 2006).

Traditional healing methods involve a holistic approach in dealing with the physical and mental illness, such as taking care of the causal factors of the illness, viz., *nazar* or evil eye which is due to external factors or people surrounding the sick or *Bhut* or evil spirits which hover around the sick from the unseen forces or spiritual influences. The traditional healer may help by mediating with God or the gods to restore balance (Khosla and Das 2019). The divine healer could also use his or her knowledge of the religious texts and scriptures to heal the patient, serving as a link between human beings and the supernatural. They may interpret the cause as messages from the ancestors and use prayers to heal the patient (Ramashankar and Sharma 2015). The divine healers may indulge in *aarti* where lamps are lit and prayers are recited for a *diety* to heal the patient; offer herbs or holy water to help the patient get rid of his/her illness (Betty 2005). Sometimes the *nazar* is taken care of by a family elder and not a temple priest or healer, where a black thread is tied around the wrist or washing the patients face with holy water or giving alms. It is through an understanding of the spiritual beliefs that underlie the nature of the illness or problem that allow the traditional healer to address the needs of the patient.

There are numerous approaches or methods that can be termed traditional healing, such as the AYUSH Approaches – – Ayurveda, Yoga, Unani, Siddha and Homeopathy. We briefly discuss Ayurveda, Yoga, Unani, and Siddha below.

Ayurveda

Ayurveda is the traditional Indian medicine that is known as the "the science of longevity" that emphasizes upon a healthy diet and a holistic way of living (Ramakrishna and Weiss 1992). In other words, it literally means the science of life – Ayu (life), and Veda (knowledge), dating back to the early Vedic civilization (about 1500 BC), as described in the classical texts of Susruta and Caraka (200 BC– 400 BC) (Moodley and Oulanova 2011). Ayurveda, according to Kumar, Bhugra and Singh (2005: 115), "avoids a strict body-mind dualism and instead emphasizes the interaction of mind and body in the causation of the human condition (health and disease)". Thus, Ayurveda adopts a holistic approach to health and illness. Health is associated with the dynamic balance of *tridoshas* (three humours: *vatha*, *pitha*, and *kapha*), and the Five Elements (ether, air, fire, water, and earth). The imbalance of *tridoshas* gives rise to various physical and mental illnesses. In a state of imbalance Ayurveda proposes that when

Hinduism and Healing in Mental Health

there is awareness of the body, then the mind can work to make it balanced (Juthani 1998). The three life forces in the body known as the *doshas* are ideally in balance and harmony with one another. Depending upon the body constitution or type or health issues, various food products are prescribed to maintain the balance (Juthani 1998). Ashtanga Ayurveda or the *bhuta*vidya, deals with the various psychological imbalances of the mind. In Ayurveda, a combination of treatments are used, including physical methods (e.g., herbs, purification through purges, ointments, dietary changes, and regular sleep); lifestyle changes (e.g., abstinence from alcohol); and moral education.

Ayurveda is a way of life that provides freedom from illness and promotes good health through prevention. The majority of the research (Bagla 2011; Mishra 2004; Shankar, Unnikrishnan and Venkatsubramanian 2007) in Ayurveda has focused on the healing properties of Ayurvedic herbs and botanical formulations, and the traditional five-step detoxification process known as *panchkanna* (Singh 2010). Other studies found that Ayurvedic treatments improved cognitive functioning (Ramu, Venkataram, Mukundan and Shankara 1992); reduce anxiety and depression (Bhargava and Singh 2013; Bhattacharya, Bhattacharya, Sairam, and Ghosal 2000); lowered stress and anxiety (Uebaba, Xu, Ogawa, Tatsuse, Wang, Hisajima, and Venkatraman 2008); and, decreased anxiety, tension, depressed mood, and insomnia and enhanced cognition (Sharma, Chandola, Singh, and Basisht 2007). Furthermore, Ayurveda helps in treating of common affective disorders (Buhrman 1997), dementia (Manyam 1999), Alzheimer's disease (Ringman, Frautschy, Cole, Masterman, and Cummings 2005), and Parkinson's disease (Nagashayana, Sankarankutty, Nampoothiri, Mohan, and Mohanakumar 2000).

Yoga

Yoga which means joining together incorporates *asanas* (physical movements), *pranayama* (breathing exercises), and *dhyana* (meditation) in its practice. It is a set of principles that emphasizes the balance between the mind and body (Mijares 2003) by training the mental and physical functions simultaneously. For example, Karma yoga and Rajayoga focus on achieving a specific state of mind or particular desirable behaviours such as working altruistically for the benefit of others within society. Simpkins and Simpkins (2011) state that Raja yoga which involves meditation and attention techniques helps in disciplining the mind and move it in a direction away from fears, worries and anxieties towards higher consciousness and enlightenment. It also provides certain *niyamas* or rules of conduct of behaviour that may lead to happiness and relief from suffering. Hatha yoga tends to involve breathing and physical postures that bring about harmony between the mind and body. The main aim of yoga then is to realize psycho-spiritual goals (Mijares 2003), bringing harmony and balance between the person and his or her mental state, physical being and spiritual environment.

The practice of Yoga is mostly used for coping, mindfulness, reducing distress and physical impairment (Park, Braun, and Siegel 2015). Specific yoga treatment known as *SudarshanKriya* Yoga has been developed for people with depression. However, despite its potential benefits for managing depressive and schizophrenic symptoms, yoga has not been widely integrated into psychotherapy due to its limited empirical support.

Several studies found that yoga interventions were effective in treating patients with major depressive disorder (Cramer, Anheyer, Lauche, and Dobos 2017; Khalsa 2004); symptoms of schizophrenia and quality of life (Cabral, Meyer, and Ames 2011; Cramer, Lauche, Langhorst, and Dobos 2013); increased physical and mental well-being, cognitive performance, reduced stress and re-incarceration rates (Wimberly and Xue 2016), and enhanced self-concept (Dubey 2011; Khosla and Singh 2019).

255

Unani

Unani is referred to as the Islamic Medicine of India. While not directly influenced by Hinduism, Unani which originated in Greece (460 BCE), and brought to India (13th century) by the Arabs and Persians has a similar philosophy as Hinduism to healing and well-being. In Unani the body is made of up of three parts: the organs (solid), humors (liquid), and pneuma (gases) the disequilibrium of which led to a diseased state (Kumar et al. 2005; see, for discussion, Moodley and Oulanova 2011).

Siddha

Siddha is an ancient system of medicine and healing originated in South India (5000 BCE) but is now practiced throughout India. Similar to Ayurveda, Siddha treatment is in restoring balance and equilibrium of the three humors (vittam, pittam, and kapham) (Moodley and Oulanova 2011). Although scarce, a few studies have examined the efficacy of Siddha meditation in the treatment of medical and psychiatric illnesses. Carruthers (1980) reported that Siddha meditation helps in the treatment of anxiety, other neurotic symptoms and psychosomatic disorders. He found that, similar to autogenic training, Siddha meditation produces a slowing of heart rate, reduction of blood pressure, and increase in motor or sensory cortical discharges in the brainstem. Kozasa et al. (2008) studied the effects of Siddha yoga in the reduction of anxiety, depression, and tension and found these traits along with an overall increase in well-being. Connell (1995) found that Siddha yoga helped in managing stress among the psychotherapists. Clinical trials to further investigate these effects are certainly warranted.

Integrating clinical and counselling psychology with indigenous healing

Indian healing traditions as yoga, meditation and breathing exercises are used widely in the West to relieve pain, anxiety and stress. The traditional Indian therapies as proposed in the Vedas basically focus on changing the unhealthy patterns of thinking, feeling and behaving. Even if the actual problem may not be cured a patient can learn to live with the problem which leads to a relief in symptoms and adaptive functioning (Khosla and Goel 2019). Sandhu (2005) incorporated the Sikh life-stress model into Western counselling which focused on causal factors of suffering, how egotism is involved in despair and stress, and how strategies can be developed to enhance coping skills. Indeed, yoga and meditation have been incorporated into the Western therapies in many different ways (Misra and Paranjpe 2012). For example, in grief counselling which uses mindfulness meditations to help patients deals with the feelings of interdependence, compassion and loss shifting consciousness from self-pity to self-acceptance, empathy for others, and improve mental health (Wada and Park 2009). Although Indian healing techniques are being used in the West, the efficacy of Western techniques on Indian clients remains unclear. Indian psychologists mention that Western psychological techniques are unsuitable for Indian clients (Arulmani 2007; Heckel and Paramesh 1974; Jain 2005; Pandey 1969). They propose that therapeutic techniques be designed in a culturally sensitive way, including the beliefs, values and other contextual in mental health care.

Mindfulness meditation and various approaches based on mindfulness are being used as interventions for treating a variety of psychological and physical problems (Chiesa and Malinowski 2011). Cognitive Behaviour Therapy (CBT) which also incorporates mindfulness in its practice (Lau and McMain 2005), is considered as a complementary process to CBT (Beck and Haigh 2014), as does the existential approach (Claessens 2009). Engaging in mindfulness meditation helps to focus on the present situation in a non-judgemental way and accept the experiences as they are (Papies, Barsalou, and Custers 2012). Brief meditation has been found to increase the white matter in the brain (Tang, Hölzel and Posner 2015), improve brain function (Jain, Khatri and Jamadar 2015), and increase attention and self-regulation (Tang et al. 2015). Also, interventions using mindfulness have been found to be effective in treating mental health problems in adults and adolescents (Khoury et al. 2013; Zoogman, Goldberg, Hoyt and Miller 2015), and alcohol misuse (Harris, Stewart, and Stanton 2017).

Future directions

Integrating the knowledge and skills from traditional healers and using that expertise in combination with a Western scientific approach would provide benefits, such as: greater insights into developing an effective health care program reduce the stigma and shame associated with seeking help for mental illness and also enhance the adjustment and acceptance in the community (Dalal 2016, Khosla and Goel 2019). Purohit (2002) conducted a survey in India and found that majority of the urban respondents (more than 90%) believed that traditional therapies effectively treat physical and mental illness. In Indian culture family and social norms play an integral role in the evolution and development of the social and psychological self. Worldviews are shaped through a communal process and not entirely individualistic as in the West. Relationships in the family and community belongingness influence the well-being of the person. The society places certain expectations from the person who is morally obliged to abide by them. Thus, the mental health practitioner needs to know the cultural norms and social structure before diagnosing or treating any illness.

More holistic treatment approaches need to be developed that focus on individual development, improving personal functioning and well-being, as well as creating harmony and a sense of compassion with the community members. Using the wisdom of the Bhagavad Gita, we can modify our thinking patterns, know our moral duties and obligations, work selflessly for the attainment of personal wellness and universal peace. Moreover, the Bhagavad Gita is very useful in developing the paradigms for various therapeutic methods and treatment strategies for effectively dealing with conflict, anxiety, depression, phobia, fear, anger, helplessness, to name but a few.

Conclusion

Hindu traditional healing practices can be incorporated into modern mental health programs and treatments in a way that can both revitalize the ancient practices and complement the modern approaches. Even though research in the field of traditional healing, yoga and meditation is still in its infancy, research consistently indicates the moderate usefulness of these techniques in therapeutic treatments. The appropriate merging of the traditional and modern healing practices has the potential to change the discourse of mental health, healing and diversity in the 21st century to more profound levels of engagement with genuine culturally positive outcomes for individuals and communities seeking mental health care.

References

Antarkar, D S (2003) 'Perspectives on Ayurveda with special reference to mental health'. In P.K. Ravindranath and SwamiPrakashananda (Eds.), *Ayurvedic and Allopathic Medicine and Mental Health*: Proceedings of the Indo–US Workshop on Traditional Medicine and Mental Health, 13–17 October 1996. Mumbai, India: Bharatiya Vidya Bhavan.

Arulmani, G. (2007) 'Counselling psychology in India: at the confluence of two traditions'. *Applied Psychology: An International Review*, 56(1): 69–82.

Bagla, P.(2011) 'Piercing the veil of Ayurveda'. *Science*, 334: 1491.

Balodhi, J. P. (1990) 'Psychotherapy based on Hindu philosophy'. *Journal of Personality and Clinical Studies*, 5(1): 51–56.

Beck, A. T., and Haigh, E. A. P. (2014) 'Advances in cognitive theory and therapy: The generic cognitive model'. *Annual Review of Clinical Psychology*, 10, 1–24. http://dx.doi.org/10.1146/annurev-clinpsy-032813-153734.

Betty, S. (2005) 'The growing evidence for 'demonic possession': What should psychiatry's response be?' *Journal of Religion and Health*, 44:13–30.

Bhargava, K. P., and Singh, N. (2013) 'Anti-Stress Activity of Ocimum Sanctum Linn'. *Indian Journal of Medical Research*, 137(3): 617–625.

Bhattacharya, S. K., Bhattacharya, A., Sairam, K., and Ghosal, S. (2000) 'Anxiolytic-Antidepressant Activity of Withania Somnifera Glycowithanolides: An Experimental Study'.*Phytomedicine*, 7(6): 463–469. https://doi.org/10.1016/S0944-7113(00)80030–6.

Buhrman, S. (1997) 'Ayurveda and strep throat'. *Protocol Journal of Botanical Medicine*, 2(2): 175–176.

Cabral, P., Meyer, H. B., and Ames, D. (2011) 'Effectiveness of Yoga Therapy as a Complementary Treatment for Major Psychiatric Disorders: A Meta-Analysis.' *The Primary Care Companion for CNS Disorders*, 13(4): 0–0. https://doi.org/10.4088/PCC.10r01068.

Carruthers, M. (1980) 'Voluntary control of the involuntary nervous system: comparison of autogenic training and siddha meditation'. In F. J. McGuigan, W. E. Sime, and J. M. Wallace (Eds.), *Stress and Tension Control* (pp. 267–275). https://doi.org/10.1007/978-1-4613-3114-8_29.

Chattopadhyay, D. (1982) 'Case for a critical analysis of the Charakha Samhita'. In D.Chattopadhyaya (Ed.), *Studies in the History of Science in India* (Vol.1). New Delhi:Centre for Studies in Civilizations.

Chekki, D. A. (1996) 'Family values and family change'. *Journal of Comparative Family Studies*, 27: 409–413.

Chiesa, A. and Malinowski, P. (2011) 'Mindfulness-based approaches: Are they all the same?' *Journal of Clinical Psychology*, 67(4): 404–424.

Chong, S. A., Verma, S., Vaingankar, J. A., Chan, Y. H., Wong, L. Y., and Heng, B. H. (2007) 'Perceptions of the public towards the mentally ill in a developed Asian country'. *Social Psychiatry and Psychiatric Epidemiology*, 42: 734–739.

Claessens, M. (2009) 'Mindfulness and existential therapy'. *Existential Analysis*, 20 (1), 109–119.

Conboy, L., Edshteyn, I., and Garivaltis, H. (2009) 'Ayurveda and Panchakarma: Measuring the Effects of a Holistic Health Intervention', *The Scientific World Journal*, 9: 272–280. doi:10.1100/tsw.2009.35.

Connell, D. M. (1995) The Relationship Between Siddha Meditation and Stress in Psychotherapists: A Transcriptional Perspective, 4576-4576.

Cramer, H.,Anheyer, D.,Lauche, R.,and Dobos, G. (2017)'A Systematic Review of Yoga for Major Depressive Disorder'. *Journal of Affective Disorders*, 213: 70–77. https://doi.org/10.1016/j.jad.2017.02.006.

Cramer, H., Lauche, R., Langhorst, J., and Dobos, G. (2013) 'Yoga for Depression: A Systematic Review and Meta-Analysis', *Depression and Anxiety*, 30(11): 1068–1083. https://doi.org/10.1002/da.22166.

Csordas, T. J. (1994) *The Sacred Self: A Cultural Phenomenology of Charismatic Healing.* Berkeley: University of California Press.

Dalal, A. K. (2016) *Cultural Psychology of Health in India: Well-being, Medicine and Traditional Health Care.* New Delhi: Sage.

Dalal, A. K. and Misra, G. (2011) *New Directions in Health Psychology.* New Delhi: Sage.

Dalal, A. K., and Pande, N. (1988) 'Psychological Recovery of Accident Victims with Temporary and Permanent Disability'. *International Journal of Psychology*, 23(1–6): 25–40. https://doi.org/10.1080/00207598808247750.

Dubey, S. N. (2011) 'Impact of yogic practices on some psychological variables among adolescents'. *Indian Journal of Community Psychology*, 7 (1): 1–7.

Easwaran, E. (Ed.) (1985) *The Bhagavad Gita.* Petaluma, CA: Nilgiri Press.

Fowler, J. (1997) *Hinduism: Beliefs and practices.* Brighton: Sussex Academic Press.

Harris, J. S., Stewart, D. G., and Stanton, B. C. (2017) 'Urge surfing as aftercare in adolescent alcohol use: A randomized control trial'. *Mindfulness*, 8:144–149. http://dx.doi.org/10.1007/s12671-016-0588-7.

Heckel, R. V. and Paramesh, C. R. (1974) 'Applied psychology in India'. *Professional Psychology*, 5(1): 37–41.

Jain, M.M, Khatri, N., and Jamadar, P.(2015) 'Improved brain Function form Meditation Following awareness Training Programme in Spiritual Medicine (ATPiSM)'. *Journal of Medical and Dental Sciences*, 4(51): 8881–8893.

Jain, A. K. (2005) 'Psychology in India'. *The Psychologist*, 18(4): 206–208.

Jayakar, K. (1994) 'Women of the Indian subcontinent'. In L. Comas-Diaz and B. Greene (Eds.), *Women of Color: Integrating Ethnic and Gender Identities in Psychotherapy* (pp. 161–181). New York: Guilford Press.

Juthani, N.V. (1998) 'Understanding and treating Hindu patients'. In G.H.Koenig, *Handbook of Religion and Mental Health* (pp.271–278). London: Academic Press

Juthani, N.V. (2001) 'Psychiatric Treatment of Hindus', *International Review of Psychiatry*, 13(2): 125–130. https://doi.org/10.1080/09540260125005.

Krishnamurthy, V. (1989) *Essentials of Hinduism*. New Delhi: Narosa.

Kakar, S. (1982) *The Analyst and the Mystic*. New Delhi: Viking.

Khalsa, S. B. (2004) 'Yoga as a therapeutic intervention: A bibliometric analysis of published research studies'. *Indian Journal of Physiology and Pharmacology*, 48 (3): 269–285.

Khosla, M. (2018a) 'A Cross- Cultural Comparison of the Traditional Healing Practices in India and Canada', The Conference on Engaging India and Canada: Challenges and Sustainable Development Goals, in conference proceedings by Shastri Indo-Canadian Institute, IIC, 8–9 June, Delhi.

Khosla, M. (2018b) 'Healing the Mind: Insights from BhagvadGita.Plenary address in the Swadeshi Indology Conference on Mind Sciences', "*Indian Culture and Psychology: A Consciousness Perspective*", University of Delhi, March 22–27.

Khosla, M. and Das, J. (2019) 'Psychological and cultural facets of traditional healing practitioners from Assam'. *Indian Journal of Psychology*, special issue: 86–97.

Khosla, M., and Goel, Y. (2019) 'Comparison of traditional healing methods and modern medical treatment practices: implications for developing integrative practices'. *International Journal of Healing and critical Mental Health* (in press).

Khosla, M., and Joshi, V. (2019) 'Understanding traditional Healing Practices'. *Indian Journal of Psychology,*in press.

Khosla, M., and Kaur, N. (2019) 'Beliefs about traditional healing in Sikh community'. *Indian Journal of Psychology*, in press.

Khosla, M., and Keya, Y. (2019) 'Inter-relation between traditional helaing and religion in the Nyshi tribe of Arunachal Pradesh'. *International Journal of Healing and Critical Mental Health,* in press.

Khosla, I., Khosla, M., and Khosla, S. (2019) 'Exploring the dynamics of temple healing and the faith in the pandit as a Messenger of God'. *Indian Journal of Psychology*, in press.

Khosla, M., Parvez, Z., and Verma, S. (2019) 'The spiritual healing of pirbabas'. *Indian Journal of Psychology,* in press.

Khosla, M., and Singh, M. (2019)'Healing through mindfulness meditation in Indian cultural context'. *Indian Journal of Psychology*, special issue: 134–140.

Khoury, B., Lecomte, T., Fortin, G., Masse, M., Therien, P., Bouchard, V., and Hofmann, S. G. (2013) 'Mindfulness-based therapy: A comprehensivemeta-analysis'. *Clinical Psychology Review*, 33,763–771. http://dx.doi.org/10.1016/j.cpr.2013.05.005.

Komiti, A., Judd, F., and Jackson, H. (2006) 'The influence of stigma and attitudes on seeking help from a GP for mental health problems: A rural context'. *Social Psychiatry Psychiatric*, 41: 738–745.

Kozasa, E. H., Santos, R. F., Rueda, A. D., Benedito-Silva, A. A., De Moraes Ornellas, F. L., and Leite, J. R. (2008) 'Evaluation of Siddha Samadhi Yoga for Anxiety and Depression Symptoms: A Preliminary Study'. *Psychological Reports,* 103(1): 271–274. https://doi.org/10.2466/pr0.103.1.271-274.

Kumar, M., Bhugra, D., and Singh, J. (2005) 'South Asian (Indian) traditional healing: Ayurvedic, Shamanic, and Sahaja therapy'. In R. Moodley and W. West (Eds.), *Integrating Traditional Healing Practices into Counseling and Psychotherapy* (pp. 113–147). Thousand Oaks, Calif: Sage.

Kumar, P. (2000) *Hindus in South Africa: Their Traditions and Beliefs*. Durban: University of Durban-Westville Press.

Kurian, G. (1986) 'Inter-generational integration with special reference to Indian families'. *Indian Journal of Social Work*, 47: 39–49.

Lau, M. A., and McMain, S. F. (2005) 'Integrating mindfulness meditation with cognitive and behavioural therapies: The challenge of combining acceptance- and change-based strategies'. *The Canadian Journal of Psychiatry*, 50 (13): 863–869.

Manyam, B. V. (1999) 'Dementia in Ayurveda'. *The Journal of Alternative and Complementary Medicine*, 5(1): 81–88. https://doi.org/10.1089/acm.1999.5.81.

Mascolo, M. F., Misra, G., and Rapisardi, C. (2004) Individual and Relational Conceptions of Self in India and the United States. New Directions for Child and Adolescent Development, 2004(104): 9–26. https://doi.org/10.1002/cd.101.

Matsumoto, D., and Juang, L. (2004) *Culture and Psychology*. California: Wadsworth.

Mijares, S. G. (2003) Modern psychology and ancient wisdom: Psychological healing practices from the world's religious traditions. Binghamton, NY: The Haworth Integrative Healing Press.

Mishra, L. C. (2004) *Scientific Basis for Ayurvedic Therapies*. New York: CRC Press.

Misra, G. and Paranjpe, A. C. (2012) 'Psychology in modern India.' In R. W. Rieber (Ed.), *Encyclopedia of the History of Psychological Theories*. New York: Springer Science.

Monier-Williams, M. (2008) A Sanskrit English Dictionary: Ayurveda. Delhi, India: Motilal Banarsidass. Corrected Edition.

Moodley, R., and Oulanova, O. (2011) 'Rhythm of the Pulse: South Asian Traditional Healers and their Healing Practices in Toronto'. *International Journal of Health Promotion and Education*, 49(3): 90–100).

Moodley, R., Lo, T. and Zhu, N. (Eds.) (2018). *Asian Healing Traditions in Counseling and Psychotherapy*. Los Angeles: Sage.

Mysorekar, U. (2006) 'Eye on religion: Clinicians and Hinduism'. *Southern Medical Journal*, 99: 441.

Nagashayana, N., Sankarankutty, P., Nampoothiri, M. R. V., Mohan, P. K., and Mohanakumar, K. P. (2000) 'Association of l-DOPA with Recovery Following Ayurveda Medication in Parkinson's Disease'. *Journal of the Neurological Sciences*, 176(2): 124–127. https://doi.org/10.1016/S0022-510X(00)00329-4.

Narendra, N. (1999) 'Mental health and spiritual values. A view from the East'. *International Review of Psychiatry*, 11: 92–96.

Padayachee, P. and Laher, S. (2014) 'South African Hindu Psychologists' Perceptions of Mental Illness'. *Journal of Religious Health*, 53: 424–437.

Pandey, R. E. (1969) 'Psychology in India'. *American Psychologist*, 24: 936–939.

Pargament, K. I. (1997) *The Psychology of Religion and Coping: Theory, Research, Practice*. New York: Guilford Press.

Park, C., Braun, T., and Siegel, T. (2015) 'Who Practices Yoga? A Systematic Review of Demographic, Health-Related, and Psychosocial Factors Associated with Yoga Practice'. *Journal of Behavioral Medicine*, 38(3): 460–471. https://doi.org/10.1007/s10865-015-9618-5.

Papies, E. K., Barsalou, L. W., and Custers, R. (2012) 'Mindful attention prevents mindless impulses'. *Social Psychological and Personality Science*, 3:291–299. http://dx.doi.org/10.1177/1948550611419031.

Purohit, S. (2002). Faith that works. Hindustan Times (20 February), Lucknow, India.

Radhey, A. (1994) *Making Sense of an Illness*. London: Sage Publications.

Rama, S. (2007) *Perennial Psychology of the Bhagvad Gita*. New Delhi: Himalayan Institute Press.

Ramakrishna, J., and Weiss, M. G. (1992) 'Health, illness, and immigration- East Indians in the United States'. *Western Journal of Medicine*, 157: 265–270.

Ramashankar, S. D., and Sharma, B. K. (2015) 'Traditional healing Practices in North East India'. *Indian Journal of History of Science*, 50(2): 324–332.

Ramisetty-Mikler, S. (1993) 'Asian Indian immigrants in America and socio-cultural issues in counseling'. *Journal of Multicultural Counseling and Development*, 21: 36–49.

Ramu, M. G., Venkataram, B. S., Mukundan, H., and Shankara, M. R. (1992) 'A Controlled Study of Ayurvedic Treatment in the Acutely Ill Patients with Schizophrenia (Unmāda): Rationale and results'. *NIMHANS Journal*, 10(1): 1–16.

Ranganathan, S. (2015) 'Rethinking "Efficacy": Ritual Healing and Trance in the Mahanubhav Shrines in India'. *Cult Med Psychiatry*, 39: 361–379.

Ringman, J. M., Frautschy, S. A., Cole, G. M., Masterman, D. L., and Cummings, J. L. (2005) 'A Potential Role of the Curry Spice Curcumin in Alzheimer's Disease'. *Current Alzheimer Research*, 2(2): 131–136.

Salagame, K. K. K. (2013) 'Perspectives on reality in Indian tradition and their implications for health and well-being.' In A. Morandi and A. N. N. Nambi (Eds.), *An Integrated View of Health and Well-being; Bridging Indian and Western Knowledge*. New York: Springer.

Sandhu, J. S. (2005) 'Asikh perspective on life-stress: Implications for counselling'. *Canadian Journal of Counselling*, 39(1): 40–51.

Saravanan, B., Jacob, M. G., Prince, M., David, A. S., and Bhugra, D. (2008) 'Perceptions about psychosis and psychiatric services: A qualitative study from Vellore, India'. *Social Psychiatry and Psychiatric Epidemiology*, 43: 231–238.

Sax, W. (2010) 'Ritual and the problem of efficacy.' In William S. Sax, Johannes Quack, and Jan Weinhold (Eds.), *The Problem of Ritual Efficacy*. New York: Oxford University Press.

Sax, W., Weinhold, J., and Scheweitzet, J. (2010) 'Ritual Healing East and West: A Comparison of Ritual Healing in the Garhwal Himalayas and "Family Constellation" in Germany'. *Journal of Ritual Studies*, 24(1): 61–77.

Sax, W. S. (2009). *God of Justice: Ritual Healing and Social Justice in the Central Himalayas*. Oxford: Oxford University Press.

Schoonover, J., Lipkin, S., Javid, M., Rosen, A., Solanki, M., Shah, S., and Craig, L.K. (2014) 'Perceptions of traditional healing for mental illness in rural Gujarat'. *Annals of Global Health*, 80: 96–102.

Shankar, B.R., Saravanan, B., and Jacob, K. S. (2006) 'Explanatory models of common mental disorders among traditional healers and their patients in rural south India'. *International Journal of Social Psychiatry*, 2: 324–332.

Sharma, H., Chandola, H. M., Singh, G., and Basisht, G. (2007) 'Utilization of Ayurveda in Health Care: An Approach for Prevention, Health Promotion, and Treatment of Disease. Part 2—Ayurveda in Primary Health Care'. *Journal of Alternative and Complementary Medicine*, 13(10): 1135–1150. https://doi.org/10.1089/acm.2007.7017-B.

Shankar, D., Unnikrishnan, P. M. and Venkatsubramanian, P. (2007) 'Need to develop inter-cultural standards for quality, safety and efficacy of traditional Indian systems of medicine'. *Current Science*, 92: 1499–1505.

Sharma, S., and Misra, G. (2009) 'Health psychology: Progress and challenges'. In G. Misra (Ed.), *Psychology in India* (Vol.4). New Delhi: Pearson.

Simpkins, A. M. and Simpkins, C. A. (2011) *Meditation and Yoga in Psychotherapy*. New Jersey: John Wiley and Sons.

Singh, R. H. (2010) 'Exploring Issues in the Development of Ayurvedic Research Methodology'. *Journal of Ayurveda and Integrative Medicine*, 1(2): 91–95.

Sinha, D., and Naidu, R. K. (1994) 'Multilayered hierarchical structure of self and not self: The Indian perspective'. In A.-M. Bouvy, F. J. R. van de Vijer, P. Voski, and P. Schmitz (Eds.), *Journeys into Cross-Cultural Psychology: Selected Papers from the Eleventh International Conference of the International Association for Cross-Cultural Psychology, Held in Liège, Belgium* (pp. 41–49). Lisse; Berwyn, PA: Swets & Zeitlinger.

Sinha, D. (1998) 'Changing perspectives in social psychology in India: A journey towards indigenization'. *Journal of Social Psychology*, 1:17–31.

Tambiah, S. J. (1979) 'A performative approach to ritual'. *Proceedings of the British Academy*, 65: 113–169.

Tang, Y.-Y., Hölzel, B. K., and Posner, M. I. (2015) 'The neuroscience of mindfulness meditation'. *Nature Reviews: Neuroscience*, 16: 213–225. doi: 10.1038/nrn3916

Tarakeshwar, N., Pargament, K.I., and Mahoney, A. (2003) 'Measures of Hindu Pathways: development and preliminary evidence of reliability and validity'. *Cultural Diversity and Ethnic Minority Journal*, 9: 316–332.

Tripathi, B. (2000) Caraka samhita of aganivesa, hindi commentary, 1 ST Edition, Published by Chaukhamba Sanskrit Pratishthan, Varansi, 108: 5/13.

Uebaba, K., Xu, F.-H., Ogawa, H., Tatsuse, T., Wang, B.-H., Hisajima, T., and Venkatraman, S. (2008) 'Psychoneuroimmunologic Effects of Ayurvedic Oil-Dripping Treatment'. *Journal of Alternative and Complementary Medicine*, 14(10): 1189–1198. https://doi.org/10.1089/acm.2008.0273.

Verma, S. K., and Verma, A. (1989) 'Manual for PGI general well-being measure. Lucknow: Ankur Psychological Agency'. VHAL. *India's Health Status*. New Delhi: Voluntary Health Association of India.

Wada, K., and Park, J. (2009) 'Integrating Buddhist psychology into grief counseling'. *Death Studies*, 33:657–683.

Wimberly, A. S., and Xue, J. (2016) 'A Systematic Review of Yoga Interventions in the Incarcerated Setting'. *Journal of Sociology & Social Welfare*, 43: 85.

Zoogman, S., Goldberg, S. B., Hoyt, W. T., and Miller, L. (2015) 'Mindfulness interventions with youth: A meta-analysis'. *Mindfulness*, 6:290–302. http://dx.doi.org/10.1007/s12671-013-0260-4.

Zysk, K.G. (1998) *Asceticism and Healing in India: Medicine in the Buddhist Monastery*. New Delhi: Motilal Banarasidas.

22

ISLAM AND HEALING IN MENTAL HEALTH

Amina Mahmood

The Muslim population is a heterogeneous group. Islam is a way of life for Muslims, and it is from their faith that many Muslims seek comfort and solace during difficult times, including when experiencing emotional distress. Thus, it becomes imperative that mental health providers educate themselves in the basics of Islamic philosophy, beliefs, and perspectives on mental health. Muslims are diverse in terms of ethnicity, culture, professional and economic backgrounds, and in their understanding and practice of their faith (Schlosser et al. 2009). Even for Muslims from a specific cultural background there is still substantial within group variability in the interpretation and practice of Islam (Schlosser et al. 2009). Culture informs the interpretation and practice of Islam (Ali et al. 2008), and the common beliefs and values of Muslims discussed in this chapter serve as a uniting factor for this diverse community.

The intersection of culture and religion sometimes makes it difficult for the lay-person to distinguish where faith ends and culture begins. This can cause disagreements on religious practice between Muslims from different cultural backgrounds, and also lead to misunderstandings by providers who are unable to distinguish a practice as being solely culture and erroneously attribute it to religion (for instance, certain *cultural* traditions in which amulets with *Quranic* verses are worn to serve as protection). Many Muslim communities in the West are comprised of diverse cultural and ethnic backgrounds, and discussions of what is cultural and acceptable within the Islamic worldview are often engaged in by *Imams* (religious leaders and *de facto* counselors to the Western Muslim communities) who seek to remind their congregations of the unity that exists within the diversity of the Muslim population.

As we explore the beliefs and values common to Muslims, and how these can be appropriately integrated into psychological interventions when working with a Muslim client it is important for the reader to recognize that there is cultural variability in how these beliefs and values manifest, that is, being aware of the intersection of multiple identities, and how this impacts practice of, and identification with faith (Schlosser et al. 2009). Islam is a way of life that a culturally diverse population follows, and as stated above this makes it challenging to distinguish between what is an "Islamic" intervention, vs. an intervention that was developed within a culture that practices Islam. Practitioners unfamiliar with Islam and its perspective on mental health and well-being may confuse where an Islamic intervention ends and the cultural intervention begins. It is important for practitioners to assess their Muslim client or patient's identification with the faith prior to offering an intervention based within a religious framework. It is also imperative for the health care provider to seek expert consultation to ensure that their well-intended attempt to provide an intervention based in their client's faith does not come across as a microaggression, particularly in today's socio-political climate when Muslim are globally marginalized, and invalidated when it comes to their faith.

Islamic scholars often remind Muslims that seeking help is encouraged by the Sunnah (prophetic tradition), and belief in God includes utilizing treatment options available to one (e.g. psychologists, psychiatrist, other mental health professionals). Seeking assistance from traditional healers, religious leaders, and engaging in indigenous healing practices has its benefits for those who believe (Moodley et al. 2008), but should not occur at the expense of ignoring science. Integration of religious and spiritual beliefs into psychotherapy is congruent with the movement towards holistic care, and the philosophy of multicultural psychology (Haque et al., 2016; Moodley et al., 2008). Islam encourages Muslims to seek treatments based in science, in addition to religious and spiritual interventions.

This chapter begins by providing the reader with a brief background on the religion of Islam, and the beliefs and values of its followers. Next, we will consider the Islamic perspective on mental health and wellness. This will be followed by a review of Islamic perspectives on treatment and healing. Case examples will illustrate the integration of indigenous Islamic healing into health and mental health care. Finally, recommendations and future directions for research, interventions, and application will be addressed.

Islam: History, philosophy and demographics

The word "Islam" originates from the root word *"salaam"* in Arabic which means "peace," "to submit," or "to surrender." A Muslim is one who follows Islam, or rather one who chooses to submit to, or surrender to the will of *Allah* (the Arabic word for God). Muslims believe that prophets and messengers have been revealing the message of Islam to humankind since the beginning, starting with Adam (peace and blessings be upon him[1]).

The Prophet Muhammad (pbuh), began receiving the message of Islam through the archangel Gabriel in the Arabian Peninsula (present-day Saudi Arabia). These revelations are believed by Muslims to be the continuation and finalization of the message of the Prophets in the Judeo-Christian traditions. The compilation of these revelations, believed to be the direct words of God, comprises the holy book of Islam: the *Qur'an*. The *Qur'an* serves as the primary source of guidance for Muslims, and focuses on economic, legal, and social guidance and mores. The second source of guidance for Muslims comes from Prophet Muhammad's (pbuh) life (*Sunnah*) and sayings (*Hadith*). Muslims believe that Prophet Muhammad (pbuh) epitomized the *Qur'an's* message, and it is through his lived example that Muslims are able to better understand how to live their faith. The *Qur'an* and *Hadith* combine to form the basis of Islamic law, which is a guidance to Muslims on how to live within the boundaries of their faith.

There are five basic tenets or pillars of Islam that are agreed upon by all Muslims, regardless of their sectarian affiliation. The first pillar is: *Tawhid*. This is the belief in the oneness of Allah, and of Prophet Muhammad (pbuh) being the last messenger. The second pillar of Islam is Salat (prayer). Muslims are required to pray five times a day (before sunrise, midday, late afternoon, sunset, and at night). Physical movement is incorporated into the prayers (similar to movements in a gentle yoga class). The prayers are structured and require Muslims to recite certain verses of the *Qur'an*, after which one may engage in personal supplication.

The third pillar is *zakat* (charity). There are numerous verses in the *Qur'an* and sayings of the Prophet Muhammad (pbuh) that remind Muslims to be charitable. As a pillar of Islam, *zakat* refers to the requirement of donating 2.5% of one's wealth to charity annually. This is a requirement for those who can afford to give, and the calculations of the *zakat-able* amount considers accrued debt, and annual living expenses. The fourth pillar of Islam is *sawm* (fasting). All Muslims who are healthy and able to do so (children are exempt) are required to fast (abstain from food or drink during the daylight hours) during the month of Ramadan, the 9th month of the Islamic lunar calendar. The physical element of fasting reminds Muslims of those in the world who are suffering or living in poverty. The greater challenge of fasting is to improve one's character, and abstain from negative behavior, e.g., lying, gossiping, backbiting, arguing, speaking rudely to others (hard to do when one is hungry!). The month of Ramadan is a time of reflection and spiritual growth.

The fifth pillar of Islam is the *Hajj*, i.e., the pilgrimage to Makkah, Saudi Arabia. Muslims are required to complete the *hajj* once in their lifetimes, if their life circumstances allow them to do so. The *hajj* commemorates Allah's command to Abraham to sacrifice his son Ishmael. The *hajj* is a transformative and cleansing experience for Muslims. If done with pure intentions Muslims believe that the *hajj* cleanses them of all their past errors and sins and allows them a fresh start in life.

It is pertinent to address the major division amongst Muslims: the Sunnis and the Shi'ites. This division began as a political one, pertaining to leadership, after the Prophet Muhammad's (pbuh) death. A segment of the Muslim population believed that leadership of the Muslim community was intended for his son-in-law and cousin Ali (Armstrong 2000). This group eventually became known as the "Shi'ite (party) of Ali." The majority within the Muslim community believed that the leadership of the community ought to be determined via consensus. This majority is referred to as Sunni.

Ultimately this political division led to the first civil war in Islam, in Karbala. After the events of the battle of Karbala (located in modern-day Iraq) in 680 CE Shi'ism was consolidated as a religious sect and gradually the political rift resulted in theological differences by the ninth century. As time progressed off-shoots of Shi'ism emerged. The reason for further division continued to be the issue of leadership (Mahmood 2006). A notable characteristic of the Shi'ite sect is the focus on social justice and activism. This is emphasized due to the history of persecution and oppression experienced by the Shi'ites from the Sunni, and the brutality with which they were treated during the events of Karbala. The Shi'ites continue to be the minority today, with approximately 15% of the Muslim population identifying as Shi'ite, and the 85% majority as Sunni (Esposito and Mogahed 2007). The commonalities that hold Muslims together are greater than the differences between sects. Values common to Muslims are briefly discussed below.

The Qur'an states:

> And turn not thy cheek away from people in [false] pride, and walk not haughtily on earth: for, behold, God does not love anyone who, out of self-conceit, acts in a boastful manner. Hence, be modest in thy bearing, and lower thy voice … .
>
> *(The Qur'an[2] 31:18–19)*

Modesty (*hijab*) is valued highly by the Muslim community and signifies more than just the headscarf for Muslim women. Modesty of behavior is equally as important, as modesty in dress for all Muslims. Muslims are encouraged to interact with modesty and kindness towards others. Modesty also plays a role in cross-gender interactions, which are influenced by cultural norms. Attaining knowledge and education is the imperative duty of each and every Muslim. Muslims are encouraged to utilize their education to serve humanity.

The emphasis within Islamic teachings is to nurture and strengthen the family. For example, with regards to parents it is stated:

> And do good unto [thy] parents. Should one of them, or both, attain to old age in thy care, never say 'Ugh' to them or scold them, but [always] speak unto them with reverent speech, and spread over them humbly the wings of thy tenderness … .
>
> *(The Qur'an 17: 23–24)*

Muslims are encouraged to work together for the well-being of their family, and by extension the local communities in which they reside. Islam emphasizes fairness and justice. Muslims should stand up against injustice and oppression, and work towards creating a fair and just society that empowers and strengthens its members. It is this injunction that guides Muslims to create and work for not-for-profit organizations, choose careers that benefit humanity, and volunteer their time for the benefit of society at large.

Today, Islam is the world's fastest growing religion in the world, and its followers (Muslims) comprise approximately one-fifth of the world's population (Esposito and Mogahed 2007; Pew Research Center 2015). Recent estimates suggest 1.6 billion of the world's population is Muslim (Pew Research Center, 2015). Contrary to stereotype the majority of the Muslim population is located outside of the Middle East. Only one in five of the world's Muslims have Arab origins (Esposito and Mogahed 2007). The largest Muslim populations reside in the countries of Indonesia, Bangladesh, Pakistan, India, and Nigeria (Esposito and Mogahed 2007; Pew Research Center 2015). These countries are diverse in their ethnic backgrounds and cultural traditions. Although arbitrary boundaries have been set by the Western world on what constitutes the "Muslim world," in today's global economy, with increased global communication, history of colonialism, and migration, Muslims are present in every corner of the globe. The global Muslim population is diverse in ethnicity, race, culture, traditions, professional, and economic backgrounds. The commonality that ties this population together is their faith: Islam.

Islamic perspectives on mental health and wellness

Islam is a way of life and Islamic teachings via the *Qur'an* and Hadith provide guidance for tackling life's challenges. These challenges can be social, economic, interpersonal, medical or psychological. As seen in the previous section, Muslims value education. Islam encourages Muslims to engage in scholarship to attain a better understanding of the world and discover solutions for problems. From the 8th to the 14th centuries, science and scholarship flourished within the Muslim world (Haque 2004). Muslim scholars built upon and expanded Greek philosophy and this led to the development of basic psychological principles that continue to be utilized in our current practice (Haque 2004).

Health and wellness are viewed holistically by Muslims (Haque and Keshavarzi 2014; Hodge and Nadir 2008). There is typically no separation between the psychological and the physical. One's mental health influences the physical well-being and vice versa, and the symptoms are often identified both within the physical and psychological realm. Compartmentalization of symptoms is primarily a Western phenomenon. The current trend amongst Western health practices is a return towards a more integrative and holistic perspective and application of health and wellness. Challenges such as illness, whether psychological or physical, and other hardships one experiences are often viewed by Muslims as a test of patience and perseverance, and a way to further purify and strengthen one's faith. This concept is beautifully illustrated by the Sufi poet Rumi's words: "If you are irritated by every rub, how will your mirror be polished?"

Mental health and wellness is viewed as a state when one's spirituality and faith is congruent with Islamic teachings (Utz 2011), whereas mental illness occurs due to incongruence (Inayat 2005), that is, distancing oneself from the faith and its practices. The seat of psychological distress in Islamic scholarship is the heart (Inayat 2005), and it is the purification of the heart that eases distress. It is important to briefly review contributions of Islamic scholars to the field of psychology.

Haque (2004) explores the expansion of Islamic psychological theory and scholarship from the 8th to the 14th centuries. Haque (2004) notes that these early Muslim scholars contemplated the nature of self and human nature, and built further upon the work of Greek philosophers by integrating Islamic perspectives (Al-Issa 2000). These scholars include amongst others Al-Balkhi, a ninth-century physician, who is the first to make a distinction between psychological and medical disorders (Badri 2013). In his translation of Al-Balkhi's manuscript *"The Sustenance of the Soul"* Badri (2013) describes Al-Balkhi's perspective that psychological stressors and illness is inevitable, and each person has varying levels of resources available to cope with these stressors. Al-Balkhi's approach to psychological health encourages prevention and a strengths-based approach for treatment (Badri 2013). Al-Balkhi makes a distinction between psychological stressors that are transient and a response to stressful life events, versus those symptoms that are chronic and medically based (Badri 2013).

Al-Razi, another ninth-century Muslim scholar and physician wrote extensively on psychology. His work in the discipline (*"Razi's Traditional Psychology"*) has been translated by Arberry (2007), and discusses coping with and treating various moral and psychological concerns (Haque 2004). Al-Razi's scholarship recommends utilizing cognitive strategies to modify behavior, and to engage in behaviors that improve one's overall psychological strengths (Arberry 2007).

Ibn Sina (known as Avicenna to the Western world), an 11th-century scholar, wrote about the mind-body connection and treating psychological conditions (Haque 2004). Another 11th-century Muslim scholar influential in Islamic psychology is Al-Ghazali. He conceptualized psychological distress as a result of being distant from God (Keshavarzi and Haque 2013). Keshvarzi and Haque (2013) expound on Al-Ghazali's conceptualization of the human soul which consists of: *nafs* (the ego), *aql* (cognition), *ruh* (the spirit), and *qalb* (the heart). These elements are intertwined and influence our behaviors and psychological condition. The goal to achieve optimal psychological development is via increasing positive thoughts and behaviors (Keshavarzi and Haque 2013).

The reader is encouraged to review Haque (2004) for a summary of early scholarship by Muslim scholars in the area of psychology that continues to influence the practice of psychology and medicine today. For instance, Al-Balkhi proposed cognitive behavior therapy in the ninth century! As scholarship and treatises in the area of psychology were being written, treatment facilities were also created for the care of the psychologically ill. The first psychiatric hospital dates to the early 9th century and was located in Baghdad, Iraq (Al-Issa 2000). Treatments provided included secular (music therapy), physical (medicines and herbs), and religious (prayers and meditation) (Al-Issa 2000). This confirms the norm within Islam to utilize and integrate best practices when providing treatment. The scholarship summarized here follows a modern-day rational-cognitive, behavioral, and strengths-based theoretical approach to conceptualizing psychological distress. The scholars were ahead of their time in determining the contribution of our cognitive faculties to mental health and identifying the mind-body connection.

Next, causes of psychological distress based on Al-Ghazali's theory of the soul will be described briefly. As mentioned previously in this chapter, Al-Ghazali conceptualizes four aspects of the human soul. This includes: *nafs* (the ego), *aql* (cognition or the intellect), *ruh* (the spirit, the unconscious), and *qalb* (the heart) (Keshavarzi and Haque 2013). He also equates psychological distress with distancing oneself from God (Keshavarzi and Haque 2013). Within Islamic tradition the heart or the *qalb* is viewed as the seat of psychological well-being, and many traditional healing practices pertain to purifying and cleansing the heart in order to alleviate psychological distress. Al-Ghazali conceptualizes the heart as influencing the nafs, aql and ruh and vice versa (Keshavarzi and Haque 2013). Since the four aspects of the human soul work together and are heavily influenced by the heart, targeted interventions to the heart will impact the entire soul. The concept of *irada* (will) or the motivation to change is necessary for the healing process (Haque 2004). The *Qur'an* states in Surah 13 verse 11: "Verily, God does not change men's condition unless they change their inner selves… ." This verse highlights the importance of taking initiative and motivation to change. It is difficult to make progress in treatment with a client who lacks insight into their own behavior or has no desire to change. Per Islamic teachings this verse provides the individual with hope that once they make an intention to change God will assist them in healing. Some Muslim clients may present to the clinician with explanations of psychological distress that the clinician is unfamiliar with. These concerns may include: *jinn* possession, the evil eye/*hasad* (envy), feeling that they are being punished for past sins (Keshavarzi and Haque 2013), and being affected by sorcery/magic (Thomas et al. 2015). These concerns are briefly explained here.

Muslims believe that God created humans, angels, and the *jinn*. The *jinn* are a supernatural being that have the ability to present themselves physically to humans, and according to Islamic traditions may also literally occupy and take over the human body. The *Qur'an* itself makes mention of the *jinn* as part of God's creation. *Jinn*, like humans, follow different religions, some can be naughty and destructive (think: poltergeist). The *jinn* mythology is common in Middle East and South Asia. Sudden changes in behavior of an individual, in particular, psychoses is traditionally attributed to *jinn* possession in some Muslim communities. For instance, onset of schizophrenia may often go undiagnosed and untreated in communities which attribute symptoms to *jinn* possession.

There is a strong belief among Muslims about the evil eye (*hasad*). This intersects with cultural beliefs in the Middle East. For instance, in Turkey it is common to see blue eye figurines and amulets that purportedly serve as protection from the evil eye. Similarly, in the South Asian sub-continent black string is tied to newborns and children for protection. These practices find their origin in culture rather than religion. Per Islamic teachings, protection is to be sought from God, and God alone. Figurines created by humans do not have the power to provide protection. Muslims believe that it is possible for someone's envy to either intentionally or unintentionally harm someone. For instance, someone who is progressing well in their personal and professional life finds themselves unexpectedly beset by obstacles. This individual may be perplexed and attribute the obstacles to someone's evil eye or envy towards them, resulting in psychological distress. Traditionally, when congratulating someone or appreciating the blessings one has received Muslims will attribute the good fortune to God and seek protection from God for these blessings.

Muslims believe that obstacles and challenges they face in life on earth serve a cleansing and purifying purpose. For example, an individual struggling with illness may explain this as punishment for past mistakes and errors. It is traditionally believed that being cleansed of one's sins on earth will prevent one from the punishment of hell-fire on the day of judgement. Some Muslims may attribute their psychological distress to sorcery or magic. The *Qur'an* Surah 113 verses 4–5 asks Muslims to seek refuge: "from the evil of all human beings bent on occult endeavors, and from the evil of the envious when he envies." The reference to magic here is contextual to the time frame in which this Surah was revealed. Asad (2003) states in the explanation that this phraseology is familiar to the Arabs and referenced a time before Islam, when magic and sorcery was practiced to wish ill upon others.

The causes of psychological distress listed above are those that Muslims may be hesitant to bring to a mainstream mental health care provider. However, knowledge of these is beneficial in strengthening the therapeutic relationship for clients who attribute their distress to these concerns. Being informed of these concerns will assist the clinician in accurate diagnoses within a culturally aware framework. For a discussion of contemporary and emerging psychological concerns that Muslim clients seek psychotherapy see: Ali et al. (2004); Ali (2006); Ali et al. (2008), Mahmood (2006); and Mahmood (2013). These concerns include anxiety, depression, substance use, relationship concerns, Muslim identity development, gender and sexuality, racism, and Islamophobia.

Islamic healing practices

Muslims believe in the healing power of the *Qur'an*, and their prayers or supplications to God. Healing practices within an Islamic framework utilize Qur'anic verses, prescriptions for specific prayers (depending on the nature of the distress), seeking repentance, and meditative practice. These interventions are generally prescribed by a leader within the religious community, for instance, the Imam, Sufi Shaykh, community leader, trusted elder, or alternative medication providers (such as, Hakims, see next paragraph). These healers are sometimes sought in conjunction with mainstream health providers, and at times serve as a conduit for the client to seek a mental health care provider. Seeking these healers is determined by intersecting identities of culture, religion, and social class.

Research suggests that Muslims are open to seeking treatment from non-Muslim providers given that these providers are familiar with Islamic beliefs and values (Kelly et al. 1996). Depending on cultural background Muslims may consider seeking assistance from traditional healers. Research conducted in the U.A.E (Thomas et al. 2015) and Pakistan (Farooqi, 2006) suggests that Muslim clients will often utilize multiple treatment modalities. For instance, they will seek out psychiatric consultation and a traditional healer concurrently. Traditional healers may include: Imams, a highly regarded teacher of religion, or a Sufi shaykh. Sufism is a mystical branch of Islam. Any Muslim can practice Sufism. The focus in Sufism is on spiritual growth. Sufi orders typically have a shaykh or teacher who serves as a guide to members of that order. Members within the community that are regarded as possessing spiritual and religious knowledge, for instance, community elders, and healers who practice alternative medicine, such as, Hakims (homeopathic providers) may also be consulted (Note: These practitioners utilize homeopathic, Ayurvedic and/or Greek medicine (also known as Unani [Unan/Yunan = Greece in Urdu/Hindi/Persian] Medicine), and are popular in South Asia, and South Asian diasporas around the world. Within a Muslim context Hakims will incorporate Quranic ayahs and prescribe special prayers as part of the healing process, in addition to the herbal remedies offered).

The heart plays a central role in Islamic tradition as the seat of psychological and emotional well-being. It is imperative that Islamic interventions for mental health and wellness focus upon purifying and cleansing the heart. In the previous section, we learned that psychological distress is often viewed within Islam as straying from the faith. Critical scholarship in the area of psychology was reviewed that recognizes the inevitability of psychological distress and differentiates between minor transient psychological and emotional stressors as opposed to chronic conditions that require professional health care interventions. Additionally, some traditional conceptualizations of psychological distress were identified. The reader is encouraged to keep this is in mind as we explore healing practices within a religious framework.

Research suggests that traditional healers within Muslim communities recognize their boundaries of competence and refer clients to professional medical and psychological treatment as necessary (Thomas et al. 2015). A brief description of some commonly used healing methods within the Islamic framework are listed below. Cultural, educational, social class, nature of religious and spiritual identification are a few variables that determine which traditional healing strategy or strategies are considered important for the Muslim client. Islamic healing methods are sought for distress attributed to jinn possession, the evil eye/envy, sorcery/magic, or a belief that one is being punished for their previous sins.

Muslims believe in the healing power of the *Qur'an* and prayer, and that: "*God does not burden any human being with more than he is well able to bear... .*" (Qur'an 2:286). There are certain surahs in the Qur'an that Muslims will turn to during distress. Muslims believe that reading, reciting or listening to these surahs in conjunction with prayer and supplication to God for assistance will ease pain and suffering. For example, Surah Rehman is believed to have healing properties. *Ayat-ul-Kursi* a verse in the *Qur'an* is utilized to ease fear, anxiety, and increase one's sense of safety. Muslims also may engage in supplementary prayers beyond the five mandated ones to ease their fears and anxiety. The *Tahajjud* prayer is another strategy often prescribed by Imams and other traditional healers to ease psychological distress. This prayer occurs during the last third of the night, and those who practice it vouch for its relaxation and meditative effects. Farooqi (2006) notes preliminary research that Tahajjud prayer has helped in reducing depressive symptoms for those who practice it. *Ruqyah* is a practice that is specifically prescribed by an Imam or a traditional healer who is an expert in the practice. This practice refers to prescribing specific chapters or verses in the *Qur'an* in conjunction with specific supplications (*duas*) in a particular sequence to ease to their suffering (Utz 2011). Prescription of the verses is dependent upon the diagnosis or concern being expressed, and the individual is encouraged to engage in evidence-based treatments concurrently (Utz 2011).

Consider the case of Ayesha, a multiracial married, hijab-wearing, Muslim female, health care professional in her 30s, with two children under the age of six. She presented to treatment with concerns regarding mood instability (bipolar disorder). In treatment Ayesha's belief in the power of prayer as healing was utilized by encouraging Ayesha to pray regularly with the reminder of the primary responsibility to take care of her health (psychological and/or medical) first and foremost. This was helpful for Ayesha during times depressive episodes which prevented her from praying regularly. Ayesha was reminded of God's compassion, mercy, and understanding of our struggles. Ayesha was reminded that psychological challenges can serve as a route to grow spiritually, and that challenges are placed to help us come closer to God. Psychoeducation was provided within a faith-based context by sharing some of the early Islamic scholarship on psychological disorders. Utilizing prayer and focusing on her blessings was helpful to Ayesha. However, she also sought out treatment with a psychiatrist, while concurrently seeking out herbal remedies that would aid in symptom stabilization (this is consistent with our discussion here that maintains some Muslim clients will seek alternative healing methods simultaneously while navigating the Western health care system).

Dhikr (meditation) is often employed to relieve stress and anxiety. Meditation is a practice integral to Islam. Prophet Muhammad (pbuh) would retreat to meditate for long periods of time, and it was during a meditative state that he received his first revelation. Sufi traditions have incorporated the tradition of meditation within their practice, however the typical Muslim tends to engage in a brief form of meditation or dhikr at the end of their daily prayers, time permitting. A *tasbih* (prayer beads) can be utilized to assist with this dhikr. Healers from various traditions have utilized prayer beads as a tool for meditation (Wernik 2009). Using the tasbih to engage in remembrance of God (dhikr) is believed to have calming and healing properties. The dhikr can focus on certain attributes of God, for instance: The Most Merciful, The Protector, The Source of Peace. Dhikr can also focus on certain verses of the *Qur'an*. The determination of the focus of the dhikr, and amount of time engaged in dhikr can be made by consulting a religiously knowledgeable person, an Imam or traditional healer.

The mystical tradition of Islam has structured practices that are designed to ease psychological distress. Haque and Keshavarzi (2014) detail interventions from the Sufi tradition and make recommendations for integrating these interventions into treatment. Sufi practices are designed to cleanse the heart and soul. Sufi practices include dhikr and meditation, ruqyah, prayers and supplication to God (see descriptions in previous section), and *muraqabah*. *Muraqabah* is a specific form of contemplative meditation practiced within Sufism, although empirical evidence is needed to assess its benefits (Haque et al. 2016) it is a practice that is regularly engaged in by those on the Sufi path. The structure of this meditation exercise may vary depending on the Sufi order one follows; however, the purpose is to cleanse the heart, and strengthen one's relationship with God to ease pain and suffering.

Psychological distress believed to be caused by previous mistakes or sins can be alleviated via repentance. Muslims believe that repenting for one's wrongdoing is purifying, and brings one closer to God (Utz 2011). A structured prescription for repentance is provided within Islamic teachings. The steps include: ceasing participation in the wrong or sinful behavior or activity; seeking forgiveness from God (there are specific supplications and prayers one can make to do so); regretting errors made; intentional decision to cease the behavior or practice; and asking for forgiveness or recompensing those who have been harmed by one's actions or behaviors (Utz 2011). Engaging in this act of repentance is necessary to relieve one of psychological distress. Consider, Ahmed, a 21-year-old Pakistani American Muslim male, moderately religious, and a senior in college experiencing an increased level of anxiety and depression and questioning his faith. Ahmed disclosed engaging in alcohol use for the past two years, and routinely visiting clubs and bars–both activities frowned upon within his Pakistani culture, and Muslim faith. Ahmed reported attempting to alleviate his distress by turning to prayer and attending meetings of the Muslim Student Association on campus. Ahmed's symptoms were addressed within a solution focused therapy approach, integrated with an Islamic framework focused on repentance. Strategies for repentance included bringing oneself closer to the faith by avoiding alcohol, clubs, bars, and sexual activity. It was also helpful to reframe "being" Muslim as "becoming" Muslim. This shift highlights the teaching that one is constantly in the process of bettering oneself spiritually and physically, and acknowledges mistakes are inevitable.

Future directions

Research on interventions with Muslims is limited. The research literature on the Muslim population is limited but growing within the discipline of psychology. An area of need in the literature is to examine the effectiveness of spiritually integrated interventions with the Muslim population. Haque et al. (2016) identify the development of culturally appropriate models for treatment that incorporate Islamic teachings, however, empirical investigation in this area is lacking. A recommendation is that rather than modifying Western models of psychological treatment and interventions to fit the Islamic perspective, we should study the works of Al-Ghazali, Al-Razi, and Al-Balkhi. These scholars identified cognitive reframing, behavior modification, mindfulness, strengths and solution-based approaches within a context and framework familiar to Muslims. These scholars also identified interventions, principles of which are incorporated in modern-day psychology. The most powerful tool we have today in working with our Muslim clients is to remind them of the contributions their faith has made to our profession.

Conclusion

Islam has a long history of science and scholarship in many disciplines, including psychology. Early Islamic scholarship explored rational-cognitive, behavioral, and mindfulness-based approaches to treatment within an Islamic framework. Muslims in the 9th century established psychiatric hospitals and conducted research on treatments that would effectively cure and manage psychological distress. Ultimately, Muslims believe God is the one who grants health and wellness. Thus, integrating religious and spiritual interventions into treatment is beneficial for those who identify strongly with their faith. More recently there has been increased interest among Muslim mental health providers to build upon past Islamic knowledge and integrate Islamically based interventions into treatment. Organizations such as the Institute of Muslim Mental Health (www.muslimmentalhealth.com), and The Family & Youth Institute (www.thefyi.org), are building upon the base of Islamic scholarship by investing in further research and development of Islamically based interventions for the Muslim client. This work is extremely important given that for many Muslims their faith is a source of strength and healing. This chapter provided a brief overview of Islamically based healing practices. As mental health providers, we should be cognizant of our clients' intersectional identities in the treatment room. Western-based secular interventions have received significant attention in research literature; however, this does not discount on invalidate the effectiveness of incorporating or integrating healing practices based within our clients' spiritual or faith-based traditions. We may be surprised that if we allow ourselves, with our clients' permission to incorporate a healing tradition based in their faith it may positively impact the treatment process significantly facilitating change which would have otherwise been hampered if the client's faith identity was ignored.

Notes

1 When referring to the messengers and prophets, Muslims will typically say this phrase either in Arabic or their primary language. In English texts the acronym is *pbuh*, followed in parentheses after the name. This will be utilized from this point on in the chapter as needed.
2 The trans-literated version of the *Qur'an* used in the text is that of Muhammad Asad (2003). This reference can be located under the reference list. The numeric notation identifies the surah and the verses of the *Qur'an*, e.g. in this case Surah 31, verses 18 and 19.

References

Ali, S. R. (2006) Psychology and Sunni Muslims. In E. T. Dowd and S. L. Nielsen (Eds.), *The Psychologies of Religion: Working with the Religious Client* (pp. 221–236). New York: Springer.

Ali, S. R., Liu, W. M. and Humedian, M. (2004) Islam 101: Understanding the Religion and Therapy Implications. *Professional Psychology: Research and Practice*, 35: 635–642.

Ali, S. R., Mahmood, A., Moel, J., Hudson, C. and Leathers, L. (2008) A Qualitative Investigation of Muslim and Christian Women's Views of religion and Feminism in Their Lives. *Cultural Diversity and Ethnic Minority Psychology*, 14: 38–46.

Al-Issa, I. (2000) Mental Illness in Medieval Islamic Society. In I. Al-Issa (Ed.), *Al-Junun: Mental Illness in the Islamic World* (pp. 43–70). Madison, CT: International Universities Press.

Arberry, A. J. (2007) *Razi's Traditional Psychology (Abu Bakr Muhammad ibn Zakariya al Razi)*. Damascus: Islamic Book Service.

Armstrong, K. (2000) *Islam: A Short History*. New York: Random House.

Asad, M. (2003) *The Message of the Qur'an*. Bristol: The Book Foundation.

Badri, M. (2013) *Abu Zayd al-Balkhi's Sustenance of the Soul: The Cognitive Behavior Therapy of a 9th Century Physician*. Herndon, VA: The International Institute of Islamic Thought.

Esposito, J. L. and Mogahed, D. (2007) *Who Speaks for Islam? What a Billion Muslims Really Think*. New York: Gallup Press.

Farooqi, Y. N. (2006) Traditional Healing Practices Sought by Muslim Psychiatric Patients in Lahore, Pakistan. *International Journal of Disability, Development and Education*, 53: 401–415.

Haque, A. (2004) Psychology from Islamic Perspective: Contributions of Early Muslim Scholars and Challenges to Contemporary Muslim Psychologists. *Journal of Religion and Health*, 43: 357–377.

Haque, A. and Keshavarzi, H. (2014) Integrating Indigenous Healing Methods in Therapy: Muslim Beliefs and Practices. *International Journal of Culture and Mental Health*, 7: 297–314. doi: 10.1080/17542863.2013.794249.

Haque, A., Khan, F., Keshavarzi, H. and Rothman, A. E. (2016) Integrating Islamic Traditions in Modern Psychology: Research Trends in the Last 10 years. *Journal of Muslim Mental Health*, 10: 75–100. http://dx.doi.org/10.3998/jmmh.10381607.0010.107.

Hodge, D. R. and Nadir, A. (2008) Moving Toward Culturally Competent Practice with Muslims: Modifying Cognitive Therapy with Islamic Tenets. *Social Work*, 53: 31–41.

Inayat, Q. (2005) Islam, Divinity, and Spiritual Healing. In R. Moodley and W. West (Eds.), *Integrating Traditional Healing Practices into Counseling and Psychotherapy* (pp. 159–169). Multicultural Aspects of Counseling and Psychotherapy, Series 22. Thousand Oaks, CA: Sage.

Kelly, E. W., Aridi, A. and Bakhtiar, L. (1996) Muslims in the United States: An Exploratory Study of Universal and Mental Health Values. *Counseling and Values*, 40: 206–218.

Keshavarzi, H. and Haque, A. (2013) Outlining a Psychotherapy Model for Enhancing Muslim Mental Health Within an Islamic Context. *The International Journal for the Psychology of Religion*, 23: 230–249. doi: 10.1080/10508619.2012.712000.

Mahmood, A. (2006) Psychology and Shia Muslims. In E. T. Dowd and S. L. Nielsen (Eds.), *The Psychologies in Religion: Working with the Religious Client* (pp. 237–252). New York: Springer.

Mahmood, A. (2013) Feminist multicultural Counseling Psychology with American Muslim Women. In C. Z. Enns and E. N. Williams (Eds.), *The Oxford Handbook of Feminist Multicultural Counseling Psychology* (pp. 221–239). New York: Oxford University Press.

Moodley, R., Sutherland, P., and Oulanova, O. (2008) Traditional Healing, the Body and Mind in Psychotherapy. *Counselling Psychology Quarterly*, 21: 153–165.

Pew Research Center. (2015) *The Future of World Religions: Population Growth Projections, 2010–2050.* Retrieved from www.pewforum.org/2015/04/02/religious-projections-2010–2050/.

Schlosser, L. Z., Ali, S. R., Ackerman, S. R. and Dewey, J. J. H. (2009) Religion, Ethnicity, Culture, Way of life: Jews, Muslims, and Multicultural Counseling. *Counseling and Values*, 54: 48–64.

Thomas, J., Al-Qarni, N. and Furber, S. W. (2015) Conceptualising Mental Health in the United Arab Emirates: The Perspective of Traditional Healers. *Mental Health, Religion, and Culture*, 18: 134–145, http://dx/doi.org/10.1080/136746.2015.1010196.

Utz, A. (2011) *Psychology from the Islamic Perspective.* Riyadh, Saudi Arabia: International Islamic Publishing House.

Wernik, U. (2009) The use of prayer beads in psychotherapy. *Mental Health, Religion, and Culture*, 12: 359–368.

23

JUDAISM AND MENTAL HEALTH

Devora Shabtai and David H. Rosmarin

A growing body of empirical research has indicated that basic spiritual/religious practices and beliefs are associated with enhanced psychological functioning and emotional well-being (e.g., Smith, McCullough and Poll 2003), and serve as very common and helpful methods of coping with distress (see Pargament 1997). In turn, mental health professionals have become increasingly more aware of the religious and spiritual needs of their patients and have displayed willingness to integrate spirituality and religious variables into clinical care for a variety of mental health symptoms and disorders (e.g., Rosmarin et al. 2015). These advancements are particularly meaningful in light of burgeoning literature highlighting the need for clinicians to adopt a multicultural approach when working with members of diverse ethnic groups (e.g., Sue and Sue 2013), including religious populations (e.g., Cornish, Wade, Tucker, and Post 2014). However, research and clinical guidelines for working with Jewish populations remains sparse, since the majority of examinations on religion and mental health has been conducted with Christian populations. Therefore, in this chapter, we (1) survey traditional Judaic attitudes toward mental health and treatment and discuss how these attitudes have developed over time, (2) explore the components of traditional Jewish culture, practice, and belief which intersect with mental health; and (3) discuss implications for clinical practice and treatment with members of the Jewish population.

Religion and multicultural psychology

Psychologically speaking, religion is thought to function in similar ways to culture in that it impacts the broader context of an individual's life (Cohen and Rozin 2001). Notably, relationships between religion and mental health functioning have been found to vary based on the distinct worldview, beliefs, and behaviors that characterize the faith (e.g., Rosmarin, Pirutinsky, Pargament, and Krumrei 2009). To these ends, an approach to religion is part and parcel of multicultural psychology.

Employing a multicultural approach is particularly salient for clinicians working with members of the Jewish population who not only represent a distinct ethnicity and culture, but who adhere to specific norms, practices, and worldviews (see Schnall 2006). Promoting cultural awareness of the Jewish population in a clinical context is especially valuable given literature documenting that clinical work has been negatively impacted by a variety of misconceptions regarding Jewish attitudes and behaviors (Ribner and Kleinplatz 2007). It has been documented that these misunderstandings have not only impeded clinical work (e.g., Ribner 2004) but also have historically led Jewish individuals to seek out clergy over clinicians (Feinberg and Feinberg 1986; Schnall et al. 2014). Furthermore, sociocultural identity and religious beliefs and practices have been correlated with psychological functioning among the Jewish population in various ways (e.g., Pirutinsky and Rosmarin, 2018), and in turn, competent clinical practice with Jewish individuals necessitates familiarity with the unique variables that often frame the backdrop and context in which a Jewish client emerges in treatment (Schnall 2006).

Progress in this area is especially warranted given research which has been documented that rates of mental health issues are at least comparable to the general population, and may even be prone to higher levels of depression (Levav et al. 1997) and anxiety (McGowan 2012) than individuals of other religions. Though Jews represent less than 2 percent of the global population, there are nevertheless 14 million Jews worldwide, existing in virtually every country around the world (Pew Research Center 2013). Cultivating awareness of the unique features of the Jewish faith is therefore warranted from a public health standpoint and thought to be necessary not only for establishing an effective therapeutic alliance (Schlosser 2006), but also for becoming familiar with the Jewish practices and norms which may be directly relevant during the course of treatment (e.g., Ribner 2004).

It is important to note that Jewish religiosity spans a wide spectrum of degrees of observance from

> the Orthodox whose entire way of life is governed by Jewish law and their meticulous adherence to its tenets, to the other extreme where there are those Jews who are entirely secular, observing none of the practices so rigorously, [and] in between are all the shades of religious practice and observance.
>
> *(Spitzer 2003: 19)*

Given the clinical focus of this book and the current chapter, we will focus on traditional Jewish beliefs, practices, and culture since Orthodox Jewish individuals tend to have more specific cultural-religious needs in the context of clinical care, relative to their non-Orthodox counterparts.

Jewish attitudes to mental health and treatment

In order to understand relationships between Judaism and mental health, it is important to first explore the attitudinal backdrop and broader interactions between these two domains.

Traditional Judaic approaches to healing

Throughout time, medicine and health have played a predominant role in the Judaic worldview (Bleich 2000; Rosner 2013). For example, rabbinic sages have interpreted the biblical verse "Be exceedingly heedful of yourselves" (Deuteronomy 4:15) to refer to the imperative to preserve one's health (see Flancbaum 2001 for a review). Similarly, the verse "you shall not stand idly by the blood of your neighbor" (Leviticus 19:16) has led Jewish sages to conclude that saving a life is paramount and takes precedence over any other religious law (see Levin 2013). To this end, Jewish Oral Law (*Talmud*) itself contains medical prescriptions (see Spitzer 2002).

Along these lines, the role of the physician from a traditional Jewish worldview has been one of considerable discussion in rabbinic literature. For example, the Talmud (Bava Kama 46B) asserts "whoever is in pain, let that person go to a physician" (cited in Flancbaum 2001).

Nonetheless, in traditional Judaic doctrine the physician's role is framed as a religious consideration in which the physician has obtained *permission* to heal, based upon from rabbinic interpretations of biblical verses such as "you shall love your neighbor as yourself" (Leviticus 19:18, see Spitzer 2003). Along similar lines, the Code of Jewish Law documented that the physician is "acting as God's agent" (cited in Spitzer 2003: 63). The very notion that a physician has been given a "license to heal" by rabbinic leaders based on biblical sources, reflects that healing is framed as a religious consideration within the traditional Judaic worldview. It is in this light that Jewish approaches to mental health treatment must be considered.

Traditional Judaic approaches to mental health

Judaism has long recognized the significance of mental health (see Flancbaum 2001) and classic Judaic sources have documented observations of symptoms of mental illness. For example, the Bible itself describes King Saul as experiencing what seems to be depression, and notes that he sought out a harp player to bring emotional solace (1 Samuel 16:23). The Talmud (Pesachim 119a) also illuminated that King David's psalms were often a means by which he attempted to express feelings of sadness and emotional pain. References to mental health are also abound throughout the Talmud, including one description that the "Godly presence does not rest in a spirit of melancholy" (Shabbat 30b). The Judaic liturgy, too, contains a daily prayer for *Refuat Hanefesh*, or healing the spirit (emotions), in addition to physical health. To this end, it has been argued that "psychiatric illnesses are accorded the same standing in [Jewish law] as physiological illnesses, and are classified in the same manner with regard to violation of Sabbath and other prohibitions in matters requiring [life saving]" (Flancbaum 2001: 150).

Several attempts to identify specific references to psychotherapeutic processes have pointed to rabbinic interpretations on the verse in Proverbs (12:25) "anxiety in the heart of a person causes dejection, but a good word will turn it into joy." Some have understood this verse to suggest that there is a benefit in the "talking cure" of psychotherapy, by relating one's worry to others (Talmud, Sanhedrin 100b) in order to seek counsel (Rashi 12:25). Another classic Jewish text espouses that a "person needs a wise physician to endeavor on his behalf. If he can prescribe a remedy for the body, good, if not, he should provide a remedy for his soul" (*Zohar* Deuteronomy 299a). Another depiction of psychotherapeutic approaches to addressing symptoms of emotional distress appears in the 11th century classic devotional text *Duties of the Heart* which elucidates Jewish philosophical principles regarding human thought and emotion (Ibn Pekuda, trans. 1970; Rosmarin, Pargament and Mahoney 2009). In this work, Ibn Pekuda (1970) points to a spiritually-based approach of enhancing trust in God as a therapeutic strategy for reducing anxiety and depression and increasing emotional well-being. Recently, empirical research that has examined methods for increasing trust in God as well as their clinical benefits, and cognitive mechanisms by which these beliefs are functionally tied to mental health (discussed later in this chapter).

Contemporary Jewish attitudes to mental health

In the mid-20th century, several theorists discussed relationships between psychology and Judaism. The bulk of this literature documented fundamental clashes between psychology and Jewish religious thought, most notably classic psychoanalytic theory and traditional Judaic axioms (see Spero 2000). In particular, many have pointed to Freud's characterization of religion as linked to neurosis, and other fundamental psychodynamic concepts such as determinism as playing a "significant role in causing Orthodox Judaism to distance itself from psychiatry and psychology which were perceived as another threat to their belief system" and in turn, has significantly reduced the Jewish community's "use of mental health services in contrast to their use of general medical services" (Feinberg and Feinberg 1986: 82). When trying to ascertain Judaism's broader attitude toward mental health treatment, it is therefore essential to consider the particular theoretical orientation being employed, as each represent the underlying approach to psychopathology that will be informed by a Judaic worldview in varied ways (see Spero 2000).

Despite these inherent tensions between modern psychology and Judaism, recent efforts to integrate and understand Jewish faith with psychological science have been fruitful. For example, several successful efforts have integrated Jewish practices, idioms, and beliefs into cognitive behavioral theory and intervention (Krumrei, Pirutinsky, and Rosmarin 2013). The cognitive behavioral approach in particular has been found to be a synergistic framework for integrating the religious and spiritual beliefs of Jewish clients into the course of clinical work (see Rosmarin et al. 2011 for a review). More broadly, these advancements have demonstrated the importance of incorporating elements of Jewish religion and culture into clinical practice, and have identified the ways in which Jewish religiosity has the potential to play a direct role in mediating cognitive processes associated with mental health functioning in this community.

Jewish religiosity and mental health

It is critical for the provision of culturally sensitive clinical work that mental health practitioners be aware of various features of traditional Jewish life that may be relevant to clinical targets of counselling. Thus, in this section, we survey some of this literature and surmise the most relevant features of Jewish culture, Jewish practice, and Jewish beliefs in relation to mental health.

Jewish sociocultural identity and mental health

While degrees of observance, beliefs, and customs may vary considerably among Jews, individuals across the spectrum of affiliation are thought to share a common history, sociocultural/ ethnic identity, and basic customs (see Schnall 2006). For example, regardless of degrees of practice, according to the US National Survey in 2013, all Orthodox Jews and most non-Orthodox Jews (73%) reported a strong sense of belonging to the Jewish people, and both Orthodox (98%) and non-Orthodox Jews (94%) report they are "proud to be Jewish." Eighty percent of Jews across the full spectrum of affiliation report that being Jewish is somewhat to very "important to them" (where nine in ten Orthodox Jews report it is very important to them).

Several basic features of Jewish sociocultural identity have been found to associate with emotional well-being. For example, the Judaic focus on interpersonal connection and involvement that often permeates Jewish communal life is thought to foster an enhanced sense of belonging and social support- a key component of broader mental health functioning (Pirutinsky and Mancuso 2011). The central ethical teaching "Love your neighbor as yourself" (Leviticus 19:18) and the precept "all members of the Jewish religion share communal responsibility for each other's welfare" (Babylonian Talmud, Tractate *Shavuoth* 39A) tend to underscore the norms practiced in Jewish communities. For example, members tend to engage in communal good deeds, and establish numerous charitable and support institutions (e.g., to provide meals for the sick, assist families in need of financial or emotional support (Loewenthal and Rogers 2004). Notably, one study among members of an ultra-Orthodox community in the United Kingdom uncovered that more than half of its members consistently volunteer for at least one support community – an amount seven times greater than participation of London's broader population (Holman and Holman 2002). Similarly, members of the Jewish community share in each other's celebrations and tragedies (Greenberg and Witzum, 2013). For example, when an individual loses a family member, there is a "built in" support system (*shiva* home). Judaism espouses many interpersonal laws and emphasizes *Chesed* (acts of lovingkindness) and *Tzedakah* (charity). Visiting the sick, helping someone in need, comforting mourners, bringing happiness to brides and grooms on their wedding day are not just viewed as interpersonal niceties, but are concrete commandments.

Another aspect of Jewish identity relates to community. The life cycle of birth, *brith* (circumcision), *bar/bat mitzvah*, and marriage are central times of celebration in Jewish life and fellow community members typically join together to support each other during these events (see Greenberg and Witzum 2013 for a review). More regularly, coming together for Sabbath and holiday meals and synagogue worship is also commonplace within these tight-knit communities (see Holliman and Wagner 2015). Along these lines, Orthodox Jewish communities, in particular, are often tight-knit and geographically close in proximity to a synagogue (Huppert et al., 2007; Pirutinsky, Schechter, Kor and Rosmarin 2015). Many Jewish communities across the spectrum of denomination throughout the world are also connected through families and broader networks of acquaintances (see Loewenthal and Rogers 2004). This extended network is particularly meaningful in light of findings that strengthened interpersonal connections utilized by religious individuals in times of distress has been found to be beneficial to psychological functioning (see Rosmarin, Pargament, Krumrei, and Flannely 2009). A study by Dubow, Pargament, Boxer, and Tarakeshwar (2000) found that Jewish ethnic identity often serves as a resource for coping with life stressors, and similarly religious beliefs and spiritual support (forms of positive religious coping) were found to relate to positive affect among Jews who recently experienced a major life stressor (Loewenthal, MacLeod, Goldblatt, Lubitsh, and Valentine 2000). One finding in particular points to the deeply embedded role of culture on mental health functioning: A study by Pirutinsky, Schechter, Kor, and Rosmarin (2015) identified that among Jews who maintain positive cultural and religious values surrounding family life, large family size was *not* tied to anxiety/depression, stress, family satisfaction or communication when compared to the broader population.

However, several aspects of Jewish culture and practice have also been implicated in increased emotional distress among this population. For example, Jewish religious life is uniquely characterized by its emphasis on traditional marriage and family building (see Fox, Schnall, and Pelcovitz 2013). Especially among the Orthodox communities, raising children is characterized as a fulfillment of the commandment "Be fruitful and multiply" (Genesis 1:28) and Orthodox Jews on average have double the amount of children as compared to the general population (Loewenthal and Rogers 2004), especially due to religious prescriptions around the use of birth control and family planning (see Holliman and Wagner 2015). This emphasis placed on family life can pose a significant challenge to the emotional functioning of those who lack family (see Greenberg and Witzum, 2013). For example, experiencing infertility has been found to have a distinct negative impact on emotional health among Jewish individuals given religious norms and values surrounding conceiving children and raising families (see Pirutinsky et al. 2015).

Relatedly, financial pressures associated with Jewish religious life have also been found to be significantly higher than implicated as psychological stressors as well (Pirutinsky et al. 2015). For example, the cost of tuition for private religious education has been found to range from $7,000 to over $20,000 per Jewish child per year in the United States, and the aggregate cost of raising a Jewish child from 0–18 years of age has been estimated at $781,500 (approximately three times the cost of raising a child in the broader population in the United States; see Pirutinsky et al. 2015). One study documented both financial difficulties as well as disagreements over education of children to be psychosocial stressors among families in Orthodox families in the United States (Schnall, Pelcovitz, and Fox 2013).

Jewish religious practices/beliefs and mental health

A growing body of research has consistently linked traditional Jewish religious practices and beliefs with psychological functioning, across a broad spectrum of observance (e.g., Rosmarin, Pargament, and Mahoney 2009). Contrary to theories posited by several early psychological leaders (Freud, 1907/1943), the majority of the extant literature has indicated that Jewish religious practices and beliefs are tied to enhanced psychological functioning including lower levels of worry and anxiety (Rosmarin et al. 2011) and depressive symptoms (Pirutinsky and Rosmarin, 2018). Researchers have identified variables that directly associate with mechanisms involved in psychological functioning, most notably among them Jewish religious coping (Rosmarin, Pirutinsky, Pargament, and Krumrei 2009) and trust/mistrust in God (Rosmarin, Pargament, and Mahoney 2009). These findings have pointed to what is arguably among the most theoretically and clinically rich relationship between Jewish religiosity and mental health functioning- namely, that Jewish practices, worldviews, and perspectives play a key role in mediating the causal pathways themselves of emotional reactions to life stressors (e.g., Krumrei, Pirutsinsky, and Pargament 2012; Rosmarin et al. 2011). Below we summarize several specific Jewish religious variables that have been studied.

Jewish religious coping

It has been well established in the broader population that religious coping - the process of drawing upon religious practices and beliefs during times of distress or perceived threat – is positively tied to emotional well-being (Pargament 1997). Religious coping has been found to involve both positive and negative strategies. Positive religious coping involves benevolent religious appraisals (e.g., perceiving daily events as part of God's plan), seeking spiritual support, and spiritual connection (e.g., trying to build a stronger spiritual connection with God or others). Conversely, negative religious coping strategies involve reappraisals of God's powers (e.g., concluding that some things are beyond God's control), passive religious deferral (e.g., not doing anything and expecting God to solve all of one's problems), and interpersonal religious discontent (e.g., arguments with members of one's religious community; Pargament, Smith Koenig, and Perez 1998).

Drawing upon this body of work, Rosmarin and colleagues (2009b) developed the 16–item Jewish Religious Coping Scale (JCOPE) which assessed for basic aspects of Jewish practice and belief. A series of studies consistently uncovered associations between positive, or adaptive forms of Jewish religious coping (e.g. I talk to my rabbi, I look for a stronger connection with God, I try to see how God may be trying to teach me something,) and lower levels of anxiety, worry, and depression. Conversely, they discovered that negative, or maladaptive Jewish religious coping (e.g., questioning God's power) – also known as "spiritual struggles" – is tied to higher degrees of emotional distress (Rosmarin, Pargament, Krumrei, and Flannely 2009). Along similar lines, Pirutinsky and colleagues (2011) established that engaging in negative religious coping strategies (e.g., "I got mad at God," "I questioned whether God could really do anything") is a reliable predictor of future depressive symptoms.

One finding in particular helps point to the theoretical underpinnings of these relationships. Rosmarin, Pargament, and Flannelly (2009) discovered that while negative religious coping tends to associate with poorer mental (as well as physical) health among many, it was found that experiencing high levels of spiritual struggles was tied to *enhanced* mental health for Orthodox Jews. Though this finding has not been replicated to date, researchers suggested that Orthodox Jews have distinct culture-specific worldviews, such as perceiving spiritual struggle as an opportunity for post-traumatic spiritual growth, which may mediate processes that are tied to mental health functioning. Along similar lines, Pirutinsky and Rosmarin (2018) found that Jewish religious practice was associated with lower degrees of depression specifically for those individuals who also reported high degrees of *intrinsic religiosity*- or religious engagement that is rooted in internal motivations, beliefs, and values (Allport and Ross 1967). This finding similarly provides insight into the pathway by which Jewish religious practice buffers against psychopathology- namely that religious practices confer emotional benefits for those who possess deeply embedded religious values and values, rather than those who are motivated by external factors (e.g., social pressures).

Many of the relationships between Jewish religiosity and mental health have been found to bear relevance across the spectrum of affiliation. For example, Rosmarin, and associates (2017) discovered that positive religious coping predicted higher subjective well-being and negative religious coping predicted lower subjective well-being, greater depression, and elevated anxiety among a large sample of Jews. Researchers found that the specific way in which religiosity was measured did *not* moderate relationships between religious coping and mental health, suggesting that religious coping associates with mental health across the entire spectrum of religious involvement for Jews (Rosmarin, Carp, Pirutinsky, and Kor 2017).

Taken together, it is now recognized that drawing upon Jewish religious belief and behavior can confer both solace and support to Jewish individuals, especially during times of worry and distress. Specifically, engaging in spiritual actions such observance of the Sabbath and performing good deeds is thought to cultivate one's sense of spiritual purpose in life and put daily struggles in the context of higher purpose. Along similar lines, efforts to strengthen one's personal connection with God through practices such as prayer may foster positive emotions such as hope and gratitude and in turn mitigate distress.

Trust in God

Another body of research has established links between Jewish religious beliefs about God and emotional well-being. Rosmarin and colleagues (2009) hypothesized that one fundamental tenet of Jewish faith known as trust in God – a cognitive state involving core beliefs in God's benevolence, love, and omniscience – would be especially salient to the mental health of Jewish individuals. In a series of studies by Rosmarin et al. (2009), a measure of trust in God was designed and administered alongside measures of anxiety, depression, and happiness. The broader findings reflected that trust in God is linked with lower levels of anxiety and depression. Researchers also discovered that *mistrust* in God – or negative beliefs that God is weak, cruel, and either unable or unwilling to assist in times of crisis – is correlated with increased anxiety and depression and to lower levels of overall happiness (Rosmarin, Pargament, Krumrei, and Flanelly 2009). Along similar lines, both constructs of trust in God and religious coping were found to work where trust in God *triggered* positive religious coping strategies and were associated with lower levels of depressive symptoms, whereas mistrust in God incurred the opposite effect (Krumrei, Pirutinsky, and Rosmarin 2013).

Following up on the above studies, Rosmarin and colleagues (2011) explored potential explanatory mechanisms by which trust in God associates with reduced emotional distress. Researchers placed the variable trust in God within the context of cognitive theory, and suggested that during stressful situations or perceived threats, embedded beliefs about God are triggered that either mitigate or promote context-specific cognitions that lead to distress (Rosmarin et al. 2011). Specifically, they discovered that cognitions about God mediates a known variable in anxiety – "intolerance of uncertainty" – or the inability to deal with the unknown- which in turn makes a person more likely to feel anxious when confronted by a perceived threat. Specifically, positive core beliefs about God, such as the belief that He is directly involved in daily affairs, fosters more optimistic appraisals and, increases one's cognitive capacity to tolerate uncertainty, thereby reducing emotional distress. Conversely, mistrust in God is thought to serve as a cognitive filter which highlights negative events and in turn triggers anxiety and distress during times of uncertainty and stress (Rosmarin et al. 2011). While it has often been perceived that Jewish religious activity refers to behavioral actions and practices (e.g., prayer), this research on trust in God has highlighted the unique impact of *internal* spiritual processes in Jewish mental health functioning and indicates that that internal religious states and beliefs play an active role in mediating distress for Jewish individuals. More specifically, positive beliefs regarding God's power and benevolence as well as the belief that there is a purpose behind life's ward against maladaptive cognitions (see Pirutinsky and Rosmarin, 2018).

Clinical practice with Jewish individuals

Barriers to mental health treatment

Despite the prevalence of mental health concerns among Jewish individuals (Bilu and Witzum 1997), Jews, especially Orthodox, have historically been hesitant to pursue mental health treatment and are more prone to denying symptoms of psychological distress (Spitzer 2003). For example, one study found that over 82 percent of Jewish mental health clinicians thought that the psychological needs of Jewish people in their communities were not being properly addressed, despite the fact that there was a high need for these services (Feinberg and Feinberg 1985). As reviewed above, the belief that treatment may be misaligned with religious beliefs may be a significant barrier toward pursuing treatment among Orthodox Jews (Schnall 2006). Perhaps for these reasons, religious Jews are more likely to consult a rabbi or religious figure on matters of mental health (Huppert et al. 2007), or a therapist who would be attuned to their religious needs and beliefs (Greenberg and Witzum 2013).

Research has implicated several culture-specific barriers among Jews in regards to treatment seeking, most notably family-centric stigma toward mental health treatment (Pirutinsky et al. 2010). That is, the traditional Jewish community's focus on family building, which is a profound concern for this population (Loewenthal and Rogers 2004), can serve as a barrier to entering treatment. One study in particular highlights the distinct cultural considerations characterizing attitudes toward mental health among members of this community, Pirutinsky and colleagues (2010) uncovered that while attribution to biological roots of mental illness has tended to reduce stigma among the general population, attributing mental health symptoms to biological causes *exacerbates* stigmatization among Orthodox Jews.

Despite this ambivalence, Jewish individuals and leaders have become increasingly more open to treatment in recent years. A 25-year follow-up study uncovered a *decrease* in general social mistrust of the mental health field and decreased belief that Judaism and psychology are in conflict, as compared to findings from the 1985 needs assessment of barriers to utilizing clinical services in the Orthodox community (Schnall et al. 2014). Recent studies have documented that rabbis are becoming increasingly more encouraging of seeking mental health treatment, even among communities where this was previously not the case (Greenberg and Shefler 2008). However, Orthodox Jews in particular continue to prefer clinicians who are sensitive to

Judaism and Mental Health

traditional Jewish ideology and practice (see Holliman and Wagner 2015). Awareness of basic Jewish religious practice and law is therefore thought to be necessary for ensuring clinically sensitive work with Jewish individuals (Haimov-Kochman, Rosenak, Orvieto, and Hurwitz 2010).

Attending to Jewish religious precepts in clinical practice

Traditional Judaism espouses both ideological beliefs that are meant to guide and inform one's worldview as well as delineates specific ways in which a person is to conduct virtually every aspect of life (Huppert, Siev, and Kushner, 2007). These *Mitzvoth* and *Halakhot* (precepts) are delineated in the *Torah* (Old Testament) and commonly referred to as biblical or written law, and have been interpreted by Jewish leaders, referred to as the oral law, and further organized in Jewish legal works collectively referred to as rabbinic law (see Spitzer 2003 for a review). To this end, traditional or Orthodox Jewish affiliation is characterized by strict adherence to the full corpus of biblical and rabbinic mandates including laws of the Sabbath, *Kashruth* (Jewish dietary laws), and *Taharath Ha'Mishpakha* (laws of family purity) which govern sexuality and inter-gender relationships.

Given the complexity and detailed scope of traditional Jewish laws, those unfamiliar with the relevance of these laws across many arenas of daily life may find it difficult to properly conceptualize the culture-specific framework in which symptoms may occur in, distinguish normative religious practices from pathology, and understand the potential mandates and prohibitions that might clash with traditional interventions. As Jewish psychiatrist and theorist Spero (2000: 152–153) noted:

> The fate of religious ritual, mannerism, and belief under the lens of the psychological or psychiatric diagnostician is one of the perennial issues in the psychology and religion literature. The notion that a rogue or even well intentioned diagnostician might conceivably evaluate religious behavior or thought as irrational, abnormal, or perverse on the grounds of categorical appraisal by contemporary diagnostic criteria continued to generation a good deal of anxiety among both the professional as well as religious [Jewish] population.

A prime example of this is seen in the work of Huppert and colleagues (2007) who identified that obtaining familiarity with Jewish norms are necessary in effectively work with religious Jewish clients with Obsessive Compulsive Disorder. Researchers explained that as adherence to normative traditional Jewish law requires meticulousness and attentiveness, those unfamiliar with Orthodox Judaism can misinterpret as scrupulosity (Huppert et al. 2007; Pirutinsky, Rosmarin, and Pargament 2009).

Along similar lines, some degree of familiarity with Jewish religious practices is often necessary for clinical work, since standard interventions for certain symptomologies may inadvertently impinge upon religious mandates. For example, religious prescriptions govern virtually every aspect of the sexual relationship (Pirutinsky et al. 2014), and to this end some secular clinical intervention to target sexual dysfunction are at odds with Jewish religious practice, such as the prohibition against extra-vaginal ejaculation- a common technique to treat premature ejaculation (Ribner 2004). To this end, Ribner (2004) highlighted the importance of consulting with rabbinic figures when treating religious Jewish patients, as well as competence in modifying standard techniques. Along similar lines, it is important for practitioners to consider the degree to which several sensitive issues relevant to mental health such as suicide, abortion, homosexual behavior, as well as other sexual relationships and behaviors intersect with Jewish religious mandates and values (see Flancbaum 2001 for review).

While it is outside the scope of this chapter to delineate each clinically relevant Jewish practice and custom, it is important for practitioners to be at least partially familiar that some Jewish laws may be relevant to various aspects of clinical practice, such as those described above. This awareness is essential for attaining therapeutic progress, both to ensure delivery of culturally appropriate services, and to facilitate case conceptualization and an understanding of presenting concerns as well as their roots.

Future directions

While the degree to which Jewish cultural and/or religious variables intersect with mental health functioning differs for each client across the spectrum of affiliation and intrinsic commitment, maintaining respect for and awareness of the potential relevance of Jewish variables is a crucial component of providing culturally competent treatment to members of this population. To these ends, we provide several suggestions to facilitate culturally sensitive care to members of the broader Jewish community.

Firstly, the above findings highlight the significance of displaying respect for Jewish beliefs, practices, and cultural norms throughout the course of treatment (Rosmarin et al. 2009; Schnall 2006). Similarly, clinicians should reflect upon their own assumptions and embedded biases against Jewish religious faith and practice, especially in light of the tendency for practitioners to confuse religious behavior and commitment with pathology (see Papovsky 2010). Practitioners should maintain awareness that for the Jewish individual (and Orthodox in particular), the gamut of life decisions (e.g., marriage and courtship, education, location, family planning and marital issues) will intersect with Jewish identity and worldview (see Holliman and Wagner 2015; Pirutinsky et al. 2014). This Jewish identity should be considered at every stage of the treatment process, and the client's own value system should be consistently be used as a guide in navigating decisions, as consistent with culturally competent practice (Holliman and Wagner 2015). Along similar lines, given research that adherence to Jewish religious law has, at times, been found to associate with emotional distress, it is important for practitioners to evaluate and address religious conflicts within the course of treatment, as well as to consider the client's own value system broader commitment to religious doctrine when navigating such conflicts rather than utilize one's own value system (Holliman and Wagner 2015). We must underscore the importance practitioners being willing to consult with the client's rabbi, especially in matters where secular psychotherapeutic practice may overtly clash with Jewish law or belief; we further underscore the importance of incorporating rabbinic guidance into the treatment process for those who wish to do so (Huppert et al. 2007). Furthermore, as discussed, Jewish identity as well as Jewish religious practices and beliefs intertwine with virtually every aspect of and daily life for a Jewish individual (especially Orthodox; see Pirutinsky et al. 2014), and in turn it is quite possible that the spectrum of presenting problems will interact with Jewish cultural life or Jewish belief and practice to varying degrees. It is therefore imperative for practitioners working with Jewish individuals to conduct a thorough clinical assessment of religious variables across domains of belief and practice at the onset of treatment, and to explore which Jewish religious laws may be relevant and significant to the individual in relation to both mental health (Rosmarin et al. 2009) and treatment modality (e.g., Ribner 2004).

Second, given the findings above demonstrating Jewish religiosity can have positive as well as negative effects on mental health and functioning for individuals with an embedded Judaic beliefs and worldview (e.g., Rosmarin et al. 2011), practitioners should consider the psychological effects of Jewish beliefs and practices on presenting symptoms. For example, Rosmarin and colleagues (2010) implemented a randomized control study utilizing Jewish variables on a sample of Jewish individuals undergoing symptoms of psychological distress. More specifically, they designed a spiritually-based intervention which incorporates uniquely Jewish material and rituals (e.g., Jewish prayer and Jewish teachings), and found that the spiritually-based intervention conferred significant decreased stress, worry, and depression (Rosmarin, Pargament, Pirutinsky, and Mahoney 2010). This advancement is particularly valuable given findings that many individuals in the broader population have expressed explicit interest in drawing upon and integrating their religious beliefs, culture, idioms, and customs within the course of clinical treatment (Rosmarin, Pargament, and Robb 2010). To these ends, practitioners should be open to harnessing Jewish religious belief and practice as resources in the treatment process. Such an approach is vital to ensure that this population receives proper clinical care (Witzum and Buchbinder 2001).

Conclusion

If progress is to be achieved in bridging these gaps and providing culturally sensitive and competent clinical work, it is necessary that practitioners understand and respect that a traditional Jewish individual often "brings to the therapeutic relationship a unique set of historical and hence, personal experiences, as well as a lifestyle governed by a comprehensive body of distinct guidelines" (Spero 2000: 4). The progressive decrease in social mistrust of the mental health field points to the fact that the time is ripe to continue efforts to build bridges between mental health practitioners, Jewish individual clients, and the Jewish community at large. Research has found that many counsellors and practitioners are not spiritual/religious and therefore desensitized to the spiritual needs and interests of their clients and unaware as to how to incorporate these variables into the treatment process (Rosmarin, Pargament, and Robb 2010). However, it is important to note that the provision of spiritually competent care could be accomplished regardless of the practitioner's personal degree of religious/spiritual involvement (Rosmarin, Green, Pirutinsky, and McKay 2013).

The scientific advancements in Judaism and mental health that we have reviewed above are promising, but there is still much progress to be made. There are many unanswered questions regarding how Jewish culture and practice are functionally tied to mental health, which areas of culture are salient across Jewish subgroups, and how Jewish beliefs and practices can be integrated into clinical interventions for various clinical targets. We hope that the coming years will see further advancements in these important arenas.

References

Bilu, Y. and Witztum, E. (1993) 'Working with Jewish Ultra-Orthodox Patients: Guidelines for a Culturally Sensitive Therapy', *Culture, Medicine and Psychiatry*, 17(2): 197–233.

Cohen, A.B. and Rozin, P. (2001) 'Religion and the Morality of Mentality', *Journal of Personality and Social Psychology*, 81(4): 697–710.

Cornish, M. A., Wade, N. G., Tucker, J. R. and Post, B. C. (2014) 'When Religion Enters the Counseling Group: Multiculturalism, Group Processes, and Social Justice', *Counseling Psychologist*, 42(5): 578.

Dubow, E. F., Pargament, K. I., Boxer, P. and Tarakeshwar, N. (2000) 'Initial Investigation of Jewish Early Adolescents' Ethnic Identity, Stress and Coping', *Journal of Early Adolescence*, 20(4): 418–441.

Feinberg, S. S. and Feinberg, K. G. (1986) 'The Rabbis View: The State of Mental Health Needs in the Jewish Community,' *Tradition: A Journal of Orthodox Jewish Thought*, 22(1): 82–94.

Feinberg, S. S. and Feinberg, K. G. (1985) 'An Assessment of the Mental Health Needs of the Orthodox Jewish Population of Metropolitan New York', *Journal of Jewish Communal Service*, 62: 29–39.

Flancbaum, L (2001) *"And You Shall Live by Them"*: *Contemporary Jewish Approaches to Medical Ethics.* Pennsylvania: Mirkov Publications.

Freud, S. (1943) *A General Introduction to Psychoanalysis.* New York: Garden City Publishing.

Greenberg, D. and Witztum, E. (2013) 'Challenges and Conflicts in the Delivery of Mental Health Services to Ultra-Orthodox Jews', *Asian Journal of Psychiatry*, 6: 71–73.

Haimov-Kochman, R., Rosenak, D., Orvieto, R. and Hurwitz, A. (2010) 'Infertility Counseling for Orthodox Jewish Couples', *Fertility and Sterility*, 93:1816–1819.

Holliman, R. P. and Wagner, A. A. (2015) 'Responsive Counseling in Jewish Orthodox Communities', *Journal of Counselor Practice*, 6(2): 56.

Holman, C. and Holman, N. (2002) *Torah, Worship and Acts of Loving-kindness: Baseline Indicators for the Charedi Community in Stamford Hill.* Leicester: De Montfort University.

Huppert, J. D., Siev, J. and Kushner, E. S. (2007) 'When Religion and Obsessive–Compulsive Disorder Collide: Treating Scrupulosity in Ultra-Orthodox Jews', *Journal of Clinical Psychology*, 63: 925–941.

Ibn Pekuda, B. (1970) *Duties of the Heart* (M. Hymanson, Trans.), Jerusalem: Feldheim. (Original work published circa 1080).

Krumrei, E. J., Pirutinsky, S. and Rosmarin, D. H. (2013) 'Jewish Spirituality, Depression, and Health: An Empirical Test of a Conceptual Framework', *International Journal of Behavioral Medicine*, (3): 327.

Levav, I., Kohn, R., Golding, J. M. and Weissman, M. M. (1997) 'Vulnerability of Jews to Affective Disorders', *American Journal of Psychiatry,* 154(7): 941–947.

Loewenthal, K. M. and Rogers, M. B. (2004) 'Culture-Sensitive Counselling, Psychotherapy and Support Groups in the Orthodox-Jewish Community: How They Work and How They Are Experienced', *International Journal of Social Psychiatry,* 50(3): 227–240.

Loewenthal, K. M., MacLeod, A. K., Goldblatt, V., Lubitsh, G., and Valentine, J. D. (2000) 'Comfort and Joy? Religion, Cognition, and Mood in Protestants and Jews Under Stress', *Cognition and Emotion,* 14: 355–374.

Margolese, H. C. (1998) 'Engaging in Psychotherapy with the Orthodox American Jew', *Journal of Psychotherapy*, 52: 37–53.

Pargament, K. I. (1997) *The Psychology of Religion and Coping: Theory, Research, Practice.* New York: The Guilford Press.

Pargament K. I., Smith B. W., Koenig H. G. and Perez L. (1998) 'Patterns of Positive and Negative Religious Coping with Major Life Stressors', *Journal for the Scientific Study of Religion*, 374: 710–724.

Pew Research Center (2013) *A Portrait of Jewish Americans.* Washington, DC: Pew Research Center.

Pirutinsky, S. (2009) 'Conversion and Attachment Insecurity Among Orthodox Jews', *International Journal for the Psychology of Religion*, 19(3): 200–206.

Pirutinsky, S. and Mancuso, A. F. (2011) 'Social Identity, Satisfaction with Life, and Self-Esteem', *Graduate Student Journal of Psychology*, 13: 39–44.

Pirutinsky, S. and Rosmarin, D. H. (2018) 'Protective and Harmful Effects of Religious Practice on Depression Among Jewish Individuals with Mood Disorders', *Clinical Psychological Science*, 6(4): 601.

Pirutinsky, S., Rosen, D. D., Shapiro Safran, R. and Rosmarin, D. H. (2010) 'Do Medical Models of Mental Illness Relate to Increased or Decreased Stigmatization of Mental Illness Among Orthodox Jews?' *Journal of Nervous and Mental Disorders*, 198: 508–512.

Pirutinsky, S., Rosmarin, D. H., Pargament, K. I. and Midlarsky, E. (2011) 'Does Negative Religious Coping Accompany, Precede, or Follow Depression Among Orthodox Jews?' *Journal of Affective Disorders*, 132(3): 401–405.

Pirutinsky, S., Schechter, I., Kor, A. and Rosmarin, D. H. (2015) 'Family size and Psychological Functioning in the Orthodox Jewish Community', *Mental Health, Religion and Culture*, 18(3): 218–230.

Popovsky, R. M. A. (2010) 'Special Issues in the Care of Ultra-Orthodox Jewish Psychiatric Inpatients', *Transcultural Psychiatry*, 47(4): 647–672.

Ribner, D. S. (2004) 'Ejaculatory Restrictions as a Factor in the Treatment of Haredi (Ultraorthodox) Jewish Couples', *Archives of Sexual Behavior*, 33(3):303–308.

Ribner, D. S. and Kleinplatz, P. J. (2007) 'The Hole in the Sheet and Other Myths about Sexuality and Judaism', *Sexual and Relationship Therapy*, 22(4): 445.

Rosmarin, D. H., Forester, B. P., Shassian, D. M., Webb, C. A. and Bjorgvinsson, T. (2015) 'Interest in Spiritually Integrated Psychotherapy Among Acute Psychiatric Patients', *Journal of Consulting and Clinical Psychology*, (6): 1149.

Rosmarin, D. H., Forester, B. P., Shassian, D. M., Webb, C. A. and Björgvinsson. T. (2015) 'Interest in Spiritually Integrated Psychotherapy Among Acute Psychiatric Patients', *Journal of Consulting and Clinical Psychology*, 83(6): 1149–1153.

Rosmarin, D. H., Green, D., Pirutinsky, S. and McKay, D. (2013) 'Attitudes Toward Spirituality/ Religion Among Members of the Association for Behavioral and Cognitive Therapies', *Professional Psychology: Research and Practice*, 44(6): 424–433.

Rosmarin, D. H., Krumrei, E. J. and Andersson, G. (2009) 'Religion as a Predictor of Psychological Distress in Two Religious Communities', *Cognitive Behaviour Therapy*, 38: 54–64.

Rosmarin, D. H., Pargament, K. I, Krumrei, E. J. and Flannelly, K. J. (2009) 'Religious coping Among Jews: Development and Initial Validation of the JCOPE', *Journal of Clinical Psychology*, 65: 1–14.

Rosmarin, D. H., Pargament, K. I. and Mahoney, A. (2009) 'The Role of Religiousness in Anxiety, Depression and Happiness in a Jewish Community Sample: A Preliminary Investigation', *Mental Health Religion and Culture*, 12(2): 97–113.

Rosmarin, D. H., Pargament, K. I., Pirutinsky, S. and Mahoney, A. (2010) 'A Randomized Controlled Evaluation of a Spiritually Integrated Treatment for Subclinical Anxiety in the Jewish Community, Delivered via the Internet, *Journal of Anxiety Disorders*, 24(7): 799–808.

Rosmarin, D. H., Pargament, K. I., and Robb, H. 2010) 'Introduction to Special Series: Spiritual and Religious Issues in Behavior Change', *Cognitive and Behavioral Practice*, 17 (pagination unspecified).

Rosmarin, D. H., Pirutinsky, S., Carp, S., Appel, M. and Kor, A. (2017) 'Religious Coping across a Spectrum of Religious Involvement among Jews', *Psychology of Religion and Spirituality*, 9(1): S96–S104.

Rosmarin, D. H., Pirutinsky, S., Pargament, K. I. and Krumrei, E. J. (2009) 'Are Religious Beliefs Relevant to Mental Health among Jews?, *Psychology of Religion and Spirituality*, 1: 180–190.

Rosner, F. (2013) 'History of Jews in Medicine and Healthcare, in Judaism and Health'. In J. Levin and M. F. Prince (Eds.), *A Handbook of Practical, Professional, and Scholarly Resources* (pp. 1–7). Woodstock, VT: Jewish Lights. Publishing.

Schlosser, L. Z. (2006) 'Affirmative Psychotherapy for American Jews', *Psychotherapy: Theory, Research, Practice, Training*, 43: 424–435.

Schnall, E. (2006) 'Multicultural Counseling and the Orthodox Jew', *Journal of Counseling and Development*, 84(3): 276–282.

Schnall, E., Kalkstein, S., Gottesman, A., Feinberg, K., Schaeffer, C. B. and Feinberg, S. S. (2014) 'Barriers to Mental Health Care: A 25-Year Follow- Up Study of the Orthodox Jewish Community', *Journal of Multicultural Counseling and Development*, 42(3): 161–173.

Schnall, E., Pelcovitz, D. and Fox, D. (2013) 'Satisfaction and Stressors in a Religious Minority: A National Study of Orthodox Jewish Marriage', *Journal of Multicultural Counseling* and Development, 41(1): 4–20.

Smith, T. B., McCullough, M. E. and Poll, J. (2003) 'Religiousness and Depression: Evidence for a Main Effect and the Moderating Influence of Stressful Life Events', *Psychological Bulletin*, 129(4): 614–636.

Spero, M. (2000) 'Psychiatry, Psychotherapy, and Halacha: A Torah Perspective on the Philosophy of Behavior Change'. In F. Rosner and J. D. Bleich (Eds.), *Jewish Bioethics* (pp. 239–258). Hoboken, NJ: Ktav Publishing House.

Spitzer, J. (2003) *Caring for Jewish Patients.* Oxford: Radcliffe Medical Press.

Sue, D. W. and Sue, D. (2013) *Counseling the Culturally Diverse: Theory and Practice (6th ed.).* New York: John Wiley.

Witzum, E. and Buchbinder, J. T. (2001) 'Strategic Culture Sensitive Therapy with Religious Jews', *International Review of Psychiatry*, 13(2): 117–124.

PART E

Special populations and culture in mental health

24

CULTURE, MENTAL HEALTH, AND CHILDREN AND ADOLESCENTS

Dominika A. Winiarski, Nisha Dogra, and Niranjan Karnik

This chapter tries to understand children and their mental health within cultural contexts. We thus begin with the construct of culture. The definition of culture by *the Association of American Medical Colleges* emphasizes patient-centeredness and applicability to clinical situations.

> *Culture is defined by each person in relationship to the group or groups with whom he or she identifies. An individual's cultural identity may be based on heritage as well as individual circumstances and personal choice. Cultural identity may be affected by such factors as race, ethnicity, age, language, country of origin, acculturation, sexual orientation, gender, socioeconomic status, religious/spiritual beliefs, physical abilities and occupation, among others.*
>
> *These factors may affect behaviours such as communication styles, diet preferences, health beliefs, family roles, lifestyle, rituals and decision-making processes. All of these beliefs and practices, in turn, can influence how patients and health care professionals perceive health and illness, and how they interact with one another.*
>
> *(the Association of American Medical Colleges 1999: 25)*

It suggests that individuals draw upon a range of resources and that, through the interplay of external and internal meanings, they themselves construct a sense of identity and unique culture. It particularly recognises that both patients and professionals bring a complex individual self to the consultation. In cases where children are the patients, this definition is helpful to providers as it also allows for children and their parents to understand the origins of their culture independently. Although children and their parents must be viewed as interacting parts of the family system, each part (i.e., each parent, each child) has his or her own diverse experiences and is shaped uniquely by the external environment. Thus, if parents, children, and in some cases the provider, are not on the same page when identifying treatment goals or the source of the familial discord, it is imperative to take a step back and evaluate each person's cultural perspective.

This chapter begins by considering how children are viewed across different cultures. We then consider how various factors related to culture influence child mental health, and the relevance of the family in the child mental health field. We briefly review the taxonomy of child mental health problems and how these are manifested within the different systems in which a child functions (e.g., family, school, cultural environment, etc.). We then suggest how to conduct culturally appropriate assessment and make management and treatment plans before concluding the possible direction of future work.

Constructing children across cultures

How does culture shape the views on childhood and roles of children, and are these views static or temporal? In fact, the term childhood is non-specific and relates to a varying range of years in human development in different contexts. Developmentally, it refers to the period between infancy and adulthood. However, it is arguable that it is a sociological concept rather than a biological phenomenon, and thus accordingly has changed over time as the views of children have changed. As our understanding of children and childhood is historically, culturally and politically influenced, it is useful to consider the concept of childhood as a dynamic process. The concept of childhood changes in response to ongoing dynamic societal changes. The perspectives and views of children held within any given culture are important, as they influence whether and how children are understood and prioritized by politicians, health providers, lawyers, social workers, educationalists, families and others.

Understanding the period of childhood defined by developmental age as opposed to chronological age and the meanings given to these age-related groupings are neither fixed nor universal. Childhood as a definition and its components are subject to the changing values, definitions and expectations within society. The historian Philippe Ariès (1962) argued that in early modern Europe, the concept of childhood did not functionally exist and that children were merely small adults. This view has been challenged over time. For example, in the 19th century in the United Kingdom, a movement began to challenge the idea that children should work. In parallel, the United States developed its first set of child labour laws with the passage of the New York State Child Labour Law of 1886. Just two years later, the American Medical Association developed a paediatric subsection, which was eventually developed into the American Paediatric Society (Perera 2014). Similarly, Chicago established the first juvenile court in 1899. This court was charged with examining legal cases, while keeping in mind the importance of considering the unique needs of children and their relative immature developmental state. It is perhaps no coincidence that as social reformers succeeded in bringing to light the treatment of children and the importance of viewing childhood as a vulnerable and critical developmental period, the scientific discipline of child development rapidly expanded through the work of individuals like G. Stanley Hall, Lev Vygotsky, Jean Piaget, John Bowlby, and Urie Bronfenbrenner. Despite this social reformation and academic paradigm shift, in many countries, many children today are still in the position where they must work to help support themselves and their families.

Although children's roles in society were slowly changing in individual societies at the turn of the 20th century, the conceptualization of children's rights was first recognised internationally by the Geneva Declaration of the Rights of the Child (1924) when it was adopted by the League of Nations. In 1989, the United Nations Convention on the Rights of the Child (CRC or UNCRC) was adopted and has since been ratified by 195 countries (UN 1989). The Convention has 54 articles that cover all aspects of a child's life and set out the civil, political, economic, social and cultural rights that all children everywhere are entitled to. It also explains how adults and governments must work together to make sure all children can enjoy all their rights. The Convention changed the way children are viewed and treated. Specifically, children are now viewed as human beings with a distinct set of rights instead of as passive objects of care and charity, and children have more of an active role in pursuing these rights. Four of the 54 articles are known as overarching general principles.

- Non-discrimination (Article 2): The Convention applies to all children whatever their ethnicity, gender, religion, language, abilities, whatever they think or say, no matter what type of family they come from, whatever their circumstances.
- Best interest of the child (Article 3): A child's best interests must be a top priority in all decisions and actions that affect children. All adults should do what is best for children and should think about how their decisions will affect children. Determining what is in children's best interests should take into account children's own views and feelings.
- Right to life, survival and development (Article 6): Children have the right to life and governments must do all they can to ensure children survive and develop to their fullest potential. The right to life and survival guarantees the most basic needs such as nutrition, shelter or access to healthcare. Overall development – physical, emotional, educational, social and spiritual – is the goal of many of the rights in the Convention.
- Right to be heard (Article 12): Every child has the right to express their views, feelings and wishes in all matters affecting them, and to have their views considered and taken seriously.

There are also optional protocols, which governments can decide whether or not to ratify: These include the optional protocol on the sale of children, child prostitution and child pornography, the optional protocol on the involvement of children in armed conflict, and the optional protocol on a mechanism for children to file a complaint to the UN when they feel that their rights have been encroached on and their country's legal system can provide no acceptable avenue for recourse.

Because the value and meaning of childhood and adolescence vary significantly across different cultures, countries vary considerably in terms of how these rights, principles, and protocols are interpreted and implemented. Despite presenting numerous safeguards for children, the UNCRC does not directly address the role that cultural variation plays in shaping child *development*. There is no specific mention that the concepts of children and childhood in relation to chronological and developmental age are not universal, and thus defining childhood and its relative components is dependent upon the changing values and sociocultural variations of a given society as discussed above. The notion of social equality in the contemporary western world has led to the idea that children are entitled to sociocultural and moral rights. Children belong to a group in society with rights and are worthy of moral consideration (Paul 2007). Nevertheless, children are still viewed as in need of protection from a range of social, psychological and physical harms, and are still restricted in terms of engaging in certain behaviours that are socially and legally permissible for adults. For example, children in most western cultures cannot vote, drive, consent to sexual encounters, smoke, drink alcohol and marry. These activities are restricted until a particular age and vary across different societies, reflecting how children are viewed differently across different contexts. The tension resides inevitably between the views of children and childhood and the rights that children are then afforded. For example, the period of adolescence is often viewed as one of "storm and stress" (Hall 1904) given the rapid rate of psychosocial growth experienced by youth at this time, and yet adolescents also experience disconnect between their biological and social maturity, which has been hypothesized to result in the development of delinquent behaviour (Moffitt 1993).

Children's access to mental health care in cultural contexts

Culture as a wider concept and as a unique entity as defined by the AAMC (see above) influences the way in which mental health and mental health needs are viewed, and how individuals from different cultures make sense of certain symptoms and behaviours. Stigma of child mental health problems is as pervasive as stigma of adult presentations of mental suffering and this can strongly influence the way in which children with mental health issues and their families are perceived (Corrigan 2004). This can also then impact whether parents bring their children for an evaluation, and what kinds of services they feel comfortable with. It has also been argued that members of minority groups would have better access to services if their providers were culturally like themselves (for example, Traylor et al, 2010 found that when same race providers were available there was likely to be patient/provider concordance). Less research has been done with children's preferences. Dogra et al. (2007) found that Guajarati adolescents and their parents valued professional characteristics more than demographic ones in their preferences for providers.

Another important factor to consider is that children and adolescents may have little choice in the kinds of care they receive, given that they are dependent on their families. This may be especially true for younger children in cultures where soliciting the opinions of children is not widely accepted. Thus, one can view families as the mediating variable between culture and utilization of mental health care for children. Families are unique cultures within themselves, and their definitions and compositions are changing and dynamic. Parents bring different experiences of being parented themselves to the new relationship with their own children. This influence will depend on the structure of the family – if it is a nuclear or extended family. Child rearing practices are influenced by cultures and these culturally embedded parenting practices also define what is seen as normal or abnormal in childhood behaviours. Therefore, balancing between a respect for individual differences within cultural contexts and a need to standardize a core set of criteria for defining normal and abnormal behaviour for mental health services is a key challenge for providers.

The third factor to consider is a potential cultural mismatch between children and their caretakers, which may affect presentations to mental health services. This cultural mismatch can occur because of differences in acculturation that can occur when families move to a new country (see discussion below) or as a result of changes in cultural norms with the passage of time (i.e., differences in opinion between parents and their children on appropriate ways for children to express their individuality through clothing and/or curfew).

The fourth factor to consider is the variation in children's relationships with parents in different cultural contexts. The number of children who develop secure relationships with their caregivers is proportionately similar across cultures at around two-thirds, suggesting that attachment is a universal phenomenon (Mesman et al. 2016). However, different cultures may value different characteristics in children, which may reflect differences as to how attachment behaviours are interpreted. It is often stated that 'western cultures' value independence, emotional openness and sociability. However, these values are not necessarily promoted in other cultures (for a pioneering discussion on individualistic versus collectivistic cultures, see Triandis 1988) and mental health professionals must be aware of unique cultural presentations of mental health problems that exist in the group they are working with (Triandis 1996).

The last factor to consider includes peer relationships with other children and environmental characteristics that shape children's developmental trajectories. Bronfenbrenner's (1979) ecological model is useful to understand the multiple layers in children's development: the microsystem, mesosystem, exosystem, and macrosystem. The microsystem is at the level of the relationships in which the child is actively involved, for example, with parents, siblings and peers. These interactions inevitably depend on the sociocultural context and the child's characteristics or personality. The mesosystem describes how the different components of the microsystem come together such as, clubs and schools. The exosystem is the wider local community such as the neighbourhood. The macrosystem is usually more remote but may still be a major social influence, for example, through socioeconomic policy on child rearing, education and health policies, and wider sociocultural contexts. It is worth noting that different factors may be important at various stages of the child's life, as is illustrated in the case example below.

Case Study: Mark (age 17)

Mark grew up in a middle-class household as an only child. His parents both worked in stable jobs through his middle school years. When he began high school, he recalls that they lived in a nice house in a suburban area. He is unsure why it happened, but he recalls that his parents started using drugs. They moved from alcohol and pills to methamphetamines. Both parents lost their jobs and soon were unable to make payments on their home. The bank foreclosed on the home and the family was evicted when Mark was age 16. He decided that he was better off on his own and left his parents, who continued their drug use. Mark moved into a youth homeless shelter in the city and decided to try to complete his high school diploma in the hopes of getting a job and being able to secure his own apartment. He does not feel that his biological family is supportive of him and feels that his friends are more like his family at this point in his life.

Bronfenbrenner's theory is especially salient when conceptualizing a case like Mark's because it illustrates the interplay between each of the different systems currently shaping his developmental trajectory. Some adverse family factors may be mitigated by external factors that come into play as children get older (e.g., peer support). When developmentalists discuss the concept of resilience (Masten 2014), they are effectively exploring how the different systems outlined above interact to shape adaptive outcomes in the context of adversity. Although Mark does not believe that his biological parents are a source of support, the interaction between Mark's personal characteristics of determination and a strong work ethic, coupled with his peer network (microsystem) interact with the homeless shelter system (exosystem). Given the interactions between these systems, Mark is able to continue going to school and plans on living independently in the near future.

Taxonomy of child mental health problems and culture

The American Psychiatric Association's *Diagnostic and Statistical Manual of Psychiatric Disorders, Fifth Edition* (*DSM 5*; 2013) and the World Health Organization's *International Classification of Diseases, Tenth Edition* (*ICD 10*; WHO 2004) are consensus documents that represent the taxonomy of psychiatric phenomena. These documents generally do not represent child and adolescent phenomena well. Most of the research that these documents draw on is focused on the psychiatric experiences of adults. These gaps are further compounded when examining issues of race/ethnicity, class, sexual orientation, disability, and religion. All these diverse elements of experience cross-cut into the developmental trajectories and impact development and developmental psychopathology in a variety of ways.

Neurodevelopmental disorders are one area of notable exception within the *DSM 5* and *ICD 10*. This spectrum of disorders including autism, ADHD and other neurodevelopmental phenomena are the major domain where child psychiatric phenomena receive explicit attention and focus. Nevertheless, here again we see a lack of attention to sociocultural elements of experience. For example, it is clear that while ADHD has an element of neurodevelopmental process to its origins and that there are likely a host of biological factors that play a part in its development, it is also true that the expression of this disorder has significant sociocultural components. The United States has nearly double the rate of expression of ADHD over the United Kingdom (Russell et al. 2014), and yet are these societies so different that this difference would be rooted in a biogenetic explanation? It seems highly unlikely and it is more reasonable to conclude this difference represents variance in the sociocultural context of the expression of ADHD; and differential investments in early childhood care, primary education, and other key social disparities likely explain why there is such a large difference in diagnosis of ADHD. In addition, when evaluating adaptive behaviours (for example, in the context of giving an autism diagnosis), it is important to consider that some assessments of adaptive behaviour do not necessarily consider different experiences that children may have as a function of their cultural background (e.g., knowing how to properly answer a telephone).

Another additional factor to consider in the taxonomy of psychiatric disorders is that childhood antecedents of major psychiatric phenomena have rarely been included in the DSM or ICD architecture. With the exception of the trauma–spectrum disorders, very few psychiatric diagnoses make explicit note of earlier events or injuries that have a relationship to the unfolding psychiatric phenomena. Charles Nemeroff and his colleagues (2003) have documented an important case where these experiences intertwine. In their study of pharmacological interventions for major depression, they identified a subpopulation with the depressed cohort of women who had early childhood sexual trauma. This subpopulation proved to have a form of depression that was resistant to traditional pharmacological approaches but that tended to respond more favourably to treatment with psychotherapy. Their finding, along with numerous studies from the famous Dunedin Study, which has followed the lives of 1,037 babies born between 1972 and 1973 (e.g., Poulton et al. 2015; Silva 1990), prove that there are strong linkages between early childhood experiences and a later onset of psychiatric illness.

This line of work has produced a significant new subfield of Adverse Childhood Experiences (ACEs) research. ACEs have proven to be robust predictors of not only psychiatric disorders but to also predict the severity and impact of medical disorders. The remarkable finding in the ACEs literature is that there is a dose response to ACEs exposure (Felitti et al. 1998; Edwards et al. 2005; Felitti 2009; Gilbert et al. 2015). In other words, the more adverse childhood experiences that individuals face, the worse the outcomes for medical and psychiatric disorders. Previous scholars have postulated that ACEs mediate the relationship between chronic socioeconomic disadvantage and poorer educational and socioemotional outcomes later in life (e.g., McLoyd 1998). Chronic stress has also been linked to behavioural problems and other adverse outcomes via physiological dysregulation (Allwood et al. 2011; Popma et al. 2007; Sondeijker et al. 2007; Gunnar and Donzella 2002) and differences in brain development (Malter-Cohen et al. 2013; van Harmelen et al. 2013; Maheu et al. 2010).

The major gap that persists in the current research on ACEs is a means of incorporating the impact of sociocultural factors into the modelling of ACEs. Minorities and the socially vulnerable are more likely to face ACEs; and face higher exposure to ACEs in the dose response models. This higher presence of adversity is linked to long histories of racism, subjugation, and abuse that members of historically marginalized populations have experienced (Thoits 2010). Researchers have been slow to adopt intersectional models that can capture more than one dimension of sociocultural experience along with the experience of ACEs. This represents one of the next major frontiers of research on child mental health and culture.

Integrating culture in mental health care for children

Balancing respect for variation and the need for universality is, therefore, the core challenge for child psychiatry across cultures. To contend with this dilemma, we have favoured a cultural sensibility approach in our teaching and research (Dogra and Karnik, 2003; Karnik and Dogra, 2010). The stance of cultural sensibility attempts to place the clinician in a position of learning about the cultural situation of the child and his/her family and trying to use the clinical space for gaining the important information that will help guide culturally sensitive treatment. A great deal of additional information about the life of the child can also be gained by looking at the artefacts, toys and the nature of play that the child engages with in his/her everyday life (Mukherji 1997). Culture plays a critical role in how and when children begin to play, such as dictating at what age a child will be encouraged to play, and shaping the kinds of games that males and females are allowed to/expected to play (DiPietro 1981).

The challenge comes from the fact that children are dynamic beings, whose developmental trajectory is subject to have a large degree of variability of behaviours. The attentive clinician must, therefore, not only be careful to observe the child, but also to have a view of the family and the degree to which it is a part of a broader cultural milieu.

It is more effective to have a principle-based approach as suggested by Dogra et al. (2017) to ensure that cultural issues are taken on board for *all* families. There are several reasons for why this approach is most successful:

- In general, this approach prevents clinicians from assuming that variables relevant to one patient/family are universal for all individuals who appear to be from the same racial/ethnic/cultural background.
- This approach should prevent stereotyping of the young person and his/her family.
- This approach enables the clinicians to provide quality care irrespective of which factor diversity may be related to.
- This approach operates on the central philosophy that young people and their families all bring perspectives which need to be taken into account early on in the case conceptualization and later when determining the most appropriate treatment.

The following guidelines for working with diverse patient populations were developed from a review of the relevant literature in the field (e.g., Whaley and Davis 2007; Sue and Sue 1990) as well as from our own clinical experiences in working with diverse patient populations from different cultural backgrounds. This is not an exhaustive list of guidelines, but in general, clinicians should consider the following when working with diverse patient populations as a whole:

(1) The need to reflect on their own biases and prejudices to ensure that these do not consciously or subconsciously justify lesser quality care for some patients.
(2) As many factors influence the individual's understanding of mental health and mental health services, at the outset of any assessment the patient's understanding of what they think is going to happen should be checked. Their explanation or understanding for how things are may be very useful for the interventions that are planned.
(3) Do not be afraid of asking if you are not sure – you just need to ensure you ask respectfully without judgement. Cultural genograms are one way to help guide the conversation in a sensitive way (Hardy and Laszloffy 1995).
(4) Do not be intimidated into avoiding difficult questions just because someone is from a visibly different background. Respecting someone's culture does not mean avoiding difficult

issues. For example, a family may disclose during a session that they believe it is permissible to physically punish their children when they misbehave. This issue cannot go unaddressed. The parents may not believe that their actions constitute child abuse as they themselves were raised in a culture where physical punishment was acceptable and may be surprised to hear from you as the provider that these actions are reportable (in most western cultures). Having this uncomfortable, but important, dialogue may open the door for a sincere discussion of how cultural differences impact family dynamics (see guideline 11 below).

(5) Do not assume that because someone superficially looks as though they may be from a similar background that this means they view the world in a similar way.

(6) Do not assume that because the last person from a particular background believed that mental illness is caused by spirits so too will the next patient from a similar background.

(7) If there are a number of treatment options, do not assume which option the individual will choose. Discuss all the options and ensure the patient and/or family are able to make an informed choice. Different people will need different levels of explanations and time. Working with interpreters can increase the time needed.

(8) It should be emphasized that currently there is no strong evidence that one type of approach is more effective than another. However, recent research with mental health adult patients revealed their preference for approaches which were consistent with the definition of diversity used above.

In addition, the following guidelines are particularly important when working specifically with children and their families:

(9) Bear in mind that just as you are making an assessment, so too is the young person and their family. Their views of you will be influenced by the range of factors discussed above. Again, remember that especially as the child grows older, they may have very different views than that of their parents.

(10) Ensure that you do get the child's (who is your patient) perspective. At times of distress and stress, family members may speak for the child and make choices that they would make for themselves rather than think about what the child might truly want.

(11) Provide psychoeducation on how differences in rates of acculturation can influence family dynamics. One widely accepted model views acculturation across four axes: marginalization, separation, assimilation, and integration (Berry 1997).

The following case study illustrates how clinicians can integrate the aforementioned guidelines when working with families from diverse cultural backgrounds.

Case Study: Jyoti (age 15)

Jyoti is 15 years old. Her father was born in India but grew up in England. Her mother came to England as an adult after getting married. Jyoti's parents are fairly traditional and allow her twin brother greater freedom than Jyoti, in terms of his social life. He is allowed out with mixed groups of friends whereas Jyoti is only allowed to go to events where there will be no boys. Additionally, Jyoti is under pressure to continue with further education. Jyoti would like to leave school and get an apprenticeship. Jyoti's mother has recently noticed that Jyoti has superficial cuts on her wrists. Jyoti was unwilling to discuss this with her mother and accused her mother of invading her privacy. Jyoti's parents disagree about the meaning of this self-harming behaviour, with her father feeling it is best ignored but her mother feeling this might reflect deeper problems and needs addressing.

In assessing Jyoti, the practitioner will need to ensure that all perspectives are heard, and assumptions not made about the family. For example, rather than making assumptions about gender roles within Jyoti's family, the clinician should specifically ask the family to discuss their views on this subject (guideline 3). Relatedly, as discussed in the 11th guideline above, the clinician may wish to specifically discuss levels of acculturation among each individual of the family. If, for example, Jyoti is integrated into the English culture, whereas her parents still view themselves as separate from the dominant culture, this may be a source of tension in their relationship. Likewise, it is important for the clinician to be frank about the risks of self-harming behaviour (guideline 4), and to address this issue with both parents with Jyoti's permission. Lastly, as discussed in guideline 7, it will be important to clearly delineate each treatment option to both parents and to Jyoti so that each person understands the treatment risks and benefits, and the family can jointly decide whether the treatment approach they select is in line with their personal and cultural values.

The skill is to take each perspective (i.e., both parents, the child, and if relevant, other members of the family) into account and identify a plan that is acceptable to all parties but is also based in good practice and the evidence available. Clinicians must always remember that their duty is to ensure that the child's best interests are met. The clinician must always remember that the child is the patient, and if necessary, this point must be re-iterated to the parents.

Future directions

This chapter has provided a broad overview of the intersection of child and adolescent mental health and the study of sociocultural factors. The field is broad and varied, and there are significant gaps in the clinical treatment and research literature. There is much to be done to advance this field.

First, there is a need to better incorporate intersectional models into our research. Just as the AAMC integrates many variables in the definition of culture, so too do theories based on the intersectional model allow us to consider the effects of race/ethnicity, gender identity, sexual orientation, disability and socioeconomic status as part of the ways that children and families develop and change over time. Traditional research models have usually looked at one of these axes, whereas intersectional models tend to try to incorporate multiple dimensions and are better at recognising the heterogeneity of human experience.

Second, as we advance mental health research there is a need to use the tools of population health to study the ways that sociocultural factors impact mental health of children and families. Aside from demographics, systems of care and data systems generally do not capture the complex nature of sociocultural research. We need to integrate sociocultural research into the existing systems, and this may entail changing the underlying framework of these systems.

Finally, this research will better inform our existing interventions. This recognition of the need to better tailor interventions to specific populations is growing in tandem with the expansion of population health data systems. These complex data systems allow for the integration of the intersectional models into new iterations of existing psychotherapies, thus providing a framework for researchers to develop more targeted, culturally sensitive interventions for youth and their families.

Conclusion

In this chapter, we illustrated the importance of integrating a careful cultural analysis into clinical work with children and their families. We discussed how clinicians should prioritize framing their case conceptualizations in a way that emphasizes patient-centeredness by engaging children (and, where applicable, their families) in a meaningful discussion on their cultural values, rather than being guided by assumptions and stereotypes. Although the roles that children ascribed to children have dramatically changed over the centuries, it is now well-understood that youth develop as part of an intricately interconnected and dynamic system that is heavily influenced by cultural variables, and the astute clinician should carefully evaluate each of these systems when working to diagnose and treat a child or adolescent.

References

Allwood, M., Handwerger, K., Kivlighan, K. T., Granger, D., and Stroud, L. R. (2011) 'Direct and Moderating Links of Salivary Alpha-Amylase and Cortisol Stress-Reactivity to Youth Behavioral and Emotional Adjustment', *Biological Psychology*, 88(1): 57–64.

American Psychiatric Association (2013) *Diagnostic and Statistical Manual of Mental Health Disorders, Fifth Edition*. Washington, DC: American Psychiatric Association.

Ariès, P. (1962) *Centuries of Childhood: A Social History of Family Life*. New York: Vintage.

Association of American Medical Colleges (1999) *Report III Contemporary Issues in Medicine: Communication in Medicine-Spirituality, Cultural Issues and End of Life Care*. Washington, DC: Association of American Medical Colleges.

Berry, J. W. (1997) 'Immigration, Acculturation, and Adaptation', *Applied Psychology*, 46(1): 5–34.

Bronfenbrenner, U. (1979) 'Contexts of Child Rearing: Problems and Prospects', *American Psychologist*, 34(10): 644–850.

Corrigan, P. (2004) 'How Stigma Interferes with Mental Health Care', *American Psychologist*, 59(7): 614–625.

DiPietro, J. A. (1981) 'Rough and Tumble Play: A Function of Gender', *Developmental Psychology*, 17(1): 50–58.

Dogra, N., Cooper, S. and Lunn, B. (2017) *Ten Teachers: Psychiatry*. 2nd edition London: Hodder Stoughton.

Dogra, N. and Karnik, N. (2003) 'First-Year Medical Students' Attitudes Toward Diversity and its Teaching: An investigation at One US Medical School', *Academic Medicine*, 78(11): 1191–1200.

Dogra, N., Vostanis, P., Abuateya, H. and Jewson, N. (2007) 'Children's Mental Health Services and Ethnic Diversity: Gujarati Families' Perspectives of Service Provision for Mental Health Problems', *Transcultural Psychiatry*, 44(2): 275–291.

Edwards, V. J., Anda, R. F., Dube, S. R., Dong, M., Chapman, D. F., Felitti, V. J. (2005) 'The Wide-Ranging Health Consequences of Adverse Childhood Experiences', in Kendall-Tackett, K. and Giacomoni, S. (Eds.) *Victimization of Children and Youth: Patterns of Abuse, Response Strategies*. Kingston, NJ: Civic Research Institute.

Felitti, V. (2009) 'Adverse Childhood Experiences and Adult Health', *Academic Pediatrics* 9(3):131–132.

Felitti, V. J., Anda, R. F., Nordenberg, D., Williamson, D. F., Spitz, A. M., Edwards, V., Koss, M. P., and Marks, J. S. (1998) 'Relationship of Childhood Abuse and Household Dysfunction to Many of the Leading Causes of Death in Adults: The Adverse Childhood Experiences (ACE) Study', *American Journal of Preventative Medicine*, 14(4):245–258.

Geneva Declaration of the Rights of the Child (1924) www.un-documents.net/gdrc1924.htm Accessed 22 February 2018.

Gilbert, L. K., Breiding, M. J., Merrick, M. T., Parks, S. E., Thompson, W. W., Dhingra, S. S., and Ford, D. C. (2015) 'Childhood Adversity and Adult Chronic Disease: An Update from Ten States and the District of Columbia', *American Journal of Preventative Medicine*, 48(3):345–349.

Gunnar, M. R., and Donzella, B. (2002) 'Social Regulation of the Cortisol Levels in Early Human Development', *Psychoneuroendocrinology*, 27(1–2): 199–220.

Hall, G. S. (1904). *Adolescence: Its Psychology and Its Relations to Physiology, Anthropology, Sociology, Sex, Crime, Religion and Education (vols 1 & 2)*. Englewood Cliffs, NJ: Prentice-Hall.

Hardy, K. V., and Laszloffy, T. A. (1995) 'The Cultural Genogram: Key to Training Culturally Competent Family Therapists', *Journal of Marital and Family Therapy*, 21(3): 227–237.

Karnik, N. and Dogra, N. (2010) 'The Cultural Sensibility Model for Children and Adolescents: A Process-Oriented Approach', *Child and Adolescent Psychiatric Clinics of North America*, 19(4): 719–738.

Maheu, F. S., Dozier, M., Guyer, A. E., Mandell, D., Peloso, E., Poeth, K., Jenness, J., Lau, J.Y. F., Ackerman, J. P., Pine, D. S., and Ernst, M. (2010) 'A Preliminary Study of Medial Temporal Lobe Function in Youths With a History of Caregiver Deprivation and Emotional Neglect', *Cognitive, Affective, & Behavioral Neuroscience*, 10(1): 34–49.

Malter-Cohen, M., Jing, D.,Yang, R. R.,Tottenham, N., Lee, F. S., and Casey, B. J. (2013) 'Early-Life Stress Has Persistent Effects on Amygdala Function and Development in Mice and Humans', *Proceedings of the National Academy of Sciences of the United States of America*, 110(45): 18274–18278.

Masten, A. S. (2014) 'Global Perspectives on Resilience in Children and Youth', *Child Development*, 85(1): 6–20.

McLoyd, V. C. (1998) 'Socioeconomic Disadvantage and Child Development', *American Psychologist*, 53(2): 185–204.

Mesman, J., van IJzendoorn, M. H., and Sagi-Schwarz, A. (2016) 'Cross-Cultural Patterns of Attachment', *Handbook of Attachment: Theory, Research, and Clinical Applications, 3rd ed.* (pp. 852–877). New York: Guilford.

Minuchin, P. (2002) 'Cross-Cultural Perspectives: Implications for Attachment Theory and Family Therapy', *Family Process*, 41(3): 546–550.

Moffitt,T. E. (1993) 'A Developmental Taxonomy', *Psychological Review*, 100(4): 674–701.

Mukherji, C. (1997) 'Monsters and Muppets: The History of Childhood and Techniques of Cultural Analysis,' in E. Long (Ed.) *From Sociology to Cultural Studies*. Malden, MA: Blackwell Publishers.

Nemeroff, C., Heim, C.,Thase, M. E., Klein, D., Rush, A. J., Schatzberg A., Ninan, P.T., McCullough, J. P., Weiss, P. M., Dunner, D. L., Rothbaum, B. O., Kornstein, S., Keitner, G., and Keller, M. B. (2003) 'Differential Responses to Psychotherapy Versus Pharmacotherapy in Patients with Chronic Forms of Major Depression and Childhood Trauma', *Proceedings of the National Academy of Sciences of the United States of America*, 100(24):14293–14296.

Paul, M. (2007) 'Rights', *Archives of Disease in Childhood*, 2(8):720–725.

Perera, F. (2014) 'Science as an Early Driver of Policy: Child Labor Reform in the Early Progressive Era, 1870–1900', *American Journal of Public Health*, 104(10): 1862–1871.

Popma, A., Doreleijers, T. A. H., Jansen, L. M. C.,Van Goozen, S. H. M.,Van Engeland, H., and Vermeiren, R. (2007) 'The Diurnal Cortisol Cycle in Delinquent Male Adolescents and Normal Controls', *Neuropsychopharmacology*, 32(7):1622–1628.

Poulton, R., Moffitt,T. E., and Silva, P.A. (2015) 'The Dunedin Multidisciplinary Health and Development Study: Overview of the First 40 Years, With an Eye to the Future,' *Social Psychiatry and Psychiatric Epidemiology*, 50(5):679–693.

Ronzoni, P. and Dogra, N. (2012) 'Children, Adolescents and Their Carers' Expectations of Child and Adolescent Mental Health Services (CAMHS)', *International Journal of Social Psychiatry*, 58(3):328–336.

Russell, G., Rodgers, L. R., Ukoumunne, O. C., and Ford, T. (2014). 'Prevalence of Parent-Reported ASD and ADHD in the UK: Findings from the Millennium Cohort Study', *Journal of Autism and Developmental Disorders*, 44(1): 31–40.

Silva, P.A. (1990) 'The Dunedin Multidisciplinary Health and Development Study: A 15 Year Longitudinal Study', *Paediatric and Perinatal Epidemiology*, 4(1): 76–107.

Sondeijker, F. E. P. L., Ferdinand, R. F., Oldehinkel, A. J.,Veenstra, R.,Tiemeier, H., Ormel, J., and Verhulst, F. C. (2007) 'Disruptive Behaviors and HPA-Axis Activity in Young Adolescent Boys and Girls from the General Population', *Journal of Psychiatric Research*, 41(7): 570–578.

Sue, D.W. and Sue, D. (1990) *Counseling the Culturally Different: Theory and Practice*. Oxford: John Wiley.

Thoits, P. A. (2010) 'Stress and Health: Major Findings and Policy Implications', *Journal of Health and Social Behavior*, 51(1): S41–S53.

Traylor A. H., Schmittdiel J. A., Uratsu C. S., Mangione C. M., Subramanian U. (2010). The Predictors of Patient–Physician Race and Ethnic Concordance: A Medical Facility Fixed-Effects Approach. *Health Service Research*, 45(3): 792–805.

Triandis, H. (1988) 'Collectivism v. Individualism: A Reconceptualisation of a Basic Concept in Cross-Cultural Social Psychology' in Christopher Bagley and Gajendra K.Verma (Eds.), *Cross-cultural Studies of Personality, Attitudes and Cognition* (pp. 60–95). London: Palgrave Macmillan.

Triandis, H. C. (1996) 'The Psychological Measurement of Cultural Syndromes', *American Psychologist*, 51(4): 407

UN General Assembly (1989) *Convention on the Rights of the Child (vol. 1577)*. United Nations, Treaty Series.

van Harmelen, A. L., van Tol, M. J., Demenescu, L. R., van der Wee, N. J. A., Veltman, D. J., Aleman, A., van Buchem, M. A., Spinhoven, P., Pennix, B. W. J. H., and Elzinga, B. M. (2013) 'Enhanced Amygdala Reactivity to Emotional Faces in Adults Reporting Childhood Emotional Maltreatment', *Social Cognitive and Affective Neuroscience*, 8(4): 362–369.

Whaley, A. L. and Davis, K. E. (2007) 'Cultural Competence and Evidence-Based Practice in Mental Health Services: A Complementary Perspective', *American Psychologist*, 62(6): 563–574.

World Health Organization (1996) ICD-10: International Statistical Classification of Diseases and Related Health Problems: 10th revision, 2nd ed. Geneva: World Health Organization.

25

CULTURE, MENTAL HEALTH, AND OLDER PEOPLE

Amanda Grenier and Blessing Ojembe

Mental health among older people, and especially older people from racialized and ethnic minority groups, is under studied, and policies and practices in this domain are known to have significant gaps.[1] While studies on mental health tend to take a population level view, little is known about mental health among racialized or ethnic minority older people (Birren et al. 2013; Hansson et al. 2012; Nguyen 2011). The tendency to overlook mental health in later life may result from the assumption that mental health and decline are a normal part of aging, the belief that mental health issues resolve as one moves across the life course and into late life, and/or the stigma associated with mental health.[2] However, although there is a developing literature on the mental health of racialized and ethnic minority people (Hansson et al. 2012), the existing body of research on aging, and on the health differences among racialized or ethnic minority populations suggests that there are notable differences when compared to the general population, and that mental health issues may extend and/or worsen in later life.

Attention to mental health among older people from racialized and ethnic minority groups is an important area for research given the importance of achieving broad frameworks of health in later life (Beard et al. 2016), and population trends whereby racialized and visible minority populations represent growing numbers of the aging population. In Canada for example, the context where we live and work, visible minority seniors (65 and over) accounted for 12.6% (691,175) of the population (Statistics Canada, 2016). Canada also has the highest proportion of foreign-born persons compared to other G8 nations and until 2131, the proportion of foreign-born Canadians is expected to increase four times faster than the rest of the population (Laher 2017). While there is a growing literature that documents mental health among racialized and ethnic minority groups, most of it is written in the context of the United States (Jang et al. 2007; Paniagua and Yamada, 2013) where social policies and systems differ from the Canadian and other international contexts with more formalised public models of health care and/or social services. Further, while key sources on mental health and the life course exist, how mental health issues may persist and/or develop into late life among racialized or ethnic minority older people is an under-developed area of research (see Clarke et al. 2011; George 1999).

The approach to mental health among older people in general limits the available knowledge on the mental health of racialized and ethnic minority older people. Responses to older people and to mental health have long been criticised as overly medicalised domains of research and practice (Estes and Binney 1989; Foucault 2003; Kaufman et al. 2004; Szasz 1997). This means

301

that when the mental health of older people does receive attention, it is primarily from a medical or professional focus (Knight et al. 1992; Lebowitz and Niederehe 1992; Zarit and Zarit 2011). Understandings of how intersecting social locations and histories may affect life course trajectories related to mental health among older people are less well acknowledged (and especially in mainstream service environments) (George 1993; Knight 1992). Yet, extending the insights of critical sociological perspectives and research on health barriers among racialized groups can help to understand mental health among racialized and ethnic minority older people. There is a need for social sciences approaches that are sensitive to the interplay between social structures, contexts, and culture with regard to mental health in late life.

This chapter takes a critical life course perspective to explore the subject of mental health among racialized older people and older people from visible ethnic minority communities. Our suggestion is that the mental health of older people must be understood and addressed within a broader social, cultural, political and economic context. This means that the mental health of racialized and ethnic minority older people, although often treated on an individual level, and often from a biomedical approach, occurs within a social and cultural context, and is experienced. As such, it is best understood through relationships, social locations, cultural contexts, and the economic and political conditions within which people live. This includes for example, the impacts of traumatic life course trajectories, differences in cultural practices, reluctance to seek assistance due to stigma, and/or language barriers that affect access to care. It is this link between the individual, the socio-political environment, culture and structured responses – whether they be institutional, organisational or systemic – that are of utmost importance.

This chapter begins by sketching the groundwork for the literature on mental health among older racialized and ethnic minority older people and among older people in general. It begins by outlining definitions of mental health and culture, how mental health may vary within and between cultures, and how different viewpoints impact how mental health is understood and approached. Next, it situates the theoretical approach for the analysis in a critical life course perspective and sketches the details of two illustrative case vignettes. It then employs these examples as a means to highlight the intersection between social locations of race and ethnicity and mental health within a social, cultural, and global context. It does this by drawing attention to four inter-related challenges, including: health disparities, im/migration, barriers to care, and family dynamics. Building on these, it outlines key issues for research, policy and practice.

Mental health in a social and cultural context

The definition of mental health with regard to older people and/or in later life can vary. Mental health can refer to a diagnosis, to a particular condition, as well as a broad concept of well-being. While the definition of mental health has long been defined in relation to mental illness as an absence of psychopathologies, a number of authors, particularly those writing from a life span perspective employ a broad definition of mental health. Westerhof and Keyes (2010: 110) for example, articulate three components of health which include feelings of happiness and satisfaction (emotional well-being), positive individual functioning and self-realization (psychological well-being) and positive societal function in terms of being of social value (social well-being). Within the literature there is also a distinction made between the timing of the mental health issue. In clinical sub-populations, this is often articulated through discussions of two groups, one who have aged with a mental health issue (i.e., depression or schizophrenia), and another who develop this issue after about age 50. Although such discussions are often discussed through age, the issue is less about chronological age and more about diagnosis, needs, and/or how these may change over time. Our interest is in the less developed area of research on how mental health viewed from a broad perspective, may vary over time for older people from racialized and ethnic minority groups as a result of social location, and relationships and structures, including policies and organisational practices.

Cultural approaches to the study of mental health

The notion of culture has been used in a range of ways where older people from racialized and ethnic minority groups are concerned. An important distinction is that of culture as shaping mental health, and mental health as differently affecting particular groups. The idea of a cultural analysis of mental health outlines how mental health is not individual but created within (and by) the social or cultural context within which one lives (Alvi and Zaidi 2017). This line of thinking provides a direct contrast to the biomedical approach to mental health, including classification, diagnosis and treatment, and how such powerful practices can lead to experiences such as stigma (Clarke et al. 2011; Conner et al. 2010; Corrigan 2000; George 1999). Most notably, cultural readings of mental health draw attention to the difference between professional and lay perspectives, how professional practices may result in oppression, and how social and cultural relations can shape experiences of mental health, and in particular, experiences of shame or stigma. At the same time, a cultural analysis of mental health also draws attention to the importance of shared narratives and community-based connections among people with mental health issues (Carr et al. 2004).

The conflation of culture with cultural differences

The notion of culture however, when used in relation to racialized and ethnic minority groups, is sometimes conflated with cultural differences. In this context, the experiences of racialized or ethnic minority groups are often treated *as* culture, and more specifically as representative of cultural differences. This understanding tends to draw attention to how mental health may vary across and between cultures, groups, cultural contexts, or how particular groups may be more affected by the stigma of mental health than others. This is not to suggest that the analysis of difference is not important. Rather, that in this case, social locations are conflated with culture, and ethnic and cultural minority groups are considered as homogeneous entities for the purposes of comparison. As such, an approach that conflates culture with cultural differences glosses over how social locations such as race, ethnicity, income, sexual orientation, and ability, when experienced in a particular cultural context, can shape experiences of mental health. It also overlooks how the experiences of particular individuals or groups may vary within a given culture at any particular point in time. While there is a paucity of literature on mental health among racialized older people, the contrast between the cultural readings of mental health (culture as causing mental health) and readings of racial and ethnic minority differences as culture (differences between groups), reveals a major gap in knowledge and practice. A question that becomes important from a critical life course perspective is how the social and cultural context may produce mental health issues, in particular, when experienced through encounters that are traumatic or discriminatory.

Critical life course perspective

This chapter takes a critical perspective of the life course that considers how life is structured and experienced (Baars et al. 2013; Dannefer and Settersten 2010; Grenier 2012). Such an analysis draws together the analysis of social relations, political and economic conditions (Estes,

Biggs and Phillipson 2003; Estes 1993; Minkler and Estes 1991) with the interpretive (Cole, Ray and Kastenbaum 2010) and cultural analysis of aging and late life (Twigg and Martin 2015). This perspective is used to explore taken-for-granted assumptions and how interpretations and responses to aging may enable and/or constrain the lives of older people. Insights offer a lens to consider the neglect of mental health among racialized and ethnic minority older people and how ideas that are common place with regard to older people and racialized or ethnic minority groups make their way into the studies of aging and/or inform health and social care practices (or not) (see Estes, Biggs and Phillipson 2003; Grenier 2012; Hendricks 2004). The concern when exploring contemporary experiences of aging, particularly among disadvantaged groups, is that without proper recognition of the intersections between risk, insecurities, and appropriately designed preventative efforts, the lives of a growing number of older people may become characterized by precarity rather than by the dominant positive frameworks of health and success (Grenier and Phillipson 2018).

A critical life course perspective on aging suggests that research and practice should explore and account for how the social and cultural context may impact the mental health of racialized older people and older people from ethnic minority groups. In this section we situate experiences of mental health within a socio-political context. To do this, we present two case illustrations to highlight the intersections of mental health, social, cultural, economic and political issues. In each, we draw on a broad conceptualisation of mental health to highlight how trajectories and social conditions can affect everyday lives. The case examples (and names) are fictitious, based on research in Canada, but also applicable across a range of international contexts. The two vignettes reveal the intersections of im/migration, poverty, health and mental health, and the need for care. Each story also highlights how mental health is embedded in social relations and experienced within a cultural context, interwoven with life trajectories, interpersonal relationships, and encounters with social structures. This includes, but is not limited to, the practical and emotional difficulties faced by older immigrants as a result of a lack of acceptance of foreign certificates, temporary employment or joblessness.[3] Both stories involve foreign-born older people experiencing mental health alongside social issues of housing, health, shifting social policies and programming, and a reliance on family care.

Vignette 1: Mr Sandhu is a 70-year-old South Asian man. His family im/migrated to Canada when he was in his mid-thirties to find a 'better life'. Mr Sandhu had always had off and on challenges with his mental health. For many years he struggled to find full time employment and his family moved often to afford the rent. He began using substances with a group of men he met on a work contract. His substance use came to affect his relationship, and once their children were adults, Mrs Sandhu decided to move in with her sister. Mr Sandhu became depressed, stopped working altogether, increased use of alcohol and drugs, and after a few months was evicted from his apartment. He began sleeping rough and using shelter services. His health began to fail, and estranged from his family, Mr Sandhu had nowhere to go and needed care. He agreed to attend a substance use treatment facility and for the social worker to put his name on a waiting list for older men. After ongoing treatment, two years of living between emergency shelter, the hospital and the street, he finally accepted to live in a residential setting for men with substance issues.

Vignette 2: Mrs Zhang is a Mandarin speaking woman (aged 80), widowed, who lives in a semi-urban city in Ontario, and her two grown children have moved to a different city to find work. She was not feeling herself both physically and emotionally but has not had very good luck in finding a service provider. She delays seeking medical treatment and does not want to tell her two children because she does not want them to worry. She decides not to go out and begins ordering everything into the house and stops meeting with her friends. She becomes depressed, and her health worsens until she experiences a fall and ends up in hospital. Once in care, the family learn that her health and mental state are fragile, and she will require regular care. The family do not want people to know about the failing health of their mother and attempt to hire a live-in caregiver. However, similar to the health system, Mrs Zhang experiences language barriers that result in frustration for Mrs Zhang and her caregiver. Neither of the children can move back to provide care and Mrs Zhang does not want to move across the country. As a last resort, the family decide on placement, but are feeling extremely guilty and shame about not being able to care for their mother.

The two case illustrations draw attention to the relationship between how lives are structured and experienced. They outline complex trajectories of im/migration including precarious work, realities of migration whereby families may live in separate parts of the country, and the health disparities resulting from disadvantage. They highlight how mental health needs that may be long-standing, such as the case of Mr Sandhu, or acquired later in life, such as Mrs Zhang, may shift as one enters late life, and requires care. They also reveal the impacts long-term stress may have on families, as well as how policies that rely on family care may be unrealistic as a result of family conflict (Mr Sandhu), or where this conflicts with geographic realities or cultural expectations (Mrs Zhang). The literature on health among racialized and ethnic minority groups, and older people who are foreign-born, suggests the presence of complex intersections between policy structures of im/migration and care, the impacts of unstable labour over time, and how barriers to care may worsen disparities in health, and likely mental health, over time (also see Ahmed et al. 2016; Koehn et al. 2013; Lahaie et al 2013).

Mental health among racialized and ethnic minority older people

This section aims to connect the issues highlighted in the case vignettes with the existing related literature on health and care among racialized and ethnic minority older people. Although there is a need for further study, insights from the literature help to situate the analysis of mental health from a critical life course perspective. This section explores four issues that can affect the mental health of older people from racialized and ethnic minority groups: health disparities, trajectories of im/migration, barriers to care, and family dynamics.

Health disparities. The literature on health disparities among people from ethnic minority groups and im/migrants holds insights for research and practice on mental health among older people (Koehn et al 2013). A review conducted by Nazroo (2003) suggests that social and economic inequalities are fundamental causes of ethnic inequalities in health, and that understanding racism is key to understanding ethnic inequalities across the life course. Studies on health disparities tend to focus on comparisons of population health (Marmot and Wilkinson, 2005). The life course is also considered to impact health disparities, either by means of early exposure (Braveman and Barclay 2009) or an accumulation of disadvantage or deficits over time (see Dannefer 2003; Ferraro and Shippee 2009; O'Rand 1996). Lessons here, although they have not always been considered in relation to older people, is that older people from racialized and ethnic minority groups may have health disparities related to socio-economic conditions, experiences of disadvantage, and racism that are important to well-being, and may change (or worsen) over time (Basavarajappa 1999; Coloma and Pino 2016). Here, for example, research focuses on the healthy immigrant effect whereby im/migrants tend to be healthier than the Canadian-born population at their time of arrival, but may experience diminished health as a result of adjustment to a new environment, stress or other health behaviours (McDonald and Kennedy 2004; Ng et al. 2011; Vang et al. 2015). Here, where Mr Sandhu's experience reveals how precarious employment affected employment, created family strain and contributed to homelessness, the case of Mrs Zhang reveals how delays in seeking medical care resulted in a health and mental health crisis. Our concern is how social locations, life course trajectories, and experiences such as discrimination may impact mental health of this group.

Trajectories of im/migration. The literature on health inequalities and precarity among older im/migrants also highlights how trajectories such as im/migration may affect the mental health of older people from racialized and ethnic minority groups. The health disparities literature suggests that im/migration can impact human capital, as well as economic and health outcomes (Ciobanu et al. 2016; Koehn et al. 2013; Nazroo 2003). Ferrer et al. (2017) for example, outline how immigration policy, and more specifically the live-in caregiver program, can impinge on the everyday lives of racialized older people (also see Hyer and Sohnle 2014). In the literature on precarity among older im/migrants, the emphasis turns to the impacts of insecurity and experiences of vulnerability among racialized and ethnic minority older people (see Allison 2012; Ciobanu and Hunter 2017; Gavanas and Calzada 2016; Grenier et al. 2017; Paret and Gleeson 2016). For example, writing about older im/migrants, Banki (2013:), outlines how "precarity of residence does not suggest imminent deportation from a country, but its very real possibility... legal status affects the ability to secure stable work" (PAGE 450-451) . Paret and Gleeson (2016) stress the experiences of older im/migrants as uncertain, unpredictable, terror, and loss. Here, the literature aligns with stress as a determinant of social disparities in health (Pearlin et al. 2005). Where Mr Sandhu's case reveals this intersection between the stress of im/migration, employment, family and housing, Mrs Zhang's case highlights the long-term implications of language barriers with regard to health and inclusion. Although not all racialized older people or people from ethnic minority groups have im/migrated, and differences will exist depending on generation, this emerging literature on insecurity, stress, and vulnerability provides key insights with regard to thinking about mental health.

Barriers to care

Research also points to the challenges older people from racialized or ethnic minority groups have with accessing care and mental health services (Dastjerdi et al. 2012; Guruge et al. 2015; Hyman 2004; Koehn 2009; Koehn et al. 2016; Lai and Surood 2013). Here, social locations such as age, race and ethnicity are considered to affect access to care, through a lack of knowledge about programs, language barriers (i.e. a lack of proficiency in English), exclusion from the labour force, and/or experiences of discrimination and racism within health structures (Koehn et al. 2013; Lightman and Gingrich 2013). While there is a developing literature on barriers to services among ethnic minority groups, there is much less attention to older people (Phillips et al. 2000; Woodward et al. 1992). One of the main identified barriers to mental health treatment among racialized and ethnic minority groups is stigma, which prevents people from seeking mental health treatment, can lead to terminating treatment, and thus likely increase disparities among racialized and ethnic minority older people (Clement et al. 2015; Conner et al. 2010; Corrigan 2004; Gary 2005; Snowden 2003). For example, evidence from a study on stigma and attitudes of older Americans showed that African Americans are more likely than their white counterparts not to seek mental health services due to fear of stigma and discrimination (Conner et al. 2010). Language proficiency for those without English or French was also identified as a barrier to seeking service (Derose et al.

2007), as were cultural barriers, the cost of treatment, and proximity to treatment location (Choi and Gonzalez 2005). Both case vignettes reference the stigma of mental health and/or seeking assistance, and how this plays out differently as a result of financial resources (e.g., precarious employment, no benefits, etc), precarity in other aspects of one's life (e.g., family, housing), cultural expectations (e.g., mental health as a private issue) and/or barriers to care (e.g., language). Where suggestions to reduce barriers to mental health treatment focus on the importance of integrating cultural values and beliefs, as well as the retention of bilingual or bicultural staff as a means to convey acceptance and discourage mistrust by racialized and minority older people, efforts must also focus on understanding mental health issue within the context of an older person's life, and how family dynamics and structural features such as policies or practices may also affect outcomes.

Family relations and expectations

In Canada for example, research on older immigrant ethnic and minority groups has shown that family relationships can affect health and mental health (McDonald 2011; Wakabayashi 2010; Wu and Penning 2015). Here, although more research is needed, positive family relations may provide a supportive buffer, with family conflict potentially worsening health or mental health. For example, dysfunctional family dynamics (e.g., interaction and relational patterns) were identified as contributing to deteriorating mental health among Asian immigrant in Canada (Alvi and Zaidi 2017). For instance, in a family where the older person perceives their role or position as a provider, and not seeking support, there is a tendency to withhold information about their mental health from the family. As a result, a mental health issue may progress to more serious concern as was the case with Mrs Zhang. There is also the issue of caregiver stress (either as a giver or as a receiver) and how challenges can arise from giving or receiving care. This is particularly the case where the impacts of economic disadvantage, policy restrictions and a shortage of care may overlap to affect the mental health of older people and their families – precisely the situations where precarity is considered to intersect in late life. The case vignettes illustrate how mental health must be contextualized in the context of policies on care and family dynamics. Mr Sandhu had few options for support as a result of the policy emphasis on family care, his lack of family network or private resources, and mental health needs. Where Mrs Zhāng had the resources, her children were geographically unable to provide care, and the breakdown of care as a result of linguistic challenges resulted in additional family stress because cultural and family values conflicted with the care option suitable for her level of need.[4] Together, disparities in health, trajectories of im/migration, barriers to care, and family relations may contribute to mental health issues as well as make it difficult for racialized and minority older adults to access treatment and other forms of care.

Future directions

This chapter used a critical life course perspective to reflect on mental health among older people from racialized and ethnic minority communities. Throughout, it suggested the need to recognize and consider a broad approach to mental health among older people from racialized and ethnic minority groups. It argued that the mental health of older people from racialized and ethnic minority groups must be understood and addressed within a broader social, cultural, political and economic context, including how health may worsen over time as a result of disadvantage. Through two examples, we highlighted how lives, relationships, social locations, cultural contexts, and the economic and political conditions within which older people live, can impact mental health. We also stressed the need to link current approaches with an analysis of the socio-political environment, and institutional or organisational structures of care.

Together, the analysis of the intersection between structures, culture and experience lead to three inter-related suggestions to build knowledge and insight to improve policies and practices for racialized older people and older people from ethnic minority communities: First, to better understand life-long mental health trajectories, including the identification of key transitional turning points. Second, to develop programs that prevent inequality, address structural barriers, and are non-stigmatizing. Third, to understand cumulative disadvantage and the relationship between disadvantage, stress, and trauma.

Understanding inequality and mental health trajectories

The existing and related literature on mental health for older racialized and ethnic minority older people suggests the need to understand how mental health may worsen as a result of inequality, at particular transitional moments, or through negative encounters with systems that are discriminatory, or do not adequately respond to needs. In the case of mental health, this means understanding change over time in the context of declining forms of social protection. There is a pressing need to better understand mental health trajectories as structured and experienced in a particular social, political and economic context, as well as how mental health issues may unfolding across the life course and into late life through the stress related to intersecting forms of disadvantage such as poverty, insecure labour, discrimination and im/migration.

Preventing inequality, disadvantage, and precarity

The existing and emerging trends on health disparities, barriers to care, and discrimination draw attention to the need for responses that prevent disadvantage, inequality, and racism across institutional and organisational structures and programs. At the structural level, there is a need to prevent discrimination in policy and service structures and identify the unique needs that may be experienced by particular groups. At the local or service level there is a need to ensure that older people can access care, feel comfortable doing so, and will be understood from their social locations and life experiences. With most of the literature focused on health, there is a serious need to understand and address how lessons may extend to mental health among older people from racialized and ethnic minority groups. Without reliable research and knowledge, the mental health challenges that are experienced by older racialized and ethnic minority people are difficult to address. Here, however, there is also a need to differentiate between the particular severe mental health needs of under-served and disadvantaged populations, and a broad view of mental health often described as general well-being. Both are worthy of attention in moving forward as a means to correct previous disadvantage and to better prepare for a diverse aging population.

The impacts of stress, discrimination, and trauma

The impacts of stress, discrimination and trauma are outlined across the health and mental health literature on the experiences of racialized and ethnic minority older people. While most tends to focus on individual health or stress, perhaps as a result of the biomedicalization of aging and mental health, there is a need to more closely consider the impacts of trauma and institutionalized racism on mental health. Here, lessons from the social determinants of health suggest the importance of the psychological impacts of inequality, disadvantage experienced by particular groups, and racism over time. In social gerontology, the attention to cumulative disadvantage suggests that experiences of disadvantage, insecurity and vulnerability may have cumulative effects on health, and thus likely mental health over time. Incorporating a lens which considers cultural shocks and experiences of racism as trauma can inform understandings of mental health across the life course and into late life. Take for example, how access to meaningful and well-paid labour, or the availability of public supports for care could alter the experiences of older people, and in particular groups who may rely most on public services. Prevention of poverty and disadvantage by means of access to the labour force, housing, and care would serve to mitigate the stress of structural barriers that currently compound the lives of disadvantaged older people from racialized and ethnic minority groups. A structural approach to preventing inequality could then be combined with a trauma informed approach to services as a means to address the mental health needs of older people from racialized and ethnic minority groups. This approach shifts the focus from cultural differences or individualized challenges to identifying and addressing the impacts of particular trajectories and/or experiences of racism and discrimination that affect health and mental health in everyday relationships and encounters.

Conclusion

This chapter engaged in a critical perspective to mental health among racialized older people and older people from visible ethnic minority communities. It began with a sketch of key issues in the literature on mental health among older racialized and ethnic minority older people and outlined two illustrations to draw attention to the intersection between race, ethnicity and culture. Drawing on a critical life course perspective, it suggested that the mental health of older people must be understood and addressed within a broader social, cultural, political and economic context. This means that the mental health of older racialized and ethnic minority older people is not an individual level phenomenon but must be understood in the social, cultural, and global context, and in relation to the circumstances within which mental health is experienced and/or lived. And based on this, the chapter concludes that there is a need to recognize mental health among older people from racialized and ethnic minority groups, to understand the trajectories and dynamics that impact mental health, to develop programs and responses that address existing barriers to care, and to heal the traumatic impacts of damaging structural relations and discriminatory policies and practices.

Acknowledgements

The authors wish to thank Stephanie Hatzifilalithis for her assistance with formatting the paper and the references. The lead author wishes to thank the donors of the Norman and Honey Schipper Chair at the University of Toronto and Baycrest, and the Social Sciences and Humanities Research Council of Canada for funding on precarity.

Notes

1 In Canada, The *Employment Equity Act* defines as visible minorities "persons, other than Aboriginal persons, who are non-Caucasian in race or non-white in colour". The visible minority population consists mainly of the following groups: South Asian, Chinese, Black, Filipino, Latin American, Arab, Southeast Asian, West Asian, Korean and Japanese.

2 There is also a tendency to conflate mental health issues with other conditions such as dementia, although this is the subject of another paper.

3 Foreign born older people often speak about barriers to employment whereby Canadian employers demand Canadian experience in order to be hired or gain entry to the first job in Canada. This demand for 'Canadian experience' means that it is difficult to gain employment, both initially upon arrival, and over time, as the lack of experience continues to accumulate over time, and where there is a gap between perceptions of how much 'Canadian experience' a person should have relative to their age and occupation

4 Here, the option of residential care or care provided by the family for persons with high level needs can be considered to create additional stress for families. Although home care services are available in Canada, they tend to top out depending on the program at about 12–14 hours per week, meaning that this form of care is less of an option for older people who require high levels of care, and do not have the available kin care to fill in the remaining hours of the week.

References

Ahmed, S., Shommu, N. S., Rumana, N., Barron, G. R., Wicklum, S., and Turin, T. C. (2016) Barriers to access of primary healthcare by immigrant populations in Canada: A literature review. *Journal of Immigrant and Minority Health, 18*(6): 1522–1540. http://dx.doi.org/10.1007/s10903-015-0276-z.

Allison, A. (2012) Ordinary refugees: Social precarity and soul in 21st century Japan. *Anthropological Quarterly, 85*(2): 345–370. https://doi.org/10.1353/anq.2012.0027.

Alvi, S. and Ziadi, A. U. (2017) Invisible voices: An intersectional exploration of quality of life for elderly South Asian immigrant women in a Canadian sample. *Journal of Cross Cultural Gerontology, 32*(2):147–170. https://doi.org/10.1007/s10823-017-9315-7.

Baars, J., Dohmen, J., Grenier, A., and Phillipson, C. (Eds.) (2013) *Ageing, meaning and social structure: Connecting critical and humanistic gerontology.* Policy Press. https://doi.org/10.1332/policypress/9781447300908.001.0001.

Banki, S. (2013) Precarity of place: A complement to the growing precariat literature. *Global Discourse, 3*(3–4): 450–463. https://doi.org/10.1080/23269995.2014.881139.

Basavarajappa, K. G. (1999) Distribution, Inequality and Concentration of Income Among Older Immigrants in Canada, 1990 (No. 129). Retrieved from Statistics Canada http://publications.gc.ca/collections/Collection/CS11-0019-129E.pdf.

Beard, J. R., Officer, A., De Carvalho, I. A., Sadana, R., Pot, A. M., Michel, J. P., … and Thiyagarajan, J. A. (2016) The World report on ageing and health: a policy framework for healthy ageing. *The Lancet, 387*(10033): 2145–2154. https://doi.org/10.1016/S0140-6736(15)00516-4.

Birren, J. E., Cohen, G. D., Sloane, R. B., Lebowitz, B. D., Deutchman, D. E., Wykle, M., and Hooyman, N. R. (Eds.) (2013) *Handbook of mental health and aging.* San Diego, CA: Academic Press.

Braveman, P., and Barclay, C. (2009) Health disparities beginning in childhood: a life-course perspective. *Pediatrics, 124*(Supplement 3): S163-S175. https://doi.org/10.1542/peds.2009-1100D.

Carr, S., Beresford, P., and Webber, M. (2004) *Social perspectives in mental health: Developing social models to understand and work with mental distress.* London: Jessica Kingsley Publishers.

Choi, N. G., and Gonzalez, J. M. (2005) Barriers and contributors to minority older adults' access to mental health treatment: Perceptions of geriatric mental health clinicians. *Journal of Gerontological Social Work, 44*(3–4): 115–135. https://doi.org/10.1300/J083v44n03_08.

Ciobanu, R. O., Fokkema, T., and Nedelcu, M. (2016) Ageing as a migrant: vulnerabilities, agency and policy implications. *Journal of Ethnic and Migration Studies, 43*(2), 164–181. https://doi.org/10.1080/1369183X.2016.1238903.

Ciobanu, R. O., and Hunter, A. (2017) Older migrants and (im) mobilities of ageing: An introduction. *Population, Space and Place, 23*(5): e2075. https://doi.org/10.1002/psp.2075.

Clarke, P., Marshall, V., House, J., and Lantz, P. (2011) The social structuring of mental health over the adult life course: advancing theory in the sociology of aging. *Social Forces, 89*(4), 1287–1313. https://doi.org/10.1093/sf/89.4.1287.

Clement, S., Schauman, O., Graham, T., Maggioni, F., Evans-Lacko, S., Bezborodovs, N., Morgan, C., Rüsch, N., Brown, J. S. L., and Thornicroft, G. (2015) What is the impact of mental health-related stigma on help-seeking? A systematic review of quantitative and qualitative studies. *Psychological Medicine, 45*(1), 11–27. https://doi.org/10.1017/S0033291714000129.

Cole, T. C., Ray, R. E, and Kastenbaum, R. (Eds.) (2010) *A guide to humanistic studies in aging: What does it mean to grow old.* Baltimore: John Hopkins University Press.

Coloma, R. S., and Pino, F. L. (2016) "There's hardly anything left": Poverty and the economic insecurity of elderly Filipinos in Toronto. *Canadian Ethnic Studies*, *48*(2): 71–97. https://doi.org/10.1353/ces.2016.0014.

Conner, K. O., Copeland, V. C., Grote, N. K., Koeske, G., Rosen, D., Reynolds III, C. F., and Brown, C. (2010) Mental health treatment seeking among older adults with depression: the impact of stigma and race. *The American Journal of Geriatric Psychiatry*, *18*(6): 531–543. https://doi.org/10.1097/JGP.0b013e3181cc0366.

Conner, K. O., Copeland, V. C., Grote, N. K., Rosen, D., Albert, S., McMurray, M. L., Reynolds, C. F., Brown, C., and Koeske, G. (2010) Barriers to treatment and culturally endorsed coping strategies among depressed African-American older adults. *Aging and Mental Health*, *14*(8): 971–983. https://doi.org/10.1080/13607863.2010.501061.

Corrigan, P. W. (2004) How stigma interferes with mental health care. *American Psychologist*, *59*(7): 614. https://doi.org/10.1037/0003-066X.59.7.614.

Corrigan, P. W. (2000) Mental health stigma as social attribution: Implications for research methods and attitude change. *Clinical Psychology: Science and Practice*, 7(1): 48–67. https://doi.org/10.1093/clipsy.7.1.48.

Dannefer, D. (2003) Cumulative advantage/disadvantage and the life course: Cross fertilizing age and social science theory. The Journals of Gerontology Series B: *Psychological Sciences and Social Sciences*, *58*(6): S327-S337. https://doi.org/10.1093/geronb/58.6.S327

Dannefer, D., and Settersten, R. A. (2010) *The study of the life course: Implications for social gerontology*. The SAGE handbook of social gerontology (pp. 3–19). https://doi.org/10.4135/9781446200933.n1.

Dastjerdi, M., Olson, K., and Ogilvie, L. (2012) A study of Iranian immigrants' experiences of accessing Canadian health care services: A grounded theory. *International Journal for Equity in Health*, *11*. https://doi.org/10.1186/1475-9276-11-55.

Derose, K. P., Escarce, J. J., and Lurie, N. (2007) Immigrants and health care: sources of vulnerability. *Health Affairs*, *26*(5): 1258–1268. https://doi.org/10.1377/hlthaff.26.5.1258.

Estes, C. L. (1993). The long-term care crisis: Elders trapped in the no-care zone. Newbury Park, CA: Sage Publications.

Estes, C. L., Biggs, S. and Phillipson, C. (2003) *Social theory, social policy and ageing: A critical introduction*. Maidenhead: Open University Press.

Estes, C. L., and Binney, E. A. (1989) The biomedicalization of aging: Dangers and dilemmas. *The Gerontologist*, *29*(5): 587–596. https://doi.org/10.1093/geront/29.5.587.

Ferraro, K. F., and Shippee, T. P. (2009) Aging and cumulative inequality: How does inequality get under the skin? *The Gerontologist*, *49*(3): 333–343. https://doi.org/10.1093/geront/gnp034.

Ferrer, I., Grenier, A., Brotman, S., and Koehn, S. (2017) Understanding the experiences of racialized older people through an intersectional life course perspective. *Journal of Aging Studies*, *41*: 10–17. https://doi.org/10.1016/j.jaging.2017.02.001.

Foucault, M. (2003) *Madness and civilization*. London: Routledge. https://doi.org/10.4324/9780203164693.

Gary, F. A. (2005) Stigma: Barrier to mental health care among ethnic minorities. *Issues in Mental Health Nursing*, *26*(10): 979–999. https://doi.org/10.1080/01612840500280638.

Gavanas, A., and Calzada, I. (2016) Multiplex migration and aspects of precarization: Swedish retirement migrants to Spain and their service providers. *Critical Sociology*, *42*(7–8): 1003–1016. https://doi.org/10.1177/0896920516628306.

George, L. K. (1993) Sociological perspectives on life transitions. *Annual Review of Sociology*, *19*(1): 353–373. https://doi.org/10.1146/annurev.so.19.080193.002033.

George, L. K. (1999) Life-course perspectives on mental health. In C. S. Aneshensel, J. C. Phelan and A. Bierman (Eds.), *Handbook of the sociology of mental health* (pp. 565–583). Boston, MA: Springer. https://doi.org/10.1007/0-387-36223-1_27.

Grenier, A. (2012) *Transitions and the lifecourse: Challenging the Constructions of 'growing old'*. Bristol: Policy Press. https://doi.org/10.2307/j.ctt1t89dvf.

Grenier, A., and Phillipson, C. (2018) Precarious aging: Insecurity and risk in late life. *Hastings Center Report*, *48*: S15-S18. https://doi.org/10.1002/hast.907.

Grenier, A., Phillipson, C., Rudman, D. L., Hatzifilalithis, S., Kobayashi, K., and Marier, P. (2017) Precarity in late life: Understanding new forms of risk and insecurity. *Journal of Aging Studies*, *43*: 9–14. https://doi.org/10.1016/j.jaging.2017.08.002.

Guruge, S., Thomson, M. S., and Seifi, S. G. (2015) Mental health and service issues faced by older immigrants in Canada: A scoping review. *Canadian Journal on Aging*, *34*(4): 431–444. https://doi.org/10.1017/S0714980815000379.

Hansson, E. K., Tuck, A., Lurie, S., and McKenzie, K. (2012) Rates of mental illness and suicidality in immigrant, refugee, ethnocultural, and racialized groups in Canada: a review of the literature. *The Canadian Journal of Psychiatry*, 57(2): 111–121. https://doi.org/10.1177/070674371205700208.

Hendricks, J. (2004) Public policies and old age identity. *Journal of Aging Studies*, 18(3): 245–260. https://doi.org/10.1016/j.jaging.2004.03.007.

Hyer, L. A., and Sohnle, S. (2014) *Trauma among older people: Issues and treatment.* New York: Routledge. https://doi.org/10.4324/9781315787046.

Hyman, I. (2004) Setting the Stage: Reviewing Current Knowledge on the Health of Canadian Immigrants: What Is the Evidence and Where Are the Gaps? *Canadian Journal of Public Health*, 95(3), 14–18. https://doi.org/10.1007/BF03403658.

Jang, Y., Kim, G., Hansen, L., and Chiriboga, D. A. (2007) Attitudes of older Korean Americans toward mental health services. *Journal of the American Geriatrics Society*, 55(4): 616–620. https://doi.org/10.1111/j.1532-5415.2007.01125.x.

Kaufman, S. R., Shim, J. K., and Russ, A. J. (2004) Revisiting the biomedicalization of aging: Clinical trends and ethical challenges. *The Gerontologist*, 44(6): 731–738. https://doi.org/10.1093/geront/44.6.731.

Knight, B. G. (1992) *Older adults in psychotherapy: Case histories.* Newbury Park CA: Sage Publications.

Knight, B. G., Kelly, M., and Gatz, M. (1992) Psychotherapy and the older adult. In D. K. Freedheim (Ed.), *The history of psychotherapy: A century of change* (pp. 528–551). Washington, DC: American Psychological Association. https://doi.org/10.1037/10110-014.

Koehn, S. (2009) Negotiating candidacy: ethnic minority seniors' access to care. *Ageing and Society*, 29(4): 585–608. http://dx.doi.org/10.1017/S0144686X08007952.

Koehn, S., Habib, S., and Bukhari, S. (2016) S 4 AC case study: Enhancing underserved seniors' access to health promotion programs. *Canadian Journal on Aging/La Revue canadienne du vieillissement*, 35(1): 89–102. https://doi.org/10.1017/S0714980815000586.

Koehn, S., Neysmith, S., Kobayashi, K., and Khamisa, H. (2013) Revealing the shape of knowledge using an intersectionality lens: results of a scoping review on the health and health care of ethnocultural minority older adults. *Ageing and Society*, 33(3): 437–464. https://doi.org/10.1017/S0144686X12000013.

Lahaie, C., Earle, A., and Heymann, J. (2013) An uneven burden: Social disparities in adult caregiving responsibilities, working conditions, and caregiver outcomes. *Research on Aging*, 35(3): 243–274. https://doi.org/10.1177/0164027512446028.

Laher, N. (2017) Diversity, Aging, and Intersectionality in Ontario Home care: Why we need an intersectional approach to respond to home care needs. Wellesley Institute, Toronto, ON.

Lai, D. W. L., and Surood, S. (2013) Effect of service barriers on health status of aging South Asian immigrants in Calgary, Canada. *Health and Social Work*, 38(1): 41–50. https://doi.org/10.1093/hsw/hls065.

Lebowitz, B. D., and Niederehe, G. (1992) Concepts and issues in mental health and aging. In *Handbook of mental health and aging* (pp. 3–26). San Diego, CA: Academic Press. https://doi.org/10.1016/B978-0-12-101277-9.50005-X.

Lightman, N. and Gingrich, L. G. (2013) The intersecting dynamics of social exclusion: Age, gender, race and immigrant status in Canada's labour market. *Canadian Ethnic Studies* 44(3): 121–145. Canadian Ethnic Studies Association. https://doi.org/10.1353/ces.2013.0010.

Marmot, M., and Wilkinson, R. (Eds.) (2005) *Social determinants of health.* Oxford: Oxford University Press. https://doi.org/10.1093/acprof:oso/9780198565895.001.0001.

McDonald, L. (2011) Theorising about ageing, family and immigration. *Ageing and Society*, 31: 1180–1201. https://doi.org/10.1017/S0144686X11000511.

McDonald, T. J. and Kennedy, S. (2004) Insights into the 'healthy immigrant effect': health status and health service use of immigrants to Canada. *Social Science and Medicine*, 59 (8): 1613–1627. https://doi.org/10.1016/j.socscimed.2004.02.004.

Minkler, M., and Estes, C. L. (Eds.) (1991) *Critical perspectives on aging: The political and moral economy of growing old.* Amityville, NY: Baywood.

Nazroo, J. (2003) The structuring of ethnic inequalities in health: Economic position, racial discrimination, and racism, *American Journal of Public Health* 93(2): 277–284. https://doi.org/10.2105/AJPH.93.2.277.

Ng, E., Pottie K., Spitzer D. (2011) Official language proficiency and self-reported health among immigrants to Canada. Health Reports 2011; 22(4): 15–23. https://doi.org/10.1177/0017896913511809.

Nguyen, D. (2011) Acculturation and perceived mental health need among older Asian immigrants. *The Journal of Behavioral Health Services and Research*, 38(4): 526–533. https://doi.org/10.1007/s11414-011-9245-z.

O'Rand, A. M. (1996) The precious and the precocious: Understanding cumulative disadvantage and cumulative advantage over the life course. *The Gerontologist*, *36*(2): 230–238. https://doi.org/10.1093/geront/36.2.230.

Paniagua, F. A. and Yamada, A. M. (Eds.) (2013) *Handbook of multicultural mental health: Assessment and treatment of diverse populations*. San Diego, CA: Academic Press.

Paret, M., and Gleeson, S. (2016) Precarity and agency through a migration lens. *Citizenship Studies*, *20*(3–4): 277–294. https://doi.org/10.1080/13621025.2016.1158356.

Pearlin, L. I., Schieman, S., Fazio, E. M., and Meersman, S. C. (2005) Stress, health, and the life course: Some conceptual perspectives. *Journal of health and Social Behavior*, *46*(2): 205–219. https://doi.org/10.1177/002214650504600206.

Phillips, K. A., Mayer, M. L., and Aday, L. A. (2000) Barriers to care among racial/ethnic groups under managed care: Ethnic minorities continue to encounter barriers to care in the current managed care–dominated US health care system. *Health Affairs*, *19*(4): 65–75. https://doi.org/10.1377/hlthaff.19.4.65.

Snowden, L. R. (2003) Bias in mental health assessment and intervention: Theory and Evidence. *American Journal of Public Health*, *93*(2): 239–243. https://doi.org/10.2105/AJPH.93.2.239.

Statistics Canada. (2016) Seniors. Retrieved from http://www.statcan.gc.ca/pub/11402-x/2012000/chap/seniors-aines/seniors-aines-eng.htm.

Szasz, T. S. (1997) *The manufacture of madness: A comparative study of the inquisition and the mental health movement*. Syracuse University Press.

Twigg, J., and Martin, W. (2015) The challenge of cultural gerontology. *The Gerontologist*, *55*(3): 353–359. https://doi.org/10.1093/geront/gnu061.

Vang, Z., Sigouin, J., Flenon, A., and Gagnon, A. (2015) The healthy immigrant effect in Canada: A systematic review. *Population Change and Lifecourse Strategic Knowledge Cluster Discussion Paper Series/Un Réseau stratégique de connaissances Changements de population et parcours de vie Document de travail*, *3*(1): 4.

Wakabayashi, C. (2010) Effects of immigration and age on health of older people in the United States. *Journal of Applied Gerontology*, *29*(6): 697–719. https://doi.org/10.1177/0733464809353602.

Westerhof, G. J., and Keyes, C. L. (2010) Mental illness and mental health: The two continua model across the lifespan. *Journal of Adult Development*, *17*(2): 110–119. https://doi.org/10.1007/s10804-009-9082-y.

Woodward, A. M., Dwinell, A. D., and Arons, B. S. (1992) Barriers to mental health care for Hispanic Americans: A literature review and discussion. *The Journal of Mental Health Administration*, *19*(3): 224–236. https://doi.org/10.1007/BF02518988.

Wu, Z., and Penning, M. (2015) Immigration and loneliness in later life. *Ageing and Society*, *35*(1): 64–95. https://doi.org/10.1017/S0144686X13000470.

Zarit, S. H., and Zarit, J. M. (2011) *Mental disorders in older adults: Fundamentals of assessment and treatment*. New York: Guilford Press.

26

CULTURE, MENTAL HEALTH, AND IMMIGRANTS

Rachel Tribe and Claire Marshall

Migrating can be a complex and challenging experience. Displacement from one country to another where voluntary or forced migrants may find their representations and meanings of mental health and illness to be challenged and defined differently, can be a perplexing experience (Tribe 2002). This means that mental health practitioners may have service users/ clients who are migrants accessing services. For example, in a meta-analysis, Cantor-Graee and Seltton (2005) found that people who had migrated were two to five times more likely to have a diagnosis of psychosis than for people who are not migrants. Whilst the number of people who were detained under the Mental Health Act in the United Kingdom are skewed towards people from Black, Asian and Minority Ethnic (BAME) backgrounds, many of whom will have migratory histories. A similar finding was found in relation to the people who were reported as being in crisis and accessed services later than those without migratory backgrounds (Fernando 2014). Several scholars have discussed issues relating to institutional racism in mental health services (Fernando 2014, 2017). The prevalence of mental health issues in the country of migration has been found to be different to that found in the country of origin (Stuart et al. 1998). Therefore, mental health services need to be culturally and linguistically accessible and appropriate if they are to meet the needs of all members of our communities including people who have migrated.

This chapter will examine different types of migration, detail the reasons people migrate and the potential psychological experiences relating to this. These will include issues relating to identity and well-being, belonging in a changing world with increasing issues of nationalism (Balibar 1991; Mavroudi 2010) where post truth has currency. The issue of negotiating transitions as well as individual and community meaning-making will be reviewed in relation to the experience of mobility and change. Issues relating to working with an interpreter or cross-culturally will also be discussed.

Migration and the socio-cultural-political context

The term migrant is always developed and exists in a socio-cultural-political context where political power plays and the vagaries of the wider national and international politics are played out. The relationship between high, middle and low income countries is also ever present and may play a role in definitions and perceptions of migration, as will issues of colonialism and power (Fernando 2014). Some politicians have used the term migrant in negative ways and have presented a problematized image of migrants and the need to stem immigration for their own agenda (Fernando 2014; Geddes and Scholten 2016). Many have linked it in a range of ways to the problems of/within what they define as 'their' country. Social identity theorists such as Tajfel and Turner, (1979) attempt to delineate in the loosest sense what and who are represented or designated as preferred citizens and who are not, thereby setting up in its loosest sense a notion of 'in' or 'out' groups. This can polarise opinion and has the potential to lead to what has been called outgroup derogation (Hewstone et al. 2002) in which a group who are labelled as an 'out' group are seen as threatening in some way to those who define themselves as the 'in' group. By doing this, politicians, media or other groups are trying to establish a discourse around migration, which frequently also problematizes issues of diversity, race, culture, religion, class and ethnicity in particular ways (Migration Observatory 2016). McIntyre et al. (2016) have noted that a lack of social identification is linked with a heightened risk of developing both depression and anxiety, and that interventions designed to assist people feeling they are part of groups and not socially excluded may be able to play a role in ameliorating these negative effects. Therefore, mental health practitioners need to be aware of the wider context and issues which migrants may face with.

The language in relation to 'migration' or 'migrant' in itself may tell us something about how diversity is viewed, and furthermore how issues of institutional racism (Newland, Patel and Senapati 2015), the positioning of race (Bell 2013), nationalism (Mavroudi 2010) and neo-colonialism (Tribe 2014) are played out. The legal, psychological and political positioning of migrants may be different given the terms – what they have been named/labelled. The term 'alien' is used in several countries, including the United Kingdom and the United States, whereas the term 'foreign national' is used in Canada to define someone who is not a national, and other countries use the term 'foreigner'. The connotations of these word appear to emphasize a discourse of difference and a lack of similarity with people defined as 'nationals'. Whilst politicians in some lower- and middle-income countries have defined their nationals who temporarily migrate to high-income countries to seek work due to world-wide financial disparities as 'Heroes', for example, in the Philippines (Nicolas 2011). Many of these 'heroes', who are a sub-group of migrants will financially support their families in the country of origin, although family separation caused by international financial disparities may not be conducive to family cohesion, continuity or well-being.

The structural inequalities lens focusses on the economic and social determinants of health and the cumulative disadvantages. For example, many older Black and Minority Ethnic people (BME) are living with higher levels of poverty, inferior housing and their access to benefits and pensions are less than older people who are white (Joseph Rowntree Foundation 2004). A lack of access to health care and the cultural appropriateness and accessibility of services for a number of marginalized groups has been raised by a number of authors (Bhugra and Bhui 2018). Racial discrimination and linguistic barriers (Tribe and Jalonen, 2020) are identified as major issues for some migrants. All of these factors can be negative indicators for optimal mental health.

Different types of migration

Types of migration have been defined in various ways, but the major demarcation is between involuntary or forced migrants and voluntary migrants. Voluntary migrants make a decision to move to another country, within some constraints of the country they wish to move to and are usually able to arrange when they will migrate. They can take some time to prepare themselves psychologically, although this does not mean that the transition will not be enormous and may be stressful (Christodoulidi 2010). The new country may bring about a series of challenges, some of which may not have been anticipated, for example racism; the different presentation of age, gender, family roles, sexuality and sexual orientation, disability, race, class, religion; and attitudes to and understanding of mental health. So-called voluntary migrants may have or choose to move due to work, family, economic, health, personal, geo-political reasons, disasters, education or other reasons. This may sometimes be less of a choice than it would appear, for example, if not migrating means unemployment, the inability to provide for children, or poverty. The latter has been referred to as voluntary but reluctant migration. Forced migrants are people who have been forced to flee from their home country due to war, international or national geopolitics or other reason, including asylum seekers, refugees, internally displaced people and people who have been trafficked (Patel, Tribe and Yule 2018).

The term migrant covers a diverse range of people from the highly paid and supported worker moving for a multinational company to a refugee, to an older adult who migrates to be closer to their relatives. Their journeys from pre-migration, migration and post-migration experiences are likely to be very different. And their needs regarding mental health will be diverse. For example, the multinational employee may face a different psychological journey, receiving a formal briefing and ongoing financial and emotional support for the individual and their family before moving and whilst settling in a second country. This varies significantly from people migrating in older age who might not speak the language of the new country and may have restricted social capital and networks.

Family members may hold a range of views about the move and may find different issues challenging. Children often adapt more quickly than adults and may gain literacy in a different language or adapt to cultural mores more quickly. This can put children into the role of taking on adult roles within the family prematurely and it can also lead to the infantalising of parents (Douglas 2017) who may take longer to learn a new language or to adapt. This can perturbate or alter family dynamics in unexpected ways. Adults may find themselves dependent on their children to negotiate systems and translate, this is not conducive to development for children and can upset the family dynamics and well-being in unexpected ways. It can also lead to adult migrants feeling socially excluded.

Social exclusion and mental well-being of immigrants

There is increasing evidence that social exclusion and adversity may result in an increased risk of mental health difficulties with migrants as well as an interactive relationship between the two phenomena (Hjern et al. 2004; Mckenzie et al. 2006). Although definitions of social exclusion within the mental health literature have been criticised for being loosely defined theoretically and methodologically, most emphasize the lack of participation in social activities as the core characteristic of the mental health service users (Morgan et al, 2007).

There is an intricate and complex interplay between culture and mental well-being or health. The positive contributions many migrants bring to a community are frequently conveniently forgotten, or the person becomes re-labelled as belonging to the country when it is beneficial to the country or they win plaudits for the country or are seen as having the potential to do so. We need to avoid what Maldonado-Torres (2016) and a number of other post-colonial theorists call a hierarchy of difference. Dustmann and Frattini (2014) estimated that between 1995 and 2011, European immigrants to Britain made a positive financial contribution of over US$6.4 billion. Many countries have actively sought out migrants with particular skills, for example people with computer skills. Countries to do this have included the United States,

Canada, Australia and Israel (Refugee Council 2018). Migrants who possess desirable educational or professional qualifications and are geographically mobile have been found to draw upon transnational networks as a source of social capital and support, they are not limited to place, and a sense of inclusion can refer to international networks (Kindler et al, 2015). This access to resources can be beneficial to their well-being and resiliency. These factors are likely to impact upon issues of identity, belonging, stability and consistency at the individual, familial, community, national or international level.

The role of social support and good networks in promoting positive mental health and resilience and reducing or buffering stress was reviewed by Kessler, Price, Wortman. (1985). Loneliness and the lack of support networks are indicated as being detrimental to good mental health (Wang et al, 2018)). Some migrants may be at an increased risk of being isolated due to racism and potential marginalization. Some migrants will have family members living in a range of countries and may not have access to a family support network, although this will vary across communities (Lane and Tribe 2017). Social networks were found to play a useful role for migrants in the early settlement process, assisting with practical issues and giving support particularly to some degree buffering the negative effects of limited cultural and economic capital, as well as a lack of a stable legal status (Kindler et al. 2015).

Migratory transitions and identity

The transition for any migrant is a complex practical and psychological process to be negotiated (Bhugra and Gupta 2011). As stated earlier, many people with skills are perceived as 'desirable' and are asked or choose to re-locate to a country different from that of their birth. Although, often seen as a more privileged group, voluntary migrants may in theory be free to return to their country of origin, but this may not always be straightforward. Whilst it is often assumed that voluntary migrants will have fewer issues relating to the psychological experience of migration, it can be a very challenging transition with multiple differences to negotiate (Christodoulidi 2010). In addition to differences in language, culture and practical differences, migration can lead to changes in perception of identity at the individual, familial, cultural and societal level (Bell 2013). Migrants perceived as different owing to skin colour may be subject to racism and micro aggressions either overtly or covertly (Migration Observatory 2016). The migratory transition can perturbate or lead to changes for an individual, family system and their sense of community (Bhugra and Gupta 2011; Patel et al. 2018) and adversely affect mental health and well-being. Therefore, practitioners need to be cognisant of the challenge in the sense of well-being and identity among immigrants.

There are a range of theoretical models around transition, culture and migration. These have included the acculturation, alternation, assimilation, fusion and multicultural models (Lafromboise et al. 1993), as well as what has been labelled the blended model of biculturalism where migrants are seen to preserve a positive heritage and cultural identity whilst also developing a positive identity through membership of the majority culture (Phinney and Devich-Navarro 1997). How an individual negotiates a transition between two (or more) countries or cultures is likely to be an individual experience which will be mediated by a wide range of factors. Breakwell (1986, 2011) developed identity process theory (IPT) in relation to identity formation across the life-span, with an emphasis upon the underlying psychological and social processes. The latter may gain particular resonance when identity is felt to be challenged, for example when a significant life transition, is experienced, which questions their previous self-concept. Migration may be one such social transition that poses a threat to an individual's identity, sense of self and subsequent well-being and mental health.

Culture, migration, and mental health

The way culture has evolved in high-income countries from the naïve (at best) view of culture being something that was related to migrants or people from 'other countries' as a form of 'othering' towards a more considered and refined understanding which has begun to recognizes a variety of ways of being and views of the world (Tribe and Tunariu 2018) and also encourages clinicians in high-income countries to question their own cultural constructions and the limits of their generalizability. The so-called cultural norm within high-income countries was frequently assumed to be the white western (Fernando 2014; Sashidharan 2001; Tribe 2007) usually male perspective (and often young and able –bodied) within the wider societal and mainstream mental health context (Condor 1991).

It could be argued that all mental health work should foreground culture, as everyone is influenced knowingly or unknowingly by aspects of 'their' culture and cultural identity. Whilst the cultural identity that an individual develops or selects is multi-layered, may be flexible, and will be subject to influences throughout the life-span. Culture can also be reified as something sacrosanct and unquestionable in ways that can be detrimental to people and their human rights and the principles of social justice and equity, for example in relation to prescribed gender roles, sexuality and how mental distress is managed. Lewis-Fernandez et al. (2015), the chair of the Culture Subgroup of the Gender and Culture Study Group of the *DSM-5*, writes:

> Culture is an interpretive framework for symptoms, signs, behaviors which are transmitted, revised, and recreated within families and society. They affect boundaries between normality and pathology, thresholds of tolerance, coping, and interpretations of need for help, awareness of the impact of culture may reduce misdiagnosis. Culture may help determine support and resilience, by contrast, it may contribute to vulnerability and stigma. It helps shape the clinical encounter and affects help-seeking choices, adherence, course, recovery.
>
> *(Lewis-Fernandez et al. 2014: 136)*

Discrimination on any grounds is likely to have an adverse effect on mental health, this may include, but not limited to racial discrimination (Chakraborty and McKenzie 2002), gender discrimination (Bondi and Burman 2001), discrimination on account of sexuality (Broadway-Horner 2017), disability (Smith 2016) or age discrimination (Lane and Tribe 2017), and class (Williams et al. 1997). Intersectionality where different forms of discrimination intersect, and which examines the macro (institutional or contextual) as well as the micro (the interpersonal) power relationships (Kelly 2009) may be at play and effect someone labelled as a migrant. At the macro level, intersectionality can illustrate some of the conjoined forms of structural oppression and how inequalities may be entrenched in socio-cultural-political systems. For example, it has been found that Black, Asian and Minority Ethnic (BAME) families use fewer health and social welfare services and are less aware of what support is available (Ahmad 2000; Shah 2008). At the micro level this may mean individuals not accessing services or finding them inappropriate to their needs.

Mental health, identity, and social context

Mental health can never be viewed in a vacuum, and the importance of contextual factors are being increasingly recognized. Kindler et al. (2015) in a review of the European literature noted that in addition to racism, many migrants may initially suffer lack of income, poorer housing and lack of social capital, at least initially. These and other contextual factors that have been identified as detrimental to mental health include the following factors; approximately two-fifths of people in low income households come from migrant or BAME communities (The Poverty Site 2017). Common mental disorders are twice as frequent among the poor as among the rich (WHO 2001). Requirements for mental health services are very varied, and pre-migratory health, reasons for migration, age, explanatory health beliefs, help-seeking behaviour, selected idioms of distress, health status and language may all play a part.

Stuart et al. (1998) working in Australia found that the prevalence of biomedical mental disorders varied in different migrant groups, but these findings were differed markedly to the rates reported in their countries of origin, which proposed that the differences appeared to be related to their migration journey and the hardships experienced in advance of migration. Having said that migrants are an extremely diverse group and no simple generalisations should be made. People who choose to migrate often possess flexibility of mind, optimism, flexible thinking and considerable resilience which may bode well for good mental health. As the Department of Health Mental health: Migrant Health Guide (2017: 1) notes "Most migrants do not have mental health problems, some may be at increased risk as a result of their experiences prior to, during, or after migration to the UK". Below may illustrate such an example.

A case of Toshio

Toshio spoke repeatedly of never considering that he was Japanese until he moved abroad to study English and then to work. Having lived in a fairly monocultural society, he found on coming to Canada that his identity was in question and he found this an unsettling experience which affected his well-being in that many of his cognitive schemas and world views were challenged, as his social context, conventions and the way people related to him were all different. The cultural norms and ways of behaving in some situations were new and challenging and he felt unsure of the appropriate protocols and expected behaviours. This coupled with his lack of confidence in his spoken English felt very anxiety-provoking and infantilizing. These experiences made him question his sense of self, of his perceived place in the world and his identity. He sought out therapeutic support. After some time and reflection, establishing more connections to the new country and a better understanding of cultural conventions, things changed. Toshio was able to make sense of these differences and he was able to see the experience of living in another country for a period of time as ultimately a positive one and enriching one.

The above example illustrates how identity may be assumed and prescribed and how migration can prove challenging in unexpected and quite fundamental ways which may affect well-being and mental health, clinicians need to be sensitive to this and consider this in their work.

Mental health, migration, and culture

With regard to mental health there may also be a range of explanatory health models: how people understand their health and well-being, may not fit with western constructions and might include possession by spirits / jinn, notions of causality and heredity may be diverse (Summerfield 2012). There are diverse idioms of distress: the way psychological distress is presented may be culturally located, for example through somatic symptoms (Tribe 2007). Whilst help-seeking behaviours, (how and from where might help be) will vary and might include talking with elders, indigenous healers, rituals and very different pathways to care for example (Fernando 2017; Tribe and Lane 2017a,b).

The *Diagnostic Statistical Manual Fifth Edition* (*DSM-5* 2013) and the *International Classification of Disease* (*ICD* 2011), which are used to diagnose mental illnesses and frequently determine who received care, were developed within high-income countries for specific purposes (e.g., insurance reimbursement use in the United States). The issue of how culture has been considered within them has a contentious and complex background and earlier versions were consistently criticised for not dealing with issues of culture adequately (Mezzich et al. 1996; Fernando 2014). The *DSM IV* and *DSM 5* (APA 2000, 2013) took a little more account of cultural differences and contained the Cultural Formulated Interview (CFI) and then the Outline for Cultural Formulation (OCF) with the objective of giving a framework for mental health practitioners to categorise materials obtained as part of assessment, formulation and intervention work. However, it is not without its critics (Bredström 2017; Ecks 2016).

Our understanding of some manifestations and interpretations of mental health will be influenced and co-produced by a number of factors including what is defined as culture. As Summerfield (2002: 248) writes:

> The Diagnostic Statistical Manual (DSM) and the International Classifications of Diseases (ICD) are not, as some imagine, atheoretical and purely descriptive nosologies with universal validity. They are western cultural documents, carrying ontological notions of what constitutes a real disorder, epistemological ideas about what counts as scientific evidence, and methodological ideas as to how research should be conducted.

People from BAME communities, including migrants and people ascribed marginalized status (by a dominant group) are known to access mental health services less than other groups (Bhugra and Gupta 2011). This lack of use may be interpreted by service providers as there being no requirement for services or in some cases or a view that people from certain communities 'look after their own', though this is frequently a view which may be a racist stereotype, which in fact lead each family to decide how they manage mental health issues individually (Katabama, et al. 2004; Tribe 2017). The need for equitable access to health for migrants formed a resolution at the World Health Assembly in 2008. How services are offered is also an issue. For example what has been labelled horizontal equity, which means the same service is offered to everyone, may not be the best way forward, since research shows that vertical equity which means tailoring services to meet particular requirements may be more effective (Oliver and Moossias 2004). Practitioners and commissioners of services need to consider innovative ways of using psychological theory and practices which foreground the requirements of service users and communities. Doing this may benefit all members of our society particularly those with a migrant or dual cultural heritage.

Key issues to consider when working with interpreters

In addition, some migrants will not have had the opportunity to learn the language of the country to which they migrate, though many will be bilingual or have English as a mother tongue. Therefore, some people will benefit from having an interpreter provided. Equal opportunities legislation means that access to services (including mental health) should not be prevented by a lack of language proficiency. There are courses available on working effectively with interpreters which may help prepare clinicians in this task. Comprehensive guidelines on working with interpreters in mental health can be located via the British Psychological Society (Tribe and Thompson 2017) and a short film on this topic is available via YouTube at www.youtube.com/watch?v=k0wzhakyjck.

More experienced practitioners have reported that many positive aspects of working with an interpreter (Tribe and Thompson 2009). These include improved clinical care and service users/clients saying that they feel understood (Angelelli ~~2004~~2019). In a systematic review, Karliner et al. (2007) found that the use of a professional interpreter can improve care for patients without language barriers. Working proficiently in partnership with interpreters is a skill that practitioners need to acquire may be the only way that some migrants are able to access services.

Major issues to consider when working with an interpreter are assessing the need to conduct a language audit for the geographical area served by any clinic or practice and considering how this service is prepared to meet the needs of this population (Tribe and Thompson 2017). If the referral pattern of the service or practice does not reflect the local geographical population, it is important to consider why this might be and what might need to be done to change this.

Undertaking formal briefing and de-briefing of interpreters for the task of working within mental health are essential (Tribe and Thompson 2017). The briefing would include the purpose of the meeting, the different roles, the boundaries of each role, whilst the interpreter / cultural broker would inform the practitioner of any cultural issues which they need to be cognisant of. It is important that this time is not rushed and appropriately allocated for this task. This briefing also allows the practitioner and interpreter to meet, develop a rapport and discuss ways of 'working together' as a team. Whilst the de-briefing at the end of the session is to offer support and supervision as appropriate. Interpreters have not had the training of becoming practitioners, with little prior clinical supervision. Thus, there is a duty of care towards them by the organisation and individual practitioner (Tribe 2002). In particular, the practitioner needs to be aware of the potential danger of vicarious traumatisation for interpreters when working with traumatic material.

The practitioner always needs to be sensitive to the change in dynamics when working with an interpreter. It is critical to keep in mind issues of confidentiality and trust, which is particularly pertinent when working with mental health service users/experts by experience from small or divided language communities. Also, practitioners may need to formally clarify the professional boundaries of the interpreter's role. It may be useful to clearly state that the practitioner alone holds clinical or organisational responsibility for the consultation. It is important to develop an open and collaborative working relationship based on trust and mutual respect (Tribe and Thompson 2017). Practitioners can find working with interpreters challenging at first but an enriching one. It can provide many positive aspects including understanding diverse cultural constructions around mental health and well-being, perhaps developing a critical evaluation of western constructions of mental health and issues relating to their generalisability. On a practical level it can lead to thinking and considering the language used in their own practice. It can also provide time for reflection when the words are being interpreted. If using any psychometric measures in session, extreme caution is needed, as they may never have been validated for diverse groups and any results obtained may not be meaningful (International Test Commission Guidelines on Test Adaptation 2000). Best practice would mean that a practitioner offers an interpreter in situations where one family member has good English, but others do not.

Future directions

There has been a move towards the homogenisation of mental health across cultures, this has largely come from high-income countries hoping to impose their ways of working onto lower income countries, without due attention to the rich traditions frequently located in low- and middle-income countries, (Fernando 2014; Summerfield 2012; Tribe 2014). Global mental health is a highly contested area, where differentials of power and resources are an issue. Whilst there are some counter-flows from low- and middle-income countries to high-income countries, this flow is relatively small, this may be for several reasons including power imbalances and racism. The way that global mental health is frequently practiced has been considered to be a kind of medical imperialism or neo-colonialism (Fernando 2014; Summerfield 2012; Tribe 2014). Many countries contain a range of cultures within them and there is much that could be learned from how mental health is considered in them that could be used as resources within high-income countries. Migrant communities can contribute to the development of more culturally appropriate and informed services in a range of ways.

Conclusion

Whilst, training of all mental health practitioners needs to foreground issues of cultural diversity and to develop a more critical understanding of current practices, rather than viewing cultural diversity (or any form of diversity) as additional extras, which is often the case at present (Fernando 2017; Tribe 2014). All clinicians need to actively promote anti discriminatory practices which foreground the lived experiences and meaning of clients with migratory histories and not ignore these experiences or assume that they understand them. It is also important to remember that migration is part of a person's identity but not their identity. Further research is also required which adequately considers issues relating to migration and which foregrounds cultural diversity and mental health. Clinicians should also consider the socio-cultural and historical context which have given rise to potential marginalization and how these may relate to mental health.

References

Ahmad, W. I. U. (2000) *Ethnicity, Disability and Chronic Illness*. Buckingham: Open University Press.
American Psychiatric Association (2013) *Diagnostic and Statistical Manual of Mental Disorders – V (5th Edition)*. Washington, DC: American Psychiatric Association.
Angelelli, C. V., (2019) *Healthcare Interpreting Explained*. London: Routledge.
Balibar, E. (1991) Racism and Nationalism. In P. Spencer and H. Wollman (Eds.), *Nations and Nationalism: A Reader* (pp. 161–72). Edinburgh: Edinburgh University Press.
Bell, D. (2013) Bearing Black. *Journal for Social Action in Counselling & Psychology*, 5(1). https://www.researchgate.net/publication/276121494_Bearing_Black
Bhugra, D. and Bhui, K. (2018) *The Textbook of Cultural Psychiatry*. Cambridge: Cambridge University Press.
Bhugra, D. and Gupta, S. (Eds.) (2011) *Migration and Mental Health*. Cambridge: Cambridge University Press.
Blue, I. (2000) Individual and contextual effects on mental health status in São Paulo, Brazil. *Revista Brasileira de Psiquiatria*, 22(3): 116–123.
Bondi, L. and Burman, E. (2001) Women and mental health: A Feminist review, *Feminist Review*, 68: 6–33.
Breakwell, G. M. (1986) *Coping with Threatened Identities*. London: Methuen.
Breakwell, G. M. (2011) Empirical approaches to social representation and identity processes: 20 years on. *Papers on Social Representations*, 20(17):1–17
Bredström, A. (2017) Culture and context in mental health diagnosing: Scrutinizing the DSM-5 revision. *Journal of Medical Humanities*, 188(2): 142–143.
Broadway-Horner, M. (2017) Ageing, Sexual Orientation and Mental Health: Lesbian, Gay, Bisexual, Transgendered and Intersex Older People. In P. Lane and R. Tribe (Eds.), *Anti-Discriminatory Practice in Mental Health for Older People* (pp. 232–257). London: Jessica Kingsley.
Cantor-Graae, E. and Selten, J-P. (2005) Schizophrenia and migration: A meta-analysis and review. *American Journal of Psychiatry*, 162(1): 12–24.
Chakraborty, A. and McKenzie, K. (2002) Does racial discrimination cause mental illness? *British Journal of Psychiatry*, 180(6): 475–477.
Christodoulidi, F (2010) *The therapist's experience in a 'foreign country': a qualitative inquiry into the effect of mobility for counsellors and psychotherapists*. PhD thesis, University of Manchester.

Condor, S. (1991) Sexism in psychological research: A brief note. *Feminism & Psychology*, 1(3): 430–434.

Collins dictionary (2018) Fake news. www.collinsdictionary.com/dictionary/english/fake-news.

Crenshaw, K. (1989) Demarginalizing the intersection of race and sex: A black feminist critique of antidiscrimination doctrine, feminist theory and antiracist politics. University of Chicago Legal Forum: 1, art. 8. Available at: http://chicagounbound.uchicago.edu/uclf/vol1989/iss1/8.

Department of Health (2018) www.gov.uk/guidance/mental-health-migrant-health-guide/

Department of Health Mental health: Migrant Health Guide (2017) www.gov.uk/guidance/mental-health-migrant-health-guide

Douglas, A. (2017) The Big Read, York: British Psychological Society.

Du Bois, W. E. B. (1989) *The Souls of Black Folks*. New York: Penguin

Dustmann, C. and Frattini, T. (2014) The fiscal effects of migration to the UK. *The Economic Journal*, 124: 593–643

Ecks, S. (2016) The strange absence of things in the "culture" of the DSM-V *Canadian Medical Association Journal*, 188(2): 142–143.

Fernando, S. (2014) *Mental Health Worldwide: Culture, Globalization and Development*. London: Palgrave Macmillan.

Fernando, S. (2017) *Institutional Racism in Psychiatry and Clinical Psychology Race Matters in Mental Health*. London: Palgrave Macmillan.

Geddes, A. and Scholten, P. (2016) *The Politics of Migration and Immigration in Europe*. London: Sage.

Hewstone, M., Rubin, M., and Willis, H. (2002) Intergroup bias. *Annual Review of Psychology*, 53: 575–604.

Herek, G.M, Gillis, J. R., Cogan, J. C., and Glunt, E. K. (1997) Hate crime victimization among lesbian, gay and bisexual adults: Prevalence correlates, and methodological issues. *Journal of Interpersonal Violence*. 12: 195–215.

Hjern, A., Wicks, S. and Dalman, C. (2004) Social adversity contributes to high morbidity in psychoses in immigrants – a national cohort study in two generations of Swedish residents. *Psychological Medicine*, 34: 1025 -1033.

ICD-11, The 11th Revision of the International Classification of Diseases www.who.int/classifications/icd

International Test Commission Guidelines on Test Adaptation April 21 (2000) Available from www.intestcom.org/Guidelines/test+adaptation.php.

Joseph Rowntree Foundation (2004) www.jrf.org.uk/report/black-and-minority-ethnic-older-peoples-views-research-findings.

Karliner LS, Jacobs EA, Chen AH, et al. (2007) Do professional interpreters improve clinical care for patients with limited English proficiency? A systematic review of the literature. *Health Services Research* 42(2): 727–54.

Katabama, S., Ahmade, W., Bhaka, P., Baker, R. and Parker, G. (2004) Do they look after their own? *Health and Social Care in the Community*, 12(5): 396–406.

Kelly, U. A. (2009) Integrating intersectionality and biomedicine in health disparities research. *Advances in Nursing Science,* 32(2): E42–E56. doi:10.1097/ANS.0b013e3181a3b3fc

Kessler, R. C., Price, R. H. and Wortman, C. B. (1985) Social factors in psychopathology: Stress, social support and coping processes. *Annual Review of Psychology*, 36: 531–572.

Kindler, M. with Ratchev, V. and Piechowska, M. (2015) Social networks, social capital and migrant integration at local level European literature review www.birmingham.ac.uk/Documents/college-social-sciences/social-policy/iris/2015/working-paper-series/IRiS-WP-6-2015.pdf.

Lafromboise, T., Coleman, H. L. K., and Gerton, J. (1993) Psychological impact of biculturalism; Evidence and theory *Psychological Bulletin*, 114(3): 395–411.

Lane, P. and Tribe, R. (2017) *Anti-discriminatory Practice in Mental Helath for Older People*. London: Jessica Kingsley Publications.

Lane, P., Tribe, R., and Hui, R. (2010) Intersectionality and the mental health of elderly chinese women living in the UK. *International Journal of Migration, Health and Social Care*, 6(4): 34–41.

Lewis-Fernández, R., Aggarwal, N. K., Bäärnhielm, S., Rohlof, H., Kirmayer, L. J., Weiss, M. G., … Lu, F. (2014) Culture and psychiatric evaluation: operationalizing cultural formulation for DSM-5. *Psychiatry*, 77(2): 130–154. http://doi.org/10.1521/psyc.2014.77.2.130.

Maldonado-Torres, N. (2016) *Outline of ten theses on coloniality and decoloniality. Foundation franz fanon.* Retrieved from http://franzfanonfoundation-foundationfranzfanon.com/IMG/pdf/maldonado-torres_outline_of_ten_theses-10.23.16_.pdf.

Mavroudi, F. (2010) Nationalism, the nation and migration: Searching for purity and diversity. *Space and Polity*, 14(3): 219–233.

McIntyre, J. C., Elahi, A., and Bentall, R. P. (2016) Social identity and psychosis: Explaining elevated rates of psychosis in migrant populations. *Social and Personality Psychology Compass*, 10(11): 619–633.

McKenzie, K. and Harpham, T. (Eds.) (2006) *Social Capital and Mental Health*. London: Jessica Kingsley.

Mezzich, J., Kleinman, A., Fabrega, H., Parron, D. (1996) *Culture and Psychiatric Diagnosis A DSM-IV Perspective*. Washington D.C.: American Psychiatric Association

Mezzich, J. E., Kirmayer, L. J, Kleinman, A., Fabrega, H. Jr, Parron, D. L, Good, B. J, Lin, K. M., Manson, S. M. (1999) The place of culture in DSM-IV. *Journal of Nervous and Mental Disorder*, 187(8): 457–464.

Migration Observatory (2016) www.migrationobservatory.ox.ac.uk/wp-content/uploads/2016/04/Report-Migration_News.pdf.

Morgan, C., Burns, T. Fitzpatrick, R., Pinfold, V. Priebe, S. (2007) Social exclusion and mental health conceptual and methodological review. *The British Journal of Psychiatry*, 191(6): 477–483.

Newland, J., Patel, N., and Senapati, M. (2015) Professional and Ethical Practice in a Multi-ethnic Society. In R. Tribe, and J. Morrissey, (Eds.) *The Handbook of Professional and Ethical Practice for Psychologists, Psychotherapists & Counsellors* (2nd ed).. London: Brunner-Routledge.

Nicolas, I. M. (2011) *Heroes and Heroines from the Homeland: Migration from a Philippine Perspective*, paper Presented at the 16th International Metropolis Conference, 'Migration Futures: Perspectives on Global Changes,' Azores Islands.

Oliver A and Moossias, E. (2004) Equity of access to health care; outlining the foundations for action. *Journal of Epidemiology & Community Health*, 58(8): 655–658.

Oxford Dictionary (2018) Post-truth. https://en.oxforddictionaries.com/definition/post-truth.

Patel, N., Tribe, R., and Yule, B. (2018) British Psychological Society Guidelines on Responding to Refugees and asylum seekers in the UK: Guidelines for Psychologists.

Phinney, J., and Devich-Navarro, M. (1997) Variations in bicultural identification among African American and Mexican American adolescents. *Journal of Research on Adolescence* 7: 3–32.

Refugee Council, (2018) www.refugeecouncil.org.uk.

Sashidharan, S. P. (2001). Institutional racism in British psychiatry. *Psychiatric Bulletin*, 25: 244–247.

Shah, A. (2008) 'Estimating the absolute number of cases of dementia and depression in the black and minority ethnic elderly population in the UK.' *International Journal of Migration, Health and Social Care*, 4(2): 4–15.

Smith, P. (2016) *Disability and Culture an Inter Professional perspective*. London: Common Ground Publishing.

Stuart, G. W., Klimidis S., and Minas I. H. (1998) The treated prevalence of mental disorder amongst immigrants and the Australian-born: community and primary-care rates. *International Journal of Social Psychiatry*, 44: 22–34.

Summerfield, D. (2002) Mental health of refugees and asylum – seekers, commentary *Advances in Psychiatric Treatment*, 8: 247–248.

Summerfield, D. (2012) How scientifically valid is the knowledge base of global mental health. *British Medical Journal*, 336 (7651): 992–994.

Summerfield, D. (2012) Afterword: Against "global mental health". *Transcultural Psychiatry*, 49 (3) 1–12.

Tajfel, H., and Turner, J. C. (1979) An Integrative Theory of Intergroup Conflict. In W. G. Austin, and S. Worchel (Eds.), *The Social Psychology of Intergroup Relations* (pp. 33–37). Monterey, CA: Brooks/Cole.

The Poverty Site, (2017) www.better-health.org.uk/resources/weblinks/poverty-site-low-income-and-ethnicity.

Thompson, K., Tribe, R. and Zlotowitz, S. (Eds.) (2018) *British Psychological Society Guidance for Psychologists on Working in Partnership with Community Organisations*. Leicester: BPS publications.

Tribe, R. (2002) Mental health and refugees. *Advances in Psychiatric Treatment*, 8(4): 240–248.

Tribe, R. (2007) Health Pluralism – a more appropriate alternative to western models of therapy in the context of the conflict and natural disaster in Sri Lanka? *Journal of Refugee Studies*, 20(1): 21–36.

Tribe, R. (2014) Culture, politics and global mental health: Deconstructing the global mental health movement: Does one size fits all? *Disability and the Global South*, 1(2): 251–265.

Tribe, R. (2014) Race and Cultural Diversity: The Training of Psychologists and Psychiatrists. In R. Moodley and M. Ocampo (Eds.), *Critical Psychiatry and Mental Health: Exploring the work of Suman Fernando in Clinical Practice* (pp. 134–144). London: Routledge.

Tribe, R. and Jalonen, A. (2020) Working with refugees and asylum seekers. In: D. Bhugra, (Eds.) *Oxford Textbook of Migrant Psychiatry*. Oxford: Oxford University Press.

Tribe, R. and Lane, P. (2017a) Caring for Carers. In P. Lane and R. Tribe (Eds.), Anti-*Discriminatory Practice When Working in Mental Health with Older People*. London and Philadelphia: Jessica Kingsley.

Culture, Mental Health, and Immigrants

Tribe, R. and Lane, P. (2017b) Ageing, ethnicity and mental health. In P. Lane and R. Tribe. (Eds.) *Anti-discriminatory practice when working in mental health with older people*. London: Jessica Kingsley.

Tribe, R. and Thompson, K. (2009) Opportunity for development or necessary nuisance? The case for viewing working with interpreters as a bonus in therapeutic work. *International Journal of Migration, Health and Social Care,* 5(2): 4–12.

Tribe, R. and Thompson, K. (2017) British Psychological Society Guidelines on Working with Interpreters www.bps.org.uk/.

Tribe, R. and Patel, N. (2007) Refugees and asylum seekers. *The Psychologist*, 20(3): 149–151.

Tribe, R and Tunariu, A. D. (2018) Psychological Interventions and Assessments. In D. Bhugra and K. Bhui (Eds.), *The Textbook of Cultural Psychiatry* (pp. 458–471). Cambridge: Cambridge University Press.

YouTube. Working with Interpreters in Mental Health https://www.youtube.com/watch?v=k0wzhakyjck.

Williams, D. R., Yu, Y., and Jackson, J. S. (1997) Racial differences in physical and mental health socio-economic status, stress and discrimination *Journal of Health Psychology* 2(3): 335–335.

World Health Organization. (2001) The World Health Report, Mental Health, New Understanding, New Hope. Geneva: WHO.

World Health Organization. (2011) *The ICD-10 classification of mental and behavioural disorders: Clinical descriptions and diagnostic guidelines*. Geneva: World Health Organization.

27
CULTURE, MENTAL HEALTH, AND REFUGEES

Sophie C. Yohani

Throughout history, humans have migrated from their birth lands due to a variety of *push* or *pull* factors. Forced migration, often associated with natural or human made *push* factors, have rendered people homeless requiring them to live in exile, in limbo, or to reestablish themselves in new homelands. Host communities have had mixed attitudes towards people seeking refuge, ranging from acceptance to hostility, which undoubtedly influences the well-being of refugees already challenged by uprooting. It wasn't until the end of the Second World War, when Europe, in disarray and confronted with large numbers of displaced people, that coordinated efforts to protect forced migrants were addressed at the United Nations Refugee Convention in 1951 (UN 1951). The United Nations High Commissioner for Refugees (UNHCR) was subsequently formed with the primary purpose to defend the rights and well-being of refugees (UNHCR 2010). The principles of protecting and supporting forced migrants are embedded within the definition of a refugee, according to the UNHCR's 1967 amendment to Article 1 of the United Nations Convention:

> A person who owing to a well-founded fear of being persecuted for reasons of race, religion, nationality, membership of a particular social group or political opinion, is outside the country of his nationality and is unable or, owing to such fear, is unwilling to avail himself of the protection of that country; or who, not having a nationality and being outside the country of his former habitual residence as a result of such events, is unable or, owing to such fear, is unwilling to return to it.
>
> *(UNHCR, 2007)*

Despite UNHCR's mandate to seek and ensure action at the international level in order to protect refugees and seek permanent solutions to resolve global refugee problems UNHCR 2010), fast forward to 2017, the international community has reached a crisis state, with over 68.5 million displaced people worldwide, 25.4 million of which are refugees (UNHCR 2018). Conflicts in Afghanistan, Democratic Republic of Congo, Myanmar, Sudan and Syria accounted for the recent rise in forced migrants (UNHCR 2018). More recently, large groups of people are regularly displaced and rendered homeless due to environmental factors (IOM 2014). Changes in the patterns of forced migration have challenged the UNHCR's task to ensure the rights and responsibilities towards refugees are upheld by host countries, rendering this population more vulnerable than ever to ongoing human rights violations and associated mental health challenges.

This chapter focuses on refugees as a population who, due to forced movement, encounter a variety of unique experiences in relation to mental health and well-being. It begins by critically discussing how recent international patterns of forced migration influence perceptions of refugees, which contribute to the way mental health of refugees is understood. By reviewing current research and conceptual models, the chapter examines the main discourses on mental health of refugees, the nature of challenges they encounter, and restoration of well-being. Throughout the chapter, a case is used to illustrate how a young person navigates aspects of the refugee experience and mental health supports. The focus is on the experiences of refugees due to human factors, namely conflicts (e.g., civil wars, gang violence, etc.), although environmental degradation can be associated with conflicts. Recommendations for future practice, training and research are provided.

How refugees are understood across cultures

"Juliet Suffers from Post-Traumatic Stress Disorder (PTSD)!" while Xeno-Racism Veiled

As a child, Juliet lived with her parents and eight older siblings in an East African country prior to moving to a refugee camp in a neighboring country. Her parents and five siblings were killed during a civil war in her country of origin, and she was subsequently raised by her brother and his wife in the refugee camp. When Juliet was 14-years, her brother and his family were given asylum in Canada. Juliet remained alone for four years in the refugee camp before reuniting with her brother and his family at age 18-years. During her time alone in the refugee camp, Juliet experienced many challenges, including witnessing deaths of people she knew and ongoing harassment and death threats because of her ethnic origin and gender. Within six months of her arrival in Canada, Juliet was placed under the government's Social Services care after experiencing conflict with her brother and his wife. Juliet was referred for psychological counselling three months later due to sleep difficulties and recurring nightmares that deemed her in need of psychological support. She was believed to suffer from Post-Traumatic Stress Disorder (PTSD). However, Juliet initially preferred to talk about her experiences of discrimination since arriving in Canada. Despite years of waiting to be reunited with her family members, her experiences had been disappointing, and she felt unwelcome. At school and in the community, she had felt marginalized and had often heard comments such as "go home to Africa." Juliet was frustrated and deeply saddened by her experiences.

Understanding Juliet and her experiences requires more than a medical diagnosis. An understanding of the global patterns of conflict, movement, and restrictions placed on asylum seekers and refugees is important to counteract existing misperceptions and understand the anti-refugee discourse and its impacts on well-being. Given that recent forced migrants and refugees are primarily from the Global South, prevailing racialized attitudes and stereotypes relating to people from these regions are embedded within views of refugees. Such attitudes drive how refugees and the refugee experience are understood and represented, resulting in misconceptions and misrepresentations that contribute to their marginalization and mental well-being. In her analysis of European migration policies, Fekete (2001) noted how the wording of migratory movements from "overpopulated" and "socially insecure countries with weaker economies" overtly demonstrated the emerging anti-refugee discourse at the end of the 20th century (2001: 23). Quoting Sivanandan, Fekete cautioned the rise of xeno-racism as a driving force behind perceptions of refugees and asylum seekers:

> A racism that is not just directed at those with darker skins, from the former colonial territories, but at the newer categories of the displaced, the dispossessed and the uprooted, who are beating at western Europe's doors, the Europe that helped to displace them in the first place. It is a racism, that is, that cannot be colour-coded, directed as it is at poor whites as well, and is therefore passed off as xenophobia, a "natural" fear of strangers. But in the way it denigrates and reifies people before segregating and/or expelling them, it is a xenophobia that bears all the marks of the old racism. It is racism in substance, but "xeno" in form. It is a racism that is meted out to impoverished strangers even if they are white. It is xeno-racism.
>
> *(Sivanandan, cited in Fekete 2001: 23–24)*

Two decades later, xeno-racism is reflected in discussions regarding the number and relocation of refugees worldwide and overall hostility towards receiving them, particularly in Western nations. By focusing on the scale of the refugee crisis and economic impacts, Western nations, as seen in Europe, have argued they cannot handle an influx of refugees and asylum seekers (Joris et al. 2018). Despite the perception that most refugees migrate to Western nations, 85% of refugees tend to remain in neighboring countries resulting in extremely high numbers in some temporary resettlement in host countries (UNHCR 2017). For example, Turkey, with 3.5 million, currently hosts the highest number of refugees (UNHCR, 2017). Other countries hosting a high number of refugees include Ethiopia (791,600), Iran (979,400), Uganda (940,800), Lebanon (1 million) and Pakistan (1.4 million) (UNHCR, 2017). In striking contrast, and contrary to what is believed, refugees who are resettled in Western countries are only a fraction of these numbers, with only 100,000 refugees permanently resettled in 2017.

Xeno-racism contributes to misrepresentations regarding refugee experiences and identities. Few people are aware of the aforementioned definition of a refugee, and this renders refugees vulnerable to stereotypes centered on binaries of being either a victim or perpetrator in relation to the violence they experienced or a hero in relation to violence they escaped. To illustrate, consider a relatively recent newspaper heading stating "Refugees Go from Surviving War to Fighting PTSD" (Brenner, 2016). This heading, along with images of Syrian refugees, could convey a particular perspective. That is, refugees are welcomed in host and resettlement countries *if* they are exclusively seen as *helpless victims* of a medical condition and in need of support and refuge while constructing them as lacking personal agency. Anthropologist Jackson (2013:91) noted the stigmatization of refugee experiences in writing that focuses on losses rather than capturing their full lived experience:

> As long as we think of refugees as solely victims, we do a grave injustice to the facts of the refugee experience, for loss is always countermanded by actions- albeit imaginative, magical, and illusory – to regain some sense of balance between the world within and the world without

Since the September 11, 2001 attacks in the United States and the rise in wars against terrorism, refugees are often treated with suspicion, driven by perceptions of them as perpetrators and / or potentially violent offenders (Piwowarczyk and Keane 2007). Hostility towards refugees is documented in research demonstrating racism towards refugees (O'Connell 2005; Haslam and

Holland 2012) and, more recently, islamophobia experienced by Muslim refugees resettling in Western nations (Every and Perry 2014). There is considerable evidence that racism and other forms of discrimination and marginalization contribute to mental health challenges in refugees and other racialized groups (Williams and Mohammed 2009). Other subtler forms of stigmatization are reflected in the discourse that paints all refugees as traumatized. A less prevalent image is that of the refugee as a hero. While notable in its attention to the resilience of humans in the face of adversity, this view is problematic in its dismissal of challenges that refugees experience in their new contexts or the responsibility of host countries to facilitate appropriate integration.

Getting to know Juliet: Fighting for her agency and autonomy

When first seen, Juliet presented as guarded and described numerous stress-related complaints, including stomach aches, heart palpitations, headaches and difficulty falling asleep. Despite these obvious challenges, Juliet also presented as a resilient young woman who described a personal history of persistence, determination and compassion. In fact, she was upset that her caseworkers appeared to treat her as a helpless and seemed to oversee the fact that she had fended for herself in a refugee camp. She often reported feeling displaced and frustrated by the slow step-wise process of moving towards independent living prescribed by the Social Services department. As the therapeutic relationship with her counsellor developed, Juliet became more relaxed and shared her experiences of living in the refugee camp and since arriving in Canada. Juliet experienced a number of internal conflicts around feelings of guilt regarding what she perceived was expected of her as "a good girl" within her family and community and her need for autonomy and self-direction, which she developed while alone in the refugee camps. She also acknowledged the desire for connection with her family and the pain of having been "left behind" by them, and her resulting isolation. Juliet experienced considerable turmoil, which manifested itself physically and through feelings of sadness and grief.

As suggested in the initial view of Juliet as a victim with PTSD, polarized views of refugees as either victims without agency, dangerous perpetrators, or heroic individuals, suggest simplistic understandings of the varied historical, contextual and human survival response to mass violence and dislocation. While she did experience some trauma symptoms, Juliet's life suggests a complex and layered experience requiring an equally complex understanding that recognizes agency while also attending to marginalization and a variety of responses to extreme conditions often faced in the refugee experience – some which can become maladaptive in new living contexts. For example, Juliet's assertive attitude (which had caused conflict with her family members) and ability to seek out assistance, supported her while living alone in a refugee camp.

Current knowledge of refugee mental health

A distinction is often made between refugees and immigrants, although there are instances when these lines are less clear. Immigrants typically migrate to seek economic betterment and future prospects for their families. Implied here is an assumption of *choice* to migrate, even though there may be multiple economic, social, or even cultural push factors contributing to the decision. Refugees, on the other hand, have little choice in the process of migration and enter permanent resettlement countries after a series of stages that range from flight from country of origin, time in a refugee camp, and/or asylum in more than one country (Prendes-Lintel 2001). Asylum seekers have not been granted refugee status. This distinction in terms is relevant to mental health practice because *choice* is an underlying factor in adaptation and acculturation to new contexts (Berry 2001), and lack of choice about migration has been associated with increased acculturation stress (Berry and Hou 2016).

There has been a proliferation of research on mental health of refugees since the study of Cambodians living in refugee camps on the border of Thailand provided the first large scale report on the mental health of refugees (Mollica et al. 1993). Subsequently, the mental health community has reflected two main perspectives regarding how mental health of refugees should be understood and redressed. A medical approach seeks to classify responses within Western diagnostic systems (i.e. DSM and ICD systems) and intervene using trauma-focused evidence-based approaches (McHugh and Barlow 2010). A humanistic perspective critiques the medicalization of normal responses to 'abnormal' experiences and advocates for contextualized and localized psychosocial responses (Summerfield 2004). More recently, a third perspective is emerging that combines aspects of both, based on ecological systems and intersectional theories (Hass 2018). Details of each approach and its contributions to understanding refugee mental health follow.

Medical approach documents prevalence and rates of mental health challenges

The overall trend in refugee mental health, driven by the medical approach, has been to focus on the consequences of exposure to and experience of traumatic events. Methods for assessing and documenting experiences are often quantitative, involving tools designed to assess a variety of mental disorders and related constructs. Studies frequently identify Post-Traumatic Stress Disorder (PTSD) as one of the main mental health challenges faced by refugees, albeit with much variation; with rates ranging anywhere between 9 and 30%, with the average being 15% (see de Jong et al. 2001; Fazel et al. 2005; Priebe et al. 2016; Steel et al., 2009). The highest predictor for PTSD is personal violation, especially torture (Steel et al., 2009). Studies also identify depression, anxiety, substance abuse disorders, and somatization as other mental health challenges experienced by refugees (Betancourt et al. 2017; Turrini et al. 2017). This pattern of frequently assessing for and identifying PTSD is also reflected in child and youth populations (Yohani, 2015). For example, a systematic review of the literature (Colucci et al. 2012) reported wide-ranging prevalence rates for PTSD, depression, and suicide among refugee youth. Likewise, Fazel and colleagues (2005) found PTSD rates among children with refugee status in Western countries were between 7 and 17%.

Given the overemphasis of trauma and PTSD in the refugee mental health literature, concerns have been raised that these studies label refugees and feed into the aforementioned perceptions of refugees as traumatized victims without agency, or dangerous because they are traumatized and therefore unpredictable in their behavioral responses. Another newspaper headline stating, "Refugees at Risk of Infection and Post-Traumatic Stress Disorder" (Coghlan 2015) highlights this concern. Other critiques of the use of the Western diagnostic classification system to assess trauma challenge the cross-cultural validity of concepts such as trauma, PTSD, and even depression, and the appropriateness of applying associated measures across cultures (Foster 2001; Summerfield 2004). Attempts to address this have been made by translating measures such as the Harvard Refugee Trauma Questionnaire prior to using with different cultural groups (e.g. de Fouchier et al. 2012; Mollica et al. 2001). While confirming the mental health community's large emphasis on assessing for mental disorders and PTSD in particular, the evidence of relatively lower rates of PTSD has been important in dispelling myths that all refugees are traumatized (Silove et al. 2017).

Humanistic approach sheds a human rights perspective on refugee mental health

The humanistic camp, in their critique of medicalized approaches to refugee mental health, highlight the need for a socio-political understanding of refugee experiences. That is, mental health responses need to be understood in relation to human rights violations and, in the case of mass violence and conflict, the destruction and destabilization of societal structures. The human rights violations experienced by refugees often extend beyond conflict zones into new settings, resulting in cumulative trauma as noted in the previous section rather than discrete time periods implied in some diagnostic formulations. Summerfield (2004) in his critique of PTSD noted that refugees themselves provide evidence for an expanded understanding of refugee trauma in that they tend to focus on social, physical, and material needs in clinical settings. These concerns may be overlooked by clinicians who do not recognize that the physical, social, material, and spiritual are intricately linked in cultures that view the individual from a holistic perspective.

Studies in resettlement countries show that mental health is influenced by pre- and post-migration experiences, and social determinants such as housing, employment, social exclusion/inclusion, and racism are critical for understanding the mental health of refugees (Kirmayer et al. 2011; Li et al. 2016; Riley et al. 2017; Yohani et al. 2019). As an example, in Canada, policies that accept refugee families using Western concepts of family units (i.e. immediate family) create the separation of family members as seen in the Case of Juliet. A compelling outcome of studies that focus on documenting rates of mental health disorders amongst refugees has been to highlight the impact of the post-migration environment on mental health. Along with previously mentioned research documenting impacts of racism and discrimination, are studies that show how restrictive policies for screening, processing, and service provision for asylum seekers further exacerbate symptoms of PTSD and depression in refugees (Asgary and Segar 2011; Robjant et al. 2004).

Ecological systems highlights contextual and intersectional factors in refugee mental health

A third, more recent perspective on refugee mental health, attends to contextual and intersectional factors that pose risks for developing mental health challenges and documents protective factors that may serve as buffers. These studies, frequently focused on resilience, are grounded in socio-ecological theories, primarily influenced by Bronfebrenner's (1992) ecological systems model. Studies on resilience document factors such as social supports, family bonds, and community connectedness as critical sites for understanding and responding to the mental health of refugee children (Betancourt and Khan 2008) and adults (e.g. Sim et al. 2019). In particular, Ungar's work highlighting resilience as involving a process that requires both macro system-level supports and the individual's ability to navigate and negotiate resources at the micro-level provides an important context for understanding refugee well-being (see Ungar 2011, 2018). While this has been a welcome direction in the refugee mental health discourse, recent concerns have been raised about the swing to overemphasize strengths without attending to the real challenges of historically marginalized groups within conflict and resettlement settings (Denov and Akeeson, 2017) and addressing issues such as stigmatization of mental health challenges (Shannon et al. 2015).

By steering the discussion away from either a medical or humanistic approach to refugee mental health, Silove (1999) had previously proposed attending to both by focusing on populations that need different types of care in post-conflict and resettlement settings. Existing research appears to support this notion, with most refugees responding to social supports, and a sub-group struggling with complex forms of PTSD (Nygaard et al. 2017) and severe mental illness such as schizophrenia (Anderson et al. 2015), requiring formal mental health supports. Other recent studies have highlighted the unique needs of groups, such as women facing gender-based violence (McMorrow and Saksena 2017). Proposing a step-wise community care model for refugees, Silove, Ventevogel and Rees (2017) recommend implementing social programs to address general levels of distress, while identifying and referring those with unique and severe mental healthcare needs to specialist services. The Adaptation and Development After Persecution and Trauma model illustrates this perspective by attending to the multiple psychosocial issues, stressors, and resources influencing communities that have experienced mass violence in conflict and post-conflict settings (Silove 2013). Silove identifies five psychosocial systems believed to incorporate the need for: (1) safety and security (2) bonds and networks (3), establishment of roles and identity, (4) justice, and (5) existential meaning and coherence. Extreme trauma and the refugee experience involving dislocation, flight, and resettlement challenge these adaptive and interdependent systems and can contribute to mental health difficulties (Silove 2013). Therefore, social and mental health difficulties are responses that occur when there are inadequate individual or social supports to facilitate adaptation after traumatic experiences. Silove and colleagues' (2017) community care model provides a useful framework for addressing these five psychosocial systems in primary, secondary, and tertiary prevention work with refugees.

Miller and Rasmussen's (2017) ecological model also attends to the social environments of refugees and the impact of daily stressors on mental health. Stressors such as isolation from family and other sources of support, unemployment, and unsafe living conditions contribute to mental health outcomes such as PTSD. Interventions aimed at reducing daily stressors are seen as avenues for addressing mental health rather than individualized trauma-focused interventions. This model also attends to specific subpopulations that need attending to due to historical marginalization and therefore increased vulnerability (i.e. women, children, seniors). These two ecological models show promise as contemporary models for understanding refugee mental health as they are based on an understanding of human agency while attending to external threats that can destabilize individual and social well-being.

Approaches to addressing mental health in refugees

Western vs. Indigenous systems of healing

Also operating within Western mental health models are studies that focus on interventions for addressing the mental health of refugees. While there is consensus that crisis-type interventions in the immediate aftermath of violence are not efficacious (Rodin and van Ommerman 2009), the general view is to utilize evidence-based interventions for the treatment of PTSD and other trauma-related disorders with refugees including Cognitive Behavioral Therapy (Buhman et al. 2016) and Narrative Exposure Therapy (Nuner et al. 2004). The Inter-Agency Standing Committee (IASC) *Guidelines for Mental Health and Psychosocial Support in Emergency Settings* (2007), UNHCR's (2013) *Operational Guidance for Mental Health and Psychosocial Support Programming for Refugee Operations*, and the World Health Organization's (2015) *mhGAP Humanitarian Intervention Guide (mhGAP- HIG)* currently serve as guidelines for implementing mental health supports for refugees outside countries of permanent resettlement.

A number of researchers have called for the inclusion of Indigenous knowledge systems into refugee mental health care responses. For example, Wessells (1999) cautioned that using Western lenses alone to understand experiences such as trauma and loss creates the risk of marginalizing local voices and cultural traditions, disempowering communities, and limiting healing. Despite this, Indigenous perspectives on the mental health of refugees from the various regions they represent remain understudied in mainstream mental health and even the refugee mental health literature. Likewise, there is little documentation of cross-cultural perceptions of trauma; likely because the term 'trauma' itself is a fairly recent concept that has become centered in Western mental health literature in the past 40 years. Counter-concerns are often raised regarding limited evidence of the effectiveness of Indigenous healing methods (Silove 1999). However, such concerns, when raised within a Western knowledge system, are themselves problematic and limited by the discourse within which the questions are asked. Cohen in this volume highlights the link between colonialism and suppression of Indigenous knowledge systems, and how these themes continue to play out in mental health practices whereby Eurocentric idioms of distress and healing are often valued over Indigenous models. Not surprisingly then, this is mirrored in refugee mental health literature.

Refugee counselling models

There are very few comprehensive counselling or intervention models focusing on refugees. The multilevel model of refugee counselling (MLM) is a promising framework that takes into consideration socio-political histories, trauma, losses associated with forced migration, cultural conceptualizations of mental illness, and resettlement stressors to develop culturally responsive interventions (Bemak and Chung 2008). Although this model is built on Western practices, it attempts to meet the various cultural and practical needs of refugees. The MLM consists of four levels of intervention that can be applied concurrently or independently. Level I: *mental health education* acknowledges the importance of familiarizing and increasing comfort with the psychotherapy process. Level II: *psychotherapy* consists of the counsellor developing an intervention plan based on the information collected at Level I. The literature on interventions used with refugee populations emphasizes the importance of using a range of modalities to address the diverse mental health needs, cultural worldviews, and manifestations of psychological concern (Ehntholt and Yule 2006). Thus, the interventions developed at this stage will integrate both Western and culturally relevant techniques. Level III: *cultural empowerment* takes into consideration the inherent difficulties in adapting to a new culture and the need for counsellors to advocate on behalf of their clients. Level IV: *integration of Western and Indigenous healing methodologies* if clients express interest in traditional healing methods or if their social network or socio-cultural background recommends it. Returning to Juliet's case, one can see elements of the MLM model, particularly Levels III and IV.

Juliet follows her dreams to reconnect to community

Counselling with Juliet utilized a developmental approach, focusing simultaneously on addressing her losses and traumatic stress-related symptoms and strengthening important skills that build on her resilience to prevent future victimization as a young woman in a new cultural context. Although she was being supported to achieve independent living, recognizing African cultural values of family and community connection, an important goal was also to find ways to reconnect Juliet back to her community in a manner that was safe and empowering for her. All counselling sessions were conducted in Swahili, Juliet's first language, and ongoing reference to cultural understandings and personal interpretations of experiences were incorporated in all work. The clinician consulted a number of times with a cultural broker from Juliet's ethno-cultural community without disclosing Juliet's identity.

One approach to working with Juliet involved exploring her dreams to give her a sense of her own internal wisdom towards her healing. This was identified because of the prominence of nightmares in her presentation, the fear they perpetuated, and the recognition of dreams within her culture. Using dreams as messengers, Juliet told her story of a repetitive dream where she sees dead bodies and hears crying. From this dream, Juliet was able to address her grief of losing her parents and siblings at a young age, and later being separated from her brother's family when he migrated to Canada. She was able to express both anger and sorrow she had been holding for a long time. Over the course of her counselling sessions, Juliet began having a different type of dream - dreams of herself singing spiritual songs. By following this dream, Juliet was able to give voice to her need for spiritual and social connection, and this led to supporting Juliet to reconnect to her ethno-cultural community by joining a church choir in her African community. Re-entering her community was an important step for Juliet to begin reconnecting to her culture, while reestablishing her identity and supports in a manner that was safe for her and socially acceptable within her community. Although it was a long journey towards reunification with her family, this was eventually achieved as Juliet understood and worked on grief associated with her traumatic losses with the support of her counsellor and church community.

Community-based healing approaches

Ethnographic approaches to understanding the mental health experiences of refugees provide some insight into how they perceive their mental health and well-being. These studies highlight cultural practices and spirituality as areas of interest and concern for refugee groups, both in conceptualizing mental health and pathways for coping and even recovery (Denov 2008, 2010; Mukamana and Brysiewicz 2008; Okraku and Yohani in press). Furthermore, studies within post-conflict settings show a variety of psychosocial and Indigenous responses. These include community development approaches to address daily life needs (UNHCR 2018), sociotherapy as seen with genocide survivors in Rwanda (Ritchers et al. 2008), testimony-based approaches (case vignette below) and the use of cleansing rituals with former child soldiers in Sierra Leone (Denov 2010), all which focus on restoration of relationships and reconnecting people to family and community. These studies provide insight into some of the Indigenous approaches to address healing after mass violence and uprooting, and the need for more research to better understand the range of Indigenous practices that support refugee mental health and well-being.

Healing through community commemoration ceremonies

In resettlement countries, migrants often facilitate cultural continuity and community support through the formation of community associations. For refugee communities, such groups can be important mechanisms for supporting healing as well. The Memory Keepers Association (MKA) is one such group in Canada that was formed specifically to attend to the issues and needs of survivors of the 1994 genocide against Tutsi of Rwanda. MKA provides Edmonton-based supports for survivors, works collaboratively with the broader Rwandan community, and organizes annual commemoration activities. During the commemoration ceremony, members of the survivor community who are ready, share their stories of loss and survival. These powerful testimonies are used to honor the memory of lost loved ones, to facilitate an individual's healing by truth-telling in the presence of witnesses, to support collective healing through the shared experience of witnessing, to educate about genocide, and to challenge counter-stories (denials of genocide). MKA in Edmonton has been working with the municipal government to create a commemoration plaque, thereby establishing a concrete location for members to congregate and remember their loved ones within then new country.

Future directions

The refugee experience is multifaceted. The resettlement process is equally complex. In most parts of the world, where recent civil unrest and conflict have taken place, there are complex social and political histories associated with these conflicts - which include colonialism whose impacts continue to reverberate to present-day experiences. Beyond the current emphasis on documenting the types and prevalence of mental health disorders experienced by refugees or documenting the types of protective factors, situating this knowledge within the unique socio-cultural contexts and histories of their lives is necessary – as these are often reflected in the concerns, meanings, and narratives of people who have been forced to migrate. Clinical training on refugee mental health should expand beyond identification of trauma and other mental health disorders, to facilitate an understanding of these complexities, and counteract the development of fixed and simplistic views of the experience of mass violence, conflict, and dislocation. Introducing holistic approaches to addressing mental health will counter notions that promote clinical treatment of the individual as the main pathway for addressing mental health. Training that encourages ongoing reflection on self, the profession, and broader influences on research and practice is important to uncover and unpack racialized, stereotyped and colonialized assumptions inherent in refugee mental health work. Likewise, practice relating to the mental health of refugees needs to apply both clinical and socio-cultural aspects of wellness. This includes incorporating practices that utilize cultural resources (Laurence et al. 2003), such as working with Indigenous healers (Bemak and Chung 2008) and community cultural brokers (Brar-Josan and Yohani 2014; Raval 2005). Finally, as noted earlier, there is a critical need for more research that examines concepts of mental health, wellness and trauma from diverse cultures represented by refugee groups. These will help elucidate the various healing approaches available for promoting mental wellness and addressing challenges.

Conclusion

Refugees encounter unique experiences in relation to mental health and well-being. Throughout the chapter, a case is used to illustrate how a young person navigates aspects of the refugee experience and mental health supports. The chapter critically discusses how changing patterns of forced migration evoke racialized attitudes and perceptions of refugees, and shape how they are received in temporary and permanent resettlement countries. By reviewing current research and conceptual models, the chapter examines the main discourses on mental health of refugees, the nature of challenges they encounter, and restoration of well-being.

References

Anderson, K. K., Cheng, J., Susser, E., McKenzie, K. J., and Kurdyak, P. (2015) 'Incidence of Psychotic Disorders among First-Generation Immigrants and Refugees in Ontario', *CMAJ*, 187(9): E279–E286.

Asgary, R. and Segar, N. (2011) 'Barriers to Healthcare Access among Refugee Asylum Seekers', *Journal of Healthcare for the Poor and Underserved*, 22: 506–522.

Bemak, F. and Chung, R. C. (2008) 'Counseling and Psychotherapy with Refugees'. In P. B. Pedersen, J. G. Draguns, W. J. Lonner, and J. E. Trimble (Eds.), *Counseling across Cultures* (6th ed., pp. 307–324). Thousand Oaks, CA: Sage.

Betancourt, T, S. and Khan, K. T. (2008) 'The Mental Health of Children Affected by Armed Conflict: Protective Processes and Pathways to Resilience', *International Review of Psychiatry*, 20: 317–328.

Betancourt, T. S., Newnham, E. A., Birman, D., Lee, R., Ellis, B. H., and Layne, C. M. (2017) 'Comparing Trauma Exposure, Mental Health Needs, and Service Utilization across Clinical Samples of Refugee, Immigrant, and US-Origin Children', *Journal of Traumatic Stress*, 30(3): 209–218.

Berry, J. W. (2001) 'A Psychology of Immigration', *Journal of Social Issues*, 57: 615–631.

Berry, J, W. and Hou, F. (2016) 'Immigrant Acculturation and Wellbeing in Canada', *Canadian Psychology*, 57: 254–264.

Brar-Josan, N. and Yohani, S. C. (2014) 'A Framework for Counsellor-Cultural Broker Collaboration', *Canadian Journal of Counselling & Psychotherapy*, 48(2): 81–99.

Brenner, Y. (2016, February 19) 'Refugees Go from Surviving War to Fighting PTSD'. Aljazeera America. Retrieved from http://america.aljazeera.com/articles/2016/2/19/refugees-go-from-surviving-war-to-fighting-ptsd.html.

Bronfebrenner, U. (1992) *Ecological Systems Theory*. London: Jessica Kingsley.

Buhman, C. B., Nordentoft, M., Ekstroem, M et al. (2016) 'The Effect of Flexible Cognitive-Behavioral Therapy and Medical Treatment, Including Anti-Depressants on Post-Traumatic Stress Disorder and Depression in Traumatized Refugees: Pragmatic Randomized Controlled Clinical Trail', *British Journal of Psychiatry*, 208: 252–259.

Coghlan, A. (2015, September 7) 'Refugees at Risk of Infection and Post Traumatic Stress Disorder', *New Scientist. Retrieved from* https://www.newscientist.com/article/dn28136-refugees-at-risk-of-measles-and-post-traumatic-stress-disorder/.

Colucci, E., Szwarc, J., Minas, H., Paxton, G., and Guerra, C. (2012) 'The Utilisation of Mental Health Services by Children and Young People from a Refugee Background: A Systematic Literature Review', *International Journal of Culture and Mental Health*, 7: 86–108.

de Fouchier, C., Blanchet, A., Hopkins, W., Bui, E., Ait-Aoudia, M., and Jehel, L. (2012) 'Validation of a French Adaptation of the Harvard Trauma Questionnaire among Torture Survivors from Sub-Saharan African Countries', *European Journal of Psychotraumatology*, 3(1), 19225.

de Jong, J. T., Komproe, I. H., van Ommeren, M. et al. (2001) 'Lifetime Events and Post Traumatic Stress Disorder in 4 Postconflict Settings', *JAMA*, 286: 555–562.

Denov, M. (2008) 'Girl Soldiers and Human Rights: Lessons from Angola, Mozambique, Sierra Leone and Northern Uganda', *The International Journal of Human Rights*, 5(12): 813–836.

Denov, M. (2010) 'Coping with the Trauma of War: Former Child Soldiers in Post-Conflict Sierra Leone', *International Social Work*, 53(6): 791–806.

Denov, M. and Akeeson, B. (2017) *Children Affected by Armed Conflict. Theory, Method, Practice.* New York: Columbia University Press.

Ehntholt, K. A. and Yule, W. (2006) 'Practitioner Review: Assessment and Treatment of Refugee Children and Adolescents Who Have Experienced War-Related Trauma', *Journal of Child Psychology and Psychiatry*, 47: 1197–1210.

Every, D. and Perry, R. (2014) 'The Relationship Between Perceived Religious Discrimination and Self-Esteem for Muslim Australians', *Australian Journal of Psychology*, 66: 241–248.

Fazel M., Wheeler J., and Danesh J. (2005) 'Prevalence of Serious Mental Disorder in 7000 Refugees Resettled in Western Countries: A Systematic Review', *Lancet*, 365(9467): 1309–1314.

Fekete, L. (2001) 'The Emergence of Xeno-Racism', *Race & Class*, 43(2): 23–40.

Foster, R. P. (2001) 'When Immigration is Trauma: Guidelines for the Individual and Family Clinician', *American Journal of Orthorpschiatry*, 71: 153–170.

Haslam N. and Holland E. (2012) 'Attitudes Towards Asylum Seekers: The Australian Experience'. In D. Bretherton and N. Balvin (Eds.), *Peace Psychology in Australia* (pp. 107–120). Boston, MA: Springer.

Hass, G. (2018) 'Understanding Psychopathology in Immigrant Population'. In J. N. Butcher and J. M. Hooley (Eds.), *APA Handbook of Psychopathology: Psychopathology: Understanding and Treating Adult Mental Disorders* (pp. 149–165). New York: American Psychological Association.

Honwana, A. (1997) 'Healing for Peace: Traditional Healers and Post-War Reconstruction in Southern Mozambique', *Peace and Conflict: Journal of Peace Psychology*, 3(3): 293–305.

Inter-Agency Standing Committee (IASC) (2007) *IASC Guidelines for Mental Health and Psychosocial Support in Emergency Settings*. Geneva: Inter-Agency Standing Committee.

International Organization for Migration (IOM) (2014) *IOM Outlook on Migration, Environment and Climate Change.* Geneva: International Organization for Migration.

Jackson, M. (2013) *The Politics of Storytelling. Violence. Variations on a Theme by Hannah Ardent* (2nd ed.). Copenahgen, Denmark: Museum Tusculanum Press.

Joris, W., d'Haenens, L., Van Gorp, B., and Mertens, S. (2018) 'The Refugee Crisis in Europe: A Frame Analysis of European Newspapers'. In S. F. Krishna-Hensel (Ed.), *Migrants, Refugees, and the Media* (pp. 59–80). London: Routledge.

Kirmayer, L. J., Narasiah, L., Munoz, M., Rashid, M., Ryde, A. G., Guzder, J., Hassan, G., Roussea, C., Pottie, K. (2011) 'Common Mental Health Problems in Immigrants and Refugees: General Approach in Primary Healthcare', *Canadian Medical Association Journal*, 183: E967.

Laurence J., Kirmayer, L. J., Groleau, D., Guzder, J., Blake, C., and Jarvis, E. (2003) 'Cultural Consultation: A Model of Mental Health Service for Multicultural Societies', *Canadian Journal of Psychiatry*, 48(3): 145–153.

Li, S. S., Liddell, B. J., and Nickerson, A. (2016) 'The Relationship between Post-Migration Stress and Psychological Disorders in Refugees and Asylum Seekers', *Current Psychiatry Reports*, 18: 82.

McHugh, R. K. and Barlow, D. H. (2010) 'The Dissemination and Implementation of Evidence-Based Psychological Treatments: A Review of Current Efforts', *American Psychologist*, 65(2), 73–84.

McMorrow, S. and Saksena, J. (2017) 'Voices and Views of Congolese Refugee Women: A Qualitative Exploration to Inform Health Promotion and Reduce Inequities', *Health Education & Behavior*, 44(5): 769–780.

Miller, K. and Rasmussen, A. (2017) 'The Mental Health of Civillians Displaced by Armed Conflict: An Ecological Model of Refugee Distress', *Epidemeological Psychiatry Science*, 26: 129–138.

Mollica, R. F., Donelan, K., and Tor, S. (1993) 'The Effect of Trauma and Confinement on Functional Health and Mental Health Status of Cambodians Living in Thailand–Cambodia Border Camps', *JAMA*, 270: 581–586.

Mollica, R. F. Sarajlic, N., Chernoff, M. et al. (2001) 'Longitudinal Study of Psychiatric Symptoms, Disability, Mortality, and Emigration among Bosnian Refugees', *JAMA*, 286: 546–554.

Mukamana, D. and Brysiewicz, P. (2008) 'The Lived Experience of Genocide Rape Survivors of Rwanda', *Journal of Nursing Scholarship* 40(4): 379–384.

Nuner, F., Schauer, M., Klaschik, C, et al. (2004) 'A Comparison of Narrative Exposure Therapy, Supportive Counselling, and Psychoeducation for Treating Posttraumatic Stress Disorder in an African Refugee Settlement', *Journal of Consulting Clinical Psychology*, 72: 579.

Nygaard, M., Sonne, C., and Carlsson, J. (2017) 'Secondary Psychotic Features in Refugees Diagnosed with Post Traumatic Stress Disorder: A Retrospective Cohort Study', *BMC Psychiatry*, 17: 5.

O'Connell, M. (2005) 'Economic Forces and Anti-Immigrant Attitudes in Western Europe: A Paradox in Search for an Explanation', *Patterns of Prejudice*, 39: 60–74.

Okraku, O. and Yohani, S. (in press). 'Resilience in the Face of Adversity: A Focused Ethnography of Liberian Former Girl Child Soldiers Living in Ghana' *Journal of International Migration & Integration*.

Piwowarczyk, L. A. and Keane, T. M. (2007) 'Impact of September 11 on Refugees and Those Seeking Asylum' *Transcultural Psychiatry*, 44: 566–580.

Prendes-Lintel, M. (2001) 'A Working Model in Counseling Recent Refugees'. In J. G. Ponterotto, J. M. Casas, L. A. Suzuki, and C. M. Alexander (Eds.), *Handbook of Multicultural Counseling* (2nd ed.) (pp.729–752). Thousand Oaks, CA: Sage.

Priebe, S., Giacco, D., and El-Nagib, R. (2016) *Public Health Aspects of Mental Health among Migrants and Refugees: A Review of the Evidence on Mental Health Care of Refugees, Asylum Seekers, and Irregular Migrants in the WHO European Region.* Copenhagen: WHO Regional Office for Europe.

Raval, H. (2005) 'Being Heard and Understood in the Context of Seeking Asylum and Refuge: Communicating with the Help of Bilingual Co-Workers', *Clinical Child Psychology and Psychiatry*, 10: 197–216.

Riley, A., Varner, A., Ventevogel, P. Hassan, M., and Whelton-Mitchell, C. (2017) 'Daily Stressors, Trauma Exposure, and Mental Health among Stateless Rohingya Refugees in Bangaladesh', *Transcultural Psychiatry*, 54(3): 304–331.

Ritchers, A., Dekker, C., and Scholte, W. C. (2008) 'Community Based Sociotherapy in Byumba, Rwanda', *Intervention*, 6: 100–116.

Robjant, K., Hassan, R., and Katona, C. (2004) 'Mental Health Implications of Detaining Asylum Seekers: Systematic Review', *British Journal of Psychiatry*, 1994: 306–312.

Rodin, D. and van Ommerman, M. (2009) 'Commentary: Explaining Enourmous Variation in Rates of Disorder in Trauma-Focused Psychiatric Epidemiology after Major Emergencies', *International Journal of Epidemeology*, 38: 1045–1048.

Shannon, P. J., Wieling, E., Simmelink-McCleary, J., and Becher, E. (2015) 'Beyond Stigma: Barriers to Discussing Mental Health in Refugee Populations', *Journal of Loss and Trauma*, 20(3): 281–296.

Silove, D. (1999) 'The Psychosocial Effects of Torture, Mass Human Rights Violations, and Refugee Trauma: Toward an Integrated Conceptual Framework', *The Journal of Nervous and Mental Disease*, 187(4): 200–207.

Silove, D. (2013) 'The ADAPT Model: A Conceptual Framework for the Mental Health and Psychosocial Programming in Post Conflict Settings', *Intervention*, 11: 237–248.

Silove, D., Ventevogel, P., and Rees, S. (2017) 'The Contemporary Refugee Crisis: An Overview of Mental Health Challenges'. *World Psychiatry*, 16: 130–139.

Sim, A., Bowes, L., and Gardner, F. (2019) 'The Promotive Effects of Social Support for Parental Resilience in a Refugee Context: A Cross-Sectional Study with Syrian Mothers in Lebanon', *Prevention Science*, 1–10.

Steel, Z., Chey, T., and Silove, D. (2009) 'Association of Torture and Other Potentially Traumatic Events with Mental Health Outcomes among Populations Exposure to Mass Conflict and Displacement' *JAMA*, 302: 537–549.

Summerfield, D. A. (2004) 'Cross-Cultural Perspectives on the Medicalization of Human Suffering'. In G. M. Rosen (Ed.), *Posttraumatic Stress Disorder: Issues and Controversies* (pp. 233–245). Chichester: Wiley.

Turrini, G., Purgato, M., Ballette, F., Nosè, M., Ostuzzi, G., and Barbui, C. (2017) 'Common Mental Disorders in Asylum Seekers and Refugees: Umbrella Review of Prevalence and Intervention Studies', *International Journal of Mental Health Systems*, 11(51): 1–14.

Ungar, M. (2011) 'The Social Ecology of Resilience: Addressing Contextual and Cultural Ambiguity of a Nascent Construct'. *American Journal of Orthopsychiatry* 81(1):1– 17. https://doi.org/10.1111/j.1939-0025.2010.01067.x.

Ungar, M. (2018) 'Systemic Resileince: Princples and Processes for a Science of Change in Contexts of Adversity'. *Ecology and Society*, 23(4): 34. https://doi.org/10.5751/ES-10385–230434.

United Nations. (1951) *Convention and Protocol Relating to the Status of Refugees*. Retrieved from www.unhcr.org/3b66c2aa10.html.

United Nations High Commissioner for Refugees (UNHCR) (2007) *Basic Facts: Refugee*. Retrieved from http://ukr.unhcr.org.ua/unhcr_mol/main.php?article_id=83&view=full.

United Nations High Commissioner for Refugees (UNHCR) (2010) Convention and Protocol Relating to the Status of Refugees. Retrieved from www.unhcr.org/3b66c2aa10.

United Nations High Commissioner for Refugees (UNHCR) (2013) *Operational Guidance. Mental Health and Psychosocial Support Programming for Refugee Operations.* Geneva: United Nations High Commissioner for Refugees.

United Nations High Commissioner for Refugees (UNHCR). (2017) *Figures at a Glance. Statistical Yearbook*. Retrieved from www.unhcr.org/figures-at-a-glance.html.

United Nations High Commissioner for Refugees (UNHCR) (2018) *Community-Based Protection and Mental Health & Psychosocial Support*. Geneva: United Nations High Commissioner for Refugees.

Wessells, M. G. (1999) 'Culture, Power, and Community: Intercultural Approaches to Psychosocial Assistance and Healing'. In K. Nader, N. Dubrow, and B. A. Stamm (Eds.), *Honoring Differences, Cultural issues in the Treatment of Trauma and Loss* (pp. 267–282). Philadelphia, PA: Brunner/Manzel.

Williams, D. R. and Mohammed, S. A. (2009) 'Discrimination and Racial Disparities in Health: Evidence and Needed Research', *Journal of Behavioral Medicine*, 32: 20–47.

World Health Organization (2015) *mhGAP Humanitarian Intervention Guide (mhGAP-HIG): Clinical Management of Mental, Neurological, and Substance Use Conditions in Humanitarian Emergencies'*, Geneva: World Health Organization.

Yohani, S. C. (2015) 'Applying the ADAPT Psychosocial Model to War Affected Children and Adolescents', *SAGE Open July-September*, 1–18.

Yohani, S., Kirova, A., Georgis, R., Gokiert, R., Mejia, T., and Chiu, Y. (2019) 'Cultural Brokering with Syrian Refugee Families with Young Children: An Exploration of Challenges and Best Practices in Psychosocial Adaptation', *Journal of International Migration & Integration*. Published on-line January 25, 2019 at https://doi.org/10.1007/s12134-019-00651-6

PART F

Culture and mental health in a global context

28

CULTURE AND MENTAL HEALTH IN BRAZIL

Francisco Ortega and Leandro David Wenceslau

Major debates in psychiatry gravitate around controversies on the universality or specificity of mental disorders and their symptoms. Global Mental Health (GMH) initiatives have lent new meaning to these polemics. Critics accuse GMH of exporting a Western model of illness and treatment, underrating the role of practitioners of traditional therapies, ignoring cultural variability in comprehending and responding to mental suffering, and medicalizing distress and ignoring its social and economic causes in low and middle-income countries (Summerfield 2012).

Central aspect of this controversy involves cultural aspects of mental health care. This chapter explores the role of culture within mental health policies and practices in Brazil. We argue that despite the existence of ethnic, racial, gender and religious differences several scholars define cultural uniformity as the main characteristic of Brazilian people. The singularity and difference of the process of cultural identity constitution in Brazil and the favor of class stratification and socioeconomic inequality over cultural diversity account for the low relevance of the cultural dimension for the Brazilian mental health field, here called the 'silencing of culture'.

After an overview of the history of mental health and of the Indigenous and traditional healers and healing in the country, we examine the possible historical roots of this process and some recent experiences in public mental health care in the country, which incorporate cultural analysis. The development of cultural analyses within Brazilian mental health may enrich our understanding of the complexity of the issues involving the care of mental health in global times.

Demographics and brief history of mental health in Brazil

The Federative Republic of Brazil is the largest country in South America, and the fifth largest country in terms of population and size. The current population estimate for 2018 is 210.87 million. Brazil's census addresses ethnicity and race by categorizing people mainly by skin color. Brazilians are asked to report whether they believe they are white, black, brown, yellow, or Indigenous. The results of the census indicated that 92 million (48%) Brazilians were white, 83 million (44%) were brown, 13 million (7%) were black, 1.1 million (0.50%) were yellow and 536,000 (0.25%) were Indigenous. This method of classifying race is controversial within Brazil, and the Brazilian Institute of Geography and Statistics (IBGE) has been criticized for continuing to use it.[1]

341

Brief history of mental health care in Brazil

In colonial times mental health patients in precarious financial conditions were allowed to wander in the streets, the countryside and other public spaces. This fact aroused criticisms and complaints by more educated sectors of the population. Those who exhibit violent behavior were placed in hospitals and prisons at their treatment was degrading. Hospitals part of *Irmandades das Santas Casas de Misericórdia* sheltered these patients under very poor sanitary conditions and they were all mixed up without concern for their individual conditions. Mental health professionals were inexistent and most care was provided by healers of all types, including catholic priests (especially Jesuits) (Machado et al. 1978; Resende 1990).

In 1830, the newly created Society of Medicine and Surgery launches a new slogan: "the madmen the asylum". The asylum, considered at the time the main therapeutic instrument of psychiatry, represented a hygienic and disciplinary criticism to the institutions of enclosure and an instrument to deal with deviant population (Machado et al. 1978). Inspired by the French model, the first national public mental asylum, the *Hospício Dom Pedro II* in Rio de Janeiro was inaugurated in 1852. The rise of the asylum in Brazil did not directly result in the management of madness by the medical body and in the institutionalization of psychiatry in Brazil (Meyer, 2017). With the proclamation of the Republic in 1889 the asylum became the exclusive responsibility of medical institutions. This period was defined by the medicalization of madness, treated in asylums and agricultural colonies (Fonte 2012; Resende 1990).

The 1920s are characterized by the influence of eugenic principles in Brazilian psychiatry. In 1923 the Brazilian League of Mental Hygiene (LBHM) was constituted and advanced eugenic, xenophobic, anti-liberal and racist actions and discourses (Costa 2007).

During the 1940s and 1950s several public psychiatric hospitals were established in the country. However, the situation at those institutions was chaotic, defined by total abandonment and an excess of hospitalized patients. In the 1960s the military government enabled the emergence of a "madness industry" (Fonte 2012) which privatized mental health care. In the 1970s the madness industry underwent heavy criticism due to the violence, mistreatment and torture practiced in Brazilian asylums.

The rise of the psychiatric reform was linked to the Brazilian health care reform initiated at the end of the 1970s and resulted from a significant social mobilization (Fleury, 2011). For the health care reform, the issue of citizenship merged with that of universal health care access and culminated in the creation of the Brazilian Unified Health System (SUS, *Sistema Único de Saúde*) in the Constitution of 1988 (Paim et al. 2011).

The Brazilian psychiatric reform originated in 1978 in the context of the re-democratization of the country. Mental health workers, together with trade unions and left-wing politicians, advanced the so-called 'anti-asylum struggle' movement in 1987 and criticized the collaboration of the psychiatric establishment with the dictatorship. Also in 1989, the first Psychosocial Care Center (*Centro de Atenção Psicossocial* – CAPS) was established in São Paulo and in the same year some psychiatric hospitals were closed down. The key historical milestone in the Brazilian Psychiatric Reform is the Caracas Declaration (1990), which set up the guidelines for the shift in mental health care from a hospital-oriented system to primary health care, promoting alternative, community-centered treatment. In 2001, the Psychiatric Reform Law was approved, which guards the protection and rights of those with mental disorders and redirects the model of care in mental health.

The theoretical framework of the Brazilian psychiatry reform corresponds to the so-called Psychosocial Care Paradigm. Although frequently reduced to the shift of mental health care services model from asylums to community mental health care, it is considered an epistemological turn in the mental health field. Human suffering is addressed in its complexity as part of a psychosocial dynamics which explores the sociopolitical mechanisms underlying the labels of normality and sanity (Yasui, Luzio and Amarante 2016).

Indigenous and traditional healers and healing

Anthropologist Eduardo Menéndez (2003) describes a plurality of care practices common to several Latin American countries. In addition to biomedicine, they comprise "alternative practices" (New Age and related practices, which rely on the care supplied by Bioenergy and New Religion healers), "non-biomedical" academic traditions (acupuncture, Chinese and Ayurveda medicines), and the proper "traditional", "Indigenous" or "popular" healing practices. The latter rely on the work of traditional healers such as sorcerers and shamans, and also on healers from Neopentecostals and charismatic religions. Traditional, Indigenous or popular healing practices include healers from Afro-Brazilian religions and healing practices within Spiritism. Hence, we will briefly describe in this section Indigenous, Afro-Brazilian, Kardecist Spiritist and Neopentecostal healing practices and traditions.

Although Indigenous peoples constitute a relatively small proportion of the total Brazilian population (between 0.02% and 0.04%), their presence is prominent in the social imaginary, as well as in public policies resulting from their constitutional rights to territory, health and culture (Langdon and Garnelo 2017). To analyze Indigenous healing, Brazilian anthropologists draw on the notion of models of *autoatención* (self-care models), i.e. "the representations and practices used by the population at individual and social levels to diagnose, explain, attend, control, alleviate, endure, cure, solve or prevent processes that affect their health in real or imaginary terms" (Menendez 2003: 198). Practices of *autoatención* within Indigenous contexts include healing, initiation, puberty and funeral rites. They also comprise massages, medicinal herbs, baths, and biomedical practices. Indigenous healing engages not only *curandeiros* (traditional healers) and *rezadores* (traditional prayers) but also Neopentecostal churches and Spiritist centers (Silva, Langdon and Ribas 2013).

In the Amazonian context shamanism plays a special role as privileged healing practice. It constitutes a widespread knowledge expressed through shared practices that reflect cultural notions of body and personhood. Healers, called *pajés* or *sacacas* circulate between different worlds and relate to different beings that can cause illnesses (Scopel, Dias-Scopel and Langdon 2015).

Indigenous people in Brazil appropriate and articulate the therapeutic options available according to their needs. Such medical pluralism assumes contact zones between biomedical and Indigenous practices: contexts of *intermedicalidade* (intermedicality) that stresses the agency of Indigenous people in the construction of sociomedical realities (Langdon and Garnelo 2017).

Despite the existence since 2002 of a National Policy for Healthcare of Indigenous Peoples, it does not really engage with their healing traditions. Those policies are marked "by a high degree of standardization of rigid prescriptive technical norms, whose strictly biomedical nature makes them impervious to local contexts and singularities" (Langdon and Garnelo 2017: 461). Moreover, there is a widespread understanding among professionals and policymakers that Indigenous cultures and healing traditions constitute an obstacle to proper biomedical health care delivery.

Therefore, primary care interventions for Indigenous peoples largely reproduce reductionist biomedical understandings of individual personhood and corporeality. This is particularly relevant for the mental health field. Indigenous peoples perceive mental suffering not as individual biological conditions but as physic-moral afflictions provoked by social conflicts, taboo-break or vulnerability to spirit assaults (Silva, Langdon and Ribas 2013). Beyond biomedical accounts, highly prevalent mental health problems among Indigenous communities in Brazil such as alcohol abuse or suicide call for complex explanations that presuppose the knowledge of the cultural, social, economic and political background and the inclusion of Indigenous healing practices (Langdon and Garnelo 2017).

Candomblé and *Umbanda* are the more popular Afro-Brazilian religions. *Candomblé* originated at the beginning of the 19th century among enslaved Africans who were transferred to Brazil during the slave trade (Mota and Bonfim 2011). *Umbanda* emerged at the beginning of the 20th century and blends Candomblé with Roman Catholicism, Spiritism, and Indigenous beliefs.

Debates around the legitimacy and legality of alternative healing practices, such as Candomblé and Umbanda accompany the process of institutionalization of Brazilian medicine since its establishment around 1830. By the end of nineteenth century the question of "quackery" was a hotly debated issue in medical journals. Candomblé, Umbanda, Kardecist Spiritism and homeopathy, now typified as magical healing practices, were considered as threat to the social order and repressed by the police (Almeida, Oda and Dalgalarrondo 2007; Puttini 2008). During the first half of the twentieth century the phenomena of trance and possession aroused great interest of the Brazilian psychiatric community, generating diverse postures. Mostly considered them as harmful to mental health, fraud, and exploitation of public credulity. Particularly the psychiatric community in Rio de Janeiro and São Paulo emphasized the role of mediumistic religions as a cause of madness, while some psychiatrists in Bahia and Pernambuco advanced a more anthropological and nuanced vision (Almeida, Oda and Dalgalarrondo 2007).

Candomblé and Umbanda's notion of health assumes the balance between various instances: body-mind-social-spiritual or *muntu-muntuê-bantu-ntu*. Both religions aim at reestablishing the *axé [/ nguzu]* vital force in the followers and other visitors of the *terreiro*. At the origin of any disease are situations of vulnerability, which indicate that the body is open, being able to lose *axé* and receive negative energies. The dichotomy between spiritual and organic illness is a dynamic and flexible frontier. Treatments can range from the use of herbal remedies, rites and sacrifices of cleansing and purification, to blessings and offerings to the *orishas* (Rabelo, Motta and Nunes 2002). Afro-Brazilian healing traditions also exhibit a therapeutic pluralism that includes the biomedical model and it is common in Brazil that users of public or private health services resort to Candomblé or Umbanda practices, during or even after treatment. The religious alternative is seen as an enhancer of medical treatment (Mota and Trad 2011).

Kardecist Spiritism shares with Candomblé and Umbanda the centrality of trance experiences. Kardecist spiritism was created by the French educator Allan Kardec, in 1857 and it arrived in Brazil around 1860. Today, Brazil brings together the largest number of spiritists in the world. It is the third largest religious group in the country, after Catholics and Neopentecostals, and has around 3.8 million believers. It is a middle-class religion, strongly associated with the practice of charity. Spiritists maintain asylums, orphanages, and schools for poor people.

In 19th century Brazil the intellectual and scientific community sought to purge any reference to religion and spirituality. There were cases of criminalization of mediums, labelled as "profiteers", "fraudsters" or mentally ill. Thus, the conflict within the medical body was intense; while some tolerated Spiritist doctrine and sought to study and even use Spiritist therapy in the treatment of their patients, others simply labelled Spiritist practices as mere quackery (Almeida, Oda and Dalgalarrondo 2007).

Specifically regarding madness and accompanying the institutionalization of Brazilian psychiatry Spiritist institutions developed therapies based on the belief that spiritual entities would have the capacity to intervene in the natural course of the disease (Jabert 2011). For kardecism, all mental disorders were understood as deviations from reason or morality, being explained as resulting from the persecutory action of disincarnated spirits. In this sense, the best treatment strategy to be employed would be the use of a medium who would seek to persuade the obsessing spirit to abandon the persecution of the alienated. As a result of these precepts, followers of kardecism eventually sponsored the creation of several asylums for the treatment of the alienated in Brazil in the first half of the twentieth century (Jabert 2011; Rabelo, Motta, and Nunes 2002).

Neopentecostal religion is Brazil's second largest religion after Catholicism. Twenty-five percent of Brazilians are Protestants, of which 19% are followers of Neopentecostal denominations. Although it does not form a homogenous movement, Neopentecostalism is based on the Theology of Prosperity and Health, which has subverted the logic of so-called salvation religions. Through the magicization of its rituals, it rehabilitated the body as the place of the manifestation of divine intervention. Neopentecostal religion and healing practices share some elements with Afro-Brazilian religions, such as the central role of religious trance, in which the body is taken by one or several spiritual entities. Well-being of the body and war on disease are central elements for Neopentecostal healing practices. The ritual of exorcism aims at extirpating the disease and healing the body. As a result, demons - often linked to entities of Afro-Brazilian religions - that cause the disease are expelled from it. Healing in this way is not just casting out demons. It is part of a broader project of liberation that involves a reorientation of life according to the principles of faith (Rabelo, Motta and Nunes 2002).

Cultural representations of illness and wellness in Brazil

There is abundant evidence that culture contributes to structural inequalities and the distribution of health problems and resources in a population. It also influences cause, course and outcome of mental disorders, as well as explanations for mental distress. Additionally, it determines individual and family coping and adaptation to illness and recovery, and provides support for the clinician-patient relationship and tools to the clinician to interpret symptoms that lead to appropriate and culturally meaningful interventions (Kirmayer and Swartz 2014).

Hence the interest in studies that assess these interventions, for example involving community-based leaders, groups, and health workers and adaptation of protocols to specific local characteristics. Although Brazil boasts an important production of qualitative studies in mental health (Souza et al. 2012), the analyses of cultural differences and cultural competence have so far not impacted the field in a relevant way.

In fact, Brazil, a continental country with one single 'official' language and with a history of migration, strong assimilation and miscegenation tends to think of itself as having a homogeneous national cultural identity which downplays and/or naturalizes racial, ethnic, gender and religious diversity.

In his book *O povo brasileiro* (The Brazilian People) Brazilian anthropologist Darcy Ribeiro (2000) defines "cultural uniformity" as the most important consequence of the formation process of the Brazilian people as an ethnically homogeneous nation, a national ethnicity that integrates cultural, racial, ethnic and regional differences. Despite its cultural uniformity, Brazil is a deeply stratified society. For him, fundamental divisions are not those of culture, ethnicity of language, but those of class. Several scholars have criticized Ribeiro's idealized view of Brazilian ethnic unity. They have stressed Brazil's multifaceted diversity of Indigenous and of former slaves - the *quilombos* - as well as that of the believers in a multitude of religious denominations, and of people of Japanese and Arab descent among others. The issue of miscegenation is the most contested matter, since some scholars see in Ribeiro's writings on race the reproduction of the "most authoritarian standards of patriarchy and the ideology of whiteness" (Nascimento 2007: 56). Thus, an extensive body of research seems to undermine the ideal of cultural and

Francisco Ortega et al.

ethnic uniformity and stresses the presence of ethnic, racial, gender and religious differences and their embodiment in modes of exclusion and segregation (Burdick 1999; Kulick 1997).

The ongoing debate around racial differences, identity politics and multiculturalism in Brazil reverberate in Brazilian mental health care and policies.[2] To tackle the place of cultural differences within mental health one has to go back to Ribeiro himself, who did not negate the existence of cultural differences; he simply says that they underlie (or are secondary to) the more fundamental difference, i.e. the class difference. And precisely the Brazilian Psychiatric Reform which emerged in the context of the resistance to the military dictatorship and the following process of re-democratization, echoes Ribeiro's argument and privileges class stratification and socioeconomic inequality to cultural diversity. Hence, if Brazilian Psychiatric Reform took Marxist psychiatry seriously and did not exhibit the same enthusiasm for multicultural psychiatry, this has to do with the difference and singularity of the process of national identity constitution in Brazil.

Sociocultural debates that challenge the question of racial democracy have so far not informed the field of mental health care in the country and there is no discussion of care policies which consider gender, ethnic or race differences. Despite the existence of special health care policies for socially vulnerable populations (black, Indigenous and LGBT populations), they occupy a marginal place, with weak legal basis and minor financing support, contributing to worse health outcomes for these populations (Boccolini and Souza Junior 2016; Werneck 2016).

The 'silencing' of culture

Notwithstanding the existence of special health care policies for socially vulnerable populations in SUS, the significance of 'cultural differences' for causes, courses and outcomes as well as cultural explanations for mental distress were incorporated neither into mental health policies nor into professionals' practice. Thus, Lima and Oliveira Nunes complain of the

> inadequacy of the psychological techniques (…) due to the psychological structure of the users, the unusual expressions of suffering, the socioeconomic conditions of the population, and especially the users' distance from an intimate and introspective style to express emotions and feelings.
>
> *(Lima and Oliveira Nunes 2006: 300)*

Scholars criticize psychological approaches that focus exclusively on subjective and intersubjective dimensions, which deprives health conditions from its social and cultural determinants (Ibid.). In this framework, cultural diversity is frequently negated, naturalized or relativized. There is often contempt toward popular beliefs and culture, regarded as obscurantist, rough, and less sophisticated (Oliveira Nunes 2009).

The most obvious example of the 'silencing' of culture is the issue of religious beliefs and practices and their role within mental health services and interventions. From an academic point of view, there is still very little research being conducted on religion and mental health in Brazil and it lacks consistent articulation between empirical data and theoretical analysis (Dalgalarrondo 2007). The significance of religious practices as therapeutic agency among Brazilian urban popular classes has been acknowledged in the literature (Redko 2003). In spite of these findings mental health professionals tend to adopt reductionist views of the relationship between religious beliefs and behaviors and mental distress (Oliveira Nunes 2009; Lima and Oliveira Nunes 2006).

Mental health professionals report the necessity of cultural adaptation to deal with users from the lower classes, given their scarce symbolic, cognitive and communicative resources. The underlying sociopolitical and cultural issues are seldom addressed, and professionals acknowledge their prejudices when dealing with lower classes. On the other hand, individuals from the popular classes find alternative ways to deal with their mental distress in Pentecostal churches and Umbanda centers. Those therapeutic alternatives are more attuned to their notions of personhood and ways to alleviate the manifestations of suffering and distress (Fonseca 2009).

Contemporary mental health practices in Brazil

Despite the neglect of cultural diversity there has been, since the 1980s, an ongoing problematization and concern with the mental distress of the popular classes. The debate around the social and cultural differences between professionals and service users basically orbited around the notion of the '*nervoso*'. *Doença dos nervos* was considered the most common cultural idiom of distress among Brazilian lower classes. It emphasized social and cultural dimensions of mental suffering (Duarte 1988).

As an illustration of *doença de nervos*, 22 interviews were conducted by a psychologist in a primary care facility in Natal, a big city in Northeast Brazil with Maria, a 38-year-old married woman and housewife with a specific complaint of *doença de nervos*. Her anxieties were associated to her financial situation and the existential insecurity. During the first interviews the professional notices a diffuse condition and Maria's attempt to clarify her feelings. "When I go to sleep, I feel that thing shaking, I shudder ...", and she continues, "I just know that I was falling asleep (…) and I wake up because of this tremble that I feel, (…) and I get a lethargy (*leseira*) in my head, I can't even explain it" (Traverso-Yépez and Medeiros 2004: 98).

Doença de nervos is precisely characterized by the multiplicity of symptoms, which brings different sensations that disturb and interfere in Mary's daily routine. When Mary started to speak freely about her suffering her narrative evolved from focusing on symptoms multiplicity to an attention to family relationships, domestic and everyday life. The dialogical process generated narratives in which suffering was progressively associated to the social and structural limitations of her life-context. Although they are structural problems of difficult solution it is important to emphasize the importance of this dialogical practice, in which the participant can be actively involved in producing changes in her daily life. This case study ratifies the considerations of *doença de nervos* as a complex problem, which brings significant suffering to the complainant in a context of profound socio-structural constraints.

Brazilian scholars argue that the expression of mental distress as located in the body and articulated through the idiom of the *doença de nervos* defied professionals' assumptions that located suffering within the individual subject, at the level of her feelings, desires and thoughts. Professionals frequently assumed that popular classes shared the same world view, had the same representations of health, disease and personhood. As a consequence, social problems tended to be psychologized, leaving aside the sociocultural, historical and political determinants of their behavior (Lima and Oliveira Nunes 2006).

We would like in the last part of this section to describe briefly two experiences of intercultural competence and sensitization which take into account the diversity of symbolic and therapeutic systems, as well as conceptions of mental suffering: the role of the community health workers (ACS, *agentes comunitários de saúde*) and the Community Therapy (CT, *terapia comunitária* or *terapia comunitaria integrativa*). They are experiences of primary mental health care that valorize local culture and favor the constitution and strengthening of local support networks.

Community health workers

Community health workers (ACS) have a leading role within the Family Health Strategy (ESF, Estratégia Saúde da Família), the primary health care model adopted by SUS (Brasil 2012). The ACS should enable the interaction between ESF teams and communities and must live in the territory they assist. They carry out regular home visits, monitor health indicators, and develop health promotion and disease prevention, mainly through educational practices.

Community health workers assume the role of mediators between local cultural idioms and lifestyles and biomedical knowledge. This role makes the ACS a social actor who mobilizes contradictions and at the same time establishes a deep dialogue between these two worldviews. (Lara, Brito, and Rezende 2012).

ACS know personally everyone they care for personally, where and how they live, and which are their major health complaints. Through home visits and health education groups, ACS draw on their knowledge of the cultural idioms, customs and local or private beliefs of the community to facilitate the communication with health professionals. That guidance often demands some form of translation between biomedical and popular worldviews (Lara, Brito, and Rezende 2012). ACS therefore exhibit important intercultural competence that turns them indispensable actors to effectively engage with patients' and communities' cultural backgrounds, values and beliefs. However, this mediation role also leads to situations in which upholding this dual identity brings uncertainty and difficulties. On the one hand, ACS have incorporated into their practice principles and strategic tools in line with the psychiatric reform and the expansion of mental health in primary care. On the other hand, community workers have major difficulties in dealing with mental health issues. They show prejudice regarding mental disorders and, although they recognize the importance of working with patients and their families, they do not feel prepared to provide adequate care (Waidman, Costa, and Paiano 2012).

Community therapy

Brazilian Community Therapy (CT) or was initiated in the 1990s by psychiatrist Adalberto Barreto in Fortaleza, Northeastern Brazil. Its theoretical basis is rooted in systemic theory, communication theory, Paulo Freire's pedagogy, cultural anthropology and resilience theories (Barreto 2005).

Each Community Therapy session – also called *roda* – consists of six phases: welcoming, selecting a theme, contextualization, problematization, closing and appreciation. Every stage has a specific progression and sequence of actions, leading participants to observe themselves through accounts of personal experiences (Barreto, 2005). After the welcoming, in which the rules of CT are explained and some jokes or engaging exercises are introduced, one topic is chosen through a vote among the possible issues raised by the participants. During the contextualizing step, the person who proposed the topic is invited to give more details about her situation and feelings.

Problematization starts with the CT therapist's key question addressed to the group for discussion. Everyone may become aware of the many possible outcomes and solutions, promoting resilience and self-esteem. The closing ritual and appreciation phases will consolidate links between participants and highlight what they have learnt from the group. The evaluation enables the facilitators to have a critical view on the session and collect data for further research. (Barreto 2005).

It is important to highlight that CT is a social intervention addressed to the community that has demonstrated efficacy in mental health promotion within primary mental health care, and helps mental health professionals to grasp the emotional conflicts within individuals, families and community. It constitutes a privileged space to convey social support, strengthen emotional bonds, consolidate social networks, diminish social exclusion and stigma and enhance individual and group resilience (Rocha et al. 2013).

As an illustration, 14 CAPS users with severe mental disorders and 8 relatives participated in weekly CT sessions, which took place in a CAPS in João Pessoa, Northeast of Brazil. Among the main problems related by the users were family conflicts, abandonment, rejection, stigma, financial difficulties and low self-esteem resulting in lack of motivation and social withdrawal. The participation in CT sessions was very important since it positively influenced the individual self-perception. One participant states, "Here I feel important, because people listen to me and respect me when I have something to speak" (Ferreira Filha and Carvalho 2010: 237). CT contributes to the social inclusion of participants, improving family and affective relationships and reducing stigma. Asked if the CT changed their life, a participant observed, "therapy helped me to get rid of my shame, because I learned from others that I should be not ashamed of my illness" (Ibid. 238).

Mental, physical and spiritual balance is achieved through a systemic approach, that draws on the participants' beliefs and cultural values. The experience of developing CT in CAPS produced good therapeutic outcomes after two years of its introduction. Participants consider CT a cozy space, where everyone shares her feelings and which values the individual history and cultural identity, restoring self-esteem and self-confidence.

Respect for cultural diversity and the multiplicity of contexts and local knowledges and practices are therefore among the main features of CT. It valorizes the cultural heritage of Indigenous, African, Oriental and European ancestors. Moreover, CT mobilizes local cultural resources which contribute to its success, attracting people to take part in the *roda* and disinhibiting participants to express their suffering. Those resources strengthen community and social bonds and help participants to resignify their suffering. Music and traditional sayings are CT's fundamental tools to embrace pain, stimulate resilience and to provide a feeling of belonging and inclusion in the community (Oliveira and Ferreira Filha 2011).

Future directions

Diverse political, socioeconomic and cultural factors within Brazilian society point to the need of a closer attention to cultural determinants in mental health policies and practices. Among them one can mention the following three: First, the growing number of migrants and refugees in Brazil from Haiti, Syria, Colombia, Republic of Congo, Bolivia and, more recently, Venezuela demands the development of intercultural and structural competences when dealing with the mental suffering of that population. Beyond the situation of poverty, social suffering and structural violence common to both migrants and poor Brazilians, there are cultural specificities when dealing with the mental health of migrants and refugees that have to be addressed by professionals and policies in the country.

Second, the already mentioned issue of Indigenous mental health. Despite the existence of policies for mental health care of Indigenous people in Brazil, there are cultural aspects involved in mental health care of that population that demand special attention from mental health professionals and policies. Research conducted on the issue of mental health in Indigenous contexts is still very incipient and requires stronger epistemological reflection to substantiate the complexity of the intercultural dialogue. There is also the need to recognize ethnic and cultural diversities in the epistemological framework used in mental health. The category of mental health and the psychic/subjective/psychological aspects of patients are themselves constructions that belong to Western explanatory models (Batista and Zanello 2016).

Finally, the public awareness of the persistence of structural racism and racial-based inequities underlying class differences in Brazil. As already mentioned, there is an extensive body of research that highlights the presence of ethnic, racial, gender and religious differences and their embodiment in modes of exclusion and segregation within Brazilian society. Inflamed debates around affirmative action in Brazil have fueled issues of racial differences, identity politics and multiculturalism that reverberate in Brazilian mental health care and policies. As examined above, even if the Psychiatric Reform explicitly condemns discrimination against Blacks, Indigenous and LGBT populations, there is no discussion of mental health care policies to address gender, ethnic or race differences.

Conclusion

This chapter examined the issue of culture and mental health in Brazil. Developing strategies of intercultural competence can assist mental health practitioners to interpret symptoms in ways that lead to appropriate and culturally meaningful interventions. Mental health interventions are more accessible, acceptable and effective when they are culturally adapted. Patients can integrate cultural explanations to communicate their distress in intelligible and social meaningful ways (Kirmayer and Swartz 2014).

The political and epistemological orientation of the psychiatric reform, which reverberate the interpretations of 'cultural uniformity' of Brazilian cultural matrices, is based on the recognition of and attention to class and economic inequalities as main determinants of mental illness. This orientation does not necessarily ignore, but at first puts in the background racial, ethnic and religious issues, at least when compared to the importance given to multiculturalism and cultural differences in Global Mental Health debates. The latter usually focus on cultural adaptation of diagnostic and interventional tools (Patel 2014) and seem to ignore how severe poverty and deep social inequalities pervade the lives of the majority of people in the 'non-Western world' and are major determinants of their mental suffering.

At the same time, recent experiences of mental health care in primary care examined here through the work of ACS and CT result in relevant, and not necessarily conflicting, exceptions to the "silencing" of culture within the Brazilian Psychiatric Reform. They constitute local paths for the insertion of cultural issues into mental health care in the Global South, not focused on ethnic diversity, but committed to addressing human life in its multiple dimensions.

Notes

1 http://worldpopulationreview.com/countries/brazil-population.
2 Training and accreditation in Brazil for psychologists, psychiatrists, nurses and other professionals is similar to the United States and Canada.

References

Almeida Angélica A. Silva de, Oda, Ana Maria G. R., Dalgalarrondo. (2007) "O olhar dos psiquiatras brasileiros sobre os fenômenos de transe e possessão". *Revista de Psiquiatria Clínica*, *34*(1): 34–41.
Barreto, A. (2005). *Terapia Comunitária passo a passo*. Fortaleza: Grafica LCR.
Batista, Marianna Queiróz, Zanello, Valeska. (2016) "Saúde mental em contextos indígenas: Escassez de pesquisas brasileiras, invisibilidade das diferenças." *Estudos de Psicologia (Natal)*, *21*(4): 403–414.
Boccolini, C. S., and de Souza Junior, P. R. B. (2016) Inequities in healthcare utilization: Results of the Brazilian National Health Survey, 2013. *International Journal for Equity in Health*, *15:* 150.
Brasil (2012) Ministério da Saúde. Secretaria de Atenção à Saúde. Departamento de Atenção Básica. *Política Nacional de Atenção Básica*. Brasília: Ministério da Saúde.

Burdick, J. (1999) What is the color of the Holy Spirit? Pentecostalism and black identity in Brazil. *Latin American Research Review*, *34*(2): 109–131.

Costa, J. F. (2007) *História da Psiquiatria no Brasil: um corte ideológico*. Rio de Janeiro: Garamond.

Dalgalarrondo, P. (2007) "Estudos sobre religião e saúde mental realizados no Brasil: histórico e perspectivas atuais". *Revista de psiquiatria clínica*, *34* (1): 25–33.

Duarte, L. F. D. (1988) *Da vida nervosa nas classes trabalhadoras urbanas*. Rio de Janeiro: Jorge Zahar.

Ferreira Filha M. O., Carvalho M. A. P. (2010) "A Terapia Comunitária em um Centro de Atenção Psicossocial: (des)atando pontos relevantes". *Rev Gaúcha Enferm, 31*(2): 232–9.

Fonseca, M. L. G. (2009) "Diferenças Culturais Entre Profissionais de Saúde e Clientela Acerca do Nervoso: Da Distância à Compreensão da Diversidade". *Rev. APS, 12*(4): 468–477.

Fonte, Eliane Maria Monteiro da. (2012) "Da institucionalização da loucura à reforma psiquiátrica: As sete vidas da agenda pública em saúde mental no Brasil." *Estudos de Sociologia*, *1*(18). https://periodicos.ufpe. br/revistas/revsocio/article/view/235235.

Fleury, S. (2011) Brazil's health-care reform: Social movements and civil society. *The Lancet*, *377*(9779): 1724–1725.

Jabert, Alexander. (2011) "Estratégias populares de identificação e tratamento da loucura na primeira metade do século XX: Uma análise dos prontuários médicos do Sanatório Espírita de Uberaba." *História, Ciências, Saúde –Manguinhos*, *18*(1): 105–120.

Kirmayer, L. J., and Swartz, L. (2014) Culture and global mental health. In V. Patel, H. Minas, A. Cohen, and M. J. Prince, (Eds.), *Global mental health: Principles and practice* (pp. 41–62). New York: Oxford University Press.

Kulick, D. (1997) The gender of Brazilian transgendered prostitutes. *American Anthropologist*, *99*(3): 574–585.

Langdon, Esther Jean, and Garnelo, Luiza. (2017) "Articulación entre servicios de salud y "medicina indígena": Reflexiones antropológicas sobre política y realidad en Brasil." *Salud Colectiva*, *13*(3): 457–470.

Lara, M. O., Brito, M. J. M., and Rezende, L. C. (2012) "Aspectos culturais das práticas dos Agentes Comunitários de Saúde em áreas rurais". *Revista da Escola de Enfermagem da USP*, *46*(3): 673–680.

Lima, M. and Oliveira Nunes, M. (2006) "Práticas psicológicas e dimensões de significação dos problemas de saúde mental". *Psicologia Ciência e Profissão*, *26*(2): 294–311.

Machado, Roberto, Ángela Loureiro, Rogério Luz, and Kátia Muricy. (1978) *Danação Da Norma: Medicina Social e Constituição da Psiquiatria no Brasil*. Rio de Janeiro: Graal.

Menéndez, Eduardo L. (2003) "Modelos de atención de los padecimientos: De exclusiones teóricas y articulaciones prácticas." *Ciência & Saúde Coletiva*, *8*(1): 185–207.

Meyer, Manuella. (2017) *Reasoning against madness: Psychiatry and the state in Rio de Janeiro, 1830–1944*. Rochester, NY: University of Rochester Press.

Mota, Clarice Santos and Bonfim, Leny Trad. (2011) "A gente vive para cuidar da população: Estratégias de cuidado e sentidos para a saúde, doença e cura em terreiros de candomblé." *Saúde e Sociedade*, *20*(2): 325–337.

Nascimento, E. L. (2007) *The sorcery of color. Identity, race, and gender in Brazil*. Philadelphia: Temple University.

Oliveira, D. S. T., and Ferreira Filha M. O. (2011) "Contribuição dos recursos culturais para a Terapia Comunitária Integrativa na visão do terapeuta". *Revista Gaúcha de Enfermagem*, *32*(3):524–30.

Oliveira Nunes, M. (2009) "O silenciamento da cultura nos (con)textos de cuidado em saúde mental". *Cadernos Brasileiros de Saúde Mental*, *1*(2): 38–47.

Paim, J., Travassos, C., Almeida, C., Bahia, L., and Macinko, J. (2011). The Brazilian health system: History, advances, and challenges. *The Lancet*, *377* (9779): 1778–1797.

Patel, V. (2014) Why mental health matters to global health. *Transcultural Psychiatry*, *51*:777–789.

Pinezi, Ana K. M. and Jorge, Érica F. C. (2014) "Doença, saúde e terapias: Aproximações e distanciamentos entre o candomblé e o neopentecostalismo." *Caminhos*, *12*(1): 65–78.

Puttini, Rodolfo Franco. (2008) "Curandeirismo e o campo da saúde no Brasil." *Interface – Comunicação, Saúde, Educação*, *12*(24): 87–106.

Rabelo, M. C., Motta, S. R. and Nunes, J. R. (2002) "Comparando experiências de aflição e tratamento no candomblé, pentecostalismo e espiritismo". *Religião e Sociedade*, *22*(1): 93–121.

Redko, C. (2003) Religious construction of a first episode of psychosis in urban Brazil. *Transcultural Psychiatry*, *40*(4): 507–530.

Resende, Heitor. (1990) "Política de saúde mental no Brasil: Uma visão histórica". In: Silvério Almeida Tundis e Nilson do Rosário Costa (Eds.), *Cidadania e loucura: Políticas de saúde mental no Brasil* (pp. 15–73). Petrópolis: Vozes.

Ribeiro, D. (2000) *The Brazilian people: The formation and meaning of Brazil.* Gainesville: University Press of Florida.

Rocha, I. A., Pinto de Sá, A. N., Braga, L. A. V., Ferreira Filha, M. O., and Dias, M. D. (2013) Community integrative therapy: Situations of emotional suffering and patients' coping strategies. *Revista Gaúcha de Enfermagem, 34*(2):155–162.

Scopel, Daniel, Dias-Scopel, Raquel Paiva, and Langdon, Esther Jean. (2015) "Intermedicalidade e protagonismo: A atuação dos agentes indígenas de saúde Munduruku da Terra Indígena Kwatá-Laranjal, Amazonas, Brasil". *Cadernos de Saúde Pública, 31*(12): 2559–2568.

Silva, Antonio de Carvalho, Langdon, Esther Jean, Ribas, Dulce Lopes. (2013) "Fatores estruturais e as práticas de autoatenção das famílias com parentes com transtornos mentais: Contexto Kaiowá e Guarani do Mato Grosso do Sul. Brasil." *Tempus - Actas de Saúde Coletiva,* 7(4): 149–168.

Souza, L. G. S., Menandro, M. C. S., Couto, L. L. M., Schimith, P. B., and Lima, R. P. (2012) "Saúde mental na estratégia saúde da família: Revisão da literatura brasileira". *Saúde e Sociedade, 21*: 1022–34.

Summerfield, D. (2012) Afterword: Against 'global mental health'. *Transcultural Psychiatry, 49*: 519–30.

Traverso-Yépez, Martha, Medeiros, Luciana Fernandes De. (2004) "Tremendo diante da vida: Um estudo de caso sobre a doença dos nervos." *Interações, 9*(18): 87–108.

Waidman, M. A. P., Costa, B., and Paiano, M. (2012) Community health agents' perceptions and practice in mental health. *Revista da Escola de Enfermagem da USP, 46*(5): 1170–1177.

Werneck, J. (2016) "Racismo institucional e saúde da população negra". *Saúde e Sociedade, 25*(3): 535–549.

Yasui, S., Luzio, C., and Amarante, P. (2016) From manicomial logic to territorial logic: Impasses and challenges of psychosocial care. *Journal of Health Psychology, 21*(3): 400–408.

29

CULTURE AND MENTAL HEALTH IN CHILE

Cristina Pastén Peña and Leonor Villacura Avendaño

Mental health is a topic that, in Chile, is constantly changing. Since the colonial times in which the moral concept was the basis of all mental disorders to communitarian modern approaches nowadays aimed toward reinsertion, there have been numerous changes and diverse paradigms and theories have been developed that have revolutionized the way of thinking and working in mental health in Chile.

The purpose of this research is to give a brief review through the mental health development in Chile in order to clarify the different cultural influences that it has continuously had. Therefore, the history of mental health in this country will be addressed as well as the cultural influence and the colonialism, the cultural representations that have been around mental disorders and health concept, the current process of professional training of people who work in mental health and finally the present and future practices and researches that are expected in this subject.

Demographics and brief history of mental health in Chile

According to the 2017 census, Chile is a country that has 17,574,003 inhabitants from which 8,972,014 are women and 8,601,989 are men. Population under 14 years old belongs to 3,523,750 inhabitant (1,789,035 men and 1,725,715 women); people between 15 and 64 years old represent the majority of population making a total of 12,046,997 inhabitants (6,107,018 women and 5,939,979 men); while elders above 65 years old reach 2,003,256 inhabitants. The elder group has a larger difference between gender, women reach 1,139,281 inhabitants and only are men 863,975 (Ministerio de Economía 2017).

The population is distributed in the 16 existing regions in Chile; however the Metropolitan Region (where the capital of the country, Santiago de Chile, is located,) concentrates the largest number of inhabitants reaching the figure of 7,112,808 (Ministerio de Economía 2017).

Regarding mental health, there is a prevalence of psychiatric disorders nationwide of 22,6% (Retamal, Markkula and Peña 2016). According to Vicente, Saldivia and Pihán (2016), the World Health Organization (WHO) places Chile between the countries with the highest burden of mobility due to psychiatric disorders (23.2%) in the world. Major depression and alcohol abuse disorders are between the first and second place in disabilities attributed to adults. Almost a third of population above 15 years have suffered a psychiatric disorder and 22.2% have experienced

353

during past year. Anxiety, major depression and abuse alcohol disorders are the most predominant despite of this, only 38.5% of the diagnosed people receive some type of care in the context of mental health in primary health care (Vicente, Saldivia and Pihán 2016).

In children and teenagers, the prevalence of psychiatric disorders is 22.5%, 19.3% for boys and 25.8% for girls, among them stand out disruptive and anxiety disorders. Disruptive disorders tend to affect more to children between 4 and 11 years than between 12 and 18, however, the latest suffer more anxiety disorders (Vicente, Saldivia and Pihán 2016).

On the other hand, suicide is a relevant nationwide problem. According to Errázuriz et al. (2015), suicide rates substantially increased between 2000 and 2009. Meanwhile in 2000 there were 9.6 deaths for suicide every 100,000 people (16.6 men and 2.7 women), in 2009 this rate increased to 12.7 (20.8 men and 5.0 in women).

In the case of teenagers, the suicide rate was of 7 every 100,000 which is in accordance with WHO suicide rate between 10 and 19 years. It is projected that for 2020 this figure will reach 12 every 100,000 inhabitants (WHO 2014; Echávarri, Maino, Fischman, Morales and Barros 2015).

This chapter is not intended to explain the causes of the figures above mentioned but rather to understand the context. In other words, how mental health in Chile has been understood and its treatment has been developed through the Chilean history and present.

In the young 19th-century colonial Chile, moral was an important concept. During this period, the idea of 'moral degeneration' was added locking mentally ill people in 'lunatic asylums' because it was believed that they suffered a kind of moral disturbance that was producing the existent symptomatology (Alarcón 1976).

According to Aburto (1994), the English physician William Benham was employed in 1875 by the Chilean government to take charge of 'Casa de Orate', the first mental hospital in the country. He stated that mentally ill people during Colony were burnt like sorcerers, whipped, chained and caged. The mentally ill person in that time was not treated as a human being who suffered but treated as an animal.

On the contrary, Álvarez (2006) notes that the mentally ill people in the Colony faced with serious situations but not to that level of torture. According to this author, in those times were three types of ill people. The 'furious insane' who ended chained in jails where they were beaten with sticks and forced to receive cold showers. The 'horny women' who were locked in religious nunneries. Finally, the 'quiet insane', men and women who were locked for life in their own houses, isolated from any member of the family and away from any outside contact. Nevertheless, if the ill person was wealthy, families chose to send him/her to San Andrés Locos Hospital, located in Lima, Peru.

After the colonial period, Fuentealba (2013) describes three stages in the history of psychiatry in Chile. The first stage, named 'Asylum Era' (1852–1952) stand out 'Casa de Orates de Nuestra Señora de los Ángeles' like one of the first specialized in mental health institutions which worked between 1852 and 1891 and it is considered the predecessor of the psychiatric institution in Chile.

With the settlement of this institution, the division of three groups above mentioned banished, however, a lot of the methods and treatments continue in a similar way such as the enchainment of unquiet ill people (Álvarez 2006). As well as colonial period institution, 'Casa de Orates' had a moral and disciplinary control to groups of people especially marginalized population.

According to Fuentealba (2013), the main treatments of 'Casa de Orates' essentially consist of moral and physical practices. Physical treatments like Hydrotherapy (i.e., tepid baths, showers, swimming with temperatures of 30°C to 32°C and with durations of approximately 2.5 hours), the bromides, camphor and antipyrine were used as sedatives and the trional, sulfonal and chloral hydrate as hypnotics. Moral treatments were mainly used in melancholic and maniac disorders that were made up of isolation, family daybreak, performing some work in the asylum or any activity that contributed to the good health of the patient such as shoemaking, carpentry and sewing.

At the same time, Carrasco (2018) states that this institution began the incorporation of psychiatric methods imported from European clinics, thus differentiating itself from its colonial predecessors. For example, 'Casa de Orates' stands out for being the first institution in Chile that includes psychotherapy as a way of working with patients (Carrasco 2018). This will be used again later by the Psychiatric Institute or as it was formerly called 'National Asylum' (Carrasco 2018). This institution (which full name was and is Psychiatric Institute Dr. José Horwitz Barak) started in 1858 due to high demand in Casa de Orates and the national need of its expansion (Medina 2001).

The high demand of psychiatric hospitalization was a serious problem. At the beginning, Casa de Orates had 30 beds and few years later increased up to 100 beds. At that time, it is when the need arises to build the previously mentioned Psychiatric Institute. This is the beginning of the second stage of the psychiatric History in Chile in which starts the medical specialty of psychiatry itself (Fuentealba 2013).

Despite the construction of the Psychiatric Institute, there were still lack of beds being a persistent problem. According to Medina (2001), it is estimated that at those times (even with the Psychiatric Institute built) in a room of 3x4 meters 17 ill people slept without a bed, with just some straw on the asphalt floor. Furthermore, here was a serious shortage of caregivers and for this reason, room doors were closed at 19:00 and open at 7:00 next day, during this time ill people had no supervision.

With the purpose of improving these conditions, around 1920 the deputy director of Casa de Orates, Dr. Jerónimo Letelier Grez, modified its internal operation (Medina 2001). Three sections were settled: Psychiatric Hospital for voluntary and observational admissions. Asylum for dangerous and antisocial mad people and Temperance asylum for alcohol and drug addicts. It is important to underline that more than the half of patients were admitted for alcoholism (Aburto 1994).

In 1927 it was decided to build a new psychiatric institution at the outskirts of the city of Santiago, one of the farmhouses that in those times was not an urban area (Medina 2001). That institution has continued its operation until today and it is known as 'Hospital Sanatorio El Peral' and is responsible for receiving patients from the José Horwitz Psychiatric Institute considered unrecoverable (Chamorro 2005; Gómez 2017). Likewise, As in the institutions described above, the historical testimonies of patients and officials indicate that the living conditions of the residents were extremely poor since they were characterized by misery, overcrowding and low sanitary standards (Gómez 2017).

A new policy that achieved a greater connection with the community and improved ill people life conditions then started (Chamorro 2005). The therapeutic approach was changed and started to focus on the work to reintegrate patients to society, in that patient care no longer consists solely of pharmacological treatments (Gómez 2017). The physical treatments and moral conceptions of mental illness that had been dragging on since colonialism have been left behind. According to Fuentealba (2013), since the 1970's Chile has been operating from Community Psychiatry. This change in psychiatry was driven by Italian antipsychiatry movements that proposed new forms of treatment focusing on the outpatient, group work and the acquisition of socio–labor tools.

This approach continues to the present, and it is used in diverse public and private mental health institutions in Chile. Moreover, the State provides hospital care to people with acute and chronic mental health struggles, but also provides phycological outpatient health care to people with less complex issues in COSAM (i.e., Community Centers of Mental Health), as well as various prevention programs. Professions in mental health services include not only psychiatrists but also other health professionals such as, psychologists and occupational therapists.

Despite these improvements, there are still people without coverage at present. According to the OECD, Chile is reported as one of the countries with the lowest public contribution to mental health (Jiménez and Radiszcz 2012). In 2010, only 8% GDP was spent to mental health services in Chile, in contrast to countries like United States where 17.6% GDP was allocated to the mental health services (Jiménez and Radiszcz 2012). It is alarming to see that depression, anxiety and suicides are problems that are growing catastrophically in our society.

Indigenous approach to health and illness in Chile

The indigenous community in Chile is heterogeneous since there are diverse ethnicities that compose it, which leads to mental health traditions being mixed with diverse cultures prior to colonialism (Gavilán et al. 2017). It is beyond a scope of this chapter to illustrate the characterization of each mental health concept and system from the diverse indigenous ethnic groups. However, it is important to highlight that Mapuche culture represents 9% of Chilean population and consists in 83.3% of indigenous population in Chile (Ministerio de Desarrollo Social 2015). Accordingly, this chapter is focused on the history and health concepts related to Mapuche people.

Regarding the Mapuche people's history, this indigenous community inhabit a wide territory between Santiago and Chiloe before Spaniards people arrived. From that time and for decades of Chilean government (1598–1881), Mapuches lived self-governing under their own rules and laws, living out of the extern government domination (Bengoa 2011).

During the 19th century, a massive European immigration proliferated towards the south of the country. The government, under a Eurocentric approach, encouraged European migration to the southern vacant lands as a way to 'civilize' the territories with less population. Around 1850, the first German settlers arrived in Valdivia (i.e., the territory most densely populated by Mapuches), Concepción, and Llanquihue (León 2007). In 1866 an attempt was made to occupy territories further south of the country with the result of bloody clashes between the Chilean Army and the natives. From that date until 1881 there was a period of very sharp border wars that was called the 'Pacification of the Araucanía' (Bengoa 2011).

This conflict officially ended in 1883 with the refoundation of Villarica city. In 1884 the process of filing the Mapuches to reservations began. Between 1884 and 1927, 3,000 reservations were built, giving a total of 500,000 hectares to a little less than 100,000 indigenous people, which led a high number of people, living without land. According to León (2007), this conflict left negative consequences to Mapuches. Their military capacity was diminished; traditional circuits of economical exchange were cut and politic alliances that lasted centuries keeping their autonomy were weakened. For this reason, a complex indigenous conflict started lasting to these days.

According to Bengoa (2011), Mapuche people is still the most discriminated, marginalized and poor social group of the country since there have been little acknowledgement and recognition and little efforts for repairment of the committed historic damage. However, this has failed to erase the Mapuche culture of the Chilean territories. Mapuches hold a strong identity who kept their traditions and language alive and continue to study their culture with high regard.

According to Mapuche culture, the concept of health is linked to the balance. When a person breaks the laws of nature produces an imbalance which is lived by the individual through an illness (Díaz, Pérez, González and Simon 2004). According to Díaz et al. (2004), there are several forces that generate imbalance: the Weda newen (negatives forces controlled by people called daufe and kalku who manipulate these energies to generate harm in specific people), los Weda pülli (referred to all negative non-human spirits that flow in nature) and the Weda küruf (spirits that affect people who are already unbalanced).

Unbalance in various formats is understood as illness that affects the spiritual and physical part of people. To address unbalance, four types of healers are recognized in Mapuche culture: Machi, Lawenche, Ngütamchefe and Püñeñelchefe. It is difficult to establish boundaries among the healers who were specialized in mental health because in the Mapuche culture it is not clear the division between body and soul as it is in the positive Western World. Nevertheless, Machi was the only one who connects spirits, therefore the closest to mental health, while Lawenche was specialized in herbs, Ngütamchefe in bone form and their position and Püñeñelchefe in labour (Díaz et al. 2004).

From the public health policies, attempts have been made to consider these concepts within the framework of intercultural health policies. In 1996, a working framework emerged by the Ministry of Health that boosted the Special Health Program and Indigenous People aimed to carry out intercultural technics (Hasen 2012). In addition to intercultural initiatives, Government efforts for intercultural policies are shown in an exhaustive study of the situation in health issues of the Mapuche population (Hasen 2012).

Despite these attempts, the question remains if an intercultural approach to mental health is in premise. According to Hasen (2012), the key would be in the training of people who work as a link between the Western world and the wisdom of indigenous cultures. Critical scholars like Olea (2013) point that current mechanisms of health in Mapuche people tend to be focused on health care and domestication rather than truly understanding sociocultural, historic and structural determinations that influence health in indigenous communities that would deepen the naturalization of the condition of the Mapuches as second-class citizens.

Colonialism and evolution of mental health practices in Chile

The trace of colonialism in mental health practices in Chile is undeniable. First, there is 'Casa de Orates' that inherits the moral role of charity institutions of mental health of Colonial times. On the other side, it is important to highlight that innovations in mental health practices in Casa de Orates such as, the aforementioned incorporation of psychotherapy, were not ideas born in Chile but they were brought from the outside by foreign physicians like William Benham, an Englishman financed by the Government of Chile to perform as house physician and who eventually would be in charge of Casa de Orates. Other Chilean physicians like Dr. Carlos Sazié (successor of Dr. Benham), were sent to Europe in order to study mental health practices (Carrasco 2018).

According to Jimena Carrasco (2018), a consequence of the colonial expansion of Europe is the generation of the idea that colonizer countries are in the center of the world, leading them in the thought that all the other countries are Otherized, as if Others are 'discovered' by colonizers. These elements make possible the existence of believing that a neutral place is where it can be observed and known, the colonizer place became that place and the colonized countries the elements that can be known.

This leads to the idea that 'true knowledge' emerge in the colonizers or, at least, through their methods and thinking schools. This is why current psychiatry has been influenced by the foreign thinking, to such an extent that is possible to question the problematic of whether there is a real Latin American psychiatry or not (Alarcón 1976).

The same happened with psychology, the discipline that arrived at Chile thanks to the collaboration of diverse people such as Germans Jörg Heinrich Schneider and Wilhelm Mann. Schneider, scholar of 'Instituto Pedagógico' (currently 'Universidad Metropolitana de Ciencias de la Educación') during the second half of the 19th century, was the one who transferred his knowledge in Psychology from Germany to create the first laboratory in Santiago of Experimental Psychology. The first nationwide one was 'Escuela Normal', Copiapó. After Schneider's retirement and death, he was replaced by Wilhelm Mann who continues in psychology and pedagogy research (Salas 2014).

Noteworth is the presence of the foreign influence even before the emergence of psychology. The first dean of the oldest university in the country, Universidad of Chile, Andrés Bello had great influences from the British psychology and philosophy. In the middle of the 19th century, French positivism had an important place between intellectuals who studied psychology in those times, outstanding authors like Comte, D'Alembert, Trugot and Saint Simon (Salas 2014).

The community approach to mental health arrived in Chile due to the influence of Italian antipsychiatry. Nowadays, many psychologists are trained in the systemic school and travel to Italy to take postgraduate degrees. That is without mentioning the general support that exists from the State of Chile towards health professionals to carry out postgraduate and specializations abroad through the Chile Scholarship system to support the study at Anglo-Saxon universities.

In this way, we can notice the strong European influence in all the development of mental health in Chile from Spanish colonialism to the full range of intellectuals influenced by German, British and French authors; the current Italian influence on community models and the continued financing of the State for professionals to specialize abroad.

Social representations of health and disease in Chile

Quoting sociologist Durkheim's concept of cultural representations where human experiences in life are socially constructed, Moscovici (1979) points out the concept of social representation to refer to the psychological organization with which each individual categorizes the diverse knowledge about something given by everyday life, but also by science and philosophy. This set of knowledge is irreducible and is, at the same time, the way in which man captures the concrete world.

Accordingly, social representations shape all our daily lives. Through languages, gestures, encounters in every interaction, socially attributed set of ideas will arise (Moscovici 1979). It also happens with health and illness; according to Flores-Guerrero (2004), the perceptions of people of good or bad health are culturally constructed. In other words, health and disease are socially represented in a collective imaginary that will vary according to the society in which we find ourselves.

In Chile, the disease is associated with death and the doctor with the avoidance of it. With the scientific advances of modernity, the doctor becomes a counselor and an expert in improving and correcting the body, which leads people to begin to have confidence in the medical diagnosis. According to Flores-Guerrero (2004), this trust began in the 19th century at the same time that the first mental health institutions in Chile were created.

With advances and confidence in medicine, the concepts of health and disease began to distance themselves from philosophy and religion. Health began to be associated with medicine and medicine with the postponement of death (Flores-Guerrero 2004), so that health means moving away from death, it is not having a medical diagnosis that brings you closer to death.

The advance in medicine with the increase to access it has managed to postpone death, giving people control over it to the point that it has become a concept of illness that is associated with bad practices in everyday life. According to Flores-Guerrero (2004:27), "it is always a surprise, an accident, and as such it becomes a clandestine fact that must be disguised, hidden and quickly overcome, so that it appears as a failure of the technique or model of modern man who can do everything" if they do not control their own illness.

In this way, disease that is a concept associated with death, is linked to bad practices in everyday life. According to the bad practice that is carried out, a certain disease will be developed. For example, according to Susan Sontag (1996), there is a social metaphor that cancer is caused by repressed emotions, especially rage (which, if not expressed, would manifest itself in a tumor of a malignant nature). Thus, the social representation of cancer would be linked to a daily bad practice that manifests one's capacity to manage rage, referring to one's faculty.

Just as there are social representations for cancer and for other physical illnesses, mental illnesses also began to have social representations. A study developed in 2005 made by the Chilean author Cristián Massad indicates that patients diagnosed with different psychiatric disorders feel excluded and stigmatized in society. According to Massad (2005), in Chile stereotypes are formed in which it is considered that any person who has a mental illness and who has been admitted to a psychiatric institution 'must be someone who hears voices' or also someone 'aggressive'. In Massad's work, many people interviewed said they were not aggressive or heard voices, however, they felt how other people treated them as if they had this symptomatology.

In the same way, in a later work on social representations and schizophrenia, Ricardo Fuentealba (2013) highlights that the patients with the diagnosis of schizophrenia in his study also had to deal with the same stereotype and that this is due to the lack of information and, even to the misinformation often circulated in the mass media. In addition, within the families of people with schizophrenia, there have been negative social representations of the disease, which makes the occurrence of the mental illness in the family to be something extremely traumatic.

Training, accreditation, licensing and certification of mental health in Chile

Regarding the history of the professionalization of psychiatry, there are three critical moments in Chile: at the end of 1820 with the first circulations of psychiatric texts; in 1927 with the first university lectureship of psychiatry; and in the 1930s with the development of medical associationism (Araya 2018).

In the first moment, the first medical texts that pose the study of the mind began to circulate as something that can be studied separately from the body which is approachable by medicine. In 1828, the Chilean newspaper 'El Mercurio' published the essay '*On moral freedom*' written by the Spanish doctor José de Passamán. This article is considered the first psychiatric writing published in Chile. In a tone of liberal political tendency, it seeks to humanize the 'madmen' under the focus of illustrated ideas, as well as raising the separation between religion and mental illness (Araya 2018). The scientification of psychiatric treatments became a public debate since it implied an attempt to secularize mental health (Araya 2018), something very different from what prevailed throughout the Asylum Era where the role of psychiatry had a character deeply religious and moralizing (Fuentealba 2013).

The second moment of the professionalization of psychiatry stands out for the creation of the independent lectureship of psychiatry in 1927 at the University of Chile, an instance that allowed legitimizing the field of study in mental health and additionally ensuring an academic space (Araya 2018). In addition, in the 1950s, psychiatry lectureships began to be taught at the

Psychiatric Hospital and in 1952, the University Psychiatric Clinic of the University of Chile was founded, as a dependency of the José Joaquín Aguirre Hospital. This network included outpatient consultation, day hospitalization, rehabilitation workshops, liaison psychiatry and other forms of treatment that surpass the conception of the asylum era. In this period, staff training was increased in universities, with special attention being paid to the prevention of alcoholism and neurosis (Fuentealba 2013).

At the same time, many doctors opted for modernization and decided to travel to Europe to learn mental health concerns and substance abuse, with the aim of formulating reforms and projects that aimed at the medicalization of asylum. Especially for those professionals the modernization of the Psychiatry in Chile this reform involved a medicalization of madness. Despite these efforts, medicalization tended to fail due to the lack of state budget and its urgency to cover infectious diseases that attack the Chilean population at that time (Araya 2018).

Continuing with Araya (2018), the third moment of the professionalization of psychiatry corresponded to psychiatric associationism, in which psychiatrists from Chile decided to work collectively for the development of psychiatric medical specialization with the purpose of legitimizing socially and strengthening their identity as medical specialists. Among the associative strategies, he highlighted the creation in 1934 of the Society of Psychiatry and Neurology and Legal Medicine, which aimed to modernize the care of mentally ill patients, consolidate the teaching of psychiatric specialization and legitimize psychiatry itself in the country. From this association, the Journal of Psychiatry and Related Disciplines emerged as its dissemination body. In addition, in 1937, the First Neuro-Psychiatric Days of the Pacific were organized in which psychiatrists from all over Latin America met.

Despite the collectivism of the 1930s and after World War II, the consolidation of American hegemony and the failure of the Latin American nationalist discourse of science and progress, the dominant discourse of Chilean psychiatry began to be reduced to scientific and technological aspects, pointing to somatic therapies and biological psychiatry (Araya 2018). This approach prevails to the present day.

Currently the training of psychiatrists is a medical specialty that can be accessed only by having the professional title of surgeon. Despite the changes in the models of mental health care and the strong influence of the community approach in the current institutions, the National Mental Health Plan of the Ministry of Health of 2017 states that the training of specialists in psychiatry has not integrated the community mental health model, so that it is still pending in the country to promote psychiatric schools to include the community approach in their training.

Regarding the training of psychologists, noteworthy is that psychology was developed in Chile as an independent discipline of psychiatry. Its development began closely linked to pedagogy with the first experimental psychology laboratory founded by Professor Romulo Peña between 1905 and 1907 at the 'Escuela Normal' of Copiapó; This laboratory initially aimed to measure student intelligence. Later, in 1908, the first experimental psychology laboratory in Santiago began its operation in the Pedagogical Institute, whose objectives were similar to those of the Escuela Normal of Copiapó (Salas and Lizama 2013).

The beginning of the psychology career, as we know it today, began with the creation of the Institute of Psychology at the University of Chile in 1941 and was aimed at the study of experimental psychology. This was the first instance in which psychology itself is studied without relating it to other disciplines (as was the case in the experimental laboratories mentioned above where psychology related to pedagogy was studied). From this institute, the first seven-semester career in Psychology at the University of Chile was founded in 1946. In 1954, the Pontifical Catholic University began to implement it and later in 1982, for the first time outside of Santiago, the Universidad de la Frontera began to teach in Temuco. The first postgraduate courses began to be taught in the '90s, the oldest being the Master in Psychology from the Pontifical Catholic University and the Master in Clinical Psychology, with the mention in Psychoanalysis from the Diego Portales University (Salas 2014).

Currently, 12 Chilean universities in both public and private have psychology program for its degree. With the title of psychologist, a person is legally authorized to work in the area of health and perform psychotherapy. However, there is an accreditation for clinical psychologists granted by the National Commission of Accreditation of Clinical Psychologists (CONAPC) that, although it is not essential when attending patients, does ensure that the professional has more training in the area.

Contemporary mental health practices

As mentioned above, mental health currently works from a community approach. This approach focuses on people who have a severe and persistent mental disorder, and the impact on their entire family and social environment. What is sought is the recovery of the person, favoring their social inclusion and the recovery of the full exercise of their rights (Ministerio de Salud 2017).

This approach is integrated and complemented with the *Model of Comprehensive Family and Community Health Care*, a central axis in mental health since 2005. Both approaches, which coexist, have three axes in current policies. First, the promotion of community mental health is emphasized; This promotion consists in deploying actions that allow the creation of environments that protect the integral and healthy development of the communities. These actions revolve around education, work, justice, transport, the environment, housing, municipalities, NGOs, among others. This model seeks to work with all these actors in order to deliver the minimum conditions so that the population can maintain their mental health (Ministerio de Salud 2017).

The second axis of work consists in prevention. Prevention from a community approach consists in knowing, promoting and supporting self-management capacities of individuals, families and communities in the face of risk conditions, such as economic vulnerability, marginalization and social exclusion. With prevention, it is sought, on the one hand, to strengthen the protective conditions of mental health that work on axis number one and, on the other, to counteract the effects of unfavorable social determinants such as, social inequality and lack of opportunities. In addition, preventive strategies seek that those who are involved maintain or recover their ability to interact with others and to participate in community, so that the family and the environment become fundamental. These strategies go beyond the symptomatology and are oriented in a change in the relations of the subject with their social conditions (Ministerio de Salud 2017).

The third axis of work issued by the Ministry of Health (Ministerio de Salud 2017) consists in direct treatment and care in mental health. This focus is on the person and aims to recover the ability to interact with others and participate in community life; Again, the family becomes a fundamental aspect. This axis also goes beyond the symptoms and is oriented towards the articulation of networks that provide basic conditions for the well-being of the users, focusing on work, housing, education, emotional ties, social relationships, among other things.

These three axes are the basis of all mental health practices in the public service in Chile. However, in the private service there are numerous guidelines and models that are not possible to describe each and every one of them in this chapter. However, it should be mentioned that in the private system there are clinics that work under these same guidelines and also others that have orientations towards particular psychological schools such as psychoanalysis, cognitive behavioral therapies, among others; There are also institutions that work from anthroposophy or with the use of complementary therapies and homeopathy. The current mental health field is extensive and offers multiple options.

Future directions

In recent years, there have been various social phenomena that have transformed ways of thinking about mental health and illness. Higher education students in our country have initiated various protests about the integration of quality of life and mental health into the education system. Our Psychology Unit of the Directorate of Student Affairs of the School of Medicine of the University of Chile has contributed from the investigation of the prevalence of mental disorders in university students, studies on profiles, crossings of sociodemographic variables, quality of the teaching-learning process, and evaluation systems.

In 2011, numerous universities, colleges and educational institutions formed a popular movement that covered most of that year and that ended in important modifications in education in Chile. In 2018, again students from higher education institutions led a new mobilization in which this time was focused on women's rights. Also, in 2018 the abortion law was approved in three cases and in 2019 the laws on gender and homoparental adoption are beginning to change towards a more inclusive and tolerant Chile. Not to mention the increase in immigration from various Latin American countries that should also be considered.

These political changes are generating cultural transformations that we still cannot analyze. The question that concerns us in the midst of all of this is how these changes will affect the mental health field of the country, how the community approach will address these sociocultural changes and how universities will modify their programs or not towards training that benefits or slows these transformations.

Chile, as mentioned at the beginning of this work, is a country with a chronic lack of attention in mental health matters. Statistics do not suggest a good future. Therefore, it is necessary to study in depth the aforementioned transformations in order to generate mental health models according to the needs of the nation and sensitive models to the continual changes of the contingency. Mental health professionals should be at the forefront of research and not be afraid when creating new avenues for the study and practice that contribute to the improvement of the mental health of all and all those who make up this State called Chile.

Conclusion

The history of mental health in Chile is marked by the deep foreign influence as well as by the chronic lack of resources. However, in the midst of this unfavorable scenario profound changes have been made in mental health models. Currently the Chilean health system is far from what it was in colonial times.

The training of professionals has also undergone numerous changes. However, today it seems not fall short of the new community models with which mental health works. Another thing that is pending is the integration of the concepts of native peoples and the development of intercultural mental health, as well as the inclusion of immigrants and cultural changes given by the modifications of the laws consistent with the demands of change of a country dissatisfied.

The demands for efficient mental health are far from being fulfilled. The lack of resources is obvious, but it is also worth asking if only that is the problem. Is the current model sufficient? Is the lack of intercultural health an isolated problem that affects a small community or could it be

Culture and Mental Health in Chile

a cross-cutting issue at the national level? Does the training of mental health professionals and personnel require modifications or perhaps a deep restructuring? These are all difficult questions to answer. The need for an in-depth study of contingencies leads again and in a circular manner to require more resources and for the authorities to put the issue of mental health as a cross-cutting priority for all areas of development.

References

Aburto Miranda, C. (1994) *Un mundo aparte. Mujeres locas y Casa de Orates de Santiago 1852–1931.* Tesis (Lic). Facultad de Historia, Geografía y Ciencia Política, Pontificia Univer sidad Católica de Chile.

Alarcón, R. (1976) Hacia una identidad de la Psiquiatría Latinoamericana. *Boletín de la Oficina Sanitaria Latinoamericana*, 109–121.

Álvarez, I. (2006) El Rey de Araucanía y la Endemoniada de Santiago: Aportes para una historia de la locura en el Chile del siglo XIX. *Persona y sociedad*, *20*(1): 105–124.

Araya, C. (2018) Aspectos de la profesionalización de la psiquiatría en Chile, siglos XIX y XX. *Autoctonía*, 146–156.

Bengoa, J. (2011) Los mapuches: Historia, cultura y conflicto. *Cahiers des Amériques latines*, *2011*(68): 89–107.

Carrasco, J. (2018) El zapato de Cenicienta: Otra versión de los inicios de la psiquiatría en Chile. *Revista de historia de la psicología*, *39*(1): 24–30.

Centro de Investigación Periodística (CIPER). (2012) *Salud mental en Chile: La otra cara del malestar social.* Retrieved from https://ciperchile.cl/2012/09/26/salud-mental-en-chile-la-otra-cara-del-malestar-social/.

Chamorro, M. G. (2005) La reconversión del Hospital psiquiátrico el Peral en Red comunitaria de Salud mental y psiquiatría. *Cuad Med Soc (Chile)*, *45*: 285–299.

Contreras, G. S. (2012) La influencia europea en los inicios de la historia de la psicología en Chile. *Interamerican Journal of Psychology*, *46*(1): 99–109.

Díaz A., Pérez, M., González, C., and Simon, J. (2004) Conceptos de enfermedad y sanación en la cosmovisión mapuche e impacto de la cultura occidental. *Ciencia y enfermería*, *10*(1): 9–16

Echávarri, O., Maino, M., Fischman, R., Morales, S., and Barros, J. (2015) Aumento sostenido del suicidio en Chile: un tema pendiente. *Temas de la Agenda Pública*, 3–14.

Errázuriz, P., Valdés, C., Vöhringer, P. A., and Calvo, E. (2015) Financiamiento de la salud mental en Chile: Una deuda pendiente. *Revista médica de Chile*, *143*(9): 1179–1186.

Flores-Guerrero, R. (2004) Salud, Enfermedad y Muerte: Lecturas desde la Antropología Sociocultural. *Revista Mad,* (10): 21–29.

Fuentealba Hernández., R. (2013) Representaciones sociales de la esquizofrenia en las redes sociales primarias de personas esquizofrénicas. Retrieved from http://repositorio.uchile.cl/handle/2250/130670

Gavilán, V., Vigueras, P., Madariaga, C., and Parra, M. (2017) Interculturalidad, tradiciones culturales y etnicidades: Tres nociones claves para comprender las políticas sanitarias en Chile. *Chungará (Arica)*, *49*(4): 477–482.

Gaete, T. (2007) Representaciones sociales de psicólogos sobre el consumo de drogas, consumidores y tratamientos: "El juicio psicológico". *Revista de psicología*, *16*(2): 53–77.

Gómez, M. (2017). De la Casa de Orates al Open Door: El paisaje en el proyecto asilar chileno, 1852–1928. *Asclepio*, *69*(2): 192.

Hasen, F. (2012) Interculturalidad en salud: Competencias en prácticas de salud con población indígena. *Ciencia y enfermería*, *18*(3): 17–24.

Jiménez, Á. and Radiszcz, E. (2012) Salud mental en Chile: La otra cara del malestar social. Retrieved from https://ciperchile.cl/2012/09/26/salud-mental-en-chile-la-otra-cara-del-malestar-social/.

León, L. (2007) Gulumapu (Araucanía): La'pacificación'y su relato historiográfico, 1900–1973. *Revista de Historia Social y de las Mentalidades*, 137–170.

Massad, C. (2005) La construcción social de las enfermedades mentales (Undergraduate Thesis). Alberto Hurtado University, Santiago de Chile.

Medina, E. (2001) De Manicomio Nacional a Hospital Psiquiátrico. *Revista chilena de neuro-psiquiatría*, *39*(1): 78–81.

Ministerio de Desarrollo Social. (2015) *Pueblo indígenas: Síntesis de resultados.* Santiago. Ministerio de Desarrollo Social.

Ministerio de Economía. Resultados Censo (2017) Retrieved from www.censo2017.cl/wp-content/uploads/2017/12/Presentacion_Resultados_Definitivos_Censo2017.pdf.

Ministerio de Salud. (2017) *Orientaciones para la implementación del modelo de atención integral de salud familiar y comunitaria.* Santiago. Ministerio de Salud.

Ministerio de Salud de Chile. (2011) *Perfil epidemiológico básico de la población mapuche residente en el área de cobertura del Servicio de Salud Araucanía Norte.* Santiago. Ministerio de Salud.

Moscovici, S. (1979) La representación social, un concepto perdido. In S. Moscovici (Ed.), *El Psicoanálisis, su imagen y su público* (pp. 27–44). Buenos Aires: Huemul.

Olea, R. (2013) Ta iñ fijke xipa rakizuameluwün. Historia, colonialismo y resistencia desde el país mapuche. Luis Cárcamo-Huechante. et al. Desde el despojo. Un agenciamiento colectivo de la historia. *Taller de letras,* (52): 195–198

Retamal C, P., Markkula, N., and Peña, S. (2016) Salud mental en Chile y Finlandia: Desafíos y lecciones. *Revista médica de Chile, 144*(7): 926–929.

Salas, G. (2014) Pasado y presente de la psicología en Chile: Profesionalización, instituciones y divulgación científica. *Historias de la psicología en América del Sur: Diálogos y perspectivas,* 100–119.

Salas, G., and Lizama, E. (2013) *Historia de la Psicología en Chile 1889–1981.* La Serena: Editorial Universidad de La Serena.

Sontag, S. (1996) *La enfermedad y sus metáforas.* Madrid: Taurus.

Vicente, B., Saldivia, S., and Pihán, R. (2016) Prevalencias y brechas hoy: Salud mental mañana. Acta bioethica, *22*(1): 51–61

30
CULTURE AND MENTAL HEALTH IN (THE GREATER) CHINA

Yu-Te Huang

Greater China refers to a geographical area known to have a thousand years of history and a massive size of territories where Chinese culture serves as a framework in shaping people's ideology and behaviors (Fan 2000). As Leung and Chen (2009) noted, Mainland China, Hong Kong, and Taiwan are culturally similar in sharing Chinese philosophies and folk religions (e.g., Confucianism, Buddhism, and Taoism). Despite the shared salience of Chinese culture, greater China is also home to diverse ethnocultural groups who have conceived of distinct concepts of and reaction to the experiences of mental illness (Parker, Gladstone and Chee 2001). Given the sizable landmass and diverse knowledge systems, it is problematic to view Chinese culture as a uniform system with a fixed set of features. Mental health professionals have been calling for incorporation of indigenous knowledge into services for those who are living with mental health issues in greater China (Leung and Chen 2009). As will be elucidated throughout this chapter, people who are shaped by Chinese cultural values appear to endorse culturally specific concepts of and reaction to mental illness issues. However, the colonization history and globalization forces also call into question any knowledge claimed to be local and authentic. As the mental health frontlines are becoming culturally diverse and complex, this chapter seeks to enhance mental health practitioners' cross-cultural competence and a critical lens in learning and applying knowledge in their helping work.

Greater China: Demographics and a brief history of mental health

Mainland China

Mainland China refers to a geopolitical area under the governance of the People's Republic of China. Mainland China has been the most populated country in the world with 1.41 billion people with an annual growth rate of only 0.59%, and Han Chinese as the predominant ethnic group. The history archives indicate that organized care for the mentally ill emerged in the Tang Dynasty (CE 618–907) (Liu et al. 2011). The first Western style psychiatric hospital, Guangzhou Brain Hospital, was established by an American missionary, John Kerr, in 1898 mainly as the means to house the homeless mentally ill (Liu et al. 2011). Moving to the People's Republic of China era in 1949, psychiatric hospitals came into place in nearly every province for the sake of protecting social security and stability (Liu et al. 2011). The

365

first National Mental Health Meeting in 1958 marked the beginning of community mental health work whereby several major cities launched preventive and treatment programs for the mentally ill. In the 1980s, a three-tier model (i.e., city, district/county, and street/town levels) was established as a model of prevention and treatment for people with psychoses (Liu et al. 2011). Later, the economic development in Mainland China led to establishment of smaller-scale mental health facilities since a large-scale mental health agency was considered less profitable. In spite of the increase in the number of mental health facilities, it was not until the late 1990s that some psychiatrists questioned the profit-driven model of the service delivery, collectively advocating for a national mental health plan (Liu et al. 2011). As a result of the meeting attended by ten Chinese Ministries and the World Health Organization held in 1999 in Beijing, the first *National Mental Health Plan* was announced by the Ministries of Health, Public Security and Civil Affairs, and China Disabled Person's Federation. In 2004, the *Proposal on Further Strengthening Mental Health Work* has become the de facto Chinese national mental health policy in setting up the directive principles of mental health services for psychological and behavioral problems (Liu et al. 2011).

Hong Kong

Although Hong Kong belongs to the People's Republic of China, its history as a British colony makes Hong Kong a unique region different from Mainland China. Hong Kong is a densely populated and compact region accommodating 7.4 million residents in a territory of 1,104 square kilometers. While repeatedly ranked as the most globalized city in the world, Hong Kong is made up predominantly by those who self-identify as Chinese (Census and Statistics Department 2016) with the British colonization (1894–1995) playing a significant part in the formation and evolution of mental health service system (Yip 1998). Here I draw on Yip's (1998) work to outline the history of Hong Kong mental health service system. During the pre-asylum period (1841–1924), the British Government did not recognize a need to build asylums for the mentally ill. The following asylum period (1925–1948) witnessed a population growth alongside a noticeable increase in people who have mental disturbance in the aftermath of the Second World War. While the government set out to build Victoria Mental Hospital to hospitalize mental patients, most inpatients received nothing but physical restrain and custodial care. A significant change marked the subsequent organization period (1948–1965) when the government assumed a greater responsibility for taking care of the mental patients. Treatment-oriented mental health services in Hong Kong developed in both government and non-government sectors, with the objectives shifting from temporary custody to treatment and hospitalization. Enactment of the Mental Health Ordinance ringed up the curtain on the rehabilitation stage (1966–1973) in which half-way houses, industrial rehabilitation farms, and psychiatric hospitals providing comprehensive services came into place. Centralized rehabilitation movement (1971–1981) followed as the government exhibited a growing resolution to catch up with the international call for mental health rehabilitation. The final stage (1982–1995) is termed the civil control versus community care. The handover of Hong Kong's sovereignty to Mainland China, a quest of social stability, incidents of public violence committed by people with psychoses, and massive population density have invoked the public concerns for psychotic patients and posed a hurdle to community-based rehabilitation movement. Currently, the Hong Kong government is committee to responding to the mental health problems, but individuals with severe mental health issues may still find it difficult to live a stigma-free life and structural discrimination against the mentally ill remains prevalent in Hong Kong (Lee, Chiu, Tsang, Chui and Kleinman 2006).

Taiwan

Taiwan, in the official term, the Republic of China, is an island adjacent to Mainland China and Hong Kong. The size of population is around 23.5 million with Han Chinese constituting the ethnic majority group. Taiwanese aboriginal people have been living in the island for approximately 5,500 years before a Han immigration began in the 17th century (Blust 1999). Among the Taiwanese indigenous communities, 16 distinct tribal lines have been recognized by the Council of Indigenous Peoples. With regard to history of mental health service, the first mental health institution was built in 1929 in Taipei (Kau and Chou 2004). The evolution of mental health policy can be divided into three stages (Wang 1997). During the establishing stage (1947–1970), there were only 63 psychiatric doctors and only four mental health asylums. Mental illness patients did not receive professional care but rather were treated along with the elders, orphanages, and people having leprosy. The expansion period (1970–1985) was marked by the rise of large psychiatric hospitals. However, most patients only received medication, which was not affordable yet for many families. As a result, some families turn to folk healing (Zhuang 1995) or sent the mentally ill to a private asylum (e.g., Hall of Dragon). Year 1985 marks the beginning of the integrating period with a nationwide service network established to address mental health issues. Incidents involving mental patients and the controversy over the private asylum added a driving force for the passage of the Mental Health Act in 1990. The launch of the National Health Insurance in 1995 made the service affordability improved. Meanwhile, people with chronic mental illness are entitled to social welfare benefits, such as income assistance, education subsidy, supplementary health care, and housing.

Chinese traditional and folk healing

According to Blowers (1996: 2), the term *indigenous* denotes "grass-roots thinking, the everyday, the commonplace, as ingrained among inhabitants of a community and a culture." Noting that the coverage of Chinese culture is enormous, this section will only concentrate on two forms of indigenous practices in relation to mental health: Chinese medicine and folk healing in Taiwan.

Chinese medicine

Chinese culture has presented a distinctive view of mental health and healing in attributing a person's mental health to the goodness of fit in the body-mind-spirit system (Chan, Ho and Chow 2002). Fundamentally differing from the Western paradigm, this holistic understanding of health emanates from Chinese classic books such as Yellow Emperor's Inner Canon and the Treaties on Cold Damage and forms the foundation of the Chinese medicine whose goals lie in enabling a person to retain the human-nature harmony (Yip 2005) and to achieve dynamic balance between one's physical, psychological, and spiritual spheres. Chinese medicine practitioners believe that when the dynamic equilibrium is restored, a person will embark on a self-healing journey (Chan et al. 2002; Ng, Chan, Ho, Wong and Ho 2006).

Chinese medicine harnesses diverse sources of ancient wisdom. The Five Elements (*Wu Xing*) theory categorizes a person's emotion, expression, organs, sensation, and spiritual system into five mutually generating and overcoming elements - metal, wood, water, fire, and earth (Yip 2005). Parallel to the Five Elements theory is the concept of Ying and Yang which stand for two forms of energy by which the universe is constituted. Inseparable yet complementing each other, Ying and Yang are in constant motion towards balance and interconnectedness (Lee, Chan, Chan, Ng and Leung 2018). Originated in this systematic and dynamic view of the nature and the human beings, Chinese medicine endorses a holistic approach to diagnosis, syndrome differentiation, and treatment of mental health problems. Applying a state-of-art four diagnostic methods, including inspection, listening and smelling examination, inquiry, and palpation (Jiang et al. 2012), Chinese medicine practitioners note the vital importance to collect comprehensive information in diagnosing and treating mental health issues.

For example, depression is classified by the Five Elements theory as metal in nature with weakness in the lungs as a root cause (Ng et al. 2006). In exploring the difference in the construct of depression between traditional Chinese medicine and Western medicine, Ng et al. (2006) found that while the Western psychiatry defines depression as a status of being emotionally low or down, depression is otherwise translated into Chinese with a reference to the stagnation syndrome, which implies that the system of emotion is "not flowing, entangled, blocked, or clogged" (Yuen, Ren, Wang and Guo 1997: 585). Ng et al. (2006) further identified three components that define the Chinese concept of depression: (1) over-attachment, which refers to an individual's obsession with things that one views as significant; (2) body-mind obstruction, which describes the obstruction and dysfunction of particular organs with which emotion is interconnected; and (3) affect-posture inhibition, which illustrates an individual's heightened self-consciousness along with uneasiness in response to other people's judgments of him or herself. Characterized by these three constructs, depression is thought to arise from disconnections across body, mind, social, and spiritual domains, rendered a condition that not only requires medical treatment but also legitimates interventions that go beyond the psychiatric medicine.

Several Hong Kong scholars (Chan et al. 2002; Ng, Chan, Leung, Chan, and Yau 2008) have been keen on the incorporation of the body-mind-spirit framework into the mental health social work. The key elements in this framework encompass: (1) the interconnections of physical, emotional, cognitive, social, and spiritual well-being; (2) the acknowledgement of the "impermanent nature of the universe" (Ng et al. 2008: 481); and (3) the restoration of the status of balance, which can not only lead to the cure of disease but also to the transcendence and growth in a person. According to this framework, physical exercise, philosophical and spiritual interventions, and alternative and complementary medicine (ACM) (e.g., herbal medicine, acupuncture, aroma therapy) can also be considered given that the emotional well-being is interconnected with other dimensions (Chan et al. 2002; Ng et al. 2008).

The use of ACM is prevalent among Chinese people with mental illness given their faith and trust in ACM, its congruence with Chinese culture, accessibility, and affordability (Hsu et al. 2008; Thirthalli et al. 2016; Wong et al. 2017). A large-scale study conducted in Hong Kong with 31,762 residents (Chung, Wong, Woo, Lo and Griffiths 2007) shows that in the 30 days preceding the survey, 1.8% reported a regular use of Traditional Chinese Medicine (TCM) in the past 6 months; 8.8% had visited a TCM practitioner, and 2.7% had used TCM over-the-counter products. A particularly interesting finding is that the use of TCM is more frequent for those with higher education. While this pattern has to do with insurance coverage, it also indicates the wide acceptance of TCM as an effective, culturally appropriate treatment option among the Chinese. Emerging studies have found the supportive evidence for the efficacy of ACM in reducing stress and improving mental health using Chinese calligraphy (Lei, Askeroth and Lee 2004), *Qigong and Tai Chi* (Chou et al. 2004; Ho et al. 2017), and aromatherapy (Lin, Chan, Ng and Lam 2007) among others.

Folk healing

Referred to as traditional or indigenous psychotherapy, folk healing has long played an important role in how the Taiwanese understand and handle their psychological distress. Essentially, the folk healing system is non-professional and non-bureaucratic in nature and its operation is dependent on the active engagement of individual, family, and community sectors (Kleinman and Sung 1979). A central figure in the folk healing practice is the person called *Dang-ki*, who is viewed as a mediumship in which a deity possesses a human to offer aid to supplicants (Lee 2016). In the eyes of believers, Dang-ki assumes the power and responsibilities for rendering general health care, psychiatric care, and crisis intervention. Kleinman and Sung (1979) offered compelling illustration for folk healing in Taiwanese society, covering its activities, rituals, problems presented and treated, and a rough profile of the clientele. In their interviews with 12 patients who sought folk healing, ten of them found the folk healing to be either partially or fully effective and reported symptomatic, behavioral, and psychological improvement following the treatment. According to their analysis, the folk healing could appear effective particularly under three conditions: (1) acute, yet naturally remitting disease (2) non-life threatening, chronic disease in which management of the illness is central to the clinical treatment; and (3) somatization of minor psychological disorders or interpersonal problems. While not many cases reported a clear sign of cure, folk healing provide local communities with an important venue for psychosocial and cultural treatments (Kleinman and Sung 1979).

To date, the use of folk healing remains an option for Taiwanese people to deal with psychological distress (Wu and Liu 2014). One large-scale study with 10,882 Taiwanese respondents (Yeh and Lin 2006) shows that in face of depressive symptoms, they would consider both professional and non-professional resources including internists and general practitioners of the Western medicine, Chinese medicine practitioners, mental health practitioners, and folk healing providers.

Colonialism and the evolution of mental health practices in greater China

Despite the long history and popularity of indigenous mental health practice, scholars from greater China have lamented the dominance of modernism and scientificism in the ways how mental health professionals understand and deal with mental illness (Lee et al. 2018). Originated in Descartes's dualistic view on mind and body, scientificism, rationalism, and individualism have occupied the center of scientific inquiries and knowledge production (Lee et al. 2018). As a result, mental health practices are directed to utilize the scientific approach to uncovering the causes of and solutions to a mental health issue at an individual level. Even though there have been growing efforts to revitalize the local and indigenous knowledge, from a postcolonial viewpoint, Western paradigm continues to shape the ways how mental illness is identified and treated in greater China (Parker et al. 2001).

Tao Tribe in Taiwan provides a particularly compelling site to reveal the colonialism in the mental health practices. Inhabiting an outlying Orchid Island of Taiwan, Tao people have historically maintained a self-sufficient economy, unique customs and cultural practices along with limited contact with people at the Taiwan main island. These contextual conditions have led them to develop a distinct view of mental illness. Tsai (2013) describes that those who are experiencing psychological distress alone usually would not be regarded as sick because the primacy of labor participation only legitimizes physical pain and bodily discomfort. As such, a mentally ill individual would perceive a need to seek mental health treatment only when his/her ability to carry out labor duties is disrupted. Also, Tao people attribute psychiatric symptoms to the power of evil spirits and/or lunar force (Tsai, 2013) and believe that these problems require solutions at a spiritual level through traditional rituals.

This indigenous understanding of mental health, however, has been dismissed by the Western psychiatry that only endorses an organic view of disease and the efficacy of biomedical treatments.

The dominance of Western medical model can be seen in the service system established by the Taiwanese Government. Tsai's (2013) ethnographic work reveals the colonialism in the case of Integration Delivery System whose objective is to diminish the disparity in healthcare resources and accessibility in remote areas through providing long-lasting injection, referral to adjacent clinics, and monthly visits by nurses and physicians to provide diagnosis and treatment. Without sufficient attention to the social cause and cultural characteristics of Tao people's mental illness, the Integration Delivery System was found to be underutilized due to patients' poor medical adherence and insensitivity to the indigenous community. A key reason for this consequence is the patients' distrust of the psychiatric medicine which disqualifies Tao people's belief in the ancestral spirit and their unique way of interpreting unpredictable phenomenon. While psychiatric medicine and the model of managed care have assumed a privileged status, dismissal of indigenous culture usually is a problematic pitfall.

Cultural representations of illness and wellness

As illustrated previously, people from a Chinese cultural background normally define wellness in the forms of harmonious interconnection and a dynamic balance across body, mind, spirit, and social relationship. One's health and wellness is thus dependent on the presence of dynamic equilibrium between diverse sometime contrasting forces (Ng et al. 2008), "balance, mutuality, change, and interdependence" (Lee et al. 2018: 34). Lee et al. (2018) use a metaphor for us to imagine this status: when riding a bicycle, one can sustain balance only when a person finds a balance between the opposite forces of steering right or left. Applying this concept to our daily life, it is important to stay energetic and restful because each side does not exist without the presence of the other. According to Lee et al. (2018), this holistic view of wellness represents a fusion of the West and the East in synthesizing the system perspective, quantum theory, integral psychology, and Daoist teaching (i.e., the Ying-Yang perspective). Moreover, the Buddhist teaching also forms a part of this viewpoint, suggesting that everything has its causes and consequences (i.e., karma). It also teaches its followers the importance of relinquishing the secular attachment given that nothing in the world is permanent and obsession of worldly things is a source of suffering.

Combing these doctrines, Lee et al. (2018) suggests that social workers should no longer view an individual and a family as the center of control who can master or solve their problems. Similarly, helping professionals should reconsider the long-held goals to maximize the individual/family's well-being, strength, and potential to actualize themselves (Lee 2005). Rather, Chinese philosophies put forth transcendence of the self and recognize the limited ability for human beings to control their lives in light of the instable nature of earthly desires. By moving beyond the self and downplaying worldly desires, a person usually can encounter inner wisdom, acquire intelligence of the nature, and derive a sense of wellness.

Training and development, accreditation, licensure, and certification processes

Following the Cultural Revolution in 1980s, social work as a profession is undergoing massive expansion in Mainland China as a result of the surging need to serve vulnerable populations, improve efficiency of public services, preclude and solve social turmoil, and maintain social orders (Wang and Yeun-Tsang 2009; Yip 2007). Meanwhile, the Chinese government also adopted the qualifying exam to qualify social workers. The 'Provisional Regulations on the Assessment of the Vocational Standards of Social Workers' outlines the criteria concerning the professional skills and competency of social workers; the 'Measures for the Implementation of the Examination Regarding Professional Qualifications of Social Workers' determined a nation-wide two-tier (i.e., assistant social worker and social worker) examination process for social workers (Wang and Yeun-Tsang 2009). Yet, the number of Mainland China's social workers who have taken and passed the licensure exams is not substantial due to limited availability of social work programs and unattractive job prospects (Shek 2017). Some imperative issues have also existed in the development of social work profession, including (1) inconsistency among government policies to institutionalize the social work profession; (2) geographic disparities of the distribution of social work jobs; and (3) mismatch between social work education and social work employment opportunities (Wu, Huang, Sun and An 2016). Given these unresolved issues, the demand for competent mental health practitioners requires responses from governmental and non-governmental sectors.

In Hong Kong, psychiatric doctors, nurses, and social workers are the primary mental health service providers (Lam et al. 2015; Yip 1998). The Econominist Intellegent Unit (2016) recently reported that the mental health system of Hong Kong have been facing the issues of inadequate mental health service access, shortage of job opportunities, and passive government actions. The recognition and monitoring of professional conducts are defined as the responsibilities of the registration boards.

The Registration Board of the Hong Kong Psychological Society was established in 1994. To register, a clinical psychologist must be a member of the Society, obtain a higher degree in psychology from an institution recognized by the Society, and complete at least one year of post-degree clinical experience in a discipline of psychology. A psychologist can select a special-ization in Clinical Psychology, Educational Psychology, Counselling Psychology, or Industrial and Organizational Psychology upon meeting respective requirements. A list of registered psychologists is publicized so that service users and institutions can verify the qualification of a service provider. Clinical psychologists with a doctoral degree can also choose to join the Hong Kong Association of Doctors in Clinical Psychology.

The Social Work Registration Board came into place under the Social Workers Registration Ordinance in 1998. Only those who have successfully registered can practice with the title of a registered social worker. Eligibility for registration include completion of an accredited social work program whose curriculum (including social work practice and non-social work core courses) meets the standard set up by the Board. Aside from the requirement on curriculum and credits, registration also requires 800 hours of field practicum, 100 hours of placement prepar-ation, and at least one placement carried out in Hong Kong.

In Taiwan, it is not until the late 1990's that the qualifying system for mental health professions became a public concern as a result of a series of natural disasters (e.g., Da-Yuan Plan Crash in 1998 and the '921 Earthquake' in 1999). In addition, the growth of suicide rates between 1997 and 2000 has pressed for improving and regulating mental health service systems (Wang, Kwan and Huang 2011). Given these situations, counselling psychologists have received a national licensure statute – the Psychologist Statute – since 2001 in charge of: (1) mandating for psychologists training; (2) administering the licensure examination and determining eligibility for professional practices; and (3) providing effective and ethical services (Wang et al. 2011).

Currently, Taiwan implements a three-pillar counselling system. Wang et al. (2011) outline the specific roles, accreditation, and licensure processes these three psychological professionals need to undertake. First, primarily providing guidance and general counselling for students at a school setting, qualified *school counsellors* need to receive a graduate level training and a teacher certificate issued by the Bureau of Education. Second, *a counselling psychologist* also needs to pass a qualifying exam and can work in various settings, such as a university, school, or community mental health center, or as a private therapist. While both types of professionals are expected to provide psychotherapy, their main responsibility is to serve clients with mild to moderate psychological distress and in need of a longer service. Last, most *clinical psychologists* practice in a hospital setting to conduct assessment and render psychotherapy for patients referred by a psychiatrist. Prior to taking a qualifying exam, a clinical psychologist is required to complete a postgraduate degree and one-year, full-time internship training.

As for social workers, Taiwan also adopts the licensure examination. Besides meeting the requirement of curriculum credits and field practicum, one needs to pass the Civil Service Special Examination for Social Welfare Workers to obtain a license or a special exam to gain the Professional Social Worker certificate. It is important to note that unlike the United States and Canada where social workers are primary group of mental health service providers, in Taiwan social workers are not permitted to provide psychological assessments and clinical therapy because Psychologist Statute commands that professional therapeutic activities are only limited to licensed psychologists (Chang 2009). Such demarcation of mental health helping activities might have rendered social workers a supplementary position when working in a mental health field. In general, social workers in Taiwan are mainly in charge of case management and community rehabilitation (Chang 2009).

Current mental health practices in greater China

Current mental health practices in greater China begin to rely on the integration of both local knowledge and the Western psychiatry. The diverse practice approaches exist and gain recognition owing to the government's support for the use of traditional Chinese medicine, investment in research, and inclusion in the coverage of health care insurance (Chang et al. 2008; Xu and Yang 2009). Given the availability and popularity of the local mental health care, some practitioners shift to embrace an integrated view of mental health in rendering a holistic formulation of a client's presenting problem. Below is a case vignette used to elucidate this integrated approach to mental health.

Jamie was a 50-year-old Chinese woman. She grew up with a constant feeling of being isolated in her family of origin, perceiving her parents to be careless towards her. As a mother of two sons, she married her husband at the age of 25 and had developed a dependent type of relationship with her husband. She came to seek professional help upon the discovery of her husband having an affair with a woman who had also got pregnant. Having persuaded Jamie to retire early, her husband had transferred most of her pension funds into his own accounts and then asked for divorce. Experiencing this devastating betrayal and loss, Jamie has suffered depressive symptoms and was being treated with antidepressant medication. However, she found the medication ineffective and continued to have a strong sense of loneliness, hurt, and sadness, feeling betrayed and abandoned. Other presenting symptoms also include crying spells, problem in sleeping, and loss of appetite.

With a reference to the Eastern paradigm that depression had exerted multifaceted effects on a person's body, mind, and spirit, Jamie's clinical condition can be tackled from an integrated approach. On the physical level, depression is manifested in the symptoms of low energy, anguish, and reduction in appetite and sleep quality. In the psychological domain, Jamie experienced sadness, feeling of guilt, and negative thoughts and emotions, and impaired self-image. In the spiritual sphere, Jamie struggled with a sense of isolation, despair, and loss of meaning. Therefore, an integrative body-mind-spirit approach to depression will aim to help Jamie restore harmony across the systems. The body movements (e.g., body tapping, or clapping-hand qigong) and Chinese medicine therapy (e.g., acupuncture) are deemed conducive to reinvigorating the flow (qi) and relieving physical symptoms. Mindfulness, expressive arts, and meditation on compassion are viable activities to enable Jamie to forgo over-attachment and develop positive self-image. Finally, spiritual growth possibly can be sought through the guided imagery of forgiveness, appreciation and gratitude journal, and therapeutic writing. Growing evidence has shown the efficacy of this body-mind-spirit approach on improving depressive clients' well-being, daily functioning, and quality of life (Ji et al. 2017; Rentala, Fong, Nattala, Chan and Konduru 2015)

Future directions

It is imperative for mental health practitioners to appreciate cultural characteristics in establishing helping relationships. Taiwanese scholars (Kuo, Hsu and Lai 2011) indicated five themes regarding the role of culture in a counselling relationship: (1) significance of counsellor's authority; (2) primacy of client-counsellor rapport and relationship; (3) centrality of collective familism; (4) observance of indigenous grief response and process; and (5) adherence to face-saving communication and interpersonal patterns. These principles thus require a practitioner to build and bolster a relationship that is not only therapeutic but also extends to a client's social connections (Kuo et al. 2011). Chong (2016) also comments on the limitation of the Western form of practitioners-client alliance when working with aboriginal communities. Often, service providers need to perform multiple roles and to seek preexisting relationships with a client in order to build rapports given that Taiwanese aboriginal people might not take these professional therapists seriously (Hsu, Yan and Tu 2012). Second, professional practices have to be culturally contextualized and kept in line with the cultural norms (e.g., respect for the elderly) and a client's everyday experiences (Chong 2016). Finally, the collectivist values and an emphasis on relationships upheld by indigenous communities require mental health professionals to locate a presenting problem within a relational context, engaging all the stakeholders, such as family members, religious leaders, and politicians in service plans.

Given cultural specificity in the manifestation and treatment of mental illness, mental health professionals therefore need to develop a critical awareness of the colonial influence of the Western knowledge. Leung and Chen (2009) emphasize the cultivation of multicultural competencies in recognizing that in the contemporary era, both clients and practitioners may have been shaped by their culture of origin and the Western dominant culture, thereby maintaining a hybrid form of cultural perspective and experience. Leung and Chen (2009) have advocated for indigenization both *from within* and *from without* (Enriquez 1993). The approach of *from without* involves modification of existing counselling models and theories by incorporating additional dimensions so as to better fit with a local cultural context. The *from within* approach guides a practitioner not to refer to any preconceived theoretical and clinical accounts but rather to seek contextual knowledge, theories, and methods originating in a cultural context, finding what is implicit in ordinary people's minds and articulate the processes and factors shaping personality, emotions, and behaviors (Blowers 1996).

Inquiry into and recognition of the intersection between mental health and culture presses for interdisciplinary collaboration. Weisz, Sandler, Durlak, and Anton (2005) have identified several mental health areas for rigorous investigations to: (1) analyze ethnicity and culture in relation to intervention selection and impact; (2) examine conditions under which programs can and cannot work; (3) specify therapeutic mechanisms that produce effects; (4) document the effect of interventions in real-world contexts; and (5) enhance accessibility and efficacy of empirically tested interventions. All of these tasks require involvement of people from diverse disciplines with distinct but complimentary training. As illustrated previously, Chinese culture has afforded a holistic framework in conceptualizing and treating a mental health issue. Hence, practitioners and researchers need to actively seek interdisciplinary knowledge and skills and develop an integrative, eclectic approach (Huang and Fang 2016; Lee et al. 2018), which encompasses evidence-based principles, scientific methods, state-of-art knowledge, a critical consciousness, and a cultural sensitivity while incorporating traditional Chinese healing approaches. Advancement in technology also open tremendous opportunities for mental health professionals to develop innovative, culturally responsive intervention and advanced evaluation approach.

Conclusion

The cultural heritage of greater China has offered a knowledge paradigm that fundamentally differs from the Western one. While recognizing the values and merits of professional knowledge stemming from both Western and Eastern traditions, mental health practitioners have to be aware of the colonial dominance and power hierarchy by which non-Western wisdoms are historically subjugated. It is only by bearing the intersection of the cultural, power, and mental health in mind that service providers will be more competent to serve clients where they are.

References

Blowers, G. H. (1996) 'The Prospects for a Chinese Psychology'. In M. H. Bond (Ed.), *Handbook of Chinese Psychology*. Oxford: Oxford University Press.

Blust, R. (1999) 'Subgrouping, Circularity and Extinction: Some Issues in Austronesian Comparative linguistics'. In E. Zeitoun and P. J. K. Li (Eds.), *Selected Papers from the Eighth International Conference on Austronesian Linguistics* (pp. 31–94). Taipei: Academia Sinica.

Brenner, M. J., Leung, P. P. Y., Sreevani, R. and Nan, J. K. M. (2018) 'Moving Out of Darkness: Application of the Integrative Body-Mind-Spirit Approach in the Treatment of Depression'. In M.Y. Lee, C. H. Y. Chan, C. H. Y. Chan, S. M. Ng, and P. P. Y. Leung (Eds.), *Integrative Body-Mind-Spirit Social Work* (pp. 257–269). New York: Oxford University Press.

Census and Statistics Department. (2016) Thematic Report: Ethnic Minorities. Retrieved from www.bycensus2016.gov.hk/data/16bc-ethnic-minorities.pdf.

Chan, C. H. Y., Ho, P. S. Y. and Chow, E. (2002) 'A Body-Mind-Spirit Model in Health', *Social Work in Health Care, 34*(3–4): 261–282.

Chang, L.-C., Huang, N., Chou, Y.-J., Lee, C.-H., Kao, F.-Y., and Huang, Y.-T. (2008) 'Utilization Patterns of Chinese Medicine and Western Medicine under the National Health Insurance Program in Taiwan: A Population-Based Study from 1997 to 2003', *BMC Health Services Research, 8*(1): 170.

Chang, R.-S. (2009) 'The Professional Development and Crisis in Psychiatric Social Work in Taiwan', *Taiwanese Social Work, 6*: 119–145.

Chong, H. H. (2016) 'The Understanding of Indigenous Peoples Towards Professional Relationships: The Case of Taiwan', *International Social Work, 59*(2): 235–245.

Chou, K. L., Lee, P. W.-H., Yu, E. C.-S., Macfarlane, D., Cheng, Y. H., Chan, S. S.-C. and Chi, I. (2004) 'Effect of Tai Chi on Depressive Symptoms amongst Chinese Older Patients with Depressive Disorders: A Randomized Clinical Trial', *International Journal of Geriatric Psychiatry, 19*(11): 1105–1107.

Chung, V., Wong, E., Woo, J., Lo, S.-V. and Griffiths, S. (2007) 'Use of Traditional Chinese Medicine in the Hong Kong Special Administrative Region of China', *The Journal of Alternative and Complementary Medicine, 13*(3): 361–368.

Enriquez, V. G. (1993) 'Developing a Filipino psychology'. In U. Kim and J. W. Berry (Eds.), *Indigenous Psychologies: Research and Experience in Cultural Context* (pp. 152–159). Newbury Park, CA: Sage.

Fan, Y. (2000) 'A Classification of Chinese Culture', *Cross Cultural Management: An International Journal, 7*(2): 3–10.

Ho, R. T. H., Wan, A. H. Y., Chan, J. S. M., Ng, S. M., Chung, K. F. and Chan, C. L. W. (2017) 'Study Protocol on Comparative Effectiveness of Mindfulness Meditation and Qigong on Psychophysiological

Outcomes for Patients with Colorectal Cancer: A Randomized Controlled Trial', *BMC Complementary and Alternative Medicine*, 17(1): 390.

Hsu, C. T., Yan, C. R. and Tu, C. C. (2012) 'Tribal Development and Community Empowerment: A Study of Pauwanese Tribe in Pingtung County', *Journal of Community Work and Community Studies*, 2(1): 29–64.

Hsu, M. C., Creedy, D., Moyle, W., Venturato, L., Tsay, S. L. and Ouyang, W. C. (2008) 'Use of Complementary and Alternative Medicine among Adult Patients for Depression in Taiwan', *Journal of Affective Disorders*, 111(2): 360–365.

Huang, Y. T. and Fang, L. (2016) 'Understanding Depression from Different Paradigms: Toward an Eclectic Social Work Approach', *British Journal of Social Work*, 46(3): 756–772.

Ji, X. W., Chan, C. H. Y., Lau, B. H. P., Chan, J. S. M., Chan, C. L. W. and Chung, K.-F. (2017) 'The Interrelationship between Sleep and Depression: A Secondary Analysis of a Randomized Controlled Trial on Mind-Body-Spirit Intervention', *Sleep Medicine*, 29: 41–46.

Jiang, M., Lu, C., Zhang, C., Yang, J., Tan, Y., Lu, A. and Chan, K. (2012) 'Syndrome Differentiation in Modern Research of Traditional Chinese Medicine', *Journal of Ethnopharmacology*, 140(3): 634–642.

Kau, L. J. and Chou, M. H. (2004) 'Community Rehabilitation Centers in Taipei City', *Taipei City Medical Journal*, 1(4): 503–511.

Kleinman, A. and Sung, L. H. (1979) 'Why Do Indigenous Practitioners Successfully Heal?', *Social Science & Medicine. Part B: Medical Anthropology*, 13(1): 7–26.

Kuo, B. C. H., Hsu, W. S. and Lai, N. H. (2011) 'Indigenous Crisis Counseling in Taiwan: An Exploratory Qualitative Case Study of an Expert Therapist', *International Journal for the Advancement of Counselling*, 33(1): 1–21.

Lam, L. C. W., Wong, C. S. M., Wang, M. J., Chan, W. C., Chen, E. Y. H., Ng, R. M. K., . . . Bebbington, P. (2015) 'Prevalence, Psychosocial Correlates and Service Utilization of Depressive and Anxiety Disorders in Hong Kong: The Hong Kong Mental Morbidity Survey (HKMMS)', *Social Psychiatry & Psychiatric Epidemiology*, 50(9): 1379–1388.

Lee, B. O. (2016) 'Transformation in Dang-ki Healing: The Embodied Self and Perceived Legitimacy', *Culture, Medicine, and Psychiatry*, 40(3): 422–449.

Lee, M. Y. (2005) 'The Complexity of Indigenization of Clinical Social Work Knowledge and Practice', *The Hong Kong Journal of Social Work*, 39(01n02): 3–31.

Lee, M. Y., Chan, C. Y., Chan, C. L. W., Ng, S. M. and Leung, P. P. Y. (2018) *Integrative Body-Mind-Spirit Social Work*. New York: Oxford University Press.

Lee, S., Chiu, M. Y. L., Tsang, A., Chui, H. and Kleinman, A. (2006) 'Stigmatizing Experience and Structural Discrimination Associated with the Treatment of Schizophrenia in Hong Kong', *Social Science & Medicine*, 62(7): 1685–1696.

Lei, T., Askeroth, C. and Lee, C. T. (2004) 'Indigenous Chinese Healing: Theories and Methods'. In J. M. Fish, J. G. Draguns and U. P. Gielen (Eds.), *Handbook of Culture, Therapy, and Healing* (pp. 191–212). Mahwah, NJ: Lawrence Erlbaum.

Leung, S. A. and Chen, P. H. (2009) 'Counseling Psychology in Chinese Communities in Asia: Indigenous, Multicultural, and Cross-Cultural Considerations', *The Counseling Psychologist*, 37(7): 944–966.

Lin, P. W. K., Chan, W. C., Ng, B. F. L. and Lam, L. C. W. (2007) 'Efficacy of Aromatherapy (Lavandula Angustifolia) as an Intervention for Agitated Behaviours in Chinese Older Persons with Dementia: A Cross-over Randomized Trial', *International Journal of Geriatric Psychiatry*, 22(5): 405–410.

Liu, J. I. N., Ma, H., He, Y. L., Xie, B. I. N., Xu, Y. F., Tang, H. Y., . . . Yu, X. I. N. (2011) 'Mental Health System in China: History, Recent Service Reform and Future Challenges', *World Psychiatry*, 10(3): 210–216.

Ng, S. M., Chan, C. L. W., Ho, D. Y. F., Wong, Y. Y. and Ho, R. T. H. (2006) 'Stagnation as a Distinct Clinical Syndrome: Comparing "Yu" (Stagnation) in Traditional Chinese Medicine with Depression', *The British Journal of Social Work*, 36(3): 467–484.

Ng, S. M., Chan, C. L. W., Leung, P. P. Y., Chan, C. H. Y. and Yau, J. K. Y. (2008) 'Beyond Survivorship: Achieving a Harmonious Dynamic Equilibrium Using a Chinese Medicine Framework in Health and Mental Health', *Social Work in Mental Health*, 7(1–3): 62–81.

Parker, G., Gladstone, G. and Chee, K. T. (2001) 'Depression in the Planet's Largest Ethnic Group: The Chinese', *American Journal of Psychiatry*, 158(6): 857–864.

Rentala, S., Fong, T. C. T., Nattala, P., Chan, C. L. W. and Konduru, R. (2015) 'Effectiveness of Body–Mind–Spirit Intervention on Well-Being, Functional Impairment and Quality of Life among Depressive Patients: A Randomized Controlled Trial', *Journal of Advanced Nursing*, 71(9), 2153–2163. doi:10.1111/jan.12677.

Shek, D. T. L. (2017) 'Editorial: A Snapshot of Social Work in the Asia-Pacific Region', *British Journal of Social Work, 47*(1): 1–8.

The Econominist Intellegent Unit. (2016). *Mental Health and Integration: Provision for Supporting People with Mental Illness: A Comparison of 15 Asia Pacific Countries*. Retrieved from www.eiuperspectives.econo-mist.com/sites/default/files/Mental_health_and_integration.pdf.

Thirthalli, J., Zhou, L., Kumar, K., Gao, J., Vaid, H., Liu, H., Hankey, A., Wang, G., Gangadhar, B. N., Nie, J.-B., and Nichter, M. (2016) 'Traditional, Complementary, and Alternative Medicine Approaches to Mental Health Care and Psychological Wellbeing in India and China', *The Lancet Psychiatry, 3*(7): 660–672.

Tsai, Y. Y. (2013) 'To Comply or Not to Comply? State Medical Governance and the "Chaos Narrative" of Tao Mentally-Disoriented People', *Taiwan: A Radical Quarterly in Social Studies, 92*: 73–140.

Wang, K. Y. (1997) 'A Review of Mental Health Policy in Taiwan: Types of Elite and the Decision-Making Process', *Chinese Journal of Mental Health, 10*(1): 29–47.

Wang, L. F., Kwan, K. L. K. and Huang, S. F. (2011) 'Counseling Psychology Licensure in Taiwan: Development, Challenges, and Opportunities', *International Journal for the Advancement of Counselling, 33*(1): 37–50.

Wang, S. B., & Yeun-Tsang, A. (2009) 'The Development of Social Work in China in the Context of Building a Harmonious Society', *China Social Sciences, 2009*: 128–140.

Weisz, J. R., Sandler, I. N., Durlak, J. A. and Anton, B. S. (2005) 'Promoting and Protecting Youth Mental Health Through Evidence-Based Prevention and Treatment', *American Psychologist, 60*(6): 628–648.

Wong, D. F. K., Cheng, C. W., Zhuang, X. Y., Ng, T. K., Pan, S. M., He, X. and Poon, A. (2017) 'Comparing the Mental Health Literacy of Chinese People in Australia, China, Hong Kong and Taiwan: Implications for Mental Health Promotion', *Psychiatry Research, 256*: 258–266.

Wu, C. S. and Liu, Y. J. (2014) 'Religious Coping in Life Difficulties: A Case Study of Taiwanese Folk Religion Female Believers', *Mental Health, Religion & Culture, 17*(2): 210–218.

Wu, S., Huang, H., Sun, F. and An, Q. (2016) 'Is Social Work Really Being Recognized? Problems with Social Work Employment Opportunities in Mainland China', *Social Work Education, 35*(2): 186–203.

Xu, J. and Yang, Y. (2009) 'Traditional Chinese Medicine in the Chinese Health Care System', *Health Policy, 90*(2): 133–139.

Yeh, Y. H. and Lin, C. H. (2006) 'A Questionnaire Study of Depression Related Help-Seeking Behavior among the General Public in Taiwan', *Formasa Journal of Mental Health, 19*(2): 125–148.

Yip, K. S. (1998) 'A Historical Review of Mental Health Services in Hong Kong (1841 To 1995)', *International Journal of Social Psychiatry, 44*(1): 46–55.

Yip, K. S. (2005) 'Chinese Concepts of Mental Health: Cultural Implications for Social Work Practice', *International Social Work, 48*(4): 391–407.

Yip, K. S. (2007) 'Tensions and Dilemmas of Social Work Education in China', *International Social Work, 50*(1): 93–105.

Yuen, Y. C., Ren, J. S., Wang, L. and Guo, K. Z. (1997) *Chinese–English Dictionary of Traditional Chinese Medicine*. Beijing, China: People's Health Publishing.

Zhuang, M. M. (1995) *A Review of Medical Service System for Mentally Ill Patients*. Taipei: Research, Development, and Evaluation Commission, Executive Yuan.

31

CULTURE AND MENTAL HEALTH IN EGYPT

Michael Elnemais Fawzy

Egypt is the most populous country in the Arab world and the third most populous country in Africa. Egypt is administratively divided into 27 governorates (regions). In spite of a large area (1,002,450 square kilometers), much of the land is covered by desert, and about 95 percent of the population is concentrated along the Nile River and its delta, which represents only 5 percent of Egypt's land area. The density in this area is valued at 1,500 inhabitant/km^2 (Materia and Riva 2011; France Diplomatie 2019).

The population is about 98 million, according to the 2018 population census (2 percent population growth rate) (Table 31.1). According to the Central Agency for Public Mobilization and Statistics (CAPMAS) and United Nations report, the unemployment rate (12.4 percent) mainly hits women (23.6 percent) and youth (33.1 percent for those 15–24 years old). The 15- to 29-year-old account for 79 percent of the total unemployed ratio while they represent 60 percent of the population of the country. The country is also characterized by an important adult illiteracy rate (around 75 percent) and discrepancies in living condition between urban and rural areas (UN 2019) (See Figure 31.1.).

Egypt ranks 115 on the Human Development Index (HDI) of 169 countries and is considered one of the medium development countries by the World Bank. The poverty is persistent and inequalities flagrant. The perspective of equitable development, whether social, economic or political, are therefore rather limited. Among the indicators of this ranking is the fact that the health needs of the population are not entirely met (UNDP 2014). Health allotments amount to 4.5 percent of the 2017–2018 budget (CAPMAS 2019). Currently, 90 percent of the population lives within 5 km of a health care unit, but the aim is to shorten the distance to 3 km for the whole population (Materia and Riva 2011). Importantly, according to the HDI report (2013), only a minority, 35 percent of the population, is satisfied with the health services (UNDP 2014).

Refugees

Bordering the Mediterranean Sea, between Libya and the Gaza Strip, the Red Sea, north of Sudan and the Asian Sinai Peninsula, Egypt became, during the 2000s, an increasingly important transit and destination country for economic migrants and asylum seekers, including Palestinians, East Africans, South Asians and, more recently, Iraqis and Syrians. Egypt draws many refugees because of its resettlement programs with the West. Cairo has one of the largest

Table 31.1 2019 Report of The Egyptian Central Agency for Public Mobilization and Statistics. (2019). Statistical Abstract. (1st ed.). Cairo, Egypt.

Population Estimate (Mil)	2019
Total	98.1
Males	50.5
Females	47.6
0–14	34.0
15–24	17.9
25–49	32.9
50–59	7.8
60–64	3.0
65+	4.4

urban refugee populations in the world. As of October 2017, the UNHCR counted 215,911 registered refugees and asylum seekers in Egypt (UNHCR 2017) (See Table 31.2.).

According to the Egypt Regional Refugee and Resilience Plan 2016–2017, refugees often suffer from loss of hope, deteriorating psychological and medical conditions, and limited livelihood opportunities. They are particularly vulnerable to poverty, insecure food supply, access to poor quality services, as well as sexual and gender-based violence, including abuse and exploitation. Refugees in Egypt do not live in camps, but among Egyptian communities across Egypt, with the most impacted governorates being Cairo, 6 October, Giza, Alexandria and Qalyubia. Hosting refugees places additional pressures on the already limited resources and services and host communities find it difficult to cope with additional competition for limited resources.

Child's place in Egyptian society

Traditionally, the roles of mothers and fathers are strictly defined, with mothers in charge of the implicit education (imitation and experience) of young children then mostly for girls, and fathers undertaking explicit education (written and oral teaching), especially for boys starting from 7 years old. The more traditional society is, the more important illiteracy is and the less explicit education is reduced.

During their early childhood, children stay in their maternal circle. During their first years, they learn through imitation. Perceived as innocent, they are rarely punished. Later, they learn, by conformism, the sense of pride and shame. They have to respect different constraints, often cultural, otherwise they would disappoint their parents or be excluded from the group (affective blackmail). Starting from the age of seven, they are expected to follow the rules and codes they previously got to know. Fathers then take the responsibility of boys' education and mothers of girls' education (Graindorge 2006).

This, however, needs to be balanced, as Egypt is a mix between tradition, modernity, religion and rites, in a context of globalization, with multiple cultural exchanges. Consequently, hybrid education forms appear, with differences between urban/rural mass population and more Occidentalized elites.

The essential elements justifying programmes in favour of early childhood are the following:

- The major role played by mothers during the first years of children, with an increased number of working mothers;
- The conformism of education (parental or at school) hampers initiatives;

Figure 31.1 UN. (2019). About Egypt. Retrieved 5 November 2019 from http://eg.one.un.org/content/unct/egypt/en/home/about-egypt.html.

- The place of religion is essential and can justify some practices and a certain rigidity in education. Teaching the Qur'an/Bible is inherent to child's education.

Violence against children

Many children in Egypt suffer various forms of violence, exploitation, human trafficking and inadequate family care. UNICEF states that the deprivation of protection is highly interconnected

Table 31.2 UNHCR. (2017). Fact sheet. Retrieved from www.unhcr.org/eg/unhcr-egypt-documents

Nationality	Asylum Seekers	Refugees	Total
Syrian	119,908	6,119	**126,027[1]**
Sudanese	18,589	16,713	**35,302**
Ethiopian	11,851	2,426	**14,277**
South Sudanese	4,778	4,664	**9,442**
Eritrean	9,327	2,335	**11,662**
Others (60 countries)	11,355	7,846	**19,201**
Total	**175,808**	**40,103**	**215,911**
Including for 2017			
New arrival	27,742, including 14,753 Syrians		
Registered	44,879, including 21,832 Syrians		

In addition, there was a 44% increase in new registrations in the first half of 2017 when compared to the same period for 2016

[1] Estimates by UNHCR and other humanitarian organizations suggest that the Syrian *refugee* population in the country could be twice that number.

to other poverty dimensions, with children deprived in protection being more likely affected by another dimension (education, health, nutrition, water and sanitation) (UNICEF 2017).

The report concludes with the necessity to mainstream protection in all programs aiming at reducing child multidimensional poverty to ensure their efficacy. Yet, violence is widespread in Egypt, with 12.4 million children having suffered or having a sibling who suffered severe physical punishment by a caregiver.

According to a study, are also of concern by National Council for Childhood and Motherhood NCCM and UNICEF on 2015:

1   emotional violence, which affected 72 percent of children in Alexandria, 76 percent in Cairo and 86 percent in Assiut;
2   neglect: one-quarter of children surveyed in Alexandria and Cairo;
3   Witness of domestic violence: 66 percent in Assiut and around 40 percent in Alexandria and Cairo.

In spite of those high figures, parents seem to have an ambivalent behaviour toward the different kinds of violence, with some parents saying they sometimes regret beating their children or perceiving emotional violence as counter-productive. This ambivalence is reflected in different studies done with, for example:

The 2006 Social Research Center/American University in Cairo research reporting that many parents used corporal punishment "under the illusion that what they do is in their child best interest (…) with the misconception that violence is necessary for good discipline".

Violence is seen as a legitimate and socially acceptable disciplinary practice by many parents, teachers, religious leaders and even children themselves. Groups at a higher risk of deprivation include children from female-headed households, or with a younger household head, with low parental educational attainment and from the poorest families (UNICEF 2015).

Addressing the social perception of violence will therefore require an important and comprehensive program toward all caregivers on positive discipline, with messages conveyed at different level (public media to one to one approaches) and provision of alternative and positive education tools to parents and caregivers. Additionally, programs offering psychosocial support need to be developed toward children and youth, in complement to specialized services for children experiencing extreme abuse and violence.

Sexual violence and harmful traditional practices

Girls are especially vulnerable in the Egyptian context, especially regarding sexual harassment, Female Genital Mutilation (FGM) and early marriage. According to the UNICEF survey done in the governorates of Cairo, Alexandria and Assiut, a majority of girls reported having experienced sexual harassment (two-thirds in Cairo). The common belief among parents and boys is that girls who are sexually harassed invite such treatment through their behaviour or clothing and that those who respond must be "enjoying the abuse" and "deserve what they get". This places girls in front of a double challenge: being responsible for provoking harassment and, at the same time, being responsible for preventing it (by staying away from men, dressing modestly, etc.) and ignoring such abuse when it happens (UNICEF 2015).

With 27.2 million of cases, Egypt has the highest number in the world of female aged 15–49 who have undergone FGM, in spite of being illegal and seen as a right violation. Despite clear threats to their health and well-being, FGM are seen as a way to "preserve" girls and their reputation and are linked to myths around girls' purity, virginity, fidelity after marriage and chastity (UNICEF 2013). Child marriage is illegal in Egypt but continues to be used as a way to control girls and to reduce the financial pressure of caring for daughters.

The national prevalence of psychiatric disorders and of substance use

The last estimated national prevalence rate of psychiatric disorders in Egypt in 2009 (18–64 years) was 17.0 percent, amounting to about 12 million of Egyptians (Ghanem, Gadellah, Meky, Mourad, and El-Kholy 2009). Mental disorders are higher in Cairo than in other sites, with a one-year prevalence rate of 18.4 percent. In Cairo, anxiety disorders are the most prevalent category of mental disorders, 7.1 percent, followed by mood disorders, 5.9 percent (Hamdi et al. 2012). These findings are in contrast to other regions in Egypt, where mood disorders were found to have a higher prevalence rate (Ghanem et al. 2009).

The lifetime prevalence of any substance use varies between 7.3 percent and 14.5 percent. The true prevalence of substance abuse is probably higher due to underreporting. The prevalence of substance use is of 13.2 percent in males and 1.1 percent in females. Prevalence increases significantly in males of Bedouin origin, in seaside governorates, in people with lower levels of education, and in people having certain types of occupations like technical or commercial jobs. The highest incidence of substance abuse, in terms of age, appears in the 15–19 age group. Cannabis is the most commonly abused substance in Egypt; alcohol is in second place, at a significantly lower rate (Hamdi et al. 2013). Because of the limited instruction and training in mental health in Egyptian medical schools, primary care doctors grossly underestimate the prevalence of mental ill health data in primary care centers in Egypt. Therefore, the previous studies depended on trained nurses, primary health care doctors, and psychiatrist who are working in Ministry of Health hospitals. Field supervisors were all experienced consultant psychiatrists for these research purposes.

As for suicide, there is significant underreporting. This is the case in Moslem countries because of stigma and traditional values. Indeed, there is no formal statistical documentation of suicide in Egypt. According to latest suicide data reported to the World Health Organization

(WHO) in 2009, the number of total deaths by suicide was 52 (Varnik 2012). The numbers are certainly much higher than that.

Mental health legislation, services and budget

Egypt has signed and ratified the United Nations Convention on the Rights of Persons with Disabilities, in 2007 and 2008, respectively. This Convention requires governments to respect, protect, and fulfill the rights of persons with psychosocial disabilities. In practice, there is an alarming mental health treatment gap, i.e., a discrepancy between the number of people who need therapy and those who actually receive it. A 2006 report by the WHO found that the treatment gap in the Middle East reaches 95 percent in the case of depression, 80 percent in the case of schizophrenia, and between 60 percent and 98 percent for epilepsy (Mental Health 2006).

Developing the 2009 Mental Health Act and its code of practice was not only a legislative process, but also an opportunity to promote public awareness of the rights of patients. Although this law has many positive aspects, it still has gaps that prevent it from completely fulfilling the Egyptian government's legal obligations with respect to mental healthcare.

The 2009 mental health legislation includes the establishment of a National Mental Health Council and a regional subsidiary council in every governorate that has inpatient mental health care under the National Mental Health Council, to monitor the country's enforcement of the 2009 mental health legislation (Loza 2010; Law 71 2009). However, the current structure, regulated by law (Article 6), weighs heavily towards officials from or affiliated with the government. Moreover, the National Mental Health Council (NMHC) is chaired by the Minister of Health himself, who should, in fact, be monitored by the Council, so a changing in this structure should be considered.

Mental health services in Egypt are provided through more than one system. First, the main provider is the General Secretariat of Mental Health, which is a part of the Ministry of Health and Population that manages 18 hospitals and centers in 14 governorates. Second, there are mental health departments in the general hospitals. In addition to these, there are psychiatric departments in the medical schools of public universities, private hospitals and not for profit non-governmental organizations (NGOs). According to the NMHC, the total number of beds in psychiatric facilities is 5,483 (2012–2013 Annual Report 2013). (See Tables 31.3 and 31.4.) Users admitted to psychiatric hospitals have sometimes been exploited; thus, patients become victims of violence, neglect, and other human rights violations (Elnemais Fawzy 2015).

In addition, there is a very serious problem with the long stay for some service users, which may extend to several years (Loza 2010). (See Table 31.5.) A database for all mental hospitals to track this type of data is being developed (2012–2013 Annual Report 2013). Although our legislation regulates involuntary admissions in hope of reducing their prevalence and preventing long, unnecessary institutional stays, the law will not be successful unless sufficient community mental health care services become available.

Table 31.3 Numbers of beds, Egyptian Mental Health Council Report 2013

Year of the Report/Number of Beds	2013	2012
Governmental hospitals	5,955	5,479
Private hospitals	1,966	1,773
Total number	7,921	7,252

Culture and Mental Health in Egypt

Table 31.4 Numbers of rates of admitted patients, Egyptian Mental Health Council Report 2013

Year of the Report/Type of Admission	2013	2012
Voluntary admission	21,291 (60%)	19,926 (64.8%)
Involuntary admission	14,287 (40%)	10,844 (35.2%)
Total admission	35,578	30,770

Table 31.5 Length of stay of patients in Abbassia psychiatric hospital (Loza, 2010)

			Duration of Stay (Years)	Total
Number (%) of	0–5	6–10	11–15 16–20 21–30	31–40 41–50 51–60 1144
patients 618		129	139 86 110	41 9 12
(54.0%)		(11.3%)	(12.2%) (7.5%) (9.6%)	(3.6%) (0.8%) (1.0%)

Mental hospitals are often based in urban areas. Their number is insufficient in areas such as Sinai, Matrouh, Hurgada, and New Waadi. Therefore, those who live in rural areas and seek to gain access to mental health care are burdened by travel and lodgings expenses, in addition to time and travel effort. In contrast, forensic psychiatric services are more centralized at Khanka, Abbassia, and Ma'amoura. The patients, especially those from rural areas, often go to traditional healers before or after seeking medical advice from the health system. Outpatient services are hospital-based. NGOs offer mostly outpatient services. Private psychiatric services are not affordable for the average Egyptian.

The Health Sector Reform Program was started in 1997 and is funded until 2018 by the United States Agency for International Development, the European Union, the World Bank, and the African Development Bank. This program is the backbone of the development of healthcare and health financing in the country, and it is a high priority at the Ministry of Health. It emphasizes family-oriented primary healthcare. However, until recently, mental health received little attention from the program and the donor community (WHO-AIMS 2006).

When the government plans and distributes the annual budget, there is a lack of attention to mental health compared to the rest of medical specialties. Okasha, Karam, and Okasha (2012) showed that Egypt has less than 1 percent allocated to mental health services of the total health budget. In addition, there is an imbalance in the distribution of resources. Most of the resources (59 percent) are spent on large institutional care, which serves a very small percentage of users rather than providing mental health services in the community or at a primary care level to reach a wider base of the population (WHO-AIMS 2006).

It can be concluded that the state still needs to assert its commitment to implement the current legislation (2009 Mental Health Act) by providing mental health care services within the network of primary health care and available in general hospitals, with improving access to medication, psychosocial interventions, and mandating community based services, rehabilitative programs and social support programs.

This strategy will decrease the costs spent on large institutional care, saving the budget needed for funding academic research which is still limited and depends on the interests of the different financing organizations. Such studies are needed to bring mental health problems to the forefront of consideration by the planners in view of the lower priority of resource allocation given to mental health. Funds also need to be redirected to fight existing stigma.

Table 31.6 Mental health resources in Egypt (Okasha et al., 2012)

	Psychiatric Beds	Psychiatrists	Psychiatric Nurses	Psychologists	Social Workers
Country	per 100,000	per 100,000	per 100,000	per 100,000	per 100,000
Egypt	13	0.9	2	0.4	0.1

Human resources development

According to WHO (2006), 5 percent of undergraduate training for medical doctors is devoted to mental health. In addition, only 5 percent of primary care physicians and 1 percent of nurses receive regular short training courses on mental health. In addition, fewer than 20 percent of primary health care physicians know the protocols that would help them in the diagnosing and managing mental disorders, and thus a very small proportion of them refer patients to mental health professionals.

The numbers of registered psychiatrists are not accurate because Egypt loses a high proportion of psychiatrists to rich Gulf countries and developed countries every year (Table 31.6). The factors influencing migration, namely the so-called push factors, have been explored. Push factors include low salaries, poor occupational safety inadequacy of supply of medicines, lack of post graduate training and continuing professional development (Jenkins et al. 2010).

Nurses, social workers, and psychologists do not have adequate mental health education in their basic training. In addition, they still have low status and lack generic skills to empower them to function in a multidisciplinary team.

Future directions

In Egypt, there is a comprehensive mental health legislation to enforce the rights of persons with mental disorders; but there is a lack of firm policy to implement it. This means that policy and legislation should be thoroughly reviewed, revised, and amended after some years of implementation. The reform needs to start now. Changes can be proposed in the light of the assessment of new mental health needs in the country, the degree of satisfaction with the legislation, improvement in the treatment of mental disorders, and international advances in the field of human rights and mental health.

The legislation should be amended to enhance adequate access to essential psychotropic drugs. Legislation and policies should define the responsibilities and authority of manufacturers, importers, wholesalers, and distributors to ensure timely delivery, safe storage, and quality control. Persons who can sell, store, and prescribe medications should also be defined. The law now applies only to patients in mental health institutions. In the future, treatment should be available in rehabilitation centers, residential centers outpatient clinics, and primary health care guaranteed by the law.

Legislative and policy reform need to be initiated to address the insufficient Child and Adolescent Mental Health Services. Such Services need to be included in the country mental health agenda. The state has an obligation to provide specialized care for children and young people in light of the overwhelming data that suggests 50 percent or more of adult mental disorders begin before age 14 (Kessler et al. 2007) and that children and adolescents with untreated mental disorders become an economic and social burden on society (Belfer 2008). Legislative and policy reform need to also be accompanied by training, awareness raising campaigns and researches, for which adequate financial resources need to be allocated as well.

Conclusion

Egypt urgently needs a national assessment of the deficiencies of its mental health system. That would provide evidence and reliable information on existing needs and the barriers to mental health care. The outputs of such an assessment can then be used in lobbying and mobilizing public opinion to rectify these conditions and to explain to the executive and legislature why amendments are necessary.

Finally, it is important to stress that no law, no matter how perfect, can alone achieve the objective of promoting the rights of persons with mental disorders if not accompanied by allocating the necessary resources and other efforts to maintain the dignity and rights of people with mental disorders.

References

Belfer, M. (2008) Child and adolescent mental disorders: The magnitude of the problem across the globe. *Journal of Child Psychology and Psychiatry*, 49(3): 226–236. Retrieved from https://doi.org/10.1111/j.1469-7610.2007.01855.x.

Elnemais Fawzy, M. (2015) Quality of life and human rights conditions in a public psychiatric hospital in Cairo. *International Journal of Human Rights in Healthcare*, 8(4): 199–217. Retrieved from https://doi.org/10.1108/ijhrh-02–2015-0006.

France Diplomatie (2019) *Présentation de l'Égypte*. Retrieved 5 November 2019, from www.diplomatie.gouv.fr/fr/dossiers-pays/egypte/presentation-de-l-egypte/.

Ghanem, M., Gadellah, M., Meky, F., Mourad, S., and El-Kholy, G. (2009) National Survey of Prevalence of Mental Disorders in Egypt-preliminary survey. *Eastern Mediterranean Health Journal*, 15(1): 65–75.

Graindorge, V. (2006) *Capitalisation de fin de mission: Appui méthodologique et pédagogique dans un programme d'action globale avec les enfants des rues*, Egypte: Caritas.

Hamdi, E., Gawad, T., Khoweiled, A., Sidrak, A., Amer, D., Mamdouh, R., et al. (2013) Life- time prevalence of alcohol and substance use in Egypt: A community survey. *Substance Abuse*, 34(2): 97–104. Retrieved from https://doi.org/10.1080/08897077.2012.677752.

Hamdi, E., Sabry, N., Refaat, O., Sedrak, A., Khoweiled, A., Abdo, H., and Emad, M. (2012) *Psychiatric morbidity in Cairo: One year prevalence. WHO EMRO Report.*

Jenkins, R., Kydd, R., Mullen, P., Thomson, K., Sculley, J., Kuper, S., et al. (2010) International migration of doctors, and its impact on availability of psychiatrists in low and middle income countries. *PLoS ONE*, 5(2): e9049. Retrieved from https://doi.org/10.1371/journal. pone.0009049.

Kessler, R., Amminger, G., Aguilar-Gaxiola, S., Alonso, J., Lee, S., and Ustun, T. B. (2007) Age of onset of mental disorders: a review of recent literature. *Current Opinion in Psychiatry*, 20(4): 359–364. Retrieved from https://doi.org/10.1097/yco.0b013e32816ebc8c.

Law for the Care of People with Mental Disorders (Law 71) (2009) *Egyptian Facts Gazette*, Cairo: Government of Egypt.

Loza, N. (2010) Integrating Egyptian mental health services into primary care: The policy maker's perspective. *International Psychiatry*, 7: 5–7.

Materia, E., and Riva, G. (2011) *Egyptian health system*. Retrieved from www.salutein- ternazionale.info/2011/11/il-sistema-sanitario-egiziano/.

Mental Health in the Eastern Mediterranean Region: *Reaching the Unreached* (2006) (pp. 108–123). Retrieved from https://applications.emro.who.int/dsaf/dsa702.pdf.

National Council for Childhood and Motherhood (NCCM) and UNICEF (2015) Violence against Children in Egypt. *A Quantitative Survey and Qualitative Study in Cairo*, Alexandria and Assiut. Egypt, Cairo. Retrieved from www.unicef.org/egypt/media/1906/file/Violence%20Against%20Children%20in%20Egypt-EN.pdf.

Okasha, A., Karam, E., and Okasha, T. (2012) Mental health services in the Arab world. *World Psychiatry*, 11(1): 52–54. Retrieved from https://doi.org/10.1016/j.wpsyc.2012.01.008.

UN (2019) *About Egypt*. Retrieved 5 November 2019, from http://eg.one.un.org/content/unct/egypt/en/home/about-egypt.html.

UNDP (2014) *HDI data by UNDP*. Retrieved from https://hdr.undp.org/g/en/data.

UNICEF (2013) *Female Genital Mutilation/Cutting: A statistical overview and exploration of the dynamics of change*. Retrieved from www.unicef.org/cbsc/files/UNICEF_FGM_report_July_2013_Hi_res.pdf.

UNICEF. (2017) *Understanding Child Multidimensional Poverty*. Retrieved from www.unicef.org/MODA-Report-Full-EN-websingle.pdf.

UNHCR. (2017) *Fact sheet*. Retrieved from www.unhcr.org/eg/unhcr-egypt-documents.

Varnik, P. (2012) Suicide in the world. *International Journal of Environmental Research and Public Health,* 9(12): 760–771. Retrieved from https://doi.org/10.3390/ijerph9030760.

WHO-AIMS Report on Mental Health System in Egypt (2006) *Cairo, Egypt*. Retrieved from www.who.int/mental_health/evidence/who_aims_report_egypt.pdf.

2012–2013 Annual Report of the Egyptian Mental Health Council. (2013) (1st ed.). Egypt: Cairo.

Report of The Egyptian Central Agency for Public Mobilization and Statistics. (2019) Statistical Abstract. (1st ed.). Egypt: Cairo.

32

CULTURE AND MENTAL HEALTH IN INDIA

Satheesh Varma M.

Since Independence in 1947, India has significantly changed in economic and social aspects. More recently, India also has taken significant strides in the measures of mental health enhancement; putting in place a robust strategic benefit of its rich cultural heritage. From the great ancient knowledge written in the form of "Upanishads" (i.e., collection of Hindu philosophical texts written between 1000 to 500 BCE) to the tremendous folk insights accessible across the country, there is a visible back up of spiritual wisdom which facilitates mental health is in operation among ordinary folks. But this long history of Indian culture as it is a benefit is also a curse in some other ways. The emotional and psychic backlog Indians carry is not synonymous with any other nations. Many at times this backlog hinders the way of progress. A deep understanding of the cultural context of mental health in India is very much essential to overcome a few of its present challenges. Policymakers and practitioners are currently taking many measures to improve the quality of mental health in India but most of these efforts are not becoming so successful because of ignoring the dynamics of collective mind and behavior of their beneficiaries.

This chapter is an effort to analyze the construct of mental health from an Indian sociocultural context. For a better understanding of readers, an account of country demographic is presented first in the chapter followed by a brief introduction of Indian cultural representations of illness and wellness. Later in this chapter, a detail description of the evolution of the Indian mental health practices and its contemporary status is provided with the discussion of sociocultural challenges in implementation and future directions.

Country demographics and mental health statistics

India is the world's second-largest country regarding population, and roughly in seven years, it is expected to overtake the people of China (United Nations 2017). According to the 2011 census, which is the most recent one since it is conducted once in ten years in India, 68.8 percent of the population is staying in rural India and 32.2 percent in urban India, with a density of 382 persons per square kilometer (Office of the Registrar General & Census Commissioner of India 2011). India also has less female ratio compared to male ratio. The literacy rate of India is 74 percent, with a significant difference between male (80.9%) and female (64.6%)

literacy rates. India has a stable workforce as 39.1 percent of the population goes for regular or marginal work. India has shown a trend of population migration with 2 percent of its entire population found to have migrated out of the country and 13 percent of the whole people out of the states as per the 2011 census. India also has a significant presence (24.4%) of highly marginalized communities (known as scheduled caste and scheduled tribe as per Indian nomenclature).

The National Mental Health Survey (NMHS) of India conducted in 2015–2016 reveals that the lifetime mental morbidity rate of India is 13.7 percent, with a range of 19.9 percent and 8.1 percent across states (Gururaj et al., 2016). The survey also reported that males, urban dwellers, middle age population in the age group of 40 to 59, people with less education and belonging to the lower and middle-income working class are more vulnerable for mental health issues. According to the survey, substance use disorders (prevalence rate = 22.44%), schizophrenia (prevalence rate = 1.40%), mood disorders (prevalence rate = 5.61%), bipolar mood affective disorders (prevalence rate = 0.50%), depressive disorders (prevalence rate = 5.25%), neurotic and stress-related disorders (prevalence rate = 3.70%), phobic and anxiety disorders (prevalence rate = 1.91%), generalized anxiety disorders (0.57%), moderate suicide risk (prevalence rate = 0.72%), high suicide risk (prevalence rate = 0.90 %) are the most occurring mental health disorders in India.

From a mental health management perspective, what is more, alarming and requires urgent attention is the treatment gap (range of 70.4% to 91.8%) for various mental health disorders. It is disconcerting to comprehend that more than 80 percent of the cases of common mental health disorders like substance use disorders and depressive disorders are often left untreated in the country, and it makes very clear that a thoughtful revision of the policies and approaches, that considers socio-cultural certainties is the need of the hour.

Indian cultural representations of illness and wellness

The core essence of Indian philosophy is the idea of endless continuity of existence and the universal law of cause and effect as known as karma (Coster 1998). The idea is that, through his actions, man can control his future. In his lower level of existence due to ignorance, man does not know how to manage the future, and he keeps himself busy by indulging in a pool of worldly desires, which invariably brings sufferings and illnesses. Ashtanga yoga, Buddhism, and Jainism identified the desire for material possessions or greed for hedonic pleasures (*Parigraha*) as the cause of mental disturbances and illness (Fisher 1997). Ayurveda, the 5,000-year-old Vedic Science of Life from India conceptualized the mind and body as one entity and regarded the body as an extension of the mind. It attributed illness as a result of wrong or unnatural usage of sense organs to attain momentary pleasures along with the accumulation of harmful emotions (Frawley 2005).

From the perspective of prevention and cure, the ancient Indian wisdom revolves around the concept of self-purification. It identified that purification of mind, as well as body, prevents illness in human beings (Marida 1990; Pandit 2001). When a person's body and mind are pure through the control of energies and urges (following the spirit of brahmacharya in all stages of life), and selfless action (called as Nishkama karma), he/she is elevated to a heightened state of well-being. It is noteworthy that recent medical research is endorsing this early knowledge about the connection between mind and body (Brower 2006; Giscombe and Black 2010) and it is also widely practiced by psychologists in the health field (Taylor 2016).

Evolution of mental health practices in India

Indigenous and traditional healing in India

In pre-colonial India, Ayurveda, Sowa Rigpa, Sidha, and Unani were the prevailing systems of medicines along with various folk medicinal practices. Ayurveda describes health as a balance between mind, body, and spirit. The diagnosis and treatment of illness are by its cause (Nidana), earlier signs (Purva- rupa), symptoms (rupa), therapeutic trials (Upashaya) and the root of its manifestation (Samprapti). Sowa Rigpa popularly known as "Amchi" is a Tibetan system of medicine popular in the Himalayan regions of India. According to this medicinal system, illness is caused by imbalances in bodily humor due to conditions such as diet, lifestyle, seasons, mental stress, etc. (Gurmeet 2004). Sidha is an ancient healing system practiced by the Siddha cult sages of Tamil Nadu, a south Indian state. The Siddha system, similar to other Indian medicinal systems also believed in the steadiness of the mind as a key to sound health (Weiss 2009). Unani is a Persian-Arab healing system patronized by Muslim rulers in India. Similar to Ayurveda, it also identified the mind and body connection, and considered illness as a natural reaction of the body to the internal and external environment (Islam 2017). All these practices followed a non-institutional community health care model, which gave attention to the prevailing socio-cultural systems. The practitioners of these medicinal systems owned a charismatic appeal in the community, and people followed their advice with utmost value.

Colonialism and mental health practices in India

Historically the Indian sub-continent was subjected to many invasions and foreign rule, and its traces are evident in the collective Indian mindset. A notable Indian Psychologist, Jai B P Sinha opined that the present collective Indian mindset is multilayered, in which composite and diverse features of every historical stage are juxtaposed one over the other (Sinha 2014).

The development of a rigid social hierarchy (the caste system) that monopolized the knowledge systems that were available only for few communities was the first social barrier that contributed to the stagnation of India's higher order socio-politico-cultural thinking. Later, continuous foreign invasions and colonial rules accelerated the disintegration.

The earlier invasions by Greeks, Scythians, Kushans and so on had made little changes in the system as all these groups comprehensively integrated and adapted to the Indian way of life, but the case of Islamic invasions was entirely different. As Islam is an altogether different form of faith and way of life, with monotheistic belief (Crane 1958), it created a distinct impact on Indian society. The Islamic invaders settled down in India and converted many of them into their religion and way of life. Over time, this created communities of Muslims in India with Indian heritage. As Muslims in India share a common ancestry, religions like Hinduism and Buddhism had a profound influence on their attitudes (Puri 2007). But this influence had also created dilemmas in the Muslim mind. In their journey to their past, they slide into areas that belong to another faith, which is different from their own. And this identity conflict halts them from a deeper integration into the general cultural fabrics of the country, like folklore and mythology, unlike in Muslim countries like Indonesia (Kakar 1996).

The British colonial rule made another enormous impact on the Indian mind. As British rulers had more economic interests in India than evangelical, its control had not caused significant social restructuring, such as the caste system (Maddison 2013). But their financial practices converted the collective Indian mindset from a master to a victim level, transforming India into one of the most impoverished, backward, illiterate and diseased societies on earth

(Tharoor 2017). Their reign in India had witnessed many human-made famines which wiped out millions (Sen 2010). Life at those times had become so uncertain that survival had become the primary objective of people and their psychosocial systems slowly converted to the attitudes of powerlessness, learned helplessness and opportunism.

Along with this to tame the Indian mind, the colonizers also introduced the Western educational system with an objective to create a secondary Indian elite class with Eurocentric worldview. This led to the development of colonial myopia in the educated youth, who believed that the pre-colonial Indian era was primitive (Shahzeb 2010). When we take into consideration the present Indian mental health policies and practices, as is similar with any other professional activities in the country, the dominant Western approach which ignores the Indian social practices and cultural milieu is evident.

The first incidence of institutional mental health care in India was reported in the time of "Muhammad Kilji", in the fifteenth century. Traditionally most of the mental health healing practices were conducted in a non-institutionalized setting with very few exceptions of the temple (Somasundaram 1973) and "Dargah" (traditional Indian Muslim shrines) healing traditions (Davar and Lohokare 2009). The concept of mental hospitals (called as "asylums" in those days) in India was introduced by the British East India Company in their early years of rule to manage mentally disturbed British soldiers in Calcutta, Mumbai, and Madras.

Later, when the British Crown succeeded the East India Company, the first Lunacy Act was enacted in 1858 that detailed the procedures for establishing mental hospitals in India (Kumar 2004). The then British empire started many mental asylums in various parts of the country under the purview of this act. These centers typically followed the custodial model of British Psychiatric practices based on the Puritan work ethics, which considered mentally disturbed people as non-productive outcasts in the society requires keeping in controlled sanctuaries for safeguarding general public. Even though the Act was amended multiple times and included many humanitarian measures in the legal system (Indian Lunacy in 1912), the core essence of the Act was not changed much (Somasundaram 1987). However, it has been argued that the treatment of mentally ill patients was significantly improved in the last periods of British rule. In 1920s and 1930s, the Ranchi European Hospital adopted radical changes in mental health management, and with this influence, the earlier custodial model was slowly changed to a curative one (Sharma 2005). For the first time in India, efforts were taken to train psychiatrists and psychiatric nurses to handle mentally ill patients, along with the introduction of psychiatric outpatient services in a few hospitals. Attempts were also made to include social science professionals like psychologists in mental health care and management.

Mental health policies and practices after Independence

At the time of Independence (i.e., August 15, 1947), the mental health facilities available in India were meager (Murthy 2011). The newly formed Indian government started its mental health practices on the recommendations made by the Bhore Committee appointed by the government under the British Rule in 1946. (Menon 2005). The most important direction of the Committee was to improve human resources in the field of mental health. Based on all the recommendations, the newly formed Government of India established the All India Institute of Mental health (now known as NIMHANS) in 1954 at Bengaluru to train psychiatric and allied professionals. Later, the Mudaliar Committee constituted to review the implementation of the Bhore Committee recommendations found a severe shortage of qualified professionals. With the Committee's suggestions, the Union government converted the Ranchi Mental Hospital in Bihar (at that time) into a fully-fledged training institute. The government also initiated formal training for Clinical Psychologists, Psychiatric Nurses and Psychiatric Social Workers at NIMHANS, Bengaluru and the Central Institute of Psychiatry, Ranchi.

Immediately after Independence, the Indian Psychiatric Society came into existence. The society considered the Indian Lunacy Act of 1912 as inappropriate and submitted a draft mental health bill to the government for consideration, but the government took 28 years to present the proposal in the parliament. After many years of deliberations in parliament, the bill was signed by the president in 1987 and implemented in 1993 (Trivedi 2009). The act made a lot of progressive changes in the mental health policy measures of the country. It offered a more humane approach to the problems of mentally ill patients, and many central and state authorities were created to safeguard their interests. But the legislation did not promote community-based mental health, and it was not supportive to widespread access to mental health care. Legal considerations were given more importance in the Act than medical, psychological, social and rehabilitative concerns.

In 1975, the World Health Organization initiated a multi-country collaborative pilot project to develop a model for integrating mental health with general health services, in collaboration with the Post Graduate Institute of Medical Education and Research (PGIMER) in Chandigarh (Roy and Rasheed 2015). The Indian Council of Medical Research (ICMR) and the Department of Science and Technology (DST) of Government of India also conducted similar studies on the feasibility of training Primary Health Centre Staff to provide mental health care (Murthy 2004). Likewise, NIMHANS, Bengaluru also started a Community Mental Health Unit in their campus and organized several training programmes to enable Primary Health Workers in selected centers to deal with mental health issues in rural areas (Isaac et al. 1982). Accumulating the experiences and knowledge acquired from these pilot programmes, the Central Council of Health and Family Welfare (CCHFW), Government of India implemented a National Mental Health Programme in 1982, a first of its kind in developing countries.

The National Mental Health Programme was based on the community psychiatry approach and hence provided minimum mental health care for all by promoting community participation. Under the programme, mental health care was integrated with general health care. Even though the development of the programme was through an extended feasibility study, its implementation was not adequate. A lot of confusion existed between the state and the central governments regarding the allocation of funds and on sharing of human resources. Psychiatrists' community showed lukewarm responses to its implementation. Considering this, NIMHANS in 1985 undertook an extensive feasibility study on the implementation of this programme within a larger population (i.e., district level) in Bellary, a backward rural district of Karnataka state popularly known as the "Bellary Model" of the District Mental Health Programme (Issac 1988). Based on the inputs from this intervention model, the Ministry of Health and Family Welfare implemented a five-year pilot District Mental Health Programme in two phases, from 1996 to 2002 in 27 districts across the country. The primary objective again was to treat the mentally ill at the community level, thereby reducing the pressure on existing mental hospitals. Twelve years later, an appraisal on the effectiveness of the programme was carried out, and it identified that due to the lack of skilled workforce and stigma about mental health in the society, the measures adopted by the programme were ineffective (Ministry of Health and Family Welfare, Government of India 2014). The programme followed the traditional psychiatric model of treatment, and the role of other allied professionals was minimal. But it is significant to note that even though the programme was not so successful in implementation, it indirectly contributed a lot to the revision of mental health practices in India (Murthy 2005). Public awareness on various mental health issues increased. It also helped to the re-revision of human rights issues on mental health, and constitution of allied legislations supporting health care like the Narcotic Drugs and Psychotropic Substances (NDPS) Act in 1985, and the Persons with Disability Act in 1995.

Contemporary mental health policies and practices in India
National mental health policy

In 2014, Ministry of Health and Family Welfare launched the "National Mental Health Policy" (MHP) with the vision of promoting mental well-being and care for illnesses to all affected persons (Roy and Rasheed 2015), including the marginalized and vulnerable population. The policy identified that untreated mental illness could result in stigma, marginalization, and discrimination, which could lead to substantial loss of human capital (Ministry of Health and Family Welfare, Government of India 2014). The policy incorporated integrated, evidence-based approach in mental health management and acknowledged the importance of the practices of medical and non-medical interventions in the prevention, care, and rehabilitation of people affected with mental illnesses by using local knowledge and practices like yoga and Ayurveda.

Indian mental health care act

On April 7, 2017, the president of India gave his consent to the new act on mental health known as the Indian Mental Health Care Act, 2017, after passing the bill in both Houses of Parliament, repealing the Mental Health Act, 1987. The Act assured every individual the right to access mental health care from state-run mental health care facilities (Ministry of Law and Justice, Government of India 2017). The new act was highly concerned about the human rights issues of mentally ill persons, and it contained a lot of provisions to protect them.

The act assured the mentally ill patients, the right to confidentiality, the right to information in the language the person can understand, the right to the restriction of the release of information, the right to access medical records, the right to legal aid and dignity. It also assured the right to community living, the right to protection from cruel, inhuman and degrading treatment and ensured medical and psychological treatment equivalent to any other physical illness, and the right to avail all medical facilities, including insurance coverage. The act also provided an individual the right to specify how to treat him/her in the event of a mental health situation and to specify who will be responsible for taking decisions on their behalf during such events. The act also restricted solitary confinement or seclusion of mentally ill patients, as physical restraint could be used only at times of emergencies with the authorization of a psychiatrist responsible for the person's treatment.

The act also laid down strict guidelines for the registration of mental health institutions in India, and it clearly stated that no person or organization should run mental health care institutions without certification from a state authority. For obtaining certification, the organization should have minimum standards of facilities with qualified professionals. This provision is essential as there are many organizations across the country providing mental health care without any facilities or expertise.

It is appreciable that after many years of Independence, India has implemented a robust Mental Health Act and drafted a stable Mental Health Policy, as one-third of the total countries in the world does not have any such legislation (Saxena, Thornicroft, Knapp and Whiteford 2007). However, it is also a hard reality that enacting a law is not just enough to improve the mental health situations. The wide treatment gap reported by the National Mental Health Survey is a serious concern. The mental health care facilities are also limited and restricted

(Francis 2014). There are only a few government-owned custodial institutions in India that can offer treatment for mentally ill patients. Private run mental hospitals, psychiatric departments in government and private general hospitals and Non-Governmental Organizations (NGO) working on general and specific mental health issues are the sources for the common man to seek help regarding mental health.

Mental health interventions, accreditation, licensure and certification processes

Mental health interventions in India commonly follow a medical model where the treatment plan in most of the cases are decided and controlled by psychiatrists. Clinical Psychologists, Psychiatric Nurses, Psychiatric Social Workers, and other allied professionals are considered to have only supporting roles in the process. Because of this, Psychiatrists and Clinical Psychologists share perturbed relationships (Singh and Singh 2006). In many places, the situation is even worse, as high levels of professional envy and ego exist between them that adversely affect the larger well-being of the patients. For example, a clinical psychologist is overcautious in referring a patient who requires pharmacotherapy to a psychiatrist.

Psychiatrists in India who had done their post-graduate level training in psychiatric medicine are registered (under the Medical Council of India) as medical practitioners. Diploma in Psychological Medicine (DPM)/Doctor of Medicine (MD) in Psychiatry, Geriatric Mental Health, Child and Adolescent Psychiatry and Diploma of National Board (DNB) in Psychiatry, are the courses in India specialized in Psychiatry (Manjunatha, Thyloth and Rao 2013). Hence medical profession is highly regulated by the Indian Medical Council Act, 1956, and guided by strong professional support from associations like the Indian Psychiatric Society; they have a better edge in professional practice by following uniform standards across the country. But, in the case of Psychology or Psychiatric Social Work Professions, there are no such practicing guidelines or regulatory bodies yet to monitor and regulate their professional practice. At present, the Rehabilitation Council of India (RCI) is the only statutory body to control professional practices in the field of Clinical and Rehabilitation Psychology (Rehabilitation Council of India 2017). The authority and scope of RCI are limited as it is only a body to regulate, standardize and monitor rehabilitation services given to persons with disabilities. Many areas of psychological practices in mental health do not come under its purview.

In India, a two-year MPhil Programme in Clinical Psychology from a few recognized institutions is the essential qualification to practice as a Clinical Psychologist (Veeraraghavan 2014). The MPhil in Clinical Psychology is an advanced Master's degree programme. At present, there are only around ten institutions offering this course. Moreover, it is a hard reality that the programme itself is becoming obsolete. The objective of a traditional university MPhil programme is to prepare the students in research skills and methodologies before the doctoral programme. Since mental health demands of India is high, it is essential to make the post-graduate degree in Clinical Psychology offered in a medical institution as a basic course for Clinical Psychology practice. At present, the Master's programme in Clinical Psychology is happening mostly in Arts and Science Colleges or Universities, where the focus is typically on dissemination of theoretical knowledge without any clinical exposure. Learning of basic theoretical foundations can occur at the undergraduate level, for which the existing degree courses are required to upgrade to Honors Programmes with rigorous training in foundation theories.

Similarly, various regulations and guidelines are required to restrict the practice of different psychological services like counseling, psychometric assessments, etc. At present, there are no regulations or clarity in the country on who can do counseling or psychometric assessments.

Many centers and individuals in India do counseling or assessments without any proper qualification, knowledge or skills, violating most of the ethical codes of professional practice. A legal body established by an act of the Parliament is very much required to regulate and monitor psychological services. Likewise, a high level of orientation about professional boundaries is also necessary to enhance collaborative professional practices. Even though psychiatric social workers or nurses have been pervasively providing psychotherapy for psychosocial support, there is little regulations for their practice.

Current challenges in Indian mental health practice

It is appreciable that presently Indian policymakers, media, and the general public are talking more about mental health issues. As there is a better understanding of mental health issues than in the past years, now it is an opportune time to redesign the policies and practices. However, there still exist many social, cultural, economic and political barriers on the road to progress.

One of the leading challenges is the social and cultural stigma existing among the people towards mental illness in India. In this era of modernization, the social stigma of mental illness is still prevalent in society. These social stigmas remarkably affect the family members of the patients (Thara and Tirupati 2000). Family members often feel mental illness as extremely shameful that influence their social status and often conceal and deny timely interventions.

The scarcity of economic resources is another big challenge for better mental health management. Many Indian households manage an event of a mental health shock by colossal borrowing, mortgaging or selling assets or livestock. Since people lack resources, spending on health care is related to the perception of its urgency and most of the mental health problems get the least priority which reduces chances of timely intervention and problem management. The government needs to subsidize mental health care services, irrespective of the income status.

Refer the following two case vignettes for the better understanding of the current mental health practice and issues in India.

Case vignette 1

Abraham is a hard-working farmer hailing from a mountainous region of Kerala in South India. His wife Mary is a homemaker. His elder son, Roy, as a young graduate had finished his Bachelor's degree in Education and was aspiring to get a government aided teaching job. Aided school teachers in Kerala are under the payroll of the government, but as an unofficial practice, recruitment is by paying huge money to the school manager. His younger daughter Annie was recently married and her husband George who is planning to start his new business is expecting Abraham to help him by paying his dowry due. As a customary practice in many parts of Kerala, marriages happen by giving large amounts as dowry by the bride's parent before the wedding day. Occasionally the groom provides the concession for paying it in installments within few years after marriage. Recently, Abraham faced severe financial problems due to crop loss. Even though he managed his financial debts by selling off some of his property, the incident caused him to lose interest at work. After the event, Abraham started experiencing intense tiredness, slow thinking, and insomnia with frequent headaches and back pain. He also started feeling low self-worth, agitation, and guilt. Recently, his friend, a neighborhood farmer had committed suicide by consuming a pesticide named "Furadan" notorious for deaths in rural Kerala and Abraham was secretly planning to follow in his friend's footsteps. For his physical symptoms, he consulted a general medical practitioner in a nearby local town, and the doctor speculated it to be a case of depression which requires emergency intervention and referred him to a psychiatric hospital in Cochin, a city 100 km away from the place. His family members were unwilling to take him for treatment as they considered his symptoms as signs of laziness and frequently bullied him for his inability to meet their desires. His wife viewed it as a wrong time and lack of God's grace and took him to a few spiritual retreat centers for divine blessing. At present, he faces the risk of committing suicide as his life has become so worst. He may do it at any moment, and it may hardly come as a one column news in local newspapers as another case of farmer suicide.

However, due to social stigma, lack of understanding and the culturally influenced mindset of adult family members considering father or husband not as a person but as their economic resource deny the right of the person to get proper treatment and support. There is considerable media coverage in India about the incidents of farmer suicides projecting it as a failure of the government's economic policies. Since reasons for death in most of these cases are attributed from both psychosocial and economic, the presenting issues can be solved by the introduction of strong community mental health support systems.

Another similar social challenge is the belief that supernatural evil forces create mental problems, and the solution is possible only through faith healing like exorcism and black magic. Faith healers are more respected in many parts of India than professional mental health service providers (Bathla et al. 2015). The mainstream mental health professionals completely oppose faith-based interventions and consider them as hurdles in their practice. But it is not wise to ignore the strong cultural beliefs of people in the treatment plan. As faith healers have mystic or divine appeal among the general public, people follow their words with compliance. It is ideal to combine, both traditional healing and mainstream practices in the intervention plan so that patients get the best mental health care, synchronized with their religious and cultural beliefs. It is appreciable to acknowledge that there are presently successful efforts adopted in various parts of the country in this stream like "Dava" (medicine) and "Dua" (prayer) Programmes (Special Correspondent – The Hindu 2014; Ravishankar 2015).

Case vignette 2

Ismail is a schizophrenic patient who is undergoing treatment under the Dava-Dua initiative set up in a famous south Indian Dargah (shrine of a Muslim saint). He came to the Dargah with his caretaker/mother a few years before as a final resort of hope, immediately after both of them were expelled from their village. He was attending the regular prayers of the shrine and survived by eating donated food and sleeping on roads. Earlier his mother was reluctant to send him to the clinic near to the Dargah as she thought his son's illness was due to the possession of evil spirits and if she takes her son to the clinic, it would be against her trust and belief in Saint's power to cure. Later the clergies of the shrine educated her that nothing wrong in taking medicines as it will have more effect when they consume it inside the shrine. Eventually, the condition of Ismail got better after taking medication and now his mother is happy that her son is earning money for primary livelihood by working in the Dava-Dua Programme's vocational training center.

In this case, the success is due to the approach of working along with the culture-based belief systems of the patients. However, it is striking to note that even after the reports of many such success stories, the majority of mental health practitioners of the country are ignorant of this model. Implementing an exogenous intervention plan without understanding the socio-cultural background of the population will not be successful. Social Science Research in India is more ideological rather than analytical (Sharma 1992) and it is more problem-focused rather than solution focused.

Future directions

India is a highly culturally sensitive society, and there exist lots of implicit and explicit societal attitudes and practices both positively and adversely affecting the mental health and well-being of ordinary folks. Understanding these attitudes and implementing suitable interventions is very much essential for the better mental health of Indians. Integrated mental health practice making use of medical, social, and cultural models are highly recommended for improving the effectiveness of Indian mental health. The integration of indigenous healing systems in the modern mental health practice would also help to improve its effectiveness. To achieve this objective both traditional healers and modern medicinal professionals need to overcome their mutual biases and require approaching mental health problems from a deep socio-cultural context. While integrating it is also important that the practitioner has to take extra caution to evade blind assumptions overlooking the effectiveness of their own systems. The intervention plans should be highly evidence-based rather than conventions.

Conclusion

India has a high potential to grow and contribute to the world with her long historical and cultural wisdom. However, the growth is complete only if her citizens enjoy better mental health and peace. Presently professional practices in Indian mental health areas are in growth pace as the policymakers are taking plenty of progressive measures. Still there exists many socio-cultural hurdles in its way to advancement. The problem is that mental health management system of the country has not completely understood and adapted to the cultural dynamics of its beneficiaries. If the policymakers and practitioner do few attitudinal changes in approach and take little more effort to understand the existing cultural background of the people and implement culturally adapted interventions, the country can grow into one of the best places to live in this world.

References

Bathla, M., Chandna, S., Bathla, J. and Kaloiya, G. S. (2015) "Faith healers in modern psychiatric practice: Results of a 4 years study." *Delhi Psychiatry Journal*, 18 (1): 48–53.
Brower, V. (2006) "Mind-body research moves towards the mainstream." *EMBO Reports*, 7(4): 358–361.
Coster, G. (1998) *Yoga and Western psychology.* New Delhi: Motilal Banarasidass.
Crane, R. I. (1958) *The history of India: Its study and interpretations.* University of Michigan: Mental Health Research Institute Staff Publications–University of Michigan.
Davar, B V, and M Lohokare (2009) "Recovering from psychosocial traumas: The pace of dargahs in Maharashtra." *Economic and Political Weekly*, 44(16): 60–67.
Fisher, M. P. (1997) *Living Religions: An encyclopedia of the world's faiths.* London: IB Tauris.
Francis, A. P. (2014) *Social work in mental health: Contexts and theories for practice.* New Delhi: SAGE Publications India.
Frawley, D. (2005) *Ayurveda and the mind: The healing of consciousness.* New Delhi: Motilal Banarasidass Publishers.
Giscombe, W. C., and Black, A. R. (2010) "Mind-body interventions to reduce risk for health disparities related to stress and strength among African American women: The potential of mindfulness-based stress reduction, loving-kindness, and the NTU Therapeutic Framework." *Complimentary Health Practice Review*, 115–131.

Gurmeet, P. (2004) "'Sowa Rigpa': Himalayan art of healing." *Indian Journal of Traditional Knowledge*, 3(2): 212–218.

Gururaj, G., et al. (2016) *National Mental Health Survey of India 2015–2016: Prevalence, pattern and outcomes.* Bengaluru: National.

Issac, M. K. (1988) "District mental health programme at Bellary." *Community Mental News*, 11: 2–16.

Isaac, M. K., Kapur, R. L., Chandrashekar, C. R., Kapur, M. and Pathasarathy, R. (1982) "Mental health delivery through rural primary care – Development and evaluation of a training programme." *Indian Journal of Psychiatry*, 24(2): 131–138.

Islam, N. M. (2017) *Chinese and Indian medicine today: Branding Asia.* Singapore: Springer Singapore.

Kakar, S. (1996) *The colours of violence.* New Delhi: Penguin Books.

Kumar, Anant (2004) "History of mental health services in India." *Journal of Personality and Clinical Studies*, 20: 171–180.

Maddison, Angus (2013) *Class structure and economic growth: India and Pakistan since the moghuls.* New York: Routledge.

Manjunatha, N., Thyloth, M. and Rao, S. (2013) "The rise of super (?sub)-specialties courses in psychiatry: Is India ready for it!" *Indian Journal of Psychiatry*, 55(4): 401–402.

Marida, K.V. (1990) *The scientific foundations of Jainism.* New Delhi: Motilal Banarasidass Publishers.

Menon, S. (2005) "Mental Health in independent India: The early years." In S. P. Agarwal, D. S. Goel, R. L. Ichhpujani, R. N .Salhan and S. Shrivastava (Eds.), *Mental Health an Indian Perspective – 1946–2003* (pp. 30–36). New Delhi: Elsevier.

Ministry of Health and Family Welfare, Government of India. (2014) *New pathways new hope: National Mental Health Policy of India.* New Delhi: Government of India Press.

Ministry of Law and Justice, Government of India (2017) "The Mental Healthcare Act 2017." In *The Gazette of India – Extraordinary*, by Government of India Ministry of Law and Justice, pp.1–51. New Delhi: Government of India Press.

Murthy, S. R. (2004) "Mental Health in the new millennium: Research strategies for India." *Indian Journal of Medical Research*, 120 (2):63–66.

Murthy, S. R. (2005) "The National Mental Health Programme: Progress and problems." In S. P. Agarwal, R. L. Goel, R. N., Ichhpujani, Salhan and S. Shrivastava (Eds.), *Mental health an Indian perspective 1946–2003* (pp. 75–91). New Delhi: Elsevier.

Murthy, S. R. (2011) "Mental health initiatives in India (1947–2010)." *THE National Medical Journal of India* 24(2): 98–107.

Office of the Registrar General & Census Commissioner, India (2011) *2011 Census Data.* New Delhi: Office of the Registrar General & Census Commissioner, India.

Pandit, B. (2001) *The Hindu mind: Fundamentals of hindu Religion and philosophy for all ages.* New Delhi: New Age Books.

Puri, B. (2007) *Muslims of India since partition.* New Delhi: Gyan Publishing House.

Ravishankar, Sandhya (2015) *India's mentally ill: On a pill and a prayer- Medicine finally joins religious therapy for thousands suffering psychological disorders in southern Tamil Nadu state.* www.aljazeera.com/indepth/features/2015/08/india-mentally-ill-pill-prayer-150830123549738.html.

Rehabilitation Council of India. (2017) "M. Phil in Clinical Psychology-Guidelines and Syllabus, Effective from Academic Year 2017–18." www.rehabcouncil.nic.in/writereaddata/M%20Phil%20Clinical%20Psychology.pdf.

Roy, S., and Rasheed, N. (2015) "The National Mental Health Programme of India." *International Journal of Current Medical and Applied Sciences*, 7(1): 7–15.

Saxena, S, G., Thornicroft, M., Knapp, and Whiteford, H. (2007) "Resources for mental health: Scarcity, inequity, and inefficiency." *The Lancet*, 370 (9590): 878–889.

Sen, S. N. (2010) *An advanced history of modern India.* New Delhi: Macmillan Publishers India.

Shahzeb (2010) "How the British influenced Indian culture." *Dawn Newspaper.* 6 June 2010. www.dawn.com/news/881307 (accessed October 22, 2017).

Sharma, S. (1992) "Social science research in India: A review." *Economic and Political Weekly*, 27(49): 2642–2646.

Sharma, S. D. (2005) "Mental health: The pre-independence scenario." In S. P. Agarwal, D. S. Goel and R. L. Ichhpujani (Eds.), *Mental health an Indian perspective-1946–2003* (pp. 25–29). New Delhi: Elsevier.

Singh, A., and Singh, S. (2006) "Psychiatrists and clinical psychologists." *Mens Sana Monographs*, 4(1): 10–13.

Sinha, J. B. P. (2014) *Psycho social analysis of Indian mindset.* New Delhi: Springer.

Somasundaram, O. (1973) "Religious treatment of mental illness in Tamilnadu." *Indian Journal of Psychiatry*, 15: 38–48.

Somasundaram, O. (1987) "The Indian lunacy act 1912: The historic background." *Indian Journal of Psychiatry*, 29(1): 3–14.

Special Correspondent – The Hindu (2014) *Dawa-dua programme gaining momentum*. 20 February 2014. www.thehindu.com/todays-paper/tp-national/tp-tamilnadu/dawadua-programme-gaining-momentum/article5708147.

Taylor, S. (2016) *Health psychology*. New Delhi: Tata McGraw-Hill.

Thara, R., and Tirupati, S. (2000) "How stigmatizing is schizophrenia in India." *International Journal of Social Psychiatry*, 46(2): 135–141.

Tharoor, S. (2017) *Inglorious empire: What the British did to India*. London: Hurst Publishers.

Trivedi, J. K. (2009) "Mental Health Act, salient features, objectives, critique and future directions". In S Gautam and S A Awasthi (Eds.), *Forensic psychiatry : clinical practice guidelines for psychiatrists in India*, pp. 11–19. Gurugram: Indian Psychiatric Society.

United Nations. (2017) *World population prospects the 2017 revision -Key findings and advance tables*. New York: United Nations.

Veeraraghavan. (2014) *Abnormal and clinical psychology*. New Delhi: Tata McGraw-Hill Education.

Weiss, R. S. (2009) *Recipes for immortality: Medicine, religion, and community in South India*. New York: Oxford University Press.

33

CULTURE AND MENTAL HEALTH IN JAMAICA

Samantha Longman-Mills, Patrice Whitehorne-Smith,
Carole Mitchell, Lester Shields and Wendel D. Abel

Mental disorders have emerged as a global public health concern with the World Health Organization declaring that mental disorders rank fourth among the global burden of disease now facing the world (Centre for Global Health Research Studies 2018). This has brought issues surrounding mental illnesses into a sharp focus and has called for a greater understanding of the socio-cultural factors influencing the development and manifestations of mental illnesses, as well as how mental health issues are addressed across societies.

This chapter examines the evolution of mental health issues and services within the Jamaican cultural context. Jamaican society has undergone several major historical transitions including, colonization, the slave trade, the abolition of slavery and independence from British rule. The social re-engineering of Jamaican culture through Indigenous genocide, the forced migration of Africans to Jamaica and the multicultural nature of contemporary Jamaican society has significant mental health implications. An outline of how these socio-historical transitions have shaped the manifestation of and perspectives on mental health is presented. Jamaican mental health services have seen a successful paradigm shift, from centralized institutional care to decentralised community-based care. However, the aetiology of mental illnesses is often attributed to spiritual factors, which influences whether spiritual or formal mental health services are sought.

Demographics and historical context of mental health in Jamaica

Jamaica is the third largest island in the Caribbean with a population of 2.9 million, with 92% being of African descent (CIA 2018). Jamaica's cultural heritage has its early roots in slavery. The first known inhabitants of Jamaica were the Tainos, however, half a century after Christopher Colombus' 'discovery' of the island for Spain, these natives were exterminated due to harsh enslavement conditions and European diseases. In 1655, the British colonized the island and via the triangular trade, captured and enslaved Africans to work on the Jamaican sugar plantations.

Slavery in the Caribbean was of a different more brutal form than that previously practiced, as its premise was that Africans were sub-human (Leary 2005; Gump 2010). The enslaved Africans endured horrific physical and psychological atrocities: they were abducted from their homeland, shackled with chains and suffered dehumanizing conditions for weeks within the holds of ships. They were branded like chattel, forced to work long hours, tortured for mild infractions, raped, beaten and as a means of preventing their many revolts, deculturated.

The enslaved Africans were stripped of their African identity and European perspectives, ideals and behaviours were enforced. African languages, rituals and values were seen as evidence of heathenism and they were prohibited from openly speaking their languages or practicing their religious rituals and were forced to adopt Christianity. Drums, which had an important ceremonial value in many African cultures, were forbidden (Hickling and Gibson 2005). They were also separated from their families and tribesmen and this further challenged the endurance of their language and rituals. Family structures were also changed: males were emasculated and marginalised within the family, while females became the head of the family and were sexually exploited by the plantation masters.

The people who exited slavery, nearly 500 years later, were no longer Africans, but rather through creolization, they became Jamaicans (Yelvington 2000). After the abolition of slavery, Indian and Chinese indentured labourers came to Jamaica to work at the plantations. Later, German, Syrian and Jewish migrants settled in Jamaica, carrying their own cultural perspectives and rituals. Jamaica became a melting pot, fusing together a variety of cultures with the interactions between all these races resulted in the miscegenation of the Jamaican people and is reflected in the Jamaican Motto "out of many, one people". The national language for Jamaica is English, with British rather than American spellings being utilized. However, the dialect, patois, which is of British and African derivative, is more frequently spoken. Christianity is the most popular religion but obeah (sorcery of African origin) is still practiced. Jamaican cuisine reflects the presence of African, British, Indian and Chinese influences. Jamaicans are a proud and determined people. They are known for their international prominence in athletics, jerk chicken, blue mountain coffee and reggae music. However, as all people are vulnerable to mental health challenges, the Jamaican people are no exception, especially with the legacy of slavery, which has left its indelible mark on the psyche of the Jamaican people. These former slaves had an elevated risk for severe mental health conditions including posttraumatic stress disorder, major depressive disorder, anxiety disorders and psychosis.

Brief history of Indigenous and traditional healers and healing

Prior to the Spanish occupation of Jamaica, the Indigenous people, the Tainos, treated the mentally ill with herbs that was mixed into their food and hung from fruit trees with the mentally ill being allowed to roam freely. This form of treatment was so successful that the Spanish colonizers ascribed the surprisingly positive results to sorcery (Beaubrun et al. 1976; Hickling and Gibson 2005). However, with the genocide of the Indigenous population such treatment became obsolete.

The British occupation of Jamaica resulted in the forcible importation and enslavement of Africans. The enslaved Africans were not deemed to be capable of developing a mental illness, and their care was the responsibility of the plantation owners, therefore behaviours characteristic of a mental illness, were seen as disobedience and would typically result in inhumane and cruel treatment, often resulting in the death of the mentally ill slave (Hickling 1988). Nonetheless, one of the earliest diagnosis that was given to enslaved Africans was drapetomania, characterized by the tendency to run away, and try to flee captivity (Cartwright 1851). It was hypothesised that this behaviour occurred because they were possessed, with the remedy being cutting off both big toes (White 2002) and 'whipping the devil out of them' (Hickling 2005).

Mentally ill slaves typically received no treatment and died from suicide, eating dirt or spent their lives incarcerated in the plantation dungeons (Hickling and Gibson 2005). However, supplemental care was provided by the African slave doctors within the confines of the plantation, and also by the 'obeah' practitioners who were not limited to a specific plantation, as they had influence within the society and were thought to be central in slave revolts (Saunders 2005). Obeah practitioners were so influential that punitive laws were implemented in 1816 to decimate and destroy their practice and influence (Hickling 1988; Saunders 2005).

Obeah as a religious practice, was not a significant religion in West Africa, however due to the slave masters' fear of it and their repeated attempts to eradicate it from Jamaican society, obeah was elevated to being the spiritual support for the enslaved Africans (Sutherland et al. 2014). Obeah practitioners allegedly communicate with the ancestral spirits, and provide herbal concoctions for drinking, rubbing, bathing or sprinkling, that was believed to result in spirits protecting or harming someone. Persons who held obeah in high esteem, typically believed that once someone works obeah on them, the only way to remove the negative hex, is to go to an obeah practitioner to get protection (Sutherland et al. 2014). Additionally, Persons who believe in obeah, often ascribe the cause of any mental health challenge to someone working obeah on them, therefore their first treatment option is not the formal mental health services but rather the acquisition of a protective potion from the obeah practitioner (Campbell-Livingston 2016). When persons have in their mental health history, attempts at treatment by an obeah practitioner, it can be assumed that only the persons for whom the treatment failed, will present to a formal mental health professional.

Traditional views of mental illnesses as being self-inflicted, due to emotional weakness, as a result of devil possession or obeah, continues to be deeply rooted in the thinking of the society; especially among those with limited education and exposure to the mentally ill (Arthur et al. 2010; Williams 2012; Abel et al. 2017). Additionally, in many instances, when treatment is sought both from a mental health professional and an obeah practitioner, there is a subjective tendency for the diagnosis and quality of service from obeah practitioners to be perceived by the patient, as being more satisfactory than that received from formal mental health practitioners (James 2012).

Colonialism and the evolution of mental health practices

British colonialism has played a central role in the evolution of mental health practices in Jamaica. After the emancipation of slaves, the care of the mentally ill was transferred from plantation owners to the government. The first Jamaican 'lunatic asylum' was established in 1776, built as an annex to the Kingston Public hospital. However, it was not until post slavery, that ex-slaves were treated there (Hickling and Gibson 2012). The asylum operated on the practice of forcible incarceration. Treatment was more custodial in nature rather than rehabilitative, with the use of chained restraints such as head locks and leg locks, with bleeding, purging and water immersion being considered treatment (Hickling and Gibson 2005). Due to the limited psychiatric treatment provided, many were condemned to long-term stays, behind closed doors, in an overcrowded environment, essentially enduring incarceration (Hickling and Maharajh 2005). The conditions to which the patients were exposed while incarcerated in the hospital were described as extremely cruel and inhumane (Hickling 1988; Hickling and Maharajh 2005; Hickling and Gibson 2012). This form of custodial care was reflective of the then European standard of treatment for the mentally ill.

In 1862, with the construction of a new mental hospital, later called the Bellevue Hospital, the colonial government assumed greater responsibility for the treatment of the increased numbers of mentally ill former slaves. However, care continued to be punitive rather than rehabilitative with restraint and incarceration representing the main therapeutic technique. Admission to the asylum occurred when an individual was arrested by police officers for perceived acts of lunacy, and then brought to court where they would be sentenced to the asylum, or if two general practitioners certified that the individual was of 'unsound mind'. The Bellevue Hospital facilitated the institutionalization of the mentally ill and the centralization of mental health care.

It was not until after independence from British rule, that transformative changes in the treatment of the mentally ill in Jamaica were instituted. It was during this period that the paradigm shift from custodial, centralized institutionalization to rehabilitative, community-based care occurred. In 1974 an amendment to the Mental Hospital Law was enacted that created the structure for integrated community-based mental health care, ending the custodial approach and downgrading the role of police officers in mental health care (Hickling and Maharajh 2005; Hickling 2010). Mental health services were no longer centralized, and were available at public or private sector health facilities such as the general hospitals, health centres, private mental health facilities (Abel 2012) and in their homes.

Cultural representations of illness and wellness

Mental illness has a significant genetic aetiology (NIMH 1998), but psychosocial factors (Shah et al. 2011; Carvalho and De Matos 2014) including economics (Lacey et al. 2016) are known to influence the development and severity of mental illnesses. As such, the culture of a nation is expected to influence the development, understanding and expression of mental illnesses. Culture influences what is considered a mental illness; whether the mentally ill are stigmatized, supported, seeks treatment, adheres to treatment; and even the type of mental illness that may develop.

Although Jamaica is classified as a upper-middle income country, it has one of the slowest growing economic rates in the world with a poverty rate of 15.9% (World Bank 2018). Also, the primary socialising agency, the family, typically employs an authoritarian parenting style, which is thought to increase the risk of negative psychological outcomes (Lipps et al. 2012). Therefore, Jamaicans are expected to be vulnerable to mental health challenges. In 2015, 4% of the Jamaican population (108,000 persons) were treated for mental health challenges with schizophrenia and depression being the most frequent diagnoses (Daley 2017).

Schizophrenia is the most severe and debilitating form of mental illness and involves faulty perceptions and a disconnection to reality. The risk for schizophrenia in Jamaican males is twice that of females, and also occurs at an earlier age in males with the overall mean age of onset being 26 years (Hickling 2008). The main psychotic features observed in Jamaica tend to be auditory and visual hallucinations, disorders of thinking, avolition as well as paranoid delusions (Hickling 2008). The age-corrected prevalence rate for schizophrenia in Jamaica, is 3.1/1000 which is comparable to that seen in developed nations (Hickling 1997). Based on the literature, this rate should have been higher considering the authoritarian parenting style typically employed by Jamaican parents, the widespread use of cannabis with its presumed psychosis inducing effects; as well as the great income inequalities demonstrated in Jamaica. But paradoxically, it is those who have left Jamaica and migrated to England, who reportedly have a tenfold increased risk of being diagnosed with schizophrenia (Hickling 1997). Migration in itself increases the risk of schizophrenia (Virupaksha et al. 2014), but this elevated rate has been attributed to the tendency of the British psychiatrists to misdiagnose people of Caribbean descent (Hickling 1997) or the distress associated with racial discrimination in Britain (Bhugra and Gupta 2010).

Nonetheless, robust evidence suggests that cultural influences within developing nations have a protective effect in relation to the course and outcome in schizophrenia (Hopper and Wanderling 2000). In the Jamaican context, persons diagnosed with schizophrenia tend to have low relapse rates due to the health policies of deinstitutionalisation and community-based mental health care (Saunders 2017). Therefore, these individuals are typically treated in general hospitals or clinics, on general wards and are reintegrated into the community upon remission; thereby eliminating some of the harmful effects associated with social alienation and withdrawal. However, it is important to note that even today, due to the cultural prominence of religiosity, schizophrenia is sometimes mistakenly believed to originate due to demon possession or obeah (sorcery). These beliefs, promote fear and avoidance of the mentally ill and may have a stigmatizing effect on the mentally ill and their families (Campbell-Livingston 2016).

As it relates to wellness, more than half of Jamaicans (57%) tend to be satisfied or very satisfied with their life; with 71% reporting participation in relaxing activities within the past week and only one in every five reported less than seven hours of sleep per day (Wilks et al. 2008). Additionally, Jamaicans tend to have a positive perception of their body with 60% feeling they were at their right body weight, while only 7.4% felt they were overweight. Despite this reported level of contentment, one in every five Jamaican also reported symptoms of depression, with the greatest depressive symptoms being seen within the 35–44 age group and among females (Wilks et al. 2008). Among outpatient clinic patients the prevalence is quoted as being as high as 29.9% (Monroe et al. 2013). These elevated depression rates challenge the 'no worries', 'Jamaica, no problem', stereotypical attitude that is often portrayed of Jamaicans, as depression is widespread in Jamaica. Among the elderly, predictors of depression were being female, low socioeconomic status, low level of cognitive functioning and older age (Gibson et al. 2013).

Depression is the most prevalent mental illness in Jamaica (WHO 2009) and this may be attributable to the challenging economic climate, the high crime and violence rates, or the stereotypical tendency to dismiss the importance of good mental health in Jamaica. However, this elevated depression rate has not translated to high suicide rates. Jamaica's suicide rate is one of the lowest in the world, with a rate or 2.2 per 100,000 in 2016, while developed nations such as the United States and Canada had a rate of 15.3 and 12.5 per 100,000, respectively, for the same year (WHO 2018). Jamaica's low suicide rate is partially attributable to the widespread practice of Christianity which is intolerant of suicide and also the emotional and economic support provided by churches. However, the risk factors for suicide include being male, a professional or senior official and being within the 25–34 age group, with the most frequently used method for suicide being hanging (Abel et al. 2012).

Substance use disorders also pose a significant concern in Jamaica, with 28 % of government GDP (Harrison 2012) being allocated to treat these disorders. The most frequently consumed licit substance in Jamaica is alcohol while cannabis is the most frequently consume illicit substance (Younger-Coleman et al. 2017). Alcohol consumption is ceremonially entrenched in Jamaican culture. Alcohol, particularly rum made from sugar cane, is widely consumed at funerals, wedding ceremonies, carnivals and other special occasions. After the death of a loved one, for 'nine-night' it is consumed nightly in a 'set-up' (staying up all night) party like gathering of friends and family members of the deceased, for nine nights after the death. This practice is of African origin and occurs to celebrate the life of the deceased and it is believed that the deceased's spirit comes on the ninth night to say goodbye. Alcohol, typically over proof white rum, is also sprinkled at gravesites during funerals, to give the deceased a 'good send-off'. Additionally, the practice of going to 'rum bars' to talk, play dominoes and drink one's problems away, is characteristic of many males. Alcohol consumption is engrained in Jamaican life as it facilitates social interactions as well as self-medicating purposes (Gibson et al. 2017).

Despite Jamaica being a transhipment port for illicit drugs from the leading world producers in South America to the leading consumers in North America (Longman-Mills et al. 2011), the frequently trafficked illicit drugs, such as cocaine and heroin are rarely used in Jamaica, due to beliefs about its harmful effects. Instead, cannabis is the illicit drug of choice. Cannabis was initially brought to Caribbean by Indian indenture labourers in the mid-nineteenth century (Reid

2005), and has become engrafted into the Jamaican culture, being widely known as 'ganja', 'sinsemilla' or 'the weed'. It is frequently used to make teas, ointments, tonics and also smoked. Jamaican folklore identifies cannabis as being effective in treating asthma, influenza, glaucoma, tuberculosis, nausea and vomiting. Its benefits are believed to include improving weight gain, as well as acting as an anti-inflammatory and an analgesic. Therefore, cannabis is seen as being beneficial and is used for its purported medicinal properties, in Rastafarian religious ceremonies and recreationally. Fifteen percent of the Jamaican population are current users of cannabis, while 28% of the Jamaican population reported that they had used cannabis at least once (Younger-Coleman et al. 2017).

Training and development, accreditation, licensure and certification processes

To effectively manage the individual and public health challenges posed by mental illnesses, a cadre of competent and professional mental health personnel are required. The key mental health practitioners in Jamaica are psychiatrists, community mental health officers, psychiatric nursing aides, social workers and psychologists. Initially, Jamaican psychiatrists were trained in the United Kingdom or North America, until 1969 when the University of the West Indies, started a Doctor of Medicine in Psychiatry programme, with its first graduates in 1975 (Hickling and Sorel 2005). Jamaican psychiatrists are medical doctors with four additional years of training in psychiatry. Successful performance on their fourth-year final examination qualifies them as a psychiatrist. Psychiatric practice, as with all medical practice, is regulated by the Medical Council of Jamaica.

Community mental health teams facilitate at home mental health care. Central to these mental health teams are Mental Health Officers (MHO). These are registered nurses who have a Bachelor's degree in nursing along with six months additional training in social work, medicine, psychopharmacology, psychiatry, psychology and management. Mental Health Officers go to the homes of the mentally ill to facilitate home care as well as crisis management. They do not initiate or change the treatment prescribed by the psychiatrist, but they can reinstate drug therapy in the event of a non-compliance, provide regular drug therapy and can initiate detention in accordance with the Mental Health Act (McKenzie 2008). Thereby, facilitating at home treatments and community-based interventions. The work of the Mental Health Officers is supported by Psychiatric Nursing Aides.

Psychiatric Nursing Aides are mental health nursing assistants. They undergo a four months training which includes basic nursing skills, and basic mental health concepts. They typically have a high school diploma but are given a matriculatory entrance examination to ensure minimum competence. They provide support to the nursing staff and work both within the community and the hospitals.

A first degree in social work is required to become a social worker. Initially, the University of the West Indies only offered a certificate in social work until 1974 when the first undergraduate degree in social work became available. Social workers are integral in protecting the mentally ill and helping them to solve problems in their everyday lives. Social work practice is not currently monitored by any regulatory body however, they are at the early stages of developing a Health Care Social Work Association that is anticipated to fulfil this role.

Training in clinical psychology at the master's level became available at the University of the West Indies in 2001, with the PhD commencing in 2002 (Hickling and Matthies 2003). The Jamaican Psychological Society certifies psychological credentials while the Council of Professions Allied to Medicine, regulate and provide licensure for psychologists.

The provision of effective and enhanced mental health services is dependent on the training of psychiatrist, psychologist, social workers, mental health officers as well as other staff in the general hospital (Abel et al. 2011a). However, a significant limitation to the current mental health system is the limited numbers of psychologists and social workers. Therefore, care for the seriously mentally ill is often from a biological approach rather than a biopsychosocial, which often results in gaps in ensuring that improvements in quality of life will be sustainable in the long term.

Contemporary mental health care practices

With burgeoning mental health challenges, it is important that appropriate and effective mental health services are available to Jamaicans. However, with its challenging economic climate, ensuring that mental health services are affordable and accessible, required creative solutions. This endeavour required a paradigm shift from institutionalized care to one that is integrative and community-based.

The current public mental health services are under the coordination of the Mental Health Unit in the Ministry of Health and are divided into four regional health authorities: Southern, South Eastern, North Eastern and Western. The Bellevue Hospital remains the only mental hospital in Jamaica, initially having 1,000 beds but this has since been reduced to 800 (Abel et al. 2011a). In addition to the Bellevue Hospital there are two designated, acute care secured psychiatric units, namely, Ward 21, the psychiatric unit at the University Hospital of the West Indies (UHWI) which has 20 beds and the psychiatric unit at the Cornwall Regional Hospital (CRH) which has 12 beds. Along with the other 23 general hospitals, they provide the mental health beds for the patients requiring treatment (Abel et al. 2011a). An important aspect of this system is that psychotic patients are treated on acute general hospital wards rather than in designated psychiatric facilities and experienced shorter hospital stays, demonstrate higher levels of treatment compliance and have better employment prospects (Hickling et al. 2000; McKenzie et al. 2004). This model has been highlighted as being effective and one to emulated (McKenzie et al. 2004).

There are also traditional inpatient ward admissions and mental health services are also available through an outpatient day hospital system. The day hospital patients receive treatment at the hospital, are monitored throughout the day, but are not admitted to the hospital. Such patients arrive at the hospital in the morning and spend the day but return to their homes in the afternoon. Patients in the day hospital are usually not acutely ill and do not require more intensive care (Abel et al. 2011a). However, upon discharge from the hospitals, additional mental health services are also available from the community mental services and teams.

Community mental health services are housed in health centres within the various communities across the island. Community mental health services, was first conceptualized at Bellevue in 1964 and over decades became established throughout the island (Abel et al. 2005). There are approximately 375 health centres which provided a variety of care, inclusive of medication management, follow-up care, counselling, and psycho-education and health promotion as well as crisis intervention (Abel et al. 2011a). Community mental health teams also go to the homes of the mentally ill to facilitate home care as well as crisis management.

Due to the integrated approach of treating patients with mental illness in primary care facilities, there has been a reduction in the number of patients admitted to the mental hospital (Abel et al. 2011b). This paradigm shift resulted in a 50% reduction in the admission rate to Bellevue Hospital between 1971 and 1988 (Hickling 1999) The success of this paradigm shift has also been partially attributed to the presence of the health centres and mental health officers, as they afford easier access and a greater availability of mental health personnel and community-based care.

Private care for the mentally ill patient is also provided on a personalized level using group homes or small residential facilities that provide opportunity for treatment (Abel et al. 2011a). The private facilities offer supervised short-term care in a home-like setting and so although in a secure facility, the atmosphere is not as clinical as that of a hospital stay. Group homes have the services of a psychiatrist and other mental health staff to ensure adequate treatment opportunities. These facilities may also offer services to other Caribbean nationals who have been sent to Jamaica for treatment but are not able to return to their homes after being discharged from hospital (Abel 2012).

Despite the strides that have been made in providing mental health services, there remains socio-cultural barriers that prevent persons from accessing care. These include limited querying of mental health by some medical professionals and the cultural stigma associated with mental health challenges. While mentally ill patients are seen at all medical facilities the querying of mental health challenges with all patients, has not been adequately integrated into the practice of all primary care physicians. Their provision of mental health services remains largely separated from that offered for other medical illnesses. Nevertheless, efforts are ongoing at the Ministry of Health to foster, through training, greater integration of mental health services into primary health care systems.

Stigma poses an additional barrier to persons accessing adequate care. Stigma is seen as the negative beliefs, attitudes and behaviours directed towards (Goffman 1963; Neuberg et al. 2000) directed towards the mentally ill. Religious beliefs, whether Christianity or obeah, are seen as supporting the stigma directed at the mentally ill. While the stigma of mental illness is not unique to Jamaica, its effects in the country continues to be a major barrier to adequate mental care (Arthur et al 2010).

Future directions

Noteworthy efforts have been made over the past decades to improve and enhance mental health services in Jamaica. There have also been mental health education campaigns, to reduce stigma and as such, it is likely that improvements will occurred within the society, as it relates to the cultural understanding of mental illnesses.

The treatment of mental illness is evolving globally and in response Jamaica continues to develop and refine its policies and practices to enhance treatment accessibility and delivery. One area of focus is the WHO Mental Health Gap Action Program (WHO 2016). This is a global capacity building program aimed at improving the services for mental, neurological and substance use disorders in low and middle income countries. The focus is on quality and accessibility of care, psychosocial assistance and medication resulting in significant increase the number of persons treated for a variety of mental illness. The thrust of the programme is the provision of training opportunities for health professionals and para-professionals as well as upgrading curricula of undergraduate and postgraduate mental health programmes (WHO 2016).

There is undoubtedly a need for greater and more consistent public education campaigns about mental health. This should include the simplifying of psychiatric terms and diagnoses to the level of lay persons, in order to build understanding across educational levels. Also, increased exposure and contact with the mentally ill may help to curb stigma (Gibson et al. 2008). However, there is also a need for the better utilization and integration of psychologists and social workers into the mental health treatment systems. This may improve the holistic treatment of patients, their prognosis as well as improving the quality of life of their families through psycho-education.

Conclusion

This chapter sought to provide a snapshot of Jamaican culture and potential mental health outcomes. It is important to note that, the legacy of slavery still has an impact on the psyche of Jamaicans. This effect has residual ripples in how Jamaicans express themselves and understand the world. It also has clear implications for how mental illnesses manifest among the Jamaican people. Therefore, in the treatment of Jamaicans it is important to retain a consciousness of the cultural context of mental illness as well as to recognize that many Jamaicans are spiritual and may possess traditional views contrary to the Western aetiological explanations of mental disorders. Many still perceive mental health challenges as a personal weakness; others view it as occurring because of demon possession or originating because someone worked obeah on them.

Jamaica has made noteworthy advances in understanding and addressing mental health challenges. The island now has a cadre of mental health professionals with clear policies and programmes to assist persons with mental illnesses. Additionally, the use of an integrated, largely community-based treatment approach has proven effective in reducing the burden of mental health care on the government, families and individuals.

Nevertheless, stigma remains a central barrier to this process, as a mental health diagnosis is perceived to be a stigmatizing label, persons may deny having a mental illness, refuse to learn about mental illnesses and may be reluctant to seek mental health assistance. As such, efforts are ongoing to improve mental health literacy, health systems and services to better meet the needs of those affected by mental illness.

References

Abel, W. (2012) 'Yes! Mental Health Services Are Available in Jamaica', *The Gleaner*, 19 September 2012. http://jamaica-gleaner.com/gleaner/20120919/health/health1.html.

Abel, W., Brown, T., Thompson, E. and Sewell, C. (2011a) 'Mental Health Services in Jamaica: From Institution to Community', *Ethnicity and Inequalities in Health and Social Care*, 4(3): 103–111. doi: 10.1108/17570981111249248.

Abel, W., McCallum, M., Hickling, F. and Gibson, R. (2005) 'Mental Health Services and Public Policy in Jamaica'. In F. Hickling and E. Sorel (Eds.), *Images of Psychiatry in the Caribbean* (pp. 297–314). Kingston, Jamaica: Stephenson's Litho Press Ltd.

Abel, W., Richards-Henry, M., Wright, E. G. and Eldemire-Shearer, D. (2011b) 'Integrating Mental Health into Primary Care an Integrative Collaborative Primary Care Model-the Jamaican Experience', *West Indian Medical Journal*, 60(4): 483–489.

Abel, W., James, K., Bridgelal-Nagassar, R., Holder-Nevins, D., Eldemire, H., Thompson, E. and Sewell, C. (2012) 'The Epidemiology of Suicide in Jamaica 2002–2010: Rates and Patterns', *The West Indian Medical Journal*, 61(5): 509–515.

Abel, W., Longman-Mills, S., Martin, J. S., Oshi, D. and Whitehorne-Smith, P. (2017) 'Does Ganja Cause Mental Illness? Perspectives from a Population-Based Assessment of Mental Health Literacy in Jamaica', *West Indies Medical Journal Open* 66. doi:10.7727/wimj.2017.209.

Arthur, C. M., Hickling, F. W., Robertson-Hickling, H., Haynes-Robinson, T., Abel, W. and Whitley, R. (2010) "Mad, Sick, Head Nuh Good': Mental Illness Stigma in Jamaican Communities', *Transcultural Psychiatry*, 47(2): 252–275. doi: 10.1177/1363461510368912.

Beaubrun, M. H., Bannister, P., Lewis, L. F., Mahy, G., Royes, K. C., Smith, P. and Wizinger, Z. (1976) 'The History of Psychiatry in the West Indies'. In G. Howell (Eds.), *World History of Psychiatry* (pp. 507–527). New York: Brunner/Mazel.

Bhugra, D. and Gupta, S. (2010) *Migration and Mental Health*. Cambridge: Cambridge University Press.

Campbell-Livingston, C. (2016) 'Mental Health Disorder or Demon Possession?', *The Gleaner*, 21 May 2016. Accessed June 20. http://jamaica-gleaner.com/article/news/20160521/mental-health-disorder-or-demon-possession.

Cartwright, S. A. (1851) 'Diseases and Peculiarities of the Negro Race'. AMS Press, INC, available at www.pbs.org/wgbh/aia/part4/4h3106t.html (Accessed June 21, 2018).

Carvalho, M. and De Matos, M. G. (2014) 'Psychosocial Determinants of Mental Health and Risk Behaviours in Adolescents', *Global Journal of Health Science*, 6(4): 22–35. doi: 10.5539/gjhs.v6n4p22.

Centre for Global Health Research Studies (2018) 'Incidence and Prevalence of Mental Disorders'. available at www.centrosaluteglobale.it/mental-health/incidence-and-prevalence-of-mental-disorders/ (Accessed July 13, 2018).

CIA. (2018) 'The World Factbook. Central America and Caribbean: Jamaica'. Central Intelligence Agency, available at www.cia.gov/library/publications/the-world-factbook/geos/jm.html (Accessed June 20, 2018).

Daley, A. (2017) 'Mental Health and Youth in Jamaica', *The Caribbean Current*. (Accessed June 21. 2018).

Gibson, R. C., Abel, W. D., White, S. and Hickling, F. W. (2008) 'Internalizing Stigma Associated with Mental Illness: Findings from a General Population Survey in Jamaica', *Pan American Journal of Public Health*, 23(1): 26–33.

Gibson, R. C., Neita, S. M., Abel, W. D., James, K. and Eldemire-Shearer, D. (2013) 'Sociodemographic Factors Associated with Depressive Symptoms among Elderly Persons from Two Communities in Kingston, Jamaica', *West Indian Medical Journal*, 62(7): 615–619. doi: 10.7727/wimj.2012.273.

Gibson, R. C., Waldron, N. K., Abel, W. D., Eldemire-Shearer, D., James, K. and Mitchell-Fearon, K. (2017) 'Alcohol Use, Depression, and Life Satisfaction among Older Persons in Jamaica', *International Psychogeriatrics*, 29(4): 663–671. doi: 10.1017/S1041610216002209.

Goffman, E. (1963) *Stigma: Notes on the Management of Spoiled Identity*. New York: Somon & Schuster.

Gump, J. (2010) 'Reality Matters: The Shadow of Trauma on African American Subjectivity', *Psychoanalytic Psychology*, 27(1): 42–54.

Harrison, J. (2012). 'Consultancy: To Conduct an Assessment of the Economic Costs of substance abuse in CARICOM Member States: Jamaica, Suriname and Trinidad and Tobago. Jamaica Report'. UWI Consulting, available at www.ncda.org.jm/images/pdf/researchday/economic.pdf (Accessed June 20, 2018).

Hickling, F. W. (1988) 'Psychiatry in the Commonwealth Caribbean: A Brief Historical Overview', *Bulletin of the Royal College of Psychiatrists*, 12(10): 434–436. doi: 10.1192/pb.12.10.434.

Hickling, F. W. (1997) 'Mental Health in the Caribbean', *Journal of Caribbean Studies* (Health and Disease) 12(1): 57–71.

Hickling, F. (1999) *Situational Needs Analysis of the Mental Health Services in Jamaica*. Kingston, Jamaica: University of the West Indies.

Hickling, F. W. (2005) 'The Epidemiology of Schizophrenia and Other Common Mental Health Disorders in the English-Speaking Caribbean', *Revista Panamericana de Salud Pública*, 18(4–5): 256–262.

Hickling, F. W. (2008) 'Psychopathology of the Jamaican People'. In F. W. Hickling, B. Matthies, K. Morgan, and R. C. Gibson (Eds.), *Perspectives in Caribbean Psychology* (pp. 32–69). Kingston, Jamaica: University of the West Indies.

Hickling, F. W. (2010) 'Psychiatry in Jamaica', *International Psychiatry*, 7(1): 9–11. doi: 10.1192/S1749367600000928.

Hickling, F. W. and Gibson, R. C. (2005) 'The History of Caribbean Psychiatry'. In Hickling, F. W. and Sorel, E. (Eds) *Images of Psychiatry: The Caribbean* (pp. 15–42). Kingston, Jamaica: University of the West Indies, Mona.

Hickling, F. and Gibson, R. C. (2012) 'Decolonization of Psychiatric Public Policy in Jamaica', *West Indian Medical Journal*, 61(4): 437–441. doi: 10.7727/wimj.2012.127.

Hickling, F. W. and Maharajh, H. (2005) 'Mental Health Legislation'. In Hickling, F. W. and Sorel, E. (Eds) *Images of Psychiatry: The Caribbean*, (pp. 43–74). Kingston, Jamaica: Stephenson's Litho Press.

Hickling, F. W. and Matthies, B. (2003) 'The Establishment of a Clinical Psychology Post-Graduate Programme at the University of the West Indies', *Caribbean Journal of Education*, 25(1): 25–36.

Hickling, F. W. and Sorel, E. (2005) 'Introduction'. In F. W. Hickling and E. Sorel (Eds.), *Images of Psychiatry* (pp. 1–14). Kingston, Jamaica: Stephenson's Litho Press.

Hickling, F. W., McCallum, M., Nooks, L. and Rodgers-Johnson, P. (2000) 'Treatment of Acute Schizophrenia in Open General Medical Wards in Jamaica', *Psychiatr Serv*, 51(5): 659–663. doi: 10.1176/appi.ps.51.5.659.

Hopper, K. and Wanderling, J. (2000) 'Revisiting the Developed Versus Developing Country Distinction in Course and Outcome in Schizophrenia: Results from Isos, the Who Collaborative Followup Project. International Study of Schizophrenia', *Schizophrenia Bulletin*, 26(4): 835–846.

James, C. (2012) 'Psychiatric Patients' Evaluation of the Efficacy of Obeah Vs. Western Medicine in Treating Their Mental Illness', *Journal of Psychology in Africa*, 22(1): 134–138. doi: 10.1080/14330237.2012.10874531.

Lacey, K. K., Powell Sears, K., Crawford, T.V., Matusko, N. and Jackson, J. S. (2016) 'Relationship of Social and Economic Factors to Mental Disorders among Population-Based Samples of Jamaicans and Guyanese', *BMJ Open*, 6(12): e012870. doi: 10.1136/bmjopen-2016–012870.

Leary, J. D. (2005) *Post Traumatic Slave Syndrome: America's Legacy of Enduring Injury and Healing*. Milwaukie, OR: Uptone Press.

Lipps, G., Lowe, G. A., Gibson, R. C., Halliday, S., Morris, A., Clarke, N. and Wilson, R. N. (2012) 'Parenting and Depressive Symptoms among Adolescents in Four Caribbean Societies', *Child & Adolescent Psychiatry & Mental Health*, 6(1): 31–42. doi: 10.1186/1753-2000-6-31.

Longman-Mills, S., González, Y., Meléndez, M., García, M., Gómez, J., Juárez, C., Martínez, E., Peñalba, S., Pizzanelli, M., Solórzano, L., Wright, G., Cumsille, F., Sapag, J., Wekerle, C., Hamilton, H., Erickson, P. and Mann, R. (2011) 'Child Maltreatment and Its Relationship to Drug Use in Latin America and the Caribbean: An Overview and Multinational Research Partnership', *International Journal of Mental Health and Addiction*, 9(4): 347–364. doi: 10.1007/s11469-011-9347-0.

McKenzie, K. (2008) 'Jamaica: Community Mental Health Services'. In A. Cohen and J. Caldas de Almeida (Eds.), *Innovative Mental Health Programs in Latin America & the Caribbean*, (pp. 79–92). Washington, DC: Pan American Health Organization.

McKenzie, K., Patel, V. and Araya, R. (2004) 'Learning from Low Income Countries: Mental Health', *British Medical Journal*, 329(7475): 1138–1140.

Monroe, C. E., Affuso, O., Martin, M. Y., Aung, M., Crossman, L. and Jolly, P. E. (2013) 'Correlates of Symptoms of Depression and Anxiety among Clinic Patients in Western Jamaica', *The West Indian Medical Journal*, 62(6): 533–542. doi: 10.7727/wimj.2012.177.

National Institute of Mental Health. (1998) *Genetics and Mental Disorders: Report of the National Institute of Mental Health's Genetics Workgroup (No. 84)*. Bethesda, MD: National Institutes of Health.

Neuberg, S., Smith, D. and Asher, T. (2000) 'Why People Stigmatize: Toward a Biocultural Framework'. In T. Heatherton, R. Kleck, M. Hebl and J. Hull (Eds.), *The Social Psychology of Stigma*, (pp. 31–61). New York: Guilford Press.

Reid, S. (2005) 'Substance Abuse'. In F. W. Hickling and E. Sorel (Eds.), *Images of Psychiatry: The Caribbean*, (pp. 197–231). Kingston, Jamaica: Stephenson's Litho Press Ltd.

Saunders, A. (2017) 'Jamaica's Schizophrenia Relapse Rate Low, Says Uwi Lecturer', *Jamaica Observer*, September 6, 2017, News.

Saunders, N. J. (2005) *The Peoples of the Caribbean: An Encyclopedia of Archeology and Traditional Culture*. Santa Barbara, CA: ABC-CLIO.

Shah, J., Mizrahi, R. and McKenzie, K. (2011) 'The Four Dimensions: A Model for the Social Aetiology of Psychosis', *British Journal of Psychiatry*, 199(1): 11–4. doi: 10.1192/bjp.bp.110.090449.

Sutherland, P., Moodley, R. and Chevannes, P. (2014) *Caribbean Healing Traditions: Implications for Health and Mental Health*. New York: Taylor & Francis.

University of the West Indies, Mona (2008) *Jamaica Health and Lifestyle Survey 2007–8*. Kingston, Jamaica.

Virupaksha, H. G., Kumar, A. and Nirmala, B. P. (2014) 'Migration and Mental Health: An Interface', *Journal of Natural Science, Biology, and Medicine*, 5(2): 233–239. doi: 10.4103/0976-9668.136141.

White, K. (2002) *An Introduction to the Sociology of Health and Illness*. London: SAGE Publications.

Wilks, R., Younger, N., Tulloch-Reid, M., McFarlane, S., & Francis, D. (2008). *Jamaica Health and Lifestyle Survey 2007–8*. Available at http://isis.uwimona.edu.jm/reports/health/JHLSII_final_may09.pdf (Accessed July 13, 2018).

World Health Organization. (2009). *WHO-AIMS Report on Mental Health System in Jamaica. Kingston, Jamaica: A Report of the Assessment of the Mental Health System in Jamaica Using the World Health Organization – Assessment Instrument for Mental Health Systems (Who-Aims)*. World Health Organization and Ministry of Health Jamaica. Available at www.who.int/mental_health/Jamaica_who_aims_report.pdf (Accessed June 21, 2018).

World Health Organization. (2016). *mhGAP intervention guide for mental, neurological and substance use disorders in non-specialized health settings: mental health Gap Action Programme (mhGAP)*. Geneva: World Health Organization.

WHO. (2018) 'Suicide Rates Per (100 000 Population)'. *World Health Organization*, Last Modified April 5th, available at www.who.int/gho/mental_health/suicide_rates_crude/en/ (Accessed June 25 2018).

Williams, D. (2012) 'Where Do Jamaican Adolescents Turn for Psychological Help?', *Child & Youth Care Forum*, 41(5): 461–477.

World Bank. (2018) 'The World in Jamaica: Context'. World Bank, available at www.worldbank.org/en/country/jamaica/overview – 1 (Accessed June 21, 2018).

Yelvington, K. (2000) 'Caribbean Crucible: History, Culture, and Globalization'. *Social Education*, 64(2): 70–77.

Younger-Coleman, N., Cumberbatch, C., Campbell, J., Ebanks, C., Williams, D., & O'Meally, V. (2017). *Jamaica National Drug Use Prevalence Survey 2016-Technical Report for the OAS/CICAD & NCDA*. Kingston, Jamaica: AOS/CICAD.

34

CULTURE AND MENTAL HEALTH IN KENYA

Elijah M. Marangu

There is large number of people who experience mental illness and yet do not receive treatment, this is commonly referred to as the 'treatment gap' (De Silva et al. 2014; Saxena, Thornicroft, Knapp, and Whiteford 2007). This 'treatment gap' is more pronounced in low- and middle-income countries where World Health Organization (WHO) estimates it to be as high as 85% in some countries (WHO 2013). In response, the Mental Health Global Action Programme (mhGAP) was initiated by WHO in 2002 to help with appraisal of current resources and future mental health needs for low- and middle-income countries (WHO 2008, 2013). Success of mhGAP and similar programmes in low- and middle-income countries is only possible if the historical, social, economic and current health care trends are contextualized and well understood (Thornicroft, Cooper, Bortel, Kakuma, and Lund 2012).

This chapter presents analysis of current approaches to mental health care in Kenya. Resisting against a background of post-colonialism and its impact on indigenous health practices, the analysis of the evolution of Kenyan health services is presented. The chapter begins by presenting brief analysis of demographics, history, including British colonialism and its impact on health care trends and practices in Kenya. Explanatory models for mental health and illness in Kenya are presented and juxtaposed against those of the larger sub-Saharan African countries. Marangu, Sands, Rolley, Ndetei, and Mansouri (2014) argued for the need to use pragmatic theoretical and methodological approaches when engaging in mental health care capacity building in low and middle-income countries like Kenya. This Chapter also urges a blended approach to mental health care, including involvement of existing useful human resources such as traditional, faith healers and other practitioners of *ethnomedicine* that are already widely consulted by their communities. The chapter ends with presentation of two case studies that should help the reader to understand how ordinary Kenyans engage with mental health providers and possible outcomes.

Demographics and brief history

Kenya is a country of nearly 45 million people (Kenya National Bureau of Statistics et al. 2015). Kenya borders South Sudan (North West), Ethiopia (North), Somalia (North East), Uganda (West) and Tanzania (South). The 536-kilometer Indian Ocean coastline houses the port of Mombasa that enables trade with some of its landlocked neighbours – Uganda, South Sudan and Rwanda.

Kenya is classified as under-developed country ranking 147 out of 177 in the Human Development Index (WorldBank 2013). Over 46% of Kenya's 45 million people live below the poverty line (Mutungi et al. 2008). With nearly 45% of the population below the age of 15 years. Kenya is heavily dependent on agriculture and tourism, making it vulnerable to seasonal droughts and political instability. Additional economic challenges include the 40% unemployment, rampant corruption among public servants, high rates of HIV/Aids and poor infrastructure, high crime rate, poverty and political instability (Kenya National Bureau of Statistics et al. 2015). Meanwhile, Kenya have failed to prioritise the mental health care of its people (Ngui, Khasakhala, Ndetei, and Roberts 2010). Kenya's neighbours, most notably Somalia and South Sudan, have experienced civil wars and political instability in recent years with significant social, political and economic impacts on Kenya. Today, Kenya is home to over 0.5 million refugees housed in many camps mainly in northern Kenya (Kenya 2015b).

Appraisal of the Kenyan health care context has to include considerations for its colonial history, recent political polarization along tribal lines, corruption and nepotism as key drivers for under-investment and prevailing poor access to health care. Kenya is a culturally and ethnically diverse country, with ethnic conflicts and deaths reported in every electoral cycle since 2007 (Kanyinga 2009). Kenya has 45 ethnic groups, the dominant ones include the Bantu speaking Kikuyu, Meru, Embu and Akamba who constitute 36% of the total population. The Luo and the Luhya living in western Kenya and Lake Victoria region constitute 27% and the Kalenjins living in the Rift Valley constitute 14%. Other smaller groups including Kisii, Mijikenda, Pokot, Turkana, Borana, Somali, Indians, Europeans and Arabs make up 23% of the population (Kenya 2008b). While the British used 'divide and conquer' strategies to play one tribe against the other to entrench their political position, post-independence Kenyan leaders appealed to ethnicity and ethnic solidarity to win and maintain power (Kanyinga 2009). A flawed system of rewarding loyal tribes with government positions and infrastructure meant that there was inequitable distribution of state resources. Historically, areas of Western Kenya and Nyanza have been under-developed because politicians from these regions were considered adversarial to sitting governments, while central and eastern Kenya fared much better with more investments in infrastructure, education and health (Ajulu 2002). It is therefore important to recognize these population dynamics when appraising the Kenyan healthcare context.

Healing practices: Role of Indigenous, traditional and faith healers

Traditional and faith healers play an important role as primary care givers in Africa (Kleinman, Eisenberg, and Good 1978), and their role pre-dates Western medical practitioners. Ndetei, Khasakhala, Kingori, Oginga, and Raja (n.d.) describe traditional and faith healers as informal health care providers, complementing Western medicine. While consumers in Kenya seek cure for their mental illness from Western-trained medical practitioners, when they consult traditional and faith healers, they are seeking cure as well as potential explanations of possible cause (Ndetei et al. n.d.). In a country like Kenya where the mental health system is under resourced in all aspects, the care gap is often plugged by traditional and faith healers (De Silva et al. 2014).

Over 42 tribes in Kenya, each has its own distinct cultural practices and values. While there are similarities in approaches to care for people with mental illness in each of the tribes, there are variations on practitioners who are considered useful in identifying causes and treatment for mental illness (Ndetei et al. n.d.). Similarly, there are variations in names used for different practitioners for each population group. Swahili is the unifying language in Kenya and the common names of practitioners include herbalist (*mganga/daktari wa kienyeji*), seer (*muonaji*), witchdoctor (*mchawi*), fortune teller (*mtabiri*) and preacher (*mhubiri*). In their study, Mutiso et al

(2018) found cultural and religious beliefs to be a barrier to accessing mental health care among Somali refugees living in Kenya and concluded that acknowledging and integrating cultural believes and practices in mental health care could enhance its access among the Somali people. Different traditional care providers often play complementary roles in care for the sick: among the Meru people of Kenya, a seer is consulted to identify the cause of the illness and refers the sick person to an herbalist for plant-based medicines, or to a preacher for prayers. On occasion, some traditional healers combine traditional and modern approaches, like appealing to the living dead as well as using the bible.

Different practitioners will adopt different approaches to treat the sick person, first there is the initial contact, where detailed history of the problem is discussed. In the majority of population groups in Kenya, mental illness is believed to be due to a curse, demonic possession or bad luck (Ndetei et al. n.d.). The initial contact serves to establish the cause of the problem before treatment regimen can be proposed, and the treatment fee can be set, ranging from monetary payment, to payment in kind with agricultural produce or domestic animals such as goats, sheep or cows. Some popular approaches to traditional treatment among Kenya's population groups include herbal roots, cleansing water, oil, incisions, bloodletting, repentance, lamb offering, exorcism, bath, ashes, prayers and use of alcohol (de Menil, Knapp, McDaid, and Njenga 2014).

Some traditional practitioners may use blended approaches to treat the mentally ill person, for example, making an incision to release evil spirits and applying medicinal portions that are believed to have healing properties. Sometimes, herbs are used but they are first prayed for to make them more potent (Menil 2014). Traditional and faith healing may occur once or entail a follow-up care plan: occasionally, the sick person may spend days or weeks with the traditional healer until the symptoms of their illness subside, very similar to hospitalisation.

The type of healing or practitioner depend on their social economic status, religion and location of residence. Urbanized population groups may frequently combine faith healing and Western medicine, while rural and nomadic communities more likely solely rely on traditional healers. Poor people living in informal settlements in the city frequently use traditional and faith healers when they are sick (Ndetei et al. n.d.). The fact that people in low- and middle-income countries like Kenya still gravitate towards traditional and faith healers may be related to current lack of transcultural content in health professional curricula because they are modelled on Western health care systems (Daar et al. 2014; Menil, Ndetei, Waruguru, Knapp, and McDaid 2014).

British colonialism and its impact on the health system in Kenya

Health care institutions and Western medical training facilities in Kenya date back to the colonial era in early 1900s. The British administrators of the new colony secured funding from the Colonial Office to set up a medical department in Nairobi, which preceded today's medical training colleges (Chaiken 1998). At the time of independence from Britain in 1963, with a population of less than 10 million people, Kenya embarked on a modernization program including reforms of the health sector. As a result, a number of large hospitals were built in Nairobi and the provinces (Chuma and Okungu 2011). This led to a reasonable network of public and private hospitals in major rural and urban centres, robust immunization, hospital care, sanitation and vector control services (Chaiken 1998). Kenya's health infrastructure has not been developed to keep up with demands of rapid population growth and with nearly 45 million people, Kenya still relies on health institutions established at independence (Carrin et al. 2007; Chuma and Okungu 2011).

At the time of independence, the Kenyan health service was based on the Western medical model where health services were tertiary based with a focus on treatment and crisis intervention, rather than focus on comprehensive treatment and prevention. During the 1980s, the primary health care model was adopted following the Alma-Ata Conference in 1978 (Muga, Kizito, Mbayah, and Gakuruh 2004), and this sought to make health care more universally available and closer to where people lived. It led to decentralization of health services and the development of health infrastructure such as, maternal and child health clinics, mobile immunization centres and family planning services to community centres (Muga et al. 2004).

The Ministry of Health in Kenya regulates and coordinates all public health services from Afya House in Nairobi. There are two main public referral hospitals in Kenya: the Kenyatta National Hospital in Nairobi; and Moi Teaching and referral hospital in Eldoret, which is located in Nairobi and the Rift Valley regions of Kenya, respectively. The Agha Khan Hospital and Nairobi Hospital are two major private hospitals both based in Nairobi. There is a countrywide network of county and sub-county hospitals that coordinate and control services for their respective administrative jurisdictions, and are responsible for generating their expenditure plans and budget requirements (Muga et al. 2004). A Human Resources in Nursing study found a shortfall of over 29,000 registered nurses to meet WHO's recommended nurse-to-population ratio in Kenya (WHO 2009). Health centres and dispensaries are often the first point of contact for consumers and they offer preventative treatment and ambulatory services at the local level (Muga et al. 2004).

Under the new Kenyan constitution promulgated in September 2010, significant administrative changes were implemented both at the national and regional level. For the first time, for example, counties under the executive direction of a governor is responsible for coordinating and delivering services, including health services at the county level. This is more suited for ensuring effective primary health care services in a system that was not as centralized previously (Kenya 2008a; Kenya 2010).

Explanatory models for mental health and illness in sub-Saharan Africa and Kenya

Africa is a diverse continent with differing explanations for causes and treatment of mental illness. Patel (1995) analyzed literature on explanatory models for mental illness from a number of sub-Saharan African countries and populations including Shona people of Zimbabwe, Xhosa people of South Africa, and populations in Ghana, Kenya, Senegal, Uganda, Botswana, Nigeria, Ethiopia and Guinea-Bissau. Patel concluded that the majority of populations in sub-Saharan Africa distinguished among mind, body and spirit, and the majority attributed the cause of certain forms of mental illness to these three constructs. Many conditions of mental illness are attributed to a human agency such as witchcraft. Other aetiological categories include a curse, 'God given', seasonality, hereditary, spirit possession, poisoning, broken taboos, infections, evil eye or 'blood boiling' (Patel 1995).

The Akan people of Ghana have a complex concept of selfhood consisting of the physical mortal part (*onipadua*), personality (*sunsum*) and the intellect (*okra*); these three have to be in balance for good physical health (Patel 1995). This is concordant with contemporary understandings of good mental health and is well grounded in primary health care principles (WHO 2009a). In a study of the impact of modernization and urbanization on explanatory models of mental illness, Patel (1995) found that increasingly people living in urban areas placed less importance on spiritual causal models; however, spiritual causal models are still held by those living in rural areas. This has implications for approaches to treatment and care that clinicians might want to take when dealing with consumers from different environments even if they have a shared culture. Patel concluded that while the analysis of explanatory models of sub-Saharan African populations reveals a rich diversity of beliefs about mental illness, key concepts of mind and body are comparable to Euro-American concepts.

Contemporary mental health practice and systems in Kenya

Using a qualitative analysis of policy documents and interviews with key stakeholders in the mental health sector, Muga and Jenkins (2010) examined the evolution of health policy in from 1965 to 1997 and found: (1) a mainly Medical Model in the 1960s and early 1970s; (2) a Primary Health Care Model in the late 1970s and 1980s; and (3) a Market Model of health care in the 1990s (Muga and Jenkins 2010).

During the1970s and early 1980s, Kenya experienced economic decline and it became apparent that it could not adequately meet the health care needs of its people. This was juxtaposed against a time when the country was experiencing the highest population growth rate in the world at 4.1% per year (Muga and Jenkins 2010). Therefore when the primary health care model was proclaimed as the correct approach to ensure access to basic mental health care in low and middle-income countries by the WHO in 1978, Kenya was one of the early adopters (Rakuom 2010). However, there was no specific mental health policy even though mental health is one of its elements (Muga and Jenkins 2010). During the 1980s, Kenya's economy declined further, the World Bank introduced Structural Adjustment Programs (SAPS), which forced the government to engage in fiscal reforms including implementing a market model for health care, where health was commoditized, and cost-sharing arrangements were introduced in all public health facilities. This meant that consumers were required to pay up to 25% of the cost of a unit of service in public health facilities (WHO 2009a).

Contemporary mental health care in Kenya can be analyzed in terms of access, resources, stigma and discrimination, specialized with respect to institutional care and alternative approaches to care. The World Health Organization launched the Mental Health Global Action Program (WHO-mhGAP) in 2002 in recognition of the increasing disease burden related to mental disorders in low and middle-income countries (WHO 2008). A key principle of WHO-mhGAP is integration of mental health services into primary health care services to ensure improved access of mental health services to majority of the population. More than 15 years after its launch, Kenya is yet to incorporate mhGAP guidelines to its mental health delivery model.

Mental health services in Kenya are provided within a catchment area that is developed around Kenya's six tier system, namely primary health care in the community setting (Level 1) to tertiary hospital (Level 6) (Rakuom 2010). A capacity for chronic and acute mental health care is only available in Kenya's three psychiatric hospitals (Mathari, Eldoret and Gilgil) with a capacity of just over 1,000 beds, meaning one bed for almost 45,000 people, far below the current global average of 17.5 beds per 100,000 population (WHO 2011), with the majority of mental health beds in Kenya are located at Mathari Hospital, a Level 6 hospital in Nairobi (Ndetei et al. 2009). The quality of mental health treatment is accessible to only a small proportion of the population who can afford these services. The medication formulary available in the primary health services essential drugs list is quite narrow and mostly limited to traditional antipsychotics (chlorpromazine, stelazine and haloperidol), an antidepressant (amitriptyline), and a sedative (diazepam) (Musyimi et al. 2017).

We present two cases: the one represents the gradual combination of both traditional and modern Westernized approaches and the other is solely relying on the Western approach to clinical issues:

Musau is 26 years old, he and his family live in a small rural town in Eastern Kenya. Musau is a third born in a family of five, his parents are peasants. Two of his elder siblings are married with their own families while his younger sister and brother are attending in college and high school respectively.

Musau dropped out of high school due to conduct and disciplinary issues, he started isolating himself and by the age of 20 had started running away from home. As is routine in this part of Kenya, Musau's parents took him to a local traditional healer (mganga) who started giving him some herbal treatment (miti), this had no impact on Musau's condition and was a constant frustration and anxiety for his parents. His uncle who lives in Nairobi suggested that he needed treatment in a hospital, took him to a clinic in Nairobi where he was assessed by a psychiatrist and was diagnosed with schizophrenia. Three months after treatment, Musau had shown much improvement although he constantly complained about the side effects of one of his medications (chlorpromazine). His parents were very happy with his improvement and reported feeling like they had a new son, for the first time, he could help with gardening and taking care of animals at home. Musau was later referred to the local sub-County hospital to continue care and monitoring of treatment by the psychiatric nurse.

This case study is a good example of how lack of mental health literacy and availability of mental health services can lead to poor choices for treatment for people with mental illness and their families. It also shows the role of age, locality and access to education as influencing the choice of mental health care. In addition to above difficulties, people like Musau have to contend with the issue of stigma related to their mental illness. Stigma and discrimination against people with mental illness in Kenya is common (Ndetei et al. 2015), while this is mostly unconscious and based on prejudicial attitudes held by the general population and based on low mental health literacy levels, it has many negative impacts for people with mental illness (Mutiso et al. 2018). Currently there is no evidence on investment by the Kenyan government in mental health literacy and mental health promotion activities that can help to counter stigma and discrimination for people with mental illness in Kenya (Jenkins et al. 2010; Ndetei et al. 2015).

Specialized mental health services such as cognitive behaviour therapy, electroconvulsive therapy and drug detoxification/rehabilitation services are provided in private and relatively expensive facilities, and mostly in major urban centres (Ngui et al. 2010). The example in the vignette below shows an example of a client in the capital city who receives specialized mental health care services from one such provider:

Rukia is 30 years old, self-employed woman working in her own small farm in the outskirts of Nairobi. Her business is flourishing as the demand for fresh produce in the city restaurants increases. Rukia is the last born in a family of four and she is the only one in the family not to complete secondary education because her parents had no money.

Rukia has self-presented to Uzima Mental Health Services based in Nairobi with history of low self-esteem, low mood, lack of sleep and lack of energy to enjoy her normal pursuits for a period of six months. She reports no previous medical or psychiatric history, she has never been in a relationship, reports to enjoy cooking and visiting her family but lately finds these activities demanding and annoying. Baseline psychometric tests undertaken at initial assessment indicated signs of depression, severe anxiety and borderline range stress level in relation to life events.

Rukia was provided with feedback on initial psychometric tests and assessment results, she agreed to a regime of cognitive behavior therapy (CBT). On completion of the agreed CBT sessions, gradual metacognition awareness was achieved as shown in repeat tests. Post treatment, Rukia

Culture and Mental Health in Kenya

reports improved productivity in her business, better engagement with family and improvements in her social life.

Rukia's case study is a good example of what prompt help seeking from qualified health care providers can do in terms of outcomes for people with highly prevalent mental health services such as anxiety and depression. However, psychological services such as the ones Rukia accessed are not available in the public health system, and due to high costs, are only affordable by a very small proportion of the Kenyan population, and those mostly living in major cities like Nairobi.

Mental health care in Kenya is conceived along two axes, public and private. Private mental health care is further divided into for-profit versus not-for-profit services, and these are mostly managed by non-governmental organizations (NGOs) and faith-based organizations (FBOs) (de Menil et al., 2014). There is also the informal sector that consists of traditional and faith healers who provide mental health care in community settings, but their services are neither regulated, documented or formally remunerated. The majority of mental health care resources in Kenya are concentrated in the three referral hospitals at Mathari, Gilgil and Moi University (Kiima and Jenkins 2010). Psychiatric nurses in Kenya primarily work in outpatient clinics in most district and provincial hospitals. There are a total of 1,114 psychiatric acute beds for the whole country based in the three main hospitals (Kiima and Jenkins 2010). Health care workers such as enrolled nurses, clinical officers and community workers provide assessment and care for people with mental health illness in primary health care settings of Kenya (Musyimi et al. 2017). However, it is not clear how their current training equips them to have the adequate knowledge, skills and attitudes necessary to provide care for people with a mental illness (Muga and Jenkins 2008). Recent constitutional changes to devolve services to county governments presents an opportunity to integrate mental health services into primary health care and move away from institutional care.

Below is a brief summary of key organizations that provide mental health services and advocacy for people with mental illness in Kenya. The government provides the bulk of mental health services. The majority (one in four psychiatric nurses and 30% of psychiatrists) of Kenya's specialists in mental health workforce are based in Mathari hospital. Each county hospital has a psychiatric in-patient unit but the bed capacity at this level varies between 5 and 22 beds (de Menil et al. 2014; Muga and Jenkins 2010).

A number of nursing homes and private clinics provide mental health services, which are owned and operated by non-governmental organizations (NGOs), faith-based organizations (FBOs) and social enterprises (Ndetei, Ongecha, Mutiso, Khasakhala, and Kokonya 2007). Kenyan health care literature distinguishes between practitioners that are established and regulated under legal statutes referred to as *formal*, and those who are unregulated and often community-based with no formal training as *informal*. The informal sector consists of traditional, faith healers, self-help groups, community-based organizations and families. Basic Needs is a UK-based non-governmental organization that support a large number of mental health consumers and carers in many Counties in Kenya (de Menil and Knapp 2015; Jenkins et al. 2012). The African Mental Health Foundation (AMHF) is engaged in mental health research and advocacy for people with mental health disorders. Private clinics such as Chiromo Lane and Avenue Nursing Home based in Nairobi, provide fee-for-mental health services (de Menil et al. 2014). In recent years, consumers have highlighted problems of human right abuses and lack of access to care for people with mental disorders in Kenya (de Menil and Knapp 2015).

Training and development, accreditation, licensure, and certification processes

Kenya's specialist mental health workforce mainly constitutes 74 psychiatrists and just under 500 psychiatric nurses (Musyimi et al. 2017). Similar findings were noted in a study undertaken in Kilifi county, Kenya where there were no psychiatrists and only two psychiatric nurses for a population of 1.2 million people (Bitta, Kariuki, Chengo, and Newton 2017). Shortages resulting from labour flight are best exemplified by Ghana, where 60% of trained doctors immigrated, mainly to the United Kingdom in the 1980s, and in 2002 47% of physician positions were unfilled in Ghana. Similarly, in South Africa, 7,000 registered nurses worked in OECD countries, while there was a shortfall of 32,000 positions for registered nurses in the country (Daniels 2008).

Through its Vision 2030, the Kenyan government through the Kenya Health Sector Strategic Plan (KHSSP) (Kenya 2015a) has projected significant growth in all health worker categories including nurses (2.1%), doctors (5.8%), psychiatrists (6.2%), social workers (11%), and occupational therapists (2.2%). The largest growth is projected to be among community health workers (300%) who will constitute majority of the health workforce in primary health care settings.

Training of psychiatrists is undertaken at the University of Nairobi's Medical School while that of nurses is undertaken at the Kenya Medical Training College in Nairobi. All trainees spend part of their training at the Mathari Hospital, a 600-bed institution for the mentally ill. On completion of their training, nurses are registered with the Nursing Council of Kenya, while doctors are registered with the Medical Practitioners and Dentists Board.

Health workers undergoing training as doctors, nurses and clinical officers (the latter are a middle-level category of health workers with roles equivalent to medical assistants, they can prescribe and supervise treatment in hospitals and health centres) have specific theoretical and clinical content on mental illness and mental health care (Ndetei et al. 2008; Ndetei et al. 2007). However, whilst a Master's level post-graduate course in psychiatry is available for doctors (Ndetei et al. 2007), other categories of health workers do not have post-graduate courses related to mental health. Recent mental health literacy survey in Kenya found no evidence of regular refresher courses on mental health care for health workers including doctors. To compound the problem, Kenya does not have a unified regulator of health professionals. Rather, each professional group has its own regulator, for example, The Nursing Council of Kenya, Clinical Officers Council, Medical and Dentists Board (Luoma et al. 2010).

Some agencies offer informal training in mental health care services such as counselling, psychosocial rehabilitation and addiction training. These agencies include Basic Needs (UK); the Africa Mental Health Foundation; Support for Addiction and Treatment in Africa (SAPTA); Liverpool Voluntary Counselling and Training (LVCT); and Kamili Organization (Kimosop, Kariuki, Mwanthi, Biwott, and Wanyonyi 2011). The Agha Khan University and tertiary hospital also engage in informal mental health training but only for their own staff (de Menil and Knapp 2015).

Future directions

Past research has found Kenya to be a country with big gaps in mental health care and very low resource levels to meet the mental health needs of its growing population. While a few researchers (Musyimi, Mutiso, Nandoya, and Ndetei 2016; Patel 1995) have explored the role of faith and traditional healers in Kenya, further research is necessary to determine the actual mental health care activities undertaken by traditional and faith healers in Kenya, including how their role fits within overall mental health care provision. It is clear that majority of Kenyans utilise services of traditional and faith healers. Thus, country mental health plans and policies should recognize and incorporate their contribution, considering it as complementary and not antagonistic to Western medical treatment.

Conclusion

It is clear from discussion in this chapter that a big gap exists between mental health resources and population needs for mental health care in Kenya. Problems of poor mental health infrastructure, resource scarcity, very low mental health specialist workforce, to low mental health literacy, out of step mental health policies and plans, and prevalent stigma and discrimination have been highlighted. And all these in a country beset by rapid population growth, poverty, very young population that is mostly unemployed, and rapid urbanization that all known risk factors for mentally illness. A great deal of work remains to be undertaken at the policy level to make restructuring of mental health services meaningful. Lack of open discussion about mental illness and the inability of public figures and politicians to advocate on behalf of people with mental illness relegates mental health services to a lower budget priority and makes it difficult to improve these services. The majority of Kenyans continue to rely on their savings to meet their health needs, with only 4.8% of Kenyans having access to health insurance (WHO 2005). Current health insurance policies do not provide coverage for mental health disorders, which means that people with mental illness or their families have to either fully fund their treatment and care except in emergency situations.

Despite these challenges, Kenya has literacy levels above 80% in the general population, an increasingly digitized environment and community ethos that not only encourages self-care but also looking after one another. These, and recent constitutional changes that have led to decentralization of power and resources to regional and rural counties are opportunities that can be leveraged to initiate mental health literacy for the general population and to train health workers on mental health care. Kenya is a regional centre, relatively more stable than most of its neighbours, in particular Somalia and South Sudan (Kenya 2012). A good number of people from these countries travel to Nairobi for specialized medical care. A working mental health system in Kenya can be a resource and model for some of these countries, essentially meeting needs of over 300 million people that live in this region.

This chapter presented the historical and modern context of mental health care in Kenya. Overall, it shows a country at crossroads from colonization and marketization of health care, traditional approaches to care and biomedical approaches, and all working together, often disharmoniously, to deliver mental health care to the sick. The role of resource scarcity, low mental health literacy, and the impact of globalization including the 'brain drain' phenomenon are highlighted as key obstacles to mental health care in Kenya.

References

Ajulu, R. (2002) 'Politicised ethnicity, competitive politics and conflict in Kenya: a historical perspective'. *African Studies, 61*(2): 251–268.

Bitta, M. A., Kariuki, S. M., Chengo, E., and Newton, C. R. (2017) 'An overview of mental health care system in Kilifi, Kenya: results from an initial assessment using the World Health Organization's Assessment Instrument for Mental Health Systems'. *International Journal of Mental Health Systems, 11*(1): 28.

Carrin, G., James, C., Adelhardt, M., Doetinchem, O., Eriki, P., Hassan, M., … Korte, R. (2007) 'Health financing reform in Kenya--assessing the social health insurance proposal'. *SAMJ-South African Medical Journal, 97*(2): 130.

Chaiken, M. (1998) 'Primary Health Care initiatives in colonial Kenya'. *World Development, 26*(9): 1701–1717.

Chuma, J., and Okungu, V. (2011) Viewing the Kenyan health system through an equity lens: implications for universal coverage. *International Journal of Equity Health, 10*:22.

Daar, A. S., Jacobs, M., Wall, S., Groenewald, J., Eaton, J., Patel, V., . . . Sunkel, C. (2014) 'Declaration on mental health in Africa: Moving to implementation'. *Global Health Action, 7*. doi:10.3402/gha.v7.24589.

Daniels, N. (2008) 'International health inequalities and global justice'. In Boylan M. (Eds.) *International Public Health Policy and Ethics. International Library of Ethics, Law, and the New Medicine, vol 42* (pp. 109–129). Dordrecht: Springer.

David Ndetei, Lincoln Khasakhala, Joyce Kingori, Alan Odinga & Shoba Raja. (n.d). The complementary role of traditional and faith healers, and potential liaisons with Western style mental health services in Kenya. *African Mental Health Foundation*. Nairobi, Kenya.

de Menil, V. P., and Knapp, M. (2015) 'Participation of psychiatric nurses in public and private mental healthcare in Kenya'. *Guest Editorial, 12*(1): 19–21. doi:10.1192/S2056474000000106.

de Menil, V. P., Knapp, M., McDaid, D., and Njenga, F. G. (2014) 'Service use, charge, and access to mental healthcare in a private Kenyan inpatient setting: the effects of insurance'. *PLOS:One*, Retrieved from https://journals.plos.org/plosone/article?id=10.1371/journal.pone.0090297.

De Silva, M. J., Lee, L., Fuhr, D. C., Rathod, S., Chisholm, D., Schellenberg, J., and Patel, V. (2014) 'Estimating the coverage of mental health programmes: a systematic review'. *International Journal of Epidemiology, 43*(2): 341–353.

Jenkins, R., Kiima, D., Njenga, F., Okonji, M., Kingora, J., Kathuku, D., and Lock, S. (2010) 'Integration of mental health into primary care in Kenya'. *World Psychiatry, 9:* 118–120.

Jenkins, R., Njenga, F., Okonji, M., Kigamwa, P., Baraza, M., and Ayuyo, J. (2012) 'Prevalence of common mental disorders in a rural district of Kenya, and socio-demographic risk factors'. *International Journal of Environmental Research and Public Health, 9(5)*:1810–1819.

Kanyinga, K. (2009) 'The legacy of the white highlands: Land rights, ethnicity and the post-2007 election violence in Kenya'. *Journal of Contemporary African Studies, 27*(3): 325–344.

Kenya National Bureau of Statistics, Ministry of Health/Kenya, National AIDS Control Council/Kenya, Kenya Medical Research Institute, Population, N. C. f., and Development/Kenya (2015) *Kenya Demographic and Health Survey 2014*. Retrieved from Rockville, MD: http://dhsprogram.com/pubs/pdf/FR308/FR308.pdf.

Kiima, D., and Jenkins, R. (2010) 'Mental health policy in Kenya—An integrated approach to scaling up equitable care for poor populations'. *International Journal of Mental Health Systems, 4*. doi:10.1186/1752-4458-4-19.

Kimosop, V., Kariuki, A., Mwanthi, C., Biwott, H., and Wanyonyi, E. (2011) 'Mental Health in Kenya; Unpacking the issues'. In International Institute of Legislative Affairs (Ed.), *Legislative Digest*. Nairobi: ILA.

Kleinman, A., Eisenberg, L., and Good, B. (1978) 'Culture, illness, and care: clinical lessons from anthropologic and cross-cultural research'. *Annals of Internal Medicine, 88*(2): 251–258.

Luoma, M., Doherty, J., Muchiri, S., Barasa, T., Hofler, K., Maniscalco, L., . . . Maundu, J. (2010) *Kenya Health System Assessment 2010*. Bethesda, MD: Health Systems 20/20 project, Abt Associates Inc.

Marangu, E., Sands, N., Rolley, J., Ndetei, D., and Mansouri, F. (2014) 'Mental healthcare in Kenya: Exploring optimal conditions for capacity building'. *African Journal of Primary Health Care and Family Medicine, 6*(1). Retrieved from https://phcfm.org/index.php/phcfm/article/view/682.

Menil, V., Ndetei, D., Waruguru, M., Knapp, M., and McDaid, D. (2014) 'A hidden face of community mental health care in Africa: Specialist care from private providers in Kenya'. *World Psychiatry, 13*(1):100–110.

Menil, V. P. d. (2014) *Under-cover in Kenya: The contribution of non-state actors tom mental health coverage.* (Doctor of Philosophy), London School of Economics, London.

Muga, and Jenkins, R. (2010) 'Health care models guiding mental health policy in Kenya 1965–1997'. *International Journal of Mental Health Systems, 4*(9). Retrieved from https://ijmhs.biomedcentral.com/articles/10.1186/1752-4458-4-9.

Muga, R., Kizito, P., Mbayah, M., and Gakuruh, T. (2004) *Overview of the Health System in Kenya*. Kenya service provision assessment (KSPA 2004) survey URL: https://dhsprogram. com/pubs/pdf/spa8/02chapter2. pdf (Accessed March 20, 2018)..

Musyimi, C. W., Mutiso, V. N., Nandoya, E. S., and Ndetei, D. M. (2016) 'Forming a joint dialogue among faith healers, traditional healers and formal health workers in mental health in a Kenyan setting: Towards common grounds'. *Journal of Ethnobiology and Ethnomedicine, 12*(1):1–8.

Musyimi, C. W., Mutiso, V. N., Ndetei, D. M., Unanue, I., Desai, D., Patel, S. G., . . . Bunders, J. (2017) 'Mental health treatment in Kenya: Task-sharing challenges and opportunities among informal health providers'. *International Journal of Mental Health Systems, 11*: 45. Retreived from https://www.ncbi.nlm.nih.gov/pmc/articles/PMC5540195/.

Mutiso, V., Warsame, A. H., Bosire, E., Musyimi, C., Musau, A., Isse, M. M., and Ndetei, D. M. (2018) 'Intrigues of Accessing Mental Health Services Among Urban Refugees Living in Kenya: The Case of Somali Refugees Living in Eastleigh, Nairobi'. *Journal of Immigrant and Refugee Studies*, 17(2): 204–221.

Mutungi, A., Harvey, S., Kibaru, J., Lugina, H., Kinoti, S., Jennings, L., and Hizza, T. B. E. (2008) 'Kenya: Assessment of Health Workforce Competency and Facility Readiness to Provide Quality Maternal Health Services'. *Operations Research Results*. Bethesda, MD: USAID.

Ndetei, D., Khasakhala, L., Kuria, M., Mutiso, V., Ongecha-Owuor, F., and Kokonya, D. (2009) 'The Prevalence of Mental Disorders in Adults in Different Level General Medical Facilities in Kenya: A Cross-sectional Study'. *Annals of General Psychiatry, 8*(1). Retrieved from www.ncbi.nlm.nih.gov/pmc/articles/PMC2631009/.

Ndetei, D., Khasakhala, L., and Omolo, J. (2008) 'Incentives for health worker retention in Kenya: An assessment of current practice'. *EQUINET, 62*, 29.

Ndetei, D., Ongecha, F., Mutiso, V., Khasakhala, L., and Kokonya, D. (2007) 'The Challenges of Human Resources in Mental Health in Kenya'. *South African Psychiatry Review, 10:* 33–36.

Ndetei, D. M., Mutiso, V., Maraj, A., Anderson, K. K., Musyimi, C., and McKenzie, K. (2015) 'Stigmatizing Attitudes toward Mental Illness among Primary School Children in Kenya'. *Social Psychiatry and Psychiatric Epidemiology*, 51(1): 73–80.

Ngui, E., Khasakhala, L., Ndetei, D., and Roberts, L. (2010) 'Mental Disorders, Health Inequalities and Ethics: A Global Perspective'. *International Review of Psychiatry, 22(3):*235–244.

Patel, V. (1995) 'Explanatory Models of Mental Illness in Sub-Saharan Africa'. *Social Science and Medicine, 40*(9): 1291–1298.

Rakuom, C. (2010) *Nursing Human Resources in Kenya*. International Centre for Human Resources in Nursing: Geneva, Switzerland. Retrieved from https://goo. gl/ZB3Zam.

Republic of Kenya. (2008a) *Laws of Kenya: The Constitution of Kenya*. Nairobi: National Council for Law Reporting. Retrieved from www.kenyalaw.org.

Republic of Kenya. (2008b) *Facts and Figures on Health-Related Indicators*. Nairobi: Ministry of Medical Services.

Republic of Kenya. (2010) *The Constitution of Kenya*. Nairobi Kenya: The National Council for Law Reporting.

Republic of Kenya. (2012) *Kenya Health Sector Strategic and Investment Plan (KHSSP): July 2013–June 2017*. Nairobi: Ministry of Health.

Republic of Kenya. (2015a) *Kenya Mental Health Policy 2015–2030 (Draft 2)*. Nairobi: Ministry of Health.

Republic of Kenya. (2015b) *Kenya National Strategy for the Prevention and Control of Non-Communicable Diseases 2015–2020*. Nairobi: Government Press.

Saxena, S., Thornicroft, G., Knapp, M., and Whiteford, H. (2007) 'Resources for Mental Health: Scarcity, Inequity, and Inefficiency'. *The Lancet, 370*(9590): 878–889.

Thornicroft, G., Cooper, S., Bortel, T. V., Kakuma, R., and Lund, C. (2012) 'Capacity Building in Global Mental Health Research'. *Harvard Review of Psychiatry, 20*(1): 13–24.

WHO (2005) *Mental Health Atlas 2005*. Geneva: World Health Organization.

WHO (2008) *Mental Health Global Action Programme (mhGAP): Scaling up care for mental, neurological and substance use disorders*. Geneva: World Health Organization.

WHO (2009a) *Improving Health Systems and Services for Mental Health*. Geneva: World Health Organization.

WHO (2009b) *Mental Health Systems In Selected Low-And Middle-Income Countries*. Geneva: World Health Organization.

WHO (2011) *Mental Health Atlas 2011*. Geneva: World Health Organization.

WHO (2013) *Mental Health Action Plan 2013–2020*. Geneva: World Health Organization.

WorldBank (2013) *Kenya Economic Update*. Retrieved from www.worldbank.org/en/country/kenya/overview.

35
CULTURE AND MENTAL HEALTH IN NIGERIA

Aneneosa A. G. Okocha, Henrietta Alika, and Olamojiba O. Bamgbose

According to the United Nations Children's Fund and World Health Organization (2009), mental health is defined as the ability to adapt to internal and external environment stressors. This definition encompasses successful adjustment to a range of innate and primordial demands epitomized by thoughts, emotions, and behaviors that are congruent with age, local and cultural norms or expectations. The foregoing definition presupposes ultimately the capability to contribute meaningfully to society via work and other endeavors.

Culture is generally defined as a shared set of customs, beliefs and values among members of a particular group or society (Sue and Sue 2016). In light of this definition, it is obvious that culture influences mental health practice. Cultural impact on mental health is exemplified by societal idiosyncratic attitudes and beliefs about mental health/illness, manner of health seeking behaviors, and types of available service and support systems (Eaton and Agomoh 2008; Lasebikan 2016). The literature in this sphere is replete with narratives regarding cultural aspects of mental health and psychotherapy practices in Nigeria (Eaton and Agomoh 2008; Lasebikan 2016; Okocha 2013; Okocha and Alika 2012). However, given that culture is dynamic (Gabriel 2016; Nnochiri 2014), and continuously buffeted by globalization, it is important to examine the status of mental health and counselling/psychotherapy practices in Nigeria within a globalizing mental health field.

This chapter discusses mental health practice in Nigeria within the country's cultural, historical and socio-political milieu. Historical development of mental health practice, including indigenous and traditional healing, as well as the cultural representations of illness and wellness are first highlighted. The discussion of training and development, accreditation and credentialing process and current contemporary mental health practices then follows. Finally, challenges and possible future development of mental health, psychotherapy and counselling services in Nigeria are emphasized.

Demographics and brief history of mental health

Nigeria, which is located on the western coast of Africa, has the largest population on the continent with approximately 206 million people (World Population Review 2020). The country consists of 250 ethnicities, of which Hausa-Fulani, Igbo, Yoruba, and Kanuri are the largest groups. Historically, mental health services in Nigeria depended solely on traditional and indigenous

422

healing methods. Around the 19th century, the British introduced Westernized treatment of mental illness, but focused on confinement in asylums, use of physical restraints, and lack of remedial treatment (Westbrook 2011). The first asylum was built in 1904 in Calabar, located in south southern Nigeria, a second asylum was established three years later in Yaba, Lagos, and a third asylum in Abeokuta in south-west Nigeria in 1914 (Jack-Ide, Uys and Middleton 2012).

In the 1950s, Nigeria's first full-time psychiatrist, Donald Cameron was hired. His arrival changed the manner in which people with mental health concerns experienced services, because he focused on treatment of symptoms (Westbrook 2011) rather than addressing the poor conditions previously provided through the British asylum systems. Almost a decade later, Yaba Lunatic Asylum was changed to Yaba Mental Hospital, which utilized orthodox medicine and therapy in the treatment of patients diagnosed with mental health concerns. A few years later, Abeokuta's Aro Mental Hospital was opened and managed under the concept of community mental health. Under this model, patients received intensive hospital support during the day but lived at home and worked in their community with identified community supports. The model, although successful, did not immediately spread out to other parts of the country or influence changes in mental health laws (Westbrook 2011). However, in the decades since, community mental health has become a significant path to delivery of services for people with mental illness, with the intent of providing accessible, affordable services to users and their families (Eaton and Agomoh 2008).

Despite the developments identified above, orthodox mental health systems in Nigeria are growing at a relatively slow pace due to a lack of adequate legislation, policies, and funding allocated towards developing relevant services. Legislatively, Nigeria's mental health system continues to practice using the Lunacy Act of 1958, as amended from the Lunacy Ordinance developed in 1916 (Oyelade, Smith, and Jarvis 2017; Westbrook 2011). The act, which was based on practices inherited through British colonialism during the 19th century, utilized archaic knowledge and practices in mental health, and inadvertently supported the dehumanization of persons with mental health needs. In 2003, a bill was proposed in the senate to repeal the Lunacy Act; however, it was withdrawn in 2009 due to inactivity (Westbrook 2011), and reintroduced in 2013 where it is yet to be passed. The bill is proposed to remove the broad definition of lunacy and replace the term with mental disorder. In addition, it would provide procedural protections to users of mental health services in respect of compulsory admission, restricted types and context of treatment, which would require facilities to meet minimum standards set forth by the Minister of Health and is intended to discourage the stigma and discrimination surrounding mental health (Jack-Ide, Uys, and Middleton 2012; Westbrook 2011).

In 1991, Nigeria adopted mental health as the ninth arm of primary health care, with responsibility falling to Local Government Areas (LGAs); however, insufficient funding affected actual integration and implementation of the policy (Armiyau 2015; Eaton and Agomoh 2008; Jack-Ide et al. 2012). The 2013 national policy for mental health services delivery evolved from the 1991 policy and if successfully implemented will ensure access to mental health support within primary health care and community services. In addition, implementation of the policy will include working partnerships with sectors of the prison, police, education, social welfare, traditional health, as well as the accreditation, training and registration bodies, and work to enhance patient welfare through prevention of mortality (Federal Ministry of Health 2013).

Mental health services within schools and higher institutions of learning also had an overhaul within the last 13 years. In 1990, the Minister of Education recommended mandatory guidance and counselling services to all students in institutions of higher education. Thereafter, in 2004, the National Policy on Education recommended guidance and counselling services for all secondary school students (Mogbo, Obumneke-Okeke, and Anyachebelu 2011). The

National Policy on Education in 2013 held the federal government responsible for provision of guidance and counselling services in schools to include counselling clinics, career resource centers, and information centers. However, the policy also recommended that these services would be offered by teachers trained in guidance and counselling services (Nigerian Educational Research and Development Council 2013) rather than full-time qualified school counsellors with a Bachelor's or Master's degree.

Indigenous and traditional healers and healing

The indigenous approach to mental health in Nigeria constitutes the native practices of the traditional healers and the spiritual/faith healers. This approach is derived from the folklore of many cultures that uses the supernatural to explain the behavior or issues of persons struggling with mental health concerns. For instance, the "babalawos" are the traditional healers amongst the Yoruba people in Nigeria, and they believe that "Shopono" deity of the earth is one of the causes of mental illness. In addition, the Ibo traditional healers, "dibias" share the view that "Agwu-ishi" (moral rectitude) regard mental illness as retributive justice for relevant offences (Egbuchulam 1989). Amongst the Hausas, traditional healers are known as "dubas." Generally, mental health disorders have often been associated with punishment from the ancestors for an act of disobedience, affliction from the spirit world, sin, or estrangement from God (Ekeopara 2009; Jegede and Okunade 1977).

With reference to the healing process, traditional healers treat the individual holistically, soul and body via specific ceremonies and the use of herbs. In terms of rituals, the spirits of the ancestors are invoked as a source of help in an attempt to foster the effectiveness of the intervention. Therapy or treatment for faith healers involves full participation of the client/person in the form of fasting, scriptural study, and evangelic prayers (Isichei 2005). The approach is very common among the African indigenous churches, especially Charismatic and Pentecostal churches that execute the so called "exorcising of the spirits."

Relationship between colonialism and the evolution of mental health practices

Nigeria was a British colony from 1901 to 1960 (Eragbe 2002) but won its independence in 1960. Prior to independence, a number of Nigerians travelled overseas especially to Europe and the United States for further education in different disciplines, including education, medical, psychiatric and psychological fields. At the same time, some Western cultural influences, such as missionaries, gradually began to pave their way for the introduction of Western models of counselling and psychotherapy to Nigeria. For example, the catholic nuns at St. Theresa's College high school in Ibadan provided an informative workshop directed at the graduating students to help them with career decisions (Okon 1983). Another source of Western influence, involved the role played by the United States Agency for International Development (USAID) in promoting counselling and psychological services in Aiyetero Comprehensive high school, Ogun state in 1967 (Makinde 1984). Other efforts include the development of the Counselling Association of Nigeria (CASSON 2010), which facilitated the provision of counselling and mental health services in Nigerian Universities via the counselling centers, as well as the training of counsellors and engagement in relevant research for the improvement of Nigerian mental health.

It should also be noted that after Nigeria's independence, some Nigerians who went abroad for further education in different fields returned and took over from the colonial masters regarding the development of the country, especially in the health services sector. One such individual was Dr. Adeoye Lambo, a prominent Western-trained psychiatrist who came back and managed the Aro psychiatric hospital in Abeokuta in western Nigeria. His contributions in the practice of psychiatry and psychotherapy, especially the integration of traditional and Western-oriented practices as well as the training of psychiatrists were significant (Isichei 2005). For example, Lambo experimented with a combination of traditional treatment of mental illness and Western Psychiatry in the first indigenous psychiatric hospital. In addition, he established his own outpatient treatment services in Aro village, at the outskirts of Abeokuta in Ogun State, Nigeria, where he pioneered the use of modern curative techniques with traditional religion and native medicines. Furthermore, he made use of traditional healers from different parts of Nigeria and sought help from farmers around the hospital to engage patients as paid laborers in their farms, while they underwent medical treatment (Jegede 2016).

Cultural representations of illness and wellness

Nigeria is a multi-ethnic nation with various cultures, traditions, customs and beliefs. These factors influence its citizens' perception of ill-health/mental health problems. In Nigeria, illness is conceptualized as a situation where the individual is unable to function optimally as a result of the dysfunction of the body system or a result of environmental challenges. Specifically, viewed via the indigenous and traditional prism, illness is seen as a direct affliction from the spirit world, probably due to the sins of the individual or that of the forefathers. This is echoed by the findings from the study of Gureje, Lasebikan, Ephraim-Oluwanuga, Olley, and Kola (2005), which indicated that one-third of the Nigerian sample believed that supernatural causation such as possession of or by evil spirits is the cause of mental illness. One tenth of their respondents believed that divine punishment from God was presented in the form of mental distress. Furthermore, a survey by Ukpong and Abasiebong (2010) showed that the attribution of mental illness to supernatural causation is not restricted to the uneducated, but also prevails among many educated persons.

Regarding wellness, this exists when a person shows a congenial or good relationship with the spirit world and when there is harmony between the individual and the environment (Abia 2012). Wellness in Nigeria also represents a condition of total effective physiological, physical and psychological functioning. This definition is in keeping with the Western world or contemporary view, which defined health/wellness as a state of comprehensive physical, mental and social well-being, and not merely the absence of disease or infirmity (World Health Organization 2009).

Training and development, accreditation, licensure, and certification process

For the most part, current mental health practice in Nigeria focuses on tertiary intervention rather than prevention. As a result, training, accreditation, licensure, and certification in most areas tend to favor a medical model of practice, although institutions of higher education have adopted a wider perspective when it comes to training. Obtaining a complete picture of training and certification requirements for mental health professionals such as psychiatrists, social workers, and counsellors (clinical and school) in Nigeria has proven to be a mammoth task, because there is no accessible unified online or written system with the information. However, using data from select universities it is possible to gain an understanding on some training routes. For example, psychiatric training at one of Nigeria's premier universities requires post-graduate studies in a Master's or doctorate, board certified examinations in the university, and a period of residency leading to fellowship examinations through the national post-graduate medical college of Nigeria, fellowship of the West African college of physicians, and the West African college of surgeons (Gureje 2011).

Social work degrees can be completed at several universities as a Bachelor's degree, although a minimum of a Master's is required for psychiatric social work. Similarly, guidance and counselling is offered as a Bachelor's degree with opportunities to complete a Master's or doctorate in counselling psychology with potential specialist offerings covering career counselling, educational and school counselling, adolescent and youth counselling, marriage and family life counselling, remedial and reformatory counselling, assessment and testing, HIV/AIDS prevention counselling, developmental psychology, clinical psychology, and educational psychology.

Information on licensure or certification was also difficult to obtain, but there is evidence to suggest that social work proficiency certification is required for membership in the Institute of Social Work of Nigeria (ISOWN, n.d.). Furthermore, the Nigerian Association of Social Workers (NAOSWS) provides open memberships for qualified social workers with degrees and experience in the field, although the association has made little impact on government policies (Okoye 2013). The Nigerian National Universities Commission accredits counselling undergraduate programs and the university faculty senates accredits counselling graduate programs (Okocha and Alika 2012). However, there is no nationally identified licensure or certification geared towards professionalization for the gamut of counselling specialties in Nigeria, despite the best efforts of the Counselling Association of Nigeria (CASSON). In 2010, CASSON began a process of trying to obtain certification and licensure for its members (Okocha and Alika 2012). On February 19, 2014, Senator Ita Enang sponsored a private bill before the senate proposing that a counselling practitioners' council of Nigeria be established. The bill has only had the first reading, however, when passed it will ensure that CASSON and counselling are viewed respectively as a legally recognized organization and profession in Nigeria (CASSON Newsletter 2010).

Integration of contemporary mental health practices and Western health care

Contemporary mental health services, including counselling and psychotherapy occur mostly in the following settings: educational institutions, mainly at the secondary school level and on a limited basis at some university counselling centers (Adeyemo 2016; Okocha 2013). In addition, psychiatric hospitals and community psychosocial rehabilitation services serve as centers for the delivery of mental health services. However, there are approximately 100 active psychiatrists in Nigeria distributed between the country's eight federal psychiatric hospitals or the twelve University Teaching Hospital Psychiatric Departments (Eaton and Agomoh 2008). Therefore, maintaining an orthodox psychiatric pathway of delivering mental health service has been quite difficult and challenging. This challenge is due to limited number of qualified psychiatric staff because of brain drain or the excessive migration of skilled workers to other countries. This migration results from globalization of the labor market, population changes in richer countries, the ability of developed countries with better resources to attract mental health specialists from poorer countries where there is limited employment (Oladeji and Gureje 2016), and where conditions of employment in this medical discipline have been less than inspiring.

Furthermore, as stated earlier, even though in 1991 Nigeria adopted mental health as its ninth arm of primary health care and introduced the 1991 national policy for mental health

(Armiyau 2015; Eaton and Agomoh 2008; Jack-Ide 2012), which was amended in 2013 (Federal Ministry of Health 2013) the policy is yet to be truly implemented. Consequently, a parlous state of mental health services is created (Bojuwoye and Mogaji 2013), a state characterized by poor implementation of existing mental health policies, delayed approval of the 2003 revised mental health bill, and insufficient data to guide planning of mental health services. In addition, it includes an absence of clear systems or structures for mental health services at the state level, and poor funding or non-existent budget for mental health needs (Abdulmalik, Kola, and Gureje 2016).

As mentioned earlier, mental health services are often practiced in "prayer houses" and traditional healing centers to address "spiritual attacks" and other healing issues. Illustrated below are case studies on how mental health, psychotherapy, and counselling services are delivered at the secondary school and university levels to elucidate the process.

The case of Ada

Background information and presenting issues

Ada is a 12-year-old girl attending a private secondary boarding school in Nigeria. Her family's social economic status could be described as middle to upper class since both parents have Bachelor's degrees and work in a bank in accounting positions. She is a middle child, with an older brother, 15 years old, a younger brother, 10 years old and a younger sister, 8 years old. The family lives in a town that is about 100 miles away from the city where Ada is attending secondary school. Ada is in her second year and is not doing well academically. She has been experiencing severe anxiety, panic attacks, disorienting dreams, inability to sleep and loss of appetite. She claims she has been bullied by a few peers who demanded that she give them some of her stored food stock, otherwise she would be beaten up. She was also verbally abused by these peers calling her negative names and she was warned not to share her negative experiences from her peers with anyone including the school authorities, otherwise she and her family would be badly hurt. Ada's problems and situation came to a head, when on being called upon by a math teacher to answer a question, she temporarily passed out.

Healing: Goals and interventions in counselling/psychotherapy

The school counsellor, Ms. Okoye, who is also an English Language teacher, has met with Ada (about three times) prior to her fainting. Her initial counselling goal with Ada was centered on providing her with tips for developing effective study habits as well as social skills and to nurture good friends that would help improve her academic standing. The school counsellor operated from a person-centered theoretical framework in building a good counselling relationship and rapport with Ada. Specifically, she used active listening and attending skills to interview and gather information from Ada regarding her situation and symptoms. She also utilized behavioral strategies such as role-playing about appropriate ways to relate with her peers and avoid negative peer pressure. Additionally, she used bibliotherapy in working with Ada in order to help attain the counselling goal. However, when Ada fainted, Ms. Okoye realized that Ada's situation was serious and consulted with Ada's parents on the phone and advised them to come and pick her up to seek medical attention outside of school. This new development led to a severe depression for Ada, who constantly cried for bringing "shame" to her family due to her ill-health and eventual dropping out of school to take care of her health issues.

Ada's parents took her to their family doctor who had a tentative diagnosis of anxiety and severe depression for Ada but encouraged them to visit one of the psychiatric hospitals to meet with a psychiatrist. The waiting time to see a psychiatrist in their state was too long due to the shortage of psychiatrists, so Ada's parents decided to seek help from one of the faith healing houses, a Pentecostal church. This was a group-based intervention that entailed praying, reading of the Bible, singing, dancing and chanting. Although, the parents derived psychological benefits from taking Ada to a faith healer, probably because it made them feel they were doing something to relieve their daughter's pain and reflected their attitude and beliefs in prayer as a panacea for mental health concerns, the approach brought no relief to Ada's health situation especially her panic attacks. In view of which, her parents took Ada to a psychiatric hospital in another state where she was treated via orthodox psychiatric methods using anti- anxiety and depression medications resulting in a substantial decrease or elimination of her symptoms.

Discussion

The above case study reflects how indigenous and orthodox mental health practices coexist in Nigeria. In fact, according to a World Health Organization (WHO) report, between 75 and 80% of humanity resort to traditional medicine for healing purposes (Isichei 2005). It also highlights the cultural prism through which Nigerians view mental health concerns and how Nigerians have been socialized to trust in spiritual belief systems, like the church, for their mental health issues, because churches are viewed as easily accessible and might be an established continuous source of community support. In some instances, Nigerians might first seek an indigenous approach to healing before engaging orthodox or contemporary methods of healing as a last resort. However, Ada's parents sought orthodox treatment first and then approached the church for support. Their particular decision-making might have been linked to their socio-economic status (middle to upper class) and education, but ultimately for most Nigerians indigenous support is more primary and an initial help-seeking pattern. Specifically, in Nigeria, research shows that the majority of patients being treated via the orthodox medical methods continue to consult with traditional/indigenous healers (Isichei 2005). Thus, it is important to intensify efforts on how both approaches could be integrated in the attempt to foster Nigerians' well-being.

The case of Abubakar

Background information and presenting issues

Abubakar is a 22-year-old male, final year student in the chemistry department at a state university. Abubakar desires to achieve a first-class honors degree, because he thinks this may be the only avenue to securing employment, a dream that is beyond the reach of most Nigerians due to the country's poor and stagnant economic situation. Abubakar comes from a low socio-economic background; his mother, a petty trader sells wares in the marketplace, and his father drives a taxi for a local transportation service. To achieve his goal of first-class honors, Abubakar decided to use psychostimulants, such as coffee, so he could stay awake, most nights, reading for various exams. On the morning of his third exam, Abubakar was rushed to the University Health Center, with sleep deprivation, burning heat and pounding pains in his head, and a disruption of his cognition, he was diagnosed with brain fag syndrome (a culturally bound syndrome commonly known in West African Psychiatry), and referred for counselling.

Healing: Goals and interventions in counselling/psychotherapy

Abubakar was admitted to the University Health Center for medical attention. However, Abubakar in consultation with his parents decided to get help from an indigenous healer and maintained that they have been told by a traditional healer that certain forces or spirits were behind Abubakar's health challenge. Thus, Abubakar was then taken to a traditional healer whom they believe can communicate with the spirits and also ensure his recovery from all his symptoms. The family's decision to seek the support of a traditional healer is probably based on a belief and culture that traditional medicine is used to maintain health and to prevent, diagnose, and improve general well-being of individuals. However, after two weeks' intervention at the indigenous healer's home, without any improvement in Abubakar's health, he decided to pursue an orthodox treatment via the university counselling services. The counsellor utilized cognitive behavior therapy (CBT) with a view to eliminating negative emotions and checking distorted thinking around fear of failure and unemployment. In addition, family members were advised to keep in touch with him, reassuring him of their love, and his ability to pass his examinations. Through counselling, Abubakar was able to relax and realize he was capable of attaining his educational goals without the excessive use of psychostimulants. He had to repeat the examination the next year, but free from anxiety and tension, he passed all his papers and was able to graduate without a reoccurrence of the brain fag syndrome.

Discussion

The university where this case study is based on had an undergraduate population of about 45,061 students (full-time and part-time) and 7,216 post-graduate students in the 2016/2017 academic session. Despite the presence of a university counselling center, as mandated by the Minister of Education in 1990 (Mogbo, Obumneke-Okeke, and Anyachebelu 2011), very few students, just under 15%, come for counselling probably due to lack of awareness about such services or lack of trust on the efficacy of counselling. However, an upsurge of service contact in students who present for counselling is observed whenever the center conducts campaigns through enlightenment promotions in the halls of residence and displays posters at strategic locations on campus.

The center has eight counsellors, who offer counselling services to students and do follow-up to ensure clients' challenges are resolved and they have adjusted appropriately to their academic environments. Similar to the case of Abubakar, clients mostly attend counselling when they have academic/career challenges, but it is note-worthy that as soon as rapport is established, clients' underlying problems are usually linked to financial problems, personal-social issues, and family problems beyond the academic or career challenges. The center also identifies and provides counselling to students who are at risk of dropping out due to poor academic performance.

To ensure that adequate counselling is provided, clients are attended to whenever they come for counselling. One of the great benefits for this service is that there are no time limits regarding the duration of counselling. Rather, the clients' needs dictate the number of counselling sessions. The center operates a 50-minute counsellor–client interactive session and most counsellors adopt a person-centered approach, although the issue presented by the counsellee, also determines the techniques and theoretical framework adopted by the counsellor. In addition to offering counselling services, the center also liaises with corporate organizations in providing scholarships for best performing students and some indigent students who excel in their studies. Furthermore, the university administration is quite supportive when it comes to student welfare and counselling services.

Abubakar's diagnosis of brain fag syndrome is not an uncommon diagnosis for mental health practice in Nigeria. The disorder, originated in 1960 when Raymond Prince, a Canadian psychiatrist working with the Yorubas in south-western Nigeria, identified a cluster of symptomology, which he termed brain fag disorder (Ayonrinde, Obuaya, and Adeyemi 2015). The syndrome was recognized in the DSM-IV-TR glossary of culture and the ICD-10 (Ayonrinde et al. 2015), however, it was noticeably absent from the DSM-V. Although, considered a diagnosis at risk of extinction, Ayonrinde et al. identified that when participants were asked to consider a diagnosis and differential diagnosis for a vignette, 37% considered brain fag syndrome, 49% anxiety disorder, 36% depressive disorder, and 30% considered somatization. From the foregoing, there is no gainsaying that in providing interventions for mental health issues, the cultural context should be evaluated alongside orthodox medicine, with a view to providing a balanced mental health intervention.

Future directions

In order to develop a positive and proactive mental health service, the Nigerian government will need to reform the mental health act, by revisiting the bill to repeal the Lunacy Act of 1958. In re-presenting and passing the bill into law, the National Assembly should seek expert advice from stakeholders in the mental health sector and include internationally recognized standards and ethics as part of best mental health practices. In addition to changing legislation, the government needs to actively implement the 2013 national policy for mental health service delivery and the National Policy on Education. Proactive implementation should include an overhaul of the current infrastructure supporting mental health services delivery. For instance, training programs need to be developed so as to enhance the skills and competencies of mental health providers at all levels of mental health service delivery – primary, secondary, and tertiary mental health care. Such training should be organized in collaboration with the Federal Ministry of Health and supervised by mental health experts including counsellors at the Master's or doctoral level, clinical psychologists, clinical psychiatric nurses, or psychiatrists. Furthermore, the government needs to allocate funding at the state and district levels to ensure proper implementation of policy requirements and availability of necessary resources and tools for psychological assessments, testing, treatment, and evaluation.

Since Nigeria is a very diverse country, emphasis should be given to multicultural issues both during training as discussed in the earlier paragraph and during the delivery of mental health services. For instance, it is important to be aware of the unique mental health needs of the elderly, persons with disabilities and other groups marginalized in Nigerian society such as the gay, lesbian and bisexual community. Thus, it is crucial that the principles of social justice and advocacy are intentionally infused into the practice of mental health in the country.

In addition to the development of orthodox mental health services, there should be laws formulated to monitor and regulate the practice of traditional indigenous healing services, which as illustrated are often the initial mental health services sought after by clients and their families in the country. These laws should take into account issues like training, documentation, quality-control, standardization and ethical issues and practice. This action if taken will go a long way to give status to traditional medicine and its potency, when compared to orthodox medicine and it will boost mental health delivery in the country. Spiritual and pastoral care should also be recognized as an additional and integral support system when dealing with people who have mental health concerns.

Unfortunately, preventative mental health services are currently absent on the national agenda, which means that counselling and its specialist areas have not been recognized as

Culture and Mental Health in Nigeria

integral to the mental health discourse. There is a need for mental health prevention to be high on the agenda as a universal right and discussed at all levels of government. This discussion should include proper utilization of counsellors and counselling specialists. However, the Nigerian government is not the only entity responsible for preventative mental health services, charity organizations, schools, and pastoral services should organize mental health initiatives with a view to enhancing the mental health of individuals in their individual unique settings in the acknowledgement that the emotional and mental constitution of individuals is vital to human performance. Preventative mental health services should include regular mental health checks as part of normal health care. These should also include enlightenment and mental health awareness interventions that are based on topics like fitness, health, eating habits, avoidance of substance abuse, stress management, personal-social relations, coping strategies when confronted with life challenges, and willingness to seek counselling even on matters like life transitions.

It is expected that technology could play an important role in the future in both the practice and delivery of preventative and remedial mental health services in Nigeria. For example, the use of technology involving, radio, television, social media and internet for educating and heightening Nigerians' awareness to mental health issues could foster a positive and accepting attitude to receiving mental health services. Furthermore, the use of meaningful mental health resources on the internet, such as the self-help mental health apps on mindfulness and meditation could be appealing to Nigerians especially the millennials and young university students who are comfortable with modern technology. In addition, in this era of globalization, Nigerian mental health educators and practitioners could benefit from possible opportunities for training and professional development, as well as collaborative research work via the internet.

Conclusion

Given the history of mental health practice in Nigeria, it is clear that the indigenous or traditional approaches and the orthodox methods will continue to be utilized by Nigerians in addressing their mental health issues, especially in light of the country's cultural beliefs, and idiosyncrasies on what constitutes mental illness and wellness. Indigenous and traditional healers of mental illness extol and believe in the intervention of the supernatural and also associate mental health disorders with ancestral and/or God's fury against perpetrators of various acts of impropriety (Ekeopara 2009; Jegede and Okunade 1977). Orthodox methods for dealing with counselling and mental health issues in Nigeria originated in the 19th century with British colonization. Additional Western influence epitomized by the work of the missionaries, targeted secondary and tertiary institutions. However, the growth of these counselling and mental health systems is relatively slow due to the lack of adequate legislation, policies, and funding. Our suggestions for a positive and proactive mental health service include improvements across the range of supports typically utilized by Nigerians with mental health concerns. Therefore, there should be a reform of legislation guiding orthodox mental health services and proper implementation of already established national policies. Additionally, traditional indigenous healing services should be regulated through laws; and spiritual and pastoral care should be recognized as an integral support system. Furthermore, counselling and mental health service professionals should be encouraged to participate in specialized training and necessary activities, including involvement in international collaborative research regarding integration of orthodox with indigenous methods in tackling mental health concerns, which will hopefully, produce evidence-based outcome. These actions if implemented will go a long way in promoting Nigerians' mental health well-being.

References

Abdulmalik, J., Kola, L., and Gureje, O. (2016) 'Mental health system governance in Nigeria: Challenges, opportunities and strategies for improvement'. *Global Mental Health*, 3(9): 1–11.

Abia, A. A. (2012) 'African belief systems and healthy living'. *International Journal of Culture and Human Development*, 4:3.

Adeyemo, D. A. (2016) 'College psychotherapy at a Nigerian University'. *Journal of College Student Psychotherapy*, 30(1): 12–14. Retrieved from https://doi.org/10.1080/87568225.2016.1105642.

Armiyau, A. Y. (2015) 'A review of stigma and mental illness in Nigeria'. *Journal of Clinical Case Report*, 5(1): 1–3.

Ayonrinde, O. A., Obuaya, C., and Adeyemi, S.O. (2015) 'Brain fag syndrome: A culture-bound syndrome that may be approaching extinction'. *British Journal of Psychiatry Bulletin*, 39: 156–161.

Azfredrick, E. C. (2015) 'Use of counseling service by school-attending adolescent girls in Nigeria'. *Journal of Child and Adolescent Mental Health*, 27(1): 1–10.

Bojuwoye, O., and Mogaji, A. A. (2013) 'Counseling and psychotherapy in Nigeria'. In R. Moodley, U. P. Gielen and R. Wu (Eds.), *Handbook of counseling and psychotherapy* (pp. 40–50). New York: Routledge.

Counselling Association of Nigeria [CASSON] (2010). *Newsletter: Consolidation on the gains of the transformation agenda*, 31: 9–10.

Eaton, J., and Agomoh, A.O. (2008) 'Developing mental health services in Nigeria: The impact of a community-based mental health awareness program'. *Social Psychiatry and Psychiatric Epidemiology*, 43: 552–558.

Egbuchulam, C. J. (1989) *Anecdotal survey on cultural beliefs and attitudes that are suspect in causing mental illness among the Ibos*. Unpublished Master's thesis, University of Jos, Jos, Nigeria.

Ekeopara, C. A. (2009) '*African traditional religion: An introduction*'. Calabar, Nigeria: Natos Affairs.

Eragbe, E. O. (2002) 'The dynamics of the evolution of Nigeria as a political unit'. In A.D. Nzemeke and E.O. Eragbe (Eds.), *Nigerian peoples and culture* (pp 36–54). Benin City: Mindex Publishing Company Limited.

Federal Ministry of Health (2013) *National policy for mental health services delivery*. Abuja: Nigeria.

Gabriel, C. (2016) *Property war in southeast: 'Never again will Igbo women be denied of their inheritance'*. Retrieved from www.vanguardngr.com/2016/09/property-war-south-east-never-will-igbo-women-denied-inheritance/.

Gureje, O. (2011) 'Nigeria'. In H. Ghodse (Ed.), *International perspectives on mental health* (pp. 41–45). London: The Royal College of Psychiatrists.

Gureje, O., Lasebikan, V. O., Ephraim-Oluwanuga, O., Olley, B. O., and Kola, L. (2005) 'Community study of knowledge of and attitude to mental illness in Nigeria'. *British Journal of Psychiatry*, 186: 436–441.

Institute of Social Work of Nigeria [ISOWN] (n. d.) Retrieved from https://isownig.org/.

Isichei, H. U. (2005) *Orthodox medicine versus alternative medicine in the management of psychiatric patients*. 23rd Inaugural Lecture, University of Jos, Jos, Nigeria.

Jack-Ide, I. O., and Uys, L. R. (2013) 'Barriers to mental health services utilization in the Niger Delta region of Nigeria: Service users' perspectives'. *Pan African Medical Journal*. Retrieved from www.panafrican-med-journal.com/content/article/14/159/full/.

Jack-Ide, I. O., Uys, L. R., and Middleton, L. E. (2012) 'A comparative study of mental health services in two African countries: South Africa and Nigeria'. *International Journal of Nursing and Midwifery*, 4(4): 50–57.

Jegede, C. O. (2016) 'The indigenous medical knowledge systems, perception and treatment of mental illness among the Yoruba of Nigeria'. *Studies in Sociology of Science*, 7(5):12–20.

Jegede, R. O., and Okunade, A. (1977) 'A comparative study of the attitudes of Nigerian student nurses and registered nurses towards mental illness'. *African Science Journal of Psychiatry*, 2: 47–50.

Lasebikan, V. O. (2016) 'Cultural aspects of mental health and mental health service delivery with a focus on Nigeria within a global community'. *Mental Health, Religion and Culture*, 19(4): 323–338.

Makinde, O. (1984) *Fundamentals of guidance and counseling*. London: Macmillan.

Mogbo, I. N., Obumneke-Okeke, I. M., and Anyachebelu, F. E. (2011) 'Implementation of guidance and counseling services in Nigerian schools'. *Journal of Emerging Trends in Educational Research and Policy Studies*, 2(5): 361–364.

Nigerian Educational Research and Development Council (2013) *National policy on education* (6th.ed.). Lagos: Nigeria, Federal Republic of Nigeria.

Nnochiri, I. (2014) *How Supreme Court voids discrimination against females in Igboland*. Retrieved from www.vanguardngr.com/2014/04/inheritance-supreme-court-voids-discrimination-females-igboland/.

Nwoko, K. C. (2009) 'Traditional psychiatric healing in Igboland'. *African Journal of History and Culture*, 1(2): 36–43.

Okocha, A. A. G. (2013) 'Counseling in Nigeria'. In T. H. Hohenshil, N. E. Amundson and S. G. Niles (Eds.), *Counseling around the world: An international handbook* (pp. 41–46). Alexandria, VA: American Counseling Association.

Okocha, A. A. G., and Alika, I. H. (2012) 'Professional counseling in Nigeria: Past, present, and future'. *Journal of Counseling and Development*, 90:362–366.

Okon, S. E. (1983) 'Guidance and counseling services in Nigeria'. *Personnel and Guidance Journal*, 67: 457–458.

Okoye, U. (2013) 'Trends and challenges of social work practice in Nigeria'. *Research Gate*: 166–174. Retrieved from www.researchgate.net/publication/267868332_Trends_and_challenges_of_social_work_practice_in_Nigeria.

Oladeji, B. D., and Gureje, O. (2016) 'Brain drain: A challenge to global mental health'. *British Journal of Psychiatry*, 13(3): 61–63.

Oyebode, F. (2004) 'Obituary: Thomas Adeoye Lambo O.B.E.' *Psychiatric Bulletin*, 28: 469.

Oyelade, O., Smith, A. A. H., and Jarvis, M. A. (2017) 'Dismissing de-escalation techniques as an intervention to manage verbal aggression within mental health care settings: Attitudes of psychiatric hospital-based Nigerian mental health nurses'. *Africa Journal of Nursing and Midwifery*, 19(2): 1–18.

Sue, D. W., and Sue, E. (2016) *Counseling the culturally diverse: Theory and practice* (7th ed.). Hoboken, NJ: John Wiley and Sons.

Ugwuegbulem, C. N., Homrich, A. M., and Kadurumba, C.U.U. (2009) *Cross cultural counseling in Nigeria*. London: Sage Publications.

Ukpong, D. I., and Abasiebong, F. (2010) 'Stigmatizing attitude toward the mentally ill: A survey in Nigerian University Teaching Hospital'. *South African Journal of Psychiatry*, 16(2): 56–60.

Westbrook, A. H. (2011) 'Mental health legislation and involuntary commitment in Nigeria: A call for reform'. *Washington University Global Studies Law Review*, 10(2): 396–418.

World Health Organization (2011) *Legal status of traditional medicine and complimentary alternative medicine: A worldwide review*. Retrieved from Who.int/medicinedocs/en/in2943e/432/html.

World Health Organization (2009) 'Improving Health Systems and Services for Mental Health'. *Mental Health Policy and Service Guidance package*. Geneva: WHO.

World Population Review (2020) *Nigeria Population 2020*. Retrieved from https://worldpopulationreview.com/countries/nigeria-population/.

36
CULTURE AND MENTAL HEALTH IN PAKISTAN

Humair Yusuf

Despite a diverse cultural heritage, Pakistani society is dominated significantly by the legacies of British colonization and state sponsored Islamization. Mental health and illness in Pakistan are similarly influenced by colonization and Islamization. The most obvious manifestation of these legacies are parallel systems of treatment: an Indigenous one based on Islamic beliefs for rural populations and a Western one, rooted in colonial infrastructure and traditions and supplemented by ongoing exposure to Western ideas, for urban populations. While existing in parallel, these two legacies interact in complex ways that appear inherently contradictory and problematic, but can also be considered adaptive and beneficial. Thus, beliefs regarding causation, coping and healing, which underlie representations of illness and ultimately shape subjective experiences of psychological distress, typically incorporate elements from both Islamic and Western traditions. For instance, while the belief that mental illness is God's punishment for sinful behaviour is widespread, paradoxically, those who have the resources to avail counselling, psychotherapy and psychiatry tend to prefer them over traditional Islamic healing based on concepts such as atonement and piety.

This chapter discusses mental health and illness in Pakistan in the context of colonial and Islamic legacies. It examines how these two legacies underlie contemporary representations of mental illness, and using vignettes from clinical cases provides insights into mental health practices in Pakistan, the challenges faced by counsellors and psychotherapists, and the limitations of the prevailing Western approaches. It concludes with suggestions to overcome these challenges and limitations as well as recommendations for research and practice.

Country demographics and history of mental health

While Pakistan's last official census was conducted in 2011, current projections estimate a population of approximately 204 million (United Nations Population Division 2019). Although there are a number of distinct ethnic groups in Pakistan it is an overwhelmingly Muslim country with 97% of the population identifying as Muslim with the remainder consisting of small minorities of Christians and Hindus. Pakistani society is strongly patriarchal, collectivist and family-oriented and the majority of the population lives in joint family residences. Income disparity is high with urban elites dominating the country's politics and economy (Federal Bureau of Statistics 2018).

The history of the region consisting of modern Pakistan can be traced back to the Indus Valley Civilization which was initially settled around 7000 BCE and evolved into a highly developed society by 4500 BCE. Since then it has been part of the Gandharan, Macedonian, Gupta and Sikh empires during which Hinduism, Buddhism, Zoroastrianism, Sikhism, variants of Hellenism and other polytheistic religions flourished (Petraglia and Allchin 2007). However, this diverse heritage has been largely forgotten and contemporary Pakistani society has been shaped to a considerable extent by Islam and British colonialism.

Islam in the region dates back to trade and limited naval incursions by Arabs in the seventh century. Invasions from Central Asia beginning in the 10th century resulted in the spread of a version of Islam influenced by Sufi traditions and the establishment of Muslim rule that continued until the arrival of the British through the East India Company in the 1600s and formally ended in 1858 with the establishment of the British Raj (Armstrong 2000; Judd 2004). Pakistan gained independence in 1947 and the state pursued a strong nationalist agenda to overcome the humiliations of colonialism. Rapid urbanization and superficial modernization resulted in traditional culture being abandoned or distorted without viable alternatives to replace it. Conservative forces framed this upheaval in religious terms, and although Pakistan declared itself an Islamic republic in 1956 it remained relatively secular. In the 1980s, however, an aggressive process of Islamization promoted by the state enabled rigid and puritanical versions of Islam. Based on the 18th-century movement led by Muhammad ibn Abdul Wahhab in Saudi Arabia, it emphasized literal interpretations of the Quran, disapproved of innovation and advocated the purging of all external influences. It became increasingly prominent and eventually displaced the relatively tolerant Sufi influenced Islam that had traditionally been practiced in the region (Wynbrandt 2009; Aslan 2011).

Like most aspects of Pakistani culture and society, mental health is dominated by its Islamic and colonial heritage. The rural population relies primarily on traditional methods based on Islamic teachings for their mental health and well-being. In contrast, the presence of colonial institutions in cities such as missionary schools, colleges and hospitals, and in particular a network of lunatic asylums dating back to 1745, exposure to Western culture through media and emigration have resulted in Western notions of mental health that prioritize psychiatry, counselling and psychotherapy amongst the urban population. However, as a result of the ongoing Islamization of Pakistani society there has been considerable interest, both in research and practice, in the incorporation of Islamic values into Western models of counselling and psychotherapy to make them more acceptable and relevant to Pakistani clients (Yusuf, Sarfraz, and Askari 2013).

Indigenous and traditional healers and healing

Islamic healing is based on the Qur'an, believed by Muslims to be the unchanged words of God revealed to the Prophet Muhammad. It instructs Muslims to "feed and clothe the insane … and tell splendid words to him" (4:5). Al-Krenawi and Graham (1999) draw on Islamic history to describe how the Prophet Muhammad treated mental illness while Haque (2004) highlights the contributions of early Islamic scholars to psychology. These include, among others, Al-Balkhi, who, in the ninth century studied anxiety, aggression, obsessions, and depression; Ibn-Sina or Avicenna, who, in the 11th century put forward psychological theories for hallucinations, insomnia, depression, and mania; and Al-Tarabi, who in the ninth century advocated the need for counselling in a manner recognizable to contemporary therapists. Youssef and Youssef (1996) describe a sophisticated understanding and management of schizophrenia in medieval Islamic society and Moodley (2000) draws attention to research by Murphy (1986) and Said (1993) who suggest that it was Ibn Khaldun in the 14th century who first suggested a connection between culture and mental illness in an attempt to explain the experiences of Bedouin who had replaced their traditional nomadic existence with a sedentary lifestyle.

Mental illness in Pakistan is often attributed to a defective relationship with God or punishment for not fulfilling religious obligations (Rizvi 1994). These beliefs are consistent with the literature on Islamic healers and healing practices (e.g., Al-Krenawi and Graham 1999) that describe mental illness in terms of God's will. Hodge (2005) describes how Muslims believe in an omnipotent God who is personally involved in worldly affairs. This omnipotence and personal involvement means that whatever happens to an individual, including mental illness, is because it has been willed by God. Healing is thus a process of moving closer to God and seeking His forgiveness through prayer, reading and reciting the Qur'an. A crucial aspect of Islamic healing is that "cures come solely from Allah" (Rassool 2015: ix) and healing can occur only through "the direct influence of Allah" (Dein, Alexander, and Napier 2008: 44).

Individuals suffering from mental illness in Pakistan often turn to healers known as pirs who trace their lineage to Sufi saints (Dein et. al. 2008). Interventions can include prayer, recitation of the Qur'an or the names of Allah, singing, dancing, playing music, blowing over the patient, drinking water that has been poured over the Qur'an, and the use of charms or amulets containing verses of the Qur'an for protection. According to Dein et al. (2008: 42), many of these practices "blur the boundaries between magic, herbal, and Islamic healing" and since saints and magic are often invoked, which implies that the healing was not the result of God's will and the assertion of his authority, many imams and religious scholars dismiss such practices as unrelated to Islam, sinful, and even heresy (Al-Daramdash 1991). Others, however, consider them "merely tools in God's hands" (Al-Krenawi and Graham 1999: 60) who mediate between individuals and God by providing advice regarding religious practices.

Gadit and Khalid (2002) describe how behaviours such as social withdrawal, aggression or infidelity may be ascribed to possession by evil spirits or jinn, in which case healing entails exorcisms that involve ritual cleansing, reading Qur'anic verses to agitate the jinn and persuade them to leave, or even a dialogue to convert the jinn to Islam. Such rituals often involve family members, thereby activating a support network that is likely to be beneficial to the client.

Pakistanis also visit shrines associated with Sufi saints who are believed to have close relationships with God and thus the ability to mediate between God and ordinary individuals. Devotion to these saints range from paying respect to them in the hope that they will mediate with God on their behalf to alleviate their suffering to actually praying to them to use their healing powers to cure afflicted individuals (Gadit and Khalid 2002).

While at a shrine individuals believe themselves to be under the Sufi's protection. Pirani, Papadopoulos, Foster and Leavey (2008) point out that remaining at the shrine provides individuals respite from stressful and problematic situations in their daily lives that are likely to be contributing to their distress. Moreover, they tend to live together in a therapeutic community in which they are accepted, have the opportunity to express their emotions without judgment or criticism and provide each other with support and empathy.

Colonialism and evolution of mental health practices

The legacy of colonization is complex and problematic for many aspects of Pakistani society and mental health is no exception. During British rule Western knowledge and education were emphasized while Indigenous traditions were discouraged and devalued, resulting in parallel healthcare systems that persist in contemporary Pakistan, especially for mental illness: a Western one for urban populations, in particular social and economic elites, and an Indigenous one for rural populations (Zaman 1991).

This dichotomy can be traced to 1745, when the British began to build lunatic asylums (renamed 'mental hospitals' in 1922) for the treatment of mental illness throughout India (Somasundaram, 1987). Initially they only admitted Europeans (Wig 2015) and even after they began to admit Indigenous populations the number of local patients remained relatively low (Mills, 2001). Described by Mubbashar (2000: 189) as "curative in their thrust and institutional in their approach" these hospitals, which were set up until the 1940s, established the parallel systems of treatment and, along with the first generation of psychiatrists who were trained in the United Kingdom (Malhotra and Chakrabarti 2015) shaped attitudes towards mental illness that remained intact after independence in 1947 (Mills 2001) resulting in an emphasis on psychiatry along with the confinement and segregation of individuals through hospitalization.

Meanwhile, as early as 1929, psychoanalysts in the sub-continent such as Berkeley Hill had highlighted the shortcomings of such approaches and proposed focusing on prevention and rehabilitation (Nizamie and Goyal 2010). Attempts were made to establish psychology as an approach to treating mental illness but since it was generally part of the philosophy curriculum in universities with courses taught by the philosophy faculty (Ansari 1967) it had a limited impact and the treatment of mental illness remained dominated by psychiatric approaches.

The beginnings of counselling and psychotherapy in Pakistan can be traced to the 1960s, when psychologists trained primarily in the United States and the United Kingdom returned to contend with a surge in rural to urban migration and the associated decline of the extended family, forcing individuals to turn to external sources to manage their distress. Simultaneously, guidance and counselling programs for women in colleges and universities as well as those entering the workplace introduced the concept of counselling for personal matters (Ibrahim and Almas 1983). Counsellors and psychotherapists, however, struggled to be accepted as legitimate mental health professionals, not only because of the stigma associated with mental illness and traditional values of relying on families to solve problems rather than seeking help from outsiders, but also because of colonial legacies that established psychiatrists' domination of treatment. Counsellors and psychotherapists were therefore forced to turn to private practice that could only be availed by elite populations who had the necessary knowledge, exposure and resources (Zaman 1991), which was paradoxically reminiscent of the colonial network of asylums that initially admitted Europeans only.

The state sponsored agenda of Islamization during the 1980s included attempts to challenge this colonial legacy in the treatment of mental illness and psychiatrists and psychologists were encouraged to develop uniquely Muslim approaches to treatment based on Islamic practices (Haque 2000). The only significant result of such efforts was an adaptation of Rational Emotive Behavioral Therapy by Rahman (1991) for Pakistanis through the identification of irrational beliefs regarding religion, deference to authority, relationships and self-esteem. In contrast the gradual yet pervasive Islamization of Pakistani society has resulted in the widespread incorporation of Islamic values into treatment for mental illness (e.g., Irfan, Saeed, Awan, Gul, Aslam and Naeem 2017). It is important to note, however, that Islamic values are being incorporated *into* Western psychiatry, counselling and psychotherapy which remain the dominant paradigm, thereby highlighting the enduring nature of the colonial legacy in the treatment of mental illness.

Cultural representations of illness and wellness

Given the extent to which colonization and Islamization have shaped contemporary Pakistani society, it is not surprising that they have significantly influenced representations of illness which are rooted in the network of meanings that an illness has in a particular culture (Good and Good 1982, in Moodley 2014). Moreover, Kleinman (1980) points out that the resources available for treatment determine which symptoms are selected and emphasized. Since in Pakistani society these resources are essentially colonial or Islamic in nature, colonial or Islamic legacies determine not just beliefs regarding causation, coping and healing but also symptomology and the subjective experience of mental illness.

There is considerable evidence that mental illness is manifested in somatic symptoms amongst Pakistanis (e.g., Bhui, King, Dein and O'Connor 2008; Dein et al. 2008; Irfan et al. 2017). Dein, Cook, Powell and Eagger (2010) highlight a particular emphasis on the biological heart, which Inayat (2005) and Irfan et al. (2017) ascribe to the influence of Sufism on Islamic beliefs in the region. In Sufi spirituality the heart is an essential element of the human psyche and where the interplay between psychological and spiritual factors is located. This notion is consistent with numerous references to diseased hearts and healing of the heart in the Qur'an, such as "In their hearts there is a disease" (2:10) or "In the remembrance of God do hearts find rest" (13:28). Consequently, distress is often labelled or described in terms of a "sinking heart" (Karuse 1989, cited in Moodley 2014:257) or an "incongruent heart" (Inayat 2005: 198).

Zaman (1997) explicitly links the expression of mental illness in terms of physical pain to the considerable stigma associated with it. Khan and Raza (1998) highlight that Pakistan is a pharmaceutically dominated society, and while the normalization of medication can be traced to the healthcare infrastructure established by the British, the focus on somatic symptoms allows mental illness to be addressed easily and without any social stigma. Moreover, in the context of the colonial legacy of treatment for mental illness being reserved for European or elite populations, it also ensures greater access to treatment for the general population. The somatization of mental illness in Pakistan is thus consistent with arguments by Pelto and Pelto (1997) that social, cultural, political, and economic factors often determine the treatment choices for individuals, who then construct representations of illness according to available resources for healing.

Mental illness in Pakistan, like in many other Muslim societies, is often considered God's punishment for sinful acts or the lack of faith, which can include doubting or questioning belief in God, neglecting religious obligations, disobeying God's instructions, or engaging in behaviour that is forbidden (e.g., Hodge 2005). Findings by Yusuf (2019) suggest that the notion of mental illness as punishment can be so powerful amongst Muslims that even when they cannot recall any impious or sinful behaviour they nevertheless believe that they must have committed a transgression that merited punishment. Moreover, many Pakistanis who are not especially religious and reject literal and punitive interpretations of Islam cannot completely set aside the notion that their suffering is a form of punishment. Such beliefs often lead feelings of resentment, guilt, shame, conflict and fatalism. Punishment for sinful behaviour is also believed to take the form of possession by spirits known as jinn who are believed to follow Iblis, the Islamic counterpart of the biblical Devil. Along with physical pain, symptoms include social withdrawal, isolation, disorientation, and incoherence, plus deviant or erratic behaviour such as aggression, infidelity, and dishonesty (Al-Kenawi and Graham 1999). Dein et al. (2008) describe how it is often the sudden appearance of the symptoms, rather than the symptoms themselves, that is attributed to possession. In their research on possession by jinn, Pirani et al. (2008) argue that giving mental illness the label of possession helps diminish the stigma experienced by individuals because, by shifting the cause of dysfunctional behaviour to external forces, they are not held personally and morally accountable and are instead considered deserving of sympathy, care, and encouragement.

Consistent with representations of illness in which beliefs regarding causation are ultimately God's punishment for lack of faith or piety, many Pakistanis attempt to find relief through turning to God and seeking forgiveness. In particular, the concept of Tawakkul, namely trusting and relying completely on God, which is emphasized repeatedly in the Qur'an can play an important part in the healing process (Hamdan 2008).

Paradoxically, given the prevalence of the belief that mental illness is punishment for sinful behaviour, Western and medical approaches, in particular psychiatry, are the preferred treatment approaches amongst Pakistanis who have the required resources, including those who describe Islam as being central to their lives and worldviews (Yusuf 2019). One possible explanation for this mismatch between beliefs regarding causation on the one hand and treatment choices on the other can be explained by the meaning and purpose to suffering provided by Islam (Hamdan 2008). And while the preference for Western approaches to treatment can be broadly attributed to Pakistan's colonial history, the dominance in Pakistan of psychiatrists, counsellors and psychotherapists trained in Western traditions, itself a colonial legacy, is likely to reinforce this preference since healthcare providers' beliefs play an important role in treatment expectations (e.g., Street, Makoul, Arora, and Epstein 2009). Other reasons for the inclination towards psychiatry, counselling and psychotherapy could be the preventive rather than curative nature of Islamic healing traditions, the feelings of defectiveness, shame and fatalism that can result from representations of mental illness based on punishment, the centrality of submission to God in Islamic healing traditions which individuals may find disempowering. However, Haque (2004) argues that Islamic societies have historically utilized contemporary knowledge and available resources for the treatment of illness and therefore taking advantage of current scientific advances and embracing biological and medical representations of distress for healing is consistent with Islamic traditions.

The contradictory aspects of representations of mental illness amongst Pakistanis can be understood as a manifestation of the tension between the rigid and puritanical Wahabi version of Islam that dominates social discourse and the more flexible and tolerant Sufi Islamic heritage along with the colonial legacies and exposure to Western culture that simultaneously shape contemporary Pakistanis' lived experiences. Moreover, rather than consider the apparently inconsistent Islamic and colonial elements of representations of illness in Pakistan as problematic, they can also be seen as adaptive and the result of a dialectical process in which Islamic beliefs regarding causation provide meaning and validate suffering, while Western counselling, psychotherapy and psychiatry provide strategies for healing that resonate with individuals and are relevant to their contemporary lives and worldviews.

Training and development, accreditation, licensure, and certification processes

Pakistan's Mental Health Act of 2001 recognizes the rights of consumers of mental health services, provides guidelines regarding treatment, and addresses complaints of misconduct or incompetence. While there is no formal accreditation, licensure, or certification process for the practice of psychology in Pakistan, organizations such as Pakistan Psychological Association and Pakistan Association for Clinical Psychologists are using this act as a basis to regulate the profession. Psychiatry, in contrast, is regulated by the College of Physicians and Surgeons Pakistan, and psychiatrists must complete specialized training modelled on British and American residency programs that leads to fellowship of the college and a license to practise.

There are a number of psychology departments in Pakistani universities offering postgraduate and doctoral degrees. Curricula are varied but tend be research focused with clinical training emphasizing psychoanalytic or cognitive-behavioural approaches. In addition, institutes affiliated with international organizations such as the British Association for Counselling and Psychotherapy offer diplomas in humanistic counselling, rehabilitation and occupational therapy.

Contemporary mental health practice

Mental health practitioners in Pakistan are typically graduates of North American or European universities or local ones that follow similar curricula. Consequently they are inclined to employ Western approaches to treatment which tends to be eclectic with elements of cognitive, narrative, client-centred, process-experiential and family systems therapy incorporated to meet client needs (Suhail 2004).

Due to the hierarchal and family-oriented nature of Pakistani society most problems, including emotional and interpersonal ones, are resolved through the advice and intervention of authority figures such as family elders. Pakistanis therefore tend to relate to mental health professionals as authority figures or elders who are expected to provide concrete solutions to their problems. As a result, interactions with mental health professionals tend to remain formal and deferential and thus very different from the therapeutic alliances typical in Western contexts. Moreover, such relationships often entail counsellors, psychotherapists and even psychiatrists engaging with family members and negotiating family relationships and hierarchies, making the establishment and maintenance of boundaries especially challenging (Zaman 1997).

The social stigma associated with mental health and illness in Pakistan presents even greater challenges. Sadruddin (2007) provides evidence that this stigma results in delays between the onset of mental illness and contact with mental health professionals. Khan and Raza (1998) argue that it underlies self-medication and treatment being limited to those who have attempted suicide, overdosed, or are suffering severe mental illness such as schizophrenia along with infrequent follow-up sessions and abrupt discontinuation of treatment.

The therapeutic journey of Omar provides an example of the current practice of counselling and psychotherapy in Pakistan. Omar was a 26-year-old who worked in a family construction business. Omar's therapy was set up by his father who, along with his mother, accompanied him to the sessions. Initially Omar sat quietly while his parents described his erratic behaviour and inability to get anything done.

By normalizing Omar's seeking of help and challenging his feelings of shame and weakness, the therapist was able to make him feel sufficiently safe in therapy to articulate his feelings of anxiety, dread and hopelessness. Omar also described being bullied in school and spending his childhood living in constant fear of his abusive and violent father. However, Omar insisted on defending his father and justifying his behaviour, and also refused to link his suffering to his early childhood experiences or explore or engage with them in any way whatsoever because he was convinced that his suffering was punishment from God.

Omar considered himself a devout Muslim who fulfilled his religious obligations and was thus unable to recall any sinful act or behaviour that would merit such punishment. Yet he insisted that "If God is punishing me then I must deserve this punishment," a belief that exacerbated his fundamental sense of shame, defectiveness and inadequacy, as well as triggered a sense of fatalism as described by Smith and Richards (2005). He resisted his therapist's attempts to challenge such thoughts or develop an alternate explanation for his distress, and eventually Omar and his therapist mutually agreed to terminate therapy since it was becoming frustrating for both of them.

Omar did, however, accept a referral to a religiously inclined therapist who incorporated religious beliefs into therapy and utilized a cognitive approach similar to that proposed by Husain and Hodge (2016) in which dysfunctional and distressing thoughts are addressed within Islamic frameworks. In contrast to the first therapist, the second one did not attempt

Culture and Mental Health in Pakistan

to challenge Omar's beliefs regarding punishment. Instead he validated Omar's beliefs, and without attempting to identify possible reasons for Omar's punishment he focused on the many references to healing and mercy in the Qur'an such as "We have sent down in the Quran such things that have healing and mercy for the believers" (17:82). Most importantly, he highlighted the concept of Tawakkal or complete submission and trust in God that is emphasized repeated in the Qur'an (8:2; 9:51; 65:38:2; 67:1–2). Omar found this approach productive and ultimately attributed the mitigation of his suffering to it:

> I understood that things happen for a reason, because they are meant to happen, because God means them to happen. Whatever happens will be for the best because it is part of God's plan. ... I left it up to God and that gave me peace.

Omar's case highlights how therapists in Pakistan have to negotiate the stigma associated with mental illness as well as the influence and involvement of clients' families in their therapy. It also provides an insight into the potentially negative impact of the hierarchal and family-oriented nature of Pakistani society and the notions of parental authority, expectations of deference and familial obligation. More importantly, however, it illustrates how Islamic beliefs can underlie psychological distress as well be a source of relief by providing meaning to suffering without addressing what Western psychology might consider its fundamental causes.

Another example is provided by Zohra, whose religious beliefs also played a role in her distress. She sought therapy for intense feelings of despair, guilt, worthlessness and hopelessness. She was 43 years old, an observant Muslim whose marriage lacked intimacy and was characterized by conflict. Divorce was not an option because, although permissible in Islam, she was unwilling to personally face or subject her family to the ensuing social stigma. Zohra was in an extramarital relationship with another man, which is considered a sin in Islam, and she consequently believed her distress was punishment for her immorality.

Zohra's therapist, who was trained in the United Kingdom and followed an emotion-focused approach, helped her understand and organize her emotional experience in terms of feelings of worthlessness based on her husband's treatment of her, failure due to her marital difficulties, hopelessness because she felt trapped in her marriage, and guilt and shame for engaging in an extramarital relationship. She proceeded to validate Zohra's needs to be respected, desired and loved, and rather than feel worthless because her husband did not fulfil these needs, or a failure for the state of her marriage, she was encouraged to feel angry at being treated badly and sad for what had been missing in her life. Moreover, the shame and guilt that Zohra felt for her extramarital relationship were reframed in terms of her asserting herself and seeking to fulfil her needs for respect, love and emotional and physical intimacy, to which she was entitled, but had been denied by her husband. Ultimately, Zohra was able to conceptualize her distress in terms of a conflict between her needs for validation and love, regarding which she reported enhanced awareness, legitimacy and entitlement, and was appropriately angry at being denied, and guilt, shame and sense of sin at embarking on a relationship with another man to fulfil her unmet physical and emotional needs. At this stage she expressed her desire to terminate therapy, which had not provided a resolution to her conflict but had enabled Zohra to differentiate the antagonistic aspects of herself and access the feelings underlying each along with their needs, which improved her ability to tolerate her distress.

During the course of Zohra's journey, her therapist attempted to probe her punitive interpretation of Islam, which emphasized ritual and obedience but appeared to lack any personal resonance or spirituality for her, and was thus a source of negative emotions. However, Zohra resisted any exploration or challenge in this regard, possibly because of the centrality of Islam to her sense of self and her worldview or the fear that engaging in such exploration would constitute a lack of faith, a major sin approaching apostacy.

Islamic beliefs were a significant factor in both Omar's and Zohra's experience distress. For Zohra, however, unlike Omar, they did not mitigate her distress or provide any relief, and instead continued to play a critical role in the conflict underlying her suffering which remained unresolved at the end of her therapy. These two vignettes highlight the inclination of therapists in Pakistan to employ primarily Western approaches, and the limitations of these approaches regarding matters of faith. They also show how counselling and psychotherapy in Pakistan can entail a parallel process of understanding mental illness from Western and Islamic perspectives simultaneously, selectively utilizing aspects of both traditions for coping and healing, and negotiating between the beliefs, values and worldviews of each tradition.

Future directions

The increased knowledge and awareness regarding mental illness in Pakistan is likely to result in greater demand for and utilization of mental health services in Pakistan. The lack of a formal accreditation, licensure, or certification process for the practice of counselling and psychotherapy in Pakistan therefore needs to be addressed urgently, ideally through the establishment of a regulatory framework with clearly defined guidelines for training, supervision and professional ethics.

Given the complex legacies of colonization and Islamization in Pakistan, their implications for representations of mental illness and the ensuing challenges for the practice of counselling and psychotherapy, the development of approaches that employ dialectical processes to enable the accommodation and integration of diverse and contradictory beliefs are of critical importance. For instance, along with Islamically modified cognitive therapy, which addresses dysfunctional thoughts by constructing statements based on Islamic concepts, narrative or emotion-focused approaches that incorporate religious beliefs and values in clients' narratives and emotional struggles could be explored. Other related directions for research and practice could be dual interventions as described by Moodley and Sutherland (2010) that employ traditional Islamic healing in conjunction with counselling and psychotherapy in a manner that could provide the benefits of both traditions, or entirely new paradigms, possibly from faith-based rather than psychological perspectives, that allow individuals to critically examine and interrogate their beliefs and make their religion personally relevant and meaningful to them and not a source of distress.

Similarly, the hierarchal and family-oriented nature of Pakistani society needs to be addressed in counselling and psychotherapy. This could entail the development of culturally appropriate codes of conduct that enable the creation of boundaries along with therapeutic approaches that allow individuals space to challenge notions of familial deference and obligation without guilt and harness families as a source of genuine support for individuals.

Conclusion

The legacies of colonialism and Islamization play a significant role in shaping the experiences and representations of mental illness in Pakistan. These two legacies interact in complex ways that pose difficulties for counselling and psychotherapy, but their interactions also suggest directions for coping and healing. While approaches that are rooted exclusively in either Islamic or Western traditions are likely to be inadequate for addressing the mental health needs of Pakistani clients, this chapter highlights the importance of developing genuinely syncretic

Culture and Mental Health in Pakistan

approaches that incorporate both legacies along with the treatment opportunities afforded by such approaches.

References

Al-Daramdash, H. (1991) *The Koran as a Treatment Tool for People who are Attacked by Satan*. Cairo: Daar Wali Al-Islamih Press.

Al-Krenawi, A. and Graham, J. R. (1999) 'Social Work and Koranic Mental Health Healers', *International Social Work*, 42(1): 53–65.

Ansari, Z. A. (1967) *Teaching and Research in Pakistan*. Islamabad: National Institute of Psychology.

Armstrong, K. (2000) *Islam: A Short History*. London: Phoenix Press.

Aslan, R. (2011) *No God but God: The Origins, Evolution, and Future of Islam*. New York: Random House.

Bhui, K., King, M., Dein, S. and O'Connor, W. (2008) 'Ethnicity and Religious Coping with Mental Distress', *Journal of Mental Health*, 17(2): 141–151.

Dein, S., Alexander, M. and Napier, A. D. (2008) 'Jinn, Psychiatry and Contested Notions of Misfortune among East London Bangladeshis', *Transcultural Psychiatry*, 45(1): 31–55.

Dein, S., Cook, C.C.H., Powell, A. and Eagger, S. (2010) 'Religion, Spirituality and Mental Health', *Psychiatrist*, 34: 63–64.

Federal Bureau of Statistics (2018) *Statistical Yearbook 2018,* Islamabad: Government of Pakistan.

Gadit, A. and Khalid, N. (2002) *State of Mental Health in Pakistan: Service, Education and Research*. Karachi: Madinat-al-Hikmah.

Good, B. J. and Good, M. J.D. (1982) 'Towards a Meaning-Centred Analysis of Popular Illness Categories: `Fright-illness' and `Heat distress' in Iran', in A. Marsella and G. M. White (Eds.), *Cultural Conceptions of Mental Health and Therapy*. Dordrecht: Reidel.

Hamdan, A. (2008) 'Cognitive Restructuring: An Islamic Perspective', *Journal of Muslim Mental Health*, 3(1): 99–116.

Haque, A (2000) 'Development of Psychology in Pakistan', in A. E. Kazdin (Ed.), *Encyclopedia of Psychology Vol. 6* (pp. 27–32). Washington DC: American Pyschological Association.

Haque, A. (2004) 'Psychology from an Islamic Perspective: Contributions of Early Muslim Scholars and Challenges to Contemporary Muslim Psychologists', *Journal of Religion and Health*, 43(4): 357–377.

Hodge, D. R. (2005) 'Social Work and the House of Islam: Orienting Practitioners to the Beliefs and Values of Muslims in the United States', *Social Work*, 50(2): 62–173.

Husain, A. and Hodge, D. R. (2016) 'Islamically Modified Cognitive Behavioral Therapy: Enhancing Outcomes by Increasing the Cultural Congruence of Cognitive Behavioral Therapy Self-Statements', *International Social Work:* 59(3), 393–405.

Ibrahim, F.A. and Almas, I. (1983) 'Guidance and Counseling in Pakistan', *International Journal for the Advancement of Counseling*, 6: 93–98.

Inayat, Q. (2005) 'Islam, Divinity, and Spiritual Healing', in R. Moodley and W. West (Eds.), *Integrating Traditional Healing Practices into Counseling and Psychotherapy* (pp.159–169). Thousand Oaks, CA: Sage.

Irfan, M., Saeed, S., Awan, N. R., Gul, M., Aslam, M. and Naeem, F. (2017) 'Psychological Healing in Pakistan: From Sufism to Culturally Adapted Cognitive Behaviour Therapy', *Journal of Contemporary Psychotherapy*, 47(2): 119–124.

Judd, D. (2004) *The Lion and the Tiger: The Rise and Fall of the British Raj, 1600–1947*. Oxford and New York: Oxford University Press.

Khan, M.M. and Reza, H. (1998) 'Benzodiazepine Self-Poisoning in Pakistan: Implications for Prevention and Harm reduction', *Journal of the Pakistan Medical Association*, 48(10): 292–295.

Kleinman A. (1980) 'Patients and Healers in the Context of Culture: An Exploration of the Borderland between Anthropology', *Medicine, and Psychiatry*. Berkeley: University of California Press.

Krause, I. B. (1989) 'Sinking Heart: a Punjabi Communication of Distress', *Social Science and Medicine*, 29(4): 563–575.

Malhotra, S. and Chakrabarti, S. (2015) *Developments in Psychiatry in India* (pp. 77–87). New Delhi: Springer India.

Mills, J. (2001) 'The History of Modern Psychiatry in India, 1858–1947,' *History of Psychiatry*, 12(48): 431–458.

Moodley, R. (2000) 'Representations of Subjective Distress in Black and Ethnic Minority Patients: Constructing a Research Agenda', *Counselling Psychology Quarterly*, 13(2): 159–174.

Moodley, R. (2014) 'Cultural Representations and Interpretations of Subjective Distress in Ethnic Minority Patients', in R. Moodley and S. Palmer (Eds.), *Race, Culture and Psychotherapy: Critical Perspectives in Multicultural Practice* (pp. 252–264). London: Routledge.

Moodley, R. and Sutherland, P. (2010) 'Psychic Retreats in Other Places: Clients who Seek Healing with Traditional Healers and Psychotherapists', *Counselling Psychology Quarterly*, 23 (3): 267–282.

Mubbashar, M. H. (2000) 'Mental Illness in Pakistan', in I. Al-Issa (Ed.), *Al-Junun: Mental Illness in the Islamic World* (pp. 187–203). Madison: International Universities Press.

Murphy, H.B.M. (1986) 'The Historical Development of Transcultural Psychiatry', in J. L. Cox (Ed.), *Transcultural Psychiatry*. London: Croom Helm.

Nizamie H.S. and Goyal N. (2010) 'History of Psychiatry in India', *Indian Journal of Psychiatry*, 52: 7–12.

Pelto, P. and Pelto, G. (1997) 'Studying Knowledge, Culture and Behaviour in Applied Medical Anthropology', *Medical Anthropology Quarterly* 11 (2): 147–163.

Petraglia, M. D. and Allchin, B. (2007) *The Evolution and History of Human Populations in South Asia: Interdisciplinary Studies in Archaeology, Biological Anthropology, Linguistics and Genetics* (Eds.). Dordrecht: Springer Science and Business Media.

Pirani, F., Papadopoulos, R., Foster, J. and Leavey, G. (2008) '"I will accept whatever is meant for us. I wait for that – day and night': The Search for Healing at a Muslim Shrine in Pakistan', *Mental Health, Religion and Culture*, 11(4): 375–386.

Rahman, N. (1991) *Rational Emotive Therapy and Its Application in Pakistan*. Presentation at the 8th Conference of the Pakistan Psychological Association, Islamabad.

Rassool, G. H. (2015) *Islamic Counselling: An Introduction to Theory and Practice*. Routledge.

Rizvi. A. A. (1994) *Muslim Traditions in Psychotherapy and Modern Trends*. Lahore: Institute of Islamic Culture.

Sadruddin, S. (2007) *Predictors of Treatment Delay in Depressive Disorders in Pakistan*, PhD Thesis, Department of Health Policy, Management and Evaluation, University of Toronto, Canada.

Said, E. W. (1993) *Culture and Imperialism*. London: Chatto and Windus.

Smith, T. and Richards, S. (2005) 'The Integration of Spiritual and Religious Issues in Racial-Cultural Psychology and Counselling', in R. Carter (Ed.), *Handbook of Racial-Cultural Psychology and Counselling* (pp. 132–163). Hoboken, NJ: John Wiley and Sons.

Somasundaram, O. (1987) 'The Indian Lunacy Act, 1912: The Historic Background', *Indian Journal of Psychiatry*, 29: 3–14.

Street Jr, R. L., Makoul, G., Arora, N. K. and Epstein, R. M. (2009) 'How Does Communication Heal? Pathways Linking Clinician–Patient Communication to Health Outcomes', *Patient Education and Counseling*, 74(3): 295–301.

Suhail, K. (2004) 'Psychology in Pakistan', *The Psychologist*, 7(11): 632–634.

United Nation Population Division (2019) *World Population Prospects*. Retrieved from https://population.un.org/wpp/.

Wig, N. N. (2015) 'The Beginnings of Psychiatry in India', in *Developments in Psychiatry in India* (pp. 3–12). New Delhi: Springer.

Wynbrandt, J. (2009) *A Brief History of Pakistan*. New York: Infobase Publishing.

Yusuf, H. (2019) *Representations of Psychological Distress Among Canadian Muslims of South Asian Origin: A Qualitative Study using the Self-regulatory Model*. Doctoral dissertation, Department of Applied Psychology and Human Development, Ontario Insitute for Studies in Education, University of Toronto.

Youssef, H. and Youssef, F., (1996) 'Evidence for the Existence of Schizophrenia in Medieval Islamic Society', *History of Psychiatry*, 7(3): 55–62.

Yusuf, H., Sarfraz, S. and Askari, L. (2013) 'Counseling and Psychotherapy in Pakistan: Colonial Legacies and Islamic Influences', in R. Moodley, U. Gielen, and R. Wu (Eds.), *Handbook of Counselling and Psychotherapy in an International Context* (pp. 226–236). New York: Routledge.

Zaman, R. M. (1991) 'Clinical Psychology in Pakistan', *Psychology and Developing Societies*, 3: 221–233.

Zaman, R.M. (1997) 'The Adaptation of Western Psychotherapeutic Methods to Muslim Societies: The Case of Pakistan', *World Psychology*, 3: 65–87.

37

CULTURE AND MENTAL HEALTH IN PERU

David M. R. Orr

This chapter contextualizes mental health in Peru today within the historical legacy of colonialism and the enduring ethno-racial inequalities to which that history gave rise. During the twentieth century, key Peruvian researchers and practitioners made important contributions to the field of cultural psychiatry. Yet mental health care remained chronically underfunded and was confronted with stark economic, gender and ethnic inequalities which have contributed significantly to experiences of poor mental health among Peruvians. Recent years have seen a new policy focus on mental health, yet significant challenges remain. Meanwhile, outside of the formal mental health sector, traditional healing retains an important presence, contrary to medical modernizers' expectations. Explanatory models and cultural concepts of distress found in Andean communities are discussed, as an important example of the indigenous approaches to mental health that remain influential for many communities within Peru.

Introduction

In November 1969, noted Peruvian novelist and anthropologist José María Arguedas took his own life after a long struggle with depression. Arguedas' novels, poetry and anthropological works explored the relationship between indigenous Quechua culture and wider Peruvian society, in a national context where the Spanish language dominated, mestizos monopolised political, economic and intellectual power, and indigenous people were mostly marginalized (a 'corralled nation', in his words). In the ensuing discussions of his life, death and intellectual legacy, the socio-emotional strains of living between the two cultures – Indigenous and mestizo – in which he had grown up, emerged as a major theme. It has sometimes been claimed that this tension was the determining factor that ultimately caused him to take his own life (Archibald 2000). Although this view drastically over-simplifies a complex confluence of factors, it highlights the widespread perception that questions of culture hold enduring significance for mental health in the Peruvian context.

Arguedas famously said of Peru that 'there is no more diverse country'. The unhappy accompaniment to this diversity has been stark and persistent inequalities along ethnic, racial and class divides – a key factor among the 'social determinants of mental health' in the country (World

445

Health Organization/Calouste Gulbenkian Foundation 2014). In order to provide key background to this reality and today's Peru, this chapter opens with a brief national history, before presenting contemporary demographics and some commentary on cultural identities. It traces historical developments in mental health care, then describes the continuing relevance of traditional healing and explores some key cultural concepts of illness and well-being. Though there is scope for only a highly selective introduction to this rich and complex subject matter, the chapter aims to convey why an understanding of those factors is essential to engagement with mental health in Peru today.

Brief history

The cultural mosaic of modern Peru has its roots in Spain's sixteenth-century invasion, which brought the Inca Empire to a sudden and violent end. The Spaniards established a new political framework which rested on the explicitly racialized division between two republics: the 'republic of Indians' and the 'republic of Spaniards'. Indigenous peoples experienced massive mortality as a result of epidemics arising from the new diseases brought from Europe, against which they had no immunity, and cultural repression as their religious beliefs were suppressed. Racial inequality and exploitation continued following independence from Spanish rule, though a significant milestone was achieved with the abolition of Afro-Peruvian slavery in 1854. As the nineteenth and twentieth centuries progressed, Peru's economic development was characterized by abrupt boom-bust cycles and regionally unbalanced growth, with wealth becoming ever more concentrated in the coastal region at the expense of the highlands and jungle areas. There, social, political and economic domination by large landowners, which in some areas reached quasi-feudal extremes, put down deep roots. Persistent failure to achieve more equitable distribution of wealth and political power led to the pronounced centralism that still characterizes Peru today.

Peasant unrest and land occupations during the 1950s and 1960s culminated in a military coup in 1968 and an Agrarian Reform which redistributed land from large landowners to peasant cooperatives. However, the reform failed to bring about lasting social consensus. Soon after the return to democratic government in 1980, discontent erupted into a vicious internal conflict. A violent uprising led by the Maoist organization *Sendero Luminoso* (Shining Path) spread from the southern highland department of Ayacucho and was met with harsh repression by state forces. The violence continued for years, leaving an estimated 69,280 people dead, and countless others bereaved, displaced and traumatised. Not all of society was equally affected; the Truth and Reconciliation Committee (TRC) established in the wake of the conflict found that 79% of the dead resided in rural zones and 75% were native speakers of indigenous languages. TRC chairman, Salomon Lerner, highlighted that earlier estimates of the number of dead had been only half the real total:

> What does it reveal about our political community to know now that 35,000 more people are missing, our brothers and sisters, and that nobody missed them?
>
> *(Lerner 2003)*

The answer, he felt, lay in persistent racism that characterized dominant structures and attitudes in the country.

Since the return of peace and democracy at the turn of the century, the Peruvian state and NGO action have greatly extended the reach of educational and social welfare programs. Yet ongoing economic, gender and ethnic inequality pose significant social challenges.

Demographics

The population of Peru was over 31.2 million in 2017 (INEI 2017). Over half of the population resides in the coastal strip (the *costa*). The next most-populated region is the Andean *sierra*, or highlands. The Amazonian jungle (the *selva*) to the east is geographically the largest of these ecological territories but the most sparsely populated, its inhabitants constituting just under 10% of the national population.

Most Peruvians readily identify as coming from the *costa*, the *sierra* or the *selva*. Beyond this, identity in Peru becomes more complex. Social researchers have shown that ethnicity in Peru is both tangled up with class and partly depends on the social situation: for example, an individual can be more or less 'indigenous' or 'white' depending on with whom they are being compared (Thorp and Paredes 2010). This is illustrated by the words of a psychologist during interviews with the author, talking about her puzzlement at being identified as *blanca* (white) by participants in a workshop on self-esteem she did in a Quechua-speaking community in the southern *sierra*:

> But I'm not white, I'm *mestiza*, I'm a mix, my family is from the *sierra* and the rest come from the north. 'No, but you're not *mestiza*, you're *de familia* [from a good family] and white.' And like that ... so it wasn't race, it was the surname, it was education. […] I learnt a huge amount in that workshop!
>
> *(cited in Orr 2004: 46)*

Ethnic identity is therefore not only multidimensional but also can be distinctly fluid, potentially shifting along a continuum according to several socially determined factors.

Language is one characteristic often used to identify indigenous people. The national census of 2017 showed that among respondents aged over five years, 17.4% of the population grew up speaking a language other than Spanish. Of these, Quechua was the native language of 13.9% (3,735,682), Aymara the native language of 1.7% (444,389), and indigenous Amazonian languages such as Ashaninka, Awajún and Shipibo-Konibo made up most of the rest (INEI 2017: 197). Indigenous languages are spoken by particularly high proportions of the population in the southern highland *departamentos* of Apurimac, Huancavelica, Ayacucho, Puno and Cusco.

The 2017 census asked for the first time about ethnic self-identification, defined in terms of 'customs and ancestry'. In response, 60.2% of respondents aged over 12 years answered that they saw themselves as 'mestizo' (mixed race), 22.3% as 'Quechua', 5.9% as 'white', 3.6% as Afro-Peruvian, 2.4% as Aymara, and 0.03% as indigenous Amazonians (INEI 2017). These figures suggest that a higher proportion of the population view themselves as indigenous than grew up speaking indigenous languages.

Since 1990, the stranglehold of white and mestizo politicians on the highest office has been broken. Legislation, civic activism and attitudes have shifted, as Peruvian society has become less tolerant of overt racism (Ministerio de Cultura n.d.). However, prejudice and discrimination remain significant, sometimes based on racial features and biology but more often on 'cultural' criteria such as education, as alluded to in the above quote. Those holding such attitudes commonly dismiss out of hand the kinds of cultural health practices and worldviews described below.

Despite the existence of important political movements representing indigenous Amazonia, such as AIDESEP and CONAP, Peru has not seen the rise to prominence of a national pan-indigenous political movement, unlike the neighbouring Andean countries of Bolivia and Ecuador (Thorp and Paredes 2010). Some in the *sierra* are wary about claiming 'indigenous' identity, feeling that it carries pejorative connotations or that it responds to outsiders' perceptions of how they should live rather than their own (García 2005). These perceptions attest to the effects of Peru's long legacy of oppression and to the continuation of social inequalities into the present-day. Many prefer to self-identify as *campesinos* (Sp. peasants), following long-standing practice among rural trade unions and the usage promoted by the reformist military government (1968–1980). This is by no means a universal view. Many identify strongly as indigenous; many others embrace their cultural heritage, but identify locally rather than as part of any national or transnational 'Quechua community' or 'indigenous alliance'. As this necessarily brief summary indicates, such questions of identity are complex. Yet a basic understanding their significance for contemporary lived experience, distilled as it is out of the starkly unequal relations between racial and ethnic groups, is essential to effective mental health practice in Peru.

History of mental health in Peru

Chronicles from the early colonial period describe the healing specialists of the Inca Empire and give some indication of their procedures. They relate that sickness was often attributed to disturbed relationships with supernatural elements, often diagnosed by divination through dreams, consultation with spiritual powers, reading the entrails of a guinea pig or llama, or other approaches (Valdivia Ponce 1975). Several descriptive terms for forms of madness are recorded in the chronicles, but – with the exception of *melancolía* (low mood) – there is comparatively little mention of how Inca society treated what today would be considered mental illnesses (Elferink 1999).

The Spaniards brought their own ideas about madness and its treatment, both religious (deriving from Catholic teachings) and medical (relying principally on Galenic humoural theory) in nature (Shuger 2012). Though what is widely considered to be the first hospital in Europe dedicated exclusively to the care of the mad had been opened in Valencia in 1410, official provision of care for the deranged in Peru – as indeed in many parts of Spain – remained basic and a number of mentally disordered individuals found themselves appearing before the Inquisition (Valdizán 1988[1918]). Though some were provided for in dedicated wings of general hospitals run by the clergy and funded by donations and alms, care for mental disorders during the period was neither extensive nor generally salubrious (Stucchi Portocarrero 2012).

In 1859 the first dedicated asylum was founded in the country, the Asilo de la Misericordia, renamed Hospital Larco Herrera in the twentieth century. Despite periodic reforms, overcrowding became a perennial problem in the Larco Herrera and led to demands for government action. Peru's first mental health law was passed in 1950 and provided for national planning for mental health at the level of the Ministry of Health. Mental health plans were drafted in succeeding decades, but, despite good intentions and isolated improvements, for the most part remained largely unimplemented. One notable achievement came with the foundation of the National Institute of Mental Health (Noguchi-Honorio Delgado) in the 1980s, which has given significant impetus to mental health research in Peru.

Over this period, some Peruvian psychiatrists considered questions of culture in their professional writings. Hermilio Valdizán (1885–1929) was the first Peruvian psychiatrist to pursue sustained study of mental health within Peruvian culture and history. His work was largely inspired by historical curiosity, but also sought – in keeping with the evolutionary theories of the time – to explain the 'degeneration' of the indigenous race, a process which he concluded could be largely attributed to narcotic addiction caused by the traditional practice of coca leaf consumption.[1] Later researchers developed the field of cultural psychiatry that he had had pioneered. Federico Sal y Rosas (1900–1974), himself a native-speaker of Quechua, explored cultural syndromes which he saw in his professional practice, such as *susto* ('fright sickness') and *sonqo-nanay* ('heart-sickness'). Carlos Seguín, meanwhile, identified the psychosocial stresses of rural-urban migration, to which he gave the name 'Psychosomatic Dysadaptation Syndrome' (Seguín 1951) – a newly labelled pathology which says much about the personal challenges for individuals of making this shift, as well as about societal anxieties over the influx of peasant families into the cities in that and succeeding decades. Despite this research tradition, however, the prominent psychiatrist Javier Mariátegui would still lament in 1988 the lack of systematic study of the mental health experiences of much of the population:

> Many Peruvians, for ethno-cultural reasons, live like foreigners in their own country. The classic references, mostly testimonies, are repeated over and over without being complemented by study in the field and analysis on the ground.
>
> *(Mariátegui 1988: 40)*

Like the TRC's finding fifteen years later that tens of thousands of deaths had gone almost unnoticed nationally, Mariátegui's view underlines the long-standing marginalization experienced by many Peruvians.

The trauma and suffering unleashed by the conflict between Shining Path and the state in the 1980–1990s led to an unprecedented acknowledgement of mental health as a focus of reconstruction efforts. The state reparations offered to some rural communities affected by the conflict commonly incorporated a psychological element, and many psychologists had been involved in gathering testimonies for the work of the TRC. Dealing with the legacy of the violence often relied on standard models of post-conflict trauma, but also led some researchers to study local understandings of the after-effects of such extreme suffering (Pedersen, Kienzler and Gamarra 2010; Theidon 2013).

The legacy of plans not implemented and opportunities not taken meant that Peru started the twenty-first century with a mental health care system that was deeply inadequate to meet levels of need. Eighty-five percent of psychiatrists were located in Lima and all but a tiny fraction of state spending on mental health went to psychiatric hospitals rather than to more accessible primary care services (Toyama et al. 2017). It is therefore not surprising that according to a series of epidemiological surveys carried out in several regions of the country, 69–85% of those reporting mental health problems had not sought care from formal services, often because of unaffordability or lack of knowledge of where to seek help (Toyama et al. 2017). There were concerns about the quality of treatment, with the Human Rights Ombudsman's Office (*Defensoría del Pueblo*) releasing a report in 2005 which criticized the lack of regulation of involuntary admission and standards obtaining in some psychiatric hospitals. The *Defensoría's* report further highlighted what it considered to be inadequate national oversight and leadership in mental health (2005: 160).

Recent years have seen mental health move up the policy agenda. Law 29889 was passed in 2012 and aimed to provide country-wide availability of mental health programs and services. Mental health care is being restructured, shifting the focus from psychiatric hospitals towards treatment in primary and secondary care facilities. Several Community Mental Health Centers (CMHCs) have been created and it is projected that 281 will be in operation nationwide by 2021 (MINSA 2018a: 50). The mental health reforms further proposed the establishment of services to help discharged psychiatric patients reintegrate into the community and extension of access to psychiatric medication by training primary care practitioners in appropriate prescribing, while mental health care has been brought within the *Seguro Integral de Salud*, the government's health insurance policy for vulnerable populations (Toyama et al. 2017). As well as the emphasis on strengthening community services, recognition of the importance of equity, gender and inter-cultural awareness and respect (*interculturalidad*) in the National Plan (MINSA 2018a) and the 2019 Mental Health Law (Law 30947) is welcome. Without clear and sustained attention to these issues, mental health challenges in Peru cannot be meaningfully tackled.

In comparison with the situation of mental health at the turn of the century, these are considerable advances. Beyond simply the fact that services have scaled up significantly, there are indications in some areas of qualitative improvements; for example, regional governments in areas where indigenous languages have a significant presence have issued decrees requiring health staff to develop competence in these languages as part of their professional training. However, the reforms must confront considerable obstacles, not least the low numbers of specialist personnel in many regions (Toyama et al. 2017). It is estimated that there are 1.4 psychiatrists per 100,000 people nationally, but this masks huge regional disparities: the figure rises to 3.2 per 100,000 in Lima. Similarly, the number of psychologists working in public health institutions varies between 41 per 100,000 and 7 per 100,000 by region, while numbers of mental health nurses, social workers and occupational therapists are also far below those needed (MINSA 2018a: 32–34).

Traditional healing

Away from the formal mental health system, traditional healing retains an important presence. Traditional healing is defined by the World Health Organization (WHO) as

> the sum total of the knowledge, skill, and practices based on the theories, beliefs, and experiences indigenous to different cultures, whether explicable or not, used in the maintenance of health as well as in the prevention, diagnosis, improvement or treatment of physical and mental illness.
>
> *(WHO 2013: 15)*

In Peru, healers in the *costa* and *sierra* draw on a shared repertoire of techniques and understandings that encompasses plant-based medicines, indigenous animism, and Catholic cosmology. Individual healers may place relatively more emphasis on one, two, or all of these elements, depending on the approach they favour, the breadth of their knowledge, and/or the claims they make of alliance with or affection for a particular saint or *apu* (Qu. mountain spirit) (Orr 2012). Healing practices in the *selva* vary between different communities but many rely on shamanic practitioners, whose use of psychoactive plants gives them access to other worlds and the ability to act against ill health or sorcery.

The term 'traditional healing' can have connotations of static or unchanging practices, as arguably implied by the WHO definition cited above. Although rich veins of continuity run through much Peruvian healing ritual, healers have always adapted to changing times and understandings. The mixing of indigenous and Catholic elements in Peruvian healing practices began early in the colonial period (Estenssoro Fuchs 2003: 385–394), despite official persecution by Catholic officials who sought to stamp out native 'idolatries'. Images of popular saints have long sat comfortably alongside invocations of the *apus*. Incorporation of novel elements has continued in modern times, from an Amazonian shaman's adoption of the power of injections into his ritual narrative (Greene 1998) to incorporation of lawyers' idioms by a highland Bolivian healer in his ceremonial appeal to the *apus* (Platt 1997). The Protestant evangelical churches which in recent decades have gained many recruits throughout Peru have proved more resistant to this kind of syncretism and are usually openly hostile to traditional healers; in

Culture and Mental Health in Peru

some Andean and Amazonian communities which have seen widespread conversions, this has led to the virtual disappearance of local traditional healers (Izquierdo 2005: 772).

The herbal knowledge of indigenous healers was renowned at the time of the arrival of the Spaniards (Valdivia Ponce 1975: 21) and the native pharmacopeia continues to occupy a prominent place in healing for both mental and physical problems. Among *campesinos*, herbal cures are often the first resort for emotional distress or agitation. Traditional ethnobotanic knowledge remains strong in some areas of the country; indeed, overharvesting in response to market demand has become a significant threat to some plant species (Bussmann and Sharon 2006). Natural hallucinogens, such as *san pedro* or *ayahuasca*, are employed to identify the source of illnesses and induce healing visions by some Amazonian shamans and northern highland healers. The potential for ethnobotanic knowledge to inform modern treatments for phys-ical and mental health issues is being investigated by research groups such as the Institute of Traditional Medicine, which seeks to map and preserve knowledge of traditional bioresources, and the Takiwasi Centre in Tarapoto, which investigates the potential of traditional Amazonian shamanic practices, including ayahuasca use, for treatment of addictions.

Traditional healers may be referred to by a range of names. The Spanish terms *curandero* (healer), *brujo* (sorcerer) or *chamán* (shaman) are generally recognised throughout society. Quechua-speakers may use other words: *hanpiq* (healer), *yachaq* (one who knows) and *paqo* (healer) are common. *Laika* indicates someone who uses his or her powers against others, often through witchcraft; however, the same individual may act sometimes as a *laika* and sometimes as a *paqo*, depending on whether s/he is aiming to heal or harm (Ricard Lanata 2007). Another key division among highland healers is between the *altomisayoq* and the *pampamisayoq*. The former is chosen by the *apus*, usually by being struck by lightning and surviving the experience. There may follow a period of initiation at the hands of an established *altomisayoq*, or, less com-monly, knowledge of how to heal may arrive suddenly, as a form of revelation (Ricard Lanata 2007: 149–159). The *altomisayoq* has the ability to communicate directly with the *apus* to entreat intervention, while the *pampamisayoq*, by contrast, lacks this special access; he or she can appeal to them through offerings, but does not invoke their presence to engage with them directly. Both may also use divination, through dreams or reading coca leaves, or diagnosis of urine or veins, to understand the causes of illness or misfortune.

Traditional medicine occupies a structurally subordinate position in relation to biomedi-cine in Peru. Practitioners within the formal health care system have openly derided indi-genous healing as superstitious and ineffective. However, contrary to medical modernizers' expectations, increased accessibility and improved provision of biomedical care have not caused traditional medicine to dwindle. Studies have shown that both forms of health care frequently co-exist, and that help-seekers commonly see them as complementary rather than contra-dictory (Blaisdell and Ødegaard 2014; Orr 2012). There is a legacy of discrimination by health professionals against poor and indigenous patients, which was particularly acute in rural com-munities (Papponet-Cantat 1995; Samuel and Frisancho 2015). Although this has yet to be fully resolved and certainly plays a part in determining therapeutic itineraries, it would be mistaken to attribute the continuing value that many Peruvians place on traditional healers solely to the disrespect with which they feel they are treated in health centres. Instead, they are strategic in selecting a favoured form of therapy, or combining approaches, according to what they think may best suit the condition or circumstances they face (Blaisdell and Ødegaard 2014). Many people consider traditional treatments to be beneficial, to have fewer harmful side-effects than pharma-ceutical medicine, or to leave them less beholden to an impersonal, and sometimes unreliable, health system (Gold and Clapp 2011; Mathez-Stiefel, Vandebroek and Rist 2012). Furthermore, as Crandon-Malamud (1993) first pointed out, sometimes making particular choices about therapeutic treatment can confer secondary social benefits. For example, appearing to comply with a doctor's prescribed treatment avoids the risk of retaliation for non-compliance through refusal to prescribe medication in the future or refusal to issue a death certificate (necessitating a costly post-mortem and laying caregivers open to accusation of contributing to the death), or seeking out healing prayers from an evangelical church holds open the possibility of membership of that church and the social opportunities that it may offer.

More so than many health conditions, mental health issues may be perceived to be the result of a range of psychological, social, biological or spiritual causes. Consequently, where to seek help amidst Peru's medical pluralism can be an open question for those affected. Serious mental disorders can prove so challenging to manage that even those sceptical about the efficacy of traditional healing sometimes resort to it, alongside seeking treatment from the formal health system (Orr 2012).

Training and registration

The Peruvian Psychiatric Association lists over 500 affiliated members (APP 2018). Membership is restricted to medically qualified individuals registered with the *Colegio Médico del Perú* and holding specialist qualification in psychiatry. In some areas of Peru, however, shortages of qualified personnel may mean that non-specialist doctors undertake clinical work that would otherwise be done by a psychiatrist. Psychologists specialising in Clinical and Health Psychology also commonly work in mental health; the minimum training required is the 10-semester psychology degree. Practising clinical psychologists must be registered with the *Colegio de Psicólogos del Perú*.

Cultural representations of illness and wellness

Peru's diverse cultural traditions offer a varied range of idioms and explanations for the experiences that biomedicine classifies as 'mental health issues'. Individuals, families and communities adopt or reject these according to their own lights. 'Western' psychiatric and psychological[2] models are unarguably influential within much of society. However, other worldviews continue to thrive alongside these understandings. Indigenous Andean views of health are broadly integrative and holistic, and *campesinos* are often willing to consider multiple aetiologies simultaneously (Orr 2012). It may make little sense from this perspective to separate out the 'spiritual', 'emotional' and 'somatic' into distinct categories, as is suggested by the way emotions such as fear or anger are understood to directly manifest in physical illnesses, such as *colerina* (anger), *susto* (fright) and *chucaque* (shame), each with its own set of physical and mental symptoms (Tapias 2015). One need not experience the emotions oneself to become sick; *susto*, for example, can be transmitted to infants through the mother's breast-milk, affecting their intellectual development or causing epilepsy (Theidon 2013: 44). For the Matsiguenka of the Amazonian Urubamba River regions too, emotions and health are inseparably connected; their verb *shinetagantsi* means both 'to be happy' and 'to be healthy' (Shepard 2002: 216). By giving rise to harmful emotions, interpersonal tensions are therefore widely considered to place the health of individuals and communities at risk. Indeed, a national survey of rural communities found that mental disorders were predominantly attributed to family difficulties or loss of loved ones (Saavedra and Uchofen-Herrera 2016). For some in indigenous communities, it may be equally important to health to remain on good terms with non-human spiritual entities through appropriate offerings.

In Andean culture, the body is seen as a relatively 'open' system, hence its perviousness to the forces of emotions and to the influence of the environment. For example, a commonly identified cause of illness or madness is the effects of 'winds' (Qu: *huayra*), which may have direct physiological effects but can also carry malign spiritual influences (Larme 1998). Another risk for humans is the loss of the 'soul', an animating form of energy known as the '*ánimo*'. This often occurs as the result of a fright, which may be occasioned by a range of triggers either supernatural or mundane, from a 'hungry earth' spirit snatching the *ánimo* of the unwary wanderer, to an actual or near-miss traffic accident. Though primarily associated with infants, who are most vulnerable to it, *susto* (Sp.), or *mancharisqa* as it is called in Quechua, can give rise to madness, mental distress or socially unacceptable behaviours in adults. A healing ceremony may be needed to call the errant *ánimo* (Greenway 1998).

Some of the most extensive work mapping cultural concepts of distress has taken place among Quechua-speaking communities in Ayacucho, as part of efforts to address the aftermath of conflict. Projects carried out in collaboration by the Universities of McGill and Cayetano Heredia made important contributions. They revealed important idioms of distress – locally meaningful ways of expressing suffering – among survivors. It is important for mental health practitioners to recognise these idioms to improve clinical communication, rapport and diagnosis, as screening and intervention for traumatic experiences should be informed by locally-relevant conceptualisations if they are to be maximally effective. Study participants spoke about the state of *pinsamientuwan* (Pedersen et al. 2008, 2010). This term means 'with thoughts' or 'worries', but at its extremes, one can become *tutal pinsamientuwan* (consumed by one's thoughts/concerns, unable to think of anything else) or *manan pinsamientuwan* (maddened, driven out of one's reason). The state of *pinsamientuwan* was closely linked to experiences of bodily pain (*nanay*), often viewed by practitioners as somatization. At the root of *pinsamientuwan* are the sources of sadness, and here an important distinction emerged between two idioms: *llaki*, corresponding to personal sorrows and internalized sadness, and *ñakary*, referring to suffering that is collective, arising from hardships shared by other community members and less closely correlated with the symptoms of *pinsamientuwan*. Cutting across both idioms were not just the violence, abuses and losses of the conflict years, but the longer-term conditions of deprivation spoken of as living *vida pobre* ('poor lives'). The significance of this is reflected in the finding that the groups most vulnerable to the psychological effects of traumatic experiences, whether defined through PTSD criteria or through local classifications of suffering, were those with reduced social networks and limited means of earning income (Pedersen et al. 2008). Local emphasis on the centrality of poverty and marginalization to psychosocial distress and mental disorder in this way is a regular finding in studies of community understandings stretching far beyond Ayacucho alone (Darghouth et al. 2006; Orr 2013).

Contemporary practice in mental health

The spread of CMHCs is making mental health treatment more readily available. Psychopharmaceutical medication is accessible in most urban areas, with costs assessed by social workers according to patients' means, but there is heavy reliance on cheaper, generic versions. Prescribing doctors are conscious of affordability constraints and how these pose difficulties for compliance with medication regimes (Claux 2018). Among psychological therapies, cognitive-behavioural approaches predominate, but some practitioners draw on psychodynamic and systems theories (Alarcón 2000; Claux 2018). Cost considerations have often limited access to psychological therapies for poorer patients, though requirements for many psychologists to perform rural service early in their careers and the new mental health reforms mitigate this to a degree.

The *Hospital Hermilio Valdizán* is Lima's specialist public psychiatric hospital. It offers treatment for psychiatric conditions and substance misuse, completing 87,379 out-patient consultations in 2017 and admitting 864 in-patients (MINSA 2018b). Apart from the provision of medication, patients may be offered cognitive-behavioural or systemic psychological therapies. Although its location in Lima means it has less trouble attracting qualified professionals than institutions in some other regions, high levels of demand and the limited socio-economic resources of many patients are an inescapable challenge for practitioners there. In this, the *Valdizán* faithfully reflects conditions faced by mental health services throughout the country.

The work on idioms of distress described earlier is now increasingly referenced in the Peruvian clinical literature. As well as informing clinical work with trauma with culturally contextualised understandings, the McGill-Cayetano Heredia collaboration gave rise to interventions rooted in community psychology and cultural perspectives, with participatory community workshops designed to support recovery of community trust and cohesion, a revalorisation of collective past history and achievements, and underpin effective collaboration in the present. These workshops encountered many challenges, including unpredictable funding streams, difficulties in embedding a shift from established hierarchical to participatory approaches, and the extent to which social bonds had broken down locally during the conflict. Nevertheless, they made an important contribution, not least in helping to restore to participants a sense of positive identity and community achievements that several had lost after so many years in which their society had known primarily violence, division and terror (Rivera-Holguin et al. 2018; Ramos and Mendoza 2008). This is one instance of creative mental health support for communities, but resilience, coping and reconciliation have been explored through different ways of meaning-making and pursuing recognition. Recognising the strengths affected individuals themselves draw on, these have taken the form of arts-based expression, political activism and community-driven ritual practice as often as formal therapy, with mental health practitioners acting as companions rather than guides (e.g. Rojas-Perez 2017).

Future directions

Mental health has moved up the agenda significantly in Peru's recent history and increased awareness of culture is to be welcomed, not least for the new respect it signals for long-marginalized identities. However, it will be important to evaluate systemically what effects the commitment to *interculturalidad* is having on practice and outcomes; careful research is needed to track how the concept and set of values are translated from policy through to the experience of the people who receive services. Growing awareness of the importance of a gender perspective on mental health is also an important development.

Perhaps the key challenge as Peruvian mental health provision expands will be to ensure expertise from experience occupies a central place at the heart of ongoing developments. If this can be achieved, with full representation of diversity made integral to the community mental health project, it will be the most effective safeguard to ensure that cultural concepts of distress and the practice of *interculturalidad* are incorporated into practice in meaningful ways.

Conclusion

The centrality of culture to mental health in Peru is widely recognised. Encouragingly, the range of widely held understandings of emotions, illness and health has been quite thoroughly

Culture and Mental Health in Peru

mapped in many Peruvian communities. However, it often remains unclear how these can best be integrated into clinical or community practice (Claux 2018), and individual practitioners may be left to find their own accommodation with the cultural concepts they encounter. The national expansion of mental health provision presents an opportunity, but there is the risk too of locally meaningful perspectives on health and well-being not being adequately taken into account. In doing so, attention must be given not only to cultural idioms and ethnopsychologies, but also to the structural inequalities so clearly identified by those living them as key contributions to incidence of psychosocial distress. An important starting-point lies in truly listening to what the individuals at the sharp edge of trauma, *llaki* and other forms of distress have to tell us about their experiences, with a historically and anthropologically-informed awareness of the social forces in which those experiences are grounded.

Acknowledgements

I am deeply grateful to the practitioners, healers and experts by experience who let me learn from them in Peru; Ines Bustamante; Grimanesa Toledo Alvarez; and the editors of this volume for their sterling work.

Notes

1 Chewing of coca leaves is a traditional indigenous practice in the Andes which has historically attracted criticism from the dominant classes. There is minimal evidence to support Valdizán's view on this matter.
2 Cognitive-behavioural and, to a much lesser extent, psychoanalytic approaches predominate among them (Alarcón 2000).

References

Alarcón, R. (2000) *Historia de la Psicología en el Perú: de la colonia a la república*. Lima: Universidad Ricardo Palma.
Archibald, P. (2000) *Imagining Modernity in the Andes*. Lewisburg, PA: Bucknell University Press.
Asociación Psiquiátrica Peruana (2018) *Relación de Asociados al 2018*. https://www.app.org.pe/pdf/asociados-app.pdf (Downloaded 4 July 2019).
Blaisdell, A. and Ødegaard, C.V. (2014) 'Losing fat, gaining treatment: a qualitative study of the uses of bio-medicine as a cure for traditional illnesses,' *Journal of Ethnobiology and Ethnomedicine*, 10:52. doi:10.1186/1746-4269-10-52.
Bussmann, R.W. and Sharon, D. (2006) 'Traditional medicinal plant use in Northern Peru: tracking two thousand years of healing culture,' *Journal of Ethnobiology and Ethnomedicine*, 2:47. doi: 10.1186/1746-4269-2-47.
Claux, J.A. (2018) *The Social Route: Peruvian psychiatrists and the politics of mental health reform*. PhD dissertation, University of Edinburgh. www.era.lib.ed.ac.uk/handle/1842/33227.
Crandon-Malamud, L. (1993) *From the Fat of Our Souls: Social change, political process, and medical pluralism in Bolivia*. Berkeley: University of California Press.
Darghouth, S., Pedersen, D., Bibeau, G. and Rousseau, C. (2006) 'Painful languages of the body: experiences of headache among women in two Peruvian communities,' *Culture, Medicine, and Psychiatry*, 30(3):271–297.
Defensoría del Pueblo (2005) *Salud mental y derechos humanos: La situación de las personas internadas en establecimientos de salud mental*. Lima: Defensoría del Pueblo.
Elferink, J.G.R. (1999) 'Mental disorder among the Incas in ancient Peru,' *History of Psychiatry*, 10:303–318.
Estenssoro Fuchs, J.C. (2003) *Del paganismo a la santidad*. Lima: IFEA.
García, M.E. (2005) *Making Indigenous Citizens: Identity, development, and multicultural activism in Peru*. Stanford: Stanford University Press.
Gold, C.L. and Clapp, R.A. (2011) 'Negotiating health and identity: Lay healing, medicinal plants, and indigenous healthscapes in highland Peru,' *Latin American Research Review*, 46(3):93–111.

Greene, S. (1998) 'The shaman's needle: development, shamanic agency, and intermedicality in Aguaruna Lands, Peru,' *American Ethnologist*, 25(4):634–658.

Greenway, C. (1998) 'Hungry earth and vengeful stars: Soul loss and identity in the Peruvian Andes,' *Social Science & Medicine*, 47(8):993–1004.

Instituto Nacional de Estadística e Informática (2017) *Perú: Perfil Sociodemográfico. Informe Principal. Censos Nacionales 2017*. https://www.inei.gob.pe/media/MenuRecursivo/publicaciones_digitales/Est/Lib1539/index.html (Downloaded 10 January 2019).

Izquierdo, C. (2005) 'When "health" is not enough: Societal, individual and biomedical assessments of well-being among the Matsigenka of the Peruvian Amazon,' *Social Science & Medicine*, 61:767–783.

Larme, A. (1998) 'Environment, vulnerability, and gender in Andean ethnomedicine,' *Social Science & Medicine,* 47(8):1005–1015.

Lerner, S. (2003) *Peruvian Commission on Truth and Reconciliation: Presentation of the Final Report*. https://revista.drclas.harvard.edu/book/peruvian-commission-truth-and-reconciliation (Downloaded 15 January 2019).

Mariateguí, J. (1988) *Salud mental y realidad nacional*. Lima: Asociación Psiquiátrica Peruana.

Mathez-Stiefel, S., Vandebroek, I. and Rist, S. (2012) 'Can Andean medicine coexist with biomedical healthcare? A comparison of two rural communities in Peru and Bolivia,' *Journal of Ethnobiology and Ethnomedicine*, 8:26. doi:10.1186/1746-4269-8-26.

Ministerio de Cultura (n.d.) *Alerta contra el racismo*. http://alertacontraelracismo.pe/informate/investigaciones (downloaded 15 January 2019).

MINSA (2018a) *Plan Nacional de Fortalecimiento de Servicios de Salud Mental Comunitaria 2018–2021*. Lima: Ministerio de Salud.

MINSA (2018b) *Plan Operativo Anual 2018: Hospital Hermilio Valdizán*. www.hhv.gob.pe/wp-content/uploads/Transparencia/Plan-Operativo/poa_2018.pdf (Downloaded 5 July 2019).

Orr, D.M.R. (2004) *Alienists in the Andes: The views of mental health professionals on culture and mental disorder in southern Peru*. Unpublished Manuscript.

Orr, D.M.R. (2012) 'Patterns of persistence amidst medical pluralism: Pathways toward cure in the southern Peruvian Andes,' *Medical Anthropology*, 31(6):514–530.

Orr, D.M.R. (2013) '"Now he walks and walks, as if he didn't have a home where he could eat": Food, healing, and hunger in Quechua narratives of madness,' *Culture, Medicine and Psychiatry*, 37(4):694–710.

Papponet-Cantat, C. (1995) 'How health care really works: The case of an Andean community in southern Cusco, Peru,' *Anthropologica*, 37(2):123–139.

Pedersen, D., Kienzler, H. and Gamarra, J. (2010) 'Llaki and ñakary: Idioms of distress and suffering among the highland Quechua in the Peruvian Andes,' *Culture, Medicine, and Psychiatry*, 34(2):279–300.

Pedersen, D., Tremblay, J., Errázuriz, C. and Gamarra, J. (2008) 'The sequelae of political violence: Assessing trauma, suffering and dislocation in the Peruvian highlands,' *Social Science & Medicine* 67:205–217.

Platt, T. (1997) 'The sound of light: Emergent communication in Quechua shamanic dialogue,'. In R. Howard-Malverde (Ed.), *Creating context in Andean cultures* (pp. 196–226). Oxford: Oxford University Press.

Ramos, M.A. and Mendoza, M. (2008) *Evaluación del proyecto fortaleciendo las redes sociales de las comunidades campesinas de Lucanas y Santiago de Vado*. Lima: Universidad Peruana Cayetano Heredia.

Ricard Lanata, X. (2007) *Ladrones de Sombra: El universe religioso de los pastores del Ausangate*. Lima: Instituto de Estudios Peruanos.

Rivera-Holguin, M., Velazquez, T., Custodio, E. and Corveleyn, J. (2018) 'Improving community mental health services for people affected by political violence in Ayacucho, Peru,' *Journal of Prevention & Intervention in the Community*, 46(1):100–112.

Rojas-Perez, I. (2017) *Mourning Remains: State atrocity, exhumations, and governing the disappeared in Peru's postwar Andes*. Stanford: Stanford University Press.

Saavedra, J.E. and Uchofen-Herrera, V. (2016) 'Percepciones sobre la atención de salud en personas con problemas autoidentificados de salud mental en zonas rurales del Perú,' *Revista Peruana de Medicina Experimental y Salud Pública* 33(4):785–793.

Samuel, J. and Frisancho, A. (2015) 'Rights-based citizen monitoring in Peru: Evidence of impact from the field,' *Health and Human Rights Journal*, 17(2):123–134.

Seguín, C. (1951) 'Síndrome psicosomático de desadaptación,' *Revista Latinoamericana de Psiquiatría*, 1:16–26.

Shepard, G. (2002) 'Three days for weeping: Dreams, emotions and death in the Peruvian Amazon,' *Medical Anthropology Quarterly*, 16(2):200–229.

Culture and Mental Health in Peru

Shuger, D. (2012) *Don Quixote in the archives: Madness in life and literature in early modern Spain.* Edinburgh: University of Edinburgh Press.

Stucchi Portocarrero, S. (2012) *Loquerías, manicomios y hospitales psiquiátricos de Lima.* Lima: Universidad Peruana Cayetano Heredia.

Tapias, M. (2015) *Embodied protests: Emotions and women's health in Bolivia.* Urbana: University of Illinois Press.

Theidon, K. (2013) *Intimate Enemies: Violence and reconciliation in Peru.* Philadelphia: University of Pennsylvania Press.

Thorp, R. and Paredes, M. (2010) *Ethnicity and the persistence of inequality: The case of Peru.* Basingstoke: Palgrave Macmillan.

Toyama, M., Castillo, H., Galea, J., Brandt, L., Mendoza, M., Herrera, V., Mitrani, M., Cutipe, Y., Cavero, V., Diez-Canseco, F. and Miranda, J.J. (2017) 'Peruvian mental health reform: A framework for scaling up mental health services,' *International Journal of Health Policy Management* 6(9):501–508.

Valdivia Ponce, O. (1975) *Hampicamayoc: Medicina folklórica y su substrato aborigen en el Perú.* Lima: Universidad Nacional Mayor de San Marcos.

Valdizán, H. (1988[1918]) *Locos de la Colonia.* Lima: Instituto Nacional de Cultura.

World Health Organization (2013) *WHO Traditional Medicine Strategy 2014–2023.* Geneva: WHO.

World Health Organization and Calouste Gulbenkian Foundation (2014) *Social Determinants of Mental Health.* Geneva: WHO.

38

CULTURE AND MENTAL HEALTH IN THE PHILIPPINES

Antover P. Tuliao, Angelica V. Ang, Melissa R. Garabiles,
Minerva D. Tuliao and Maria Cristina Samaco-Zamora

Researchers based in Western industrialized countries have often been puzzled why Filipinos and Filipino immigrants tend to underutilize mental health services and continue to patronize folk healers to address both physical and psychological ailments. Scholars note that compared to 18% of the general U.S. population (Wang et al. 2005), only 5% of Filipino Americans and Filipino immigrants to the United States sought professional mental health services, whereas 15% sought help from their lay networks and folk healers for psychological issues (Gong et al. 2003). Part of this bewilderment seems to stem from an underlying assumption that Western medical models of mental health (presumed to be 'scientific' and 'empirical') are incompatible with lay and folk models.

The goal of this chapter is to provide readers with an overview of how the 'science versus folk medicine dialectic' plays out in the Philippines. The chapter begins with a brief discussion of the Philippines's colonial history, and how it has an impact of current mental health practices. Cultural conceptualizations of mental illness and wellness, and Indigenous treatments for psychological problems will be presented. Case presentations will also highlight how the medical model and Indigenous beliefs are practised in Philippines, particularly how the two seemingly disparate paradigms are integrated. The chapter ends with a discussion of areas for future research, particularly those that would help improve mental health among Filipinos.

Country demographics and a brief history of mental health

To better understand mental health in the Philippines, it is essential to provide a geographical and historical context. Sanchez and Gaw (2007) argues that the Philippine culture is an amalgamation of different cultures. As an archipelago of 7,107 islands located in Southeast Asia (Central Intelligence Agency [CIA] 2013), the Philippine culture is influenced by the surrounding Indo-Malay, Chinese, and Islamic cultures (Majul 1966; Miclat 2000). Prior to the Spanish colonization in the 16th century, the Philippines was comprised of autonomous principalities and kingdoms (Bernad 1971). This precolonial political system influenced the Filipino tendency towards regionalism (Bernad 1971) and the heterogeneity in language, with the Philippines having eight major dialects, although Filipino and English are the main languages (CIA 2013).

Currently, there are an estimated 94 million Filipinos in the Philippines and an estimated 8 million employed in different parts of the world as short-term overseas migrant workers (Philippine Overseas Employment Agency 2008; World Health Organization [WHO] 2011). Almost half (49%) of the population lives in urban centers, and gender distributions are relatively equal (WHO 2011). Majority of the population is between the ages of 15 and 65 (62%), and 34% are below 15. The literacy rates are 84% for males and 89% for females (WHO 2011), and poverty rate is at 61% (National Statistics Office 2010).

Precolonial Philippines and the Spanish colonization

The Philippines roughly has four historical eras (Francia 2014), with each having an impact on the country's mental health: (1) precolonial, (2) Spanish colonization, (3) American colonization; and (4) post-colonial Philippines. Psychological issues and treatment during precolonial Philippines were based on magical, spiritual, and animistic beliefs (Reid 1988; Scott 2004), much of which persists to this day (discussed in later sections).

After the defeat of the local chieftain, Spain occupied Manila in 1572 and designated it as the seat of Spanish power in the Philippine Islands (Francia 2014). Three centuries of Spanish colonization significantly influenced Philippine culture, particularly in introducing Roman Catholicism. Currently, Roman Catholicism is the predominant religion (83%), followed by Islam (5%), and the rest is comprised of different Christian denominations (CIA 2013). Spain also introduced Western medicine with the establishment of Hospital Real in 1565, with other hospitals established thereafter being managed by various Catholic religious orders (Department of Health [DOH] 2014). Institutional care for the mentally ill began with the establishment of Hospicio De San Jose in 1782, which also took care of the sick, orphans, elderly, and those with special needs (Samaniego 2017). Documented accounts of mental illness included *locura o furor* (madness or rage), which was attributed to demonic possession which was consistent with lay conceptualizations of the time (Ladrido-Ignacio et al. 2017). Individuals with mental illness were brought either to the church or folk healers for purification and exorcism (Samaniego 2017).

American colonization

After Spain, the U.S. colonization from 1898 to 1946 also left an indelible mark on Philippine culture, education, political system, and mental health, particularly in the fields of psychiatry and psychology. It was during this period in 1904 that the first hospital unit dedicated to the mentally ill opened, the Insane Department of the San Lazaro Hospital (Samaniego 2017). The first Filipino psychiatrist, Elias Domingo, received his training from the U.S. and eventually headed the Insane Department of the San Lazaro Hospital (Samaniego 2017). In 1918, the City Sanitarium at San Juan del Monte was opened, and the first hospital dedicated to mental and nervous disorders (Insular Psychopathic Hospital) was established in December 18, 1928. With the establishment of the Philippine General Hospital in 1910, American physicians taught psychiatry to medical students (Samaniego 2017). It was also during this period that several physicians were sent to Harvard University to receive their psychiatry training (Samaniego 2017). Treatment of mentally ill in the early 1900s included somatic therapies (e.g., fever induction, insulin shock, and hydrotherapy), medication (e.g., barbiturates) and electroshock therapy (Samaniego 2017).

The psychology and counselling disciplines can also trace their academic lineage from the United States. Agustin Alonzo received his PhD in experimental psychology from the University of Chicago in 1926 and headed the first psychology department in the Philippines (Licuanan

1985). The first psychological clinic established in 1932 was headed by Sinforoso Padilla, PhD, an alumnus of the University of Michigan (Licuanan 1985). The Far Eastern University Psychological Clinic was established in 1933 by Jesus Perpiñan, who received his PhD in psychology from Iowa State University. Estefania Aldaba-Lim is credited as the first Filipino to receive training in clinical psychology (University of Michigan 1942), and she established the Institute of Human Relations at the Philippine Women's University in 1948 (Licuanan 1985).

Indigenous conceptualizations of psychological illness and treatment

Philippine folk conceptualizations of illnesses do not differentiate between physical and mental disorders, and Filipinos tend to conceptualize medical and psychological illnesses differently from the medical model (Araneta 1993; Tan 2008). Lay conceptualizations of physical and psychological disorders have implications for help seeking for and treatment of psychological disorders, particularly on the issue of the preference for Indigenous or folk healers. In one early study, Indigenous and folk healers were sought for 'disturbed behavior', as well as for somatic complaints that have no verified underlying medical causes (Shakman 1969). The importance of bodily symptoms without medical causes is made even more salient given that different cultural groups manifest psychological symptoms as somatic complaints (e.g., Tsai and Chentsova-Dutton 2002). Moreover, somatic symptoms are more emphasized than the affective component of depression among non-Western cultures (Tsai and Chentsova-Dutton 2002). For a thorough discussion on the Filipino traditional conceptualization of illnesses, see Tan (2008).

One core theme in the conceptualization of physical and psychological disorders implicates the role of supernatural beings and individuals with supernatural powers. Filipino Indigenous beliefs on physical and psychological illnesses stem from an animistic transpersonal worldview that human beings coexist with spirits who are not only invisible but also possess the power to either bring luck, or punishment and sickness (Bantug 1953). This model conceives the material world as inhabited by a variety of sprits living and occupying the same space as human beings (Recepcion 2007). Among the spirits, there is the Supreme Being (i.e., *Bathala*) and the lesser divinities (e.g., *diwata* or fairies, and *anito* or idols). Spirits can cause sickness or death, depending on how humans relate with them. In the same manner, there are those deities who protect men, heal the sick, and intercede for them to the *Bathala*.

Spiritual and animistic attributions of physical and psychological illnesses are still present. For instance, Edman and Kameoka's (1997) study reveal that Filipino women still attributed illnesses to spiritual causes (e.g., God, chance, witchcraft and sorcery, and spirits). Filipinos were also more likely to attribute the symptoms of dissociative disorders, depression, and other psychological illnesses to spirit possession or having offended the spirits (Ang 2018; Gingrich 2006; Tan 2008). Interestingly, there are a few Filipino psychologists who believe that disorders such as depression and narcissistic personality disorders create spiritual vulnerabilities, which attract evil spirits leading to spirit possession (Ang 2018). However, this conceptualization may not represent the views of many Western-trained Filipino psychologists (Ang 2018). Catholic images and themes also permeate the conceptualization of and expression of mental illness among Filipinos to this day. For instance, rather than being possessed by spirits, some schizophrenic delusions could involve possession of saints or the *Santo Niño* (Child Jesus; e.g., Lin et al. 1990).

Another core theme in conceptualizing physical and psychological disorders involves soul-loss, lack of balance, and pollution/contagion (Araneta 1993; Tan 2008). For instance, chronically ill elderly Filipino-American immigrants believe that the work-life imbalance, too much worrying, overworking, and elevated stress cause illnesses (Becker 2003). In addition, rapid shifts from a warm to cold environment cause illnesses, and health is maintained by keeping the body in a warm condition. Cholesterol and other toxins are thought to pollute the body, and perspiration is one way to flush these out. Behaviors such as indifference, withdrawal, irrationality, and nightmares (i.e., *bangungot*) are believed to be a result of 'soul-loss' (Araneta 1993).

Relationship problems are purported to also cause physical, as well as mental illnesses (Edman and Kameoka 1997). For instance, Filipino women living in Australia believe that the primary cause of depression is the lack of social support (Thompson et al. 2002). This prompts the attitude that mental health professionals are "not helpful … because a friend could fulfill the same role" (Thompson et al. 2002: 685). Mental illness is also perceived as a family problem that is inherited and runs in the blood (Tanaka et al. 2018). Consequently, mental illness is viewed as a problem that should be kept within the confines of the home. Emotional problems are considered transitory and relationship-related, and can be solved by talking to friends, family members, or trusted community members (Hechanova et al. 2011).

Other lay conceptualizations emphasize personal responsibility. Severe psychological problems are believed to be caused by a 'softness' or 'weakness' of character (Thompson et al. 2002) and a failure to meet cultural expectation of being resilient to challenges (Tanaka et al. 2018). Furthermore, being able to cope with one's emotional problems is also valued and is perceived to be one's own responsibility (Thompson et al. 2002). Perceived responsibility for one's own psychological wellness is one reason for the reluctance to seek professional help (Pinggolio and Mateo 2018). Furthermore, the perception that individuals with mental illness are soft and weak hinder them from receiving empathy and understanding from other people (Tanaka et al. 2018). Physical and psychological illnesses are also believed to be caused by *sumpâ* (curse) brought about by a violation of strict family values, or are caused by *gabâ*, a curse or retribution from God (Tan 2008).

There are also indications that Filipinos may consider some behaviors 'normal' that would otherwise be considered symptoms of psychological illness from a Western medical model. For instance, for the symptom of having large gaps in one's memory in dissociative disorders, 39% of the Filipino sample indicated that the symptom was still considered 'normal', 28% considered the symptom 'abnormal' only if the symptom was severe and experienced frequently, and 27% considered the symptom 'abnormal' (Gingrich 2006). Seventy-five percent of the sample also indicated that identity confusion was commonly experienced by their peers (Gingrich 2006). Gingrich (2006) argued that, because spirit possession is common and commonly accepted in the Philippine culture, some symptoms commonly associated with dissociative disorders in the West are somewhat accepted by Filipinos as normal.

Indigenous conceptualizations of wellness

Wellness is expressed as *kaginhawaan* in Filipino (Paz 2008). *Kaginhawaan* is the absence of want, a state of being at peace, and being free from problems (Paz 2008). It is also expressed as a state of feeling light and being able to breathe easily (*nakakahinga ng maluwag*; Paz 2008). Filipino conceptualizations and indicators of wellness cut across multiple domains, starting with material and financial security (Paz 2008; Samaco-Zamora and Fernandez 2016; Sycip et al. 2000). Wellness – or having a good life (*magandang buhay*) – entails having sufficient material things (e.g., having ample food, owning a house, and having livestock), adequate personal savings and wealth, having a stable household income, and finishing tertiary education, oftentimes thought of as an opportunity for upward socioeconomic mobility (Paz 2008; Sycip et al. 2000).

Economic indicators of wellness however are only secondary. Financial stability allows the family to meet basic needs, enjoy some luxuries, send children to school, and lead a comfortable life. Further, to be well means the family is worry-free, happy, and content. Having financial security assures the family's physical health. *Kaginhawaan*, therefore, is also conceptualized as family-centric (Samaco-Zamora and Fernandez, 2016). Wellness is also a product of socialization. It is important for Filipinos to take part in community celebrations and working together to achieve a goal like harvesting or building a house (Paz 2008; Samaco-Zamora and Fernandez 2016). Ladrido-Ignacio and Verzosa (2011) used the term *kapwa* to describe the Filipinos' yearning for a shared inner life, and the term *pakikipag-kapwa* or having a bond with others, including one's neighbors, community, and nature. In addition to having good relationships with the family and the community, a good relationship with God is also essential (Sycip et al. 2000). Participation in religious activities and spiritual life, having faith, attending church activities, and doing good to others are indicators of a good relationship with God. Also, when the family faces economic challenges, the family copes through prayers and turning to God (Samaco-Zamora and Fernandez 2016).

Indigenous treatments

Filipino traditional medicine has been around since the eighth century CE. Influence of traditional medicines from other countries may be traced to traders from China, India, and Persia visiting the Philippines even before the Spanish colonial era (Saydoven 2009). Traditional and complementary medicine being utilized today is an amalgamation of precolonial Indigenous practices with some influences from Ayurvedic and Chinese traditional medicine (Lagaya 2005; Saydoven 2009). The type of traditional and complementary medicine that Filipinos typically resort to complements the lay conceptualizations of physical and psychological disorders.

Filipino Indigenous healing stems from the belief that spirits can cause sickness or death. Similarly, there are also spirits who protect men, heal the sick, and intercede for them. To these deities, sacrifices and offerings are made to court favors or appease them in case of transgressions (Bantug 1953). Ancient Filipinos called upon a priestess, the *Katalonan* (as she was known among the Tagalogs or *Babaylan* among the Visayans), to invoke her gods and offer sacrifices whenever anyone fell ill. The *Katolonan* becomes the medium through which the spirit called upon possesses the priestess, communicates the prognosis and what had to be done to repair the relations between man and the spirit world (Bantug 1953; Salazar 1979).

Modern-day Indigenous healers, named after their preferred mode of treatment, include *albularyos* (herbologists), *manghihilot* (bonesetters), *mangtatawas* (those who use alum for diagnosis), and faith healers or *spiritista* (those who practice divination and folk exorcism; Salazar 1979). Healing practices also include exorcising the spirit or the witch inflicting the ailment by *hilot* (similar to acupressure or reflexology), hard patting (using the palm of the hand or a short wooden stick cut from a medicinal plant), and blowing prayers (Salazar 1979). Traditional healers also use medicinal plants for common physical ailments (Salazar 1979; Saydoven 2009). Massage and 'magnetic healing' (where the healer's hands are placed on the affected area, and the healer prays or meditates) are used to restore the normal flow and balance of life-force (Araneta 1993; Tan 2008). To relieve pain, reduce anxiety, improve state of mind, herbal medicines and massage are utilized by *manghihilot* and *albularyos* (Araneta 1993; Lagaya 2005).

Indigenous treatments in the Philippines today: The case of Mara

When Spanish colonizers brought Catholic Christianity to the Philippines, Indigenous practices were condemned as 'works of the devil' (Saydoven 2009). Indigenous healing practices however continues to survive despite the colonizing powers' efforts to suppress and supplant it (Salazar 1979). Filipinos residing in urban areas have been more exposed to the Western health care system, whereas traditional folk healers are still sought out in rural areas particularly for psychological symptoms (Valencia and Palo 1979). In general, modern-day traditional healers generally give way to medical doctors for medical diseases, but also claim the ability to heal diseases that modern medicine could not address (Salazar 1979). As discussed later, Filipinos can resort to both Indigenous and medical treatments at the same time without experiencing cognitive dissonance. However, especially in rural areas, traditional healers are sought over medical doctors. The case of Mara illustrates a present-day Indigenous approach to addressing mental health concerns (Ang 2018).

> *Mara, a 12-year-old female from the city, went to her family's hometown in Bukidnon, a rural province in the Philippines, for the summer break. Mara reported that her symptoms started when she urinated beside a large, 'mysterious' tree in the farm where she and her cousins harvested crops. The same evening, Mara became nauseous and ran a fever. Every night thereafter, Mara reported that a man would visit her, approaching her by the window of her bedroom, and he would entice her to join him. His visits would induce her 'spirit possession', somewhat similar to a delirium. During her episodes, Mara's family also reported that she would become violent and belligerent. Mara, however, had no recollection of being physically aggressive. Medical doctors were unable to diagnose the cause for her symptoms, which escalated over time. One night during one of her episodes, Mara reported that she followed the man and ate the food he offered to her. This event resulted in a two-day coma, and Mara's family thought she died. Upon waking, Mara was brought to an albularyo who made her drink an oily substance, hung her upside down, and 'beat' her (hard patting to the body using an implement like a long wooden stick) until she vomited a black substance. The albularyo told her family that the spirit possessing Mara wanted to bring her to his kingdom. For protection, the albularyo gave her a necklace to wear so the spirit could no longer trace her. Mara immediately got well, and the hallucinations and delirium stopped.*

Mental health professionals in the Philippines

The practice of psychiatry and psychotherapy in the Philippines began during the American regime. To date, Western concepts and models of psychiatry, counselling, and psychotherapy continue to influence both the training and practice of psychologists and psychiatrists in the Philippines (Della 2012; Samaniego 2017). At present, four general professions are legally recognized to provide mental health services: guidance and counselling practitioners (Guidance and Counselling Act of 2004); psychologists (Philippine Psychology Act of 2009); social workers (Republic Act [RA] 4373); and, those under the umbrella of the medical professions. Under the Guidance and Counselling Act, a licensed guidance counsellor must have a Master's degree in guidance and counselling and must have passed the licensure examination. Between 2013 and 2018, an average of 394 Filipinos a year passed the Guidance and Counselling board exams and are license-eligible. Currently, there are only 2,431 licensed guidance and counselling practitioners, which is small compared to the estimated need of 37,000 (for a primer, see www.prc.gov.ph/sites/default/files/Guidance%20Counselor_PRIMER.pdf).

Professional regulation for psychometricians and psychologists only occurred after the Philippine Psychology Act of 2009. To be license-eligible, a psychometrician must have a Bachelor's degree in psychology and must have passed the licensure exams (for a primer, see www.prc.gov.ph/sites/default/files/Psychometrician_PRIMER.pdf). Between 2014 and 2018, an average of 5,559 Filipinos passed the psychometrician licensure exam. A psychologist, on the other hand, is required to have a Master's degree in psychology and have undergone supervised clinical internship in addition to passing the psychologist licensure exam (for a primer, see www.prc.gov.ph/sites/default/files/Psychologist_PRIMER.pdf). An average of 71 Filipinos per year passed the licensure exam between 2014 and 2018. Both licensed guidance counsellors and psychologists are permitted to perform individual and group interventions and assessments. However, psychometricians are only permitted to administer and interpret psychological tests under the supervision of a licensed psychologist.

Licensed social workers are also permitted to provide individual and group interventions within organized social service institutions and using social work methods (e.g., social work counselling, provision of family and child services, and casework and groupwork; RA 4373; for primer, see https://prc.gov.ph/uploaded/documents/Social%20Worker_PRIMER.pdf). A licensed social worker needs to have at least a Bachelor's degree in social work, should have completed a minimum of 1,000 supervised case hours of practical training, and passed the licensure exam. Between 2011 and 2015, an average of 1128 Filipinos passed the social worker licensure exam per year.

In the Philippines, there are between 400 and 500 Philippine Psychiatric Association accredited psychiatrists (Samaniego 2017; also see http://ppa.philpsych.ph/all-listings/). After six years of medical school, clerkship, and internship and passing the medical board examinations, a medical doctor can specialize in psychiatry. There are 13 institutions that offer postgraduate psychiatry training in the Philippines (eight of which are based in the Philippines capital of Manila), and postgraduate residency training can range between three to four years (Samaniego 2017). New psychiatrists are awarded the Diplomate of the Specialty Board of Philippine Psychiatry after residency training and successfully passing the Diplomate Board Examination (Samaniego 2017).

Studies suggest that there are not enough mental health professionals and facilities in the Philippines. The school counsellor to client ratio is 1:800 to 1:1,000 (Villar 2000) and only 60% of primary and secondary schools have either a part-time or full-time mental health professional (WHO 2006). Research suggests that there are 0.40 psychiatrists, 0.40 psychiatric nurses, 0.14 psychologists, 0.08 social workers, and 0.08 occupational therapists per 100,000 general population (Jacob et al. 2007; WHO 2006). There are only 19 community-based psychiatric inpatient units, 15 community residential facilities, 46 outpatient mental health facilities, and four day-treatment facilities which treat 4.42 users per 100,000, majority of which are located in urban centers (Conde 2004; WHO 2006). Medical doctors (one for every 80,000) are also scarce compared to traditional healers (one for every 300), which could perpetuate the Filipino's reliance on folk medicine (WHO and DOH 2012).

In 2017, the Mental Health Act (Republic Act 11036) was passed in order to enhance mental health services. However, due to the nascency of this law and the laws professionalizing psychologists, psychometricians, and guidance counsellors, no research is yet available on how these recent changes have affected utilization of mental health services. In addition, no information is readily available for other mental health professionals, such as addiction counsellors and pastoral counsellors.

Integrating Indigenous and Western-based mental health practices

Given the impact of American colonization on Philippine education, the practice of psychiatry, counselling, and psychotherapy is patterned after Western-based mental health practices. However, the 1970s saw the rise of *Sikolohiyang Pilipino* (Filipino Psychology), which is a reaction to and a resistance towards the hegemony of Western and American psychology in the Philippines (Conaco 2005; Pe-Pua and Marcelino 2000). Virgilio G. Enriquez, the father of *Sikolohiyang Pilipino*, questioned the validity and applicability of Western psychological concepts and methodologies to Filipinos. Enriquez advocated for a truly universal and inclusive psychology through the use of culturally appropriate research methodologies and through understanding Filipino thought and experience from a Filipino perspective (Pe-Pua and Marcelino 2000).

The *Sikolohiyang Pilipino* movement has inspired other Filipino researchers and practitioners to question the applicability of Anglocentric mental health practices. The initial uncontested adoption of Western approaches such as Freudian psychoanalysis has been criticized (e.g., Marcelino 1990). There have been efforts to understand psychopathology (e.g., Gingrich 2006) and wellness (e.g., Ladrido-Ignacio and Verzosa 2011) from a Filipino perspective. There have also been steps to utilize Indigenous beliefs and practices for psychological treatment. For example, Bulatao (1982), upon noting the ease with which Filipinos enter altered states of consciousness, used techniques of hypnosis to treat those suffering from dissociative symptoms. Using a form of "psychological exorcism" (Bulatao 1982: 58), Bulatao's approach aimed to enter the world of the client "as if he too were following the folk model" (Bulatao 1982: 420) while using hypnosis to exorcise the imaginal spirits which he regarded as "thought forms" (Bulatao 1982: 420) constructed by the mind.

Adapting Western-based practices to address the needs of Filipinos

Efforts to fully indigenize psychotherapeutic approaches have been minimal. In integrating Indigenous and Western-based practices, the current trend seems to be the identification of psychotherapeutic approaches and techniques that are best suited to Filipinos. Practitioners have noted that, among the Western approaches, behavior modification, client-centered counselling (Lagmay 1984), and approaches involving the family (Tuason et al. 2012) suit the needs of the clients and accounts for the Filipino values of family belongingness and group-centeredness. Another trend is the adaptation of existing evidence-based treatments to the Filipino culture. For instance, in developing a resiliency intervention for Filipino disaster survivors, spiritual coping and addressing maladaptive thoughts about God (e.g., the disaster was a punishment from God) was included in the program given Filipinos' propensity to use spiritual coping (Hechanova et al. 2015). The intervention, however, is based on Western, contemporary cognitive-behavioral therapeutic techniques.

Western-based mental health practices are also being adapted to address issues that are endemic to the Philippine context, such as those associated with poverty, transnational migrant work, crime and trauma, and frequent natural disasters (e.g., typhoons; Tuason et al. 2012). The case of Dina exemplifies this, in particular how a 'wrap-around' care or case management addresses several issues related to the family, poverty, and transnational migrant work:

Dina is a Filipino domestic worker in Hong Kong. She has a husband and a 2-year old son who remained in the Philippines. As a first-time domestic worker, Dina experienced physical and verbal abuse from her employer for six months. She lost almost a third of her weight after eating only instant noodles every day. She also had no days off and no contact with her family during her entire stay. Dina now lives in a shelter for abused domestic workers. She filed a case against her employer but needs to stay abroad throughout the proceedings before she can return to the Philippines. Although presently safe from harm, Dina has flashbacks of the abuse. She also feels guilty for leaving her family and feels anxious about her return. Aside from offering a temporary home, the shelter also brings a Filipino psychologist twice a year to provide counselling. Using brief solution-focused therapy (a Western-based psychotherapeutic technique), the psychologist helped Dina focus on concrete steps to bounce back from the abuse and to reunite with her family. They discussed how she could regain her weight, in coordination with a local medical doctor and the shelter's resident advocate. They reviewed other resources she could access while abroad, including attending masses at church and vocational training seminars at the Philippine Consulate, attending free meditation sessions, and searching for medical and financial benefits offered by Philippine governmental agencies. They also discussed how she could reintegrate with her family from abroad. Through regular online communication, she could reintroduce herself to her son, rekindle her marital relationship, and plan how she and her husband could find new ways to earn money.

Indigenous and Western medicine practised side-by-side

Traditional practices and Western medicine can also be utilized simultaneously and in parallel with each other. There is a tacit recognition among folk healers and religious leaders that there are ailments that are beyond their practice, and would refer clients to medical doctors (Ang 2018). The same is true for psychiatrists, counsellors, and psychologists. The case of Sister Caroline illustrates how traditional and medical treatments, two seemingly incompatible healing perspectives, are used (Ang 2018):

> *Caroline is a 43-year old nun who was brought to a hospital by her fellow sisters due to observed changes in her behavior. She has become more wild, violent, and suspicious of others. The psychiatrist diagnosed Caroline with schizophrenia and prescribed antipsychotic medications which provided some temporary relief. However, Caroline's paranoia and psychosis escalated. She would complain of diabolic activity in the convent and would show prints on her arm which she claimed to be the devil's fingers. She further isolated herself from others who she believed were plotting against her. Organic brain lesions were ruled out. In addition to antipsychotic medications, Caroline was referred to a psychologist to address paranoid ideations and an exorcist to find out if evil spirits were indeed harming her. The exorcist team prayed over her as they believed she was harassed, not possessed, by evil spirits. The religious sisters and the exorcist believed that her illness created spiritual openings for these oppressions. Caroline subsequently stayed in treatment with the support of the sisters and their superior. Improved rapport with her psychiatrist led to better follow up. She continued to have poor insight but had no more violent episodes. Her impulse control likewise improved. Caroline continued to have a strong prayer life.*

Caroline's case demonstrates the healing of a patient suffering on different levels which includes the neurological, psychological, and the spiritual. The integrated healing could not have come about without addressing the neurochemical imbalance as well as without hearing how the client and the religious community conceptualized Caroline's illness. Caroline's improved cooperation with her psychiatrist may well have been a result of having a sense of validation that she was indeed experiencing demonic oppression caused by her illness.

Future directions

The need to provide mental health services to Filipinos cannot be emphasized enough. Increasing the number of and improving access to mental health professionals is needed. Moreover, the question of how best to provide these services and what gaps to address are still unanswered. Reducing perceived stigma to seeking mental health services is one area of research that can aid in increasing service utilization. In comparison to their U.S. counterparts, Filipinos still have a significantly higher perceived stigma to seeking mental health services (Tuliao 2018). Other areas of research are assessment of models and validation of measures, which are usually created in Western contexts and investigated among Western populations. Psychometric research is crucial in improving diagnosis and in understanding etiology, maintenance, and risk factors of disorders (Elhai and Palmieri 2011).

Another way to narrow the discrepancies in utilization of mental health services is through a better understanding of the lay conceptualizations of mental illness, cultural expressions of psychopathology, and culture-bound illnesses (Lopez and Guarnaccia, 2000; Sue et al. 2012). The rationale is straightforward: The type of help sought will depend on how the mental illness is defined and what the etiological attributions are. Given Filipinos' preference for lay support, spiritual leaders, and folk healers to help address mental health issues (Gong et al. 2003), it is also worthwhile to examine how these social networks can be utilized to help reduce stigma and as possible mental health paraprofessionals. Furthermore, given the centrality of family in the perceived etiology of mental illness and in wellness, it is also essential to examine how family members can be mobilized to achieve psychological health. Moreover, school counsellors can be tapped more as students are more willing to seek help from them than psychiatrists (Pinggolio and Mateo 2018).

Conclusion

The Philippines has a rich history of folklore and Western colonization that still influence conceptualizations of mental health today. As evidenced by the passing of recent mental health laws and continuing research that integrate Western and Indigenous approaches, the country shows promise in improving mental health services. The adaptation of mental health interventions illustrates the strong and continuing Western influence on the practice of Philippine mental health care. However, there are also continued attempts to increase cultural sensitivity by way of accommodating lay conceptualizations of mental health and wellness and in considering the specific socio-cultural, historical, economic, and political context of the Filipinos.

References

Ang, A. (2018) *Understanding spirit possession: A social representations approach* (Unpublished doctoral dissertation). Ateneo de Manila University, Quezon City, Philippines.

Araneta, E.G. (1993) 'Psychiatric Care of Filipino Americans'. In A.C. Gaw (Ed.), *Culture, Ethnicity, and Mental Illness* (pp. 377–411). Washington, DC: American Psychiatric Press.

Bantug, J.P. (1953) *A short history of medicine in the Philippines during the Spanish Regime, 1565 – 1898.* Colegio Médico-Far-macéutico de Filipinas. Retrieved from http://digitallibrary.ust.edu.ph/cdm/fullbrowser/collection/section5/id/49479/rv/compoundobject/cpd/49741.

Becker, G. (2003) 'Cultural Expressions of Bodily Awareness Among Chronically Ill Filipino Americans'. *Annals of Family Medicine*, 1(2): 113–118.

Bernad, M.A. (1971) 'Philippine Culture and the Filipino Identity', *Philippine Studies*,, 19(4): 573–592.

Bulatao, J. (1982) 'Local Cases of Possession and Their Cure', *Philippine Studies*,, 30: 415–425.

Central Intelligence Agency (2013). *The World Factbook: Philippines*,, Retrieved from: www.cia.gov/library/publications/the-world-factbook/geos/rp.html.

Conaco, M.C.G. (2005) 'The Development of a Filipino Indigenous Psychology'. *Philippine Journal of Psychology*, 38(2): 1–17.

Conde, B. (2004) 'Philippines Mental Health Country Profile'. *International Review of Psychiatry*,, 16(1–2):159–166.

Della, C.D. (2012) 'Culture and Psychotherapy: A Psychosocial Framework for Analysis'. *Acta Medica Philippina*, 46(1): 57–62.

Department of Health (2014) *The Department of Health Story: A Legacy of Public Health* (2nd Ed.). Tayuman and Manila: Department of Health.

Edman, J.L. and Kameoka, V.A. (1997) 'Cultural Differences in Illness Schemas: An Analysis of Filipino and American Illness Attributions'. *Journal of Cross-Cultural Psychology*, 28(3): 252–265.

Elhai, J.D., and Palmieri, P.A. (2011) 'The Factor Structure of Posttraumatic Stress Disorder: A Literature Update, Critique of Methodology, and Agenda for Future Research' *Journal of Anxiety Disorders*, 25(6): 849–854.

Francia, L.H. (2014) *A History of the Philippines: From Indios Bravos to Filipinos.* New York, NY: The Overlook Press.

Gingrich, H.J.D. (2006) 'An Examination of Dissociative Symptoms as They Relate to Indigenous Filipino Concepts'. *Social Science Diliman*, 3(1–2): 1–48.

Gong, F., Gage, S.J. and Tacata, L.A. (2003) 'Helpseeking Behavior Among Filipino Americans: A Cultural Analysis of Face and Language', *Journal of Community Psychology*, 31(5): 469–488.

Guidance and Counseling Act (2004) *Republic Act No. 9258.*

Hechanova, M.R.M., Ramos, P. and Waelde, L. (2015) 'Group-Based Mindfulness-Informed Psychological First Aid After Typhoon Haiyan'. *Disaster Prevention and Management*, 24(5): 610–618.

Hechanova, M.R.M., Tuliao, A.P. and Ang, P.H. (2011) 'If You Build It, Will They Come?: Prospects and Challenges in Online Counseling for Overseas Migrant Workers'. *Media Asia*, 38(1): 32–40.

Hechanova, M.R.M., Waelde, L.C., Docena, P.S., Alampay, L.P., Alianan, Flores, A.S. and Melgar, M.I.E. (2015) 'The Development and Initial Evaluation of *Katatagan*: A Resilience Intervention for Filipino Disaster Survivors'. *Philippine Journal of Psychology*, 48(2): 105–131.

Jacob, K.S., Sharan, P., Mirza, I., Garrido-Cumbrera, M., Seedat, S., Mari, J.J., Sreenivas, V. and Saxena, S. (2007) 'Mental Health Systems in Countries: Where Are We Now?' *The Lancet 370*, 9562: 161–1077.

Ladrido-Ignacio, L., Tan, M. and Quiring, J.S. (2017) 'Historical and Cultural Perspectives from the Philippines'. In H. Minas and M. Lewis (Eds.), *Mental Health in Asia and the Pacific* (pp. 163–174). Boston, MA: Springer.

Ladrido-Ignacio, L. and Verzosa, M.L.R. (2011) 'Focus on the Human Person: Promoting Well-being'. In L. Ladrido-Ignacio (Ed.), *Ginhawa: Well-Being in the Aftermath of Disasters.* Republic of the Philippines: Philippine Psychiatrists Association, Inc. and World Association for Psychosocial Rehabilitation.

Lagaya A.T. (2005) 'Republic of the Philippines'. In G. Bodeker, C.K. Ong, C. Grundy, G. Burford and K. Shein (Eds.), *WHO Global Atlas of Traditional, Complementary, and Alternative Medicine* (pp. 199–204). Kobe, Japan: World Health Organization Centre for Health Development.

Lagmay, A.V. (1984) 'Western Psychology in the Philippines: Impact and Response'. *International Journal of Psychology*, 19: 31–44.

Licuanan, P.B. (1985) 'Psychology in the Philippines: History and Current Trends'. *Philippine Studies*, 33: 67–86.

Lin, K.M., Demonteverde, L. and Nuccio, I. (1990) 'Religion, Healing, and Mental Health Among Filipino Americans'. *International Journal of Mental Health*, 19(3): 40–44.

Lopez, S.R. and Guarnaccia, P.J.K. (2000) 'Cultural Psychopathology: Uncovering the Social World of Mental Illness'. *Annual Review of Psychology*, 51: 571–598.

Majul, C.A. (1966) 'Islamic and Arab Cultural Influences in the South of the Philippines', *Journal of Southeast Asian History*, 7(2): 61–73.

Marcelino, E.P. (1990) 'Towards Understanding the Psychology of the Filipino'. *Women & Therapy*, 9(1–2): 105–128.

Mental Health Act (2017) *Republic Act No. 11036.*

Miclat, M.C. (2000) 'Tradition, Misconception, and Contribution: Chinese Influences in Philippine Culture'. *Humanities Diliman*, 1(2): 100–108.

National Statistics Office, Republic of the Philippines. (2010) *Philippines in figures.* Retrieved from www.census.gov.ph/data/publications/2010PIF.pdf.

Paz, C.J. (2008) 'Ginhawa: Well-Being as Expressed in Philippine Languages'. In C.J. Paz (Ed.), *Ginhawa, Kapalaran, Dalamhati: Essays on Well-being, Opportunity/Destiny, and Anguish* (pp. 3–12). Diliman, Quezon City: The University of the Philippines Press.

Pe-Pua, R. and Marcelino, E.P. (2000) 'Sikolohiyang Pilipino (Filipino Psychology): A Legacy of Virgilio G. Enriquez'. *Asian Journal of Social Psychology*, 3: 49–71.

Philippine Overseas Employment Agency (2008) *Overseas Employment Statistics,* Retrieved from www.poea.gov.ph/stats/2008_stats.pdf.

Philippine Psychology Act (2009) *Republic Act No. 10029.*

Pinggolio, J.P.R.V. and Mateo, N.J. (2018) 'Help-Seeking Behaviors of College Students: A Mixed Methods Study'. *Philippine Journal of Counseling Psychology*, 20(1): 1–12.

Recepcion, A.G. (2007) 'The Filipino Transpersonal Worldview'. *Asian Christian Review*, 1(3): 67–75.

Reid, A. (1988) *Southeast Asia in the Age of Commerce 1450–1680 Volume One: The Lands Below the Winds.* New Haven: New Haven Yale University Press.

Salazar, Z.A. (1979) *Faith healing in the Philippines: An historical perspective.* Retrieved from www.asj.epd.edu. ph/mediabox/archive/ASJ-181980/salazar.pdf.

Samaco-Zamora, M.C.F. and Fernandez, K.T.G. (2016) 'A Grounded Theory of Filipino Wellness (Kaginhawaan)'. *Psychological Studies*, 61(4): 279–287.

Samaniego, R.M. (2017) 'The Evolution of Psychiatry and Mental Health in the Philippines'. *Taiwanese Journal of Psychiatry*, 31(2): 101–114.

Sanchez, F. and Gaw, A. (2007) 'Mental Health Care of Filipino Americans', *Psychiatric Services*, 58(6): 810–815.

Saydoven, A.K. (2009) *Filipino traditional medicine.* Retrieved from www.scribd.com/doc22046305/Filipino-Traditional-Medicine-report#scribd.

Scott, W.H. (2004) *Barangay: Sixteenth-Century Philippine Culture and Society.* Quezon City: Ateneo De Manila University Press.

Shakman, R. (1969) 'Indigenous Healing of Mental Illness in the Philippines'. *International Journal of Social Psychiatry*, 15: 279–287.

Sue, S., Cheng, J.K.Y., Saad, C.S. and Chu, J.P. (2012) 'Asian American Mental Health: A Call to Action'. *American Psychologist*, 67(7): 532–544.

SyCip, L., Asis, M. and Luna, E. (2000) *The Measurement of Filipino Well-being.* Quezon City: University of the Philippines.

Tan, M.L. (2008) *Revisiting Usog, Pasma, Kulam: Traditional Theories of Health and Illness in the Philippines.* Quezon City: University of the Philippines Press.

Tanaka, C., Tuliao, M.T.R., Tanaka, E., Yamashita, T. and Matsuo, H. (2018) 'A Qualitative Study on the Stigma Experienced by People with Mental Health Problems and Epilepsy in the Philippines'. *BMC Psychiatry*, 18(1): 325. doi:10.1186/s12888-018-1902-9.

Thompson, S., Manderson, L., Woelz-Stirling, N., Cahill, A. and Kelaher, M. (2002) 'The Social and Cultural Context of Mental Health of Filipinas in Queensland'. *Australian and New Zealand Journal of Psychiatry*, 36: 681–687.

Tsai, J.L. and Chentsova-Dutton, Y. (2002) 'Understanding Depression Across Cultures'. In I. Gotlib and C. Hammen (Eds.), *Handbook of Depression* (pp. 467–491). New York: Guilford Press.

Tuason, M.T.G., Fernandez, K.T.G., Catipon, M.D.P., Trivino-Dey, L. and Carandang, M.L.A. (2012) 'Counseling in the Philippines: Past, Present, and Future'. *Journal of Counseling & Development*, 90: 373–377.

Tuliao, A.P. (2018) 'Public Stigma, Self-Stigma, and Help-Seeking Intent: A Comparison Between a U.S. and Philippines Sample'. Unpublished manuscript.

Valencia, L.B. and Palo, E.M. (1979) 'Community Responses to Mental Illness and Utilization of Traditional System of Medicine in Three Selected Study Sites in Metro Manila: Some Implications for Mental Health Planning'. *Philippine Sociological Review*, 27(2): 103–115.

Villar, I.V.G. (2000) 'Counselor Professionalization: An Imperative'. *Philippine Journal of Counseling Psychology*, 3(1), 10–16.

Wang, P.S., Lane, M., Olfson, M., Pincus, H.A., Wells, K.B. and Kessler, R.C. (2005) 'Twelve-Month Use of Mental Health Services in the United States: Results from the National Comorbidity Survey Replication', *Archives of General Psychiatry*, 62: 629–640.

World Health Organization (2006) *WHO-AIMS Report on Mental Health System in the Philippines.* Manila: World Health Organization and Department of Health.

World Health Organization (2011) *Western Pacific Country Health Information Profiles: 2011 Revision.* Geneva: Author.

World Health Organization and Department of Health (2012) *Health service delivery profile: Philippines, Manila*: World Health Organization, Western Pacific Region, Philippines Office. Retrieved from www.wpro.who.int/health_services/service_delivery_profile_philippines.pdf.

39

CULTURE AND MENTAL HEALTH IN SOUTH AFRICA

Edmarie Pretorius and Sharon Moonsamy

Culture is the lens through which an individual perceives and interprets the world (Battle 2012). Culture bears upon people's perceptions of health and wellness, their help seeking behaviours, the expression and manifestation of symptoms, their coping skills, the social support, their views about stigma, and the meaning they impart to their illness. When providing mental health services, it is thus important to understand the influence of cultural differences of the service users, between service users and mental health practitioners (MHPs) and the way mental health treatment settings are organized. Potential cultural misunderstandings, miscommunication and mistrust should not be ignored. Also, the socio-economic circumstances, political climate and environmental change contribute to additional complexities in the field of mental health care within the South African context.

The purpose of the chapter is to provide a critical analysis of Western and Indigenous cultural and traditional mental health practices in the South African context. This chapter highlights the demographics, reflects on the relationship between colonialism and the evolution of Western mental health care in the country and explains the cultural representations of illness and well-being, Indigenous and traditional practices from a South African perspective. In addition, the current mental health system, training and development in mental health care and contemporary mental health care practices in South Africa are presented. The chapter concludes with some final reflections on future research, training and practice.

Demographics in South Africa

South Africa, *the Rainbow Nation* – encapsulates the cultural and ethnic diversity of the four sub-ethnic groups – Nguni, Sotho, Shangaan-Tsonga and Venda – represented by the population of 58.78 million people in South Africa (Statistics South Africa 2019). There are numerous sub-groups within these four groups. The Zulu and Xhosa sub-groups of the Nguni group are the largest. South Africa also has 11 official languages (www.sa-venues.com/sa_languages). South African population is thus complex in its diversity of languages and cultures.

Statistics South Africa (2019) estimated the 2019 mid-year South African population at 58,78 million people spread across the nine provinces. The majority of the population (80.7%) are Black African, followed by coloured (8.8%), white (7.9%), and (2.6%) Indian or Asian.

In South Africa's political terminology, Black includes African, Coloured and Indian/Asian populations.

Colonialism and the evolution of Western mental health care in South Africa

Mental illness has been experienced and treated by Indigenous people long before the arrival of Europeans in South Africa, but mental health care in South Africa started in 1652 when the Dutch East Indian Company's first settlement occurred in the Cape of Good Hope. Gillis (2012) describes the context and development of mental health care in South Africa into three phases. The initial phase – '*expediency and confinement*' – entailed dealing with the mental illness among the settlers, the passing soldiers and sailors, with the main focus on ensuring the safety of the person and controlling aggressive or destructive behaviour. Treatment included sedatives, hypnotics and medicine to deal with agitation and toxins. Psychiatric diagnosis were non-existing and if physical causes were not identifiable, people were referred to as insane or lunatics.

Mental illness as a disease was only recognized towards the end of the 18th century when a French physician in 1808 created the term psychiatry (Gillis 2012). In South Africa, initially primitive structures adjacent to the Van Riebeeck Fort in Cape Town was used and enlarged in 1674 to care for the mentally ill. In 1699 a new hospital, bordering the Company Gardens was built where people were locked up in small overcrowded rooms. A third hospital was built in 1772, however, the demand for care increased rapidly, and the availability of space in hospitals continued to be insufficient. Eventually mentally ill people were also transferred to a Slave Lodge. Minto started no chain restraint unless solitude had been tried. He also instituted 'occupational therapy' and people started to produce crafts like mats and baskets which were sold (Gillis 2012).

The second phase, '*the psychiatric hospital era*', took place during British control between the early 19th and the beginning of the 20th centuries (Gillis 2012). In 1818, the British colonial government opened Somerset Hospital and beds were set aside for 'lunatics'. This was the only facility in the Cape Colony and people who were mentally unwell came to this facility from as far as the Eastern Cape. Over-crowdedness, mentally ill people were transferred to Robin Island in 1836. It was a prison, but then also became a shelter for lepers, lunatics and chronically ill people (Burroughs 1951). Although Valkenburg hospital was built in 1892, the facilities at Robin Island only closed in 1920. At the end of the 19th century it was evident that temporary lock-up, confinement strategies and restraint in police cells were not suitable or aligned with current ideas about mental health care (Gillis 2012).

The character of humanism, fundamental to the transformation in Europe and the French Revolution, filtered to South Africa largely controlled by the British. Copying British and American models, specific institutions called asylums were built for the mentally ill (Gillis 2012). The trend was to build hospitals with parks and gardens, where fresh air and useful occupation therapy would advance recovery of the mentally ill. The availability of treatment was still limited and no effective drugs or cures existed apart from the natural reduction of symptoms (Gillis 2012).

Between 1858 and 1974, a number of hospitals mushroomed in the Eastern Cape, KwaZulu Natal, Free State, Western Cape, Gauteng and North West Province (Gillis 2012; Sukeri, Betancourt and Emsley 2014). The different institutions were governed by *Lunacy Laws* and particular regulations relevant to the mentally ill, which fluctuated in the Boer Republics. In 1910 with Union, the responsibility for psychiatric hospitals and new legislation – the *Mental Disorders Act of 1916*, was assigned to the Department of Health. Despite the fact that mentally ill people were better housed and cared for, the approach remained custodial. Over-crowdedness, lack of effective treatment and limited resources remained as challenges (Sukeri et al. 2014).

From the beginning of the 20th century to the present marks the third phase, the '*modern period*' (Gillis 2012). The Diagnostic and Statistical Manual for Mental Disorders and the International Classifications of Diseases changed the world in ways of diagnosing and treating mental illness. Some major therapeutic developments in the 1930s was convulsion therapy, electro convulsion therapy in 1935 and insulin in 1950. In 1942, the National Health Service Commission (NHSC) was appointed to investigate the national health services and make recommendations to ensure that all people, irrespective of race and class receive adequate medical services according to their needs as a basic human right (Gillis 2012; Jeeves 2005). The NHSC proposed the delivery of health care services via nationally deployed health care centres.

When the National Party won the elections in South Africa in 1948, the apartheid government implemented racial segregation strategies and entrenched the fragmentation in health and mental health care services by creating the Bantustans, each with its own department of health and subtly manipulated control at national level (Coovadia et al. 2009). The health care system was centrally run, and subsequently access to resources and services offered to the poor were restricted (Moonsamy, Mupawose, Seedat, Mophosho and Pillay 2017).

Countrywide, health and mental health care services were discriminatory and intricately entangled with the colonial past and the apartheid regime. This strategy undermined the non-racial and all-inclusive health system advocated and proposed by the NHSC in 1942. Strict legislation enforced separate facilities and accommodation for black patients in psychiatric facilities (Gillis 2012).

The World Health Organization's Report on apartheid and mental health care in 1983 condemned the state of psychiatry and the poor hygiene standards and care levels afforded to black South Africans. In 1978, a task team of the American Psychiatric Association established that the apartheid policy resulted in discrimination of 'non-white' patients treated in mental hospitals in South Africa (Emsley 2001; Swanepoel 2011), and serious criticism was received by the Society of Psychiatrists of South Africa, for their obvious support of the racist apartheid's legislation. In 1985, the Royal College of Psychiatrists confirmed substantial evidence of discrimination based on race in the provision of mental health services and declared that it was completely unacceptable and unjust (Emsley 2001). Wu (2009) claims that a report on the asylum at Robin Island indicated that as early as 1836, white people were kept separate from the blacks. Therefore, it can be argued that the apartheid policy cemented a previously existing racist policy into mental health care.

Since 1987 the delivery of psychiatric services became the responsibility of provincial health authorities which was a major incentive because of the focus on curative services and the flexibility of more diverse venues and forms of therapy. This resulted in psychiatry to be viewed as part of general medicine which to an extent minimised the stigma attached to mental health care.

In 1991, transformation started in some psychiatric facilities and resulted in the abolishment of racial divisions when the first democratic government came into power in 1994. The national health plan for South Africa drawn up with the technical support from the World Health Organisation (WHO) and United Nations International Children's Emergency Fund (UNICEF) was published by the ANC in May 1994 and clearly articulated that a single, impartial and consolidated National Health System (NHS) should be created.

The ANC government inherited a plural health system. The public health sector, used by the majority of Black South African citizens was financed through general taxation and the private health sector, mainly serving the minority of citizens (mainly white and those who can afford private health care), was largely funded through medical aid schemes. Huge disparities between 'the haves and the have-not' exist, and Ross and Deverell (2010) describe it as a 'dual burden of disease'.

A unified, non-racial and all-inclusive public health system advocated and proposed by the NHSC in 1942, had to be established by the new government. Although the previous health system was relatively well resourced, more than 50% of the resources were allocated to the private health sector (Coovadia et al. 2009). The national public health sector provides care for approximately 84% of the South African population (Robertson, Chiliza, Janse van Rensburg and Talatala 2018), but is staffed by 30% of the medical workforce. Annual per capita spending on health in the private sector is approximately ten times that of the public sector (Coovadia et al. 2009). Large inequalities in the public health sector is evident when infrastructure, human and financial resources among the different geographical areas and levels of care are considered (Pretorius 2015). This unequal status was evident in both urban–rural and private–public contexts in South Africa.

The Department of Health (DoH 1997) published the White Paper for the transformation of the South African health system. The proposed unified NHS is based on a Primary Health Care (PHC) approach to health. It envisaged an integrated public and private health sector to correct inequalities by developing a district health system to increase access to essential health care services and provide basic health care services to all South African citizens especially deprived people in the rural areas of South Africa (Schneider, Barron and Fonn 2007).

A new era started for South African psychiatry when the *Mental Health Care Act No 17* of 2002 replaced the Mental Health Act of 1973, and implemented on 15 December 2004 (Szabo and Kaliski 2017). The Act was in line with the 1996 Constitution and showed a human rights orientation with the aim to provide humane care and required proper accountability (Szabo and Kaliski 2017). South Africa confirmed the transformation process of the existing health care system to ensure Univeral Health Coverage (UHC) inclusive of health care for people living with mental illness (PLWMI) when the National Health Insurance (MHI) White Paper was released in 2017. The implication of UHC is that all people should be able to access health care in line with their needs without encountering financial hardship. However, both health care sectors – public and private – are fragmented, poorly resourced and provide mainly hospital-based mental health care.

Cultural representations of illness and well-being

Indigenous explanatory models of illness are reckoned by many South Africans. These Indigenous explanatory models of illness include the spiritual understanding of causation, upsetting the ancestors, witchcraft and neglecting to perform rituals (Crawford and Lipsedge 2004; Meissner 2004; World Health Organization 2002). For example, De Andrade and Ross' study (2005) illustrates traditional healers' beliefs on hearing loss due to curses, ancestors, patient in the wrong place and the person's inner spirit being disturbed.

As culture and communication are intertwined, an individual will not be able to build rapport with the therapist if the therapist does not understand the ethnographic and cultural factors of the patient, as these factors give the individual its "*peoplehood*" or "*ethnic identity*" (Battle 2012:2). Race, in South Africa – given its history – is also a major factor and often determines the level of trust between people and influences help seeking behaviours. Ross and Deverell (2010: 28) state that "race and ethnicity is one component of a person's social identity, with people attaching different prioritises to this aspect".

Another aspect to be mindful of is religion, its practices and customs. South Africa has diverse religions including Christianity, Judaism, Hinduism, African religions, Islam, Buddhism, and practices of atheism. All of these are acknowledged and mostly respected by health care practitioners. These customs and practices ground the individual and their families, and should be included in interventions toward a holistic approach.

Indigenous and traditional practice from a South African perspective

In Africa, inclusive of South Africa, mental health challenges are often perceived to be the influence of ancestors or bewitchment (Sorsdahl, Flisher, Wilson and Stein 2010). Although studies on traditional healers (THs) or alternative healers (AHs) in other African countries recognize the symptoms or manifestation of severe mental illness, they strongly believe that the causes of mental illness is supernatural (Abbo 2011). A number of South African studies indicate that approximately 70% to 84% of health service users with different needs and ailments, consult with THs and AHs during their lifespan (Koen, Niehaus, Muller and Laurent 2003; National Progressive Primary Health Care Network Summary Brief 1997; Pretorius, Moonsamy and Eagle 2012).

Mufamadi (2001) claims that the cultural backgrounds of the service users and the THs and AHs are often shared and might have a distinct understanding of the service users' viewpoints on the symptoms they are experiencing and the ascribed cultural or traditional meaning of the illness. Robertson (2006) also argues that the holistic care by THs and AHs, their easier accessibility and their practicing of a more conventional and customary approach in the community, are reasons why they are consulted more frequently than biomedical MHPs.

In South Africa, THs and AHs play vital roles in primary health care in rural areas, peri-urban and urban areas. In the rural areas, THs and AHs are actively involved with community members to treat various diseases and health issues (Semenya and Potgieter 2014; Zingela, Van Wyk and Pietersen 2019). In low to middle income countries the involvement of 'non-professionals' which include THs and AHs, might become an important resource for providing mental health care (Saraceno et al. 2007).

Semenya and Potgieter's study (2014) reports that THs are confident and have sufficient knowledge and skills to 'cure' mental illness. Often part of the treatment is for the service user to stay with the TH or they visit service users regularly, for psychosocial support to address conflict areas in the life and to ensure the service user's adherence to treatment. Scholars note that provision of mental health care by THs and AHs may positively affect the individual's and the community's mental health, particularly for common mental disorders such as depression and anxiety (Meissner 2004). Peltzer, Mngqundaniso and Petros (2006) reported that mental health problems were on the list of most regular ailments THs and AHs address among 9% of their service users. They argue that if the categories of ancestral problems (22.5%) and spirit illness (21%) are categorised as mental disorders according to the western diagnostic system, the mental health problems addressed by THs and AHs will be much higher.

The Traditional Health Practitioners Bill in South Africa was promulgated by the Department of Health (2003), and THs and AHs have been recognized as health care practitioners. The implementation of the Act is accompanied by many attempts towards formalisation, regulation and professionalization of this sector. However, a number of concerns around 'professionalization' of the sector remain (Campbell-Hall et al. 2010). First, a debate exists if it is necessary to have a system fundamentally rooted in cultural and spiritual knowledge and practice regulated by the government (Wreford 2005). Second, it was and still is not clear how the interface of the two fundamentally different health care systems will take place (Devenish 2005). Third, both systems of health care are rooted in established elucidatory and discursive frameworks (Yen and Wilbraham 2003), and stem from deeply engrained beliefs within their own communities, therefore the challenge is to circumvent the imposition of one system over the other.

Freeman and Motsei (1992) delineated three possibilities: incorporation, co-operation or collaboration and complete integration. Collectively, the different stakeholders were supportive of the collaboration system where both systems remained autonomous, self-regulated and cooperative among THs, AHs and MHPs through mutual referrals (Khan and Kelly 2001). However, the reciprocal relationship between THs, AHs and medical practitioners appears to be one-sided. Although the THs and AHs are more open and willing to collaborate, they do not experience the same collaboration from medical professionals, thus collaboration remains challenging (Campbell-Hall et al. 2010).

As consultation with THs and AHs is common practice among mental health care service users, MHPs have to become more knowledgeable about the traditional and alternative medicine and embrace a holistic approach to mental health services (Pan and Zhou 2013; Zingela et al. 2019). This will require from MHPs to familiarise themselves with the belief systems of their service users, proactively incorporate traditional healing practices with the Westernized practices to promote the right of choice of the service users (Bereda 2002) and negotiate with the service user if their need is in conflict with the MHPs' belief system. Patel (2011) claims that the mutual distrust between the two health care systems and the trepidations about health care practices of traditional and alternative healers are barriers to collaboration and it hampers integrative and integral mental health care services.

A study in Port Elizabeth, Nelson Mandela Bay revealed that when THS and AHs were involved in educational workshops, it resulted in collaboration between medical and allied health professions and brought positive change in these fields (Peltzer et al. 2006). If mental health education can be replicated in a similar way (Zingela et al. 2019), it might be possible for MHPs, THs and AHs to collaboratively promote psychoeducation in mental health. Also, it is critical to address factors impeding on the collaboration such as, an inadequate health care budget, limited facilities and fewer numbers of health care practitioner to patient ratio.

According to the World Health Organization (WHO 2012) in countries where access to allopathic medicines is limited, traditional medicine is the main source of health care. Mbatha, Street, Ngcobo and Gqaleni (2012) postulate that the traditional medicine strategy for 2002–2005 by the WHO provides a framework for the promotion of traditional medicine and the integration into the national health care policies. Although South African THs and AHs are not integrated into the national health care strategies at present, partnerships amongst different health disciplines at different levels were formed with the main purpose to improve health and mental health care to function in a changing environment where the service users right of choice is acknowledged.

Current mental health system in South Africa

The South African Constitution (1996) and Section 8 of the Mental Health Care Act No 17 of 2002 require metal health services in the community. The public sector mental health system focused on a deinstitutional route since the mid-1990s (Lazarus 2005; South African National Department of Health 2012). However, a lack of funding to implement the Mental Health Care Act resulted in a disorganized process of de-institutionalization with inconsistent development of community health services and re-institutionalization in some areas (Burns 2011; Robertson and Szabo 2017; Sukeri, et al. 2014).

For example, the Gauteng Health Department used the de-institutionalization process in mental health care and implemented a disruptive strategy to save costs in 2015. Almost 1,700 people with severe psychosocial and other disabilities were transferred from the facilities of a long-term medium care hospital group which provided state-funded care for psychiatric patients for many years to either specialized psychiatric hospitals (renovated and staffed for the purpose), a government-run care and rehabilitation centre or non-governmental residential facilities (NGOs, Robertson and Makgoba 2018). Within a year of transfer, 119 (8.3%) of the people died, and 131 (9.1%) died during the 2016 calendar year (Robertson and Makgoba 2018). People transferred to a specialized psychiatric hospital were significantly more likely to have survived than those transferred to the government care centre or an NGO. The survival came at a financial cost five times higher than the cost of the original long-term medium care hospital group's facilities, and 12 times higher than an NGO. Reasons for the tragedy were lack of financial security, underestimation of the susceptibility of PLWMI and a misconception of what comprises community-based mental health care. This gloomy reality is evident in the following quote:

> *Josinah Dlamini was still in bed when she heard it. Something heavy was being dragged across the house's concrete floor. Then she could make out the sound of the front door opening, of someone stepping out into the front yard.*
>
> *She got up to see what was happening. As she got outside, she saw him; there in the early morning sunlight was her Uncle John bent over his mattress. He grabbed the mattress with both hands and then begin to pull it apart, Dlamini remembers. After that, he slept on the floor. The scene was not entirely out of place at the Dlamini home in Soweto. Uncle John who was diagnosed with schizophrenia about 9 years ago was one of the almost 1700 people who had to leave one of the long-term medium care facilities who provided state-funded care for psychiatric patients… Uncle John who has schizophrenia, went home. At the long-term medium care facility, taking medication helped to control Uncle John's symptoms. But back home, he stopped taking his daily medication. This man, whose family described him as kind and loving with a quiet demeanour/temperament began to act out in destructive and sometimes violent ways… Josinah's mother Annah, John's sister, estimates they phoned the police at least five times for help in getting him into one of these specialized wards. Each time the police would arrive with sirens blaring, scaring John, who would "disappear", Annah, remembers. "He runs fast, fast, fast. You will never catch him".*
>
> *Eventually, Josinah says frustrated police officers would utter a common refrain: "Hayi! It is the ambulance that's supposed to deal with these patients".*
>
> *But when emergency medical services arrived, they refused to take John because they weren't equipped to restrain him and could not administer medication to calm him down during the ride to the nearest specialist facility, Josinah explains. "They'd say, 'No, you need to call the police if the patient is violent'".*
>
> *(Holmes 2018)*

The inhumane and insidious re-institutionalization of PLWMI in prisons and forensic psychiatric units is most alarming (Naidoo and Mkize 2012). Also, implementation of the Act came with multiple challenges for clinicians, including the administrative burden, inadequate support to oversee and facilitate the different processes and procedures, and limited resources (Szabo and Kaliski 2017).

In South Africa, Primary Health Care (PHC) is fundamentally dependent on nursing staff and is continually mentioned in policies and plans as a way to improve attention to mental health (South African National Department of Health 2014; 2017; 2018). In the North West

Province, the integration of SMI in PHC is hindered due to the lack of community-based psychiatric nurses (Hanlon, Luitel, Kathree et al. 2014).

In relation to community-based mental health services, South African National Department of Health (2017) state that the NHI will cater for psychiatric care in hospitals from regional level and above. Although the National Mental Health Policy Framework and Strategic Plan 2013–2020 (NMHPF) postulates that community-based mental health services are the backbone of psychiatric care in conjunction with general hospital psychiatric units providing acute symptom relief, it is not clear whether these services, if perceived to be a part of the PHC, will be adequately financed under the NHI (Robertson et al. 2018). The South African National Department of Health Annual Performance Plan for 2018/19–2020/21 (South African National Department of Health 2018) does not include community-based mental health services, but only District Specialist Mental Health Teams, forensic mental health and primary mental health care under the PHC programme and it is allocated 0.6% of the total health budget. Robertson et al. (2018: 103) note that "there are no health indicators for community-based mental health services, no monitoring of illness relapse or adverse community-dwelling PLWMI, and no user-level outcome measures".

The private health sector only provides for PLWMI with either some degree of functional impairment, or those with significant family support. Their strategy is on prevention of mental disability through early detection treatment and rehabilitation of SMI. In addition, the private sector prioritise care to control symptoms and contain mental disability in an attempt to prevent relapses.

It is evident that both public and private sector care for PLWMI are not meeting the requirements of the Constitution of South Africa, UHC, and the Convention on the Rights of Persons with Disabilities. Both sectors are still hospital-centred, the public sector care is mainly in poorly resourced institutions and acute hospitalisation is the priority of the private sector. In addition, both sectors are underpinned by the shortage of financial protection for PLWMI and their service needs (Robertson et al. 2018).

Training and development in contemporary mental health practice

There has been an acute shortage of psychiatrists in South Africa. According to Gillis (2012), initially the majority of psychiatric hospitals were staffed by medical practitioners with basic but not specialized training in mental health care. They gained experience, while working in the mental health care sector. There have been a few psychiatrists who were trained overseas or practised jointly as neurologists in private practice and a few senior psychiatrists in hospitals for mentally ill-patients, who registered when the South African Medical Council instituted a specialist register.

The first academic training programme was initiated in 1949, by the University of the Witwatersrand. This spearheaded the Diploma of Psychological Medicine (based on the equivalent British qualification) and was associated with registration for a MMed degree and with specialist registration thereafter (Gillis 2012). In 1951 seven candidates graduated and a second group of seven graduated in 1952. Thereafter, similar training programmes were established at all the South African Medical Schools. Currently, approximately 20 psychiatrists are annually registered with the South African Medical Council. In 1954, the first full-time post of Professor of Psychiatry in an academic department was created in a joint appointment between the University of the Witwatersrand and the then Transvaal Provincial Department of Health. Subsequently, all academic departments at medical schools appoint professorial and other staff members in the field of specialization (Gillis 2012).

In 1961 the Fellowship of the Faculty of Psychiatry of the College of Medicine was created because a diploma was not appropriate for this important medical discipline. Psychiatry developed into a major clinical subject in the training of medical doctors and at present, it is the fifth major clinical subject in the final MBBCh examination at the majority of medical schools. In addition, psychiatric nursing training has a long history and started at the end of the 19th century. An integrated training course inclusive of psychiatric nursing was introduced for all nurses by the South African Council of Nursing. Tara Hospital in Joahnnesburg, Gauteng and Groote Schuur Hospital in Cape Town offered advanced courses in psychiatric nursing in the 1950s and 1962, respectively (Gillis 2012).

Future directions

The development of a mental health workforce within PHC and community-based mental health services is needed. This should include the provision of basic psychiatric nursing training for all nurses, establishing community-based multidisciplinary teams in line with the NDoH's manual on norms; and incorporating new posts and adequate training where required for other practitioners (e.g. clinical associates and registered counsellors).

Training of THs and AHs in Western methods in identifying common mental disorders and becoming part of the community-based multidisciplinary teams is probably part of the solution. THs mention that there is a lack of appreciation from the Western health care services for their services (Campbell-Hall et al. 2010). For collaboration to be successful, mutual respect and preparedness from both sectors is required (Wreford 2005). The development of an evidence-based model of collaboration which facilitate reciprocal collaboration at community level, is needed. A model of collaboration in Kenya, Women Fighting AIDS in Kenya (WOFAK), is a relevant example where both biomedical and traditional health care practitioners worked closely together, resulted in encouraging trust, mutual learning and improved working relationships between the two health care sectors in the same location (Anderson and Kaleeba 2002).

To achieve UHC for PLWMI, the development of guidelines describing pathways for a national programme to care for PLWMI, which consider scope of practice, task-sharing duties the NDoH standard treatment guidelines and requirements of the Mental Health Care Act, are required (Robertson et al. 2018). This might be achieved by demarcating inter-sectorial duties using the service delivery agreement negotiated at national level, and translating the pathways for a national programme to care for PLWMI into clear action steps for staff in community-based mental health services, in general hospitals for critical admissions and in specialized hospitals for people with serious mental deficiencies.

In relation to the outcomes of care, health indicators should provide quality assurance. This could be executed by initiating community-based clinical audits, doing regular surveys and include service users as one of the stakeholders in the survey and regularly monitor and assess health indicators in relation to the outcomes of care.

Conclusion

In spite of the South African constitution and health legislation, the accessible care to PLWMI under the NHI is questionable. The fact that community-based mental health services as a multidisciplinary psychiatric service is not acknowledged and financed, it is doubtful whether those most in need of mental health care will be able to access promotive, preventive, curative, rehabilitative and palliative mental health care (Robertson et al. 2018).

Culture and Mental Health in South Africa

Although community members embrace traditional explanatory models of illness, both traditional and biomedical services are used (Campbell-Hall et al. 2010; Crawford and Lipsedge 2004; Meissner 2004). Western health care practitioners have to shift from a purely biomedical debate of care towards a 'meaning centred approach' that considers diverse cultural explanations of illness to achieve a truly equitable collaborative arrangement with traditional health care practitioners (Campbell-Hall et al. 2010).

Comprehensive, integrated, coordinated and collaborative mental health services with easy access for service users are required in South Africa. There are many more THs and AHs in South Africa than MHPs and a large portion of the South African population with mental health problems consult with THs (Zingela et al. 2019). Therefore, it might be useful to engage with THs and AHs to explore workable referral pathways that might promote collaboration and co-operation on delivering essential mental health services, provide increased access to care and encourage adherence to different modalities of treatment. South Africa would then be working towards achieving basic human rights for all.

References

Abbo, C. (2011) 'Profiles and outcome of traditional healing practices for severe mental illnesses in two districts of Eastern Uganda, *Global Health Action*', 4. doi:10.3402/gha.v4i0.7117.

Anderson, S. and Kaleeba, N. (2002) *Ancient remedies, new disease: Involving traditional healers in increasing access to AIDS care and prevention in East Africa.* Geneva: UNAIDS.

Battle, D. (2012) 'Communication disorders in a multicultural and global society'. In Battle, D.E. (Ed.), *Communication disorders in multicultural and international Populations* (pp. 2–19). St. Louis, MO: Elsevier.

Bereda, J.E. (2002) *Traditional healing as a health care delivery system in a transcultural society.* MA dissertation, Pretoria University, South Africa.

Bhagwanjee, A., Petersen, I., Akintola, O. and George, G. (2008) 'Bridging the gap between VCT and HIV/AIDS treatment uptake: Perspectives of VCT and HIV/AIDS treatment service users in a mining sector workplace setting in South Africa', *African Journal of AIDS Research*, 7: 271–279.

Bradshaw, D (2008) *Determinants of health & their trends.* Chapter 4. www.hst.org.za/uploads/files/chap4_08.pdf.

Burns, J.K. (2011) 'The mental health gap in South Africa: A human rights issue', *Equal Rights Review*, 6:99–113.

Burroughs, E.H. (1951) 'History of medicine in South Africa, Cape Town', *Balkema*, 121.

Campbell-Hall, V., Petersen, I., Mjadu, S., Hosegood, V. and Flischer, A.J. (2010) 'Collaboration between traditional practitioners and primary health care staff in South Africa: Developing a workable partnership for community mental health services', *Transcultural Psychiatry*, 47(4): 610–628.

Colvin, M., Gumede, L., Grimwade, K. and Wilkinson, D. (2001) Policy Brief No 5: '*Integrating traditional healers into a tuberculosis control programme in Hlabisa, South Africa'.* Durban: Durban Medical Research Council.

Colvin, M., Gumede, L., Grimwade, K., Maher, D. and Wilkinson, D. (2003) 'Contribution of traditional healers to a rural tuberculosis control programme in Hlabisa, South Africa', *International Journal of Tuberculosis and Lung Disease,* 7: 586–591.

Coovadia, H., Jewkes, R., Barron, P., Sanders, D., and McIntyre, D. (2009) 'The health and health system of South Africa: Historical roots of current public health challenges', *The Lancet*, 374: 817–834.

Crawford, T. and Lipsedge, M. (2004) 'Seeking help for psychological distress: The interface of Zulu traditional healing and Western biomedicine', *Mental Health, Religion & Culture*, 7: 131–148.

De Andrade, V. and Ross, E. (2005) 'Beliefs and practices of black South African traditional healers regarding hearing impairment', *International Journal of Audiology*, 44: 489–499.

Devenish, A. (2005) 'Negotiating healing. Understanding the dynamics among traditional healers in KwaZulu-Natal as they engage with professionalisation', *Social Dynamics*, 31; 243–284.

Department of Health (1997) *Department of Health White paper for the transformation of the health system in South Africa.* Retrieved from www.gov.za/sites/default/files/gcis_document/201409/17910gen6670.pdf.

Department of Health (2003) *Traditional Health Practitioners Bill* (rep. No. B66-2003).

Emsley, R. (2001) 'Focus on psychiatry in South Africa', *British Journal of Psychiatry*, 178: 382–386.

Freeman, M. and Motsei, M. (1992) 'Planning healthcare in South Afrcia–Is there a role for traditional healers?' *Social Science & Medicine*, 34: 1183–1190.

Gillis, L. (2012) 'The historical development of psychiatry in South Africa since 1952', *South African Journal of Psychiatry*, 18(3): 1–14.

Hanlon, C., Luitel, N.P., Kathree, et al. (2014) 'Challenges and opportunities for implementing integrated mental health care: A district level situation analysis from five low-and middle-income countries', *PloS*, 9(2): e88437.

Holmes, T (2018) *72 hours to care : The precarious road to psychiatric help*. Retrieved from https://mg.co.za/article/2018-11-15-00-72-hour-observation-wards-care-the-precarious-road-to-psychiatric-care-mental-health/.

Khan, M. and Kelly, K. (2001) 'Cultural tensions in psychiatric nursing: Managing the interface between Western mental health care and Xhosa traditional healing in South Africa', *Transcultural Psychiatry*, 38: 35–50.

Koen, L., Niehaus, D., Muller, J. and Laurent, C. (2003) Use of traditional treatment methodsin a Xhosa schizophrenic population', *South African Medical Journal*, 93: 443.

Lazarus, R. (2005) 'Managing de-institutionalisation in a context of change: The case of Gauteng, South Africa', *South African Psychiatry Review*, 8(2): 65–69.

Mbatha, N., Street, R.A., Ngcobo, M. and Gqaleni, N. (2012) 'Sick certificates issued by South African traditional health practitioners: Current legislation, challenges and the way forward', *South African Medical Journal*, 102: 129–131.

McIntyre, D., Muirhead, D., and Gilson, L. (2002) 'Geographic patterns of deprivation in South Africa: Informing health equity analyses and public resource allocation strategies', *Health Policy and Planning*, 17 (1): 30–39.

Meissner, O. (2004) 'The traditional healer as part of the primary health care team?', *South African Medical Journal*, 94: 901–902.

Moonsamy, S., Mupawose, A., Seedat, J., Mophosho, M. and Pillay, D. (2017) 'Speech-language pathology and audiology practice in South Africa: Reflections on transformation in professional practice since the end of apartheid', *Perspectives of the ASHA Special Interest Groups,* 2(17): 30–41.

Mufamadi, J. (2001) *A group of traditional healers' perceptions of and approaches to the treatment of mental illness*. Indigenous Knowledge Conference, University of Saskatchewan, Saskatoon, Canada. Retrieved from: http://datalib.usask.ca/iportal/2007.10.17/IKC-2001/IKC-2001-Mufamadi.pdf.

Naidoo, S. and Mkize, D.L. (2012) 'Prevalence of mental disorders in a prison population in Durban, South Africa', *African Journal of Psychiatry*, 15: 30–35.

National Progressive Primary Health Care Network Summary Brief (1997) *National Progressive Primary Health Care Summary Brief of public hearings on traditional healers*. Cape Town, South Africa: National Progressive Primary Health Care Network.

Ndetei, D.M. (2007) 'Traditional healers in East Africa', *International Psychiatry*, 4:85–86.

Pan, W. and Zhou, H. (2013) 'Integrative medicine: A paradigm shift in clinical practice', *International Journal of Integrative Medicine,* 1(21). https://doi.org/10.5772/56817.

Patel, V. (2011) 'Traditional healers for mental health care in Africa', *Global Health Action*, 4. doi:10:3402/gha.v4i0.7956.

Peltzer, K., Mngqundaniso, N. and Petros, G. (2006) 'HIV/AIDS/STI/TB knowledge, beliefs and practices of traditional healers in KwaZulu-Natal, South Africa', *AIDS Care*, 18: 608–613.

Pretorius, E. (2015) 'Community Empowerment and participation: The missing link in the South African health-care system?'. In U. Brizay, R. Lutz and F. Ross (Eds.), *Sozialarbeit des Südens Band 4 Zugang zum Gesundheitswesen und Gesundheitspolitik-Access to Health Care Services and Health Policy* (pp. 301–322). Paulo Freire Verlag, Oldenburg: Deutschen Bibliothek.

Pretorius, E., Moonsamy, S., and Eagle, G. (2012) 'Clemmont Vontress's cross-cultural and humanistic-existential approaches: Their relevance to counselling diverse South African communities'. R. Moodley, L. Epp and H. Yusuf (Eds.), *Counseling across the cultural divide The Clemmont E Vontress reader* (pp. 304–318). PCCS BOOKS, Herefordshire: United Kingdom.

Robertson, B.A. (2006) 'Does the evidence support collaboration between psychiatry and traditional healers? Findings from three South African studies: Review article', *Sabinet Online*, 9: 87–90.

Robertson, I.J. and Szabo, C.P. (2017) 'Community mental health services in Southern Gauteng: An audit using district health information systems data', *South African Journal for Psychiatry*, 23:10–55.

Culture and Mental Health in South Africa

Robertson, I.J. and Makgoba, M.W. (2018) 'Mortality analysis of people with severe mental illness transferred from long-stay hospital to alternative care in the Life Esidimeni tragedy', *South African Medical Journal,* 108(10):813–817.

Robertson, L.J., Chiliza, B., Janse van Rensburg, A.B. and Talatala M. (2018) 'Towards universal health coverage for people living with mental illness in South Africa', *South African Health Review.* Retrieved from www.hst.org.za/publications/South%20African%20Health%20Reviews/Chap%2011%20Mental%20Illness%20SAHR2018.pdf.

Ross, E. and Deverell, A. (2010) *Health, illness and disability: Psychosocial processes.* Van Schaik: Pretoria.

Saraceno, B., van Ommeren, M., Batniji, R., Cohen, A., Gureje, O., Mahoney, J., Sridhar, D., and Underhill, C. (2007) 'Barriers to improvement of mental health services in low-income and middle-income countries', *The Lancet,* 370: 1164–1174.

Schneider, H., Barron, P., and Fonn, S. (2007) 'The Promise and the Practice of Transformation in South Africa's Health System in S. Buhlungu'. J. Daniel, R. Southall and J. Lutchman (Eds.), *State of the nation: South Africa 2007* (289–311). Cape Town: HSRC Press.

Semenya, S.S. and Potgieter, M.J. (2014) 'Bapedi traditional healers in the Limpopo Province, South Africa: Their socio-cultural profile and traditional healing practice', *Journal of Ethnobiology and Ethnomedicine,* 10(4):1–12.

Sorsdahl, K.R., Flischer, A. J., Wilson, Z. and Stein, D.J. (2010) 'Explanatory models of mental disorders and treatment practices among traditional healers in Mpumulanga South Africa', *African Journal of Psychiatry,* 284–290.

South African National Department of Health (2003) *Norms manual for severe psychiatric conditions,* Pretoria: NDoH.

South African National Department of Health (2012) *National Mental Health Policy Framework and Strategic Plan 2013–2020,* Pretoria: NDoH.

South African National Department of Health (2014) *The National Health Promotion Policy and Strategy 2015–2019,* Pretoria: NDoH.

South African National Department of Health (2017) *Annual Report 2017/18,* Pretoria: NDoH.

South African National Department of Health (2018) *The South African National Department of Health Annual Performance Plan for 2018/19–2020/21,* Pretoria: NDoH.

Statistics South Africa (2019) *Mid-year population estimates.* Retrieved from www.statssa.gov.za/publications/P0302/P03022019.pdf.

Statistics South Africa (2014) Retrieved from: www.education.gov.za/Portals/0/Documents/Publications/Education%20Statistics%222014.pdf?ver=2016-05-13-144159-067.

Sukeri, K., Betancourt, O.A. and Emsley, R. (2014) 'Lessons from the past: Historical perspectives of mental health in the Eastern Cape', *South African Journal of Psychology,* 20(2):34–39.

Swanepoel, M. (2011) 'Human rights that influence the mentally ill patient in South African medical law: A discussion of sections 9, 27, 30 and 31 of the Constitution", *Potchefstroom Electronic Law Journal (PELJ),* 14(7):1–20.

Szabo, C.P. and Kaliski, S.Z. (2017) 'Mental health and the law: A South African perspective', *British Journal of Psychiatry International,* 14(3): 69–71.

Thornicroft, G., Deb, T. and Henderson, C. (2016) 'Community mental health care worldwide: Current status and further developments', *World Psychiatry,* 15(3): 276–286.

World Health Organization (2002) *Traditional medicine strategy 2002–2005.* Geneva: World Health Organization.

World Health Organization (2012) *Module 6: Integrative medicine- incorporating traditional healers into public health delivery [Course].* Retrieved from: www.uniteforsight.org/effective-program-development/module6.

Wreford, J. (2005) 'Missing each other: Problems and potential for collaborative efforts between biomedicine and traditional medicine in South Africa', *Social Dynamics,* 31: 55–58.

Wu, M. (2009) 'Between universalism and racism: Tensions in theories of treatmentin South African psychiatry', *Brown Journal of History,* 95–113.

Yen, J. and Wilbraham, L. (2003) 'Discourses of culture and illness in South African mental health care and indigenous healing part 1: Western psychiatric power', *Transcultural Psychiatry,* 40: 542–561.

Zingela, Z., Van Wyk, S. and Pietersen, J. (2019) Use of traditional and alternative healers by psychiatric patients: A descriptive study in urban South Africa', *Transcultural Psychiatry,* 56(1): 146–166.

PART G

Indigenous and traditional healing in mental health

40

INDIGENOUS NORTH AMERICAN HEALING

Roderick McCormick

It is a daunting task to write a chapter on Indigenous North American Healing Practices as there is so much diversity in practices that exist amongst the many Indigenous Nations in North America. Because of the space limitations, the author will focus primarily on Canada and provide additional examples from the United States as both Canada and the United States are collectively known to Indigenous peoples as Turtle Island. Most Indigenous peoples of the two countries do not recognize the border dividing Turtle Island (North America). In addition to a shared artificial border, Indigenous peoples of Canada and the United States share a common colonial history of surviving aggressive attempts by European settlers to exterminate Indigenous cultures. A prime example of this was the use of the Residential Schools. In 1879 the Prime Minister of Canada: Sir John A. Macdonald commissioned politician Nicholas Flood Davin to study industrial schools established for American Indian students in the United States. Davin recommended that Canada follow the U.S. example of "aggressive civilization" and establish similar schools in Canada (Canada 1880).

The over 100 years of Residential Schools left a legacy that includes alcohol and drug abuse, sexual abuse, violence, harsh parenting, and depression (Bopp and Lane Jr. 2000). Many of the children sent to Residential Schools never came home as they were killed by disease, accidents, fires and even by freezing to death in their efforts to escape and return home. Many more were hurt by physical and sexual abuse within the schools. The psychological damage incurred by the students has had an intergenerational effect upon their children and grandchildren. Recently, the Canadian Health Minister Jane Philpott said the suicide rates among Indigenous youth were at least ten times higher than for the general population of young people. "It is a staggering reality, it is completely unacceptable ... there is nothing more devastating than realizing someone has reached the point of no hope", she told the emergency debate in the House of Commons (Ljunggren and Nickel 2016). Despite the many mental health problems experienced by Indigenous peoples in North America, they tend not to use the mental health services provided by the majority culture (Sue 1981). Indigenous peoples also have a higher therapy dropout rate and are less likely to respond to treatment (Trimble and Fleming 1990; More 1985; Sue 1981). Another significant obstacle to the utilization of mainstream mental health services is the lack of access to such services in rural and remote Indigenous communities. Increasingly, Indigenous peoples are recognizing that reclaiming the traditional healing practices used by them for thousands of years prior to colonization, may be the solution to provide healing to both individuals and communities.

In 2015, the Truth and Reconciliation Commission (TRC) of Canada released its report on the Indian residential school system and its impact on Aboriginal peoples. The TRC Report set out 94 action items including #22 which called upon the Canadian health care system "to recognize the value of Aboriginal healing practices and use them in the treatment of Aboriginal patients in collaboration with Aboriginal healers and Elders where requested by Aboriginal patients" (Truth and Reconciliation Canada 2015). The World Health Organization (WHO) has also recognized the importance of traditional Indigenous medicine in providing health care to vulnerable populations because of its accessibility, affordability, and cultural appropriateness (WHO 2002).

A brief history of Indigenous and traditional healing

It should be noted that there has been relatively few articles or reports published on traditional healing. Two possible reasons for this are that traditional Indigenous cultures are oral cultures and knowledge is therefore shared through the spoken word and not by writing it down. Secondly, many Indigenous tribes have cultural prohibitions about publishing details of traditional healing practices and ceremonies (McCormick 2003). Traditional healing is based on the unique cultural perspectives of different Indigenous cultures and their respective views on health and illness. These cultural beliefs and values pertaining to healing are often quite different from the beliefs and values of bio-medical healing. Spirituality, balance, harmony, nature, connectedness, cultural identity, self -knowledge, cleansing, and the use of symbols are important components of traditional healing for most Indigenous peoples (McCormick 2003).

Although many Indigenous tribes in Turtle Island (North America) maintained some ceremonies and traditional means of healing, the widespread reclamation of Indigenous healing initiatives got their beginnings in the American Indian sobriety movement in the 1970s which evolved into the Red Road Initiative (Hill 2008). This initiative is headed by Dr. Eduardo Duran and Gene Thin Elk who are also founders of the Red Road Gathering. This healing movement expanded Northward into Canada into initiatives such as the Four Worlds Development Project (Hill 2008). The "Four Worlds Development Project began as a research project based at the University of Lethbridge, and focused on supporting Canadian Aboriginal community efforts to address issues related to community healing and development. Four Worlds provided and published dozens of books, curriculum pieces, films and concept papers including the popular Sacred Tree and Walking with Grandfather" series (www.fourworlds.ca/who_history.html).

Ceremonies are central to traditional healing practice. Although there are thousands of traditional healing ceremonies used by Indigenous peoples worldwide, very few have been recorded. Some of the documented healing ceremonies in North America are the Sun Dance ceremony, the Sweat Lodge ceremony, and the Vision Quest Ceremony. Traditional healing practices such as the talking circle and smudge are also widely known and documented as well (McCormick 2003). The author will use an example from his home province to illustrate the present-day use of traditional medicine. The British Columbia First Nations Health Society conducted a province wide environmental scan on the use of traditional medicines and practices (FNHS 2010). The survey found that of the almost 300 self-identified traditional healers in the province, 58 percent were part of their community's health centre services and programs. Almost two-thirds or 62 percent of traditional healers taught their practices to others in the community. About half of the instruction was done on a one-to-one basis. In terms of elders/ traditional knowledge holders, 57 percent provided mentoring and support of health centre

Indigenous North American Healing

staff in their knowledge development. An overwhelming 90 percent of respondents wanted to see more use of traditional medicines or practices in their communities and 91 percent wanted to see traditional medicines and practices incorporated into their health programs. In terms of research 41 percent of communities are currently undertaking research in the area of traditional medicines/practice while 68 percent of communities would be willing to participate in traditional medicines/practices research (FNHS 2010).

The relationship between colonialism and its impact and resistance on the Indigenous and traditional healing practices

The main instrument of colonization in North America was the Residential Schools. By 1930, 75 percent of First Nations children between the ages of 7 and 15 years were enrolled in one of 80 such schools across the country and in the 1940s, attendance was expanded to include Inuit children as well (Stout and Kipling 2003). Over 70 percent of attendees had witnessed the abuse of others. Personal abuse was reported by many: sexual abuse (32.6%); physical abuse (79.2%); and verbal or emotional abuse (79.3%) (NAHO 2003). As the purpose of the Residential Schools was to assimilate Indigenous peoples, students were forbidden to speak their language, wear traditional clothing, or engage in any cultural or ceremonial practices. Outside of the schools it was much the same for the parents. This quote by a senior official in Indian Affairs illustrates the government policy of the time:

> The Sun Dance, the Tamanawas and the Potlach festivals help to keep alive habits and practices which are most objectionable, but, as they have religious and economic features, the department policy has been to suppress the worst features and wait for time and other influences to do the rest. This policy is having the desired effect as fast as could have been expected, although sometimes the members which had been thought to be pretty well dead will flicker up fitfully, and some Indians who have abandoned these dances and festivals revive them for a year or so.
>
> *(Department of Indian Affairs 1921)*

In spite of government attempts to eliminate these practices, traditional ceremonies such as the Vision Quest and Sweat Lodge served to re-inforce adherence to cultural values and help to remind people of the importance of keeping family and community networks strong (Lafromboise, Trimble and Mohatt 1990). In his work examining Aboriginal worldview Ross (1992: 183) states:

> All of the outlawed and denigrated facets of traditional culture – the spirit dances, the sweat lodge and pipe ceremonies, and the regular ritual offering of tobacco as a symbol of gratitude – must be seen for what they really were: tools to maintain and deepen a belief in the inter-connectedness of all things. Now that such practices are being slowly brought back, they serve a second function too, for they offer an alternative focus to that of our individualistic and materialistic value system.

The relationship between traditional healing and biomedicine is often an uneasy one. There are significant differences between these two systems of healing. Traditional healing is spiritual and holistic while biomedicine is scientific and compartmentalized. Traditional medicine has relatively simple methods of diagnosis but complex methods of treatment while biomedicine has complex methods of diagnosis but relatively limited methods of treatment.

In a journal article entitled "The Politics of Health in the Fourth World: A Northern Canadian Example", John O'Neil (1986) describes the experience of Inuit people and how colonization affected their system of traditional healing. As this example is very similar to the experience of most other Indigenous cultures in North America, it will be briefly described here. Because of the colonially introduced epidemics of infectious diseases (diphtheria, small pox, measles, influenza, and tuberculosis), anywhere between 10 and 50 percent of Inuit people in northern communities died. Because the Indigenous medicines used by Shamans were not effective with these white diseases the Inuit were forced to seek assistance from white traders and missionaries. This resulted in the Inuit shifting from a traditional health system in which each individual had been involved in all dimensions of health care, to a system controlled by outsiders (O'Neil 1986). Contributing to this substitution of cultural practices was the criminalization of Aboriginal spirituality and ceremony. In the Pacific Northwest, one of the most important ceremonies was the potlach ceremony. This important ceremony was used for the ceremonial distribution of property and gifts to affirm or reaffirm social status. Canadian Prime Minister John A. Macdonald did not see this tradition as valuable or appropriate and, under the guise of unifying the Dominion of Canada, encouraged the government to lay "an iron hand on the shoulders of the [native] people by restricting some of their non-essential, inappropriate rituals and leading them towards what he perceived as a healthier European mindset" (Cole and Chaikin 1990). The criminalization of ceremonies along with enforced attendance at Residential Schools were combined with other government programs to assimilate Aboriginal people. It is not surprising that many Aboriginal people have grown up with little knowledge of traditional healing, let alone traditional spirituality, language, and culture (Waldram 1997; O'Neil 1986).

Indigenous ways of knowing and definitions of illness and wellness

It has been argued that Indigenous traditional healing strives for the patient to reach a state of self-transcendence versus a state of self-actualization (Lafromboise, Trimble and Mohatt 1990). It is only through getting beyond the self that we are able to connect with sources of strength and healing such as family, community, culture, the land, and the creator. One medical anthropologist describes Indigenous healing as the reparation of damaged and disordered relationships (Waldram 1990). This view of self-transcendence differs from Western mental health approaches that stress the need to strengthen the self or the ego so that the individual can master their environment (McCormick 1996).

One of the hallmarks of Indigenous healing is that there is a commonly accepted belief amongst Indigenous people that the natural world contains the blueprint for how we should live our lives (McCormick 1996). As opposed to a Western hierarchical and compartmentalized cosmology that places nature at the bottom with humans having mastery over nature, an Indigenous cosmology sees god, humans and nature as equal and part of the whole of creation. Because humans are not seen as superior to nature, humans readily look to nature for direction and for healing. By including the natural and spiritual world Indigenous peoples have a broad spectrum of healing resources available to them. Western mental health approaches are sometimes viewed as restrictive in what they have to offer for healing (McCormick 1996).

Another common belief in Indigenous healing is that attaining and maintaining balance is an important part of the healing process. The Medicine Wheel model is used by many Indigenous tribes in North America to illustrate this belief. The model teaches that the mental, physical, emotional, and spiritual parts of our selves must be kept in balance to remain healthy (McCormick 1996; Bopp et al. 1984). If we do not maintain balance then we become sick.

Indigenous North American Healing

Similar to balance, Indigenous healing stresses the importance of connection to family, community, culture, the natural world, and the spiritual world. We become sick if we are disconnected. A traditional healing journey includes re-connecting to one or more of these sources of healing.

There are many other aspects of Indigenous healing that differ from mainstream healing. The following points briefly illustrate some of the additional hallmarks of Indigenous healing practices. The author recognizes that these are generalizations but merely wishes to point out some of the known differences. The means and ends of healing are often different due to differing worldviews for example Indigenous healing stresses Harmony, Inter Connection and a focus on the present while Western healing practices tend to focus on Mastery, Independence, and a focus on the future (McCormick 1996). As mentioned earlier, Western medicine has a stronger focus on diagnosis along with less treatment options, while Indigenous medicine has a stronger focus on treatment with more healing options (McCormick 2003). The Western healer takes credit for the healing, the Indigenous healer gives all credit to the creator and the relationship the patient has with their environment/creation (McCormick 2003). Traditional medicine has always seen the connection between the mind, the body, and the spirit. Western medicine is just starting to understand this connection (McCormick 2003). Finally, there exists a sacred relationship between the healer and the medicine in Indigenous healing practices.

Indigenous healing practice

This discussion will focus on the practice of Indigenous healing ceremonies to illustrate some of the theories and practices used in Indigenous healing. Some scholars have found that traditional ceremonies and traditional medicine follow a path of separation, transition, and incorporation. Separation means to separate from the present life or unhealthy way of being. Transition or transformation requires the dying of the old life and the birth of a new one. Incorporation means that the individual is incorporated or reincorporated into the community in his/her new state and new way of being. (Van Gennep 1960; McCormick 1996). An example of this can be illustrated by the Vision Quest Ceremony wherein an individual leaves her/his community and climbs up a mountain (separation). While on the mountain for 2–3 days she/he undergoes a transformation. Upon his return she/he is incorporated in their new state back into their community.

Historians such as Eliade (1958) believed that rituals and ceremonies were an enactment of a culture's mythology that is the basis of its whole existence. Mental health researchers who have worked with Indigenous peoples believe that ritual and ceremony allow Indigenous people to give expression to personal experience while at the same time connecting people with their community (Hammerschlag 1993). The Vision Quest Ceremony is said to help a person to realize the vastness of the universe, and by enabling the person to transcend himself, to realize ultimately his oneness with nature (McGaa 1989; Dugan 1985).

Some of the common therapeutic goals of Indigenous healing ceremonies are Confession, Catharsis, Abreaction, Connection, Grounding, Emotional expression, Empowerment, Balance, and Discipline (McCormick 1996; Hammerschlag 1993; Beauvais and LaBoueff 1985; LaBarre 1964; Torrey 1986; Garrett and Osborne 1995; Ross 1992; Duran and Duran 1995; Jilek 1982).

Spirituality is probably the most important component of ceremonies and traditional healing. Metaphysical or spiritual healing is universally utilized by traditional healers but is not used in the bio-medical system. In his review of healers around the world Torrey (1986) found that mental illness is universally thought to be caused by one of three things; biological events, experiential events, or metaphysical events. The first two are the foundation for biomedicine, whereas traditional healers also utilize the metaphysical or spiritual components of healing.

Case vignette

An example of an emerging healing practice involves teaching people how to use the land in healing. Canadian Indigenous communities and universities have recently experienced a growth in the offering of land-based healing courses. A recent example comes from the authors own university which recently offered an Indigenous Learning from the Land course.

This graduate level course in the Faculty of Education and Social Work provides an interdisciplinary approach to learning about the importance of learning on and with the land through Indigenous wellness practices, local language, and traditional plant medicines. Students learn how to approach the natural world with humility and openness and they learn about the different relationships they must develop to attain guidance and healing from nature. One such teaching is that provided by Mi'kmaq elder and healer Murdena Marshall who states that there are four understandings we must have in working with traditional medicines: physical knowledge of the medicine, personal connection with the medicine, respect for the medicine, an understanding of the sacred nature of medicine.

The healers and accreditation

Indigenous healers are known by many names throughout North America and the process of selection, initiation, and training varies between different tribes/nations. Three of the common specialties are the herbalist; diviner/diagnostician; and healer or medicine man (McCormick 2003). Torrey (1986) believes that in the field of mental health these specialties would be similar to pharmacist, psychologist, and psychiatrist.

The selection and initiation of healers varies from tribe to tribe. Among the Navajo a healer is usually not admitted into training until he has come to be called a "Hastin" or elder in his local community (Topper 1987). This quote by Topper provides one example of how traditional healers are selected and trained.

> This term is usually applied to a man when he is in his late thirties or early forties and has established himself in his community as a reliable worker, a dedicated parent, and a reasonably knowledgeable and capable person. At this time, if such a man shows an interest in learning a particular ceremony, is well acquainted with a medicine man, and has sufficient financial resources to pay for his training, he may become apprenticed to a local medicine man.
>
> *(Topper 1987: 218)*

The process of apprenticeship and training also varies from tribe to tribe. In most cases the medicine man is not trained formally in a school but by another medicine man (Jilek 1982). The Navajo apprenticeship to become a medicine man is complex and lengthy and can take as long as 10 years (Levy 1983). Further north amongst the Tsimshian a potential Shaman must be suddenly overcome by his 'Haleit' (medicine man's power) and transported to the verge of death through trances and visions in which his spirit aides appear to him (Torrey 1986).

Healer accreditation can be problematic in North America. Because most tribes do not have any formal certification or regulatory processes it can be difficult to know who is a healer or who has the right or authority to designate another as a healer (Waldram 1990). This is less problematic in small Indigenous communities where a healer is known by their reputation. In large urban communities it becomes more of a challenge.

Indigenous North American Healing

Training of traditional healers is also a concern due to the small number of traditional practitioners. It is very evident to many Indigenous people living in North America in search of a traditional healer that the growing demand far exceeds the supply. It is often the case that clients wishing to see a traditional healer must spend a lot of money to travel to the traditional healer (Duran and Duran 1995: 8).

Contemporary case examples and collaboration with Western medicine

The relationship between traditional medicine and biomedicine can be a risky one. Attempts to integrate the two systems would likely result in a relationship where the two partners would not be equal. It is also likely that traditional medicine would be dominated by biomedicine and regarded as an auxiliary status (Waldram 1990). If such a partnership is to work effectively then traditional healing must be part of the core and not part of the periphery. In a previous examination of traditional healing the author of this paper advocated for 'Collaboration' as opposed to 'Integration'. The full-scale integration of biomedicine and traditional healing may not be practical or even desirable (McCormick 2003).

Mental health programs and interventions that have been designed from a mainstream medical perspective do not recognize or meet the health needs of Indigenous people as they ignore the cultural, historical, and socio-political context (Smye and Mussell 2001). There are many recent examples of mental health initiatives that do respect the traditions, values and health belief systems of Indigenous peoples. One such mental health initiative that the author is familiar with is the Quu'Asa Mental Wellness Team (MWT) located on the west coast of British Columbia, Canada. The Quu'Asa MWT use mainstream, traditional, and cultural methods to increase collaboration with service providers and other mental health services throughout the region. The MWT has also been very successful in using Western approaches such as cognitive behavioural therapy with traditional teachings and approaches in a collaborative and culturally sensitive way. Most importantly, Quu'asa has been remarkably successful in reaching their goal to respectfully provide and exercise client-driven, culturally sensitive, strength-based treatment (McCormick and Green 2011).

What is perhaps one of the most successful mental health healing initiatives in Canada was initiated in the Indigenous community of Alkali Lake located in Central British Columbia. This community employed traditional healers to help its members revive traditional dances, ceremonies, and spiritual practices. Community members were introduced to cultural activities such as pow-wow dancing, sweetgrass and sweatlodge ceremonies, and drumming. The treatment strategy used by the people of Alkali Lake has been copied by other Indigenous healing centres such as Poundmaker and Round Lake. The guiding philosophy of these treatment programs has been: "Culture is treatment, and all healing is spiritual" (York 1990). The success of programs using this philosophy/strategy has been phenomenal. The community of Alkali Lake alone decreased its alcoholism rate from 95 percent to 5 percent in 10 years (McCormick 2003).

Future directions

The level of participation in traditional healing and in traditional ceremonies is growing. Research on participation has demonstrated impressive numbers. Obstacles to the survival and growth of traditional healing include the lingering effects of colonization as well as the 150 years of attempted assimilation and disempowerment of Indigenous individuals, communities and tribes/nations. Additional obstacles are: the unsupportive attitudes of bio-medical physicians and Western governments; access to limited numbers of traditional healers; and cultural appropriation (McCormick 2003).

In terms of policies, it is fair to say that the federal, provincial and state governments have done very little so far to develop appropriate policies and strategies to strengthen and protect Indigenous North American Healing practices. Twenty-five years ago the Canadian Royal Commission on Aboriginal peoples (RCAP) provided the federal government with numerous recommendations on how to reclaim and preserve traditional healing practices (RCAP: Canada 1993). Most importantly the RCAP report recognized the need for more traditional healers and the need for more culturally appropriate services and greater access to traditional healers (Royal Commission on Aboriginal Peoples 1993). Unfortunately, successive governments have not implemented these recommendations. The Canadian Standing Committee on Health recommended that medicines prepared by Aboriginal healers be exempted from legislation regarding natural health products. The Task Force on Aboriginal Peoples in Federal Corrections recognized the need for Corrections Services to provide spiritual and cultural services to Aboriginal inmates (albeit it did not recognize such services as healing interventions) (Waldram 1997). The Canadian Truth and Reconciliation Commission Calls to Action called upon the Canadian health care system to recognize the value of Aboriginal healing practices and use them in the treatment of Aboriginal patients in collaboration with Aboriginal healers and Elders where requested by Aboriginal patients (Truth and Reconciliation Canada 2015).

Ethical guidelines are needed to ensure culturally appropriate and respectful use of Indigenous healing practices. Several African and South American countries have developed ethical guidelines for their respective traditional healing organizations. The difficulty in developing guidelines for traditional healing is that such guidelines will inevitably be culturally encapsulated. Ethical guidelines will only be appropriate for use within that culture and cannot be universally applied across cultures.

A Canadian suicide prevention researcher Masecar (2006) explained the difference between Western and Indigenous science and how both can approach problems very effectively. In his words, the Western approach sees knowledge as the result of science. There is no greater "proof" than saying that there is scientific evidence for something. What is not understood is that each culture has its own form of what constitutes proof and that it is also misleading to use the term science in a general way as there are many sciences. Science is a product of the culture that developed it. Western science for example is concerned with being able to control one's environment. Indigenous science in contrast seeks to learn from and live in harmony with one's environment. The methodological approaches used in one science will not necessarily work in another science.

There is a great need for research concerning Indigenous North American Healing Practices such as the need for empirical research on the efficacy of traditional healing. Several researchers: Dauphinais, Dauphinais and Rowe (1981); Wohl (1989); McCormick (1996), refer to the lack of empirical studies in this field. One recommendation of the author is that research concerning Indigenous healing should ideally be conducted 'by Indigenous peoples' as opposed to 'on Indigenous peoples' or even 'with Indigenous peoples'. Research of this nature is a subjective exercise and should therefore be developed, delivered, managed, and owned by Indigenous peoples.

'Re-search' in an Indigenous context can also be seen as the need to search again for what we once knew. Colonization has disconnected us from traditional knowledge which kept us healthy for more than 10,000 years (McCormick 2017).

Training programs need to be developed and supported for the training of traditional healers. It would also be helpful to gather information concerning traditional healer organizations,

Indigenous North American Healing

policies, ethical guidelines, examples of legislation etc. that are used in other continents such as Africa and South America.

One organization that has helped to facilitate the development and acceptance of traditional healing can be found in New Zealand. Tikanga ā-Rongoā is the name of the Māori traditional healing partnership with the New Zealand Government. The Ministry of Health works with Māori traditional healing practitioners to support rongoā Māori within the health and disability sector. For a number of years, the Ministry has discussed with rongoā whānau – including traditional healers, Māori health providers and iwi – the role that traditional healing has with mainstream services. In December 2011, a new national rongoā governance body – Te Kāhui Rongoā Trust – was established to protect, nurture and promote rongoā Māori. There are over 600 Māori Traditional Healers offering services that are covered by the state health care system. (Ministry of Health 2014)

Conclusion

The future of Indigenous North American Healing is a bright one if certain goals can be achieved. One of these goals is to obtain government policies that would protect traditional healing from restrictive legislation and cultural appropriation. Another goal is to conduct culturally sensitive and respectful research into the efficacy of different traditional healing approaches. Yet another goal is to explore innovative ways to train traditional healers and to reclaim and share traditional healing practices while maintaining cultural integrity (McCormick 2003). The real struggle for traditional healing will be to reclaim and preserve the rich tradition of effective healing approaches that have been developed over thousands of years. Many communities have experienced the revival of old ceremonies, practices and teachings such as smudging, the sweat lodge, the use of the sacred pipe, fasting, vision quests, ceremonies for naming, healing, reconciliation, and personal or collective commitment. Some communities have been disconnected from their own healing practices and have therefore travelled to other communities and tribes across the continent to find spiritual teachers who would help them recover something of their own Indigenous spiritual teachings and practices (RCAP 1993). To cope with the high number of Mental Health Crises that occur in Indigenous Communities on Turtle Island we need to shift our energies and resources from intervention and postvention upstream to focus on prevention. The solutions to preventing Indigenous mental health crises must also come from the real experts, that is those communities and individuals who have successfully recovered from their own crisis. Government resources must shift from providing crisis intervention and post-vention to a new role of helping Indigenous communities in their efforts to rediscover, reclaim, and utilize the natural occurring healing resources, teachings and practices that work (McCormick 2017).

Traditional Indigenous healers do exist in our communities as they have for thousands of years. Traditional Indigenous healers have provided healing services to our people in the past, and can and will do so in the future. A strong traditional healing movement is occurring amongst Indigenous peoples in North America and despite the many obstacles faced by traditional healing the future for traditional healing promises to be a good one.

References

Beauvais, F. and LaBoueff, S. (1985) 'Drug and alcohol abuse intervention in American Indian communities'. *International Journal of the Addiction*, 20 (1): 139–171.

Bopp, J., Bopp, M., Brown, L., and Lane, P. (1984) *The Sacred Tree*. Lethbridge, AB: Four Worlds International Institute for Human and Community Development.

Bopp, M. and Lane Jr., P. (2000) *Nuxalk Nation Community Healing and Wellness development plan: A Comprehensive 10 Year Plan for the Healing and Development of the Nuxalk Nation*. Lethbridge, AB: Four Worlds International.

Davin, N. F. (1879) *Report on Industrial Schools for Indians and Half-Breeds*.14th March 1879. Ottawa, ON: www.google.com/url?sa=t&rct=j&q=&esrc=s&source=web&cd=&ved=2ahUKEwjh3KXA1 LzqAhUVMH0KHTYTBt4QFjAAegQIARAB&url=http%3A%2F%2Fwww.canadianshakespeares. ca%2Fmultimedia%2Fpdf%2Fdavin_report.pdf&usg=AOvVaw1B6FC6RS0enBUjQerzyM_Q.

Cole, D., and Chaikin, I. (1990) *An Iron Hand Upon the People: The Law Against the Potlatch on the Northwest Coast*. Seattle: University of Washington Press.

Dauphinais, P., Dauphinais, L. and Rowe, W. (1981) 'Effects of race and communication style on Indian perceptions of counsellor effectiveness'. *Counsellor Education and Supervision*, 21: 72–80.

Department of Indian Affairs (1921) *Annual Report of the Department of Indian Affairs for the Fiscal Year Ended March 31, 1920*. Ottawa: Thomas Mulvey.

Dugan, K.M. (1985) *The Vision Quest of the Plains Indians: Its Spiritual Significance*. Lewiston, NY: Edwin Mellin Press.

Duran, E., and Duran, B. (1995) *Native American Post-Colonial Psychology*. New York: Suny Press.

Eliade, M. (1958) *Patterns in Comparitive Religion*. Cleveland: World Publishing.

First Nations Health Society (2010) *First Nations Traditional Models of Wellness (Traditional Medicines and Practices): Environmental Scan in British Columbia* (unpublished report).

Garrett, M.W. and Osborne, W.L. (1995) 'The Native American sweat lodge as a metaphor for group work'. *The Journal for Specialists in Group Work*, 20 (1): 33–39.

Hammerschlag, C. (1993) *The Theft of the Spirit: A Journey to Spiritual Healing with Native Americans*. New York: Simon and Schulster.

Hill, L (2008) *Understanding Indigenous Canadian Traditional Health and Healing*. Doctoral dissertation, Wilfrid Laurier University, Waterloo, Ontario.

Jilek, W. (1982) *Indian Healing: Shamanic Ceremonialism in the Pacific Northwest Today*. Surrey: Hancock House.

LaBarre, W. (1964) Confessions as Cathartic Therapy in American Indian Tribes. In A. Kiev (Ed.), *Magic Faith and Healing* (pp. 36–49). New York: Free Press.

Lafromboise, T., Trimble, J. and Mohatt, G. (1990). Counselling Intervention and American Indian Tradition: An Integrative Approach. *The Counselling Psychologist*, 18: 628–654. https://doi.org/10.1177/0011000090184006

Levy, J E. (1983) Traditional Navajo Health Beliefs and Practices. In S. J. Kunitz (Eds), *Disease Change and the Role of Medicine: The Navajo Experience*, 118–145. *Berkeley*, California: The University of California Press.

Ljunggren, D. and Nickel, R. (2016, April 12) *Canada Holds Emergency Debate over Aboriginal Suicide 'Tragedy'*. Reuters World News. www.reuters.com/article/us-canada-aboriginal-suicides-idUSKCN0X927D.

Masecar, D. (2006) *What Is Working, What Is Hopeful: Supporting Community Based Suicide Prevention Strategies*. Canada: First Nations Inuit Health Branch. www.google.com/url?sa=t&rct=j&q=&esrc= s&source=web&cd=&ved=2ahUKEwi0xeur2bzqAhWRIDQIHfV1AhIQFjABegQIAxAB&url=h ttps%3A%2F%2Fmgss.ca%2Fwp-content%2Fuploads%2F2013%2F03%2Fwhat-is-working-report. pdf&usg=AOvVaw1xg84MNJ_HNOuE7E82Mo26.

McGaa, E. (1989) *Mother Earth Spirituality: Native American Paths to Healing Ourselves and Our World*. San Francisco: Harper and Row.

McCormick, R.M. (1996) Culturally Appropriate Means and Ends of Counselling as Described by the First Nations People of British Columbia. *International Journal for the Advancement of Counselling*, 18 (3): 163–172.

McCormick, R.M. (2003) *Traditional Healing Practices Monograph*. Ottawa: Aboriginal Healing Foundation.

McCormick, R and Green, H. (2011) *Quu'asa Mental Wellness Team Process Evaluation*. Unpublished report.

Ministry of Health (2014) *Tikanga ā-Rongoā*. Wellington, NZ: Government of New Zealand.

More, J.M. (1985) *Cultural Foundations of Personal Meaning: Their Loss and Recovery*. Unpublished master's thesis, University of British Columbia: Vancouver, BC.

National Aboriginal Health Organization (2003) *Regional Health Survey 2002/03 Adult Survey Highlights*. Ottawa: First Nations Centre. Retrieved from www.naho.ca/firstnations/english/regional_health.php.

O'Neil, J. (1986) 'The Politics of Health in the Fourth World: A Northern Canadian Example'. *Human Organization*, 45 (2): 119–128.

Ross, R. (1992) *Dancing with a Ghost: Exploring Indian Reality*. Markham: Octopus.

Royal Commission on Aboriginal Peoples (RCAP) (1993) *The Path to Healing: Report of the National Round Table on Aboriginal Health and Social Issues*. Ottawa: Communications Group.

Smye, V., and Mussell, B. (2001) *Aboriginal Mental Health: What Works Best*. (unpublished discussion paper)

Stout, M. and Kipling, G. (2003) *Aboriginal People, Resilience and the Residential School Legacy*. Ottawa: Aboriginal Healing Foundation.

Sue, D.W. (1981) *Counselling the Culturally Different: Theory and Practice*. Toronto: John Wiley.

Topper, M.D. (1987) The Traditional Navajo Medicine Man: Therapist, Counsellor, and Community Leader. *Journal of Psychoanalytic Anthropology*, 10: 217–249.

Torrey, E.F. (1986) *Witchdoctors and Psychiatrists: The Common Roots of Psychotherapy and its Future*. New York: Harper and Row.

Trimble, J.E. and Fleming, C.M. (1990) Providing Counselling Services for Native American Indians: Client, Counselor, and Community Characteristics. In P.B. Pederson, J.G. Draguns, W.J. Lonner, and J.E. Trimble (Eds.), *Counselling Across Cultures* (3rd ed., pp.177–204). Honolulu: University of Hawaii Press.

Truth and Reconciliation Canada (2015) *Honouring the Truth, Reconciling for the Future: Summary of the Final Report of the Truth and Reconciliation Commission of Canada*. Winnipeg: Truth and Reconciliation Commission of Canada.

van Gennep, A. (1960) *The Rites of Passage*. Chicago: University of Chicago Press.

Waldram, J. (1990) Access to Traditional Medicine in a Western Canadian City. *Medical Anthropology*, 12: 325–348.

Waldram, J. (1997) *The Way of the Pipe: Aboriginal Spirituality and Symbolic Healing in Canadian Prisons*. Peterborough, ON: Broadview Press.

Wohl, J. (1989) Cross Cultural Psychotherapy. In P.B. Pederson, JG. Draguns, W.J. Lonner, and J.E. Trimble (Eds.), *Counselling Across Cultures*. (3rd Ed.) (pp. 177–204). Honolulu: University of Hawaii Press.

World Health Organization. (2002) *WHO Policy Perspectives on Medicines. Traditional medicine: growing needs and potential, No. 2* [monograph on the Internet] pp. 1–6. Geneva: World Health Organization. http://whqlibdoc.who.int/hq/2002/WHO_EDM_2002.4.pdf.

York, G. (1990) *The Dispossessed: Life and Death in Native Canada*. London: Vintage UK.

41

INDIGENOUS AFRICAN HEALING

Olaniyi Bojuwoye

Every human society has its knowledge system with which it responds to a variety of environmental conditions including ill-health conditions or diseases (Mariach 2003). Every region of the world has a form of Indigenous knowledge system for healing, either formal or informal (Gielen, Fish and Draguns 2004). The Indigenous knowledge system for healing comprised bodies of knowledge and practices used in the diagnosis, prevention and elimination of physical, mental and social imbalance and relying exclusively on practical experiences and observations handed down from generation to generation, mostly verbally, but also, to a limited extent, in writing (World Health Organization, 2001). Indigenous healing systems are also described as knowledge systems locally developed, recognized and used by most of the inhabitants of a historical community which they believe to incorporate their health concepts and needs (Levers 2006; Mpofu 2006).

The African Indigenous knowledge systems developed for healing are integral parts of the African cultures. The African Indigenous knowledge systems represent the whole of the beliefs, attitudes, customs, methods and established practices indicative of the worldviews of the African people (Bojuwoye and Sodi 2010). Traditional African Indigenous knowledge systems have existed since time immemorial. The roots of the African Indigenous knowledge systems are traceable to the time when the foundations of the African cultures were being laid (Bojuwoye 2006). These African Indigenous knowledge systems are reflections of the ways African people perceive realities within their environments and, hence, the African worldviews which inform the cultural meaning systems and practices regarding how African people define human nature, ideal human functioning or optimal quality of life including conception of health, ill-health and health care delivery (Bojuwoye 2006). African people have drawn on these knowledge systems to solve specific developmental and environmental problems for hundreds of years (Mohamedbbai 2013).

In terms of how knowledge of traditional medicine is acquired, traditional African people developed unique ways of knowing and understanding the world around them including the visible world of animals, trees, people and cities, as well as the invisible or unseen world of spirits, powers and diseases (Oduro, Hennie, Nussbaum and Brain 2008). Main sources of knowledge for medicine or traditional health care, as claimed by traditional healers include God (acknowledged as the Creator and ultimate source of medicinal knowledge), the spirits (including the ancestral spirits through which God communicates the knowledge to humans), and, visions and dreams

496

(very vital parts of traditional medicine). Traditional healers are believed to be capable of communicating with spirits world in vision, dreams or trance to gain information for diagnosis of diseases, the causes of ill-health and also the cure). Other equally important sources of knowledge for traditional African healing are animals, plants and supernatural encounters. Through the supernatural contacts with the spirits in vision, dreams or trance, it is believed that traditional healers gain access to knowledge which, in normal circumstances may not be available to ordinary people. The acquisition of such knowledge is believed to be purely by mystical or magical power (Borokini and Lawal 2014).

Colonialism and African traditional healing practices

Although there is currently increasing recognition for the African Indigenous knowledge systems and, in particular, African traditional healing practices, many African scholars are of the view that Western invasion has been a set-back in the process of development in Africa, particularly in modes of knowledge production (Taiwo 1993; Afisi 2009). From the perspectives of these scholars, the eras of slavery, capitalism, colonialism and imperialism, neo-colonialism and all forms of dominations and exploitations that have been embedded in these eras constituted major stumbling-blocks in the actualization of African Indigenous knowledge development. The negative impact of colonialism on Indigenous African knowledge system, especially knowledge of medicine, has been described by African scholars and researchers as tremendous and irreparable loss (Feierman 2002; Millar 2004; Konadu 2008; Mapara 2009). Furthermore, Abdullahi (2011) also observes that the arrival of the Western culture and Western medicine, during the colonial period, led to cultural-ideological clash which in turn also resulted in an unequal power-relation that practically undermined and stigmatized the traditional health care system in Africa because of the over-riding power of the Western medicine. Moreover, with colonization came various aspects of Western culture, including education, religion and healing practices, all of which were imposed on African countries (Sima and West 2005). Indigenous knowledge systems were not given the chance to systematize and develop because they were considered as inferior and, therefore, marginalized. As a consequence, this area of Indigenous African knowledge was greatly impeded. In many extreme cases colonialists, across Africa, outrightly banned African traditional healing practices as these were associated with witchcraft, regarded as backwards and superstitious and, therefore, something that should be eliminated completely (Ancient-Origins 2019). For instance, the Whites-dominated South African Medical Association, in 1953, outlawed traditional medical system, while the Witchcraft Suppression Act of 1957 and the Witchcraft Suppression Amendment Act of 1970 also ruled traditional medicine unconstitutional thereby disallowing the practitioners from practising their trade in South Africa (Abdullahi 2011). Although in some African countries, during the colonial era, there were local efforts made to challenge the stigmatization and relegation of African traditional medicine, however, as Abdullahi (2011) further notes, the subjugation of traditional medicine continued in most African countries even after independence in the later half of the twenty-first century.

The theories and practices of Indigenous African medicine

Each society not only has its own culture and knowledge systems for responding to diseases and or ill-health, but also, each culture has its own unique explanatory models of health and illness that can be understood within the culture's respective worldviews (Mariach 2003; So 2005) According to Good and Good (1982), the meaning of illness for an individual is grounded in the network of meanings a particular culture has for an illness including the metaphors associated with illness and cure patterns that shape the experience of the illness and the social reactions to the sufferer. Moodley (2000) further argues that, it is the cultural perspectives that inform the understanding of the origin(s) or cause(s) of an illness and treatment(s) of such illness. Therefore, one major difference between conventional Western medicine and traditional African medicine, is the way of viewing illnesses and their treatments (Ancient-Origins 2019). Western medicine relies on natural science in its explanatory models of ill-health and treatments, whilst African medicine places high emphasis on the roles of social and spiritual conditions, power relations and societal institutional arrangements in the conceptualization of health or ideal human functioning as well as associated help-seeking behaviours (Angelique and Kyle 2001).

Furthermore, from the traditional Africa cultural perspectives, health and ill-health are multi-dimensional and are socially constructed. The multidimensional nature of health, as informed by the traditional Africa's cultures, considers each human as being represented in the physical body part, the spirit and the mind, the interpersonal part and being part of the environment (Bojuwoye 2010). When these parts are working together in harmony a person is said to be experiencing good health. Edwards (2000) also asserts that Africans view of good health is synonymous with euphoric harmonious relationships with the universe and the local ecology including plants, animals and interpersonal relationships. It is further contended that a healthy person is one who integrates with and contributes to the community and continues to work at maintaining balance, renewing order and striving to be in harmony with forces of nature impinging on him/her, whether these be humans or non-humans in the environment (Edwards 2000). For the Africans, good health consists of mental, physical, spiritual and emotional stability of oneself, family members and the community (Omonzejele 2008). Moreover, as Iroegbu (2005) notes, health amongst Africans is not based merely on how it affects the living, but also the non-living particularly the ancestors who must be perceived to stay healthy so that they can protect the living. In this connection, Setswe (1999) contends that the major focus of African medicine is the spiritual and physical well-being of people. Thus, this view of health has greater meaning, balance, connectedness and wholeness, both within each individual and also between individuals and the environment (Vontress 2000). This contention is consistent with the view of WHO (1993) that health is not just the absence of disease and infirmity, but complete physical, mental, social, occupational, and spiritual well-being.

Traditional Africa's conception of ill-health is also multidimensional as the belief is that people experience difficulties in different areas of life including the world of self (private or intrapersonal world), the world of interpersonal relationships, the world of environmental relationships and the world of spirit forces (Vontress 1996). Ill-health is disharmonious relationships or breaks in relatedness within the individual (between the body and the mind or breaks in the intrapersonal relationships), between people (interpersonal relationships) and their natural environment or other realities – spiritual entities (God and ancestral spirits) (Vontress 1996; Atherton 2007). Thus, like health, ill-health also has wider ramifications and connections with all aspects of human existence including the physical, psychological, mental, emotional, social, familial, occupational and spiritual aspects of life (Vontress 1996; Vontress 2000; Atherton 2007).

The fundamental causation of ill-health or disease is usually explained in metaphysical terms. The general believe is that ill-health or disease originates from the environment outside of the affected person and that it may be due to the actions of malevolent spiritual agents or witchcraft. Traditional African views consider disease as being caused by attacks from spirits or ancestors. Generally non-Western cultures often consider illness or disease as an affliction (Comarroff 1980). "Affliction" is also often used in place of ill-health in anthropological and ethnomedical literature to indicate not just the physical nature but also that disease or ill-health can be psychological, social and spiritual (Bojuwoye 2006). However, Kleinman (1980) contends that traditional Africa's perspective on disease or ill-health is socially constructed to indicate that ill-health has connections with several aspects of life including emotional, social, familial, occupational and spiritual. Moreover, by virtue of its social construction it must also be considered that disease or ill-health also has its origin in interpersonal relationships and not necessarily due to only organic causes. This African cultural view or theory of ill-health or disease is consistent with Dryden's (1984) assertion that some cultures view ill-health as largely extra-psychic, rather than intra-psychic and as a reflection of acute or chronic disturbances in the balance of emotional forces in the individual and important relationships system. To the Africans, therefore, the genesis of ill-health (disease or psychological disorders) may not necessarily be physical but also in the people's social realities.

Traditional healers and treatment of diseases in African traditional health care

In each Indigenous culture, certain members of the community are recognized as competent health care providers. These health care providers, otherwise referred to as traditional healers are believed to be talented and to possess awareness, knowledge, skills, values and attitudes all related to the practice of traditional medicine. According to WHO (1993), traditional healers are persons who are recognized by the communities in which they live as being competent to provide health care by using herbs, animal and or mineral substances and certain other methods based on the social, cultural and religious background as well as knowledge, attitudes and beliefs that are prevalent in the community regarding physical, mental and social well-being and the causation of disease and disability.

Traditional healers (men or women depending on the cultural groupings) usually dedicate their lives to the art of traditional healing within their communities and through long period of training, timeless experiences and wisdom help their people solve health related problems and make decisions for the well-being of people. Traditional healers, who are highly revered and respected in their communities, fulfil different social and political roles including divination, healing physical, emotional and spiritual illnesses, directing birth or death rituals, serve as security agents for their communities, counteracting witchcraft, and are custodians of their community history and cultures as well as the theories of healing.

There are many types of traditional healers depending on their areas of specialization. Most popular ones are the diviners, the herbalists, traditional birth attendants (TBA), bone setters, traditional psychiatrists, traditional paediatricians, spiritual therapists, traditional surgeons and herb sellers (Borokini and Lawal 2014) Obinna (2012) describes the role of diviners to be that of treating illnesses primarily through facilitating the direct intervention of the spirits; consulting the spirits world to obtain information about ill-health problem presented to the healers, including its causes and knowledge of the treatment of the same problem. Furthermore, the diviners also play an intermediary role between the spirits world and the physical world. The herbalists are the general practitioners who make use of herbs to treat diseases. The traditional surgeons are those responsible for circumcision and body art. Generally, it would seem that the roles of traditional healers are broader than those of Western-oriented medical doctors as the roles of traditional healers extend to advising patients in all aspects of life including physical, psychological, spiritual, moral, career and sometime legal matters (White 2015).

In terms of acquisition of knowledge, skills and values for practising traditional medicine, there are several ways by which traditional healers acquire the ability to heal. In some African cultures, the ability to heal is believed to be inherited from the healers' ancestors, while some other cultures believe that the ability is transmitted from another healers through training and initiation. In some cultures, healers are called by the ancestors. Some Southern African cultures believe that ancestors can call people to train to be traditional through inflicting some type of ill-health on the people. Whatever the method of selection of traditional healers, they usually undergo many years of apprenticeship to master the skills required in their areas of specialization.

The traditional healing process starts when a person with ill-health consults a traditional healer. The first step is diagnosis which starts with information gathering for better understanding of the patient and the presenting illness including its causes. Assessment process or information gathering about the patient involves observation and visual examination of the patient (including examination of the patient's eyes, skin or other relevant parts of the body as well as the patient's attitudes and gestures). The patient is also interviewed and through such interview information about the history of the illness including health history of the family is gained. Since it is customary for a patient to be accompanied by a close relative (or relatives) of the patient the traditional healers may also permit the relative to speak on behalf of the patient and through such means collect medical reports on the patient. Through the observation, examination, and interview the healer is able to establish the organic cause(s) of the illness. The spiritual or mystical cause(s) of the illness also need to be established and this is by divination. Divination involves consultation with the spirits about the causes of the illness and the appropriate treatment. There are various forms of divination including throwing or casting of divination chain, cowries or bones, reading and understanding of the patterns or arrangements of the falling objects and the chanting of divination poems. The traditional healer may also go into trance to consult the spirits world. Traditional African approach believes that the knowledge of medicine and therapies for treatment of diseases or for procuring health is not within ordinary human understanding and wisdom and that the acquisition of supernatural power for healing can only be through the spirits world. The healer needs to consult the spirits world to acquire the supernatural power for healing and also to gain permission of the spirits to carry out the treatment and in order not to incur the anger of the afflicting spirits.

For the actual treatment of the ill-health, this not only entails aiding physical component of human being, but may also involve the psychological, spiritual, emotional, moral, social and other components of the human being as well. Thus, African traditional medicine incorporates techniques with potential role of facilitating increased level of well-being in one or more of the levels or parts of the physical body, mind, emotion and spirit as well as interpersonal relationships (Atherton 2007). Furthermore, unlike in Western medicine with tendency to compartmentalize human experiences and to segment patients into physical, psychological and mental parts for separate treatments, African people do not divide their illness into categories of somatic or psychological, rather they express their distress as "*when part of me is ill, the whole part is ill*", irrespective of what the illness is (Buhrmann 1986: 26). Consequently, the Indigenous African medicine treats the "whole" person by directing intervention efforts at all forces considered as being responsible for ill-health by addressing both the symptoms and causes of ill-health in order to procure health, harmony or ideal human functioning (Edwards 2004; So 2005). This holistic model of healing is also responsible for describing the Indigenous African healing system as comprehensive since it is also concerned with illness prevention, health promotion and treatment or cure (Sodi, 2009). Thus, Indigenous African healing practice is not just about taking pills or herbal infusions, but it is also about making decisions, changing lifestyles or taking steps to ensure changes occur in the interpersonal, socio-economic conditions, attitudes and behaviours of people (Marks 1994; Bojuwoye and Sodi 2010). Good health, for traditional Africans, is also the result of appropriate behaviour and living in accordance with the values and norms of the traditions of the society (Iroegbu 2005).

Health care delivery strategies

African traditional health care delivery strategies are informed by the multidimensional view of health. Since health or ill-health is socially constructed, the basic health care delivery strategy of traditional African medicine is the construction of good social networks which usually involves the construction of networks not only of fellow humans but also of ancestors and deities (Bojuwoye 2010). Good health includes the viewing of an individual as a collective member of the community and as such good health includes good relations with the ancestors and the community (Iroegbu 2005). Thus, for harmony in nature and health for the people, traditional African health care delivery employs human interactions by creating activities for people to interact with one another (Shutte 1993). The human interactions are not just for the integration of the body and mind (intrapersonal harmony) but also for the integration of the individual with his/her environment (interpersonal harmony) (Artheton 2007). Thus, cultural activities usually created for the procurement of health or ideal human functioning are cere- monies which involve physical exercises and social activities such as rituals, festivals and many other activities that can create perfect settings for people to come together, commune with one another, share information and empower each other. The values of psycho–social intervention of this nature are tremendous and include education, problem-sharing or brainstorming for solutions, skill acquisition, more effective ways of coping and generation of mutual emotional support. These cultural activities are fundamentally concerned with social net-workings which are expected to result to reconstruction of physical, social and spiritual orders. As rightly noted by Ochoa de Equileor (1997), these cultural activities, are social group activities (family or community groups) for guiding and facilitating social and behavioural changes. Music, singing and dancing are powerful tools for promoting curative process. Music, singing and dancing act like forces of change and are transformative and important ingredients for healing (Vontress 1999). As music is played and people express themselves in dancing and singing, their spirits are freed from the contamination of destructive negative emotional feelings, and this in turn facilitates self-discovery and the creation of pleasant positive appreciative and affirming envir- onment (Atherton 2007). Group healing strategy as characterized by African traditional healing enhances group consciousness and solidarity promoting acceptance and appreciation of one another. Essential outcomes of group healing as espoused by African traditional healing are changes in the dynamics of human relationships from being competitive to being collaborative. Moreover, as emotions are expressed in dance, catharsis is achieved and realities from cultural perspectives are accepted as people embrace new values and behaviours in efforts to reduce deviations from existing culturally defined standards.

Contemporary Indigenous African healing

Traditional medicines are getting significant attention in global health debates. According to the report by WHO (2001), herbal medicine has become a popular form of health care as nat- ural medicinal products are gaining, increasing popularity and use worldwide. Due to the very prominent role played by African traditional health care delivery system, in 1977, the WHO gave formal recognition to it and has been encouraging African countries to make the practice more formalized to ensure quality and better service delivery (Truter 2007; WHO 2001). The WHO (2001) had also reported that some African countries are locally producing traditional medicines used for various diseases such as chronic diarrhoea, liver disorders, amoebic dysentery, consti- pation, cough, eczema, ulcers, hypertension, diabetes, menta health and HIV/AIDS in order to improve people's access to medicines. Many countries and institutions of higher learning in

Africa have put research into herbal medicine and training of traditional medical practitioners (White 2015). For instance, White (2015) reported that the Kwame Nkruma University of Science and Technology and the University of Ghana have established departments of herbal medicine and that some public hospitals in Ghana have also opened centres for herbal medicine where people can access health care.

In Nigeria, Borokini and Lawal (2014) reported that traditional herbal medicine has been receiving significant attention since early 80s when the Federal government established the Nigerian Institute for Pharmaceutical Research and Development (NIPRD). This organization is said to have developed globally accepted herbal sickle cell drug (i.e., NIPRISAN) and fixed dose combination drug for the treatment of Ebola Virus Disease (i.e., NIPRIBOL). These two drugs are results of collaboration between traditional medical practitioners and biomedical scientists. Nigerian government has developed National Policy on Traditional Medicine in 2004. In 2007, Nigeria published guidelines for registration and evaluation of traditional medicine. Furthermore, the Nigerian government has also established laboratories for research and development on herbal products.

South Africa, in 2003, drafted the Traditional Health Practitioners Bill and some sections of the Traditional Health Practitioners Act of 2004 came into operation in 2006. The Kenya Medical Research Institute has been collaborating with the country's herbalists. Many research laboratories have been established in many African countries with many traditional healers collaborating with biomedical scientists for research on African herbs for the development of new medicines to cure various ailments such as NIPRISAN.

Future directions and conclusion

African traditional medical practice has been in existence long before the arrival of colonialists and their Western-oriented medical system. With their own Indigenous knowledge Africans have been dealing with diseases and finding traditional solutions whether or not the diseases had spiritual or physical causes. African traditional medical practice is intertwined with cultural a religious beliefs and is holistic in nature, focusing on physical, psychological, social, occupational and spiritual aspects of individuals, families and communities (Truter 2007). Although Western medicine is generally accepted throughout Africa, it has not replaced but rather compliment Indigenous health approaches. African traditional healers remain central to the lives of many. The WHO (2001) estimates that 80 percent of people in Africa regularly seek the services of traditional healers. African traditional medicine is popular in Africa not only because of its cultural sensitivity but also because it is available and affordable. There has been a call for the integration of African traditional medicine with Western-oriented medicine. According to Chan (2008), a former director of the World Health Organization, integrating different cultural health initiatives would make for better public health coverage since the pooling of different cultural resources would make for utilization of the best features of each cultural system while compensating for certain weaknesses in each. To make for success of this integration both the traditional healers and Western medical practitioners will have to come together and collaborate (White 2015). For Western-oriented medical practitioners and traditional healers to work together members of the two parties must share their methods and knowledge (Borokini and Lawal 2014). Furthermore, there will be need for some form of training and regulation for traditional medicine practice in form of registration of the practitioners. Through registration it is hoped that charlatans would be eliminated while the practitioners would be placed under surveillance (Borokini and Lawal 2014). The training is necessary in order to ensure safety, quality and efficacy of traditional medicinal products, practice and to regulate practitioners (White 2015).

References

Abdullahi, A. A. (2011) 'Trends and challenges of traditional medicine in Africa'. *African Journal of Traditional, Complementary and Alternative Medicine*, 8(5): 115–123.

Adesina, S. K. (2005) *Traditional medical care in Nigeria*. Retrieved 9 October 2019 from: http://onlinenigeria.com/health/?blurb=574.

Afisi, O. T. (2009) 'Tracing contemporary Africa's conflict situation to colonialism: A breakdown of communication among natives'. *Philosophical Papers and Reviews*, 1(4): 59–66.

Ancient-Origin (2019) *Traditional African medicine and its role in healing in a modern world*. Accessed 13 September 2019 from www.ancient-origins.net/history-ancient-traditions/traditional.

Angelique, H. and Kyle, K. (2001) *Draft of Monterey declaration of critical community psychology*. Presented at the Conference on Critical Psychology, Monterey Bay, California.

Atherton, K. (2007) *Holistic healing*. Pindari Herb Farm. [Online] Accessed 21 May 2007 from http://pindariherbfarm.com/healing/holiheal.htm.

Bojuwoye, O. (2006) 'Training of professional psychologists for Africa –community psychology or community work?' *Journal of Psychology in Africa* (Special Edition on Community Psychology), 16(2): 161–166.

Bojuwoye, O. and Sodi, T. (2010) 'Challenges and opportunities to integrating traditional healing into counselling and psychotherapy'. *Counseling Psychology Quarterly*, 23(3): 281–296.

Borokini, T. I. and Lawal, I. O. (2014) 'Traditional medicine practices among the Yoruba people of Nigeria: a historical perspective'. *Journal of Medicinal Plants Studies*, 2(6): 20–33.

Buhrmann, M. V. (1986) 'Psyche and Soma: Therapeutic considerations'. In G. Sayman (Ed.), Modern South Africa in search of soul: Jungian perspectives on the wilderness within (pp. 203–218). Boston: Sigo Press.

Comaroff, J. (1980) 'Healing and the cultural order. The case of Baralong Boo Rashidi of Southern Africa'. *American Ethnologist* 7: 637–657.

Chan, M. (2008) Address at the WHO Congress on Traditional Medicine, at Beijing, People's Republic of China, 7 November 2008.

Dryden W. (1984) 'Therapeutic arenas'. In W. Dryden (Ed.), *Individual therapy in Britain* (pp. 1–22). London: Harper and Row.

Edwards, S. D. (2000). 'Developing community psychology in Zululand, South Africa'. In S. N. Madu, P. K. Baguma, and A. Ptirz (Eds). *Psychotherapy and African reality* (pp. 149–159). Pietersburg: UNN Press.

Edwards, S. D. (2004). 'The psychology of breathing'. *University of Zululand Journal of Psychology* 21(20), 26–38.

Feierman S. (2002) '*Traditional Medicine in Africa: Colonial Transformations*' New York Academy of Medicine. Reported by Carter GM. The Foundation for the Integrative AIDS Research, 2002.

Gielen, U. P., Fish, J. M. and Draguns, J. G. (2004) *Handbook of culture, therapy and healing*. Mahwah, NJ: Lawrence Erlbaum.

Good, B. J. and Good M. J. D. (1982) 'Towards a meaning-centered analysis of popular illness categories: Fright-illness and heat distress in Iran'. In A. J. Marsela and G. M. White (Eds.), *Cultural conception of mental health and therapy*. Dordrecht: Reidel.

Iroegbu, P. (2005) 'Healing insanity: Skills and expert knowledge of Igbo healers', *African Development*, 30(3): 78–92.

Kleinman, A. (1980) *Patients and healers in the context of culture*. Berkeley: University of California.

Konadu, K. (2008) 'Medicine and anthropology in twentieth century Africa: Akan medicine and encounters with (medical) anthropology' *African Studies Quarterly*, 10(2–3).

Levers, L. L. (2006) 'Traditional healing as indigenous knowledge: Its relevance to HIV/AIDS in southern Africa and the implications for counsellors'. *Journal of Psychology in Africa*, 16: 87–100.

Mapara J. (2009) 'Indigenous Knowledge Systems in Zimbabwe: Juxtaposing Postcolonial Theory' *The Journal of Pan African Studies*, 3(1):139–155.

Marks, D. F. (1994). 'Psychology role in the health of the nation'. *The Bulletin of the British Psychological Association*, 7: 119–121.

Millar, D. (2004). 'Interfacing two knowledge systems: Local knowledge and science in Africa'. Paper for the Compas panel in the conference: Bridging Scales and Epistemologies: Linking Local Knowledge with Global Science in Multi-Scale Assessments. Alexandria, March 2004.

Mariach, L. (2003) 'Psychotherapy in Africa – The mental health of indigenous and tribal peoples of Africa'. In N. S. Madu (Ed.), *Contributions to psychotherapy in Africa*. Sovenga: University of the North Press.

Mohamedbbai, G. (2013) 'Indigenous knowledge must be harvested for development. University World News'. Global Edition: 262. Accessed 9 March 2018, from www.universityworldnews.com/article.php?story=2013030712115748.

Moodley, R. (2000). 'Representation of subjective distress in black and ethnic minority patients: Constructing a research agenda'. *Counselling Psychology Quarterly*, 13(2), 159–174.

Mpofu, E. (2006) 'Majority world health care traditions intersect indigenous and complementary and alternative medicine'. *International Journal of Disability, Development and Education*, 53(4): 375–379.

Mpofu, E. (2007) 'Conduct disorder in children: Presentation, treatment options and cultural efficacy in an African setting'. *International Journal of Disability, Community and Rehabilitation* 2(1). Accessed 7 January 2018 at www.ijdcr.ca/VOL02_01_CAN/articles/mpofu.shtm12007.

Ochoa de Equileor, I. A. (1997) 'Rituals in family therapy'. In P. J. Hawkins and J. N. Nostoros (Eds.), *Psychotherapy: New perspectives on theory, practice and research*. Athens, Greece: Elinika Grammata.

Obinna, E. (2012) 'Life is a superior to wealth?: Indigenous healers in an African community, Amariri, Nigeria'. In A. Afe, E. Chitando and B. Bateye (Eds.), *African traditions in the study of religion in Africa* (pp. 137–139). Farnham: Ashgate.

Oduro, T., Hennie P., Nussbaum S. and Brain B. (2008) *Mission in an African way: A practical introduction to African instituted churches and their sense of mission*. Wellington: Christian Literature Fund and Bible Media.

Omonzejele, P. F. (2008). 'African concepts of health, disease and treatment: An ethical inquiry'. *Explore*, 4(2), 120–123.

Setswe, G. (1999). 'The role of traditional healers and primary healthcare in South Africa'. *Health, SA Gesondheld*, 4(2), 56–60.

Shutte, A. (1993) *Philosophy of Africa*. Rodenbosch: University of Cape Town Press.

Sima, R. G. and West, W. (2005) 'Sharing healing secrets. Counselors and Traditioner healers in conversation'. In R. Moodley and W. West (Eds.), *Integrating traditional healing practices into counselling and psychotherapy* (pp. 316–325). Thousand Oaks. CA: SAGE.

So, K. J. (2005) 'Traditional and cultural healing among Chinese'. In R. Moodley and W. West (Eds.), *Integrating traditional healing practices into counselling and psychotherapy* (pp. 100–111). Thousand Oaks CA: SAGE.

Sodi, T. (2009) 'Indigenous healers diagnostic and treatment methods for illness and social dysfunctions'. *Indilinga: African Journal of Indigenous Knowledge*, 8(1): 60–73.

Taiwo O. (1993) 'Colonialism and its aftermath: The crisis of knowledge production'. *Callaloo*, 16(4):891–908.

Truter, I., (2007) 'African traditional healers: Cultural and religious beliefs inter-twined in a holistic way', *SA Pharmaceutical Journal*, 60: 56–60.

Vontress, C. E. (1996) 'A personal retrospective on cross-cultural counseling'. *Journal of Multicultural Counseling and Development*, 24(3): 156–166.

Vontress, C. E. (1999) 'Interview with a traditional African healer'. *Journal of Mental Health Counseling*, 21(4):326–336.

Vontress, C. E. (2000) *Cross-cultural counselling in the 21st century: A keynote address*. Presented at the International Association for Counseling, Thessaloniki, Greece.

White, P. (2015) 'The concept of diseases and health care in African traditional religion in Ghana'. *HTS Theologies Studies/Theological Studies* 71(3). doi.org/104102/hts.v7113.2762.

World Health Organization (1993) *World health statistical manual: 1992*. Geneva: World Health Organization.

World Health Organization (2001) *Legal status of traditional medicines and complimentary alternatives: A world review*. Retrieved 12 November 2010, from: http://whqlibdoc-who.int/hq/2001/WHO-EDM-TRM.2001.2.pdf.

42

SOUTH ASIAN HEALING

Baiju Gopal

South Asia has very rich traditions of conceptualizing and dialoguing with mental illness. It is a pluralistic mix of religion, beliefs, myths, magic, and medicine developed over thousands of years. Healing practices in South Asian countries contribute to collective alternate world views about mind, psyche, self and personality, unlike Western knowledge. Ancient philosophy and epistemology of health beliefs, consciousness and psychological theories do exist as intellectual traditions in the countries of South Asia. The diversity of healing traditions is notable which are unique to the concerned geographical area and the traditions are determined by the cultural values and their evolution over ages. Referring to the Indian scenario of the complex and striking features of these healing traditions, Kakar (1982) observed that a stranger to this region can feel healing in its manifold aspects, which is a central cultural preoccupation of this region.

South Asia or Southern Asia, also known as the Indian subcontinent, comprises the sub-Himalayan countries called as the South Asian Association for Regional Countries (SAARC). South Asia is known for its diverse socio–cultural history and practices. It is the place of emergence of religions like Hinduism, Buddhism, Jainism, and Sikhism. The evolution of several languages in this region also gives an impression about the complexity of the socio–cultural dynamics which is evident in the variation of the health beliefs and traditional healing practices.

Different studies conducted by the scholars across South Asia have arrived at a consensus on the predominant role of the traditional healing practices in healing for mental illness in the Indian subcontinent. Majority of the patients consult shamans, mystics or religious healers in the different phase of the treatment process for mental illness in India (Bhugra, and Campion 1997; Charles, Manoranjitham, and Jacob 2007; Mohan 1973; Rajaram 1976). Voluntar Health Association of India (1991) points out that more than 90% of the Indian population use these services at some point in time. Zafar (2008) observed a vast majority of Pakistanis share many non-biomedical beliefs to the cause of mental illness like schizophrenia. Jhakris are the common name used for shamans in Nepal. The dynamic, synthetic and evolving tradition of Jhakris are present in healing for various ailments in Nepal (Sidky 2010). These studies and surveys pointed out that, in contrast to the West, traditional healers are often the first line of care for people with mental illness in this region (Schoonover et al. 2017).

History of Indigenous and traditional healing practices

The system of health and healing prevailing in the Indian subcontinent owes a history from the fifth century BCE to modern times. These practices can range from unorganized folk traditions of shamanic practices to sophisticated medical traditions such as Ayurveda, Unani and Siddha medical traditions. The present chapter emphasizes on the shamanic practices and the traditional forms of medical system in the South Asian region.

The shamanic practices are originated from the shared folk wisdom, beliefs and practices of native people which involve shamans, gurus and faith healers in alleviating various personal, familial, social and cultural problems. The theories and practices of this form can be identified in the proverbs, oral traditions, rituals, myths and narratives of various cult forms. Understanding this form of healing practices is crucial to analyze the accumulated socio-cultural beliefs of healing present in the communities collectively. Narayanan (2006) pointed out the origin of shamanic practices from the Indigenous communities in the pre-Aryan era while Dalal (2012) further explained its foundation outside the classic traditions of Vedas, Upanisads and the Bhagavad Gita. For instance, the etymology of the names of deities such as *Chathan, Chundalayandi, Chamundhi and Neeli* worshipped in the shamanic traditions in South India are rooted in the tribal communities which supplements the beginning of Indigenous practices outside classical and philosophical traditions (Narayanan 2006).

Ayurveda, Siddha and Unani are considered as the three major indigenized medical models practised in this region. Ayurveda, one of the oldest classification systems of disorders, is an Indigenous medicine and a way of life originated in fifth century BCE in Indian subcontinent (Kapoor 2011). The philosophy of harmonious living proposed by Ayurveda is rooted in the ancient Indian Vedic texts such as Rigveda and Atharva veda (Adhikari and Paul 2018). The classic text of Charakasamhita describes the concept, classification and treatment for various ailments. The Siddha system of medicine originated during the Indus civilization and then was popularized between 2500 and 1700 BCE, combines ancient medicinal practices, spiritual disciplines and mysticism (Augustyn et al. 2017). This system of medicine is based on *Saiva* philosophy, one out of six branches of Hindu religion. Similar to Ayurveda, it is developed through Indigenous knowledge of using natural resources for ensuring optimum health (Adhikari and Paul 2018).

The SSM is the oldest traditional treatment system generated from Dravidian culture and it is flourished in the period of Indus valley civilization (Mukherjee and Wahile 2006). The SSM is the oldest traditional treatment system generated from Dravidian culture and it is flourished in the period of Indus valley civilization (Mukherjee and Wahile 2006).

The practice of Unani is originated in Arabia in the 8th to the 13th century and travelled to the Indian subcontinent in the 12th century. It was assimilated into the culture and medical practices existing in this region (Sujatha and Abraham 2012). Through this assimilation, Unani evolved as one of the popular indigenized medical models in this region.

Although these systems of healing produce a very rich knowledge about the concept, classification, and treatment of mental illness, the mainline academic approach in mental health has maintained a fair distance from this cultural heritage. Misra (2003) argued that the colonial incursion was the main reason for this distance and even suspicion, denial, and undervaluation of this traditional wisdom, whereas Western Eurocentric knowledge of mental illness has been accepted and welcomed without scrutiny. A brief history of the colonial invasion will be helpful to understand this disparity further.

Emergence of a new knowledge of psychiatry: Resistance and anxieties

The lunatic asylums came to existence in south Asia along with colonial power. The newly imported science of mental health (psychiatry) created anxiety among the natives. In contrast to the west, the relationship between psychiatry and colonial connection is another important aspect of mental health history of south Asia.

At the end of the 18th century, lunatic asylums were established in different parts of South Asia. It was considered as the result of modern Eurocentric movement in mental health. Bynum et al (1985) observed that asylum became the pride equivalent to the steam engine, the rights of man or the spread of universal knowledge. In contrast with the other parts of the world, the colonial legacy and its interaction and integration with the modern scientific movement made the South Asian mental health scenario further complex. The emergence of the new knowledge of psychiatry and establishment of asylums posed major crises to the systems of traditional and Indigenous forms of healing. It was noted by Basu (2004a) that the medical systems like Ayurveda and Unani, which were being practised along with various localized but systematic practices that dealt with problems of the mind, was deeply affected by the coming of psychiatry in India as a modern, rational and Western set of knowledge.

But the endeavour of psychiatry was to create and legitimize the new knowledge which was unfamiliar and strange to the natives of the Indian subcontinent. Rubbing shoulders with colonialism they adopted all possible strategies to conquer the 'uncivilized' minds and sidelined the existing wisdom of the Indigenous knowledge of this region. Mills (1999) further explains the process of integration of colonialism and medical discourses through individual subjectivities. According to him, the British established various asylums in their different presidencies to cure the Indian insane using different treatment strategies such as medical treatment, scrupulous cleanliness, liberal diet, recreation and attention to all the functions of the body. The administrative report of the Lunatic Asylum of Madras presidency shows that moral management was one of the major treatment strategies applied to improve the conditions of the insane:

> *(1) Improved dietary (2) Better clothing (3) Special means for heating barracks occupied by the weakly and convalescent during cold weather months (4) General introduction of means for affording amusements to insane (5) Selected patients to be allowed to walk outside asylum walls (6) Greater attention to be paid to the feeding and clothing of lunatics when they are in transit to the asylum.*
>
> *(Report of Lunatic Asylum, Madras Presidency 1895: 5)*

The recovery or cure of the Indian insane was denoted by an exhibition of certain qualities in the individual linked to self-regulation and productivity. During the colonial period in Indian subcontinent, British medical officers made use of the therapeutic regimes developed in 19th-century Europe to determine treatment plans. The major agenda were controlling, reforming and civilizing the inmates in their sway (Mills 1999).

The resistance from the natives against the new knowledge of madness was evident in the low insanity rate reported in the asylums under British jurisdiction. The total population of the three asylums in South India namely Madras, Vizagapatnam, and Calicut in 1914 was 754, 100 and 190, respectively. W.B. Bannerman, Surgeon General of Madras Presidency expressed his deep concern about the less insanity incidence in South India when compared to Europe. His report submitted to the chief secretary of the government of Madras concluded the reason for the extremely low rate in comparison with the West lies in lack of education, scientific knowledge, and industrialism (Lunatic Asylum, Madras Presidency, 1914, pp3–5). The insanity number of inmates in other Asylum was also very low compared to the Western standard. The total asylum population of Travancore in the year 1932 was 191 (Velupillai 1940a). From the analysis of the 25 years of the Asylum report in Calicut Asylum shows that the total number of patients treated in the Lunatic Asylum from 1878 to 1902 is found to be 3103 (Gopal 2008).

Even though the resistance of the people was very passive and internal towards the emerging knowledge of psychiatry, it was very strongly reflected in their decision about mental health treatment for themselves and their relatives. One example of such resistance is evident in the case of Madhavan Iyyappan. This case also illustrates how colonialism and medical discourses were interlinked in British India.

The case of Madhavan Iyyappan

Madhavan Iyyappan was a patient admitted to Travancore Lunatic Asylum in 1889. The case was developed based on the correspondence between Madhavan Narayanan (elder brother of Madhavan Iyyappan), Diwan of Travancore (administrative head of the state), and durbar physician Esmond White. Madhavan Narayanan wanted the release of his brother from the asylum after four weeks of treatment. But, the authorities of the asylums were unwilling to let the patient go. Following this, Madhavan Narayanan filed a petition to Diwan against the asylum authorities and sought the Diwan to release his brother from the asylum. The Diwan of Travancore exchanged letters with the durbar physician Esmond White regarding the possibility of releasing Madhavan Iyyappan. The physician argued that Iyyappan was not fit enough to be discharged from the asylum. Following this, the Diwan requested that Dr. White release the patient. Madhavan Iyyappan was confined to the asylum, not for any criminal offences, the Diwan pointed out. He also stated that the patient's brother had assured to take good care so as to ensure that Madhavan Iyyappan would not trouble the public. Taking Madhavan Narayanan's promise at face value, the Diwan also argued that there was a rationale for releasing Madhavan Iyyappan from the asylum.

Responding to the Diwan's letter, Dr. White underscored the need to protect the law in the asylum practices and objected to the idea of letting Madhavan Iyyappan go with his brother. Dr. White made it unambiguously clear that admitting and discharging patients from the asylum were the duties of the doctor and that he was not ready to discharge Madhavan Iyyappan until his state was better from the medical point of view. Finally, the Diwan of Travancore informed Madhavan Narayanan that the medical officer had stated that Madhavan Iyyappan's condition was improving and that he would be discharged from the asylum once he was fit and safe to be released (Bundle 42, Cover files 1889).

An analysis of this case sheds light on the state of affairs in colonial psychiatric treatment in the 19th century in South India. It not only reveals the resistance of the patients' family towards asylum treatment but also the relationship between doctor, patients and local government in the colonial context. The physician's argument was based mainly on two points: one is that the patient was not fit to be released from the asylum. A doctor cannot allow the discharge of a patient if the latter was not deemed fit and healthy. The second argument is about protecting the rules and regulations followed in the asylum treatment. The first argument apparently reflects the anxiety of a good doctor about the well-being of his patient. One may find that the act of the durbar physician as the right act of a Good Samaritan, but the second argument showed that Dr. White was more 'concerned' about the rules and regulations. Surprisingly, he reminded the Diwan (the representative of the state) about the proper execution of the law in the asylum affairs. The words of the durbar physician show that the representatives of the colonial government had an upper hand over the psychiatric treatment in the asylum. The local state government was just a body to execute the policies of the British East India Company. The colonial rulers and their policies challenged the freedom and the rights of the patients.

The impact of colonization on Indigenous healing

The emergence of Western psychiatry engulfed the wisdom of the natives. Hochmuth (2006) explored this confrontation between Western psychiatry and the Indigenous healing traditions. He observed that one major agenda of colonial medical discourse in 19th-century Indian sub-continent was the presumed superiority of scientific medicine over Indigenous healing systems. Indigenous practitioners were regarded as shameless impostors who would not hesitate to use the most dangerous drugs and poisons on their patients. They were regarded as dangerous to the society and people, thus eradication of Indigenous medicine was considered as a way of protecting people's life (Hochmuth, 2006). It was not only eradicating Indigenous practices but also reach an extent where physically eradicating practitioners took place. M. G. S. Narayanan, a well-known historian from India, pointed out that colonial government even physically eradicated a group of shamans called Odiyans in South India. The Odiyans were considered as one of the most physically powerful people in that area with special skills in tough martial arts. One of the major arguments of colonial administrations about this assault was to protect people from the dangerous acts performed by the Odiyans (M. G. S. Narayanan, personal communication, 12 May 2006). It was believed that through a special magical act called odividya these shamans were able to flexibly transfer their soul to another individual. Although these practitioners are non-existent in the society now, the Odiyans and odividya became the subject for creative media like cinema and fictions depicting the cultural imagination of a dangerous shaman in the society.

Hochmuth (2006) from the analysis of the large documents in the Bengal context concluded that scientific medicine was not easily transplanted from the colonial centre to the Indian periphery; rather, scientific medicine was negotiated and accommodated. Based on the case studies he observed that negotiation was one of the major strategies used by the modern medical movement to conquer the beliefs of the people in this region. This negotiation resulted in overpowering the existing Indigenous way of understanding healing illnesses.

One of the major challenges faced by the British led mental health movement was the question of reaching out to people. The diversity of languages spoken in the region complicated this further. One of the major strategies adopted by psychiatry was to organize the psychiatric knowledge through vernacular languages. Publishing the knowledge of psychiatry through the magazines and journals in Bengali helped them to popularize the notions about psychiatry. Basu (2004b) argued that through this vernacularization, psychiatry opened up a new possibility of an allied science. This attempt was successful to certain extent to homogenize the plural cultural understanding about health beliefs in this region. The criteria of identification and classification of mentally ill became the major agenda of the proponents of this new science of the mind.

Theory and practice of shamanic healing methods

Much before psychiatry and modern medical movement began marching fast in this region, the different forms of healing traditions existing here, followed their own meta-theoretical framework and well laid-out practices. Considering the vastness of these practices the present section looks at shamanic and Indigenous medical practices in the Indian subcontinent.

The term shaman originated from the language spoken by the Jurchen people of ancient northern China and went places through the practices of generations of Jurchen descendants of the Manchu-Tungus people (Guo and Liang 2015). Many traditional healing practices in the region are unique because of the presence of shaman and shamanic performances or practices. One of the distinctive features of shamanic healing is described as the special ability of the shamans to get into an altered state of consciousness during the process the ritualistic healing. Voluntary and controlled trance during the process make them unique from other possessions that are uncontrollable and violent. The shamans mainly act as mediators between people and god or deity. The presence of shamans were visible in different forms of healing traditions practised in this region that included temple-based healing, ritual art form-based practices, cults and other community-based healing methods. Kakar (1982) pointed out that the conceptualization of shaman in South Asian context is very different from that of the West. Shamans in the west had been described as 'veritable idiot', 'trickster', 'outright psychotics' and genuinely ill. But shamanic practices were a part of the rural life in most part of South Asia.

Shamans act as mediators between the world of the client /people and the world of the god. In an altered state of consciousness, shamans "communicate" with his deity and understand the past, present, and future of the clients associated with the rituals. Researchers differ among themselves on whether the altered state of consciousness or trance-state is genuine or fake. Some are certain of the genuineness of this occurrence, while others portray shamans as pretentious. Others assert that shamanism has nothing to do with trance and is merely the acting out of culturally defined roles (Sidky 2010).

Instead of questioning whether the trance is real or not, there is also scope for asking questions on the connection of shamans with these traditions of healing and their deities. Repeated ritual practices, narratives, they identify themselves with the gods or goddesses. It also shows the intimate connection between the deity and the shaman which facilitate the strong beliefs of the shaman in the act of deity. Shaman's dedication and commitment to their culture and tradition also help them act as a mediator between god and people. Shaman is an individual who has made a one-time vow to the god. This intimacy with the deity facilitates shaman to speak for the god and carry the spirits of the deity.

Basilov (1999) explained the fundamental beliefs of shamanism in the South Asian context. According to him, the shamanism believes that all the surrounding world is animated, inhabited by the spirits that influence human life. The connection between human, nature, and spirits are reciprocal. The human beings are not superior but equal to other organisms existing in the universe. Since the humans are closely connected to the cosmos, it is possible for human beings to acquire some qualities of a spirit and visit the other worlds.

Recreating interdependent caste relationship is one of the unique features of shamanic tradition in Indian subcontinent. Historically, the society in Indian subcontinent by and large conforms to caste hierarchy. The power relationship between the lower caste and high caste defines the social and religious engagement of people in this region. Ishii (2017) pointed out that rituals of "lower caste" are frequently reduced to a symbolic representation of the caste hierarchy in the socio-political sphere. The number of shamanic performance revisits this caste hierarchy and reminds the communities about the need for interdependence between different castes in the society. Through a transactional network and relational divinity, the performers / practitioners involved in the act of this practice reconstruct a new model of caste relationship which has the great imaginative quality about an ideal society. The shamanic ritual art form called theyyam is a good example to elaborate the unique dynamics of caste system in the shamanic tradition.

Theyyam or theyyattam is one of the peculiar folk arts prevalent in the northern part of Kerala, South India. The attempt to harmonize the caste hierarchy is evident in this practice. According to Narayanan (1973), the theyyams are essentially forms of hero worship. When the dead heroes and martyrs are invoked through song and dance and magical symbols, the main episodes from their lives are enacted (Narayanan 1973). The common terms used for denoting this particular form of folk art are theyyam or theyyattam and thira and thirayattam. Attam means dance in Malayalam, the vernacular language of this region. Theyyam is another version for Daivam or God. Thus, theyyattam means the god's dance (Kurup 1973). According to Namboodiri (2006), the theyyam performers are mainly from the tribal group of northern Kerala. The performance styles could vary from one group to another. The main performers are from the communities of Vannan, Malayan, Panan, Velan, Mavilan, Cheruvan, Chingathan, Thuluvelan, Koppalan, Anjuran, Munnuran, Pulayan, Kalanadi, Peruvannan (Vishnunamboodiri 2006). Most of these communities are historically marginalized in the society. The dance or invocation is generally performed in the village shrines. It is also performed in the houses as ancestor worship with elaborate rite and rituals. Though the performers are from the marginalized society, including the upper caste like Brahmins bow down in front of the theyyam performers and listen carefully to the words of theyyam. This shows a different analogy, oppressed becomes the god and oppressor bow down to listen to the wisdom of the oppressed. The shamanic practices on Himalayan region are also performed by the so-called marginal caste group in the society. Only during a day of the shamanic practices, the people in the village accept the shaman as the mediator of the Devi (the mother goddess) and once the rituals are over, they will not even eat or drink from the shaman's house. He will continue as an untouchable in the society.

Although the acceptance of the shaman is temporary, it enables the society to rethink about the possibility of change in the caste stereotypes and discriminations. In that sense, the shamanic practices propose a social model, reflect the desire for freedom and rue the isolation experienced by the marginalized communities for a long time.

In most of the shamanic practices, the shaman may frequently appear to be a superior human in relation to the individuals of his or her community. The superiority generally explained in terms of the shaman's strong body, will, and commitment. Shamans are capable of performing mental efforts which are beyond the capabilities of the ordinary people in the society. For example, shamans of Siri cult in Karnataka, India, remember and recite 15,000 lines of songs, narrate the story of goddess Siri (Varghese, Gopal, and Thomas 2011). There is no documentation of the theme songs and it passes from generation to generation. The shamans during the theyyam performance in Kerala, India recite the lengthy story of the origin of that particular deity. In some of the rituals, they even walk on fire and perform the most difficult techniques in martial arts.

These abilities are generally interpreted as the capacity of the shaman to remember cultural myths and the efforts to serve as an educator who can pass traditions and wisdom on to the younger generations. This can also be looked at from the cultural expectations of society itself about the healer. Culturally, the society expects a healer who can resolve all the problems through magic. The culture itself attributes certain cognitive, physical and spiritual capacities to the healer that make them impressive and appear special to the communities.

The shaman identifies the origin of the disturbances with the help of the astrologer. More than the early family connections, other members in the community and outside family can contribute to the development of suffering. Pena kodukkal is an exceptional shamanic practice prevailing in certain region of India. In this ritual, the shaman identifies the origin of pena (spirit). If the pena (spirit) is from a dead person, the astrologer in consultation with the shaman identifies whom the spirit belongs to. During the ritual, the shaman explains certain remedies for resolving the problem. Most often, the shaman advises the family members to make a small model of the dead person and hand over to the family which he or she belongs to. Kakar (1982) explained a ritual called Sankat which is prevailing in the northern part of India. In this ritual if a close relative of the patient prays to the deity that he is ready to take the distress then the bhuta (spirit) often leaves the patients and possesses the supplicant. Through involving patients, relatives, family members and community, these practices attempt to bridge the gap between normal and abnormal members in the society. This also helps the patients to overcome feelings of isolation and moral worthlessness.

Wellness and illness presentation in the traditional medical model

The absence of body and mind divide is one of the common topics subjected to detailed analysis of the nature of the relationship between body and mind. Ayurveda, Siddha, and Unani have taken a clear stand on the development, classification and treatment of illness. According to Ayurveda, all of the functions of the body are controlled by three elements, which in ayurvedic parlance are called tridosas. They are vayu or vata, pitta and kapha or selsma (Sharma and Dash 2007). This theory of tridosas is considered as the fundamental explanation of health, ill health, and treatment in Ayurveda. Illness was defined as the result of vitiation or imbalance of the dosas. It is connected to the holistic life of the person which includes his or her lifestyle, age, occupation, food habits and state of mind.

Sujatha and Abraham (2012) differentiated the philosophical orientation, history and language expression of Ayurveda and Siddha traditions. The Siddha tradition emerged and was practised primarily in Tamil region until about the seventeenth century CE as a criticism to the Brahmanic orthodoxies. Most of the siddhars (the practitioners of Siddha traditions) belonged to the non-Brahmanic communities. But the conceptual foundation for the medicine was the same as Ayurveda. Like Ayurveda, this system also considers that all matter in the universe including the human body is composed of five fundamental elements namely, earth, water, fire, air, and sky. The food, which the human body takes and the drugs it uses are all, made of these five elements (Ministry of AYUSH, n.d.).

The unani system of medicine is built on the principles of four humours proposed by Hippocrates: blood, yellow bile, dark bile, and mucus. Human body is made up of seven standards which manage prosperity and disease condition namely, Mizaj (temperaments), Anza (organs), Quo (resources), Arkan (components), Arawh (spirits), Aklath (humours), and Afal (capacities) (Adhikari and Paul, 2018). Unani scholars believe health as the balanced function of all these components.

Training, development and accreditation issues

Planning Commission of India (1992–1997) observed that India has more than half a million traditional healers which includes all practitioners of alternate medicines (Dalal 2011). The healers' training and development, accreditation, licensure, and certification is a major issue debated in the context of integrating traditional healing practices with mainstream mental health practices. The training of Jhakris, shamans in Nepal are often done by number of teachers from different ethnic groups regardless of their ethnic background or religious affiliations. The special skills Jhakris learned from the different teachers will be applied in the healing for physical and mental illness (Sidky 2010). Although the shamanic and other folk healing practices are prominent and deep-rooted in the psyche of people, there is still lack of conviction from the governments and administrators about the legitimacy of these practices. But the traditional medical model received better attention and approval in the recent past especially in India the ministry of AYUSH (Ayurveda, Yoga, Unani, Naturopathy, and Homeopathy) was formed in 2014 to ensure the best possible development of Indigenous wisdom knowledge. Under this, the central government in India also developed guidelines for certification and licensed to practice AYUSH. There are national and state level institutions to train the professionals in AYUSH. But at the same time, there is a lack of clarity to deal with the other traditional models such as shamanism, folk healing, and other family-based practices. The practitioners of these traditions primarily get their training from the ancestors and pass it to the next generations.

Current mental health practice

The classical practitioners of Ayurveda, Unani and Siddha were well trained in their traditions of the medicine so that they have strictly and authentically followed these systems. At the same time, the exchange between the local traditional healing practitioners such as shamans and other healers is very much evident. Instead of treating them as binaries, these systems accepted the coexistence of such practices. For example, in the southern part of India, the treatment process of illness is traditionally considered as teamwork. It includes Mantravadi (shaman), Jyothyan (astrologer) and Vaidyan (Ayurvedic physician). A functional co-operation between these practitioners is very much evident in many instances of treatment (Gopal 2008). The following case demonstrates this relationship.

A 19-year-old emerging adult, Dinesh, hails from Ujire, South Karnataka, India was brought to Venkappa Nalike, a shaman who practices Kaleppune. Kaleppune is an Indigenous form of healing for various ailments in Karnataka wherein the shaman effectively mixes herbal medicine and ritual practice. The chief compliant given by the parents about the client was that he stopped talking to any one for the last two weeks after he got scared by seeing something on the way back from the workplace in a midnight. According to his parents, Dinesh got severe fever after the incident happen in the midnight. First, they have consulted an allopathic doctor in the locality and taken medicine for the fever. The fever was subsided after few days but the mental condition of not talking to anyone persisted in the patient. Since this problem was not resolved, they have again consulted a neurologist, did a CT scan as per the direction of the doctor and the results were found to be normal. Then they have consulted an astrologer in the locality and he suggested to meet Venkappa Nalike, an experienced Kaleppune practitioner. During the first consultation itself Venkappa Nalike came to the conclusion of the origin of this particular condition. According to him the patient got scared by a wandering bad spirit. He promises the patient's family that, his ancestral deities are much powerful than the wandering spirit and he will help the client to come back to the normal state of mind. He took a thread and did some prayers facing to the seat of his deities and tied on the patient's body. He also applied some bhasma (holy powder) on the forehead and both the shoulders and gave some herbal medicine to the patient to drink. Surprisingly the patient's parents testimonised an observable change in their son. This case validates the exchange between astrologer and shamans in the context of treatment for ailments. It further explains the back and forth process of the patients between the Western medical practice and traditional healing.

Poonkudil mana is also a well-known family-based ayurvedic centre in North Kerala, India. They had a fully functioning inpatient section at the house premises until 2015. Even though, the prime focus of their treatment is based on the Ayurvedic principles, they also include some prayer elements in the treatment process. One of the chief Vaidyans (physician) of the centre P.N. Namboodiri commented on this:

> *One of the important elements of the treatment is faith. Without faith, treatment will not be effective. Treatment is nothing but understanding the coolness and frustrations of the mind.*

A prayer mixed treatment would help us to understand and deal with this dynamic process of mind effectively.

(Personal communication, May 18, 2015)

The medicines used in the traditional medical models are locally available and appropriate to the environment. The prime ingredients of Siddha medicine is the appropriate combination of herbs, minerals, and metals (Sujatha 2012). A combination of medicines, medical procedures (Panchakarma), diet and activities were followed in the traditional ayurvedic treatment which is called cikitsa (Jayasundar 2012). Most of the medicines used for this treatment are primarily available locally.

An interview with Unni, a traditional healing practitioner in Kalakadu mana, North Kerala makes this perspective clearer:

> Various types of medicines were prepared at home for treating illness. Preparation of these medicines is very difficult as finding ingredients for the medicine is very time consuming. Kalakadu mana was very popular for a particular medicine for treating epilepsy. Around 25 ingredients are required for making it. Now we have stopped preparing it because of the non-availability of the ingredients and prescribe the medicine to the patients which they can buy from the shop. My ancestors were also good in preparing medicines.

(Personal communication, April 15, 2007)

Compared to the past the traditional healers are more open about the ingredients and preparation of medicines. They also occasionally refer the theory of Western medical practices while explaining the causality of mental disorders, which shows that traditional healers are aware about the need for integration.

Future directions

In South Asian countries the majority of people live in rural areas, but public health facilities and services are primarily focused in towns and cities. Traditional healers often reside and practice in villages which would be become the primarily available resort for mental health issues among common people. Since they share the same locality with the clients; Indigenous healers probably would have a better understanding about their clients' psychosocial problems (Shankar, Saravanan and Jacob 2006). The shared world view of the client, language and ethnic background act as an advantage to deal with the clients' problems.

The integration of traditional healing practices with the Western medicine is a new academic dialogue but yet to materialize in the public health practices. The majority of mainstream mental health providers are not in agreement with the concept, classification and treatment proposed by the traditional healing models but develop a singular training model based on the Western theories, On the other hand, the popular understanding of people about illness is rooted in cultural beliefs. This creates dilemma in mental health practices. In other words, the task of the therapist in every day practice is to translate the worldview of the client into a comfortable nomenclature of Western medical science (Basu 2005). This situation demands more culturally specific theories and therapeutic models accommodating the multiple voices of Indigenous knowledge. In particular, theoretical and intervention models need to evolve addressing the diverse cultural view in mental health practice. The possibilities of developing skills among practitioners to deal with the Indigenous ways of understanding health issues are pertinent.

Conclusion

South Asia holds culturally rich and diverse traditions of medical practices, shamanism, Islamic traditions and many other folk-based practices. Each of these traditions has different history and contrasting principles with other systems which make the scenario much more complex. The scholars worked in this field attempted to integrate these models with the mainline mental health practices but yet to become a reality. In this context revisiting this culturally fascinating phenomenon; understanding and interpreting it with precision and clarity will help the researchers and academicians to move on at an adequate pace.

References

Adhikari, P., Paul, B., and Satya. (2018) 'History of Indian traditional medicine: A medical inheritance'. *Asian Journal of Pharmaceutical and Clinical Research, 11*: 421. 10.22159/ajpcr.2017.v11i1.21893.

Annual Report on the Lunatic Asylums in the Madras Presidency During the Year 1895. Madras: Madras Government Press.

Annual Report on the Lunatic Asylums in the Madras Presidency During the Year (1914) Madras: Madras Government Press.

Annual Report on the Lunatic Asylums in the Madras Presidency During the Year (1915) Madras: Madras Government Press.

Augustyn, A. et al. (2017) 'Siddha medicine'. *Encyclopedia Britannica.* Retrieved from www.britannica.com/science/Siddha-medicine.

Basu, A.M. (2004a) 'A new knowledge of madness-nineteenth century Asylum Psychiatry in Bengal'. *Indian Journal of History of Science, 39*(3): 247–277.

Basu, A.M. (2004b) 'Emergence of a marginal science in a colonial city: Reading psychiatry in Bengali periodicals'. *The Indian Economic and Social History Review, 41*(2): 103–141.

Basu, A.M. (2005) 'Historicizing Indian Psychiatry'. *Indian Journal of Psychiatry, 47*: 126–129.

Basilov, V.N. (1999) 'Cosmos as everyday reality in shamanism: An attempt to formulate a more precise definition of Shamanism'. In R. Mastromattei and A. Rigopoulos (Eds.), Shamanic cosmos: From India to the north pole star (pp. 17–40). New Delhi: Venetian Academy of Indian Studies/DK Printworld.

Bhugra, J.C.D. and Campion, D. (1997) 'Experiences of religious healing in psychiatric patients in South India'. *Social Psychiatry Epidemiology, 32*(9): 215–221.

Bynum, W.F., Porter, R. and Shepherd, M. (1985) *The Anatomy of madness: Essays in the history of psychiatry. Vol II. Institutions and societies.* London: Tavistock Publications.

Charles, H., Manoranjitham, S.D., and Jacob, K.S. (2007) 'Stigma and explanatory models among people with schizophrenia and their relatives in Vellore, South India'. *International Journal of Social Psychiatry, 53*(4): 325–332.

Dalal, A.K. (2011) 'Folk wisdom and traditional healing practices: Some lessons for modern psychotherapies'. *Foundations of Indian Psychology, 2*: 21–35.

Gopal, B. (2008) *The concept of madness and its management: The Kerala scenario.* Unpublished dissertation, Department of Psychology, University of Calicut.

Guo, S. and Liang, Y. (2015) 'An investigation into the origin of the term "Shaman"'. *Sibirica: Interdisciplinary Journal of Siberian Studies, 14*:3.

Hochmuth, C. (2006) 'Patterns of medical culture in colonial Bengal, 1835–1880'. *Bulletin of the History of Medicine, 80*(1): 39–72.

Ishii, M. (2017) 'Caring for divine infrastructures: nature and spirits in a special economic zone in India'. *Ethnos, 82*(4): 690–710.

Jayasundar, R. (2012) 'Contrasting approaches to health and disease – Ayurveda and biomedicine'. *Medicine, state and society – indigenous medicine and medical pluralism in contemporary India.* Delhi: Orient Longman.

Kakar, S. (1982) *Shamans, mystics and doctors. A psychological inquiry into India and its healing traditions.* Delhi: Oxford University Press.

Kapoor, K. (2011) 'The philosophy of healing in Indian medicine'. *Foundations of Indian Psychology, Vol 2: Practical Applications: 9.* New Delhi: Pearson.

Kurup, K.K.N. (1973) *The cult of teyyam and hero worship in Kerala.* Calcutta: Indian Publications.

Mills, J.H. (1999) 'Re-forming the Indian: Treatment regimes in the lunatic asylums of British India, 1857–1880'. *The Indian Economic and Social History Review, 36* (4): 407–409.

Ministry of AYUSH (n.d.). *Siddha: Basic Concepts.* Retrieved from http://ayush.gov.in/about-the-systems/siddha/basic-concepts.

Misra, G. (2003) 'Implications of culture for psychological knowledge'. In J.W. Berry, R.C. Misra and R.C. Tripathi (Eds.), Psychology in human and social development (pp. 31–67). New Delhi: Sage.

Mohan, B. (1973) *Social psychiatry in India: A treatise on the mentally ill.* Calcutta: Minerva Associates.

Mukherjee, P. K. and Wahile, A. (2006). 'Integrated approaches towards drug development from Ayurveda and other Indian system of medicines'. *Journal of Ethnopharmacology,* 103 (1), 25–35.

Namboodiri, M.V. (2004) *Kalisangalpam Keralaparisarathil.* Chirakkal: Kerala Folklore Academy.

Nambudiri, M.V. (2005) *Teyyam Tirayudetottampattukal.* Kottayam: Current books.

Namboodiri, M.V. (2006) *Theyyavum Thirayum.* Thiruvanthapuram: Centre for Kerala Studies.

Narayanan, K. (2006) *Manthravatham Keralathil.* Kozhikode: The Mathrubhumi Printing & Publishing Co. Ltd.

Narayanan, M.G.S. (1973) *In forward of the cult of Teyyam and hero worship in Kerala.* Calcutta. Indian Publications.

Rajaram, S. (1976) Methods of management of psychiatric patient before coming to hospital. D.S.W. dissertation, Bangalore University.

SAARC (2018). *South Asian Association for Regional Cooperation.* Retrieved from http://saarc-sec.org/about-saarc.

Serial 2886/file 3634/bundle 141/year *1889Lunatics- Private, their release from the asylum*

Sidky, H. (2010) 'On the antiquity of shamanism and its role in human religiosity'. *Method & Theory in the Study of Religion, 22*(1): 68–92.

Schoonover, J., Lipkin, S., Javid, M., Rosen, A., Solanki, M., Shah, S., and Katz, C.L. (2014) 'Perceptions of traditional healing for mental illness in rural Gujarat. *Annals of global health, 80*(2): 96–102.

Sujatha, V and Abraham, L (2012) *Medical pluralism in contemporary India.* New Delhi: Orient Blackswan.

Shankar, B.R., Saravanan, B., and Jacob, K.S. (2006) 'Explanatory models of common mental disorders among traditional healers and their patients in rural south India'. *International Journal of Social Psychiatry, 52*(3): 221–233.

Sharma, R.K. and Dash, B. (2007) *Charaka Samhita.* Varanasi: Showkhamba Sankrit series office

Varghese, K.J., Gopal, B., and Thomas, T.M. (2011) 'Revisiting psychotherapeutic practices in Karnataka, India: lessons from indigenous healing methods'. *International Journal of Health Promotion and Education, 49*(3): 128–136.

Velupillai, T.K. (1940a) *The Travancore State Manual.* Vol III. Trivandrum: The Government of Travancore.

Voluntar Health Association of India (1991) *India's health status.* New Delhi: Voluntar Health Association of India.

Zafar, S.N., Syed, R., Tehseen, S., Gowani, S.A., Waqar, S., Zubair, A., and Naqvi, H. (2008) 'Perceptions about the cause of schizophrenia and the subsequent help seeking behavior in a Pakistani population – results of a cross-sectional survey'. *BMC Psychiatry, 8*(1): 56.

43

CARIBBEAN HEALING

Shivon Raghunandan and Roy Moodley

Through migration, immigration and globalization, traditional healing methods are becoming increasingly more widespread in the West. There is an emergent awareness of spirituality as a force in healing, particularly in mental health. Black and ethnic minority communities in the Caribbean and diaspora use a wide variety of traditional healing and spiritual practices, such as Voodoo, Spiritism, Espiritismo, Santeria, Spiritual Baptist, Maat and Christian Pentecostal, for treating health and mental health ailments (Bilby and Handler 2004; Blom et al. 2015; Moodley 2011). These spiritual and healing practices were particularly relevant during the colonial period when very little attention was given to the health of enslaved peoples.

Colonialism and systemic racism led to the disavowal of Caribbean healing practices which were viewed as "primitive" and "superstitious" (Gomez 2014: 97). Caribbean spiritual aetiology of mental and physical ailments is frequently dismissed by Western biomedical models (Maharajh and Parasram 1999). The dominant positivistic approach asserts, "basic science transcends culture" and argues that anti-reductionists and holistic approaches are merely placebogenic, where benefits only stem from the empathic nature of healers and sociocultural beliefs of those seeking treatment (Mommaerts and Devroey 2013: 280). Caribbean medicines and healing practices are seen as having limited empirical evidence on efficacy, validity and 'safety', which is oftentimes used to legitimize their exclusion from mainstream health care (Moodley and Sutherland 2011). However, despite the efforts to exclude these healing practices, culture-specific beliefs and traditional remedial interventions *are* widespread among culturally and spiritually diverse clients and are often the preferred choice for many clients. According to Kirmayer (2004), 20–40% of the adult population in Canada, Australia, the United Kingdom, and the United States use complementary and traditional medicines. More than half of the American population seek complementary and alternative treatments (Moodley 2013).

Western health and mental health models were developed and intended for a predominantly White, Western, Christian, male, heterosexual, cisgender population and are "essentially Eurocentric, ethnocentric, individualistic, patriarchal and social-class oriented" (Moodley 2000: 166). Consequently, Western treatment modalities often dismiss culture-specific syndromes and idioms of distress resulting in high prevalence of psychological distress and physical ailments, debilitating sense of inadequacy and low self-esteem, over-diagnosis and mis-diagnosis of mental health disorders within Caribbean communities (Sutherland, Moodley and Chevannes 2014). The underutilization and premature termination of Western mental health services by Caribbean peoples highlight the importance of understanding culturally appropriate health/mental health treatment approaches (Hutchinson and Sutherland 2013; Ojelade et al. 2014).

Since traditional healing practices have been a part of the geopolitical landscape of the Caribbean since colonialism, there has been an accumulation of knowledge over time, providing researchers with rich information on cultural practices of healing. A historical, cultural and spiritual contextualization of Caribbean healing is necessary in understanding the health and mental health of clients from the Caribbean and the diaspora (Arthur and Whitley 2015). In this chapter, we will discuss Caribbean healing practices and healers including *Obeah, Vodou, Santeria* and *Shango*. This chapter will also discuss Caribbean healing within a sociocultural, historical and geopolitical context. Implications for sensitive and culturally congruent integration of Caribbean healing beliefs and practices into Western healing frameworks will be explored. Finally, we will discuss recommendations and future directions for Caribbean healing practices.

We wish to acknowledge that the healing practices discussed below may not be faithfully represented, as much of these traditions were orally transmitted and intellectualization may fail to relay precise, sacred nuances that are only accessible through original languages, rituals and practices. In addition, we wish to acknowledge the First Peoples of the Caribbean, whose healing practices are not discussed in this chapter. However, we recognize that Indigenous Amerindians of the Caribbean founded and utilized herbal medicines and scared connections with Spirits long before colonialism (Maharajh and Parasram 1999).

Colonial history and its impacts on Caribbean healing

Many Caribbean healing practices originated in Africa and were brought to the Caribbean during the time of slavery. These practices evolved from the cruel, oppressive and dehumanizing experiences of enslaved Africans who were forced to assimilate into 'European approved' systems of existence (Maharajh and Parasram 1999; Sutherland et al. 2014). The physical and mental well-being of enslaved peoples were disregarded by colonizers, and enslaved Africans sought the remedial properties of African spiritual and folk medicines, giving birth to various healing practices still readily practiced in the Caribbean and the diaspora (Sutherland et al. 2014). Many of these practices were also coalesced with spiritual and social traditions of the First Peoples of the Caribbean, as well as the religious and spiritual traditions of Indians and European peoples. This resulted in the birth of various spiritualities and healing practices in the Caribbean, including *Obeah, Spiritism, Spiritual Baptist, Shango/Orisha, Vodou, Kali-Mai, Candomblé, Brua, Lucumi, Rastafari* and *Santeria*. Consideration of the socio-political constituents of these healing practices is key, particularly the colonial/historical trauma, oppressive, exploitative and survival underpinnings rooted in these approaches (Bilby and Handler 2004; Blom et al. 2015; Moodley 2011; Ojelade et al. 2014; Sutherland et al. 2014). Caribbean healing practices "evolved to accommodate racial discrimination and cultural marginalization" (Moodley 2011: 75). A critical socio-political and colonial consideration will therefore allow for accurate etiological (SR: aetiological or etiological?) conceptualization of health and mental health ailments and inform appropriate treatment approaches and interventions within a Caribbean context, holding the capacity to decolonize and heal from colonial/oppressive internalizations and trauma (Crosson 2015).

The adverse effects of colonization are evident in the high rates of mental health diagnoses, institutionalization and criminalization of Black, ethnic minorities and Caribbean peoples. These communities continue to have higher rates of involuntary psychiatric detainment, experience more police brutality, and are 44% more likely to be detained under the Mental Health Act compared to White clients who may present with similar psychological symptoms (Sutherland et al. 2014). Culturally incongruent Western clinicians often fail to acknowledge and consider the historical trauma and the prevailing (post-)colonial oppression of Caribbean peoples, but focus exclusively on the emotional and psychological symptoms without consideration of the geopolitical root cause of these symptoms. Consequently, the omission of a holistic spiritual approach, and the use of a predominantly Eurocentric framework may in fact be "reminiscent of colonialism and be retraumatizing" for many Caribbean clients (Sutherland and Moodley 2010: 271).

It is important to be reminded at this point that Caribbean peoples are vastly heterogeneous and as a consequence of colonialism, globalization and migration, Caribbean peoples possess diverse beliefs on health and healing including positive views on Western biomedical treatments (Hutchinson and Sutherland, 2013). A study by Arthur and Whitley (2015) show that Jamaican clients attributed the causes of their mental illnesses to cannabis, biological factors (genetics, chemical imbalances), psychological factors (stress), socio-economic determinants and spiritual and religious causes. A research by Ojelade et al. (2014) found that clients credited their mental illness to Western socialization (adopting a Western identity and disowning their cultural identity), individual behaviours and ancestral causes, and utilized personal resources, spiritual resources and Western therapy in their treatments.

Caribbean healing methods

Psychological distress and "culture-bound syndromes" are oftentimes seen as interconnecting occurrences in Caribbean health frameworks (Campinha-Bacote 1992: 11). The creolized healing traditions of the Caribbean posit that ancestral spirits/entities and deities infiltrate the daily lives of people, and ailments are partly a result of spiritual afflictions (Sutherland et al. 2014). It is believed that 'supernaturally engendered illnesses' may stem from tumultuous relationships with ancestors, disharmony with spirits and inflictions by malevolent living beings. Emotional distress and mental illness may be seen as being in disharmony and disequilibrium with Gods, Goddesses and/or Spirits and derived from nature, spiritual and/or supernatural forces (Kirmayer 2004; Moodley 2013; Moodley and Sutherland 2011). A study by Ojelade et al. (2014) showed that all participants attributed their Western-diagnosed conditions – such as anxiety, mood disorders, substance and psychotic disorders – to spiritual aetiologies.

Seeking the remedial guidance of traditional healers is therefore an acumen solution where healers are believed to have "the power to detect, eradicate or placate the offending spirit" (Sutherland 2014: 19). Healing may involve engaging spiritual powers from spirits, deities and ancestors to alleviate physical and mental ailments, and even personal misfortunes (Moodley and Bertrand 2011). Integration of body, mind and spirit is necessary when addressing psychological distress as they are believed to be interconnected and disturbance in one will inadvertently affect the other. Healing is therefore holistically guided and necessitates the integration of physical, mental and spiritual components (James 2012). Caribbean healers may thus engage the body in treatment – as is evident in ritualistic movement, dance and prescriptive exercise – and the physical body is often the access point of treatment (Blom et al. 2015).

It is also worth noting that peoples from the Caribbean and diaspora may differentiate between curing and healing. Curing is seen as symptom relief and healing is conceptualized as treating the whole being, requiring the integration of physical, mental and spiritual components (James 2012) as is practiced in *Obeah, Vodou, Santeria* and *Shango/Orisha*.

Obeah

The word *Obeah* is loosely translated as "'practitioner, herbalist', 'doctor', 'spiritual power' or 'knowledge of the arts'" (Handler and Bilby 2001: 92) and was derived from West Africa during colonialism to diagnose, heal and protect enslaved Africans from ailments and harm, including those believed to be inflicted by slave owners. Obeah was also used to regain balance and autonomy during this pre-emancipation period, as it served as an instrument of control and support (Hutchinson and Sutherland 2013; Murrell 2014; Wisecup 2013). The 'fear and intimidation' associated with Obeah was therefore a positive anti-colonial tool for enslaved Africans (Bilby and Handler 2004; Meudec 2017).

Obeah is often misconceived as an 'evil and dangerous' practice, which emanated from hegemonic colonial ideologies and fears (Handler and Bilby 2001; Wisecup 2013). Bilby and Handler (2004: 156) state that popular anti-Obeah stigmatization stems from a "colonialist and racist lens", where White European cultural conception of witchcraft and sorcery influenced the deeply–entrenched, negative views on Obeah. Obeah was considered a viable threat to colonial supremacy by colonizers, as it was believed to have the potential to reinstate political, cultural, social and individual sovereignty to enslaved Africans (Bilby and Handler 2004). For instance, enslaved Africans involved in the Jamaican slave rebellion in 1760 were believed to have used Obeah to spearhead the rebellion (Handler and Bilby 2001). Obeah was criminalized in Jamaica in 1898 and continues to be scrutinized with pervasive negative anti-Obeah ideologies in many Caribbean islands (James 2012).

Supporters fervently lobby against anti-Obeah laws and ideologies. For example, a supporter states, "these laws came about from the colonial masters and these laws were intended to suppress the African race and to suppress the spirituality that is within the African" (Bilby and Handler 2004: 166). Stigmatization remains highly pervasive, even among the Caribbean community and diaspora, attributable to internalized colonial discourse, and it is often associated with peoples from African descents, rural, elderly, creole-speaking and economically disadvantaged peoples (Crosson 2015; Meudec 2017). Secrecy in worship and practice is commonplace and Crosson (2015: 154) states, many practitioners "maintain anti-African ideologies by day, even though they might consult Obeah practitioners in desperation by night".

In the Caribbean and diaspora, Obeah is comprised of a non-monolithic set of beliefs and practices, and is centralized around the relationship between the human realm and the spirit realm (Meudec 2017; Olmos and Paravisini-Gebert 2003). It is characterized by practices involving manipulation and control of spiritual forces and divination (Bilby and Handler 2004). Obeah is a dynamic spirituality that incorporates spiritual and ancestor possession and divination, drumming, dancing, foods, scents, dreams and visions (Arthur and Whitley 2015). Obeah is believed to have abundant benefits including healing, treatment of ailments and illnesses, protection against harm, redressing harm and injury, bringing about prosperity and relief of misfortunes e.g. aiding in locating stolen belongings/properties, removal of hexes (Bilby and Handler 2004; Handler and Bilby 2001). Many Obeah practitioners believe mental illness, commonly referred to as 'madness', has spiritual aetiologies (Arthur and Whitley 2015) and Obeah healers may integrate sacred healing elements from both the spirit and medicinal realms (Handler and Bilby 2001; Murrell 2014).

Although Obeah has endured relentless colonial, legal, political and religious scrutiny, it is still widely practiced in the Caribbean and the diaspora. This indefatigability is attributed to the oral transmission of Obeah through apprenticeship, familial inheritance and self-teachings (Meudec 2017). The integration of the healing practices of Obeah into Western models of health and healing is prevalent among Caribbean peoples.

Vodou

Vodou or Voodoo is derived from the word *vodun*, meaning "spirit" and "sacred energy" and is an exceptionally intricate spirituality/religion (Eyre 2016: 133–134; Campinha-Bacote 1992; Olmos and Paravisini-Gebert 2003). Vodou traces its origins to African cultural and religious traditions with some influence from Indigenous peoples of the Caribbean (Desrosiers and Fleurose 2002). During the colonial regime, the health of enslaved Africans was neglected and there was also resistance to the harsh and unknown treatments of White physicians (Campinha-Bacote 1992). This led to the development of a dual treatment of "White medicine and Black medicine", where "the Black doctor (conjure man) dealt with conjured cases and the White doctor with physical cases" (Campinha-Bacote 1992: 12). Conjure doctors or "root doctors" utilized African-derived religious, spiritual and magical practices to cast out and/or contain spirits that inflicted illnesses. It is believed that "the conjure man permitted slaves the perception of exercising some control over their masters" (Campinha-Bacote 1992: 12).

Since colonial times, Vodou practitioners have worshiped in secrecy from fear of retaliation from colonizers, which resulted in Vodou's syncretism with medieval Roman Catholicism (Campinha-Bacote 1992; Eyre 2016). For example, Gods of Vodou (*Laos*) are often represented as Biblical figures, Spirits of African ancestors or deceased family members (Desrosiers and Fleurose 2002).

Vodou practitioners believe that all living things possess sacred *Spirit*. In African-Haitian Vodou, it is believed that *Gran Met* (God) or *Loas* (Gods of Voodoo) entrusts various spirits or deities to govern over various aspects of life (love, death, water, etc.), and these spirits/deities serve as mediums between *Gran Met/Loas* and Vodou practitioners (Campinha-Bacote 1992; Desrosiers and Fleurose 2002). Health and wellness is construed as being in harmony and goodwill with Spirits, nature and deities (Morrison and Thornton, 1999). On the other hand, the aetiology of illnesses lies in the disharmony with nature, Spirits and deities, and practitioners believe "illness or death may come to an individual via a supernatural force" (Campinha-Bacote 1992: 11; Morrison and Thornton 1999). Ailments may be caused by curses and hexes by malevolent others (Campinha-Bacote 1992; Desrosiers and Fleurose, 2002). It is important to note that because of the heterogeneity of Vodou followers along with globalization, many Vodou devotees also believe in natural causes of illnesses. For instance, depression, more accurately described as "discouragement", may be seen as the result of a Vodou curse or a consequence of worry and trauma (Desrosiers and Fleurose 2002: 514).

Vodou is considered both the cause and remedy of ailments; for example, followers of Vodou believe in the supernatural cause of illnesses ('someone put Vodou on them') but may also seek the service of a Vodou priest (*hungan* or *ougan*) or Vodou priestess (*manbo*) who serve as conduits between the Spirit world and the human world (Desrosiers and Fleurose 2002; M'eance 2014). *Hungans or manbos* may perform sacrificial rituals, thaumaturgy, divination and conjuring, and are also herbalists and root doctors (Campinha-Bacote 1992; M'eance 2014). Vodou healers report two general categories of symptomology: gastrointestinal symptoms (nausea, vomiting, diarrhea, weight loss) and behavioural symptoms (hallucinations, delusions). They may assess the cause of these physiological and psychological symptoms as resulting from either bad luck, retaliation from a spirit or possession by a spirit (M'eance 2014). Some untreated "voodoo illnesses" are believed to result in "voodoo death" (Campinha-Bacote 1992: 11).

Santeria

Santeria is believed to have derived from the religion *Ifa*, which was originally practiced by the Yoruba tribe of Western Africa (Baez and Hernandez 2001). Ifa was transmitted orally and encompassed a "vast and colorful pantheon, extensive rituals for spiritual progress, divination, healing and a vibrant musicality based on Yoruban drumming and chanting" (Baez and Hernandez 2001: 410). Like many Caribbean spiritualities, Ifa/Santeria was brought to the Caribbean during colonialism by Yoruba descendants and was feared and prohibited by European colonizers leading to its syncretism with Spanish influenced Catholicism (Brandon 1991).Yoruban deities or *Orishas* were given names of corresponding Catholic saints in efforts to conceal and protect its practices. For example, in Cuba, the deity, *Obatala* – the oldest Orisha – also known as the Father of all Orishas is syncretized with Our Lady of Mercy (Baez and Hernandez 2001). Santeria is also believed to have been influenced by the European Spiritism Movement (Brandon 1991).

Santeria also known as *La Regla De Ocha* is considered a highly established spiritual and healing system in Cuba and a complete comprehension of its intricacies may be lost when it is translated from Yoruba or Spanish. Santeria affirms the interconnectedness between living things and believe all living creatures have a spiritual constituent. Santeria further posits that specific ailments could originate from the 'evil eye', as in witchcraft by a malevolent being or inherited deficits of an individual (Hernandez-Ramdwar 2014). Followers of Santeria believe in the spiritual derivation of illnesses and believe that specific body parts are influenced by specific spirits. For example, the human head is ruled by *Obatala*. Punishment and disharmony with *Obatala* could result in mental illnesses, blindness and addictions. *Rogacion de Cabeza* (rotation of the head) is a healing practice aimed at restoring mental and spiritual abilities of those affected and is often used to treat depression, mental confusion, witchcraft and high blood pressure (Brandon 1991).

Santeria is considered "the practice of divination" and asserts that preventative and remedial treatments are directly linked to the development and maintenance of harmony with divine spirits (Hernandez-Ramdwar 2014: 103). Santeria asserts that skilled healers – known as *Santero* – possess magical abilities, particularly the high priest or *Babalawo* (Baez and Hernandez 2001). Through the guidance of *santeros*, distress, ailments and disharmony with spirits may be restored by performing sacrifices, providing offerings and utilizing herbs, plants and sacred stones (Brandon 1991; Hernandez-Ramdwar 2014).

Egwe, the Lucumi term for herbs, plants and weed is central to the practice of Santeria and believed to have *aché* (divine power and healing properties). *Aché* is also believed to have unique personalities and temperaments and is often associated with different Orishas. During colonial times, *egwe* (symbolic beads, leaves and herbs) offered protection to enslaved Africans.Wild *egwe* is believed to possess more potent healing powers and is used to treat a variety of ailments including gastrointestinal issues, syphilis, female reproductive problems and nervous disorders. A hindrance to practitioners particularly those in the Cuban diaspora is limited access to *egwe* (Brandon 1991).

Santeria's presence in Cuban health and mental health care and in the Latin diaspora is long-standing and continues to play a central role in healing in Afro-Cuban communities (Baez and Hernandez 2001). The 1959 Cuban revolution led to the migration of Cubans to North America and consequently the incursion of Santeria into North American culture (Brandon 1991). Similar to Vodou, practitioners of Santeria often use dual healing approaches and *santeros* have been known to work collaboratively and refer their patients to Western clinicians. A study cited by Hernandez-Ramdwar (2014) showed that 68% of clients who sought the treatment of traditional healers were referred by their *Santero* to Western practitioners for biomedical concerns. Dual intervention is often seen as advantageous by traditional healers.

Shango/Orisha

The colonial contextualization of Shango bares both similarities and differences to other Caribbean spiritualities. *Shango* – also commonly referred to as *Trinidad Orisha, Yoruba Orisha* or *Orisha* – traces its origins to West Africa, stemming from Yoruba spiritual and religious beliefs and practices (Bilby and Handler 2004; Hucks and Stewart 2003; Simpson 1962). Shango is also the name of the Yoruban deity, God of Thunder, and is one of the many deities worshipped by Shango followers (Glazier 2012; Simpson 1962). Shango is believed to have arrived in Trinidad in around the post-emancipation period and was a vital source of health, healing and survival for enslaved Africans and ex-slaves (Hucks and Stewart 2003; Maharajh and Parasram 1999).

Similar to other African-derived spiritualities, Shango was affiliated with "malevolence and sorcery", and rituals and practices including fortune-telling, dancing, drumming and worshipping was feared and prohibited by European colonizers (Hucks and Stewart 2003: 178). Shango worshipping was banned in Trinidad until 1951. The attempt to abolish Shango resulted in believers practicing in secrecy as well as the 'Christianization' of Shango, wherein Catholic images and symbols were syncretized with Yoruban sacred symbols and images (Hucks and Stewart 2003). For example, the deities *Elefon* and *Obalufon* have been reinterpreted and referred to as Eternal Father and Jesus in Trinidadian Shango. Additionally, *Eshu* is commonly referred to as Satan with an association to evil (Simpson 1962).

The syncretism of Yoruba spirituality and Christianity is evident in that many Shangoists also regularly attend Christian churches (Simpson 1962). Trinidadian Shango also has an intricate relationship with Spiritual Baptist, where Shango and Spiritual Baptists devotees "both adhere to salient African-derived practices such as drumming and chanting, the ring shout, possession trance, ancestral veneration, a communotheistic conception of the divine, and divination and herbalism" (Hucks and Stewart 2003: 178). Trinidadian Shango is also believed to have some Muslim syncretism, where it is believed that the Yoruba God, *Osain* is syncretized with the Muslim saint, Hossein (Simpson 1962). The influence of Indian traditions is conflicting where some believe that various East Indian ingredients are found in Shango practices (Hucks and Stewart 2003; Simpson 1962). "Ritual borrowing" from Spiritual Baptist, Kali-Mai, and Ifa traditions have also been documented in Shango (Glazier 2012: 201).

In Shango, it is believed that deities/spirits influence all facets of existence (Simpson 1962). For instance, a Shango goddess, Mother of the Earth (*Mama Laate*) whose Catholic equivalent is St. Veronica, Mother of Mount Carmel and Eve, is believed to rule over agriculture (Simpson 1962). Furthermore, similar to Obeah, Vodou and Santeria, there is a causal association between various medical and mental health issues and specific Shango deities. For example, *Osain* often associated with St. Francis, is usually summoned to treat various illnesses, particularly those believed to be caused by evil spirits. *Orisala* or *Orishala* is believed to inflict deformities and disabilities upon the children of communicants who warrant punishment. It is also believed that illnesses, misfortunes, and adversities are also associated with angry spirits of the dead (Glazier 2012; Simpson 1962).

Consequently, remedial and preventative antidotes may involve worshipping and rituals geared towards appeasing specific Orishas and ancestor spirits. Curative and preventative practices may involve sacrifices and sacred elements such as crucifixes, candles, flowers, leaves, water, oils, rosaries, cowries, kola-nuts and stones (Glazier 2012; Hucks and Stewart 2003; Simpson 1962). Charms are also regularly prescribed by Shango healers in the form of rings, bracelets, amulets and protective medicines against harmful spirits (Simpson 1962). Drums are also commonly used and is considered the most important musical instrument in Shango, and some believe the *Batta* drum is a powerful medicine with the capacity to heal illnesses inflicted by evil spirits. Rhythms, handclapping, foot stomping, animal sacrifices and dancing are also sacred and elemental in Trinidadian Shango. Furthermore, similar to some Western psychotherapeutic modalities, dreams are a critical element of healing. However, in Shango, dreams are believed to celestially divulge healing remedies and serve as warnings and counsels with mystic messages (Simpson 1962).

It is estimated that there are over 100 million followers of Orisha/Shango worldwide and Shango is said to "provide a mechanism for Caribbean people to validate their past and recover their African roots" (Glazier 2012: 199). In Trinidad and the diaspora, the influence of culturally and spiritually informed treatment modalities for both mental and physical ailments is evident. For example, mental health treatments in Trinidad constitutes a blend of Western neurobiological frameworks of illnesses as well as traditional and folk medicines and religions, wherein imams, pandits, priests and traditional healers are often first contacted for various ailments. It is believed that Shango and Spiritual (Shouter) Baptist have infiltrated psychiatry in Trinidad, even in the area of behavioural modification, whereas some behavioural modification techniques are framed within religious and cultural adherence and norms (Maharajh and Parasram 1999). This integrative treatment modality has the potential of effectively serving spiritually and culturally diverse peoples in Trinidad, the Caribbean and the diaspora.

Caribbean healers: Training and healing community

The training processes for Caribbean healers are vastly different from Western credentialization models. Novice healers are either selected by established healers or are descendants of established healers, and may learn healing methods through informal observation and/or apprenticeship (Blom et al. 2015; Reiff et al. 2003). Healers may also be chosen based on innate divination skills and talents, divine/spiritual interventions ('called to heal'), dreams and/or auspicious birthmarks (Blom et al. 2015; Glazier 2012). For example, *Mother Rita* was a prominent Jamaican healer who was believed to have descended from a line of female healers. Mother Rita's maternal grandmother was an enslaved African woman and an expert in bush medicines but gave up her practice after her conversion to Christianity. Mother Rita's mother, *Mammie Forbes*, was believed to have been visited by an angel who held "a bundle of herbs and commanded her to rise up and heal the people" (Barrett 1973: 9). Mother Rita was believed to have been taught by her mother (Mammie Forbes) but also possessed innate healing/divination skills, when as a child, she was believed to be a medium and a conduit to the spirit world (Barrett 1973).

Although the healing skills of many Caribbean healers are acquired through informal education and training, a study by Reiff et al. (2003) showed that one healer, Sra. Alicia, a healer from the Dominican Republic who resided in New York City, learned healing skills from her mother and grandmother ('the universal energy was passed'), but also later acquired formal training in Psychology and Reiki in the United States. Sra. Alicia described her experience as "to have a certificate in something I have always done" (Reiff et al. 2003: 15). Another study by Glazier (2012) showed that numerous Shango healers had advanced university degrees and were also trained as nurses, chiropractors and pharmacists.

Caribbean healers are not a homogenous group and may utilize various healing methods including herbal baths, bush medicines, 'laying of the hand', counsel, massage, telepathic healing, possessions/communication with spirits and ancestors, dream interpretations, psychic readings, exercises and Western medicines (Barrett 1973; Reiff et al. 2003). Caribbean healers often adopt a pluralistic approach to healing and often refer patients to Western health care as part of their treatment plan (Glazier 2012; Reiff et al. 2003). Payments to healers are based on monetary compensation and/or a reciprocity model, where clients may present gifts to healers and in return, healers bestow spiritual/healing treatment (Glazier 2012).

Healing often occurs in the privacy of the healer's home and/or the patient's home as many healers remain secretive about their practice from fear of perceived and/or actual repercussions (Blom 2015). Caribbean healers often have traditional full-time jobs and/or other religious and spiritual obligations making access to healers in the Caribbean and diaspora a challenge (Glazier 2012).

Caribbean healing practices in a global context

Traditional Caribbean medicines and healing practices are frequently sought out by both Caribbean and non-Caribbean individuals because of the "limitations of biomedicine and their metaphoric logic of transformation, which promises wholeness, balance and well-being" (Kirmayer 2004: 33). The synchronicity of these healing practices with the historical, cultural and spiritual tenets of Caribbean peoples make them viable remedial options for many spiritually and culturally diverse Caribbean peoples. A study by Ojelade et al. (2014) found that all participants belonging to a Yoruba belief system first sought the services of an *Orisa* priest when addressing their mental health problems prior to seeking Western therapy. Additionally, a research by James and Peltzer (2012: 95) showed that one-third of their research participants believed their mental illness was due to Obeah and many participants sought traditional healing including the use of herbs and oils, spiritual guidance, "laying of hands", and ritualistic and spiritual baths (Giordan 2009: 229). These studies demonstrate that we are in an epoch of "spiritual revolution", however, Western colonial health and mental health frameworks continue to control, manage and regulate the practice of health in a Eurocentric, ethnocentric and individualistic manner even when treating culturally and spiritually diverse peoples from the Caribbean (Giordan 2009: 229).

Western health frameworks may misconstrue culture-specific idioms of distress, resulting in inaccurate diagnoses and incongruous treatment approaches and outcomes (Blom et al. 2015; Ellis 2015). For instance, a Western-trained health professional treating a person of Jamaican heritage who presents with "obeah illness" or "mind-madness", with symptoms of speaking in tongues or communicating with spirits, may fail to consider this person's spiritual belief in the supernatural as a precursor for their distress (Ellis 2015: 85). This practitioner may eventually diagnose their Jamaican client with a schizophrenia spectrum disorder, senile dementia or dissociative identity disorder – to name a few – as characterized in the *Diagnostic and Statistical Manual – Fifth Edition* (*DSM-5*: American Psychiatric Association 2013), and use psychopharmacological treatment without critically considering the spiritual and cultural beliefs of their client (Seligman 2005). Furthermore, Western-trained health professionals may adopt an individualistic approach without consulting significant others such as family members, religious practitioners and/or Obeah healers, who may be imperative in their client's treatment.

Despite the pre-eminence of Western positivistic medical and mental health models, some African/Caribbean-influenced and Eastern medicines have been incorporated into Western health paradigms, such as ayurvedic medicine, acupuncture, homeopathy, yoga, herbal remedies, spiritual and cultural therapies (Maharajh and Parasram 1999). However, Moodley and Bertrand (2011: 87) state, once "traditional healing practices gain some legitimacy within Western health care, the healers themselves are often excluded as the authorial practitioners or sources of knowledge". Some may argue that this is exemplified in some yoga practices, where the practice of yoga has gained rapid momentum and commercialization in Western culture and is acknowledged as a good practice for stress management. However, the traditional spiritual and cultural underpinnings of yoga seem to have been largely omitted in some of its current Westernized forms. The healing practices that have been endorsed by Western health care (e.g., yoga, ayurvedic medicines, acupuncture, etc.) are primarily derived from Eastern philosophies and spiritualities, revealing the hierarchy of racism (i.e. anti-Black racism) present in Western medical and mental health sectors.

The modification of Western approaches and integration of Caribbean healing practices is conceivably the most favourable as is elucidated in Blom et al. 2015 article about the case of Mr. A. Mr. A., a 44-year-old male from Aruba residing in the Netherlands was referred for psychiatric evaluation because of anxiety, paranoia and flashbacks stemming from a past of violent involvement with a gang and a discernible fear of *Brua. Brua* is an Afro-centric religion and healing practice which bares similarities to Obeah, Vodou and Santeria. Mr. A believed that a powerful spirit possessed him, and that others tried to steal this powerful spirit at night. He also believed that one of his ancestors may have done something bad and therefore his family may have been cursed. Mr. A. often felt a black creature pressing down upon him at night and he suffered from sleep paralysis, and when he was able to move, he would inadvertently hit his wife.

Mr. A was assessed in the Netherlands and diagnosed with PTSD, anti-social personality disorder and anxiety. He was also advised and recommended to seek the counsel of a *Brua* expert to manage his fear of *Brua* and the supernatural. Mr. A., however, was committed to his Catholic faith and professed that he had never sought treatment from a traditional healer, although friends and family have encouraged the use of herbs, sacred washing of the body, prayers to saints including San Miguel and rituals involving coins and other objects. Mr. A. did attend a *montamentoe* ceremony where with the aid of an Ouija board, various spirits were summoned (Blom et al. 2015: 842–843).

In order to achieve optimal integration of Caribbean healing and Western healing practices, as in the case of Mr. A, the World Health Organization identifies four necessary conditions: support and integration of traditional healing practices along with policy and regulation of products, practices and service providers; safe and effective use of quality products and services; preservation of knowledge and increased access to services; and ongoing skills, competency and knowledge upgrades by providers (Payne-Jackson 2014). These further explicate the importance of an overarching framework of respect, preservation and accommodation of cultural and spiritual beliefs and practices of ethnic, racial, cultural and spiritually diverse peoples (Ellis 2015).

Moodley and Sutherland (2011) recommend engaging clients in dual health and mental health interventions by integrating Western forms of healing (e.g. medicines, psychotherapy) with traditional healers. A medical pluralism framework, defined as the utilization of multiple systems of healing including self-care, social supports, spiritual healing and Western therapy may be more culturally congruent for a diverse Caribbean population (Arthur and Whitley 2015; Blom et al. 2015; Moodley 2011; Ojelade et al. 2014). For example, *Psychohistoriographic Cultural Therapy (PCT)*, developed in Jamaica, integrates and considers intergenerational experiences, historical trauma, oral traditions, creative arts, and group psychotherapy to address mental health issues (Arthur and Whitley 2015). A pluralistic framework such as PCT will allow for integration of traditional healing as well as Western approaches that are adaptive and appropriate such as culturally adapted cognitive behavioural therapy (CBT) and family therapy interventions (Hutchinson and Sutherland 2013).

According to Baez and Hernandez (2001: 408), "the successful provision of culturally sensitive and culturally inclusive mental health services depends in large part on the level of congruence between the client's and the mental health practitioner's respective views of mental illness and its treatment". Baez and Hernandez (2001: 414) argue that spiritual awareness of practitioners is key in identifying "spiritual convergence and dissonance" between clients/patients and practitioners, which may determine efficacy of treatment. Therefore, the adoption of a strength-based approach to actively engage spiritually and culturally diverse peoples' in their course of treatment as well as create 'culturally sanctioned spaces' for clients/patients to explore their fears and suspicions about Eurocentric forms of treatments is necessary (Ellis 2015; Moodley and Bertrand 2011). In addition, critical awareness of systemic barriers that prevent peoples from the Caribbean from accessing traditional forms of healing, as well as microaggressions and micro-barriers within clinical and health settings is also essential.

Future directions

Inclusion and integration of safe and effective traditional healing methods with Western health and healing approaches are necessary when working with spiritually and culturally diverse peoples from the Caribbean. However, the regulation of these healing practices and integration within a Western empirical and positivist framework may be counterintuitive, wherein, sacred elements of these healing approaches may in fact be lost during the 'westernization' process (Sutherland et al. 2014). Therefore, integration should be executed within a Caribbean-centric healing framework with nonpartisanship and equitable consultation with Caribbean healers and peoples. It is also imperative that the Western approaches used in this integrative framework be researched and validated for efficacy with a Caribbean population. Furthermore, since the Caribbean population have endured relentless repercussions from colonialism, Western health care practitioners should consider social determinants of health (i.e. poverty, immigration status, racism, cultural and personal losses, etc.) in their treatment modalities and plans (Reiff et al. 2003; Hutchinson and Sutherland 2013).

Conclusion

Caribbean healing practices are grounded in Afro-centric religions and spiritualities which persevered and adapted to inhumane colonial oppression, marginalization, disowning and dislocation. The pervasive effects of colonialism have resulted in the over-diagnosis and under-diagnosis, premature termination, over-representation in psychiatric facilities (involuntary detainment) and underutilization of Western health and mental health services by peoples in the Caribbean and the diaspora. This highlights the deficiency of mainstream Western health and mental health services in meeting the needs of Caribbean and other spiritually and culturally diverse peoples.

An integrative, anti-racist, anti-oppressive, strengths-based and decolonizing practice is recommended where culturally and spiritually diverse peoples from the Caribbean and diaspora are supported in the restitution of their autonomy and self-determination, with the capacity to heal personal, spiritual, cultural and historic/colonial wounds (Hucks and Stewart 2003; Kirmayer 2004). Integration of culture-specific spiritual beliefs and practices may seem inconceivable, and well-intentioned culturally sensitive practitioners may fear saying or doing the wrong things, making therapeutic and ethical errors, and culturally appropriating these traditional practices. The recognition that Western health and mental health practices and modalities may in fact be 'the alternative' rather than the primary treatment intervention is imperative, particularly when working with racialized, marginalized and spiritually and culturally diverse peoples from the Caribbean and the diaspora.

References

American Psychiatric Association. (2013) *Diagnostic and Statistical Manual of Mental Disorders*. Arlington, VA: American Psychiatric Association.

Arthur, C. M. and Whitley, R. (2015) '"Head Take You": Casual Attributions of Mental Illness in Jamaica', *Transcultural Psychiatry*, 51(1): 115–132.

Baez, A. and Hernandez, D. (2001) 'Complementary Spiritual Beliefs in the Latino Community: The Interface with Psychotherapy', *American Journal of Orthopsychiatry*, 71(4): 408–415).

Barrett, L. (1973) 'The Portrait of a Jamaican Healer: African Medical Lore in the Caribbean', *Caribbean Quarterly*, 19(3): 6–19.

Bilby, K. M. and Handler, J. S. (2004) 'Obeah: Healing and Protection in West Indian Slave Life', *The Journal of Caribbean History*, 38(2): 153–183.

Blom, J. D., Poulina, I. T., van Gellecum, T. L. and Hoek, H. W. (2015) 'Traditional Healing Practices Originating in Aruba, Bonaire, and Curacao: A Review of the Literature on Psychiatry and Brua', *Transcultural Psychology*, 52(6): 840–860.

Brandon, G. (1991) 'The Uses of Plants in Healing in Afro-Cuban Religion, Santeria', *Journal of Black Studies*, 22(1): 55–76.

Campinha-Bacote, J. (1992) 'Voodoo Illness', *Perspectives in Psychiatric Care*, 28(1): 11–17.

Crosson, J. B. (2015) 'What Obeah Does Do: Healing, Harm, and the Limits of Religion', *Journal of Africana Religions*, 3(2): 151–176.

Desrosiers, A. and St. Fleurose, S. (2002) 'Treating Haitian Patients: Key Cultural Aspects', *American Journal of Psychotherapy*, 56(4): 508–521.

Ellis, H. A. (2015) 'Obeah-Illness Versus Psychiatrist Entities among Jamaican Immigrants: Cultural and Clinical Perspectives for Psychiatric Mental Health Professionals', *Archives of Psychiatric Nursing*, 29(2): 83–89.

Eyre, L. A. (2016) Review of the books *Healing in the Homeland: Haitian Vodou Tradition* by M. M. Armand and *Vodou Songs* by B. Hebblethwaite. The University of the West Indies, 133–138. doi: 10.1080/00086495.2016.1157252.

Giordan, G. (2009) 'The Body between Religion and Spirituality', *Social Compass,* 56 (2): 226–236.

Glazier, S. D. (2012) '"If Old Heads Could Talk": Sango Healers in the Caribbean', *Anthropologica*, 54(2): 199–209.

Gomez, P. F. (2014) 'Incommensurable Epistemologies?: The Atlantic Geography of Healing in the Early Modern Caribbean', *Small Axe*, 18(2): 95–107.

Handler, J. S. and Bilby, K. M. (2001) 'On the Early Use and Origin of the Term 'Obeah' in Barbados and the Anglophone Caribbean', *Slavery and Abolition*, 22(2): 87–100.

Hernandez-Ramdwar, C. (2014) 'La Regla De Ocha (Santeria): Afro-Cuban Healing in Cuba and the Diaspora' in Sutherland, P., Moodley, R. and Chevannes, B. (Eds.), *Caribbean Healing Traditions: Implications for Health and Mental Health* (pp. 101–112). New York: Routledge.

Hucks, T. E. and Stewart, D. M. (2003) 'Authenticity and Authority in the Shaping of the Trinidad Orisha Identity: Toward an African-Derived Religious Theory', *The Western Journal of Black Studies*, 27(3): 176–185.

Hutchinson, G. and Sutherland, P. (2013) 'Counseling and Psychotherapy in the (English-Speaking) Caribbean', in Moodley, R., Gielen, U. P. and Wu, R. (Eds.), *Handbook of Counseling and Psychotherapy in an International Context* (pp. 117–127). New York and London: Routledge.

James, C. C. A. B. and Peltzer, K. (2012) 'Traditional and alternative therapy for mental illness in Jamaica: Patients' perceptions and practitioners' attitude', *African Journal of Traditional, Complementary and Alternative Medicines*, 9(1): 94–104.

James, C. C. B. (2012) 'Psychiatric Patients' Evaluation of the Efficacy of Obeah vs. Western Medicine in Treating their Mental Illness', *Journal of Psychology in Africa,* 22(1): 134–138.

Kirmayer, L. J. (2004) 'The Cultural Diversity of Healing: Meaning, Metaphor and Mechanism', *British Medical Bulletin*, 69(1): 33–48.

Maharajh, H. D. and Parasram, R. (1999) 'The Practice of Psychiatry in Trinidad and Tobago', *International Review of Psychiatry*, 11(2–3): 173–183.

Meance, G. (2014) 'Vodou Healing and Psychotherapy', in Sutherland, P., Moodley, R. and Chevannes, B. (Eds), *Caribbean Healing Traditions: Implications for Health and Mental Health* (pp. 78–88). New York: Routledge.

Meudec, M. (2017) 'Ordinary Ethics of Spiritual Work and Healing in St. Lucia, or Why Not to Use the Term Obeah', *Small Axe*, 21(1:52): 17–32.

Mommaerts, J. and Devroey, D. (2013) 'From "Does it work?" to "What is it?": Implications for Voodoo, Psychotherapy, Pop-Psychology, Regular, and Alternative Medicine', *Perspectives in Biology and Medicine*, 56(2): 274–288.

Moodley, R. (2000) 'Representation of Subjective Distress in Black and Ethnic Minority Patients: Constructing a Research Agenda', *Counselling Psychology Quarterly*, 13(2): 159–174.

Moodley, R. (2011) 'The Toronto Traditional Healers Project: An Introduction', *International Journal of Health Promotion & Education*, 49(3): 74–78.

Moodley, R. (2013) 'Spirit-Based Healing in the Black Diaspora'. *Therapy Today* 24(6): 15–18. www.therapytoday.net.

Moodley, R. and Bertrand, M. (2011) 'Spirits of a Drum Beat: African Caribbean Traditional Healers and Their Healing Practices in Toronto', *International Journal of Health Promotion & Education*, 49 (3): 79–89.

Moodley, R. and Sutherland, P. (2011) 'Traditional and Cultural Healers and Healing: Dual Interventions in Counselling and Psychotherapy', in Moodley, R. (Ed.) *Outside the Sentence. Readings in Critical Multicultural Counselling and Psychotherapy* (pp. 105–119). Toronto and Bangalore: Centre for Diversity in Counselling and Psychotherapy.

Morrison, E. F. and Thornton, K. A. (1999) 'Influence of Southern Spiritual Beliefs on Perceptions of Mental Illness', *Issues in Mental Health Nursing*, 20(5): 443–458.

Murrell, N. S. (2014) 'Obeah: Afro-Caribbean Religious Medicine Art and Healing', Sutherland, P., Moodley, R. and Chevannes, B. (Eds.), *Caribbean Healing Traditions: Implications for Health and Mental Health* (pp. 65–77). New York: Routledge.

Ojelade, I. I., McCray, K., Meyers, J. and Ashby, J. (2014) 'Use of Indigenous African Healing Practices as a Mental Health Intervention', *Journal of Black Psychology*, 40(6): 491–519.

Olmos, M. F. and Paravisini-Gebert, E. (2003) *Creole Religions of the Caribbean: An Introduction from Vodou and Santeria to Obeah and Espiritismo*. New York and London: New York University Press.

Payne-Jackson, A. (2014) 'Caribbean Traditional Medicine: Legacy from the Past, Hope for the Future', Sutherland, P., Moodley, R. and Chevannes, B. (Eds), *Caribbean Healing Traditions: Implications for Health and Mental Health* (pp. 41–51). New York: Routledge.

Reiff, M., O'Connor, B., Kronenberg, F., Balick, M., Lohr, P., Roble, M., Fugh-Berman, A. and Johnson, K. D. (2003) 'Ethnomedicine in the Urban Environment: Dominican Healers in New York City', *Human Organization*, 62(1): 12–26.

Seligman, R. (2005) 'Distress, Dissociation, and Embodied Experience: Reconsidering the Pathways to Mediumship and Mental Health', *Ethos*, 33(1): 71–99.

Simpson, G. E. (1962) 'The Shango Cult in Nigeria and Trinidad', *American Anthropologist*, 64(6): 1204–1219.

Sutherland, P. and Moodley, R. (2010) 'Reclaiming the Spirit: Clemmont E. Vontress and the Quest for Spiritual and Traditional Healing in Counseling', in Moodley, R. and Walcott, R. (Eds.), *Counseling Across and Beyond Cultures: Exploring the Work of Clemmont E. Vontress in Clinical Practice* (pp. 263–277). Toronto: University of Toronto Press.

Sutherland, P., Moodley, R. and Chevannes, B. (2014) *Caribbean Healing Traditions: Implications for Health and Mental Health*. New York: Routledge.

Wisecup, K. (2013) 'Knowing Obeah', *Atlantic Studies*, 10(3): 406–425.

44
MĀORI INDIGENOUS HEALING PRACTICES IN AOTEAROA (NEW ZEALAND)

Rebecca Wirihana, Cherryl Smith, and Takirirangi Smith

Māori people are indigenous to Aotearoa (New Zealand). Aotearoa is a small nation made up of two distinct islands: Te-Ika-a-Maui (North Island); and Te Waipounamu (South Island), located in the South Pacific Ocean. The Māori nation forms part of wider Indigenous community located throughout the Pacific Ocean of a people who navigated the vast 'Polynesian Triangle' (Durie 2006: 4). According to Durie, the development of values, social systems and practices adapted as Māori migrated to Aotearoa. Moreover, kin-based relationships with the natural environment were premised on a complex social hierarchical structure that promoted an inherent relationship with the sacred. Social structures are made up of iwi (tribes), hapū (sub-tribes) and whānau (extended family). Māori creation stories identify Io as the original creator of potentiality, the heavens and the natural environment (Moorfield 2013). The natural environment was comprised of two primal Ariki (supernatural beings) who were considered as parental figures. The first embodied the sky (Ranginui) and the other embodied the earth (Papatūānuku). These creation stories provided the foundations for how Māori based their relationships within all facets of the natural environment and the practice associated to these narratives were passed down across generations. Essentially Māori maintain direct decent from Ranginui and Papatūānuku. Recently, an iwi based in the Whanganui region of Aotearoa successfully passed a governmental bill acknowledging the personhood of the river that flows through their tribal region (Buchan 2017). These relationships with the sacred, and the natural environment, provided the basis for the structure of Māori whānau (family), hapū (sub-tribe) and iwi (tribe/tribal) relationships within Māori communities.

Smith (2005: 10) expressed that "pre-colonial knowledge frameworks" indicated the Māori community existed in harmony with the natural environment. Māori communities were made up of tribal societies that were guided by these whakapapa kōrero (genealogical narratives), and sustained in the practice of tikanga (custom, protocol, lore). The narratives and protocols developed by Māori acknowledged and preserved the inherent spirituality of the people and recognised the integral connection between the people with the natural environment. Moreover, whakapapa kōrero were preserved in the context of an oral, performance based and creative artistic tradition and emphasised the importance of matriarchal and patriarchal balance within the Māori community (Mikaere 2003; Mildon 2012; Wirihana and Smith 2014). In summary, the purpose of this chapter is to explore the history of traditional Māori methods of healing. It then discusses the impact of colonization on these methods and explores how Māori have sought to retain traditional Māori narratives of healing within a contemporary context. To conclude, it provides a case vignette that will examine how Māori methods of healing continue to be utilised in the context of health settings today.

Brief history of traditional Māori healing

Māori methods of healing arise from the traditional knowledge systems based on whakapapa kōrero. Māori knowledge was passed down across generations using multiple methods including the practice and recitation of oral knowledge transmission such waiata (song), karakia (prayer), oriori (lullaby/lament), pepeha (tribal proverbs), pātere (chant) and whakapapa (genealogy) (Wirihana 2012). It was sustained within whānau and iwi environments using performance and martial arts including haka (dance), mau taiaha, patu and poi (a light ball on a string swung rhythmically to song). Healing, astrology and navigation were maintained by tohunga who were considered learned practitioners and scholars within the community who were specially chosen and trained across multiple disciplines including child birth, healing, navigation, astrology (Mataamua 2017).

These approaches to learning and teaching Māori knowledge through dance, chant, song and poetry formed the basis of healing methods from grief, loss and heartache (Emery, Cookson-Cox and Raerino 2015). McLachlan, Huriwai and Wirihana (2017: 49) recently demonstrated how Māori narratives can be used to facilitate healing in mental health and addictions services using Māori value cards "Whakatauki, along with whakatauaki and pepeha are part of a collection of traditional proverbs whakatauaki." Cherrington (2003) discussed the use of pūrākau (Māori creation stories) within clinical settings and demonstrated how they can be applied using therapeutic letter writing (Cherrington 2016). Knowledge, skill and community expertise was largely held by tohunga (practitioner):

> It was the role of tohunga to ensure tikanga (customs) were observed. Tohunga guided the people and protected them from spiritual forces. They were healers of both physical and spiritual ailments, and they guided the appropriate rituals for horticulture, fishing, fowling and warfare. They lifted the tapu on newly built houses and waka (canoes), and lifted or placed tapu in death ceremonies.
>
> *(Keane 2011)*

Tohunga were trained to specialize in specific areas of knowledge. For example, Mataamua (2017) advised his own ancestor was an expert in Māori astronomy. More recently, Māori healers, practitioners and scholars have compiled knowledge in a broad range of healing practices that span physical health, psychological health, rongoā (medicines/remedies), spiritual healing, mirimiri (massage), midwifery and child development (Durie 1998; Durie 2005; Ihimaera 2004; Levy and Waitoki 2017; McLachlan and Huriwai 2017; Reynolds and Smith 2012; Valentine 2009; Waiti 2014).

The basis of traditional Māori healing is founded on the premise that healing is inherently spiritual (Ahuriri-Driscoll et al. 2008; Jones 2001; Levy and Waitoki 2016). A growing dearth of knowledge regarding Māori methods of healing continues to grow at present, and diversity in practice among Māori is extensive. Durie (1998) described five primary methods of Māori healing including ritenga and karakia (rituals and incantations), rongoā (natural medicinal remedies), mirimiri (massage), wai (water) and surgical interventions. Jones (2000) acknowledged that Māori methods of healing included a "diversity of healing practices and models of integration" (p. 108), which were instituted on the basis of local whānau, hapū and iwi knowledge.

For example, as described by Mataamua (2017), the grieving process can be tracked back to the original parental separation story. Mataamua also noted specific ceremonies were used during Matariki (the Māori New Year) to further support the process of grief when "the community would gather together to mourn the dead" and many of these practices have been maintained within the Māori continue today (Mataamua 2016: 62).

Traditionally, Māori women maintained the same status as men within the tribal hierarchy. There existed multiple structured levels within the tribal system, which were represented by both sexes at each echelon. The upper levels of the structure were strategists for the tribe, the following layers were maintained by the tohunga practitioners, the third layer were directed by the upper level strategists who ensured that their aspirations for the tribe were sustained, and the final layers were teachers who groomed the next generations of leaders and strategists. The lower layers who were often survivors of inter-tribal warfare formed the lowest level of this hierarchy. This hierarchy ensured that the community existed harmoniously and, if members of the tribe perpetrated physical or sexual violence, perpetrators were punished swiftly and severely (T. Ruwhiu, personal communication, 30 November 2017).

In summary, Māori healing required that Māori maintained balance between male and female, spirit and body, sacred (or restricted) and without restriction, nature and mankind. Whakapapa kōrero and the transmission of knowledge across generations sustained the systems, methods and processes required to ensure this balance was preserved.

The impact of colonization on Māori methods of healing and Māori resistance narratives

Early colonial contact in Aotearoa began with Abel Tasman in 1642. Māori voices of these earlier experiences with colonialists are largely silent and the history records are chronicled predominantly by white male scholars. As a consequence, Māori have engaged in the process of decolonization (Tuhiwai-Smith 2003), to reassert traditional Māori knowledge contemporaneously as traditional Māori practices of healing and well-being have eroded or transformed throughout the process of colonization (Wirihana and Smith 2014).

Early missionary contact impacted substantially on Māori methods of healing as the removal of traditional carvings, a prior storehouse of knowledge, was forbidden in many areas. The Native Schools Act 1867 impacted severely on the retention of te reo Māori. Māori children who were considered as taonga (precious) and were rarely disciplined by adults were severely punished in the schools for speaking Māori, which further perpetuated the intergenerational loss of Māori knowledge and practice (Wirihana and Smith 2014). The adoption of patriarchal practices dominant in early colonial Christian communities further subjugated the role of Māori women eliminating the "sacred balance" between genders further impacting Māori well-being (Mead 1998: 22).

Māori were forcibly removed from their lands by the British Army in the land wars during 1840–1860 (Keenan 2012). The scorched earth policies of 1865 when kainga (traditional Māori homes) were "razed and crops destroyed during a campaign…seriously undermined the local Māori economy" (Ministry of Culture and Heritage 2014).

A recent research programme conducted by Te Atawhai o te Ao (Independent Māori Research Institute for Environment and Health) examined the impact of historical trauma, as a result of British colonial oppression, across four main areas: whenua (land) dislocation; sexual violence prevention; health and well-being of Māori in prisons; Māori narratives of healing and well-being (Pihama et al. 2016, 2014; Rattray 2016; Reid 2014; Reid, Varona, Fisher and Smith 2016; Wirihana and Smith 2014). The study identified that the loss of land reduced the ability to maintain financial and economic autonomy precipitating a sense of grief, loss and hopelessness (Reid, Taylore-Moore and Varona 2014). Māori men were incarcerated following the wars (Ministry of Culture and Heritage 2014). Māori women and children were left vulnerable to military rape (Ministry of Culture and Heritage 2014) exacerbating the intergenerational impact of physical and sexual violence. The isolation of Māori families in the urbanisation process further maintained cycles of sexual violence and abuse (Cavino 2016). Epigenetic research has demonstrated how experiences of trauma exacerbate health related disease among Indigenous populations (Walters et al. 2011). The study also identified that Māori communities were able to preserve traditional methods of healing as a process of resistance to colonization, which transferred orally across generations (Wirihana and Smith 2014).

The generational effects of colonization on Māori health and well-being have been immense and current Māori health statistics are evidence of the cumulative impact of these forces. The following section will seek to highlight how, regardless of the process of colonization and the subsequent effects of historical trauma, Māori resistance strategies have maintained traditional theories and practices of healing within our community.

Māori methods of healing in theory and practice

As discussed earlier, Māori healing was based on a primarily spiritual healing process (Valentine, Tassell and Flett, 2017), and incantation and ritual were used to navigate the relationship between tapu (sacred) and noa (safety), "the laws of tapu reflected the extent to which tribes had formed a reciprocal relationship with their environment and were as much about avoiding danger and exercising caution, as about religious observation and spiritual retribution" (Durie 2005: 10). All adept practitioners were fluent in the arts and practices applicable to the use of karakia, waiata, oriori and haka (Smith 2015). The use of these arts was necessary for promoting and enhancing the healing and recovery process.

Māori healing methods included the use of mirimiri (light massage), romiromi (deep massage) and rongoā (herbal medicinal ointments and medicines). All of these methods of healing were applied in the context of ritenga and karakia by adept practitioners trained from early ages to assume specific roles within their whānau, hapū and iwi. The underlying assumption that spiritual well-being was as important as physical well-being was intrinsic (Marks 2012). Thus, when engaging in healing both realms were acknowledged and addressed.

Medicinal applications included the use of specific or supplementary diets when presenting with specific problems to promote specific therapeutic benefits. During pregnancy men were responsible for ensuring their partners had primary access to the most nutritious food possible during their pregnancies. The foetal health was assessed by specialists in maternity care and if their assessment indicated that the mother had not been tended appropriately by her partner, he suffered severe consequences (T. Ruwhiu, personal communication, 8 May 2018).

Māori psychological trauma was described by Smith (2008) as patu (strike, hit, assault, kill, subdue, ill-treat) ngākau (internal organs). Trauma was understood as an embodied physiological experience, which led to mamae (ache, pain, injury wound) ngākau (internal organs, seat of affections, heart, mind, soul). When unaddressed patu ngākau had the potential to lead to pōuritanga (depression, despondency, gloom, dejection, unhappiness, sadness). Moreover, pōuritanga would be passed down to subsequent generations if it remained unaddressed in one's own lifetime (Smith 2008; Wirihana and Smith 2014).

Māori theories of psychological trauma and healing align with the research regarding intergenerational and historical trauma (Bezo and Maggi 2018; Pihama et al. 2016), which acknowledges the impact of colonization and historical trauma within Indigenous communities, and describes how these processes have exacerbated violence, trauma and abuse within the Māori community (Cavino 2016; Walters et al. 2011; Waretini-Karena 2012; Yellow Horse Brave Heart 2008). Currently, physical and sexual violence rates within the Māori community are extremely high (Pihama 2016).

Durie (1995) identified that Māori do not aspire to medicalised approaches to health that require physicians to compartmentalise the body in to specific areas and created the need for specialized treatment. Well-being for Māori is also connected to the well-being of the environment. Māori literature makes clear reference to the importance of the land in ensuring well-being. A well-known Māori whakatauki (proverb); Ko te whenua, te ukaipo. Ko te ukaipo, te whenua (*The land is our breast milk. That which gives us substance is the land.*); reflects this alliance between Māori and the land and highlights the reliance Māori had on the land traditionally.

Taitimu, Read and McIntosh (2007; 2018) examined Māori experiences of presenting with psychoses in Aotearoa. They clearly stated that this experience remains within the constructs of cultural knowledge, and that Māori who presented to mental health services were hesitant to share these interpretations within mainstream services due to fear of being further "pathologised or ignored" (2018: 153). Sadly, this concern remains prevalent for Māori presenting within the mental health services in Aotearoa, and Taitimu, Read and McIntosh (2018: 154) have advised that "clinicians need to be aware that important personal and cultural meanings of experiences labelled psychotic may be withheld due to fear of judgement or stigmatisation."

Māori psychologists in Aotearoa (Waitoki and Levy 2016) demarcate the need to engage, assess, formulate and develop treatment interventions for Māori that are based on kaupapa Māori methods of understanding illness and well-being and utilise te reo Māori me ona tikanga. Additionally, there is an inherent honouring of Māori relationships when wairua is acknowledged within the therapeutic relationship (Valentine 2016), and clinicians increase their own understandings of the dynamics the whānau environment. Le Grice, Braun and Wetherell (2017: 88) reiterated how Māori knowledge and ways of being have been "suppressed and invalidated in psychological paradigms" and that "rich and diverse networks" were pre-empted on the foundations of a "down to earth, pragmatic and humorous manner" within the Māori community.

Valentine, Tassell-Mataamua and Flett (2017: 64) state boldly that "wairua is fundamental to Māori existence and therefore, important to Māori health and well-being." Yet Valentine (2016:159), as a practising Māori psychologist in Aotearoa, voiced her experience of the need to "shed my identity to fit in with the mental health professionals, uncomfortable as it may be, necessary at times to preserve my sanity and keep my wairua safe." The statement itself is a tragic indictment on the potentially negative impact of mental health services and their approaches and environments on the well-being of Māori who present therein.

Cultural factors influencing Māori mental health presentations have been widely explored by Māori practitioners, services users, policy advisors and politicians (Ahuriri-Driscoll et al. 2008; Bennett 2009; Cherrington 2016; Durie 2003; Wepa 2018). Much is to be gained when mental health services engage with Māori mental health practitioners to develop relationships with local tribes that can inform effective service delivery for Māori who present to primary, secondary and tertiary health services.

The healers' training and development, accreditation, licensure and certification

The Tohunga Suppression Act 1907 was originally introduced to promote Māori well-being as a consequence of such epidemics as influenza. Traditional Māori practices that espoused spiritual healing were ineffective when managing the spread of contagious disease during this time. Although well-meaning and introduced with the support of prominent Māori leaders, it also served to erode traditional Māori healing methods across generations (Valentine, Tassel-Mataamua and Flett 2017) The Tohunga Suppression Act in 1907 discredited and criminalised Māori healing practices and, although Māori continued to maintain traditional methods of healing, this was largely done in their homes as a part of everyday life. For example, my grandmother taught me how to source balms from her garden and how to brew them on order to make a tonic.

The Māori renaissance during the 1970s to 1980 saw a regeneration of kaupapa Māori methods of engaging with the world. During this time Māori language revitalisation began with the creation of Kōhanga Reo (Māori Language Nests), kaupapa Māori based pre-schools, which aimed to teach te reo Māori in early childhood education. These early childhood education centres were largely developed and delivered by locally based whānau hapū and iwi. The renaissance influenced the growth of Māori methods of healing and our first openly publicised rongoā clinic was developed by Alec Phillips in Taumaranui in the heart of the Te-Ika-a-Maui (the North Island of New Zealand). Alec Phillips and a number of his tauira (students) began travelling the country meeting with whānau, hapū and iwi across marae. Marae are central to Māori communities and are iwi-based sites with traditionally carved Whare Tīpuna (House of Ancestors), or meetings houses, where formal gatherings are held.

Māori healers and health practitioners have petitioned for decades for the inclusion of kaupapa Māori based methods when working with Māori in Aotearoa (Durie 1995; Durie 1998; Levy and Waitoki 2016; Marks 2012; Pihama et al. 2014; McLachlan, Wirihana and Huriwai 2017; Wirihana and Smith 2014; Valentine, Tassell-Mataamua and Flett 2017). Durie (1995; 1998) specifically noted the importance of understanding Māori ways of being and how Māori present when physically and psychologically unwell. It is also widely understood that Māori respond well to services that are kaupapa Māori–based, as well as those that are responsive to Māori specific needs (Bennet 2009; Cherrington 2003; Curtis 2016; Levy 2017).

Māori healing, health and well-being are strongly influenced by Māori political movements and politicians. As a Māori psychologist who has been working and practising in the area of mental health and addictions for almost 20 years, I have seen Māori health advance most while under the stewardship of the Labour Party Health Minister Dame Tariana Turia. Dame Turia left the Labour Party following the highly contestable Foreshore and Seabed Act in 2004 that sought to further erode Māori foreshore and seabed rights. Dame Turia left the Labour Party and created and led the Māori Party in protest of this Act and successfully maintained her role as Minister of Health across changing party leadership. She also successfully supported and developed a dearth of Māori health services nationally within the government and non-government health sector. She and Sir Mason Durie were critical to the development of a number of Māori health workforce initiatives that have successfully trained hundreds of Māori health practitioners throughout the country.

Under The Health Practitioners Competence Assurance Act of 2003, Māori health workers and healers working in health services without formal health registration were required to either upskill or complete training programmes in their respective areas of health to formally register with a professional health association to ensure they were able to continue working within the health sector.

Sadly, traditional Māori healers do not have an acknowledged registered professional association, which allows them to practice their methods of healing officially in Aotearoa. Many healers continue to practice traditional methods of healing, but do so voluntarily and/or they rely on koha (donations, gifts, offerings) Marks (2012) noted that Māori healing knowledge was passed down across generations. Marks further noted that tohunga knowledge was held by esteemed healers within Māori communities who maintained the highest levels of sacred knowledge within whānau, hapū and iwi.

Māori health services are delivered in multiple ways across the nations. Some services provide care from marae-based settings. Some are situated within the hospitals and provide a kaupapa Māori based support service working alongside the medical professions. These services primarily support Māori engagement and provide culturally appropriate interventions as required within their settings. Kaupapa Māori–based care is provided across all levels of governmental systems within Aotearoa, and it is largely acknowledged as a requirement within Aotearoa that Māori are able to request Māori specific support when accessing governmental services. For example, in mental health services kaupapa Māori mental health services are provided in some of the major hospitals and city centres where people are able to access clinical services that are provided by a largely Māori workforce who practice across all areas of service delivery including as psychiatrists, psychologists, social workers, nurses, occupational therapists and Māori specific experts in Māori health interventions.

Case vignette[1]

Teina is a 22-year-old Māori woman who presented to mental health services with major depressive episodes with psychotic features. Her family reported she has not slept for approximately four nights and her behaviour has become increasingly bizarre during this time. Her behaviour was described as childlike and she "speaks" to her grandmother who passed away several years prior in general conversation. Her whānau have been concerned about her for several weeks now as she has been isolating herself, has a poor appetite and spends hours crying in her room alone or on her laptop. Precipitating factors include a sexual assault six months ago while she was walking home from work one night. Since this time, she has been using alcohol and cannabis excessively and has lost her job due to failing a workplace drug test. Her parents were encouraged by an extended whānau member (who is also a paediatric nurse) to admit her to hospital. They were hesitant to do so but became concerned when she started making references to suicide. Her mother lost a sister to suicide so they agreed to bring her to the hospital for a psychiatric assessment. She is fluent in te reo Māori as her parents sent her to a Kura Kaupapa Māori (Māori Language School) and is versed in tikanga within her hapū. She speaks English as a second language, but her preference is te reo Māori. Her parents, her koroua (grandfather) and her two siblings were present at her assessment.

Assessment phase

Teina and her whānau were seen by a Māori psychiatrist, a Māori psychiatric nurse and a kaiārahi Māori (kaupapa Māori practitioner) with the kaupapa Māori mental health service. Mihi whakatau (formal welcoming ceremony) and opening karakia (prayer) were provided in te reo Māori by the kaiārahi Māori before the assessment began. Once these processes were complete – the formal clinical assessment began. Each practitioner offered a brief formulation regarding their interpretation of the precipitating factors that led to Teina's presentation to her whānau and a kaupapa Māori based approach to treatment was offered.

Treatment

The kaupapa Māori mental health team offered regular contact with the kaiārahi Māori and support to attend the kaupapa Māori therapy programmes provided within their service.

Medication treatments for her depression and psychoses were discussed by the psychiatrist and monitored by the psychiatric nurse who visited Teina in her home with the kaiārahi Māori on a weekly basis initially. Once her symptoms of depression, suicide and psychoses reduced a referral to the Māori psychologist on the team (who based his practice on kaupapa Māori interventions) was encouraged to provide individual therapy. Whānau sessions and support were also provided by the kaiārahi Māori to ensure that Teina's whānau received psychoeducation regarding each specific treatment intervention provided by the team. Teina relapsed during treatment and began using cannabis heavily while she was under the mental health service. She was then supported to reduce her medications several months after she began therapy with the psychologist. She was referred to the alcohol and drug counsellor in the kaupapa Māori addictions service and began a harm reduction treatment programme. She continues to use alcohol socially, but is aware that cannabis can trigger a relapse of her symptoms of depression and psychoses. She remained abstinent from cannabis use following her second relapse. Teina remained under the care of the kaupapa Māori service for approximately three years until she was discharged back to her general practitioner for ongoing primary health care follow up. Teina has never presented to mental health services since her first presentation and has remained in contact with the service only to update them regarding her progress.

Ngā moemoeā: Dreams and aspirations for the future

Future directions will continue to promote this approach to meet with growing needs of Māori within Aotearoa. Māori are widely over-represented in mental health addictions and the growing dearth of research conducted by Māori for Māori, using kaupapa Māori theory and practice, continue to produce significant improvements for Māori who experiences these difficulties.

Future directions based on kaupapa Māori theory, research and practice could include the integration of child, youth, adult and elder services for Māori wherein the whānau as a whole are seen, supported and monitored generationally. Māori whānau continue to exist within strong generational contexts therefore service delivery must allow for assessment and treatment of the wider whānau rather than the current focus on individualised treatment.

As we head into the future it is hoped that whānau-based approaches to health care, that are guided by kaupapa Māori principles, form the basis from which services working with Māori will progress into the future. Furthermore, the growing research on the need to integrate trauma informed care approaches within health services calls for the integration of these methods in Aotearoa given the high rates of trauma experienced within the Māori community (Pihama et al. 2014; Reid et al. 2014; Wirihana and Smith 2014). Research towards this end will only serve to enhance Māori well-being, and facilitate pathways of healing from the layers of trauma Māori have experienced, and continue to experience, in Aotearoa today.

Conclusion

Due to the high prevalence rates of Māori in general and specialized mental health services it is integral that policy makers, service providers, and clinicians themselves, ensure they are working with Māori in a manner that aligns with kaupapa Māori methods of understanding health, healing and well-being. It is also incumbent on training providers to provide training to mental health clinicians that ensures that they do not render our people unsafe by virtue of *omitting* our language, culture and practices or by marginalising our values. Most importantly, there is a dire need to create spaces where our people, our values and our ways of viewing mental illness are encouraged and, as stated by Taitimu (2007: i), by integrating "Māori ways of understanding extra-ordinary experiences" we can create opportunities for mental health services to decrease tendencies to further pathologize an already stigmatised community.

Recent developments in the He Kokonga Whare research project with Te Atawhai o te Ao (Independent Māori Research Institute for Environment and Health) have highlighted the consequence of historical trauma on the Māori community (Pihama et al. 2014; Reid et al. 2014; Wirihana and Smith 2014). As highlighted in this chapter, Māori health, healing and well-being requires an understanding of the impact of historical trauma on current health and well-being – particularly within mental health and addictions services. Māori have experienced multiple generations of trauma, as a direct consequence of historical trauma, and the erosion of traditional Māori narratives of healing and well-being continue to exacerbate this process and hinder the journey of healing for Māori. In addition, this process impacts directly on Māori generational well-being. Nevertheless, Māori continue to identify the importance of utilising kaupapa Māori based knowledge in the wider health context and the associated positive outcomes have been highlighted in the context of this chapter. Dedicated Māori healers, health practitioners and health researchers have strongly contributed to this process and their work has created pathways for ongoing development and promotion of kaupapa Māori mental health and addictions services. This growth can only be seen as positive as, more and more, kaupapa Māori research indicates that by Māori for Māori solutions enhance Māori well-being and facilitate healing from mild to severe and complex mental health and addictions needs.

Note

1 This case study is fictional but is drawn from the writers' experience of working within both kaupapa Māori and mainstream mental health and addictions services.

References

Ahuriri-Driscoll, A., Baker, V., Hepi, M., Hudson, M., Mika, C., Tiakiwai, S. (2008) '*The future of rongoā Māori: Wellbeing and sustainability*'. Wellington: Ministry of Health.

Ballara, A. Pomare I. (2017, November 28) *Te Ara – the Encyclopedia of New Zealand*, Retrieved from https://teara.govt.nz/en/biographies/1p19/pomare-i.

Bennett, S. (2009) *Te huanga o te iwi Māori: Cognitive behavioural therapy for Māori clients with depression – Development and evaluation of a culturally adapted treatment programme.* Wellington; Massey University.

Bezo, B., and Maggi, S. (2018) 'Intergenerational perceptions of mass trauma's impact on physical health and well-being'. *Psychological Trauma: Theory, Research, Practice, and Policy*, 10(1): 87–94.

Buchan, K. (2017) *New Zealand: Bill Establishing River as Having Own Legal Personality Passed.* Retrieved 11 October 2017, from www.loc.gov/law/foreign-news/article/new-zealand-bill-establishing-river-as-having-own-legal-personality-passed/.

Cavino, H. (2016) 'Intergenerational sexual violence and whānau in Aotearoa/New Zealand – pedagogies of contextualisation and transformation'. *Sexual Abuse in Australia and New Zealand*, 7(1): 4–17.

Cherrington, L. (2003) 'The use of Māori mythology in clinical settings: Training issues and needs'. In L. W. Nikora, M. Levy, B. Masters, W. Waitoki, N. Te Awekotuku, and R. J. M. Etheredge (Eds.), *Proceedings of the National Māori Graduates of Psychology Symposium 2002: Making a difference* (pp. 117–120). Hamilton, NZ: Māori and Psychology Research Unit, University of Waikato.

Cherrington, L. (2016) 'Re: I just want to heal my family'. In Waitoki, W., and Levy, M. (Eds.), *Te Manu Kai i Te Mātauranga: Indigenous Psychology in Aotearoa/New Zealand* (pp. 115–124). Wellington: New Zealand Psychological Society.

Curtis, E. (2016) 'Indigenous positioning in health research: the importance of kaupapa theory informed practice'. *AlterNATIVE: An International Journal of Indigenous Peoples*, 12(4): 396–410.

Durie, M. (1995) *Counselling for Māori.* Paper presented at the New Zealand Counselling and Guidance Association Hui, Palmerston North.

Durie, M. (1998a) *Te mana, te kawanatanga*. Auckland: Oxford University Press.

Durie, M. (1998b) *Whaiora: Māori health development*. Auckland: Oxford University Press

Durie, M. (2005a) *Mauri ora: The dynamics of Māori health*. Melbourne: Oxford University Press.

Durie, M. (2005b) *Nga kahui pou: Launching Maori futures*. Wellington: Huia Publishers.

Durie, M. (2006) *Ngā tai matatū: Tides of Māori endurance*. Melbourne: Oxford University Press.

Emery, T., Cookson-C, C., and Raerino, N. (2015) 'Te waiata a Hinetitama: hearing the heartsong'. *AlterNATIVE, 11*(3): 225–239.

Ihimaera, L. (2004) *He ara ki te ao mārama: A pathway to understanding taha wairua in mental health services*. Palmerston North: Massey University.

Jones, R. (2000) Traditional Māori healing practices. *Pacific health dialog, (7)*1, 107–109.

Kahuikiwa, R., Potiki, R., Ihimaera, W., and Kaa, K. (1999) *Oriori: A Māori child is born – from conception to birth*. Auckland: Tandem.

Keane, B. (2011) 'Traditional Māori religion – ngā karakia a te Māori – Tohunga'. In *Te Ara - the Encyclopedia of New Zealand*. Retrieved 28 November 2017, from www.TeAra.govt.nz/en/traditional-maori-religion-nga-karakia-a-te-maori/page-2.

Keane, B. (2006, April 22) 'Tūmatauenga'. In *Te Ara – the Encyclopaedia of New Zealand*. Retrieved from https://teara.govt.nz/en/artwork/8257/tumatauenga.

Keenan, D. (2012, April 28) 'New Zealand wars'. In *Te Ara – the Encyclopedia of New Zealand*. Retrieved 23 March 2019 from www.TeAra.govt.nz/en/new-zealand-wars.

Kingi, T. (2018) *Maea te ora: Maori health transformations*. Wellington: Huia.

Leahy, H. (2015) *Crossing the floor: The story of Tariana Turia*. Wellington: Huia.

Le Grice, J., Braun, V., and Wetherell, M. (2017) '"What I reckon is, is that like the love you give to your kids they'll give to someone else and so and so on": Whanaungatanga and matauranga Maory in practice'. *New Zealand Journal of Psychology, 46*(3): 88–97.

Levy, M. (2016) 'Kaupapa Maori psychologies'. In M. Waitoki and M. Levy (Eds.), *Indigenous Psychologies in Aotearoa/New Zealand*. Wellington: The New Zealand Psychological Society.

Levy, M., and Waitoki, M (2016) *Te manu kai i te matauranga: indigenous psychology in Aotearoa/New Zealand*. Wellington: New Zealand Psychological Society.

King, M. (1991) *Whina: A biography of Whina Cooper*. Penguin: Auckland.

Mark, G. (2012). *Rongoā Māori (traditional Māori healing) through the eyes of Māori healers: Sharing the healing while keeping the tapu* (Unpublished doctoral thesis). Massey University, Auckland, New Zealand.

Mataamua, R. (2016, April 22) *EIT Public Lecture: Dr. Rangi Mataamua*. Retrieved from www.youtube.com/watch?v=hfuEkqz8v3k.

Mataamua, R. (2017) *Matariki: The star of the year*. Wellington: Huia.

McLachlan, A., Wirihana, R., and Huriwai, T. (2017) 'Whai tikanga: The application of a culturally relevant value centred approach'. *New Zealand Journal of Psychology, 46*: 46–54.

Mead, A. (1998) 'The sacred balance'. *He Pukenga Kōrero, 3*(2): 22–27.

Mikaere, A. (2003) *Consequences for Māori women of the colonisation of tikanga Māori*. Auckland: University of Auckland.

Mildon, C. (2012) *Essentialism of Tohuna*. A thesis completed in partial fulfilment of the requirements of the degree of Master of Indigenous Studies. Whakatane: Te Whare Wānanga ō Awanuiārangi.

Ministry of Culture and Heritage (2014, April 22) *Invasion of a pacifist settlement at Parihaka 5 November 1881*. Retrieved from https://nzhistory.govt.nz/occupation-pacifist-settlement-at-parihaka.

Ministry of Culture and Heritage. (2014, April 22) *Riwha Titokowaru*. Retrieved from https://nzhistory.govt.nz/search/site/titokowaru.

Moorfield, J. (2013) Te aka online dictionary. Retrieved from https://maoridictionary.co.nz/search?idiom=andphrase=andproverb=andloan=andhistLoanWords=andkeywords=io.

Pihama, L., Reynolds, P., Smith, C., Reid, J., Tuhiwai-Smith, L., and Te Nana, R. (2014) 'Positioning historical trauma theory'. AlterNATIVE: *An International Journal of Indigenous Peoples, 10*(3): 248–263.

Pihama, L., Te Nana, R., Cameron, N., Smith, C., Reid, J., and Southy, K. (2016) 'Maori cultural definitions of sexual violence'. *Sexual Abuse and Australia and New Zealand, 7*(1): 43–50.

Rattray, H. (2016, October) *Health and well-being of Maori after prison*. Paper presented at the He Kokonga Whare: Maori intergenerational trauma and healing workshop, Waikato, New Zealand.

Reid, J., Taylor-Moore, K., and Varona, G. (2014) 'Towards a social-structural model for understanding current disparities in Māori health and well-being'. *Journal of Loss and Trauma: International Perspectives on Stress and Coping, 10*:1–23.

Reid, J., Varona, G., Fisher, M., and Smith, C. (2016) 'Understanding Maori 'lived' culture to determine cultural connectedness and wellbeing'. *Journal of Population Research, 33*(1): 31–49.

Reynolds, P., and Smith, C. (2012) *The gift of children: Māori infertility.* Wellington: Huia.

Smith, T. (2005) *Whakapapa kōrero, tangata whenua and turangawaewae: A case study of the colonisation of indigenous knowledge.* Auckland: University of Auckland.

Smith, T. (2008) 'Knowing and ngākau'. *Indigenous Knowledge in the Pacific, 17*(2): 10–14.

Smith, T. (2012) 'Aitanga: Māori precolonial conceptual frameworks and fertility – a literature review'. In P. Reynolds and C. Smith (Eds.), *The gift of children: Māori fertility* (pp. 3–41). Wellington: Huia.

Smith, T. (2015, February) *Presentation from Dr. Takirirangi Smith.* Paper presented at the He Kokonga Whare: Māori Historical Trauma, Healing and Wellbeing Workshop with Dr. Eduardo Duran and Dr. Takirirangi Smith, Whanganui, New Zealand.

Taitimu, M. (2007). Ngā whakawhitingā: standing at the cross roads (Unpublished doctoral thesis). University of Auckland, Auckland, New Zealand.

Taitimu, M., and Read, J. (2006) 'Explanatory models of Schizophrenia'. *The British Journal of Psychiatry: The Journal of Mental Science, 189*(03): 284–285.

Taitimu, M., Read, J., and Mcintosh, T, (2018) 'Nga whakawhitinga (standing at the crossroads): How Maori understand what Western psychiatry calls "schizophrenia"'. *Transcultural Psychiatry, 55*(2): 153–177.

Tuhiwai-Smith, L. (2003) *Decolonising methodologies: Research and indigenous peoples.* Dunedin: University of Otago Press.

Waiti, J. (2014) *Whakaoranga whanau: A whanau resilience framework.* Wellington: Massey University.

Walters, A., and Seymour, F. (2017) 'Stories of survival and resilience: An enquiry into th what helps tamariki and rangatahi through whanau violence'. *New Zealand Journal of Psychology, 46*(3): 80–87.

Walters, K., Mohammed, S., Evans-Campbell, T., Beltran, R., Chae, D., and Duran, B. (2011) 'Bodies don't just tell stories, they tell histories: Embodiment of historical trauma among American Indians and Alaska Natives'. *Du Bois Review, 8*(1): 179–189.

Waretini-Karena, R. (2012) 'Takitoru: From parallel to partnership: A ritual of engagement based on Te Tiriti o Waitangi for implementing safe cultural practice in Māori counselling and social science'. *MAI Journal, 1*(1): 61–75.

Wepa, D. (2018, June 30) *Māori responsiveness.* Retrieved from www.hqsc.govt.nz/our-programmes/partners-in-care/resources/videos-maori-responsiveness/.

Wirihana, R. (2012). Ngā pūrākau o ngā wāhine rangatira Māori o Aotearoa: The stories of Māori women leaders in New Zealand (Unpublished doctoral thesis). Massey University, Auckland, New Zealand.

Wirihana, R. and Smith, C. (2014) 'Historical trauma, healing and wellbeing in Māori communities'. *MAI Journal, 3*(3): 197–210.

Valentine, H. (2009) *Kia ngāwari ki te awatea: The relationship between wairua and Māori wellbeing: A psychological perspective.* Palmerston North: Massey University Press.

Valentine, H. (2016) 'Wairuatanga'. In M. Waitoki and M. Levy (Eds.), *Indigenous Psychologies in Aotearoa/ New Zealand.* Wellington: The New Zealand Psychological Society, 155–169.

Valentine, H., Tassel-Mataamua, N., and Flett, R. (2017) 'Whakairia ki runga: The many dimensions of wairua'. *New Zealand Journal of Psychology, 46*(3): 64–71.

Yellow Horse Brave Heart, M. (2008) 'Gender Differences in the historical trauma response among the Lakota.' *Journal of Health and Social Policy,* 10(4): 1–21.

GLOSSARY

Ariki	Name for god, paramount chief, high chief
Aoteroa	Land of the long white cloud (New Zealand)
Haka	To dance, perform
Hapū	Sub-tribe
Iwi	Tribe
Kaiarahi	Guide, escort, counsellor
Kainga	Traditional Māori homes
Karakia	Prayer, incantation, ritual chant, grace
Karanga	Formal call, ceremonial call, welcome call, call
Kaumatua	Adult, elder, elderly man, elderly woman, old man – a person of status within the whānau
Kīngitanga	Kingdom, reign (of a king), dominion, majesty, nation, country
Koha	Gift, present, offering, donation
Koroua	Elderly man, old man, elder, grandfather, granduncle
Kura Kaupapa Māori	Total immersion Māori language schools
Kurawaka	Name of the place in the creation stories where the first woman was created
Māori	Indigenous peoples of Aoteroa (New Zealand)
Mamae	Painful, sore, injured, hurt, wound
Marae	Formal gathering place
Matariki	The Māori New Year as based on the rising the star cluster Matariki (Pleiades)
Mau Taiaha	Weaponry using a long carved wooden weapon
Mihi Whakatau	Speech of greeting, official welcome speech
Mirimiri	Massage, to rub, soothe
Ngatī	Prefix for a tribal group
Ngarauru kiitahi	Tribal group of the Waitootara/Whanganui area, the descendents of Rauru kiitahi
Noa	Without restraint, freely
Oriori	Lullaby
Papatūānuku	Earth mother and wife of Ranginui

Glossary

Pātere	To chant
Patu	To hit, strike, beat, assault, a club (weapon)
Pepeha	Tribal saying or proverb
Poi	A light ball on a string of varying length which is swung or twirled rhythmically to sung accompaniment
Pōuritanga	Depression, despondency, gloom, dejection, unhappiness, sadness
Pūrākau	Traditional narrative, creation stories
Rāhui	Temporary prohibition
Rarohenga	Underworld, netherworld, the place where the spirits go
Ranginui	God of the sky and husband of Papatūānuku
Ritenga	Ritual
Rohe	Boundary, district, area, border, region, land
Rongoā	Remedy, medicine, drug, cure, to treat or apply
Rongomatane	God of cultivated food
Taiao	Natural environment, world, earth, nature, country
Tane	Male, man
Tānenuiarangi	Child of Ranginui and Papatūānuku who brought about their separation
Tangaroa	God of the sea and fish
Tangata	Person, man, human being
Taonga	Treasure, anything priced, precious objects
Tapu	Sacred, prohibited, protected, set apart, under Ariki protection
Tauira	Students
Tāwhirimātea	God of winds, clouds, rain, hail, snow and storms
Te Ika a Maui	North Island of Aotearoa (New Zealand)
Te reo Māori	Māori language
Te Tai Tokerau	Northland region of the North Island
Te Waipounamu	South Island of Aotearoa (New Zealand)
Tikanga	Custom, lore, protocol
Tiakitanga	Guardianship, caring of, protection, upkeep
Tinana	Physical body
Tino Rangatiratanga	Self-determination, autonomy, sovereignty
Tipuna	Ancestor, grandparent, grandmother, grandfather
Tohunga	To be expert, proficient, adept
Tohunga Kōkōrangi	Astronomer, expert in the study of celestial bodies
Tūmatauenga	God of war and mankind
Waiata	Song, chant
Wahine	Women
Wairua	Soul, spirit,
Waka	Canoe
Wānanga	Tribal knowledge, lore, learning
Whakapapa	Genealogy, descent, lineage
Whakapapa kōrero	Genealogical narratives
Whakawhanaungatanga	Process of establishing relationships, relating well to others
Whānau	Family, extended family
Whanaunga	Relative, relation, kin, blood relation
Whānau pani	Chief mourners, bereaved family – relations of the deceased
Whakatauki	Proverbs

Glossary

Whakatauākī	Proverbs associated with an author, place of origin or audience
Whakawātea	To clear, free, dislodge, purge, get rid of
Whare	House
Whare Tīpuna	Ancestral house

INDEX

aarti (healing ceremony) 254
Abasiebong, F. 425
Abdullahi, A. A. 497
Abel, W. D. xix, 399–410
Abeokuta: Aro Mental Hospital 23, 423, 425
'abjects' 1–2
Abraham, L. 512
Aburto Miranda, C. 354
acceptance and commitment therapy
    (ACT) 230–2
acculturation xxii, xxiii, 16, 38, 232, 289, 292, 296,
    297, 317, 330: Ward's definition 162
acting White 157
Adaptation and Development after Persecution
    and Trauma 332
Adelson, L. J. 208
adharma (disharmony) 253
ADHD: sociocultural context 293–4
adolescents: 'biological' versus 'social' maturity 291;
    Gujarati 292
adverse childhood experiences (ACEs) 294
affirmative action 15, 350
Africa 35, 36
Africa MH Foundation 418
African Americans 70, 71, 85, 87, 106, 108–9, 157,
    217; former US president 108
African healing 496–504: acquisition of
    knowledge 499–500; causation of ill-health
    498–9; colonialism 497; contemporary era
    501–2; cultural activities 501; delivery strategies
    501; future directions 502; healing process 500;
    holistic approach 500; sources of knowledge
    496–7; theories and practices 497–9; treatment
    (actual) of ill-health 500; treatment of diseases
    499–500
African MH Foundation (AMHF) 417
agentes comunitários de saúde (ACS) 347, 348, 350

Aggarwal, N. K. 164
Agha Khan University and Hospital 418
agnostics 216, 218, 220–2
Ahmad, A. xii, 187–99
Ahmed, S. 11
Ajana, B. 58
Akan people (Ghana) 414
Al-Balkhi 435; 'Sustenance of Soul' 266,
    270
albularyo 462, 463
alcohol 20, 355, 403, 485, 491, 536, 537
Alegría, M. 170
Algeria 21, 97–8
Al-Ghazali: theory of soul 266–7, 270
alien (terminology) 315
Alika, H. xiv, 422–33
Ali, S. R. 268
Alkali Lake 491
Al-Krenawi, A. 435
All-India Institute of MH (NIMHANS)
    390–1allocentrism 155
Allport, G. W. 157
Alma-Ata Conference (1978) 414
Alonzo, A. 459–60
Al-Razi: *Razi's Traditional Psychology*
    266, 270
Al-Tarabi 435
alternative and complementary medicine
    (ACM) 3, 368
Álvarez, I. 354
American Atheists 219
American Counselling Association (ACA):
    advocacy competencies 72–3
American Medical Association 290
American Paediatric Society 290
American Psychiatric Association 52, 63, 77, 99,
    100, 120, 164, 472

Index

American Psychological Association (APA) 71; conference (1973) 73; 'Division 49' 107; ethical standards 73, 152; guidelines 209
American University in Cairo 380
analytic third (Ogden) 87
ANC 472–3
Ancient Greece 215, 220, 256, 265, 266
Anderson, B. 94
Ang, A.V. xi, 458–69
Angell, M. 99
angst 246n1
anthropologists/anthropology xxiii, 46, 48, 83, 87, 93, 240, 242, 328, 343, 445, 488, 498–9; comparative method 22
anti-psychiatry movement 98, 355, 358
anti-racism 98–9
Aotearoa 39, 216; British colonial oppression 532–3; Foreshore and Seabed Act (2004) 535; Health Practitioners Competence Assurance Act (20003) 535; land wars (1840–1860) 532; Māori indigenous healing 530–43; Ministry of Health 493; Native Schools Act (1867) 532; scorched earth policies (1865) 532; Te-Ika-a–Maui (North Island) 535; *Tohunga* Suppression Act (1907) 534–5
apu (mountain spirit) 450, 451
aql (cognition) 266–7
Araya, C. 360
Arguedas, J. M. 445
Ariès, P. 290
Armat, V. C. 167
Armstrong, K. 88, 233n2
Arthur, C. M. 519
Aruba 526
Asad, M. 267
asanas (physical movements, in yoga) 255
Asclepius 240
ashram (shrine) 253
Asian values 158
Assertive Community Treatment (ACT) 130
Association of American Medical Colleges (AAMC) 289, 291, 297
Asuni, T. 23
asylums 35–6, 38, 54, 92, 95, 98, 119, 366, 367, 390; phased out 96, 116, 342
atheism: cultures of healing 219–20; environmental factors 220; ethnicity and religion 217; forms of distress 223; future directions 223; gender and sexuality 217; and healing in MH 215–25; individual contexts, healing and well-being 222; intersectionality 217; many faces 216–17; and MH 220–2; negative versus positive 215; stigma 219; substance abuse 222, 223; suicide 220, 223
atheist religions 215, 216
attam (dance) 511
Austin, A. 207
Australia 35, 216, 317, 319, 461

Australian Aborigines 4, 13, 20, 25, 27
autoatención (self-care models) 343
axé (vital force) 344
Ayonrinde, O. A. 430
Ayurvedic medicine 255, 268, 388, 389, 392, 462, 506, 507, 512–14, 525–6; Five Elements 254, 367–8

babalawo (Yoruba traditional healer) 424
Babcock, J. C. 203–4
Back, L. 9
Baez, A. 526–7
Bahia 344
Bainbridge, L. 130
Balcazar, F. E. xiv, 162–73
Bamgbose, O. O. xvii, 422–33
Bang, H. 229
Banki, S. 306
Bannerman, W. B. 507
Barn, R.: 'culturalist perspective' 143
Barr, S. M. 208, 209
Barreto, A. 348
Barton, L. 163
Basic Needs (NGO) 417, 418
Basilov, V. N. 510
Basu, A. M. 507, 509
Bedouin 381, 436
Beer, D. 58
Beers, C.: *Mind That Found Itself* (1908) 116
Behavioral Risk Factor Surveillance System (USA 2014) 201
Beiser, M. 115
Beit-Hallahmi, B. 216–17
Bell, D. 14
Bellary Model 391
Bello, A. (University of Chile) 358
Bemak, F. xiv, 103–14
Benedict, R. 242
Benham, W. 354, 357
Benning, T. B. xix, 19–31
Berg-Cross, L. 72
Bertrand, M. 525
Bethel Baptist Church (Jamaica) 245
Bettez, S. C. 25
Bhabha, H. 20, 22, 27, 28, 33; hybridity theory 25, 26; *Location of Culture* (1994) 94
Bhavsar, V. 43–53
Bhugra, D. 43–53, 253
bhut (evil spirits) 254
bhuta (spirit) 512
Big 7 socio-cultural identities 3
Bilby, K. M. 520biomedicalism 129, 130, 302, 303
biomedicine 49–50, 188–90, 193, 196, 302
bio-psycho-social model 188
Black, Asian and Minority Ethnic (BAME) people 314, 318–19, 320
Black church (USA) 191

Index

black feminism (Crenshaw) 84
Black Lives Matter 107
Black and Minority Ethnic (BME) people 4, 13, 315
Blackness 12
Black psychologists 71blended model of biculturalism 317
Blom, J. D. 526
Blowers, G. H. 367
Blumenbach, J. 59
Blumer, H. 141, 143
Bockting, W. O. 202, 207–8
Bohm, D. 104
Bojuwoye, O. xvii, 496–504
Borokini, T. I. 502
Bracken, P. 48, 100
Braddock, D. L. 163
brahmacharya 388
'brain fag disorder' (Prince) 428–30
Bramadat, P. 217
Brantlinger, P. 10
Braun, V. 534
Brazil 40, 341–2; community health workers (ACS) 347, 348, 350; contemporary MH practices 347–9; cultural representations of illness and wellness 345–6; 'cultural uniformity' thesis 345–6, 350; demographics 341; Family Health Strategy (*Estratégia Saúde da Família*, ESF) 348; future directions 349–50; Indigenous MH 349; MH (historical survey) 342–3; migrants and refugees 349; National Policy for Healthcare of Indigenous Peoples (2002) 343; *nervoso* 347; psychiatric reform (1978) 342, 346, 350; Psychiatric Reform Law (2001) 342; 'silencing' of culture 341, 346–7, 350; slavery 344, 345; social exclusion and stigma 349; Society of Medicine and Surgery 342; strategies of intercultural competence 350; structural racism 350; traditional healers 343–5; trance and possession 344
Brazilian Community Therapy (CT) 347, 348–50
Brazilian Institute of Geography and Statistics (IBGE) 341
Brazilian League of Mental Hygiene (LBHM) 342
Brazilian Unified Health System 342
Breakey, W. R. 189–90
Breakwell, G. M.: identity process theory (IPT) 317
Brennan, D. 36
Breslow, A. S. 205, 208
Brewer, M. B. 157
Brewster, M. E. 217, 221
Brickman, C.: *Aboriginal populations in mind* (2003) 22
Brief COPE coping measure 206
British Columbia xix, 20, 27, 117, 486, 491
British Empire 35, 62, 390

British Psychological Society 320
Bronfenbrenner, U. 331; multiple layers in children's development 292–3
Brothers, D. 88
Brown, S. E. 165
Brown, T. H. 165
Brua 526
Buber, M. 13
Buddha 226, 227, 233, 233n1, 233n4; *Bhaisajyaguru* ('Master of Healing') 228
Buddha as Doctor: Mahayana Buddhism 228–30, 234n8–11; Theravada Buddhism 227–8, 230, 233–4n4–7
Buddhism 215, 217, 226–37; compassion towards self and others 231; future directions 232–3; Mahayana 226–31; metacognitive insight 231; and MH 227–30; mindfulness 231; schools 227–30; *suttas*, *vinaya*, *abhidhamma* 227; third-wave therapies 230–3, 234n12; Theravada 226–8; and Western therapy 230–2; wisdom and autonomy 231
Budge, S. L. 207, 208
Bulatao, J. 465
bureaucratic hierarchies 135
Burton, D. 227
Butt, H. 115
Bynum, W. F. 507
Byrd, J. A. 21

Calhoun, J. C. 61
California: Cambodian Buddhist refugees 230
Cameron, D. 423
campaign for global MH (CGMH) 44–5, 48; critics 49, 51; de-institutionalization 46–7
Campbell, D. E. 216, 217
Canada 12, 13, 130–2, 147, 166, 215, 216, 243, 244, 317, 327, 331; atheists 218; civil rights movement 15; diversity 115, 123; foreign-born older people 310n3; foreign-born persons 301; Health Professions Act 117; home care services 307, 310n4; MH nursing 115–27; Royal Commission on Aboriginal Peoples (RCAP 1993) 492; Task Force on Aboriginal Peoples in Federal Corrections 492; Theravada 226–8; Truth and Reconciliation Commission (TRC) 486, 492
Canadian Standing Committee on Health 492
Candomblé (Afro-Brazilian religion) 344
cannabis 403–4, 536, 537
Cantor-Graee, E. 314
Cape Colony 35
Cape Town 471; Groote Schuur Hospital 478
capital 32, 41, 55
capitalism 3, 34, 129, 130, 497
Caracas Declaration (1990) 342
caregiver stress 307
care management (UK) 130

Index

Caribbean 35, 37, 70; First Peoples 518; Indigenous Amerindians 518

Caribbean healing 517–29; case vignette 526; colonial history 517–29; future directions 527; global context 525–7; healing community 524–5; holistic approach 517, 519; methods 519–24; *Obeah* 520; *Santeria* 521–2; *Shango/Orisha* 523–4; stigmatization 520; training 524–5; *Vodou* 521

Carlat, D. 99

Carmichael, J. xv, 226–37

Carothers, J. C. 38–9

Carrasco, J. 355, 357

Carruthers, M. 256

Casa de Orates (Chile) 354–5, 357

case management (Canada/US) 130, 133, 134

case vignettes (A–E): Abraham (suicidal farmer in Kerala) 394–5; Abubakar ('brain fag syndrome'; mixed modern and traditional healing methods) 428–30; Ada (bullied schoolgirl, mixed modern and traditional healing methods) 427–8; African American woman (multiple-identity challenges) 165; Ahmed (repentant Pakistani American Muslim) 270; Ayesha (mother with bipolar disorder) 269; Buddha's cure of Kisa Gotami 228, 231, 234n5; Caroline (Indigenous and Western medicine side-by-side) 466; Christian healing associated with community support ministry 245; Clients A and B (social workers' failings) 131–4; David (materialism issue) 159; Dina (Western practices adapted to needs of Filipina) 465–66; Dinesh (current MH practice in India) 513–14; earthquake survivor in Nepal ('religious test', 2015) 189

case vignettes (G–L): gay Muslim experiencing depression 178–9; Grace (suicide of Jamaican preacher) 190–1; Gregory ('acting White' issue) 157; Ismail (schizophrenic patient) 395–6; Jamie (integrated mind-body-spirit approach for Chinese woman) 372–3; John (proxy kids worldview) 158; Juliet (refugee suffering from PTSD) 327, 329, 333–5; Jyoti (aged 15; self-harming) 296–7; Latino man experiencing bipolar mania 164

case vignettes (M): Madhavan Iyyappan (release-from-asylum issue 1889) 508–9; Mara (Indigenous healing in Philippines) 462–3; Maria/Mary (*doença dos nervos*) 347; Mark (aged 17, son of drug-users) 293; member of Black LGBTQ Student Alliance 146, 147; Mr A. (integration of Caribbean and Western healing) 526; Mr Sandhu (aged 70, with substance issues) 304–7, 309; Mrs Zhang (widow aged 80 in fragile health) 304–7, 309; Musau (combination of methods) 416

case vignettes (O–S): Omar (current practice in Pakistan) 440–2; peer support 169; Ramira

(Afro-Caribbean lesbian in London) 176–8; Rukia (specialised MH care) 416–17; social exclusion 166; supposed spirit-possession 244–5; Susan (power of 'other' in therapeutic relationship) 82

case vignettes (T–Z): Teina (Māori health intervention) 536–7; Terry (Filipino-American victim of crabs-in-barrel classism) 156; Toshio (Japanese migrant to Canada) 319; treatment of schizophrenic by Tibetan Lama Zopa Rinpoche 229; Uncle John (South African schizophrenic) 476; use of land in healing (North America) 490; veteran of war in Afghanistan with PTSD 146–7; woman receiving MBCT after fertility failures 231–2; Zohra (role of marital failure and religious beliefs in distress) 441–2

caste xxiv, 389, 510–11

categorization 57; as form of psycho-power 54

Césaire, A. 22, 33

Chamberlin, E. J. 24

Chan, L. xv, 151–61

Chan, M. 502

Chandigarh: Post Graduate Institute of Medical Education and Research (PGIMER) 391

Chandradasa, M. 230

Chen, P. H. 365, 373

Cherrington, L. 531

chesed (acts of loving kindness) 277

Chicago juvenile court (1899–) 290

child abuse 379–81, 487

childhood: 'chronological age' versus 'developmental age' 290; concept 290

'child' idea 61

children: access to MH care in cultural contexts 291–3; acculturation 289, 292, 296, 297; cross-cultural construction 290–1; cultural mismatch with caretakers 292; culture and MH 289–300; Egypt 378–81, 384; future directions 297; guidelines for working with diverse patient populations 295–6; integrating culture in MH care 295–7; intersectionality 289–300; parental punishment issue 296; peer relationships 292–3; principle-based approach to cultural issues 295; refugees 330–2; relationship with parents (cultural context) 292; resilience 293; self-harming behaviour 296–7; stigma 291–2; taxonomy of MH problems and culture 293–4; universality 295

Childs, P. 19

Chile: alcoholism 355; asylums 342, 345, 354, 359; children 354; colonialism and evolution of MH practices 357–8; Community Psychiatry 355; contemporary MH practices 361–2; culture and MH 353–64; demographics 353; Diego Portales University 361; future directions 362–3; history of MH 353–6, 362; Indigenous approach to health and illness 356–7; intercultural MH

362–3; *Journal of Psychiatry* 360; licensing and certification 359–61; Ministry of Health 361; 'moral degeneration' 354; National Commission of Accreditation of Clinical Psychologists (CONAPC) 361; National MH Plan (2017) 36; Pontifical Catholic University 360–1; social representations of health and disease 358–9; Society of Psychiatry (1934–) 360; suicide problem 354, 356; training and accreditation 359–62

China 158, 159, 215–18; Measures Regarding Professional Qualifications of Social Workers 371; National MH Meeting (1958–) 366; National MH Plan 366; Proposal on Strengthening MH Work (2004) 366; Regulations on Vocational Standards of Social Workers 370–1; three-tier model 366; *see also* Greater China

Chinese Exclusion Act (USA 1882) 106

Chinese medicine 367–8, 372, 462

Chiu, M. 122

choice 329–30

Chong, H. H. 373

Christianity 221, 400, 403, 406, 517, 523, 524; African context 244–5; 'being cured' versus 'being healed' 240; Bible (New English King James version) 247n9; body-soul relation 240; case studies 244; coping strategies 243; epistemological significance 246; eschatology 240; future directions 245–6; Gospels 239, 247n6, 247n10; healing (20th century) 241–2; healing (*NT* context) 241, 247n11; and healing in MH 238–49; healing traditions: context (historical and philosophical) 239–41, 247n8–10; holistic approach 243, 245, 246; intersectionality 242–5, 247n12; stigma of mental illness 238–9; theological view of wholeness (health) 238

Chung, R. C.-Y. xvii, 103–14

Civil Rights Act (USA 1964) 14, 69

civilization 1, 12, 22, 33, 36–9, 58, 61, 254, 435, 485, 506

civilizing missions 55, 56

Clark, J. 229

Clarke, J. J. 94

classificatory power 60–2

classism 151; defining 152–4; discussion in MH practice (significance) 154–6; domains (upward, downward, internalized, lateral) 154–5; future directions 159

Cleary, A. S. 39

Clements-Noelle, K. 201

clinical psychology 72, 92, 96, 99, 393, 452, 460; cultural education and training 73–4; fourth and fifth force 71–3

coercion 45, 46, 132, 155; therapeutic social control 133

Cogan, J. C. 202

Cognitive Behaviour Therapy (CBT) 230, 232, 234n12, 256–7, 332, 416, 429, 453, 455n2, 526; Islamic origins (ninth century) 266; Judaism 276

Cohen, B. M. Z. 32–42, 333

Coleman, P. G. 221

colonialism xxiv, 2–4, 9, 34, 93, 342, 357–8, 369–70; Chile 357–8; incarceration rates in asylums 35, 37

colonial psychiatry 32, 35–6, 99

Colonial Psychiatry and African Mind (McCulloch 1995) 22

colonial settler studies 19; indigeneity/MH interface 26–9

coloniality, globalization and MH 4, 7–65; coloniality, indigeneity and MH 19–31; culture and globalization of MH 43–53; empire and psychiatric expansionism 32–42; politics of GMH governance 54–65; race and culture in MH 9–18

coloniality of power (Quijano) 19

colonizer-colonized dialectic 24–5

colouring-in-the-White movement 11–12

Comas-Díaz, L. 87

Comfort, N. 219

community care 96, 99, 130–1, 334, 342, 366

Community Centers of MH (COSAM) 356

community commemoration ceremonies 334–5

Community Treatment Orders (Canada) 61

Compassion-Focused Therapy (CFT) 231

Compson, J. 232

Confucianism 215, 216

conjure doctors 521

Connell, D. M. 256

Cook, J. A. 168, 169

Copeland, M. E. 168–9

Copiapó (Chile): *Escuela Normal* 358, 360

coping profiles 206

Corrigan, P. W. 166

Council on Social Work Education (CSWE) 128

Counselling Association of Nigeria (CASSON) 424, 426

counselling: cultural education and training 73–4; fourth and fifth force 71–3

counselling psychology 69–80; future directions 75–6; research and funding 75

Craddock, N. 100

Crandon-Malamud, L. 451–2

Crenshaw, K. 84

critical life course perspective 302–5, 309

critical race theory (CRT) 10, 13–16; interest convergence 15–16; liberalist ideologies 14; permanence of racism 14; value of counter-narratives 16; white dominance 15

critical social work scholars 129, 131, 134, 136

critical theory 124

cross-cultural research 134, 136, 142

Index

Crosson, J. B. 520
Cross, W.: theory of 'Nigrescence' 74
Crow, L. 163–4
Cuba 522
cultural anthropologists 86
cultural competence: definition 119;
globalization 76; MH nursing 119–20; stages
(Papadopoulos) 119–20
cultural education and training 73–4
cultural ethical boundaries: redefinition in group
therapy race dialogues 110–11
Cultural Formulated Interview (CFI) 120–1,
164, 320
cultural identity 242; definition 162
cultural imperialism 144, 145
culturalism (Dalal) 13
culturalists 85–6
cultural psychiatry 47–8, 142
cultural psychology 87
culture xxiii, 4; conflation with race 93–5;
counselling psychology 69–80; definition
(Association of American; globalization of
MH 43–53; group psychotherapy 103–14;
implication 162; internal and external reality
87–8; interplay with MH 2; intersectionality
and MH 84–5; MH nursing 115–27; 'neither
fixed nor static' 12; oppression 143–5; 'our
shared illusion' 81; in psychiatry 92–102;
and race 93–4; resistance 85; sociological 93;
terminology 94
culture and identity in MH 5, 139–212; disability
162–73; gender 141–50; religion 187–99; sexual
orientation 174–86; social class 151–61; social
work 128–38; transgender individuals 200–12
culture and MH: children and adolescents
289–300; global context 5–6, 339–481; Chile
353–65; Egypt 377–86; Greater China 365–76;
India 387–98; immigrants 314–25; Jamaica
399–410; Kenya 411–21; Nigeria 422–33; older
people 301–13; Peru 445–57; Philippines
458–69; Pakistan 435–44; refugees 326–38;
South Africa 470–81; special populations 5,
287–338
culture and psychoanalysis 81–91; future
directions 88–9
'culture of psychiatry' 96
curandeiros (traditional healers) 343
Czech Republic 215, 218

da Silva, D. F. 55, 58
Dalai Lama, His Holiness 229, 230, 233
Dalal, A. K. 13, 251, 505
dang-ki (medium) 369
Daoism 370
Darwin and Darwinism 10, 70, 93, 220
Das, J. 252
Dauphinais, P. 492

David, King 275
Davids, C. A. F. R. 230
Davin, N. F. 485
Davis, A. 70
Dawkins, R. 219
De Andrade, V. 473
Dean, M. 61
DeAngelis, T. 73
death 228, 358
decompensation theory 177–8
Dein, S. xix, 187–99, 436, 438
Delgado, R. 14
depression 45, 71, 105, 190
Descartes, R. 95, 242, 245, 250–2, 369
determinants of health 50; Richmond and Ross
(2009) 26
detoxification process (*panchkanna*) 255
Deverell, A. 473
Dewey, L. 167
dharma 251
dhyana (meditation) 255
Diagnostic Interview Schedule (DIS) (1981) 57
Diagnostic and Statistical Manual 142, 245, 330, 472;
DSM–3 57; *DSM–4* (2000) 320, 430; *DSM–5*
(2013) 44, 99, 120, 164, 293, 294, 320, 430, 525;
Four Ds 59
Dialectical Behaviour Therapy (DBT) 230–2
dibia (Ibo traditional healer) 424
Diderot, D. 215
differential racialization concept 14
disability 2, 162–73: budgetary constraints 170;
coping strategies 167–9; diagnosing MH
163–4; empowerment 170–1; future directions
169–71; intersectionality 164–6, 170; lifestyles
169; microaggressions 166; newspaper reports
166; peer support 169; resistance 167–8; self-
determination 168, 169; social exclusion 165–7;
social model 163–4; through abandonment
167; through discrimination 167; through
elimination 166–7; through segregation 167;
'upward social comparisons' 169
divination 500, 524
Dixon, S. xviii, 238–49
Dockett, K. H. 229
doença dos nervos (Brazil) 347
Dogra, N. xvii, 289–300
Domingo, E. 459
Dominican Republic 524
double-bind 98
Dover, M. A. 144–5
drums and drumming 245, 400, 491, 520, 522–4
Dryden, W. 499
duas (supplications) 269
duba (Hausa traditional healer) 424
DuBois, W. E. B. xxiii, 70
Dunedin Study 294
Duran, B. 20

Duran, E. Dr. 20, 486
Durie, Mason Sir 530, 531, 534, 535
Durkheim, É. 358
Dustmann, C. 316
Dutch East Indies 36, 39

East India Company (VOC) 435, 471
Economist Intelligence Unit 371
Edge, D. 243
Edwards, S. D. 498
Egypt: asylum-seekers and refugees (UNHCR estimates) **380**; Child and Adolescent MH Services 384; children 378–81, 384; culture and MH 377–86; early marriage 381; education 378; future directions 384–5; General Secretariat of MH 382; general statistics *379*; harmful traditional practices 381; Health Sector Reform Program (1997–) 383; Health Sector Reform Program (1997–) 383; human resources development 384; mental hospitals 383; MH beds (2013) **382**; MH legislation, services, budget 382–4; MH Act (2009) 382, 383; MH patients (2012–2013) **383**; MH patients (length of stay 2010) **383**; MH resources **384**; Ministry of Health 381–3; National MH Council (NMHC) 382; population statistics **378**; psychiatric disorders 381–2; refugees 377–8; Regional Refugee and Resilience Plan (2016–2017) 378; sexual violence 381; substance abuse 381–2; suicide 381–2; treatment gap 382; violence against children 379–81
Eldoret psychiatric hospital 414, 415
Eliade, M. 489
Elk, G. T. 486
Ellis, S. xix, 174–86
El Mercurio 359
Elnemais Fawzy, M. xvi, 377–86
EMERALD programme 56–7
employment: Canadian experience demanded 310n3; precarious 306, 307
Employment Equity Act (Canada) 309n1
Enang, Senator I. 426
Engel, G. L. 96
Enlightenment 92, 188
Enriquez, V. G. 464–5
epilepsy 252, 382, 452, 514
epistemological psychiatry 246
epistemology 28, 50
Ermine, W.: ethical space concept 25
Ernst, W. 36
Essandoh, P. K. 72
essentialism 24, 25
Esterson, A. 98
ethical boundaries 110–11
Ethiopia 328
ethnicity 2; in psychiatry 95; psycho-social 93; and religion 217

ethnocultural transference (Comas-Díaz and Jacobsen) 87
Etowa, J. xv, 115–27
eugenics 3, 10, 38, 48, 133, 342
Eurocentrism 3, 4, 9, 16, 19, 82–4, 527
evidence-based medicine (EBM) 45–50, 75, 99, 135, 169, 269, 330, 332, 374, 392, 396, 431, 478
evidence-based treatments (EBTs) 3, 465
evil eye 120, 252, 267, 522
exorcism 193, 241, 345, 459, 466

Fabris, E. 61
faith-based organizations (FBOs) 417
faith-healing 513–14
Faith Matters survey (2006) 216
Fall or Adam and Eve story 239, 240, 247n8
family 16, 23, 47, 51, 82, 83, 94, 104, 111, 118, 121, 134, 151, 158–9, 175, 222–3, 228, 277, 280, 281, 289, 292, 295, 315, 317–19, 402, 437, 440, 461, 508; adverse factors for child development 293
family care: unreliability 304–5
family of choice 176, 180
family dynamics 158, 296, 302, 305, 307, 316
Family & Youth Institute 271
Fanon, F. xxii, 20, 21, 25–8, 33, 39, 70, 129; 'alienation' and 'disalienation' 97; *Black Skin White Masks* (1952) 22; critical psychiatry 97–100
Far Eastern University Psychological Clinic 460
Farooqi, Y. N. 269
Fazel, M. 330
Fekete, L. 327–8
Female Genital Mutilation (FGM) 381
feminine psychology 86
feminism 11, 12, 14–16, 74, 84, 86, 87, 132, 176, 228
Ferber, A. L. 10
Fernando, S. xix, xxiv, 2, 28; 'medication revolution' 96–7; *MH Worldwide* (2014) 100; 'new racisms' 93; *Race, Culture, and MH* (1991) 24; race and culture in psychiatry 92–102
Ferrari, M. xvi, 226–37
Ferrer, I. 306
fifth force (social justice counselling) 72–3
First Nations (Canada) 4, 26–7, 37, 487
Fisher, D. 168
Fitzgerald, K. 203–4
Flannelly, K. J. 278
Flett, R. 534
Flores-Guerrero, R. 358–9
forced migration 316, 326
Fordham, S. 157
'foreign national' (terminology) 315
Fortaleza (Brazil) 348
Foucault, M. xxiii, 21, 35, 54, 135, 188; 'great confinement' 95–6; *Madness and Civilization*

(1961) 1; 'master of madness' figure 60; power
   'relationship of force' 55
fourth force (multicultural psychology) 71–3
Four World Development Project 486
France 36, 97, 215, 217, 218
Frattini, T. 316
Freeman, A. 14
Freeman, M. 475
Freese, R. 206
Freire, P. 348
Freud, S. 22, 23, 116, 220, 465; atheism 190;
   religion linked to neurosis 275
Fromm, E. 85–6
Fuentealba Hernández, R. 354–5, 359
Fullagar, S. 1

Gadit, A. 436
Galen 92, 448
Galen, L. W. 222
Galton, F. 38–9
Garabiles, M. R. xvi, 458–69
Gauteng Health Department 475–6, 478
Gaw, A. 458
Gelwick, R. 28
gender 141–50, 217, 454; oppression 143–5
gender diversity: terminology 201
gender minority stress and resilience (GMSR)
   model 208
genderqueer 200–1, 207
Genie, V. 221
genocide xxiv, 3, 10, 13
Ghana 502; brain drain 418
gift-giving 111
Gilgil psychiatric hospital 415, 417
Gillis, J. R. 202
Gillis, L. 471
Gingrich, H. J. D. 461
glass ceiling 15–16
Glazier, S. D. 524
Gleeson, S. 306
Global Atheist Convention (2010) 219
Global Burden of Disease project 48
global context 339–481; Brazil 341–52; Chile
   353–64; Egypt 377–86; Greater China 365–76;
   India 387–98; Jamaica 399–410; Kenya 411–21;
   Nigeria 422–33; Pakistan 435–44; Peru 445–57;
   Philippines 458–69; South Africa 470–81
Global Index of Religiosity and Atheism (2012,
   2016) 218
globalization 3, 34, 43–53, 422, 426; coloniality
   and MH 4, 7–65
global MH (GMH) 44–5, 142, 341, 350;
   background in evidence-based medicine 45–6;
   campaigns for and against 43–4; critics 47–8;
   cultural psychiatry 47–8; 'deeper problems'
   48–9; definitions 43–4; governance 54–65;
   historicist view 44; implementation 45

Global South 2, 4, 32–4, 39–41, 60, 62, 97, 99, 129,
   132, 327; official narrative of Western psychiatry
   35–6; psychologies 3
Gone, J. 25
Gonzales, L. 166
good governance (IMF/WB) 61–2
Good, B. J. 497–8
Goodman, R. 207
Good, M. J. D. 497–8
Gopal, B. xii, 505–16
Gordon, H. L. 38
Gorman, R. 58
Graham, J. R. 435
'Grand Challenges in Global MH' (Collins et al.
   2011) 44
Greater China: Chinese medicine 367–8;
   colonialism and evolution of MH practices
   369–70; cultural representations of illness and
   wellness 370; culture and MH 365–76; current
   MH practices 372–3; demographics 365–7;
   depression 368; future directions 373–4; history
   of MH 365–7; holistic approach 367–8, 370,
   372, 374; Indigenous knowledge 365; licensure
   and certification processes 370–2; multicultural
   competence 373; Taiwanese folk healing 368–9;
   training and development 370–1
Grenier, A. xi, 301–13
group psychotherapy 103–14; key factors in
   addressing race 105–11; acknowledging racial
   identity 107–8; encouraging race dialogues
   105–6; facilitating emotionally-charged race
   dialogues 108–9; group psychotherapists
   as role models 109; incorporating political
   countertransference 109–10; racial interpersonal process as core element 106–7
group therapists: acceptance of gifts 111; cultural
   responsiveness 111; role models 109; self-
   disclosure 111; *see also* therapists
Guralnik, O. 85
Gureje, O. 425
guru-chela relationship 253
Guruge, S. 115
Guthrie, R. V. 70
Guzder, J. xv, xxii–xxv

Haiti 50, 521
haleit (traditional healer's power) 490
Hall, S. xxii, 95
Handler, J. S. 520
hapū (sub-tribe) 530, 531, 533, 535, 536, 541
Haque, A. 266, 270, 435, 439
Harappa community 254
Hardt, M. 34
Harley, D. 132
Harnack, A. 238
Harney, S. 54
Harris, S. 223

Harvard Refugee Trauma Questionnaire 330
Harvard University 459
hasad (envy) 267
Haslam, M. 229
Hatzenbuehler, M. L.: Psychological Mediation
   Framework 177
Headrick, D. R. 35
healing *see* Indigenous healing
Health Resources and Services Administration
   (HRSA) 136
He Kokonga Whare research project 538
Helms, J. E. 74; racial interaction patterns 106
help-seeking 118–19
herbal medicine 499–502, 513, 518, 521, 522
Herek, G. M. 202
Hernandez, D. 526–7
Hernandez-Ramdwar, C. 522
Heuer, J. R. 69–80
Hickling, F.: dialectics 23; psycho-historiographic
   model 23, 27
Hill, B. 437
Hinduism 217, 219–20, 226, 250–61; Ayurveda
   254–5, 506; coping 252–3; future directions
   257; *guru-chela* relationship 253; healing 252–3;
   holistic approach 250–7; illness representations
   251–2; integrating psychology with Indigenous
   healing 256–7; Karma and Dharma 251; MH
   perceptions 251–2; ritual healing 253; *Siddha*
   256, 389, 506, 512–14; stigma and shame 257;
   texts and scriptures 250, 251, 254, 256, 257;
   traditional healing 254–7; yoga 255–6
Hindu texts: *Bhagavad Gita* 250, 251, 257, 506;
   Charakasamhita 506; *Upanishads* 387, 506
Hindus 191–2
Hippocrates 512
Hispanic community 82, 83
historicism 62
historicity 55
Hitchens, C. 219
Ho, Y. C. S. xx, 151–61
Hochmuth, C. 509
Hodge, D. R. 440
Holbach, Baron d' 215
Holliday, B. G. 71, 72
Holmes, A. L. 71, 72
Holmes, T. 476
Holocaust 3, 13, 85
Holy Spirit 241, 243–5, 247n11
homelessness 117, 167, 170
Hong Kong 365, 366; body-mind-spirit
   framework 368; training and certification
   371; MH Ordinance 366; Social Workers
   Registration Ordinance (1998) 371; Victoria
   Mental Hospital 366
Hong Kong Association of Doctors in Clinical
   Psychology 371
Hong Kong Psychological Society (1994–) 371

horizontal equity versus vertical equity 320
Horney 85–6
Horwitz, A. V.: *Social Control of Mental Illness*
   (1982) 133
Hou, F. 115
Howard, K. 207
Howell, A. 59–60
Huang, Y. T. xx, 365–76
Hudson, C. C. 118
Hughes, B. 163–4
Hughes, J. M. 93
human capital 306, 392
Human Development Index (HDI) 377
human rights 86, 417, 473, 479; SMI 132
humility 27
Hunsberger, B. 221
Huppert, J. D. 281
Huriwai, T. 531
Husain, A. 440
Hutson, H. R. 167

Ibn Khaldun 436
Ibn Pekuda, B.: *Duties of Heart* 275
Ibn Sina ('Avicenna') 266, 435
Ibrahim, F. A. 69–80; training model for
   clinicians 73
Ibrahim, M. 36, 39
Icarus Project 168
identity 74–6, 84, 318–19
identity process theory (IPT) 317
ideology 9, 10
Ifa religion 521–2
Illich, I. 188
immigrant, refugee, ethnocultural and racialized
   (IRER) groups 118–19, 122–4; barriers to
   accessing health care 115–16
immigrants: children (adaptability) 316; computer
   skills 316–17; culture and MH 314–25; culture,
   migration, MH 317–18; depression and anxiety
   315; future directions 321–2; institutional
   racism 314, 315, 323; interpreters (key issues)
   320–1; intersectionality 318–19; MH, identity,
   social context 318–19; MH, migration, culture
   319–20; migratory transitions and identity
   317; othering 318; resilience 317; social
   exclusion and mental well-being 316–17; social
   networks 317; social support 317; stigma 318;
   well-being 317
immigration 3, 4, 9, 13, 16, 59, 60, 87, 88, 95, 105,
   109, 115, 118, 130, 356, 362, 367, 517, 527
immigration trajectories 306
impairment 163–4; WHO definition 163
imperialism 10, 36; definition (Childs and
   Williams) 34
Inayat, Q. 438
India 35, 40, 57–8, 83, 217, 250–61; Bhore
   Committee (1946) 390; case vignettes 394–5;

Index

Central Council of Health and Family Welfare (CCHFW) 391; colonialism and MH practices 389–90; Communal MH Unit 391; cultural representation of illness and wellness 388; culture and MH 387–98; Dava-Dua initiative 395; demographics 387–88; Department of Science and Technology (DST) 391; District MH Programme 391; farmer suicides 394–5; future directions 396; human rights 392, 393; Indigenous and traditional healing 389, 396; licensure and certification processes 393–4; Lunacy Act (1858) 390; (1912) 390, 391; Medical Council Act (1956) 393; MH Act (1987) 391, 392; MH Care Act (2017) 392–3; MH interventions and accreditation 393–4; MH policies (post-Independence) 390–2; MH practice (current challenges) 394–6; MH statistics 388; Ministry of AYUSH (2014–) 512–13; Ministry of Health and Family Welfare 391; Mudaliar Committee 390; Narcotic Drugs and Psychotropic Substances Act (1985) 391; National MH Policy (2014–) 392; National MH Programme (1982) 391; National MH survey (NMHS) 388, 392; Persons with Disability Act (1995) 391; stigma 392, 394, 395; suicide 394; treatment gap 388, 392–3

Indian Council of Medical Research 391

Indian Psychiatric Society 391, 393

indigeneity 19–31: future directions 28

Indigenous: definition (Blowers) 367; and 'indigeneity': terminology 19–20; knowledge 3, 4, 332–3; MH 21–2; paradigms 26–7

Indigenous healing 2, 6, 483–543: African 496–504; Caribbean 517–29; Māori 530–43; North American 485–95; South Asian 505–16; *see also* religion and healing

Indigenous mind 37–8, 41; 'native mind' 33; views of colonial psychiatrists 37

individualism 83, 129, 369

individuals 2, 12, 14, 25, 38, 39, 44, 47, 128, 131–6, 144, 151–9, 162–71, 177, 220, 222, 243, 274–83, 436, 442, 525; transgender 200–12

Indonesia 36, 47, 389

infant mortality 20

infants 83–4

Institute of Muslim MH 271

institutional racism xix, xxii, 24, 93, 100, 314, 315

institutional structures 26, 98

intellectual atheism 215, 216, 220, 223

Inter-Agency Standing Committee (IASC) 332

interest convergence 15–16

intergenerational conflict 158

intermedicalidade (intermedicality) 343

internalized homophobia (Sophie) 176, 177

International Association for Group Psychotherapy 110

International Federation of Social Workers 128

International Hearing Voices Movement 168

International Labour Organization 19–20

International Monetary Fund 56, 61–2

International Round Table for Counselling 76

interpersonalists 85–6

interpreters 296, 320–1

intersectionality xxii, 14, 20, 72, 74–7, 86, 124; Crenshaw 84, 145; culture and MH 84–5; MH nursing 122; religion 195–6

intersubjectivity 86, 87

intolerance of uncertainty 280

intra-psychic level of analysis 21

Inuit people 487, 488

irada (will) 267

Ireland, D. 36

Irfan, M. 438

Irmandades das Santas Casas de Misericórdia 342

Iroegbu, P. 498

Isaac, R. J. 167

Ishii, M. 510

Islam 195, 220, 262–72, 389; beliefs and values 263–5; community leaders 268; 'culture' versus 'religion' 262; five pillars 263–4; future directions 270; healing practices 268–71; *hijab* (modesty) 264; history, philosophy, demographics 263–5; holistic approach 265; meditation (*dhikr*) 269–70; mystical tradition 270; Pakistan 435–44; perspectives on MH and wellness 265–8; prayer 269; psychiatry (first hospital, Baghdad, ninth century) 266, 271; psychology 266, 271; repentance 270; scholarship 265–6, 271; Sufism 268, 270; Sunnis and Shi'ites 264

Islamic empire 92, 94

Islamic texts: *Ayat-ul-Kursi* 269; *Hadith* 263, 265; *Qur'an* 263–5, 267–9, 271n2, 379, 436, 438, 439, 441; *Sunnah* 263; *Surah Rehman* 269

Israel 317

Ivemark, B. 11

iwi (tribe) 493, 530, 531, 533, 535–6

Jackson, J. F. 16

Jackson, M. 328

Jacobsen, F. 87

Jainism 215, 217

Jalal, F. H. 76

Jamaica 23, 27, 247n12, 520, 525; accreditation, licensure and certification 404–5; asylums (1776–) 401–2; Bellevue Hospital 401–2, 405; colonialism and evolution of MH practices 401–2; community care 402, 405–6; contemporary MH practices 405–6; Cornwall Regional Hospital (CRH) 405; Council of Professions Allied to Medicine 404; cultural representations of illness and wellness 402–4; culture and MH 399–410; demographics 399; depression and anxiety 400, 402, 403; future directions 406–7; Health Care Social Work Association (prospective) 404; historical context 399–400; history of Indigenous and traditional healers 400–1; holistic approach 406–7; Mental Hospital Law (1974 amendment) 402; MH Act 404; MH Gap Action Programme (WHO) 406; MH Officers (MHO) 404; Ministry of Health 406; Ministry of Health, MH Unit 405; private MH facilities 406; Psychiatric Nursing Aides 404; PTSD 400; schizophrenia 402–3; slave rebellion (1760) 520; slavery 399–401, 407; stigma 402, 403, 406, 407; substance abuse 403–4, 406; suicide 400, 403; training and development 404–5

Jamaican Psychological Society 404
James, C. C. A. B. 525
Japan 83–4, 215, 216, 218
Japanese Americans 106, 134
Japanese Canadians 133–4
Jarvis, G. E. xiv, 215–25
Jenkins, R. 415
Jesudason, S. 165
Jewish Religious Coping Scale (JCOPE) 278
Jews 192; community volunteering 276–7; family-building 277, 280; pride in Jewishness 276; rites of passage 277; Sabbath and synagogue 277, 279
jhakri (Nepalese shaman) 505, 512
Ji-Gong (Seon Buddhist monk) 229
jinn 267, 319, 438
João Pessoa (Northeast Brazil) 349
Johannesburg: Tara Hospital 478
Johnson, S. B. 75
Johnstone, M. xvi, 128–38
Jones 531
Jones, N. xvii, 162–73
Jonikas, J. A. 168, 169
Joseph, A. J. 33
Judaism 273–85; attending to Jewish religious precepts in clinical practice 281–2; barriers to MH treatment 280–1; clinical practice with Jewish individuals 280–1; Code of Jewish Law 275; contemporary attitudes to MH 275–6; depression and anxiety 274, 275, 277–9, 283; dietary laws 281; family purity laws 281; financial pressures of religious life 277–85; future directions 282–3; Hebrew Bible 274–5, 277, 281; intrinsic religiosity 279; need for practitioners to consult client's rabbi 282; psalms 275; rabbinic guidance 275, 275, 281, 282; *Refuat Hanefesh* (prayer for healing emotions) 275; religion and multicultural psychology 273–4; religious beliefs and MH 278–80; religious coping 278–9; role of physician 274–5; sociocultural identity and MH 276–8; stigma towards MH treatment 280; *Talmud* (Oral Law) 274–6; *Torah* 281; traditional approaches to

healing 274–5; traditional approaches to MH 275; trust in God 275, 279–80
Jung, C. G. 22
Jurchen people (China) 509–10

Kabbat-Zinn, J. 230
kaginhawaan (wellness) 461–2
kaiārahi Māori (*kaupapa* Māori practitioner) 536
Kakar, S. 505, 510–12
Kaleppune (herbal medicine and ritual practice) 513
Kamli Organization 418
Kant, I. 37, 59
kanya-kanya syndrome 156
Kaplan, R. M. 75
karakia (Māori prayer/incantation) 531, 533, 536, 541
Kardecist Spiritism 343–5
karka-karka syndrome 156
Karliner, L. S. 321
karma 229, 233, 250, 252, 370, 388; explained 251
Karnataka 511, 513
Karnik, N. xvii, 289–300
Katz, M. 201
kaupapa 534–8, 538n
Keane, B. 531
Keller, R. C. 37–9; *Colonial Madness* (Keller 2007) 22; 'instrumental agency' 193
Kenya 38–9; accreditation, licensure and certification 418; brain drain 419; case vignettes 416–17; Clinical Officers Council 418; colonial impact on health system 413–14; contemporary MH systems 415–17; culture and MH 411–21; demographics 411–12; depression and anxiety 416–17; ethnomedicine 411; faith healers 411–13, 417–19; 'formal' versus 'informal' practitioners 417; future directions 418–19; HDI ranking 412; health insurance access 419; historical context 412; market model 415; medical model 415; Medical Practitioners and Dentists Board 418; MH hospital beds (lack of capacity) 415; MH and illness (explanatory models) 414–15; mhGAP (WHO) 411, 415; Ministry of Health 414; nursing homes and private clinics 417; nursing shortage 414; primary health care 414, 415, 417; refugees 412, 413; stigma 416, 419; traditional healers 412–13; training and development 418; Vision 2030 project 418
Kenya Health Sector Strategic Plan (KHSSP) 418
Kenya Medical Research Institute 502
Kenyan Constitution (2010) 414
Kerala 394–5, 510–11, 513
Keshvarzi, H. 266, 270
Kessler, R. C. 317
Keyes, C. L. 302
Khalfa, J. 97–8

Index

Khalid, N. 436
Khan, A. H. xi, 238–49
Khan, M. M. 438, 440
Khan, N. G. 69–80
Khosla, M. xvi, 250–61
Kierkegaard, S. A. 246n1
Killick, E. xiv, 250–61
Kindler, M. 318–19
Kingsley Hall 98
Kingston Public Hospital 401
Kirmayer, L. J. 48, 51, 122, 517
Kisa Gotami 228, 231
Kleinman, A. 369, 438, 499; 'category fallacy' 196
Kloet, J. D. 222
knowledge production 48–51
knowledge structures 48–51
Kobor, P. C. 75
Koenig, H. G. 188; *Handbook of Religion and Health* (2012) 220
Kōhanga Reo (Māori Language Nests) 535
Kohn, M. L. 158
Kor, A. 277
Kozasa, E. H. 256
Kraepelin, E. 47, 58, 99; comparative anthropological psychology 38
Kremlin, E. 242
Krumrei, E. J. 278
Kumar, M. 253
Kura Kaupapa Māori (Māori Language School) 535
Kuruppuarachchi, K. A. L. A. 230
Kymlicka, W. 12

labels 46, 135
Ladrido-Ignacio, L. 462
Laing, R. D. 98
Lamb, H. R. 167
Lambo, T. A. Dr. 425, 459; village system 23–4; decolonized psychology 27
Lancet 48
land 534
land-based healing 490
language gap 121–3, 315, 316
lateral classism: four worldviews 152, 155–9; crabs-in-barrel mentality 156; materialism 158–9; proxy kids 158; selling out 157
Latin America 19
Laungani, P. 83, 250
Lavie-Ajayi, M. 135, 136
Lawal, I. O. 502
Layton, L.: normative unconscious processes 84
Lazarus 110
Le Grice, J. 534
Leach, M. M. 221
Lee, E. x, xxii, 128–38
Lee, K. C. 231
Lee, M. Y. 370

Leighton, A. H. 93
Leininger, M., 121; cultural care diversity 119; Inquiry Guide for Kinship and Social Factors (2002) 120
Leong, F. T. L. 75–6
Lerner, S. 446
lesbian, gay and bisexual (LGB) persons 174–86, 217; adolescence 175; depression 176–8; health care bias 175; identity-concealment 176–7; outness 207, 208; stigmatization 175–9; suicidality 175, 208
Letelier Grez, J. Dr. 355
Leung, S. A. 76, 365, 373
Lévy-Bruhl, L. 23
Levitt, H. M. 204
Lewis, J. 88
Lewis-Fernández, R. 318
Lijtmaer, R. M. xviii, 81–91
Lima 449, 450; *Hospital Hermilio Valdizán* 454; San Andrés Locos Hospital 354
Lima, M. 346
Liu, W. M. xx, 151–61
live-in caregiver 306
Liverpool Voluntary Counselling and Training 418
Lloyd, M. 163
Lo, H. 121
Lombardi, E. L. 201
Longman-Mills, S. xviii, 399–410
low-and middle-income countries (LAMIs or LMICs) xxiii, 45, 46, 47, 50, 51, 56

Macdonald, Sir John 485, 488
madness: making and managing 57–9
Madras Presidency: *Report of Lunatic Asylum* (1895) 507
Mahmood, A. xi, 262–72
Mahone, S. 37
Mahoney, A. 253
Maitra, Begum 24, 28
Making MH Global Development Priority (2016) 56
Maldonado-Torres, N. 316
mamae (pain) 533
Mann, T. 49
Mann, W. 358
mansa (awareness) 252
Maori: oral knowledge transmission 531; pre-colonial knowledge framework 530
Māori healing 530–43; accreditation, licensure, certification 534–6; case vignette 536–7; depression 533, 537; dreams and aspirations for future 537–8; history 531–2; holistic approach 533, 534; impact of colonization 532–3; *ngā moemoeā* 537; resistance narratives 532–3; theory and practice 533–4, 537; training and development 534–6
Māori language 532, 534–6, 542

Index

marae (Māori gathering place) 535, 536, 541
Marangu, E. M. xiv, 411–21
Mariátegui, J. 449
māristāns (Islamic hospitals) 92
Marks 535
Marsella, A. 70
Marshall, C. xiii, 314–25
Marshall, M. (Mi'kmaq elder and healer) 490
Marx, K. 220
Marx, R. 201
Marxism 215, 217
Marxist psychiatry 346
Masecar, D. 492
Masinde, E. 39
Massad, C. 359
Mataamua, R. 531, 532
materialism 158–9
Mbatha, N. 475
McCannell, K. 142
McConnell, E. A. 180
McCormick, R. xviii, 485–95
McFarland, M. R. 121
McIntosh, T. 534
McIntyre, J. C. 315
McLachlan, A. 531
McLeod, J. 33–4
Mead, M. 242
Medical Colleges 289, 291
medical imperialism 32, 40, 196
medical power 44, 96
medication 146–7; critiques 99; mandatory administration 61
Medina, E. 355
Meerwijk, E. L. 201
Meier, S. C. 203–4
Memmi, A. 33
Memory Keepers Association (MKA) 334–5
Mendenhall, E. 49–50
Menéndez, E. 343
mental health (MH): Acts 36, 39; community governance 60, 62; cultural approaches 303; culture and intersectionality 84–5; current global paradigm 2–4; definitions 43–4; education 333; Indigenous and traditional healing, 6, 483–543; theory and practice 1
mental illness: biological view challenged 98; feared 166; sociogenic basis 20, 21; Western explanatory models and conceptualizations 20–1
mental patients' liberation movement 168
mental status (*ahara* and *vihara*) 253
mestizos/mestizas 445, 446
Meyer, I. H. 205; minority stress theory 176–8
Meyer, O. L. 121, 123
MH Commission of Canada (MHCC) 122
MH practitioners (MHPs) 470

MH professionals: intersectionality and identity 74–5
MH treatment gap (mhGAP) xxii, 45, 51–2, 56, 57; e-mhGAP 60; *mhGAP Humanitarian Intervention Guide* (WHO) 332
Michonski, J. 203–4
microaggressions 14, 16, 107, 144–6, 153, 177, 180, 204, 263, 527
migration: context 314–15; types 315–16
Miller, K. 332
Miller, L. L. 54–65
Mills, C. 54–65
Mills, J. 35, 36
Mills, J. H. 507
mind: and body 95, 242, 245, 344, 368, 388, 512; 'multiplying of possible surfaces' 55
Mindfulness-Based Cognitive Therapy (MBCT) 230–2
Mindfulness-Based Stress Reduction (MBSR) 230
minority stress theory (MST) 176–8
'Minto' 471
Mio, J. S. 73
Mitchell, C. xii, 399–410
Mizock, L. xv, 200–12
Mngqundaniso, N. 474
Mochon, D. 222
modern magic 194–5
Modernist Buddhism 230–2
Mohamed Abdullah Hassan 39
Molina, K. M. xv, 162–73
Monteiro, L. M. 232
Montréal: Transcultural Psychiatry Research Unit 69
Moodley, R. x, xxii, 9–18, 94, 250–61, 435, 442, 498, 517–29
Moonsamy, S. xviii, 470–81
Moore, J. T. 221
'moral therapy' 116
Morton, G.: *Crania Americana* (1839) 59
Moscovici, S. 358
Moten, F. 54
Mother Rita 524
Motsei, M. 475
Movement for Global MH (MGMH) 32, 36, 39–40, 56, 57, 187; critiques of psychiatry 99–100
Mubbashar, M. H. 437
Mueser, K. T. 205–6
Muga, R. 415
multiculturalism 2, 4, 11–12, 13, 95, 100
multicultural psychology 273–4; fourth force 70–4
multilevel model (MLM) of refugee counselling 333–4
Mulvany, J. 163
muntu-muntuê-bantu-ntu (body-mind-social-spiritual) 344
muraqabah (contemplative meditation) 270

Murphy, A. 230
Murphy, H. B. M. 435
Muslims 97–8, 105, 110, 178–80, 191–2, 329
Musten, R. F. 232
Mutiso, V. 412–13

nafs (ego) 266–7
Nair, R. das 178
Nairobi 413, 416, 419; Afya House 414; Agha
    Khan Hospital 414; Kenya Medical Training
    College 418; Kenyatta National Hospital 414;
    Mathari Hospital 415, 417, 418; Moi Teaching
    Hospital 414, 417; private clinics 417; *Uzima
    Mental Health Services* 416
Nakash, O. 135, 136
Namboodiri, P. N. 513–14
Nanamoli, B. 233n2
Narayanan, K. 510–11
Narayanan, M. G. S. 505, 509
Narrative Exposure Therapy 332
Natal (Brazil) 347
National Association of Social Workers (USA)
    136
National Empowerment Center 168
National Household Survey (Canada 2011)
    216, 220
National Institute of MH (NIMH) 136
National Psychiatric Morbidity Study (England
    2013) 222
Native Americans 4, 13
Nature 44, 219
Navajo 490
nazar (evil eye) 254
Nazroo, J. 305
Ndetei, D. M. 412
Negri, A. 34
Nemeroff, C. 294
Nemoto, T. 201–2
Neo-Buddhism 227, 230
neoliberalism: attack on MH care 129–36;
    dominant governing principles 135; social
    control of racialized mentally ill 132–4;
    workfare-as-welfare 131–2, 135
Neopentecostalism 343–5, 347
Nepal 505, 512
Netherlands 36, 526
New Atheism 218–19, 221, 223
New England Journal of Medicine 99
new historicity 22–3
New Kadampa Tradition (NKT) 229
New Public Management (NPM) 130, 133
New York City 153, 524
New York State Child Labour Law (1886) 290
New Zealand *see* Aotearoa
Ng, S. M. 368
ngākau (internal organs) 533
NGOs 56, 99, 361, 382, 383, 417, 476

Nigeria 23–4, 27; accreditation, licensure,
    certification 425–6; asylums 423; brain drain
    426; case vignettes 427–30; colonialism and
    evolution of MH practices 424–5; community
    mental health 423; contemporary MH
    practices 426–7; cultural representations of
    illness and wellness 425, 431; culture and
    MH 422–33; demographics 422; depression
    and anxiety 428, 430; Federal Ministry of
    Health 430; future directions 430–1; history
    of MH 422–4; Indigenous healing 424, 430,
    431; Lunacy Act (1958) 423, 430; MH policy
    (1991, 2013) 423, 427–8, 430; MH services
    in schools and colleges 423–4; Ministry of
    Health 423; National Education Policy 423–24,
    430; National Policy on Traditional Medicine
    (2004) 502; preventative MH services 430–1;
    role of technology 431; stigma 423; training
    and development 425–6, 430, 431; university
    teaching hospitals (psychiatric departments) 426
Nigerian Association of Social Workers 426
Nigerian Institute for Pharmaceutical Research
    and Development 502
Nigerian National Universities Commission 426
niyamas (rules of conduct) 255
Nkwenkwe, N. 39
noa (safety) 533
non-binary: terminology 200–1
non-dominant groups: definition 244
non-religious people ('nones') 215, 216, 218,
    221, 223
normality 57–9
North Africa 36–40
North America 142–3
North American Indigenous healing 485–95;
    accreditation 490–1; case vignette 490;
    collaboration with Western medicine 491;
    contemporary case examples 491; definitions
    of illness and wellness 488–9; future directions
    491–3; hallmarks 488–9; history 486–7; holistic
    approach 487; impact of colonialism 487–8;
    Medicine Wheel model 488–9; practice 489–90;
    self-transcendence 488, 489; spirituality 489,
    491; 'uneasy' relationship with biomedicine 487,
    491; Vision Quest Ceremony 486, 487, 489;
    ways of knowing 488–9
Northern Territory 20
nursing 115–27; artful use of self in therapeutic
    relationship 121; causation and prevalence
    118; collecting information 120–1; cultural
    competence 119–20; cultural considerations
    117–19; cultural formulation interview
    120–1; cultural negotiation 121; future
    directions 122–3; historical background
    116–17; intersectionality 122; presentation and
    help-seeking 118–19
Nursing Council of Kenya 418

Index

Obeah 400–1, 403, 406, 407, 520, 523, 525; criminalized (1898) 520
Obsessive Compulsive Disorder 281
O'Callaghan, E. M. 16
Ochoa de Equileor, I. A. 501
odividya (magical act) 509
Odiyans (group of shamans) 509
Ogbu, J. U. 157
Oh, A. 231
Ojelade, I. I. 519, 525
Ojembe, B. xii, 301–13
Okocha, A. A. G. xi, 422–33
older people: African Americans 306; barriers to care 306–7, 309; conflation of culture with cultural differences 303; critical life course perspective 302–5, 309; cultural approaches to study of MH 303; culture and MH 301–13; depression 302; family relations and expectations 307; future directions 307–9; health disparities 305–6; impacts of stress, discrimination, trauma 308–9; intersectionality 304–5, 309; language barriers 305–7; MH (definitions) 302; MH 'must be contextualized' 307, 309; MH among racialized and ethnic minorities 305–7; MH in social and cultural context 302–3, 309; preventing inequality, disadvantage, precarity 308; schizophrenia 302; social determinants of health 308–9; social locations 302–3, 306–8; stigma associated with MH 301, 303, 306; trajectories of immigration 306; understanding inequality and MH trajectories 308; well-being (emotional, psychological, social) 302
Oliveira Nunes, M. 346
Omi, M. 93
O'Neil, J. 488
Ontario 208; service utilization 122
Operario 201–2
oppression: determinant of MH 145–7; five faces (Young) 144–8; future directions 147–8; gender, culture and 143–5
Orr, D. M. R. xiii, 445–57
Orr, J.: *Panic Diaries* (2006) 55–7
Ortega, F. xiv, 341–52
Osazuwa, S. 9–18
othering 11, 33, 34, 37, 82, 85, 88, 89, 98, 243, 244, 357
Ott, M. Q. 206
Outline for Cultural Formulation (OCF) 320
Overmars, D. 25
Owens, T. xix, 200–12
Oxford House 170

Padilla, S. 460
pajés (healers) 343
pakikipagkapwa-tao (how to treat others in Filipino culture) 156

Pakistan 268, 328; accreditation, licensure, certification 439–40, 442; anxiety 440; asylums (later 'mental hospitals') 437; case vignettes 440–2; College of Physicians and Surgeons 439; colonialism and evolution of MH practices 436–7, 442; contemporary MH practice 440–2; cultural representations of illness and wellness 437–9; demographics 434; future directions 442–3; history of MH 434; Indigenous and traditional healers 435–6; Islamization 434, 435, 437–8; Mental Health Act (2001) 439; MH 435–44; somatization of MH 438; stigma 437, 438, 440–1; training and development 439; women 437
Pakistan Association for Clinical Psychologists 439
Pakistan Psychological Association 439
Pantalone, D. W. 206
Papadopoulos, I. 119–20
Parekh, B. 13
parents and parenting 133–4, 157, 158, 220, 289, 316, 402, 416, 440, 485, 513, 536; Egypt 378, 380, 381
pareshani (problem or physical trouble) 253
Paret, M. 306
Pargament, K. I. 241, 253, 278
parigraha (hedonic pleasures) 388
Parish, S. L. 163
Passamán, J. de 359
Pastén Peña, C. xiii, 353–64
Patel, V. 45, 414–15
Paterson, K. 163–4
Paul, St. (apostle) 241, 247n5
Pedersen, P. 71–2
Pelto, G. 438
Pelto, P. 438
Peltzer, K. 474, 525
pena (spirit) 511
Peña, R. 360
pena kodukkal (shamanic practice) 511
Penner, H. H. 233n2
Penson, W. J. 39
Pentecostal churches 180, 241, 245, 343–5, 347, 424, 428
people of colour 11, 14, 16, 63, 71, 107, 132, 151, 157
People with Disability Australia 163
Perez, R. M. 181
Perpiñan, J. 460
Perry, B. L. 132, 134
person-in-social environment (PIE) 129
Peru: Asilo de la Misericordia (later Hospital Larco Herrera) 448; asylums 448, 449; 'body' in Andean culture 453; *campesinos* ('peasants') 448, 451, 452; coca-leaf consumption 448, 445n1; *Colegio de Psicólogos* 452; Community Mental Health Centers (CMHCs) 449, 453; contemporary MH practice 453–4; cultural representations

of illness and wellness 452–3; culture and MH 445–7; *Defensoría del Pueblo* (Human Rights Ombudsman's Office) 449; demographics 447–8; depression 445; educational attainment 447; epidemiological surveys 449; ethnic identity 447–8; future directions 454–5; history 446; holistic approach 452; Inca Empire 446, 448; Institute of Traditional Medicine 450; *interculturalidad* (inter-cultural awareness) 450, 454; *llaki* (sorrows) 453, 455; language demography 447; MH history 448–50; mental health laws: (1950) 448; (2012) 449; (2019) 450; Ministry of Health 448; National Institute of Mental Health 448; National Plan 450; native pharmacopeia 450; number of MH professionals 450; *pinsamientuwan* 453; racism 446, 447; *Seguro Integral de Salud* (health insurance) 449; slavery 445; traditional healing 450–2; training and registration 452; Truth and Reconciliation Committee (TRC) 446, 449

Peruvian Psychiatric Association 452
Petersen, K. S. 135
Petros, G. 474
Philip, St. (apostle) 241
Philippine Psychiatric Association 464
Philippine Psychology Act (2009) 463–4
Philippines: American colonization 459–60; case vignettes 462–3, 465–6; culture and MH 458–69; demographics 458–9; family 461–2, 465, 467; folk healers 458–60, 464, 466; future directions 466–7; geographical and historical context 458; Guidance and Counselling Act (2004) 463–4; Hospicio de San José (1782–) 459; Indigenous conceptions: psychological illness 460–1; treatments 462–3; wellness 461–2; Insular Psychopathic Hospital (1928–) 459; integration of Indigenous and Western MH practices 464–6; Mental Health Act (2017) 464; MH professionals 463–4; pre-colonial 459; religion 459, 462; Spanish colonization 459, 462; San Lazaro Hospital: Insane Department (1904–) 459; stigma 466–7
Philippine Women's University: Institute of Human Relations (1948–) 460
Phillips, A. 535
Philpott, J. 485
phrenology 59
Pickren, W. E. 75–6
Pieterse, J. N.: cultural hybridity 92
Pihán, R. 353
Pinel, P. 37
Pio, E. 234n7
Pirani, F. 436, 438
Pirutinsky, S. 277–80
Planning Commission of India 512
Plich, J. J. 239–40
Plöderl, M. 207

pneumatikos (spiritual man) 247n5
Polanyi, M.: 'epistemic totalitarianism' 28
political atheism 215, 216, 223
political countertransference: in race dialogues 109–10
political empathy (Lavie-Ajayi and Nakash) 136
politics: GMH governance 54–65
Pols, H. 36
Ponterotto, J. G. 76
Pope, K. S. 110–11
Porot, A. 38
Portera, A. 105
Porterfield, A. 241
positivism 14, 20, 27, 28, 189, 190, 193, 358, 517
post-colonial canon 28
post-colonial context 23
post-colonial continuation 36
post-colonial discourse 25
post-colonial studies 20, 21, 26, 27, 28–9
post-colonial theory 19, 20, 28; essence 25; Indigenous MH 21–2; *see also* postcolonial theory
post-traumatic growth (PTG) 192
post-traumatic stress disorder (PTSD) 118, 192, 453, 526; TGD 203; war trauma 146–7
(post)colonial MH contexts 24, 28
postcolonial theory 32–42; hyphen deliberately dropped 33; and MH 33–4
Potgieter, M. J. 474
potlach ceremony 487, 488
Pottinger, A. 121
Poundmaker healing centre 491
pōuritanga (depression) 533
poverty 21, 40, 45, 70, 85, 94, 109, 118, 131, 144, 151–9, 162, 203, 264, 304, 349, 377, 378, 380, 402, 412, 453, 459, 465
power-knowledge relations 1–2
power relations 10–11, 22, 25, 26, 27, 55, 82, 84, 122, 131–5, 497, 498, 510
pranayama (breathing exercises, in yoga) 255
prasadam (offering to God) 253
presentation 118–19
Pretorius, E. xiii–xiv, 470–81
Price, R. H. 317
Prince, M. 45
Prince, R. 430
professional associations 71, 74, 76
progressivist narratives 22
pseudo science 3, 10–12
psychiatric expansionism 32–42
Psychiatric Institute Dr José Horwitz Barak 355
psychiatrists 20, 43, 117, 195
psychiatry 12, 242, 507–8; background and current practice 95–7; after colonial withdrawal 23–4; critiques: Fanon 97–8; medication 99; MGMH 99–100; USA and UK 98–9; efforts to come into line with medicine 48–9; expansionism

32–42; 'found wherever there is power' (Foucault) 54; Latin America 358; 'must be political' (Fanon) 98; origin as discipline 92; race and culture in 92–102; rupture with spirituality 189–90; terminology (1808–) 471; universality 100; Western (official narrative in Global South) 35–6

Psychiatry and Empire (Mahone and Vaughan 2007) 22

psychikos (natural man) 247n5

psychoanalysis 121, 455n2; culture and 81–91; culture-free 81–2; Eurocentric view 82–4; inclusion of culture and race 85–7

psychoanalytic anthropology 83

Psychohistoriographic Cultural Therapy (PCT) 526

psychological anthropology 87

Psychological Mediation Framework (PMF) 177

psychologists 152–3, 159–60

psychology 3; Latin America 358; tensions with Judaism 275–6, 280

psychopathology 21, 129, 147, 465, 467

psychopharmaceutical medication 32, 453

psycho-power 55, 58, 60, 62

Psychosocial Care Center (*Centro de Atenção Psicossocial* (CAPS) 342, 349

Psychosocial Care Paradigm 342–3

psychosocial support 332, 381, 394, 476

'Psychosomatic Dysadaptation Syndrome' (Seguín 1951) 449

psychotherapy 28, 83, 333; 'no longer politically neutral' (Lavie-Ajayi and Nakash) 135

psy-disciplines 54, 92; technologies of security and governance 59–62

psy-entific rationale 55

Puckett, J. A. 204

Puliampatti (Tamil Nadu) 245

Pulice-Farrow, L. 204

Pupavac, V.: 'therapeutic governance' 62

Purohit, S. 257

Putnam, R. D. 216, 217

qalb (heart) 266–8

qigong 368, 372

quality of life 151, 153, 166, 167, 187, 252–3

Quayson, A. 33

Quebec: Hotel Dieu 116

Quechua 445, 447, 448, 453

Quijano, A. 19

quilombos (Brazil) 345

Quu'Asa Mental Wellness Team (MWT) 491

race 2, 4, 81; configurations 9–18; conflation with culture 93–5; origins of term 10; physical 93; resistance 85; social construction 10–11; terminology 93

race and culture in MH practices 5, 67–138; counselling psychology 69–80; group psychotherapy 103–14; nursing 115–27; psychiatry 92–102; psychoanalysis 81–91; social work 128–38

race dialogues 103–6; emotionally-charged (in group psychotherapy) 108–9; key issues 105

racial healing 111

racial identity: key element in group psychotherapy 107–8

racial interpersonal process 106–7

racism 9–16, 26, 40, 75, 81, 86, 89, 94–5, 98, 103–11, 118, 143, 155, 176–80, 243, 268, 294, 305–9, 314–18, 322, 350, 446–7, 517, 526, 527; permanence 14

radical feminism 14

Raghunandan, S. xviii, 517–29

Rahmaan, A. 229

Rahman, N. 437

Ranchi Mental Hospital 390

randomized control trials (RCTs) 3, 48, 51, 283

rape 201, 533

Rasmussen, A. 332

Rational Emotive Behavioral Therapy 437

Ratts, M. J. 72

Ravaud, J. F. 166

Raza, H. 438, 440

Read, J. 534

reality: and culture 87–8; internal and external 87–8

recovery approach 97

Red Road Gathering 486

Red Road Initiative 486

reductionism 20, 21, 26, 346

Reed, A. M. 61

Rees, S. 332

refugees 88, 187, 232; agency and autonomy 329; case vignette 327, 329, 333–5; children 330–2; community-based 334; cross-cultural understanding 327–8; culture and MH 326–38; counselling models 333; ecological systems 331–2; Egypt 377–8; future directions 335; healing approaches 332–35; holistic approaches 335; human rights perspective on MH 331; humanistic approach 331; versus 'immigrants' 329–30; intersectionality 331–2; MH (current knowledge) 329–30; MH challenges (prevalence and rates) 330; PTSD 327–32; resilience 331, 333; stigmatization 328, 331; through community commemoration ceremonies 334–5; UNHCR definition 326; Western versus Indigenous systems 332–3, 335

Registered Psychiatric Nurse (RPN) 117

Rehabilitation Council of India (RCI) 393

Reicherter, D. 230

Reiff, M. 524

Reisner, S. L. 204, 206

Index

religion 187–99; charismatic church 190–1; coping (positive and negative) 191–2; emergence in MH 189; future directions 196; intersectionality 195–6; and MH 188–91; and MH across cultures 192–4; and MH systems 194–5; overview of MH findings 188–9; resilience 188–9; suicide 188, 190–1

Religion and Ethnicity in Canada (Bramadat and Seljak 2009) 217

religion and healing in MH 5, 213–85; atheism 215–25; Buddhism 226–37; Christianity 238–49; Hinduism 250–61; Islam 262–72; Judaism 273–85; *see also* Indigenous healing

religious atheists 219–20, 223

Religious Landscape Study (Pew 2014) 216, 218

Research Domain Criteria (RDoC) 46

Research Institute for Environment and Health) 532

Residential Schools (Canada) 485, 487, 488

resilience 179–81

resistance 21–2, 32, 40, 136, 167–8; culture and race 85

rezadores (traditional prayers) 343

Ribeiro, D. 345–6; *O povo brasileiro* (*Brazilian People*) (2000) 345

Ribner, D. S. 281

Richard, T. 11

Richards, S. 440

Richmond, M.: *Social Diagnosis* (1917) 130

Riggs, D. W.: decompensation theory 177–8

Rio de Janeiro 344; *Hospício Dom Pedro II* (1852–) 342

ritenga (Māori ritual) 531, 533

rlung (psychic wind) 233

Roberts, D. 165

Robertson, L. J. 477

Robertson, M. 21

roda (CT session) 348, 349

Roets, G. 131

Roland 83

rongoā (Māori medicines) 531, 533, 535

rongoā Māori 492

rongoā whānau 493

Rood, B. A. 206

Rose, N. 59, 60

Rosmarin, D. H. xiii, 273–85

Ross, C. E. 221–2

Ross, E. 473

Ross, R. 487

Rossman, H. K. 207

Roth, W. D. 11

Rothberg, M. 21

Round Lake healing centre 491

Royal College of Psychiatrists (UK) 189, 472

ruh (spirit) 266–7

rule of law 55, 61–2

Rumi (Sufi poet) 265

Rungreangkulkij, S. 230

rural areas 153, 254, 377, 383, 391, 414, 463, 473, 474, 485, 510, 514

Rwandan genocide 13, 334–5

Ryle, G. 95

sacacas (healers) 343

Sadowsky, J. 23–4, 35, 37, 38; *Imperial Bedlam* (1999) 22

Sadruddin, S. 438

Said, E. W. 20, 27, 28, 33; *Culture and Imperialism* (1993/1994) 94, 435; *Orientalism* (1978) xxii, 21–2

Saiva philosophy 506

Sal y Rosas, F. (1900–1974) 448–9

Saldivia, S. 353

Samaco-Zamora, M. C. xvi, 458–69

San Francisco 201, 229–30

San Juan del Monte 459

Sanchez, F. 458

Sánchez, F. J. 203

Sandhu, J. S. 256

sankat ritual 511–12

Santeria 521–2, 523

santeros (healers) 522

Santiago de Chile: Hospital Sanatorio El Peral (1927–) 355; Laboratory of Experimental Psychology 358

São Paulo 342, 344

sarx (flesh) 247n5

Satheesh Varma M. xviii, 387–98

Sazié, Dr C. 357

Schechter, I. 277

Scheff, T. 98

schizophrenia 39, 98, 133, 194, 267, 359, 382, 416, 466, 476, 505, 525

Schneider, J. H. 358

scientific racism 48, 70, 71

security 59–62

Seguín, C. 449

self-reflexivity 22, 27

self-sufficiency 133; neoliberal value 134

Seljak, D. 217

Seltton, J-P. 314

Semenya, S. S. 474

Semlyen, J. xv, 174–86

Sendero Luminoso (Shining Path) 446, 449

Seng, J. S. 74

Setswe, G. 498

Sevelius, J. M. 201

severely mentally ill (SMI) people 129–36; own voice 'dismissed and pre-empted' 134, 135; social control 131–2

sexual orientation 174–86; asylum-seekers 180–1; double jeopardy 178; future directions 181–2; gay-affirmative therapy 181; intersectionality 174, 177, 178–9, 182; and MH 175–6; removal

from *DSM* (1973) 174, 175; risk, resilience and protective factors 179–81; theoretical perspectives (minority stress) 176–8
Shabtai, D. xiii, 273–85
Shakespeare, T. 163
shaman: origin of term 509
shamanism 254, 343, 450, 488; 505–16; theory and practice 509–12
shame 166, 203, 204, 394, 438, 440, 441, 452
Shango/Orisha 523–4
Shapiro, L. 168
Sharp, C. 203–4
Sharpe, C. 62
Shields, L. xvi, 399–410
Shin, R. Q. 76
shiva home 277
Shonin, E. 230
Shorter, A. 244
Shorter, E. 92
Siddha system of medicine (SSM) 256, 389, 506, 512–14
Sikhs 252–3, 256
Sikolohiyang Pilipino (Filipino Psychology) 464–5
Silove, D. 331–2
Silver, C. F. 217
Simpkins, A. M. 255
Simpkins, C. A. 255
Singer, B. C. J. 59–60
Singh, A. A. 205
Singh, J. 253
Singleton, M. 244
Sinha, J. B. P. 389
Sioux 22–3
Sivanandan 328
slave trade 13, 344, 399
slavery 9, 10, 55, 59, 61, 145, 157, 243, 399–401, 407, 446, 497, 517–29
Smith, B. 84
Smith, C. xii, 530–43
Smith, L. 152
Smith, T. 440
Smith, T. xix, 530–43
Smitherman, G. 157
So, D. 72
social anthropology 93
social capital 123, 316, 317, 319
social class 2, 151–61, 345, 346, 347; awareness 153–4; classification problems 151–2; defining 152–4; intersectionality 153, 155–6, 159; terminology 151
Social Class and Classism Consciousness Model (SCCC) 154, 158
Social Class Worldview Model (SCWM) 153
social context 84–5, 87, 130, 318–19
social control 32, 35, 37, 39, 90, 129, 131–2, 154, 215; racialized mentally ill 132–4

social determinants of health (SDH) 47, 51, 115, 117–19, 122–4, 128, 143, 445, 527
social exclusion 143, 144, 165, 166–7, 177, 331, 361, 349; immigrants 316–17
social identity theorists 315
socialization 73, 162, 462, 519
social justice 124, 128, 129
social justice counselling: fifth force 72–3, 75–7
social marginalization: everyday process 135
social media 3, 45, 106, 109, 110, 170, 206, 431
social networks 43, 118, 159, 206, 220, 222, 317, 333, 349, 453, 467, 501
social problems 76, 129, 141, 347, 514
social status 151, 158, 394, 488
social support 50, 123, 155, 157, 180–1, 203, 206–8, 230, 253, 276, 317, 331, 349, 383, 461, 470, 526; *see also* psychosocial support
social therapy (Fanon) 98
social work 128–38; 'core profession' 136; definition 128; future directions 135–6; marginalized populations in community MH 130–1
social workers 463, 464
soft coercion 132, 133; norm in MH practice 133
soft power tactics 134–5
Solomon, P. 169
Solomos, J. 9
soma (body) 247n5
Sontag, S. 359
Sophie, J. 176
South Africa 39, 418; alternative healers (AHs) 474, 475, 478, 479; Annual Performance Plan (2018–2021) 477; apartheid 472; asylums 471, 475; biomedical approach 474, 478, 479; case vignette 476; College of Medicine (Faculty of Psychiatry) 478; colonialism and evolution of Western MH care 470–3; community care 475–7; Convention on Persons with Disabilities 477; cultural representations of illness and wellness 473–4, 479; culture and MH 470–81; current MH system 475–7; demographics 470–4; Department of Health (DoH/NDoH) 471, 473, 477, 478; depression and anxiety 474; future directions 478–9; Indigenous and traditional practice 474–5; 'meaning centred approach' 479; Mental Disorders Act (1916) 471; Mental Health Care Act (2002) 473, 475–6, 478; MH practitioners (MHPs) 470, 474, 475, 479; National Health Insurance (NHI) 473, 477, 478; National Health Service Commission (NHSC 1942) 472, 473; National Health System (NHS) 472; National MH Policy Framework 2013–2020 (NMHPF) 477; National Party 472; people living with mental illness (PLWMI) 473, 476–8; primary health care (PHC) 473, 474, 476–8; private health sector 472–3, 477; Society of Psychiatrists 472; Somerset Hospital

Index

(1818–) 471; race 473; religion 474; traditional healers (THs) 474, 475, 478, 479; Traditional Health Practitioners Act (2003) 474; (2004) 502; training and development 477–8; Universal Health Coverage (UHC) 473, 477, 478; Witchcraft Suppression Act (1957, amended 1970) 497; WHO Report (1983) 472

South African Constitution (1996) 473, 475, 477

South African Council of Nursing 478

South African Medical Association 497

South African Medical Council 477

South Asia 267; asylums 507–8

South Asian Association for Regional Countries (SAARC) 505

South Asian healing 505–16: case vignettes 508–9, 513–14; concepts of wellness and illness 512; current MH practice 513–14; faith healers 506; future directions 514–15; history 506; impact of colonialism 509; number of practitioners 512; resistance and anxieties 507–8; shamanic healing methods (theory and practice) 509–12; shamanism 505–16; training, development, accreditation 512–13

South-East Asia 228, 232, 233

sovereign incarceration (Howell) 60

Soviet Union 217

Sowa Rigpa 389

special populations and culture in MH 5, 287–338; children and adolescents 5, 289–300; immigrants 5, 314–25; older people 5, 301–13; refugees 326–38

Speight, S. L. 74–5

Spero, M. 281

spirit possession 192–4, 244, 460, 461, 463

spirits 369, 425, 438, 450, 462, 497, 498, 500, 511–13, 519, 521, 524–6

spirituality: emergence in MH 189; and MH 188–9; rupture with psychiatry 189–90

Spitzer, J. 274

Spivak, G. 20, 27, 28, 33; *Can the subaltern speak?* (1988) 21–2

Sra Alicia (healer) 524

stagnation syndrome 368

state control 129, 133

statistics 57–8

stigma xxiv, 117, 119, 121, 122, 366

stigmatization 134, 144, 145, 168

Stiker, H. J. 166

Stocking, G. 22

Stoler, A. L. 55

Stroman, D. F. 168

structural inequalities 74, 315, 345, 455

structural violence 26, 51–2, 349

Stuart, G. W. 319

Suarez-Balcazar, Y. 163

subaltern studies 26

Sudarshan Kriya Yoga (for people with depression) 255

Sue, D. W. 166

Sufism, 435, 436, 438, 439

Sugano, E. 201–2

suicide 20, 26, 40, 536, 537; IPT general theory 208, 485, 492

'suicide by cop' (SbC) 167

Sujatha, V. 512

Sullivan, H. S. 85–6

Sumari, M. 76

Summerfield, D. 49, 196, 320, 331; 'new missionaries' 40

Sung, L. H. 369

Support for Addiction and Treatment in Africa 418

Sustainable Development Goals (SDGs) 56

Sutherland, P. 442, 526

Swartz, S. 35, 37, 38

swastha (my own self that is situated) 252

sweat lodge ceremony 486, 487, 491, 493, 494

Szasz, T.: *Myth of Mental Illness* (1962) 98

taboo 178, 179, 189, 343, 414; social class 151, 152, 159

Tainos 399, 400

Taitimu, M. 534

Taiwan (Republic of China) 365, 367; Civil Service Examination for Social Welfare Workers 372; 'clinical psychologists' 372; 'counselling psychologists' 371–2; Council of Indigenous Peoples 367; folk healing 368–9; MH Act (1990) 367; National Health Insurance (1995–) 367; 'school counsellors' 371; suicide 371; training and certification 371–2

Tajfel, H. 315

Takatāpui wahine 174

Tan, M. L. 460

Tan, P. 234n5

Tang, N. 84

Tao people (Taiwan) 369–70, 373

tapu (sacred) 533

Tarakeshwar, N. 253

Tarapoto (Peru): Takiwasi Centre 450

tasbih (prayer beads) 269

Tasman, A. 532

Tassell-Mataamua, N. 534

Tatz, C. 20

Taumaranui 535

Taylor, C. 217

Te Atawhai o te Ao (Independent Māori Research Institute for Environment and Health) 532, 538

Teghtsoonian, K. 136

Te Kāhui Rongoā Trust 493

Temuco (Chile): Universidad de la Frontera 361

terapia comunitária (community therapy) 347–50

te reo Māori (Māori language) 532, 534–6, 542

Testa, R. J. 208

'therapeutic community' approaches 98
therapeutic relationship 82, 87, 117; artful use of self (MH nursing) 121
therapists 70, 72, 75, 82, 86–7, 89–90, 131–5; ability to engage 84–5; anger and discomfort 83; 'participant observer' 86; *see also* group therapists
theyyam or *theyyattam* (Kerala folk art) 510–11
Thich Nhat Hanh 230, 233
thira 511
thirayattam 511
third space 25
Thomas, P. 100
Thomson, M. S. 115
'thorny problem' 9
Thurner, M. 19
Tibet 227, 229, 233, 389
tikanga (Māori customs) 531, 534, 536
Tikanga ā-Rongoā 493
Timimi, S. 100
tohunga (Māori practitioner) 531–2, 535–6
Tomlinson-Clarke, S. 76
Topper, M. D. 490
Torres Strait Islander people 27
Torrey, E. F. 489, 490
traditional birth attendants (TBA) 499
Traditional Chinese Medicine (TCM) 367–8, 372, 462
traditional healing 2, 27; Africa 195; South Africa 195; WHO definition 450; *see also* Indigenous healing
trance 500, 510
transcultural psychiatry 142, 242
Transcultural Psychiatry Society (TCPS) 98
transcultural psychology 69–70
transference and countertransference 87, 88
transgender people 142, 145; definition 200
transgender or gender diverse (TGD): anxiety 203–5; background 200–1; collective action 205; community connectedness 207–9; coping profiles 206; 'coping' versus 'resilience' (Meyer) 205; coping with transphobia 204–6; culture and MH 200–12; depression 203–5; future directions 209; MH difficulties 202–4; microaggressions 204; minority stress model 207; outness 207–8; resilience 205, 208; stigma 202–9; substance abuse 203, 204, 206; suicide ideation (SI) 203, 204, 208
transnational feminist scholars 132
transphobia 201–2, 209; internalized 202–4; protective and coping factors 204–6
Transvaal Provincial Department of Health 477
trauma xxiii–xxiv, 85, 86, 89, 118, 123, 134, 537; historical 518, 519, 526, 532–4, 538; social 88; socio-historical 20
Travancore 508
Treharne, G. J.: decompensation theory 177–8
Tribe, R. xvii, 314–25

tridosa (three elements) 512
tridoshas (three humours) 254–5
Trinidad 523, 524
Tsai, Y.Y. 369–70
Tsimshian people 490
Tuliao, A. P. xii, 458–69
Tuliao, M. D. xvi, 458–69
Turia, Dame Tariana 535
Turkey 267, 328
Turner, J. C. 315
Turtle Island 485, 493
Tuskegee experiment (1932–1972) 106
Two Accounts of Journey through Madness (Barnes and Berke 1971) 98
tzedakah (charity) 277

Ukpong, D. I. 425
Umbanda (Afro-Brazilian religion) 344, 347
UN Convention on Rights of Child (CRC/UNCRC, 1989) 290; optional protocols 291; overarching principles 291
UN Convention on Rights of Persons with Disabilities 382
UN High Commissioner for Refugees (UNHCR) 326, 328, 332, 334, **380**
Unani (Greek medicine) 256, 268, 389, 506, 507, 512, 513
Ungar, M. 331
UNICEF 379–80, 381, 422, 472
United Arab Emirates (UAE) 194–5
United Kingdom 36, 130, 166, 189, 193, 215, 243, 246, 276–7, 290, 294, 315, 319; Atheist Bus Campaign (2008–2009) 218–19; census (2001) 95; critiques of psychiatry 98–9; 'new ethnicities' 95
United Kingdom: MH Act 190–1, 314
United Nations 76
United States 13, 19, 21, 57, 70, 71, 72, 74, 76, 83, 85, 87, 130, 166, 167, 170, 215–23, 253, 277–78, 294, 301, 315, 316, 320; 'aggressive civilization' 485; census (1840) 58, 61; civil rights movement 14, 15, 69; critiques of psychiatry 98–9; diversity issues 104–5; immigration 104–5; US Department of Health and Human Sciences (DHSS) 162; US Health and Retirement Study 165; USAID 424
universalism 24–5, 40, 54; versus particularism 25
Universities of McGill and Cayetano Heredia 453, 454
University of Chile 358, 359, 362
University of Chile: Institute of Psychology 360
University Hospital of West Indies (UHWI) 405
University of Lethbridge 486
University of Nairobi: Medical School 418
University of West Indies 404
Unni (traditional healer, Kerala) 514

Index

Valdizán, H. (1885–1929) 448, 455n1
Valentine, H. 534
Vasquez, M. J. T. 75–6, 110–11
Vaughan, M. 37
Ventevogel, P. 332
Ventriglio, A. 43–53
Vera, E. M. 74–5
Verzosa, M. L. R. 462
Vicente, B. 353
Vietnam 230
Vietnamese 131–2
Vilain, E. 203
Villacura Avendaño, L. xv, 353–64
Vine Deloria Jr.: *Jung and Sioux Traditions* (2009) 22–3
violence 144; against children (Egypt) 379–81
visible minorities 301; definition 309n1
vision quest ceremony 486, 487, 489, 493
Vodou 50, 521, 523
voluntary migrants 315–17
Vontress, C. E. 70

wairua (soul, spirit) 534, 542
Waldram, J. B.: *Revenge of the Windigo* (2004) 22
Walker, R. 25
Wang, L. F. 371–2
Ward, C. 162
Warner, D. F. 165
Watson, N. 163
Weber, M. 220
Weber, S. R. 221
Weir, L. 59–60
Weisz, J. R. 373
well-being 44, 46, 129, 252, 276–9, 368
Wenceslau, L. D. xv, 341–2
Wessells, M. G. 332
Westerhof, G. J. 302
Wetherell, M. 534
whakapapa kōrero (Māori genealogical narratives) 530–2
whānau (family) 530, 531, 533–6, 542
White, E. 508–9
White, P. 502
white feminists 15–16
white homogeneity myth 11–12
Whitehorne-Smith, P. xvii, 399–410
Whitley, R. xviii, 48, 215–25, 519
Whole Person Healing 245, 247n12
Wig, N. N. 35
Wilkinson, P. J. 221
Williams, C. 9

Williams, C. C. xii, 141–50
Winant, H. 93
Winiarski, D. A. xiii, 289–300
Wirihana, R. xvii, 530–43
witchcraft 194, 497, 499, 520
Wittkower, E. 69
Witwatersrand University 477
Wohl, J. 492
women xxiii, 15–16, 20, 89, 115, 116, 123, 142, 143, 147, 217, 242–43, 264, 332, 353, 354, 362, 377, 437, 460, 461, 499, 532, 533; early childhood sexual trauma 294
Women Fighting AIDS in Kenya (WOFAK) 478
Woodrum, T. D. xix, 200–12
workfare-as-welfare (Roets) 131–2
World Bank 56, 61–2, 415
World Health Assembly (2008) 320
World Health Organization (WHO) 32, 36, 39–40, 44, 45, 48, 122, 332, 353, 366, 384, 391, 399, 414, 415, 422, 428, 475, 486, 498, 499, 501, 502, 526; definition of MH 238, 243; *International Classification of Diseases (ICD)* 46, 99, 293, 294, 320, 330, 430, 472; quality of life (QOL) instrument 187; world health report (2000) 56
world wars 85, 106, 116, 134, 242
Wortman, C. B. 317
writing to transgress 25–6
Wu, M. 472

xeno-racism 327, 328, 336

Yaba Mental Hospital 423
Yin and Yang 367, 370
Yip, K. S. 366
yoga 191, 231, 250, 255–7, 263, 388, 392, 512, 525–6
Yohani, S. C. xix, 326–38
Yoruba 521–3, 525
Young, I. M.: five faces of oppression 144–8
Young, R. J. C. 97–8
Youssef, H. and Youssef, F. 435
Youth-MOVE 168
Yusuf, H. xiv, 435–44

Zafar, S. N. 505
Zagzebski, L. T. 233
Zaman, R. M. 438
Zane, N. 121, 123
Zuckerman, P. 218, 220

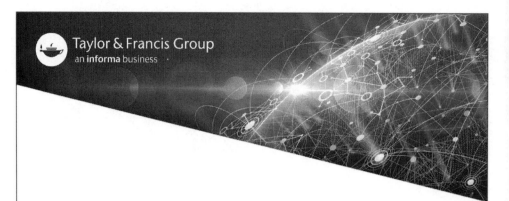